Examining Ethics

Corporations That Give Back to Communities (*Ch 1*)
Beyond Ethical Codes (*Ch 2*)
How Much Is Too Much for CEO Pay? (*Ch 7*)
Dealing with Dishonesty (*Ch 8*)
Marketing Tobacco Products Around the World (*Ch 13*)
Who Is Reading Your E-Mail? (*Ch 17*)
Do Big Corporations "Cook the Books"? (*Ch 18*)
What Is a Predatory Lender? (*Ch 19*)
An Investment Too Good to Be True! (*Ch 20*)

Exploring Business

Social Responsibility Goes to School (*Ch 2*)
Getting Ready for Exporting (*Ch 3*)
Procter & Gamble: Optimism Led the Way Even When It Was Not the Best of Times (*Ch 5*)
Incubators Nurture Web Businesses (*Ch 6*)
What Companies Look for in a Leader (*Ch 7*)
HR Secrets of the Container Store (*Ch 10*)
Dealing with Workplace Stress (*Ch 11*)
White-Collar Contract Issues at Boeing (*Ch 12*)
South Beach Markets Healthy and Hip (*Ch 13*)
Nike Swings Away from the Swoosh (*Ch 14*)
FedEx Custom Critical Coddles Customers (*Ch 15*)
Microsoft Reshapes Its Public Image (*Ch 16*)
Evaluating Inventory (*Ch 18*)
A Case of "Too Much" Consumer Credit (*Ch 19*)
Finance 101: The Basics of How to Get Financing for a Business (*Ch 20*)
Do You Want to Be a Millionaire? (*Ch 21*)

Talking Technology

Looking for a Good Investment? Try a Computer Industry (*Ch 1*)
Building Trust into Global e-Commerce (*Ch 3*)
Privacy on the Internet (*Ch 4*)
The AOL/Time Warner Merger (*Ch 5*)
High-Tech Teen Entrepreneurs (*Ch 6*)
Web-Based Outsourcing (*Ch 8*)
Cisco Systems' Phenomenal Growth (*Ch 9*)
Log On and Learn (*Ch 10*)
Digging Deeper into Buying Behavior (*Ch 13*)
Customers Set Their Own Prices at Priceline (*Ch 14*)
How Stores Are Battling Online Rivals (*Ch 15*)
Sampling Builds Online Beauty Business (*Ch 16*)
The Importance of Standardization (*Ch 17*)
Investing Online (*Ch 21*)
Online Career Planning (*Appendix A*)

Video Cases

Motorola's Total Commitment to Employees (*Ch 1*)
Home Depot's Social Responsibility Agenda (*Ch 2*)
Dat'l Do-It Cooks Up Hot Exports (*Ch 3*)
Blackboard.com: The Future of Educational Technology (*Ch 4*)
IMCO Recycling, Inc. (*Ch 5*)
Entrepreneurial Spirit Is Firm Foundation for Pelzel Construction (*Ch 6*)
Southwest Managers Help the Airline Soar (*Ch 7*)
T.G.I. Friday's Organizes for Global Expansion (*Ch 8*)
Saturn Listens to Its Customers (*Ch 9*)
Recruiting Goes High-Tech with Career Mosaic and Headhunter.net (*Ch 10*)
Motivation Is the Recipe for Success at Harbor Sweets (*Ch 11*)
Management and Unions Team Up at Xerox (*Ch 12*)
1-800-Flowers Keeps Its Business in Bloom (*Ch 13*)
Product Development Keeps Gillette on the Cutting Edge (*Ch 14*)
Dash.com Rewards Loyal Online Shoppers (*Ch 15*)
The Ups and Downs of Dot-Com Advertising (*Ch 16*)
CSX Transportation: From "Iron Horse" to High Technology (*Ch 17*)
Office Depot, Inc. (*Ch 18*)
Why Stokes Interactive Needs Bank Financing (*Ch 19*)
Physician Sales & Service Sets Long-Term Goals (*Ch 20*)
DLJdirect: A Firm That Knows the Value of Customer Service (*Ch 21*)

Strategic Cases

Orbis Demonstrates Global Social Responsibility (*Part I*)
Awards.com: A Company That Deserves an Award! (*Part II*)
E*Trade Trades on Smart Management, Organization, and Operations (*Part III*)
The Challenge of Human Resources Management at Motorola (*Part IV*)
K'NEX Connects with Its Target Market (*Part V*)
United Parcel Service (*Part VI*)
Worldlyinvestor.com: The One Source for Global Information (*Part VII*)

PRIDE | HUGHES | KAPOOR

business

SEVENTH EDITION

business

SEVENTH EDITION

William M. Pride
Texas A & M University

Robert J. Hughes
Dallas County Community Colleges

Jack R. Kapoor
College of DuPage

Houghton Mifflin Company Boston New York

To Nancy, Allen, and Michael Pride

To my mother, Barbara Y. Hughes; and my wife, Peggy

To my parents, Ram and Sheela; my wife Theresa; and my children, Karen, Kathy, and Dave

Executive Editor: George T. Hoffman
Senior Development Editor: Susan M. Kahn
Marketing Manager: Steven W. Mikels
Senior Project Editor: Cathy Labresh Brooks
Production/Design Coordinator: Jodi O'Rourke
Senior Manufacturing Coordinator: Marie Barnes

Cover design: Diana Coe
Cover illustration: © 2000 by Adam Cohen.

Text credits begin on page A73.
Photo credits begin on page A76.

Printed in the U.S.A.

Library of Congress Control Number: 2001131540

ISBN
Student text: 0-618-11594-3
Library edition: 0-618-11593-5

123456789-VH-05 04 03 02 01

Brief contents

contents

3 Exploring Global Business 67

Part II Trends in Business Today 101

4 Navigating the World of e-Business 102

9 Producing Quality Goods and Services 237

Part IV Human Resources 269

10 Attracting and Retaining the Best Employees 270

Part VI Information for Business Strategy and Decision Making 477

17 Acquiring, Organizing, and Using Information 478

18 Using Accounting Information 511

Part VII Finance and Investment 543

19 Understanding Money, Banking, and Credit 544

20 Mastering Financial Management 577

21 Understanding Securities Markets and Investments 607

APPENDIX A Careers in Business A1

APPENDIX B Risk Management and Insurance A17

APPENDIX C Business Law, Regulation, and Taxation A31

Preface

Leading the Way! These three words describe the seventh edition of Pride/Hughes/Kapoor, *Business.* While there are many introduction to business textbooks that claim to be number one in the marketplace, we believe that the sixth edition of *Business* sold more books than any one of our competitors. We thank you for your support. Certainly, comments and suggestions made by professors and reviewers who teach the course, our national advisory panel, and students who take the course have helped to make each of the six editions of *Business* better than the last. And yet, what's more important than how well the sixth edition sold, are the changes we've made to make the seventh edition even better. As authors, we are especially proud of this edition because these important changes were made with two goals in mind: *Student Success* and *Great Teaching.*

Leading The Way to Student Success!

Students deserve the most up-to-date textbook and package available. The Pride/Hughes/Kapoor, *Business* learning package begins with a thoroughly revised, beautifully designed textbook that invites students into the study of business and helps them to become satisfied, successful, and enthusiastic by providing the content coverage that is important in today's ever-changing business world. In addition we provide real-world examples that reinforce text material and career information in every chapter.

When students purchase the new edition of *Business,* they get more than a textbook. Shrink-wrapped with every text, the total learning package includes

- A set of audio review CDs that contain ten to fifteen minutes of review material for each chapter in the text.
- The Real Deal UpGrade CD (starting in January 2002), which contains video and interactive material to reinforce text content.
- The *News You Can Use Career Guide*—a supplement created in partnership with *U.S.News & World Report*—written to help students explore job opportunities and chart a course for career success.

At the same time that we offer a thoroughly revised text and the best learning package in the marketplace, students also get a great low price. **The seventh edition of *Business,* available in convenient looseleaf format that allows flexible use of the text, is priced 1/3 less than our full-length competitors.**

Leading The Way to Great Teaching!

Our objective has always been to provide both students and instructors with a textbook and package that is relevant, accurate, and as interesting as business itself. To that end, we worked hard to make sure that this new edition of *Business* maintains the same tradition of providing quality instructional materials based on our own classroom experiences. You should know that all three authors teach college-level courses. Collectively, we have over sixty-five years of experience teaching Introduction to Business, and two of the three authors teach multiple sections of Introduction to Business every semester. New ideas and important changes to both the textbook and the instructional package are based on our own experiences in the classroom. You should also know that we are the ones who revise the *Business* text with the help of comments and suggestions from other professors, reviewers, our national advisory board, and students, and a very committed team of professionals at our publisher—Houghton Mifflin. Finally, you should know that the authors either write each component or are heavily involved in each component of our instructional package. We think that our classroom experience and personal involvement in the publishing process make a difference and help to create a textbook that is truly *Leading the Way!*

As you choose a new Introduction to Business textbook, we invite you to compare different textbooks and instructional packages to find a better value. To make the decision process easier, we describe in the next several sections the distinctive features that make the seventh edition of *Business* the right choice for you and your students.

New to This Edition

Suggestions from both educators and students who have used previous editions have been incorporated into the seventh edition. Here are some of the new ways that we make business accessible and relevant.

- This edition includes a new chapter on e-Business (Chapter 4), which covers numerous e-business concepts illustrated with a number of real-world, familiar companies, brands, and products. In addition, e-business issues are thoroughly integrated throughout the text in boxed features, examples, and discussions at appropriate points.
- Each chapter in this edition contains a new feature entitled *Using the Internet,* which highlights one or more web sites that are relevant to the chapter's content.
- A new feature—end-of-part strategic cases accompanied by videos—deals with issues that come from multiple chapters within each part, thus requiring students to integrate concepts within the framework of real-world examples.
- To keep the book to a manageable length we took the recommendation of reviewers and moved the coverage of risk management and insurance to an appendix. We also combined the material on business law, regulation, and taxation into one appendix.
- All of the boxed features in this edition are new. Each boxed feature focuses on one of the following areas: Adapting to Change, Examining Ethics, Exploring Business, Going Global, and Talking Technology. These boxed features are discussed further in the next section.
- All chapters begin with opening vignettes called *Inside Business.* Each Inside Business is new to this edition. Examples of featured companies include AOL/Time Warner, Yahoo!, General Electric, Nokia, Arthur Andersen, and Qualcomm. A related feature at the end of each chapter, *Return to Inside Business,* provides additional information about the organization profiled in the opening vignette and poses questions to stimulate class discussion.
- With this edition there are new technology-based supplements including a set of audio review CDs, the Real Deal UpGrade CD that contains video and interactive self-test material for students, and a CD-ROM for instructors.

Exciting Boxed Features

To help highlight today's important issues, we have included a variety of boxed features. Five types of boxes appear throughout the book: Adapting to Change, Examining Ethics, Exploring Business, Going Global, and Talking Technology.

Adapting to Change

Nothing is more certain in today's business environment than change. And the changes taking place are dramatic. Although viewpoints vary considerably about the nature of such changes, business people must deal with both the benefits and challenges of these changes. The workplace changes on which we focus fall into several broad areas, including cultural diversity, total quality management, and changes in business practices. Specific topics include

- e-Business Is Here to Stay (Chapter 1)
- Intellectual Capital: A New Kind of Asset (Chapter 5)
- Collegehire.com's Approach to College Recruiting (Chapter 10)
- The Changing Roles of Men and Women in the Workplace (Chapter 11)
- Copyright Laws vs. the Internet (Chapter 17)

Examining Ethics

Following up on the ethical coverage provided in Chapter 2, Being Ethical and Socially Responsible, the Examining Ethics features are designed to develop students' abilities to think critically about typical ethical dilemmas that can arise in business. To encourage classroom discussion, discussion questions are provided at the end of each Examining Ethics feature. Examples of topics discussed are

- Corporations That Give Back to Communities (Chapter 1)
- How Much Is Too Much for CEO Pay? (Chapter 7)
- Dealing with Dishonesty (Chapter 8)
- Marketing Tobacco Products Around the World (Chapter 13)
- Who Is Reading Your E-Mail? (Chapter 17)
- Do Big Corporations "Cook the Books"? (Chapter 18)

Exploring Business

The Exploring Business series examines a wide range of organizations and contemporary topics that include business trends, social issues, success stories, and personal applications for students. Selected topics include

- Procter & Gamble: Optimism Led the Way Even When It Was Not the Best of Times (Chapter 5)
- What Companies Look for in a Leader (Chapter 7)
- Nike Swings Away from the Swoosh (Chapter 14)
- Microsoft Reshapes Its Public Image (Chapter 16)
- Finance 101: The Basics of How to Get Financing for a Business (Chapter 20)
- Do You Want to Be a Millionaire? (Chapter 21)

Going Global

This series of boxes, together with Chapter 3, Exploring Global Business, is designed to enhance students' awareness of the globalization of the business world. Sample boxed features include

- Business Ethics Around the World (Chapter 2)
- Satisfying Employees Around the World (Chapter 11)
- Swatch Watches Its Product Mix (Chapter 14)
- Making Convenience Stores More Convenient in Japan (Chapter 15)
- International Accounting Standards (Chapter 18)
- Just Say the Word "Russia" to Investors and They Shudder! (Chapter 20)

Talking Technology

Both consumers and businesses are aware of the impact that technology has had on the way we do business. The topics covered in this boxed feature describe some of the latest, state-of-the-art applications that promise to change the way we live. Selected topics include

- Privacy on the Internet (Chapter 4)
- High-Tech Teen Entrepreneurs (Chapter 6)
- Cisco Systems' Phenomenal Growth (Chapter 9)
- How Stores Are Battling Online Rivals (Chapter 15)
- Sampling Builds Online Beauty Business (Chapter 16)
- Investing Online (Chapter 21)

Effective Pedagogical Aids

As we invite students to study business, this text provides the pedagogical tools that will help make their first business course a success. The following features in the text have been evaluated and recommended by reviewers with years of teaching experience.

Part Introductions

Each of the text's seven parts begins with a concise description of the materials to follow. From the outset of each part, students are exposed to upcoming content and develop a better understanding of the chapters' content within the text.

Learning Objectives

A student with a purpose will learn more effectively than a student wandering aimlessly. Each chapter of *Business* contains clearly stated learning objectives signaling important concepts to be mastered. The learning objectives are reinforced as they appear in the margins of the text and serve as the chapter summary's organizing framework. To aid instructors, questions in the *Test Bank* are keyed to the learning objectives.

Inside Business

Chapter-opening Inside Business features introduce the theme of each chapter and focus on pertinent activities of real organizations, such as Dell, Barnes & Noble, and Hewlett-

Packard. The decisions and activities of these organizations not only demonstrate what companies are actually doing, but also make the materials in each chapter relevant and absorbing. When students become involved in the chapter material, critical thinking and active participation replace passive acceptance, and real learning takes place.

Introductory Chapter Overview

The opening paragraphs of each chapter offer an informal chapter preview, while also providing a smooth transition from the Inside Business section. Students can quickly grasp the major topics in the chapter and the sequence in which they are covered. When students are ready to review, each introductory paragraph also serves as a useful reminder of chapter content.

Margin Notes

Two types of margin notes help students understand and retain important concepts. First, to aid students in building a basic business vocabulary, the definition of each *key term* is placed in the margin near the introduction of the term in the text. Second, each *learning objective* is positioned at the beginning of the section where it is discussed. This easy reference to terms and objectives helps reinforce the learning of business fundamentals.

Stimulating Writing Style

One of our major objectives in *Business* is to communicate to students our enthusiasm for business in a direct, engaging manner. Throughout the book we have used a lucid writing style that builds interest and facilitates students' understanding of the concepts discussed. To ensure that the text is stimulating and easy for students to use, we have given special attention to word choice, sentence structure, and the presentation of business language.

Real-World Examples and Illustrations

Numerous real-world examples drawn from familiar organizations and recognizable products are used in each chapter. What services does e-Bay provide its users? How did SBC Communications win the National Minority Supplier Development Council's "Corporation of the Year" award? What is included on a personal balance sheet and personal income statement? Why do people invest in stocks and mutual funds? Contemporary examples such as these catch students' attention and enable them to apply the concepts and issues of each chapter. The Spotlight feature highlights up-to-date fun facts, and the content-based photo captions provide continual, eye-catching examples.

Return to Inside Business

This end-of-chapter feature helps students tie theory and practice together. The Return to Inside Business feature offers additional information about the organization profiled at the beginning of the chapter to reinforce the application of specific principles. At the end of each Return to Inside Business feature, there are questions that can be used for classroom discussion. Suggested answers are included in the *Instructor's Resource Manual.*

Complete End-of-Chapter Review Materials

We provide the practical applications that make a business course so valuable for students. Each end-of-chapter summary, based on the chapter's learning objectives, reviews important ideas. A list of key terms with page references and a complete set of review questions reinforce the learning of chapter definitions and concepts. Discussion questions encourage careful consideration of selected issues by asking students to engage in critical thinking and writing about chapter topics.

Video Cases

A video case in each chapter focuses on recognizable organizations. The cases offer descriptions of current business issues and activities, allowing students to consider the real-world implications associated with the concepts covered in the chapter. Related questions suitable for class discussion or individual assignment follow each case. Sample case titles include

- Blackboard.com: The Future of Educational Technology (Chapter 4)
- Saturn Listens to Its Customers (Chapter 9)
- Motivation Is the Recipe for Success at Harbor Sweets (Chapter 11)
- 1-800-FLOWERS Keeps Its Business in Bloom (Chapter 13)
- The Ups and Downs of Dot-Com Advertising (Chapter 16)
- Why Stokes Interactive Needs Bank Financing (Chapter 19)

Building Skills for Career Success

Each chapter ends with the section Building Skills for Career Success. All exercises in this section provide detailed introductory material along with a student assignment. The five exercises include Exploring the Internet, Developing Critical Thinking Skills, Building Team Skills, Researching Different Careers, and Improving Communication Skills. Suggested answers for each student assignment are included in the *Instructor's Resource Manual.*

Glossary

A glossary containing nearly 750 fundamental business terms from the text appears at the end of the book. The glossary serves as a convenient reference tool to reinforce students' learning of basic business vocabulary.

Complete Package of Support Materials

Accompanying the seventh edition of *Business* is a support package that focuses on generating enthusiasm in your class, inspiring student success, increasing the effectiveness of instructors, and helping students to learn and apply business concepts.

For Instructors to Plan, Present, and Assess More Effectively

New HMClassPrep™ CD-ROM This instructor's CD provides a variety of teaching resources in electronic format allowing for easy customization to meet specific instructional needs. Files included on the CD include PowerPoint, Word files from the *Instructor's Resource Manual,* and selected videos.

Online/Distance Learning Support Instructors can create and customize online course materials to use in distance learning, distributed learning, or as a supplement to traditional classes. The *Blackboard Course Cartridge* and *WebCT e-Pack* that accompany the text include a variety of study aids for students as well as course-management tools for instructors.

Instructor's Web Site This password-protected site includes valuable tools to help instructors design and prepare for the course. The contents include the Teaching Idea Exchange, FAQs about teaching Introduction to Business, sample syllabi, PowerPoint slides that can be downloaded, Word files from the *Instructor's Resource Manual,* and more.

PowerPoint Slide Presentations PowerPoint slides have been specially developed for this edition of *Business.* The package contains over 500 slides, providing a complete lecture for each chapter, including key figures from the text as well as new illustrations. Instructors with Microsoft PowerPoint can use these presentations as is, or they may edit, delete, and add to them to suit their specific class needs. For those without PowerPoint software, a reader is provided so that the slides may be viewed.

Videos There are seven new part-ending videos to support the part-ending cases. In addition there are twenty-one video modules, one for each chapter, to help instructors bring lectures to life by providing thought-provoking insights into real-world companies, products, and issues. Each chapter module includes four segments: a chapter overview, two key concept segments, and a segment supporting the end-of-chapter video case. A complete description of each chapter's series of video segments is provided in the *Video Guide.*

Video Guide This guide is designed to help instructors integrate text content with the video series. A video preview and description of each of the four segments (overview, two separate concept segments, and the video case) are provided for each chapter video. Similar information is provided for each part video. Multiple-choice questions that can be used for classroom discussion or testing are also provided.

Instructor's Resource Manual The comprehensive two-volume *Instructor's Resource Manual,* written by the text's authors, features the following items for each chapter:

- Note from the authors
- Learning objectives
- Brief chapter outline
- Guide for using the transparency acetates
- Comprehensive lecture outline (including transparency cross references, suggestions on where video material can be used, suggested answers to Examining Ethics feature questions, and At Issue debate features for class discussion)
- Supplemental lecture
- Answers to the text review questions, discussion questions, and case questions
- Suggested answers for Building Skills for Career Success exercises
- Two chapter quizzes with answer keys
- Answer key for transparency class exercise and quiz

In addition, the *Instructor's Resource Manual* provides general information that instructors can use to integrate the text into their courses, suggestions for planning the course, sample syllabi, and FAQs about teaching Introduction to Business.

Test Bank Written and class-tested by the text's authors, the *Test Bank* contains over 3,000 items. Each chapter contains a variety of essay, true/false, and multiple-choice questions. An item-information column in the *Test Bank* specifies details about each question, such as learning objective tie-in, learning level (knowledge or application), answer, and text page reference. More specific information about different types of test questions appears in the introduction to the *Test Bank.*

HMTesting This electronic version of the printed *Test Bank* allows instructors to generate and change tests easily. The program includes an online testing feature by which instructors can administer tests via their local area network or over the Web. It also has a gradebook feature that lets users set up classes, record and track grades from tests or assignments, analyze grades, and produce class and individual statistics.

Transparencies The instructional package includes 300 color transparencies—some drawn from the text and over 150 from outside sources. Supplemental transparencies for each chapter include a chapter outline, a class exercise useful for stimulating class discussion, a debate issue excellent for generating fast-paced class interaction, and a multiple-choice chapter quiz. Additional transparencies for each chapter include definitions and figures not found in the text.

For Students to Enhance Knowledge and Application Skills

New Student CDs A set of Audio Review CDs contains short chapter summaries that highlight key concepts and terms. These CDs are ideal for students who learn best by listening and students on the go. The Real Deal UpGrade CD (available in January 2002) includes interactive self-tests, video clips, and other tools for review.

News You Can Use Career Guide Created in partnership with *U.S.News & World Report,* this reader compiles useful information, advice, and articles that will help students explore career options.

Student Web Site This valuable resource includes a research center linking to other sites of interest for business students; the end-of-chapter Exploring the Internet exercises with links to the assigned sites, and any updates that are necessary to keep the exercises current; links to the companies highlighted in Inside Business, boxed features, and cases; online self-tests that give students immediate feedback on their progress; an online version of the e-business chapter that is continually updated; career-related information and links; and more.

Study Guide Written by Kathryn Hegar of Mountain View College, the *Study Guide* is a self-help tool for students to use in learning definitions, concepts, and relationships in each chapter. Based on student feedback, the exercises and questions have been designed to be especially useful for self-evaluation and review purposes. For each chapter in the text, the *Study Guide* provides key terms, matching questions, true/false questions, multiple-choice questions, short-answer and analytical questions, and an answer key.

***It's Strictly Business* Telecourse Guide, Third Edition** For those students enrolled in the It's Strictly Business Telecourse, this guide provides the necessary correlation between the video lessons and the textbook, including assignments, learning objectives, key terms, text focus points, video focus points, and practice tests.

***The Ultimate Job Hunter's Guidebook,* Third Edition** This practical, how-to handbook by Susan Greene (Greene Marketing and Advertising) and Melanie Martel (New Hampshire Technical Institute) is a concise manual containing abundant examples, practical advice, and exercises related to each of the job hunter's major tasks: conducting a self-assessment, preparing résumés and cover letters, targeting potential employers, obtaining letters of recommendation, filling out job applications, interviewing, and starting a new job. The guide also covers current topics of interest such as online job hunting, handling rejection, networking, evaluating job offers, negotiating salary, and looking ahead to future opportunities. It also includes numerous success stories to inspire students.

A Special Note to Students and Instructors

We have worked very hard to bring you a text and support package that will successfully address a variety of needs. Since a text should always be evaluated by the students and instructors who use it, we would welcome and sincerely appreciate your comments and suggestions. Please feel free to contact us.

William M. Pride
Department of Marketing
Texas A & M University
College Station, TX 77843
w-pride@tamu.edu

Robert J. Hughes
Division of Business and Professions
Dallas County Community Colleges
12800 Abrams
Dallas, TX 75243
rjh8410@dcccd.edu

Jack R. Kapoor
Division of Business
College of DuPage
22nd & Lambert Streets
Glen Ellyn, IL 60137
kapoorj@cdnet.cod.edu

Acknowledgments

We wish to express a great deal of appreciation to Brahm Canzer at John Abbot College who provided expert advice in helping us develop technology-related materials for the text and supplements. We thank Kathryn Hegar of Mountain View College for developing the *Study Guide*. We are grateful to Charlie Cook of the University of West Alabama for developing the PowerPoint slides. We thank Bob Woelfle of the R. Jan LeCroy Center for Educational Telecommunications of the Dallas County Community College District for his role in developing materials related to the Telecourse. Finally we wish to thank the following people for technical assistance: Adele Lewis, Clarissa Sims, Colette Williams, Reagan Ladd, Tonia Goddard, Kathryn O'Connor, Cheri Coppock, Stephanie Matthews, Marian Wood, Theresa and Dave Kapoor, David Pierce, Karen Guessford, Patricia Thomas, Kathryn Thumme, and Karen Tucker.

A special Faculty Advisory Board assisted us in making decisions both large and small throughout the entire development process of the text and the instructional package. For being "on-call" and available to answer questions and make valuable suggestions, we are grateful to those who participated:

Maria Aria
Camden County College

Gloria Bemben
Finger Lakes Community College

Gary Cutler
Dyersburg State Community College

Brian Davis
Weber State University

Keith Harman
National-Louis University

Jianwen Liao
Robert Morris College

Kathleen Lorencz
Oakland Community College

Robert Reinke
University of South Dakota

Warren Schlesinger
Ithaca College

David Sollars
Auburn University Montgomery

Elizabeth White
Orange County Community College

For the generous gift of their time and for their thoughtful and useful comments and suggestions, we are indebted to the following reviewers of this and previous editions. Their suggestions have helped us improve and refine the text as well as the whole instructional package.

David V. Aiken
Hocking College

Phyllis C. Alderdice
Jefferson Community College

Marilyn Amaker
Orangeburg-Calhoun Technical College

Harold Amsbaugh
North Central Technical College

Carole Anderson
Clarion University

James O. Armstrong, II
John Tyler Community College

Ed Atzenhoefer
Clark State Community College

Harold C. Babson
Columbus State Community College

Xenia P. Balabkins
Middlesex County College

Gloria Bemben
Finger Lakes Community College

Charles Bennett
Tyler Junior College

Robert W. Bitter
Southwest Missouri State University

Mary Jo Boehms
Jackson State Community College

Stewart Bonem
Cincinnati Technical College

James Boyle
Glendale Community College

Steve Bradley
Austin Community College

Lyle V. Brenna
Pikes Peak Community College

Tom Brinkman
Cincinnati Technical College

Robert Brinkmeyer
University of Cincinnati

Harvey S. Bronstein
Oakland Community College

Edward Brown
Franklin University

Joseph Brum
Fayetteville Technical Institute

Janice Bryan
Jacksonville College

Howard R. Budner
Manhattan Community College

Clara Buitenbos
Pan American University

C. Alan Burns
Lee College

Frank Busch
Louisiana Technical University

Joseph E. Cantrell
DeAnza College

Brahm Canzer
John Abbot College

Don Cappa
Chabot College

Robert Carrel
Vincennes University

Richard M. Chamberlain
Lorain County Community College

Bruce H. Charnov
Hofstra University

Lawrence Chase
Tompkins Cortland Community College

Michael Cicero
Highline Community College

William Clarey
Bradley University

Robert Coiro
LaGuardia Community College

Don Coppa
Chabot College

Robert J. Cox
Salt Lake Community College

Bruce Cudney
Middlesex Community College

Andrew Curran
Antonelli Institute of Art and Photography

Rex R. Cutshall
Vincennes University

John Daily
St. Edward's University

Helen M. Davis
Jefferson Community College

Harris D. Dean
Lansing Community College

Wayne H. Decker
Memphis State University

William M. Dickson
Green River Community College

M. Dougherty
Madison Area Technical College

Sam Dunbar
Delgado Community College

Robert Elk
Seminole Community College

Pat Ellebracht
Northeast Missouri State University

John H. Espey
Cecil Community College

Carleton S. Everett
Des Moines Area Community College

Frank M. Falcetta
Middlesex County College

Thomas Falcone
Indiana University of Pennsylvania

Janice Feldbauer
Austin Community College

Coe Fields
Tarrant County Junior College

Carol Fischer
University of Wisconsin—Waukesha

Gregory F. Fox
Erie Community College

Michael Fritz
Portland Community College at Rock Creek

Fred Fry
Bradley University

Eduardo F. Garcia
Laredo Junior College

Arlen Gastineau
Valencia Community College

Carmine Paul Gibaldi
St. John's University

Edwin Giermak
College of DuPage

R. Gillingham
Vincennes University

Robert Googins
Shasta College

W. Michael Gough
DeAnza College

Cheryl Davisson Gracie
Washtenaw Community College

Joseph Gray
Nassau Community College

Michael Griffin
University of Massachusetts—Dartmouth

Ricky W. Griffin
Texas A & M University

Stephen W. Griffin
Tarrant County Junior College

Roy Grundy
College of DuPage

John Gubbay
Moraine Valley Community College

Rick Guidicessi
Des Moines Area Community College

Ronald Hadley
St. Petersburg Junior College

Carnella Hardin
Glendale Community College

Aristotle Haretos
Flagler College

Richard Hartley
Solano Community College

Carolyn Hatton
Cincinnati State University

Sanford Helman
Middlesex County College

Victor B. Heltzer
Middlesex County College

Ronald L. Hensell
Mendocino College

Leonard Herzstein
Skyline College

Donald Hiebert
Northern Oklahoma College

Nathan Himelstein
Essex County College

L. Duke Hobbs
Texas A & M University

Charles Hobson
Indiana University Northwest

Marie R. Hodge
Bowling Green State University

Gerald Hollier
University of Texas—Brownsville

Jay S. Hollowell
Commonwealth College

Townsend Hopper

Joseph Hrebenak
Community College of Allegheny County—Allegheny

James L. Hyek
Los Angeles Valley College

James V. Isherwood
Community College of Rhode Island

Charleen S. Jaeb
Cuyahoga Community College

Sally Jefferson
Western Illinois University

Jenna Johannpeter
Belleville Area College

Gene E. A. Johnson
Clark College

Carol A. Jones
Cuyahoga Community College

Pat Jones
Eastern New Mexico University

Robert Kegel
Cypress College

Isaac W. J. Keim, III
Delta College

George Kelley
Erie Community College

Marshall Keyser
Moorpark College

Betty Ann Kirk
Tallahassee Community College

Edward Kirk
Vincennes University

Karl Kleiner
Ocean County College

Clyde Kobberdahl
Cincinnati Technical College

Robert Kreitner
Arizona State University

Patrick Kroll
University of Minnesota, General College

Kenneth Lacho
University of New Orleans

John Lathrop
New Mexico Junior College

R. Michael Lebda
DeVry Institute of Technology

George Leonard
St. Petersburg Junior College

Marvin Levine
Orange County Community College

Chad Lewis
Everett Community College

William M. Lindsay
Northern Kentucky University

Carl H. Lippold
Embry-Riddle Aeronautical University

Thomas Lloyd
Westmoreland County Community College

Paul James Londrigan
Mott Community College

Kathleen Lorencz
Oakland Community College

Fritz Lotz
Southwestern College

Robert C. Lowery
Brookdale Community College

Anthony Lucas
Community College of Allegheny County—Allegheny

Sheldon A. Mador
Los Angeles Trade and Technical College

Gayle J. Marco
Robert Morris College

John Martin
Mt. San Antonio Community College

Irving Mason
Herkimer County Community College

John F. McDonough
Menlo College

Catherine McElroy
Bucks County Community College

L. J. McGlamory
North Harris County College

Charles Meiser
Lake Superior State University

Ina Midkiff-Kennedy
Austin Community College—Northridge

Edwin Miner
Phoenix College

Linda Morable
Richland College

Charles Morrow
Cuyahoga Community College

T. Mouzopoulos
American College of Greece

W. Gale Mueller
Spokane Community College

C. Mullery
Humboldt State University

Robert J. Mullin
Orange County Community College

Patricia Murray
Virginia Union University

Robert Nay
Stark Technical College

James Nead
Vincennes University

Jerry Novak
Alaska Pacific University

Gerald O'Bryan
Danville Area Community College

Larry Olanrewaju
Virginia Union University

David G. Oliver
Edison Community College

John R. Pappalardo
Keene State College

Dennis Pappas
Columbus Technical Institute

Roberta F. Passenant
Berkshire Community College

Clarissa M. H. Patterson
Bryant College

Constantine Petrides
Manhattan Community College

Donald Pettit
Suffolk County Community College

Norman Petty
Central Piedmont Community College

Joseph Platts
Miami-Dade Community College

Gloria D. Poplawsky
University of Toledo

Greg Powell
Southern Utah University

Fred D. Pragasam
SUNY at Cobleskill

Peter Quinn
Commonwealth College

Kimberly Ray
North Carolina A&T State University

Kenneth Robinson
Wesley College

John Roisch
Clark County Community College

Rick Rowray
Ball State University

Jill Russell
Camden County College

Karl C. Rutkowski
Pierce Junior College

Martin S. St. John
Westmoreland County Community College

Ben Sackmary
Buffalo State College

Eddie Sanders, Jr.
Chicago State University

P. L. Sandlin
East Los Angeles College

Nicholas Sarantakes
Austin Community College

Marilyn Schwartz
College of Marin

Jon E. Seely
Tulsa Junior College

John E. Seitz
Oakton Community College

J. Gregory Service
Broward Community College—North Campus

Lynne M. Severance
Eastern Washington University

Dennis Shannon
Belleville Area College

Richard Shapiro
Cuyahoga Community College

Raymond Shea
Monroe Community College

Lynette Shishido
Santa Monica College

Anne Smevog
Cleveland Technical College

Carl Sonntag
Pikes Peak Community College

Russell W. Southall
Laney College

John Spence
University of Southwestern Louisiana

Nancy Z. Spillman
President, Economic Education Enterprises

Richard J. Stanish
Tulsa Junior College

Jeffrey Stauffer
Ventura College

E. George Stook
Anne Arundel Community College

W. Sidney Sugg
Lakeland Community College

Lynn Suksdorf
Salt Lake Community College

Richard L. Sutton
University of Nevada—Las Vegas

Robert E. Swindle
Glendale Community College

William A. Syvertsen
Fresno City College

Raymond D. Tewell
American River College

George Thomas
Johnston Technical College

Judy Thompson
Briar Cliff College

William C. Thompson
Foothill Community College

Karen Thomas
St. Cloud University

James B. Thurman
George Washington University

Patric S. Tillman
Grayson County College

Jay Todes
North Lake College

Charles E. Tychsen
Northern Virginia Community College—Annandale

Ted Valvoda
Lakeland Community College

Robert H. Vaughn
Lakeland Community College

Frederick A. Viohl
Troy State University

C. Thomas Vogt
Allan Hancock College

Loren K. Waldman
Franklin University

Stephen R. Walsh
Providence College

John Warner
The University of New Mexico—Albuquerque

W. J. Waters, Jr.
Central Piedmont Community College

Philip A. Weatherford
Embry-Riddle Aeronautical University

Jerry E. Wheat
Indiana University, Southeast Campus

Benjamin Wieder
Queensborough Community College

Ralph Wilcox
Kirkwood Community College

Larry Williams
Palomar College

Paul Williams
Mott Community College

Steven Winter
Orange County Community College

Wallace Wirth
South Suburban College

Nathaniel Woods
Columbus State Community College

Gregory J. Worosz
Schoolcraft College

Marilyn Young
Tulsa Junior College

Many talented professionals at Houghton Mifflin have contributed to the development of *Business,* Seventh Edition. We are especially grateful to Charlie Hartford, George Hoffman, Steve Mikels, Susan Kahn, Fred Burns, Jodi O'Rourke, and Cathy Brooks. Their inspiration, patience, support, and friendship are invaluable.

The Environment of Business

In Part I of *Business,* we begin first with an examination of the world of business. Second, we discuss the responsibilities of business as part of our society. Then we explore the increasing importance of international business.

1 Exploring the World of Business

LEARNING OBJECTIVES

1. Discuss your future in the world of business.
2. Define *business* and identify potential risks and rewards.
3. Describe the two types of economic systems: capitalism and command economy.
4. Identify the ways to measure economic performance.
5. Outline the four types of competition.
6. Summarize the development of America's business system.
7. Discuss the challenges that American businesses will encounter in the future.

This year, General Electric was chosen as America's most admired corporation for the third year in a row.

General Electric: America's Most Admired Company

Each year for the last eighteen years, *Fortune* magazine has created a list of America's most admired companies. The process begins by identifying the companies that have the highest sales revenue. This year 1,025 U.S. companies and U.S. subsidiaries of foreign-held enterprises were placed on the *Fortune* list. Corporate executives then vote on the top companies in their respective industries to help *Fortune* create a "most admired" list for practically every industry—entertainment, trucking, and medical products, to name a few. Eight specific criteria that include innovation, quality of management, employee talent, financial soundness, use of corporate assets, long-term investment value, social responsibility, and quality of products and services are used to help determine the best of the best. Then the list of top ten companies is chosen by securities analysts, corporate board members, and executives. This year, General Electric was chosen as America's Most Admired Corporation. What makes this year's award even more important is that this year is the fourth year in a row that General Electric has won this coveted award.

By now, you may be asking yourself: How could a company that makes light bulbs win this prestigious award? Although most of us know General Electric, or simply GE, as a manufacturer of light bulbs, the company is also a corporate giant consisting of over twenty different core businesses. It all started back in 1878 when Thomas Edison founded the Electric Light Company. A merger with the Thomson-Houston Electric Company before the turn of the century created the General Electric Corporation—the name we know today. This new company invented and manufactured electrical devices that ranged from the small filaments that are still used in light bulbs to the first steam turbine generator powerful enough to supply electricity to an entire city. Since then GE has expanded into many other areas of business that range from broadcasting to financial services to silicone manufacturing. The company even built the first nuclear power plant.

While General Electric is admired by many business executives and enjoys tremendous financial success, America's most admired company is not one to sit back and rest on past performance. A program of lofty standards, called *growth initiatives,* is used to examine every facet of production and service. One growth initiative, called the *Sixth Sigma,* is a rigid process of defining, measuring, analyzing, improving, and controlling quality. Because of the Sixth Sigma, managers and employees are empowered to improve on every product the company sells, from jet engines to medical equipment.

Another growth initiative states GE's firm resolution to become the global leader in each of its core business areas. Although lesser companies often want to just sell their products or services around the world, GE doesn't just stop with selling its products or services. This award-winning company also helps the people in other nations develop their resources including raw materials and "intellectual capital." For example, GE employs over thirty thousand people and has made large investments in building manufacturing plants in Mexico. America's Most Admired Corporation is also urging its suppliers to build facilities in Mexico. And GE's global commitment doesn't stop with Mexico. Currently, the firm employs over 340,000 employees in 100 different countries around the globe.

So what if the company wins an award and is recognized as a global leader? Has time and money been invested well? Consider the following facts. The company has paid quarterly dividends to stockholders every year since 1899. One share of General Electric purchased before 1926 is now worth $245,760. Maybe, what's more important is the fact that General Electric is the "darling" of Wall Street. Financial analysts continue to recommend the stock as a "best bet" for the future.[1]

In today's competitive business environment, it's common to hear of profitable companies. It is less common to hear of profitable companies that are held in high regard by their competitors. That's what is so astonishing about General Electric being chosen by *Fortune* magazine as America's Most Admired Corporation for four years in a row. What's even more astonishing is that General Electric doesn't just concentrate on earning profits. The company is committed to giving back resources to the communities in which it operates. Its public service program, Elfun, consists of more than 40,000 GE employees and retirees who have just donated an annual record of 1.3 million volunteer hours working for community service projects such as food and renovation programs for the poor and also supporting mentoring programs at schools to help students and teachers in science, engineering, and math. In reality, General Electric is an excellent example of what American business should be doing.

Perhaps the most important characteristic of our economic system is the freedom of individuals to start a business, to work for a business, and to buy or sell ownership shares in the business. While business always entails risks, it can also have its rewards. For Michael Dell, the chairman, CEO, and founder of Dell Computer Corporation, there has been the satisfaction of succeeding in a very competitive industry—not to mention some very substantial financial rewards.

Within certain limits, imposed mainly to ensure public safety, the owners of a business can produce any legal good or service they choose and attempt to sell it at the price they set. This system of business, in which individuals decide what to produce, how to produce it, and at what price to sell it, is called **free enterprise.** Our free-enterprise system ensures, for example, that Dell Computer can buy parts from Intel, software from Lotus Development Corporation, and manufacture its own computers. Our system gives Dell's owners and stockholders the right to make a profit from the company's success; it gives Dell's management the right to compete with Compaq and IBM; and it gives computer buyers the right to choose.

free enterprise the system of business in which individuals are free to decide what to produce, how to produce it, and at what price to sell it

In this chapter, we look briefly at what business is and how it got that way. First, we discuss your future in business and explore some important reasons for studying business. Then we define *business,* noting how business organizations satisfy needs and earn profits. Next we examine how capitalism and command economies answer four basic economic questions. Then our focus shifts to how the nations of the world measure economic performance and the four types of competitive situations. Next we go back into American history for a look at the events that helped shape today's business system. We conclude this chapter with a discussion of the challenges that businesses face.

Your Future in the World of Business

LEARNING OBJECTIVE

1 Discuss your future in the world of business.

What do you want?
Why do you want it?
Write it down!

During a segment on the Oprah Winfrey television show, Joe Dudley, one of the world's most successful Black business owners, gave the above advice to anyone who wants to succeed in business. And his advice is an excellent way to begin our discussion of what free enterprise is all about. What's so amazing about Dudley's success is that he grew up in a rural farmhouse with no running water and began his career selling Fuller Brush products door-to-door. He went on to develop his own line of hair-care products and open a chain of beauty schools and beauty supply stores. Today, Dudley is president of Dudley Products, Inc.—one of the largest minority-owned companies in the nation. Not only a successful business owner, he is the winner of the Horatio Alger Award—an award given to outstanding individuals who have succeeded in the face of adversity.[2]

Opportunity! It's only eleven letters, but no other word provides a better description of the current business environment. While many people would say that Joe Dudley was just lucky or happened to be in the right place at the right time, the truth is that he became a success because he had a dream and worked hard to turn his dream into a reality. He would be the first to tell you that you have the same opportunities that he had. In fact, employment opportunities for entry-level workers, investment opportunities, and career advancement opportunities have never been greater. However, people who are successful must adapt to changes in their environment. Consider just some of the changes that have occurred since the previous edition of *Business* was published.

All work and no play? Not for this entrepreneur. Jeff Bonforte, founder and CEO of idrive.com, knows that starting a high-tech company is hard work and requires long hours, but that it can be a lot of fun. It can also be very rewarding. Bonforte is now worth an estimated $5 to $10 million.

- Today the economy is healthy and we have experienced the longest period of sustained economic growth in our history.
- There is a large increase in the number of new, start-up companies especially in the technology and information industries.
- The increased use of the Internet has created new jobs that did not exist even three years ago.
- Unemployment numbers are at record lows and employers are now recruiting new employees.
- An increasing number of people work at home for all or part of the work week.

For the person that has the required abilities and skills, it is an excellent time to start a career. And yet, employers and our capitalistic economic system are more demanding than ever before. Ask yourself: What can I do that will make employers want to pay me a salary? What skills do I have that employers need? With these two questions in mind, we begin the next section with another basic question: Why Study Business?

Why Study Business?

Education is a unique purchase—one of the few things you can buy that will last your lifetime. It can't rust, corrode, break down, or wear out. Education can't be stolen, burned, repossessed, or destroyed. Education is a purchase that becomes a permanent part of you. Once you have it, no one can take it away.[3]

In this section, we explore what you may expect to get out of this business course and text. You will find at least four quite compelling reasons for studying business.

To Become a Better-Informed Consumer and Investor

The world of business surrounds us. You cannot buy a home, a new Trans Am from the local Pontiac dealer, a Black & Decker sander at the Home Depot, a pair of jeans at the Gap, or a hot dog from a street vendor without entering a business transaction. These and thousands of similar transactions describe the true nature of the American business system.

Using the Internet

Your Internet connection to more business information begins at **Houghton Mifflin's College Division** web site. Enter the web site URL **http://www.college.hmco.com.** Select the student tab and then go to "Business." Select the text web site or the resource center to find quick access to business journals and web sites that explore many topics discussed in the text chapters and more. This site will simplify your search for information on the Internet. Use it often to keep up to date with current developments in the fast-paced world of business.

spotLight

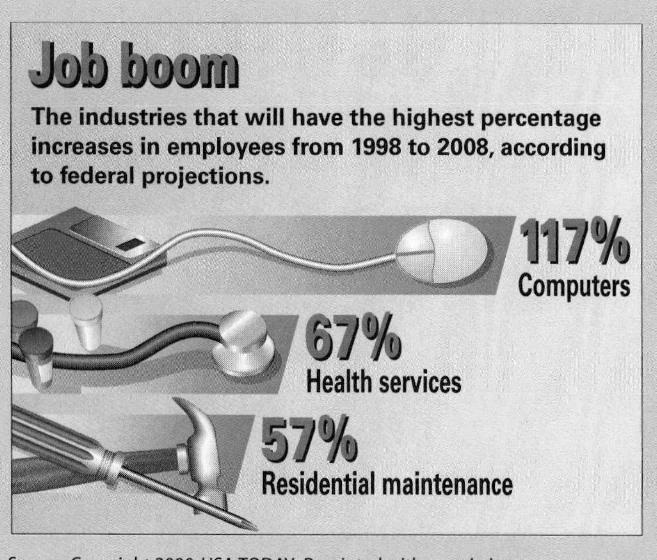

Source: Copyright 2000, USA TODAY. Reprinted with permission.

Because you will no doubt engage in business transactions almost every day of your life, one very good reason for studying business is to become a more fully informed consumer. Your knowledge of business will enable you to make intelligent buying decisions and to spend your money more wisely. This same basic understanding of business will also make you a better-informed investor.

For Help in Choosing a Career What do you want to do with the rest of your life? Someplace, sometime, someone has probably asked you that same question. And like many people, you may find it a difficult question to answer. This business course will introduce you to a wide array of employment opportunities. In private enterprise, these range from small, local businesses owned by one individual to large companies like American Express and Marriott International that are owned by thousands of stockholders. There are also employment opportunities with federal, state, county, and local governments and with not-for-profit organizations like the Red Cross and Save the Children. For help deciding what career might be right for you, read Appendix A: Careers in Business. Also, you might want to read information about researching a career and the steps necessary to perform a job search that are posted on the web site that accompanies this edition of *Business.* To view this information:

1. Make an Internet connection and go to http://college.hmco.com/business/
2. Locate the Student Center site and click to enter.
3. Then scroll down on the Student Center page and click on *career section.*

One thing to remember as you think about what your ideal career might be is that a person's choice of a career is ultimately just a reflection of what he or she values and holds most important. Because people have different values, they choose different careers; what will give one individual personal satisfaction may not satisfy another. For example, one person may dream of becoming a millionaire before the age of thirty. Another may choose a career that has more modest monetary rewards but that provides the opportunity to help others. One person may be willing to work long hours and seek additional responsibility in order to get promotions and pay raises. Someone else may prefer a less demanding job with little stress and more free time. What you choose to do with your life will be based on what you feel is most important.

To Be a Successful Employee Deciding on the type of career you want is only a first step. To get a job in your chosen field and to be successful at it, you will have to develop a plan, or road map, that ensures that you have the skills and knowledge the job requires. Today's employers are looking for job applicants who can *do something,* not just fill a spot on an organizational chart. You will be expected to have both the technical skills needed to accomplish a specific task and the ability to work well with many types of people in a culturally diverse work force. These skills, together with a working knowledge of the American business system, can give you an inside edge when you are interviewing with a prospective employer.

This course, your instructor, and all the resources available at your college or university can help you acquire the skills and knowledge you will need for a successful career. But don't underestimate your part in making your dream a reality. It will take hard work, dedication, perseverance, and time management to achieve your goals. Time management is especially important because it will help you accomplish the tasks that you consider most important. As an added bonus, it is also a skill that employers value. Communication skills are also important. Today, most employers are looking for employees who can compose a business letter and get it in mailable form. They also want employees who can talk with customers and use e-mail to communicate to people within and outside of the organization. Employers will also be interested in any work experience you may have had in cooperative work/school programs, during summer vacations, or in part-time jobs during the school year. These things can make a difference when it is time to apply for the job you really want.

Home or office? Today more and more successful employees—like Carla Patterson, a field representative for Nebraska's Department of Economic Development—are working at home.

To Start Your Own Business Some people prefer to work for themselves, and they open their own businesses. To be successful, business owners must possess many of the same skills that successful employees have. And they must be willing to work hard and put in long hours.

It also helps if your small business can provide a product or service that customers want. For example, Mark Cuban started a small Internet company called Broadcast.com that now provides hundreds of live and on-demand audio and video programs ranging from rap music to sporting events to business events over the Internet. This new, high-tech startup company quickly became a major player in electronic business or what many refer to as e-business. **E-business** is the organized effort of individuals to produce and sell, for a profit, the products and services that satisfy society's needs *through the facilities available on the Internet.* When Cuban sold Broadcast.com to Yahoo! Inc., he became a billionaire. Today he is an expert on how the Internet and e-business will affect society in the future and believes that many small technology firms will fail over the next ten years. According to Cuban, there is a real need for all companies—not just technology companies—to provide something that their customers want. If they don't do that, their company could very well fail.[4] For more information on how two very successful firms use e-business, read the Adapting to Change boxed feature.

e-business the organized effort of individuals to produce and sell, for a profit, the products and services that satisfy society's needs through the facilities available on the Internet

Unfortunately, many small-business firms fail; 70 percent of them fail within the first five years. The material in Chapter 6 and selected topics and examples throughout this text will help you decide whether you want to open your own business. Before proceeding to the next section, take a few minutes to familiarize yourself with the text by reading the material below.

Special Note to Students

It's important to begin reading this text with one thing in mind: *this business course doesn't have to be difficult.* In fact, we've done everything possible to eliminate the problems that students encounter in a typical class. All the features in each chapter have been evaluated and recommended by instructors with years of teaching experience. In addition, business students were asked to critique each chapter component. Based on this feedback, the text includes the following features:

Adapting to change

E-Business Is Here to Stay

ALL ACROSS THE GLOBE, E-BUSINESS IS changing the way in which companies process purchasing orders, ship merchandise, and handle customer requests. And for companies that use e-business to increase productivity and sales, profits also increase. While doing business electronically used to be reserved for only high-tech companies, over the last few years it has become apparent that those companies that refuse to join the e-business revolution will be left behind. Consider how e-business is changing the way that Charles Schwab and Wal-Mart do business.

Charles Schwab Discount Brokerage

Today, Charles Schwab is recognized as one of the most successful discount firms in the brokerage business. The reason for this success is based on two concepts: customer service and the use of technology. Technology enables investors to not only trade online but also to research potential investments online. Back in 1975, when Schwab opened his first office, employees were taught that customer service was a top priority. To help ensure that employees were willing to help the firm's customers get top quality service, his employees were paid salaries, not commissions–a practice unheard of in the brokerage business. As a result, employees were able to spend more time with customers helping them learn how to make investment decisions. When the technology became available, it was possible for the company to extend this same philosophy to investors who wanted to trade online. Today, both stock market rookies and experienced investors use the Schwab system to trade stocks online at reduced commissions. More importantly, these same investors use research tools provided online to learn more about the financial fundamentals required to become better investors.

Wal-Mart

When the late Sam Walton opened his first Wal-Mart store in 1962, company growth was his primary objective. In order to succeed he implemented all of the emerging technology available at the time. Over the years, his objective was achieved; Wal-Mart became the number 1 retailer in the world employing over 1,140,000 employees in almost 4,000 stores. Although the road to success has been phenomenal, it has not been without a few bumps along the way. During the mid-1990s, for example, the retailer experienced inventory problems and a sales slump. According to some analysts, it almost seemed like the retail giant lost its competitive edge. Corporate executives investigating the problem discovered that both managers and employees were not as technology-literate as they should be. They also discovered that just because the technology had been made available, it didn't mean that the managers and employees were using it. To remedy the problem both managers and employees received advanced training which eventually enabled Wal-Mart to correct problems and increase sales. Today, the company owns an elite information system which can automatically transmit data via satellite to all stores and corporate headquarters. Inventory is no longer an issue; suppliers are connected to the network and receive orders immediately. Wal-Mart recently expanded its network by adding an online ordering system for consumers. Wal-Mart.com is a virtual store and a complete companion to its physical stores.

E-Business: A Career Perspective

Companies who have the willingness to make the e-business conversion create extraordinary opportunities and have incredible advantages over their competitors. And while it's obvious e-business is here to stay, the largest stumbling block for companies using improved technology is not purchasing the new equipment, but training people or finding people who can use it. Today, companies are looking for employees who have the computer skills required to not only use new technology, but also improve on existing technology. In fact, many employers believe skilled talent is indispensable. Excellent jobs are available for those who have a vision on how to use improved technology.

- *Learning objectives* appear at the beginning of each chapter. All objectives signal important concepts to be mastered within the chapter.
- *Inside Business* is a chapter-opening case that highlights how successful companies do business on a day-to-day basis. These short cases were chosen to illustrate the key concepts and ideas described in each chapter.
- *Margin notes* are used throughout the text to reinforce both learning objectives and key terms.
- *Boxed features* highlight ethical behavior, change in the workplace, global issues, and the impact of technology. In addition, a boxed feature entitled Exploring Business highlights a wide range of contemporary business issues.

- *Spotlight* features highlight interesting facts about business and society and often provide a real-world example of an important concept within a chapter.
- *Using the Internet* features provide useful web addresses that relate to chapter material.
- *End-of-chapter materials* provide questions about the opening case, a chapter summary, a list of key terms, review and discussion questions, and a video case. The last section of every chapter is entitled Building Skills for Career Success and includes exercises devoted to exploring the Internet, developing critical thinking skills, building team skills, researching different careers, and improving communication skills.

In addition to the text, a number of student supplements will help you explore the world of business. We're especially proud of two items that are available with this edition of *Business.* The set of student CDs packaged with every new text purchased through your college bookstore will help you review important concepts with audio material that you can use at your convenience. We're also proud of the web site that accompanies this edition. Here you will find a computerized study guide, along with many other tools designed to help ensure your success in this course. If you want to take a look at the Internet support materials available for this edition of *Business,* go to: http://college.hmco.com/business and click on Text Web Sites.

As authors, we realize that you are our customers. We want you to be successful. And we want you to appreciate business and how it affects your life as an employee and a consumer. Since a text should always be evaluated by the students and instructors who use it, we would welcome and sincerely appreciate your comments and suggestions. Please feel free to contact us by using one of the following e-mail addresses:

Bill Pride	w-pride@tamu.edu
Bob Hughes	rjh8410@dcccd.edu
Jack Kapoor	kapoorj@cdnet.cod.edu

LEARNING OBJECTIVE

2 Define *business* and identify potential risks and rewards.

Business: A Definition

business the organized effort of individuals to produce and sell, for a profit, the goods and services that satisfy society's needs

Business is the organized effort of individuals to produce and sell, for a profit, the goods and services that satisfy society's needs. The general term *business* refers to all such efforts within a society (as in "American business") or within an industry (as in "the steel business"). However, *a business* is a particular organization, such as Dudley Products, Inc., American Airlines, Inc., or Cracker Barrel Old Country Stores. To be successful, a business must perform three activities. It must be organized. It must satisfy needs. And it must earn a profit.

The Organized Effort of Individuals

For a business to be organized, it must combine four kinds of resources: material, human, financial, and informational. *Material* resources include the raw materials used in manufacturing processes, as well as buildings and machinery. For example, Sara Lee Corporation needs flour, sugar, butter, eggs, and other raw materials to produce the food products it sells worldwide. In addition, this Chicago-based company needs human, financial, and informational resources. *Human* resources are the people who furnish their labor to the business in return for wages. The *financial* resource is the money required to pay employees, purchase materials, and generally keep the business operating. And *information* is the resource that tells the managers of the business how effectively the other resources are being combined and used (see Figure 1.1).

Today, businesses are usually classified as one of three specific types. *Manufacturing businesses* are organized to process various materials into tangible goods, such as delivery trucks or towels. For example, Intel produces computer chips that are in turn sold to companies that manufacture computers. *Service businesses*

figure 1.1

Combining Resources
A business must effectively combine all four resources to be successful.

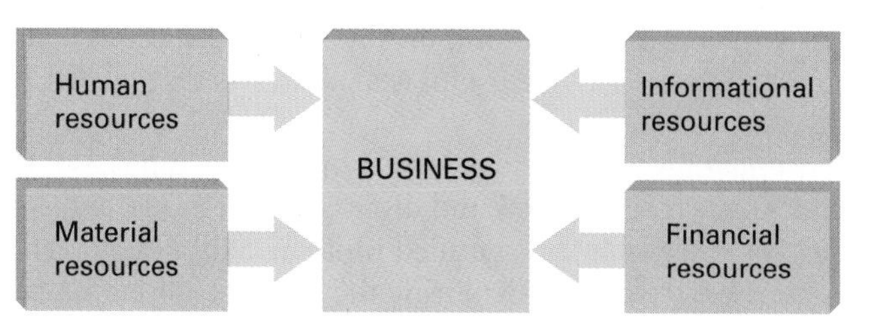

produce services, such as haircuts, legal advice, or tax preparation. And some firms—called *marketing intermediaries*—are organized to buy products from manufacturers and then resell them. Sony Corporation is a manufacturer that produces stereo equipment, among other things. These products may be sold to a marketing intermediary such as Kmart Corporation, which then resells them to consumers in its retail stores. **Consumers** are individuals who purchase goods or services for their own personal use.

consumers individuals who purchase goods or services for their own personal use

Satisfying Needs

The ultimate objective of every firm must be to satisfy the needs of its customers. People generally don't buy goods and services simply to own them; they buy products and services to satisfy particular needs. People rarely buy an automobile solely to store it in a garage; they do, however, buy automobiles to satisfy their need for transportation. Some of us may feel this need is best satisfied by an air-conditioned BMW with stereo compact-disc player, automatic transmission, power seats and windows, and remote-control side mirrors. Others may believe a Ford Focus with a stick shift and an AM radio will do just fine. Both products are available to those who want them, along with a wide variety of other products that satisfy the need for transportation. To satisfy their customers' needs for information, Ford has joined up with Microsoft's *Carpoint* web site http://carpoint.msn.com/home/New.asp to help consumers find decision-critical information about their products and dealers from the comfort, convenience, and privacy of their own homes and offices. Ford and Microsoft hope to transform the site into a complete build-to-order system that will link customer orders for options directly with their supplier system. This way, customers get the products they want and Ford reduces the risks associated with guessing the inventories of cars its dealers should stock.[5]

And you think you've got books! For a company like Amazon.com, books are a way of life. In this warehouse facility, employees process orders and ship books to satisfy customers' needs.

When firms lose sight of their customers' needs they are likely to find the going rough. But when businesses understand their customers' needs and work to satisfy those needs, they are usually successful. Arkansas-based Wal-Mart Stores, Inc., provides the products its customers want and offers excellent prices. This highly successful discount-store organization continues to open new stores in the United States, Argentina, Brazil, Canada, China, Germany, and Mexico.

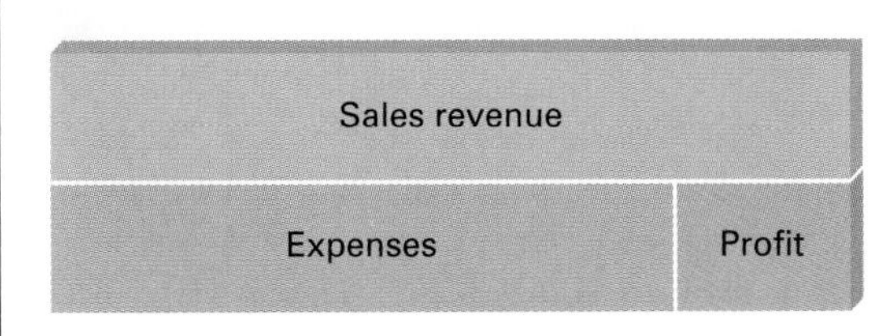

figure 1.2

The Relationship Between Sales Revenue and Profit
Profit is what remains after all business expenses have been deducted from sales revenue.

Business Profit

A business receives money (sales revenue) from its customers in exchange for goods or services. It must also pay out money to cover the expenses involved in doing business. If the firm's sales revenue is greater than its expenses, it has earned a profit. More specifically, as shown in Figure 1.2, **profit** is what remains after all business expenses have been deducted from sales revenue. (A negative profit, which results when a firm's expenses are greater than its sales revenue, is called a *loss.*)

profit what remains after all business expenses have been deducted from sales revenue

The profit earned by a business becomes the property of its owners. So in one sense, profit is the reward business owners receive for producing goods and services that consumers want.

Profit is also the payment that business owners receive for assuming the considerable risks of ownership. One of these is the risk of not being paid. Everyone else—employees, suppliers, and lenders—must be paid before the owners. A second risk that owners run is the risk of losing whatever they have invested into the business. A business that cannot earn a profit is very likely to fail, in which case the owners lose whatever money, effort, and time they have invested. Internet-based book and CD retailer Amazon.com Inc. currently spends over $115 million each month to keep the company on track toward the eventual day when the firm will sell enough merchandise to generate profits for its shareholders. To date, Amazon's six years of operating losses total more than $1.2 billion, scaring away some who fear the firm will never reach the promised profit goals set by visionary founder Steve Bezos.[6] When a business is profitable, some businesses choose to give back a portion of their profits to the communities they serve. For information on how three different companies help children, read the Examining Ethics boxed feature.

To satisfy society's needs, and make a profit, a business must operate within the parameters of a nation's economic system. In the next section, we describe two different types of economic systems and how they affect not only businesses but also the people within a nation.

LEARNING OBJECTIVE

3 Describe the two types of economic systems: capitalism and command economy.

Types of Economic Systems

Economics is the study of how wealth is created and distributed. By *wealth* we mean anything of value, including the products produced and sold by business. *How wealth is distributed* simply means "who gets what." The way in which people deal with the creation and distribution of wealth determines the kind of economic system, or **economy,** that a nation has.

economics the study of how wealth is created and distributed

economy the system through which a society answers the two economic questions—how wealth is created and distributed

Over the years, the economic systems of the world have differed in essentially two ways: (1) the ownership of the factors of production and (2) how they answer four basic economic questions that direct a nation's economic activity. **Factors of production** are the resources used to produce goods and services. There are four such factors:

factors of production natural resources, labor, capital, and entrepreneurship

- *Natural resources*—elements in their natural state that can be used in the production process. Typical examples include crude oil, forests, minerals, land, water, and even air.

Examining Ethics

Corporations That Give Back To Communities

... McDonald's and Ronald McDonald House Charities are committed to continuing our efforts in support of children and families around the world.... We remain dedicated to one of McDonald's fundamental values, which is to give back to communities we serve.

JACK GREENBERG, MCDONALD'S CHAIRMAN AND CEO

BECAUSE OF ITS CONCERN FOR THE WELL BEING and education of children, its environmental programs in recycling, reducing waste, and conserving energy, *Fortune* magazine ranked McDonald's number 1 in social responsibility–one of eight criteria used to select America's Most Admired Corporation for 1999. Is the recognition deserved? Before you answer this question, consider the following.

Today, McDonald's is viewed as a pioneer in recognizing the need for social responsibility in the corporate world, but the firm's history of social responsibility began with one project–a Ronald McDonald house. Back in 1974, McDonald's created a home-away-from-home for families of seriously ill children receiving treatment at nearby hospitals in Philadelphia. Named in honor of the clown that is the firm's symbol of happiness, McDonald's is now responsible for establishing over 200 Ronald McDonald houses in 32 countries and has awarded more than $225 million in grants to children's programs worldwide. What a success story!

While many people think that corporations are only interested in earning profits, McDonald's is not alone in its desire to give back part of their profits to communities. In fact, many business organizations are giving back resources to the communities they serve. Some corporate responsibility programs even go the extra mile and get their customers involved. One such program–Campbell Soup Company's Labels for Education program has been in operation for over twenty-six years. This program provides a way for people in the community to help local schools by collecting Campbell Soup product labels. Once enough labels are collected, then the school can redeem the labels for computers, software, sports equipment, research materials, and other types of equipment that the school needs. Like the Campbell Soup Labels for Education program, the Randalls/Tom Thumb Good Neighbor Program involves the firm's customers. Customers apply for a Reward Card which allows them to receive special discounts on select merchandise purchased in either a Randalls or Tom Thumb grocery story. At the time of application, customers can designate any nonprofit youth organization to receive cash donations based on the dollar value of the customers' total purchases.

Issues to Consider

1. As a stockholder, do you feel it is right for management to use corporate funds to sponsor social responsibility programs?
2. Is it ethical for a corporation to promote the sale of their products or services in return for a corporate promise to contribute to youth-oriented programs?

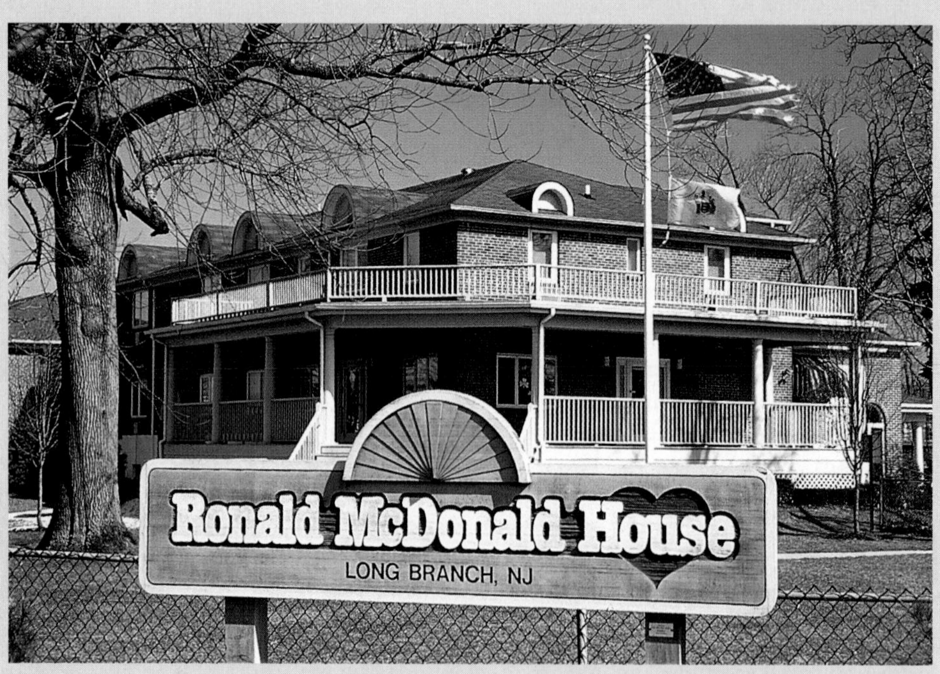

- *Labor*—human resources such as managers and workers.
- *Capital*—money, facilities, equipment, and machines used in the operation of organizations. While most people think of capital as just money, it can also be the manufacturing equipment on a Ford automobile assembly line or a computer used in the corporate offices of Ace Hardware.
- *Entrepreneurship*—the willingness to take risks and the knowledge and ability to use the other factors of production efficiently. An **entrepreneur** is a person who risks his or her time, effort, and money to start and operate a business.

entrepreneur a person who risks time, effort, and money to start and operate a business

A nation's economic system significantly affects all the economic activities of its citizens and organizations. This far-reaching impact becomes more apparent when we consider that a country's economic system provides answers to four basic economic questions.

1. What goods and services—and how much of each—will be produced?
2. How will these goods and services be produced?
3. For whom will these goods and services be produced?
4. Who owns and who controls the major factors of production?

capitalism an economic system in which individuals own and operate the majority of businesses that provide goods and services

market economy an economic system in which businesses and individuals decide what to produce and buy, and the market determines quantities sold and prices

mixed economy an economy that exhibits elements of both capitalism and socialism

Capitalism

Capitalism is an economic system in which individuals own and operate the majority of businesses that provide goods and services. Capitalism stems from the theories of the eighteenth-century Scottish economist Adam Smith. In his book *Wealth of Nations,* published in 1776, Smith argued that a society's interests are best served when the individuals within that society are allowed to pursue their own self-interest.

Adam Smith's laissez-faire capitalism is based on four fundamental issues. First, Smith argued that the creation of wealth is properly the concern of private individuals, not of government. Second, the resources used to create wealth must be owned by private individuals. Smith argued that the owners of resources should be free to determine how these resources are used. They should also be free to enjoy the income, profits, and other benefits they might derive from the ownership of these resources. Third, Smith contended that economic freedom ensures the existence of competitive markets that allow both sellers and buyers to enter and exit as they choose. This freedom to enter or leave a market at will has given rise to the term *market economy.* A **market economy** (sometimes referred to as a *free-market economy*) is an economic system in which businesses and individuals make the decisions about what to produce and what to buy, and the market determines how much is sold and at what prices. Finally, in Smith's view, the role of government should be limited to providing defense against foreign enemies, ensuring internal order, and furnishing public works and education. With regard to the economy, government should act only as rule maker and umpire.

In other words, Smith believed that each person should be allowed to work toward his or her *own* economic gain, without interference from government. The French term *laissez faire* describes Smith's capitalistic system and implies that there shall be no interference in the economy. Loosely translated, it means "let them do" (as they see fit).

Saturn: A true success story. There are no guarantees that Saturn will be successful just because it operates in a capitalistic society. However, companies like Saturn that produce goods and services that customers *really* want have a much better chance of being successful.

Capitalism in the United States

Our economic system is rooted in the laissez-faire capitalism of Adam Smith. However, our real-world economy is not as "laissez faire" as Smith would have liked because government participates as more than umpire and rule maker. Ours is, in fact, a **mixed economy,** one that exhibits elements of both capitalism and socialism.

In today's economy, the four basic economic questions discussed at the beginning of this section of Chapter 1 are answered through the interaction of households, businesses, and governments. The interactions among these three groups are shown in Figure 1.3.

Households Households are consumers of goods and services, as well as owners of some of the factors of production. As *resource owners,* the members of households provide businesses with labor, land, buildings, and capital. In return, businesses pay wages, rent, and dividends and interest, which households receive as income.

As *consumers,* household members use their income to purchase the goods and services produced by business. Today almost two-thirds of our nation's total production consists of **consumer products:** goods and services purchased by individuals for personal consumption. (The remaining one-third is purchased by businesses and governments.) This means that consumers, as a group, are the biggest customer of American business.

consumer products goods and services purchased by individuals for personal consumption

Businesses Like households, businesses are engaged in two different exchanges. They exchange money for resources and use these resources to produce goods and services. Then they exchange their goods and services for sales revenue. This sales revenue, in turn, is exchanged for additional resources, which are used to produce and sell more goods and services. So the circular flow of Figure 1.3 is continuous.

Along the way, of course, business owners would like to remove something from the circular flow in the form of profits. And households try to retain some income as savings. But are profits and savings really removed from the flow? Usually not! When the economy is running smoothly, households are willing to invest their savings in businesses. They can do so directly, by buying ownership shares in businesses or by lending money to businesses. They can also invest indirectly, by placing their savings in bank accounts; banks then invest these savings as part of their normal business operations. In either case, savings usually find their way back into the circular flow in order to finance business activities.

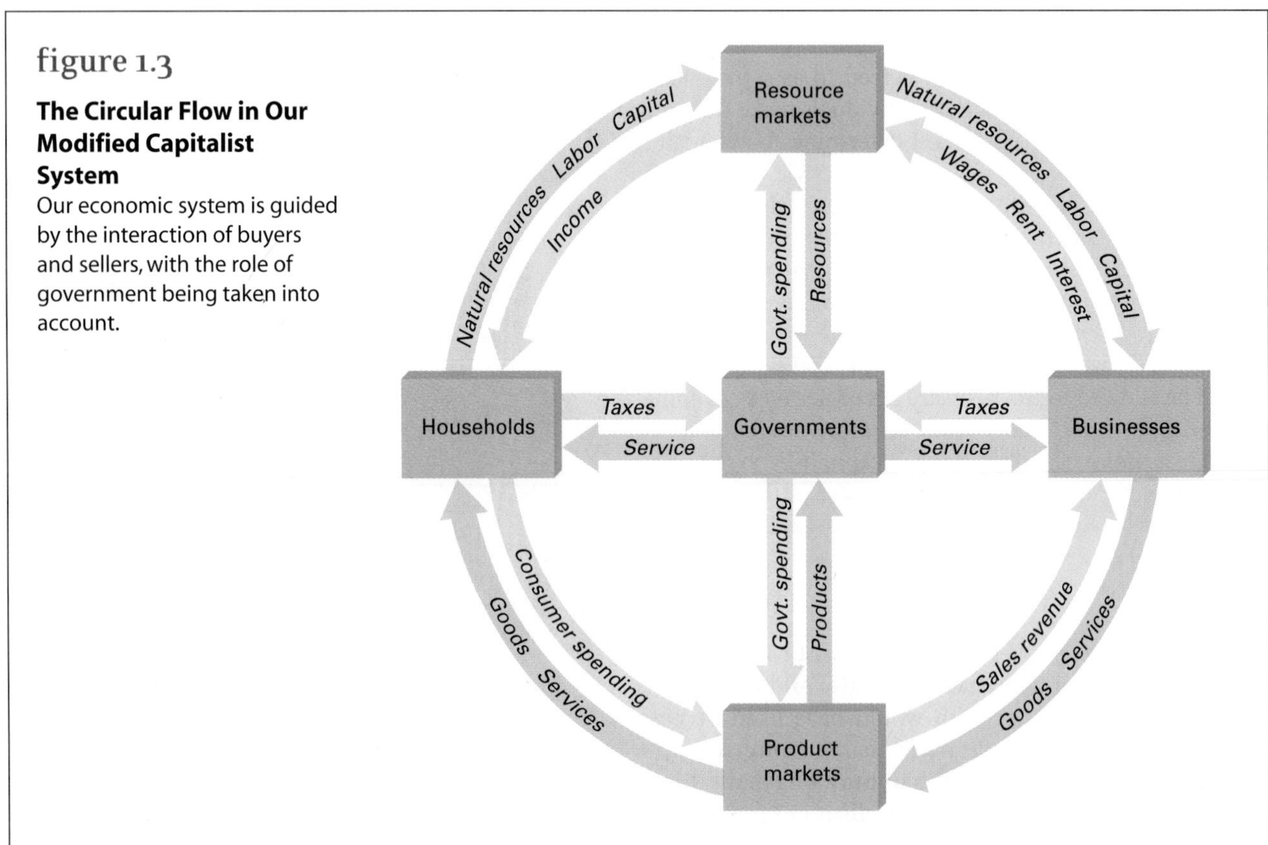

figure 1.3

The Circular Flow in Our Modified Capitalist System

Our economic system is guided by the interaction of buyers and sellers, with the role of government being taken into account.

When business profits are distributed to business owners, these profits become household income. (Business owners are, after all, members of households.) And, as we saw, household income is retained in the circular flow as either consumer spending or invested savings. So business profits, too, are retained in the business system, and the circular flow is complete. How, then, does government fit in?

spotLight

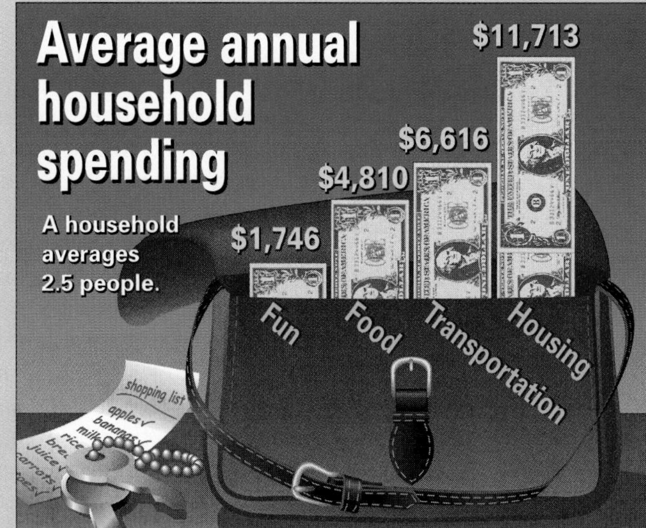

Source: Copyright 2000, USA TODAY. Reprinted with permission.

Governments The framers of our Constitution desired as little government interference with business as possible. At the same time, the Preamble to the Constitution sets forth the responsibility of government to protect and promote the public welfare. Local, state, and federal governments discharge this responsibility through regulation and the provision of services. Government regulations of business are discussed in detail in various chapters of this book. The numerous services are important but either (1) would not be produced by private business firms or (2) would be produced only for those who could afford them. Typical services include national defense, police and fire protection, education, and construction of roads and highways. To pay for all these services, governments collect a variety of taxes from households (such as personal income taxes and sales taxes) and from businesses (corporate income taxes).

Figure 1.3 shows this exchange of taxes for government services. It also shows government spending of tax dollars for resources and products required to provide these services. In other words, governments, too, return their incomes to the business system through the resource and product markets.

Actually, with government included, our circular flow looks more like a combination of several flows. And in reality it is. The important point is that, together, the various flows make up a single unit—a complete economic system that effectively provides answers to the basic economic questions. Simply put, the system works.

Command Economies

Before we discuss how to measure a nation's economic performance, we look quickly at another economic system called a command economy. A **command economy** is an economic system in which the government decides what goods and services will be produced, how they will be produced, who gets available goods and services, and what prices will be charged. The answers to all four basic economic questions are determined, at least to some degree, through centralized government planning. Today, two types of economic systems—*socialism* and *communism*—serve as examples of command economies.

command economy an economic system in which the government decides what will be produced, how it will be produced, who gets what is produced, and the prices of what is produced

Socialism In a *socialist* economy, the key industries are owned and controlled by the government. Such industries usually include transportation, utilities, communications, banking, and industries producing important materials such as steel. Land, buildings, and raw materials may also be the property of the state in a socialist economy. Depending on the country, private ownership of smaller businesses is permitted to varying degrees. People usually may choose their own occupations, but many work in state-owned industries.

What to produce and how to produce it are determined in accordance with national goals, which are based on projected needs and the availability of resources—at least for government-owned industries. The distribution of goods and services—who gets what—is also controlled by the state to the extent that it controls rents and wages. Among the professed aims of socialist countries are the equitable distribution of income, the elimination of poverty, the distribution of social services (such as medical care) to all who need them, and elimination of the economic waste that supposedly accompanies capitalistic competition.

Britain, France, Sweden, and India are democratic countries whose economies include a very visible degree of socialism. Other, more authoritarian countries may actually have socialist economies; however, we tend to think of them as communist because of their almost total lack of freedom.

Communism If Adam Smith was the father of capitalism, Karl Marx was the father of communism. In his writings during the mid-nineteenth century, Marx advocated a classless society whose citizens together owned all economic resources. All workers would then contribute to this *communist* society according to their ability and would receive benefits according to their need.

Since the breakup of the Soviet Union and economic reforms in China and most of the eastern European countries, the best remaining examples of communism are North Korea and Cuba. Today these so-called communist economies seem to practice a strictly controlled kind of socialism. Almost all economic resources are owned by the government. The basic economic questions are answered through centralized state planning, which sets prices and wages as well. In this planning, the needs of the state generally outweigh the needs of individual citizens. Emphasis is placed on the production of goods the government needs rather than on the products that consumers might want, so there are frequent shortages of consumer goods. Workers have little choice of jobs, but special skills or talents seem to be rewarded with special privileges. Various groups of professionals (bureaucrats, university professors, and athletes, for example) fare much better than, say, factory workers.

LEARNING OBJECTIVE

4 Identify the ways to measure economic performance.

Measuring Economic Performance

productivity the average level of output per worker per hour

One way to measure a nation's economic performance is to assess its productivity. **Productivity** is the average level of output per worker per hour. An increase in productivity results in economic growth because a larger number of goods and services are produced by a given labor force. Although U.S. workers produce more than many workers in other countries, the rate of growth in productivity has declined in the United States and has been surpassed in recent years by workers in Japan and the United Kingdom. Productivity improvements are expected to improve dramatically as more economic activity is transferred onto the Internet, reducing costs for servicing customers and handling routine ordering functions between businesses. The resulting time and money savings allow businesses to increase their profits and turn their efforts to other business opportunities. We discuss productivity in detail in Chapter 9.

Economic Indicators

gross domestic product (GDP) the total dollar value of all goods and services produced by all people within the boundaries of a country during a one-year period

In addition to productivity, a measure called gross domestic product can be used to measure the economic well-being of a nation. **Gross domestic product (GDP)** is the total dollar value of all goods and services produced by all people within the boundaries of a country during a one-year period. For example, the value of automobiles produced by employees in both an American-owned General Motors plant and a Japanese-owned Toyota plant *in the United States* are both included in the GDP for the United States. The U.S. gross domestic product was $9,256.1 billion in 1999.[7]

inflation a general rise in the level of prices

The gross domestic product figure facilitates comparisons between the United States and other countries, since it is the standard used in international guidelines for economic accounting. It is also possible to compare the GDP for one nation over several different time periods. This comparison allows observers to determine the extent to which a nation is experiencing economic growth. To make accurate comparisons of the GDP for different years, we must adjust the dollar amounts for inflation. **Inflation** is a general rise in the level of prices. By using inflation-adjusted figures, we are able to measure the *real* gross domestic product for a nation. In effect, it is now possible to compare the products and services produced by a nation in constant dollars—dollars that will purchase the same amount of goods and services. Figure 1.4 depicts the GDP

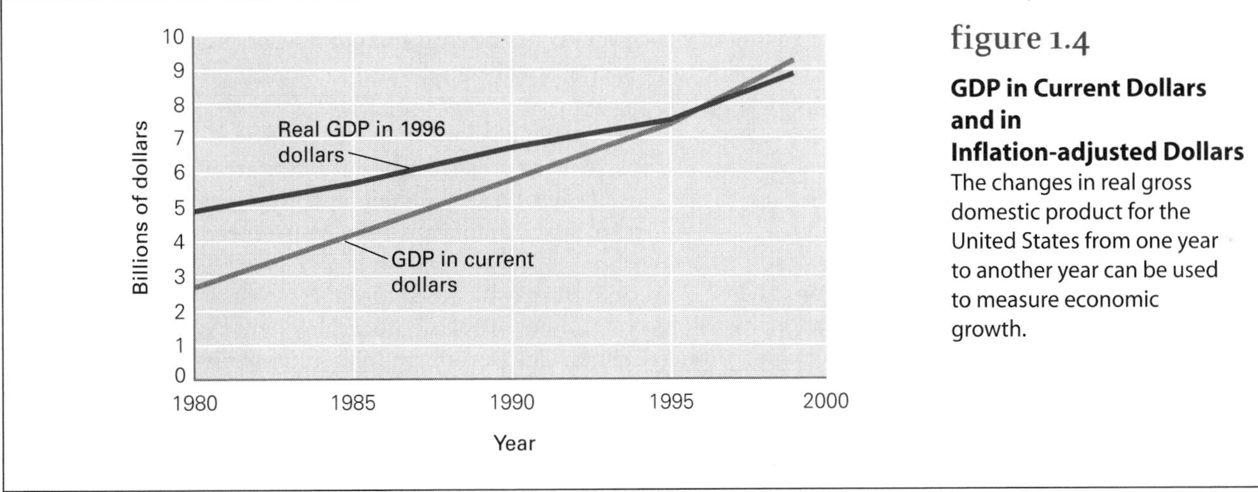

figure 1.4

GDP in Current Dollars and in Inflation-adjusted Dollars

The changes in real gross domestic product for the United States from one year to another year can be used to measure economic growth.

Source: U.S. Department of Commerce web site (www.doc.gov) on May 8, 2000.

of the United States in current dollars and the *real* GDP in inflation-adjusted dollars. Note that between 1980 and 1999, America's real GDP grew from $4,900.9 billion to $8,848.2 billion.

In addition to gross domestic product, there are other economic measures that can be used to evaluate a nation's economy. Although there are many economic measures, some of the more significant terms are described in Table 1.1. Like the GDP, these measures can be used to compare one economic statistic over different periods of time. For current statistical information about the government, you may want to access the U.S. Department of Commerce web site (www.doc.gov/).

The Business Cycle

A nation's economy fluctuates rather than grows at a steady pace every year. These fluctuations are generally referred to as the **business cycle,** that is, the recurrence of periods of growth and recession in a nation's economic activity. The changes that result

business cycle the recurrence of periods of growth and recession in a nation's economic activity

table 1.1 Common Measures Used to Evaluate a Nation's Economic Health

Economic Measure	Description
1. Balance of Trade	The total value of a nation's exports minus the total value of its imports over a specific period of time.
2. Consumer Price Index	A monthly index that measures the changes in prices of approximately three hundred goods and services purchased by a typical consumer.
3. Inflation Rate	An economic statistic that tracks the increase in prices of goods and services over a period of time. This measure is usually calculated on a monthly or annual basis.
4. Prime Interest Rate	The lowest interest rate that banks charge their most creditworthy customers.
5. Producer Price Index	A monthly index that measures prices at the wholesale level.
6. Productivity Rate	An economic measure that tracks the increase and decrease in the average level of output per worker.
7. Unemployment Rate	The percentage of a nation's labor force unemployed at any time.

from either growth or recession affect the amount of products and services that consumers are willing to purchase, and as a result the amount of products and services produced. Generally, the business cycle consists of four states: prosperity, recession, depression, and recovery.

During *prosperity,* unemployment is low and total income is relatively high. As long as the economic outlook remains prosperous, consumers are willing to buy products and services. In fact, businesses often expand and offer new products and services during prosperity in order to take advantage of the consumer's increased buying power.

recession two consecutive three-month periods of decline in a country's gross domestic product

Economists define a **recession** as two consecutive three-month periods of decline in a country's gross domestic product. Because unemployment rises during a recession, total buying power declines. The pessimism that accompanies a recession often stifles both consumer and business spending. As buying power decreases, consumers tend to become more value-conscious and reluctant to purchase frivolous items. In response to a recession, many businesses focus on the products and services that provide the most value to their customers.

depression a severe recession that lasts longer than a recession

monetary policies Federal Reserve's decisions that determine the size of the supply of money in the nation and the level of interest rates

fiscal policy government influence on the amount of savings and expenditures; accomplished by altering the tax structure and by changing the levels of government spending

Economists define a **depression** as a severe recession that lasts longer than a recession. A depression is characterized by extremely high unemployment rates, low wages, reduced purchasing power, lack of confidence in the economy, and a general decrease in business activity. To offset the effects of recession and depression, the federal government uses both monetary and fiscal policies. **Monetary policies** are the Federal Reserve's decisions that determine the size of the supply of money in the nation and the level of interest rates. Through **fiscal policy,** the government can influence the amount of savings and expenditures by altering the tax structure and changing the levels of government spending.

federal deficit a shortfall created when the federal government spends more in a fiscal year than it receives

national debt the total of all federal deficits

Although the federal government collects almost $2 trillion in annual revenues, the government spends more than it receives in most years, resulting in the **federal deficit.** Since 1980, there has been a federal deficit every year except 1998 and 1999. The total of all federal deficits is called the **national debt.** Today, the U.S. national debt is about $5.6 trillion or about $21,000 for every man, woman, and child in the United States.

Some experts believe that effective use of monetary and fiscal policies can speed up recovery and even eliminate depressions from the business cycle. *Recovery* is the movement of the economy from depression or recession to prosperity. High unemployment rates decline, income increases, and both the ability and the willingness to buy rise. Greater demand for products and services results.

Types of Competition

LEARNING OBJECTIVE

5 Outline the four types of competition.

Our free-market economic system ensures that businesses make the decisions about what to produce, how to produce it, and what price to charge for the product. Mattel Inc., for example, can introduce new versions of its famous Barbie doll, license the Barbie name, change the doll's price and method of distribution, and attempt to produce and market Barbie in other countries or over the Internet at www.mattel.com. Our system also allows customers the right to choose between Mattel's products and those produced by competitors.

competition rivalry among businesses for sales to potential customers

Competition like that between Mattel and other toy manufacturers is a necessary and extremely important by-product of a free-market economy. Because many individuals and groups can open businesses, there are usually a number of firms offering similar products. In other words, business firms must compete with each other for sales. Business **competition,** then, is essentially a rivalry among businesses for sales to potential customers. In a free-market economy, competition works to ensure the efficient operation of business. Competition also ensures that a firm will survive only if it serves its customers well. Economists recognize four different degrees of competition, ranging from ideal, complete competition to no competition at all. These are pure competition, monopolistic competition, oligopoly, and monopoly.

Pure Competition

Pure competition is the market situation in which there are many buyers and sellers of a product, and no single buyer or seller is powerful enough to affect the price of that product. Note that this definition includes several important ideas. First, we are discussing the market for a single product—say, bushels of wheat. Second, all sellers offer essentially the same product for sale; a buyer would be just as satisfied with seller A's wheat as with that offered by seller B or seller Z. Third, all buyers and sellers know everything there is to know about the market (including, in our example, the prices that all sellers are asking for their wheat). And fourth, the overall market is not affected by the actions of any one buyer or seller.

pure competition the market situation in which there are many buyers and sellers of a product, and no single buyer or seller is powerful enough to affect the price of that product

When pure competition exists, every seller should ask the same price that every other seller is asking. Why? Because if one seller wanted 50 cents more per bushel of wheat than all the others, that seller would not be able to sell a single bushel. Buyers could—and would—do better by purchasing wheat from the competition. On the other hand, a firm willing to sell below the going price would sell all its wheat quickly. But that seller would lose sales revenue (and profit), because buyers are actually willing to pay more.

In pure competition, then, sellers—and buyers as well—must accept the going price. But who or what determines this price? Actually, everyone does. The price of each product is determined by the actions of *all buyers and all sellers together,* through the forces of supply and demand.

The Basics of Supply and Demand

The **supply** of a particular product is the quantity of the product that *producers are willing to sell at each of various prices.* Producers are rational people, so we would expect them to offer more of a product for sale at higher prices and to offer less of the product at lower prices, as illustrated by the supply curve in Figure 1.5.

supply the quantity of a product that producers are willing to sell at each of various prices

The **demand** for a particular product is the quantity that *buyers are willing to purchase at each of various prices.* Buyers, too, are usually rational, so we would expect them—as a group—to buy more of a product when its price is low and to buy less of the product when its price is high, as depicted by the demand curve in Figure 1.5. This is exactly what happens when the price of wheat rises dramatically. People buy other grains or do without and reduce their purchases of wheat. They buy more wheat only when the price drops.

demand the quantity of a product that buyers are willing to purchase at each of various prices

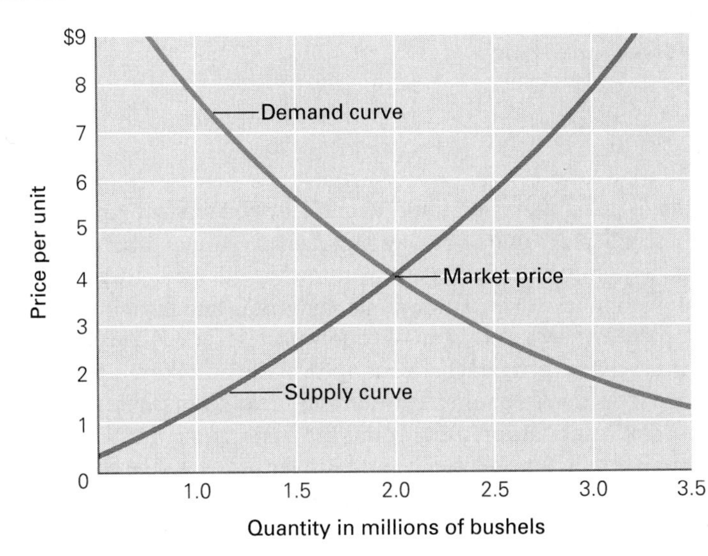

figure 1.5

Supply Curve and Demand Curve

The intersection of a supply curve and a demand curve indicates a single price and quantity at which suppliers will sell products and buyers will purchase them.

The Equilibrium, or Market, Price There is always one certain price at which the demanded quantity of a product is exactly equal to the produced quantity of that product. Suppose producers are willing to *supply* 2 million bushels of wheat at a price of $4 per bushel, and buyers are willing to *purchase* 2 million bushels at a price of $4 per bushel. In other words, supply and demand are in balance, or *in equilibrium,* at the price of $4. Economists call this price the market price. The **market price** of any product is the price at which the quantity demanded is exactly equal to the quantity supplied. If suppliers produce 2 million bushels, then no one who is willing to pay $4 per bushel will have to go without wheat, and no producer who is willing to sell at $4 per bushel will be stuck with unsold wheat.

market price the price at which the quantity demanded is exactly equal to the quantity supplied

In theory and in the real world, market prices are affected by anything that affects supply and demand. The *demand* for wheat, for example, might change if researchers suddenly discovered that it offered a previously unknown health benefit. Then buyers would demand more wheat at every price. Or, the *supply* of wheat might change if new technology permitted the production of greater quantities of wheat from the same amount of acreage. Other changes that can affect competitive prices are shifts in buyer tastes, the development of new products, fluctuations in income due to inflation or recession, or even changes in the weather that affect the production of wheat.

Pure competition is quite rare in today's world. Some specific markets (such as auctions of farm products) may come close, but no real market totally exhibits perfect competition. Many real markets, however, are examples of monopolistic competition.

Monopolistic Competition

monopolistic competition a market situation in which there are many buyers along with a relatively large number of sellers who differentiate their products from the products of competitors

Monopolistic competition is a market situation in which there are many buyers along with a relatively large number of sellers. The various products available in a monopolistically competitive market are very similar in nature, and they are all intended to satisfy the same need. However, each seller attempts to make its product different from the others by providing unique product features, an attention-getting brand name, unique packaging, or services such as free delivery or a "lifetime" warranty. For example, Hanes originally differentiated L'eggs pantyhose from numerous competing brands through unique branding and packaging.

product differentiation the process of developing and promoting differences between one's products and all similar products

Product differentiation is the process of developing and promoting differences between ones products and all similar products. It is a fact of life for the producers of many consumer goods, from soaps to clothing to personal computers. An individual producer like Hanes sees what looks like a mob of competitors, all trying to chip away at its market. By differentiating each of its products from all similar products, the producer obtains some limited control over the market price of its product. Under pure competition, the price of all pantyhose brands would simply be the market price of all similar pantyhose products.

Oligopoly

oligopoly a market situation (or industry) in which there are few sellers

An **oligopoly** is a market situation (or industry) in which there are few sellers. Generally these sellers are quite large, and sizable investments are required to enter into their market. For this reason, oligopolistic industries tend to remain oligopolistic. Examples of oligopolies are the automobile, car rental, and farm implement industries.

Because there are few sellers in an oligopoly, each seller has considerable control over price. At the same time, the market actions of each seller can have a strong effect on competitors' sales. If General Motors, for example, reduces its automobile prices, Ford, Chrysler, Toyota, and Nissan usually do the same to retain their market shares. As a result, similar products eventually have similar prices. In the absence of much price competition, product differentiation becomes the major competitive weapon; this is very evident in the advertising of the major auto manufacturers. For instance, when General

Motors began offering low-interest financing for all of its cars, Ford, Chrysler, and Toyota also launched competitive financing deals.

How do you spell monopoly? This is one word that Bill Gates and the folks at Microsoft know how to spell. Embroiled in multiple lawsuits and legal battles, Microsoft argues that it has become one of the most successful companies in the world because it operates in a capitalistic society that encourages business firms to pursue excellence. On the other hand, opponents argue that Microsoft is too successful and takes advantage of its monopoly position in the computer software industry.

Monopoly

A **monopoly** is a market (or industry) with only one seller. Because only one firm is the supplier of a product, it would seem that it has complete control over price. However, no firm can set its price at some astronomical figure just because there is no competition; the firm would soon find it had no customers or sales revenue, either. Instead, the firm in a monopoly position must consider the demand for its product and set the price at the most profitable level.

Classic examples of monopolies in the United States are public utilities. Each utility firm operates in a **natural monopoly,** an industry that requires a huge investment in capital and within which any duplication of facilities would be wasteful. Natural monopolies are permitted to exist because the public interest is best served by their existence, but they operate under the scrutiny and control of various state and federal agencies. While many public utilities are still classified as natural monopolies, there is increased competition in many industries. For example, the breakup of AT&T has increased the amount of competition in the telecommunications industry. And there have been increased demands for consumer choice when choosing a company that provides electrical service to both homes and businesses.

A legal monopoly—sometimes referred to as a *limited monopoly*—is created when the federal government issues a copyright, patent, and trademark. A copyright, patent, or trademark exists for a specific period of time and can be used to protect the owners of written materials, ideas, or product brands from unauthorized use by competitors that have not shared in the time, effort, and expense required for their development. Because Microsoft owns the copyright on its popular Windows software, it enjoys a limited monopoly position. Competitors cannot take the windows software, change the name, and sell it as their product without Microsoft's approval.

monopoly a market (or industry) with only one seller

natural monopoly an industry requiring huge investments in capital and within which duplication of facilities would be wasteful and thus not in the public interest

Except for natural monopolies and monopolies created by copyrights, patents, and trademarks, federal laws prohibit both monopolies and attempts to form monopolies. A recent amendment to the Sherman Antitrust Act of 1890 made any such attempt a criminal offense, and the Clayton Antitrust Act of 1914 prohibited a number of specific actions that could lead to monopoly. The goal of these and other antitrust laws is to ensure the competitive environment of business and thereby to protect consumers. Although both the Sherman and Clayton acts were enacted many years ago, they still provide a legal basis for encouraging competition and the possible breakup of a company that has a monopoly position. In fact, the Sherman act provided the legal basis for the recent court case involving the United States Department of Justice vs. Microsoft. Although Judge Thomas Penfield Jackson issued "findings of fact" stating Microsoft used its monopoly in personal computer (PC) operating systems to stifle competition to the detriment of consumers, Microsoft has responded through appeals to higher courts. Microsoft is likely to argue that it enjoys industry dominance because consumers choose their products voluntarily and that the court has no right to remove its proprietary right to continue selling its products that have contributed to American technological dominance in the PC field globally.[8]

The Development of American Business

LEARNING OBJECTIVE

6 Summarize the development of America's business system.

Our American business system developed together with the nation itself. Both have their roots in the knowledge, skills, and values that the earliest settlers brought to this country. Refer to Figure 1.6 for an overall view of the relationship between our history, the development of our business system, and some major inventions that influenced them both.

figure 1.6

Time Line of American Business
Notice that invention and innovation naturally led to changes in transportation. This trend in turn caused a shift to more of a manufacturing economy.

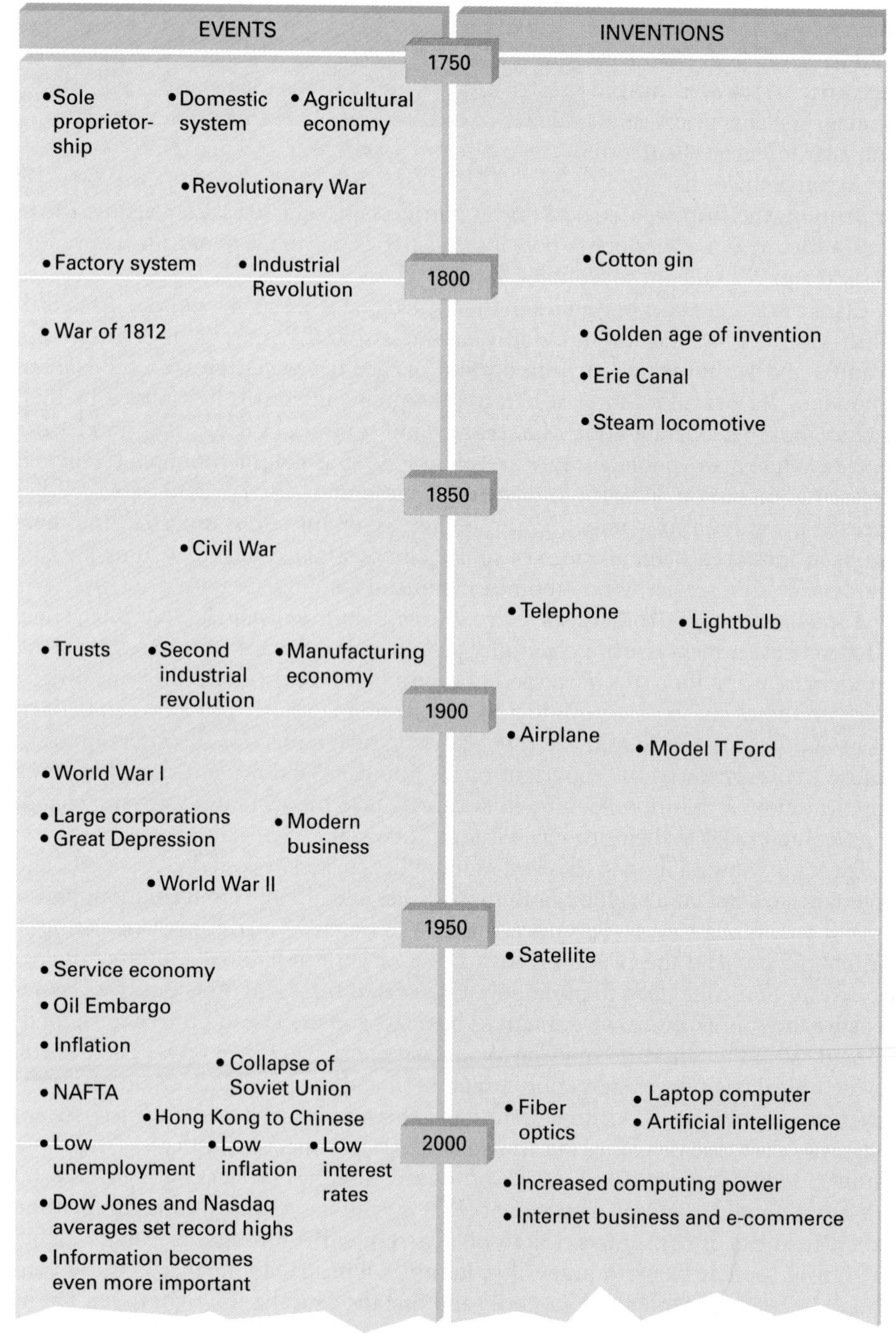

The Colonial Period

The first settlers in the New World were concerned mainly with providing themselves with basic necessities—food, clothing, and shelter. Almost all families lived on farms, and the entire family worked at the business of surviving.

The colonists did indeed survive, and eventually they were able to produce more than they consumed. They used their surplus for trading, mainly by barter, among themselves and with the English trading ships that called at the colonies. **Barter** is a system of exchange in which goods or services are traded directly for other goods and/or services—without using money. As this trade increased, small-scale business enterprises began to appear. Most of these businesses produced farm products. Other industries that had been founded by 1700 were shipbuilding, lumbering, fur trading, rum manufacturing, and fishing. International trade with England grew, but British trade policies heavily favored British merchants.

barter a system of exchange in which goods or services are traded directly for other goods and/or services—without using money

As late as the Revolutionary War period, 90 percent of the population were still living on farms and were engaged primarily in activities to meet their own needs. Some were able to use their skills and their excess time to work under the domestic system of production. The **domestic system** was a method of manufacturing in which an entrepreneur distributed raw materials to various homes, where families would process them into finished goods. The goods were then offered for sale by the merchant entrepreneur.

domestic system a method of manufacturing in which an entrepreneur distributed raw materials to various homes, where families would process them into finished goods to be offered for sale by the merchant entrepreneur

The Industrial Revolution

In 1790 a young English apprentice mechanic named Samuel Slater decided to sail to America. At this time, British law forbade the export of machinery, technology, and skilled workers. To get around the law, Slater painstakingly memorized the plans for Richard Arkwright's water-powered spinning machine, which had revolutionized the British textile industry, and left England disguised as a farmer. A year later, he set up a textile factory in Pawtucket, Rhode Island, to spin raw cotton into thread. Slater's ingenuity resulted in America's first use of the **factory system** of manufacturing, in which all the materials, machinery, and workers required to manufacture a product are assembled in one place. The Industrial Revolution in America was born.

factory system a system of manufacturing in which all the materials, machinery, and workers required to manufacture a product are assembled in one place

The invention of the cotton gin in 1793 by Eli Whitney greatly increased the supply of cotton for the textile industry. And by 1814 Francis Cabot Lowell had established a factory in Waltham, Massachusetts, to spin, weave, and bleach cotton, all under one roof. In doing so, Lowell seems to have used a manufacturing technique called specialization. **Specialization** is the separation of a manufacturing process into distinct tasks and the assignment of different tasks to different individuals. The purpose of specialization is to increase the efficiency of industrial workers; Lowell's workers were able to produce 30 miles of cloth each day.

specialization the separation of a manufacturing process into distinct tasks and the assignment of different tasks to different individuals

The three decades from 1820 to 1850 were the golden age of invention and innovation in machinery. Elias Howe's sewing machine became available to convert materials into clothing. The agricultural machinery of John Deere and Cyrus McCormick revolutionized farm production. At the same time, new means of transportation greatly expanded the domestic markets for American products. The Erie Canal was opened in the 1820s. Soon afterward, thanks to Robert Fulton's engine, steamboats could move upstream against the current and use the rivers as highways for hauling bulk goods. During the 1830s and 1840s, the railroads began to extend the existing transportation system to the West carrying goods and people much farther than was possible by waterways alone.

Many business historians view the period from 1870 to 1900 as the second industrial revolution; certainly, many characteristics of our modern business system took form during these three decades. In this period, for example, the nation shifted from a farm economy to a manufacturing economy. The developing coal and oil industries provided fuel for light, heat, and energy. During this time, the United States became not only an industrial giant but a leading world power as well.

Early Twentieth Century

Industrial growth and prosperity continued well into the twentieth century. Henry Ford's moving automotive assembly line, which brought the work to the worker, refined the concept of specialization and helped spur on the mass production of consumer goods. By the 1920s the automobile industry had begun to influence the entire economy. The steel industry, which supplies materials to the auto industry, grew along with it. The oil and chemical industries grew just as fast. And the emerging airplane and airline industries promised convenient and faster transportation.

Fundamental changes occurred in business ownership and management as well. The largest businesses were no longer owned by one individual; instead, ownership was in the hands of thousands of corporate shareholders who were willing to invest in—but not to operate—a business.

Certain modern marketing techniques are products of this era, too. Large corporations developed new methods of advertising and selling. Time payment plans made it possible for the average consumer to purchase costly durable goods such as automobiles, appliances, and home furnishings. Advertisements counseled the public to "buy now and pay later." Capitalism and our economy seemed strong and healthy, but it was not to last.

The Great Depression

The Roaring Twenties ended with the sudden crash of the stock market in 1929 and the near collapse of the economy. The Great Depression that followed in the 1930s was a time of misery and human suffering. The unemployment rate varied between 16 and 25 percent in the years 1931 through 1939, and the value of goods and services produced in America fell by almost half. People lost their faith in business and its ability to satisfy the needs of society without government interference.

After Franklin D. Roosevelt became president in 1933, the federal government devised a number of programs to get the economy moving again. In implementing these programs, the government got deeply involved in business for the first time. Many business people opposed this intervention, but they reluctantly accepted the new government regulations.

Recovery and Beyond

The economy was on the road to recovery when World War II broke out in Europe in 1939. The need for vast quantities of war materials—first for our allies and then for the American military as well—spurred business activity and technological development. This rapid economic pace continued after the war, and the 1950s and 1960s witnessed both increasing production and a rising standard of living. **Standard of living** is a loose, subjective measure of how well-off an individual or a society is, mainly in terms of want-satisfaction through goods and services.

standard of living a loose, subjective measure of how well-off an individual or a society is, mainly in terms of want-satisfaction through goods and services

The Late Twentieth Century

In the mid-1970s, however, a shortage of crude oil led to a new set of problems for business. As the cost of petroleum products increased, a corresponding increase took place in the cost of energy and the cost of goods and services. The result was inflation at a rate well over 10 percent per year during the early 1980s. Interest rates also increased dramatically, so both businesses and consumers reduced their borrowing. Business profits fell as the consumer's purchasing power was eroded by inflation and high interest rates. By the mid-1980s, many of these problem areas showed signs of improvement. Unfortunately, many managers now had something else to worry about—corporate mergers and takeovers. In addition, a large number of bank failures, coupled with an increasing number of bankruptcies, again made people uneasy about our business system.

By the 1990s, the U.S. economy began to show signs of improvement and economic growth. Unemployment numbers, inflation, and interest—all factors that affect business—were now at record lows. In turn, business took advantage of this economic prosperity to invest in information technology, cut costs, and increase flexibility and efficiency. (To see the excellent returns that investments in information technology have provided, read the Talking Technology boxed feature.) These changes in our economy have led some economists to believe that we now have a *New Economy* fueled by faster economic growth and increased demand for new products. If there exists a centerpiece of the New Economy, then the Internet is surely it. Initially created in America and now part of a globally connected telecommunications network of people and organizations around the world, the Internet is still dominated by American commercial interests including computer hardware, software, and Internet content providers. As further evidence of the financial health of the new economy, the stock market has enjoyed the longest period of sustained economic growth in our history. Both the Dow Jones Industrial Average and the Nasdaq Stock Index—two measures that investors use to measure stock market performance—have reached record highs. For individual

Talking Technology

Looking for a Good Investment? Try a Computer Industry

JUST SAY THE WORD *COMPUTERS* TO investors, and they sit up and take notice. When *Fortune* magazine released their report card on corporate America in the spring of 2000, three different computer industries were bunched at the very top when ranked on return to shareholders. Check out the numbers below–they're guaranteed to get your attention.

Fortune Ranking	Specific Industry	Return to Shareholders for One Year
1	Computer Peripherals	80.1 percent
3	Computer and Data Services	47.3 percent
6	Computers and Office Equipment	28.5 percent

In addition to the top industry rankings above, three major corporations that were leaders in the computers and office equipment industry were also among the top twenty corporations in the first *Fortune* 500 list of the twenty-first century. Let's look at this year's winners.

International Business Machines

Ranked Number 6 on *Fortune's* list of top twenty, IBM–sometimes referred to as Big Blue–markets over 40,000 products and is the world's largest computer firm. It is a major provider of technical support to business accounts. Today, IBM is promoting its networking products and has intensified sales of its stand-alone computer parts. Based in Armonk, New York, IBM has 291,000 employees with sales revenues of more than $87 million in 1999. Chairman and CEO Louis Gerstner, Jr., became head of IBM in 1993.

Hewlett-Packard Company

Ranked number 13 on *Fortune's* list of top twenty corporations, Hewlett-Packard is the world's second largest computer company and is based in Palo Alto, California. Today HP is re-creating itself as a speedy Internet specialist providing web servers, software, and services to corporate customers. With more than 29,000 products on the market, it had sales revenues that total nearly $50 million for 1999. It employs approximately 124,000 employees. Appointed by the board in 1999, Carleton S. "Carley" Florina is the first woman CEO and president of a top *Fortune* 500 Corporation–"not a bad way to start a new century."

Compaq Computer Corporation

Ranked number 20 on *Fortune's* list of top twenty corporations, Compaq is the third largest computer firm in the world. This Houston-based company has 71,000 employees and generated revenues of $38.5 million in 1999. It was the first company to introduce a computer based on Intel's 386 computer chip in 1986. Their laptop computer was an immediate success in 1988. Today, personal computers account for over half of its sales. Its primary head-to-head competitor is Dell Computer, and both companies are challenging each other for the top spot among PC makers. In 1999, Compaq chose Michael D. Capellas as president and CEO.

investors, it has been a bumpy ride at times, but the financial rewards have justified the added risk of investing in stocks and mutual funds. As we enter a new millennium, many of those same economists and investors are wondering how long it will last.

The New Millennium

Quick test! Answer the following questions:

1. Do you own a cell phone?
2. Do you own a computer or use a computer at work?
3. How much time do you spend surfing the Internet?

Three quick questions, but they serve as a crude measuring stick to determine the importance of information technology in the world today. As we begin the new millennium, information technology will continue to fuel the new economy. There will be more investment spending on information technology and Internet usage will increase at even faster rates. The importance of e-business—a topic that we will continue to explore throughout this text—will increase dramatically. In addition to information technology, the growth of service businesses and increasing opportunities for global trade will also impact the way American firms do business in the twenty-first century. Because they employ over half of the American work force, service businesses are a very important component of our economy. As a result, service businesses must find ways to improve productivity and cut costs while at the same time providing jobs for even a larger portion of the work force.

American businesses are beginning to realize that to be successful, they must enter the global marketplace. In short, American firms must meet the needs not only of American consumers but also of foreign consumers. And foreign firms are now selling record amounts of products and services to American consumers. Indeed, the world—as far as business is concerned—is becoming smaller. (Both our service economy and our place in the global marketplace are discussed more fully later in the text.)

The Challenges Ahead

LEARNING OBJECTIVE

7 Discuss the challenges that American businesses will encounter in the future.

There it is—the American business system in brief. When it works well, it provides jobs for those who are willing to work, a standard of living that few countries can match, and many opportunities for personal advancement. But, like every other system devised by humans, it is not perfect. Our business system may give us prosperity, but it also gave us the Great Depression of the 1930s and the economic problems of the 1970s and the late 1980s.

Obviously, the system can be improved. It may need no more than a bit of fine-tuning, or it may require more extensive overhauling. Certainly there are plenty of people who are willing to tell us exactly what *they* think the American economy needs. But these people provide us only with conflicting opinions. Who is right and who is wrong? Even the experts cannot agree.

The experts do agree, however, that several key issues will challenge our economic system over the next few decades. Some of the questions to be resolved:

- How much government involvement in our economy is necessary for its continued well-being? In what areas should there be less involvement? In what areas, more?
- How can we encourage economic growth and at the same time continue to conserve natural resources and protect our environment?

Today it seems that everyone is wired. One of the fastest growing segments of the economy is telecommunications. At this career fair, a human resource specialist for CellNet Data Systems talks with a job applicant about the qualities and skills necessary for success in high-tech companies.

- How can we meet the challenges of managing culturally diverse work forces to meet the needs of a culturally diverse marketplace?
- How can we evaluate the long-term economic costs and benefits of existing and proposed government programs?
- How can we hold down inflation and yet stimulate the economy to provide jobs?
- How can we preserve the benefits of competition in our American economic system?
- How can we meet the needs of the less fortunate?
- How can we make American manufacturers more productive and more competitive with foreign producers who have lower labor costs?
- How can we best market American-made products in foreign nations?
- How can we ensure that domestic business organizations will keep pace with the technological advancements of firms in other countries?
- How can we finance additional investment spending on information technology?
- How can we encourage an entrepreneurial spirit in large, established corporations?

The answers to these questions are anything but simple. In the past, Americans have always been able to solve their economic problems through ingenuity and creativity. Now, as we begin the twenty-first century, we need that same ingenuity and creativity not only to solve our current problems but also to compete in the global marketplace.

According to economic experts, if we as a nation can become more competitive, we may solve many of our current domestic problems. As an added bonus, increased competitiveness will also enable us to meet the economic challenges posed by other industrialized nations of the world. The way we solve these problems will affect our own future, our children's future, and that of our nation. Within the American economic and political system, the answers are ours to provide.

The American business system is not perfect by any means, but it does work reasonably well. We discuss some of its problems in Chapter 2, as we examine the role of business as part of American society.

RETURN TO Inside Business

ACCORDING TO MANAGEMENT EXPERTS, a business must do two things to be successful. First, it must put the customer first–by listening, understanding, and providing customer service. Second, a company–both its managers and employees–must act with speed and flexibility. The General Electric Company scores A+ on both counts. For the past four years, General Electric has received *Fortune* magazine's Most Admired Corporation Award because of its ability to see an opportunity and turn it into a product or service that its customers want.

What does the future hold for GE? Well, to begin with, the General Electric Company is not one to sit back and rest on past performance. Like most large firms, GE is concerned about sales and profits, but corporate management realizes that sales and profits will increase when a business meets customer needs. To that end, corporate management is always looking for ways to meet customer needs and at the same time perfect the methods it uses for generating ideas, planning, and product manufacturing. This huge corporate giant is on the lookout for ways to expand its core businesses. For example, one of GE's most aggressive growth initiatives is to develop methods for conducting e-business within its core businesses. Until the beginning of 1999, GE's use of the Internet was almost nonexistent. At that time, GE's chief executive officer, Jack Welch, and its board of directors decided that the company needed to use the Internet to attract new customers. General Electric's new e-business strategy not only attracted new customers, generating millions of dollars in sales revenue, it evolved into a system that enabled the company to offer innovative services to its existing customers. To see how America's Most Admired Corporation uses the Internet to meet customer needs and increase sales, go to www.ge.com.

Questions

1. Today General Electric is one of the largest and most respected firms in the world. What factors led to GE's success?
2. It would be easy for General Electric to sit back and rest on past performance. After all, it is the Most Admired Corporation in America and the darling of Wall Street. And yet, Jack Welch and other corporate managers want to maintain their position in a very competitive business world. What steps is General Electric taking to maintain their market leadership?

chapter Review

SUMMARY

1 Discuss your future in the world of business.

Opportunity! It's only eleven letters, but no other word provides a better description of our current business environment. And yet, employers and our capitalistic economic system are more demanding than ever before. As you begin this course, ask yourself: What can I do that will make employers want to pay me a salary? What skills do I have that employers need? By studying business, you can become a better-informed consumer and investor. By introducing you to a wide range of employment opportunities, a business course can also help you decide on a career. The kind of career you choose will ultimately depend on your own values and what you feel is most important in life. But deciding on the kind of career you want is only a first step. To get a job in your chosen field and to be successful at it, you will have to develop a plan, or road map, that ensures you have the skills and knowledge the job requires. A sound working knowledge of business can also enable you to start your own business.

2 Define *business* and identify potential risks and rewards.

Business is the organized effort of individuals to produce and sell, for a profit, the goods and services that satisfy society's needs. Four kinds of resources—material, human, financial, and informational—must be combined to start and operate a business. The three general types of businesses are manufacturers, service businesses, and marketing intermediaries. Profit is what remains after all business expenses are deducted from sales revenue. It is the payment that owners receive for assuming the risks of business—primarily the risks of not receiving payment and of losing whatever has been invested in the firm. Most often, a business that is operated to satisfy its customers earns a reasonable profit.

3 Describe the two types of economic systems: capitalism and command economy.

Economics is the study of how wealth is created and distributed. An economy is a system through which a society decides those two issues. An economic system must answer four questions: What goods and services will be produced? How will they be produced? For whom will they be produced? Who owns and who controls the major factors of production? Capitalism (on which our economic system is based) is an economic system in which individuals own and operate the majority of businesses that provide goods and services. Capitalism stems from the theories of Adam Smith. Smith's pure laissez-faire capitalism is an economic system in which these decisions are made by individuals and businesses as they pursue their own self-interest. In a laissez-faire capitalist system, the factors of production are owned by private entities, and all individuals are free to use their resources as they see fit; prices are determined by the workings of supply and demand in competitive markets; and the economic role of government is limited to protecting competition.

Our economic system today is a mixed economy. Although our present business system is essentially capitalist in nature, government takes part, along with households and businesses. In the circular flow (Figure 1.3) that characterizes our business system, households and businesses exchange resources for goods and services, using money as the medium of exchange. Government collects taxes from businesses and households and purchases products and resources with which to provide services.

In a command economy, government, rather than individuals, owns the factors of production and provides the answers to the three other economic questions. Socialist and communist economies are—at least in theory—command economies. In the real world, however, communists seem to practice a strictly controlled kind of socialism.

4 Identify the ways to measure economic performance.

One way to evaluate the performance of an economic system is to assess changes in productivity, which is the average level of output per worker per hour. Gross domestic product (GDP) can also be used to measure a nation's economic well being and is the total dollar value of all goods and services produced by all people within the boundaries of a country during a one-year period. This figure facilitates comparisons between the United States and other countries, since it is the standard used in international guidelines for economic accounting. It is also possible to adjust GDP for inflation and thus to measure real GDP. In addition to gross domestic product, there are other economic indicators that can be used to measure a nation's economy. These include a nation's balance of trade, consumer price index, inflation rate, prime interest rate, producer price index, productivity rate, and unemployment rate.

A nation's economy fluctuates rather than grows at a steady pace every year. These fluctuations are generally referred to as the business cycle. Generally, the business cycle consists of four states: prosperity, recession, depression, and recovery. Some experts believe that effective use of monetary policy (the Federal Reserve's decisions that determine the size of the supply of money) and fiscal policies (the government's influence on the amount of savings and expenditures) can speed up recovery and even eliminate depressions for the business cycle.

5 Outline the four types of competition.

Competition is essentially a rivalry among businesses for sales to potential customers. In a free-market economy, competition works to ensure the efficient and effective operation of business. Competition also ensures that a firm will survive only if it serves its customers well. Economists recognize four degrees of competition. Ranging from most to least competitive, the four degrees are pure competition, monopolistic competition, oligopoly, and monopoly. The factors of supply and demand generally influence the price that consumers pay producers for goods and services.

6 Summarize the development of America's business system.

Since its beginnings in the seventeenth century, American business has been based on private ownership of property and freedom of enterprise. And from this beginning, through the Industrial Revolution of the early nineteenth century, to the phenomenal expansion of American industry in the nineteenth and early twentieth centuries, our government maintained an essentially laissez-faire attitude toward business. However, during the Great Depression of the 1930s, the federal government began to provide a number of social services to its citizens. Government's role in business has expanded considerably since that time.

During the 1970s a shortage of crude oil led to higher prices and inflation. Business profits fell as the consumer's purchasing power was eroded by inflation and high interest rates. By the mid-1980s, corporate mergers and takeovers, bank failures, and an increasing number of bankruptcies made people uneasy about our business system. By the 1990s, the U.S. economy began to show signs of improvement and economic growth. Unemployment numbers, inflation, and interest—all factors that affect business—were now at record lows. Fueled by investment in information technology, the stock market enjoyed the longest period of sustained economic growth in our history. As we enter the new millennium, information technology will continue to fuel a new economy. Increased use of the Internet and e-business are now changing the way that firms do business in the twenty-first century. Other factors that affect the way firms do business include the increasing importance of services and global trade.

7 Discuss the challenges that American businesses will encounter in the future.

Today, American businesses face a number of significant challenges. Among the issues to be contended with are the level of government involvement in business; the extent of business's environmental and social responsibilities; the effective management of cultural diversity in the workplace; the problem of holding down inflation while stimulating the economy; competition with foreign producers; technological innovation; and the problem of encouraging the entrepreneurial spirit in large, established corporations. If we as a nation can become more competitive, we may solve many of our domestic economic problems. As an added bonus, increased competitiveness will enable us to meet the challenges posed by foreign nations.

KEY TERMS

You should now be able to define and give an example relevant to each of the following terms:

free enterprise (4)
e-business (7)
business (9)
consumers (10)
profit (11)
economics (11)
economy (11)
factors of production (11)
entrepreneur (13)
capitalism (13)
market economy (13)
mixed economy (13)
consumer products (14)
command economy (15)
productivity (16)
gross domestic product (GDP) (16)
inflation (16)
business cycle (17)
recession (18)
depression (18)
monetary policies (18)
fiscal policy (18)
federal deficit (18)
national debt (18)
competition (18)
pure competition (19)
supply (19)
demand (19)
market price (20)
monopolistic competition (20)
product differentiation (20)
oligopoly (20)
monopoly (21)
natural monopoly (21)
barter (23)
domestic system (23)
factory system (23)
specialization (23)
standard of living (24)

REVIEW QUESTIONS

1. What reasons would you give if you were advising someone to study business?
2. What factors affect a person's choice of careers?
3. Describe the four resources that must be combined to organize and operate a business. How do they differ from the economist's factors of production?
4. What distinguishes consumers from other buyers of goods and services?
5. Describe the relationship among profit, business risk, and the satisfaction of customers' needs.
6. What are the four basic economic questions? How are they answered in a capitalist economy?
7. Describe the four fundamental issues required for a laissez-faire capitalist economy.
8. Why is the American economy called a mixed economy?
9. Based on Figure 1.3, outline the economic interactions between government and business in our business system. Outline those between government and households.
10. How does capitalism differ from socialism and communism?
11. Define gross domestic product. Why is this economic measure significant?
12. Choose three of the economic measures described in Table 1.1 and describe why these indicators are important when measuring a nation's economy.
13. Identify and compare the four forms of competition.
14. Explain how the equilibrium, or market price, of a product is determined.
15. Trace the steps that led from farming for survival in the American colonial period to today's mass production.

16. What do you consider the most important challenges that will face people in the United States in the years ahead?

DISCUSSION QUESTIONS

1. What factors caused American business to develop into a mixed economic system rather than some other type of system?
2. Does an individual consumer really have a voice in answering the basic economic questions?
3. Is gross domestic product a reliable indicator of a nation's standard of living? What might be a better indicator?
4. Discuss this statement: "Business competition encourages efficiency of production and leads to improved product quality."
5. In our business system, how is government involved in answering the four basic economic questions? Does government participate in the system or interfere with it?

VIDEO CASE

Motorola's Total Commitment to Employees

Because everyone wants to find the "perfect" position, choosing a career can be a traumatic experience, to say the least. Many job applicants express concern about being hired to work in dead-end positions with no potential. They worry that employers may be more concerned about finding someone willing to work for low wages than about helping employees grow professionally. If you have had similar concerns, take heart: some firms do value employees and the contributions they make to their operations. One such firm is Motorola. A leading provider of wireless communications, semiconductors, and advanced electronic systems, Motorola credits its employees with making it the largest producer of cellular phones, pagers, and mobile radios in the world.

How important are employees to Motorola's success? According to Robert Galvin, the chairman of Motorola's executive committee, people are the firm's most important asset. Given this attitude, it is not surprising that very few employees leave Motorola until they reach retirement age. The firm was one of the first major corporations to offer a cafeteria for employees, and its profit-sharing plan has served as a model for other companies. But there is something more to Motorola's ability to retain people beyond its above-average compensation, medical benefits, and company-sponsored day-care centers. The secret to attracting and keeping some of the best people in the industry is Motorola's commitment to making people the most effective employees they can be.

For Motorola, the employment process begins with recruiting people who have the emotional, psychological, and physical skills the organization needs. But recruiters also look for employees who can think creatively and who can use their mental agility in decision making. Once hired, employees are not just encouraged to develop professionally to reach their career potential; they are expected to do so. All employees are required to take at least five days of training each year. Workers who do poorly on reading and mathematics tests enroll in remedial classes. Manufacturing workers attend classes in quality control, idea sharing, and teamwork. And all employees can take courses in product design, risk taking, and managing change. In short, Motorola is willing to invest both time and money to provide its employees with state-of-the-art training programs.

Although Motorola—or for that matter any organization—may use financial, material, or informational resources to accomplish its goals, people are the ones who get the job done. As Robert Galvin points out, people in an organization like Motorola have one fundamental purpose, and that is to provide total customer satisfaction. The ability to provide total customer satisfaction, which depends on Motorola's most important asset—its dedicated employees—is what has enabled Motorola to maintain its leadership position in the very competitive electronics industry.[9]

Questions

1. To be successful, most businesses use material, financial, human, and informational resources. Robert Galvin, chairman of Motorola's executive committee, has said that people are his firm's most important asset. Do you think human resources are really that important?
2. Motorola's state-of-the-art training programs cost the company both time and money. As a stockholder in this corporation, would you feel this is a good use of corporate assets? Why or why not?
3. Motorola's recruiters look for people who can think creatively and use their mental agility in decision making. In your own words, describe what you think "creative thinking" and "mental agility" mean. Why would these traits be important to a firm like Motorola?
4. Once hired, Motorola's employees are not just encouraged to develop professionally to reach their career potential; they are expected to do so. Would you want to work for a company like Motorola? Explain your answer.

Building skills for career success

1. Exploring the Internet

The World Wide Web, or web, is a global network of corporate, government, institutional, and individual computers accessible to users who can connect to its grid. Your school or firm is most likely connected to the Web, or you may have private access through a commercial service provider like America Online.

To familiarize you with the wealth of information available through the Internet and its usefulness to business students, this exercise focuses on information services available from a few popular "search engines" used to explore the web. Each of the remaining chapters in the text also contains an Internet exercise that is in some way associated with the topics covered in the chapter. After completing these exercises, you will not only be familiar with a variety of sources of business information, you will also be better prepared to locate information you might need in the future.

To use one of these search engines, enter its "Internet address" in your web browser or choose from a list of search engines that may be posted on your school's startup screen. Ask your teacher or technician for help if you have any trouble. The addresses of some search engines are as follows:

http://www.altavista.com
http://www.yahoo.com
http://www.lycos.com

Visit the text web site for updates to this exercise.

Assignment

1. Examine the way in which two search engines present categories of information on their opening screens. Explore the articles in the business and economics categories. Which search engine was better to use, in your opinion? Why?
2. Think of a business topic you would like to know more about; for example, "gross domestic product" or another concept introduced in this chapter. Using your preferred search engine, explore a few articles and reports provided on your topic. Briefly summarize your findings.

2. Developing Critical Thinking Skills

Under capitalism, competition is a driving force that allows the market economy to work, affecting the supply of goods and services in the marketplace and the prices consumers pay for those goods and services. Have you thought about how competition has a daily impact on your life and your buying habits? Let's see how competition works by pretending you want to buy a new car.

Assignment

1. Brainstorm the following questions:
   a. How will you decide on the make and model of car you want to buy, where to buy the car, and how to finance it?
   b. How is competition at work in this scenario?
   c. What are the pros and cons of competition as it affects the buyer?
2. Record your ideas.
3. Write a summary of the key points you learned about how competition works in the marketplace.

3. Building Team Skills

Over the past few years, employees have been expected to function as productive team members instead of working alone. People often believe they can work effectively in teams, but this is not always true. Being an effective team member requires skills that encourage other members to participate in the team endeavor. College classes that function as teams are more interesting and more fun to attend, and students generally learn more about the topics in the course. If your class is to function as a team, it is important to begin building the team early in the semester. One way to begin creating a team is to learn something about each student in the class. This helps team members feel comfortable with each other and fosters a sense of trust.

Assignment

1. Find a partner, preferably someone you do *not* know.
2. Each partner has five minutes to answer the following questions:
   a. What is your name and where do you work?
   b. What interesting or unusual thing have you done in your life? (Do not talk about work; rather, focus on things like hobbies, travel, family, and sports.)
   c. Why are you taking this course and what do you expect to learn? (Satisfying a degree requirement is not an acceptable answer.)
3. Introduce your partner to the class. Use one to two minutes, depending on the size of the class.

4. Researching Different Careers

In this chapter, *entrepreneurship* is defined as the willingness to take risks and the knowledge and ability to use the other factors of production efficiently. An *entrepreneur* is a person who risks his or her time, effort, and money to start and operate a business. Often people believe these terms apply only to small business operations, but recently employees with entrepreneurial attitudes have advanced more rapidly in large companies.

Assignment

1. Go to the local library or use the Internet to research how large firms, especially corporations, are rewarding employees who have entrepreneurial skills.
2. Find answers to the following questions:
   a. Why is an entrepreneurial attitude important in corporations today?
   b. What makes an employee with an entrepreneurial orientation different from other employees?
   c. How are these employees being rewarded, and are the rewards worth the effort?
3. Write a two-page report that summarizes your findings.

5. Improving Communication Skills

Most jobs today require good writing skills. Written communications in the workplace range from the simple task of jotting down telephone messages to the more complex tasks of writing memos, newspaper articles, policy manuals, and technical journals. Regardless of the type of communication, the writer must convey the correct information to the reader in a clear, concise, and courteous manner. This involves using effective writing skills, which can be improved through practice. You can begin improving your skills by writing in a journal on a regular basis.

Assignment

1. Each week during the semester, write your thoughts and ideas in a journal. Include business terms you learned during the week and give an example of how each term is used in the business world. Also, do one of the following:
   a. Ask someone, preferably a person working in business, a question based on a topic in the class assignment for the week. Record the answers, and comment on your perceptions about the topic.
   b. Read a newspaper article relating to a topic covered in the class assignment for the week. Summarize your thoughts on the topic in your journal, specifically discussing what you learned.
2. Ask your instructor for guidelines and due dates for the completed journal and the summary you will prepare at the end of the semester.

Being Ethical and Socially Responsible

2

LEARNING OBJECTIVES

1 Understand what is meant by *business ethics*.

2 Identify the types of ethical concerns that arise in the business world.

3 Discuss the factors that affect the level of ethical behavior in organizations.

4 Explain how ethical decision making can be encouraged.

5 Describe how our current views on the social responsibility of business have evolved.

6 Explain the two views on the social responsibility of business and understand the arguments for and against increased social responsibility.

7 Discuss the factors that led to the consumer movement and list some of its results.

8 Analyze how present employment practices are being used to counteract past abuses.

9 Describe the major types of pollution, their causes, and their cures.

10 Identify the steps a business must take to implement a program of social responsibility.

It's not easy to set one standard that applies everywhere.

Doing What's Legal and What's Right at Texas Instruments

More countries, more ethical questions. That was the challenge Texas Instruments (TI) faced as it expanded from its Texas headquarters to acquire companies and open operations in more than two dozen nations. A leading manufacturer of sophisticated computer chips and industrial control equipment, Texas Instruments (http://www.ti.com) had forty thousand plus employees in offices and factories stretched across four continents. Even as global sales pushed TI's revenues toward $10 billion, top management worried about maintaining universally high ethical standards while staying on the right side of local laws and customs. Carl Skooglund, TI's former vice president and director of ethics, observed that "it's not easy to set one standard that applies everywhere. We are facing a variety of issues that we really never had to think about before and a large part of the company's continued success in the global market depends on how we come to grips with these issues."

Still, TI wasn't starting from scratch in handling ethical issues. The company had published its first ethics booklet in 1961 and issued periodic updates as government regulations and business practices changed. However, as TI became involved with an ever-larger international network of suppliers, partners, competitors, distributors, customers, and mergers, employees at all levels were increasingly dealing with more complex ethical problems. Despite TI's traditional reliance on employee empowerment, management found that employees needed and wanted more support in handling ethical questions.

So TI created an Ethics Office, consisting of five senior corporate managers, to monitor and approve company-wide ethics plans, compliance, and disciplinary actions. TI's Ethics Director, reporting to the Ethics Office, was appointed to see that company policies and procedures stayed in line with high ethical standards. These policies and procedures covered various situations where ethical questions arise, including conflicts of interest, purchasing, and gifts. The company also launched a training program, "Decision Making in the New TI," to reinforce the vital role of corporate ethics and values in every business activity.

Even with the written code of ethics and training, TI realized that employees would sometimes be confronted with tough ethical problems that had to be resolved *quickly*. That's why the firm created the "TI Ethics Quick Test," seven principles printed on a convenient pocket-size card that employees could review whenever they needed to: (1) Is the action legal? (2) Does it comply with our values? (3) If you do it, will you feel bad? (4) How will it look in the newspaper? (5) If you know it's wrong, don't do it! (6) If you're not sure, ask. (7) Keep asking until you get an answer.

By reaffirming its long-time commitment to ethics and integrity throughout periods of global expansion and acquisitions, TI has earned stakeholder trust—and successfully boosted sales and profits within a dynamic and often uncertain business environment.[1]

Obviously, organizations like Texas Instruments want to be recognized as responsible corporate citizens. Such companies recognize the need to harmonize their operations with environmental demands and other vital social concerns. Not all firms, however, have taken steps to encourage a consideration of social responsibility and ethics in their decisions and day-to-day activities. Some managers still regard such business practices as a poor investment, in which the cost is not worth the return. Other managers—indeed, most managers—view the cost of these practices as a necessary business expense, similar to wages or rent.

Most managers today, like those at TI, are finding ways of balancing a growing agenda of socially responsible activities with the drive to generate profits. This also happens to be a good way for a company to demonstrate its values and to attract like-minded employees, customers, and stockholders. In a highly competitive business environment, an increasing number of companies are, like TI, seeking to set themselves apart by developing a reputation for ethical and socially responsible behavior.

We begin this chapter by defining *business ethics* and examining ethical issues. Next we look at the standards of behavior in organizations and how ethical behavior can be encouraged. We then turn to the topic of social responsibility. We compare and contrast two present-day models of social responsibility and present arguments for and against increasing the social responsibility of business. After that, we examine the major elements of the consumer movement. We discuss how social responsibility in business has affected employment practices amd environmental concerns. Finally, we consider the commitment, planning, and funding that go into a firm's program of social responsibility.

Business Ethics Defined

LEARNING OBJECTIVE

1 Understand what is meant by *business ethics*.

Ethics is the study of right and wrong and of the morality of the choices individuals make. An ethical decision or action is one that is "right" according to some standard of behavior. **Business ethics** is the application of moral standards to business situations. Recent court cases involving unethical behavior have helped make business ethics a matter of public concern. In one such case, Copley Pharmaceutical, Inc., pled guilty to federal criminal charges (and paid a $10.65 million fine) for falsifying drug manufacturers' reports to the Food and Drug Administration. In another much-publicized case, lawsuits against tobacco companies have led to $246 billion in settlements, although there has been only one class-action lawsuit filed on behalf of ill smokers. That case, Engle vs. R J Reynolds, could cost tobacco companies an estimated $500 billion. In another similar effort, 28 cities and counties brought class-action suits against gun manufacturers in 1999. The suits seek to recover governments' expenses related to police protection, emergency services, and enforcement of local gun-control ordinances. Housing authorities around the country also are planning to file class-action suits against gun-makers, holding them liable for unnecessary and preventable handgun violence.[2]

ethics the study of right and wrong and of the morality of the choices individuals make

business ethics the application of moral standards to business situations

Ethical Issues

LEARNING OBJECTIVE

2 Identify the types of ethical concerns that arise in the business world.

Ethical issues often arise out of a business's relationship with investors, customers, employees, creditors, or competitors. Each of these groups has specific concerns and usually exerts pressure on the organization's managers. For example, investors want management to make sensible financial decisions that will boost sales, profits, and returns on their investments. Customers expect a firm's products to be safe, reliable, and reasonably priced. Employees demand to be treated fairly in hiring, promotion, and compensation decisions. Creditors require accounts to be paid on time and the accounting information furnished by the firm to be accurate. Competitors expect the firm's competitive practices to be fair and honest.

Guns, violence, and accountability. Federal, state, and local law enforcement authorities across the country are trying to make the gun industry more responsible. Here, Andrew Cuomo, Secretary of Housing and Urban Development, speaks to the press after a HUD meeting about taking legal action against gun manufacturers. The firearm manufacturers must design safer childproof guns, increase firearm safety, and pay compensatory and punitive damages caused by gun violence or face new national lawsuits.

Businesspeople face ethical issues every day, and some of these issues can be difficult to assess. Although some types of issues arise infrequently, others occur regularly. Let's take a closer look at several ethical issues.

Fairness and Honesty

Fairness and honesty in business are two important ethical concerns. Besides obeying all laws and regulations, businesspersons are expected to refrain from knowingly deceiving, misrepresenting, or intimidating others. The consequences of failing to do so can be expensive. Recently, for example, the German automobile firm of Bayerische Motoren Werke AG (BMW) received a court order to pay $2 million to a U.S. buyer because it had failed to inform him that his car paint had been damaged and retouched. Testimony showed that about one thousand other Americans had also unknowingly bought touched-up BMWs.[3]

In another case, Prudential Insurance Company agreed to pay a record fine of $35 million for misleading sales practices. This settlement followed a series of accusations of fraud and misrepresentation that have plagued the company for a decade.[4]

Organizational Relationships

A businessperson may be tempted to place his or her personal welfare above the welfare of others or the welfare of the organization. Relationships with customers and coworkers often create ethical problems. Unethical behavior in these areas includes taking credit for others' ideas or work, not meeting one's commitments in a mutual agreement, and pressuring others to behave unethically.

Conflict of Interest

Conflict of interest results when a businessperson takes advantage of a situation for his or her own personal interest rather than for the employer's interest. Such conflict may occur when payments and gifts make their way into business deals. A wise rule to remember is that anything given to a person that might unfairly influence that person's business decision is a bribe, and all bribes are unethical.

For example, Nortel Networks Corporation does not permit its employees, officers, and directors to accept any gifts, or to serve as directors or officers of any organization which might supply goods or services to Nortel Networks. However, Nortel employees may work part-time with firms that are not competitors, suppliers, or customers.

Communications

Business communications, especially advertising, can present ethical questions. False and misleading advertising is illegal and unethical, and it can infuriate customers. Sponsors of advertisements aimed at children must be especially careful to avoid misleading messages. Advertisers of health-related products must also take precautions to guard against deception when using such descriptive terms as "low fat," "fat free," and "light." In fact the Federal Trade Commission has issued guidelines on the use of these labels.

Factors Affecting Ethical Behavior

LEARNING OBJECTIVE

3 Discuss the factors that affect the level of ethical behavior in organizations.

Is it possible for an individual with strong moral values to make ethically questionable decisions in a business setting? What factors affect a person's inclination to make either ethical or unethical decisions in a business organization? Although the answers to these questions are not entirely clear, three general sets of factors do appear to influence the standards of behavior in an organization. As shown in Figure 2.1, the sets consist of individual factors, social factors, and opportunity.

Several individual factors influence the level of ethical behavior in an organization. How much an individual knows about an issue is one factor: a decision maker with a greater amount of knowledge regarding a situation may take steps to avoid ethical problems, whereas a less-informed person may unknowingly take action that leads to an ethical quagmire. An individual's moral values and central, value-related attitudes also clearly influence his or her business behavior. Most people join organizations to accomplish personal goals. The types of personal goals an individual aspires to and the manner in which these goals are pursued have a significant impact on that individual's behavior in an organization.

A person's behavior in the workplace is, to some degree, determined by cultural norms, and these social factors vary from one culture to another. For example, in some countries it is acceptable and ethical for customs agents to receive gratuities for performing ordinary, legal tasks that are a part of their jobs, whereas in other countries these practices would be viewed as unethical and perhaps illegal. The actions and decisions of coworkers is another social factor believed to shape a person's sense of business ethics. For example, if your coworkers make long-distance telephone calls on company time and at company expense, you might view that behavior as acceptable and ethical because everyone does it. The moral values and attitudes of "significant others"—spouses, friends, and relatives, for instance—can also affect an employee's perception of what is ethical and unethical behavior in the workplace. Even the Internet presents new challenges for firms whose employees enjoy easy access to sites through convenient high-speed connections at work. An employee's behavior online can be viewed as offensive to coworkers and possibly lead to lawsuits against the firm, if employees conduct unethical behavior on controversial web sites not related to their job. As a result, research by Websense and the Center for Internet Studies reveal that nearly two out of three companies nationwide have disciplined employees, and nearly one out of three have fired employees for Internet misuse in the workplace.[5]

Opportunity refers to the amount of freedom an organization gives an employee to behave unethically if he or she makes that choice. In some organizations, certain company policies and procedures reduce the opportunity to be unethical. For example, at some fast-food restaurants, one employee takes your order and receives your payment and another fills the order. This procedure reduces the opportunity to be unethical because the person handling the money is not dispensing the product, and the person giving out the product is not handling the money. The existence of an ethical code and the importance management places on this code are other determinants of opportunity (codes of ethics are discussed in more detail in the next section). The

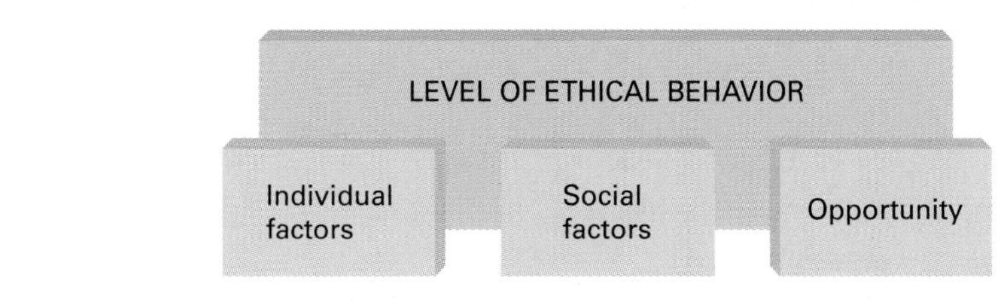

figure 2.1

Factors That Affect the Level of Ethical Behavior in an Organization

Source: Based on O. C. Ferrell and Larry Gresham, "A Contingency Framework for Understanding Ethical Decision Making in Marketing," *Journal of Marketing*, summer 1985, p. 89.

Going Global

Business Ethics Around the World

When U.S. companies cross national borders to buy or sell, they quickly discover that local ethical and legal standards governing payoffs, pollution, and human rights can be oceans apart from U.S. standards. Remaining competitive while sidestepping ethical and legal problems is a major challenge—especially in the Internet age, when media reports of violations can reach investors and other stakeholders throughout the world in a matter of minutes.

Bribery and Corruption

In some countries, government officials, suppliers, and distributors routinely seek payoffs in exchange for completing transactions. However, under the Foreign Corrupt Practices Act, U.S. companies operating abroad cannot legally pay bribes, although they can make small payments under certain conditions. Even as more countries crack down on payoffs, Motorola and a few other U.S. businesses are using software to analyze invoices and payments and spot possible payoffs. Gifts from suppliers to U.S. companies are also a problem. Here's how United Technologies handles gifts: "Every year we write to vendors, saying that we don't want gifts, we want good service," says United Technologies' head ethics officer.

Pollution

Environmental controls in many countries are far less stringent than in the United States. Should U.S. companies comply with local environmental standards rather than applying the stronger U.S. standards? BP Amoco, like a growing number of global giants, has set minimum environmental-protection standards for all its operations, regardless of location. Still, maintaining these standards in every country can be difficult—especially when joint venture partners are involved. Rather than withdraw from global joint ventures, as some firms have done, BP Amoco is continuing to work with partners to improve compliance with standards.

Human Rights

U.S. positions on labor issues and other human rights issues often differ from the accepted positions in other countries—leaving U.S. companies caught in the middle. Nike, for example, has been criticized for tolerating low wages in some overseas factories that make its shoes and apparel. The company finally forced its Indonesian suppliers to raise wages, with Nike absorbing much of the increase. "They are independent businesses, but we take responsibility," says Dusty Kidd, Nike's director of labor practices.

degree of enforcement of company policies, procedures, and ethical codes is a major force affecting opportunity. When violations are dealt with consistently and firmly, the opportunity to be unethical is reduced.

Now that we have considered some of the factors believed to influence the level of ethical behavior in the workplace, let's explore what can be done to encourage ethical behavior and to discourage unethical behavior.

Encouraging Ethical Behavior

LEARNING OBJECTIVE

4 Explain how ethical decision making can be encouraged.

Most authorities agree there is room for improvement in business ethics. A more problematic question is, Can business be made more ethical in the real world? The majority opinion on this issue suggests that government, trade associations, and individual firms can indeed establish acceptable levels of ethical behavior.

The government can encourage ethical behavior by legislating more stringent regulations. But rules require enforcement, and the unethical businessperson frequently seems to "slip something by" without getting caught. Increased regulation may help, but it surely cannot solve the entire ethics problem.

Trade associations can and often do provide ethical guidelines for their members. These organizations, which operate within particular industries, are in an excellent position to exert pressure on members that stoop to questionable business practices. However, enforcement and authority vary from association to association. And because trade associations exist for the benefit of their members, harsh measures may be self-defeating.

Codes of ethics that companies provide to their employees are perhaps the most effective way to encourage ethical behavior. A **code of ethics** is a written guide to acceptable and ethical behavior as defined by an organization; it outlines uniform policies, standards, and punishments for violations. Because employees know what is expected of them and what will happen if they violate the rules, a code of ethics goes a long way toward encouraging ethical behavior. However, codes cannot possibly cover every situation. Companies must also create an environment in which employees recognize the importance of complying with the written code. Managers must provide direction by fostering communication, actively modeling and encouraging ethical decision making, and training employees to make ethical decisions.

code of ethics a guide to acceptable and ethical behavior as defined by an organization

During the 1980s, an increasing number of organizations created and implemented ethics codes. In a recent survey of *Fortune* 1000 firms, 93 percent of the

Examining Ethics

Beyond Ethical Codes

POSTING A CODE OF ETHICS IS JUST THE first step in encouraging ethical behavior. Studies show that many employees see unethical behavior such as sexual harassment and discrimination in their organizations but they fail to report these problems. Although such violations can result in legal action and damaging publicity, many organizations don't give employees all the tools and support they need to deal with ethical problems.

After formulating a code of ethics, companies should develop ethics training courses geared to the issues employees face on the job. "[Employees are] the ones who will be able to identify what problems exist and what things can be done better," stresses Jacquelyn Gates, vice president for ethics, compliance, and diversity at Verizon.

Lockheed Martin, for example, created a game called "The Ethics Challenge" based on real-life ethical problems confronting its employees. Managers and supervisors can select specific problems from the game when they train employees. "It was a pretty big gamble to take something as serious as ethics training and make it into a game," notes Tracy C. Dougherty, director of ethics communication and training. "But we wanted to so something unusual that stood out from all the other training that our employees get. Our sense is that it is an effective tool to increase ethics awareness."

In addition, companies must periodically review and update their ethics training programs to reflect changes in industry practices and government regulations. In the health-care field, for example, hospitals used to give doctors rewards for referring patients—a custom now considered both unethical and illegal. This is only one of several changes that Colorado's HealthONE hospital system incorporated into its ethics training program.

Issues to Consider

1. How can a company find out whether its employees are getting the message about ethics?
2. What can a company do to encourage employees to report suspected ethics violations?

figure 2.2

Defining Acceptable Behavior: TI's Code of Ethics

Texas Instruments encourages ethical behavior through an extensive training program and a written code of ethics and shared values.

TEXAS INSTRUMENTS CODE OF ETHICS

"One of TI's greatest strengths is its values and ethics. We had some early leaders who set those values as the standard for how they lived their lives. And it is important that TI grew that way. It's something that we don't want to lose. At the same time, we must move more rapidly. But we don't want to confuse that with the fact that we're ethical and we're moral. We're very responsible, and we live up to what we say."

Tom Engibous, President and CEO
Texas Instruments,1997

We Respect and Value People By:

Treating others as we want to be treated.

- Exercising the basic virtues of respect, dignity, kindness, courtesy and manners in all work relationships.
- Recognizing and avoiding behaviors that others may find offensive, including the manner in which we speak and relate to one another and the materials we bring into the workplace, both printed and electronically.
- Respecting the right and obligation of every TIer to resolve concerns relating to ethics questions in the course of our duties without retribution and retaliation.
- Giving all TIers the same opportunity to have their questions, issues and situations fairly considered while understanding that being treated fairly does not always mean that we will all be treated the same.
- Trusting one another to use sound judgment in our use of TI business and information systems.
- Understanding that even though TI has the obligation to monitor its business information systems activity, we will respect privacy by prohibiting random searches of individual TIers' communications.
- Recognizing that conduct socially and professionally acceptable in one culture and country may be viewed differently in another.

We Are Honest By:

Representing ourselves and our intentions truthfully.

- Offering full disclosure and withdrawing ourselves from discussions and decisions when our business judgment appears to be in conflict with a personal interest.
- Respecting the rights and property of others, including their intellectual property. Accepting confidential or trade secret information only after we clearly understand our obligations as defined in a nondisclosure agreement.
- Competing fairly without collusion or collaboration with competitors to divide markets, set prices, restrict production, allocate customers or otherwise restrain competition.
- Assuring that no payments or favors are offered to influence others to do something wrong.
- Keeping records that are accurate and include all payments and receipts.
- Exercising good judgment in the exchange of business courtesies, meals and entertainment by avoiding activities that could create even the appearance that our decisions could be compromised.
- Refusing to speculate in TI stock through frequent buying and selling or through other forms of speculative trading.

Source: Courtesy of Texas Instruments.

companies that responded reported having a formal code of ethics. Some companies are now even taking steps to strengthen their codes. For example, to strengthen its accountability, the Healthcare Financial Management Association recently revised its code to designate contact persons who handle reports of ethics violations, to clarify how its board of directors should deal with violations of business ethics, and to guarantee a fair hearing process. S.C. Johnson & Son, makers of Pledge, Drano, Windex, and many other household products, is another firm that recognizes it must behave in ways the public perceives as ethical; its code includes expectations for employees and its commitment to consumers, the community, and society in general. Included in the ethics code of electronics giant Texas Instruments are issues relating to policies and procedures; laws and regulations; relationships with customers, suppliers, and competitors; conflicts of interest; handling of proprietary information; and code enforcement. (see Figure 2.2.).

Assigning an ethics officer who coordinates ethical conduct gives employees someone to consult if they aren't sure of the right thing to do. An ethics officer meets with employees and top management to provide ethical advice, establishes and maintains an anonymous confidential service to answer questions about ethical issues, and takes action on ethics-code violations.

Sometimes, even employees who want to act ethically may find it difficult to do so. Unethical practices can become ingrained in an organization. Employees with high personal ethics may then take a controversial step called whistle blowing. **Whistle blowing** is informing the press or government officials about unethical practices within one's organization. Whistle blowing could have averted disaster and prevented needless deaths in the *Challenger* space-shuttle disaster, for example. How could employees have known about life-threatening problems and let them pass? Whistle blowing, on the other hand, can have serious repercussions for employees: those who "blow whistles" sometimes lose their jobs.

whistle blowing informing the press or government officials about unethical practices within one's organization

When firms set up anonymous hotlines to handle ethically questionable situations, employees may actually be more likely to engage in whistle blowing. When firms instead create an environment that educates employees and nurtures ethical behavior, fewer ethical problems arise, and ultimately the need for whistle blowing is greatly reduced.

It is difficult for an organization to develop ethics codes, policies, and procedures to deal with all relationships and every situation. When no company policy or procedures exists or applies, a quick test to determine if a behavior is ethical is to see if others—coworkers, customers, suppliers—approve of it. Ethical decisions will always withstand scrutiny. Openness and communication about choices will often build trust and strengthen business relationships. Table 2.1 provides some general guidelines for making ethical decisions.

table 2.1 Guidelines for Making Ethical Decisions

1. **Listen and learn.**
   Recognize the problem or decision-making opportunity that confronts your company, team, or unit. Don't argue, criticize, or defend yourself—keep listening and reviewing until you are sure you understand others.
2. **Identify the ethical issues.**
   Examine how coworkers and consumers are affected by the situation or decision at hand. Examine how you feel about the situation and understand the viewpoint of those involved in the decision or in the consequences of the decision.
3. **Create and analyze options.**
   Try to put aside strong feelings such as anger or desire for power and prestige and come up with as many alternatives as possible before developing an analysis. Ask everyone involved for ideas about which options offer the best long-term results for you and the company. Which option will increase your self-respect even if, in the long run, things don't work out the way you hope?
4. **Identify the best option from your point of view.**
   Consider it and test it against some established criteria, such as respect, understanding, caring, fairness, honesty, and openness.
5. **Explain your decision and resolve any differences that arise.**
   This may require neutral arbitration from a trusted manager or taking "time out" to reconsider, consult, or exchange written proposals before a decision is reached.

Source: Tom Rusk with D. Patrick Miller, "Doing the Right Thing," *Sky* Delta Airlines, Aug. 1993, pp. 18–22.

Social Responsibility

social responsibility the recognition that business activities have an impact on society and the consideration of that impact in business decision making

Social responsibility is the recognition that business activities have an impact on society and the consideration of that impact in business decision making. Obviously, social responsibility costs money. It is perhaps not so obvious—except in isolated cases—that social responsibility is also good business. Customers eventually find out which firms are acting responsibly and which are not. And, just as easily as they cast their dollar votes for a product produced by a company that is socially responsible, they can vote against the firm that is not.

Consider the following examples of organizations that are attempting to be socially responsible:

- Union Carbide Corporation, a worldwide chemical company, recognizes that good corporate citizenship is essential to its success. The firm encourages and supports community involvement through a number of programs. For example, the Union Carbide Foundation, a $20 million charitable trust, was established to enhance the corporation's commitment to be an involved citizen in the communities where its employees work and live. The foundation makes grants in three primary areas: education, diversity, and environmental protection. One of the foundation's programs sponsors teachers attending Keystone Science School where they learn the best ways to teach environmental science to middle and high school students. In Kanawha County, West Virginia, schools, support of the Bold Education Achievement through Math and Science (BEAMS) program resulted in an increased number of students taking elective high school and college math and science courses. At Boston University's Center on Work and Family, a grant helps professors study effects of the nation's changing workplace demographics. As an organization, Union Carbide applies the same dedication to communities as it does to its relationships with its customers and employees. Union Carbide recognizes that its future success depends on developing strong relationships with all three audiences.[6]
- During the past one hundred years, AT&T has built a tradition of supporting education, health and human services, the environment, public policy, and the arts in communities it serves. In 1999, the AT&T Foundation donated $45 million to nonprofit organizations in communities throughout the United States and around the world. Also included in the AT&T Foundation are AT&T Cares, a company-wide program through which employees volunteered more than 400,000 hours of community service in 1999, and the AT&T Learning Network, an online program connecting teachers, schools, and parents to the technology tools they need to help improve teaching and learning. Since 1911, AT&T has been a sponsor of the Telephone Pioneers of America, the world's largest, industry-based volunteer organization consisting of nearly 800,000 employees and retirees from the telecommunications industry.[7]
- In a week-long Habitat for Humanity homebuilding project in Manila, the Philippines, more than thirty Dow Chemical Company employees volunteered their time and talent to construct new homes for the poor. Dow completed construction of four new classrooms to expand the Herbert Dow School in Guaruja, Brazil, to add space for increasing enrollment. The school now accommodates 720 students.[8]
- The U.S. based Arthur Andersen LLP Foundation (Arthur Andersen is one of the Big Five accounting firms) supports higher-education programs with a special emphasis on business education. It offers special support for nonprofit organizations that assist individuals who may not have equal access to educational opportunities. In addition, the Foundation matches gifts made by its partners and employees to their alma maters. In 1999, these funds exceeded $4 million. Also in 1999 *Working Mother* magazine recognized the firm as one of the "100 Best Companies for Working Mothers" for its efforts to help parents balance the challenges of career and family.[9]

- ConAgra, Inc., America's second largest food company, developed the Feeding Children Better program to attack childhood hunger. Through an innovative partnership between ConAgra, America's Second Harvest, (the nation's largest domestic charitable hunger relief organization), and Tufts University Center on Hunger and Poverty, the company made a multimillion dollar commitment to help solve the problem. According to Bruce Rohde, chairman and chief executive officer of ConAgra, Inc., the Feeding Children Better program is a strategic approach to improve the charitable food distribution system in the United States. As a leading food company, ConAgra has a unique ability to make an impact on childhood hunger.[10]

Giving back. Social responsibility may cost money, but it is also good business. Margaret McEntire, who started Candy Bouquets in her garage, sets aside 10 percent of profits for employees' tuition. Now she wants Congressional help in donating her franchises to inner-city operators.

- The Shell Oil Company Foundation is one of the nation's largest company-sponsored foundations. Created in 1953, the Foundation is funded by donations from Shell Oil Company and its subsidiaries. The Foundation contributes only to nonprofit organizations in the United States, and supports a broad range of charitable endeavors in health and human services, culture and the arts, and other community activities. For example, in 1998, the Shell Houston Open golf tournament donated a record $2.6 million to local children's charities. Since Shell assumed the sponsorship of this tournament in 1992, more than $10 million has been donated to charities. In addition, the Foundation funds university programs, including Doctoral Fellowships, Faculty Career Initiation Funds, Career Counseling Grants, Matching Gifts, and secondary education.[11]
- The General Electric Company employees and the GE Fund have supported 120 United Way campaigns with more than $20 million. GE employees and retirees support United Way agencies by building playgrounds, collecting supplies for food banks, renovating homeless shelters and serving as Big Brothers and Big Sisters. Through herSource.com, GE Medical Systems provides comprehensive breast cancer information helping women make more informed decisions, raise awareness, and drive home the importance of early detection. Furthermore, the GE Fund invented the corporate matching gift program, now used by more than 1,000 corporations worldwide. Since 1954, when the GE Fund began matching employee and retiree contributions, companies have donated more than $2 billion in matching gifts to colleges, universities and other educational institutions.

GE and its employees have made a strong commitment to their communities. Whether it is volunteering over one million hours of annual service to young people, supporting innovative programs in education, or helping provide community service, the GE people are making a difference on a global scale. GE, its employees, the GE Fund, and GE Elfun (a global organization of GE employees and retirees) contribute more that $90 million annually to support education, the arts, the environment and human service organizations worldwide.[12]

These are just a few illustrations from the long list of companies that attempt to behave in socially responsible ways. In general, people are more likely to want to work for and buy from such organizations.

The Evolution of Social Responsibility in Business

LEARNING OBJECTIVE

5 Describe how our current views on the social responsibility of business have evolved.

Business is far from perfect in many respects, but its record of social responsibility today is much better than in past decades. In fact, present demands for social responsibility have their roots in outraged reactions to the abusive business practices of the early 1900s.

During the first quarter of the twentieth century, businesses were free to operate pretty much as they chose. Government protection of workers and consumers was minimal. As a result, people either accepted what business had to offer or they did without. Working conditions were often deplorable by today's standards. The average workweek in most industries exceeded sixty hours, no minimum-wage law existed, and employee benefits were almost nonexistent. Work areas were crowded and unsafe, and industrial accidents were the rule rather than the exception. To improve working conditions, employees organized and joined labor unions. But during the early 1900s, businesses—with the help of government—were able to use court orders, brute force, and even the few existing antitrust laws to defeat union attempts to improve working conditions.

caveat emptor a Latin phrase meaning "let the buyer beware"

During this period, consumers were generally subject to the doctrine of **caveat emptor,** a Latin phrase meaning "let the buyer beware." In other words, "what you see is what you get," and if it's not what you expected, too bad. Although victims of unscrupulous business practices could take legal action, going to court was very expensive and consumers rarely won their cases. Moreover, no consumer groups or government agencies existed to publicize their consumers' grievances or to hold sellers accountable for their actions.

table 2.2 Early Government Regulations That Affected American Business

Government Regulation	Major Provisions
Interstate Commerce Act (1887)	First federal act to regulate business practices; provided regulation of railroads and shipping rates
Sherman Antitrust Act (1890)	Prevented monopolies or mergers where competition was endangered
Pure Food and Drug Act (1906)	Established limited supervision of interstate sale of food and drugs
Meat Inspection Act (1906)	Provided for limited supervision of interstate sale of meat and meat products
Federal Trade Commission Act (1914)	Created the Federal Trade Commission to investigate illegal trade practices
Clayton Antitrust Act (1914)	Eliminated many forms of price discrimination that gave large businesses a competitive advantage over smaller firms

Prior to the 1930s, most people believed that competition and the action of the marketplace would in time correct abuses. Government therefore became involved in day-to-day business activities only in cases of obvious abuse of the free-market system. Six of the more important business-related federal laws passed between 1887 and 1914 are described in Table 2.2. As you can see, these laws were aimed more at encouraging competition than at correcting abuses, although two of them did deal with the purity of food and drug products.

The collapse of the stock market on October 29, 1929, triggered the Great Depression and years of dire economic problems for the United States. Factory production fell by almost one-half, and up to 25 percent of the nation's work force was unemployed. Before long, public pressure mounted for government to "do something" about the economy and about worsening social conditions.

Using the Internet

The Business for Social Responsibility Organization web site provides a good overview of business ethics and proper social behavior. Be sure to explore the Global Business Responsibility Resource Center, the organization's gateway to useful reports, research, and links to related sites. **http://www.bsr.org/.**

Soon after Franklin Roosevelt was inaugurated as president in 1933, he instituted programs to restore the economy and to improve social conditions. Laws were passed to correct what many viewed as the monopolistic abuses of big business, and various social services were provided for individuals. These massive federal programs became the foundation for increased government involvement in the dealings between business and society.

As government involvement has increased, so has everyone's awareness of the social responsibility of business. Today's business owners are concerned about the return on their investment, but at the same time most of them demand ethical behavior from employees. In addition, employees demand better working conditions, and consumers want safe, reliable products. Various advocacy groups echo these concerns and also call for careful consideration of our earth's delicate ecological balance. Managers must therefore operate in a complex business environment—one in which they are just as responsible for their managerial actions as for their actions as individual citizens. Interestingly, today's high technology and Internet-based firms fare relatively well when it comes to environmental issues, worker conditions, the representation of minorities and women in upper management, animal testing, and charitable donations. According to the New York watch-group called the *Council on Economic Priorities*, which examines more than seven hundred of the country's largest companies annually, these new economy firms tend to rate better than average but are not immune from criticism.[13]

Two Views of Social Responsibility

LEARNING OBJECTIVE

6 Explain the two views on the social responsibility of business and understand the arguments for and against increased social responsibility.

Government regulation and public awareness are *external* forces that have increased the social responsibility of business. But business decisions are made *within* the firm—and, there, social responsibility begins with the attitude of management. Two contrasting philosophies, or models, define the range of management attitudes toward social responsibility.

The Economic Model

According to the traditional concept of business, a firm exists to produce quality goods and services, earn a reasonable profit, and provide jobs. In line with this concept, the **economic model of social responsibility** holds that society will benefit most when business is left alone to produce and market profitable products that society needs. The economic model has its origins in the eighteenth century, when businesses were owned primarily by entrepreneurs or owner-managers. Competition was vigorous among small firms, and short-run profits and survival were the primary concerns.

economic model of social responsibility the view that society will benefit most when business is left alone to produce and market profitable products that society needs

Exploring Business

Social Responsibility Goes to School

SOCIAL RESPONSIBILITY CAN TAKE MANY forms—including flying lessons. Through Young Eagles, underwritten by S.C. Johnson, Phillips Petroleum, Lockheed Martin, Jaguar, and other corporations, 22,000 volunteer pilots have taken a half million youngsters on free flights designed to teach flying basics and inspire excitement about flying careers. Young Eagles is just one of a growing number of education projects undertaken by businesses building solid records as good corporate citizens.

Education programs often link social responsibility with corporate self-interest. For example, Bayer and Merck, two major pharmaceuticals firms, promote science education as a way of enlarging the pool of future employees. Students who visit the Bayer Science Forum in Elkhart, Indiana, work alongside scientists conducting a variety of experiments. And workshops created by the Merck Institute for Science Education show teachers how to put scientific principles into action through hands-on experiments.

Computer giant Hewlett-Packard promotes science and technology education by pairing students with employees who serve as mentors by e-mail for class projects. As many as 1,500 employees are corresponding with middle school and high school students to discuss projects as diverse as building a bicycle pump or investigating computer careers. "We're investing in our own future," comments Marsh Faber, Hewlett-Packard's education marketing manager for general-purpose products.

Businesses around the world see education projects as a way to make a difference in the markets they serve. As one example, Natura Cosmeticos, a Brazilian cosmetics firm, has teamed up with the Abrinq Foundation for Children's Rights to fund dozens of programs that boost elementary school students' self-confidence and skills. In addition, the firm's "Pedagogic Journeys" project supports teacher training for new schools in rural areas. As another example, Japan-based Toyota is sponsoring teacher grants in the United States to promote mathematics and science education. Whether they're teaching flying, science, or self-confidence, all these education projects are giving corporations the opportunity to showcase their commitment to social responsibility in a very tangible way.

To the manager who adopts this traditional attitude, social responsibility is someone else's job. After all, stockholders invest in a corporation to earn a return on their investment, not because the firm is socially responsible, and the firm is legally obligated to act in the economic interest of its stockholders. Moreover, profitable firms pay federal, state, and local taxes that are used to meet the needs of society. Thus, managers who concentrate on profit believe they fulfill their social responsibility indirectly, through the taxes paid by their firms. As a result, social responsibility becomes the problem of government, various environmental groups, charitable foundations, and similar organizations.

The Socioeconomic Model

In contrast, some managers believe they have a responsibility not only to stockholders but also to customers, employees, suppliers, and the general public. This broader view is referred to as the **socioeconomic model of social responsibility.** It places emphasis not only on profits but also on the impact of business decisions on society.

socioeconomic model of social responsibility the concept that business should emphasize not only profits but also the impact of its decisions on society

Recently, increasing numbers of managers and firms have adopted the socioeconomic model, and they have done so for at least three reasons. First, business is dominated by the corporate form of ownership, and the corporation is a creation of society. If a corporation doesn't perform as a good citizen, society can and will demand changes. Second, many firms have begun to take pride in their social responsibility records, among them Starbucks Coffee, Hewlett-Packard, Colgate-Palmolive, and Coca-Cola. Each of these companies is a winner of a Corporate Conscience Award in the areas of environmental concern, responsiveness to employees, equal opportunity, and community involvement. And, of course, many other corporations are much more socially responsible today than they were ten years ago. Third, many businesspeople believe it is in their best interest to take the initiative in this area. The alternative may be legal action brought against the firm by some special-interest group; in such a situation, the firm may lose control of its activities.

The Pros and Cons of Social Responsibility

Business owners, managers, customers, and government officials have debated the pros and cons of the economic and socioeconomic models for years. Each side seems to have four major arguments to reinforce its viewpoint.

Arguments for Increased Social Responsibility Proponents of the socioeconomic model maintain that a business must do more than simply seek profits. To support their position, they offer the following arguments:

1. Because business is a part of our society, it cannot ignore social issues.
2. Business has the technical, financial, and managerial resources needed to tackle today's complex social issues.
3. By helping resolve social issues, business can create a more stable environment for long-term profitability.
4. Socially responsible decision making by firms can prevent increased government intervention, which would force businesses to do what they fail to do voluntarily.

These arguments are based on the assumption that a business has a responsibility not only to stockholders but also to customers, employees, suppliers, and the general public.

Arguments against Increased Social Responsibility Opponents of the socioeconomic model argue that business should do what it does best: earn a profit by manufacturing and marketing products that people want. Those who support this position argue as follows:

1. Business managers are primarily responsible to stockholders, so management must be concerned with providing a return on owners' investments.
2. Corporate time, money, and talent should be used to maximize profits, not to solve society's problems.
3. Social problems affect society in general, so individual businesses should not be expected to solve these problems.
4. Social issues are the responsibility of government officials who are elected for that purpose and who are accountable to the voters for their decisions.

These arguments are obviously based on the assumption that the primary objective of business is to earn profits and that government and social institutions should deal with social problems.

Table 2.3 compares the economic and socioeconomic viewpoints in terms of business emphasis. Today few firms are either purely economic or purely socioeconomic in outlook; most have chosen some middle ground between the two extremes. However, our society generally seems to want—and even to expect—some degree of social

table 2.3 A Comparison of the Economic and Socioeconomic Models of Social Responsibility as Implemented in Business

Economic Model Primary emphasis is on			Socioeconomic Model Primary emphasis is on
1. Production	M	G	1. Quality of life
2. Exploitation of natural resources	I	R	2. Conservation of natural resources
3. Internal, market-based decisions	D	O	3. Market-based decisions, with some community controls
4. Economic return (profit)	D	U	4. Balance of economic return and social return
5. Firm's or manager's interest	L	N	5. Firm's and community's interests
6. Minor role for government	E	D	6. Active government involvement

Source: Adapted from Keith Davis, William C. Frederick, and Robert L. Blomstrom, *Business and Society: Concepts and Policy Issues* (New York: McGraw-Hill, 1980), p. 9. Used by permission of McGraw-Hill Book Company.

responsibility from business. Thus, within this middle ground, businesses are leaning toward the socioeconomic view. In the next several sections, we look at some results of this movement in four specific areas: consumerism, employment practices, concern for the environment, and implementation of social responsibility programs.

Consumerism

consumerism all activities undertaken to protect the rights of consumers

Consumerism consists of all activities undertaken to protect the rights of consumers. The fundamental issues pursued by the consumer movement fall into three categories: environmental protection, product performance and safety, and information disclosure. Although consumerism has been with us to some extent since the early nineteenth century, the consumer movement became stronger in the 1960s. It was then that President John F. Kennedy declared that the consumer was entitled to a new "bill of rights."

LEARNING OBJECTIVE

7 Discuss the factors that led to the consumer movement and list some of its results.

The Six Basic Rights of Consumers

President Kennedy's consumer bill of rights asserted that consumers have a right to safety, to be informed, to choose, and to be heard. Two additional rights added in the last decade are the right to consumer education and to courteous service. These six rights are the basis of much of the consumer-oriented legislation that has been passed during the last forty years. These rights also provide an effective outline of the objectives and accomplishments of the consumer movement.

The Right to Safety The consumers' right to safety means that the products they purchase must be safe for their intended use, must include thorough and explicit directions for proper use, and must be tested by the manufacturer to ensure product quality and reliability. There are several reasons why American business firms must be concerned about product safety. Federal agencies such as the Food and Drug Administration and the Consumer Product Safety Commission have the power to force businesses that make or sell defective products to take corrective actions. Such actions include offering refunds, recalling defective products, issuing public warnings, and reimbursing consumers—all of which can be expensive. Business firms should also be aware that consumers and the government have been winning an increasing number of product-liability lawsuits against sellers of defective products. Moreover, the amount of the awards in these suits has been steadily increasing. Fearing the outcome of numerous lawsuits filed around the nation, tobacco giants Philip Morris and R. J. Reynolds, which for decades had denied that cigarettes cause illness, began negotiating in 1997 with state attorneys general, plaintiffs' lawyers, and antismoking activists. The tobacco giants proposed sweeping curbs on their sales and advertising practices and the payment of

You have a right to know. The government-mandated Surgeon General's warning on tobacco products is one way the right to be informed is ensured.

hundreds of billions of dollars in compensation. Yet another major reason for improving product safety is the consumer's demand for safe products. People will simply stop buying a product they believe is unsafe or unreliable.

spotLight

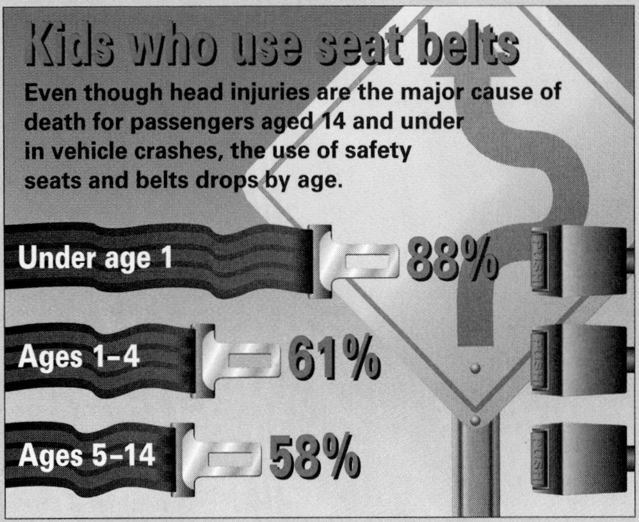

Kids who use seat belts

Even though head injuries are the major cause of death for passengers aged 14 and under in vehicle crashes, the use of safety seats and belts drops by age.

Under age 1 88%

Ages 1-4 61%

Ages 5-14 58%

Source: Copyright 2000, USA TODAY. Reprinted with permission.

The Right to Be Informed The right to be informed means that consumers must have access to complete information about a product before they buy it. Detailed information about ingredients and nutrition must be provided on food containers, information about fabrics and laundering methods must be attached to clothing, and lenders must disclose the true cost of borrowing the money they make available to customers who purchase merchandise on credit.

In addition, manufacturers must inform consumers about the potential dangers of using their products. Manufacturers that fail to provide such information can be held responsible for personal injuries suffered because of their products. For example, Maytag provides customers with a lengthy booklet that describes how they should use an automatic clothes washer. Sometimes such warnings seem excessive, but they are necessary if user injuries (and resulting lawsuits) are to be avoided.

The Right to Choose The right to choose means that consumers must have a choice of products, offered by different manufacturers and sellers, to satisfy a particular need. The government has done its part by encouraging competition through antitrust legislation. The greater the competition, the greater the choice available to consumers.

Competition and the resulting freedom of choice provide additional benefits for customers by reducing prices. For example, when electronic calculators were initially introduced, they cost over $200. Thanks to intense competition and technological advancements, calculators today can be purchased for less than $10.

The Right to Be Heard This fourth right means that someone will listen and take appropriate action when customers complain. Actually, management began to listen to consumers after World War II, when competition between businesses that manufactured and sold consumer goods increased. One way firms got a competitive edge was to listen to consumers and provide the products they said they wanted and needed. Today businesses are listening even more attentively, and many larger firms have consumer relations departments that can be easily contacted via toll-free phone numbers. Other groups listen, too. Most large cities and some states have consumer affairs offices to act on citizens' complaints.

Additional Consumer Rights In 1975 President Gerald Ford added to the consumer bill of rights the right to consumer education, which entitles people to be fully informed about their rights as consumers. In 1994 President Bill Clinton added a sixth right: the right to service, which entitles consumers to convenience, courtesy, and responsiveness from manufacturers and sellers of consumer products.

Major Consumerism Forces

The major forces in consumerism are individual consumer advocates and organizations, consumer education programs, and consumer laws.

Consumer advocates, such as Ralph Nader, take it upon themselves to protect the rights of consumers. They band together into consumer organizations, either independently or under government sponsorship. Some organizations, such as the National Consumers' League and the Consumer Federation of America, operate nationally, whereas others are active at state and local levels. They inform and organize other consumers, raise issues, help businesses develop consumer-oriented programs, and pressure lawmakers to enact consumer protection laws. Some consumer advocates and organizations encourage consumers to boycott products and businesses to which they have objections. Today the consumer movement has adopted corporate-style marketing and addresses a broad range of issues. Current campaigns include efforts (1) to curtail the use of animals for testing purposes, (2) to reduce liquor and cigarette billboard advertising in low-income, inner-city neighborhoods, and (3) to encourage recycling.

Educating consumers to make wiser purchasing decisions is perhaps one of the most far-reaching aspects of consumerism. Increasingly, consumer education is becoming a part of high school and college curricula and adult education programs. These programs cover many topics—for instance, what major factors should be considered when buying specific products, such as insurance, real estate, automobiles, appliances and furniture, clothes, and food; the provisions of certain consumer protection laws; and the sources of information that can help individuals become knowledgeable consumers.

Major advances in consumerism have come through federal legislation. Some laws enacted in the last forty years to protect your rights as a consumer are listed and described in Table 2.4. Most businesspeople now realize that they ignore consumer issues only at their own peril. Managers know that improper handling of consumer complaints can result in lost sales, bad publicity, and lawsuits.

Employment Practices

LEARNING OBJECTIVE

8 Analyze how present employment practices are being used to counteract past abuses.

We have seen that managers who subscribe to the socioeconomic view of business's social responsibility, together with significant government legislation enacted to protect the buying public, have broadened the rights of consumers. The last four decades have seen similar progress in affirming the rights of employees to equal treatment in the workplace.

minority a racial, religious, political, national, or other group regarded as different from the larger group of which it is a part and that is often singled out for unfavorable treatment

Everyone should have the opportunity to land a job for which he or she is qualified and to be rewarded on the basis of ability and performance. This is an important issue for society, and it also makes good business sense. Yet, over the years, this opportunity has been denied to members of various minority groups. A **minority** is a racial, religious, political, national, or other group regarded as different from the larger group of which it is a part and that is often singled out for unfavorable treatment.

The federal government responded to the outcry of minority groups during the 1960s and 1970s by passing a number of laws forbidding discrimination in the workplace. (These laws are discussed in Chapter 10 in the context of human resources management.) Now, thirty-eight years after passage of the first of these (the Civil Rights Act of 1964), abuses still exist. An example is the disparity in income levels for whites, blacks, and Hispanics, as illustrated in Figure 2.3 on page 54. Lower incomes and higher unemployment rates also characterize Native Americans, handicapped persons, and women. Responsible managers have instituted a number of programs to counteract the results of discrimination. As part of his "Digital Divide" campaign tour President Clinton visited many communities to bring attention to the fact that a gap exists between those Americans fortunate enough to be participating in Internet and high-technology industries and those who have been left out. He called on Silicon Valley business executives in the Palo Alto area of California in particular to accept the challenge and social responsibility to educate Americans rather than to import skilled workers to fill vacant jobs.[14]

table 2.4 Major Federal Legislation Protecting Consumers Since 1960

Legislation	Major Provisions
Federal Hazardous Substances Labeling Act (1960)	Required warning labels on household chemicals if they are highly toxic
Kefauver-Harris Drug Amendments (1962)	Established testing practices for drugs and required manufacturers to label drugs with generic names in addition to trade names
Cigarette Labeling Act (1965)	Required manufacturers to place standard warning labels on all cigarette packages and advertising
Fair Packaging and Labeling Act (1966)	Called for all products sold across state lines to be labeled with net weight, ingredients, and manufacturer's name and address
Motor Vehicle Safety Act (1966)	Established standards for safer cars
Wholesome Meat Act (1967)	Required states to inspect meat (but not poultry) sold within the state
Flammable Fabrics Act (1967)	Extended flammability standards for clothing to include children's sleepwear in sizes 0 to 6X
Truth in Lending Act (1968)	Required lenders and credit merchants to disclose the full cost of finance charges in both dollars and annual percentage rates
Child Protection and Toy Act (1969)	Banned toys with mechanical or electrical defects from interstate commerce
Credit Card Liability Act (1970)	Limited credit card holder's liability to $50 per card and stopped credit card companies from issuing unsolicited cards
Fair Credit Reporting Act (1971)	Required credit bureaus to provide credit reports to consumers regarding their own credit files; also provided for correction of incorrect information
Consumer Product Safety Commission Act (1972)	Established the Consumer Product Safety Commission
Trade Regulation Rule (1972)	Established a "cooling-off" period of 72 hours for door-to-door sales
Fair Credit Billing Act (1974)	Amended the Truth in Lending Act to enable consumers to challenge billing errors
Equal Credit Opportunity Act (1974)	Provided equal credit opportunities for males and females and for married and single individuals
Magnuson-Moss Warranty-Federal Trade Commission Act (1975)	Provided for minimum disclosure standards for written consumer product warranties for products that cost more than $15
Amendments to Equal Credit Opportunity Act (1976, 1994)	Prevented discrimination based on race, creed, color, religion, age, and income when granting credit
Fair Debt Collection Practices Act (1977)	Outlawed abusive collection practices by third parties
Drug Price Competition and Patent Restoration Act (1984)	Established an abbreviated procedure for registering certain generic drugs
Orphan Drug Act (1985)	Amended the original 1983 Orphan Drug Act and extended tax incentives to encourage the development of drugs for rare diseases
Nutrition Labeling and Education Act (1990)	Required the FDA to review current food labeling and packaging focusing on nutrition label content, label format, ingredient labeling, food descriptors and standards, and health messages
Telephone Consumer Protection Act (1991)	Prohibited the use of automated dialing and prerecorded-voice calling equipment to make calls or deliver messages
Consumer Credit Reporting Reform Act (1997)	Placed more responsibility for accurate credit data on credit issuers; required creditors to verify that disputed data are accurate and to notify a consumer before reinstating the data

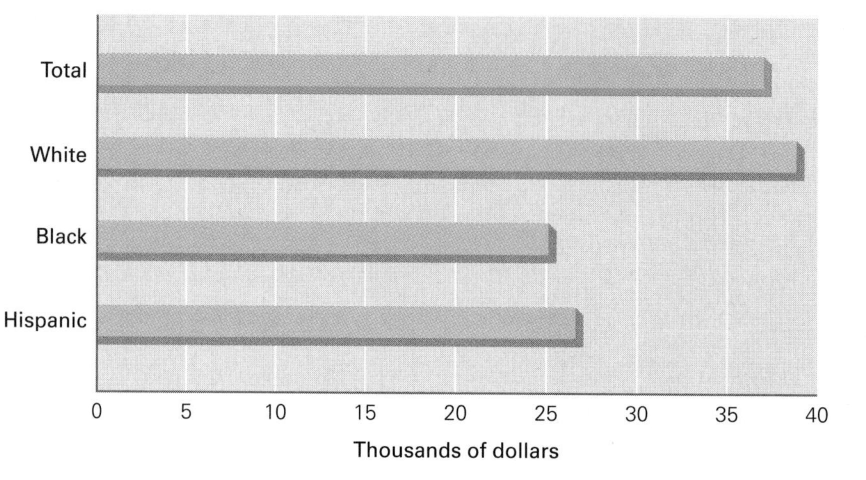

figure 2.3

Comparative Income Levels

The chart shows the median household incomes of the total population and of white, black, and Hispanic workers in 1997. (Hispanic persons may be of any race.)

Source: U.S. Bureau of the Census, *Statistical Abstract of the United States*, 1999, p. 474.

Affirmative Action Programs

affirmative action program a plan designed to increase the number of minority employees at all levels within an organization

An **affirmative action program** is a plan designed to increase the number of minority employees at all levels within an organization. Employers with federal contracts of more than $50,000 per year must have written affirmative action plans. The objective of such programs is to ensure that minorities are represented within the organization in approximately the same proportion as in the surrounding community. If 25 percent of the electricians in a geographic area in which a company is located are black, then approximately 25 percent of the electricians it employs should also be black. Affirmative action plans encompass all areas of human resources management: recruiting, hiring, training, promotion, and pay.

Unfortunately, affirmative action programs have been plagued by two problems. The first involves quotas. In the beginning, many firms pledged to recruit and hire a certain number of minority members by a specific date. To achieve this goal, they were forced to consider only minority applicants for job openings; if they hired nonminority workers, they would be defeating their own purpose. But the courts have ruled that such quotas are unconstitutional even though their purpose is commendable. They are, in fact, a form of discrimination called reverse discrimination.

The second problem is that although most such programs have been reasonably successful, not all businesspeople are in favor of affirmative action programs. Managers not committed to these programs can "play the game" and still discriminate against workers. To help solve this problem, Congress created (and later strengthened) the **Equal Employment Opportunity Commission (EEOC),** a government agency with power to investigate complaints of employment discrimination and power to sue firms that practice it.

Equal Employment Opportunity Commission (EEOC) a government agency with power to investigate complaints of employment discrimination and power to sue firms that practice it

The threat of legal action has persuaded some corporations to amend their hiring and promotional policies, but the discrepancy between men's and women's salaries has not really been affected, as illustrated in Figure 2.4. For more than thirty years, women have consistently earned only about 60 cents for each dollar earned by men.

Training Programs for the Hard-Core Unemployed

hard-core unemployed workers with little education or vocational training and a long history of unemployment

For some firms, social responsibility extends far beyond placing a help-wanted ad in the local newspaper. These firms have assumed the task of helping the **hard-core unemployed:** workers with little education or vocational training and a long history of unemployment. In the past, such workers were often routinely turned down by personnel managers, even for the most menial jobs.

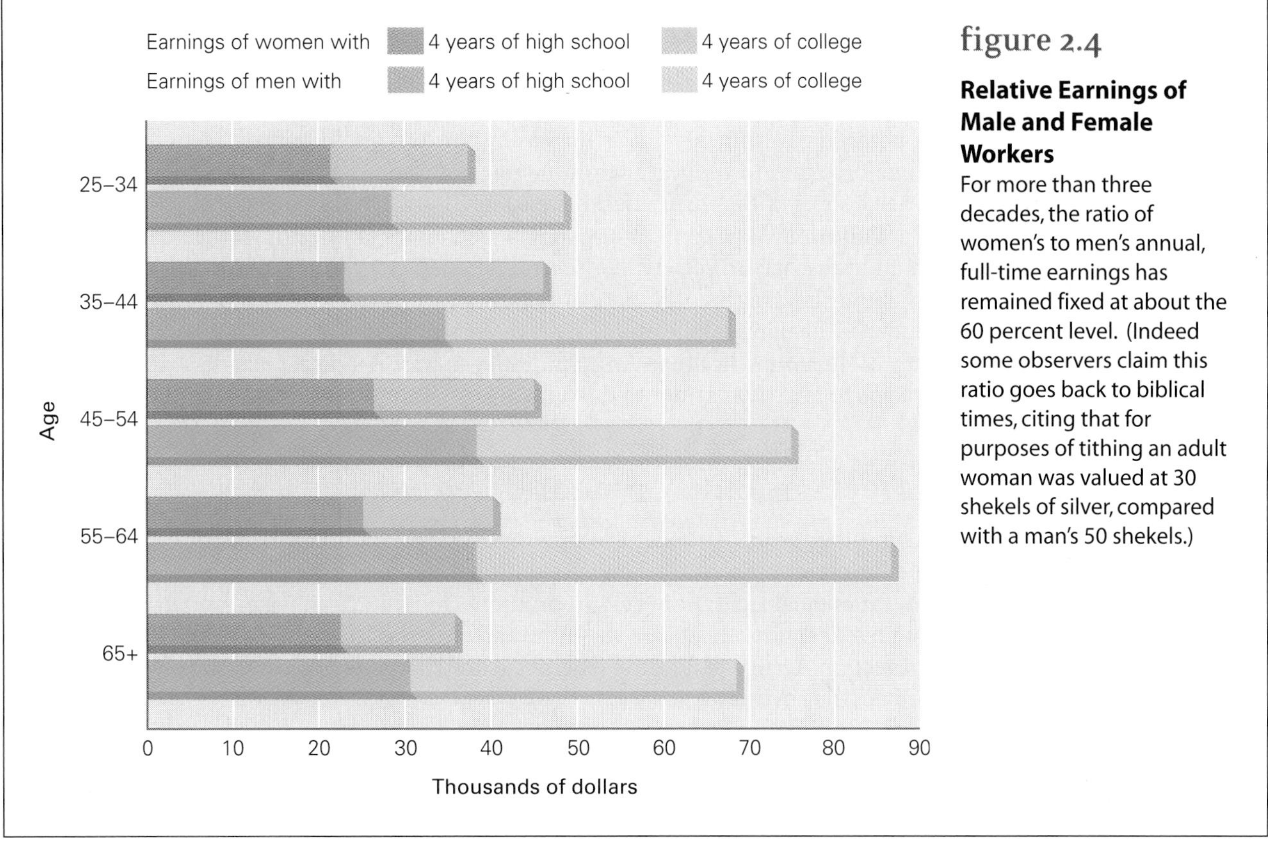

figure 2.4

Relative Earnings of Male and Female Workers
For more than three decades, the ratio of women's to men's annual, full-time earnings has remained fixed at about the 60 percent level. (Indeed some observers claim this ratio goes back to biblical times, citing that for purposes of tithing an adult woman was valued at 30 shekels of silver, compared with a man's 50 shekels.)

Source: U.S. Bureau of the Census, *Statistical Abstract of the United States*, 1999, p. 482.

Obviously, such workers require training; just as obviously, this training can be expensive and time-consuming. To share the costs, business and government have joined together in a number of cooperative programs. One particularly successful partnership is the **National Alliance of Business (NAB),** a joint business-government program to train the hard-core unemployed. The NAB is sponsored by participating corporations, whose executives contribute their talents to do the actual training. The government's responsibilities include setting objectives, establishing priorities, offering the right incentives, and providing limited financing.

National Alliance of Business (NAB) a joint business-government program to train the hard-core unemployed

Training where it's most needed. Preparing workers with little education or vocational training can be expensive and time-consuming. To share the training costs, business and government have joined together in cooperative programs. In a San Jose, California, homeless shelter, Rick Franco and others take a Cisco Systems computer training class.

Concern for the Environment

LEARNING OBJECTIVE

9 Describe the major types of pollution, their causes, and their cures.

The social consciousness of responsible business managers, the encouragement of a concerned government, and an increasing concern on the part of the public have led to a major effort to reduce environmental pollution, conserve natural resources, and reverse some of the worst effects of past negligence in this area.

pollution the contamination of water, air, or land through the actions of people in an industrialized society

Pollution is the contamination of water, air, or land through the actions of people in an industrialized society. For several decades, environmentalists have been warning us about the dangers of industrial pollution. Unfortunately, business and government leaders either ignored the problem or weren't concerned about it until pollution became a threat to life and health in America. Today Americans expect business and government leaders to take swift action to clean up our environment—and to keep it clean.

Effects of Environmental Legislation

As in other areas of concern to our society, legislation and regulations play a crucial role in pollution control. The laws outlined in Table 2.5 reflect the scope of current environmental legislation: laws to promote clean air, clean water, and even quiet work and living environments. Of major importance was the creation of the Environmental Protection Agency (EPA), the federal agency charged with enforcing laws designed to protect the environment.

table 2.5 **Summary of Major Environmental Laws**

Legislation	Major Provisions
National Environmental Policy Act (1970)	Established the Environmental Protection Agency (EPA) to enforce federal laws that involve the environment
Clean Air Amendment (1970)	Provided stringent automotive, aircraft, and factory emission standards
Water Quality Improvement Act (1970)	Strengthened existing water pollution regulations and provided for large monetary fines against violators
Resource Recovery Act (1970)	Enlarged the solid-waste disposal program and provided for enforcement by the EPA
Water Pollution Control Act Amendment (1972)	Established standards for cleaning navigable streams and lakes and eliminating all harmful waste disposal by 1985
Noise Control Act (1972)	Established standards for major sources of noise and required the EPA to advise the Federal Aviation Administration on standards for airplanes
Clean Air Act Amendment (1977)	Established new deadlines for cleaning up polluted areas; also required review of existing air-quality standards
Resource Conservation and Recovery Act (1984)	Amended the original 1976 act and required federal regulation of potentially dangerous solid-waste disposal
Clean Air Act Amendment (1987)	Established a national air-quality standard for ozone
Oil Pollution Act (1990)	Expanded the nation's oil spill prevention and response activities; also established the Oil Spill Liability Trust Fund
Clean Air Act Amendments (1990)	Required that motor vehicles be equipped with onboard systems to control about 90 percent of refueling vapors

When they are aware of a pollution problem, many firms respond to it rather than wait to be cited by the EPA. But other owners and managers take the position that environmental standards are too strict. (Loosely translated, this means that compliance with present standards is too expensive.) Consequently, it has often been necessary for the EPA to take legal action to force firms to install antipollution equipment and clean up waste storage areas.

Experience has shown that the combination of environmental legislation, voluntary compliance, and EPA action can succeed in cleaning up the environment and keeping it clean. However, much still remains to be done.

Water Pollution The Clean Water Act has been credited with greatly improving the condition of the waters in the United States. This success comes largely from the control of pollutant discharges from industrial and waste water treatment plants.[15] Although the quality of our nation's rivers, lakes, and streams has improved significantly in recent years, many of these surface waters remain severely polluted. Currently, one of the most serious water-quality problems results from the high level of toxic pollutants found in these waters.

Among the serious threats to people posed by water pollutants are respiratory irritation, cancer, kidney and liver damage, anemia, and heart failure. Toxic pollutants also damage fish and other forms of wildlife. In fish, they cause tumors or reproductive problems; shellfish and wildlife living in or drinking from toxin-infested waters have also suffered genetic defects.

The task of water cleanup has proved to be extremely complicated and costly because of pollution runoff and toxic contamination. And yet, improved water quality is not only necessary; it is also achievable. Consider Cleveland's Cuyahoga River. A few years ago the river was so contaminated by industrial wastes that it burst into flames one hot summer day! Now, after a sustained community cleanup effort, the river is pure enough for fish to thrive in.

Another serious issue is acid rain, which is contributing significantly to the deterioration of coastal waters, lakes, and marine life in the eastern United States. Acid rain forms when sulfur emitted by smokestacks in industrialized areas combines with moisture in the atmosphere to form acids that are spread by winds. The acids eventually fall to the earth in rain, which finds its way into streams, rivers, and lakes. The acid rain problem has spread rapidly in recent years, and experts fear the situation will worsen if the nation begins to burn more coal to generate electricity. To solve the problem, investigators must first determine where the sulfur is being emitted. The expenses that this vital investigation and cleanup entail are going to be high. The human costs of having ignored the problem so long may be higher still.

Air Pollution Aviation emissions are a potentially significant and growing percentage of greenhouse gases that contribute to global warming. Aircraft emissions are potentially significant for several reasons. First, jet aircraft are the main source of human emissions deposited directly into the upper atmosphere, where they may have a greater warming effect than if they were released at the earth's surface. Second, carbon dioxide—the primary aircraft emission—is the main focus of international concern. For example, it survives in the atmosphere for nearly one hundred years and contributes to global warming, according to the Intergovernmental Panel on Climate Change. The carbon dioxide emissions from worldwide aviation roughly equal those of some industrialized countries. Third, carbon dioxide emissions, combined with other gases and particles emitted by jet aircraft, could have two to four times as great an effect on the atmosphere as carbon dioxide alone. Fourth, the Intergovernmental Panel recently concluded that the rise in aviation emissions due to growing demand for air travel would not be fully offset by reductions in emissions achieved solely through technological improvements. Experts in the U.S. General Accounting Office interviewed, as well as the report of the Intergovernmental Panel, have cited several options for better understanding and mitigating the impact of aviation on the atmosphere as the industry grows. These options include (1) continuing research to improve the scientific understanding of aviation's effects on the global atmosphere as a basis for guiding the

Would you want to breathe this air? In addition to its adverse impact on human health and animal life, air pollution inflicts considerable global economic damage. The task of cleaning the air, such as that around this steel plant in Volta Redunda, Brazil, is complicated and costly—but must be mandatory to save our planet.

development of aircraft and engine technology to reduce them, (2) promoting more efficient air traffic operations through the introduction of new technologies and procedures, and (3) expanding the use of regulatory and economic measures to encourage reductions in emissions.[16]

Usually two or three factors combine to form air pollution in any given location. The first factor is large amounts of carbon monoxide and hydrocarbons emitted by motor vehicles concentrated in a relatively small area. The second is the smoke and other pollutants emitted by manufacturing facilities. These two factors can be partially eliminated through pollution-control devices on cars, trucks, and smokestacks.

A third factor that contributes to air pollution—one that cannot be changed—is the combination of weather and geography. The Los Angeles basin, for example, combines just the right weather and geographic conditions for creating dense smog. Los Angeles has strict regulations regarding air pollution. Even so, Los Angeles still struggles with air pollution problems because of uncontrollable conditions.

How effective is air pollution control? The EPA estimates that the Clean Air Act and its amendments will eventually result in the removal of 56 billion pounds of pollution from the air each year, thus measurably reducing lung disease, cancer, and other serious health problems caused by air pollution[17] Other authorities note that we have already seen improvement in air quality. A number of cities have cleaner air today than they did twenty-five years ago. Numerous chemical companies have recognized that they must take responsibility for operating their plants in an environmentally safe manner; some now devote considerable capital to purchasing antipollution devices. However, air levels of sulfur dioxide and nitrogen dioxide—the main components of acid rain—continue to increase. Although one might think that Internet-based home-shopping would help reduce air pollution by cutting back the need for consumers to drive their cars to shopping malls, there has been an *increase* in air pollution due to the addition of delivery vehicles, according to Lynne Elvins of SustainAbility, a London-based consulting group.[18]

spotLight

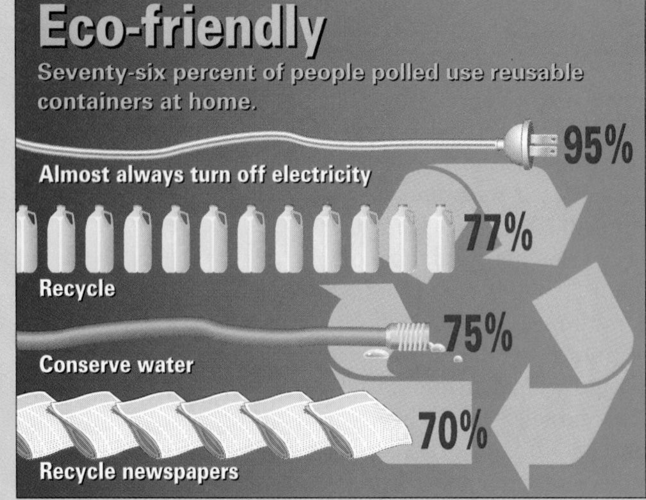

Source: Copyright 2000, USA TODAY. Reprinted with permission.

Land Pollution Air and water quality may be improving, but land pollution is still a serious problem in many areas. The fundamental issues are (1) how to restore damaged or contaminated land at a reasonable cost and (2) how to protect unpolluted land from future damage.

The land pollution problem has been worsening over the past few years, as modern technology has continued to produce increasing amounts of chemical and radioactive waste. U.S. manufacturers produce an estimated 40 to 60 million tons of contaminated oil, solvents, acids, and sludges each year. Service businesses, utility companies, hospitals, and other industries also dump vast amounts of wastes into the environment.

Individuals in the United States contribute to the waste disposal problem, too. A shortage of landfills, owing to stricter regulations, makes garbage disposal a serious problem in some areas. Incinerators help solve the landfill shortage problem, but they bring with them their own problems. They reduce the amount of garbage but also leave tons of ash to be buried—ash that often has a higher concentration of toxicity than the original garbage. Other causes of land pollution include strip-mining of coal, nonselective cutting of forests, and the development of agricultural land for housing and industry.

Land pollution still a serious hazard. Congress created a $1.6 billion Superfund to help pay the costs of cleaning up land laced with chemicals and toxic wastes. Here, EPA scientists check soil for arsenic at a Superfund site in California.

To help pay the enormous costs of cleaning up land polluted with chemicals and toxic wastes, Congress created a $1.6 billion Superfund in 1980. Originally, money was to flow into the Superfund from a tax paid by 800 oil and chemical companies that produce toxic waste. The EPA was to use the money in the Superfund to finance the cleanup of hazardous waste sites across the nation. To replenish the Superfund, the EPA had two options: it could sue companies guilty of dumping chemicals at specific waste sites, or it could negotiate with guilty companies and thus completely avoid the legal system. During the 1980s, officials at the EPA came under fire because they preferred negotiated settlements. Critics referred to these settlements as "sweetheart deals" with industry. They felt the EPA should be much more aggressive in reducing land pollution. Of course, most corporate executives believe that cleanup efficiency and quality might be improved if companies were more involved in the process.

Since the Superfund was established, the EPA has spent about $17.7 billion, yet 42 percent of the nation's 1,400 most severely contaminated hazardous waste sites need cleanups.[19]

Noise Pollution Excessive noise caused by traffic, aircraft, and machinery can do physical harm to human beings. Research has shown that people who are exposed to loud noises for long periods of time can suffer permanent hearing loss. The Noise Control Act of 1972 established noise emission standards for aircraft and airports, railroads, and interstate motor carriers. The act also provided funding for noise research at state and local levels.

Noise levels can be reduced by two methods. The source of noise pollution can be isolated as much as possible. (Thus, many metropolitan airports are located outside the cities.) And engineers can modify machinery and equipment to reduce noise levels. If it is impossible to reduce industrial noise to acceptable levels, workers should be required to wear earplugs to guard against permanent hearing damage.

Who Should Pay for a Clean Environment?

Governments and businesses are spending billions of dollars annually to reduce pollution—over $35 billion to control air pollution, $25 billion to control water pollution, and $12 billion to treat hazardous wastes.

To make matters worse, much of the money required to purify the environment is supposed to come from already depressed industries, such as the chemical industry. And a few firms have discovered it is cheaper to pay a fine than to install expensive equipment for pollution control.

Who, then, will pay for the environmental cleanup? Many business leaders offer one answer—tax money should be used to clean up the environment and to keep it clean. They reason that business is not the only source of pollution, so business should not be forced to absorb the entire cost of the cleanup. Environmentalists disagree. They believe the cost of proper treatment and disposal of industrial wastes is an expense of doing business. In either case, consumers will probably pay a large part of the cost—either as taxes or in the form of higher prices for goods and services.

Perhaps, as a study by the Boston Consulting Group suggests, e-business can help provide a solution satisfactory to all participants through a reduction in paper usage for newspapers and catalogs. The study estimates that by 2003, use of the Internet will result in a two million-ton annual decline in newsprint consumption in the U.S. alone as consumers shift their search for information to online sources. The savings and social benefits increase when the costs of pollution for delivery of print-based newspapers and catalogs are factored in.[20]

Implementing a Program of Social Responsibility

LEARNING OBJECTIVE

10 Identify the steps a business must take to implement a program of social responsibility.

A firm's decision to be socially responsible is a step in the right direction—but only the first step. The firm must then develop and implement a program to reach this goal. The program will be affected by the firm's size, financial resources, past record in the area of social responsibility, and competition. But above all, the program must have the firm's total commitment or it will fail.

Developing a Program of Social Responsibility

An effective program for social responsibility takes time, money, and organization. In most cases, developing and implementing such a program will require four steps: securing the commitment of top executives, planning, appointing a director, and preparing a social audit.

Commitment of Top Executives Without the support of top executives, any program will soon falter and become ineffective. For example, the Boeing Company's Ethics and Business Conduct Committee is responsible for the ethics program. The committee is appointed by the Boeing Board of Directors and its members include the company chairman and chief executive officer, president and chief operating officer, presidents of the operating groups, and senior vice presidents. As evidence of their commitment to social responsibility, top managers should develop a policy statement that outlines key areas of concern. This statement sets a tone of positive support and will later serve as a guide for other employees as they become involved in the program.

Planning Next a committee of managers should be appointed to plan the program. Whatever form their plan takes, it should deal with each of the issues described in the top managers' policy statement. If necessary, outside consultants can be hired to help develop the plan.

Appointment of a Director After the social responsibility plan is established, a top-level executive should be appointed to implement the organization's plan. This individual should be charged with recommending specific policies and helping individual departments understand and live up to the social responsibilities the firm has assumed. Depending on the size of the firm, the director may require a staff to handle the program on a day-to-day basis. For example, at the Boeing Company, the director of Ethics and Business Conduct administers the ethics and business conduct program.

The Social Audit At specified intervals, the program director should prepare a social audit for the firm. A **social audit** is a comprehensive report of what an organization has done, and is doing, with regard to social issues that affect it. This document provides the information the firm needs to evaluate and revise its social responsibility program. Typical subject areas include human resources, community involvement, the quality and safety of products, business practices, and efforts to reduce pollution and improve the environment. The information included in a social audit should be as accurate and as quantitative as possible, and the audit should reveal both positive and negative aspects of the program.

social audit a comprehensive report of what an organization has done, and is doing, with regard to social issues that affect it

Today, many companies listen to concerned individuals within and outside the company. For example, the Boeing Ethics Line listens to and acts on concerns expressed by employees and others about possible violations of company policies, laws, or regulations such as improper or unethical business practices, as well as health, safety, and environmental issues. Employees are encouraged to communicate their concerns, as well as ask questions about ethical issues. The Ethics Line is available to all Boeing employees, including Boeing subsidiaries. It is also available to concerned individuals outside the company.

Funding the Program

We have noted that social responsibility costs money. Thus, just like any other corporate undertaking, a program to improve social responsibility must be funded. Funding can come from three sources:

1. Management can pass the cost on to consumers in the form of higher prices.
2. The corporation may be forced to absorb the cost of the program, if, for example, the competitive situation does not permit a price increase. In this case, the cost is treated as a business expense, and profit is reduced.
3. The federal government may pay for all or part of the cost through tax reductions or other incentives.

RETURN TO Inside Business

TEXAS INSTRUMENTS HAD BEEN preaching and practicing ethical decision-making for decades—even before its aggressive global expansion. But new markets brought new ethical challenges, so TI moved beyond its written code of ethics to create new employee tools and training for ethical decision-making. The company also appointed an ethics director (currently Jack Swindle) and a compliance officer (currently Hector Cardenas) to report to a new senior-level Ethics Office charged with monitoring and enforcing ethics policies and practices.

Organization-wide surveys help TI confirm that employees remain aware of the firm's strong commitment to ethics. TI's ethics initiatives have also received public recognition, winning three business ethics awards and serving as a model for other companies. By using every opportunity to reinforce high ethical standards, TI has forged a reputation as a principled leader in its industry and in the communities where it operates.

Questions

1. Why would other companies prefer to do business with an acknowledged ethics leader such as Texas Instruments?
2. Should TI require all its suppliers and distributors to act in accordance with the company's high ethical standards? Explain your answer.

chapter Review

SUMMARY

1 Understand what is meant by *business ethics.*

Ethics is the study of right and wrong and of the morality of choices. Business ethics is the application of moral standards to business situations.

2 Identify the types of ethical concerns that arise in the business world.

Ethical issues arise often in business situations out of relationships with investors, customers, employees, creditors, or competitors. Businesspeople should make every effort to be fair, to consider the welfare of customers and others within the firm, to avoid conflicts of interest, and to communicate honestly.

3 Discuss the factors that affect the level of ethical behavior in organizations.

Individual, social, and opportunity factors all affect the level of ethical behavior in an organization. Individual factors include knowledge level, moral values and attitudes, and personal goals. Social factors include cultural norms and the actions and values of coworkers and significant others. Opportunity factors refer to the amount of leeway that exists in an organization for employees to behave unethically if they so choose.

4 Explain how ethical decision making can be encouraged.

Governments, trade associations, and individual firms can all establish guidelines for defining ethical behavior. Governments can pass stricter regulations. Trade associations provide ethical guidelines for their members. Companies provide codes of ethics—written guides to acceptable and ethical behavior as defined by an organization—and create an atmosphere in which ethical behavior is encouraged. An ethical employee working in an unethical environment may resort to whistle blowing to bring a questionable practice to light.

5 Describe how our current views on the social responsibility of business have evolved.

In a socially responsible business, management realizes its activities have an impact on society and considers that impact in the decision-making process. Before the 1930s, workers, consumers, and government had very little influence on business activities; as a result, business leaders gave little thought to social responsibility. All this changed with the Great Depression. Government regulations, employee demands, and consumer awareness combined to create a demand that businesses act in socially responsible ways.

6 Explain the two views on the social responsibility of business and understand the arguments for and against increased social responsibility.

The basic premise of the economic model of social responsibility is that society benefits most when business is left alone to produce profitable goods and services. According to the socioeconomic model, business has as much responsibility to society as it has to its owners. Most managers adopt a viewpoint somewhere between these two extremes.

7 Discuss the factors that led to the consumer movement and list some of its results.

Consumerism consists of all activities undertaken to protect the rights of consumers. The consumer movement has generally demanded—and received—attention from business in the areas of product safety, product information, product choices through competition, and in the resolution of complaints about products and business practices. Although concerns over consumer rights have been around to some extent since the early nineteenth century, the movement became more powerful in the 1960s when President John F. Kennedy initiated the consumer "bill of rights." The six basic rights of consumers include the right to safety, the right to be informed, the right to choose, the right to be heard, and the rights to consumer education and courteous service.

8 Analyze how present employment practices are being used to counteract past abuses.

Legislation and public demand have prompted some businesses to correct past abuses in employment practices—mainly with regard to minority groups. Affirmative action and training of the hard-core unemployed are two types of programs that have been used successfully.

9 Describe the major types of pollution, their causes, and their cures.

Industry has contributed to the noise pollution and the pollution of our land and water through the dumping of wastes, and to air pollution through vehicle and smokestack emissions. This contamination can be cleaned up and controlled, but the big question is, Who will pay? Present cleanup efforts are funded partly by government tax revenues, partly by business, and, in the long run, by consumers.

10 Identify the steps a business must take to implement a program of social responsibility.

A program to implement social responsibility in a business begins with total commitment by top management. The program should be carefully planned, and a capable director should be appointed to implement it. Social audits should be prepared periodically as a means of evaluating and revising the program. Programs may be funded through price increases, reduction of profit, or federal incentives.

KEY TERMS

You should now be able to define and give an example relevant to each of the following terms:

ethics (37)
business ethics (37)
code of ethics (41)
whistle blowing (43)
social responsibility (44)
caveat emptor (46)
economic model of social responsibility (47)
socioeconomic model of social responsibility (48)
consumerism (50)
minority (52)
affirmative action program (54)
Equal Employment Opportunity Commission (EEOC) (54)
hard-core unemployed (54)
National Alliance of Business (NAB) (55)
pollution (56)
social audit (61)

REVIEW QUESTIONS

1. Why might an individual with high ethical standards act less ethically in business than in his or her personal life?
2. How would an organizational code of ethics help ensure ethical business behavior?
3. How and why did the American business environment change after the Great Depression?
4. What are the major differences between the economic model of social responsibility and the socioeconomic model?
5. What are the arguments for and against increasing the social responsibility of business?
6. Describe and give an example of each of the six basic rights of consumers.
7. There are more women than men in the United States. Why, then, are women considered a minority with regard to employment?
8. What is the goal of affirmative action programs? How is this goal achieved?
9. What is the primary function of the Equal Employment Opportunity Commission?
10. How do businesses contribute to each of the four forms of pollution? How can they avoid polluting the environment?
11. Our environment *can* be cleaned up and kept clean. Why haven't we simply done so?
12. Describe the steps involved in developing a social responsibility program within a large corporation.

DISCUSSION QUESTIONS

1. When a company acts in an ethically questionable manner, what types of problems are caused for the organization and its customers?
2. How can an employee take an ethical stand regarding a business decision when his or her superior has already taken a different position?
3. Overall, would it be more profitable for a business to follow the economic model or the socioeconomic model of social responsibility?
4. Why should business take on the task of training the hard-core unemployed?
5. To what extent should the blame for vehicular air pollution be shared by manufacturers, consumers, and government?
6. Why is there so much government regulation involving social responsibility issues? Should there be less?

VIDEO CASE

Home Depot's Social Responsibility Agenda

Home Depot is a home-improvement superstore chain that does everything on a large scale—including putting its corporate muscle behind a focused social responsibility agenda. Founded in 1978, Home Depot quickly became a major force in home-improvement retailing. These days, the company operates more than 1,000 stores across North America, employs 201,000 people, and rings up more than $38 billion in annual sales. Home Depot is an aggressive competitor, laying claim to more than 14 percent of the $140 billion U.S. market for home-improvement retailing. In the face of industry consolidation, the company has been able to stay well ahead of its nearest rival, Lowes Companies (the number 2 chain).

But just because the chain is big doesn't mean it's uncaring and impersonal. On the contrary: cofounders Bernard Marcus and Arthur Blank have fostered a corporate culture that puts a premium on meaningful social responsibility. Every year, Home Depot donates more than $10 million to charitable projects that benefit the communities in which the company does business. Rather than scatter its philanthropic resources, the company has chosen to concentrate on three broad areas: affordable housing, youth at risk, and the environment.

"The Home Depot Social Responsibility Report" on the company's Web site is a public report of exactly how the company distributes its annual charitable contributions. In one recent year, Home Depot provided support to dozens of housing groups, including more than 100 Habitat for Humanity construction projects and many local groups, such as The Clearwater Neighborhood Housing Services and the New Orleans Neighborhood Development Foundation. The chain also incorporates social responsibility into its business practices. For example, it will buy lumber and wood products only from suppliers that do not log from endangered forests, and it ships products strapped to environmentally-friendly pallets that can be reused multiple times.

On a more personal level, Home Depot strongly encourages all employees to get involved in the community through volunteerism and civic activities. On any given day, a small army of Home Depot volunteers may be wielding paintbrushes to fix up a family shelter, planting trees to spruce up an inner-city park, or nailing joists to support the interior of a Habitat for Humanity house.

Home Depot also strives to apply social responsibility to its employment practices, with the aim of assembling a workforce that is both diverse and reflective of the population in the markets it serves. Nonetheless, the chain recently settled a class action gender discrimination lawsuit brought by women employees, who charged that they were paid less than men, awarded fewer pay raises, and promoted less often.

As part of the settlement, Home Depot was required to establish a formal system to ensure that employees can notify management when they are interested in being considered for advancement. In announcing the settlement, the chain stressed that it was not admitting to wrongdoing. In fact, it defended its position, saying the store "provides opportunities for all of its associates to develop successful professional careers and is proud of its strong track record of having successful women involved in all areas of the company." Following the settlement, the company installed a $10 million automated system for recruiting and evaluating job candidates. Within two years, the company had boosted the number of female managers by 30 percent and boosted the number of minority managers by 20 percent. However, more recently, former and current employees have filed a number of lawsuits charging the company with racial, gender, and age discrimination.

Looking ahead, Home Depot believes that social responsibility can and should be an integral part of its business operations. Knowing that its customers feel good about buying from a company that actively commits resources to social issues, the chain remains committed to its focused strategy of philanthropy and volunteerism. This commitment extends throughout the company, fueled by top-level support from the cofounders and reinforcement from a corporate culture that places great value on being part of the solution, not part of the problem.[21]

Questions

1. In addition to making contributions to groups that address affordable housing, youth at risk, and the environment, what other social issues might Home Depot choose to support that fit well with its business direction?
2. As a publicly traded company, how can Home Depot justify budgeting more than $10 million annually for philanthropic causes?
3. In light of the class action gender discrimination settlement, what actions might Home Depot take to further strengthen the rights of its employees to equal treatment in the workplace?

Building skills for career success

1. Exploring the Internet

Socially responsible business behavior can be as simple as donating unneeded older computers to schools, mentoring interested learners in good business practice, or supplying public speakers to talk about career opportunities. Students, as part of the public at large, perceive a great deal of information about a company, its employees, and its owners by the positive social actions taken and perhaps even more by those actions not taken. Microsoft donates millions of dollars of computers and software to educational institutions every year. Some consider this level of corporate giving insufficient given the scale of the wealth of the corporation. Others believe that firms have no obligation to give back any more than they wish and that recipients should be grateful. Visit the text web site for updates to this exercise.

Assignment

1. Select any firm involved in high technology and the Internet such as Microsoft or IBM. Examine their Web site and report their corporate position on social responsibility and giving as they have stated it. What activities are they involved in? What programs do they support and how do they support them?
2. Search the Internet for commentary on business social responsibility, form your own opinions and then evaluate the social effort demonstrated by the firm you have selected. What more could the firm have done?

2. Developing Critical Thinking Skills

Recently an article entitled, "Employees Coming to Terms with Moral Issues on the Job" appeared in a big city newspaper. It posed the following situations:

- You are asked to work on a project you find morally wrong.
- Important tasks are left undone because a coworker spends more time planning a social event than working on a proposal.
- Your company is knowingly selling defective merchandise to customers.

Unfortunately, many employees currently are struggling with such issues. The moral dilemmas that arise when employees find their own ethical values incompatible with the work they do every day are causing a lot of stress in the workplace, and, furthermore, these dilemmas are not being discussed. There exists an ethics gap. You may have already faced a similar situation in your workplace.

Assignment

1. In small groups with your classmates, discuss your answers to the following questions:
   a. If you were faced with any of the above situations, what would you do?
   b. Would you complete work you found morally unacceptable, or would you leave it undone and say nothing?
   c. If you spoke up, what would happen to you or your career? What would be the risk?
   d. What are your options?
   e. If you were a manager rather than a lower-level employee, would you feel differently and take a different approach to the issue? Why?
2. In a written report, summarize what you learned from this discussion.

3. Building Team Skills

A firm's code of ethics outlines the kind of behavior expected within the organization and serves as a guideline for encouraging ethical behavior in the workplace. It reflects the rights of the firm's workers, shareholders, and consumers.

Assignment

1. Working in a team of four, find a code of ethics for a business firm. Start the search by asking firms in your community for a copy of their codes, by visiting the library, or by searching and downloading information from the Internet.
2. Analyze the code of ethics you have chosen and answer the following questions:
   a. What does the company's code of ethics say about the rights of its workers, shareholders, consumers, and suppliers? How does the code reflect the company's attitude toward competitors?
   b. How does this code of ethics resemble the information discussed in the chapter? How does it differ?
   c. As an employee in this company, how would you personally interpret the code of ethics? How might the code influence your behavior within the workplace? Give several examples.

4. Researching Different Careers

Business ethics has been at the heart of many discussions over the years and continues to trouble employees and shareholders. Stories about dishonesty and wrongful behavior in the workplace appear on a regular basis in newspapers and on the national news.

Assignment

Prepare a written report on the following:

1. Why can it be so difficult for people to do what is right?
2. What is your personal code of ethics? Prepare a code outlining what you believe is morally right. The document should include guidelines for your personal behavior.
3. How will your code of ethics affect your decisions about
   a. the types of questions you should ask in a job interview?
   b. selecting a company in which to work?

5. Improving Communication Skills

Businesses with programs of social responsibility provide a wealth of services to groups in their communities, such as schools, libraries, city governments, and service and civic organizations. If you are not aware of the businesses in your community that are doing this, you might be surprised at what is happening.

Assignment

1. Identify several businesses in your community that are providing services to local institutions and organizations.
2. Prepare a table using the following columns to indicate what services they provide, what the impact of these services has been on your community, and in what ways they make a difference to the organization or institution receiving the services:

    - Column 1: Name of company providing services
    - Column 2: Types of services provided
    - Column 3: Organizations or institutions receiving services
    - Column 4: Impact in the community
    - Column 5: Difference within the organization

3. Summarize your philosophy of business's social responsibility. As an employee, how would you feel about helping your company fulfill its social responsibility within the community? Why? Is that a fair job requirement? Explain.

Exploring Global Business

3

LEARNING OBJECTIVES

1 Explain the economic basis for international business.

2 Discuss the restrictions nations place on international trade, the objectives of these restrictions, and their results.

3 Outline the extent of international trade and identify the organizations working to foster it.

4 Define the methods by which a firm can organize for, and enter, international markets.

5 Describe the various sources of export assistance.

6 Identify the institutions that help firms and nations finance international business.

JLG's annual international sales outpaced the entire company's annual sales level of five years earlier.

inside business

JLG's Global Business Is Up in the Air

In any work environment, it's important that when employees go up, they must be able to come down—safely. That's the business of JLG Industries (http://www.jlg.com), a leading manufacturer of aerial work platforms and lifts. At its world headquarters in McConnellsburg, Pennsylvania, JLG makes heavy-duty, movable devices designed to lift workers and equipment as high as 150 feet off the ground.

More than one-quarter of JLG's $720 million in annual sales comes from international sales, mainly to European distributors that rent the devices to shipyards, construction firms, and other businesses. JLG began exporting in the 1970s, just a few years after founder John L. Grove started the business to commercialize the aerial lifts he invented in his garage. Because JLG's lifts can cost $110,000 or more, international sales were initially slow.

As word spread about the safety and convenience benefits of JLG's lifts, however, overseas businesses began to buy. In addition, the practice of renting instead of buying became more prevalent. Soon rental yards were popping up to cater to the needs of construction companies and other businesses that wanted to use aerial platforms for as short a period as half a day or as long as two years. To handle this global expansion, JLG opened factories in Scotland and Australia. But when the U.S. economy took a dip in 1991, JLG's sales and profits also dipped. The company quickly decided to close its overseas factories and concentrate on the U.S. market.

During the next few years, JLG rebuilt its domestic operations by improving productivity, which cut costs and let the company cut prices, as well. Year after year, the company boosted domestic sales, and then used that strong base to reenter the global marketplace. By the end of the 1990s, JLG's annual international sales had outpaced the entire company's annual sales level of five years earlier. The company's goal is to double international sales by moving more aggressively into growing global markets. Three joint ventures to form overseas dealerships (in the Netherlands, Thailand, and Brazil) are helping JLG get firmly established in Europe, Asia, and South America. The company has also set up sales and service offices to work with customers in South Africa, Italy, and Scotland.

JLG is building a reputation as a good global corporate citizen, as well. Concerned about pollution, the company recently unveiled a new lift powered by a fuel cell instead of a diesel engine. Although the cost of operating this new lift is higher than the cost of operating a traditional lift, JLG's management sees the technology becoming less expensive as fuel cells start showing up in cars and other consumer products. Meanwhile, JLG continues to roll out new products and enter new markets, raising lift sales to new heights around the world.[1]

JLG is just one of a growing number of U.S. companies, large and small, that are doing business with firms in other countries. Some companies, like JLG, sell to firms in other countries; others buy goods around the world to import into the United States. Whether they buy or sell products across national borders, these companies are all contributing to the volume of international trade that is fueling the global economy.

Theoretically, international trade is every bit as logical and worthwhile as interstate trade between, say, California and Washington. Yet nations tend to restrict the import of certain goods for a variety of reasons. For example, in the early 1990s the United States restricted the import of Chinese wrenches and steel pipe because they were made by forced labor.

In spite of such restrictions, international trade has increased almost steadily since World War II. Many of the industrialized nations have signed trade agreements intended to eliminate problems in international business and to help less-developed nations participate in world trade. Individual firms around the world have seized the opportunity to compete in foreign markets by exporting products and increasing foreign production, as well as by other means.

In an international education policy statement in 2000, President Clinton declared, "To continue to compete successfully in the global economy and to maintain our role as a world leader, the United States needs to ensure that its citizens develop a broad understanding of the world, proficiency in other languages, and knowledge of other cultures. America's leadership also depends on building ties with those who will guide the political, cultural, and economic development of their countries in the future."[2]

We describe international trade in this chapter in terms of modern specialization, whereby each country trades the surplus goods and services it produces most efficiently for products in short supply. We also explain the restrictions nations place on products and services from other countries and present some of the possible advantages and disadvantages of these restrictions. We then describe the extent of international trade and identify the organizations working to foster it. We describe several methods of entering international markets and the various sources of export assistance available from the federal government. Finally, we identify some of the institutions that provide the complex financing necessary for modern international trade.

LEARNING OBJECTIVE

1 Explain the economic basis for international business.

The Basis for International Business

International business encompasses all business activities that involve exchanges across national boundaries. Thus, a firm is engaged in international business when it buys some portion of its input from, or sells some portion of its output to, an organization located in a foreign country. (A small retail store may sell goods produced in some other country. However, because it purchases these goods from American distributors, it is not engaged in international trade.)

international business all business activities that involve exchanges across national boundaries

Using the Internet

"Our Mission: To Help U.S. Business Succeed, Globally." That's the stated goal for the International Trade Administration of the U.S. Department of Commerce and given that one out of every ten Americans owes his/her job to exports, it is clear just how important trade is to America and why it is encouraged. You will find a variety of useful information related to international business and trade at the ITA web site, located at **http://www.ita.doc.gov/**. The site has links to statistics, industry analysis, trade laws, and answers to often-asked trade questions.

Absolute and Comparative Advantage

Some countries are better equipped than others to produce particular goods or services. The reason may be a country's natural resources, its labor supply, or even customs or a historical accident. Such a country would be best off if it could *specialize* in the production of such products, because it can produce them most efficiently. The country could use what it needed of these products and then trade the surplus for products it could not produce efficiently on its own.

Saudi Arabia has thus specialized in the production of crude oil and petroleum products; South Africa, in diamonds;

Exploiting absolute advantage. Kuwait has long specialized in the production of crude oil and petroleum products at oil refineries such as this one. Because of their natural oil reserves, Kuwait and other countries in the Middle East enjoy an absolute advantage—their ability to produce petroleum products more efficiently than countries in any other area of the world.

absolute advantage the ability to produce a specific product more efficiently than any other nation

and Australia, in wool. Each of these countries is said to have an absolute advantage with regard to a particular product. An **absolute advantage** is the ability to produce a specific product more efficiently than any other nation.

One country may have an absolute advantage with regard to several products, whereas another country may have no absolute advantage at all. Yet it is still worthwhile for these two countries to specialize and trade with each other. To see why this is so, imagine you are the president of a successful manufacturing firm, and you can accurately type ninety words per minute. Your assistant can type eighty words per minute but would run the business poorly. You thus have an absolute advantage over your assistant in both typing and managing. But you cannot afford to type your own letters because your time is better spent in managing the business. That is, you have a comparative advantage in managing. Within a nation, a **comparative advantage** is the ability to produce a specific product more efficiently than any other product.

comparative advantage within a nation, the ability to produce a specific product more efficiently than any other product

Your assistant, on the other hand, has a comparative advantage in typing because he or she can do that better than managing the business. So you spend your time managing, and you leave the typing to your assistant. Overall, the business is run as efficiently as possible, because you are each working in accordance with your own comparative advantage.

The same is true for nations. Goods and services are produced more efficiently when each country specializes in the products for which it has a comparative advantage. Moreover, by definition, every country has a comparative advantage in *some* product. The United States has many comparative advantages—in research and development, high technology industries, and identifying new markets, for instance. California-based Yahoo Inc. is considered a pioneer in the development of Internet search software. As growth in Internet usage accelerates globally, firms with experience and a proven product can exploit the comparative advantage they enjoy over local firms in foreign markets who might just be getting started in the commercial areas of the Internet. So far Yahoo has expanded operations to twenty countries worldwide.[3]

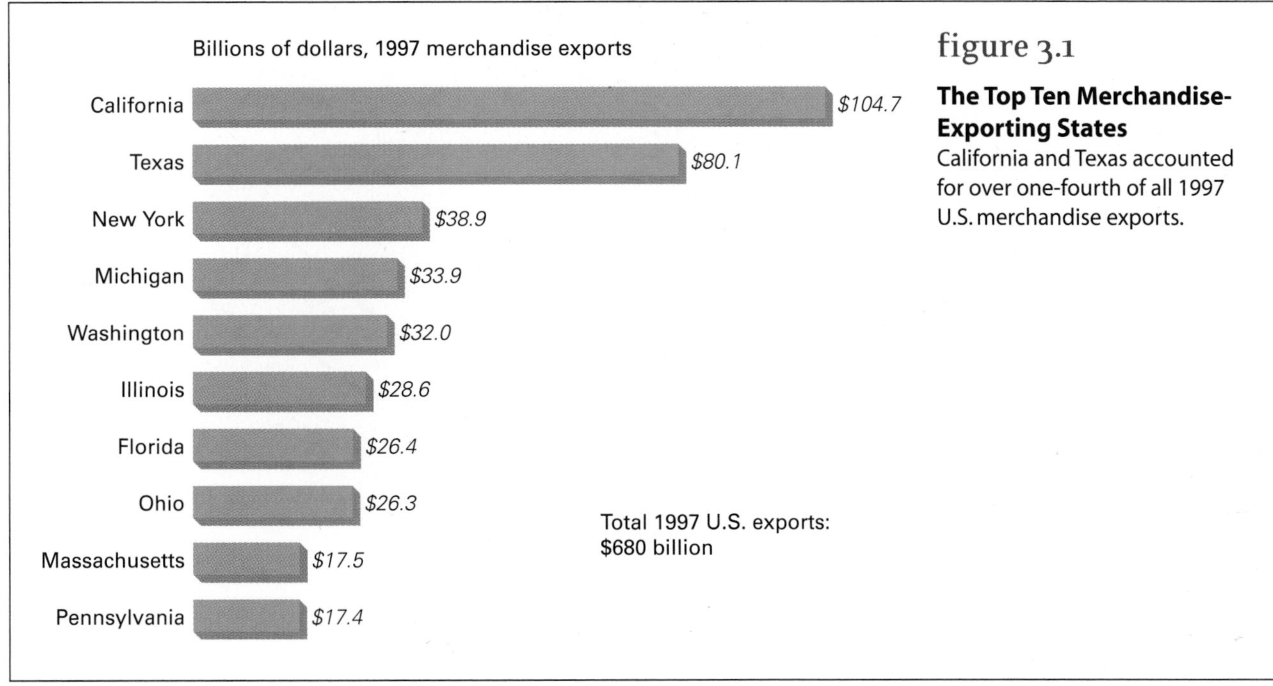

figure 3.1

The Top Ten Merchandise-Exporting States

California and Texas accounted for over one-fourth of all 1997 U.S. merchandise exports.

Source: *Review,* Federal Reserve Bank of St. Louis, January–February 2000, p. 4.

Exporting and Importing

Suppose the United States specializes in producing corn. It will then produce a surplus of corn, but perhaps it will have a shortage of wine. France, on the other hand, specializes in producing wine but experiences a shortage of corn. To satisfy both needs—for corn and for wine—the two countries should trade with each other. The United States should export corn and import wine. France should export wine and import corn.

Exporting is selling and shipping raw materials or products to other nations. The Boeing Company, for example, exports its airplanes to a number of countries for use by their airlines. Figure 3.1 shows the top ten merchandise-exporting states in this country.

exporting selling and shipping raw materials or products to other nations

Importing is purchasing raw materials or products in other nations and bringing them into one's own country. Thus, buyers for Macy's department stores may purchase rugs in India or raincoats in England and have them shipped back to the United States for resale.

importing purchasing raw materials or products in other nations and bringing them into one's own country

Importing and exporting are the principal activities in international trade. They give rise to an important concept called the balance of trade. A nation's **balance of trade** is the total value of its exports *minus* the total value of its imports, over some period of time. If a country imports more than it exports, its balance of trade is negative and is said to be *unfavorable.* (A negative balance of trade is unfavorable because the country must export money to pay for its excess imports.) In 1999 the United States imported $1,030 billion worth of merchandise and exported $683 billion worth. It thus had a trade deficit of $347 billion. A **trade deficit** is a negative balance of trade (see Figure 3.2). However, as shown in Figure 3.3, the United States has consistently enjoyed a large and rapidly growing surplus in services. For example, in 1999 the United States imported $200 billion worth and exported $275 billion worth of services, thus creating a favorable balance of $75 billion.[4]

balance of trade the total value of a nation's exports minus the total value of its imports, over some period of time

trade deficit a negative balance of trade

On the other hand, when a country exports more than it imports, it is said to have a *favorable* balance of trade. This has consistently been the case for Japan over the last two decades or so.

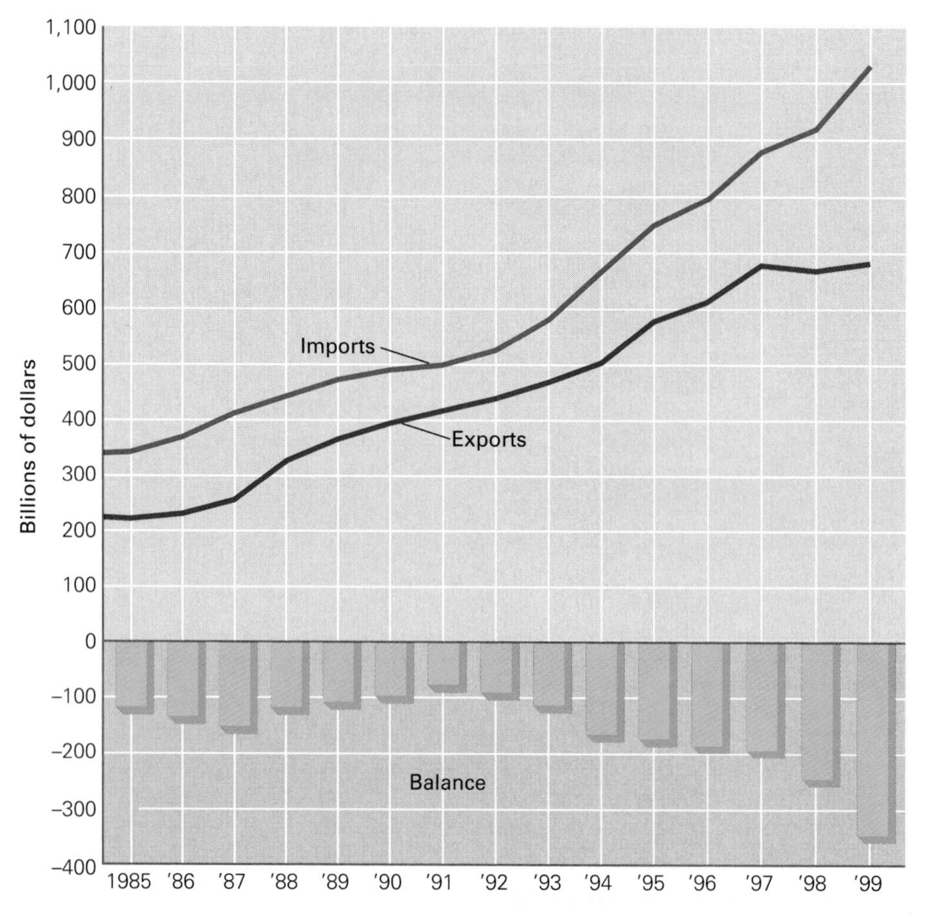

figure 3.2

U.S. International Trade in Goods

If a country imports more goods than it exports, the balance of trade is negative, as it was in the United States in 1999.

Source: U.S. Department of Commerce, International Trade Administration, http://www.ita.doc.gov/td/industry/otea/usfth/aggregate/H99t01.txt, May 15, 2000.

balance of payments the total flow of money into the country minus the total flow of money out of the country, over some period of time

A nation's **balance of payments** is the total flow of money into the country *minus* the total flow of money out of the country, over some period of time. Balance of payments is thus a much broader concept than balance of trade. It includes imports and exports, of course. But it also includes investments, money spent by foreign tourists, payments by foreign governments, aid to foreign governments, and all other receipts and payments.

A continual deficit in a nation's balance of payments (a negative balance) can cause other nations to lose confidence in its economy. A continual surplus may indicate that the country encourages exports but limits imports by imposing trade restrictions. As Figure 3.4 shows, the United States has consistently suffered a deficit in its balance of payments since 1992. A bright spot for the U.S. global trade position is the stellar growth of worldwide Internet commerce projected to reach $6.8 trillion by 2004 according to Forrester Research Inc. Although North America currently represents the vast majority of activity, Asian-Pacific and Western European countries are expected to make great strides in the race to catch up over the next few years.[5]

Restrictions to International Business

LEARNING OBJECTIVE

2 Discuss the restrictions nations place on international trade, the objectives of these restrictions, and their results.

Specialization and international trade can result in the efficient production of want-satisfying goods and services on a worldwide basis. As we have noted, international business is generally increasing. Yet the nations of the world continue to erect barriers to free trade. They do so for reasons ranging from internal political and economic pressures to simple mistrust of other nations. We examine first the types of restrictions that are applied and then the arguments for and against trade restrictions.

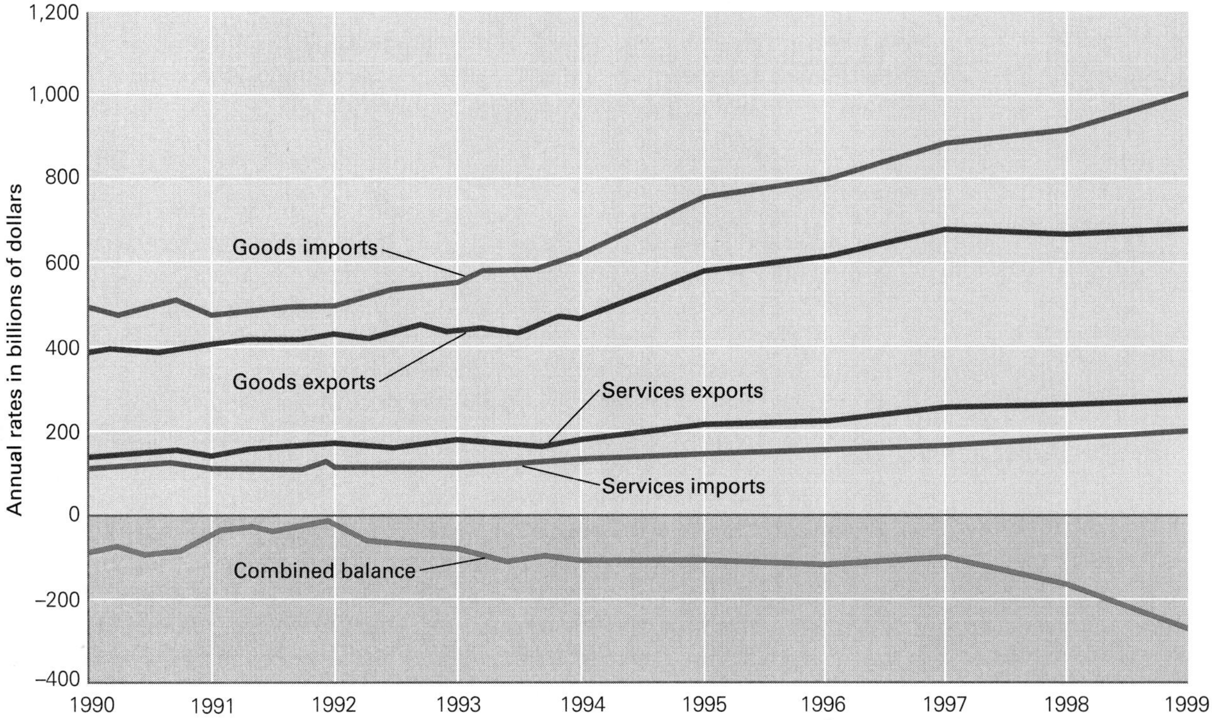

Annual rates in billions of dollars
1,200
1,000
800
600
400
200
0
−200
−400
1990
1991
1992
1993
1994
1995
1996
1997
1998
1999
Goods imports
Goods exports
Services exports
Services imports
Combined balance

figure 3.3

U.S. International Trade in Goods and Services and the Combined Balance

Even though the United States has a positive balance of trade in services, the combined effect is still a deficit in our balance of trade.

Source: U.S. Department of Commerce, International Trade Administration, http://www.ita.doc.gov/td/industry/otea/usfth/aggregate/H99t02.txt, May 16, 2000.

1989
1990
1991
1992
1993
1994
1995
1996
1997
1998
1999
−350
−300
−250
−200
−150
−100
−50
0
50
Deficit in billions of dollars

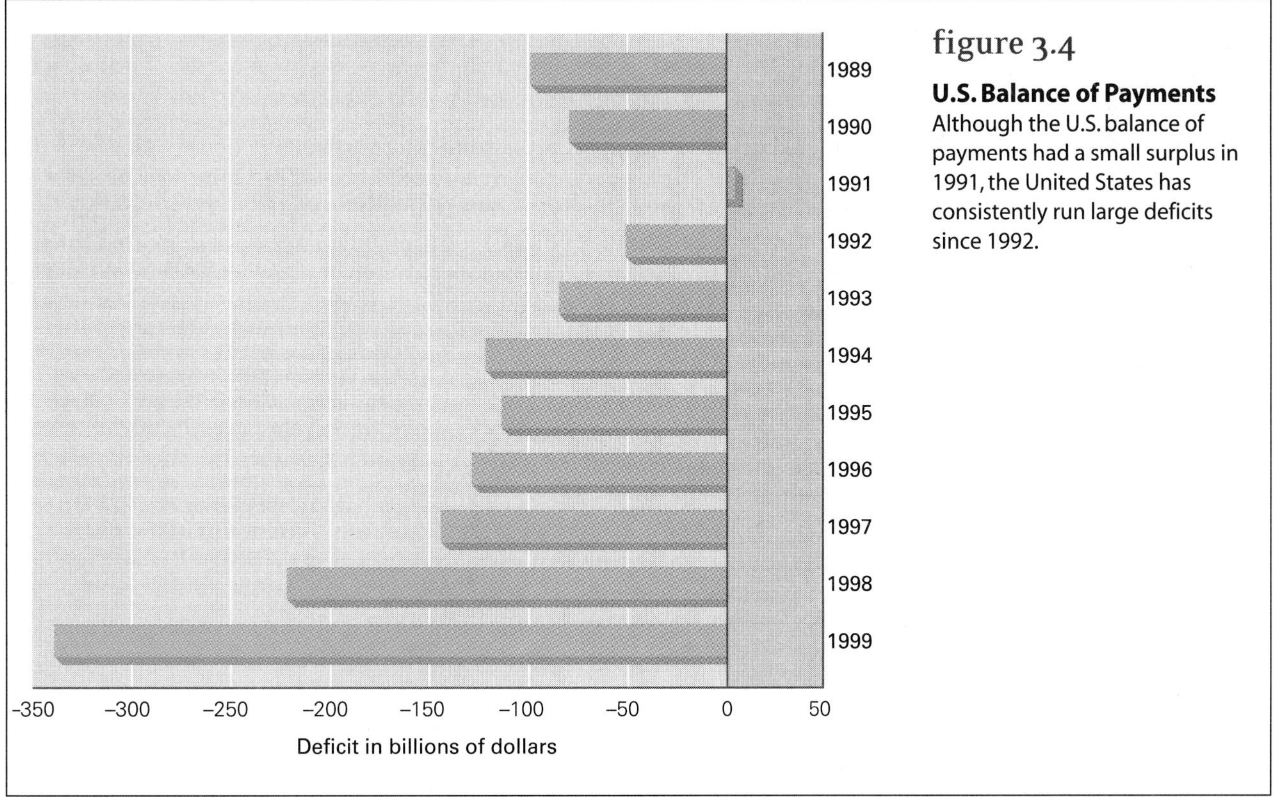

figure 3.4

U.S. Balance of Payments

Although the U.S. balance of payments had a small surplus in 1991, the United States has consistently run large deficits since 1992.

Source: U.S. Department of Commerce, Bureau of Economic Analysis web site at http://www.bea.doc.gov/bea/di/bopa/bop1-2.htm, May 19, 2000.

Types of Trade Restrictions

Nations are generally eager to export their products. They want to provide markets for their industries and to develop a favorable balance of trade. Hence, most trade restrictions are applied to imports from other nations.

import duty (tariff) a tax levied on a particular foreign product entering a country

Tariffs

Perhaps the most commonly applied trade restriction is the customs (or import) duty. An **import duty** (also called a **tariff**) is a tax levied on a particular foreign product entering a country. The two types of tariffs are revenue tariffs and protective tariffs; both have the effect of raising the price of the product in the importing nations, but for different reasons. *Revenue tariffs* are imposed solely to generate income for the government. For example, the United States imposes a duty on Scotch whiskey solely for revenue purposes. *Protective tariffs*, on the other hand, are imposed to protect a domestic industry from competition by keeping the price of competing imports level with or higher than the price of similar domestic products. Because fewer units of the product will be sold at the increased price, fewer units will be imported. The French and Japanese agricultural sectors would both shrink drastically if their nations abolished the protective tariffs that keep the price of imported farm products high. Today U.S. tariffs are the lowest in history, with average tariff rates on all imports under 4 percent.

dumping exportation of large quantities of a product at a price lower than that of the same product in the home market

Some countries rationalize their protectionist policies as a way of offsetting an international trade practice called dumping. **Dumping** is exportation of large quantities of a product at a price lower than that of the same product in the home market. Thus, dumping drives down the price of the domestic item. Recently, for example, the Pencil Makers Association, which represents eight U.S. pencil manufacturers, charged that low-priced pencils from Thailand and the People's Republic of China were being sold in the United States at less than fair value prices. Unable to compete with these inexpensive imports, several domestic manufacturers had to shut down.[6] To protect themselves, domestic manufacturers can obtain an antidumping duty through the government to offset the advantage of the foreign product. In 2000, for example, the U.S. Department of Commerce imposed preliminary antidumping duties on carbon steel products from the United Kingdom.[7]

nontariff barrier a nontax measure imposed by a government to favor domestic over foreign suppliers

Nontariff Barriers

A **nontariff barrier** is a nontax measure imposed by a government to favor domestic over foreign suppliers. Nontariff barriers create obstacles to the marketing of foreign goods in a country and increase costs for exporters. The following are a few examples of government-imposed nontariff barriers:

import quota a limit on the amount of a particular good that may be imported into a country during a given period of time

embargo a complete halt to trading with a particular nation or in a particular product

foreign-exchange control a restriction on the amount of a particular foreign currency that can be purchased or sold

currency devaluation the reduction of the value of a nation's currency relative to the currencies of other countries

- An **import quota** is a limit on the amount of a particular good that may be imported into a country during a given period of time. The limit may be set in terms of either quantity (so many pounds of beef) or value (so many dollars' worth of shoes). Quotas may also be set on individual products imported from specific countries. Once an import quota has been reached, imports are halted until the specified time has elapsed.
- An **embargo** is a complete halt to trading with a particular nation or in a particular product. The embargo is used most often as a political weapon. At present, the United States has import embargoes against Cuba and Iraq—both as a result of extremely poor political relations.
- A **foreign-exchange control** is a restriction on the amount of a particular foreign currency that can be purchased or sold. By limiting the amount of foreign currency importers can obtain, a government limits the amount of goods importers can purchase with that currency. This has the effect of limiting imports from the country whose foreign exchange is being controlled.
- A nation can increase or decrease the value of its money relative to the currency of other nations. **Currency devaluation** is the reduction of the value of a nation's currency relative to the currencies of other countries.

  Devaluation increases the cost of foreign goods, while it decreases the cost of domestic goods to foreign firms. For example, suppose the British pound is worth \$2. Then an American-made \$2,000 computer can be purchased for £1,000. But if the United Kingdom devalues the pound so that it is worth only $1, that same computer will cost £2,000. The increased cost, in pounds, will reduce the import of American computers—and all foreign goods—into England.

On the other hand, before devaluation, a £500 set of English bone china costs an American $1,000. After the devaluation, the set of china will cost only $500. The decreased cost will make the china—and all English goods—much more attractive to U.S. purchasers.

- Bureaucratic red tape is more subtle than the other forms of nontariff barriers. Yet it can be the most frustrating trade barrier of all. A few examples are unnecessarily restrictive application of standards and complex requirements related to product testing, labeling, and certification.

Another type of nontariff barrier is related to cultural attitudes. Cultural barriers can impede acceptance of products in foreign countries. For example, illustrations of feet are regarded as despicable in Thailand. When customers are unfamiliar with particular products from another country, their general perceptions of the country itself affect their attitude toward the product and help determine whether they will buy it. Because Mexican cars have not been viewed by the world as being quality products, Volkswagen, for example, may not want to advertise that some of its models sold in the United States are made in Mexico.[8] Many retailers on the Internet have yet to come to grips with the task of designing an online shopping site that is attractive and functional for all global customers. According to a study by Forrester Research, 46 percent of all orders to U.S. based sites placed by people living outside the United States went unfilled due to process failures. Given that the Forrester study suggests that the average web site gets 30 percent of its traffic and 10 percent of its orders from non-U.S. customers, the results suggest an enormous loss of potential export sales will continue until web sites better reflect local buyer culture and behavior.[9]

This dog could save your life. Products are banned because they may pose health and safety hazards. In Oahu, Hawaii, Department of Agriculture beagle "Cagney" sniffs luggage from arrivals from Asia for illegal fruit, vegetables, and meat.

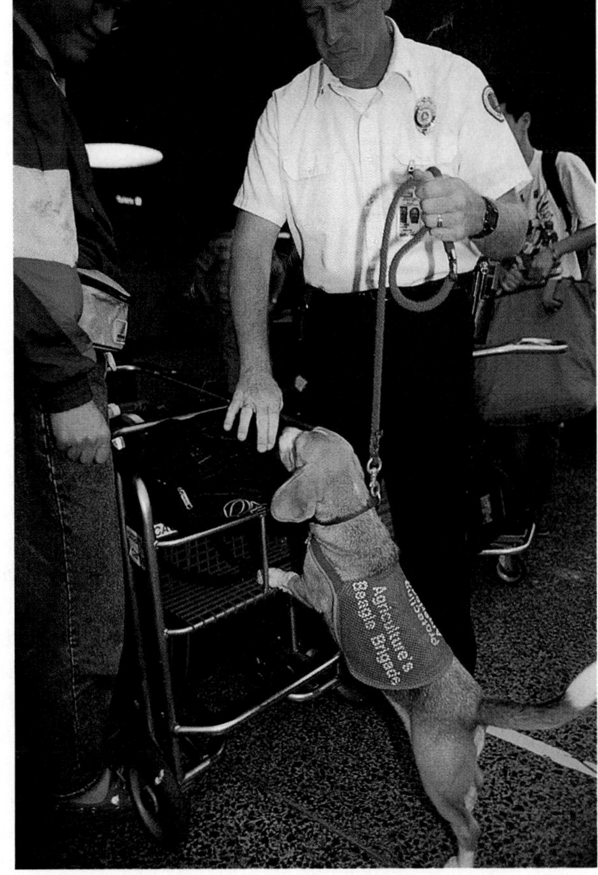

Reasons for Trade Restrictions

Various reasons are advanced for trade restrictions either on the import of specific products or on trade with particular countries. We have noted that political considerations are usually involved in trade embargoes. Other frequently cited reasons for restricting trade include the following:

- *To equalize a nation's balance of payments.* This may be considered necessary to restore confidence in the country's monetary system and in its ability to repay its debts.
- *To protect new or weak industries.* A new, or *infant,* industry may not be strong enough to withstand foreign competition. Temporary trade restrictions may be used to give it a chance to grow and become self-sufficient. The problem is that once an industry is protected from foreign competition, it may refuse to grow and "temporary" trade restrictions will become permanent. For example, a recent report by the General Accounting Office (GAO), the congressional investigative agency, has accused the federal government of routinely imposing quotas on foreign textiles without "demonstrating the threat of serious damage" to U.S. industry. The GAO said the Committee for the Implementation of Textile Agreements sometimes applies quotas even though it cannot prove the textile industry's claims that American companies have been hurt or jobs eliminated.

- *To protect national security.* Restrictions in this category generally apply to technological products that must be kept out of the hands of potential enemies. For example, strategic and defense-related goods cannot be exported to unfriendly nations.
- *To protect the health of citizens.* Products may be embargoed because they are dangerous or unhealthy (for example, farm products contaminated with insecticides).
- *To retaliate for another nation's trade restrictions.* A country whose exports are taxed by another country may respond by imposing tariffs on imports from that country.
- *To protect domestic jobs.* By restricting imports, a nation can protect jobs in domestic industries. However, protecting these jobs can be expensive. For example, U.S. consumers spend about $25 billion a year to protect jobs in the textile and apparel industry—about $50,000 annually per job.[10] And to protect 9,000 jobs in the U.S. carbon steel industry costs $6.8 billion, or $750,000 per job.[11]

Reasons Against Trade Restrictions

Trade restrictions have immediate and long-term economic consequences—both within the restricting nation and in world-trade patterns. These include

- *Higher prices for consumers.* Higher prices may result from the imposition of tariffs or the elimination of foreign competition, as described above. For example, imposing quota restrictions and import protections adds $25 billion annually to U.S. consumers' apparel costs by directly increasing costs for imported apparel.
- *Restriction of consumers' choices.* Again, this is a direct result of the elimination of some foreign products from the marketplace and of the artificially high prices that importers must charge for products that *are* still imported.
- *Misallocation of international resources.* The protection of weak industries results in the inefficient use of limited resources. The economies of both the restricting nation and other nations eventually suffer because of this waste.
- *Loss of jobs.* The restriction of imports by one nation must lead to cutbacks—and the loss of jobs—in the export-oriented industries of other nations. Furthermore, trade protection has a significant effect on the composition of employment. U.S. trade restrictions—whether on textiles, apparel, steel, or automobiles—benefit only a few industries while harming many others. The gains in employment accrue to the protected industries and their primary suppliers, and the losses are spread across all other industries. A few states gain employment, but many other states lose employment.

The Extent of International Business

LEARNING OBJECTIVE

3 Outline the extent of international trade and identify the organizations working to foster it.

Restrictions or not, international business is growing. Although the worldwide recession of 1991 slowed the rate of growth, globalization is a reality of our time. Since the end of World War II, the proportion of trade as a share of global income has risen from 7 percent to 21 percent. In the United States, international trade now accounts for over one-fourth of gross domestic product. As trade barriers decrease, new competitors enter the global marketplace, creating more choices for consumers and new opportunities for job seekers. International business will grow along with the expansion of commercial use of the Internet. By 2003 more than two-thirds of all Internet users will log on from outside the United States. The non-American share of e-commerce is expected to reach 56 percent, more than doubling the 26 percent share in 1998. Meanwhile, European consumer e-commerce is expected to grow from $5.6 billion in 1998 to $430 billion by 2003, and Japanese online buying is expected to expand twentyfold over five years from $3.2 billion in 1999 to $63.4 billion in 2004. The numbers clearly suggest opportunities for firms with an online global capability.[12]

The World Economic Outlook for Trade

While the U.S. economy has been growing steadily over the last nine years and is recording the longest peacetime expansion in the nation's history, the economies of some of our major trading partners have been sluggish. This weakness of economies overseas is the major reason behind the growth of our trade deficit in the last eight years. Now, with the new wave of market-oriented economies in Eastern Europe and Asia, international experts predict global economic growth of 3.5 percent to 4 percent for the next two decades.[13] At this rate of growth, world production of goods and services will double by the year 2020. Figure 3.5 shows the growth rate of world real GDP since 1970.

Perhaps even more impressive is that inflation has been falling in almost every major region of the world. For example, in South America, the declines have been spectacular. The International Monetary Fund (IMF), an international bank with more than 150 member nations, estimates that inflation rates in the developed industrial countries have fallen from 4.3 percent in 1991 to an estimated 2.0 percent in 2000. In the developing economies, the inflation slowdown has been even greater, from about 13 percent per year in 1991 to about four percent in 2000. Hence, a favorable economic outlook for trade in the new millenium (see Figure 3.6).

Pretty as a picture. Globalization represents a huge opportunity for all countries and businesses. One giant economy on the South Asian subcontinent—India—is expected to grow rapidly. Here, Kodak products are for sale on a wooden boat at the Dal Lake in Kashmir, India.

Canada and Western Europe Our leading export-import partner, Canada, is projected to show the fastest growth. The inflation rate in Canada is about half of the U.S. rate, and our exports to Canada are booming. However, economies in Western Europe have been growing slowly. Only the United Kingdom enjoyed good economic growth in 2000 with the lowest level of unemployment in 20 years; the economies of Germany, Greece, Denmark, Switzerland, and Italy all grew less than two percent.

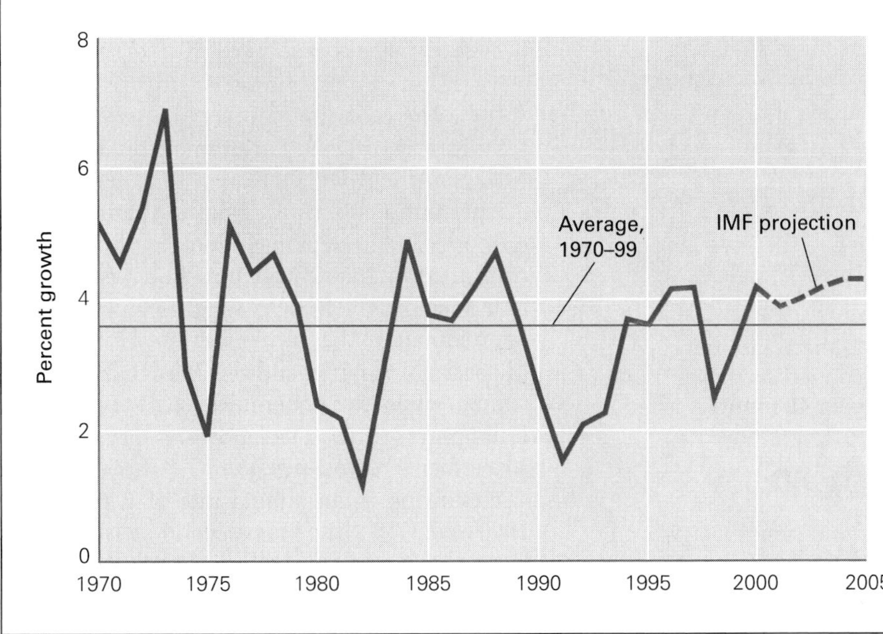

figure 3.5

Growth of World Real GDP Since 1970

Even though the economies of some of our major trading partners have been weak, with the new market-oriented economies in Eastern Europe and Asia, global economic growth is expected to grow at about 4 percent annually.

Source: *The World Economic Outlook: The International Monetary Fund.* Reprinted with permission from the International Monetary Fund.

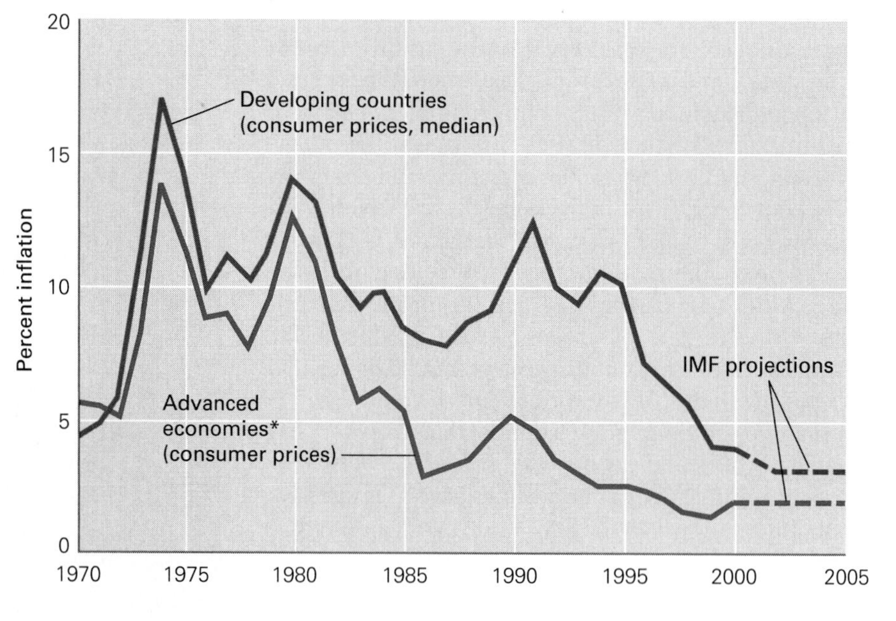

figure 3.6

Annual Inflation Rates in Developing and Advanced Economies*

Inflation rate has been falling in almost every major region of the world and is expected to remain low in the near future.

*Advanced economies include the United States, Japan, Germany, France, Italy, United Kingdom, and Canada. Developing economies include most countries in Africa, Asia, the Middle East, and South America.

Source: *The World Economic Outlook: The International Monetary Fund.* Reprinted with permission from the International Monetary Fund.

Mexico and South America Our second largest export-import partner, Mexico, suffered its sharpest recession ever in 1995, but its growth rate in 2000 was about 4.5 percent. In general, the Latin American economies grew more rapidly in 1999 than in the preceding two years. Most of the increase occurred because of Argentina's recovery from recession in 1995. The economies of the other major countries in the region—Brazil, Chile, Colombia, and Venezuela—continue their upward trend in 2000. More rapid growth of about 4.0 percent is projected for the region.

Japan The recovery of the Japanese economy from recession remains weak. After falling in 1997 and 1998, real GDP increased during the first half of 1999, but it declined by 4 percent again during the second half of the year. However, improvements in corporate profits, industrial production, and business confidence is expected.

spotLight

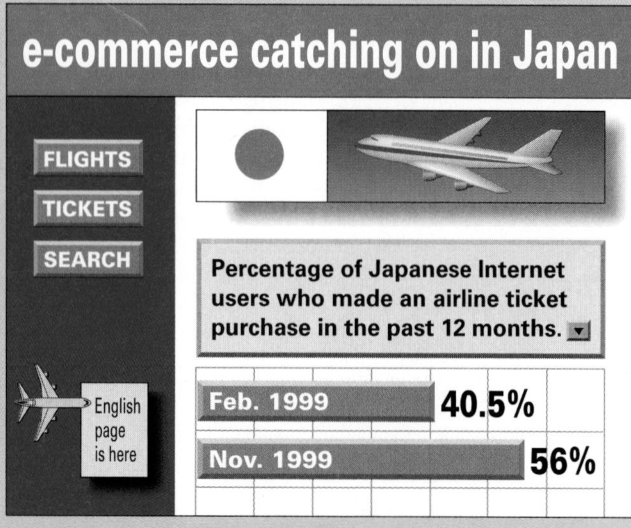

Source: Associated Press, February 24, 2000.

Asia The economic recovery in Asia increased significantly in 1999. For example, in Korea and Malaysia, the GDP increased 10.5 percent and 5.5 percent, respectively. Even in the hardest hit economy in the region, Indonesia, the recovery continued in 2000. Growth in Korea is expected to moderate somewhat to about 7 percent, and be approximately the same rate in Hong Kong, Malaysia, Singapore, and the Taiwan Province of China, while the economies of Indonesia, the Philippines, and Thailand are projected to strengthen by 3 to 5 percent.

Growing at an annual rate of 7 percent in 1999 and 2000, the Chinese economy is by far the largest of the emerging Asian markets. China's inflation fell from an estimated 10 percent in 1996 to less than one percent in 1999: however, prices may increase marginally in 2000. Although inflation is down and economic growth continues, China faces several challenges. Perhaps the biggest will be tackling the inefficiency of China's state-owned enterprises. Many of these enterprises lose money every year and reforming them will be politically difficult. Unemployment and underemployment are major problems in China, and state-run businesses employ millions. However, China's prospective membership in the World Trade Organization is likely to add momentum to the structural reforms.

Storm in a coffee cup? American businesses realize that the Chinese economy is the largest of the emerging Asian markets. Drinking coffee is gaining popularity in China and Starbucks gourmet coffee has recently taken this new marketplace by storm.

The two giant economies on the South Asian subcontinent, India and Pakistan are each expected to grow about 6 percent in 2000. Economic growth in Australia and New Zealand is expected to be about 4 percent.

Central and Eastern Europe and Russia After World War II, trade between the United States and the communist nations of Central and Eastern Europe was minimal. The United States maintained high tariff barriers on imports from most of these countries and also restricted its exports. But since the disintegration of the Soviet Union and the collapse of communism, trade between the United States and Central and Eastern Europe has expanded substantially.

The countries that made the transition from communist to market economies quickly have recorded positive growth for several years; those that did not continue to struggle. Among the nations that have enjoyed several years of positive economic growth are the member countries of the Central European Free Trade Association (CEFTA): Hungary, the Czech Republic, Poland, Slovenia, and the Republic of Slovakia.

Russia has been one of the countries whose transition to a market economy has been difficult. However, Russia's economic performance in 1999 was much better than expected. For example, GDP increased by 3 percent rather than remaining flat and inflation was lower than anticipated. The reform efforts in Russia and most other countries of the former Soviet Union continue to lag behind schedule. In Ukraine and Belarus, economic growth remains slow while in Kazakhstan the economy is growing at about 3 percent annual rate.

In central Europe and the Baltics economy is expanding. In Hungary and Poland, GDP is growing between 4.5 to 5 percent. Recovery is expected in the Czech Republic after three years of weak economic growth. Economies in the Slovak Republic, Estonia, Latvia, and Lithuania are expected to recover quite rapidly in 2001.

U.S. exports to Central and Eastern Europe and Russia will increase, as will U.S. investment in these countries, as demand for capital goods and technology opens new markets for U.S. products. There has already been a substantial expansion in trade between the United States and the Czech and Slovak Federal Republic, Hungary, and Poland.

Exports and the U.S. Economy Globalization represents a huge opportunity for all countries—rich or poor. The fifteenfold increase in trade volume over the past forty years has been one of the most important factors in the rise of living standards

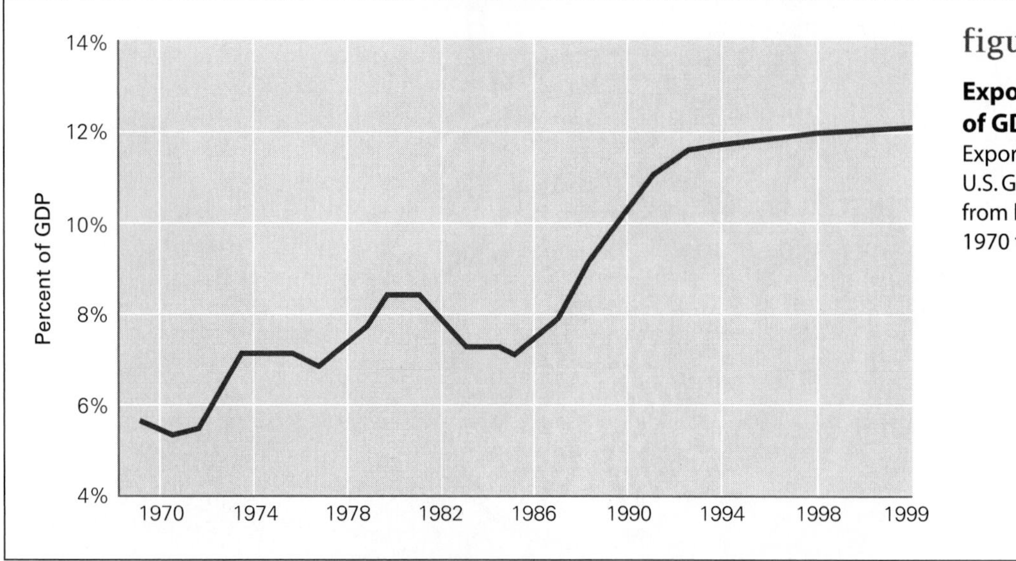

figure 3.7

Exports as Percentage of GDP

Exports as a percentage of U.S. GDP have increased from less than 6 percent in 1970 to 12 percent today.

Source: U.S. Department of Commerce; and Federal Reserve Bank of St. Louis, February 2000.

around the world.[14] During this time, exports have become increasingly important to the U.S. economy. As Figure 3.7 shows, exports as a percentage of U.S. gross domestic product have more than doubled since 1970. And our exports to developing and newly industrialized countries are on the rise. Table 3.1 shows the value of U.S. merchandise exports to, and imports from, each of the nation's ten major trading

Talking Technology

Building Trust into Global e-Commerce

GLOBAL E-COMMERCE IS SET TO EXPLODE, as more people log onto the Internet and more businesses launch web sites to sell to individuals and organizations. Thanks to the speed and convenience of online transactions, buyers and sellers can connect even when they're in another country or continent. Yet online identities can be hidden, stolen, and forged, so how do participants who are oceans apart learn to trust in the integrity of online transactions?

The answer, for a growing number of online businesses, is to arrange for encrypted digital certificates verifying that the user is who it says it is. For example, http://www.schwab.com is actually the site of stockbroker Charles Schwab. Verisign, one of the largest digital certificate suppliers in the world, authenticates and issues 400 such certificates every day. Says CEO Stratton Sclavos: "The notion of trust differs from country to country, but the Internet breaks down geographic borders, and you have to have some commonality," Sclavos explains. Verisign's technology is being used in twenty countries outside the United States, including Korea, Japan, Ireland, France, and Germany.

Business-to-business transactions—especially financial transactions, which can entail millions of dollars—require particularly powerful and secure authentication technology. Because of recent changes in U.S. law, digital certification firms such as CyberTrust can now export 128-bit cryptography software to approved international customers. Transactions encrypted with this software are extremely secure: only one "key" out of many billions of possible keys will unlock the code.

China, like many other countries, is moving ahead with digital certification as part of its infrastructure for e-commerce. The People's Bank of China recently arranged for Entrust Technologies, Sun Microsystems China, and Beijing Data Systems to work on digital certificates covering the central bank's interactions with businesses and consumers. Projections indicate that China's Web-surfing population will grow beyond 40 million within the next two years. Digital certification will help build trust between the millions of Chinese buyers and sellers who are joining their global counterparts online.

table 3.1 Value of U.S. Merchandise Exports and Imports, 1999

Rank/Trading Partner	Exports ($ billions)	Rank/Trading Partner	Imports ($ billions)
1 Canada	166.2	1 Canada	198.3
2 Mexico	86.9	2 Japan	131.4
3 Japan	57.5	3 Mexico	109.7
4 United Kingdom	38.3	4 China	81.8
5 Germany	26.8	5 Germany	55.1
6 South Korea	23.0	6 United Kingdom	39.2
7 Netherlands	19.4	7 Taiwan	35.2
8 Taiwan	19.1	8 South Korea	31.3
9 France	18.9	9 France	25.9
10 Singapore	16.2	10 Singapore	22.4

Source: U.S. Department of Commerce, International Trade Administration, http://www.ita.doc.gov/td/industry/otea/usfth/aggregate/H99t06.txt, May 20, 2000.

partners. Note that Canada, Mexico, and Japan are the best customers for our exports; however, Japan is our second most important source of imports. Figure 3.8 shows the U.S. goods export and import shares in 1999. Major U.S. exports and imports are manufactured goods, agricultural products, and mineral fuels. Note again that approximately 46 percent of our exports and 43 percent of our imports were from the same three leading trading partners.

Many more U.S. firms need to take advantage of the almost limitless potential in exporting. At present, only one-third of all U.S. companies export. About fifty of these companies account for more than 40 percent of the country's exports. No industrial nation has greater potential for export expansion than the United States, and a mere 15 percent growth in export sales would put 1 million Americans to work.

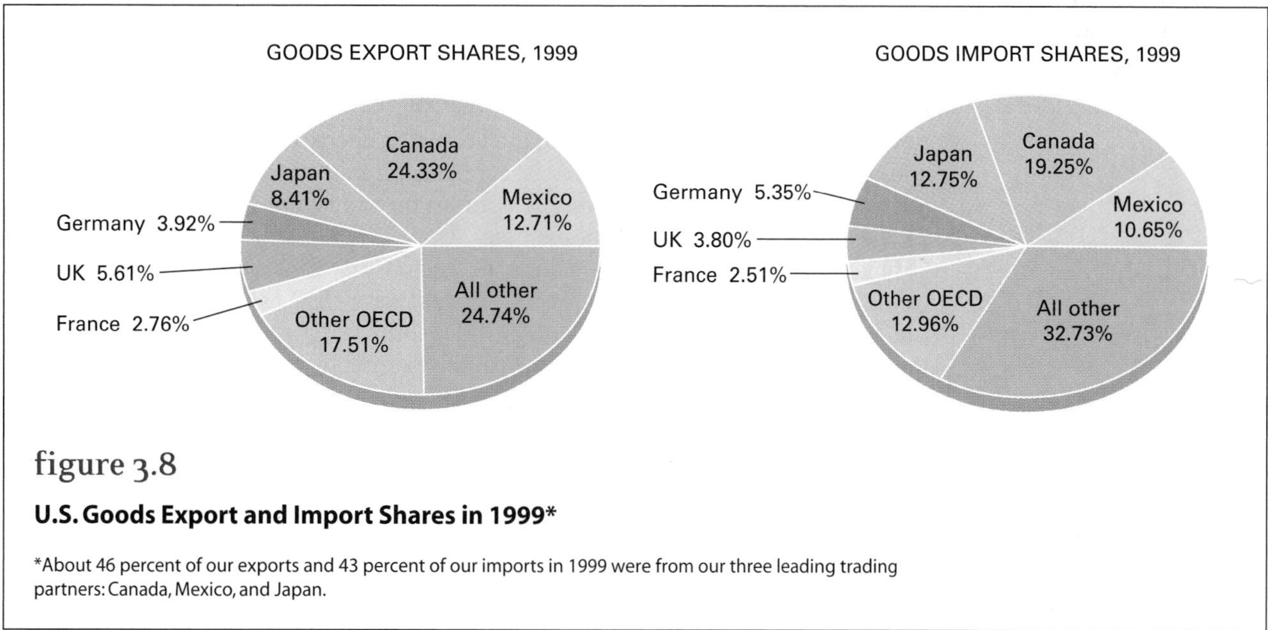

figure 3.8

U.S. Goods Export and Import Shares in 1999*

*About 46 percent of our exports and 43 percent of our imports in 1999 were from our three leading trading partners: Canada, Mexico, and Japan.

Source: The Federal Reserve Bank of St. Louis, *National Economic Trends,* April 2000, p. 18.

The General Agreement on Tariffs and Trade and the World Trade Organization

General Agreement on Tariffs and Trade (GATT) an international organization of 132 nations dedicated to reducing or eliminating tariffs and other barriers to world trade

At the end of World War II, the United States and twenty-two other nations organized the body that came to be known as GATT. The **General Agreement on Tariffs and Trade (GATT)** was an international organization of 132 nations dedicated to reducing or eliminating tariffs and other barriers to world trade. These 132 nations accounted for 90 percent of the world's merchandise trade. GATT, headquartered in Geneva, Switzerland, provided a forum for tariff negotiations and a means for settling international trade disputes and problems. *Most-favored-nation status (MFN)* was the famous principle of GATT. It meant that each GATT member nation was to be treated equally by all contracting nations. MFN therefore assured that any tariff reductions or other trade concessions were automatically extended to all GATT members. From 1947–1994, the body sponsored eight rounds of negotiations to reduce trade restrictions. Three of the most fruitful were the Kennedy Round, the Tokyo Round, and the Uruguay Round.

The Kennedy Round (1964-1967) In 1962 the U.S. Congress passed the *Trade Expansion Act.* This law gave President John F. Kennedy the authority to negotiate reciprocal trade agreements that could reduce U.S. tariffs by as much as 50 percent. Armed with this authority, which was granted for a period of five years, President Kennedy called for a round of negotiations through GATT.

These negotiations, which began in 1964, have since become known as the *Kennedy Round.* They were aimed at reducing tariffs and other barriers to trade in both industrial and agricultural products. The participants succeeded in reducing tariffs on these products by an average of more than 35 percent. They were less successful in removing other types of trade barriers.

The Tokyo Round (1973-1979) In 1973 representatives of approximately one hundred nations gathered in Tokyo for another round of GATT negotiations. The *Tokyo Round* was completed in 1979. The participants negotiated tariff cuts of 30 to 35 percent, which were to be implemented over an eight-year period. In addition, they were able to remove or ease such nontariff barriers as import quotas, unrealistic quality standards for imports, and unnecessary red tape in customs procedures.

The Uruguay Round (1986-1993) In 1986 the *Uruguay Round* was launched to extend trade liberalization and to widen the GATT treaty to include textiles, agricultural products, business services, and intellectual-property rights. This most ambitious and comprehensive global commercial agreement in history concluded overall negotiations on December 15, 1993, with delegations on hand from 109 nations. Calling the 22,000-page agreement "truly momentous," U.S. Vice President Albert Gore said it will "bring the global trading system into the twenty-first century." Gore noted that in developed countries alone, the agreement could raise GDP as much as 3.5 percent in the coming decade. The agreement included provisions to lower tariffs by greater than one-third, to reform trade in agricultural goods, to write new rules of trade for intellectual property and services, and to strengthen the dispute-settlement process. These reforms were expected to expand the world economy by an estimated $200 billion annually.

World Trade Organization (WTO) powerful successor to GATT that incorporates trade in goods, services, and ideas

The Uruguay Round also created the **World Trade Organization (WTO)** on January 1, 1995. The WTO was established by GATT to oversee the provisions of the Uruguay Round and resolve any resulting trade disputes. Membership of the WTO obliges member nations to observe GATT rules. The WTO has judicial powers to mediate among members disputing the new rules. It incorporates trade in goods, services, and ideas, and exerts more binding authority than GATT.

International Economic Communities

economic community an organization of nations formed to promote the free movement of resources and products among its members and to create common economic policies

The primary objective of WTO is to remove barriers to trade on a worldwide basis. On a smaller scale, an **economic community** is an organization of nations formed to promote the free movement of resources and products among its members and to create common economic policies. A number of economic communities now exist. Table 3.2 lists the members of the four most familiar ones.

The European Union (EU), also known as the *European Community* and the *Common Market,* was formed in 1957 by six countries—France, the Federal Republic of Germany, Italy, Belgium, the Netherlands, and Luxembourg. Its objective was freely conducted commerce among these nations and others that might later join. As shown in Table 3.2, nine more nations have joined the EU. (Cyprus, Poland, Hungary, the Czech Republic, Slovenia, and Estonia have begun formal negotiations to join EU; Latvia, Lithuania, Slovakia, Romania, and Bulgaria have requested membership as well.)

A second community in Europe, the *European Economic Area (EEA),* became effective in January 1994. This pact consists of Austria, Finland, Iceland, Norway, Sweden, and the fifteen member nations of the European Union. The EEA, encompassing an area inhabited by 370 million people, allows for the free movement of goods throughout all seventeen countries.

The *North American Free Trade Agreement (NAFTA)* joined the United States with its first- and second-largest trading partners, Canada and Mexico. Implementation of NAFTA on January 1, 1994, created a market of about 374.2 million people. This market consists of Canada (population 27.3 million), the United States (254.5 million), and Mexico (92.4 million). Given the estimated annual output for this trade area of $7 trillion, NAFTA has major implications for developing business opportunities in the United States.[15]

table 3.2 Members of Major International Economic Communities

European Union and OPEC have been in existence for decades but NAFTA and AFTA are new international economic communities.

European Union (EU)	North American Free Trade Agreement (NAFTA)	ASEAN Free Trade Area (AFTA)	Organization of Petroleum Exporting Countries (OPEC)
France	United States	Brunei	Venezuela
Germany	Canada	Indonesia	Algeria
Italy	Mexico	Malaysia	Libya
Belgium		Philippines	Iraq
Netherlands		Singapore	Iran
Luxembourg		Thailand	United Arab Emirates
United Kingdom		Vietnam	Ecuador
Ireland			Nigeria
Denmark			Gabon
Greece			Saudi Arabia
Portugal			Kuwait
Spain			Qatar
Austria			Indonesia
Finland			
Sweden			

Source: U.S. Department of Commerce, International Trade Administration, http://www.ita.doc.gov/td/industry/otea/usfth/aggregate/H99t06.txt, May 20, 2000.

Promoting the free movement of resources. The European Union (EU), also known as the Common Market and the European Community, was formed in 1957 by six countries. Now its 15-nation members gather for talks at the EU Commission building in Brussels, Belgium. Current topics include freeing trade in agriculture and curtailing greenhouse gases to protect the planet from global warming.

NAFTA is built on the Canadian Free Trade Agreement (FTA), signed by the United States and Canada in 1989, and on the substantial trade and investment reforms undertaken by Mexico since the mid-1980s. Initiated by the Mexican government, formal negotiations on NAFTA began in June 1991 between the three governments. The support of NAFTA by President Bill Clinton, past U.S. presidents Ronald Reagan and Jimmy Carter, and Nobel Prize-winning economists provided the impetus for U.S. congressional ratification of NAFTA in November 1993. NAFTA will gradually eliminate all tariffs on goods produced and traded among Canada, Mexico, and the United States to provide for a totally free trade area by 2009.

The *Association of Southeast Asian Nations (ASEAN),* with headquarters in Jakarta, Indonesia, was established in 1967 to promote political, economic, and social cooperation among its seven member countries: Indonesia, Malaysia, Philippines, Singapore, Thailand, Brunei, and Vietnam. In January 1992, ASEAN agreed to create a free trade area known as the ASEAN Free Trade Area (AFTA). AFTA countries have a population of more than 400 million people, and their trade totals $250 billion.

The *Pacific Rim,* referring to countries and economies bordering the Pacific Ocean, is an informal, flexible term generally regarded as a reference to East Asia, Canada, and the United States. At a minimum, the Pacific Rim includes Canada, Japan, the People's Republic of China, Taiwan, and the United States. It may also include Australia, Brunei, Cambodia, Hong Kong/Macau, Indonesia, Laos, North Korea, South Korea, Malaysia, New Zealand, the Pacific Islands, the Philippines, Russia (or the Commonwealth of Independent States), Singapore, Thailand, and Vietnam.

The *Commonwealth of Independent States (CIS)* was established in December 1991 as an association of eleven republics of the former Soviet Union: Russia, Ukraine, Belarus (formerly Byelorussia), Moldova (formerly Moldavia), Armenia, Azerbaijan, Uzbekistan, Turkmenistan, Tajikistan, Kazakhstan, and Kirgizstan (formerly Kirghiziya). The Baltic states did not join. Georgia maintained observer status before joining the CIS in November 1993.

In the Western Hemisphere, the *Caribbean Basin Initiative (CBI)* is an inter-American program led by the United States to give economic assistance and trade preferences to Caribbean and Central American countries. CBI provides duty-free access to the U.S. market for most products from the region and promotes private sector development in member nations.

The *Organization of Petroleum Exporting Countries (OPEC)* was founded in 1960 in

spotLight

Source: U.S. Bureau of the Census, Foreign Trade Division, and Federal Reserve Bank of Dallas, 2000.

Making China a "Normal" Trade Partner

ONE OF THE MOST BOISTEROUS TRADE FIGHTS OF recent years ended when the U.S. Congress voted on granting China permanent normal trade relations (PNTR). U.S. businesses were already exporting more than $12 billion worth of aircraft, electrical equipment, and other goods to China—and importing over $80 billion worth of toys, apparel, and other items. This lopsided balance of trade was due to restrictions such as high tariffs and complex licensing requirements imposed by China.

Until this vote, Congress had reviewed China's trade status every year, debating its progress on improving human rights and opening markets to U.S. businesses. Granting China PNTR status would end this yearly review and put China on an equal footing with other U.S. trading partners, smoothing the way for the country's entry into the World Trade Organization.

U.S. businesses such as Ford, Intel, and Wal-Mart favored PNTR because they wanted to buy more from and sell more to China. They saw China's huge population and growing prosperity fueling ever-stronger demand for many goods and services, including telecommunications. "Sometime this year or next year, China will become the second-largest wireless market, behind the United States, but ahead of Japan," said the president of AT&T's China operation.

However, unions were concerned about losing jobs if U.S. manufacturers opened plants in China to take advantage of the country's lower wages. Tens of thousands of apparel jobs moved to Mexico following the signing of the North American Free Trade Agreement, and unions worried that PNTR could touch off a similar shift to China. Also, human rights activists feared that China would no longer feel U.S. pressure to reform its practices. This argument was countered by business leaders such as Jacques Nasser, Ford's CEO, who said that "if we really do want to progress in human rights within China, one of the ways to do that is to actually open up trade."

Finally, after a lengthy debate, the House of Representatives and the Senate approved PNTR for China. Next on China's agenda: WTO membership. (As of January 2001, China was moving closer to its goal of joining the WTO but it still could be a few more months before it becomes a member.)

response to reductions in the prices that oil companies were willing to pay for crude oil. The organization was conceived as a collective bargaining unit to provide oil-producing nations with some control over oil prices.

Finally, the *Organization for Economic Cooperation and Development (OECD)* is a group of twenty-four industrialized market-economy countries of North America, Europe, the Far East, and the South Pacific. OECD, headquartered in Paris, was established in 1961 to promote economic development and international trade.

Methods of Entering International Business

LEARNING OBJECTIVE

4 Define the methods by which a firm can organize for, and enter, international markets.

A firm that has decided to enter international markets can do so in several ways. We shall discuss several different methods. These different approaches require varying degrees of involvement in international business. Typically, a firm begins its international operations at the simplest level. Then, depending on its goals, it may progress to higher levels of involvement.

Licensing

licensing a contractual agreement in which one firm permits another to produce and market its product and use its brand name in return for a royalty or other compensation

Licensing is a contractual agreement in which one firm permits another to produce and market its product and to use its brand name in return for a royalty or other compensation. For example, Yoplait yogurt is a French yogurt licensed for production in the United States. The Yoplait brand maintains an appealing French image, and in return, the U.S. producer pays the French firm a percentage of its income from sales of the product.

Licensing is especially advantageous for small manufacturers wanting to launch a well-known domestic brand internationally. For example, all Spalding sporting products are licensed worldwide. The licensor, the Questor Corporation, owns the Spalding name but produces no goods itself. The German firm of Lowenbrau has used licensing agreements, including one with Miller in the United States, to increase its beer sales worldwide without committing capital to building breweries.[16]

Licensing thus provides a simple method of expanding into a foreign market with virtually no investment. On the other hand, if the licensee does not maintain the licensor's product standards, the product's image may be damaged. Another possible disadvantage is that a licensing arrangement may not provide the original producer with any foreign marketing experience.

Exporting

A firm may also manufacture its products in its home country and export them for sale in foreign markets. Like licensing, exporting can be a relatively low-risk method of entering foreign markets. Unlike licensing, however, it is not a simple method; it opens up several levels of involvement to the exporting firm.

At the most basic level, the exporting firm may sell its products outright to an *export/import merchant,* which is essentially a merchant wholesaler. The merchant assumes all the risks of product ownership, distribution, and sale. It may even purchase the goods in the producer's home country and assume responsibility for exporting the goods. An important and practical issue for domestic firms dealing with foreign customers is securing payment. This is a two-sided issue which reflects the mutual concern rightly felt by both parties to the trade deal: the exporter would like to be paid before shipping the merchandise whereas the importer would obviously prefer to know they have received the shipment before releasing any funds. Neither side wants to take the risk of fulfilling their part of the deal only later to discover that the other side has not. The result would lead to legal costs and complex lengthy dealings wasteful of everyone's resources.

This mutual level of mistrust is in fact good business sense and has been around since the beginning of trade centuries ago. The solution then, was as it still is today, for both parties to use a mutually trusted "go-between" who can assure that the payment is held until the merchandise is in fact delivered according to the terms of the trade contract. The go-between representatives employed by the importer and exporter are still, as they were in the past, the local domestic banks involved in international business.

In Vietnam do as the Vietnamese do. American companies, such as Federal Express, are slowly tiptoeing back into Vietnam. Memories of a disastrous war and failed business ventures linger. The cultural differences are immense. In order to succeed, American management and marketing methods will have to be adapted to Vietnamese culture.

Here's a simplified version about how it works. After signing contracts detailing the merchandise sold and terms for its delivery, an importer will ask his local bank to issue a **letter of credit** for the amount of money needed to pay for the merchandise. The letter of credit is issued "in favor of the exporter", meaning that the funds are tied specifically to the trade contract involved. The importer's bank forwards the letter of credit to the exporter's bank, which also normally deals in international transactions.

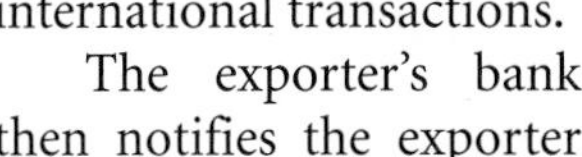

The exporter's bank then notifies the exporter that a letter of credit has been received in their name and they can go ahead with the shipment. The carrier transporting the merchandise provides the exporter with evidence of the shipment in a document called a **bill of lading.** The exporter signs over title to the merchandise (now in transit) to their bank by delivering a signed copy of the bill of lading and letter of credit.

In exchange, the exporter issues a **draft** from the bank, which orders the importer's bank to pay for the merchandise. The draft, bill of lading, and letter of credit are sent from the exporter's bank to the importer's bank. Acceptance by the importer's bank leads to the return of the draft and it's sale by the exporter to its bank, meaning the exporter receives cash and the bank assumes the risk of collecting the funds from the foreign bank. The importer is obliged to pay his bank upon delivery of the merchandise and the deal is complete.

In most cases, the letter of credit is part of a lending arrangement between the importer and their bank and of course, both banks earn fees for the issuing of letters of credit, drafts, and handling the import/export services for their clients. Furthermore, the process incorporates the fact that both importer and exporter will have different local currencies and might even negotiate their trade in a third currency. The banks look after all of the necessary exchanges. For example, the vast majority of international business is negotiated in U.S. dollars even though the trade might be between countries other than the U.S. So although the importer may end up paying for the merchandise in their local currency, and the exporter might receive payment in another local currency, the banks involved will exchange all necessary foreign funds in order to allow the deal to take place.

The exporting firm may instead ship its products to an *export/import agent,* which for a commission or fee arranges the sale of the products to foreign intermediaries. The agent is an independent firm—like other agents—that sells and may perform other marketing functions for the exporter. The exporter, however, retains title to the products during shipment and until they are sold.

An exporting firm may also establish its own *sales offices,* or *branches,* in foreign countries. These installations are international extensions of the firm's distribution system. They represent a deeper involvement in international business than the other exporting techniques we have discussed—and thus they carry a greater risk. The exporting firm maintains control over sales, and it gains both experience and knowledge of foreign markets. Eventually, the firm might also develop its own sales force to operate in conjunction with foreign sales offices.

letter of credit issued by a bank upon request of an importer stating that the bank will pay an amount of money to a stated beneficiary

bill of lading issued by the transport carrier to the exporter to prove merchandise has been shipped

draft is issued by the exporter's bank, ordering the importer's bank to pay for the merchandise thus guaranteeing payment once accepted by the importer's bank

Exploring Business

Getting Ready for Exporting

"A LOT OF COMPANIES ARE AFRAID TO export, but you have to export to live in this global economy," advises Ingeborg Hegenbart, an international trade finance expert with SouthTrust Bank. With careful planning, even the smallest business can profitably sell its goods or services abroad. Experts suggest getting ready by following these steps:

Prepare your company. You'll need funds and staff, consultants, or partners to research potential markets, understand customer needs and priorities, identify distributors or customers, investigate government regulations, evaluate shipping alternatives, promote in new markets, fill orders, and collect payments. Is your firm equipped to handle all these activities?

Prepare your product. Determine the customer needs and government regulations your product must satisfy to be sold in the targeted country. Also be sure to protect your legal rights to the product and the brand in that nation. What paperwork is needed to begin selling your product there?

Develop a plan. Know exactly what you want to achieve by exporting–and be sure these goals fit with the company's overall goals. Next, lay out the actions you will take to reach these goals. Finally, compare the costs with the projected profits. Is an investment in exporting the best use of your firm's resources?

Network. In addition to tapping government sources, approach your bank, your suppliers, and other business contacts with questions about exporting. Get ideas from global trade events; talk to firms that have struggled as well as firms that have succeeded with exporting. What do you need to know–and who can you ask?

Learn about the culture. SouthTrust Bank's Hegenbart believes exporters need a basic understanding of the countries they are targeting. By studying the culture, you can avoid offending potential customers and be in a better position to compete with global rivals. What local customs and practices should you know about?

Be flexible. The world market can change at any time. You must be ready to handle shifts in currency valuation, regulations, economic conditions, competition, and any other changes that might come up. Can your firm adapt?

Joint Ventures

A *joint venture* is a partnership formed to achieve a specific goal or to operate for a specific period of time. A joint venture with an established firm in a foreign country provides immediate market knowledge and access, reduced risk, and control over product attributes. However, joint-venture agreements established across national borders can become extremely complex. As a result, joint-venture agreements generally require a very high level of commitment from all the parties involved.

A joint venture may be used to produce and market an existing product in a foreign nation or to develop an entirely new product. Recently, for example, Archer Daniels Midland Company (ADM), one of the world's leading food processors, entered into a joint venture with Gruma SA, Mexico's largest corn flour and tortilla company. Besides a 22 percent stake in Gruma, ADM also received stakes in other joint ventures operated by Gruma. One of them will combine both companies' U.S. corn flour operations, which account for about 25 percent of the U.S. market. ADM also has a 40 percent stake in a Mexican wheat flour mill. ADM's joint venture increased its participation in the growing Mexican economy where ADM already produces corn syrup, fructose, starch, and wheat flour.[17] And in order to share expertise, risk and benefit from quicker development of new products in the fast-paced world of the Internet, iPlanet was formed as a joint venture between Sun Microsystems and Netscape Communications in March 1999 to develop e-commerce platforms. The alliance operates independently of the parent firms with its own management and goals.[18]

Totally Owned Facilities

At a still deeper level of involvement in international business, a firm may develop *totally owned facilities,* that is, its own production and marketing facilities in one or more foreign nations. This *direct investment* provides complete control over operations, but it carries a greater risk than the joint venture. The firm is really establishing a subsidiary in a foreign country. Most firms do so only after they have acquired some knowledge of the host country's markets.

Direct investment may take either of two forms. In the first, the firm builds or purchases manufacturing and other facilities in the foreign country. It uses these facilities to produce its own established products and to market them in that country and perhaps in neighboring countries. Firms such as General Motors, Union Carbide, and Colgate-Palmolive are multinational companies with worldwide manufacturing facilities. Colgate-Palmolive factories are becoming *Euro-factories,* supplying neighboring countries as well as their own local markets.[19]

A second form of direct investment in international business is the purchase of an existing firm in a foreign country under an arrangement that allows it to operate independently of the parent company. When Sony Corporation (a Japanese firm) decided to enter the motion-picture business in the United States, it chose to purchase Columbia Pictures Entertainment Inc., rather than start a new motion-picture studio from scratch.[20]

Strategic Alliances

Strategic alliances, the newest form of international business structure, are partnerships formed to create competitive advantage on a worldwide basis. They are very similar to joint ventures. The number of strategic alliances is growing at an estimated rate of about 20 percent per year. In fact, in the automobile and computer industries, strategic alliances are becoming the predominant means of competing. International competition is so fierce and the costs of competing on a global basis so high that few firms have all the resources needed to do it alone. Thus individual firms that lack the internal resources essential for international success may seek to collaborate with other companies.

strategic alliance a partnership formed to create competitive advantage on a worldwide basis

An example of such an alliance is the New United Motor Manufacturing, Inc. (NUMMI), formed by Toyota and General Motors to make Chevrolet Novas and Toyota Tercels. This enterprise united the quality engineering of Japanese cars with the marketing expertise and market access of General Motors.[21]

Trading Companies

A **trading company** provides a link between buyers and sellers in different countries. A trading company, as its name implies, is not involved in manufacturing or owning assets related to manufacturing. It buys in one country at the lowest price consistent with quality and sells to buyers in another country. An important function of trading companies is taking title to products and performing all the activities necessary to move the products from the domestic country to a foreign country. For example, large grain-trading companies operating out of home offices in both the United States and overseas control a major portion of the world's trade in basic food commodities. These trading companies sell homogeneous agricultural commodities that can be stored and moved rapidly in response to market conditions. The best-known U.S. trading company is Sears World Trade, which specializes in consumer goods, light industrial items, and processed foods.[22]

trading company provides a link between buyers and sellers in different countries

Countertrade

In the early 1990s, many developing nations had major restrictions on converting domestic currency into foreign currency. Exporters therefore had to resort to barter agreements with importers. **Countertrade** is essentially an international barter transaction in which goods and services are exchanged for different goods and services. Examples include Saudi Arabia's purchase of ten 747 jets from Boeing with payment in crude oil; Philip Morris's sale of cigarettes to Russia in return for chemicals used to make fertilizers; and Iraq's barter of crude oil for warships from Italy.

countertrade an international barter transaction

The volume of countertrade is growing. Given the importance of countertrade as a means of financing world trade, prospective exporters will undoubtedly have to engage in this technique from time to time to gain access to international markets.

table 3.3 **The Ten Largest U.S. Multinational Corporations**

		REVENUE		
1999 Rank	**Company**	**Foreign Revenue (In Millions)**	**Total (In Millions)**	**Foreign as Percent of Total**
1	ExxonMobil	$115,464	$160,883	71.8
2	IBM	50,377	87,548	57.5
3	Ford Motor	50,138	162,558	30.8
4	General Motors	46,485	176,558	26.3
5	General Electric	35,350	111,630	31.7
6	Texaco	32,700	42,433	77.1
7	Citigroup	28,749	82,005	35.1
8	Hewlett-Packard	23,398	42,370	55.2
9	Wal-Mart Stores	22,728	165,013	13.8
10	Compaq Computer	21,174	38,525	55.0

Source: http://www.forbes.com.

Multinational Firms

multinational enterprise a firm that operates on a worldwide scale, without ties to any specific nation or region

A **multinational enterprise** is a firm that operates on a worldwide scale without ties to any specific nation or region. The multinational firm represents the highest level of involvement in international business. It is equally "at home" in most countries of the world. In fact, as far as the operations of the multinational enterprise are concerned, national boundaries exist only on maps. It is, however, organized under the laws of its home country.

Table 3.3 lists the ten largest U.S. multinational corporations; Table 3.4 shows the ten largest public companies outside the United States. Notice that seven of the foreign-based multinational companies are located in Japan. Table 3.5 shows the ten largest foreign and U.S. public multinational companies; the ranking is based on a composite

table 3.4 **The Ten Largest Multinational Corporations Outside the United States**

2000 Rank	**Company**	**Business**	**Country**	**Revenue ($ in Millions)**
1	DaimlerChrysler	automobiles	Germany	151,632
2	Mitsui & Co	trading	Japan	123,706
3	Mitsubishi	trading	Japan	122,883
4	Toyota Motor	automobiles	Japan	120,697
5	Itochu	trading	Japan	113,808
6	Royal Dutch/Shell Group	energy sources	Netherlands/ United Kingdom	105,366
7	Sumitomo	trading	Japan	99,860
8	Nippon Tel & Tel	telecom	Japan	97,658
9	Marubeni	trading	Japan	95,796
10	BP Amoco	energy sources	United Kingdom	83,566

Source: http://www.forbes.com.

table 3.5 The Ten Largest Foreign and U.S. Multinational Corporations

2000 Rank	Company	Business	Country	Revenue ($ in Millions)
1	Citigroup	financial services	United States	82,005
2	General Electric	electricity and electronics	United States	111,630
3	Exxon Mobil	energy	United States	160,883
4	Bank of America	banking	United States	51,632
5	Royal Dutch/ Shell Group	energy	Netherlands	105,366
6	Ford Motor	automobiles	United States	162,558
7	HSBC Group	banking	United Kingdom	39,348
8	General Motors	automobiles	United States	176,558
9	International Business Machines	computer systems	United States	87,548
10	American International Group	insurance	United States	40,656

Source: http://www.forbes.com.

score reflecting each company's best three out of four rankings for sales, profits, assets, and market value. Table 3.6 on page 92 describes steps in entering international markets.

According to the chairman of the board of Dow Chemical Company, a multinational firm of U.S. origin, "The emergence of a world economy and of the multinational corporation has been accomplished hand in hand."[23] He sees multinational enterprises moving toward what he calls the "anational company," a firm that has no nationality but belongs to all countries. In recognition of this movement, there have already been international conferences devoted to the question of how such enterprises would be controlled.

Sources of Export Assistance

LEARNING OBJECTIVE

5 Describe the various sources of export assistance.

In September 1993, President Bill Clinton announced the *National Export Strategy (NES)* to revitalize U.S. exports. Under the NES, the *Trade Promotion Coordinating Committee (TPCC)* assists U.S. firms in developing export promotion programs. The export services and programs of the nineteen TPCC agencies can help American firms compete in foreign markets and create new jobs in the United States. An overview of selected export assistance programs follows.

- *U.S. Export Assistance Centers (USEACs):* USEACs are federal export assistance offices. They provide assistance in export marketing and trade finance by integrating in a single location the counselors and services of the U.S. and Foreign Commercial Services of the Department of Commerce, the Export-Import Bank, the Small Business Administration, and the U.S. Agency for International Development: (http://www.doc.gov).
- *International Trade Administration (ITA), U.S. Department of Commerce:* ITA offers assistance and information to exporters through its units, which include (1) domestic and overseas commercial officers, (2) country experts, and (3) industry experts. Each unit promotes products and offers services and programs for the U.S. exporting community: (http://www.ita.doc.gov/tic).
- *U.S. and Foreign Commercial Services (US&FCS):* To help U.S. firms compete more effectively in the global marketplace, the US&FCS has a network of trade specialists in sixty-seven countries worldwide. US&FCS offices provide

table 3.6 Steps in Entering International Markets

Step	Activity	Marketing Tasks
1	Identify exportable products	Identify key selling features Identify needs that they satisfy Identify the selling constraints that are imposed
2	Identify key foreign markets for the products	Determine who the customers are Pinpoint what, when they will buy Do market research Establish priority, or "target," countries
3	Analyze how to sell in each priority market (methods will be affected by product characteristics and unique features of country/market)	Locate available government and private-sector resources Determine service and back-up sales requirements
4	Set export prices and payment terms, methods, and techniques	Establish methods of export pricing Establish sales terms, quotations, invoices, and conditions of sale Determine methods of international payments, secured and unsecured
5	Estimate resource requirements and returns	Estimate financial requirements Estimate human resources requirements (full- or part-time export department or operation?) Estimate plant production capacity Determine necessary product adaptations
6	Establish overseas distribution network	Determine distribution agreement and other key marketing decisions (price, repair policies, returns, territory, performance, and termination) Know your customer (use U.S. Department of Commerce international marketing services)
7	Determine shipping, traffic, documentation procedures and requirements	Determine methods of shipment (air or ocean freight, truck, rail?) Finalize containerization Obtain validated export license Follow export-administration documentation procedures
8	Promote, sell, and be paid	Use international media, communications, advertising, trade shows, and exhibitions Determine the need for overseas travel (when, where, how often?) Initiate customer follow-up procedures
9	Continuously analyze current marketing, economic, and political situations	Recognize changing factors influencing marketing strategies Constantly re-evaluate

Source: U.S. Department of Commerce, International Trade Administration, Washington, D.C.

information on foreign markets, agent/distributor location services, and trade leads, as well as counseling on business opportunities, trade barriers, and prospects abroad.

- *Export Legal Assistance Network (ELAN)*: ELAN is a nationwide group of attorneys with experience in international trade who provide free initial consultations to small businesses on export-related matters.
- *Advocacy Center*: The Advocacy Center, established in November 1993, facilitates high-level U.S. official advocacy to assist U.S. firms competing for major projects and procurements worldwide. The center is directed by the Trade Promotion Coordinating Committee: (http://www.ita.doc.gov/advocacy)
- *Commerce Business Daily (CBD)*: CBD is published daily by the Department of Commerce. It lists foreign business opportunities and information on federal programs and activities that support U.S. exports, including information on

overseas markets and industry trends. The CBD maintains a computerized calendar of U.S. government-sponsored domestic and overseas trade events. Telephone: 1-800-USA-TRADE; e-mail: tic@ita.doc.gov; Internet home page: http://www.ita.doc.gov/tic.

- *Trade Information Center*: This information center was established as a comprehensive source for U.S. companies seeking information on federal programs and activities that support U.S. exports, including information on overseas markets and industry trends. This center maintains a computerized calendar of U.S. government-sponsored domestic and overseas trade events. Telephone: 1-800-USA-TRADE; e-mail: tic@ita.doc.gov; Internet home page: http://www.ita.doc./gov.
- *Economic Bulletin Board (EBB)*: EBB is a daily resource for business, economic, and trade information. A firm can connect to this vast collection of information and download trade leads, market research reports, and the Commerce Business Daily via computer. Subscription costs are low and vary, depending on which information you wish to access. For more information, call 1-800-STAT-USA (1-800-782-8872).
- *STATUSA/Internet* (http://www.sta-usa.gov): A comprehensive collection of business, economic, and trade information available on the web. Through this site a firm can access the NTDB, daily trade leads and economic news, *Commerce Business Daily,* and the latest economic press releases and statistical series from the federal government. For more information on this low cost service, call 1-800-STAT-USA (1-800-782-8872).
- *STAT-USA/Fax*: This fax-on-demand service provides instant hard copy of business and economic information from the federal government. All releases are available twenty-four hours a day, seven days a week. The most popular fax documents include the daily trade leads and numerous U.S. government economic press releases. For more information, call 1-800-STAT-USA (1-800-782-8872).
- *TRADESTATS*: A comprehensive source for U.S. export and import data, both current and historical. Maintained by the Commerce Department's Office of Trade and Economic Analysis, this web site contains total U.S. trade statistics by country and commodity, state and metropolitan area export data, and trade and industry statistics. Much of this data are downloadable. The web site address is http://www.ita.doc.gov/tradestats.
- *Selected SBA market research-related general resources*: The Small Business Administration publishes many helpful guides to assist small and medium-sized companies, including: *Marketing for Small Business: An Overview, Researching Your Market, Breaking into the Trade Game,* or the videos *Marketing: Winning Customers with a Workable Plan, or The Basics of Exporting.* Contact the Small Business Answer Desk, 1-800-U-ASK-SBA (1-800-827-5722).
- *National Trade Data Bank (NTDB)*: The NTDB contains international economic and export promotion information supplied by over twenty U.S. agencies. Data are updated daily on the Internet (http://www.azexport.com/programs/ntdb.htm) and updated monthly on CD-ROM. The CD-ROM version is available for use at over 1,000 libraries throughout the country. The NTDB contains data from the Departments of Agriculture (Foreign Agriculture Service), Commerce (Bureau of Census, Bureau of Economic Analysis, International Trade Administration, and National Institute for Standards and Technology), Energy, and Labor (Bureau of Labor Statistics); the Central Intelligence Agency; the Export-Import Bank; the Federal Reserve System; the U.S. International Trade Commission; the Overseas Private Investment Corporation; the Small Business Administration; and the U.S. Trade Representative.

These and other sources of export information enhance the business opportunities of U.S. firms seeking to enter expanding foreign markets. Another vital entry factor is financing.

Financing International Business

LEARNING OBJECTIVE

6 Identify the institutions that help firms and nations finance international business.

International trade compounds the concerns of financial managers. Currency exchange rates, tariffs and foreign-exchange controls, and the tax structures of host nations all affect international operations and the flow of cash. In addition, financial managers must be concerned both with the financing of their international operations and with the means available to their customers to finance purchases.

Fortunately, along with business in general, a number of large banks have become international in scope. Many have established branches in major cities around the world. Thus, like firms in other industries, they are able to provide their services where and when they are needed. In addition, financial assistance is available from U.S. government and international sources.

Several of today's international financial organizations were founded many years ago to facilitate free trade and the exchange of currencies among nations. Some, such as the Inter-American Development Bank, are internationally supported and focus on developing countries. Others, like the Export-Import Bank, are operated by one country but provide international financing.

The Export-Import Bank of the United States

Export-Import Bank of the United States an independent agency of the U.S. government whose function it is to assist in financing the exports of American firms

The **Export-Import Bank of the United States** is an independent agency of the U.S. government whose function it is to assist in financing the exports of American firms. *Eximbank*, as it is commonly called, extends and guarantees credit to overseas buyers of American goods and services, and guarantees short-term financing for exports. It also cooperates with commercial banks in helping American exporters offer credit to their overseas customers. Recently the Eximbank provided credit to Saudi Arabia in a $4 billion contract awarded to AT&T to update the Saudis' communication system.

Multilateral Development Banks

multilateral development bank (MDB) an internationally supported bank that provides loans to developing countries to help them grow

A **multilateral development bank (MDB)** is an internationally supported bank that provides loans to developing countries to help them grow. The most familiar is the World Bank, which operates worldwide. Four other MDBs operate primarily in Central and South America, Asia, Africa, and Eastern and Central Europe. All five are supported by the industrialized nations, including the United States.

The *Inter-American Development Bank (IDB)* was created in 1959 by ten Latin American countries and the United States. Twenty-six Latin American and fifteen other countries now own the bank, which is headquartered in Washington, D.C. The IDB makes loans and provides technical advice and assistance to countries.

With fifty-two member nations, the *Asian Development Bank (ADB)* promotes economic and social progress in Asian and Pacific regions. The U.S. government is the second-largest contributor to the ADB's capital, after Japan. Recently the ADB approved $903 million in loans to China for environmental protection, natural resource conservation, and poverty reduction.

The *African Development Bank (AFDB)* was established in 1963 with headquarters in Abidjan, Ivory Coast. Its members include fifty African and twenty-six non-African countries. The AFDB's goal is to foster the economic and social development of its African members. The bank pursues this goal through loans, research, technical assistance, and the development of trade programs.

Established in 1990 to encourage reconstruction and development in the Eastern and Central European countries, the London-based *European Bank for Reconstruction and Development (EBRD)* has more than forty members. Its loans are geared toward developing market-oriented economies and promoting private enterprise.

The International Monetary Fund

The **International Monetary Fund (IMF)** is an international bank with more than 150 member nations that makes short-term loans to developing countries experiencing balance-of-payment deficits. This financing is contributed by member nations, and it must be repaid with interest. Loans are provided primarily to fund international trade.

International Monetary Fund (IMF) an international bank with more than 150 member nations that makes short-term loans to developing countries experiencing balance-of-payment deficits

RETURN TO inside Business

THE FIRST TIME JLG INDUSTRIES entered the global business market, a slowing U.S. economy forced it to retrench and focus only on domestic sales. During the past few years, however, JLG has returned to its pursuit of international sales. JLG redesigned its lifts to suit the global rental market, standardizing control and component layouts and streamlining product maintenance. Now, using exporting, joint ventures, and totally-owned facilities, JLG's aerial lifts and platforms are available on six continents.

JLG's global sales revenues top $200 million, and the company sees more potential for growth in the years ahead. JLG recently expanded by acquiring Ohio-based Gradall Industries, adding new industrial equipment to the product line offered at its 600 facilities around the world. And there's no ceiling in sight for JLG's high-flying global sales.

Questions

1. Why would JLG form a joint venture to open a dealership in Thailand, rather than selling to an established local dealership?
2. Was JLG a multinational firm the first time it entered the global marketplace? Is it a multinational firm today?

chapter Review

SUMMARY

1 Explain the economic basis for international business.

International business encompasses all business activities that involve exchanges across national boundaries. International trade is based on specialization, whereby each country produces those goods and services that it can produce more efficiently than any other goods and services. A nation is said to have a comparative advantage relative to these goods. International trade develops when each nation trades its surplus products for those in short supply.

A nation's balance of trade is the difference between the value of its exports and the value of its imports. Its balance of payments is the difference between the flow of money into and out of the nation. Generally, a negative balance of trade is considered unfavorable.

2 Discuss the restrictions nations place on international trade, the objectives of these restrictions, and their results.

In spite of the benefits of world trade, nations tend to use tariffs and nontariff barriers (import quotas, embargoes, and other restrictions) to limit trade. These restrictions are typically justified as being needed to protect a nation's economy, industries, citizens, or security. They can result in the loss of jobs, higher prices, fewer choices in the marketplace, and the misallocation of resources.

3 Outline the extent of international trade and identify the organizations working to foster it.

World trade is generally increasing. Trade between the United States and other nations is increasing in dollar value but decreasing in terms of our share of the world market. The General Agreement on Tariffs and Trade (GATT) was formed to dismantle trade barriers and provide an environment in which international business can grow. Today the World Trade Organization (WTO) and various economic communities carry on that mission.

4 Define the methods by which a firm can organize for, and enter, international markets.

A firm can enter international markets in several ways. It may license a foreign firm to produce and market its products. It may export its products and sell them through foreign intermediaries or its own sales organization abroad, or it may sell its exports outright to an export/import merchant. It may enter into a joint venture with a foreign firm. It may establish its own foreign subsidiaries. Or it may develop into a multinational enterprise. Generally, each of these methods represents an increasingly deeper level of involvement in international business, with licensing being the simplest and the development of a multinational corporation the most involved.

5 Describe the various sources of export assistance.

Many government and international agencies provide export assistance to U.S. and foreign firms. The export services and programs of the nineteen agencies of the U.S. Trade Promotion Coordinating Committee (TPCC) can help U.S. firms compete in foreign markets and create new jobs in the United States. Sources of export assistance include U.S. Export Assistance Centers, the International Trade Administration, U.S. and Foreign Commercial Services, Export Legal Assistance Network, Advocacy Center, National Trade Data Bank, and other government and international agencies.

6 Identify the institutions that help firms and nations finance international business.

The financing of international trade is more complex than that of domestic trade. Institutions such as the Eximbank and the International Monetary Fund have been established to provide financing and ultimately to increase world trade for American and international firms.

KEY TERMS

You should now be able to define and give an example relevant to each of the following terms:

international business (69)
absolute advantage (70)
comparative advantage (70)
exporting (71)
importing (71)
balance of trade (71)
trade deficit (71)
balance of payments (72)
import duty (tariff) (74)
dumping (74)
nontariff barrier (74)
import quota (74)
embargo (74)
foreign-exchange control (74)
currency devaluation (74)
General Agreement on Tariffs and Trade (GATT) (82)
World Trade Organization (WTO) (82)
economic community (83)
licensing (86)
letter of credit (87)
bill of lading (87)
draft (87)
strategic alliance (89)
trading company (89)
countertrade (89)
multinational enterprise (90)
Export-Import Bank of the United States (94)
multilateral development bank (MDB) (94)
International Monetary Fund (IMF) (95)

REVIEW QUESTIONS

1. Why do firms engage in international trade?
2. What is the difference between an absolute and a comparative advantage in international trade? How are both types of advantages related to the concept of specialization?
3. What is a favorable balance of trade? In what way is it "favorable"?
4. List and briefly describe the principal restrictions that may be applied to a nation's imports.
5. What reasons are generally given for imposing trade restrictions?
6. What are the general effects of import restrictions on trade?
7. Define and describe the major objectives of the World Trade Organization (WTO) and the international economic communities.
8. Which nations are the principal trading partners of the United States? What are the major U.S. imports and exports?
9. The methods of engaging in international business may be categorized as either direct or indirect. How would you classify each of the methods described in this chapter? Why?
10. In what ways is a multinational enterprise different from a large corporation that does business in several countries?
11. List some key sources of export assistance. How can these sources be useful to small business firms?
12. In what ways do Eximbank, multilateral development banks, and the IMF enhance international trade?

DISCUSSION QUESTIONS

1. The United States restricts imports but, at the same time, supports the WTO and international banks whose objective is to enhance world trade. As a member of Congress, how would you justify this contradiction to your constituents?
2. What effects might the devaluation of a nation's currency have on its business firms? on its consumers? on the debts it owes to other nations?
3. Should imports to the United States be curtailed by, say, 20 percent to eliminate our trade deficit? What might happen if this were done?
4. When should a firm consider expanding from strictly domestic trade to international trade? When should it consider becoming further involved in international trade? What factors might affect the firm's decisions in each case?
5. How can a firm obtain the expertise needed to produce and market its products in, for example, the EU?

VIDEO CASE

Dat'l Do-It Cooks Up Hot Exports

In the early 1980s, Christopher Way started cooking up fiery datil pepper sauces for his seafood restaurant in St. Augustine, Florida, and placed a jar of the sauce on each table. Little did he know that the theft of those jars by his customers would lead to the founding of a global business!

Day in and day out, Way noticed that his customers were taking home the jars of datil sauce. He reasoned that, if his customers liked the sauce enough to steal it, he would give them a chance to buy it. So in 1983, Way founded Dat'l Do-It to create and sell sauces and relishes made from the datil pepper, one of the hottest peppers in the world—slightly less fiery than the blistering habanero pepper.

Way's timing was excellent: his product introductions caught the wave of an upsurge of public interest in hotter-tasting foods. His sauces were also unique in that datil peppers are grown only in the St. Augustine area. Because not all tastebuds are alike, Way decided to offer his foods in a range of intensities. Dat'l Do-It Pepper Jelly was on the mild end of the scale, while Devil Drops was on the volcanic end.

Although Way originally cooked up his datil-based sauces in the kitchen of his restaurant, he knew that the recipes would have to be adapted for mass production. So he sent all his recipes to a food chemist in Atlanta, who converted them to formulas for use by a commercial food-manufacturing plant. The adapted formulas were designed both to taste good and to lengthen the shelf life of the sauces. To supply the manufacturer with enough datils to cook up truckloads of fiery sauces, Way hired farmers to grow hundreds of bushels of peppers per season. Within a few years, he would be supplementing the output of these outside growers by establishing a Dat'l Do-It corporate farm with the capacity to produce up to 20,000 pounds of peppers per season.

Once Way had a full line of products ready, he needed to get them to customers with a taste for fiery foods. He soon found that getting new products onto grocery-store shelves can be both time-consuming and costly. Even though a vice president of the giant Winn-Dixie supermarket chain liked Dat'l Do-It sauces and wanted to carry the line, Way was able to get his products into only a few of the stores. "There's so little profit from gourmet products, and the grocery stores operate in high-profit items," Way says. "The 'gourmet' or specialized food arena is still a really difficult market to get into."

Despite the challenges, Dat'l Do-It's annual sales continued to grow. By 1993 sales were just below $500,000, and the company was breaking even. Way next decided to expand into retailing. He opened a Dat'l Do-It Hot Shop in St. Augustine to sell his sauces and made plans to franchise similar shops around the South. He also opened small kiosks in high-traffic shopping malls during the Christmas shopping season and started a mail-order division to reach customers all over the United States.

Then Kodo Matsumoto, an experienced exporter based in St. Petersburg, Florida, suggested that Way try exporting Dat'l Do-It products to Japan. Studies showed that the Japanese people enjoyed hot foods, and Matsumoto had successfully introduced a variety of products to the Japanese market. But Way couldn't simply put his foods into a box and ship them to Japan. He first had to modify the ingredients and the labeling to comply with stringent Japanese regulations. He also had to rely on Matsumoto for guidance in navigating the complex customs and practices of the Japanese distribution system, which has traditionally been geared toward protecting locally made products.

Thanks to Matsumoto's expert knowledge of the Japanese market, Way has been able to expand his exports year after year. In fact, Way is so encouraged about prospects for international sales that he changed the sign at the Dat'l Do-It farm to read "World Headquarters." The Dat'l Do-It Web site (http://www.datldoit.com) also carries the "Worldwide Headquarters" logo, emphasizing the company's ability to ship anywhere on the planet. The site offers a complete product catalog plus recipes, tourism links for the company's hometown of St. Augustine, an e-mail newsletter, and more. No doubt Dat'l Do-It will undergo more global expansion as Way cooks up new plans for his company in the coming years.[24]

Questions

1. What kinds of trade restrictions would make it difficult for Christopher Way to export his products to Japan?
2. What financial change might affect the cost of Dat'l Do-It products in Japan, thereby influencing demand?
3. To circumvent trade restrictions, should Way invest in a manufacturing plant in Japan? Explain your answer.

Building Skills for Career Success

1. Exploring the Internet

A popular question debated among firms actively involved on the Internet is whether or not there exists a truly global Internet-based customer, irrespective of any individual culture, linguistic, or nationality issues. Does this Internet-based universal customer see the Internet and products sold there in pretty much the same way? If so, then one model might fit all customers. For example, although Yahoo.com translates its web pages so that it is understood around the world, its look might be considered pretty much the same regardless of which international site you use. Is this good strategy or should the sites reflect local customers differently?

Visit the text web site for updates to this exercise.

Assignment

1. Examine a web site like Yahoo (http://www.yahoo.com) and its various international versions that operate in other languages around the world. Compare their similarities and differences as best you can, even if you don't understand the individual languages.
2. After making your comparison, do you now agree that there are indeed universal Internet products and customers? Explain your decision.

2. Developing Critical Thinking Skills

Suppose you own and operate an electronics firm that manufactures transistors and integrated circuits. As foreign competitors enter the market and undercut your prices, you realize your high labor costs are hindering your ability to compete. You are concerned about what to do and are open for suggestions. Recently, you have been trying to decide whether to move your plant to Mexico where labor is cheaper.

Assignment

1. Questions you should consider in making this decision include the following:
   a. Would you be better off to build a new plant in Mexico or to buy an existing building?
   b. If you could find a Mexican electronics firm similar to yours, would it be wiser to try to buy it than to start your own operation?
   c. What are the risks involved in directly investing in your own facility in a foreign country?
   d. If you did decide to move your plant to Mexico, how would you go about it? Are there any government agencies that might offer you advice?
2. Prepare a two-page summary of your answers to these questions.

3. Building Team Skills

The North American Trade Agreement between the United States, Mexico, and Canada went into effect on January 1, 1994. It has made a difference in trade among the countries and has affected the lives of many people.

Assignment

1. Working in teams and using the resources of your library, investigate NAFTA. Answer the following questions:
   a. What are NAFTA's objectives?
   b. What are its benefits?
   c. What impact has NAFTA had on trade, jobs, and travel?
   d. Some Americans were opposed to the implementation of NAFTA. What were their objections? Have any of these objections been justified?
   e. Has NAFTA influenced your life? How?
2. Summarize your answers in a written report. Your team should also be prepared to give a class presentation.

4. Researching Different Careers

Today firms around the world need employees with special skills. In some countries, such employees are not always available, and firms must then search abroad for qualified applicants. One way they can do this is through global workforce databases. As business and trade operations continue to grow globally, you may one day find yourself working in a foreign country, perhaps for an American company doing business there or for a foreign company. In what foreign country would you like to work? What problems might you face?

Assignment

1. Choose a country in which you might like to work.
2. Research the country. NTDA (National Trade Data Bank), a CD-ROM computer program, is a good place to start. Find answers to the following questions:
   a. What language is spoken in this country? Are you proficient in it? What would you need to do if you are not proficient?
   b. What are the economic, social, and legal systems like in this nation?
   c. What is its history?
   d. What are its culture and social traditions like? How might they affect your work or your living arrangements?
3. Describe what you have found out about this country in a written report. Include an assessment of whether you would want to work there and the problems you might face if you did.

5. Improving Communication Skills

Working in a foreign country, even for a short time, can significantly affect your career. While there are benefits, there may also be many obstacles to overcome. How would you deal with the obstacles, and would it be worth the trouble? If you could work in another country for at least three years, how would it affect your career?

Assignment

1. Read newspaper articles and periodicals to find answers to the following questions:
   a. What would be the benefits of working in a foreign country for a three-year period? How might it advance your career?
   b. What obstacles might this experience present? How would you deal with them?
2. Compare the benefits with the obstacles and record the findings in your journal.

strategic case I

Orbis Demonstrates Global Social Responsibility

Saving the eyesight of millions is an enormous aspiration—one that has become a reality, thanks to Orbis. Houston ophthalmologist Dr. David Paton founded Orbis as a nonprofit organization in 1982. Realizing that most eye conditions need not progress to blindness, he was looking for a way to train health professionals around the world in the diagnosis and treatment of sight-threatening eye conditions. Dr. Paton envisioned an airplane outfitted as a mobile eye hospital—complete with operating room and state-of-the-art medical equipment—flying to developing countries so specialists could demonstrate new techniques and share their knowledge with local medical professionals.

The first Orbis plane was a DC-8 donated by United Airlines and modified to accommodate diagnostic and surgical equipment, thanks to grants and donations from various sources. Then, as now, volunteer ophthalmologists, nurses and assistants, flight personnel, mechanics and engineers, and administrative specialists staffed the Orbis plane. In its first two years, the Orbis DC-8 visited 24 countries, concentrating on teaching the latest surgical techniques.

When the plane visited Malawi, Orbis discovered that only two local ophthalmologists were available to treat the entire population of 7 million. As a result, Orbis management decided to expand the organization's focus beyond surgical procedures. Today, its volunteers work with local medical technicians, nurses, assistants, and public health officials on a wide range of eyecare training, treatment, and community health programs aimed at blindness prevention.

Keeping the Orbis Plane Flying

All these programs and country visits require both supplies and money. As a nonprofit organization, Orbis would not be able to survive without the volunteers who staff the plane and the generous donations of money and products from numerous corporations, philanthropic foundations, government agencies, and individuals. For example, when Orbis determined that it needed a new plane to replace its aging DC-8, it received contributions toward the purchase and conversion of a wide-body DC-10, launched in 1994. Alcon Laboratories, Johnson & Johnson, Pharmacia, and other medical products manufacturers have given Orbis free supplies for years. United Airlines, another long-time contributor, has donated pilot training, tickets, and various support services. Contributions of products and services represent nearly one-third of Orbis's funding.

To raise the rest of the money needed to keep the plane flying, Orbis organizes fundraising events and programs around the world. In addition to direct mail campaigns, Orbis has raised money by holding galas and award dinners, and partnering with corporations to encourage employee contributions. Orbis also receives cash donations from many companies, including Berkshire, Hathaway, Standard Chartered Bank, Wells Fargo Bank, and Deloitte Touche Tohmatsu, as well as from philanthropic foundations established by companies or executives. Fundraising activities bring in money, but they also cost money. About 20 percent of Orbis's budget is devoted to fundraising, while more than 76 percent of the budget is spent on surgical training, blindness prevention education, and related programs.

Different Countries, Different Approaches

Over the years, Orbis has brought its blindness prevention expertise to countries in Asia, Eastern Europe, Africa, and Latin America, in hospital-based sessions as short as three days and plane-based programs as long as three weeks in duration. The organization adapts its training and educational programs to the different needs and conditions in each country, taking language and culture into consideration as well.

Orbis uses various types of public awareness programs in different countries to spread the message of early detection and treatment. For example, in India, Orbis arranged public parades in New Delhi and Mumbai, during which school children marched with handmade posters inspired by the phrase "From Darkness Into Light." Orbis also ran advertisements in local newspapers (underwritten by pharmaceutical companies) and distributed posters and mailings encouraging people to donate their corneas. Thanks to this campaign, thousands of people signed up with the Eye Bank Association of India to donate their corneas.

Training Thousands, Reaching Millions

Since its founding in 1982, Orbis has trained more than 50,000 medical specialists in 80 countries and treated the eyecare conditions of more than 23,000 patients. Still, Orbis's management and volunteers are keenly aware that 180 million people around the globe are either blind or at risk of becoming blind.

The organization recently joined with the World Health Organization and 20 other groups to launch Vision 2020. This ambitious program targets the five causes of blindness that are most easily addressed with today's ophthalmic expertise. By the conclusion of this program in 2020, the groups hope to save the eyesight of 100 million people. Day by day, year by year, Orbis and its staff, volunteers, and donors are taking steps to make that ambitious goal a reality.

Questions

1. How does the Orbis team use the four resources in carrying out its sight-saving mission?
2. How does Orbis apply specialization in operating its flying eyecare facility?
3. By donating services to Orbis, is United Airlines following the economic or socioeconomic model of social responsibility?
4. If Orbis pays local publications for advertisements in India, how does this transaction affect the U.S. balance of trade and balance of payments?

Trends in Business Today

In Part II of *Business* we look at several trends that influence how and where business is conducted. First we investigate the exploding world of e-business. Then we move to a very practical aspect of business: how businesses are owned. Issues related to ownership are particularly interesting in today's world where large global businesses that are restructuring, acquiring other firms, and/or selling off divisions coexist with small businesses that are continually starting up, being acquired, going public, and/or failing. Finally, because the majority of businesses are small, we look at specific issues related to small business.

4 Navigating the world of e-business

LEARNING OBJECTIVES

1. Define and explain the meaning of e-business.
2. Explore the basic framework of e-business.
3. Identify and explain fundamental models of e-business.
4. Discuss the social and legal concerns of e-business.
5. Explore the growth, future opportunities, and challenges of e-business.

Only 15 years after its founding, AOL entered the new millenium as the world's leading online service firm.

AOL and Time Warner Team Up

DIFFICULT AS IT MAY BE to comprehend today, America Online (AOL), Inc. started out in 1985 as simply one of many service firms providing customers with a way to connect to the Internet. Remarkably, only fifteen years after its founding, AOL entered the new millennium as the world's leading online service firm, with more than 20 million paying subscribers and a phenomenal growth in revenue. Since merging with the world's leading media company, Time Warner Inc., AOL has clearly transformed itself into an Internet colossus. With combined revenues of $36 billion, the new firm, AOL Time Warner Inc., is being touted as the "world's first media and communications company of the Internet age."

The union of AOL and Time Warner illustrates how partnerships and mergers between firms can benefit Internet-related businesses. By merging, AOL has enhanced its delivery of Internet content, since it can now offer customers some of Time Warner's rich variety of entertaining and informative products, such as CNN online news services. By the same token, Time Warner has found a partner that can deliver its content to a large existing audience–the audience AOL has built up through mergers and acquisitions, as well as through the introduction of its internally developed products and services.

According to AOL's research, 70 percent of online consumers regularly or occasionally receive their news through the Internet. The synergy of the fit between AOL and Time Warner thus becomes even more obvious. With the merger, both parties have made considerable progress in their efforts to expand their e-businesses. AOL's exclusive Time Warner content, which may attract new customers, gives the company a major competitive advantage over other Internet service providers that lack access to the same content. The merger may also increase the number of consumers of Time Warner's magazines (*InStyle, Time, Sports Illustrated, People, Teen People,* and *Entertainment Weekly)* and other products including music (Atlantic Records, Rhino Records, Warner Bros. Records), cable television (TNT, Cartoon Network, Turner Classic Movies, CNN, HBO), films (Warner Bros., New Line Cinema), and all the accompanying web sites. Furthermore, the variety of communications products–such as telephone service through cable, e-commerce products, and cross-promotion of a variety of consumer products–will generate many new opportunities for growth.[1]

AOL is an example of a firm that can trace its history only as far back as the start of commercial activity on the Internet. Like other well-known e-business firms, such as Yahoo, e-Bay, and MP3, AOL owes its very existence to the Internet. Quite simply, without the Internet, there would be no AOL, Yahoo, e-Bay, or MP3.

Most firms, on the other hand, have developed, or will develop, an Internet presence by transferring some of their business practices to the Internet. This was the route taken by Time Warner, which found opportunities by placing some of its entertainment and information content online. Providing services to customers on the Internet delivers added value to a firm's customers, an important goal for any business. For reasons we will examine more closely in this chapter, virtually all businesses will eventually find themselves conducting a growing proportion of their affairs on the Internet.

The fundamental division between businesses that invented themselves on the Internet, such as AOL, and previously established firms that have transferred only some of their activities to the Internet, such as the Gap, is a distinguishing characteristic of e-business. Firms with no history but the one defined on the Internet make their business decisions with a clear focus on the online world. There is no concern for interfering with other established business activity. On the other hand, firms like the Gap are very concerned about how development on the Internet will affect their current retail store sales, costs, customer relations, and so forth.

This chapter examines the development of both types of businesses and provides a structure for understanding how and why business activities that are finding their way onto the Internet will change the way businesses function in the future. We also take a closer look at how firms conduct business on the Internet and what growth opportunities may be available to both new and existing firms. But before exploring this new and exciting arena for business competition, let's begin by building a framework that can help you understand how all of this came about.

LEARNING OBJECTIVE

1 Define and explain the meaning of e-business.

Defining e-Business

e-business (electronic business) the organized effort of individuals to produce and sell, for a profit, the products and services that satisfy society's needs through the facilities available on the Internet

In Chapter 1, we defined *business* as the organized effort of individuals to produce and sell, for a profit, the products and services that satisfy society's needs. In a simple sense then, **e-business,** or **electronic business,** can be defined as the organized effort of individuals to produce and sell, for a profit, the products and services that satisfy society's needs *through the facilities available on the Internet.* And just as we distinguished between any *individual business* and the general term *business,* which refers to all such efforts within a society, we recognize both the individual *e-business,* such as AOL, and the general concept of *e-business.* IBM's e-business web site (http://www.ibm.com/ebusiness) defines e-business as the transformation of key business activities through the use of Internet technologies.[2] It is the transformation of these key business activities, like buying and selling products and services, building better supplier and customer relationships, and improving general business operations, that has stimulated so much excitement about this new and rapidly evolving business environment.

e-commerce buying and selling activities conducted online

Sometimes people use the term *e-commerce* instead of *e-business.* In a strict sense, *e-business* is used when one is speaking about all business activities and practices conducted on the Internet by an individual firm or industry. On the other hand, **e-commerce** is a part of e-business; the term refers only to buying and selling activities conducted online. These activities may include identifying suppliers, selecting products or services, making purchase commitments, completing financial transactions, and obtaining service.[3] We generally use the term *e-business* because of its broader definition and scope.

Organizing e-Business Resources

As noted in Chapter 1, to be organized, a business must combine *human, material, informational,* and *financial resources.* This is true of e-business, too (see Figure 4.1), but in this case, the resources may be highly specialized. For example, people who can

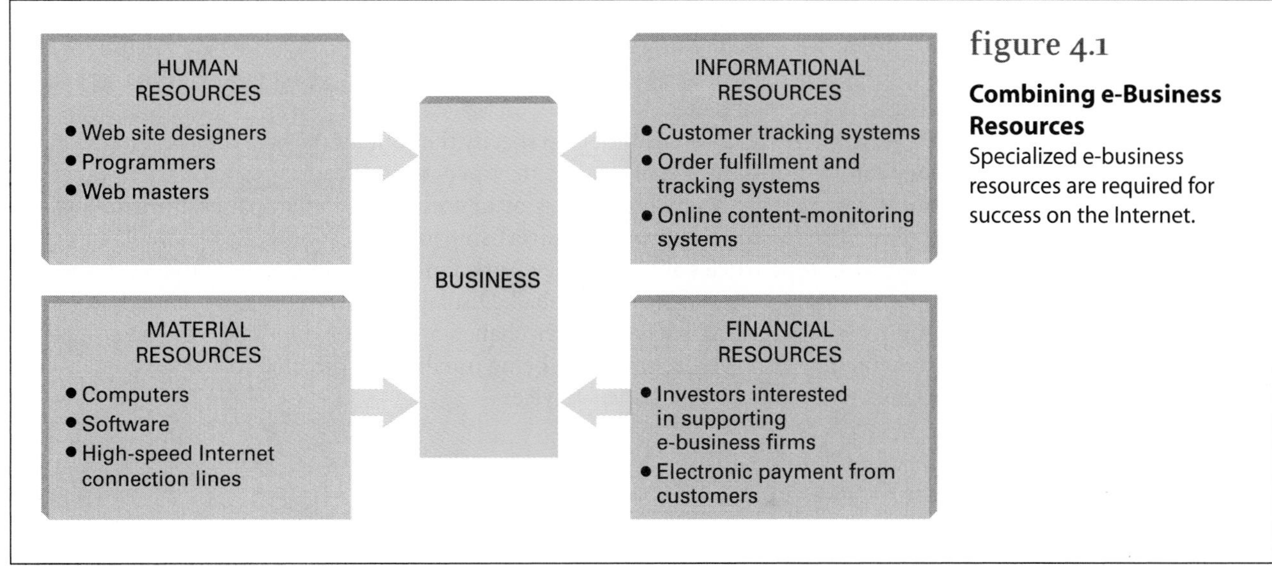

figure 4.1

Combining e-Business Resources
Specialized e-business resources are required for success on the Internet.

design, create, and maintain web sites are only a fraction of the specialized human resources required by businesses considering an Internet presence. Material resources must include specialized computers, equipment, software, and high-speed Internet connection lines. Computer programs that track the efficiency of the firm's web site operations and that offer insight into customers' interactions with the web site are generally among the specialized informational resources required. Financial resources, the money required to start and maintain the firm and allow it to grow, usually reflect greater participation by individual entrepreneurs and venture capitalists, instead of conventional financial sources like banks.

Satisfying Needs Online

The Internet has created some new customer needs, and e-businesses can satisfy these needs, as well as more traditional ones, in a way that would not be possible in conventional business practices. For example, among the products and services AOL offers its customers are Internet access, browsers, chat rooms, databases, and exclusive Time Warner entertainment content. Amazon.com gives customers anywhere in the world access to the same virtual store of books, videos, and CDs. And at e-Bay's global auction site, customers can, for a small fee, buy and sell almost anything. Even your college's web site satisfies informational needs for people interested in courses and educational programs. In each of these examples, customers receive a value-added service through the Internet.

Internet users can now access print media, such as newspapers and magazines, and radio and television programming at a time and place convenient to them. In addition to offering such a wide selection of content, the Internet provides the opportunity for *interaction*. In other words, communication is now an active two-way street between the online program and the viewer. In contrast to the passive situation they encounter with traditional media, customers can respond to Internet programming by requesting more information about a product or posing specific questions, which may lead to a purchase decision. In any case, the ability

spotLight

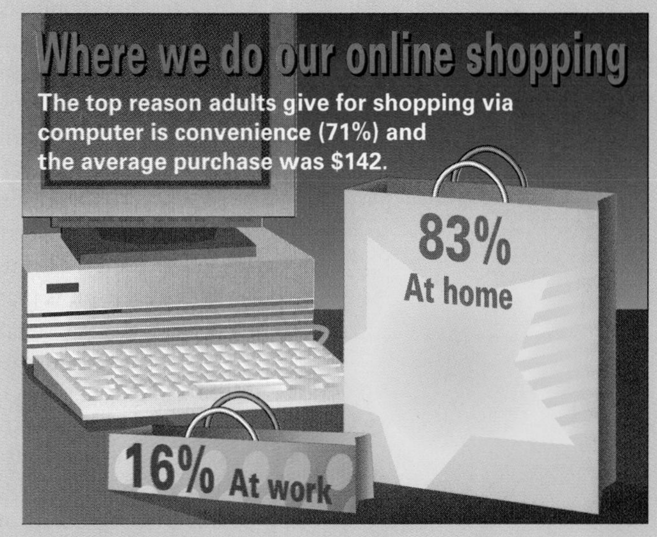

Source: Copyright 2000, USA TODAY. Reprinted with permission.

to engage the viewer in two-way communication means e-businesses can enjoy a more involved, and therefore more valuable viewer. CNN.com and other news-content sites encourage dialogue among viewers in chat rooms and exchanges with the writers of articles posted to the site.

The Internet allows customers to specify the content they are offered. For example, they can custom-design daily online newspapers and magazines with articles that are of interest to them. Knowing what is of interest to an individual customer allows an Internet firm to direct appropriate advertising to that customer. For example, someone wanting to read articles about the New York Yankees might be a potential customer for products and services related to baseball. Displaying only advertising that is likely to be of interest to the viewer has a greater chance of resulting in a sale. For the advertiser, knowing that its advertisements are being intelligently directed to the most likely customers represents a value-added service.

Creating e-Business Profit

Firms can increase their profits by either increasing sales revenue or reducing expenses through a variety of e-business activities.

Revenue Growth. Online merchants can reach a global customer base twenty-four hours a day, seven days a week; the opportunity to shop on the Internet is virtually unrestricted. The removal of barriers that might keep customers from conventional stores is a major factor in increasing sales revenue potential for e-businesses, as firms like Amazon.com, Barnesandnoble.com, and Disney.com have demonstrated.

Intelligent informational resource systems are another major factor in generating sales revenue for Internet firms. Such systems store information about each customer's purchases, along with a variety of other information about the buyer's preferences. Using this information, the system can assist the customer in making a purchase decision the next time he or she visits the web site. For example, if the customer has bought a Shania Twain or Garth Brooks CD in the past, the system might suggest CDs by similar artists.

Interestingly, customers may use a web site simply to browse and delay purchasing until they are in the firm's physical store. For instance, when buying clothing, customers often consider it critical to try on a garment before purchasing it. A site like Gap.com thus serves not only online customers but also those who eventually come to Gap stores to finalize their selection. Similarly, Toyota.com can provide basic comparative information for shoppers so that they are better prepared for their visit to an automobile showroom. Thus, while some customers in certain situations may not make a purchase online, the existence of the firm's web site and the services it provides may lead to increased sales in the firm's physical store.

revenue stream a source of revenue flowing into a firm

A fundamental concern for online firms is how to select, develop, and nurture sources of revenue. Each source of revenue flowing into the firm is referred to as a **revenue stream**. Since revenue streams provide the dollars needed to operate the firm, they are a major issue for any business. Furthermore, the simple redirection of existing revenue to an online stream is not desirable. For example, shifting revenues earned from customers inside a real store to revenues earned by those customers online does not create any real new revenue for the firm. Web-based businesses might not see sufficient new revenues generated to offset the high start-up costs of going online for a long time. Investors examine the feasibility of reaching targeted revenue projections laid out in the e-business plan and evaluate the current and long-term value of the firm based on their assessment of these numbers. This orientation helps explain why e-businesses like Amazon.com can command high investor confidence in the absence of any real profit during the start-up phase. Investors take a longer-term view, looking to the expected level of profit that will hopefully materialize when the firm reaches its full potential and settles down to stable revenue streams and expenses.

Typically, e-business revenue streams are created by the sale of products and services, by advertising placed on web pages, and by subscription fees charged for access to online services and content. For example, Hoover's Online (www.hoovers.com), a comprehensive source for company and industry information, makes some of its online content free for anyone who visits the site, but more detailed data is available only by paid subscription. In addition, it receives revenue from companies that are called *sponsors*, who advertise their products and services on Hoover's web site.

Many Internet firms that distribute news, magazine and newspaper articles, and similar content generate revenue primarily from advertising sponsors and commissions earned from sellers of products linked to the site. Online shopping malls now provide communities of related vendors of electronic equipment, computer hardware and software, health foods, fashion items, and other products. Sites like Petopia.com focus on the large market for pet supplies. WebMD and other health-related sites provide information about remedies, disease, and other health topics and issues. In many cases, the vendors share online sales revenues with the site owners.

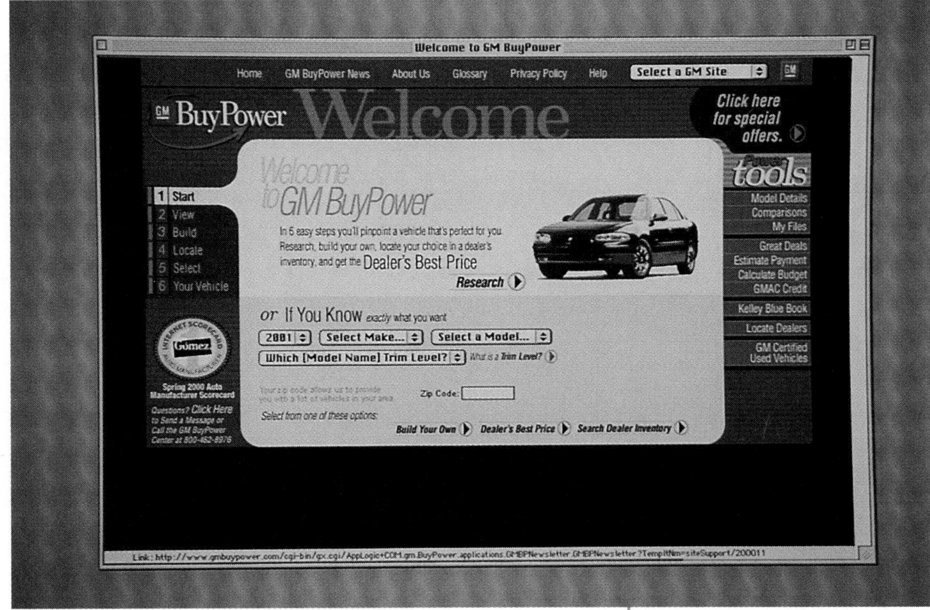

Want to buy a car? General Motors sure hopes so. To help increase sales, GM has created one of the comprehensive web sites in the automobile industry that provides information to potential car buyers 24 hours a day, 7 days a week.

Expense Reduction. Expense reduction is the other major way in which e-business can help increase profitability. Providing online access to information customers want can reduce the cost of dealing with customers. For example, most airlines provide updated scheduling and pricing information, as well as promotional material, on their web sites. This reduces the costs of dealing with customers through a call center operated by employees and of mailing brochures, which may be outdated within weeks or easily misplaced by customers. SprintPCS (www.sprintpcs.com) is just one company that maintains an extensive web site where potential customers can learn more about cell phone products and services, and current customers can access personal account information, send e-mail questions to customer service, and purchase additional products or services. With such extensive online services, SprintPCS probably does not have to maintain as many physical store locations as it would without these services.

We examine more examples of how e-business contributes to profitability throughout this chapter, especially as we focus on some of the business models for activity on the Internet.

A Framework for Understanding e-Business

LEARNING OBJECTIVE

2 Explore the basic framework of e-business.

The Internet was originally conceived as an elaborate military communications network that would allow vital messages to be transmitted in the event of war. Should one center of the network be destroyed, the system was designed to ensure that an alternative route could be found in the remaining network, thus allowing messages to be communicated to decision centers.

Before 1994, the U.S. National Science Foundation, the agency that funded and regulated the use of the Internet, restricted its use to noncommercial activities, such

figure 4.2

The Three Primary Groups of e-Businesses
Most firms overlap into more than one area of e-business.

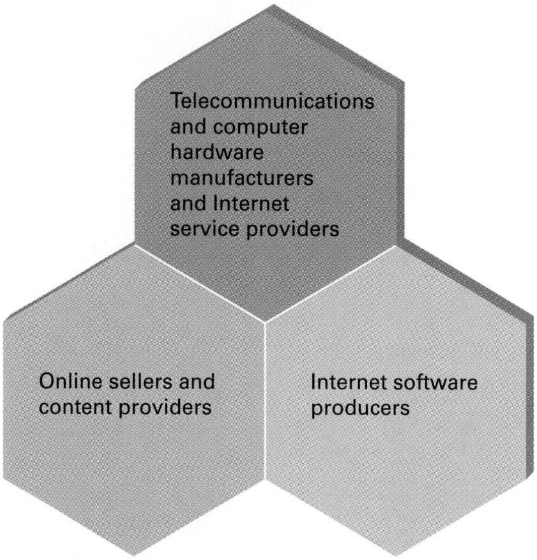

as e-mail communication and the sharing of data among university researchers. However, as the potential commercial benefits of the Internet became increasingly obvious, a growing list of commercially interested groups demanded that the doors be opened to business activity. At about the same time, new technology emerged that simplified the use of the Internet and allowed the addition of multimedia content. This multimedia environment of audio, visual, and text data came to be known as the **World Wide Web** (or, more simply, **the web**).

World Wide Web (the web) the Internet's multimedia environment of audio, visual, and text data

The Internet can be envisioned as a large network of computers connected by cables and satellites, which pass small, standardized packets of electronic data from one station to another until they are delivered to their final destination. In a sense, the Internet is the equivalent of the telephone network that was created almost one hundred years ago. However, instead of transmitting just voice communication, the Internet can transfer a variety of multimedia data at high speed around the world. To be transferred over the Internet, data need to be **digitized**, which means converted to a type of signal that the computers and telecommunications equipment that make up the Internet can understand.

digitized data that has been converted to a type of signal that the computers and telecommunications equipment that make up the Internet can understand

Most firms involved in e-business today fall more or less into one of three primary groups as defined by their e-business activities (see Figure 4.2):

- Telecommunications and computer hardware manufacturers and Internet service providers
- Internet software producers
- Online sellers and content providers

In this section we examine these three groups and also look at how e-business facilitates both global and small business operations.

Telecommunications and Computer Hardware Manufacturers and Internet Service Providers

The telecommunications and computer hardware manufacturers that helped build the Internet, together with Internet service providers, supply the physical infrastructure of the industry today. Lucent Technologies, Cisco Systems, and Nortel Networks produce most of the telecommunications hardware that allows the Internet to work. Companies such as IBM, Apple, Dell, Compaq, and Gateway produce many of the computers used by consumers; and companies such as Sun, IBM, and Hewlett-Packard manufacture servers that control corporate computer networks. Internet service providers (ISPs), which buy their technological capability from the makers of telecommunications hardware, provide customers with the necessary technology to connect to the Internet through various phone plugs and cables. This last link to the Internet is the shortest, but typically the slowest, in the global electronic network. As phone lines are replaced by faster cable and fiber-optic connections, speed for home users will gradually improve to levels enjoyed by businesses in city centers where the telecommunications infrastructure has already been upgraded. AOL is the largest and best-known ISP, but hundreds of smaller ISPs in both urban and rural areas also provide access to the Internet.

Internet Software Producers

Producers of software that provides the functional capability to do things on the Internet are the second primary group of e-business firms that have emerged since the start of online commercial activity. Searching the Internet, browsing web sites, sending e-mail messages, shopping or viewing multimedia content online—all these activities require specialized computer programs. Browser software is the single most basic product for user interaction on the Internet. Currently, the dominant browser is Microsoft's Internet Explorer, followed well back by AOL's Netscape Communicator. Not many years ago in the short history of the Internet, the ranking of these two browsers was just the opposite, Netscape was the dominant leader.

Online Sellers and Content Providers

The third primary group of e-businesses consists of all the firms that customers actually interact with on web sites. The Internet would still be limited to communication between individuals and among groups of special-interest researchers were it not for the activity of online sellers and content providers. In this area of e-business, we have just begun to see the development of strategies for reaching out to existing and new customers.

As noted earlier, some e-businesses, such as AOL and e-Bay, owe their existence to the Internet. They offer products and services that can be found only online. In contrast, other firms—among them the Gap, Nike, Martha Stewart, and Gear—have moved only some of their business practices to the Internet. They use the Internet simply to provide information and supplement their regular business activities.

Although it is rather uncertain what content and activities will eventually make their way to the Internet, it is clear that what we are experiencing today is dominated by the movement of current business practice and behavior to the Internet. Time Warner's decision to merge with AOL is a case in point. By arranging for online distribution of content that was formerly distributed through the old technology of magazines, radio, and television, Time Warner has found new opportunities for revenue growth. Similarly, traditional shopping behavior

No Gap in information here! The Gap uses their Internet web site not only to increase sales, but also to provide information to would-be customers.

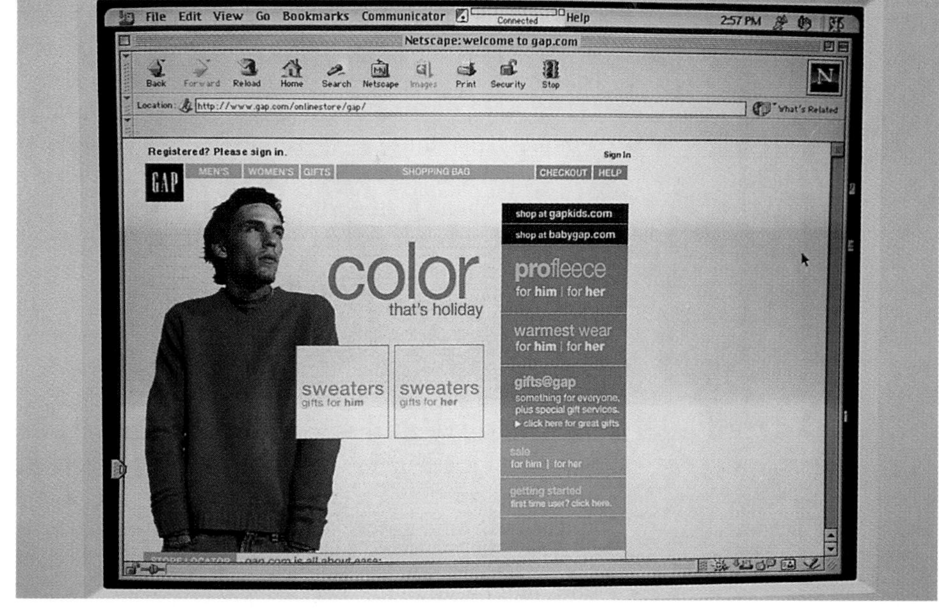

has been transferred to a virtual environment in which cyberspace retailers can provide more information to customers and have a greater degree of influence on the customer's decision. The Internet is jammed with shopping, as anyone who has entered the keyword *shop* on a search engine like Yahoo has discovered.

The greatest area for entrepreneurial adventure on the Internet is in the production of some service or content. Anyone with a good idea that might appeal to a globally distributed audience stands a chance of successfully launching an e-business. As the short history of the Internet indicates, we are only at the beginning of new and exciting applications that can be delivered online. According to Timothy Draper, an insider in the world of e-business and the managing director of Draper Fisher Jurvetson, a West Coast venture capital firm, "The Internet has opened the world up and that means everyone's now going to be part of the world economy."[4]

Global e-Business

All three primary groups of e-business firms are in a race to capture global business revenues. Telecommunications firms are competing to build the infrastructure in countries all over the world, and in many cases, they are skipping technological stepping-stones. For example, in areas of poor countries where telephone poles have never existed, ground-based wireless systems are now providing instant state-of-the-art communication. In many places, Internet service providers and software producers like AOL are competing against better-known local firms. And online sellers and content producers see no limits to penetrating markets anywhere in the world that customers want their products.

The ability to customize content for individual customer needs makes the Internet an adaptable tool for global enterprise. Consider Berlitz's web site (http://www.berlitz.com), which allows anyone in the world to jump quickly to a web site designed in the viewer's preferred language. By clicking on the appropriate icon, viewers can move forward to a web site created to meet their needs in their own language. Once there, the viewer can examine Berlitz's wide range of products and services, including multimedia language learning material, online translation services, and referrals to local Berlitz classroom-based instruction services. This global strategy, which reaches out to the world and yet allows for viewer customization, is at the heart of e-business.

Small e-Business

According to a report prepared by Access Markets International (AMI) Partners and *Inc.* magazine, an estimated 600,000 small U.S. businesses sold their products and services on e-business sites in 1999, up 50 percent from 400,000 in 1998. During the same period, small-business online transactions and purchases grew more than 1,000 percent, rising from $2 billion to $25 billion. Andy Bose, president and CEO of AMI, believes this growth in the small-business market segment will lead to small-business online purchases of $118 billion by 2001. Interestingly, the report also found that about 1 million small businesses planned to participate in online auctions in 2000 and that 1.3 million were interested in pooling with other small businesses to buy online in groups to obtain better prices for products and services. However, a significant number of small firms—six out of ten, according to Bose—were reluctant to sell their own products online because of security concerns, the technological challenges, and the belief that their products were unsuited for online selling.[5]

Although global-scale firms dominate e-business, the remarkable thing about the Internet is how accessible it is to small businesses. The relatively low cost of going online means that the Internet is open to thousands of small businesses seeking opportunities to grow internationally. In some cases, small firms have found a niche service or product to sell online. Special online shopping malls bring shoppers a wide selection of unique crafts and artistic creations from small businesses. And many small online magazines, or **e-zines,** as they are often called, have recently found their special audiences through the virtual world of online publishing. In fact, many small publications that began online have gone on to create print versions of their e-zines.

e-zines small online magazines

Writers like Stephen King and recording artists like Sarah McLachlan have discovered that they can earn higher profits by dealing directly with customers online rather than through conventional middlemen such as wholesalers and retail distributors. The Internet has given even unknown artists a new venue for finding an audience; after reading or listening to a sample of their work, newfound fans can order books or CDs directly or download and create their own copies. Software producers like MP3 and Napster are only two of the firms challenging the traditional methods of entertainment distributors. Both firms are at the center of legal concerns over ownership of distribution rights to content on the Internet. Interestingly, Sarah McLachlan was an early financial supporter of MP3 and earned substantial gains as an investor. However, the music industry in general feels threatened by the loss of distribution control.

LEARNING OBJECTIVE

3 Identify and explain fundamental models of e-business.

Fundamental Models of e-Business

One way to get a better sense of how businesses are adapting to the opportunities available on the Internet is to identify e-business models. A **business model** represents a group of shared characteristics and behaviors in a business situation. For example, large food stores share a similar business model when it comes to their selection of merchandise, their organizational structure, their employee job requirements, and, often, their financing needs. Each of the models discussed below represents a primary descriptive characteristic for many e-businesses. The models focus attention on the identity of a firm's customers, the users of the Internet activities, the uniqueness of the online product or service, and the firm's degree of online presence.

business model a group of shared characteristics and behaviors in a business situation

Business-to-Business Model

Many e-businesses can be distinguished from others simply by their customer focus. For instance, some firms use the Internet mainly to conduct business with other businesses. These firms are generally referred to as having a **business-to-business**, or **B2B, model**. Currently, the vast majority of e-business is B2B in nature.

business-to-business (B2B) model firms that conduct business with other businesses

When examining B2B practice, two clear types emerge. In the first type, the focus is simply on facilitating sales transactions between businesses. For example, Dell manufactures computers to specifications that customers enter on the Dell web site. The vast majority of Dell's online orders are from corporate clients who are well informed about the products they need and are looking for fairly priced, high-quality computer products that will be delivered quickly. Basically, by building only what is ordered, Dell reduces storage and carrying costs and rarely is stuck with unsold older technology. By dealing directly with Dell, customers eliminate costs associated with the wholesalers and retailers they would otherwise have to pay, thereby helping reduce the price they pay for equipment.

A second, more complex type of B2B model involves the relationships and procedures used by companies and their suppliers, which often are numerous, geographically dispersed, and difficult to manage. Suppliers today commonly make bids on products and services they wish to offer, learn about conditions under which business will be conducted, which rules and procedures to follow, and so forth. Likewise, firms seeking specific items can now ask for bids on their web sites and choose suppliers that make their offers through the online system. For example, the online leader in the auto industry, Ford Motor Company, links 30,000 auto-parts suppliers and 6,900 dealers in its network, resulting in an estimated \$8.9 billion savings each year on transaction costs, materials, and inventory. In addition, Ford expects to earn approximately \$3 billion from the fees it charges for use of its supplier network.[6]

Given the magnitude of Ford's cost savings, it is all the more surprising that the savings come primarily from the elimination of manual labor and the errors created by the repetitive entry of data by employees. For example, under the old system, Ford

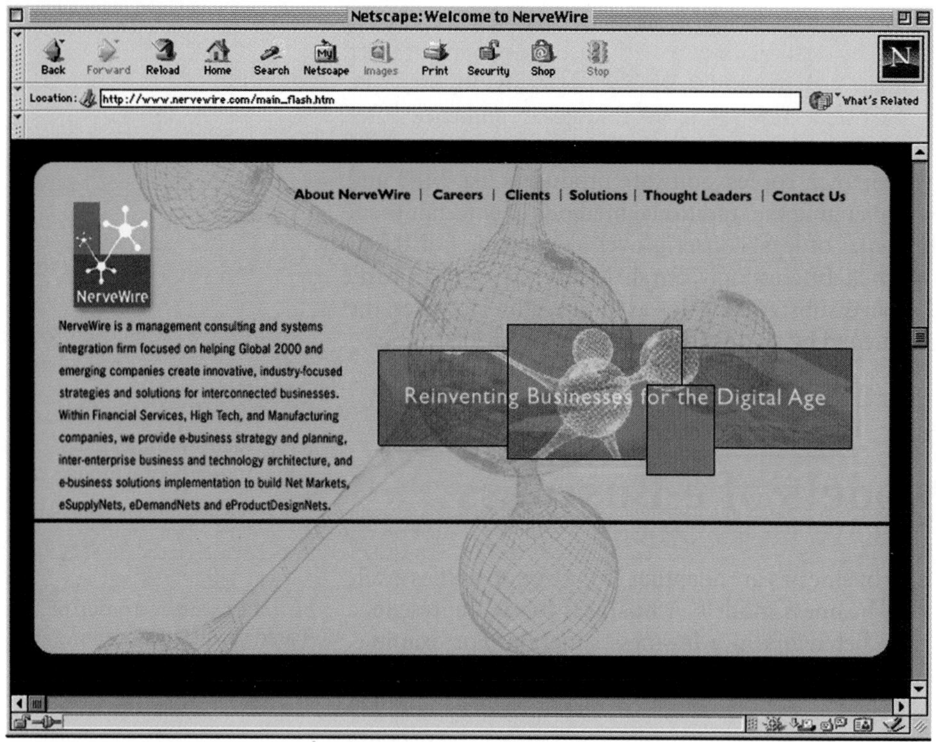

NerveWire can help get the job done. Begun in 1999, NerveWire is a management consulting firm focused on helping emerging companies in the financial, high tech, and manufacturing industries sell their products or services to other businesses online using the B2B model.

might fax an order for parts to a supplier. The supplier would fill out another order form and send a copy to Ford for confirmation. The data would have to be entered in each company's computer system each step of the way. However, under the new system, the supplier has access to Ford's inventory of parts and can place bids for parts online. Ford eliminates the labor costs of data entry and much of the order-processing costs by connecting suppliers to the system.

Similarly, the supplier system at General Motors is expected to eliminate the costs of processing more than 100,000 annual purchase orders, which average $125 each.[7] Given the substantial savings from such networks, it is no wonder that many other manufacturers and their suppliers are beginning to use the same kind of system. Using the system reduces costs and creates a simpler structure for suppliers to use when dealing with each of the manufacturers. The suppliers are able to use the system to bid on work and to monitor their dealings with the manufacturers. Their activities are streamlined with those of their customers. There is less separation between the buyer and the seller, as suppliers become part of the production strategy designed by the companies they serve.

Although managing the activities between a firm and its suppliers is an established business strategy that existed before the Internet came along, it is a focal point of e-business activity for many firms. This is due mostly to the savings and improvements that can be realized by changing current business processes and practices to better ones that are structured around a web site. The result is not only cost savings but also the establishment and control of standard procedures of operation clearly visible through the firm's web site.

Business-to-Consumer Model

business-to-consumer (B2C) model firms that focus on conducting business with individual buyers

In contrast to the customer focus of the B2B model, firms like Amazon.com and e-Bay are clearly focused on individual buyers and so are referred to as having a **business-to-consumer**, or **B2C, model**. In a B2C situation, understanding how consumers behave online is critical to the firm's success. Will consumers use web sites merely to simplify and speed up comparison shopping and end up buying at a traditional store? What sorts of products and services are best suited for online consumer shopping, and which are simply not good choices at this stage of online development? (The case of whether stock trading is improved by moving online is examined in Adapting to Change.) Although an enormous amount of research has been done to answer these and other questions about consumer shopping behavior in traditional stores, relatively little has been done to date about online consumer behavior. No doubt, as more consumers make use of online environments, an increasing amount of research will help explain how best to meet their needs.

In addition to providing round-the-clock global access to their products and services, online B2C firms often make a special effort to build long-term relationships with

Adapting to change

Online Stock Trading: A Change for the Better?

ONLINE STOCK TRADING PROVIDED BY many brokerage firms, including Charles Schwab, TD Waterhouse Group, and E-Trade Group, allows individuals to open a trading account by depositing a sum of money and providing a short personal profile of their financial position. In brief, online customers are able to execute their trades directly through the user-friendly web pages these firms provide. As stocks are bought and sold, the brokerage firms earn revenue through commissions. They also earn revenue by lending money to the online customer to buy more stocks; the stocks held in the customer's account secure the loans.

On the surface, the arrangement appears to be a good one for customers seeking personal control over their stock trading and for brokerage firms looking for ways to further satisfy a niche of investors. However, in the isolation of cyberspace, what is not clear is just how different any individual investor's behavior would be from that expressed in conjunction with a real financial advisor. As traditional methods for conducting business change in the online environment, it is important to question whether change is necessarily best for all parties. On reflection, one might find that the old method is preferable for some clients and the new one for others. The result most likely will not be the elimination of the traditional method, but the addition of a new one, thus allowing greater choice for all.

customers. The thinking behind this is that customers should be valued not only for the sale at hand but also for their long-term contribution to the firm's profitability. The cost incurred in earning a customer's trust is high, but if a firm gains a loyal customer for life, that customer's repeated purchases will repay the investment many times over. Many financial models that attempt to evaluate the real value of a dot.com business make use of estimates of the long-term value of the current customer base.

The Internet has enhanced the ability of firms to build good customer relationships. One factor contributing to this enhanced ability is specialized software that allows sellers to track the decisions customers make as they navigate a web site. Using the resulting data on buying preferences and customer profiles, management can make well-informed decisions about how best to serve the customer. This approach can also enhance inventory decisions, buying selections, and decisions in many other managerial areas. In essence, this is Amazon.com's selling approach. By tracking and analyzing customer data, Amazon can provide individualized service to its customers.

Social and Legal Concerns

LEARNING OBJECTIVE

4 Discuss the social and legal concerns of e-business.

The social and legal concerns of an e-business extend beyond those shared by all businesses. In addition to the issues presented in Chapter 2, e-businesses must deal with the special circumstances of operating in a new frontier—one without borders and without much in the way of control by government or any organization. For better or worse, the world of e-business is an emerging industry with great opportunities for customers and businesses—but with equally great concern about human behavior.

Ethics and Social Responsibility

Socially responsible and ethical behavior by individuals and businesses on the Internet is a major concern. As discussed in Chapter 2, opportunity is a primary factor in determining whether people will behave unethically or illegally. Unfortunately, the Internet provides a shelter of anonymity and detachment for both individuals and firms. These factors may explain why certain behaviors have surfaced. For example, an ethically questionable practice in cyberspace is the unauthorized access and use of information discovered through computerized tracking of users once they are connected to the Internet. Essentially, a user may visit a web page and unknowingly receive a small piece of software code called a **cookie**. This connection may allow the sender to track where the user goes on the Internet and to measure how long the user stays at any particular site. Although this ability may produce valuable customer information, it can also be viewed as an invasion of privacy, especially since users may not even be aware that their movements are being monitored.

cookie a small piece of software sent by a web site that tracks an individual's Internet use

The special circumstances of social interaction in an online environment are also a matter of increasing concern. For example, in some cases, people engaging in online chat rooms will reveal personal information that they would never reveal in face-to-face settings. The online social environment, which encourages a false sense of privacy and security, tends to change an individual's behavior. People may buy things, say things, and do things they otherwise would not because of the effect of the virtual environment. But none of this should be surprising. People behave differently when they are on vacation, at a party, or watching a baseball game in a stadium. The environment has an effect on us, whether it is a physical environment or one created in cyberspace.

A variety of issues about privacy and the distribution of questionable online content, such as pornographic and hate literature, will remain issues of concern in the foreseeable future. Most ISPs and browsers allow users to block out web sites identified as adult in nature, and many chat rooms are supervised so that unacceptable language or behavior can be terminated. Nonetheless, given the openness of the Internet and the relative absence of regulation, online users will have to develop their own strategies for handling difficult ethical and social situations.

computer viruses software codes that are designed to disrupt normal computer operations

copyright control of content ownership

Security Concerns

Because the Internet today is often regarded as an unregulated frontier, both individual and business users must be particularly aware of online risks and dangers. **Computer viruses,** which can originate anywhere in the world, are software codes designed to disrupt normal computer operations. Their potentially devastating effects have given rise to a software security industry. Ken Norton's antivirus program, distributed by Symantec(http://www.symantec.com), is only one of several well-known products that help screen out incoming files containing unwanted viruses, such as the infamous *LoveBug* that emerged in the spring of 2000. As long as undesirable data can be easily transmitted, viruses and other forms of online harassment will remain a security issue and a business opportunity for firms like Symantec, which must continuously revise software to deal with newly issued viruses.

No love lost here. Aki Su, marketing manager of Ultimate PC & Mac Gallery in Hong Kong, caught the "I Love You" bug with a security program. Unfortunately, many computers users were not so lucky. The fact that the virus affected computers around the world illustrates just how popular computers, e-mail, and the Internet have become.

A major concern for businesses that use the Internet to distribute content is control of ownership, or **copyright**. Most affected by this issue are the music and publishing industries. Both have had to deal with new technologies that have allowed individuals to make copies of their content. The music industry has had to contend with unauthorized replication and distribution of content through audiotape and CD technologies. Now, with software provided by such firms as MP3 (http://www.mp3.com) and Napster(http://www.napster.com), any Internet user can create a file of a song online and then send it to someone else, without ever paying the copyright owner. As far as the music industry is concerned, every copy of a song passed along freely on the Internet represents lost sales revenue from a customer who would otherwise make a purchase. To achieve a better degree of control over the distribution of their content, music companies have begun to sign distribution contracts with firms like MP3 and Napster.

Talking Technology

Privacy on the Internet

WHO'S WATCHING WHEN PEOPLE SURF the Internet? Online privacy has become a hot issue as companies sort out the ethical, legal, and management issues. DoubleClick, an online advertising network, is one of the firms at the eye of the privacy storm. The company has collected data on the habits of millions of web surfers, recording which sites they visit and which ads they click on. DoubleClick insists the profiles are anonymous and are used to better match surfers with appropriate ads. However, after the company announced a plan to add names and addresses to its database, it was forced to back down because of public concerns over invasion of online privacy.

DoubleClick isn't the only firm gathering personal data about people's Internet activities. People who register at Yahoo! are asked to list date of birth, among other details. Amazon.com, e-Bay, and other sites also ask for personal information. As Internet usage increases, however, surveys show that people are troubled by the amount of information being collected and who gets to see it.

One way management can address these concerns is to post a privacy policy on the web site. The policy should explain exactly what data the company collects and who gets to see the data. It should also allow people a choice about having their information shared with others and indicate how people can opt out of data collection. Walt Disney, IBM, and other companies support this position by refusing to advertise on web sites that have no posted privacy policies.

In addition, companies can offer web surfers the opportunity to review and correct information that has been collected, especially medical and financial data. In the off-line world, consumers are legally allowed to inspect credit and medical records. In the online world, this kind of access can be costly and cumbersome, because data are often spread across several computer systems. Despite the technical difficulties, government agencies are already working on Internet privacy guidelines, which means companies will need internal guidelines, training, and leadership to ensure compliance.

Government Regulation

For the most part, government regulators have come to view the Internet as just an extension of regular business activity of firms operating in their jurisdictions. To the extent that online business activities resemble traditional business activities, the same rules and regulations apply whether businesses exist entirely or only partially online. Thus, for example, when selling products online to customers who live in areas where governments levy a sales tax, firms must collect the tax and remit it to the local governments. Online firms are thereby prevented from gaining a competitive advantage over traditional "bricks-and-mortar" firms located in jurisdictions with sales taxes. When online business first began, government control over the charging of sales taxes was lax, and many bricks-and-mortar merchants located in highly taxed jurisdictions lost revenues as their customers avoided the sales tax by ordering products online. This was especially true for expensive items that could readily be delivered by courier, such as notebook computers and software. What online businesses and government regulators have discovered is that the unique opportunities and activities presented by the online environment are not always covered by existing regulations, resulting in a lack of sufficient rules and restrictions.

Another area of concern is the sale and distribution of restricted products like pharmaceuticals. In most jurisdictions, to obtain a restricted drug from a pharmacist, a person must present a doctor's prescription. The Internet allows anyone to obtain medications online and, in some cases, with only a claim to a prescription and a credit card. It is, however, the legal responsibility of the online pharmacist to verify the validity of the order and to look for abusive patterns, such as doctors prescribing unusually large quantities of certain drugs for one patient. Nonetheless, the fact that pharmaceuticals can be bought online with relatively little difficulty opens the way for their being subsequently sold into the illicit drug market.

Although it should be emphasized that most firms attempt to ensure that their online activity is fair and legal, the Internet presents a great opportunity for illegal activity in which profit is a major motivator. In the absence of stricter government control, legal and ethical issues in the online environment will become even more pronounced as more firms move their traditional businesses to the Internet.

The U.S. Government Electronic Commerce Policy site (http://www.ecommerce.gov) provides current information about regulations related to online business both within the United States and internationally. It is the definitive portal, or gateway to the Internet, for such information, which is understandable since U.S. commercial interests dominate Internet business.

The Future of e-Business: Growth, Opportunities, and Challenges

LEARNING OBJECTIVE

5 Explore the growth, future opportunities, and challenges of e-business.

Since the advent of commercial activity on the Internet, developments in e-business have been rapid and formidable. Forrester Research, Inc., a research firm located in Cambridge, Massachusetts, predicts that global Internet commerce will soar to $6.8 trillion by 2004, up substantially from earlier growth estimates. Although most of this activity will remain a North American phenomenon, growth is also expected to explode in some Asian-Pacific and Western European countries.[8]

Measurements of Growth

Measurements of e-business growth not only illustrate the magnitude and scope of how much has happened in just a few short years but also indicate trends for the future. According to a study prepared by Strategis Group, a market research and consulting firm based in Washington, D.C., more than 61 percent of U.S. home Internet users went online every day in 1999—often several times a day—compared with 57 percent in 1998 and 46 percent in 1997. Home users spent an average of 7.2 hours a week online, about the same as in 1998, which suggests a stable pattern of use. Men who use the Internet still outnumber women slightly, but the growth in the number of female users has risen steadily. In 1997, only 16.5 percent of women were using the Internet; by late 1999, that figure was up to 49 percent. The average Internet user's age has risen steadily as well, to 40 years, up from 38.6 years in 1997. The number of Internet users making purchases online nearly doubled between 1998 and 1999, going from 27 million to 52 million.[9]

Using the Internet

What do e-business players read to keep up to date on other people, ideas, and trends in the fast-paced world of e-business? Although there has been an information explosion due to the Internet, the answer is likely to include the following:

Wired: **www.wired.com**
Fast Company: **www.fastcompany.com**
Worth: **www.worth.com**
The Industry Standard: **www.thestandard.com**
CNET News: **www.news.com/**
ZDNet: **www.zdnet.com**

Indicative of just how new e-business is, the U.S. Department of Commerce did a survey of online consumer spending for the first time during the last three months of 1999. According to the survey, consumers bought a record $5.4 billion worth of merchandise online, primarily from Amazon.com, Barnesandnoble.com, and e-Toys, confirming the importance of online retail shopping.[10]

According to a Neilsen/NetRatings survey, 130 million people can access the Internet from home, and some 80 million did in April 2000. In comparison with the home market, 35 million users had access to the Internet at their places of work, and nearly 31 million of them actively used the Internet. Both groups of users spent about thirty minutes per session and viewed an average of thirty-five pages. The primary difference between these groups was in the number of sessions per month; those at work connected an average of thirty-eight times per month, twice the number of those at home.[11]

Global Internet users spent an average of 7.6 hours online in March 2000, up from 7.17 hours in January 2000. U.S. and Canadian Internet users spent the most time on the Internet in March, with a combined average of nearly 13 hours per visitor, while users in Europe spent on average just over 5 hours.[12]

Ratings of the popularity of web sites vary depending on the country and the research firms' methodology. Because users' preferences change over time, these ratings, like those of television and radio shows, have meaning only if they are current. According to Media Metrix, AOL is currently on top with more than 59 million "unique visitors." A unique visitor is a person who visits a site at least once during the month; repeat visits by the same person are not counted. AOL is followed by Yahoo with 48 million unique visitors, Microsoft sites with 46 million, Lycos with 32 million, and Excite@home with 28 million.[13]

The Internet will continue to offer great opportunities for growth to both existing bricks-and-mortar firms and those that exist exclusively online. Firms that simply adapt existing business models to an online environment will continue to dominate development. Books, CDs, clothing, hotel accommodations, car rentals, and travel reservations are products and services well suited to online buying and selling. These commodities will continue to be sold in the traditional way, as well as in a more cost-effective and efficient fashion over the Internet. To date, only a fraction of businesses have ventured into the e-business arena. Certainly, development of e-business has just begun.

The most exciting prospect for businesses and customers is not the conversion of existing processes to e-business processes, but the creation of altogether new and unique products and services.

spotLight

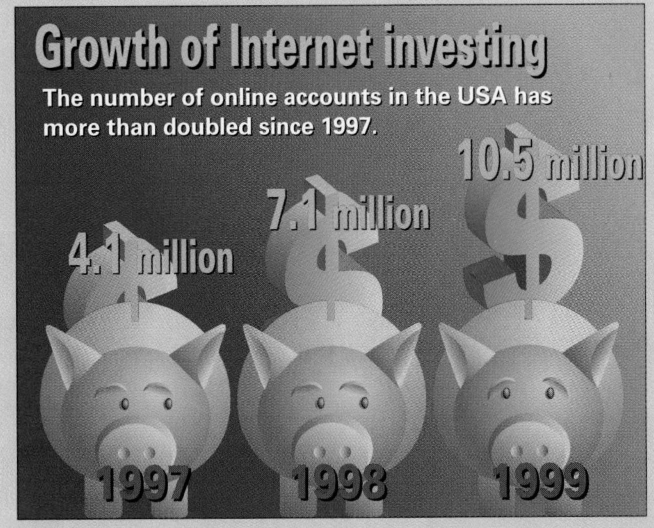

Source: Copyright 2000, USA TODAY. Reprinted with permission.

Do you Yahoo? One of the reasons why people are spending more time on the Internet is that search engines like Yahoo! make it easy. Here, a group of Yahoo! employees are discussing new ideas to make the search engine even more valuable to Internet users.

As noted earlier, MP3 and Napster are only two of the firms providing software for the distribution of music directly to customers. Also now emerging are independent online music webcasters, which are presented to users as online radio stations. So, in addition to enabling existing radio stations to find a global audience for their product, the technology exists for independent producers to set up their own unique radio webcasting stations. And given the rapidly developing technologies available through wireless communications, webcast radio will very shortly become as commonplace as any local radio station received in the customer's physical broadcast area. Netscape's webcast radio services (http://radio.netscape.com) provides information about how private and public webcast can be created.

Convergence of Technologies

convergence of technologies the overlapping capabilities and the merging of products and services into one fully integrated interactive system

As webcast radio illustrates, the borders of telecommunications technologies for electronic distribution of sound, images, and text have become less clear. Today, we can send and receive e-mail from pagers, interact with the Internet from a small screen on a cell phone, and even have visually active telephone conversations. This phenomenon of overlapping capabilities and the merging of products and services into one fully integrated interactive system is referred to as the **convergence of technologies.** This convergence may well lead to interactive television programs, which would allow viewers to select their preferences in the way a program is presented. Viewers of a cooking show, for example, might be able to select whether they would prefer instructions for regular or nonfat cooking. The profile of the viewer's personal tastes and preferences could be maintained, so that the next time the viewer watched the cooking show, the profile would be automatically entered and the appropriate data provided on the screen.

Online Communities

online communities groups of individuals or firms that want to exchange information, products, or services over the Internet

Online communities, which are made up of groups of individuals or firms that want to exchange information, products, or services over the Internet, are a phenomenon that is likely to grow. One example of a thriving online community is iVillage.com, a commercial site for women (see Going Global on page 120). Other online communities include buyers' groups, such as OnVia.com, a site that caters to the small-business market. Small businesses can use this site to search out other businesses that might provide a needed product or service, and they can also make use of automated bidding agents that will locate the best deals. Online learning communities continue to evolve as sites in a wide variety of fields, allowing people who share an interest or concern to communicate with each other. Geocities.com is only one portal to a huge selection of online communities.

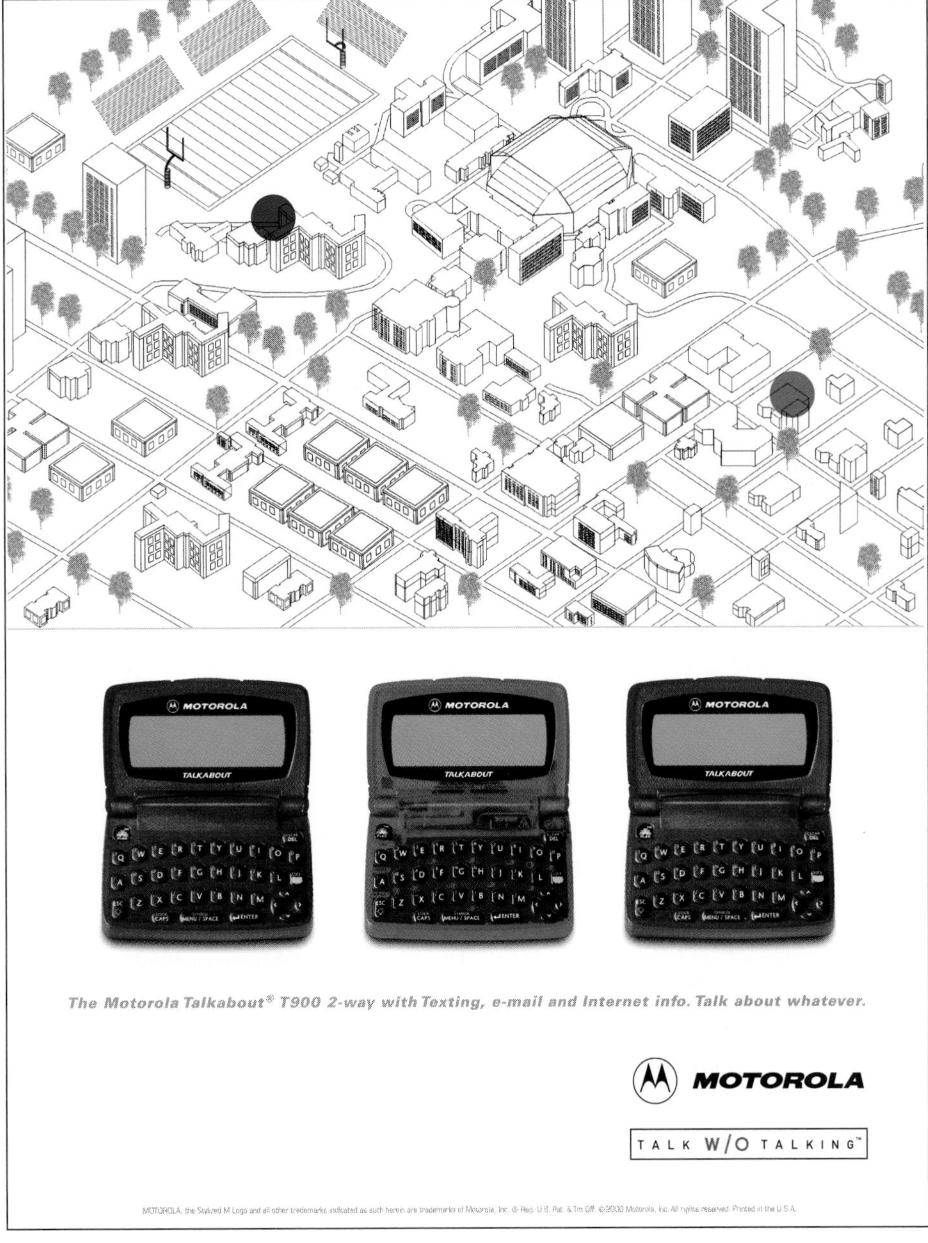

Talk! Talk! Talk! Today, people receive e-mail from pagers, access the Internet with cell phones, and can even see each other when talking over the telephone. These trends will continue because of the convergence of technologies.

Partnering Online

While opportunities for independent e-business effort will continue, online partnerships, which can be of benefit to both large and small firms, are likely to be increasingly common. By playing a role within a larger entity, small firms can enjoy competitive advantage and access to marketable items, thereby increasing their rate of market penetration. A review of the major e-business sites, including those of IBM, Microsoft, and Oracle, indicates that the e-business approach taken by these firms involves local geographic partnerships.

Many Internet firms have been able to realize rapid growth through partnerships with smaller firms. For example, Amazon.com pays its web-site partners a commission on items bought by users whom the partners send to Amazon. Suppose an online learning community made up of students of Spanish and small vendors of related products and services had a link on its web page that took viewers to Amazon.com. By connecting with Amazon.com, the site can earn revenue and at the same time satisfy users who might not find what they are looking for within the learning community's limited selection. The learning community's range of products is thus automatically

Going Global

iVillage: A Global Community for Women

CREATING A WEB SITE THAT FOCUSES ON the lifestyles and interests of one group of viewers is a popular e-business strategy. In many ways, iVillage.com, a site that caters to women who are mostly college-educated and twenty to fifty years old, is a logical extension of a print-based magazine strategy. Here, women can find information and advice on such topics as health, family, education, business, and career. Chat rooms and links to related sites make iVillage a portal for women on the Internet. Like similar online communities, such as Martha Stewart's (http://www.marthastewart.com), iVillage earns revenues through advertising placed on the site by other firms and through its own online shopping service, which offers daily special promotions. The relationship with the audience is a long-term one; gift-giving ideas and online learning about everything from gardening to nutrition provide a reason for viewers to visit the site regularly. Maintaining a reason for viewers to return to iVillage is the challenge for site managers. Future possibilities for iVillage include spin-off web sites focusing on more narrowly defined target audiences, like single lifestyle interests such as fashion.

extended to the wide selection carried by Amazon, and both Amazon and the learning community benefit.

This chapter has presented an overview of the fast-paced, emerging world of e-business. Throughout the text, you will find more e-business references and examples as they apply to the different aspects of business, such as management, marketing, and finance. Chapter 17 covers the more technological side of e-business, focusing on topics like web pages and standards for communications, Internet-based software, and the communications system that makes up the Internet. In Chapters 5 and 6 we examine issues related to forms of business ownership and special considerations surrounding small business.

RETURN TO Inside Business

BECAUSE CUSTOMERS CAN CHANGE Internet service providers with relative ease, they have begun to see little differentiation among these firms except with respect to price. Being able to offer its customers Time Warner content allows AOL to avoid competing with other Internet service providers on the basis of price alone. This major competitive advantage changes how the battle for customers will be fought. Internet service providers will focus attention not on price, but on the value-added services they can offer their customers. Whether online services are in the form of entertainment content or access to specialized communications and software, customers will find a growing selection of services being offered by Internet service providers as each seeks to attract and keep customers.

AOL and Time Warner will continue to make news regularly as they bring new products to the Internet.

Questions

1. What content would you put online to attract customers to AOL?
2. Besides lowering prices, what would you do to help AOL retain customers?

chapter Review

SUMMARY

1 Define and explain the meaning of e-business.

E-business, or electronic business, can be defined as the organized effort of individuals to produce and sell, for a profit, the products and services that satisfy society's needs through the facilities available on the Internet. The term *e-business* refers to all business activities and practices conducted on the Internet by an individual firm or industry. On the other hand, *e-commerce* is a part of e-business; the term refers only to online buying and selling activities, including identifying suppliers, selecting products or services, making purchase commitments, completing financial transactions, and obtaining service. The human, material, information, and financial resources that any business requires are highly specialized for e-business. New customer needs created by the Internet as well as traditional ones can be satisfied in unique ways by e-business. By using a variety of e-business activities firms can increase sales revenue and reduce expenses in order to increase profits.

2 Explore the basic framework of e-business.

Most firms involved in e-business fall more or less into one of three primary groups as defined by their e-business activities: (1) telecommunications and computer hardware manufacturers and Internet service providers, which together supply the physical infrastructure of the Internet; (2) producers of Internet software, which provide the ability to do things on the Internet; and (3) online sellers and content providers. The Internet would still be limited to communication between individuals and among groups of special-interest researchers were it not for the activity of online sellers and content producers. In this area of e-business, we have just begun to see the development of online strategies for reaching out to existing and new customers. The special characteristics of e-business provide increased opportunity for firms to reach global markets and for small businesses to start up and grow.

3 Identify and explain fundamental models of e-business.

E-business models focus attention on the identity of a firm's customers, the users of the Internet activities, the uniqueness of the online product or service, and the firm's degree of online presence. Many e-businesses can be distinguished from others simply by their customer focus. Firms that use the Internet mainly to conduct business with other businesses are generally referred to as having a business-to-business, or B2B, model. Currently, the vast majority of e-business is B2B in nature. In contrast to the focus of the B2B model, firms like Amazon.com and e-Bay are clearly focused on individual buyers and so are referred to as having a business-to-consumer, or B2C, model.

4 Discuss the social and legal concerns of e-business.

The social and legal concerns of an e-business extend beyond those shared by all businesses. E- businesses must deal with the special circumstances of operating in a new frontier—one without borders and with limited control by government or any other organization. As a result, consumers, businesses, and the government are all learning how to deal with issues related to ethics, social responsibility, security, and regulation.

5 Explore the growth, future opportunities, and challenges of e-business.

Since the advent of commercial activity on the Internet, developments in e-business have been rapid and formidable. Although most commercial online activity will remain a North American phenomenon, growth is also expected to explode in some Asian-Pacific and Western European countries. As online activity increases, the creation of new products and services, the convergence of technologies, and online communities also grows. While opportunities for independent e-business effort will continue to grow, online partnerships, which can be of benefit to both large and small firms, are also likely to increase. By playing a role within a larger entity, small firms can enjoy competitive advantage and access to marketable items, thereby increasing their rate of market penetration. Larger firms like Amazon.com have already realized the benefits of partnering with small businesses.

KEY TERMS

You should now be able to define and give an example relevant to each of the following terms.

e-business (electronic business) (104)
e-commerce (104)
revenue stream (106)
World Wide Web (the web) (108)
digitized (108)
e-zines (110)
business model (111)
business-to-business (B2B) model (111)
business-to-consumer (B2C) model (112)
cookie (114)
computer viruses (114)
copyright (114)
convergence of technologies (118)
online communities (118)

REVIEW QUESTIONS

1. What are the major characteristics that define e-business?
2. How does e-business differ from e-commerce?
3. How do e-businesses generate revenue streams?
4. What roles do telecommunications firms and Internet service providers play in e-business?
5. How do software producers contribute to e-business?
6. What does the term *content providers* mean?
7. Why does e-business represent a global opportunity to reach customers?
8. What are the two fundamental e-business models?
9. Give an example of an unethical use of the Internet by a business or an individual.
10. What has been the general level of involvement of governments in e-business to date?
11. What does *convergence of technologies* mean?
12. What are online communities?
13. How can partnering with other e-businesses help firms compete on the Internet?

DISCUSSION QUESTIONS

1. Can advertising provide enough revenue for an e-business to succeed in the long run?
2. How can small businesses compete against large-scale e-businesses?
3. What distinguishes the B2B and B2C e-business models?
4. Discuss some of the social, ethical, and legal issues facing e-business.
5. Discuss the role of government and regulatory agencies in e-business.
6. Describe the growth of e-business since the start of commercial activities on the Internet.

VIDEO CASE

Blackboard.com: The Future of Educational Technology

Welcome to the future where learning has no limits, where education is powered by Blackboard.com. Formed in 1997 in Washington, D.C., by a group of young entrepreneurs, Blackboard has become one of the leading companies in connecting the Internet to the $800 billion a year education market. Now less than five years after its incorporation date, Blackboard is influencing the way people teach and learn not only in the United States but around the world.

According to industry analysts, Blackboard.com is the leading provider of e-learning platforms in the academic market and sits at the intersection of two large and fast-growing markets: the Internet and education. The company's vision is to transform the Internet into a powerful environment for teaching and learning. To accomplish its vision, Blackboard has established computer software that allows colleges, universities, and commercial education providers to distribute their online courses and educational materials to more than one-half million users around the globe.

Here's how the Blackboard educational computer platform works for college courses. Any teacher can access Blackboard's software programs and put their course materials online for free. Once the course is available, students from all over the globe can access Blackboard's computer network via the Internet, obtain information about the course, and register for the course at the host college or university. Once registered, students can then read announcements, obtain course assignments, participate in chat rooms and discussion forums, and even test online. By using the Internet, students and instructors can also communicate with each other. And both students and instructors can take advantage of a number of specialized sites within the Blackboard platform that provide access to news, articles, tutorials, research, and reference tools including Internet search engines.

Any new company needs financing to begin operations, and Blackboard.com is no exception. Fifty million dollars of start-up capital for Blackboard.com was provided by a number of recognized companies that include America Online, The Aurora Funds, Dell Computer Corporation, Merrill Lynch, and numerous venture-capital firms that thought the potential profits justified the risk of investing in a small start-up firm like Blackboard.com. Once it began operations, Blackboard.com created sales revenues by charging licensing fees for its services to more than 3,000 colleges, universities, publishers, and commercial education providers.

What does the future hold for a technology company like Blackboard.com. Simple answer: The future looks bright! According to Michael Chasen, president and cofounder, "We definitely see a time in which every teacher believes that the Internet is as key a tool as a textbook in their class for teaching and learning." And for the folks at Blackboard.com, that's pretty exciting.[14]

Questions

1. Blackboard.com began operations in 1997. Now, according to industry analysts, it is the leading provider of e-learning platforms in the academic market. What factors led to Blackboard.com's phenomenal success?
2. According to the material in this chapter, the Internet has created new opportunities for e-businesses to satisfy customer needs. How does Blackboard.com satisfy the needs of students? Of colleges, universities, and commercial education providers?
3. More than 3,000 colleges and universities now offer college courses online. Would this type of educational program appeal to you? Explain your answer.

Building skills for career success

1. Exploring the Internet

To thrive, all web sites need visitors. Without the revenue that comes from firms that buy banner advertising on web sites or the subscription fees paid by viewers, the necessary cash to create, maintain, and grow would simply not exist. What attracts viewers varies according to their lifestyles, age, gender, and information requirements. Many online communities focus on the interests of a selected target audience. MarthaStewart.com and iVillage.com are two well-known sites catering mostly to college-educated women interested in leisure, parenting, business, nutrition, and the like. However, these are only two sites in a sea of choice. Visit the text web site for updates to this exercise.

Assignment

1. Identify and describe two or more web sites with content that attracts you and keeps you returning on a regular basis.
2. How would you describe the target audience for these sites?
3. What advertisements are typically displayed?

2. Developing Critical Thinking Skills

Although the variety of products available to online shoppers is growing quickly, many people are reluctant to make purchases over the Internet. For a variety of reasons, some individuals are uncomfortable with using the Internet for this purpose, while others do so easily and often. The considerations involved in making a business-to-business purchase decision differ from those involved in making a personal purchase. However, the experience of buying office supplies from Staples.com for a business might influence an individual to visit other online sites to shop for personal items.

Assignment

1. Which sorts of products or services do you think would be easy to sell online? What kinds of things do you think would be difficult to purchase online? Explain your thinking.
2. Have you ever purchased anything over the Internet? Explain why you have or have not.
3. Explain how the considerations involved in buying office supplies from Staples.com for a business might differ from those involved in making a personal purchase.

3. Building Team Skills

An interesting approach taken by Yahoo.com and several other web sites is to provide viewers with the tools needed to create a personal web page or community. Yahoo.com's GeoCities site (http://geocities.yahoo.com/home) provides simple instructions for creating a site and posting your own content, such as articles and photographs. Yahoo earns money by selling banner advertising, which is visible to viewers of all the different communities that Yahoo hosts free of charge.

Assignment

1. Working in a group, examine some of the GeoCities communities and personal web pages. Discuss which sites you think work well and which do not. Explain your reasoning.
2. Develop an idea for your own web site. Draw a sketch of how you would like the site to appear on the Internet. You may use ideas that look good on other personal pages.
3. Who is your target audience, and why do you think they will want to visit the site?

4. Researching Different Careers

The Internet offers a wide assortment of career opportunities in business, as well as in Internet-related technologies. As firms seek opportunities online, new e-businesses are springing up every day. In many cases, these firms want people with a fresh outlook on how e-business can succeed, and they prefer individuals without preconceived notions about how to proceed. Web site managers, designers, creative artists, and content specialists are just a few of the positions available. Many large online job sites, such as Monster.com, can help you find out about employment opportunities in e-business and the special skills required for various jobs.

Assignment

1. Summarize the positions that appear to be in high demand in e-business.
2. What are some of the special skills required to fill these jobs?
3. What salaries and benefits are typically associated with these positions?
4. Which job seems most appealing to you personally? Why?

5. Improving Communication Skills

Describing web sites in summary form can be difficult because of the mix of information involved. A useful exercise is to create a table, which can serve not only as an organizational tool for the information but also as a means of quick comparison.

Assignment

1. Create a table that will compare ten web sites you have visited. Place the title of one type of information at the head of each column. For example, you might start with the firm's name in the first column, the type of product it sells online in the second column, and so forth.
2. Enter short descriptive data in each column.
3. Write a descriptive summary of the table you have prepared, identifying a few of the outstanding characteristics listed in the data.

choosing a form of business ownership

5

LEARNING OBJECTIVES

1 Describe the advantages and disadvantages of sole proprietorships.

2 Explain the different types of partners and the importance of partnership agreements.

3 Describe the advantages and disadvantages of partnerships.

4 Summarize how a corporation is formed.

5 Describe the advantages and disadvantages of a corporation.

6 Discuss the purpose of an S-corporation, limited liability company, government-owned corporation, and other special forms of business ownership.

7 Explain how growth from within and growth through mergers can enable a business to expand.

The Hewlett-Packard way of doing business made it famous as a progressive, well-managed company.

inside business

Hewlett-Packard: The Company That Invented Silicon Valley

WHEN YOU HEAR THE name Hewlett-Packard, you immediately think of a large global corporation. But today's corporate giant was created by two Stanford University classmates—Bill Hewlett and David Packard—with only $538 and a garage in Palo Alto, California. Encouraged by their professor and mentor, Frederick Terman, these two young entrepreneurs began a small partnership that led to the development of Silicon Valley.

When Hewlett and Packard first started the company, they weren't even sure what they wanted to manufacture. But, with a toss of a coin, their partnership, Hewlett-Packard Company, was formed on January 1, 1939 and invention began. By the end of 1940, they had eight products on the market, and annual sales totaling $34,000. To celebrate their success, they gave each of their three employees a $5 Christmas bonus. In 1942 they built their first 10,000 square foot building but designed it so that it could be used as a grocery store if their electronics business failed. The business was incorporated in 1947, issued stock for the first time in November of 1957, and was listed as No. 460 on *Fortune* magazine's top 500 in 1962.

From the beginning, the two partners created a corporate culture that stressed trust and openness where all employees were treated equally. The company also became known as a great place to work because of its relaxed working environment and consensus approach to manufacturing and marketing of every new product. In short, the HP way of doing business made it famous as a progressive, well-managed company. So much so, that most employees remained with this "granddaddy of technology" company for an average of eleven years—an amazing feat considering the high employee turnover in other firms in the computer electronics industry. And because of committed employees coupled with the HP way of doing business, Hewlett-Packard continued to grow with more inventions, mergers, acquisitions, and joint-venture operations.

Today, dubbed as the "company that invented Silicon Valley," Hewlett-Packard has over 124,000 employees and manufactures and markets more than 29,000 products. It is recognized as the second largest computer company in the world and is currently No. 13 on the *Fortune* 500 list. It is also the first *Fortune* 500 company to appoint a female as president and chief executive officer.

Carleton (Carly) S. Fiorina was named president and chief executive officer of Hewlett-Packard on July 17, 1999. Educated at Stanford University, the University of Maryland, and MIT's Sloan School, she made her way up the corporate ranks at AT&T and Lucent Technologies. As the first woman to run a top-tier 500 giant, *Fortune* magazine has called her the most powerful woman in American business.

Ms. Fiorina is the first outsider to be brought in as head of Hewlett-Packard, and only the fifth CEO in its company history. After joining Hewlett-Packard, she immediately made a whirlwind tour of all of its facilities, conferring with executives, managers, and employees to explain that her goals are to preserve the best of the past. However, she has made it clear that she is totally focused on improving sales revenues and profits, providing total customer satisfaction, and making HP the company that makes the Internet work for its customers. For more information about what's happening at Hewlett-Packard, log on to its web site at www.hp.com.[1]

Although IBM is the largest computer company in the world, Hewlett-Packard's 124,000 managers and employees would like to see their company become No. 1. They are optimistic that HP will not only be able to maintain its position in the volatile computer industry, but increase its sales revenues, profits, and its share of the volatile computer market. While operating in a very competitive industry that has undergone tremendous change over the past twenty years, the firm has continued to provide a quality product that is known around the world. What's their secret of success?

To answer that question, let's quickly review the definition of business given in Chapter 1. A *business* is the organized effort of individuals to produce and sell, for a profit, the goods and services that satisfy society's needs. Hewlett-Packard—or for that matter, any other successful business—is a practical example of that definition. The first and most important step for all businesses—sole proprietorships, partnerships, corporations, or some special form of business ownership—is to produce products or services their customers want.

Many people dream of opening a business, and one of the first decisions they must make is what form of ownership to choose. We begin this chapter by describing the three common forms of business ownership: sole proprietorships, partnerships, and corporations. We discuss how these types of businesses are formed and note the advantages and disadvantages of each. Next we consider several types of business ownership usually chosen for special purposes, including S-corporations, limited liability companies, government-owned corporations, not-for-profit corporations, cooperatives, joint ventures, and syndicates. We conclude the chapter with a discussion of how businesses can grow through internal expansion or through mergers with other companies.

LEARNING OBJECTIVE

1 Describe the advantages and disadvantages of sole proprietorships.

Sole Proprietorships

A **sole proprietorship** is a business that is owned (and usually operated) by one person. Although a few sole proprietorships are large and have many employees, most are small. Sole proprietorship is the simplest form of business ownership and the easiest to start. In most instances, the owner (the *sole* proprietor) simply decides he or she is in business and begins operations. Some of today's largest corporations, including Ford Motor Company, H. J. Heinz Company, and J. C. Penney Company, started out as tiny—and, in many cases, struggling—sole proprietorships.

sole proprietorship a business that is owned (and usually operated) by one person

As you can see in Figure 5.1, there are more than 16.9 million sole proprietorships in the United States. They account for 73 percent of the country's business firms. Sole proprietorships are most common in retailing, service, and agriculture. Thus, the clothing boutique, corner grocery, and television repair shop down the street are likely to be sole proprietorships. The current shortage of highly sought after knowledge

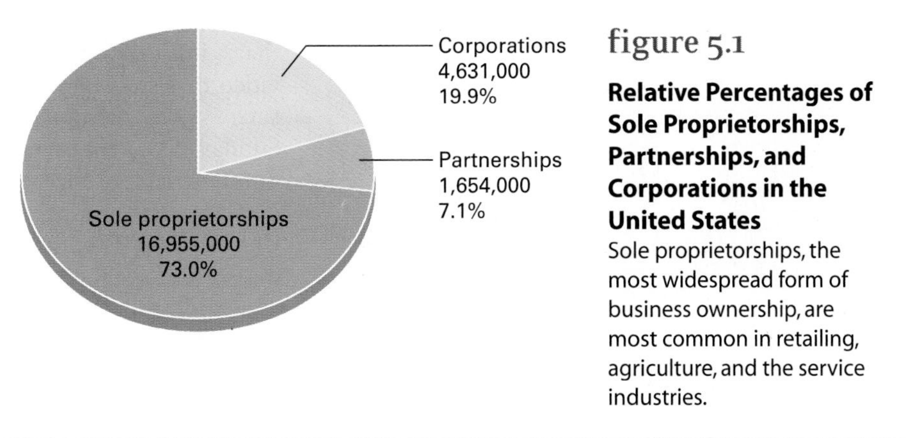

figure 5.1

Relative Percentages of Sole Proprietorships, Partnerships, and Corporations in the United States

Sole proprietorships, the most widespread form of business ownership, are most common in retailing, agriculture, and the service industries.

Source: U.S. Bureau of the Census, *Statistical Abstract of the United States,* 119th ed., Washington, D.C., 1999, p. 545.

workers in Internet-related information technology industries has created an enormous opportunity for individuals to start up their own consulting services firms by working on a contractual basis for various clients. Skilled Internet web site designers, e-commerce programmers, software trainers, and many others have found that they are better off working for themselves. Not only can they pick and choose which job assignments to accept, they have also found that they can earn more money by not working exclusively for one firm as a salaried employee.

Advantages of Sole Proprietorships

Most of the advantages of sole proprietorships arise from the two main characteristics of this form of ownership: simplicity and individual control.

Ease of Start-Up Sole proprietorship is the simplest and cheapest way to start a business. Start-up requires no contracts, agreements, or other legal documents. Thus, a sole proprietorship can be, and most often is, established without the services of an attorney. Certain types of businesses, such as restaurants or catering services, that are regulated in the interest of public safety may require a state or city license. But beyond that, a sole proprietor pays no special start-up fees or taxes. Nor are there any minimum capital requirements.

If the enterprise does not succeed, the firm can be closed as easily as it was opened. Creditors must be paid, of course. But generally, the owner does not have to go through any legal procedure before hanging up an "Out of Business" sign.

Retention of All Profits Because all profits become the personal earnings of the owner, the owner has a strong incentive to succeed. This direct financial reward attracts many entrepreneurs to the sole proprietorship form of business and, if the business succeeds, is a source of great satisfaction.

Flexibility A sole proprietor is completely free to make decisions about the firm's operations. Without asking or waiting for anyone's approval, a sole proprietor can switch from retailing to wholesaling, move a shop's location, open a new store, or close an old one.

A sole proprietor can also respond to changes in market conditions much more quickly than the partnership or corporate forms of business. Suppose the sole proprietor of an appliance store finds that many customers now prefer to shop on Sunday afternoons. He or she can make an immediate change in business hours to take advantage of that information (provided that state laws allow such stores to open on Sunday). The manager of a store in a large corporate chain like Best Buy Company or Circuit City may have to seek the approval of numerous managers and company officials before making such a change. Furthermore, a sole proprietor can quickly switch suppli-

A picture of success. Sometimes a picture is worth a thousand words. This entrepreneur is proud of the business he started because it meets the needs of customers by selling camera supplies and film developing services.

ers to take advantage of a lower price, whereas such a switch could take weeks in a more complex business.

Possible Tax Advantages The sole proprietorship's profits are taxed as personal income of the owner. Thus, a sole proprietorship does not pay the special state and federal income taxes that corporations pay. (As you will see later, a corporation's profits may be taxed twice. A sole proprietorship's profits are taxed only once.) Owners of a sole proprietorship do have to make estimated quarterly tax payments to the federal government.

Secrecy Sole proprietors are not required by federal or state governments to publicly reveal their business plans, profits, or other vital facts. Therefore, competitors cannot get their hands on this information. Of course, sole proprietorships must report certain financial information on their personal tax forms.

spotLight

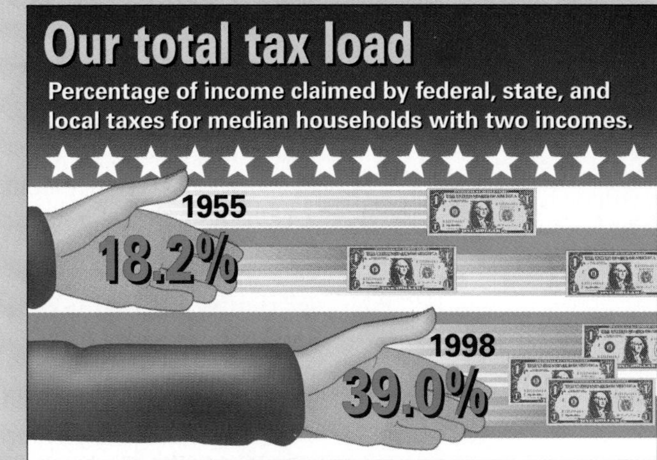

Source: Copyright 2000, USA TODAY. Reprinted with permission.

Disadvantages of Sole Proprietorships

The disadvantages of a sole proprietorship stem from the fact that these businesses are owned by one person. Some capable sole proprietors experience no problems. Individuals who start out with few management skills and little money are most at risk.

Unlimited Liability **Unlimited liability** is a legal concept that holds a business owner personally responsible for all the debts of the business. There is legally no difference between the debts of the business and the debts of the proprietor. If the business fails or if the business is involved in a lawsuit and loses, the owner's personal property—including savings and other assets—can be seized (and sold if necessary) to pay creditors.

unlimited liability a legal concept that holds a business owner personally responsible for all the debts of the business

Unlimited liability is perhaps the major factor that tends to discourage would-be entrepreneurs with substantial personal wealth from using this form of business organization.

Lack of Continuity Legally, the sole proprietor *is* the business. If the owner dies or is declared legally incompetent, the business essentially ceases to exist. In many cases, however—especially when the business is a profitable enterprise—the owner's heirs take it over and either sell it or continue to operate it.

Lack of Money Banks, suppliers, and other lenders are usually unwilling to lend large sums to sole proprietorships. Only one person—the sole proprietor—can be held responsible for repaying such loans, and the assets of most sole proprietors are usually limited. Moreover, these assets may already have been used as the basis for personal borrowing (a home mortgage or car loan) or for short-term credit from suppliers. Lenders also worry about the lack of continuity of sole proprietorships: who will repay a loan if the sole proprietor dies? Finally, many lenders are concerned about the large number of sole proprietorships that fail—a topic discussed in Chapter 6.

The limited ability to borrow money can prevent a sole proprietorship from growing. It is the main reason many business owners, when in need of relatively large amounts of capital, change from the sole proprietorship to the partnership or corporate form of ownership.

Limited Management Skills Later in this text, you will see that managers perform a variety of functions in such areas of business as finance, marketing, human resources management, and operations. The sole proprietor is often the sole manager—in addition to being the only salesperson, buyer, accountant, and, on occasion, janitor.

Even the most experienced business owner is unlikely to have expertise in all these areas. Consequently, unless he or she obtains the necessary expertise by hiring employees, assistants, or consultants, the business can suffer in the areas in which the owner is less knowledgeable. For the many sole proprietors who cannot hire the help they need, there just aren't enough hours in the day to do everything that needs to be done. This usually means long hours each day, six-day or seven-day work weeks, few days off, and limited vacation time.

Difficulty in Hiring Employees The sole proprietor may find it hard to attract and keep competent help. Potential employees may feel there is no room for advancement in a firm whose owner assumes all managerial responsibilities. And when those who *are* hired are ready to take on added responsibility, they may find the only way to do so is to quit the sole proprietorship and go to work for a larger firm or start up their own businesses. The lure of higher salaries and increased benefits may also cause existing employees to change jobs.

Beyond the Sole Proprietorship

Like many others, you may decide the major disadvantage of a sole proprietorship is the limited amount that one person can do in a workday. One way to reduce the effect of this disadvantage (and retain many of the advantages) is to have more than one owner. To see why two sole proprietors decided to form a partnership, read Exploring Business.

Exploring Business

Procter & Gamble: Optimism Led the Way Even When It Was Not the Best of Times

William Procter owned a candle-making business; James Gamble owned a soap business. When the two young sole proprietors married sisters, their father-in-law convinced them that they should merge their business and form a partnership. He reasoned that a partnership would stand a much better chance of weathering the economic problems that small businesses were experiencing in the United States. In fact, the United States was experiencing a financial panic. Banks were closing and concerns for the economy ran deep throughout the nation. So, in 1837, with the optimism of young entrepreneurs, they formed a partnership and called it Procter & Gamble and set out to compete with fourteen other soap and candle-makers in Cincinnati, Ohio. Twelve years later, by 1859, their partnership was one of the largest companies in Cincinnati with annual sales of $1 million and eighty employees. And during the Civil War their business continued to grow because Procter & Gamble won government contracts to supply soap and candles to the troops. The fact that soldiers brought their Procter & Gamble products home to their families when the war ended helped build brand recognition. Then in 1879, P&G introduced Ivory, the "floating" soap. By 1890, Procter & Gamble had grown into a multimillion dollar corporation selling more than thirty different products. With the invention of the electric light bulb, candles were phased out of their product line in the 1920s, but their research laboratory was cranking out one innovative product after another. Then in the 1930s, Procter & Gamble used radio advertising to sponsor soap operas and at the same time strengthen its share of the market for consumer products.

Today, Procter & Gamble is a global corporation that manufactures and markets more than three hundred brands of consumer goods with operations in more than seventy countries. Worldwide sales to over five billion customers totaled $10.6 billion for 1999–the latest year for which complete financial results are available. Still don't believe how successful this corporation is? Every home in America has at least one product bearing the Procter & Gamble trademark. Open your kitchen cabinets; maybe you will find Crisco or Folgers coffee. Go into your laundry room; there you may see Tide or Bounce. How about Crest toothpaste or Charmin in your bathroom? And, oh yes, look at the baby's bottom. It was Procter & Gamble that introduced Pampers–the disposable diaper! Not too bad for two optimistic entrepreneurs that formed a partnership in "not the best of times." For more information on Procter & Gamble and the products it produces, visit its web site at: www.pg.com.

Partnerships

LEARNING OBJECTIVE

2 Explain the different types of partners and the importance of partnership agreements.

Throughout our lives, we form partnerships with family members, friends, and spouses. Business partnerships do not usually entail as much affection as these other relationships, but to some people they are equally natural. A person who would not think of starting and running a business alone may enthusiastically seize the opportunity to enter into a business partnership.

The U.S. Uniform Partnership Act defines a **partnership** as a voluntary association of two or more persons to act as co-owners of a business for profit. For example, in 1983, two young African-American entrepreneurs named Janet Smith and Gary Smith started Ivy Planning Group–a company that provides strategic planning and performance measurement for clients. Today, the company has evolved into a multimillion dollar company that has hired a diverse staff of employees and provides cultural diversity training for *Fortune* 500 firms and other large organizations. In recognition of its efforts, Ivy Planning Group was chosen by *Black Enterprise* for its Emerging Company of the Year Award for the year 2000.[2]

partnership a voluntary association of two or more persons to act as co-owners of a business for profit

There are approximately 1.7 million partnerships in the United States. As shown in Figure 5.2, partnerships account for about $1,042 billion in receipts. Note, however, that this form of ownership is much less common than the sole proprietorship or the corporation. In fact, as Figure 5.1 shows, partnerships represent only about 7 percent of all American businesses.

Although there is no legal maximum on the number of partners a partnership may have, most have only two. Large accounting, law, and advertising partnerships, however, are likely to have multiple partners. Often, a partnership represents a pooling of special managerial skills and talents; at other times, it is the result of a sole proprietor's taking on a partner for the purpose of obtaining more capital.

Types of Partners

All partners are not necessarily equal. Some may be active in running the business, whereas others may have a limited role.

General Partners

A **general partner** is a person who assumes full or shared responsibility for operating a business. General partners are active in day-to-day business operations, and each partner can enter into contracts on behalf of the other partners. He or she also assumes unlimited liability for all debts, including debts incurred by any other general partner without his or her knowledge or consent. A **general partnership** is a business co-owned by two or more general partners who are liable for everything the business does.

general partner a person who assumes full or shared responsibility for operating a business

general partnership a business co-owned by two or more general partners who are liable for everything the business does

Although a partnership pays no income tax, each partner is taxed on his or her share of the profit—in the same way a sole proprietor is taxed. To avoid future liability, a general partner who withdraws from the partnership must give notice to creditors, customers, and suppliers.

Limited Partners

A **limited partner** is a person who contributes capital to a business but who has no management responsibility or liability for losses beyond his or her investment in the partnership. A **limited partnership** is a business co-owned by one or more general partners who manage the business and limited partners who invest money in it. Limited partnerships may be formed to finance real estate, oil and gas, motion-picture, and other business ventures. Typically, the general partner or partners collect management fees and a percentage of profits and income. Limited partners receive income, a portion of profits, and tax benefits.

limited partner a person who contributes capital to a business but has no management responsibility or liability for losses beyond the amount he or she invested in the partnership

limited partnership a business co-owned by one or more general partners who manage the business and limited partners who invest money in it

Because of potential liability problems, special rules apply to limited partnerships. These rules are intended to protect customers and creditors who deal with limited partnerships. For example, prospective partners in a limited partnership must file a formal declaration, usually at their county courthouse, that describes the essential

figure 5.2

Total Sales Receipts of American Businesses

Although corporations account for only 19.9 percent of U.S. businesses, they bring in 88.8 percent of the sales receipts.

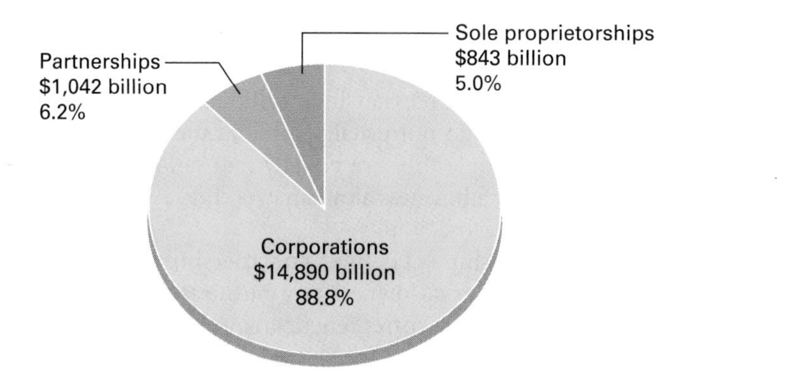

Source: U.S. Bureau of the Census, *Statistical Abstract of the United States,* 119th ed., Washington, D.C., 1999, p. 545.

details of the partnership and the liability status of each partner involved in the business; some states require that the same type of information be filed with the secretary of state. At least one general partner must be responsible for the debts of the limited partnership. Also, the limited partner's name must not appear in the partnership's name.

master limited partnership (MLP) a business partnership that is owned and managed like a corporation but taxed like a partnership

A special type of limited partnership is referred to as a master limited partnership. A **master limited partnership (MLP)** is a business partnership that is owned and managed like a corporation but taxed like a partnership. This special ownership arrangement has at least two advantages when compared with the more traditional partnership and corporate forms of ownership. First, units of ownership in MLPs can be sold to investors to raise capital and are often traded on organized security exchanges. Because MLP units can be traded on an exchange, investors can sell their units of ownership at any time, hopefully for a profit. Second, profits from MLPs are reported as personal income. MLPs thus avoid the double taxation paid on corporate income. Two MLPs you may recognize are the world-famous Boston Celtics basketball team and Bloomberg, the publisher of financial news.

The Partnership Agreement

Articles of partnership are an agreement listing and explaining the terms of the partnership. Although both oral and written partnership agreements are legal and can be enforced in the courts, a written agreement has an obvious advantage: it is not subject to lapses of memory.

Figure 5.3 shows a typical partnership agreement. The partnership agreement should state who will make the final decisions, what each partner's duties will be, and the investment each partner will make. The partnership agreement should also state how much profit or loss each partner receives. Finally, the partnership agreement should state what happens if a partner wants to dissolve the partnership or dies. The breakup of a partnership can be as complicated and traumatic as a divorce, and it is never too early to consider what could happen in the future. Although the people involved in a partnership can draft their own agreement, most experts recommend consulting an attorney.

When entering into a partnership agreement, partners would be wise to let a neutral third party—a consultant, an accountant, a lawyer, or a mutual friend—assist with any disputes that might arise. With no intense personal stake in the dispute, a third party can look beyond personal opinion and emotions to seek the best solution for the partnership. Each partner should agree to abide by the third party's decisions.

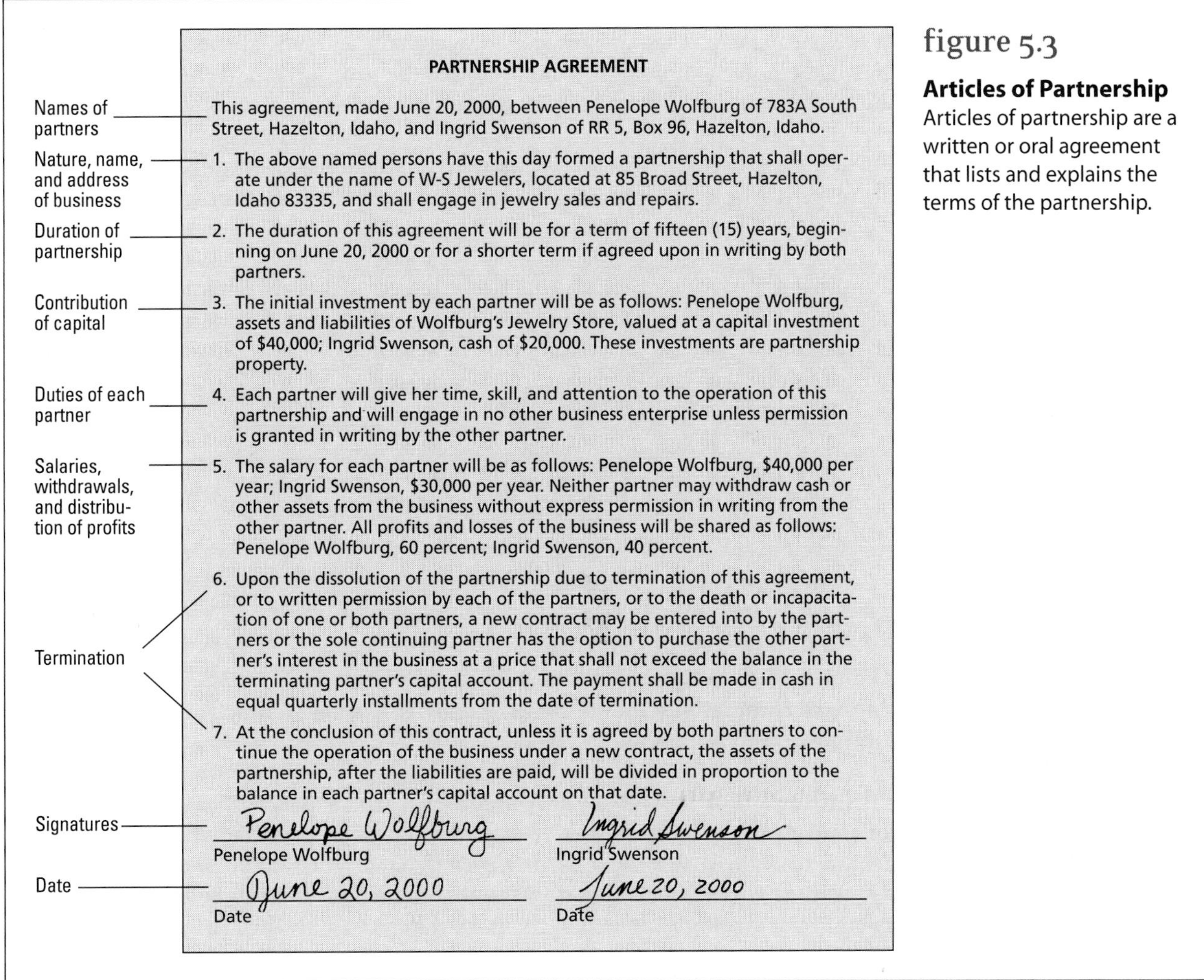

PARTNERSHIP AGREEMENT

This agreement, made June 20, 2000, between Penelope Wolfburg of 783A South Street, Hazelton, Idaho, and Ingrid Swenson of RR 5, Box 96, Hazelton, Idaho.

1. The above named persons have this day formed a partnership that shall operate under the name of W-S Jewelers, located at 85 Broad Street, Hazelton, Idaho 83335, and shall engage in jewelry sales and repairs.
2. The duration of this agreement will be for a term of fifteen (15) years, beginning on June 20, 2000 or for a shorter term if agreed upon in writing by both partners.
3. The initial investment by each partner will be as follows: Penelope Wolfburg, assets and liabilities of Wolfburg's Jewelry Store, valued at a capital investment of $40,000; Ingrid Swenson, cash of $20,000. These investments are partnership property.
4. Each partner will give her time, skill, and attention to the operation of this partnership and will engage in no other business enterprise unless permission is granted in writing by the other partner.
5. The salary for each partner will be as follows: Penelope Wolfburg, $40,000 per year; Ingrid Swenson, $30,000 per year. Neither partner may withdraw cash or other assets from the business without express permission in writing from the other partner. All profits and losses of the business will be shared as follows: Penelope Wolfburg, 60 percent; Ingrid Swenson, 40 percent.
6. Upon the dissolution of the partnership due to termination of this agreement, or to written permission by each of the partners, or to the death or incapacitation of one or both partners, a new contract may be entered into by the partners or the sole continuing partner has the option to purchase the other partner's interest in the business at a price that shall not exceed the balance in the terminating partner's capital account. The payment shall be made in cash in equal quarterly installments from the date of termination.
7. At the conclusion of this contract, unless it is agreed by both partners to continue the operation of the business under a new contract, the assets of the partnership, after the liabilities are paid, will be divided in proportion to the balance in each partner's capital account on that date.

Penelope Wolfburg — Penelope Wolfburg   Ingrid Swenson — Ingrid Swenson

June 20, 2000 — Date   June 20, 2000 — Date

figure 5.3

Articles of Partnership
Articles of partnership are a written or oral agreement that lists and explains the terms of the partnership.

Source: Arnold J. Goldman and William D. Sigismond, *Business Law,* 4th ed. Copyright © 1996, 2000 by Houghton Mifflin Company. Reprinted with permission.

Advantages of Partnerships

Partnerships have many advantages. The most important are described below.

LEARNING OBJECTIVE

3 Describe the advantages and disadvantages of partnerships.

Ease of Start-up

Like sole proprietorships, partnerships are relatively easy to form. The legal requirements are often limited to registering the name of the business and purchasing any necessary licenses or permits. It may not even be necessary to prepare written articles of partnership, although doing so is generally a good idea.

Availability of Capital and Credit

Because partners can pool their funds, a partnership usually has more capital available than a sole proprietorship does. This additional capital, coupled with the general partners' unlimited liability, can form the basis for a better credit rating. Banks and suppliers may be more willing to extend credit or grant larger loans to such a partnership than to a sole proprietor.

This does not mean that partnerships can borrow all the money they need. Many partnerships have found it hard to get long-term financing simply because lenders worry about the possibility of management disagreements and lack of continuity. But, in general, partnerships have greater assets and stand a better chance of obtaining the loans they need.

Retention of Profits As in a sole proprietorship, all profits belong to the owners of the partnership. The partners share directly in the financial rewards and therefore are highly motivated to do their best to make the firm succeed. As noted, the partnership agreement should state how much profit or loss each partner receives.

Personal Interest General partners are very concerned with the operation of the firm—perhaps even more so than sole proprietors. After all, they are responsible for the actions of all other general partners, as well as for their own.

Combined Business Skills and Knowledge Partners often have complementary skills. The weakness of one partner—in manufacturing, for example—may be offset by another partner's strength in that area. Moreover, the ability to discuss important decisions with another concerned individual often relieves some pressure and leads to more effective decision making.

Possible Tax Advantages Like sole proprietors, partners are taxed only on their share of the profits. They do not pay the special taxes (such as state and federal income taxes) imposed on corporations.

Disadvantages of Partnerships

Although partnerships have many advantages when compared with sole proprietorships and corporations, they also have some disadvantages, which anyone thinking of forming a partnership should consider.

Unlimited Liability As we have noted, each general partner has unlimited liability for all debts of the business. Each partner is legally and personally responsible for the debts and actions of any other partner, even if that partner did not incur those debts or do anything wrong. General partners thus run the risk of having to use their personal assets to pay creditors. Limited partners, however, risk only their original investment.

Lack of Continuity Partnerships are terminated if any one of the general partners dies, withdraws, or is declared legally incompetent. However, that partner's ownership share can be purchased by the remaining partners. For example, the partnership agreement may permit surviving partners to continue the business after buying a deceased partner's interest from his or her estate. But if the partnership loses an owner whose specific management or technical skills cannot be replaced, it is not likely to survive.

Mission impossible? Not really! L. Scott Perry and Junichiro Miyazu shake hands to celebrate an agreement between AT&T and Nippon Telegraph and Telephone to form a partnership to manage communications networks for multinational companies. Like many partnerships, this one represents a combination of business skills, knowledge, and management expertise.

Effects of Management Disagreements According to *Inc.* magazine, there are seven events that can destroy a partnership—see Table 5.1.[3] Notice that each of the seven events involves one partner doing something that disturbs the other partner(s). This human factor is especially important because business partners—with egos, ambitions, and money on the line—are especially susceptible to friction. If the division of responsibilities among several partners is to be successful and

table 5.1 Seven Trigger Points That Can Destroy a Partnership

1. A partner that is going through a divorce.
2. A partnership that is experiencing growth pains because of rapid growth.
3. A partner brings a spouse or a relative into the business.
4. A partner that wants to withdraw more money from the business.
5. A partner makes sexual advances toward another partner.
6. A partner experiences serious medical problems.
7. A partner begins doing business on the side with the partnership's customers.

Source: Reprinted with permission, *Inc.* magazine, February 2001. Copyright 1998 by Gruner + Jahr USA Publishing, 38 Commercial Wharf, Boston, MA 02110. *Inc.* is a registered trademark of Gruner + Jahr Printing and Publishing.

if partners are to work together as a team, they must have trust in each other. When partners begin to disagree about decisions, policies, or ethics, distrust may build and get worse as time passes—often to the point where it is impossible to operate the business successfully.

Frozen Investment It is easy to invest money in a partnership, but it is sometimes quite difficult to get it out. This is the case, for example, when remaining partners are unwilling to buy the share of the business that belongs to a partner who retires or wants to relocate to another city. To avoid such difficulties, the partnership agreement should include some procedure for buying out a partner.

In some cases, a partner must find someone outside the firm to buy his or her share. How easy or difficult it is to find an outsider depends on how successful the business is and how willing existing partners are to accept a new partner.

Beyond the Partnership

The main advantages of a partnership over a sole proprietorship are the added capital and management expertise of the partners. However, some of the basic disadvantages of the sole proprietorship also plague the general partnership. One disadvantage in particular—unlimited liability—can cause problems. A third form of business ownership, the corporation, overcomes this disadvantage.

Corporations

LEARNING OBJECTIVE 4
Summarize how a corporation is formed.

Perhaps the best definition of a corporation was given by Chief Justice John Marshall in a famous Supreme Court decision in 1819. A corporation, he said, "is an artificial being, invisible, intangible, and existing only in contemplation of the law." In other words, a **corporation** is an artificial person created by law, with most of the legal rights of a real person. These include the rights to start and operate a business, to buy or sell property, to borrow money, to sue or be sued, and to enter into binding contracts. Unlike a real person, however, a corporation exists only on paper.

corporation an artificial person created by law, with most of the legal rights of a real person, including the rights to start and operate a business, to buy or sell property, to borrow money, to sue or be sued, and to enter into binding contracts

There are 4.6 million corporations in the United States. They comprise only about 20 percent of all businesses, but they account for 88.8 percent of sales revenues. Table 5.2 on page 136 lists the ten largest U.S. industrial corporations, ranked according to sales.

Corporate Ownership

The shares of ownership of a corporation are called **stock.** The people who own a corporation's stock—and thus own part of the corporation—are called **stockholders,** or sometimes *shareholders.* Once a corporation has been formed, it may sell its stock to

stock the shares of ownership of a corporation

stockholder a person who owns a corporation's stock

table 5.2 The Ten Largest U.S. Industrial Corporations, Ranked by Sales

Rank 1999	Rank 1998	Company	Sales ($ millions)	Profits ($ millions)	Assets ($ millions)
1	1	GENERAL MOTORS Detroit	189,058.0	6,002.0	273,921.0
2	3	WAL-MART STORES Bentonville, Ark.	166,809.0	5,377.0	70,245.0
3	4	EXXON MOBIL Irving, Texas	163,881.0	7,910.0	144,521.0
4	2	FORD MOTOR Dearborn, Mich.	162,558.0	7,237.0	276,229.0
5	5	GENERAL ELECTRIC Fairfield, Conn.	111,630.0	10,717.0	405,200.0
6	6	INTL. BUSINESS MACHINES Armonk, N.Y.	87,548.0	7,712.0	87,495.0
7	7	CITIGROUP New York	82,005.0	9,867.0	716,900.0
8	10	AT&T New York	62,391.0	3,428.0	169,406.0
9	8	PHILIP MORRIS New York	61,751.0	7,675.0	61,381.0
10	9	BOEING Seattle	57,993.0	2,309.0	36,147.0

Source: *Fortune* 500, © 2000 Time Inc., April 17, 2000, p. F-1.

individuals. It may also issue stock as a reward to key employees in return for certain services, or as a return to investors (in place of cash payments).

close corporation a corporation whose stock is owned by relatively few people and is not sold to the general public

A **close corporation** is a corporation whose stock is owned by relatively few people and is not sold to the general public. As an example, Mr. and Mrs. DeWitt Wallace owned virtually all the stock of Reader's Digest Association, making it one of the largest corporations of this kind. A person who wishes to sell the stock of a close corporation generally arranges to sell it *privately,* to another stockholder or a close acquaintance.

open corporation a corporation whose stock is bought and sold on security exchanges and can be purchased by any individual

Although founded in 1922 as a close corporation, the Reader's Digest Association became an open corporation when it sold stock to investors for the first time in 1990. An **open corporation** is one whose stock is bought and sold on security exchanges and can be purchased by any individual. General Motors Corporation, the largest industrial company in the United States, is an example. Most large firms are open corporations, and their stockholders may number in the hundreds of thousands, or even millions. For example, General Motors has about 600,000, Walt Disney has over 650,000, and AT&T has just over 3 million.

Forming a Corporation

incorporation the process of forming a corporation

The process of forming a corporation is called **incorporation.** Although you may think that incorporating a business guarantees success, it does not. There is no special magic about placing the word *Incorporated* or the abbreviation *Inc.* after the name of a business. Unfortunately, like sole proprietorships or partnerships, incorporated businesses can go broke. The decision to incorporate a business should therefore be made only after carefully considering whether the corporate form of ownership suits your needs better than the sole proprietorship or partnership forms.

If you decide the corporate form is the best form of organization for you, most experts recommend that you begin the incorporation process by consulting a lawyer to be sure all legal requirements are met. While it may be possible to incorporate a business without legal help, it is well to keep in mind the old saying, "A man who acts as his own attorney has a fool for a client." Unfortunately, this can be true for business owners when they start a business. Table 5.3 lists some aspects of starting and running a business that may require legal help.

Where to Incorporate

A business is allowed to incorporate in any state it chooses. Most small and medium-sized businesses are incorporated in the state where they do the most business. The founders of larger corporations, or of those that will do business nationwide, often compare the benefits that various states provide to corporations.

table 5.3 Aspects of Business That May Require Legal Help

1. Choosing either the sole proprietorship, partnership, or corporate form of ownership
2. Constructing a partnership agreement
3. Establishing a corporation
4. Registering a corporation's stock
5. Obtaining a trademark, patent, or copyright
6. Filing for licenses or permits at the local, state, and federal levels
7. Purchasing an existing business or real estate
8. Leasing real estate or equipment
9. Hiring employees and independent contractors
10. Handling labor disputes and customer lawsuits
11. Extending credit and collecting debts
12. Handling bankruptcy and reorganization

Source: Adapted from Seth Godin, ed., *1997 Business Almanac*. Copyright © 1996 by Houghton Mifflin Company.

Some states are more hospitable than others, and some offer fewer restrictions, lower taxes, and other benefits to attract new firms. Delaware offers the most lenient tax structure, and a huge number of firms (more than 75,000) have incorporated there, even though their corporate headquarters may be located in another state.

The growth of Internet-based businesses and e-commerce has complicated the question about business location even further. Online sales are supposed to be charged state and local taxes just like sales from catalog retailers. Any business with a physical location (an office, store, warehouse, etc.) in a state where a purchase is made must charge that state's sales tax on the purchase. If there is no physical presence and no sales tax is collected, the customer is supposed to pay a "use tax" to his or her state, which is usually the same percentage as the sales tax. So the customer cannot avoid paying a local tax. Currently, there are more than 36,000 state and local taxing jurisdictions in the United States, and about 7,000 of them impose sales and use taxes. To help simplify the complexity of what taxes to charge and remit to local governments, several states have joined together to form the Streamlined Sales Tax Project. The goal is to overhaul the existing sales tax system and create a simplified system fair to all participants. Until a national policy is agreed to, online buyers and sellers will have to cope with the complex task of tax compliance.[4]

An incorporated business is called a **domestic corporation** in the state in which it is incorporated. In all other states where it does business, it is called a **foreign corporation.** Sears, Roebuck, for example, is incorporated in New York, where it is a domestic corporation. In the remaining forty-nine states, Sears is a foreign corporation. A corporation chartered by a foreign government and conducting business in the United States is an **alien corporation.** Volkswagen, Sony Corporation, and the Royal Dutch/Shell Group are examples of alien corporations.

domestic corporation a corporation in the state in which it is incorporated

foreign corporation a corporation in any state in which it does business except the one in which it is incorporated

alien corporation a corporation chartered by a foreign government and conducting business in the United States

The Corporate Charter Once a "home state" has been chosen, the incorporator(s) submit *articles of incorporation* to the secretary of state. If the articles of incorporation are approved, they become the firm's corporate charter. A **corporate charter** is a contract between the corporation and the state, in which the state recognizes the formation of the artificial person that is the corporation. Usually the charter (and thus the articles of incorporation) includes the following information:

corporate charter a contract between the corporation and the state, in which the state recognizes the formation of the artificial person that is the corporation

- Firm's name and address
- Incorporators' names and addresses
- Purpose of the corporation
- Maximum amount of stock and types of stock to be issued
- Rights and privileges of stockholders
- Length of time the corporation is to exist

Each of these key details is the result of decisions the incorporators must make as they organize the firm—before they submit the articles of incorporation. Let's look at one such area: stockholders' rights.

common stock stock owned by individuals or firms who may vote on corporate matters, but whose claims on profit and assets are subordinate to the claims of others

preferred stock stock owned by individuals or firms who usually do not have voting rights, but whose claims on dividends are paid before those of common-stock owners

dividend a distribution of earnings to the stockholders of a corporation

proxy a legal form listing issues to be decided at a stockholders' meeting and enabling stockholders to transfer their voting rights to some other individual or individuals

board of directors the top governing body of a corporation, the members of which are elected by the stockholders

corporate officers the chairman of the board, president, executive vice presidents, corporate secretary and treasurer, or any other top executive appointed by the board of directors

Stockholders' Rights There are two basic types of stock. Owners of **common stock** may vote on corporate matters. Generally, an owner of common stock has one vote for each share owned. The owners of **preferred stock** usually have no voting rights, but their claims on dividends are paid before those of common-stock owners.

Perhaps the most important right of owners of both common and preferred stock is to share in the profit earned by the corporation through the payment of dividends. A **dividend** is a distribution of earnings to the stockholders of a corporation. Other rights include examining corporate records, voting on changes to the corporate charter, and attending the corporation's annual stockholders' meeting, where they may exercise their right to vote.

Because common stockholders usually live all over the nation, very few may actually attend a corporation's annual meeting. Instead, they vote by proxy. A **proxy** is a legal form listing issues to be decided and enabling stockholders to transfer their voting rights to some other individual or individuals. The stockholder can register a vote and transfer voting rights simply by signing and returning the form.

Organizational Meeting As the last step in forming a corporation, the incorporators and original stockholders meet to elect their first board of directors. (Later, directors will be elected or re-elected at the corporation's annual meetings.) The board members are directly responsible to the stockholders for the way they operate the firm.

Corporate Structure

The organizational structure of most corporations is more complicated than that of a sole proprietorship or partnership. In a corporation, both the board of directors and the corporate officers are involved in management.

Board of Directors As an artificial person, a corporation can act only through its directors, who represent the corporation's owners. The **board of directors** is the top governing body of a corporation, and, as we noted, directors are elected by the stockholders. Board members can be chosen from within the corporation or from outside it.

Directors who are elected from within the corporation are usually its top managers—the president and executive vice presidents, for example. Those elected from outside the corporation are generally experienced managers or entrepreneurs with proven leadership ability and/or specific talents the organization seems to need. In smaller corporations, majority stockholders usually serve as board members.

The major responsibilities of the board of directors are to set company goals and develop general plans (or strategies) for meeting those goals. They are also responsible for the firm's overall operation.

Corporate Officers **Corporate officers** are appointed by the board of directors. The chairman of the board, president, executive vice presidents, corporate secretary, and treasurer are all corporate officers. They help the board make plans, carry out strategies established by the board, hire employees, and manage day-to-day business activities.

spotLight

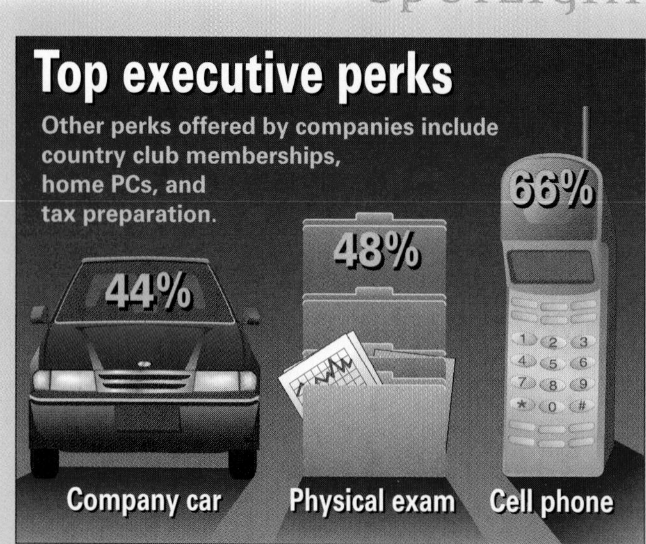

Source: Copyright 2000, USA TODAY. Reprinted with permission.

Periodically (usually each month), they report to the board of directors. And, at the annual meeting, the directors report to the stockholders. In theory, then, the stockholders are able to control the activities of the entire corporation through its directors (see Figure 5.4).

Above-average growth made this building possible. To control a large fast-food chain like Taco Bell it takes more than a building. It takes talented managers and employees. The first restaurant was opened in 1962 by Glen Bell. Taco Bell now has 6,800 restaurants in 17 different countries.

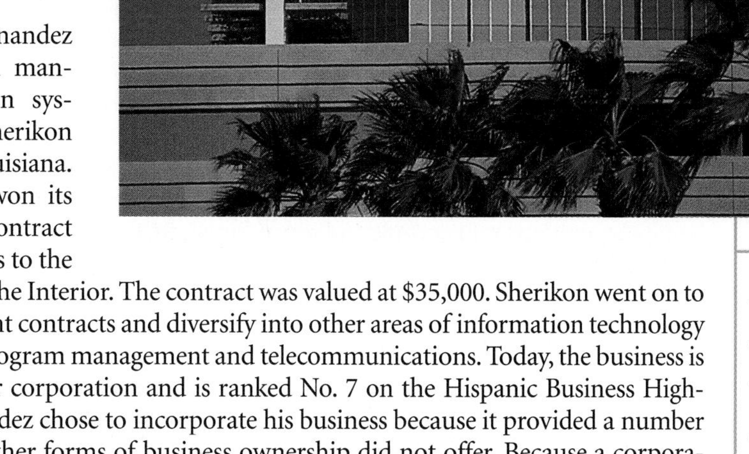

Advantages of Corporations

In 1884, Ed Fernandez began a one-person management information systems firm named Sherikon that was based in Louisiana. In 1984, Sherikon won its first government contract for computer services to the U.S. Department of the Interior. The contract was valued at $35,000. Sherikon went on to win more government contracts and diversify into other areas of information technology including medical program management and telecommunications. Today, the business is a multimillion dollar corporation and is ranked No. 7 on the Hispanic Business High-Tech 50.[5] Mr. Fernandez chose to incorporate his business because it provided a number of advantages that other forms of business ownership did not offer. Because a corporation is an artificial person or legal entity, it has some definite advantages when compared with other forms of ownership.

limited liability a feature of corporate ownership that limits each owner's financial liability to the amount of money she or he has paid for the corporation's stock

Limited Liability One of the most attractive features of corporate ownership is **limited liability.** With few exceptions, each owner's financial liability is limited to the amount of money she or he has paid for the corporation's stock. This feature arises from the fact that the corporation is itself a legal being, separate from its owners. If a corporation fails, creditors have a claim only on the corporation's assets, not on the owners' personal assets.

LEARNING OBJECTIVE

5 Describe the advantages and disadvantages of a corporation.

Ease of Raising Capital The corporation is by far the most effective form of business ownership for raising capital. Like sole proprietorships and partnerships, corporations can borrow from lending institutions. However, they can also raise additional sums of money by selling stock. Individuals are more willing to invest in corporations than in other forms of business because their liability is limited and they can sell their stock easily—hopefully for a profit. Information on the process a corporation uses to sell stock and why investors purchase that stock is provided in Chapters 20 and 21.

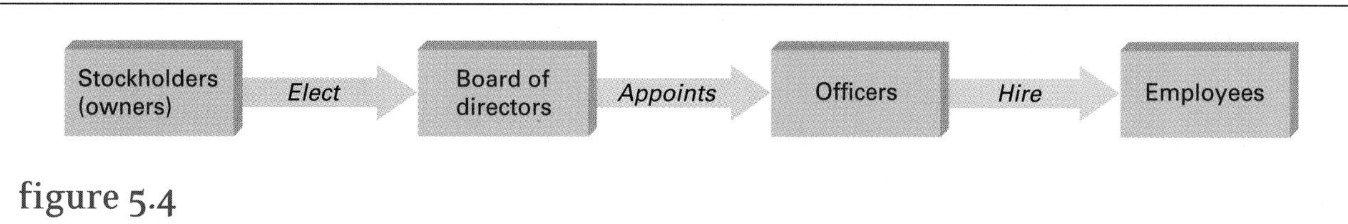

figure 5.4

Hierarchy of Corporate Structure

Stockholders exercise a great deal of influence through their right to elect the board of directors.

Using the Internet

Where can you find out more about starting and managing a business? The Small Business Administration web site explores a variety of business topics that are beneficial to new businesses as well as those currently in operation. Answers to typical questions such as which legal form is best and how to get financing are provided as well as a help desk where you can submit written questions about any specific concerns. Your gateway to the SBA is at **http://www.sbaonline.sba.gov/.**

Ease of Transfer of Ownership A telephone call to a stockbroker is all that is required to put stock up for sale. Willing buyers are available for most stocks, at the market price. Ownership is transferred when the sale is made, and practically no restrictions apply to the sale and purchase of stock issued by an open corporation.

Perpetual Life Since it is essentially a legal "person," a corporation exists independently of its owners and survives them. Unless its charter specifies otherwise, a corporation has perpetual life. The withdrawal, death, or incompetence of a key executive or owner does not cause the corporation to be terminated. Sears, Roebuck, which started as a partnership in 1886 and incorporated in 1906, is one of the nation's largest retailing corporations, even though its original owners, Richard Sears and Alvah Roebuck, have been dead for decades.

Specialized Management Typically, corporations are able to recruit more skilled, knowledgeable, and talented managers than proprietorships and partnerships. This is because they pay bigger salaries and are large enough to offer considerable opportunity for advancement. Within the corporate structure, administration, human resources, finance, marketing, and operations are placed in the charge of experts in these fields. To see how some corporations value people and recruit intellectual capital, read Adapting to Change.

Disadvantages of Corporations

Like its advantages, many of a corporation's disadvantages stem from its legal definition as an artificial person or legal entity. The most serious disadvantages are described below. (See Table 5.4 for a comparison of some of the advantages and disadvantages of a sole proprietorship, partnership, and corporation.)

Difficulty and Expense of Formation Forming a corporation can be a relatively complex and costly process. The use of an attorney is usually necessary to complete the legal forms and apply to the state for a charter. Charter fees, attorney's fees, registration costs associated with selling stock, and other organizational costs can amount to thousands of dollars for even a medium-sized corporation. The costs of incorporating, in terms of both time and money, discourage many owners of smaller businesses from forming corporations.

table 5.4 Some Advantages and Disadvantages of a Sole Proprietorship, Partnership, and Corporation

	Sole Proprietorship	General Partnership	Regular Corporation
Protecting against liability for debts	Difficult	Difficult	Easy
Raising money	Difficult	Difficult	Easy
Ownership transfer	Difficult	Difficult	Easy
Preserving continuity	Difficult	Difficult	Easy
Government regulations	Few	Few	Many
Formation	Easy	Easy	Difficult
Income taxation	Once	Once	Twice

Source: Nicholas Siropolis, *Small Business Management,* Sixth Edition. Copyright © 1996 by Houghton Mifflin Company. Reprinted with permission.

Adapting to change

Intellectual Capital: A New Kind of Asset

TODAY, MANY MANAGEMENT EXPERTS agree that corporate success is not based on *just* selling a product or providing a service; it requires the ideas of people to invent new products and services, to organize the manufacturing processes, and to find new markets in a very competitive environment. This idea-generating brainpower–knowledge, skills, innovation, and creativity–is so important that it is often referred to as "intellectual" capital. Just like machinery and buildings, intellectual capital is a resource that often fuels a growing enterprise. In fact, today's new economy considers people power not simply as just a tool; it's a main resource that keeps the organization from experiencing stagnation.

People Are Our Most Important Asset

Today, organizations want open-minded members to fully participate in brainstorming sessions that sizzle with excitement, create synergy and trust, and generate innovations and solutions. Although managers for large corporations used to move slowly and gradually initiate changes, today's business managers must make decisions at lightning speed because of e-business and e-mail. Also, the amount of new business start-ups makes it essential for managers to constantly evaluate their competition and customer base to survive. All involved must instantly assess situations and plan using entrepreneurial skills traditionally associated with small business owners. The ability to envision the future and face the challenge of constant change are forces that empower the entire organization.

Recruiting Intellectual Capital

Organizations, especially in the high-tech sector, are pulling out all stops to obtain intellectual capital. In place of traditional signing bonuses or parking spaces, corporate recruiters are using lavish items that include trips to Mexico and even Porsche automobiles. And companies are giving up to $15,000 to existing employees for successful referrals that lead to hiring new employees with the "right stuff." Retaining brainpower is as high a priority as acquiring it. One popular reward used by many corporations is stock options. Employees, who once worked solely for wages, are now placing more emphasis on ownership and want to not only reap the benefits of being part of a successful company but also the financial rewards that result when a company's stock values increase in value.

Government Regulation A corporation must meet various government standards before it can sell its stock to the public. Then it must file many reports on its business operations and finances with local, state, and federal governments. In addition, the corporation must make periodic reports to its stockholders about various aspects of the business. Also, its activities are restricted by law to those spelled out in its charter.

Double Taxation Unlike sole proprietorships and partnerships, corporations must pay a tax on their profits. In addition, stockholders must pay a personal income tax on profits received as dividends. Corporate profits are thus taxed twice—once as corporate income and a second time as the personal income of stockholders.

Lack of Secrecy Because open corporations are required to submit detailed reports to government agencies and to stockholders, they cannot keep their operations confidential. Competitors can study these corporate reports and then use the information to compete more effectively. In effect, every public corporation has to share some of its secrets with its competitors.

Other Types of Business Ownership

LEARNING OBJECTIVE

6 Discuss the purpose of an S-corporation, limited liability company, government-owned corporation, and other special forms of business ownership.

Although most businesses are organized for the purpose of earning profits, some are organized for special purposes. Among them are S-corporations, limited liability companies, government-owned corporations, not-for-profit corporations, cooperatives, joint ventures, and syndicates.

S-Corporations

S-corporation a corporation that is taxed as though it were a partnership

If a corporation meets certain requirements, its directors may apply to the Internal Revenue Service for status as an S-corporation. An **S-corporation** is a corporation that is taxed as though it were a partnership. In other words, the corporation's income is taxed only as the personal income of stockholders.

Becoming an S-corporation can be an effective way to avoid double taxation while retaining the corporation's legal benefit of limited liability. Moreover, stockholders can personally claim their share of losses incurred by the corporation to offset their own personal income.

To qualify for the special status of an S-corporation, a firm must meet the following criteria:

1. No more than seventy-five stockholders are allowed.
2. Stockholders must be individuals, estates, or certain trusts.
3. There can be only one class of outstanding stock.
4. The firm must be a domestic corporation.
5. There can be no nonresident alien stockholders.
6. All stockholders must agree to the decision to form an S-corporation.

Limited Liability Companies

limited liability company (LLC) a form of business ownership that provides limited liability protection and is taxed like a partnership

In addition to the traditional forms of business ownership already covered, a new and promising form of ownership called a limited liability company has been approved in all 50 states—although each state's laws may differ. A **limited liability company (LLC)** is a form of business ownership that combines the benefits of a corporation and a partnership while avoiding some of the restrictions and disadvantages of those forms of ownership. Chief advantages of an LLC are

1. It is taxed like a partnership and thus avoids the double taxation imposed on most corporations.
2. Like a corporation, it provides limited liability protection. An LLC thus extends the concept of personal-asset protection to small business owners.

Although many experts believe the limited liability company is nothing more than a variation of the S-corporation, there is a difference. An LLC is not restricted to seventy-five stockholders—a common drawback of the S-corporation. LLCs are also less restricted than S-corporations in terms of who can become an owner and who can make management decisions. Although the owners of an LLC must file articles of organization with their state's secretary of state, they are not hampered by lots of IRS rules and government regulations that apply to corporations. As a result, experts are predicting that LLCs may become one of the most popular forms of business ownership available.

Government-Owned Corporations

government-owned corporation a corporation owned and operated by a local, state, or federal government

quasi-government corporation a business owned partly by the government and partly by private citizens or firms

A **government-owned corporation** is owned and operated by a local, state, or federal government. The Tennessee Valley Authority (TVA), the National Aeronautics and Space Administration (NASA), and the Federal Deposit Insurance Corporation (FDIC) are all government-owned corporations. They are operated by the U.S. government. Most municipal bus lines and subways are run by city-owned corporations.

A government corporation usually provides a service the business sector is reluctant or unable to offer. Profit is secondary in such corporations. In fact, they may continually operate at a loss, particularly if they are involved in public transportation. Their main objective is to ensure that a particular service is available.

It's a good feeling to help others help themselves! Debbie Vincent and a team of all-women volunteers are taking part in Habitat for Humanity's First Ladies Build Project. Habitat for Humanity—a not-for-profit corporation—was formed to provide homes for qualified, low-income people who could not afford housing without some extra help.

In certain cases, a government will invite citizens or firms to invest in a government corporation as part owners. A business owned partly by the government and partly by private citizens or firms is called a **quasi-government corporation.** COMSAT (Communications Satellite Corporation), the Federal National Mortgage Association (Fannie Mae), and the Student Loan Marketing Association (Sallie Mae) are examples of quasi-government corporations.

Not-for-Profit Corporations

A **not-for-profit corporation** is a corporation organized to provide a social, educational, religious, or other service, rather than to earn a profit. Various charities, museums, private schools, and colleges are organized in this way, primarily to ensure limited liability. Habitat for Humanity is a not-for-profit corporation and was formed to provide homes for qualified, low-income people who could not afford housing. Even though this corporation may receive more money than it spends, any surplus funds are "reinvested" in building activities to provide low-cost housing. It is a not-for-profit corporation because its primary purpose is to provide a social service. Other examples include the Public Broadcasting System (PBS), the Girl Scouts, and the Red Cross.

not-for-profit corporation a corporation organized to provide a social, educational, religious, or other service, rather than to earn a profit

Occasionally, some not-for-profit organizations are inspired with entrepreneurial zeal. The Children's Television Workshop, for example, netted $7.7 million a few years ago by licensing Sesame Street products. In the same year, the New York Museum of Modern Art sold air rights in Manhattan for $17 million to allow the construction of a private forty-four-story residential tower. Tax-free income from the sale helped finance a new wing, doubling the size of the museum.

Cooperatives

A **cooperative** is an association of individuals or firms whose purpose is to perform some business function for its members. The cooperative can perform its function more effectively than any member could by acting alone; thus, members benefit from its activities. For example, cooperatives purchase goods in bulk and distribute them to members; thus the unit cost is lower than it would be if each member bought the goods in a much smaller quantity.

cooperative an association of individuals or firms whose purpose is to perform some business function for its members

Although cooperatives are found in all segments of our economy, they are most prevalent in agriculture. Farmers use cooperatives to purchase supplies, to buy services such as trucking and storage, and to process and market their products. Ocean Spray Cranberries, Inc., for example, is a cooperative of some seven hundred cranberry growers and more than one hundred citrus growers spread throughout the country. Other examples of cooperatives include Missouri-based Farmland Industries and Florida-based Sunkist Growers.

Joint Ventures

joint venture an agreement between two or more groups to form a business entity in order to achieve a specific goal or to operate for a specific period of time

A **joint venture** is an agreement between two or more groups to form a business entity in order to achive a specific goal or to operate for a specific period of time. Both the scope of the joint venture and the liabilities of the people or businesses involved are usually limited. Once the goal is reached or the period of time elapses, the joint venture is dissolved.

Corporations, as well as individuals, may enter into joint ventures. A number of joint ventures were formed by major oil producers in the 1970s and 1980s to share the extremely high cost of exploring for offshore petroleum deposits. More recently, Walt Disney formed a joint venture with Pixar Animation Studios to create movies over the next ten years. Finally, Volkswagen has formed a joint venture with Chinese automaker Shanghai Automotive Industry Corporation to manufacture and market a new small automobile. With its $15,000 price tag and small one liter engine, the car is specifically designed for the Chinese market.[6]

Syndicates

syndicate a temporary association of individuals or firms organized to perform a specific task that requires a large amount of capital

A **syndicate** is a temporary association of individuals or firms organized to perform a specific task that requires a large amount of capital. The syndicate is formed because no one person or firm is willing to put up the entire amount required for the undertaking. Like a joint venture, a syndicate is dissolved as soon as its purpose has been accomplished.

Syndicates are most commonly used to underwrite large insurance policies, loans, and investments. To share the risk of default, banks have formed syndicates to provide loans to developing countries. Stock brokrage firms usually join together in the same way to market a new issue of stock. For example, Morgan Stanley and other Wall Street firms formed a syndicate to sell shares of stock in United Parcel Service (UPS). The initial public offering was the largest in U.S. history—too large for Morgan Stanley to handle without help from other Wall Street firms. (An *initial public offering* is the term used to describe the first time a corporation sells stock to the general public.)

Corporate Growth

LEARNING OBJECTIVE

7 Explain how growth from within and growth through mergers can enable a business to expand.

Growth seems to be a basic characteristic of business, at least for firms that can obtain the capital needed to finance growth. One reason for seeking growth has to do with profit: a larger firm generally has greater sales revenue and thus greater profit. Another reason is that in a growing economy, a business that does not grow is actually shrinking relative to the economy. A third reason is that business growth is a means by which some executives boost their power, prestige, and reputation.

Should all firms grow? Certainly not until they are ready. Growth poses new problems and requires additional resources that must first be available and must then be used effectively. The main ingredient in growth is capital—and, as we have noted, capital is most readily available to corporations. Thus, to a great extent, business growth means corporate growth.

Growth from Within

Most corporations grow by expanding their present operations. Some introduce and sell new but related products—for example, Palm Computing hand-held electronic devices, Nintendo's electronic games, or Motorola's Startac cellular phone. Others expand the sale of present products to new geographic markets or to new groups of consumers in geographic markets already served. Currently, Wal-Mart serves customers in forty-nine states, Argentina, Brazil, Canada, China, Germany, and Mexico and has long-range plans for expanding into additional international markets.

Sometimes a corporation wants to give something back. Although Oracle Corporation has experienced tremendous growth, it is more than a company that earns profits. As evidence of its commitment to help communities, Oracle donated $100 million to furnish schools with computers. In this picture, sixteen-year-old Brandon Biggers demonstrates a new, donated computer for Larry Ellison, chairman and CEO of Oracle and Colin Powell, the U.S. Secretary of State.

Growth from within, especially when carefully planned and controlled, can have relatively little adverse effect on a firm. For the most part, the firm continues to do what it has been doing, but on a larger scale. Because this type of growth is anticipated, it can be gradual and the firm can usually adapt to it easily. For instance, Larry Ellison, Chairman and CEO of Oracle Corporation of Redwood City, California, built the firm's annual revenues up from a mere $282 million in 1988 to an estimated $9.7 billion today—an incredible increase of more than 3,350 percent. Much of that growth has taken place since 1994 as Oracle capitalized on its global leadership in Internet software in addition to its base in information management software. Measuring growth in terms of employees and markets, Oracle now has more than 23,000 employees in 144 countries in addition to the 21,000 working in the United States.[7]

Growth Through Mergers and Acquisitions

Another way a firm can grow is by purchasing another company. The purchase of one corporation by another is called a **merger.** An *acquisition* is essentially the same thing as a merger, but the term is usually used in reference to a large corporation's purchases of other corporations. Although most mergers and acquisitions are friendly, hostile takeovers also occur. A **hostile takeover** is a situation in which the management and board of directors of the firm targeted for acquisition disapprove of the merger, usually because their company will become a subsidiary of the purchasing firm and they will have to give up control.

When a merger or acquisition becomes hostile, a corporate raider—another company or a wealthy investor—may make a tender offer or start a proxy fight to gain control of the target company. A **tender offer** is an offer to purchase the stock of a firm targeted for acquisition at a price just high enough to tempt stockholders to sell their shares. Corporate raiders may also initiate a proxy fight. A **proxy fight** is a technique used to gather enough stockholder votes to control the targeted company.

If the corporate raider is successful and takes over the targeted company, existing management is usually replaced. Faced with this probability, existing management may try the following techniques (sometimes referred to as "poison pills," "shark repellents," or "porcupine provisions") to maintain control of the firm and avoid the hostile takeover:

1. Issue a new class of preferred stock that gives stockholders the right to redeem their shares at a premium *after* the corporate raider assumes control of the company.

merger the purchase of one corporation by another

hostile takeover a situation in which the management and board of directors of the firm targeted for acquisition disapprove of the merger

tender offer an offer to purchase the stock of a firm targeted for acquisition at a price just high enough to tempt stockholders to sell their shares

proxy fight a technique used to gather enough stockholder votes to control the targeted company

2. Allow existing stockholders to purchase new stock at a discounted price well below the market value of existing stock. This increases the number of outstanding shares and makes a hostile takeover more expensive for the corporate raider.
3. Give "golden parachute" contracts to top executives, thus ensuring that the corporate raider will find it very expensive to get rid of top management.
4. Adopt a supermajority provision, which requires at least a two-thirds or three-fourths majority of votes cast by stockholders to ratify a takeover by an outsider.
5. Create staggered terms for the corporation's board members. This makes it more difficult for the corporate raider to install a new board sympathetic to the takeover attempt.
6. Use leveraged recapitalization to make the company less attractive. *Leveraged recapitalization* means that the corporation obtains a large amount of debt capital and then makes large cash distributions to existing stockholders.
7. Find a "white knight"—a friendly corporation willing to take over the targeted company. Generally, the white knight agrees to keep existing management and allow the acquired firm to continue operating as an independent unit.

Whether mergers are friendly or hostile, they are generally classified as *horizontal, vertical,* or *conglomerate* (see Figure 5.5).

Horizontal Mergers A *horizontal merger* is a merger between firms that make and sell similar products or services in similar markets. The merger between Exxon and Mobil is an example of a horizontal merger because both firms are in the petroleum industry. This type of merger tends to reduce the number of firms in an industry—and thus may reduce competition. For this reason, each merger may be reviewed carefully by federal agencies before it is permitted.

Firms may use horizontal mergers to accomplish goals other than growth. For example, the major goal of many of the mergers in the Internet service provider industry that occurred in the late 1990s and first part of the twenty-first century was to acquire new customers. In many cases, it was actually less costly to buy another Internet service provider (and its existing subscribers) than obtain new users by advertising, free promotional items, and more traditional methods of selling.

figure 5.5

Three Types of Growth by Merger

Today mergers are classified as horizontal (firms in similar markets), vertical (firms at different but related levels) or conglomerate (firms in completely unrelated industries).

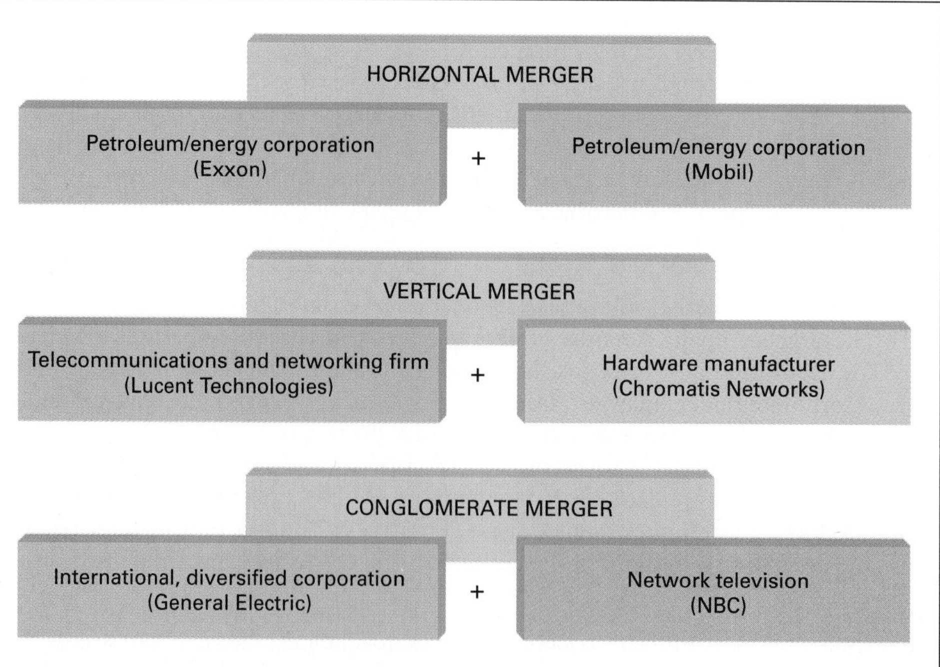

Vertical Mergers A *vertical merger* is a merger between firms that operate at different but related levels in the production and marketing of a product. Generally, one of the merging firms is either a supplier or a customer of the other. A vertical merger occurred when Lucent Technologies agreed to purchase Chromatis Networks. At the time, Lucent needed optical networking equipment to compete with Cisco and other networking firms. Rather than buy the equipment it needed, Lucent simply bought the company—Chromatis Networks—that produced the state-of-the-art equipment it needed to remain competitive in the ever-changing computer networking industry.

Conglomerate Mergers A *conglomerate merger* takes place between firms in completely unrelated industries. One of the largest conglomerate mergers in recent history occurred when General Electric (a diversified international firm) purchased NBC (network television). The General Electric/NBC merger was a friendly merger because it enlarged the base from which General Electric receives its sales revenue. It also allowed NBC to have the financial backing it needed to compete against ABC, CBS, Fox, and cable television.

Current Merger Trends

Economists, financial analysts, corporate managers, and stockholders still hotly debate whether takeovers are good for the economy—or for individual companies—in the long run. But one thing is clear: there are two sides to the takeover question. Takeover advocates argue that in companies that have been taken over, the purchasers have been able to make the company more profitable and productive by installing a new top management team and by forcing the company to concentrate on one main business. Takeover advocates also point out that proceeds from the sale of subsidiaries and divisions not aligned with the parent company's main business have been used either to pay off debt or to enhance the company.

Takeover opponents argue that takeovers do nothing to enhance corporate profitability or productivity. These critics argue that threats of takeovers have forced managers to devote valuable time to defending their companies from takeover, thus robbing time from new product development and other vital business activities. This, they believe, is why U.S. companies are less competitive with companies in such countries as Japan, Germany, and South Korea, where takeovers rarely occur. Finally, the opposition argues that the only people who benefit from takeovers are investment bankers, brokerage firms, and takeover "artists," who receive financial rewards by manipulating U.S. corporations, rather than by producing tangible products or services.

Most experts now predict that mergers and acquisitions during the first part of the twenty-first century will be the result of cash-rich companies looking to acquire businesses that will enhance their position in the marketplace. Analysts also anticipate more mergers that involve companies or investors from other countries. Regardless of the companies involved or where the companies are from, future mergers and acquisitions will be driven by solid business logic, the

Lucent Technologies and Octel Communications: a merger that makes dollars and sense. When New Jersey-based Lucent Technologies acquired Octel Communications, more than 1,000 employees celebrated by forming the company's logo, the "Innovation Ring." The acquisition gives Lucent a major entrance into Silicon Valley and the West Coast through Octel's messaging products.

desire to compete in the international marketplace, and the explosion of information technology. For example, in the race to gain technological expertise in the highly specialized optical networking field, the Microelectronics Group of Lucent Technologies acquired Herrmann Technology, Inc., a privately held company based in Dallas, Texas, for approximately $450 million of Lucent stock. This type of acquisition is a common strategy used by larger firms like Lucent to fill technology or manufacturing capacity gaps in their own operations. On the reverse side of this strategic coin, many small businesses that can be easily integrated into a large firm like Lucent, are more than happy to become an operational division and thereby grow at a rate which would not be likely to occur if they remained smaller independent businesses. In exchange, their owners generally receive some cash, but are also compensated with shares of stock in the larger corporation.[8] For more information about one merger driven by solid business logic and the explosion of information technology, read Talking Technology.

Experts also predict that less borrowed money (sometimes referred to as debt capital) will be used to pay for mergers and acquisitions. When considering possible merger deals, bankers and lenders today seem far more skeptical than they were in the

Talking Technology

The AOL/Time Warner Merger

AMERICA ONLINE, THE INTERNET service provider for over 21 million homes, is known for buying other companies. In the past six years, it has acquired twenty-two other businesses, including CompuServe, Netscape, ICQ, MovieFone, and MapQuest. On January 10, 2000, it announced plans to purchase giant Time Warner. On January 11, 2001, the AOL/Time Warner merger was approved by the federal government. To date, this mega-deal was the largest merger ever approved by the government.

Why the Merger Makes Sense

For America Online this merger makes complete sense. The combination of AOL and Time Warner created a corporation that is worth an estimated $250 billion with annual sales revenues of $36 billion. It also employs over 80,000 people. Although AOL once focused on giving personal computer users access to the Internet through its purchases of other businesses, it now offers products and services using other types of equipment including television and telephones. Today, AOL sells long-distance telephone service, publishes digital city guides, sells movie tickets, and operates Internet music channels. It has also invested in online travel services, online education, PC maker Gateway, and satellite TV supplier DirecTV.

For Time Warner, the merger also makes sense. Although Time Warner is involved in more traditional media such as publishing, news, and television networks, and owns the second largest cable television company with million of subscribers, it has not been able to acquire the cutting-edge technology needed to compete with more innovative competitors. According to management experts, its bureaucratic management lacks the momentum necessary to keep up with constant change. On the other hand, AOL is famous for its creative management and believes this merger is just the solution for Time Warner's stagnation. Simply put, combining the resources of both companies will result in drastically different methods of packaging, distributing, and marketing information and entertainment and create one very aggressive company ready to take on all competitors.

The Government's Approval Process

When large mergers take place, the U.S. Senate holds hearings to examine evidence prepared by the U.S. Justice Department's antitrust division and the Federal Trade Commission. Before a merger is permitted, it must be established that a newly formed corporation will not stifle competition or reduce diversity in the marketplace. In this case, the primary concern was that AOL/Time Warner would control a large percentage of cable and television networks, and it might be tempted to block distribution of non-AOL/Time Warner content. AOL has guaranteed Congress that competitors will be allowed to use its television networks and cable systems and content will not be restricted.

1980s and 1990s. In the old days, corporate raiders could borrow enough money to purchase the target company. They would then dismantle the company and sell off different parts—a process called **divestiture**—to make a quick profit or to raise cash to make loan payments.

Finally, experts predict more leveraged buyouts in the future. A **leveraged buyout (LBO)** is a purchase arrangement that allows a firm's managers and employees or a group of investors to purchase the company. (LBO activity is sometimes referred to as taking a firm "private.") To gain control of a company, LBOs usually rely on borrowed money to purchase stock from existing stockholders. The borrowed money is later repaid through the company's earnings, sale of assets, or money obtained from selling more stock.

Whether they are sole proprietorships, partnerships, corporations, or use some other form of business ownership, most U.S. businesses are small. In the next chapter, we focus on these small businesses. We examine, among other things, the meaning of the word *small* as it applies to business and the place of small business in the American economy.

divestiture the process of dismantling a company and selling off different parts

leveraged buyout (LBO) a purchase arrangement that allows a firm's managers and employees or a group of investors to purchase the company

RETURN TO Inside Business

BILL HEWLETT AND DAVID PACKARD'S philosophy of working quickly, inventing something significant, and creating a relaxed working environment has enabled Hewlett-Packard Company to grow from a partnership that began in a garage in Palo Alto, California, to a global corporation. However, along the way, these two entrepreneurs created a business organization with lots of divisions, 124,000 employees, multiple products, and annual sales of over $49 billion.

With this record of success, many experts wonder if Hewlett-Packard can continue to grow while meeting the challenges of the future. The answer to that question may be determined to some extent by Hewlett-Packard's new CEO Carleton (Carly) S. Fiorina. The first woman to run a top-tier *Fortune* 500 company, Ms. Fiorina has already realized that to move this global corporation forward requires not only hard work, but also a vision of where the corporation is going. Fortunately, the company has a rich sixty-year heritage to build on. And the future does look bright. She has already begun to reorganize this corporate giant into an organization that will focus on creating new and improved technology that will meet the needs of customers. Ms. Fiorina is also launching an advertising campaign to send a clear message that Hewlett-Packard is ready to provide the state-of-the-art computer equipment that customers will need to use the Internet and other computer applications in the future.

Questions

1. Hewlett-Packard evolved from a partnership into a corporation with stockholders, board members, managers, and employees. Why do you think this form of ownership is appropriate for a company like Hewlett-Packard?
2. With its inventions, mergers, acquisitions, and joint ventures, Hewlett-Packard's 124,000 employees manufacture and market more than 29,000 technology products. Based on this information, is size an advantage or disadvantage for Hewlett-Packard?
3. Hewlett-Packard is currently the second largest computer company in the world. It has over 124,000 employees and manufactures and markets more than 29,000 technology products. Simply put, it is a corporate giant. Would you want to work for a company like Hewlett-Packard? Why or why not?

chapter Review

SUMMARY

1 Describe the advantages and disadvantages of sole proprietorships.

In a sole proprietorship, all business profits become the property of the owner, but the owner is also personally responsible for all business debts. Sole proprietorship is the simplest form of business to enter, control, and leave. It also has possible tax advantages. Perhaps for these reasons, seventy-three percent of all American business firms are sole proprietorships. Sole proprietorships nevertheless have disadvantages, such as unlimited liability and limits on one person's ability to borrow or to be an expert in all fields.

2 Explain the different types of partners and the importance of partnership agreements.

Like sole proprietors, general partners are responsible for running the business and for all business debts. Limited partners receive a share of the profit in return for investing in the business. However, they are not responsible for business debts beyond the amount they have invested. It is also possible to form a master limited partnership (MLP) and sell units of ownership to raise capital. Regardless of the type of partnership, it is always a good idea to have a written agreement (or articles of partnership) setting forth the terms of a partnership.

3 Describe the advantages and disadvantages of partnerships.

Although partnership eliminates some of the disadvantages of sole proprietorship, it is the least popular of the major forms of business ownership. The major advantages of a partnership include ease of start-up, availability of capital and credit, retention of profits, personal interest, combined skills and knowledge, and possible tax advantages. According to *Inc.* magazine, there are seven events that can destroy a partnership. The effects of management disagreements are one of the major disadvantages of a partnership. Other disadvantages include unlimited liability (in a general partnership), lack of continuity, and frozen investment.

4 Summarize how a corporation is formed.

A corporation is an artificial person created by law, with most of the legal rights of a real person, including the right to start and operate a business, to own property, and to enter into contracts. With the corporate form of ownership, stock can be sold to individuals to raise capital. Stock can also be issued as a reward to key employees or given to investors in place of cash payments.

The process of forming a corporation is called incorporation. Most experts believe the services of a lawyer are necessary when making decisions about where to incorporate and about obtaining a corporate charter, holding an organizational meeting, and all other legal details involved in incorporation. In theory, stockholders are able to control the activities of the corporation because they elect the board of directors who appoint the corporate officers.

5 Describe the advantages and disadvantages of a corporation.

Perhaps the major advantage of the corporate form is limited liability; stockholders are not liable for the corporation's debts beyond the amount they paid for its stock. Other important advantages include ease of raising capital, ease of transfer of ownership, perpetual life, and specialized management. A major disadvantage of the corporation is double taxation: all profits are taxed once as corporate income and again as personal income, since stockholders must pay a personal income tax on the profits they receive as dividends. Other disadvantages include: difficulty and expense of formation, government regulation, and lack of secrecy.

6 Discuss the purpose of an S-corporation, limited liability company, government-owned corporation, and other special forms of business ownership.

S-corporations are corporations that are taxed as though they were partnerships but that enjoy the benefit of limited liability. To qualify as an S-corporation, a number of criteria must be met. A limited liability company (LLC) is a form of business ownership that provides the limited liability of a corporation but is taxed like a partnership. In comparison with an S-corporation, an LLC has fewer restrictions. Government-owned corporations provide particular services, such as public transportation, to citizens. Not-for-profit corporations are formed to provide social services, rather than to earn profits. Three additional forms of business ownership are the cooperative, joint venture, and syndicate. All are used by their owners to meet special needs, and each may be owned by either individuals or firms.

7 Explain how growth from within and growth through mergers can enable a business to expand.

A corporation may grow by expanding its present operations or through a merger—the purchase of another corporation. Although most mergers are friendly, hostile takeovers also occur. A hostile takeover is a situation in which the management and board of directors of the firm targeted for acquisition disapprove of the merger. Mergers are generally classified as horizontal, vertical, or conglomerate mergers.

While economists, financial analysts, corporate managers, and stockholders debate the merits of mergers, some trends should be noted as we enter the next century. First, experts predict that future mergers will be the result of cash-rich companies looking to acquire businesses that will enhance their position in the marketplace. Second, more mergers are likely to involve foreign companies or investors. Third, there will be less debt financing. Fourth, mergers will be driven by business logic, the desire to compete in the international marketplace, and the explosion of information technology. Finally, more leveraged buyouts are expected.

KEY TERMS

You should now be able to define and give an example relevant to each of the following terms:

sole proprietorship (127)
unlimited liability (129)
partnership (131)
general partner (131)
general partnership (131)
limited partner (131)
limited partnership (131)
master limited partnership (MLP) (132)
corporation (135)
stock (135)
stockholder (135)
close corporation (136)
open corporation (136)
incorporation (136)
domestic corporation (137)
foreign corporation (137)
alien corporation (137)
corporate charter (137)
common stock (138)
preferred stock (138)
dividend (138)
proxy (138)
board of directors (138)
corporate officers (138)
limited liability (139)
S-corporation (142)
limited liability company (LLC) (142)
government-owned corporation (142)
quasi-government corporation (142)
not-for-profit corporation (143)
cooperative (143)
joint venture (144)
syndicate (144)
merger (145)
hostile takeover (145)
tender offer (145)
proxy fight (145)
divestiture (149)
leveraged buyout (LBO) (149)

REVIEW QUESTIONS

1. What is a sole proprietorship? What are the major advantages and disadvantages of this form of business ownership?
2. How does a partnership differ from a sole proprietorship? Which disadvantages of sole proprietorship does the partnership tend to eliminate or reduce?
3. What is the difference between a general partner and a limited partner?
4. What issues should be included in a partnership agreement? Why?
5. Explain the difference between
   a. An open corporation and a close corporation
   b. A domestic corporation, a foreign corporation, and an alien corporation
   c. A government-owned corporation, a quasi-government corporation, and a not-for-profit corporation
6. Outline the incorporation process and describe the basic corporate structure.
7. What rights do stockholders have?
8. What are the primary duties of a corporation's board of directors? How are directors elected?
9. What are the major advantages and disadvantages associated with the corporate form of business ownership?
10. How do an S-corporation and a limited liability company differ from the usual open or close corporation?
11. Why are cooperatives formed? Explain how they operate.
12. In what ways are joint ventures and syndicates alike? In what ways do they differ?
13. Describe the three types of mergers.
14. What is a hostile takeover? What can management do to prevent a hostile takeover?

DISCUSSION QUESTIONS

1. If you were to start a business, which ownership form would you choose? What factors might affect your choice?
2. Why might an investor choose to become a limited partner in a business instead of purchasing the stock of an open corporation?
3. Discuss the following statement: "Corporations are not really run by their owners."
4. What kinds of services do government-owned corporations provide? How might such services be provided without government involvement?
5. Is growth a good thing for all firms? How does management know when a firm is ready to grow?
6. Assume that a corporate raider wants to purchase your firm, dismantle it, and sell the individual pieces. What could you do to avoid this hostile takeover?

VIDEO CASE

IMCO Recycling, Inc.

IMCO Recycling, Inc., is the largest aluminum-recycling company in the world. The company processes more than a billion pounds of aluminum each year. IMCO buys used aluminum beverage cans and aluminum scrap on the open market. In most cases, however, the company processes customer-owned aluminum and returns it to customers in molten form or as ingots ready for reuse. Because of IMCO's recycling efforts, manufacturers can reduce material costs and at the same time conserve natural resources.

When IMCO Recycling was first organized, management chose the corporate form of ownership for two reasons. First, it takes a lot of capital to start a recycling company. With the corporate form of ownership, individuals and institutional investors (financial institutions, mutual funds, pension funds, and insurance companies) provide financing when they purchase shares of ownership. Today IMCO has several thousand individual investors who own approximately 33 percent of the corporation. The remaining 67 percent is owned by institutional investors and the firm's management.

The second reason management chose the corporate form of ownership was to shield stockholders from potential liability problems arising from safety, environmental, and legal issues. With few exceptions, the stockholders' liability in an incorporated business is limited to the amount of money they paid for their stock. Without having to risk their personal assets, stockholders were willing to supply the capital IMCO needed to grow into its current leadership position in the aluminum-recycling industry.

Once the decision to incorporate and sell stock was made, IMCO's management spent a lot of time and money incorporating the business, obtaining Security and Exchange Commission approval to sell common stock to the general public, and getting listed on the New York Stock Exchange. To begin the incorporation process, the company's managers hired a law firm to deal with legal and taxation issues and to ensure that limited liability shielded stockholders' personal assets. Then, before it could sell shares to the general public, IMCO had to obtain approval from the Security and Exchange Commission (SEC). To do so, it had to submit detailed disclosure information about the company, including its management, financial history, and future projections. Once SEC approval was obtained, it was possible to apply for listing on the New York Stock Exchange (NYSE). Again, before even one share of the company's stock could be sold on the NYSE, information about the company and its finances had to be submitted and approved. This was an especially important step because listing on the NYSE provides a market for stockholders who want to buy or sell IMCO's stock.

Since incorporation in 1985, IMCO Recycling has grown into a large corporation with annual sales in excess of $800 million. It now has sixteen U.S. subsidiaries and affiliates, and, like many American companies responding to new opportunities and the pressure of worldwide competition, it has entered the international marketplace. Currently, IMCO owns 50 percent of a joint venture that operates two recycling plants in Germany. In addition, IMCO is building a new plant in Wales. While IMCO's success can be attributed to many factors, the decision to incorporate is the most important one. Incorporation attracted the stockholders who provided the financing needed to turn a company into a giant in the recycling industry.[9]

Questions

1. Compared with a sole proprietorship or partnership, the corporation is a far more effective form of business ownership for raising capital. Why would an investor consider purchasing stock in a company that is incorporated?
2. Limited liability limits each stockholder's financial liability to the amount of money she or he has paid for a corporation's stock. How important is this concept to investors?
3. For most corporations that want to incorporate, it takes two to three years to obtain SEC approval and get a company's stock listed on the New York Stock Exchange. Do you think the benefits of incorporation and a listing on the New York Stock Exchange are worth the time and effort? Why, or why not?

Building skills for career success

1. Exploring the Internet

The arguments about mergers and acquisitions often come down to an evaluation of who benefits and by how much. Sometimes the benefits include access to new products, talented management, new customers, or new sources of capital. Often the debate is complicated by the involvement of firms based in different countries. Nationalists will argue any loss of a domestic company can never be considered good. This is why many industries have regulations and restrictions on mergers. For example, the banking, telecommunications, and broadcasting industries are all subject to regulations about who can control a firm in the industry and to what degree ownership can be concentrated.

The Internet is a fertile environment for information and discussion about mergers. The firms involved will provide their view about who will benefit and why it is either a good thing or not. Journalists will report facts and offer commentary as they see the future result of any merger, and of course chat rooms located on web sites of many journals promote discussion about the issues. Visit the text web site for updates to this exercise.

Assignment

1. Using an Internet search engine such as AltaVista or Yahoo!, locate two or three sites providing information about a recent merger (use a keyword like "merger").
2. After examining these sites and reading journal articles, report the information about the merger such as the value, the reasons behind the action, and so forth.
3. Based on your assessment of the information you have read do you think the merger is a good idea or not for the firms involved, the industry, and for society as a whole? Explain your reasoning.

2. Developing Critical Thinking Skills

Suppose you are a person who has always dreamed of owning a business but never had the money to open one. Since you were old enough to read a recipe, your mother allowed you to help in the kitchen. Most of all, you enjoyed baking and decorating cakes. You liked using your imagination to create cakes for special occasions. By the time you were in high school, you were baking and decorating wedding cakes for a fee. After high school, you started working full time as an adjuster for an insurance company. Your schedule now allows little time for baking and decorating cakes. Recently, you inherited $250,000 and changes at your job have created undue stress in your life. What should you do?

Assignment

1. Discuss the following points:
   a. What options are available to you?
   b. What specific factors must you consider in starting a business versus working for another firm?
   c. What form of ownership would be best for your business?
   d. What advantages and disadvantages apply to your preferred form of business ownership?
2. Prepare a two-page report summarizing your findings.

3. Building Team Skills

Using the scenario in Exercise 2, suppose you have decided to quit your job as an insurance adjuster and open a bakery. Your business is now growing, and you have decided to add a full line of catering services. This means more work and responsibility. You will need someone to help you, but you are undecided about what to do. Should you hire an employee or find a partner? If you add a partner, how will you organize the business and what will you need to do to create a legal partnership?

Assignment

1. In a group, discuss the following questions:
   a. What are the advantages and disadvantages of adding a partner versus hiring an employee?
   b. Assume that you have decided to form a partnership. What articles should be included in a partnership agreement?
   c. How would you go about finding a partner?
2. Summarize your group's answers to these questions and present them to your class.
3. As a group, prepare an articles of partnership agreement. Be prepared to discuss the pros and cons of your group's agreement with other groups from your class, as well as to examine their agreements.

4. Researching Different Careers

Many people spend their entire lives working in jobs they do not enjoy. Why is this so? Often, it is because they have taken the first job they were offered without giving it much thought. How can you avoid having this happen to you? First, you should determine your "personal profile" by identifying and analyzing your own strengths, weaknesses, things you enjoy, and things you dislike. Second, you should identify the types of jobs that fit your profile. Third, you should identify and research the companies that offer those jobs.

Assignment

1. Take two sheets of paper and draw a line down the middle of each sheet, forming two columns on each page. Label column 1 Things I Enjoy or Like to Do; column 2, Things I Do Not Like Doing; column 3, My Strengths; and column 4, My Weaknesses.
2. Record data in each column over a period of at least one week. You may find it helpful to have a relative or friend give you input.
3. Summarize the data and write a profile of yourself.
4. Prepare a list of jobs that fit your profile. Take your profile to a career counselor at your college or to the public library and ask for help in identifying jobs that fit your profile. Your college may offer testing to assess your skills and personality. The Strong-Campbell Interest Inventory and the Meyers-Briggs personality indicator can help you assess the kind of work you may enjoy. The Internet is another resource.
5. Research the companies that offer the type of jobs that fit your profile.
6. Write a report on your findings.

5. Improving Communication Skills

If businesses are to succeed, they must continually change. Change takes many forms. Every week, newspapers report on companies taking steps to organize into larger units or to downsize into smaller units. This chapter has discussed several strategies that effect change in organizations. They include mergers and acquisitions, hostile takeovers, divestitures, and leveraged buyouts.

Assignment

1. Read articles illustrating how one or more of these strategies has caused an organization to change.
2. Write a two-page report covering the following:
   a. Explain in your own words what led up to this change.
   b. How will this change affect
      - the company itself
      - its consumers
      - its employees
      - its industry
   c. What opportunities does this change create, and what problems do you forecast?

Small Business, Entrepreneurship, and Franchises

6

LEARNING OBJECTIVES

1. Define what a small business is and recognize the fields in which small businesses are concentrated.
2. Identify the people who start small businesses and the reasons why some succeed and many fail.
3. Assess the contributions of small businesses to our economy.
4. Judge the advantages and disadvantages of operating a small business.
5. Explain how the Small Business Administration helps small businesses.
6. Appraise the concept and types of franchising.
7. Analyze the growth of franchising and franchising's advantages and disadvantages.

Looking for community, this entrepreneur finds herself Businesswoman of the Year.

inside business

Latino.Com Builds Web Community and Business

Searching for a sense of community far from home led Lavonne Luquis to an online business opportunity. Born in Puerto Rico, Luquis was working as a newspaper reporter in Washington state when she started surfing the Internet looking for sites with a Latino flavor. She didn't find any, so she took the entrepreneurial plunge. Drawing on her journalism background, her experience of helping to manage a family business, and what she learned working at an advertising agency, she launched her highly-targeted web site in 1995.

Luquis originally envisioned LatinoLink.com as a news and information site for Spanish-speaking people in the United States. Transferring her knowledge of print media to the Internet, she concentrated on providing quality content for a select audience, including news articles and reviews of other Latino Internet sites. She forged content agreements with Netscape, Yahoo! and other Internet businesses and planned to support the site through the sale of online ads to companies that wanted to reach Hispanic consumers.

However, LatinoLink initially attracted fewer visitors and advertisers than its founder had hoped. One challenge was figuring out how to satisfy her online audience's hunger for more interaction. E-mail messages indicated that LatinoLink visitors wanted to do more than read about issues and developments within the community—they wanted to be able to discuss ideas online. This feedback persuaded Luquis to add chat technology and special-interest bulletin boards so visitors could exchange messages. Soon her audience was growing month after month as more visitors logged on to join the community.

Luquis also faced the challenge of changing some misconceptions about her audience. "The perception among those on Wall Street, marketers, and business-minded people in general has been that Hispanics don't go online, Hispanics don't own computers, Spanish speakers are exotic beings who are not interested in the Internet," she says. In reality, research shows that 36 percent of Hispanic households in the United States use the Internet. Over time, as her audience grew and her site attracted coverage in the *Wall Street Journal* and other publications, Luquis signed IBM, AT&T, Microsoft, Banco Popular de Puerto Rico, and many other firms as advertisers.

Response has been so strong that Luquis expanded her site into Latino.com (http://www.latino.com), a bilingual web portal designed as a comprehensive Internet gateway to Hispanic news, arts, sports, business, and finance, complete with community-building features such as a job bank. Luquis's entrepreneurial success has been recognized by the U.S. Hispanic Chamber of Commerce, which named her National Hispanic Businesswoman of the Year, and by *Hispanic Business* magazine, which included her in its listing of "100 Most Influential Hispanics." While searching for community, this entrepreneur founded a business and helped others find a sense of community, as well.[1]

Lavonne Luquis's Latino.com web portal business has experienced considerable growth during the last six years. That kind of growth is unusual even for the rapidly expanding Internet industry. In fact, most businesses start small, and those that survive usually stay small. They provide a solid foundation for our economy—as employers, as suppliers and purchasers of goods and services, and as taxpayers.

In this chapter, we do not take small businesses for granted. Instead, we look closely at this important business sector—beginning with a definition of small business, a description of industries that often attract small businesses, and a profile of some of the people who start small businesses. Next we consider the importance of small businesses in our economy. We also present the advantages and disadvantages of smallness in business. We then describe services provided by the Small Business Administration, a government agency formed to assist owners and managers of small businesses. We conclude the chapter with a discussion of the pros and cons of franchising, an approach to small-business ownership that has become very popular in the last twenty-five years.

LEARNING OBJECTIVE

1 Define what a small business is and recognize the fields in which small businesses are concentrated.

Small Business: A Profile

The Small Business Administration (SBA) defines a **small business** as "one which is independently owned and operated for profit and is not dominant in its field." How small must a firm be not to dominate its field? That depends on the particular industry it is in. The SBA has developed the following specific "smallness" guidelines for the various industries.[2]

small business one that is independently owned and operated for profit and is not dominant in its field

- *Manufacturing*—a maximum of 500 to 1,500 employees, depending on the products manufactured
- *Wholesaling*—a maximum of 100 employees
- *Retailing*—maximum yearly sales or receipts ranging from $5 million to $21 million, depending on the industry
- *General construction*—average annual receipts ranging from $13.5 million to $17 million, depending on the industry
- *Special trade construction*—annual sales ranging up to $7 million
- *Agriculture*—maximum annual receipts of $0.5 million to $9 million
- *Services*—maximum annual receipts ranging from $2.5 million to $21.5 million, depending on the type of service

The SBA periodically revises and simplifies its small-business size regulations.

Annual sales in the millions of dollars may not seem very small. However, for many firms, profit is only a small percentage of total sales. Thus, a firm may earn only $30,000 or $40,000 on yearly sales of $1 million—and that *is* small in comparison to the profits earned by most medium-sized and large firms. Moreover, most small firms have annual sales well below the maximum limits in the SBA guidelines.

The Small-Business Sector

A surprising number of Americans take advantage of their freedom to start a business. There are, in fact, about 23 million businesses in this country. Only just over 14,000 of these employ more than 500 workers—enough to be considered large.

Interest in owning or starting a small business has never been greater than it is today. During the last decade, the number of small businesses in the United States has increased 49 percent, and for the last few years, new business formation in the United States has broken successive records. During 1998, there were 898,000 new firms—a 1.5 percent increase over the record 889,000 in 1997.[3] Furthermore, part-time entrepreneurs have increased fivefold in recent years; they now account for one-third of all small businesses.[4]

Statistically, over 70 percent of new businesses can be expected to fail within their first five years.[5] The primary reason for these failures is mismanagement resulting from a lack of business know-how. The makeup of the small-business sector is thus constantly changing. In spite of the high failure rate, many small businesses succeed modestly. Some, like Apple Computer, Inc., are extremely successful—to the point where they can no longer be considered small. Taken together, small businesses are also responsible for providing a high percentage of the jobs in the United States. According to some estimates, the figure is well over 50 percent.

Industries That Attract Small Businesses

Some industries, such as auto manufacturing, require huge investments in machinery and equipment. Businesses in such industries are big from the day they are started—if an entrepreneur or group of entrepreneurs can gather the capital required to start one.

By contrast, a number of other industries require only a low initial investment and some special skills or knowledge. It is these industries that tend to attract new businesses. Growing industries, such as outpatient care facilities, are attractive because of their profit potential. However, knowledgeable entrepreneurs choose areas with which they are familiar, and these are most often the more established industries.

Small enterprise spans the gamut from corner newspaper vending to the development of optical fibers. The owners of small businesses sell gasoline, flowers, and coffee to go. They publish magazines, haul freight, teach languages, and program computers. They make wines, movies, and high-fashion clothes. They build new homes and restore old ones. They fix appliances, recycle metals, and sell used cars. They drive cabs and fly planes. They make us well when we are ill, and they sell us the products of corporate giants.

The various kinds of businesses generally fall into three broad categories of industry: distribution, service, and production. Within these categories, small businesses tend to cluster in services and retailing. Table 6.1 shows the fifteen fastest growing types of small businesses.

table 6.1 Fastest Growing Types of Small Businesses, 1995–1996

Business	Employment Increase (thousands)	Employment Increases (%)
Miscellaneous Retail Establishments	54.7	24.6
Transportation Services	5.8	13.3
Meat Markets and Freezer Provisioners	6.7	12.9
Masonry, Stonework, and Plastering	49.2	11.7
Building Materials and Garden Supplies	3.9	10.5
Top, Body, and Upholstery Repair Shops	20.7	10.1
Furniture and Home Furnishings Stores	50.6	10.1
Used Merchandise Stores	10.3	9.9
Retail Nurseries and Garden Stores	8.8	9.7
Fresh Fruits and Vegetables	10.3	9.6
Automotive Repair Shops	12.8	9.5
Mailing, Reproduction, Stenographic	27.2	9.4
General Automotive Repair Shops	22.3	9.3
Engineering, Accounting, Research	74.8	9.1
Medical and Dental Laboratories	18.0	9.0
Total, Top 15 Industries	376.1	10.8

Source: From *The State of Small Business: A Report of the President*, Washington, D.C., U.S. Government Printing Office, 1998, p. 38

Exploring Business

Incubators Nurture Web Businesses

WHAT DO IDEALAB, HOTBANK, AND eHatchery have in common? All are business incubators for Internet start-ups, supplying office space and equipment, administrative support, expert advice, and financing to help dot-coms become operational. In exchange, each web business gives the incubator an equity stake—up to 50 percent. When one of these start-ups becomes profitable or offers stock to the public, the incubator also shares in the rewards.

Idealab (http://www.idealab.com), one of the earliest Internet incubators, helped to launch CarsDirect.com and GoTo.com. Expanding from California to a branch in New York City's Silicon Alley, Idealab's main focus is commercializing the business ideas of founder Bill Gross. "Our companies are like our children—we will do anything to make them succeed," Gross says. More than four dozen firms have been in Idealab's care, with at least two reporting profits.

At Atlanta's eHatchery (http://www.ehatchery.com), founder Jeff Levy emphasizes speed because "you can assume that there are ten other groups of very smart people out there trying to do the same thing." When Ari Straus set out to develop his web business idea, he expected the process to take about nine months. However, with eHatchery's help—and access to its e-commerce software—Straus's business, Fig-Leaves.com, was up and running in less than three months. Small businesses also help each other in the incubator environment, the way Straus and his staff helped the owners of Simply Collectible and VetExchange, two start-ups at eHatchery.

Boston-based I-Group Hotbank (http://www.igroup.com), created by the Japanese firm Softbank and U.S. partners Intercontinental Group, provides tech-ready office space as well as $1 to 2 million in cash. In today's crowded web start-up field, incubators offer yet another benefit for entrepreneurs: Savvy mentors with contacts. Explains Ellen Roy, a managing director: "We can help you get above the clutter, get you to the people you need to see." Paul Ognibene, founder of ClubTools.com, is delighted with the mentoring at this incubator. "That's the best part," he says. "It's not the money or the building. It's the adviser, a guy who's already built a billion-dollar business who basically goes with me whenever I need him."

Distribution Industries This category includes retailing, wholesaling, transportation, and communications—industries concerned with the movement of goods from producers to consumers. Distribution industries account for approximately 33 percent of all small businesses. Of these, almost three-quarters are involved in retailing, that is, the sale of goods directly to consumers. Clothing and jewelry stores, pet shops, bookstores, and grocery stores, for example, are all retailing firms. Slightly less than one-quarter of the small distribution firms are wholesalers. Wholesalers purchase products in quantity from manufacturers and then resell them to retailers.

Service Industries This category accounts for over 48 percent of all small businesses. Of these, about three-quarters provide such nonfinancial services as medical and dental care; watch, shoe, and TV repairs; hair-cutting and styling; restaurant meals; and dry cleaning. About 8 percent of the small service firms offer financial services, such as accounting, insurance, real estate, and investment counseling. An increasing number of self-employed Americans are running service businesses from home.

Production Industries This last category includes the construction, mining, and manufacturing industries. Only about 19 percent of all small businesses are in this group, mainly because these industries require relatively large initial investments. Small firms that do venture into production generally make parts and subassemblies for larger manufacturing firms or supply special skills to larger construction firms.

The People in Small Businesses: The Entrepreneurs

LEARNING OBJECTIVE

2 Identify the people who start small businesses and the reasons why some succeed and many fail.

Small businesses are typically managed by the people who started and own them. Most of these people have held jobs with other firms and could still be so employed if they wanted. Yet owners of small businesses would rather take the risk of starting and operating their own firms, even if the money they make is less than the salaries they might otherwise earn.

An entrepreneur's dream. Many entrepreneurs such as David Du Tran are driven by the desire to be their own bosses, do what they want to do, and turn passions into profit-making businesses. Tran, who escaped Saigon in 1979 with his wife and six children, owns several food-related small businesses in Westminster, California, and is a self-made multimillionaire.

Researchers have suggested a variety of personal factors as reasons why people go into business for themselves. One that is often cited is the "entrepreneurial spirit"—the desire to create a new business. For example, Nikki Olyai always knew she wanted to create and develop her own business. Her father, a successful businessman in Iran, was her role model. She came to the United States at the age of seventeen, lived with a host family in Salem, Oregon, attending high school there. Undergraduate and graduate degrees in computer science led her to start Innovision Technologies while she held two other jobs to keep the business going, and took care of her four-year-old son. In 2000, Nikki Olyai was honored by the Women's Business Enterprise National Council's "Salute to Women's Business Enterprises" as one of 11 top successful firms. Innovision Technologies specializes in information technology, systems analysis and assessment, project management and quality assurance. In 1999, her firm was ranked #195 on the *Inc.* 500 list of America's fastest growing, privately-held companies. For three consecutive years, her firm was selected as a "Future 50 of Greater Detroit Company."[6] Other factors, such as independence, the desire to determine one's own destiny, and the willingness to find and accept a challenge, certainly play a part. Background may exert an influence as well. In particular, researchers think that people whose families have been in business (successfully or not) are most apt to start and run their own businesses. Those who start their own businesses also tend to cluster around certain ages—more than 70 percent are between 24 and 44 years old (see Figure 6.1).[7]

Finally, there must be some motivation to start a business. A person may decide she has simply "had enough" of working and earning a profit for someone else. Another may lose his job for some reason and decide to start the business he has always wanted rather than seek another job. Still another person may have an idea for a new

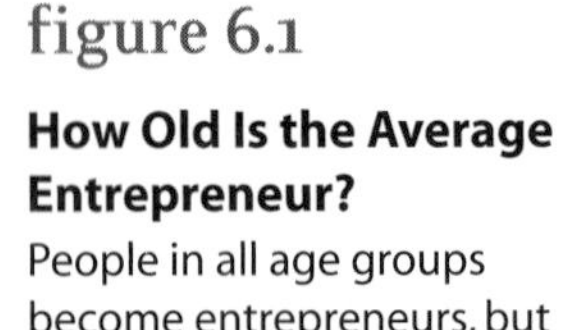
figure 6.1

How Old Is the Average Entrepreneur?

People in all age groups become entrepreneurs, but more than 70 percent are between 24 and 44.

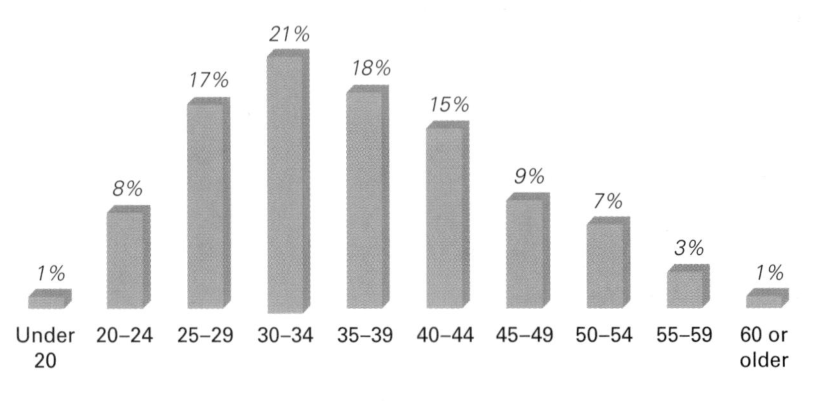

Source: Data developed and provided by the NFIB Foundation and sponsored by the American Express Travel Related Services Company, Inc.

product or a new way to sell an existing product. Or the opportunity to go into business may arise suddenly, perhaps as a result of a hobby, as was the case with Cheryl Strand. Strand started baking and decorating cakes from her home while working full-time as a word processor at Clemson University. Her cakes became so popular that she soon found herself working through her lunch breaks and late into the night to meet customer demand.

After deciding to start her own business, Strand contacted the Clemson University Small Business Development Center. The center helped her prepare for the business start-up and develop a loan package—complete with a detailed business plan and financial statements for presentation at local banks. Strand obtained the $10,000 she needed. Since then, Cakes by Cheryl has doubled in size and increased sales by approximately 56 percent per year. It now offers fresh breads, deli sandwiches, a tempting line of baked goods, and catering and carry-out services.[8]

Cheryl Strand is one of a growing number of women who are small business owners. Women are 51 percent of the U.S. population, and according to the SBA, they owned at least 50 percent of all small businesses in 2000. Women already own 66 percent of the home-based businesses in this country, and the number of men in home-based businesses is growing rapidly.

The SBA estimates women-owned businesses provide 15.5 million jobs and employ 35 percent more workers in the United States than the *Fortune* 500 companies worldwide. Furthermore, 7.7 million women-owned businesses in the United States have proven they are more successful; over 40 percent have been in business for 12 years or more. According to Dun and Bradstreet, women-owned businesses are financially sound and creditworthy and their risk of failure is lower than average.[9]

In some people, the motivation to start a business develops slowly, as they gain the knowledge and ability required for success as a business owner. Knowledge and ability—especially management ability—are probably the most important factors involved. A new firm is very much built around the entrepreneur. The owner must be able to manage the firm's finances, its personnel (if there are any employees), and its day-to-day operations. He or she must handle sales, advertising, purchasing, pricing, and a variety of other business functions. The knowledge and ability to do so are most often acquired through experience working for other firms in the same area of business.

Why Small Businesses Fail

Small businesses are prone to failure. Capital, management, and planning are the key ingredients in the survival of a small business, and also the most common reasons for failure. Businesses can experience a number of money-related problems. It may take several years before a business begins to show a profit. Entrepreneurs need to have not only the capital to open a business but also the money to operate it in its possibly lengthy start-up phase. One cash-flow obstacle often leads to others. And a series of cash-flow predicaments usually ends in a business failure. This scenario is all too often played out by small and not-so-small start-up Internet firms that fail to meet their financial backer's expectations and so are denied a second wave of investment dollars to continue their drive to establish a profitable online firm. For example, in one month alone Digital Entertainment Network shut its video streaming site, clothing distributor boo.com closed after spending more than $100 million in only six months of business, and healthshop.com shut its doors completely after failing to meet their investor's expectations.[10]

Many entrepreneurs lack the management skills required to run a business. Money, time, personnel, and inventory all need to be effectively managed if a small business is to succeed. Starting a small business requires much more than optimism and a good idea.

Success and expansion sometimes lead to problems. Frequently entrepreneurs with successful small businesses make the mistake of overexpansion. But fast growth often results in dramatic changes in a business. Thus, the entrepreneur must plan carefully and adjust competently to new and potentially disruptive situations.

Every day, and in every part of the country, people open new businesses. Though many will fail, others represent well-conceived ideas developed by entrepreneurs who have the expertise, resources, and determination to make their businesses succeed. As these well-prepared entrepreneurs pursue their individual goals, our society benefits in many ways from their work and creativity. Such billion-dollar companies as Apple Computer, McDonald's Corporation, and Procter & Gamble are all examples of small businesses that expanded into industry giants.

The Importance of Small Businesses in Our Economy

LEARNING OBJECTIVE

3 Assess the contributions of small businesses to our economy.

This country's economic history abounds with stories of ambitious men and women who turned their ideas into business dynasties. The Ford Motor Company started as a one-man operation with an innovative method for industrial production. L.L. Bean, Inc., can trace its beginnings to a basement shop in Freeport, Maine. Both Xerox and Polaroid began as small firms with a better way to do a job.

Providing Technical Innovation

Invention and innovation are part of the foundations of our economy. The increases in productivity that have characterized the past two hundred years of our history are all rooted in one principal source: new ways to do a job with less effort for less money. Studies show that the incidence of innovation among small-business workers is significantly higher than among workers in large businesses. Small firms produce two and a half times as many innovations as large firms, relative to the number of persons employed.

According to the U.S. Office of Management and Budget, more than half the major technological advances of the twentieth century originated with individual inventors and small companies. Even just a sampling of those innovations is remarkable:

- Air conditioning
- Airplane
- Automatic transmission
- Ball-point pen
- Double-knit fabric
- FM radio
- Heart valve
- Helicopter
- Instant camera
- Insulin
- Jet engine
- Penicillin
- Personal computer
- Power steering
- Xerography
- Zipper

spotlight

Source: Copyright 2000, USA TODAY. Reprinted with permission.

Perhaps even more remarkable—and important—is that many of these inventions sparked major new U.S. industries. More often, a small business innovation contributes to an estab-lished industry by adding some valuable service, as demonstrated by San Mateo, California, makeoverstudio.com. The firm's free Internet service allows users to upload a digital photo of themselves and then experiment with the latest product styles and colors available from cosmetic vendors who license the products. Customers can change their hair and lipstick color a thousand different ways with just a click of their mouse.

Created by Lori Von Rueden, the firm earns a percentage of online sales generated at each site when customers purchase the products that have delivered their online look.[11]

We may soon be seeing more innovations from small firms because of funding increases in the Small Business Innovation Research Program (SBIR). Under this program, federal agencies with large research and development (R&D) budgets must direct certain amounts of their R&D contracts to small businesses. Since the inception of the program in 1983, small firms have received almost $5 billion in federal R&D awards.

Creating employment opportunities for senior citizens. Small businesses have traditionally provided the thrust to keep our nation's economy running smoothly and prosperously. Vita Needle Co., which employs workers whose average age is 73, is a manufacturer of veterinary, human, and industrial needles. Small firms such as this generate virtually all new jobs while large companies continue to downsize.

Providing Employment

Small firms have traditionally added more than their proportional share of new jobs to the economy. In 1998, the U.S. economy created over three million new jobs. Seven out of the ten industries that added the most new jobs were small-business dominated industries. Small businesses creating the most new jobs in 1997 included engineering and management services and special trade contractors. The amusement and recreation services, the fastest growing small business dominated industry, increased employment by 7.6 percent in 1997. Small firms hire a larger proportion of employees who are younger workers, older workers, women, or workers who prefer to work part-time. Furthermore, small businesses provide 67 percent of workers with their first jobs and initial on-the-job training in basic skills. According to the SBA, small businesses represent 99.7 percent of all employers, employ 53 percent of the private work force, and provide virtually all of the net new jobs added to our economy.[12]

Small businesses thus contribute significantly to solving unemployment problems. Table 6.2 shows the types of small businesses that are generating the most new jobs.

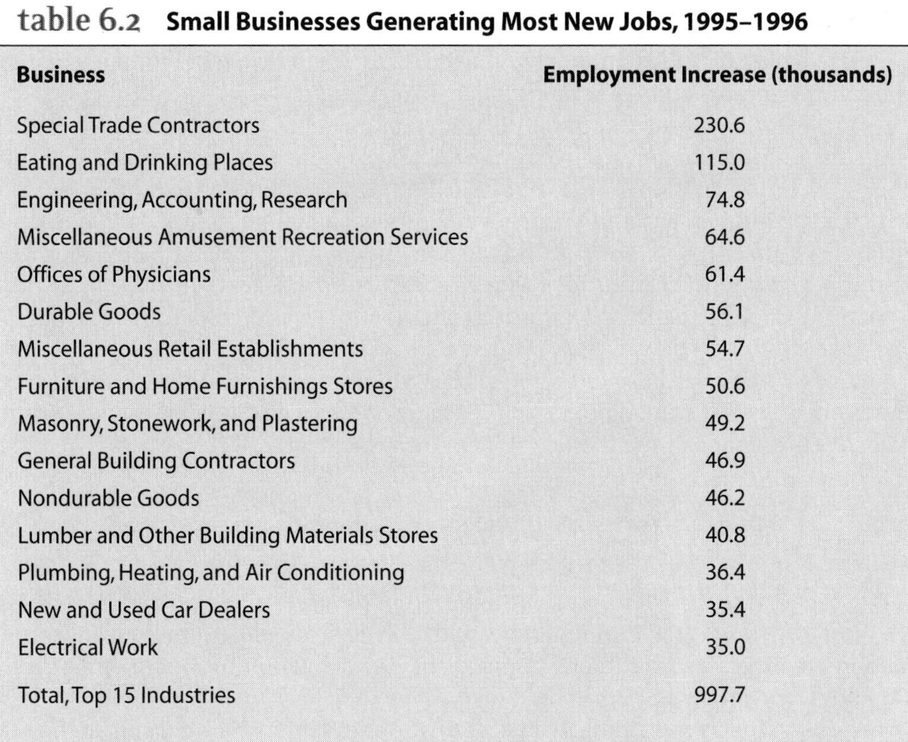

table 6.2 Small Businesses Generating Most New Jobs, 1995–1996

Business	Employment Increase (thousands)
Special Trade Contractors	230.6
Eating and Drinking Places	115.0
Engineering, Accounting, Research	74.8
Miscellaneous Amusement Recreation Services	64.6
Offices of Physicians	61.4
Durable Goods	56.1
Miscellaneous Retail Establishments	54.7
Furniture and Home Furnishings Stores	50.6
Masonry, Stonework, and Plastering	49.2
General Building Contractors	46.9
Nondurable Goods	46.2
Lumber and Other Building Materials Stores	40.8
Plumbing, Heating, and Air Conditioning	36.4
New and Used Car Dealers	35.4
Electrical Work	35.0
Total, Top 15 Industries	997.7

Source: Adapted from *The State of Small Business: A Report of the President*, Washington, D.C., U.S. Government Printing Office, 1998, p. 36.

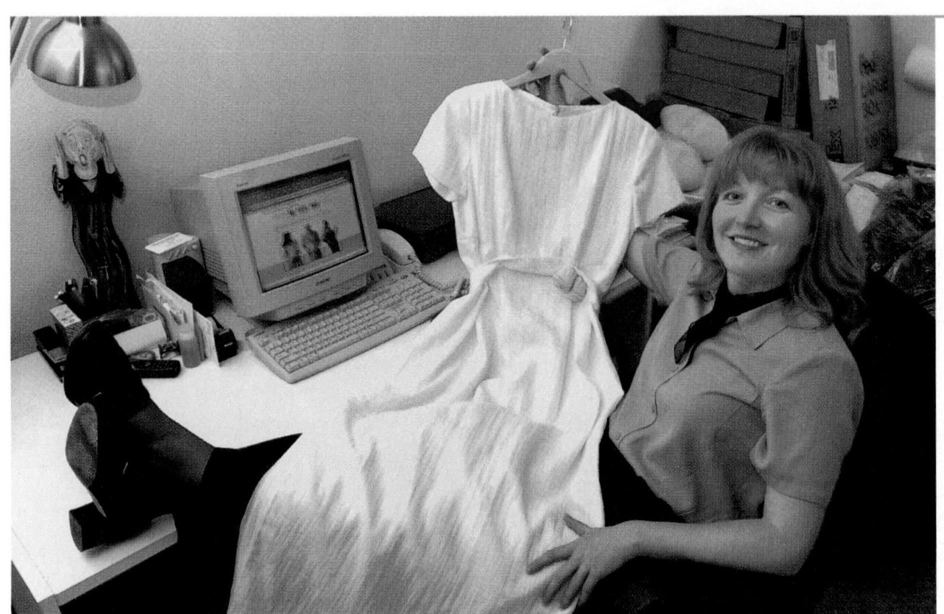

Meeting customer needs. Lorraine Vorsky shows off the most popular item she sells on her Internet business aimed at pregnant executives: a wedding dress. Vorsky says that "even if someone is pregnant, she wants to have a nice wedding." Such special groups of customers create almost perfect markets for small companies.

Providing Competition

Small businesses challenge larger, established firms in many ways, causing them to become more efficient and more responsive to consumer needs. A small business cannot, of course, compete with a large firm in all respects. But a number of small firms, each competing in its own particular area and its own particular way, together have the desired competitive effect. Thus, several small janitorial companies together add up to reasonable competition for the no-longer-small ServiceMaster.

Filling Needs of Society and Other Businesses

By their nature, large firms must operate on a large scale. Many may be unwilling or unable to meet the special needs of smaller groups of consumers. Such groups create almost perfect markets for small companies, which can tailor their products to these groups and fill their needs profitably. A prime example is a firm that modifies automobile controls to accommodate handicapped drivers.

Small firms also provide a variety of goods and services to each other and to much larger firms. Sears, Roebuck purchases merchandise from approximately 12,000 suppliers—and most of them are small businesses. General Motors relies on more than 32,000 companies for parts and supplies and depends on more than 11,000 independent dealers to sell its automobiles and trucks. Large firms generally buy parts and assemblies from smaller firms for one very good reason: it is less expensive than manufacturing the parts in their own factories. This lower cost is eventually reflected in the price that consumers pay for their products.

It is clear that small businesses are a vital part of our economy and that, as consumers and as members of the labor force, we all benefit enormously from their existence. Now let us look at the situation from the viewpoint of the owners of small businesses.

The Pros and Cons of Smallness

LEARNING OBJECTIVE

4 Judge the advantages and disadvantages of operating a small business.

Do most owners of small businesses dream that their firms will grow into giant corporations—managed by professionals—while they serve only on the board of directors? Or would they rather stay small, in a firm where they have the opportunity (and the responsibility) to do everything that needs to be done? The answers depend on the personal characteristics and motivations of the individual owners. For many, the advantages of remaining small far outweigh the disadvantages.

Talking Technology

High-Tech Teen Entrepreneurs

THE INTERNET HAS BECOME A SMALL-business on-ramp for teenaged entrepreneurs. Start-up costs are relatively small: A computer, a modem, a phone line, and an Internet domain name. Yet the rewards–and the opportunities–can be extremely large.

Just ask Michael Furdyk, Michael Hayman, and Albert Lai. As teens, the three collaborated on MyDesktop.com, a web site loaded with help tips for software and computer games. Within two years, the site was drawing a million visitors monthly and bringing in $30,000 from ad revenues. The content and the traffic caught the eye of Internet.com, which bought the company for more than $1 million down, thousands of stock options, and additional cash payments based on growth. The entrepreneurs immediately began working on a second web-based business, BuyBuddy.com. "It is an e-commerce site that we hope to make into a market player now that we have more experience and contacts," says Hayman.

Or ask Cameron Johnson, the teen who started the SurfingPrizes.com site. Web surfers can earn money for every hour they're logged on through the site which exposes them to ads from companies such as Discover Card, Ask Jeeves, Tickets.com, and Warner Brothers. More than 25,000 surfers have already signed up. What's Johnson's next move? "We will hopefully be able to file for an IPO very shortly," he says, referring to plans to sell stock in the company.

High-tech teen entrepreneurship is definitely exploding. "There's not a period in history where we've seen such a plethora of young entrepreneurs," comments Nancy F. Koehn, associate professor of business administration at Harvard Business School. Still, teen entrepreneurs face unique pressures in juggling their schoolwork, their social life, and their high-tech workload. Some ultimately quit school, while others quit or cut back on their business activities. Melissa Sconyers, a web designer, chose to shrink her workload: "I had lost touch with my friends. I had to remember I am a teenager."

Advantages of Small Business

Small-business owners with limited resources often must struggle to enter competitive new markets. They also have to deal with increasing international competition. However, they enjoy several unique advantages.

Personal Relationships with Customers and Employees For those who like dealing with people, small business is the place to be. The owners of retail shops get to know many of their customers by name and deal with them on a personal basis. Through such relationships, small-business owners often become involved in the social, cultural, and political life of the community.

Relationships between owner-managers and employees also tend to be closer in smaller businesses. In many cases. the owner is a friend and counselor as well as the boss.

These personal relationships provide an important business advantage. The personal service small businesses offer to customers is a major competitive weapon—one that larger firms try to match but often cannot. In addition, close relationships with employees often help the small-business owner keep effective workers who might earn more with a larger firm.

Ability to Adapt to Change Being his or her own boss, the owner-manager of a small business does not need anyone's permission to adapt to change. An owner may add or discontinue merchandise or services, change store hours, and experiment with various price strategies in response to changes in market conditions. And through personal relationships with customers, the owners of small businesses quickly become aware of changes in people's needs and interests, as well as in the activities of competing firms.

A personal tour. Service firms such as this travel agency require a low initial capital investment. Knowledgeable entrepreneurs, such as this expert travel agent, who choose areas with which they are familiar, can provide personal service to their customers. Such personal service encourages the customer loyalty on which small businesses thrive.

Simplified Recordkeeping Many small firms need only a simple set of records. Recordkeeping might consist of a checkbook, a cash-receipts journal in which to record all sales, and a cash-disbursements journal in which to record all amounts paid out. Obviously, enough records must be kept to allow for producing and filing accurate tax returns.

Independence Small-business owners don't have to punch in and out, bid for vacation times, take orders from superiors, or worry about being fired or laid off. They are the masters of their own destinies—at least with regard to employment. For many people, this is the prime advantage of owning a small business.

Other Advantages According to the Small Business Administration, the most profitable companies in the United States are small firms that have been in business for more than ten years and employ fewer than twenty people. Small-business owners also enjoy all the advantages of sole proprietorships, which are discussed in Chapter 5. These include being able to keep all profits, the ease and low cost of going into business and (if necessary) going out of business, and being able to keep business information secret.

Disadvantages of Small Business

Personal contacts with customers, closer relationships with employees, being one's own boss, less cumbersome recordkeeping chores, and independence are the bright side of small business. In contrast, the dark side reflects problems unique to these firms.

Risk of Failure As we have noted, small businesses (especially new ones) run a heavy risk of going out of business—about two out of three close their doors within the first five years. Older, well-established small firms can be hit hard by a business recession, mainly because they do not have the financial resources to weather an extended difficult period.

Limited Potential Small businesses that survive do so with varying degrees of success. Many are simply the means of making a living for the owner and his or her family. The owner may have some technical skill—as a hair stylist or electrician, for example—and may have started a business to put this skill to work. Such a business is unlikely to grow into big business. Also, employees' potential for advancement is limited.

Limited Ability to Raise Capital Small businesses typically have a limited ability to obtain capital. Figure 6.2 shows that most small-business financing comes out of the owner's pocket. Personal loans from lending institutions provide only about one-fourth of the capital required by small businesses. More than two-thirds of all new firms begin with less than $10,000 in total capital, according to Census Bureau and Federal Reserve surveys. In fact, almost half of new firms begin with less than $5,000, usually provided by the owner or family members and friends.[13] Recognizing the

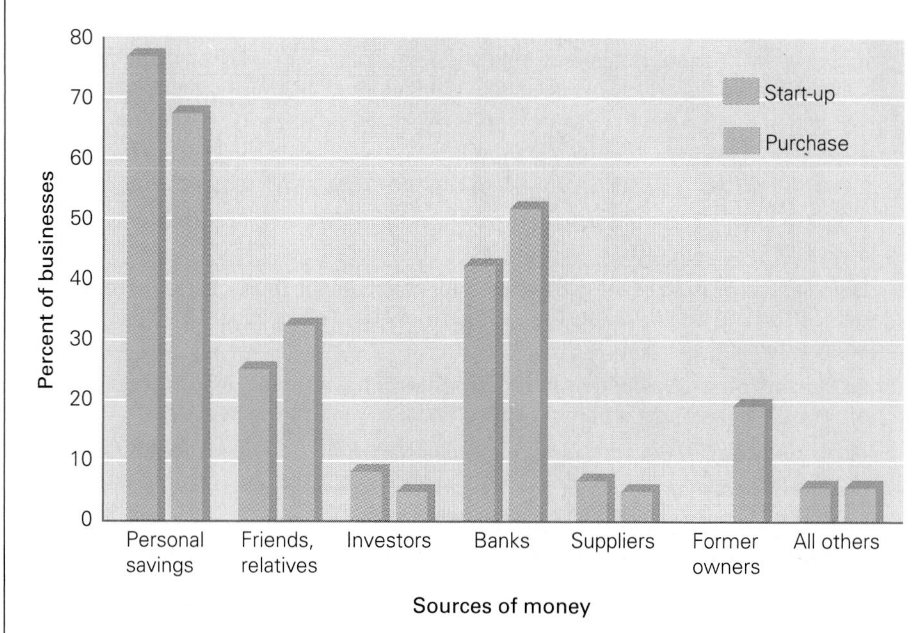

figure 6.2

Sources of Capital for Entrepreneurs

Small businesses get financing from various sources; the most important is personal savings.

Source: Data developed and provided by the NFIB Foundation and sponsored by the American Express Travel Related Services Company, Inc.

opportunity to capitalize on the needs of small businesses with limited cash, firms like bigstep.com provide small businesses with the opportunity to create their own web site for free, a service that generally would cost about $250 a month from other web site service firms. Backed by partnerships with Sun Microsystems, the Washingtonpost.com and Newsweek Interactive, bigstep.com makes its money from sponsorships and fees for optional services.[14] Fortunately for small businesses today the Internet provides a powerful yet relatively inexpensive communication tool for reaching customers, suppliers, and employees. According to a recent Arthur Andersen study, about 88 percent of small businesses now have computers and 39 percent have networks. Given the advantages of the Internet, it is not surprising that in 2000, 53 percent of small businesses have a web page, as compared to 32 percent in 1998. More than 85 percent say they use the Internet, up from 65 percent in 1998, to e-mail and research products. About 40 percent say they use the Internet to purchase goods and services, and 23 percent say they also sell products and services.[15]

Although every person who considers starting a small business should be aware of the hazards and pitfalls we have noted, a well-conceived business plan may help avoid the risk of failure. The U.S. government is also dedicated to helping small businesses make it. It expresses this aim most actively through the Small Business Administration.

Developing a Business Plan

Lack of planning can be as deadly as lack of money to a new small business. Planning is important to any business, large or small, and should never be overlooked or taken lightly. A **business plan** is a carefully constructed guide for the person starting a business. It also serves as a concise document that potential investors can examine to see if they would like to invest or assist in financing a new venture.

business plan a carefully constructed guide for the person starting a business

Table 6.3 shows the ten sections a business plan should include. When constructing a business plan, the businessperson should strive to keep it easy to read, uncluttered, and complete. Like other busy executives, officials of financial institutions do not

table 6.3 Components of a Business Plan

1. **Introduction** Basic information such as name and address of the business, nature of the business, statement of the business's financial needs (if any), and statement of confidentiality (to keep important information away from potential competitors)
2. **Executive summary** Summary of the entire business plan (a convenience for busy investors), including a justification stating why the business will succeed
3. **Industry analysis** Examination of the potential customer, current competitors, and business's future
4. **Detailed description of the business** Information on the products or services to be offered, size and location of the business, personnel and office equipment needed, and brief history of the business
5. **Production plan** Description and cost analysis of the manufacturing process, plus an outline of the raw materials, physical plant, and heavy machinery needed
6. **Marketing plan** Discussion of pricing, promotion, distribution, and product forecasts
7. **Organizational plan** Description of the form of ownership of the venture and responsibilities of all members of the organization
8. **Assessment of risk** Evaluation of the weaknesses of the business and how the company plans to deal with these and other business problems
9. **Financial plan** Summary of the investment needed, forecasts of sales, cash-flow forecasts, breakeven analysis, estimated balance sheet, and sources of funding
10. **Appendix** Supplementary information such as market research results, copies of leases, and supplier price lists

Source: Adapted from Robert D. Hisrich and Michael P. Peters, *Entrepreneurship*, 3rd ed. (Homewood, Ill.:BPI/Irwin, 1995), pp. 119–127.

Using the Internet

So How Do You Write a Good Business Plan?

The Internet is a great source of information for learning how to write a proper business plan. The Small Business Administration, for example, provides a selection of links to sites with samples of good business plan writing and suggestions for entrepreneurs to consider. You can connect to these links at **http://www.sba.gov/hotlist/bplan.html.**

have the time to wade through pages of extraneous data. The business plan should answer the four questions banking officials and investors are most interested in: (1) What exactly is the nature and mission of the new venture? (2) Why is this new enterprise a good idea? (3) What are the businessperson's goals? (4) How much will the new venture cost?

The great amount of time and consideration that should go into creating a business plan will probably end up saving time later. For example, Sharon Burch, who was running a computer software business while earning a degree in business administration, had to write a business plan as part of one course. Burch has said, "I wish I'd taken the class before I started my business. I see a lot of things I could have done differently. But it has helped me since I've been using the business plan as a guide for my business."[16]

Accuracy and realistic expectations are crucial to an effective business plan. It is unethical to deceive loan officers, and it is unwise to deceive yourself.

LEARNING OBJECTIVE

5 Explain how the Small Business Administration helps small businesses.

The Small Business Administration

Small Business Administration (SBA) a governmental agency that assists, counsels, and protects the interests of small businesses in the United States

The **Small Business Administration (SBA)**, created by Congress in 1953, is a governmental agency that assists, counsels, and protects the interests of small businesses in the United States. It helps people get into business and stay in business. The agency provides assistance to owners and managers of prospective, new, and established small businesses. Through more than one hundred offices throughout the nation, the SBA provides both financial assistance and management counseling. It helps small firms bid for and obtain government contracts, and it helps them prepare to enter foreign markets.

SBA Management Assistance

Statistics show that most failures in small business are related to poor management. For this reason, the SBA places special emphasis on improving the management ability of the owners and managers of small businesses. The SBA's Management Assistance Program is extensive and diversified. It includes free individual counseling, courses, conferences, workshops, and a wide range of publications. Recently the SBA provided management and technical assistance to nearly 850,000 small businesses through its 950 Small Business Development Centers and 11,500 volunteers from the Service Corps of Retired Executives.[17]

Management Courses and Workshops The management courses offered by the SBA cover all the functions, duties, and roles of managers. Instructors may be teachers from local colleges and universities or other professionals, such as management consultants, bankers, lawyers, and accountants. Fees for these courses are quite low. The most popular such course is a general survey of eight to ten different areas of business management. In follow-up studies, businesspeople may concentrate in depth on one or more of these areas, depending on their particular strengths and weaknesses. The SBA occasionally offers one-day conferences. These conferences are aimed at keeping owner-managers up-to-date on new management developments, tax laws, and the like.

The SBA also invites prospective owners of small businesses to workshops at which management problems and good management practices are discussed. A major goal of these sessions is to emphasize the need for sufficient preparation before starting a new venture. Sometimes the sessions convince eager but poorly prepared entrepreneurs to slow down and wait until they are ready for the difficulties that lie ahead.

Service Corps of Retired Executives (SCORE) a group of retired businesspeople who volunteer their services to small businesses through the SBA

SCORE The **Service Corps of Retired Executives (SCORE)** is a group of 11,500 retired businesspeople who volunteer their services to small businesses through the SBA. The collective experience of SCORE volunteers spans the full range of American enterprise. These volunteers have worked for such notable companies as Eastman Kodak, General Electric, IBM, and Procter & Gamble. Experts in areas of accounting, finance, marketing, engineering, and retailing provide counseling and mentoring to entrepreneurs.

A small-business owner who has a particular problem can request free counseling from SCORE. An assigned counselor visits the owner in his or her establishment and, through careful observation, analyzes the business situation and the problem. If the problem is complex, the counselor may call on other volunteer experts to assist. Finally, the counselor offers a plan for solving the problem and helping the owner through the critical period.

Scoring with SCORE. A SCORE volunteer advises a young couple about their business. Any small business owner can request free counseling from retired businesspeople who volunteer their services through the SBA.

Consider the plight of Elizabeth Halvorsen, a mystery writer from Minneapolis. Her husband had built up the family advertising and graphic arts firm for seventeen years when he was called in 1991 to serve in the Persian Gulf War. The only one left behind who could run the business was Mrs. Halvorsen, who admittedly had no business experience. Enter SCORE. With a SCORE management expert at her side, she kept the business on track.[18]

Help for Minority-Owned Small Businesses Americans who are members of minority groups have had difficulty entering the nation's economic mainstream. Raising money is a nagging problem for minority business owners, who may also lack adequate training. Members of minority groups are, of course, eligible for all SBA programs, but the SBA makes a special effort to assist those who want to start small businesses or expand existing ones. For example, the Minority Business Development Agency awards grants to develop and increase business opportunities for members of racial and ethnic minorities.

Helping women become entrepreneurs is also a special goal of the SBA. Emily Harrington, one of nine children, who was born in Manila, the Philippines. She arrived in the United States in 1972 as a foreign exchange student. Convinced that there was a market for hard-working, dedicated minorities and women, she launched Qualified Resources, Inc. *Inc.* magazine selected her firm as one of "America's Fastest Growing Private Companies" just six years later. Harrington credits the U.S. Small Business Administration for giving her the technical support that made her first loan possible. Finding a SCORE counselor who worked directly with her, she refined her business plan until she got a bank loan. Before contacting the SBA, Harrington was turned down for business loans "by all the banks I approached," even though she worked as a manager of loan credit and collection for a bank. Now, Emily Harrington is SBA's Year 2000 winner of the local, regional, and national Small Business Entrepreneurial Success Award for Rhode Island, the New England region, and the nation! For several years in a row, QRI was named one of the fastest-growing private companies in Rhode Island. Harrington's annual revenue was nearly $10 million in 1999.

Small Business Institute (SBI) a group of senior and graduate students in business administration who provide management counseling to small businesses

Small Business Institutes A **Small Business Institute (SBI)** is a group of senior and graduate students in business administration who provide management counseling to small businesses. SBIs have been organized on almost 520 college campuses as another way to help business owners. The students work in small groups guided by faculty advisers and SBA management-assistance experts. Like SCORE volunteers, they analyze and help solve the problems of small-business owners at their business establishments.

Small Business Development Center (SBDC) university-based group that provides individual counseling and practical training to owners of small businesses

Small Business Development Centers A **Small Business Development Center (SBDC)** is a university-based group that provides individual counseling and practical training to owners of small businesses. SBDCs draw from the resources of local, state, and federal governments; private business; and universities. These groups can provide managerial and technical help, data from research studies, and other types of specialized assistance of value to small businesses. In 1997 there were over 1000 SBDCs, located primarily at colleges and universities. Recently, SBDCs provided services to more that 600,000 small businesses that created 93,000 jobs, and generated $98 billion in sales and $584 million in tax revenues.[19]

SBA Publications The SBA issues management, marketing, and technical publications dealing with hundreds of topics of interest to present and prospective managers of small firms. Most of these publications are available from the SBA free of charge. Others can be obtained for a small fee from the U.S. Government Printing Office.

SBA Financial Assistance

Small businesses seem to be constantly in need of money. An owner may have enough capital to start and operate the business. But then he or she may require more money to finance increased operations during peak selling seasons, to pay for required pollution-control equipment, to mop up after a natural disaster such as a flood, or to finance an expansion. The SBA offers special financial-assistance programs that cover all these situations. However, its primary financial function is to guarantee loans to eligible businesses.

Regular Business Loans Most of the SBA's business loans are actually made by private lenders such as banks, but repayment is partially guaranteed by the agency. That is, the SBA may guarantee that it will repay the lender up to 90 percent of the loan if the borrowing firm cannot repay it. Guaranteed loans may be as large as $750,000. The average size of an SBA-guaranteed business loan is $208,000 and its average duration is about eight years.

Small Business Investment Companies **Venture capital** is money that is invested in small (and sometimes struggling) firms that have the potential to become very successful. In many cases, only a lack of capital keeps these firms from rapid and solid growth. The people who invest in such firms expect that their investments will grow with the firms and become quite profitable.

venture capital money that is invested in small (and sometimes struggling) firms that have the potential to become very successful

The popularity of these investments has increased over the past fifteen years, but most small firms still have difficulty in obtaining venture capital. To help such businesses, the SBA licenses, regulates, and provides financial assistance to Small Business Investment Companies. A **Small Business Investment Company (SBIC)** is a privately owned firm that provides venture capital to small enterprises that meet its investment standards. SBICs are intended to be profit-making organizations. The aid the SBA offers allows them to invest in small businesses that would not otherwise attract venture capital.

Small Business Investment Company (SBIC) privately owned firm that provides venture capital to small enterprises that meet its investment standards

We have discussed the importance of the small-business segment of our economy. We have weighed the advantages and drawbacks of operating a small business as compared with a large one. But is there a way to achieve the best of both worlds? Can one preserve one's independence as a business owner and still enjoy some of the benefits of "bigness"? Let's take a close look at franchising.

LEARNING OBJECTIVE

6 Appraise the concept and types of franchising.

Franchising

A **franchise** is a license to operate an individually owned business as if it were part of a chain of outlets or stores. Often the business itself is also called a franchise. Among the most familiar franchises are McDonald's, H & R Block, AAMCO Transmissions, GNC (General Nutrition Centers), and Dairy Queen. Many other franchises carry familiar names; this method of doing business has become very popular in the last thirty years or so. It is an attractive means of starting and operating a small business.

franchise a license to operate an individually owned business as though it were part of a chain of outlets or stores

What Is Franchising?

Franchising is the actual granting of a franchise. A **franchisor** is an individual or organization granting a franchise. A **franchisee** is a person or organization purchasing a franchise. The franchisor supplies a known and advertised business name, management skills, the required training and materials, and a method of doing business. The franchisee supplies labor and capital, operates the franchised business, and agrees to abide by the provisions of the franchise agreement. Table 6.4 lists some items that would be covered in a typical franchise agreement.

franchising the actual granting of a franchise

franchisor an individual or organization granting a franchise

franchisee a person or organization purchasing a franchise

Types of Franchising Arrangements

Franchising arrangements fall into three general categories. In the first approach, a manufacturer authorizes a number of retail stores to sell a certain brand name item. This franchising arrangement, one of the oldest, is prevalent in sales of passenger cars

table 6.4 McDonald's Conventional Franchise Agreement as of April 2000

McDonald's (Franchisor) Provides	Individual (Franchisee) Supplies
1. Nationally recognized trademarks and an established reputation for quality	1. Total investment of approximately $432,800 to $715,150, which includes initial franchise fee of $45,000
2. Designs and color schemes for restaurants, signs, and equipment	2. Approximate cash requirement of 25 to 40 percent of total investment
3. Specifications for certain food products	3. A minimum of 4 percent of gross sales annually for marketing and advertising
4. Proven methods of inventory and operations control	4. Payment of a service fee of 4 percent of monthly gross sales to McDonald's
5. Bookkeeping, accounting, and policies manuals specially geared toward a franchised restaurant	5. Payment of a variable rent percent of monthly gross sales to McDonald's based on McDonald's investment and/or sales
6. A franchise term of up to 20 years	6. Kitchen equipment, seating, decor, lighting, and signs in conformity with McDonald's standards (included in total investment figure)
7. Formal training program completed on a part-time basis in approximately 18-24 months in a McDonald's restaurant	7. Taxes, insurance, and maintenance costs on the restaurant building and land
8. Five weeks of classroom training, including two weeks at Hamburger University	8. Commitment to assuring high-quality standards and upholding McDonald's reputation
9. Ongoing regional support services and field service staff	
10. Research and development of labor-saving equipment and methods	
11. Monthly bulletins, periodicals, or meetings to inform franchisees about management and marketing techniques	
12. Site selection (purchase or lease) and development, including building	

Source: *"McDonald's Conventional Franchise Agreement as of April 2000," from McDonald's Franchising*, McDonald's Corporation, Oak Brook, IL, April 27, 2000. Used with permission from McDonald's Corporation.

and trucks, farm equipment, shoes, paint, earth-moving equipment, and petroleum. About 90 percent of all gasoline is sold through franchised, independent, retail service stations, and franchised dealers handle virtually all sales of new cars and trucks. In the second type of franchising arrangement, a producer licenses distributors to sell a given product to retailers. This arrangement is common in the soft-drink industry. Most national manufacturers of soft-drink syrups—the Coca-Cola Company, Dr. Pepper/Seven-Up Companies, Pepsico, Royal Crown Companies, Inc.—franchise independent bottlers who then serve retailers. In a third form of franchising, a franchisor supplies brand names, techniques, or other services instead of a complete product. Although the franchisor may provide certain production and distribution services, its primary role is the careful development and control of marketing strategies. This approach to franchising, which is the most typical today, is used by Holiday Inns, the Howard Johnson Company, AAMCO Transmissions, McDonald's, Dairy Queen, Avis, the Hertz Corporation, KFC (Kentucky Fried Chicken), and SUBWAY, to name but a few.

The Growth of Franchising

LEARNING OBJECTIVE

7 Analyze the growth of franchising and franchising's advantages and disadvantages.

Franchising, which began in the United States around the time of the Civil War, was originally used by large firms, such as the Singer Sewing Company, to distribute their products. Franchising has been steadily increasing in popularity since the early 1900s, primarily for filling stations and car dealerships; however, this retailing strategy has experienced enormous growth since the mid-1970s. The franchise proliferation has generally paralleled the expansion of the fast-food industry. As Table 6.5 on page 173 shows, three of *Entrepreneur* magazine's top-rated franchises for 2000 were in this category.

spotLight

Buying a franchise

The average investment in a franchise, including fees and additional expenses, is $143,260. The cost including fees, expenses, etc., is. . .

Less than $100,000	43%
More than $100,000	41%
Don't know/ no answer	14%

Source: Copyright 2000, USA TODAY. Reprinted with permission.

Of course, franchising is not limited to fast foods. Hair salons, tanning parlors, and dentists and lawyers are expected to participate in franchising arrangements in growing numbers. Franchised health clubs, pest exterminators, and campgrounds are already widespread, as are franchised tax preparers and travel agencies. The real estate industry has also experienced a rapid increase in franchising.

Also, women-owned franchises are growing. For example, in 1994 the LubePro oil change service licensed its first female-owned franchise. Franchisors like Precision Tune and Creative Colors International are starting a trend toward courting female franchisees in traditionally male-oriented businesses.[20]

"Dual-branded" franchises, in which two franchisors offer their products together, are a new small-business trend. For example, pleased with the success of sixty-six restaurants that carry both Carl's Jr. and Green Burrito brands, franchisors CKE Restaurants and GB Foods will open at least sixty more dual-branded units in each of the next four years.[21] Also, an agreement between franchisors Doctor's Associates, Inc., and TCBY Enterprises Inc., now allows franchisees to sell SUBWAY sandwiches and TCBY yogurt in the same establishment.

Are Franchises Successful?

Franchising is designed to provide a tested formula for success, along with ongoing advice and training. The success rate for businesses owned and operated by franchisees is significantly higher than the success rate for other independently owned small businesses. In a recent nationwide Gallup poll of 944 franchise owners, 94 percent of franchisees indicated they were very or somewhat successful, only 5 percent believed they were very unsuccessful or somewhat unsuccessful, and 1 percent did not know.[22]

Despite these impressive statistics, franchising is not a guarantee of success for either franchisees or franchisors. Too rapid expansion, inadequate capital or management skills, and a host of other problems can cause failure for both franchisee and franchisor. Thus, for example, the Dizzy Dean's Beef and Burger franchise is no longer in business.

table 6.5 *Entrepreneur's* Top Ten Franchises in 2000

1999 Rank	Franchisor	Minimum Start-up	Franchising Since
1	McDonald's	$433,800–$1,400,000	1955
2	SUBWAY	$66,200–$175,000	1974
3	Jackson Hewitt Tax Service	$49,400–$74,900	1986
4	7-Eleven Convenience Stores	$12,500 + (Varies)	1964
5	Jiffy Lube Int'l Inc.	$174,000–$194,000	1979
6	Snap-On Tools	$121,500–$209,000	1991
7	Mail Box Etc.	$117,500–$199,200	1980
8	Radio Shack	$59,300	1968
9	Sonic Drive-in Restaurants	$530,800–$672,800	1959
10	GNC Franchising Inc.	$125,000–$268,700	1988

Source: "The Top Ten Franchises for 2000," *Entrepreneur*, January 2000, pp. 195–245.

adapting to change

Supporting Diversity in Franchising

FRANCHISING IS ATTRACTING MORE women and minority business owners in the United States than ever before. One reason is continued economic growth. which provides more financing options for entrepreneurs seeking to buy franchises. Another reason is that special outreach programs designed to encourage franchisee diversity have developed. Franchisors such as Wendy's, McDonald's, Burger King, and Church's Chicken all have special corporate programs to attract minority and women franchisees. Just as important, successful women and minority franchisees are willing to get involved by offering advice and guidance to new franchisees.

Herman Petty, the first black McDonald's franchisee, remembers that the company provided a great deal of help while he worked to establish his first units. In turn, Petty traveled to help other black franchisees, and he invited new franchisees to gain hands-on experience in his Chicago restaurants before starting their own establishments. Petty also organized a support group, the National Black McDonald's Operators Association, to help black franchisees in other areas. Today, this support group has 33 local chapters and more than 330 members across the country. "We are really concentrating on helping our operators to be successful both operationally and financially," says Craig Welburn, the McDonald's franchisee who leads the group.

Eyeing the boom in women entrepreneurs, Church's Chicken has launched a major initiative to attract more women franchisees. "If we want women to view restaurant franchising as a real and exciting opportunity, it is up to us to educate them about every aspect of franchise ownership, from skill requirements and marketing support to opportunities for creativity and community involvement," says president Hala Moddelmog. As a result, she spearheaded the company's Professional Mentoring Program to provide in-person and online mentoring for women interested in restaurant franchising. "I see the mentoring program as a safety net, so to speak, an opportunity for new entrepreneurs to work with existing women franchisees who know the benefits and pitfalls," Moddelmog explains. She adds that "the idea of a mentor, a peer who wants you to succeed, can be a great motivator."

Advantages of Franchising

Franchising plays a vital role in our economy and may soon become the dominant form of retailing. Why? Because franchising offers advantages to both the franchisor and the franchisee.

To the Franchisor The franchisor gains fast and well-controlled distribution of its products without incurring the high cost of constructing and operating its own outlets. The franchisor thus has more capital available to expand production and to use for advertising. At the same time, it can ensure, through the franchise agreement, that outlets are maintained and operated according to its own standards.

The franchisor also benefits from the fact that the franchisee—a sole proprietor in most cases—is likely to be very highly motivated to succeed. The success of the franchise means more sales, which translate into higher royalties for the franchisor.

To the Franchisee The franchisee gets the opportunity to start a business with limited capital and to make use of the business experience of others. Moreover, an outlet with a nationally advertised name, such as Radio Shack, McDonald's, or Century 21 Real Estate, has guaranteed customers as soon as it opens.

If business problems arise, the franchisor gives the franchisee guidance and advice. This counseling is primarily responsible for the very high degree of success enjoyed by franchises. In most cases, the franchisee does not pay for such help.

The franchisee also receives materials to use in local advertising and can take part in national promotional campaigns sponsored by the franchisor. McDonald's and its franchisees, for example, constitute one of the nation's top twenty purchasers of advertising. Finally, the franchisee may be able to minimize the cost of advertising, supplies, and various business necessities by purchasing them in cooperation with other franchisees.

Disadvantages of Franchising

Franchising flexibility. SUBWAY continues to grow by encouraging franchisees to match their products to the needs of each market. Even though submarine sandwiches, salads, chips, and soft drinks always top the menu, Subway management recognizes that tastes and customs vary from country to country. That's why franchisees such as this one in Jerusalem are allowed to use their creativity in adding menu items suited to local tastes.

The main disadvantage of franchising affects the franchisee, and it arises because the franchisor retains a great deal of control. The franchisor's contract can dictate every aspect of the business: decor, design of employee uniforms, types of signs, and all the details of business operations. All Burger King french fries taste the same because all Burger King franchisees have to make them the same way.

Contract disputes are the cause of many lawsuits. For example, in 1994 nine 7-Eleven franchisees filed a lawsuit against their franchisor; the Southland Corporation, alleging violation of franchise agreements. The franchisees charged that Southland failed to advertise, remodel stores, and provide other support services.[23] In 1997 Rekha Gabhawala, a Dunkin' Donuts franchisee in Milwaukee, alleged that the franchisor was forcing her out of business so that the company could profit by reselling the downtown franchise to someone else; the company, on the other hand, alleged that Gabhawala breached the contract by not running the business according to company standards.[24] Other franchisees claim that contracts are unfairly tilted toward the franchisors. Yet others have charged that they lost their franchise and investment because their franchisor would not approve the sale of the business when they found a buyer.

To arbitrate disputes between franchisors and franchisees, the National Franchise Mediation Program was established in 1993 by thirty member firms, including Burger King Corporation, McDonald's Corporation, and Wendy's International Inc. Negotiators have since resolved numerous cases through mediation. In 1997 Carl's Jr. brought in one of its largest franchisees to help set its system straight, making most franchisees happy for the first time in years. The program also helped Pepsico settle a long-term contract dispute and renegotiate its franchise agreements.[25]

Because disagreements between franchisors and franchisees have increased in recent years, many franchisees have been demanding government regulation of franchising. In 1997, to avoid government regulation, some of the largest franchisors proposed a new self-policing plan to the Federal Trade Commission.

Franchise holders pay for their security, usually with a one-time franchise fee and continuing royalty and advertising fees, collected as a percentage of sales. As Table 6.4 shows, a McDonald's franchisee pays an initial franchise fee of $45,000, an annual fee of 4 percent of gross sales (for advertising), and a monthly fee of 4 percent of gross sales. In Table 6.5 you can see how much money a franchisee needs to start a new franchise for selected organizations. In some fields, franchise agreements are not uniform: one franchisee may pay more than another for the same services.

Even success can cause problems. Sometimes a franchise is so successful that the franchisor opens its own outlet nearby, in direct competition—although franchisees may fight back. For example, a court recently ruled that Burger King could not enter into direct competition with the franchisee because the contract was not specific on the issue.[26] A spokesperson for one franchisor contends that the company "gives no geographical protection" to its franchise holders and thus is free to move in on them. Thus, in a 1994 Taco Bell case, the court ruled that the language of the contract specifically gave the franchisor permission to enter into competition with its own Taco Bell franchisee.[27]

Franchise operators work hard. They often put in ten- and twelve-hour days, six days a week. The International Franchise Association advises prospective franchise purchasers to investigate before investing and to approach buying a franchise cautiously. Franchises vary widely in approach as well as in products. Some, like Dunkin' Donuts and Baskin-Robbins, demand long hours. Others, like Great Clips hair salons and Albert's Family Restaurants, are more appropriate for those who don't want to spend many hours at their stores.

Global Perspectives in Small Business

For small American businesses, the world is becoming smaller. National and international economies are growing more and more interdependent as political leadership and national economic directions change and trade barriers diminish or disappear. Globalization plus instant worldwide communications are rapidly shrinking distances at the same time they are expanding business opportunities. According to a recent Arthur Andersen study, the Internet is increasingly important to small business strategic thinking with more than 50 percent of those surveyed indicating that the Internet represented their most favored strategy for growth—a 17 percent increase from the year before. This was more than double the next favored choice, strategic alliances reflecting the opportunity to reach both global as well as domestic customers.[28]

The Small Business Administration offers help to the nation's small-business owners who want to enter the world markets. The SBA's efforts include counseling small firms on how and where to market overseas, matching U.S. small-business executives with potential overseas customers, and helping exporters secure financing. The agency brings small U.S. firms into direct contact with potential overseas buyers and partners.

International trade will become more important to small-business owners as they face unique challenges in the new century. Small businesses, which are expected to remain the dominant form of organization in this country, must be prepared to adapt to significant demographic and economic changes in the world marketplace.

This chapter ends our discussion of American business today. From here on, we shall be looking closely at various aspects of business operations. We begin, in the next chapter, with a discussion of management—what management is, what managers do, and how they work to coordinate the basic economic resources within a business organization.

RETURN TO Inside Business

LAVONNE LUQUIS STARTED LATINOLINK as a community-building web site for Hispanic people in the United States. Although the site initially resembled a magazine, with news and articles, it quickly evolved into Latino.com, a comprehensive Internet portal for the Latino community. In addition to news stories written by staff members and articles drawn from outside publications, the site invites audience interaction through free e-mail, online chat, and daily polls about timely subjects. Latino.com now attracts more than 400,000 visitors every month, with most coming back to the site at least once a week.

Luquis spends her work day deciding which news stories to post on the site, talking with advertisers about the audience, and dealing with crises, such as the night the site's computer equipment crashed. Despite the ups and downs of running a growing business, she says that without the available technology of the Internet, "I truly believe I wouldn't have my own company." As Latino.com continues to attract a larger audience and more advertisers, Luquis sees even more community-minded expansion in the future: "We intend to be a cultural town square reflecting the common interests and rich heterogeneity of the Latino community," she says.

Questions

1. Why do you think Lavonne Luquis would be unable to have her own company if the Internet didn't exist?
2. As a small business owner operating in the dynamic Internet environment, what advantages do you think Luquis has when battling larger competitors?

chapter Review

SUMMARY

1 Define what a small business is and recognize the fields in which small businesses are concentrated.

A small business is one that is independently owned and operated for profit and is not dominant in its field. There are about 23 million businesses in this country, and more than 90 percent of them are small businesses. Small businesses employ more than one-half of the nation's work force, even though about 70 percent of new businesses can be expected to fail within five years. More than half of all small businesses are in retailing and services.

2 Identify the people who start small businesses and the reasons why some succeed and many fail.

Such personal characteristics as independence, desire to create a new enterprise, and willingness to accept a challenge may encourage individuals to start small businesses. Various external circumstances, such as special expertise or even the loss of a job, can also supply the motivation to strike out on one's own. Poor planning and lack of capital and management experience are the major causes of small business failure.

3 Assess the contributions of small businesses to our economy.

Small businesses have been responsible for a wide variety of inventions and innovations, some of which have given rise to new industries. Historically, small businesses have created the bulk of the nation's new jobs. Further, they have mounted effective competition to larger firms. They provide things that society needs, act as suppliers to larger firms, and serve as customers of other businesses, both large and small.

4 Judge the advantages and disadvantages of operating a small business.

The advantages of smallness in business include the opportunity to establish personal relationships with customers and employees, the ability to adapt to changes quickly, independence, and simplified recordkeeping. The major disadvantages are the high risk of failure, the limited potential for growth, and limited ability to raise capital.

5 Explain how the Small Business Administration helps small businesses.

The Small Business Administration was created in 1953 to assist and counsel the nation's millions of small-business owners. The SBA offers management courses and workshops; managerial help, including one-to-one counseling through SCORE and ACE; various publications; and financial assistance through guaranteed loans and SBICs. It places special emphasis on aid to minority-owned businesses, including those owned by women.

6 Appraise the concept and types of franchising.

A franchise is a license to operate an individually owned business as though it were part of a chain. The franchisor provides a known business name, management skills, a method of doing business, and the training and required materials. The franchisee contributes labor and capital, operates the franchised business, and agrees to abide by the provisions of the franchise agreement. There are three major categories of franchise agreements.

7 Analyze the growth of franchising and franchising's advantages and disadvantages.

Franchising has grown tremendously since the mid-1970s. The franchisor's major advantage in franchising is fast and well-controlled distribution of products, with minimal capital outlay. In return, the franchisee has the opportunity to open a business with limited capital, to make use of the business experience of others, and to sell to an existing clientele. For this, the franchisee must usually pay both an initial franchise fee and a continuing royalty based on sales. He or she must also follow the dictates of the franchise with regard to operation of the business.

Worldwide business opportunities are expanding for small businesses. The Small Business Administration assists small-business owners in penetrating foreign markets. The next century will present unique challenges and opportunities for small-business owners.

KEY TERMS

You should now be able to define and give an example relevant to each of the following terms:

small business (157)
business plan (167)
Small Business Administration (SBA) (168)
Service Corps of Retired Executives (SCORE) (169)
Small Business Institute (SBI) (170)
Small Business Development Center (SBDC) (170)
venture capital (171)
Small Business Investment Company (SBIC) (171)
franchise (171)
franchising (171)
franchisor (171)
franchisee (171)

REVIEW QUESTIONS

1. What information would you need to determine whether a particular business is small according to SBA guidelines?
2. Which two areas of business generally attract the most small businesses? Why are these areas attractive to small business?
3. Distinguish among service industries, distribution industries, and production industries.
4. What kinds of factors encourage certain people to start new businesses?
5. What are the major causes of small-business failure? Do these causes also apply to larger businesses?
6. Briefly describe four contributions of small business to the American economy.
7. What are the major advantages and disadvantages of smallness in business?
8. What are the major components of a business plan? Why should an individual develop a business plan?
9. Identify five ways in which the SBA provides management assistance to small businesses.
10. Identify two ways in which the SBA provides financial assistance to small businesses.
11. Why does the SBA concentrate on providing management and financial assistance to small businesses?
12. What is venture capital? How does the SBA help small businesses obtain it?
13. Explain the relationships among a franchise, the franchisor, and the franchisee.
14. What does the franchisor receive in a franchising agreement? What does the franchisee receive? What does each provide?
15. Cite one major benefit of franchising for the franchisor. Cite one major benefit of franchising for the franchisee.

DISCUSSION QUESTIONS

1. Most people who start small businesses are aware of the high failure rate and the reasons for it. Why, then, do some take no steps to protect their firms from failure? What steps should they take?
2. Are the so-called advantages of small business really advantages? Wouldn't every small-business owner like his or her business to grow into a large firm?
3. Do average citizens benefit from the activities of the SBA, or is the SBA just another way to spend our tax money?
4. Would you rather own your own business independently or become a franchisee? Why?

VIDEO CASE

Entrepreneurial Spirit Is Firm Foundation for Pelzel Construction

As the founder and CEO of an extremely successful, high-profile construction company in Austin, Texas, Mary Guerrero-Pelzel has built her small business from the ground up. She started out handling finances and scheduling for a general contractor. When she told the owner that she wanted to work in the field rather than remain in the office, he responded, "A woman can't do that." This response certainly didn't stop Pelzel. She quickly decided to harness her entrepreneurial drive to stop working for that contractor and establish her own company, Pelzel Construction. Since 1982, Pelzel has been her own boss, going into the field to supervise construction projects and to motivate staff and subcontractors to work as a team.

Pelzel Construction's first assignment was to build a two-story, 12,000-square-foot executive office building in Austin, working with a budget of nearly $1 million. "By the time I had finished that, I had $1.8 million under construction," says Pelzel, looking back. Her tenacity, dedication to quality, and attention to detail helped her win more and more projects. She also worked hard to earn the trust of her subcontractors by paying them as promised. And being a woman in a traditionally male-dominated industry brought her added visibility.

Not long after Pelzel started her business, an economic downturn slowed local construction spending. Pelzel reacted with flexibility, keeping her company afloat by learning to diversify into other types of projects. Over the years, she has sought out construction work on a wide variety of projects, including residential housing, office buildings, warehouse facilities, schools, fire stations, and churches. As her company developed a reputation in the construction industry, Pelzel was able to bid successfully on contracts for even larger municipal projects, including the construction of the Aus-Tex Printing and Mailing building—a $2.7 million construction project—and work on the local convention center—a $1.4 million construction project.

One of Pelzel's largest and most visible projects was an $11 million contract to build the west runway at the Austin-Bergstrom International Airport, which opened in 1999. With twenty-five gates, the new airport covers more than 4,100 acres and serves many more air travelers than the current airport. Although the city of Austin maintains official goals for hiring minority and women contractors on municipal construction projects, Pelzel Construction was relatively small and therefore had little chance of being awarded such an immense contract on its own. To win the contract, Pelzel teamed up with Hensel Phelps Construction and formed the Pelzel/Phelps joint venture, received certification as a minority joint venture, and entered the winning bid on the runway project.

When Pelzel takes off her hard hat after a long day on the job, she is active in industry groups and in the community. She served as the first woman president of a trade association covering thirteen counties in central Texas, and she was the first woman to head Austin's Construction Advisory Committee. Her entrepreneurial efforts have been recognized by the Hispanic Chamber of Commerce, which named her "Businesswoman of the Year" in 1992. In addition, *Hispanic* magazine and NationsBank (now Bank of America) honored Pelzel with an Adelante Award in 1996, citing her leadership, her business success, and her contributions to the community. Working from the ground up, Pelzel has built a construction business that is poised for even more success and prominence in the years ahead.[29]

Questions

1. In light of Pelzel's success, would it be a good idea for her to franchise her name and methods? Explain your answer.
2. This chapter cites five advantages of small business. Which of these seem to apply to Pelzel Construction?
3. This chapter cites three disadvantages of small business. Which of these is likely to be the biggest problem for Pelzel in the coming years?

Building skills for career success

1. Exploring the Internet

Perhaps the most challenging difficulty for small businesses is operating with scarce resources, especially people and money. To provide information and point small-business operators in the right direction, many Internet sites offer helpful products and services. Although most are sponsored by advertising and may be free of charge, some charge a fee, and others are a combination of both. The Small Business Administration within the U.S. Department of Commerce provides a wide array of free information and resources. You can find your way to the SBA through:

http://www.sbaonline.sba.gov
http://www.sba.gov

Visit the text web site for updates to this exercise.

Assignment

1. Describe the various services provided by the SBA site.
2. What sources of funding are there?
3. What service would you like to see improved? How?

2. Developing Critical Thinking Skills

Small businesses play a vital role in our economy. They not only contribute to technological innovation and to the creation of many new jobs; they also ensure that customers have an alternative to the products and services offered by large firms. In addition, by making parts for large firms at a cost lower than the large firms could make the parts themselves, they help keep the lid on consumer prices. Regardless of our need for them, many small businesses fail within their first five years. Why is this so?

Assignment

1. Identify several successful small businesses in your community.
2. Identify one small business that has failed.
3. Gather enough information about these businesses to answer the following questions:
   a. What role do small businesses play in your community?
   b. Why are they important?
   c. Why did the business fail?
   d. What was the most important reason for its failure?
   e. How might the business have survived?
4. Summarize what you have learned about the impact of small businesses on your community. Give the summary to your instructor.

3. Building Team Skills

A business plan is a written statement that documents the nature of a business and how that business intends to achieve its goals. Although entrepreneurs should prepare a business plan *before* starting a business, the plan also serves as an effective guide later on. The plan should concisely describe the business's mission, the amount of capital it requires, its target market, competition, resources, and production plan, marketing plan, organizational plan, assessment of risk, and financial plan.

Assignment

1. Working in a team of four students, identify a company in your community that would benefit from using a business plan, or create a scenario in which a hypothetical entrepreneur wants to start a business.
2. Using the resources of the library or the Internet and/or interviews with business owners, write a business plan incorporating the information in Table 6.3
3. Present your business plan to the class.

4. Researching Different Careers

Many people dream of opening and operating their own businesses. Are you one of them? To be successful, entrepreneurs must have certain characteristics; their profiles generally differ from those of people who work for someone else. Do you know which personal characteristics make some entrepreneurs succeed and others fail? Do you fit the successful entrepreneur's profile? What is your potential for opening and operating a successful small business?

Assignment

1. Use the resources of the library or the Internet to establish what a successful entrepreneur's profile is and to determine whether your personal characteristics fit that profile. Internet addresses that can help you are:

   http://www.smartbiz.com/sbs/arts/ieb1.html
   http://www.sba.gov. See Starting Your Business and FAQ's (Frequently Asked Questions)

   These sites have quizzes online that can help you assess your personal characteristics. The Small Business Administration also has helpful brochures.
2. Interview several small business owners. Ask them to describe the characteristics they think are necessary for being a successful entrepreneur.
3. Using your findings, write a report that includes the following:
   a. A profile of a successful small-business owner
   b. A comparison of your personal characteristics with the profile of the successful entrepreneur
   c. A discussion of your potential as a successful small-business owner

5. Improving Communication Skills

Franchising is a method of doing business that has grown steadily in popularity since the early 1900s. It offers entrepreneurs who want to start a business certain opportunities and advantages. If you started a business, would a franchise be an option?

Assignment:

1. Choose a franchise business in your community, preferably one of those listed in Table 6.5.
2. Investigate the business by interviewing the franchise owner. Ask the following questions:
   a. Why did you decide to open a franchise business?
   b. What are the advantages or disadvantages of having a franchise agreement over opening a new business or buying an existing business?
   c. When you were deciding whether to become a franchisee, what were some of your major concerns? What type of research did you do?
   d. What key things does the franchisor provide for you? What are your obligations to the franchisor?
   e. What advice would you give a person who was thinking about becoming a franchisee?
3. Write a two-page report summarizing the information you have gathered.

Awards.com: A Company That Deserves an Award!

The Stanley Cup, the Oscar, and the Olympic gold medal are some of the most famous awards in sports and entertainment. But it is the millions of awards and trophies that ordinary individuals receive in recognition of some achievement that is the heart of the $7 billion-a-year awards industry. For every sports achievement, every business accomplishment, or every team success, there is typically an award or a trophy. Just think for a moment and remember the time you received a trophy for winning the school spelling bee or for participating in Little League. There's a pretty good chance that your trophy came from a small retail business. Until recently, that's the way trophies were sold—by small retailers that served the needs of people who live in local communities.

Now Awards.com, an online resource for more than 2,500 awards and recognition products, is trying to change an entire industry dominated by small brick and mortar operations often referred to as mom and pop retailers. The company is an Internet company and sells not only trophies and plaques, but all kinds of recognition items ranging from pencils to clothing to lead crystal. Because Awards.com carries a large variety of awards, trophies, and medals, it can provide delivery within two days. The company can also process customized orders quickly because of its "trophy builder application" software program that allows customers to put together any number of combinations of colors, materials, and styles to create a personalized award. To make its merchandise even more appealing, it has partnered with three major sports leagues that allow for the use of team logos from major baseball, soccer, and hockey teams on trophies and awards sold by Awards.com. By contrast, most of its competitors offer limited choices because they carry small inventories. And if you want to customize any trophy or award purchased from a local retailer, you usually have to wait at least two weeks for your delivery.

Start-Up: The Right Environment and Good Decisions

Today, Awards.com is taking advantage of the current upsurge of retailers selling merchandise online. Giga Information Group, Inc. of Cambridge, Massachusetts projects that there will be 2.2 million small businesses operating over the Internet by 2002, up from 385,000 in 1999. The increase in the number of Internet firms will create larger online sales revenue says well-known research firm Forrester Inc., also of Cambridge, Massachusetts. It believes online retail sales will reach $184 billion by 2004. But to turn impressive statistics into reality, the founders of Awards.com, Michael Hamilton and Warren Struhl, knew that they would need vision, skills, and financial backing to reach millions of potential customers through the Internet.

From the start, Hamilton and Struhl were careful to make the right decisions that would ensure that their company would be positioned to compete against the mom and pop operations. Financing was obtained from investors who could see how a corporation like Awards.com could become the dominant player in the awards and recognition industry. Then a corporate name had to be chosen. Consider the name that was finally chosen—Awards.com. This name is definitely a plus because customers who want to purchase an award online don't have to think very hard when they see the www.awards.com web address. Just by looking at the name, potential customers can figure out what type of business this is and what type of products the company sells. It is also very easy to remember for customers who want to return to the web site.

Hamilton and Struhl also knew that the Awards.com web site would have to be easy to use and provide more than just a picture of a trophy or recognition award. To keep customers from leaving its web site, designers and computer programmers worked hard to make the pages on the Awards.com web site visually appealing, easy to navigate, interesting, and informative. For instance, there are hot buttons that allow customers to view information about motivation, employee morale, how to give an award, and the importance of recognition. There's even an "Awards Advisor" section that begins, "We're here to help you inspire someone."

For Awards.com, one of the ironies of life was that a company that sells trophies and awards to recognize others had to toot its own horn. To attract customers, Awards.com launched an aggressive $10 million marketing campaign that mailed catalogs featuring over 750 products to a large target audience and almost 200,000 "mini catalogs" to baseball, softball, and soccer coaches. Additionally, the company placed print ads in national magazines such as *Forbes* and *Business Week*.

Setting an Example

In some ways Awards.com is a Cinderella story. The company is an excellent example of how entrepreneurs with a vision can compete and win in an industry typically dominated by small mom and pop operations. And yet, for Hamilton and Struhl, managing Awards.com is more than just a way to become the world's next dot-com zillionaire. This is one company that really practices what it preaches. It is quick to recognize the work that others perform to make the world a better place. In 2000, Awards.com bestowed its 'HERO' award twice. The first HERO award was given to Dr. Leonard Green on behalf of the Corporate Angel Network (CAN), for his nineteen years of providing terminally ill patients with air transportation to different treatment hospitals. The second HERO award was given to WorldByNet.com—a multilingual software company that provided the transportation needed to bring a Polish infant named Kamil Suska to Houston, Texas. Once in Houston, doctors operated on little Kamil's severe birth defect. According to Hamilton, "we applaud the concern and the compassion shown by WorldByNET.com for Kamil. It is our goal to promote recognition and reward in all walks of life, and we feel that the entire World-ByNet.com team exemplifies the values that the HERO Award stands for."

Questions

1. You are a Little League soccer coach. The kids on your team expect trophies at the end of the season. Would you purchase trophies from Awards.com or would you use a smaller, local retailer? Explain your answer.
2. Michael Hamilton and Warren Struhl chose to incorporate their business. Why do you think they chose the corporate form of ownership?
3. Today, Awards.com sells over 2,500 different items, which makes it the largest online one-stop shop for awards and motivational and promotional merchandise. What factors have led to this dot-com's success?

Management and organization

part III

This part of the book deals with the organization—the "thing" that is a business. We begin with a discussion of the management functions involved in developing and operating a business. Then we analyze the organization itself, to see what makes it tick. Next we put the two together, to examine the part of a business that is directly concerned with manufacturing finished products.

7 Understanding the Management Process

Suddenly they had a company to run—and the cofounders realized that their passion for the Internet and their entrepreneurial instincts weren't enough to guide Yahoo! through the growing pains of the coming years.

LEARNING OBJECTIVES

1 Define what management is.

2 Describe the four basic management functions: planning, organizing, leading and motivating, and controlling.

3 Distinguish among the various kinds of managers, in terms of both level and area of management.

4 Identify the key management skills and the managerial roles.

5 Explain the different types of leadership.

6 Discuss the steps in the managerial decision-making process.

7 Describe how organizations benefit from total quality management.

8 Summarize what it takes to become a successful manager today.

inside Business

Managing World Wide Web Growth at Yahoo!

When Jerry Yang and David Filo starting compiling and posting a list of favorite web sites at the dawn of the Internet age, they never imagined that Yahoo! (http://www.yahoo.com) would quickly develop into one of the world's most successful e-businesses. At the time, the two were working on Ph.D. degrees at Stanford University. However, they wound up spending more time on their web directory than on their studies. Soon their directory contained so many links—and was attracting so many visitors—that the university's computer system could barely keep up with the traffic. This was the first clue that their hobby could become a real business.

The second clue came when corporate dealmakers and venture capitalists heard about the ever-growing list and tracked down Filo and Yang to talk about the directory's future. This strong interest convinced the two to write a business plan, incorporate under the Yahoo! name, hire their first employee (who helped with the business plan), and obtain $1 million in venture capital funding to get underway.

Suddenly they had a company to run—and the cofounders realized that their passion for the Internet and their entrepreneurial instincts weren't enough to guide Yahoo! through the growing pains of the coming years. Searching for a seasoned, professional manager, they signed high-tech veteran Timothy Koogle as CEO to take the lead in planning and organizing the new firm. The three began prioritizing business activities and creating a flat organization to foster open communication among the rapidly-expanding employee ranks.

Since hiring Koogle, Filo and Yang have both assumed the title of Chief Yahoo but play very different roles in the company. Filo uses his technical skills to oversee technological advances at Yahoo!. In contrast, Yang uses his conceptual and interpersonal skills to serve as "everything from technical visionary to chief strategist to corporate spokesman and cheerleader to Washington lobbyist to the company's conscience," according to John Hennessy, Stanford University's provost.

Despite competitive pressures, the cofounders and the CEO have been able to steer the company through successive years of profitable growth. Yet they have the insight to realize that motivating the staff doesn't mean pushing everyone to the limit all the time. "It's our responsibility—not just Dave and me, but all of the management team—to know when to push harder, and when to be realistic and pull back," Jerry Yang says. This is the kind of managerial know-how that keeps Yahoo! at the forefront of Internet businesses.[1]

The challenges at Yahoo! are proof that management can be one of the most exciting and rewarding professions available today. Managers of both small and large firms play an important part in shaping the world we live in. Depending on its size, a firm may employ a number of specialized managers who are responsible for particular areas of management, such as marketing, finance, and operations. That same organization also includes managers at several levels within the firm. For a company like Yahoo!, what is important is not the number of managers it employs but the ability of these managers to achieve the organization's goals. As you will see in this chapter, today's managers wear many hats and perform a variety of different jobs.

In this chapter, we define *management* and describe the four basic management functions of planning, organizing, leading and motivating, and controlling. Then we focus on the types of managers with respect to levels of responsibility and areas of expertise. Next we focus on the skills of effective managers and the different roles managers must play. We examine several styles of leadership and explore the process by which managers make decisions. We also describe how total quality management can improve customer satisfaction. We conclude the chapter with a discussion of what it takes to be a successful manager today.

What Is Management?

LEARNING OBJECTIVE

1 Define what management is.

management the process of coordinating people and other resources to achieve the goals of the organization

Management is the process of coordinating people and other resources to achieve the goals of the organization. As we saw in Chapter 1, most organizations make use of four kinds of resources: material, human, financial, and informational (see Figure 7.1).

Material resources are the tangible, physical resources an organization uses. For example, General Motors uses steel, glass, and fiberglass to produce cars and trucks on complex machine-driven assembly lines. A college or university uses books, classroom buildings, desks, and computers to educate students. And the Mayo Clinic uses beds, operating room equipment, and diagnostic machines to provide health care.

Perhaps the most important resources of any organization are its *human resources*—people. In fact, some firms live by the philosophy that their employees are their most important assets. One such firm is Southwest Airlines. Southwest treats its employees with the same respect and attention that it gives its passengers. Southwest selectively seeks employees with upbeat attitudes and promotes from within its own ranks 80 percent of the time. And when it's time for making decisions, everyone who will be affected is encouraged to get involved in the process. In an industry in which deregulation, extreme price competition, and fluctuating fuel costs have eliminated several major competitors Southwest keeps on growing and making a profit because of its valuable employees.

Financial resources are the funds the organization uses to meet its obligations to investors and creditors. A 7-Eleven convenience store obtains money from customers

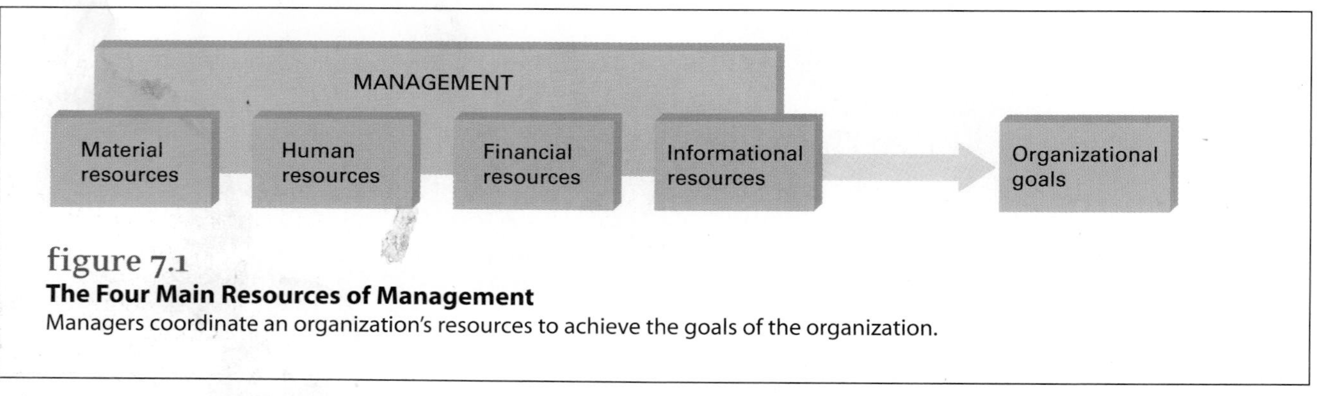

figure 7.1
The Four Main Resources of Management
Managers coordinate an organization's resources to achieve the goals of the organization.

at the check-out counters and uses a portion of that money to pay its suppliers. Citicorp, a large New York bank, borrows and lends money. Your college obtains money in the form of tuition, income from its endowments, and state and federal grants. It uses the money to pay utility bills, insurance premiums, and professors' salaries.

Finally, many organizations increasingly find they cannot afford to ignore *information*. External environmental conditions—including the economy, consumer markets, technology, politics, and cultural forces—are all changing so rapidly that a business that does not adapt will probably not survive. And, to adapt to change, the business must know what is changing and how it is changing. Most companies gather information about their competitors to increase their knowledge about changes in their particular industries and learn from other companies' failures and successes.

It is important to realize that the four types of resources described above are only general categories of resources. Within each category are hundreds or thousands of more specific resources. It is this complex mix of specific resources—and not simply "some of each" of the four general categories—that managers must coordinate to produce goods and services.

Another interesting way to look at management is in terms of the different functions managers perform. These functions have been identified as planning, organizing, leading and motivating employees, and controlling. We look at each of these management functions in the next section.

Basic Management Functions

LEARNING OBJECTIVE

2 Describe the four basic management functions: planning, organizing, leading and motivating, and controlling

Gordon Bethune, a high school dropout who went on to become an airplane mechanic, took control of down-and-out Continental Airlines in 1994. When he arrived he found a disjointed operation that had caused Continental to rank last in almost every Department of Transportation performance measure, such as on-time performance, lost baggage, and cancelled flights. Using a combination of clever incentives and discussions with many employees, Bethune changed the attitude and actions of workers, including the baggage handlers and gate agents. Today, as the fifth largest U.S. airline, 50,000 employees work together to board 140,000 travellers onto 502 airplanes, making 2,172 flights every day, and these Continental employees look happy while doing their work. By using many highly effective management skills, Bethune has dramatically turned Continental into a well-run, profitable, and congenial organization.[2]

Management functions like those described above do not occur according to some rigid, preset timetable. Managers don't plan in January, organize in February, lead and motivate in March, and control in April. At any given time, managers may engage in a number of functions simultaneously. However, each function tends to lead naturally to others. Figure 7.2 provides a visual framework for a more detailed discussion of the four basic management functions. How well managers perform these key functions determines whether a business is successful.

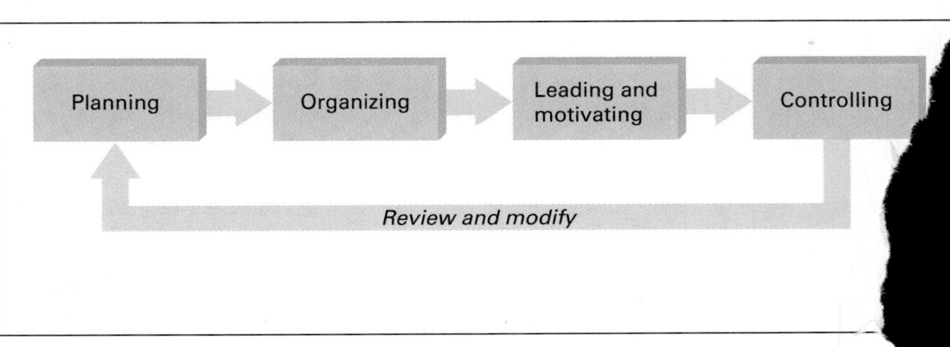

Understanding management functions. Continental Airlines Chairman and CEO Gordon Bethune understands not only basic management functions, but also how to integrate these functions—planning, organizing, leading, and controlling—to improve Continental Airlines' revenues and profits and to win customer satisfaction awards. Here he presents the model for a new airport concourse that Continental should finish building in 2002.

Planning

Planning, in its simplest form, is establishing organizational goals and deciding how to accomplish them. It is often referred to as the "first" management function because all other management functions depend on planning. Organizations like Nissan, Houston Community Colleges, and the U.S. Secret Service begin the planning process by developing a mission statement.

An organization's **mission** is a statement of the basic purpose that makes this organization different from others. Yellow Freight Systems' mission statement is: "Pick it up on time, deliver it on time, and don't bust it."[3] Houston Community College System's mission is to provide an education for local citizens. The mission of the Secret Service is to protect the life of the president. Once an organization's mission has been described in a mission statement, the next step is to develop organizational goals and objectives, usually through strategic planning. **Strategic planning** is the process of establishing an organization's major goals and objectives and allocating the resources to achieve them.

tablishing organiza-
eciding how to

the basic
niza-

Establishing Goals and Objectives

A **goal** is an end result that the organization is expected to achieve over a one-to-ten-year period. For example, GM's goal for its subsidiary, General Motors Retail Holdings, is to buy 5 to 10 percent of its franchised dealerships over the next ten years.[4] An **objective** is a specific statement detailing what the organization intends to accomplish over a shorter period of time. Compared with goals, objectives have a much narrower time frame—usually one year or less. Compaq, for example, set an objective of selling 60 percent of its business PC's direct to business customers (instead of through resellers) within a single year.[5]

Goals and objectives can deal with a variety of factors, such as sales, company growth, costs, customer satisfaction, and employee morale. Whereas a small manufacturer may focus primarily on sales objectives for the next six months, Exxon Corporation may be more interested in goals for the year 2005. Finally, goals are set at every level of the organization. Every member of the organization—the president of the company, the head of a department, and an operating employee at the lowest level—has a set of goals he or she hopes to achieve.

The goals developed for these different levels must be consistent with one another.
owever, it is likely that some conflict will arise. A production department, for example,
ay have a goal of minimizing costs. One way to do this is to produce only one type of
oduct and offer "no frills." Marketing, on the other hand, may have a goal of maxi-
ing sales. And one way to implement this goal is to offer prospective customers a
range of products with many options. As part of his or her own goal setting, the
ger who is ultimately responsible for *both* departments must achieve some sort of
e between conflicting goals. This balancing process is called *optimization*.
he optimization of conflicting goals requires insight and ability. Faced with the
ting-versus-production conflict just described, most managers would probably
opt either viewpoint completely. Instead, they might decide on a reasonably

Setting tasty organizational goals. Some of Ben & Jerry's goals focus on using ingredients that have not been directly or indirectly treated with chemicals. This goal is so important to both the company and its customers that it is stated directly on the product's label.

diverse product line offering only the most widely sought-after options. Such a compromise would seem to be best for the organization as a whole.

Establishing Plans to Accomplish Goals and Objectives

Once goals and objectives have been set for the organization, managers must develop plans for achieving them. A **plan** is an outline of the actions by which the organization intends to accomplish its goals and objectives. Just as it has different goals and objectives, the organization also develops several types of plans.

plan an outline of the actions by which the organization intends to accomplish its goals and objectives

strategy an organization's broadest set of plans, developed as a guide for major policy setting and decision making

An organization's **strategy** is its broadest set of plans, developed as a guide for major policy setting and decision making. These plans are set by the board of directors and top management and are generally designed to achieve the long-term goals of the organization. Thus, a firm's strategy defines what business the company is in or wants to be in and the kind of company it is or wants to be. When the U.S. Surgeon General issued a report linking smoking and cancer, top management at Philip Morris Companies recognized that the company's very survival was being threatened. Executives needed to develop a strategy to diversify into nontobacco products.

The Internet has introduced new challenges to traditional strategic thinking that have worked well for a long time. For example, reluctant to move from a face-to-face sales approach to a less personal web site approach, Allstate is now taking what some consider small, catch-up steps by creating an Internet presence to support their established salesforce and channels. Firms like eCoverage.com with exclusive web-based strategies are expected to take a big share of the estimated $4 billion Internet insurance sales market.[6]

In addition to strategies, most organizations also employ several narrower kinds of plans. A **tactical plan** is a smaller-scale plan developed to implement a strategy. Most tactical plans cover a one-to-three-year period. If a strategic plan will take five years to complete, the firm may develop five tactical plans, one covering each year. Tactical plans may be updated periodically as conditions and experience dictate. Their more limited scope permits them to be changed more easily than strategies. In an attempt to fulfill its strategy of diversification, Philip Morris developed individual tactical plans to purchase several nontobacco-related companies such as General Foods, Kraft Foods, and Miller Brewing.

tactical plan a smaller-scale plan developed to implement a strategy

An **operational plan** is a type of plan designed to implement tactical plans. Operational plans are usually established for one year or less and deal with how to accomplish the organization's specific objectives. Assume that after Philip Morris purchased Kraft Foods, managers adopted the objective of increasing sales of Kraft's Cheez Whiz by 5 percent the first year. A sales increase of this size does not just happen, however. Management must develop an operational plan that describes certain activities the firm can undertake over the next year to bring about the increased sales. Specific components of the Kraft Cheez Whiz operational plan might include newspaper and television advertising, reduced prices, and coupon offers—all designed to increase consumer sales.

operational plan a type of plan designed to implement tactical plans

Regardless of how hard managers try, sometimes business activities don't go as planned. Today most corporations also develop contingency plans along with strategies, tactical plans, and operational plans. A **contingency plan** is a plan that outlines alternative courses of action that may be taken if the organization's other plans are disrupted or become ineffective. Remember that one reason for Philip Morris's purchase of Kraft was

contingency plan a plan that outlines alternative courses of action that may be taken if the organization's other plans are disrupted or become ineffective

to diversify into nontobacco products. If it became impossible to purchase Kraft, Philip Morris could fall back on contingency plans to purchase other nontobacco companies.

Organizing the Enterprise

organizing the grouping of resources and activities to accomplish some end result in an efficient and effective manner

leading the process of influencing people to work toward a common goal

motivating the process of providing reasons for people to work in the best interests of the organization

directing the combined processes of leading and motivating

controlling the process of evaluating and regulating ongoing activities to ensure that goals are achieved

After goal setting and planning, the second major function of the manager is organization. **Organizing** is the grouping of resources and activities to accomplish some end result in an efficient and effective manner. Consider the case of an inventor who creates a new product and goes into business to sell it. At first, she will probably do everything herself—purchase raw materials, make the product, advertise it, sell it, and keep her business records up-to-date. Eventually, as business grows, she will find that she needs help. To begin with, she might hire a professional sales representative and a part-time bookkeeper. Later she might need to hire full-time sales staff, other people to assist with production, and an accountant. As she hires new personnel, she must decide what each person will do, to whom that person will report, and generally how that person can best take part in the organization's activities. We discuss these and other facets of the organizing function in much more detail in the next chapter.

Leading and Motivating

The leading and motivating function is concerned with the human resources within the organization. Specifically, **leading** is the process of influencing people to work toward a common goal. **Motivating** is the process of providing reasons for people to work in the best interests of the organization. Together, leading and motivating are often referred to as **directing.**

We have already noted the importance of an organization's human resources. Because of this importance, leading and motivating are critical activities. Obviously, different people do things for different reasons—that is, they have different *motivations*. Some are primarily interested in earning as much money as they can. Others may be spurred on by opportunities to get ahead in an organization. Part of the manager's job, then, is to determine what factors motivate workers and to try to provide those incentives in ways that encourage effective performance.

Quite a bit of research has been done on both motivation and leadership. As you will see in Chapter 11, research on motivation has yielded very useful information. Research on leadership has been less successful. In spite of decades of study, no one has discovered a general set of personal traits or characteristics that makes a good leader. Later in this chapter, we discuss leadership in more detail.

Motivating employees. Some organizations provide recreational facilities such as this one to create a satisfying work environment. Employees who are physically fit and who enjoy competing in sports together are likely to be effective team players at work as well.

Controlling Ongoing Activities

Controlling is the process of evaluating and regulating ongoing activities to ensure that goals are achieved. To see how controlling works, consider a rocket launched by NASA to place a satellite in orbit. Do NASA personnel simply fire the rocket and then

Exploring Business

What Companies Look for in a Leader

COMPANIES KNOW THAT THE MOST IMPORTANT leadership qualities don't show up on a résumé. So what are they looking for in a leader? One key characteristic is the ability to empower rather than order employees to do their jobs. General Electric's Jack Welch, a very successful CEO, was famous for pushing empowerment deep into the organization. He made GE a nimble and responsive global competitor by allowing managers and employees, not just top executives, to decide how to solve problems and achieve objectives.

Effective empowerment depends on the leader and the employees building mutual respect, trust, and commitment. This suggests a second key characteristic of leadership: the ability to communicate by fostering an ongoing dialogue rather than issuing mandates. For example, Richard Branson, CEO of London-based Virgin Group, reads and responds to every message he receives from employees. Whether he's on the road visiting business facilities or hosting his yearly company-wide party, Branson listens carefully to gripes as well as ideas. This kind of open communication has helped Branson fix problems—and jump on opportunities such as starting a mobile-phone unit.

A third key quality of leadership is the ability to inspire employees by articulating a compelling vision. Larry Ellison, CEO of Oracle, is known for making bold statements about where his software company should be headed. Excited by Ellison's ideas, employees at all levels enthusiastically dive into uncharted waters—giving Oracle a head start in young but promising markets such as e-commerce. "We decided five years ago to bet the ranch on the Internet," he recently observed, "and it looks like a good bet."

Clearly, leaders require the ability to empower, communicate, and inspire. But they also must have the technical, conceptual, and interpersonal skills needed to be effective managers in any organization.

check back in a few days to find out whether the satellite is in place? Of course not. The rocket is constantly monitored, and its course is regulated and adjusted as needed to get the satellite to its destination.

The control function includes three steps (see Figure 7.3). The first is *setting standards* with which performance can be compared. The second is *measuring actual performance* and comparing it with the standard. And the third is *taking corrective action* as necessary. Notice that the control function is circular in nature. The steps in the

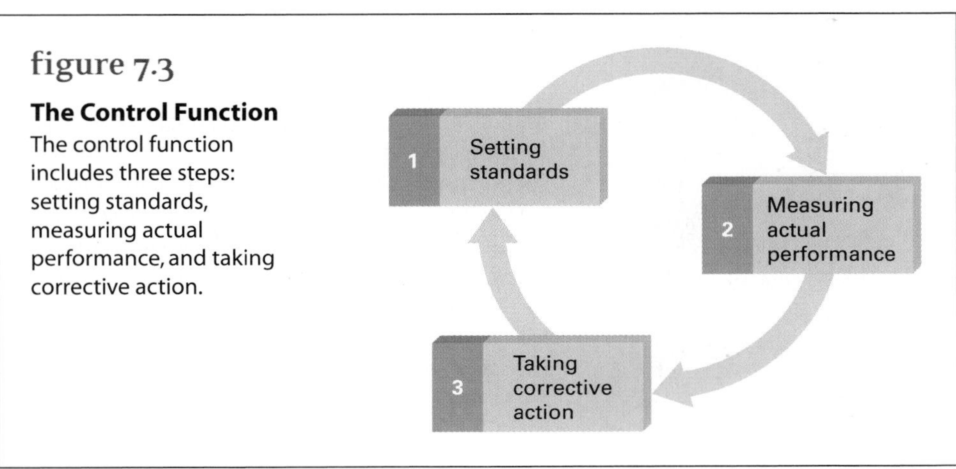

figure 7.3

The Control Function

The control function includes three steps: setting standards, measuring actual performance, and taking corrective action.

control function must be repeated periodically until the goal is achieved. For example, suppose that United Airlines establishes a goal of increasing its profit by 12 percent next year. To ensure that this goal is reached, United's management might monitor its profit on a monthly basis. After three months, if profit has increased by 3 percent, management might be able to assume that plans are going according to schedule. Probably no action will be taken. However, if profit has increased by only 1 percent after three months, some corrective action would be needed to get the firm on track. The particular action that is required depends on the reason for the small increase in profit.

Kinds of Managers

LEARNING OBJECTIVE

3 Distinguish among the various kinds of managers, in terms of both level and area of management.

Managers can be classified in two ways: according to their level within the organization, and according to their area of management. In this section, we use both perspectives to explore the various types of managers.

Levels of Management

For the moment, think of an organization as a three-story structure (as illustrated in Figure 7.4). Each story corresponds to one of the three general levels of management: top managers, middle managers, and first-line managers.

top manager an upper-level executive who guides and controls the overall fortunes of the organization

middle manager a manager who implements the strategy and major policies developed by top management

first-line manager a manager who coordinates and supervises the activities of operating employees

Top Managers

A **top manager** is an upper-level executive who guides and controls the overall fortunes of the organization. Top managers constitute a small group. In terms of planning, they are generally responsible for developing the organization's mission. They also determine the firm's strategy. It takes years of hard work, long hours, and perseverance, as well as talent and no small share of good luck, to reach the ranks of top management in large companies. Common job titles associated with top managers are president, vice president, chief executive officer (CEO), and chief operating officer (COO).

Middle Managers

Middle management probably comprises the largest group of managers in most organizations. A **middle manager** is a manager who implements the strategy developed by top managers. Middle managers develop tactical plans and operational plans, and they coordinate and supervise the activities of first-line managers. For example, Alan Lacy, President of Services Operation at Sears, Roebuck and Company and a member of the corporate office of the chief executive, heads the renewed online efforts to make Sears "the premier clicks-and-mortar retailer in America."[7] Titles at the middle-management level include division manager, department head, plant manager, and operations manager.

spotLight

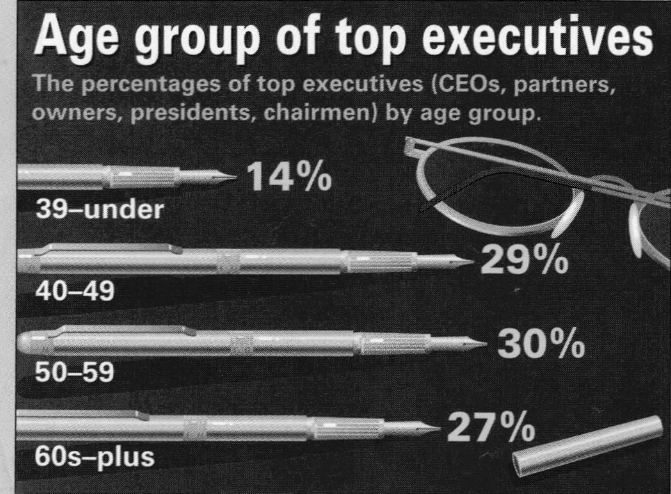

Source: Copyright 2000, USA TODAY. Reprinted with permission.

First-Line Managers

A **first-line manager** is a manager who coordinates and supervises the activities of operating employees. First-line managers spend most of their time working with and motivating their employees, answering questions, and solving day-to-day problems. Most first-line managers are former operating employees who, owing to their hard work and potential, were promoted into management. Many of today's middle and top managers began their careers on this first management level. Common titles for first-line managers include office manager, supervisor, and foreman.

figure 7.4

Management Levels Found in Most Companies

The coordinated effort of all three levels of managers is required to implement the goals of any company.

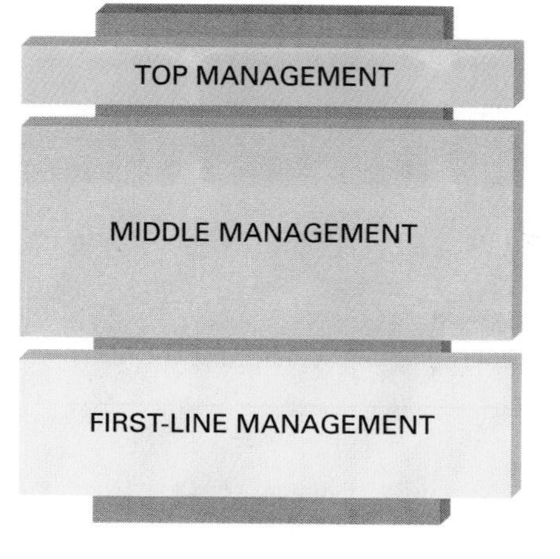

Areas of Management

Organizational structure can also be divided into areas of management specialization (see Figure 7.5). The most common areas are finance, operations, marketing, human resources, and administration. Depending on its mission, goals, and objectives, an organization may include other areas as well—research and development, for example.

Financial Managers A **financial manager** is primarily responsible for the organization's financial resources. Accounting and investment are specialized areas within financial management. Because financing affects the operation of the entire firm, many of the CEOs and presidents of this country's largest companies are people who got their "basic training" as financial managers.

financial manager a manager who is primarily responsible for the organization's financial resources

Examining Ethics

How Much Is Too Much for Ceo Pay?

HOW MUCH IS TOO MUCH FOR EXECUTIVE compensation and incentives? When a company is doing well, stakeholders rarely complain about top managers' compensation packages. Look at Cisco Systems, which makes servers and other equipment for Internet operations. Because Cisco's sales and profits have been solid, CEO John Chambers' total yearly pay of $121.7 million–among the healthiest pay packages in the United States–hasn't raised many eyebrows.

But what about high CEO pay for a company with flagging fortunes? Consider William Farley's compensation package as CEO of apparel-maker Fruit of the Loom. From 1996 to 1998, Farley took home more than $40 million in salary, bonuses, and stock options–even though the company lost more than $100 million during the same period. In addition, the company loaned Farley $103 million from 1994 through 1999. Meanwhile, Fruit of the Loom was having major financial problems. In 1999, it announced losses of $576 million, then filed for bankruptcy just months after forcing Farley out as CEO. Should Farley have been earning and borrowing so much while his firm was in trouble?

Stephen Hilbert, CEO of the financial services firm Conseco, has also been criticized for taking hefty loans while his company struggled. Hilbert had enlarged the company through a series of acquisitions of health-care insurers and finance companies. Along the way, he borrowed $178 million from the company to buy its stock. But cash became tight and Conseco faltered, sending the stock price tumbling. The company loaned Hilbert another $23 million so he could avoid having to sell his Conseco shares. After Hilbert left in early 2000, he paid back the $23 million from the $72.5 million severance package he received. But should he have been able to borrow so much and get such a huge severance package when Conseco was not doing well?

Issues to Consider

1. Is a CEO's job more difficult when a company is in trouble? Do you think a CEO deserves a larger compensation package during such periods?
2. What should the role of the board of directors be in evaluating financial incentives for a company's top executives? Should other stakeholders have a say in this decision?

figure 7.5

Areas of Management Specialization

Other areas may have to be added, depending on the nature of the firm and the industry.

operations manager a manager who manages the systems that convert resources into goods and services

marketing manager a manager who is responsible for facilitating the exchange of products between the organization and its customers or clients

human resources manager a person charged with managing the organization's human resources programs

administrative manager a manager who is not associated with any specific functional area but who provides overall administrative guidance and leadership

Operations Managers An **operations manager** manages the systems that convert resources into goods and services. Traditionally, operations management has been equated with manufacturing—the production of goods. However, in recent years many of the techniques and procedures of operations management have been applied to the production of services and to a variety of nonbusiness activities. Like financial management, operations management has produced a large percentage of today's company CEOs and presidents.

Marketing Managers A **marketing manager** is responsible for facilitating the exchange of products between the organization and its customers or clients. Specific areas within marketing are marketing research, product management, advertising, promotion, sales, and distribution. A sizable number of today's company presidents have risen from the ranks of marketing management.

Human Resources Managers A **human resources manager** is charged with managing the organization's human resources programs. He or she engages in human resources planning; designs systems for hiring, training, and evaluating the performance of employees; and ensures that the organization follows government regulations concerning employment practices. Some human resources managers are making effective use of technology. For example, over 7,500 companies post job openings on jobs.com which attracts about two million visitors monthly.[8]

Administrative Managers An **administrative manager** (also called a *general manager*) is not associated with any specific functional area but provides overall administrative guidance and leadership. A hospital administrator is an example of an administrative manager. He or she does not specialize in operations, finance, marketing, or human resources management but instead coordinates the activities of specialized managers in all these areas. In many respects, most top managers are really administrative managers.

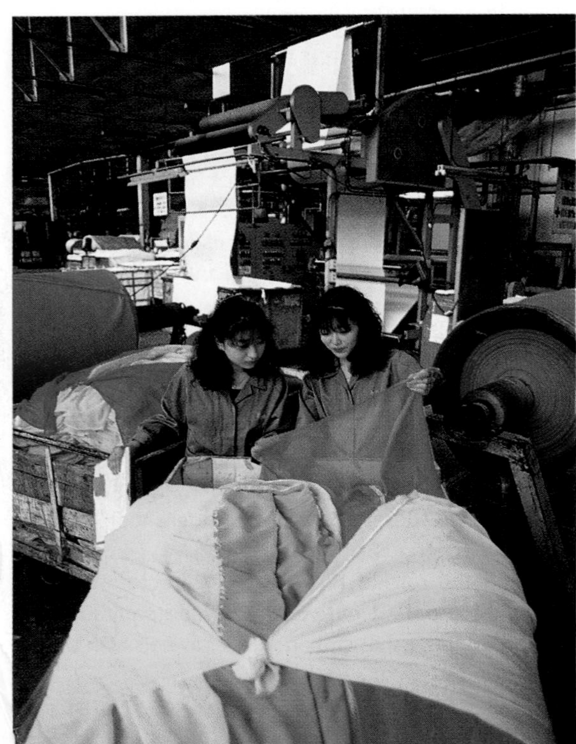

Operations management can be beautiful. These operations managers at a textile mill in Kyoto, Japan, examine production output to assess the accuracy of their production processes. If they find flaws in the fabric, they will have to determine when in the production process they occurred and then make the necessary adjustments to improve quality.

Whatever their level in the organization and whatever area they specialize in, successful managers generally exhibit certain key skills and are able to play certain managerial roles. But, as we shall see, some skills are likely to be more critical at one level of management than at another.

What Makes Effective Managers?

LEARNING OBJECTIVE

4 Identify the key management skills and the managerial roles.

In general, effective managers are those who (1) possess certain important skills and (2) are able to use these skills in a number of managerial roles. Probably no manager is called on to use any particular skill *constantly* or to play a particular role *all the time.* However, these skills and abilities must be available when they are needed.

Key Management Skills

The skills that typify effective managers tend to fall into three general categories: technical, conceptual, and interpersonal.

technical skill a specific skill needed to accomplish a specialized activity

Technical Skills

A **technical skill** is a specific skill needed to accomplish a specialized activity. For example, the skills engineers and machinists need to do their jobs are technical skills. First-line managers (and, to a lesser extent, middle managers) need the technical skills relevant to the activities they manage. Although these managers may not have to perform the technical tasks themselves, they must be able to train subordinates, answer questions, and otherwise provide guidance and direction. A first-line manager in the accounting department for the Hyatt Corporation, for example, must be able to perform computerized accounting transactions *and* be able to help employees complete the same accounting task. In general, top managers do not rely on technical skills as heavily as do managers at other levels. Still, understanding the technical side of a business is an aid to effective management at every level.

conceptual skill the ability to think in abstract terms

Conceptual Skills

Conceptual skill is the ability to think in abstract terms. Conceptual skill allows the manager to see the "big picture" and to understand how the various parts of an organization or an idea can fit together. These skills are useful in a wide range of situations, including the optimization of goals described earlier. They are usually more useful for top managers than for middle or first-line managers.

interpersonal skill the ability to deal effectively with other people

Interpersonal Skills

An **interpersonal skill** is the ability to deal effectively with other people, both inside and outside the organization. Examples of interpersonal skills are the ability to relate to people, understand their needs and motives, and show genuine compassion. One reason why Mary Kay Ash, founder of Mary Kay Cosmetics, has been so successful is her ability to motivate her employees and to inspire their loyalty and devotion to her vision for the firm. And although it is obvious that a CEO like Mary Kay Ash must be able to work with employees throughout the organization, what is not so obvious is that middle and first-line managers must also possess interpersonal skills. For example, a first-line manager on an assembly line at Procter & Gamble must rely on employees to manufacture Tide laundry detergent. The better the manager's interpersonal skills, the more likely the manager will be able to lead and motivate those employees. When all other things are equal, the manager able to exhibit these skills will be more successful than the arrogant and brash manager who doesn't care about others.

Managerial Roles

Research suggests that managers must, from time to time, act in ten different roles if they are to be successful.[9] (By *role* we mean a set of expectations that one is expected to fulfill.) These ten roles can be grouped into three broad categories: decisional, interpersonal, and informational.

spotLight

Source: Copyright 2000, USA TODAY. Reprinted with permission.

decisional role a role that involves various aspects of management decision making

Decisional Roles As you might suspect, a **decisional role** is one that involves various aspects of management decision making. The decisional role can be subdivided into the following four specific managerial roles. In the role of *entrepreneur*, the manager is the voluntary initiator of change. For example, a manager for Coca-Cola who develops a new strategy or expands the sales force into a new market is playing the entrepreneur's role. A second role is that of *disturbance handler*. A manager who settles a strike is handling a disturbance. Third, the manager also occasionally plays the role of *resource allocator*. In this role, the manager might have to decide which departmental budgets to cut and which expenditure requests to approve. The fourth role is that of *negotiator*. Being a negotiator might involve settling a dispute between a manager and a worker assigned to the manager's work group.

interpersonal role a role in which the manager deals with people

Interpersonal Roles Dealing with people is an integral part of the manager's job. An **interpersonal role** is one in which the manager deals with people. Like the decisional role, the interpersonal role can be broken down according to three managerial functions. The manager may be called on to serve as a *figurehead*, perhaps by attending a ribbon-cutting ceremony or taking an important client to dinner. The manager may also have to play the role of *liaison* by serving as a go-between for two different groups. As a liaison, a manager might represent his or her firm at meetings of an industrywide trade organization. Finally, the manager often has to serve as a *leader*. Playing the role of leader includes being an example for others in the organization as well as developing the skills, abilities, and motivation of employees.

informational role a role in which the manager either gathers or provides information

Informational Roles An **informational role** is one in which the manager either gathers or provides information. The informational role can be subdivided as follows. In the role of *monitor*, the manager actively seeks information that may be of value to the organization. For example, a manager who hears about a good business opportunity is engaging in the role of monitor. The second informational role is that of *disseminator*. In this role, the manager transmits key information to those who can use it. As a disseminator, the manager who heard about the good business opportunity would tell the appropriate marketing manager about it. The third informational role is that of *spokesperson*. In this role, the manager provides information to people outside the organization, such as the press, television reporters, and the public.

LEARNING OBJECTIVE

5 Explain the different types of leadership.

Leadership

leadership the ability to influence others

Leadership has been broadly defined as the ability to influence others. A leader has power and can use it to affect the behavior of others. Leadership is different from management in that a leader strives for voluntary cooperation, whereas a manager may have to depend on coercion to change employee behavior.

Formal and Informal Leadership

Some experts make a distinction between formal leadership and informal leadership. Formal leaders have legitimate power of position; that is, they have *authority* within an organization to influence others to work for the organization's objectives. Informal leaders usually have no such authority and may or may not exert their influence in support of the organization. Both formal and informal leaders make use of several kinds of power, including the ability to grant rewards or impose punishments, the possession of expert knowledge, and personal attraction or charisma. Informal leaders who identify with the organization's goals are a valuable asset to any organization. On the other hand, a business can be brought to its knees by informal leaders who turn work groups against management.

Styles of Leadership

Which leadership style works best? Highly effective General Electric CEO Jack Welch was known for his use of the authoritarian leadership style. However, other companies can be just as successful with laissez-faire or democratic leaders in the top position.

For many years, leadership was viewed as a combination of personality traits, such as self-confidence, concern for people, intelligence, and dependability. Achieving a consensus on which traits were most important was difficult, however, and attention turned to styles of leadership behavior. In the last few decades, several styles of leadership have been identified: authoritarian, laissez-faire, and democratic.[10] The **authoritarian leader** holds all authority and responsibility, with communication usually moving from top to bottom. This leader assigns workers to specific tasks and expects orderly, precise results. The leaders at United Parcel Service employ authoritarian leadership. At the other extreme is the **laissez-faire leader,** who gives authority to employees. With the laissez-faire style, subordinates are allowed to work as they choose with a minimum of interference. Communication flows horizontally among group members. Leaders at Apple Computer are known to employ a laissez-faire leadership style in order to give employees as much freedom as possible to develop new products. The **democratic leader** holds final responsibility but also delegates authority to others, who participate in determining work assignments. In this leadership style, communication is active both upward and downward. Employee commitment is high because of participation in the decision-making process. Managers for both Wal-Mart and Saturn have used the democratic leadership style to encourage employees to become more than just rank-and-file workers.

authoritarian leader one who holds all authority and responsibility, with communication usually moving from top to bottom

laissez-faire leader one who gives authority to employees and allows subordinates to work as they choose with a minimum of interference; communication flows horizontally among group members

democratic leader one who holds final responsibility but also delegates authority to others, who help determine work assignments; communication is active upward and downward

Which Managerial Leadership Style Is Best?

Today most management experts agree that no one "best" managerial leadership style exists. Each of the styles described above—authoritarian, laissez-faire, and democratic—has advantages and disadvantages. For example, democratic leadership can motivate employees to work effectively because they are implementing *their own* decisions. On the other hand, the decision-making process associated with democratic leadership takes time that subordinates could otherwise be devoting to the work itself.

Although hundreds of research studies have been conducted to prove which leadership style is best, there are still no definite conclusions. The "best" leadership seems to occur when the leader's style matches the situation. Actually, each of the three leadership styles can be effective in the right situation. The style that is *most* effective depends on the interaction among the employees, the characteristics of the work situation, and the manager's personality.

LEARNING OBJECTIVE

6 Discuss the steps in the managerial decision-making process.

Managerial Decision Making

Decision making is the act of choosing one alternative from among a set of alternatives.[11] In ordinary, everyday situations, our decisions are made casually and informally. We encounter a problem, mull it over for a way out, settle on a likely solution, and go on. Managers, however, require a more systematic method for solving complex

decision making the act of choosing one alternative from among a set of alternatives

Experience helps in making good managerial decisions. Ellen M. Hancock is Chairman and CEO of Exodus Communications, an Internet hosting company. Previously she worked at IBM, National Semiconductor, and Apple. With this experience, she has learned valuable lessons in making highly effective managerial decisions. Her philosophy is to delegate authority so the people who are closest to a problem can tackle it, and do it quickly.

problems in a variety of situations. As shown in Figure 7.6, managerial decision making involves four steps: (1) identifying the problem or opportunity, (2) generating alternatives, (3) selecting an alternative, and (4) implementing and evaluating the solution.

Identifying the Problem or Opportunity

A **problem** is the discrepancy between an actual condition and a desired condition—the difference between what is occurring and what one wishes would occur. For example, a marketing manager at Campbell Soup Company has a problem if sales revenues for Campbell's Hungry Man frozen dinners are declining (the actual condition). To solve this problem, the marketing manager must take steps to increase sales revenues (desired condition). Most people consider a problem to be "negative"; however, a problem can also be "positive." A positive problem should be viewed as an "opportunity."

problem the discrepancy between an actual condition and a desired condition

Although accurate identification of a problem is essential before the problem can be solved or turned into an opportunity, this stage of decision making creates many difficulties for managers. Sometimes managers' preconceptions of the problem prevent them from seeing the situation as it actually is. They produce an answer before the proper question has ever been asked. In other cases, managers overlook truly significant issues by focusing on unimportant matters. Also, managers may mistakenly analyze problems in terms of symptoms rather than underlying causes. Disney Corporation management has reorganized its efforts at its 72 percent owned GO.com portal to the Internet after losses and general criticism for its earlier failure to capitalize on its strong brand name recognition. Interestingly, the Disney.com site is number 1 among entertainment sites, and its fully owned ESPN.com sports portal is also very successful, demonstrating the importance of clear brand recognition and synergy with existing brands found outside the Internet.[12]

Effective managers learn to look ahead so that they are prepared when decisions must be made. They clarify situations and examine the causes of problems, asking whether the presence or absence of certain variables alters a given situation. Finally, they consider how individual behaviors and values affect the way problems or opportunities are defined.

Generating Alternatives

After a problem has been suitably defined, the next task is to generate alternatives. Generally, the more important the decision, the more attention is devoted to this stage. Managers should be open to fresh, innovative ideas as well as to more obvious answers.

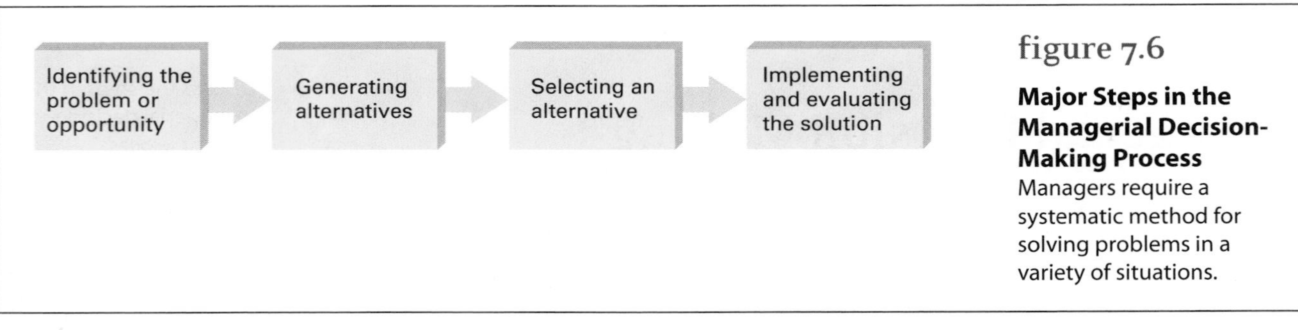

figure 7.6

Major Steps in the Managerial Decision-Making Process

Managers require a systematic method for solving problems in a variety of situations.

Certain techniques can aid in the generation of creative alternatives. Brainstorming, commonly used in group discussions, encourages participants to come up with as many new ideas as possible, no matter how outrageous. Other group members are not permitted to criticize or ridicule. Another approach to generating alternatives, developed by the U.S. Navy, is called "Blast! Then Refine." Group members tackle a recurring problem afresh, erasing from their minds all solutions and procedures tried in the past. The group then re-evaluates its original objectives, modifies them if necessary, and devises new solutions to the problem. Other techniques—including trial and error—are also useful in this stage of decision making.

Using the Internet

The American Management Association web site is an excellent reference tool for researchers, offering a variety of reports and statistics related to managers and management from both an American and an international perspective. The AMA home page is located at **http://www.amanet.org/index.htm** and the reports and statistical area can be accessed from there.

Selecting an Alternative

A final decision is influenced by a number of considerations, including financial constraints, human and informational resources, time limits, legal obstacles, and political factors. Managers must select the alternative that will be most effective and practical under the circumstances. At times two or more alternatives, or some combination of alternatives, will be equally appropriate.

Managers may choose solutions to problems on several levels. The word *satisfice* has been coined to describe solutions that are only adequate and not the best possible. When they lack time or information, managers often make decisions that satisfice, even though this is not the most productive approach in the long run. Whenever possible, managers should try to investigate alternatives carefully and select the one that best solves the problem. Critics of London-based Virgin Group have pointed out that the firm's Internet effort has been a poorly developed strategy so far. Nonetheless, Richard Branson, the firm's charismatic entrepreneur and owner intends to spend millions of dollars on this alternative to make Virgin.com one of the megaportals of the United Kingdom, providing a hub for navigating the company's many businesses.[13]

Implementing and Evaluating the Solution

Implementation of a decision requires time, planning, preparation of personnel, and evaluation of the results. Managers must usually deal with unforeseen consequences as well, even when they have carefully considered the alternatives.

The final step in managerial decision making entails evaluating the effectiveness of a decision. If the alternative that was chosen removes the difference between the actual condition and the desired condition, the decision is judged effective. If the problem still exists, managers may

- Decide to give the chosen alternative more time to work.
- Adopt a different alternative.
- Start the problem identification process all over again.

Failure to evaluate decisions adequately may have negative consequences. Kelloggs purchased Lender's Bagels in 1995 for $466 million. After four years of lackluster performance, Kelloggs sold Lender's to Aurora Foods for $275 million! Better evaluation by Kelloggs may have prevented this loss.[14]

LEARNING OBJECTIVE

7 Describe how organizations benefit from total quality management.

Managing Total Quality

The management of quality is a high priority in some organizations today. Major reasons for a greater focus on quality include foreign competition, more demanding customers, and poor financial performance resulting from reduced market shares and higher costs. Over the last few years, several U.S. firms have lost the dominant, competitive positions they had held for decades.

Total quality management is a much broader concept than just controlling the quality of the product itself (which is discussed in Chapter 9). **Total quality management (TQM)** is the coordination of efforts directed at improving customer satisfaction, increasing employee participation, strengthening supplier partnerships, and facilitating an organizational atmosphere of continuous quality improvement. For total quality management programs to be effective, management must address each of the following components:

total quality management (TQM) the coordination of efforts directed at improving customer satisfaction, increasing employee participation, strengthening supplier partnerships, and facilitating an organizational atmosphere of continuous quality improvement

- *Customer satisfaction*—Ways of improving customer satisfaction include producing higher quality products, providing better customer service, and showing customers that the company really cares about them.
- *Employee participation*—Employee participation can be increased by allowing employees to contribute to decisions, to develop self-managed work teams, and to assume responsibility and accountability for improving the quality of their work.
- *Strengthening supplier partnerships*—Developing good working relationships with suppliers can help ensure that the right supplies and materials will be delivered on time at a lower cost.
- *Continuous quality improvement* should not be viewed as achievable through one single program that has a target objective. A program based on continuous improvement has proved to be the most effective long-term approach. A spokesperson for BI, a business improvement service company, emphasized the importance of continuous improvement by stating that the company's winning of the 1999 Malcolm Baldrige National Quality Award was an important destination on the firm's quality journey.[15]

Although many factors influence the effectiveness of a total quality management program, two issues are crucial. First, top management must make a strong commitment to a TQM program by treating quality improvement as a top priority and giving it frequent attention. Firms that establish a total quality management program but then focus on other priorities will find that their quality improvement initiatives will fail. Second, management must coordinate the specific elements of a TQM program so that they work in harmony with each other.

Managing total quality. Producing high-quality products on a consistent basis requires diligent product inspection. Here, workers at the Rawlings baseball factory in Costa Rica inspect products. If a major league player strikes out, it won't be the ball's fault.

Although not all U.S. companies have total quality management programs, these programs provide many benefits. Overall financial benefits include lower operating costs, higher return on sales and on investments, and an improved ability to use premium pricing rather than competitive pricing. Additional benefits include faster development of innovations, improved ability to compete in global markets, higher levels of customer retention, an enhanced reputation, and a more productive and better-satisfied workforce.

What It Takes to Become a Successful Manager Today

LEARNING OBJECTIVE

8 Summarize what it takes to become a successful manager today.

Everyone hears stories about the corporate elite who make salaries in excess of $1 million a year, travel to and from work in chauffeur-driven limousines, and enjoy lucrative pension plans that provide for a luxurious lifestyle even after they retire. Although management can obviously be a very rewarding career, what is not so obvious is the amount of time and hard work that managers invest to achieve the impressive salaries and perks that may come with the job.

A Day in the Life of a Manager

Organizations don't pay managers to look good behind expensive wooden desks. Organizations pay for performance. As we already pointed out in this chapter, managers coordinate the organization's resources. They also perform the four basic management functions: planning, organizing, leading and motivating, and controlling. And managers make decisions and then implement and evaluate those decisions. This heavy workload requires that managers work long hours, and most don't get paid overtime for work in excess of forty hours a week. Typically, the number of hours increases as managers move up the corporate ladder.

Make no mistake about it: today's managers work hard in tough, demanding jobs. The pace is hectic. Managers spend a great deal of time talking with people on an individual basis. The purpose of these conversations is usually to obtain information or to resolve problems. (Remember, a problem can be either negative or positive and is a discrepancy between an actual condition and a desired condition). In addition to talking

adapting to change

Management Skills for the Internet Age

WHAT SKILLS DO MANAGERS NEED IN the Internet age? The three general categories of management skills—interpersonal, conceptual, and technical—still apply. However, managers must now adjust their skills within each category to be effective in an environment marked by fast-moving competitive, regulatory, and technological developments as well as increasing competitive pressures.

Technical skills. Although managers aren't expected to be hands-on experts in building or programming web sites, they must have an understanding of how the Internet and related technological trends can affect their organizations and the environment in which they operate. This is such an important priority that both Ford and Delta Air Lines have offered all their managers and employees a low-price deal on a computer and Internet access so they can get better acquainted with e-business.

Conceptual skills. Seeing the big picture is more critical—and more difficult—in the Internet age. Consider how planning is affected. Traditionally, planning meant setting an orderly progression of steps to meet objectives and establishing a schedule to track movement toward completion. In the Internet age, however, managers must be ready for any change at any time. To be effective, managers must be able to switch gears instantly and improvise to keep workers moving in the right direction, even when the future may be momentarily unclear.

Interpersonal skills. Relationships online can start or end at the click of a mouse, so managers need top-notch interpersonal skills to connect with customers, suppliers, distributors, and other key stakeholders. Because many projects cross departmental and geographic lines, managers also need to know how to manage people with multiple skills in multiple locations.

Perhaps the only constant in the Internet age is change—which means managers must change, as well. "We're just going to keep adding skills," observes John Putzier, president of the Society for Human Resources Management's High-Tech Net. "We're coming up with new functions every day. Everything's being redefined."

with individuals, a manager often spends a large part of the workday in meetings with other managers and employees. In most cases, the purpose of the meetings—some brief and some lengthy—is to resolve problems. And if the work is not completed by the end of the day, the manager usually packs unfinished tasks in a briefcase and totes them home to work on that night.

Perhaps in no managerial job is the workload more demanding than in those connected with the Internet and dot-com start-ups. In response to their personal experiences of burnout, Steve Baldwin and Bill Lessard launched a New York-based web site aptly called Netslaves (located at http://www.disobey.com/netslaves). The two are driven to demythologize the media image of work in the Internet industry and provide a forum for other managers to exchange stories about difficulties working in a dot-com world.[16]

Personal Skills Required for Success

To be successful in today's competitive business environment, you must possess a number of different skills. Some of these skills—technical, conceptual, and interpersonal skills—were discussed earlier in this chapter. But you also need to develop some "personal" skills in order to be successful. For starters, oral and written communication skills, computer skills, and critical thinking skills may give you the edge in getting an entry-level management position.

- *Oral communication skills.* Because a large part of a manager's day is spent conversing with other managers and employees, the ability to speak *and* listen is critical for success. For example, oral communication skills are used when a manager must make sales presentations, conduct interviews, perform employee evaluations, and hold press conferences.
- *Written communication skills.* Managers must be able to write. The manager's ability to prepare letters, e-mails, memos, sales reports, and other written documents may spell the difference between success and failure.
- *Computer skills.* Today many managers have a computer at their fingertips. Most employers do not expect you to be an expert computer programmer, but they do expect that you should know how to use a computer to prepare written and statistical reports and communicate with other managers and employees in the organization.
- *Critical thinking skills.* Employers expect managers to use the steps for effective managerial decision making that were described earlier in this chapter. They also expect managers to use their critical thinking skills to ensure that they identify the problem correctly, generate reasonable alternatives, and select the "best" alternative to solve an organization's problem.

The Importance of Education and Experience

Although most experts agree that management skills must be learned on the job, the concepts that you learn in business courses lay the foundation for a successful career. In addition, successful completion of college courses or obtaining a degree can open doors to job interviews and career advancement.

Most applicants who enter the world of work do not have a wealth of work experience. And yet there are methods that you can use to "beef up" your résumé and to capitalize on the work experience you do have. First, obtain summer jobs that will provide opportunities to learn about the field you wish to enter when you finish your formal education. If you choose carefully, part-time jobs during the school year can also provide work experience that other job applicants may not have. (By the way, some colleges and universities sponsor cooperative work/school programs that give students college credit for job experience.) Even with a solid academic background and relevant work experience, many would-be managers still find it difficult to land the "right" job. Often they start in an entry-level position to gain more experience and eventually—after years on the job—reach that "ideal" job. Perseverance does pay!

We include this practical advice not to frighten you but to provide a real-world view of what a manager's job is like. Once you know what is required of managers today—and how competitive the race is for the top jobs—you can decide whether a career in management is right for you.

In the next chapter, we examine the organizing function of managers in some detail. We look specifically at various organizational forms that today's successful businesses use. Like many factors in management, how a business is organized depends on its goals, strategies, and personnel.

RETURN TO inside Business

THANKS TO CAREFUL PLANNING, organizing, leading, and controlling, Yahoo! has evolved well beyond the simple list of web sites that cofounders Jerry Yang and David Filo began compiling as graduate students at Stanford. Today, Yahoo! boasts an astounding 145 million registered users. It has twenty-two country-specific sites stretching from Argentina to Japan and attracts nearly fifty million visitors every month. Although most of Yahoo!'s revenue comes from advertising, its online shopping center is a growing profit center, ringing up millions of dollars worth of sales every day.

Still, the cofounders and CEO Tim Koogle know they can't slow down any time soon. Looking ahead, the three want to make the most of new technologies such as Internet voice communication and wireless Internet access. "We have a strong belief about where the Internet is going and have to make sure we don't rest on our laurels," explains Yang. He and his colleagues are constantly setting new objectives and crafting strategies to keep Yahoo! on track toward its mission–which is, in Yang's words, to offer "services that make the Web a bigger part of people's lives."

Questions

1. Which of the basic management functions are cofounders Filo and Yang emphasizing? Which functions are CEO Koogle's focus?
2. Which key management skills are especially important for a fast-growing Internet business such as Yahoo?

chapter Review

SUMMARY

1 Define what management is.

Management is the process of coordinating people and other resources to achieve the goals of the organization. Managers are concerned with four types of resources—material, human, financial, and informational.

2 Describe the four basic management functions: planning, organizing, leading and motivating, and controlling.

Managers perform four basic functions. Management functions do not occur according to some rigid, preset timetable, though. At any time, managers may engage in a number of functions simultaneously. However, each function tends to lead naturally to others. First, managers engage in planning—determining where the firm should be going and how best to get there. Three types of plans, from the broadest to the most specific, are strategies, tactical plans, and operational plans. Managers also organize resources and activities to accomplish results in an efficient and effective manner, and they lead and motivate others to work in the best interests of the organization. In addition, managers control ongoing activities to keep the organization on course. There are three steps in the control function: setting standards; measuring actual performance; and taking corrective action.

3 Distinguish among the various kinds of managers, in terms of both level and area of management.

Managers—or management positions—may be classified from two different perspectives. From the perspective of level within the organization, there are top managers, who control the fortunes of the organization; middle managers, who implement strategies and major policies; and first-line managers, who supervise the activities of operating employees. From the viewpoint of area of management, managers most often deal with the areas of finance, operations, marketing, human resources, and administration.

4 Identify the key management skills and the managerial roles.

Effective managers tend to possess a specific set of skills and to fill three basic managerial roles. Technical, conceptual, and interpersonal skills are all important, though the relative importance of each varies with the level of management within the organization. The primary managerial roles can be classified as decisional, interpersonal, or informational.

5 Explain the different types of leadership.

Managers' effectiveness often depends on their styles of leadership—that is, their ability to influence others, either formally or informally. Leadership styles include the authoritarian "do-it-my-way" style, the laissez-faire "do-it-your-way" style, and the democratic "let's-do-it-together" style.

6 Discuss the steps in the managerial decision-making process.

Decision making, an integral part of a manager's work, is the process of developing a set of possible alternative solutions to a problem and choosing one alternative from among the set. Managerial decision making involves four steps: managers must accurately identify problems, generate several possible solutions, choose the solution that will be most effective under the circumstances, and implement and evaluate the chosen course of action.

7 Describe how organizations benefit from total quality management.

Total quality management (TQM) is the coordination of efforts directed at improving customer satisfaction, increasing employee participation, strengthening supplier partnerships, and facilitating an organizational atmosphere of continuous quality improvement. To have an effective total quality management program, top management must make a strong, sustained commitment to the effort and must be able to coordinate all of the program's elements so that they work in harmony. Overall financial benefits of TQM include lower operating costs, higher return on sales and investment, and an improved ability to use premium pricing rather than competitive pricing.

8 Summarize what it takes to become a successful manager today.

Organizations pay managers for their performance. Managers coordinate resources. They also plan, organize, lead, motivate, and control. They make decisions that can spell the difference between an organization's success and failure. To complete their tasks, managers work long hours at a hectic pace. To be successful, they need personal skills (oral and written communication skills, computer skills, and critical-thinking skills), an academic background that provides a foundation for a management career, and practical work experience.

KEY TERMS

You should now be able to define and give an example relevant to each of the following terms:

management (186)
planning (188)
mission (188)
strategic planning (188)
goal (188)
objective (188)
plan (189)
strategy (189)
tactical plan (189)
operational plan (189)
contingency plan (189)
organizing (190)
leading (190)
motivating (190)
directing (190)
controlling (190)
top manager (192)
middle manager (192)
first-line manager (192)
financial manager (193)
operations manager (194)
marketing manager (194)
human resources manager (194)
administrative manager (194)
technical skill (195)
conceptual skill (195)
interpersonal skill (195)
decisional role (196)
interpersonal role (196)
informational role (196)
leadership (196)
authoritarian leader (197)
laissez-faire leader (197)
democratic leader (197)
decision making (197)
problem (198)
total quality management (TQM) (200)

REVIEW QUESTIONS

1. Define the term *manager* without using the word *management* in your definition.
2. What is the mission of a neighborhood restaurant? of the Salvation Army? What might be reasonable objectives for these organizations?
3. What does the term *optimization* mean?
4. How do a strategy, a tactical plan, and an operational plan differ? What do they all have in common?
5. What exactly does a manager organize, and for what reason?
6. Why are leadership and motivation necessary in a business in which people are paid for their work?
7. Explain the steps involved in the control function.
8. How are the two perspectives on kinds of managers—that is, level and area—different from each other?
9. In what ways are management skills related to the roles managers play? Provide a specific example to support your answer.
10. Compare and contrast the major styles of leadership.
11. Discuss what happens during each of the four steps of the managerial decision-making process.
12. What are the major benefits of a total quality management program?
13. What personal skills should a manager possess in order to be successful?

DISCUSSION QUESTIONS

1. Does a healthy firm (one that is doing well) have to worry about effective management? Explain.
2. Which of the management functions, skills, and roles do not apply to the owner-operator of a sole proprietorship?
3. Which leadership style might be best suited to each of the three general levels of management within an organization?
4. According to this chapter, the leadership style that is *most* effective depends on the interaction among the employees, the characteristics of the work situation, and the manager's personality. Do you agree or disagree? Explain your answer.
5. Do you think people are really as important to an organization as this chapter seems to indicate?
6. As you learned in this chapter, managers often work long hours at a hectic pace. Would this type of career appeal to you? Explain your answer.

VIDEO CASE

Southwest Managers Help the Airline Soar

In 1967 Texas businessman Rollin King and lawyer Herb Kelleher established Air Southwest Company. Originally, King and Kelleher planned to fly only within Texas, linking Dallas, San Antonio, and Houston with low-priced, frequent flights. In 1971 the company—renamed Southwest Airlines—made its debut flight between Dallas and San Antonio. Over the years, Southwest grew beyond the borders of the Lone Star State, garnering fame for on-time flights, low fares, and excellent customer service. With 2,650 flights a day to fifty-eight cities, 30,000 employees, and 91 million bags of peanuts served a year, Southwest rings up more than $5 billion in annual ticket sales—and its profit margins are three times higher than the industry average.

When Southwest was a small upstart company, Kelleher rejected most elements of what he termed the "Darth Vader School of Management"—bureaucracy, hierarchy, titles, and unquestioning obedience to a powerful leader in total command. In Kelleher's view and in the view of his airline, requiring multiple sign-offs, second-guessing people's decisions, and refusing to allow managers the freedom to innovate are all marks of an outdated and ineffectual management style. Southwest does not want mindless obedience from its managers (or the rest of its workforce). It does want originality and proactivity. This attitude is reflected in the company's mission: "Dedication to the highest quality of customer service delivered with a sense of warmth, friendliness, individual pride, and company spirit."

Long before "empowerment" became a business buzzword, Southwest Airlines liberated its first-line managers from centralized policies, maintaining as few rules and regulations as possible. First-line managers have not only the freedom but the responsibility to take initiative and make decisions without having to check first with upper-level management or corporate headquarters. If an automatic ticketing machine isn't working properly or the lights in a gate area are out, a manager can try to repair them. If a passenger is lost, a manager can walk that passenger to the correct gate. If a passenger is stranded, a manager can even take that passenger home for the night.

By empowering employees to make their own decisions and try new ideas without fear of repercussion and by treating them as people, not merely workers, managers strive to make working at Southwest a positive experience for all employees. A Southwest Information Systems manager reports that he always tries to give his employees every opportunity to implement their visions and work through situations on their own. He believes that leadership "is a service in the organization, as opposed to an egotistical exercise." At Southwest Airlines' Chicago Reservations Center, the operations supervisor always finds time to help her coworkers. She rearranges employees' schedules so that they have time to go to a child's school play and helps them resolve problems with customers at the ticket counter. These first-line managers, and others like them throughout the airline, employ a management style that is more coach than boss, more mentor than superior.

Still prisoners of the old myth of autocratic leadership, many executives of organizations with more traditional management styles are dubious about Southwest Airlines. Southwest's style, however, has contributed to uncommon employee loyalty and extraordinary business success. The airline's high-flying customer satisfaction record has landed it on the top of the Airline Quality Rating study for four of the last five years. Now Southwest is planning for future growth by supplementing its short-haul operations with more long-distance flights between U.S. cities. Looking ahead, Southwest's spirit of empowerment will keep it soaring to new heights long after CEO Kelleher retires.[17]

Questions

1. What type of leadership style appears to be used at Southwest Airlines?
2. In what ways does the type of leadership employed at Southwest Airlines facilitate total quality management at this organization?
3. Most of the managers discussed in the case are at what level of management?

Building Skills for Career Success

1. Exploring the Internet

Most large companies at one time or another call on a management consulting firm for a variety of services, including employee training, help in the selection of an expensive purchase such as a computer system, recruitment of employees, and direction in reorganization and strategic planning.

Large consulting firms generally operate in the global marketplace and can provide information and assistance to companies considering entry into foreign countries or business alliances with foreign firms. They use their web pages, along with magazine-style articles, to celebrate their achievements and to present their credentials to clients. The business student can acquire an enormous amount of up-to-date information in the field of management by perusing these sites.

Assignment

1. Explore each of the following web sites:

   Andersen Consulting: http://www.ac.com
   KPMG Peat Marwick: http://www.kpmg.com
   Ernst and Young: http://www.ey.com
   Pricewaterhouse: http://www.pw.com

2. Judging from the articles and notices posted, what are the current areas of activities of one of these firms?
3. Explore one of these areas in more detail by comparing postings from each firm's site. For instance, if "global business opportunities" appears to be a popular area of management consulting, how has each firm distinguished itself in this area? Who would you call first for advice?
4. Given that consulting firms are always trying to fill positions for their clients and to meet their own recruitment needs, it is little wonder employment postings are a popular area on their sites. Examine these in detail. Based on your examination of the site and the registration format, what sort of recruit are they interested in?

2. Developing Critical Thinking Skills

As defined in the chapter, an organization's mission is a statement of the basic purpose that makes the organization different from others. Clearly, a mission statement, by indicating the purpose of a business, directly affects the company's employees, customers, and stockholders.

Assignment

1. Find the mission statements of three large corporations in different industries. The Internet is one source of mission statements. For example, you might search these sites:

   http://www.kodak.com
   http://www.benjerry.com
   http://www.att.com

2. Compare the mission statements on the basis of what each reflects about the philosophy of the company and its concern for employees, customers, and stockholders.
3. Which company would you like to work for and why?
4. Prepare a report on your findings.

3. Building Team Skills

Over the past few years, an increasing number of employees, stockholders, and customers have been demanding to know what their company is about. As a result, more companies have been taking the time to analyze their operations and to prepare a mission statement, which focuses on the purpose of the company. The mission statement is becoming a critical planning tool for successful companies. To make effective decisions, employees must understand the purpose of their company.

Assignment

1. Divide into teams and write a mission statement for one of the following types of businesses:

   - Food service, restaurant
   - Banking
   - Airline
   - Auto repair
   - Cabinet manufacturing

2. Discuss your mission statement with other teams. How did the other teams interpret the purpose of your company? What is the mission statement saying about the company?
3. Write a one-page report on what you learned about developing mission statements.

4. Researching Different Careers

A successful career requires planning. Without a plan, or roadmap, you will find it very difficult, if not impossible, to reach your desired career destination. The first step in planning is to establish what your career goal is. You must then set objectives and develop plans for accomplishing those objectives. This kind of planning takes time, but it will pay off later.

Assignment

Complete the following statements:

1. My career goal is to ______________________________.
   This statement should encapsulate what you want to accomplish over the long run. It may include the type of job you want and the type of business or industry you want to work in. Examples include
   - My career goal is to work as a top manager in the food industry.
   - My career goal is to supervise aircraft mechanics.
   - My career goal is to win the top achievement award in the advertising industry.
2. My career objectives are to ______________________________
   ____.
   Objectives are benchmarks along the route to a career destination. They are more specific than a career goal. A statement about a career objective should specify what you want to accomplish, when you will complete it, and any other details that will serve as criteria against which you can measure your progress. Examples include
   - My objective is to be promoted to supervisor by January 1, 20xx.
   - My objective is to enroll in a management course at Main College in the spring semester, 20xx.
   - My objective is to earn an A in the management course at Main College in the spring semester, 20xx.
   - My objective is to prepare a status report by September 30 covering the last quarter's activities by asking Charlie in Quality Control to teach me the procedures.
3. Exchange your goal and objectives statements with another class member. Can your partner interpret your objectives correctly? Are the objectives concise and complete? Do they include criteria against which you can measure your progress? If not, discuss the problem and rewrite the objective.

5. Improving Communication Skills

Being an efficient, productive employee in the workplace today requires certain personal and managerial skills. Without proficiency in these skills, promotions and other rewards are unlikely to be forthcoming. To be competitive, employees must periodically assess their skill levels and, when necessary, work to improve them. How do your personal and managerial skills measure up?

Assignment

1. Rate yourself and have at least two other people rate you on the skills listed in the table.
2. Prepare a plan for improving your weak areas. The plan should specify exactly how, where, and by when you will accomplish your goal. It should also include criteria for measuring your level of improvement.

Skills Assessment

	Below average	Average	Above average	Specific examples
Personal skills Oral communication skills				
Written communication skills				
Computer skills				
Critical thinking skills				
Managerial skills Conceptual skills				
Technical skills				
Interpersonal skills				
Decision-making skills				

creating a flexible organization

8

LEARNING OBJECTIVES

1. Understand what an organization is and identify its characteristics.
2. Explain why job specialization is important.
3. Identify the various bases for departmentalization.
4. Explain how decentralization follows from delegation.
5. Understand how the span of management describes an organization.
6. Understand how the chain of command is established by using line and staff management.
7. Describe the four basic forms of organizational structure: bureaucratic, matrix, cluster, and network.
8. Summarize how corporate culture, intrapreneurship, committees, coordination techniques, informal groups, and the grapevine affect an organization.

Nokia's flexible organizational structure fosters open communication, teamwork, and creativity.

inside business

Nokia Dials Up Organizational Flexibility

How can a company successfully shift from producing rubber boots and toilet paper to making mobile phones and wireless web appliances? Nokia's answer is organizational flexibility. Founded in Finland in 1865, Nokia has spent the past decade transforming itself into a focused, high-tech telecommunications powerhouse. Now the 55,000-employee firm rings up $20 billion in annual sales, selling more mobile phones than any other company in the world.

Ten years ago, however, Nokia was struggling when Jorma Ollila, a rising management star, was assigned to head its infant mobile-phone business. Although today this thriving business is the cornerstone of the company's prosperity, at the time it was both demoralized and disorganized. Ollila jumped right in, traveling around listening to employees and discussing his ideas for the unit. Then he reorganized the research and development department so the unit's products would be ready for new digital communication standards. This successful turnaround catapulted Ollila into the CEO slot a year later.

When Ollila became CEO, Nokia was in the process of selling its rubber and paper businesses—and was ripe for change. Ollila quickly redirected the company's efforts into cutting-edge telecommunications, including handheld devices for Internet access. Over the years, he has realigned the top hierarchy and pushed responsibility ever deeper into the ranks of up-and-coming managers. "We are a company that likes to grow from within and give power and leverage to young people, and that has been our strength," Ollila says.

Under Ollila, Nokia's organizational structure fosters open communication, teamwork, and creativity. The CEO wants to "send a very strong signal that this is a meritocracy, and this is a place where you are allowed to have a bit of fun, to think unlike the norm, where you are allowed to make a mistake." Employees definitely get the message. Tony Mitchell, a Nokia production manager in Fort Worth, Texas, comments: "That's unique to Nokia—the freedom a group is allowed to take. There are certain shared systems we keep as standard, but you're allowed to be creative."

Keeping the entire organization pointed in the right direction takes a clear, inspiring vision. Unlike other companies, where senior management defines and articulates the vision, Nokia's vision is shaped by company-wide dialogue—from the bottom up. First, managers in local areas meet to discuss their ideas for the coming year's priorities. They send their recommendations up the line, where top managers extract the main points to form a comprehensive vision that is disseminated throughout the organization.

More than just a slogan, each year's vision provides a sense of purpose for the Nokia organization, showing employees what's important and where the company wants to go in the coming months. Ollila says the current vision is "to put the Internet into every pocket." And Nokia has the organization to make it happen.[1]

To survive and to grow companies like Nokia must constantly look for ways to improve their methods of doing business. Managers at Nokia, like those at many other organizations, deliberately reorganized the company to help it achieve its goals and objectives and to create satisfying products that will foster long-term customer relationships.

When firms are organized, or reorganized, the focus is sometimes on achieving low operating costs. In other cases, as in the case of Nokia, the emphasis is on providing high-quality products to ensure customer satisfaction. The way a firm is organized influences its performance. Thus, the issue of organization is important.

We begin this chapter by examining the business organization—what it is and how it functions in today's business environment. Next we focus one by one on five characteristics that shape an organization's structure. We discuss job specialization within a company; the grouping of jobs into manageable units or departments; the delegation of power from management to workers; the span of management; and the establishment of a chain of command. Then we step back for an overall view of four approaches to organizational structure: the bureaucratic structure, the matrix structure, the cluster structure, and the network structure. Finally, we look at the network of social interactions—the informal organization—that operates within the formal business structure.

LEARNING OBJECTIVE

1 Understand what an organization is and identify its characteristics.

What Is an Organization?

We used the term *organization* throughout Chapter 7 without really defining it, mainly because its everyday meaning is close to its business meaning. Here, however, let us agree that an **organization** is a group of two or more people working together to achieve a common set of goals. A neighborhood dry cleaner owned and operated by a husband-and-wife team is an organization. IBM, Rubbermaid, and Home Depot, which employ thousands of workers worldwide, are also organizations in the very same sense. Although each corporation's organizational structure is vastly more complex than that of the dry-cleaning establishment, all must be organized if they are to achieve their goals.

organization a group of two or more people working together to achieve a common set of goals

An inventor who goes into business to produce and market a new invention hires people, decides what each will do, determines who will report to whom, and so on. These activities are the essence of organizing, or creating, the organization. One way to create that "picture" is to create an organization chart.

Large and small organizations. All organizations—from small businesses like Uncle Sol's Sandwich Shop to large corporations like Polaroid—must be organized to achieve their goals. Organization charts can help businesses to define positions and clarify reporting relationships.

figure 8.1

A Typical Corporate Organization Chart

A company's organization chart represents the positions and relationships within an organization and shows the managerial chains of command.

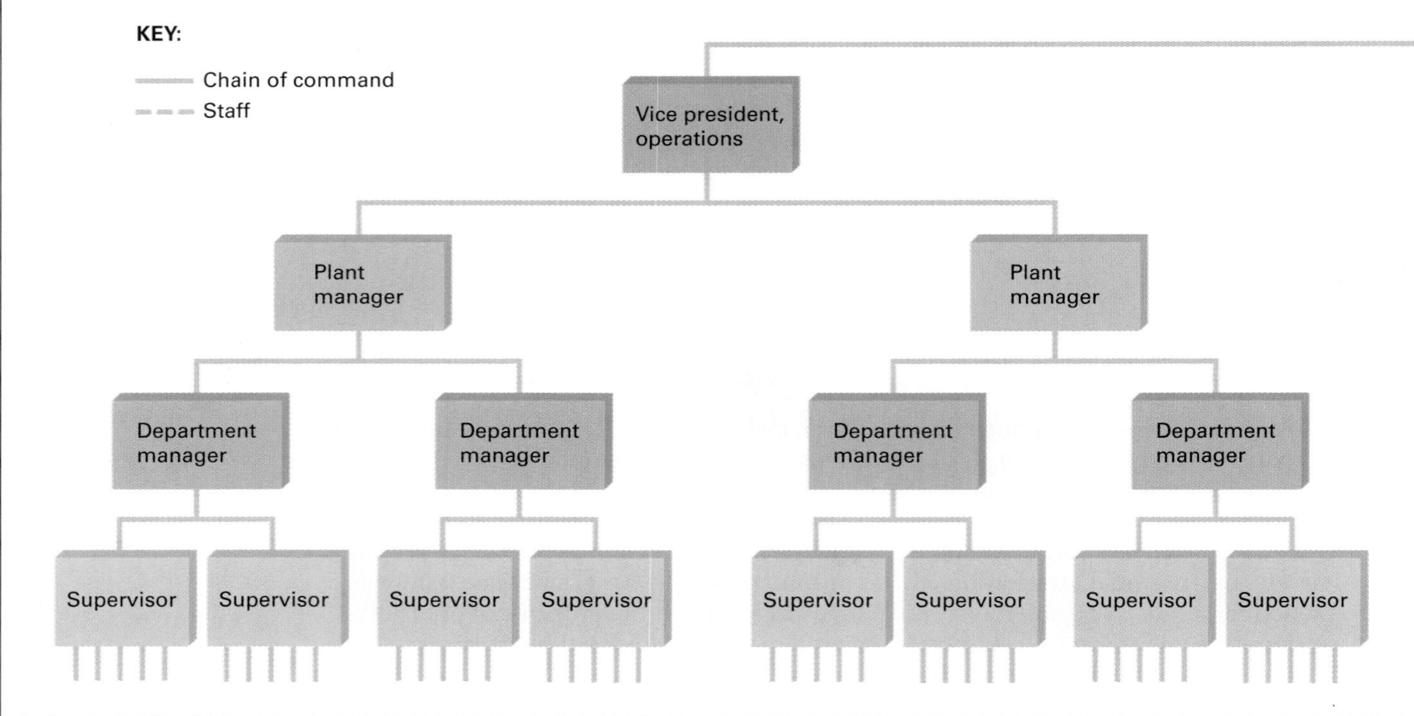

Developing Organization Charts

organization chart a diagram that represents the positions and relationships within an organization

chain of command the line of authority that extends from the highest to the lowest levels of an organization

An **organization chart** is a diagram that represents the positions and relationships within an organization. An example of an organization chart is shown in Figure 8.1. What does it tell us?

Each rectangle in the chart represents a particular position or person in the organization. At the top of the chart is the president; at the next level are the vice presidents. The solid vertical lines connecting the vice presidents to the president indicate that the vice presidents are in the chain of command. The **chain of command** is the line of authority that extends from the highest to the lowest levels of the organization. Moreover, each vice president reports directly to the president. Similarly, the plant managers, regional sales managers, and accounting department manager report directly to the vice presidents. The chain of command can be short or long. For example, at Royer's Roundtop Cafe, an independent restaurant in Roundtop, Texas, the chain of command is very short. Bud Royer, the owner, is responsible only to himself and can alter his hours or change his menu quickly. On the other hand, the chain of command at McDonald's is long. Before making certain types of changes, a McDonald's franchisee seeks permission from regional management which, in turn, seeks approval from corporate headquarters.

Notice in the chart that the connections to the directors of legal services, public affairs, and human resources are shown as broken lines; these people are not part of the direct chain of command. Instead, they hold *advisory*, or *staff*, positions. This difference will be examined later in the chapter, when we discuss line and staff positions.

Most smaller organizations find organization charts useful. They clarify positions and reporting relationships for everyone in the organization, and they help managers

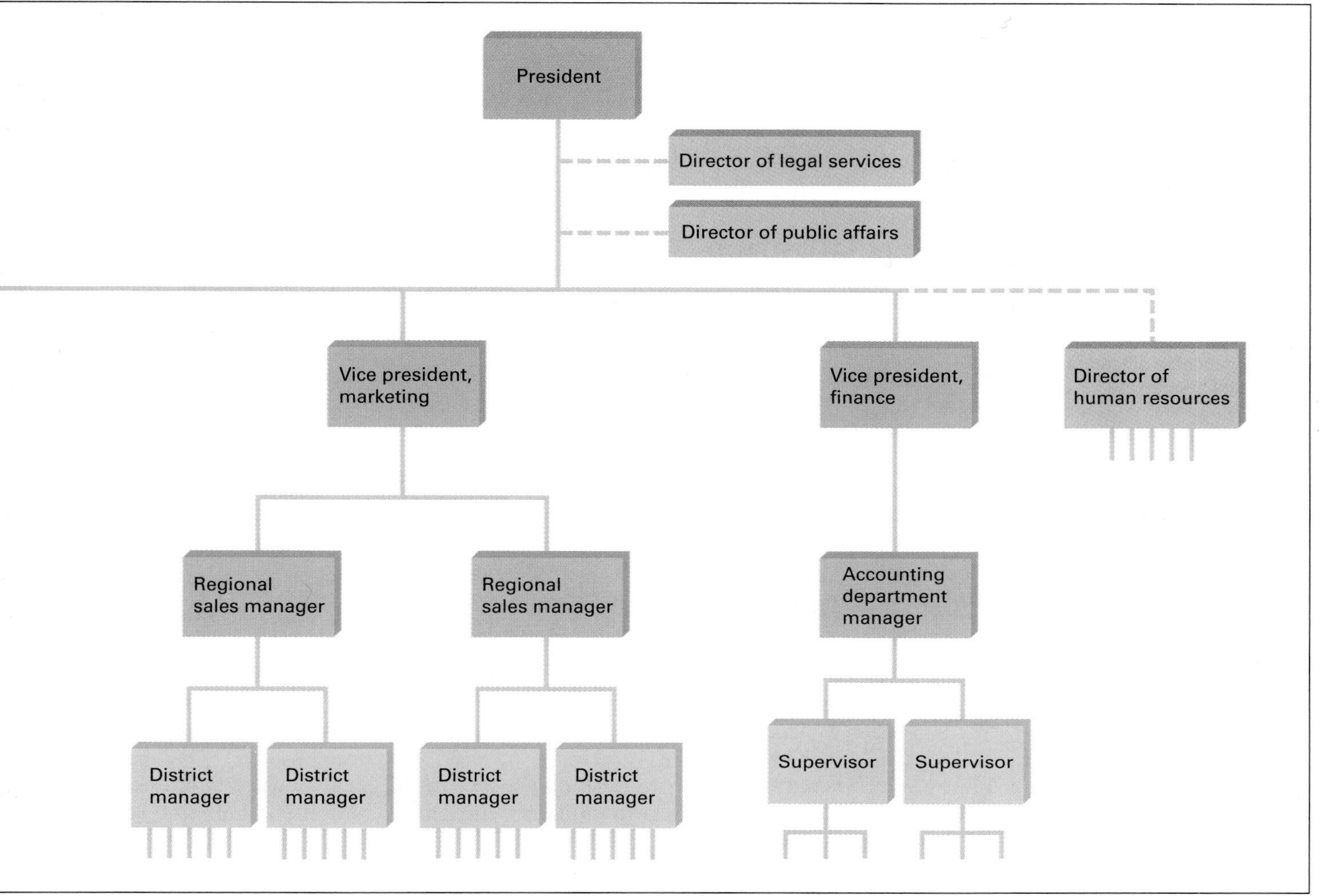

track growth and change in the organizational structure. For two reasons, however, many large organizations, such as Exxon, Kellogg, and Procter & Gamble, do not maintain complete, detailed charts. First, it is difficult to accurately chart even a few dozen positions, much less the thousands that characterize larger firms. And, second, larger organizations are almost always changing one part of their structure or another. An organization chart would probably be outdated before it was completed.

Five Steps For Organizing a Business

When a firm is started, management must decide how to organize the firm. These decisions are all part of five major steps that sum up the organizing process. The five steps are:

1. Divide the work that is to be done by the entire organization into separate parts, and assign those parts to positions within the organization. This step is often called *job design*.
2. Group the various positions into manageable units, or departments. This step is called *departmentalization*.
3. Distribute responsibility and authority within the organization. This step is called *delegation*.
4. Determine the number of subordinates who will report to each manager. This step creates the firm's *span of management*.
5. Establish the organization's chain of command by designating the positions with direct authority and those that are support positions.

In the next several sections, we discuss major issues associated with these steps.

Job Design

LEARNING OBJECTIVE

2 Explain why job specialization is important.

In Chapter 1, we defined *specialization* as the separation of a manufacturing process into distinct tasks and the assignment of different tasks to different people. Here we are extending that concept to *all* the activities performed within the organization.

Job Specialization

job specialization the separation of all organizational activities into distinct tasks and the assignment of different tasks to different people

Job specialization is the separation of all organizational activities into distinct tasks and the assignment of different tasks to different people. Adam Smith, the eighteenth-century economist whose theories gave rise to capitalism, was the first to emphasize the power of specialization in his book *The Wealth of Nations.* According to Smith, the various tasks in a particular pin factory were arranged so that one worker drew the wire for the pins, another straightened the wire, a third cut it, a fourth ground the point, and a fifth attached the head. Using this method, Smith claimed, ten men were able to produce 48,000 pins per day. Before specialization, they could produce only 200 pins per day because each worker had to perform all five tasks!

The Rationale for Specialization

For a number of reasons, some job specialization is necessary in every organization. First and foremost is the simple fact that the "job" of most organizations is simply too large for one person to handle. In a firm like Chrysler Corporation, thousands of people are needed to manufacture automobiles. Others are needed to sell the cars, to control the firm's finances, and so on.

Second, when a worker has to learn only a specific, highly specialized task, that individual should be able to learn to do it very efficiently. Third, the worker who is doing the same job over and over does not lose time changing from one operation to another, as the pin workers probably did when each was producing a complete pin. Fourth, the more specialized the job, the easier it may be to design specialized equipment for those who do it. And finally, the more specialized the job, the easier it is to train new employees when an employee quits or is absent from work.

Job specialization. Production line workers, such as the one at this vacuum cleaner production facility, engage in job specialization, which in turn results in production efficiency.

Alternatives to Job Specialization

Unfortunately, specialization can have some negative consequences as well. The most significant drawback is the boredom and dissatisfaction many employees feel when they do the same job over and over. Monotony can be deadening. Bored employees may be absent from work frequently, may not put much effort into their work, and may even sabotage the company's efforts to produce quality products.

To combat these problems, managers often turn to job rotation. **Job rotation** is the systematic shifting of employees from one job to another. For example, a worker may be assigned to a different job every week for a four-week period and then return to the first job in the fifth week. The idea behind job rotation is to provide a variety of tasks so that workers are less likely to get bored and dissatisfied.

job rotation the systematic shifting of employees from one job to another

At Canadian Life, a life insurance company, job rotation is employed for senior management. Over 80 percent of senior managers are in different roles than they were four years ago. A spokesperson said that the company's job rotation program is an essential part of the firm's positioning as a strong global competitor. Job rotation heightens employees' motivation and involvement, increases their career satisfaction and commitment to stay with a company, and gives them a better understanding of strategic issues.[2]

Two other approaches—job enlargement and job enrichment—can also provide solutions to the problems caused by job specialization. These topics, along with other methods used to motivate employees, are discussed in Chapter 11.

LEARNING OBJECTIVE

3 Identify the various bases for departmentalization.

Departmentalization

After jobs are designed, they must be grouped together into "working units," or departments. This process is called departmentalization. More specifically, **departmentalization** is the process of grouping jobs into manageable units. Several departmentalization bases are commonly used. In fact, most firms use more than one. Today the most common bases for organizing a business into effective departments are by function, by product, by location, and by type of customer.

departmentalization the process of grouping jobs into manageable units

departmentalization by function grouping jobs that relate to the same organizational activity

By Function

Departmentalization by function groups jobs that relate to the same organizational activity. Under this scheme, all marketing personnel are grouped together in the marketing department, all production personnel in the production department, and so on. An example of a firm that recently organized based on function is the Iomega Corporation. Its departments include sales and marketing, product development, manufacturing and operations, corporate marketing, finance, legal, human resources, corporate strategy, and customer service and applications.[3]

Most smaller and newer organizations base their departmentalization on function. Supervision is simplified because everyone is involved in the same kinds of activities, and coordination is fairly easy. The disadvantages of this method of grouping jobs are that it can lead to slow decision making and that it tends to emphasize the department rather than the organization as a whole.

Departmentalization based on function. Many organizations employ departmentalization based on function. Company mailrooms, such as the one shown here, are derived from functional departmentalization.

By Product

departmentalization by product grouping activities related to a particular product or service

Departmentalization by product groups activities related to a particular good or service. This approach is often used by older and larger firms that produce and sell a variety of products. Each department handles its own marketing, production, financial management, and human resources activities.

Departmentalization by product makes decision making easier and provides for the integration of all activities associated with each product. However, it causes some duplication of specialized activities—such as finance—from department to department. And the emphasis is placed on the product rather than on the whole organization.

Microsoft recently reorganized to create two new product groups. The Desktop Applications Division, which produces Windows applications such as Office, became part of the Platforms and Applications Group. The Interactive Media Group manages multimedia games, consumer CD-Roms, the Microsoft Network, and hardware.

By Location

departmentalization by location grouping activities according to the defined geographic area in which they are performed

Departmentalization by location groups activities according to the defined geographic area in which they are performed. Departmental areas may range from whole countries (for international firms) to regions within countries (for national firms) to areas of several city blocks (for police departments organized into precincts). Departmentalization by location allows the organization to respond readily to the unique demands or requirements of different locations. Nevertheless, a large administrative staff and an elaborate control system may be needed to coordinate operations in many locations. In order to function at top speeds, computers that run the Internet need to be as close to users as possible. The further away they are located, the slower the transmission speed. To meet the demand for storage of large installations of computers, older buildings such as hotels and warehouses located in the downtown core of major cities are being refurbished with the latest technology and staff to run the new economy as web-hosting centers.[4]

By Customer

departmentalization by customer grouping activities according to the needs of various customer populations

Departmentalization by customer groups activities according to the needs of various customer populations. A local Chevrolet dealership, for example, may have one sales staff to deal with individual consumers and a different sales staff to work with corporate fleet buyers. The obvious advantage of this approach is that it allows the firm to deal efficiently with unique customers or customer groups. The biggest drawback is that a larger-than-usual administrative staff is needed.

Combinations of Bases

Many organizations use more than one of these departmentalization bases. For example, General Motors has realigned its divisions on the bases of small-vehicle and large-vehicle product groups. Each GM division, in turn, is departmentalized by function. Pontiac, for example, has its own marketing, finance, and human resources groups. Production groups might be further departmentalized by plant location. Similarly, a divisional marketing group might be divided in such a way that one unit handles consumer sales and another handles fleet and corporate sales.

Take a moment to examine Figure 8.2. Notice that departmentalization by customer is used to organize New-Wave Fashions, Inc., into three major divisions: men's clothing, women's clothing, and children's clothing. Then functional departmentalization is used to distinguish the firm's production and marketing activities. Finally, location is used to organize the firm's marketing efforts.

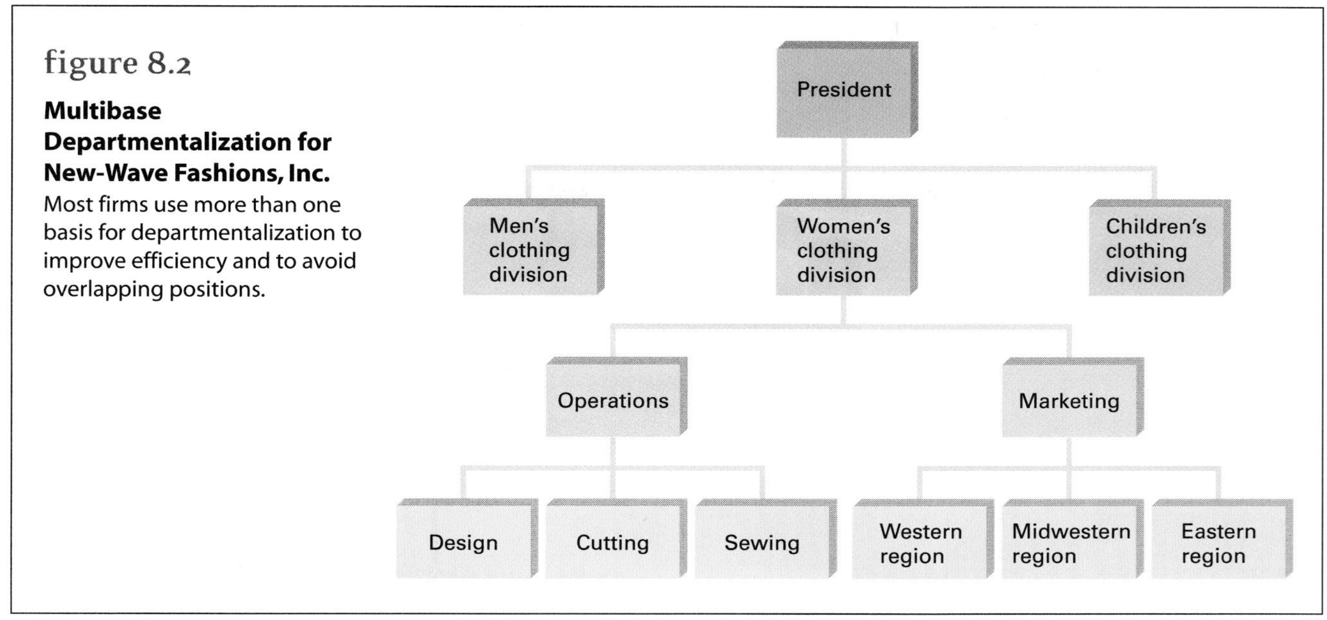

figure 8.2
Multibase Departmentalization for New-Wave Fashions, Inc.
Most firms use more than one basis for departmentalization to improve efficiency and to avoid overlapping positions.

Delegation, Decentralization, and Centralization

LEARNING OBJECTIVE
4 Explain how decentralization follows from delegation.

The third major step in the organizing process is to distribute power in the organization. **Delegation** assigns part of a manager's work and power to other workers. The degree of centralization or decentralization of authority is determined by the overall pattern of delegation within the organization.

delegation assigning part of a manager's work and power to other workers

Delegation of Authority

Because no manager can do everything, delegation is vital to the completion of a manager's work. Delegation is also important in developing the skills and abilities of subordinates. It allows those who are being groomed for higher-level positions to play increasingly important roles in decision making.

Steps in Delegation The delegation process generally involves three steps (see Figure 8.3). First, the manager must *assign responsibility*. **Responsibility** is the duty to do a job or perform a task. In most job settings, a manager simply gives the worker a job to do. Typical job assignments might range from having a worker prepare a report on the status of a new quality-control program to placing the person in charge of a special task force. Second, the manager must *grant authority*. **Authority** is the power, within the organization, to accomplish an assigned job or task. This might include the power to obtain specific information, order supplies, authorize relevant expenditures, and make certain decisions. Finally, the manager must *create accountability*. **Accountability** is the obligation of a worker to accomplish an assigned job or task.

responsibility the duty to do a job or perform a task

authority the power, within the organization, to accomplish an assigned job or task

accountability the obligation of a worker to accomplish an assigned job or task

Note that accountability is created but that it cannot be delegated. Suppose you are an operations manager for Delta Air Lines and are responsible for performing a specific task. You, in turn, delegate this task to someone else. You nonetheless remain accountable to your immediate supervisor for getting the task done properly. If the other person fails to complete the assignment, you—not the person—will be called on to account for what has become *your* failure.

THE DELEGATION PROCESS

Manager
1 Assign responsibility
2 Grant authority
3 Assign accountability
Worker

figure 8.3

Steps in the Delegation Process

To be successful, a manager must learn how to delegate. No one can do everything alone.

Barriers to Delegation For several reasons, managers may be unwilling to delegate work. One reason was just stated—the person who delegates remains accountable for the work. Many managers are reluctant to delegate simply because they want to be sure the work gets done properly. Another reason for reluctance to delegate stems from the opposite situation. The manager fears the worker will do the work so well that he or she will attract the approving notice of higher-level managers and will therefore become a threat to the manager. Finally, some managers don't delegate because they are so disorganized they simply are not able to plan and assign work effectively.

decentralized organization an organization in which management consciously attempts to spread authority widely in the lower levels of the organization

centralized organization an organization that systematically works to concentrate authority at the upper levels of the organization

Decentralization of Authority

The general pattern of delegation throughout an organization determines the extent to which that organization is decentralized or centralized. In a **decentralized organization**, management consciously attempts to spread authority widely across various organization levels. Coca-Cola has decentralized its global operations. A spokesperson said that Coke has to think local and act local. In the past too many decisions had to be approved at the Atlanta headquarters where precious time was lost. Now, more responsibility and accountability will be in the hands of local executives around the world.[5] A **centralized organization**, on the other hand, systematically works to concentrate authority at the upper levels. For example, many publishers of college-level textbooks are centralized organizations, with authority concentrated at the tops of these companies.

spotLight

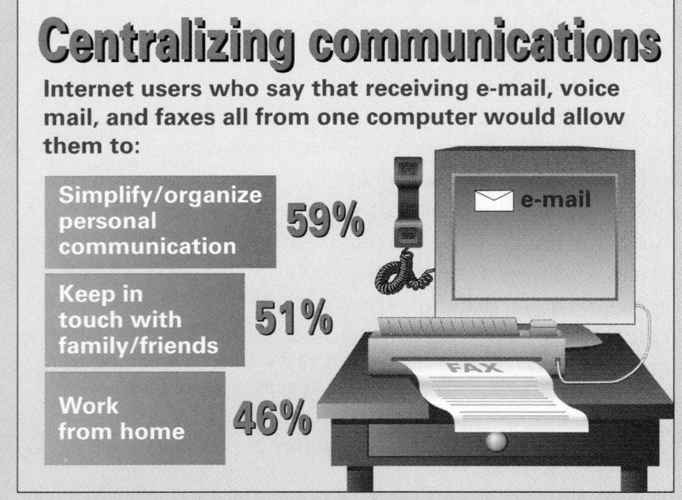

Source: Copyright 2000, USA TODAY. Reprinted with permission.

A variety of factors can influence the extent to which a firm is decentralized. One is the external environment in which the firm operates. The more complex and unpredictable this environment, the more likely it is that top management will let lower-level managers make important decisions. After all, lower-level managers are closer to the problems. Another factor is the nature of the decision itself. The riskier or the

Talking Technology

Web-Based Outsourcing

WEB-BASED OUTSOURCING IS THE ULTImate in decentralization. Increasingly, companies are contracting with suppliers to handle a particular activity, such as technology or personnel management, via the Internet. This allows a fast-growing company to concentrate on its main business, rather than being distracted by support functions that don't directly contribute to competitive advantage or profitability.

Allegiance Telecom, a Dallas-based telephone company, was expanding so rapidly that management had difficulty keeping up with all the human resources tasks to support hundreds of new hires per month. Then the company signed on with Online Benefits (http://www.online-benefits.com), a web-based company specializing in benefits management. Allegiance employees can quickly and conveniently learn about their employer's profit-sharing program or check on different insurance options, simply by signing onto a special password-protected web site. Now Allegiance's yearly outlay is about one-quarter of what it would have spent to keep a benefits manager on staff, and employees are satisfied because they can get fast answers to their questions.

Technology has become a hot area for web-based outsourcing as more companies outsource the use of specialized software for accounting and finance, sales force management, database management, and other tasks. Sunburst Hospitality, a hotel operator, recently contracted with USinternetworking to gain access to sophisticated financial software. By outsourcing, Sunburst avoids the headaches and staff problems associated with implementing current and upgraded versions of the software. Best of all, Sunburst's costs are predictable because it pays one fixed monthly fee for access to the software.

Not every activity can or should be outsourced, however. Experts advise companies not to outsource any activity that is absolutely critical to success. In addition, companies should analyze and address major problems before outsourcing a particular activity. In the end, outsourcing is not a way to get rid of an activity, it's just a more decentralized method of managing it. That's why companies need to work with suppliers who have skilled personnel, top-notch practices, and compatible cultures.

more important the decision, the greater the tendency to centralize decision making. A third factor is the abilities of lower-level managers. If these managers do not have strong decision-making skills, top managers will be reluctant to decentralize. And, in contrast, strong lower-level decision-making skills encourage decentralization. Finally, a firm that has traditionally practiced centralization or decentralization is likely to maintain that posture in the future. According to a Jupiter Communications study the need for human intervention, helping online customers, rises substantially from 8 percent at low price levels to nearly 30 percent as the product price crosses the $100 point. If e-commerce efforts at firms establishing Internet customer services are to succeed, decentralization of authority to the level of the online service representative must be in place.[6]

In principle, neither decentralization nor centralization is right or wrong. What works for one organization may or may not work for another. Kmart Corporation and McDonald's have both been very successful—and both practice centralization. By the same token, decentralization has worked very well for General Electric and Sears. Every organization must assess its own situation and then choose the level of centralization or decentralization that will work best.

LEARNING OBJECTIVE

5 Understand how the span of management describes an organization.

span of management (or span of control) the number of workers who report directly to one manager

The Span of Management

The fourth major step of organizing a business is establishing the **span of management** (or **span of control**), which is the number of workers who report directly to one manager. For hundreds of years, theorists have searched for an ideal span of management. When it became apparent that there is no perfect number of subordinates for a manager to supervise, they turned their attention to the more general issue of whether the span should be wide or narrow. This issue is complicated by the fact that the span of management may change from one department to another department within the same organization. For example, the span of management at Federal Express varies within the company. Departments in which workers do the same tasks on a regular basis—customer service agents, handlers and sorters, couriers, and the like—usually have a span of management of fifteen to twenty employees per manager. Groups performing multiple and different tasks are more likely to have smaller spans of management consisting of five or six employees.[7] Thus, Federal Express uses a wide span of control in some departments and a narrow span of control in others.

Wide and Narrow Spans of Control

A *wide* span of management exists when a manager has a larger number of subordinates. A *narrow* span exists when the manager has only a few subordinates. Several factors determine the span that is better for a particular manager (see Figure 8.4). Generally, the span of control may be wide when (1) the manager and the subordinates are very competent, (2) the organization has a well-established set of standard operating procedures, and (3) few new problems are expected to arise. The span should be narrow when (1) workers are physically located far from one another, (2) the manager has much work to do in addition to supervising workers, (3) a great deal of interaction is required between supervisor and workers, and (4) new problems arise frequently.

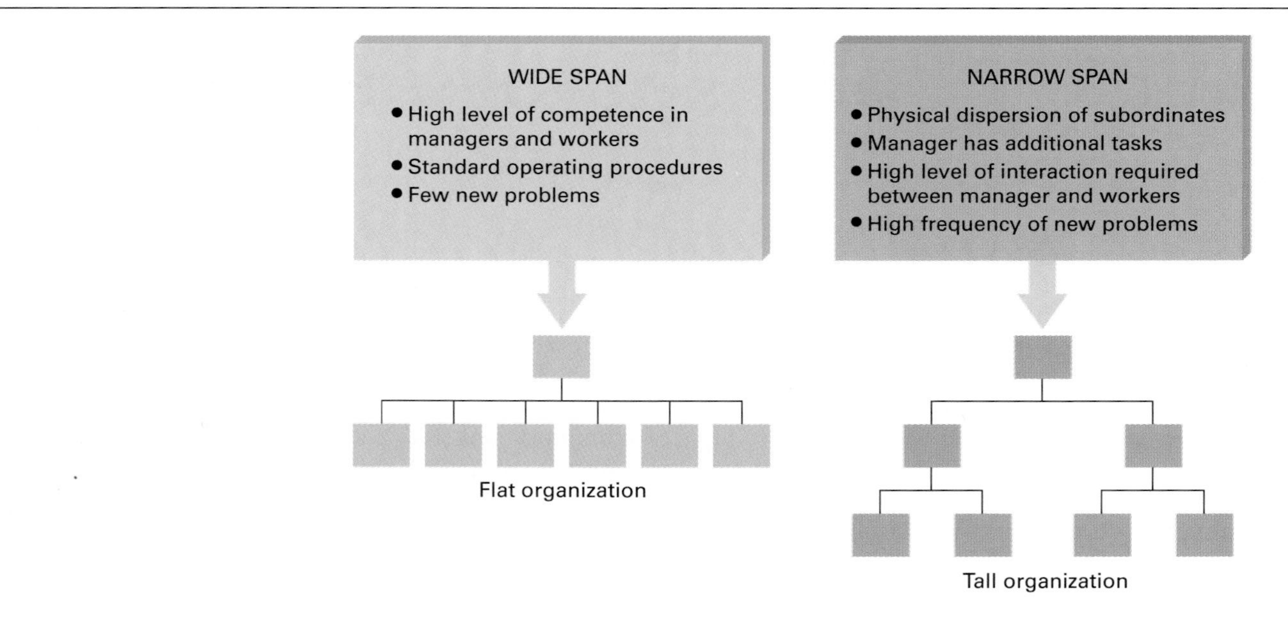

figure 8.4

The Span of Management

Several criteria determine whether a firm uses a wide span of management, in which several workers report to one manager, or a narrow span, in which a manager supervises only a few workers.

Organizational Height

The span of management has an obvious impact on relations between managers and workers. It has a more subtle but equally important impact on the height of the organization. **Organizational height** is the number of layers, or levels, of management in a firm. The span of management plays a direct role in determining the height of the organization, as shown in Figure 8.4. If spans of management are wider, fewer levels are needed and the organization is *flat*. If spans of management are generally narrow, more levels are needed and the resulting organization is *tall*.

In a taller organization, administrative costs are higher because more managers are needed. And communication among levels may become distorted because information has to pass up and down through more people. Although flat organizations avoid those problems, their managers may have to perform more administrative duties simply because there are fewer managers. Wide spans of management may also require managers to spend considerably more time supervising and working with subordinates.

Using the Internet

Andersen Consulting is a leader that firms turn to for advice about reorganization of current structures and processes. A strategic alliance with Microsoft will drive the firm further into the specialized consulting services field of helping clients adapt to e-business. You can learn more about Andersen's activities as well as their client's reorganization efforts in the new economy beginning at their home page **http://www.ac.com/**.

organizational height the number of layers, or levels, of management in a firm

Chain of Command: Line and Staff Management

LEARNING OBJECTIVE

6 Understand how the chain of command is established by using line and staff management

Establishing the chain of command is another step in organizing a business. It reaches from the highest to the lowest levels of management. A **line management position** is part of the chain of command; it is a position in which a person makes decisions and gives orders to subordinates to achieve the goals of the organization. A **staff management position,** by contrast, is a position created to provide support, advice, and expertise to someone in the chain of command. Staff managers are not part of the chain of command but do have authority over their assistants (see Figure 8.5).

line management position a position that is part of the chain of command and that includes direct responsibility for achieving the goals of the organization

staff management position a position created to provide support, advice, and expertise within an organization

Line and Staff Positions Compared

Both line and staff managers are needed for effective management, but the two kinds of positions differ in important ways. The basic difference is in terms of authority. Line managers have *line authority*, which means they can make decisions and issue directives that relate to the organization's goals.

Staff managers seldom have this kind of authority. Instead, they usually have either advisory authority or functional authority. *Advisory authority* is simply the expectation that line managers will consult the appropriate staff manager when making decisions. Functional authority is stronger, and in some ways it is like line authority. *Functional authority* is the authority of staff managers to make decisions and issue directives, but only about their own areas of expertise. For example, a legal adviser for Nike can decide whether to retain a particular clause in a contract, but not what price to charge for a new product. Contracts are part of the legal adviser's area of expertise; pricing is not.

spotlight

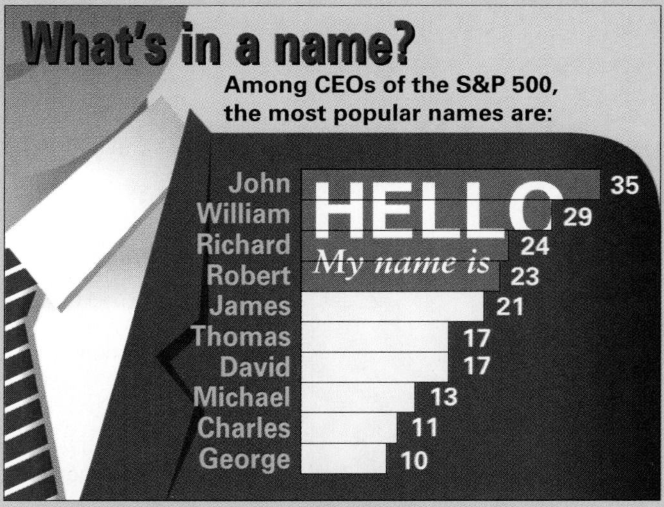

Source: Copyright 2000, USA TODAY. Reprinted with permission.

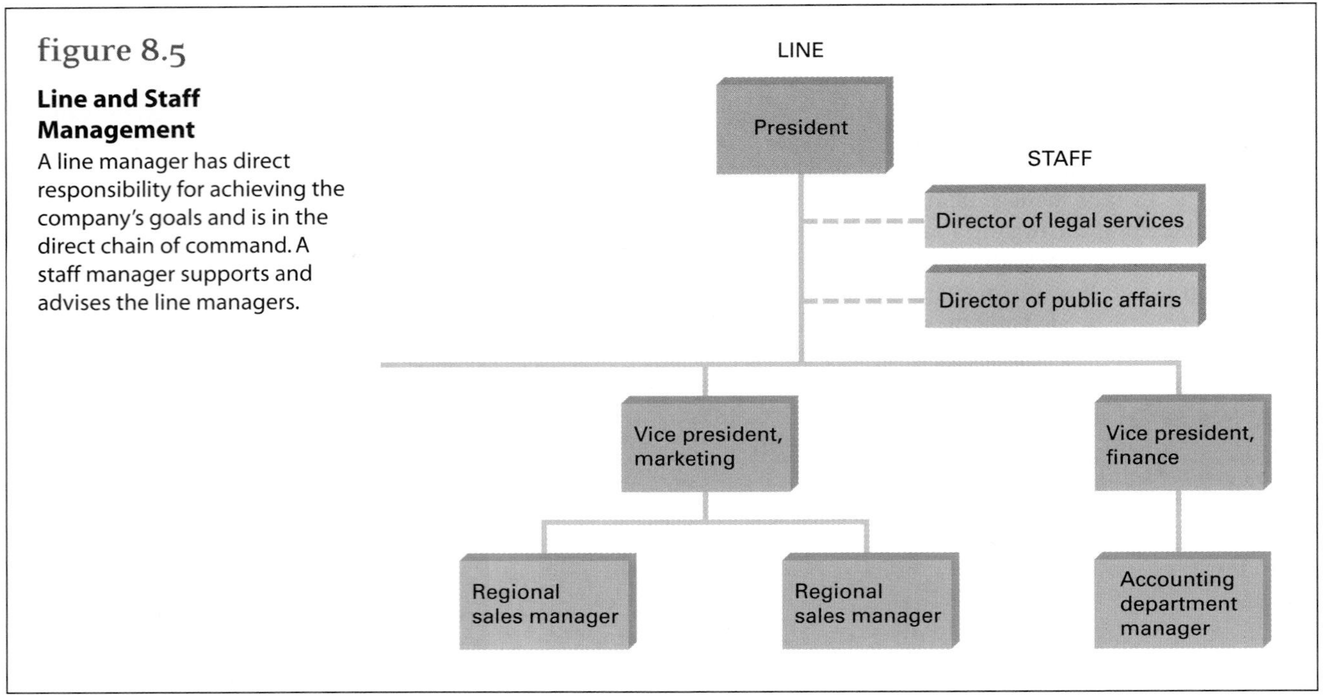

figure 8.5

Line and Staff Management

A line manager has direct responsibility for achieving the company's goals and is in the direct chain of command. A staff manager supports and advises the line managers.

Line-Staff Conflict

For a variety of reasons, conflict between line managers and staff managers is fairly common in businesses. Staff managers often have more formal education and are sometimes younger (and perhaps more ambitious) than line managers. Line managers may perceive staff managers as a threat to their own authority and thus may resent them. For their part, staff managers may become annoyed or angry if their expert recommendations—in public relations or human resources management, for example—are not adopted by line management.

table 8.1 **Five Characteristics of Organizational Structure**

Dimension	Purpose
Job design	To divide the work performed by an organization into parts and assign each part a position within the organization.
Departmentalization	To group various positions in an organization into manageable units. Departmentalization may be based on function, product, location, customer, or a combination of these bases.
Delegation	To distribute part of a manager's work and power to other workers. A deliberate concentration of authority at the upper levels of the organization creates a centralized structure. A wide distribution of authority into the lower levels of the organization creates a decentralized structure.
Span of management	To set the number of workers who report directly to one manager. A narrow span has only a few workers reporting to one manager. A wide span has a large number of workers reporting to one manager.
Line and staff management	To distinguish between those positions that are part of the chain of command and those that provide support, advice, or expertise to those in the chain of command.

Fortunately, there are several ways to minimize the likelihood of such conflict. One way is to integrate line and staff managers into one team working together. Another is to ensure that the areas of responsibility of line and staff managers are clearly defined. Finally, line and staff managers can both be held accountable for the results of their activities.

Before studying the next topic—forms of organizational structure—you may want to review the five organization-shaping characteristics that we have just discussed. See Table 8.1 for a summary.

Forms of Organizational Structure

LEARNING OBJECTIVE

7 Describe the four basic forms of organizational structure: bureaucratic, matrix, cluster, and network.

Up to this point, we have focused our attention on the major characteristics of organizational structure. In many ways, this is like discussing the important parts of a jigsaw puzzle one by one. Now it is time to put the puzzle together. In particular, we discuss four basic forms of organizational structure: bureaucratic, matrix, cluster, and network.

The Bureaucratic Structure

bureaucratic structure a management system based on a formal framework of authority that is carefully outlined and precisely followed

The term *bureaucracy* is often used in an unfavorable context, to suggest rigidity and red tape. This image may be negative, but it does capture some of the essence of the bureaucratic structure.

A **bureaucratic structure** is a management system based on a formal framework of authority that is carefully outlined and precisely followed. A bureaucracy is likely to have the following characteristics:

1. A high level of job specialization
2. Departmentalization by function
3. Formal patterns of delegation
4. A high degree of centralization
5. Narrow spans of management, resulting in a tall organization
6. Clearly defined line and staff positions, with formal relationships between the two

Perhaps the best examples of contemporary bureaucracies are government agencies and colleges and universities. Consider the very rigid and formal college entrance and registration procedures. The reason for such procedures is to ensure that the organization is able to deal with large numbers of people in an equitable and fair manner. We may not enjoy them, but regulations and standard operating procedures pretty much guarantee uniform treatment.

Another example of a bureaucratic structure is the U.S. Postal Service. Like colleges and universities, the post office relies on procedures and rules to accomplish the organization's goals. However, the postal service has streamlined some of its procedures and

Have you ever stood in line at a bureaucratic-structured organization? These individuals are standing in line at the Department of Motor Vehicles in New York City. A frequent complaint about bureaucratic-structured organizations is that the emphasis is on procedures and rules rather than on customer service.

initiated new services in order to compete with Federal Express, United Parcel Service, and other delivery services. As a result, customer satisfaction has begun to improve.

The biggest drawback to the bureaucratic structure is its lack of flexibility. A bureaucracy has trouble adjusting to change and coping with the unexpected. Because today's business environment is dynamic and complex, many firms have found that the bureaucratic structure is not an appropriate organizational structure. Interestingly, the Internet brings a new way of looking at the rigidity of bureaucratic structures. According to Eric Schmitt, an analyst at Forrester Research Inc., organizations are in the midst of changing the way they do business as they adapt their corporate structure to an online presence based on Internet interaction with customers and suppliers. For example, Cisco Systems Inc. uses Ariba Inc.'s software to run its online purchasing system, which directs its 20,000 employees' interactions with more than 3,000 suppliers. Besides helping to standardize interaction processes, the result has been an estimated 10 percent to 20 percent savings.[8]

The Matrix Structure

matrix structure an organizational structure that combines vertical and horizontal lines of authority, usually by superimposing product departmentalization on a functionally departmentalized organization

cross-functional team a group of employees from different departments who work together on a specific project

The matrix structure is one of the more complex types of organizational structure. When the matrix structure is used, individuals report to more than one superior at the same time. The **matrix structure** combines vertical and horizontal lines of authority. The matrix structure occurs when product departmentalization is superimposed on a functionally departmentalized organization. In a matrix organization, authority flows both down and across.

To understand the structure of a matrix organization, first consider the usual functional arrangement, with people working in departments such as engineering, production, finance, and marketing. Now suppose we assign people from these departments to a special group that is working on a new project as a team. This team is called a **cross-functional team.** Frequently, cross-functional teams are charged with the responsibility of developing new products. For example, Ford Motor Company assem-

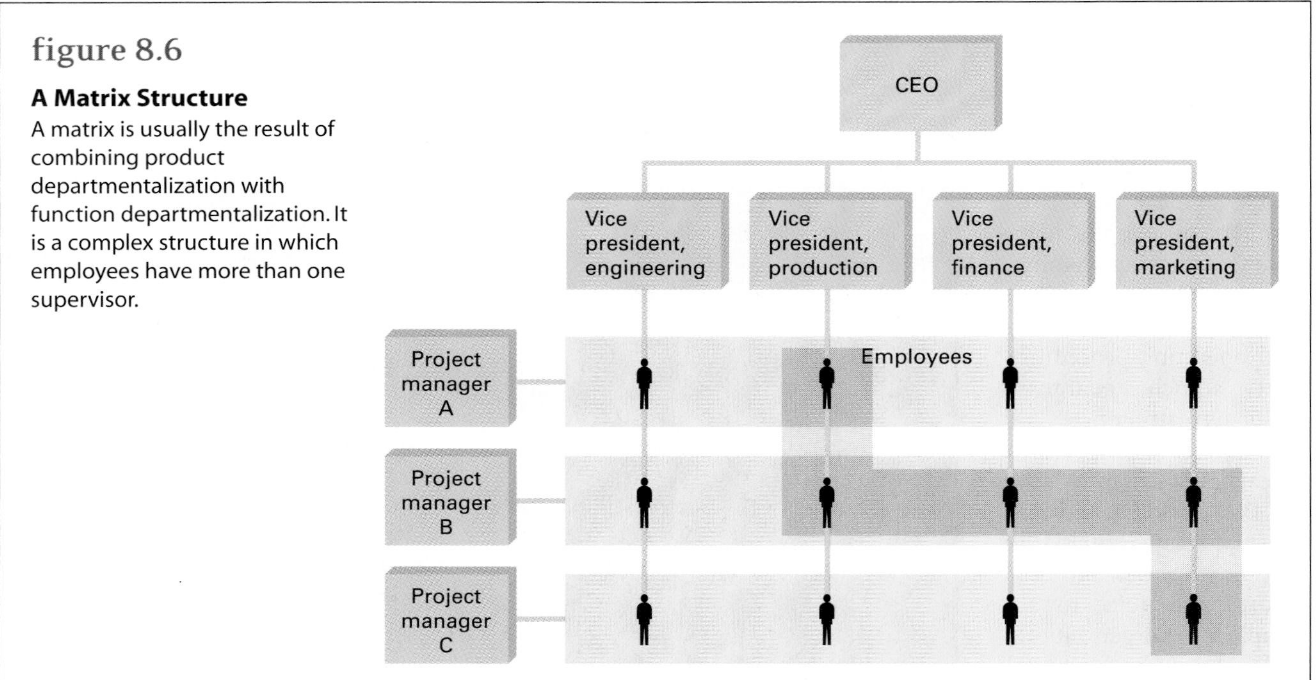

figure 8.6

A Matrix Structure

A matrix is usually the result of combining product departmentalization with function departmentalization. It is a complex structure in which employees have more than one supervisor.

Source: Ricky W. Griffin, *Management*, 6th ed. Copyright © 1999 by Houghton Mifflin Company. Adapted with permission.

bled a special project team to design and manufacture its global cars. The manager in charge of a team is usually called a *project manager*. Any individual who is working with the team reports to *both* the project manager and the individual's superior in the functional department (see Figure 8.6)

Cross-functional team projects may be temporary, in which case the team is disbanded once the mission is accomplished, or they may be permanent. These teams are often empowered to make major decisions. When a cross-functional team is employed, prospective team members may receive special training, because effective teamwork can require skills different from those needed when working alone. For cross-functional teams to be successful, team members must be given specific information on the job each is required to perform. The team must also develop a sense of cohesiveness and maintain good communications among its members.

Matrix structures offer several advantages over other organizational forms. Added flexibility is probably the most obvious advantage. The matrix structure also can increase productivity, raise morale, and nurture creativity and innovation. In addition, employees experience personal development through doing a variety of jobs.

The matrix structure also has some disadvantages. Having employees report to more than one supervisor can cause confusion about who is in charge in various situations. Like committees, teams may take longer to resolve problems and issues than individuals working alone. Other difficulties include personality clashes, poor communication, undefined individual roles, unclear responsibilities, and finding ways to reward individual and team performance simultaneously. Because more managers and support staff may be needed, a matrix structure may be more expensive to maintain than other forms of organizational structure.

The Cluster Structure

A **cluster structure** is a type of business that consists primarily of teams with no or very few underlying departments. This type of structure is also called *team* or *collaborative*. In this type of organization, team members work together on a project until it is finished, and then the team may remain intact and be assigned another project or team members may be reassigned to different teams, depending on their skills and the needs of the organization. In a cluster organization the operating unit is the team and remains relatively small. If a team becomes too large, it can be split into multiple teams or individuals can be assigned to other existing teams.

cluster structure an organization that consists primarily of teams with no or very few underlying departments

The cluster organizational structure has both strengths and weaknesses. Keeping the teams small provides the organization with the flexibility necessary to change directions quickly, to try new techniques, and to explore new ideas. Some employees in these types of organizations express concerns regarding job security and the increased amount of stress that arises due to the fact that changes occur rapidly.[9]

The Network Structure

In a **network structure** (sometimes called a *virtual organization*) administration is the primary function performed, and other functions such as engineering, production, marketing, and finance are contracted out to other organizations. Frequently, a network organization does not manufacture the products that it sells. This type of organization has only a few permanent employees consisting of top management and a few hourly clerical workers. Leased facilities and equipment as well as temporary workers are increased or decreased as the needs of the organization change. Thus, there is rather limited formal structure associated with a network organization.

network structure an organization in which administration is the primary function and most other functions are contracted out to other firms

An obvious strength of a network structure is flexibility which allows an organization to quickly adjust to changes. Some of the challenges faced by managers in network structured organizations include controlling the quality of work performed by other organizations, low morale and high turnover among hourly workers, and the vulnerability associated with relying on outside contractors.[10]

LEARNING OBJECTIVE

8 Summarize how corporate culture, intrapreneurship, committees, coordination techniques, informal groups, and the grapevine affect an organization.

Additional Factors That Influence an Organization

As you might expect, other factors in addition to those already covered in this chapter affect the way a large corporation operates on a day-to-day basis. To get a "true picture" of the organizational structure of a huge corporation like Marriott, for example, which employs over 143,000 people,[11] you need to consider the topics discussed in this section.

Corporate Culture

corporate culture the inner rites, rituals, heroes, and values of a firm

Managers do not perform their jobs in a vacuum. Most managers function within a corporate culture. A **corporate culture** is generally defined as the inner rites, rituals, heroes, and values of a firm. An organization's culture can have a powerful influence on how its employees think and act. It can also determine how the public perceives the organization. At E-trade, the online brokerage, the CEO believes that corporate culture is crucial for catapulting his firm to success. He spends considerable time and resources crafting a culture for the Internet age that may seem downright bizarre and yet at times brilliant. He wants his company to be filled with people who are wildly creative, arch-competitive, and so closely knit that they are almost family. To make his executives move faster, the CEO held a one-day Formula One race. To create a light atmosphere, he had his employees carry rubber chickens or wear propeller beanies. To create familylike bonding, he had his managers attend a cooking school that required them to depend on each other to whip up gourmet meals.[12]

Corporate culture is generally thought to have a very strong influence on a firm's performance over time. Hence it is useful to be able to assess a firm's corporate culture.

Examining Ethics

Dealing with Dishonesty

WHAT IS THE EFFECT OF CORPORATE culture on employee honesty? This is a major issue in today's hotly competitive business world, where a "win-at-all-costs" climate can inadvertently encourage employees to cut ethical corners. Padded expense accounts and travel reimbursements are two other areas where managers may turn a blind eye when employees fudge the figures.

Dishonesty is a problem in all sizes and types of organizations, although employees believe that small-business leaders have more integrity, according to a recent survey. Leadership is critical: Creating a culture of honesty starts at the top, where corporate values are molded. Corporate attitudes toward honesty are reinforced as the employees watch the leaders at work. This is often easier in smaller organizations, where employees can "see the day-to-day decisions made by a leader," says polling expert Jeff Marr. "The values of the leadership are more visible and under scrutiny," Marr adds.

Paul Orfalea, the founder of the Kinko's business services chain, learned first-hand what a difference leadership can make. Years ago, Orfalea had to confront a manager who was caught stealing. The manager said he was driven by the stress of a family crisis, so Orfalea took pity and didn't fire him—which angered other Kinko's managers and employees. "Here they were playing by the rules," recalls Orfalea, "and I let this guy who stole continue to work for us. My unwillingness to take action screwed up the working environment at several stores."

Although this incident occurred twenty years ago, Orfalea never forgot the lesson he learned: "I realized from that experience that I couldn't let my heart rule my mind if I were to succeed in business," he says. "I'm tougher now. I'm more consistent. I'm still nice, but I don't tolerate lying and stealing. As for that manager, he stole again. That time, I fired him."

Issues to Consider

1. Under what circumstances, if ever, do you think it is appropriate for an employee to be dishonest at work? Explain your answer.
2. As a small-business leader, what would you do to discourage dishonesty in your organization?

Common indicators include the physical setting (building, office layouts, and so on); what the company itself says about its corporate culture (in its advertising and news releases, for example); how the company greets its guests (does it have formal or informal reception areas?); and how employees spend their time (working alone in an office most of the time or spending much of the day working with others).

Corporate culture. Some organizations' corporate cultures allow for casual attire and meetings in informal settings. This isn't what most people expect an annual meeting to look like, but these board members of M.E.D.I.C.O., an international nonprofit medical association, are discussing serious business.

Goffee and Jones have identified four distinct types of corporate cultures (see Figure 8.7). One is called the *networked culture*, characterized by a base of trust and friendship among employees, a strong commitment and feeling of loyalty to the organization, and a relaxed and informal environment. The *mercenary culture* embodies the feelings of passion, energy, sense of purpose, and excitement for one's work. The term *mercenary* does not imply that employees are motivated to work only for the money, but this is part of it. In this culture employees are very intense, focused, and determined to win. In the *fragmented culture*, employees do not necessarily become friends, and they work "at" the organization, not "for" it. Employees have a high degree of autonomy, flexibility, and equality. The *communal culture* combines the positive traits of the networked culture and the mercenary culture—those of friendship, commitment, high focus on performance, and high energy. People's lives revolve around the product in this culture, and success by anyone in the organization is celebrated by all.[13]

Sociability	Low Solidarity	High Solidarity
High	**Networked Culture** • Extrovert energized by relationships • Tolerant of ambiguities and have low needs for structure • Can spot politics and act to stop "negative" politics • Consider yourself easygoing, affable, and loyal to others	**Communal Culture** • You consider yourself passionate • Strong need to identify with something bigger than yourself • You enjoy being in teams • Prepared to make sacrifices for the greater good
Low	**Fragmented Culture** • Are a reflective and self-contained introvert • Have a high autonomy drive and strong desire to work independently • Have a strong sense of self • Consider yourself analytical rather than intuitive	**Mercenary Culture** • Goal-oriented and have an obsessive desire to complete tasks • Thrive on competitive energy • Keep "relationships" out of work—develop them only to achieve your goals • Keep things clear-cut and see the world in black and white

figure 8.7 **Types of Corporate Cultures**

Source: "Types of Corporate Culture," from *The Character of a Corporation* by Rob Goffee and Gareth Jones. Copyright © 1998 by Rob Goffee and Gareth Jones. Reprinted by permission of HarperCollins Publishers, Inc.

Adapting to change

[illegible]ging Organizational [illegible]nge

[illegible]DAY'S HIGHLY DYNAMIC, FIERCELY [illegible]titive global business environment, man[illegible] [illegible]t every level must be prepared to serve as [illegible]aders within the organization. But what [illegible]ney be seeking to change—and how?

[illegible]anagement expert Peter F. Drucker urges man[illegible]s to follow a policy he calls "organized abandon[illegible]nt." This entails systematically examining prod[illegible]cts, services, processes, partnerships, and every other activity to weed out those that no longer contribute to organizational performance. Do this with an eye to the future, so the company stays in shape for the challenges and opportunities of tomorrow as well as today.

Next, change leaders should regularly examine every activity to determine which can be improved, how they can be improved, and by how much. It's important for managers to set specific goals for improvement in key areas—and then push for improvement year after year. These kinds of changes can transform the company and lead to new businesses, Drucker notes.

Change leaders should also pay close attention to environmental changes, such as demographic shifts and industry disturbances, which can open up promising opportunities for new products and new profits. Making changes to respond to environmental shifts may not be speedy or easy, however. This is why managers must remain champions of change throughout the inevitable ups and downs of planning, testing, implementation, and fine-tuning—a sometimes lengthy process.

As difficult as change leadership may be, MIT professor Peter Senge believes it's vital. Without change, he says, organizations stagnate. If employees aren't encouraged to change by innovating or taking risks, they're likely to lose the passion and commitment that makes work satisfying and meaningful. Organizations should therefore strive to make change leadership an integral part of the corporate culture.

Some experts believe that cultural change is needed when the company's environment is changing significantly, when the industry is becoming more competitive, when the company's performance is mediocre, when the company is growing rapidly, or when the company is about to become a truly large organization. Organizations of the future will look quite different from those of today. In particular, experts predict that tomorrow's business firms will be made up of small task-oriented work groups, each with control over its own activities. These small groups will be coordinated through an elaborate computer network and held together by a strong corporate culture. Businesses operating in the fast-changing environment of the Internet require leadership that supports trust and risk-taking. Creating a culture of trust in an organization can lead to increases in growth, profit, productivity, and job satisfaction. A culture of trust can help retain the best people, inspire customer loyalty, develop new markets, and increase creativity. Critics suggest that IBM inadvertently developed a culture that punished those that took good risks and then failed in their endeavors. As a result, up to the early 1990s the organization became bureaucratic and people gradually stopped taking competitive risks to avoid failure. Today IBM's leadership approach is vastly different, reflecting the new age of creative thinking about the ways to manage organizations.[14]

Intrapreneurship

intrapreneur an employee who pushes an innovative idea, product, or process through the organization

Since innovations and new product development are important to companies, and entrepreneurs are among the most innovative people around, it seems almost natural that an entrepreneurial character would prominently surface in many of today's larger organizations. An **intrapreneur** is an employee who takes responsibility for pushing an innovative idea, product, or process through the organization.[15] An intrapreneur possesses the confidence and drive of an entrepreneur but is allowed to use organizational resources for idea development. For example, Art Fry, inventor of the colorful Post-it notes that Americans can't live without, is a devoted advocate of intrapreneurship.

Nurturing his note-pad idea at Minnesota Mining and Manufacturing for years, Fry speaks highly of the intrapreneurial commitment at 3M. Fry indicates that an *intrapreneur* is an individual who doesn't have all the skills to get the job done and thus has to work within an organization, making use of its skills and attributes.

Committees

Today business firms use several types of committees that affect organizational structure. An **ad hoc committee** is created for a specific short-term purpose, such as reviewing the firm's employee benefits plan. Once its work is finished, the ad hoc committee disbands. A **standing committee** is a relatively permanent committee charged with performing a recurring task. A firm might establish a budget review committee, for example, to review departmental budget requests on an ongoing basis. Finally, a **task force** is a committee established to investigate a major problem or pending decision. A firm contemplating a merger with another company might form a task force to assess the pros and cons of the merger. When Equinix, of Redwood City, California, needed to build thirty fortified Internet hubs around the world costing $1.2 billion, it hired San Francisco–based Bechtel Corporation to do the complicated and very detailed construction. The century-old, globally experienced Bechtel construction firm also contracted with online grocer Webvan Group of Foster City, California, to build twenty-six warehouses for a $1 billion. (In each of these cases, task force committees were needed to select and then oversee the integration of the work carried out by Bechtel into the individual firms' organizations and operations.)[16]

ad hoc committee a committee created for a specific short-term purpose

standing committee a relatively permanent committee charged with performing some recurring task

task force a committee established to investigate a major problem or pending decision

Committees offer some advantages over individual action. Their several members are, of course, able to bring more information and knowledge to the task at hand. Furthermore, committees tend to make more accurate decisions and to transmit their results through the organization more effectively. However, committee deliberations take much longer than individual actions. In addition, unnecessary compromise may take place within the committee. Or the opposite may occur, as one person dominates (and thus negates) the committee process.

Coordination Techniques

A large organization is forced to coordinate organizational resources to minimize duplication and to maximize effectiveness. One technique is simply to make use of the **managerial hierarchy,** which is the arrangement that provides increasing authority at higher levels of management. One manager is placed in charge of all the resources that are to be coordinated. That person is able to coordinate them by virtue of the authority accompanying that position.

managerial hierarchy the arrangement that provides increasing authority at higher levels of management

Resources can also be coordinated through rules and procedures. For example, a rule can govern how a firm's travel budget is to be allocated. This particular resource, then, would be coordinated in terms of that rule.

In complex situations, more sophisticated coordination techniques may be called for. One approach is to establish a liaison. A liaison is a go-between—a person who coordinates the activities of two groups. Suppose General Motors is negotiating a complicated contract with a supplier of steering wheels. The supplier might appoint a liaison whose primary responsibility is to coordinate the contract negotiations. Finally, for *very* complex coordination needs, a committee could be established. Suppose General Motors is in the process of purchasing the steering-wheel supplier. In this case, a committee might be appointed to integrate the new firm into General Motors' larger organizational structure.

The Informal Organization

So far, we have discussed the organization as a more or less formal structure consisting of interrelated positions. This is the organization that is shown on an organization chart. There is another kind of organization, however, that does not show up on any

informal organization the pattern of behavior and interaction that stems from personal rather than official relationships

informal group a group created by the members themselves to accomplish goals that may or may not be relevant to the organization

chart. We define this **informal organization** as the pattern of behavior and interaction that stems from personal rather than official relationships. Firmly embedded within every informal organization are informal groups and the notorious grapevine.

Informal Groups An **informal group** is created by the group members themselves to accomplish goals that may or may not be relevant to the organization. Workers may create an informal group to go bowling, form a union, get a particular manager fired or transferred, or have lunch together every day. The group may last for several years or only a few hours.

Employees join informal groups for a variety of reasons. Perhaps the main reason is that people like to be with others who are similar to themselves. Or it may be that the goals of the group appeal to the individual. Others may join informal groups simply because they have a need to be with their associates and to be accepted by them.

Informal groups can be powerful forces in organizations. They can restrict output, or they can help managers through tight spots. They can cause disagreement and conflict, or they can help boost morale and job satisfaction. They can show new people how to contribute to the organization, or they can help people get away with substandard performance. Clearly, managers should be aware of these informal groups. Those who make the mistake of fighting the informal organization have a major obstacle to overcome.

grapevine the informal communications network within an organization

The Grapevine The **grapevine** is the informal communications network within an organization. It is completely separate from—and sometimes much faster than—the organization's formal channels of communication. Formal communication usually follows a path that parallels the organizational chain of command. By contrast, information can be transmitted through the grapevine in any direction—up, down, diagonally, or horizontally across the organizational structure. Subordinates may pass information to their bosses, an executive may relay something to a maintenance worker, or there may be an exchange of information between people who work in totally unrelated departments.

Grapevine information may be concerned with topics ranging from the latest management decisions, to the results of today's World Series game, to pure gossip. It can be important or of little interest. And it can be highly accurate or totally distorted.

How should managers treat the grapevine? Certainly they would be making a big mistake if they tried to eliminate it. People working together, day in and day out, are going to communicate. A more rational approach is to recognize the existence of the grapevine as a part—though an unofficial part—of the organization. For example, managers should respond promptly and aggressively to inaccurate grapevine information to minimize the damage that such misinformation might do. Moreover, the grapevine can come in handy when managers are on the receiving end of important communications from the informal organization.

In the next chapter, we apply these and other management concepts to an extremely important business function: the production of goods and services.

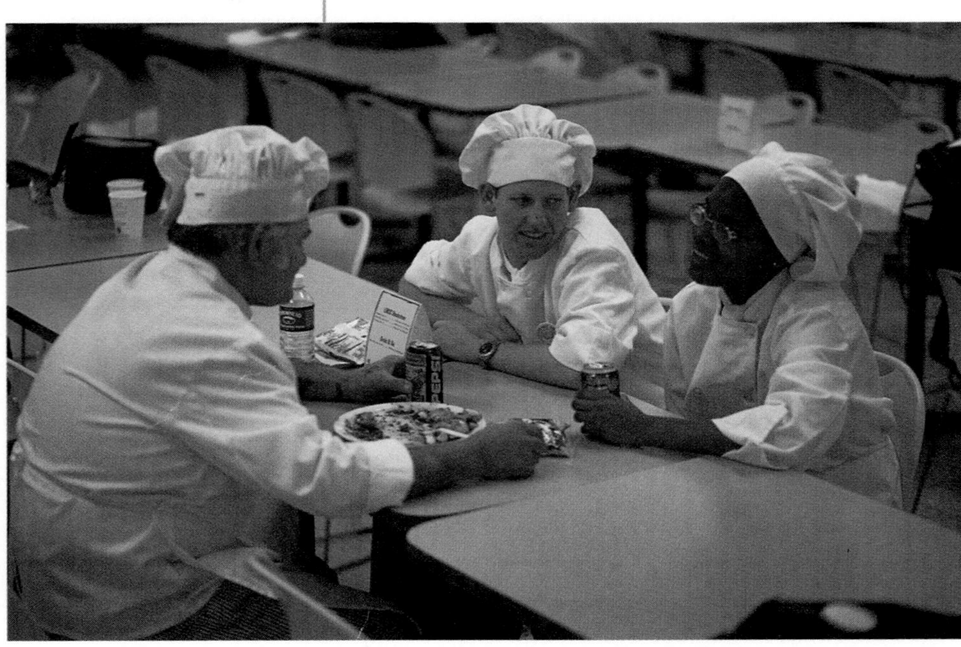

The grapevine at work. Informal communication through the grapevine can have both negative and positive effects on an organization. These hospital cooks gathered in the hospital's cafeteria might be planning next week's menu, gossiping about a co-worker, or even discussing the latest hit movie.

RETURN TO Inside Business

JORMA OLLILA TOOK NOKIA from toilet paper to telecommunications, reinventing the company as a global market leader in mobile phones and Internet access. His top-down support for organizational flexibility and empowerment keeps the firm nimble so it can jump on new opportunities and quickly adapt to local conditions around the world.

In fact, the hierarchy can be so flexible that new employees are sometimes unsure of the formal lines of authority. "People who join Nokia spend a few months trying to figure it out," observes one Nokia human resources manager. "You really have to figure out a network of people to get things done."

If he sees no hope of achieving a growth rate of 25 percent a year, one of Ollila's few ironclad rules is to divest himself of those businesses that are unable to grow at that pace. Another is that certain top managers must retain final decision-making authority on key issues, such as product design, to ensure consistency. With a few standard rules, a flexible organization, and a roster of talented employees, Nokia is continuing its drive to secure the products and markets of tomorrow.

Questions

1. What role does corporate culture play in Nokia's organizational flexibility?
2. How important are informal groups likely to be in flexible organizations such as Nokia?

chapter Review

SUMMARY

1 Understand what an organization is and identify its characteristics.

An organization is a group of two or more people working together to achieve a common set of goals. The relationships among positions within an organization can be illustrated by means of an organization chart. Five specific characteristics—job design, departmentalization, delegation, span of management, and chain of command—help determine what an organization chart and the organization itself look like.

2 Explain why job specialization is important.

Job specialization is the separation of all the activities within an organization into smaller components and the assignment of those different components to different people. Several factors combine to make specialization a useful technique for designing jobs, but high levels of specialization may cause employee dissatisfaction and boredom. One technique for overcoming these problems is job rotation.

3 Identify the various bases for departmentalization.

Departmentalization is the grouping of jobs into manageable units. Typical bases for departmentalization are by function, product, location, or customer. Because each of these bases provides particular advantages, most firms—especially larger ones—use a combination of different bases in different organizational situations.

4 Explain how decentralization follows from delegation.

Delegation is the assigning of part of a manager's work to other workers. It involves the following three steps: (a) assigning responsibility, (b) granting authority, and (c) creating accountability. A decentralized firm is one that delegates as much power as possible to people in the lower management levels. In a centralized firm, on the other hand, power is systematically retained at the upper levels.

5 Understand how the span of management describes an organization.

The span of management is the number of workers who report directly to a manager. Spans are generally characterized as wide (many workers per manager) or narrow (few workers per manager). Wide spans generally result in flat organizations (few layers of management); narrow spans generally result in tall organizations (many layers of management).

6 Understand how the chain of command is established by using line and staff management.

A line position is one that is in the organization's chain of command, or line of authority. A manager in a line position makes decisions and gives orders to workers to achieve the goals of the organization. On the other hand, a manager in a staff position provides support, advice, and expertise to someone in the chain of command. Staff positions may carry some authority, but it usually applies only within staff areas of expertise.

7 Describe the four basic forms of organizational structure: bureaucratic, matrix, cluster, and network.

There are four basic forms of organizational structure. The bureaucratic structure is characterized by formality and rigidity. With the bureaucratic structure, rules and procedures are used to ensure uniformity. The matrix structure may be visualized as product departmentalization superimposed on functional departmentalization. With the matrix structure, an employee on a cross-functional team reports to both the project manager and the individual's supervisor in a functional department. A cluster structure is an organization that consists primarily of teams with very few underlying functional departments. In an organization with a network structure, the primary function performed internally is administration and other functions are contracted out to other firms.

8 Summarize how corporate culture, intrapreneurship, committees, coordination techniques, informal groups, and the grapevine affect an organization.

Corporate culture, the inner rites, rituals, heroes, and values of a firm, is thought to have a very strong influence on a firm's performance over time. An intrapreneur is an employee in an organizational environment who takes responsibility for pushing an innovative idea, product, or process through the organization. Additional elements that influence an organization include the use of committees and development of techniques for achieving coordination among various groups within the organization. Finally, both informal groups created by group members and an informal communication network called the grapevine may affect an organization and its performance.

KEY TERMS

You should now be able to define and give an example relevant to each of the following terms:

organization (211)
organization chart (212)
chain of command (212)
job specialization (214)
job rotation (215)
departmentalization (215)
departmentalization by function (215)
departmentalization by product (216)
departmentalization by location (216)
departmentalization by customer (216)
delegation (217)
responsibility (217)
authority (217)
accountability (217)
decentralized organization (218)
centralized organization (218)
span of management (or span of control) (220)
organizational height (221)
line management position (221)
staff management position (221)
bureaucratic structure (223)
matrix structure (224)
cross-functional team (224)
cluster structure (225)
network structure (225)
corporate culture (226)
intrapreneur (228)
ad hoc committee (229)
standing committee (229)
task force (229)
managerial hierarchy (229)
informal organization (230)
informal group (230)
grapevine (230)

REVIEW QUESTIONS

1. In what way do organization charts create a picture of an organization?
2. What is the chain of command in an organization?
3. What determines the degree of specialization within an organization?
4. Describe how job rotation can be used to combat the problems caused by job specialization.
5. What are the major differences among the four departmentalization bases?
6. Why do most firms employ a combination of departmentalization bases?
7. What three steps are involved in delegation? Explain each.
8. How does a firm's top management influence its degree of centralization?
9. How is organizational height related to the span of management?
10. What are the key differences between line and staff positions?

11. Contrast the bureaucratic and matrix forms of organizational structure.
12. What are the differences between the cluster structure and the network structure?
13. What is corporate culture? Describe the major types.
14. Which form of organizational structure would probably lead to the strongest informal organization? Why?
15. How may the managerial hierarchy be used to coordinate the organization's resources?

DISCUSSION QUESTIONS

1. Explain how the five steps of the organizing process determine the characteristics of the resulting organization. Which steps are most important?
2. Which kinds of firms would probably operate most effectively as centralized firms? As decentralized firms?
3. How do decisions concerning span of management, the use of committees, and coordination techniques affect organizational structure?
4. How might a manager go about formalizing the informal organization?

VIDEO CASE

T.G.I. Friday's Organizes for Global Expansion

The first T.G.I. Friday's restaurant opened for business in New York City in 1965. It was not, however, until a group of Texas businessmen opened a franchise in Dallas in 1972 that the T.G.I. Friday's we know today—with its Tiffany lamps, antiques and memorabilia, striped awnings, and huge menu—came into existence. By 1972 T.G.I. Friday's was on its way to becoming a nationwide chain. In 1989 it launched its first foray into Asia, and by 1992 it was operating not just in Korea, but in Mexico, Spain, and Great Britain as well. Today Friday's serves its famous Loaded Potato Skins, Spicy Buffalo Wings, and Mocha Mud Pie in 638 restaurants located in 52 countries. With this kind of growth—and $1.5 billion in worldwide sales—came the need to restructure T.G.I. Friday's organization into smaller, more manageable divisions.

In the United States, Friday's divided its organization into four geographic regions: West, Midwest, Northeast, and Southeast. Each region is headed by a vice president of operations who is responsible for about eighty restaurants. About half these are franchises and half are company-owned. Because Friday's executives are located in the geographic area they serve and are available to the restaurants there, they know more about their customers and are better able to meet their needs.

Friday's fifth region—its international one—includes over 165 restaurants in every corner of the world, from Iceland to Ireland to India and many places in between. Although franchisees within specific geographic areas manage their own restaurants, T.G.I. Friday's sends teams from the United States to teach them how to select new employees, where to get the food they need, and how to provide the fun and friendly atmosphere for which Friday's is known. Once restaurants are up and running, however, the regional franchisees are responsible for making their restaurants successful.

Many companies with a global presence modify their products to meet the needs of local cultures. T.G.I. Friday's, however, doesn't change much from country to country or culture to culture. What is important to the restaurant chain is to bring American culture with it wherever it goes, as well as to preserve Friday's own culture of service and fun. As one observer put it, "T.G.I. Friday's oozes apple pie and Chevrolet." When Friday's opened its first restaurant in New Delhi, India, for example, the menu included Friday's usual mix of American, Italian, and Mexican specialties, though to suit local tastes, it had more than the usual number of vegetarian dishes. In the five Japanese T.G.I. Friday's restaurants, fourteen of sixty-nine menu items are geared to local tastes. "If we serve too many Japanese dishes, our atmosphere will suffer," explains Tetsuya Emura, the president of T.G.I. Friday's Japan. "If we serve too few, we won't get the business, so we settled on 20 percent of the menu."

T.G.I. Friday's is just one restaurant division of Carlson Restaurants, its parent company. One of Carlson's other divisions, Star Concepts, operates a series of upscale restaurants. These include Star Canyon, a three-restaurant chain featuring Texas-style food and decor, and Taqueria Canonita, two restaurants reminiscent of Mexico's marketplace taquerias. Overseeing the management of all these restaurant divisions is Wally Doolin, Carlson's CEO, who has an unconventional view of the relationship between headquarters and the divisions. "We give a level of service that makes our guests recognize the difference," notes Doolin. "As an extension of that, our store employees and managers should expect the same thing from the corporate office. This may sound strange, but I think too much credit is given to CEOs for things they're not directly controlling."[17]

Questions

1. What type of departmentalization basis is T.G.I. Friday's using? Explain your answer.
2. T.G.I. Friday's is currently undergoing considerable global expansion. To what extent is such expansion likely to force T.G.I. Friday's to change its organizational departmentalization?
3. Does Carlson Restaurants have a centralized or decentralized organization? How do you know?

Building skills for career success

1. Exploring the Internet

After studying the various organizational structures described in this chapter and the reasons for employing them, you may be interested in learning about the organizational structures in place at large firms. As noted in the chapter, departmentalization is typically based on function, product, location, and customer. Many large firms successfully use a combination of these organizational strategies. You can gain a good sense of which organizational theme prevails in an industry by looking at several corporate sites. Visit the text web site for updates to this exercise.

Assignment

1. Explore the web site of any large firm you believe is representative of its industry and find its organization chart or a description of its organization. Create a brief organization chart from the information you have found. (You may choose one of the consulting firms listed in the Internet exercise for Chapter 7).
2. Describe the firm's organizational division.

2. Developing Critical Thinking Skills

A firm's culture is a reflection of its most basic beliefs, values, customs, and rituals. Because it can have a powerful influence on how employees think and act, this culture can also have a powerful influence on a firm's performance. The influence may be for the better, of course, as in the case of Southwest Airlines, or it may be for the worse, as in the case of a bureaucratic organization whose employees feel hopelessly mired in red tape. When a company is concerned about mediocre performance and declining sales figures, its managers would do well to examine the cultural environment to see what might be in need of change.

Assignment

1. Analyze the cultural environment in which you work. (If you have no job, consider your school as your workplace, and your instructor as your supervisor.) Ask yourself and your coworkers (or classmates) the following questions and record the answers:
   a. Do you feel your supervisors welcome your ideas and respect them even when they may disagree with them? Do you take pride in your work? Do you feel your work is appreciated? Do you think the amount of work assigned to you is reasonable? Are you adequately compensated for your work?
   b. Are you proud to be associated with the company? Do you believe what the company says about itself in its advertisements? Are there any company policies or rules, written or unwritten, that you feel are unfair? Do you think there is an opportunity for you to advance in this environment?
   c. How much independence do you have in carrying out your assignments? Are you ever allowed to act on your own, or do you feel you have to consult with your supervisor on every detail?
   d. Do you enjoy the atmosphere in which you work? Is the physical setting pleasant? How often do you laugh in an average workday? How well do you get along with your supervisor and coworkers?
   e. Do you feel the company cares about you? Will your supervisor give you time off when you have some pressing personal need? If the company had to downsize, how do you think you would be treated?
2. Using the responses to these questions, write a two-page paper describing how the culture of your workplace affects your performance and the overall performance of the firm. Point out the cultural factors that have the most beneficial and negative effects. Include your thoughts on how negative effects could be reversed.

3. Building Team Skills

An organization chart is a diagram showing how employees and tasks are grouped and how the lines of communication and authority flow within an organization. These charts can look very different depending on a number of factors, including the nature and size of the business, the way it is departmentalized, its patterns of delegating authority, and its span of management.

Assignment

1. Working in a team, use the following information to draw an organization chart:

   The KDS Design Center works closely with two home-construction companies, Amex and Highmass. KDS's role is to help customers select materials for their new homes and to ensure that their selections are communicated accurately to the builders. The company is also a retailer of wallpaper, blinds, and drapery. The retail department, the Amex accounts, and the Highmass accounts make up KDS's three departments.

   The company has the following positions:
   President
   Executive vice president
   Managers, 2
   Appointment coordinators, 2
   Amex coordinators, 2
   Highmass coordinators, 2
   Consultants/designers for the Amex and Highmass accounts, 15
   Retail positions, 4
   Payroll and billing personnel, 1
2. After your team has drawn the organization chart, discuss the following:
   a. What type of organizational structure does your chart depict? Is it a bureaucratic, matrix, cluster, or network structure? Why?

b. How does KDS use departmentalization?
c. To what extent is authority in the company centralized or decentralized?
d. What is the span of management within KDS?
e. Which positions are line positions and which are staff? Why?

3. Prepare a three-page report summarizing what the chart revealed about relationships and tasks at the KDS Design Center and what your team learned about the value of organization charts. Include your chart in your report.

4. Researching Different Careers

In the past, company loyalty and ability to assume increasing job responsibility usually assured advancement within an organization. While the reasons for seeking advancement (the desire for a better-paying position, more prestige, and job satisfaction) have not changed, the qualifications for career advancement have. In today's business environment, climbing the corporate ladder requires packaging and marketing yourself. To be promoted within your company, or be considered for employment with another company it is wise to improve your skills continually. By taking workshops and seminars, or enrolling in community college courses, you can keep up with the changing technology in your industry. Networking with people in your business, or community can help you find a new job. Most jobs are filled through personal contacts. Who you know can be important.

A list of your accomplishments on the job can reveal your strengths and weaknesses. Setting goals for improvement helps to increase your self-confidence.

Be sure to recognize the signs of job dissatisfaction. It may be time to move to another position or company.

Assignment

Are you prepared to climb the corporate ladder? Do a self-assessment by analyzing the following areas and summarize the results in a two-page report.

a. Skills
  - What are your most valuable skills?
  - What skills do you lack?
  - Describe your plan for acquiring new skills and improving your skills.

b. Networking
  - How effectively are you using a mentor?
  - Are you a member of a professional organization?
  - In which community, civic, or church groups are you participating?
  - Whom have you added to your contact list in the last six weeks?

c. Accomplishments
  - What achievements have you reached in your job?
  - What would you like to accomplish? What will it take for you to reach your goal?

d. Promotion or New Job
  - What is your likelihood for getting a promotion?
  - Are you ready for a change? What are you doing or willing to do to find another job?

5. Improving Communication Skills

Delegation of authority involves giving another person responsibility for performing a task and the authority, or power, needed to accomplish the task. The person doing the delegating, however, remains responsible, or accountable, for seeing that the job is done properly. Delegating work is important not only because it is often the only way a manager can accomplish everything that needs to be accomplished; it also gives lower-level employees the opportunity to improve their skills. For a variety of reasons, managers sometimes fail to delegate authority. They may feel their subordinates are not competent to perform the work properly, or they may feel their subordinates are too competent, in which case they would pose a threat to the manager. And some managers are simply too disorganized to delegate their work.

Assignment

1. Arrange an interview with the manager of a business in your community. Prepare a list of questions you will ask in the interview. They should focus on the following topics:
   a. What is the general pattern of delegation in the company?
   b. To what extent is the organization centralized or decentralized?
   c. How much work does this manager delegate? What are the kinds of tasks delegated?
   d. What are the benefits of delegating work? What are the drawbacks?
   e. Does this manager experience any difficulties in delegating? If so, what are they? Has the manager thought of any ways to resolve them?
2. Write a two-page report on the results of your interview.

Producing Quality Goods and Services

9

LEARNING OBJECTIVES

1. Explain the nature of production.
2. Outline how the conversion process transforms raw materials, labor, and other resources into finished products or services.
3. Describe how research and development lead to new products and services.
4. Discuss the components involved in planning the production process.
5. Explain the four major areas of operations control: purchasing, inventory control, scheduling, and quality control.
6. Discuss the increasing role of computers, robotics, and flexible manufacturing in the production process.
7. Outline the reasons for recent trends in productivity.

Imagine having to cook dinner for millions of people. Well, that's what the people at Campbell Soup do every day.

inside business

Campbell Soup's Really Cooking!

Imagine having to cook dinner for millions of people. Well, that's what the people at Campbell Soup do every day. And while Campbell's Soup along with the company's other products that include Prego, V-8, Godiva, Franco-American, and Pepperidge Farm are often included on a customer's grocery shopping lists, the company's products don't grow on trees or in fields ready for packaging. How does Campbell Soup do it? Many people believe that the company simply hires a lot of people who stand over stoves and cook individual food items, but nothing could be further from the truth. In reality, it takes sophisticated manufacturing processes to convert raw materials into the products that you see on store shelves. These same manufacturing processes also have to maintain the high-quality standards that customers expect when they purchase Campbell Soup products.

Although it is known today for its high-tech approach to producing food items, the Campbell Soup company started as a small firm in Camden, New Jersey. It all began with a handshake between Joseph Campbell, a fruit merchant, and Abraham Anderson, a tin icebox manufacturer, back in 1869. Original products included canned tomatoes, vegetables, jellies, soups, condiments, and minced meats—all produced by hand, one can at a time—and sold from a horse-drawn wagon. Then in 1897, a company chemist developed a process for removing water from canned soup. This new-fangled manufacturing process gave Campbell Soup a tremendous advantage over competitors: it could sell its condensed soup for substantially less than its competitors. When consumers discovered that the original five varieties of soup were of the highest quality, as well as inexpensive, the soups were an instant success. In fact, one of the original varieties—tomato soup—still ranks as one of the top ten grocery items sold in the United States today.

Although one of the most successful companies at the beginning of the 1900s, the company had to continue to innovate and improve its manufacturing processes to meet increased demand for its products. By 1904, the product line for soup had been expanded to 21 different varieties and the company was selling 40,000 cans of soup each week. It became one of the first companies in the United States to achieve national distribution of a food product. About this time, new manufacturing facilities were built in Toronto and Sacramento to produce an ever-larger number of new products. To save on manufacturing costs, the company even began to make its own cans.

Since then, the Campbell Soup company along with those well-known red and white labels and its "m'm! m'm! good" advertising slogans have become symbols recognized not only in the United States but throughout the world. Today, Campbell Soup has a reputation as a company that has conservative managers who are always seeking more efficient methods of manufacturing a wide array of products. Management is also quick to realize the importance of the firm's 125,000 employees and work to make sure that all employees feel like they are part of a team. Along the way, Campbell Soup has also grown into a corporate giant with products sold in over 120 countries, annual sales of over $6.5 billion, profits of more than $1.3 billion a year, and a 285.7 percent return on owners' equity in 1999—not bad for a company that makes its products "m'm! m'm! good!"[1]

No company illustrates this chapter's content—the production of quality goods and services—better than the Campbell Soup Company. Companies like Campbell Soup that are in the food-processing business take all kinds of raw materials—meat, chicken, vegetables, pasta, flour, sugar, spices—and transform them into soups, sauces, beverages, biscuits, cupcakes, and other food items that are sold around the globe. Campbell Soup is one of the most respected food manufacturers in the world. And yet even Campbell Soup must constantly look for ways to improve its methods of doing business. As a result, executives, managers, and workers continue to tinker with Campbell Soup's production system, make improvements where needed, and change the firm's recipes to adjust for regional tastes. But regardless of how the system is changed, the goal is still the same: produce a product that people want.

We begin this chapter with an overview of operations management—the activities involved in the conversion of resources into products. In this section, we also discuss competition in the global marketplace and careers in operations management. Next, we describe the conversion process that makes production possible and also note the growing role of services in our economy. Then we examine more closely three important aspects of operations management: developing ideas for new products, planning product design and production facilities, and effectively controlling operations after production has begun. Next we discuss changes in production as a result of automation, robotics, and computer-aided manufacturing. We close the chapter with a look at productivity trends and ways productivity can be improved.

What Is Production?

LEARNING OBJECTIVE

1 Explain the nature of production.

Have you ever wondered where a new pair of Levi jeans comes from? Or a new JVC 35-inch color television, Izod pullover, or Uniroyal tire for your car? Even factory service on a Compaq notebook computer or a Magnavox VCR would be impossible if it weren't for the activities described in this chapter. In fact these products and services and millions of others like them wouldn't exist if it weren't for production activities.

Let's begin this chapter by reviewing what an operating manager does. In Chapter 7, we described an *operation manager* as a person who creates and manages systems that convert resources and raw materials into goods and services. This area of management is usually referred to as **operations management**; it consists of all the activities managers engage in to produce goods and services.

operations management all activities managers engage in to produce goods and services

To produce a product or service successfully, a business must perform a number of specific activities. For example, suppose an organization like BMW has an idea for a new sport-utility vehicle called the X5, which will cost in excess of $45,000. Marketing research must determine not only if customers are willing to pay the price for this product but also what special features they want. Once it has been determined that there is a market for this type of automobile, BMW's operations managers must turn the concept into reality.

BMW's managers cannot just push the "start button" and immediately begin producing the new automobile. Production must be planned. As you will see, planning takes place both *before* anything is produced and *during* the production process.

Managers must also concern themselves with the control of operations to ensure that the organization's goals are achieved. For a product like BMW's X5 sport-utility vehicle, control of operations involves a number of important issues, including product quality, performance standards, the amount of inventory of both raw materials and finished products, and production costs.

We discuss each of the major activities of operations management later in this chapter. But, first, let's take a closer look at American manufacturers and how they compete in the global marketplace.

Competition in the Global Marketplace

After World War II, the United States became the most productive country in the world. For almost thirty years, until the late 1970s, its leadership was never threatened. By then, however, manufacturers in Japan, Germany, Great Britain, Italy, Korea, Sweden, and other industrialized nations were offering U.S. firms increasing competition. Once the leader in just about everything, U.S. firms lost market share in a number of vital industries, including steel, cement, building products, manufacturing equipment, farm machinery, and electronics. U.S. manufacturers quickly realized that "Made in the U.S.A." did not guarantee sales in foreign nations. Even to maintain market share, they would be forced to compete in an ever-smaller world to meet the needs of more demanding customers.

In an attempt to regain a competitive edge on foreign firms, U.S. manufacturers have taken another look at the importance of improving quality and meeting the needs of their customers. The most successful U.S. firms have also focused on the following:

1. Reducing production costs by selecting suppliers that offer higher-quality raw materials and components at reasonable prices
2. Replacing outdated equipment with state-of-the-art manufacturing equipment
3. Using computer-aided and flexible manufacturing systems that allow a higher degree of customization
4. Improving control procedures to help ensure lower manufacturing costs
5. Building new manufacturing facilities in foreign countries where labor costs are lower

Although competing in the global economy is a major challenge, it is a worthwhile pursuit. For most firms, it is not only profitable; it is also an essential activity that requires the cooperation of everyone within the organization. To see how one of America's most admired corporations—Rubbermaid—is selling products abroad, read Going Global.

Manufacturing products around the globe. AT&T's roots stretch back to 1875 with founder Alexander Graham Bell's invention of the telephone. Since then it has grown to become a huge global company that not only sells telecommunications services, but also manufactures equipment all over the world so that customers can obtain information—voice, video, or data—in any form that is useful to them.

Careers in Operations Management

Although it's hard to provide information about specific career opportunities in operations management, some generalizations do apply to this management area. First, you must appreciate the manufacturing process and the steps required to produce a product or service. A basic understanding of the difference between an analytic process and a synthetic process is essential. An **analytic process** breaks raw materials into different component parts. For example, a barrel of crude oil refined by Kerr-McGee—an Oklahoma-based chemical and energy company—can be broken down into gasoline, jet fuel, oil and lubricants, and many other petroleum by-products. A **synthetic process** is just the opposite of the analytic one; it combines raw materials or components to create a finished product. Black & Decker uses a synthetic system when it combines plastic, steel, rechargeable batteries, and other components to produce a cordless drill.

Once you understand that operations managers are responsible for producing tangible products or services that customers want, you must determine how you fit into the production process. Today's successful operations managers must

Going Global

The World According to Rubbermaid

WHETHER YOU LIVE IN THE UNITED States, Canada, Japan, Europe, or South America, take a closer look at that dustpan you use to sweep up the dirt from your floors. Chances are that it is made by Rubbermaid. This typical household item that we casually toss into the garage or the pantry has a history all its own. James Caldwell, a rubber chemist, and his wife played around with a new process of using novel dyes that could transform plain rubber objects into dazzling colors. In 1933, they used this new process to create their very first product—the "Rubbermaid" dustpan. Soon, more kitchen and bath products were developed including a drain board, a soap dish, and a sink stopper. When Horatio Ebert, co-owner of the Wooster Rubber Company, discovered their products, he asked Caldwell to join his company. Over the next ten years, more innovative household items were added to the Rubbermaid line, and under Caldwell's leadership as president and general manager, Rubbermaid corporation developed into a company known for innovation, product quality, and customer satisfaction.

Rubbermaid's Commitment to Quality

Today, what makes Rubbermaid a special corporation is its commitment to quality. Improving over five thousand everyday products—mops, storage boxes, toys, desk organizers, and so on—that most people take for granted may not seem important, but to Rubbermaid's employees this commitment is the "stuff that dreams are made of." Two examples illustrate Rubbermaid's level of commitment to details.

According to one story, Rubbermaid's CEO was walking along a New York street one day when he heard a doorman grumbling as he tried to sweep dirt into a Rubbermaid dustpan. He asked the man what was wrong, and the answer persuaded the executive that the lip where the dustpan meets the floor was too thick to catch the dirt. Not long after that, shoppers were buying redesigned Rubbermaid dustpans in stores all over the world.

Another example further illustrates Rubbermaid's commitment to doing things right. Several times a week, Rubbermaid's employees visit stores that sell the company's products. If they find a lid that doesn't fit or even a wrinkled label, they buy the defective product, bring it back to headquarters in Wooster, Ohio, and call a meeting to deal with the problem. In fact, all Rubbermaid employees—not just top management—are encouraged to make suggestions or propose changes that will improve the company's products.

Going Global at Rubbermaid

Rubbermaid began selling products overseas in the 1960s. Then, an International Division was established in 1986. In 1994, Rubbermaid Japan Inc. was formed, a European headquarters was opened in Brussels, Belgium, and an Asian headquarters was established in Hong Kong. In 1999, the Newell corporation purchased Rubbermaid for $6 billion and formed Newell Rubbermaid, Inc. Today, global sales account for just over 20 percent of Rubbermaid's total sales revenues and the company markets its products in multilingual packaging with easy-to-understand pictures that cut across language barriers.

1. Be able to motivate and lead people
2. Understand how technology can make a manufacturer more productive and efficient
3. Appreciate the control processes that help lower production costs and improve product quality
4. Understand the relationship between the customer, the marketing of a product, and the production of a product

If operations management seems like an area you might be interested in, why not do more career exploration? You could take an operations management course if your college or university offers one, or you could obtain a part-time job during the school year or a summer job in a manufacturing company.

analytic process a process in operations management in which raw materials are broken into different component parts

synthetic process a process in operations management in which raw materials or components are combined to create a finished product

LEARNING OBJECTIVE

2 Outline how the conversion process transforms raw materials, labor, and other resources into finished products or services.

utility the ability of a good or service to satisfy a human need

form utility utility created by converting raw materials, people, finances, and information, into finished products

The Conversion Process

To have something to sell, a business must convert resources into goods and services. The resources are materials, finances, people, and information—the same resources discussed in Chapters 1 and 7. The goods and services are varied, ranging from heavy manufacturing equipment to fast food. The purpose of this conversion of resources into goods and services is to provide utility to customers. **Utility** is the ability of a good or service to satisfy a human need. Although there are four types of utility—form, place, time, and possession—operations management focuses primarily on form utility. **Form utility** is created by converting raw materials, people, finances, and information into finished products.

But how does the conversion take place? How does Ford convert steel and glass, money from previous auto sales and stockholders' investments, production workers and managers, and economic and marketing forecasts into automobiles? How does Aetna Life and Casualty convert office buildings, insurance premiums, actuaries, and mortality tables into life insurance policies? They do so through the use of a conversion process like the one illustrated in Figure 9.1. As indicated by our Aetna Life and Casualty example, the conversion process is not limited to manufacturing products. The conversion process can also be used to produce services.

INPUTS
- Concept for an automobile
- Financing

CONVERSION
- Design and product specifications
- Purchase of steel, glass, engines, stereo equipment, etc.
- Hiring of employees

OUTPUTS
- Completed automobile

figure 9.1

The Conversion Process

The conversion process converts resources such as materials, finances, and people into useful goods, services, and ideas. It is a crucial step in the economic development of any nation.

The Nature of the Conversion

The conversion of resources into products and services can be described in several ways. We limit our discussion here to three: the focus or major resource used in the conversion process, its magnitude of change, and the number of production processes employed.

Focus By the *focus* of a conversion process we mean the resource or resources that comprise the major or most important *input*. For a bank like Citibank, financial resources are the major resource used in the conversion process. A refiner such as Texaco concentrates on material resources. A college or university is primarily concerned with information. And a barbershop focuses on the use of human resources.

Magnitude of Change The *magnitude* of a conversion process is the degree to which the resources are physically changed. At one extreme lie such processes as the one by which the Clorox Corporation produces Glad Wrap. Various chemicals in liquid or powder form are combined to form long, thin sheets of plastic Glad Wrap. Here the original resources are totally unrecognizable in the finished product. At the other extreme, American Airlines produces *no* physical change in its original resources. The airline simply provides a service and transports people from one place to another.

Number of Production Processes A single firm may employ one production process or many. In general, larger firms that make a variety of products use multiple production processes. For example, General Electric manufactures some of its own products, buys other merchandise from suppliers, and operates a credit division, an insurance company, and a medical equipment division. Smaller firms, by contrast, may use one production process or very few production processes. For example, Texas-based Advanced Cast Stone, Inc. manufactures one basic product: building materials made from concrete.

The Increasing Importance of Services

The application of the basic principles of operations management to the production of services has coincided with a dramatic growth in the number and diversity of service businesses. In 1900 only 28 percent of American workers were employed in service firms. By 1950 this figure had grown to 40 percent, and by the end of 1999, it had risen to 80 percent.[2] By any yardstick, service firms have become a dominant part of our economy. In fact, the American economy is now characterized as a service economy (see Figure 9.2). A **service economy** is one in which more effort is devoted to the production of services than to the production of goods.

This rapid growth is the primary reason for the increased use of production techniques in service firms. The managers of restaurants, laundries, real estate agencies, banks, movie theaters, airlines, travel bureaus, and other service firms have realized that they can benefit from the experience of manufacturers and construction firms. And yet the production of services is very different from the production of manufactured goods in the following four ways:

spotlight

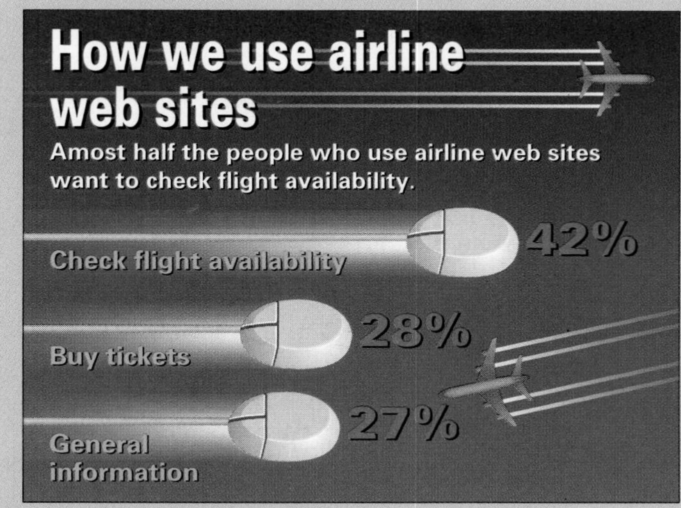

Source: Copyright 2000, USA TODAY. Reprinted with permission.

service economy an economy in which more effort is devoted to the production of services than to the production of goods

1. Services are consumed immediately and, unlike manufactured goods, cannot be stored. For example, a hair stylist cannot store completed haircuts like a manufacturer stores microwave ovens.
2. Services are provided when and where the customer desires the service. In many cases, customers will not travel as far to obtain a service as they would to purchase a manufactured product.
3. Services are usually labor intensive because the human resource is often the most important resource used in the production of services.
4. Services are intangible, and it is therefore more difficult to evaluate customer satisfaction.[3]

Although it is often more difficult to measure customer satisfaction, today's successful service firms work hard at providing the services customers want. Compared with manufacturers, service firms often listen more carefully to customers and respond more quickly to the market's changing needs. The Internet is a growing force in the service sector. According to Forrester Research Inc., 37 percent of all online buyers request customer service while shopping online. In order to provide efficient and effective services, large-scale Internet enterprises and *Fortune* 500 companies conducting e-business tend to adopt operational support software such

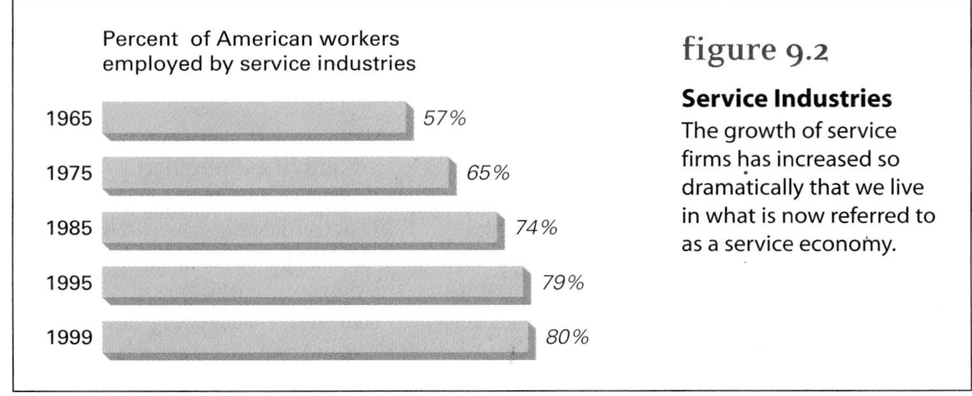

figure 9.2

Service Industries

The growth of service firms has increased so dramatically that we live in what is now referred to as a service economy.

Source: Bureau of Labor Statistics, *Monthly Labor Review*, March 2000, p. 76.

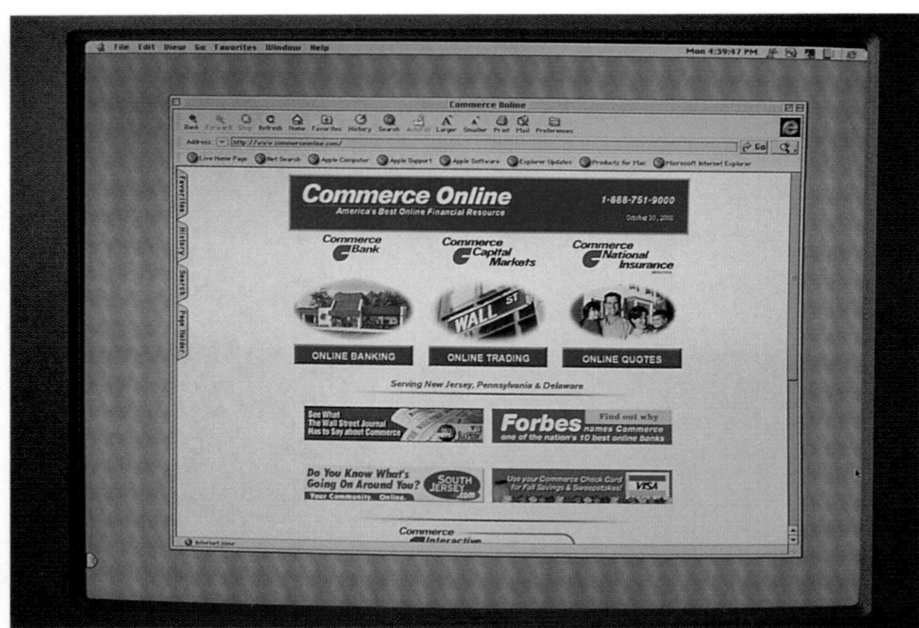

Online investment services you can bank on. The rapid growth of Internet banking and investment services can be attributed in part to the fact that online banks, brokerage firms, and other financial companies work hard at providing the services their customers need and want.

as the one from Silknet/Kana Communications Inc. These software programs assist operators handling multiple chats with online customers. Built-in functions, such as quick triggers, which launch prerecorded replies to customers, allow operators to increase their efficiency.[4]

Now that we understand something about the production process that is used to transform resources into goods and services, we can consider three major activities involved in operations management. These are product development, planning for production, and operations control.

Where Do New Products and Services Come from?

LEARNING OBJECTIVE

3 Describe how research and development lead to new products and services.

No firm can produce a product or service until it has an idea. In other words, someone must first come up with a new way to satisfy a need—a new product or an improvement in an existing product. Starbucks' milkshake–like coffee drink, Honda's ergonomically designed motorcycle, and Hewlett-Packard's color printer all began as an idea. And the quest for new ideas that lead to new products goes on. Already there are companies that are developing video cell phones, electronic wall paper, and even a robot dog.[5] While no one can predict with 100 percent accuracy what type of products will be available in the next five years, it is safe to say that companies will continue to introduce new products that will change the way we take care of ourselves, interact with others, and find the information and services we need.

Research and Development

How did we get VCRs, personal computers, and compact-disc players? We got them the same way we got light bulbs and automobile tires: from people working with new ideas. Thomas Edison created the first light bulb and Charles Goodyear discovered the vulcanization process that led to tires. In the same way, scientists and researchers working in businesses and universities have produced many of the newer products we already take for granted.

These activities are generally referred to as research and development. For our purposes, **research and development (R&D)** is a set of activities intended to identify new ideas that have the potential to result in new goods and services.

research and development (R&D) a set of activities intended to identify new ideas that have the potential to result in new goods and services

Today business firms use three general types of R&D activities. *Basic research* consists of activities aimed at uncovering new knowledge. The goal of basic research is scientific advancement, without regard for its potential use in the development of goods and services. *Applied research*, in contrast, consists of activities geared to discovering new knowledge with some potential use. *Development and implementation* are research activities undertaken specifically to put new or existing knowledge to use in producing goods and services. The 3M Company has always been known for its development and implementation research activities. At the end of the twentieth century, the company had developed more than 50,000 products designed to make people's lives easier. Does a company like 3M quit innovating because it has developed successful products? No, not at all! Just recently, the 3M company used development and implementation when it combined its transdermal drug delivery system with the drug nitroglycerin to create the smallest daily nitroglycerin patch in the world. This new product is called Minitran.™ For heart patients, this is a major breakthrough that makes their lives easier while enabling them to take the medicine they need to live a normal life.[6]

The quest to cure Alzheimer's disease. Research scientists at New Jersey–based Nymox Pharmaceutical Corporation have worked since 1989 on the development of drugs that can be used to treat Alzheimer's disease and other brain disorders. Ultimately the goal of the company's research and development employees is to find a cure for these devastating diseases.

Product Extension and Refinement

When a brand-new product is first marketed, its sales are zero and slowly increase from that point. If the product is successful, annual sales increase more and more rapidly until they reach some peak. Then, as time passes, annual sales begin to decline, and they continue to decline until it is no longer profitable to manufacture the product. (This rise-and-decline pattern, called the *product life cycle*, is discussed in more detail in Chapter 14.)

If a firm sells only one product, when that product reaches the end of its life cycle, the firm will die too. To stay in business, the firm must, at the very least, find ways to refine or extend the want-satisfying capability of its product. Consider television sets. Since they were first introduced in the late 1930s, television sets have been constantly *refined*, so that they now provide clearer, sharper pictures with less dial adjusting. They are tuned electronically for better picture control and can even compensate for variations in room lighting and picture-tube wear. During the same time, television sets were also *extended*. There are color as well as black-and-white sets, television-only sets, and others that include VCRs and digital clocks. There are even television sets that allow their owners to access the Internet. And, the latest development, high-definition, or digital, televisions, are already available. Although initial prices are high, the improved picture will convince some consumers to bite the bullet and buy a new set.

Each refinement or extension results in an essentially "new" product whose sales make up for the declining sales of a product that was introduced earlier. For example, Jell-O was introduced to the public in 1897 and was acquired by Kraft Foods in 1925. One of Kraft Foods' newer products, Jello Pudding Snacks, is still based on Jell-O and produces sales of more than $100 million annually. For most firms, extension and refinement are expected results of their development and implementation effort. Most often, they result from the application of new knowledge to existing products. For instance, improved technology affects the content companies can distribute on the Internet. The Disney Corporation currently has a clear advantage over competitors since much of its content is animation. Animation is the easiest non-still content to transfer to the Internet and the vast majority of Internet users only have access to narrow-bandwidth which delivers a reasonable quality image of animation. As bandwidth access expands, Disney is expected to be ready with a vault full of prerecorded film and video content.[7]

Planning for Production

LEARNING OBJECTIVE

4 Discuss the components involved in planning the production process.

Only a few of the many ideas for new products, refinements, and extensions ever reach the production stage. But for those ideas that do, the next step is planning for production. Planning for production involves three major phases: design planning, facilities planning and site selection, and operational planning.

Design Planning

When the R&D staff at Compaq recommended to top management that the firm produce and market an affordable notebook computer, the company could not simply swing into production the next day. Instead, a great deal of time and energy had to be invested in determining what the new computer would look like, where and how it would be produced, and what options would be included. These decisions are a part of design planning. **Design planning** is the development of a plan for converting a product idea into an actual product. The major decisions involved in design planning deal with product line, required capacity, and use of technology.

design planning the development of a plan for converting a product idea into an actual product

product line a group of similar products that differ only in relatively minor characteristics

Product Line

A **product line** is a group of similar products that differ only in relatively minor characteristics. During the design-planning stage, management must determine how many different product variations there will be. A computer manufacturer like Compaq Computers needs to determine how many different models to produce and what major options to offer. A restaurant chain like Pizza Hut must decide how many menu items to offer.

An important issue in deciding on the product line is to balance customer preferences and production requirements. For this reason, marketing managers play an important role in making product-line decisions. Once the product line has been determined, each distinct product within the product line must be designed. **Product design** is the process of creating a set of specifications from which the product can be produced. When designing a new product, specifications are extremely important. For example, product engineers for Whirlpool Corporation must make sure that a new frost-free refrigerator keeps food frozen in the freezer compartment. At the same time, they must make sure that lettuce and tomatoes don't freeze in the crisper section of the refrigerator. The need for a complete product design is fairly obvious; products that work cannot be manufactured without it. But services should be carefully designed as well, and *for the same reason.* To see how one company, Cisco Systems, provides both products and services, read Talking Technology.

product design the process of creating a set of specifications from which a product can be produced

capacity the amount of products or services that an organization can produce in a given time

Required Capacity

Capacity is the amount of products or services that an organization can produce in a given period of time. (The capacity of an automobile assembly plant, for instance, might be 500,000 cars per year.) Operations managers—again working with the firm's marketing managers—must determine the required capacity. This in turn determines the size of the production facility. Capacity of a production plant is vitally important. If the facility is built with too much capacity, valuable resources (plant, equipment, and money) will lie idle. If the facility offers insufficient capacity, additional capacity may have to be added later, when it is much more expensive than in the initial building stage.

Capacity means about the same thing to service businesses. For example, the capacity of a restaurant like the Hard Rock Cafe is the number of customers it can serve at one time. Like the manufacturing facility described above, if the restaurant is built with too much capacity—too many tables and chairs—valuable resources will be wasted. If the restaurant is too small, customers may have to wait for service; if the wait is too long, they may leave and choose another restaurant.

Use of Technology

During the design-planning stage, management must determine the degree to which *automation* will be used to produce a product or service. Here, there is a tradeoff between high initial costs and low operating costs (for automation) and low initial costs and high operating costs (for human labor). Ultimately, management must choose between a labor-intensive technology and a capital-intensive technology. A **labor-intensive technology** is a process in which people must do most of the work. Housecleaning services and the New York Yankees baseball team, for example, are labor intensive. A **capital-intensive technology** is a process in which machines and equipment do most of the work. A Motorola automated assembly plant is capital intensive.

labor-intensive technology a process in which people must do most of the work

capital-intensive technology a process in which machines and equipment do most of the work

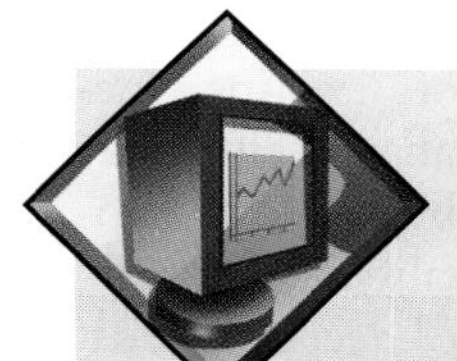

Talking Technology

Cisco Systems' Phenomenal Growth

QUESTION: IS CISCO SYSTEMS A MANUFACTURER or a service provider?
Answer: Both! Simply put, Cisco does it all—whatever the customer needs.

Back in 1984 a Stanford University professor named Leonard Bosack wanted his computer lab network to talk to the computer network at the graduate school of business, where his wife worked. He teamed up with other Stanford professors and developed a piece of equipment called a router that allowed data signals from one computer network to be directed to another. After this initial success, the professors formed Cisco Systems and talked some of their colleagues into working on expanding the technology in return for the hope of money in the future. From their first sale of one network router in 1986, through management changes and acquisitions of other technology companies, Cisco now sells over 150 different products to ease the flow of traffic on the Internet. These same products generate sales in excess of $21 billion a year. The company's hardware sales come mainly from routers, network switches, and servers that permit dial-up networking required by Internet service providers. Recently, it has expanded into selling video transmission equipment and cable modems. And last, but not least, it sells the software that enables all their equipment to work smoothly as a system.

Why Is Cisco So Successful?

Cisco offers its customers a total network solution. Before a business client can purchase hardware or software, it must meet with Cisco engineers to determine what type of system the customer needs. This type of customer service begins at the top of the Cisco organization and is very important to John Chambers, Cisco's CEO since 1985. With his leadership, Cisco has become the fastest growing, most profitable company in the history of the computer industry. His customer service methods have been recognized as some of the best in business today. In fact, many executives from other corporations, such as GE (recognized as the best-managed company in the United States by *Fortune* magazine) visit Cisco to study and learn how it provides outstanding customer service. Says Chambers, "I have no love for technology for technology's sake—only solutions for customers. When it comes to customers, we will do whatever it takes to win them. The word *"NO"* to us just means we have to come back." He really *does* believe in customer service and practices what he preaches. On top of his administrative duties, Chambers personally spends more than 30 hours per week with customers.

Another reason for Cisco's success is that it has acquired more than fifty companies since its inception and plans on maintaining momentum by buying twenty more in the immediate future. Cisco says it isn't just buying businesses; it's obtaining existing technology and much needed engineers for future research and development. Still another reason for Cisco's success is that it outsources 75 percent of its manufacturing to other companies who produce its products under strict quality control measures. For Cisco, buying other companies and outsourcing are the least expensive ways to provide for the firm's expansion and have contributed to its almost unheard of short-time growth into a company worth more than $480 billion and currently ranked No. 146 on the *Fortune* 500.

Cisco's Need for Knowledge Workers

For Cisco Systems, one of its biggest problems is recruiting knowledge workers—the people who can design, build, and maintain networks. To help guarantee that Cisco has the qualified personnel it needs, the company has initiated the Cisco Networking Academy. This program, which entails four semesters of course work, enables students to take the Cisco Certified Networking Associate (CCNA) exam upon completion. A student that has passed the CCNA exam possesses the basic talent and skills that are now in such demand throughout the computer industry.

Facilities Planning and Site Selection

Once initial decisions have been made about a new product line, required capacity, and the use of technology, it's time to determine where the products or services are going to be produced. Initially, managers must decide whether they will build a new plant or refurbish an existing factory. Generally, a business will choose to produce a new product in an existing factory as long as (1) the existing factory has enough capacity to handle customer demand for both the new product and established products, and (2) the cost of refurbishing an existing factory is less than the cost of building a new one.

A team effort! Often people and machines can team up to produce a product more efficiently and at lower costs. Here an employee works with a machine to produce paper at a recycling plant.

After exploring the capacity of existing factories, management may decide to build a new production facility. Once again, a number of decisions must be made. Should all the organization's production capacity be placed in one or two large facilities? Or should it be divided among several smaller facilities? In general, firms that market a wide variety of products find it more economical to have a number of smaller facilities. Firms that produce only a small number of products tend to have fewer but larger facilities.

In determining where to locate production facilities, management must consider a number of variables, including the following:

- Geographic locations of suppliers of parts and raw materials
- Locations of major customers for their company's products
- Transportation costs to deliver finished products to customers
- The cost of both land and construction required to build a new production facility
- Local and state taxes, environmental regulations, and zoning laws that could affect a new production facility
- The amount of financial support offered by local and state governments
- Special requirements, such as great amounts of energy or water used in the production process
- Quality of life for employees and management
- Availability and cost of skilled and unskilled labor

It may, of course, be impossible to find the perfect location for a production facility. In fact, the choice of a location often involves balancing the most important variables for each production facility. Before making a final decision about where a proposed plant will be located and how it will be organized, two other factors—human resources and plant layout—should be examined.

Human Resources Several issues involved in facilities planning fall within the province of the human resources manager. Thus, at this stage, human resources and operations managers work closely together. For example, suppose a U.S. firm like Reebok International wants to lower labor costs by constructing a sophisticated production plant in China. The human resources manager will have to recruit managers and employees with the appropriate skills, perhaps even arranging for their transfer to China, or develop training programs for local workers, or do both. Human resources managers can also obtain and provide valuable information on availability of skilled workers in various areas, wage rates, and other factors that may influence choices of the use of technology and plant location.

plant layout the arrangement of machinery, equipment, and personnel within a production facility

Plant Layout **Plant layout** is the arrangement of machinery, equipment, and personnel within a production facility. Three general types of plant layout are used (see Figure 9.3 on page 249).

The *process layout* is used when different operations are required for creating small batches of different products or working on different parts of a product. The plant is arranged so that each operation is performed in its own particular area. Once the task in one area is completed, the work in process is moved to another area. An auto repair facility at a local Buick dealership provides an example of a process layout. The various operations might be engine repair, body work, wheel alignment, and safety inspection. Each operation is performed in a different area. A particular car "visits" only those areas performing the kinds of work it needs.

A *product layout* (sometimes referred to as an assembly line) is used when all products undergo the same operations in the same sequence. Work stations are arranged to match the sequence of operations, and work flows from station to station. An assembly line is the best example of a product layout. For example, Massachusetts-based ACT Manufacturing uses a product layout to produce printed circuit boards.

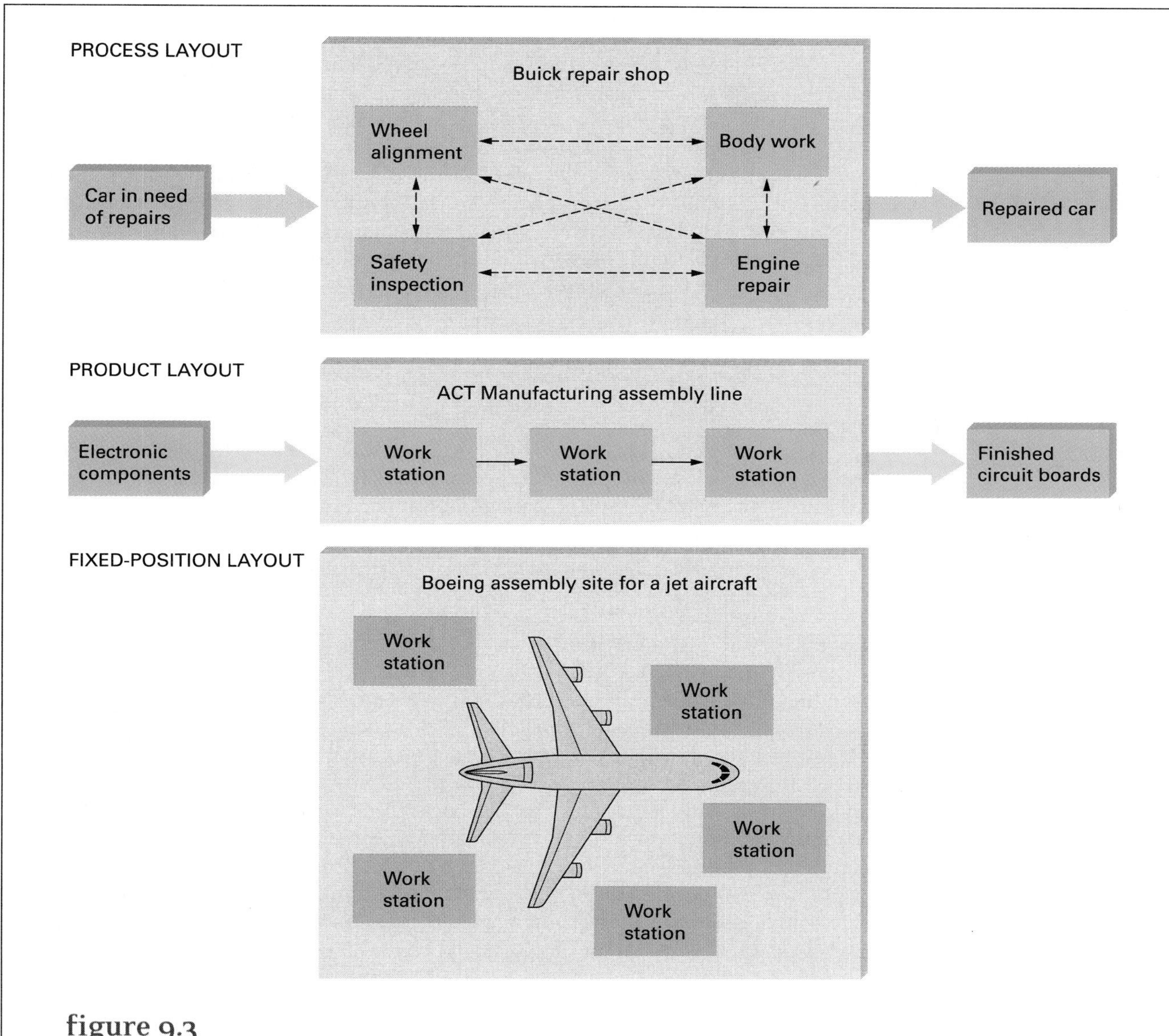

figure 9.3

Facilities Planning

The process layout is used when small batches of different products are created or worked on in a different operating sequence. The product layout (assembly line) is used when all products undergo the same operations in the same sequence. The fixed-position layout is used in producing a product too large to move.

A *fixed-position layout* is used when a very large product is produced. Aircraft manufacturers and shipbuilders apply this method because of the difficulty of moving a large product like an airliner or ship. The product remains stationary while people and machines are moved as needed to assemble the product. Boeing, for example, uses the fixed-position layout to build 777 jet aircraft at its Everett, Washington, manufacturing facility. When a fixed-position layout is used, it is much easier to move people and machines around the airliner than to move the plane during the production process.

Operational Planning

Once the product has been designed and a decision made to use an existing production facility or build a new one, operational plans must be developed. The objective of operational planning is to decide on the amount of products or services each facility will produce during a specific period of time. Four steps are required.

planning horizon the period during which a plan will be in effect

Step 1: Selecting a Planning Horizon A **planning horizon** is simply the time period during which a plan will be in effect. A common planning horizon for production plans is one year. Then, before each year is up, management must plan for the next.

A planning horizon of one year is generally long enough to average out seasonal increases and decreases in sales. At the same time, it is short enough for planners to adjust production to accommodate long-range sales trends. Firms that operate in a rapidly changing business environment with many competitors may find it best to select a shorter planning horizon to keep their production planning current.

Step 2: Estimating Market Demand The *market demand* for a product is the quantity that customers will purchase at the going price. This quantity must be estimated for the time period covered by the planning horizon. The sales forecasts and projections developed by marketing managers are the basis for market-demand estimates.

Step 3: Comparing Market Demand with Capacity The third step in operational planning is to compare the projected market demand with the facility's capacity to satisfy that demand. Again, demand and capacity must be compared for the same time period. One of three outcomes may result: demand may exceed capacity, capacity may exceed demand, or capacity and demand may be equal. If they are equal, the facility should be operated at full capacity. But if market demand and capacity are not equal, adjustments may be necessary.

Step 4: Adjusting Products or Services to Meet Demand Adjustments to production schedules are more common than most production managers would like. The biggest reason for changes to a firm's production schedule is changes in the amount of products or services that a company sells to its customers. For example, Houston-based Image Plastics Corporation (IPC) manufactures plastic beverage cups that are sold to airlines and larger mugs that can be screen-printed to promote a company or a company's products or services. If IPC obtains a large contract to provide promotional mugs to a fast-food chain like Whataburger or McDonald's, the company may need to work three shifts a day, seven days a week until the contract is fulfilled. Unfortunately, the reverse is also true. If the company's sales force doesn't generate new sales, there may only be enough work for the employees on one shift. It may also be necessary to reduce the number of days that these employees work to two or three days a week until new customers are found for the company's products. Specific suggestions used to adjust for increased or reduced demand for a company's products or services are described below.

When market demand exceeds capacity, several options are available to the firm. Production of products or services may be increased by operating the facility overtime with existing personnel or by starting a second or third work shift. For manufacturers, another response is to subcontract a portion of the work to other producers. If the excess demand is likely to be permanent, the firm may expand the current facility or build another facility.

Some firms occasionally pursue another option: ignore the excess demand and allow it to remain unmet. For several years, the Adolph Coors Company used this strategy. A mystique gradually developed around Coors beer because it was not available in many parts of the country. When the firm's brewing capacity was finally expanded, an eager market was waiting.

What happens when capacity exceeds market demand? Again, there are several options. To reduce output temporarily, workers may be laid off and part of the facility shut down. Or the facility may be operated on a shorter-than-normal workweek for as long as the excess capacity persists. To adjust to a permanently decreased demand, management may shift the excess capacity of a manufacturing facility to the production of other goods or services. The most radical adjustment is to eliminate the excess capacity by selling unused facilities.

Operations Control

We have discussed the development of a product idea and the planning that translates that idea into the reality. Now we push the "start button," begin the production process, and examine four important areas of operations control: purchasing, inventory control, scheduling, and quality control (see Figure 9.4).

LEARNING OBJECTIVE

5 Explain the four major areas of operations control: purchasing, inventory control, scheduling, and quality control.

Purchasing

Purchasing consists of all the activities involved in obtaining required materials, supplies, and parts from other firms. Levi Strauss must purchase denim cloth, thread, and zippers before it can produce a single pair of jeans. Similarly, Nike, Inc., must purchase leather, rubber, cloth for linings, and laces before manufacturing a pair of athletic shoes. For all firms, the purchasing function is far from routine, and its importance should not be underestimated. For some products, purchased materials make up more than 50 percent of their wholesale costs.[8] To improve their purchasing system aerospace giants Boeing, BAE Systems, Lockheed Martin, and Raytheon jointly developed an online exchange that will link more than 37,000 suppliers, hundreds of airlines, and national governments into a single web-based marketplace for parts estimated to be worth more than $400 billion in sales. It will also reduce administrative costs and speed procurement for the private and government aerospace and defense concerns worldwide.[9]

purchasing all the activities involved in obtaining required materials, supplies, and parts from other firms

The objective of purchasing is to ensure that required materials are available when they are needed, in the proper amounts, and at minimum cost. To achieve this objective, management must select suppliers carefully. Generally, the company with purchasing needs and suppliers must develop a working relationship built on trust. For example, Harvard Manufacturing, a Hispanic-owned business in Texas, Cherokee Nation Industries, a Native American firm in Oklahoma, and Pacific Network, an African-American-owned business in California formed a joint venture to market

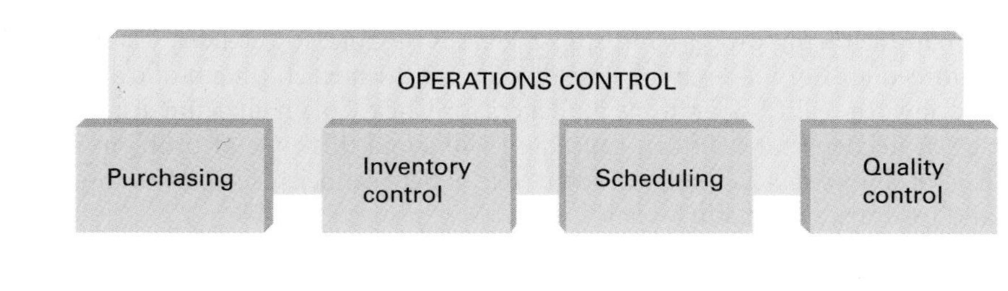

figure 9.4

Four Aspects of Operations Control

Implementing the operations control system in any business requires the effective use of purchasing, inventory control, scheduling, and quality control.

their products to SBC Communications and other large corporations. While you probably recognize SBC Communications as the telecommunications company that does business in nearly half of the United States, you may not recognize the three suppliers that formed the joint venture. All three firms are small companies that wanted to sell products and services to SBC. Each company found that SBC was reluctant to give large contracts to small companies because they didn't have enough locations, inventory, and resources to meet the purchasing needs of a large corporation. But when the three companies formed a joint venture and established a larger business entity, SBC began buying telecommunications equipment from the joint venture. The joint venture is working and sales for Harvard Manufacturing, Cherokee Nation, and Pacific Network have increased. At the same time, SBC Communications has found a supplier that can meet its purchasing needs.[10] Incidentally, SBC Communications won the National Minority Supplier Development Council's "Corporation of the Year" award for its efforts to do business with minorities in 1999. At the time of the award, SBC spent $1.3 billion annually or 20 percent of its purchasing budget with 550 different minority firms controlled by minorities, women, or disabled veterans.[11]

Purchasing personnel should constantly be on the lookout for new or back-up suppliers, even when their needs are being met by their present suppliers, because problems like strikes and equipment breakdowns can cut off the flow of purchased materials from a primary supplier at any time.

The choice of suppliers should result from careful analysis of a number of factors. The following are especially critical:

- *Price*—Comparing prices offered by different suppliers is always an essential part of selecting a supplier. Even tiny differences in price add up to enormous sums when large quantities are purchased.
- *Quality*—Purchasing specialists are always challenged to find the "best" materials at the lowest price. Although the goal is not necessarily to find the highest quality available, purchasing specialists always try to buy materials at a level of quality in keeping with the type of product being manufactured. The minimum acceptable quality is usually specified by product designers.
- *Reliability*—An agreement to purchase high-quality materials at a low price is the purchaser's dream. But such an agreement becomes a nightmare if the supplier doesn't deliver. Purchasing personnel should check the reliability of potential suppliers, including their ability to meet delivery schedules.
- *Credit terms*—Purchasing specialists should determine if the supplier demands immediate payment or will extend credit. Also, does the supplier offer a cash discount or reduction in price for prompt payment?
- *Shipping costs*—One of the most overlooked factors in purchasing is the geographic location of the supplier. Low prices and favorable credit terms offered by a distant supplier can be wiped out when the buyer must pay the shipping costs. Above all, the question of who pays the shipping costs should be answered before any supplier is chosen.

Inventory Control

Can you imagine what would happen if a Coca-Cola manufacturing plant ran out of the company's familiar red and white aluminum cans? It would be impossible to complete the manufacturing process and ship the cases of Coke to retailers. Management would be forced to shut the assembly line down until the next shipment of cans arrived from a supplier. In reality, operations managers for Coca-Cola realize the disasters that a shortage of needed materials can cause and will avoid this type of problem if at all possible. The simple fact is that shutdowns are expensive because costs such as rent, wages, and insurance must still be paid.

Operations managers are concerned with three types of inventories. A *raw-materials inventory* consists of materials that will become part of the product during the production process. The *work-in-process inventory* consists of partially completed products. The *finished-goods inventory* consists of completed goods.

Associated with each type of inventory are a *holding cost*, or storage cost, and a *stock-out cost*, the cost of running out of inventory. *Inventory control* is the process of managing inventories in such a way as to minimize inventory costs, including both holding costs and potential stock-out costs. Today, computer systems are being used both to control inventory levels and to record costs. In both large and small firms, computer-based systems keep track of inventories, provide periodic inventory reports, and alert managers to impending stock-outs.

inventory control the process of managing inventories in such a way as to minimize inventory costs, including both holding costs and potential stock-out costs

One of the most sophisticated methods of inventory control used today is materials requirements planning. **Materials requirements planning (MRP)** is a computerized system that integrates production planning and inventory control. One of the great advantages of an MRP system is its ability to juggle delivery schedules and lead times effectively. For a complex product like an automobile or airplane, it is virtually impossible for individual managers to oversee the hundreds of parts that go into the finished product. But a manager using an MRP system can arrange both order and delivery schedules so that materials, parts, and supplies arrive when they are needed.

materials requirements planning (MRP) a computerized system that integrates production planning and inventory control

Two extensions of materials requirements planning are used by manufacturing firms today. The first is known as *manufacturing resource planning*. The primary difference between the two systems is that materials requirements planning involves just production and inventory personnel whereas manufacturing resource planning involves the entire organization. Thus, manufacturing resource planning, often referred to as *MRP II*, provides a single common set of facts that can be used by all of the organization's managers to make effective decisions. The second extension of materials requirements planning is known as *enterprise resource planning* or just *ERP*. The primary difference between ERP and the above methods of controlling inventory and production is that ERP software is more sophisticated and can monitor not only inventory and production processes, but quality, customer satisfaction, and even such variables as inventory at a supplier's location. While MRP and MRP II are used to monitor activities at one firm, ERP can be used to monitor activities at more than one firm.

Because large firms can incur huge inventory costs, much attention has been devoted to inventory control. The "just-in-time" system being used by some businesses is one result of all this attention. A **just-in-time inventory system** is designed to ensure that materials or supplies arrive at a facility just when they are needed so that storage and holding costs are minimized. The just-in-time system requires considerable cooperation between the supplier and the customer. The customer must specify what will be needed, when, and in what amounts. The supplier must be sure the right supplies arrive at the agreed-upon time and location.

just-in-time inventory system a system designed to ensure that materials or supplies arrive at a facility just when they are needed so that storage and holding costs are minimized

Without proper inventory control, it is impossible for operations managers to schedule the work required to produce goods that can be sold to customers.

Scheduling

Scheduling is the process of ensuring that materials and other resources are at the right place at the right time. The materials and resources may be moved from the warehouse to the work stations; they may move from station to station along an assembly line; or they may arrive at work stations "just in time" to be made part of the work in process there. For finished goods, scheduling involves both movement into finished-goods inventory and shipment to customers to fill orders.

scheduling the process of ensuring that materials and other resources are at the right place at the right time

As our definition implies, both place and time are important to scheduling. (This is no different from, say, the scheduling of classes. You cannot attend your classes unless you know both where and when they are held.) The *routing* of materials is the sequence of work stations that the materials will follow. Assume that Drexel-Heritage—one of America's largest and oldest furniture manufacturers—is scheduling production of an oval coffee table made from cherry wood. Operations managers would route the needed materials (wood, screws, packaging materials, and so on) through a series of individual work stations along an assembly line. At each work station, a specific task would be performed and then the partially finished coffee table would move to the next work station. Once all work is completed, Drexel can either

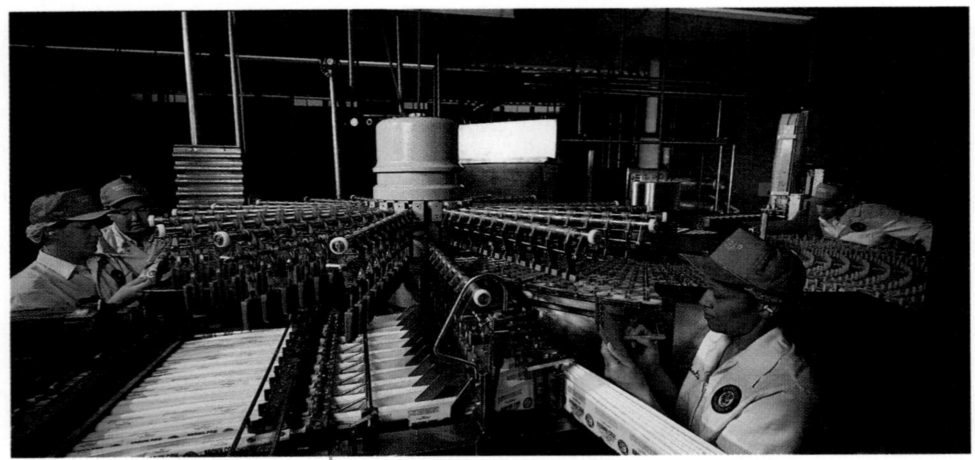

Making ice cream is serious business. Scheduling is part of a sophisticated production process used to manufacture ice cream bars. To create one of the world's coolest desserts, milk, sugar, chocolate, vanilla, and other ingredients are combined in a series of steps in just the right order and at just the right time to create the finished product.

store the completed coffee table in a warehouse or ship it to a retailer. When routing materials, operations managers are especially concerned with the sequence of production. For the coffee table, the top and legs must be cut to specifications before the wood is finished. (If the wood was finished before being cut, the finish would be ruined and the coffee table would have to be restained.)

When scheduling production, managers are also concerned with timing. The *timing* function specifies when the materials will arrive at each station and how long they will remain there. For the cherry coffee table, it may take workers thirty minutes to cut the table top and legs and another thirty minutes to drill the holes and assemble the table. Before packaging the coffee table for shipment, it must be finished with cherry stain and allowed to dry. This last step may take as long as three days depending on weather conditions and humidity.

Whether or not the finished product requires a simple or complex production process, operations managers are responsible for monitoring schedules—called *follow-up*—to ensure that the work flows according to a timetable. For complex products, many operations managers prefer to use Gantt charts or the PERT technique.

Gantt chart a graphic scheduling device that displays the tasks to be performed on the vertical axis and the time required for each task on the horizontal axis

Scheduling Through Gantt Charts

Developed by Henry L. Gantt, a **Gantt chart** is a graphic scheduling device that displays the tasks to be performed on the vertical axis and the time required for each task on the horizontal axis. A Gantt chart that describes the activities required to build three dozen golf carts is illustrated in Figure 9.5. As you see in the figure, completed tasks can also be shown on a Gantt chart, so actual progress can be monitored against planned activities. Gantt charts are not particularly suitable for scheduling extremely complex situations. Nevertheless, using them forces a manager to plan the steps required to get a job done and to specify time requirements for each part of the job.

PERT (Program Evaluation and Review Technique) a scheduling technique that identifies the major activities necessary to complete a project and sequences them based on the time required to perform each one

Scheduling Control via PERT

Another technique for scheduling a process or project and maintaining control of the schedule is **PERT (Program Evaluation and Review Technique)**. To use PERT, we begin by identifying all the major *activities* involved in the project. For example, the activities involved in producing your textbook include editing the manuscript, designing the book, obtaining cost estimates, marking the manuscript for typesetting, setting type, and carrying out other activities. The completion of each of these activities is an *event*.

Next we arrange the events in a sequence. In doing so, we must be sure that an event that must occur before another event in the actual process also occurs before that event on the PERT chart. For example, the manuscript must be edited before the type is set. Therefore, in our sequence, the event "edit manuscript" must precede the event "set type."

critical path the sequence of production activities that takes the longest time from start to finish

Next we use arrows to connect events that must occur in sequence. We then estimate the time required for each activity and mark it near the corresponding arrow. The sequence of production activities that takes the longest time from start to finish is called the **critical path**. The activities on this path determine the minimum time in which the process can be completed. These activities are the ones that must be scheduled and controlled carefully. A delay in any one of them will cause a delay in completion of the project as a whole.

Figure 9.6 is a PERT diagram for the production of this book. The critical path runs from event 1 to event 4 to event 5. It then runs through events 6, 8, and 9 to the

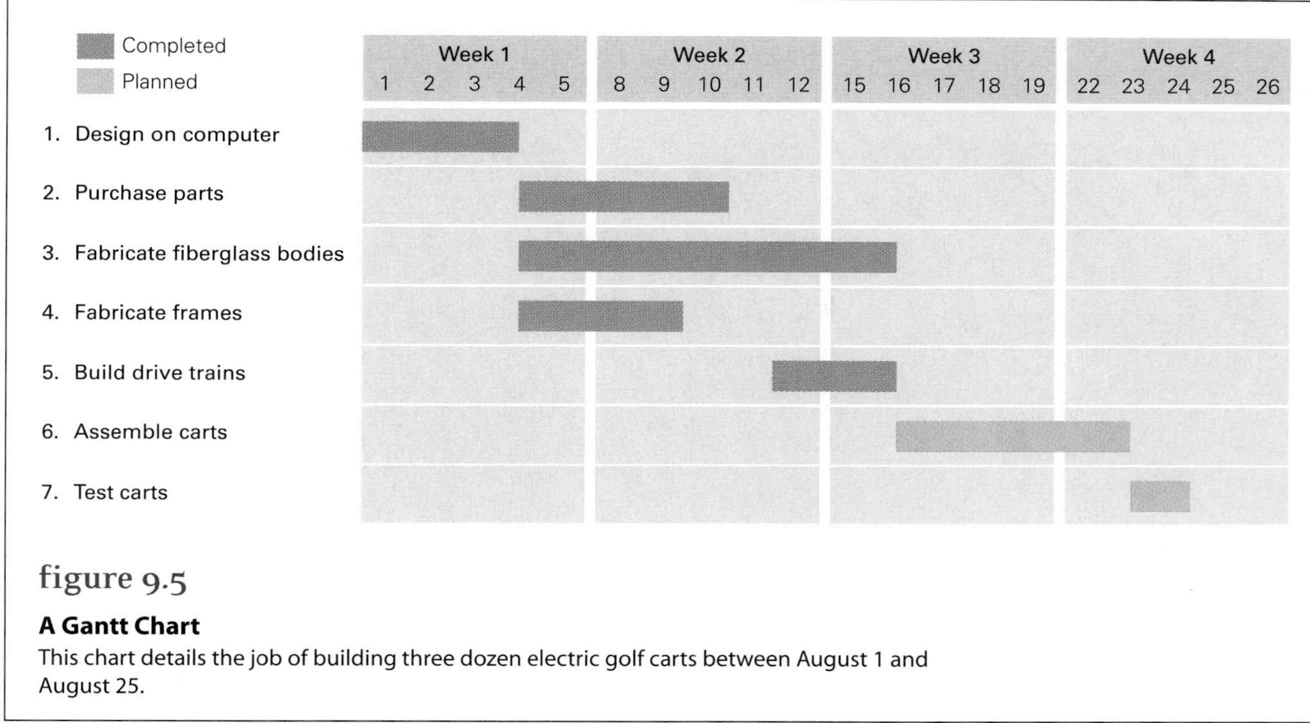

figure 9.5

A Gantt Chart

This chart details the job of building three dozen electric golf carts between August 1 and August 25.

Source: Robert Kreitner, *Management,* 8th ed. Copyright © 2001 by Houghton Mifflin Company. Reprinted with permission.

finished book at event 10. Note that even a six-week delay in preparing the cover will not delay the production process. However, *any* delay in an activity on the critical path will hold up publication. Thus, if necessary, resources could be diverted from cover preparation to, say, make up of pages or preparing film negatives for the printer.

Quality Control

Quality control is the process of ensuring that goods and services are produced in accordance with design specifications. The major objective of quality control is to see that the organization lives up to the standards it has set for itself on quality. Some firms, such as Mercedes-Benz and Neiman Marcus, have built their reputations on quality. Customers pay more for their products in return for assurances of high quality. Other firms adopt a strategy of emphasizing lower prices along with reasonable (but not particularly high) quality.

quality control the process of ensuring that goods and services are produced in accordance with design specifications

Many U.S. firms use two systems to gather statistical information about the quality of their products. **Statistical process control** (SPC) is a system that plots data on control charts and graphs to see if the production process is operating as it should and pinpoint problem areas. **Statistical quality control** (SQC), a similar technique, is a set of specific statistical techniques used to sample both work in progress and finished products. A firm can use the information provided by both these to correct problems in the production process and improve the quality of its products.

statistical process control (SPC) an information-gathering system that plots data on control charts and graphs to identify and pinpoint problems in product quality

statistical quality control (SQC) a set of techniques used to sample both work in progress and finished products to find problems in the production process and improve product quality

Increased effort is also being devoted to **inspection,** which is the examination of the quality of work in process. Inspections are performed at various times during production. Purchased materials may be inspected when they arrive at the production facility. Subassemblies and manufactured parts may be inspected before they become part of a finished product. And finished goods may be inspected before they are shipped to customers. Items that are within design specifications continue on their way. Those that are not within design specifications are removed from production.

inspection the examination of the quality of work in process

The method of inspection depends on the item being examined. *Visual inspection* may be sufficient for products like furniture or rug-cleaning services. General Electric

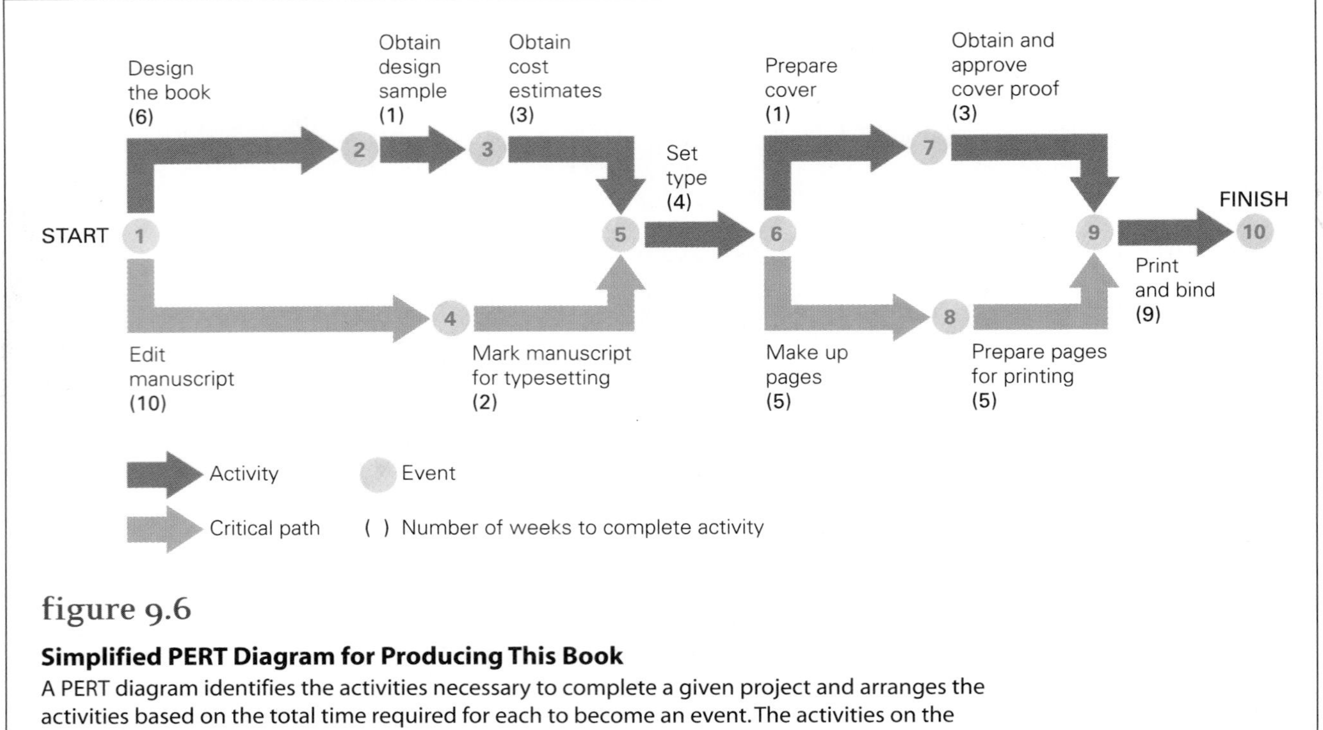

figure 9.6

Simplified PERT Diagram for Producing This Book

A PERT diagram identifies the activities necessary to complete a given project and arranges the activities based on the total time required for each to become an event. The activities on the critical path determine the minimum time required.

may test one or two light bulbs from every hundred produced. At the other extreme, complete *x-ray inspection* may be required for the vital components of airplanes.

Improving Quality Through Employee Participation Historically, efforts to ensure quality increased the costs associated with making that good or service. For that reason, quality and productivity were viewed as conflicting: one was increased at the other's expense. Over the years, more and more managers have realized that quality is an essential "ingredient" of the good or service being provided. Viewed in this light, quality becomes an overall approach to doing business and is the concern of all members of the organization. This view of quality provides several benefits. The number of defects decreases, which causes profits to increase. Making products right the first time reduces many of the rejects and much of the rework. And making the employees responsible for quality eliminates the need for inspection. An employee is indoctrinated to accept full responsibility for the quality of his or her work.

quality circle a group of employees who meet on company time to solve problems of product quality

Because of increased global competition, American manufacturers have adopted a goal that calls for better quality in their products. As noted in Chapter 7, a *total quality management (TQM)* program coordinates the efforts directed at improving customer satisfaction, increasing employee participation, strengthening supplier partnerships, and facilitating an organizational atmosphere of continuous quality improvement. Firms like American Express, AT&T, Motorola, and Hewlett-Packard have all used TQM to improve product quality and ultimately customer satisfaction.

The use of a **quality circle,** a group of employees who meet on company time to solve problems of product quality, is another way manufacturers are achieving better quality at the operations level. Quality circles have been used successfully in such companies as IBM, the Northrop Grumman Corporation, and Compaq Computers.

Using the Internet

There are several web-based gateway sources of information and journals devoted to quality management and production issues such as the National Association of Manufacturers (**http://www.nam.org/**), *Quality Digest* (**http://www.qualitydigest.com/**), and *Industry Week* (**http://www.iwgc.com/**).

World Quality Standards: ISO 9000 and ISO 14000 Different companies have different perceptions of quality. Without a common standard of quality, however, customers may be at the mercy of manufacturers and vendors. As the number of companies competing in the world marketplace has increased, so has the seriousness of this problem. To deal with it, the International Organization for Standardization (a nonprofit organization in Geneva, Switzerland, with a membership of ninety-five countries), brought together a panel of quality experts to define what methods a company must use to produce a quality product.

In 1987 the panel published the ISO 9000 (*ISO* is Greek for "equal"), which sets the guidelines for quality management procedures that businesses must use to receive certification. This certification, issued by independent auditors, serves as evidence that a company meets the standards for quality control procedures in manufacturing design, production processes, product testing, training of employees, recordkeeping, and correction of defects.

Although certification is not a legal requirement to do business globally, the organization's ninety-five member countries have approved the ISO standards. In fact, ISO 9000 is so prevalent in the European Community that many customers refuse to do business with noncertified companies. As an added bonus, companies completing the certification process often discover new, cost-efficient ways of improving their existing quality control programs.

As a continuation of this standardization process, the International Organization for Standardization has developed ISO 14000. ISO 14000 is a series of international standards for incorporating environmental concerns into operations and product standards. As with ISO 9000 certification, ISO 14000 requires that a company's procedures be documented by independent auditors. It also requires that a company develop an environmental management system that will help it achieve environmental goals, objectives, and targets. For many companies, certification is necessary because their competitors are certified or their customers refuse to do business with a firm that doesn't have ISO 14000 certification.

The Impact of Computers and Robotics on Production

LEARNING OBJECTIVE

6 Discuss the increasing role of computers, robotics, and flexible manufacturing in the production process.

Automation, a development that has been revolutionizing the workplace, is the total or near-total use of machines to do work. The rapid increase in automated procedures has been made possible by the microprocessor, a silicon chip that led to the production of desktop computers. In factories, microprocessors are used in robotics and in computer manufacturing systems.

Robotics

robotics the use of programmable machines to perform a variety of tasks by manipulating materials and tools

Robotics is the use of programmable machines to perform a variety of tasks by manipulating materials and tools. Robots work quickly, accurately, and steadily. For example, at Engineering Concepts Unlimited, a small Indiana manufacturer of palm-sized electronic engine controllers, robots finish one unit every three to four seconds by placing parts in holes, putting boards in a rack, flipping them over, and soldering connections. With a few employees and only four robots, the company has annual sales in excess of $1 million. Robots are especially effective in tedious, repetitive assembly line jobs like this, as well as in handling hazardous materials. They are also useful as artificial "eyes" that can be used to check the quality of products as they are being processed on the assembly lines. And miniature buglike robots can be used to inspect spaces too small for humans to enter.

To date, the automotive industry has made the most extensive use of robotics, but robots have also been used to mine coal, inspect the inner surfaces of pipes, assemble computer components, provide certain kinds of patient care in hospitals, and clean and guard buildings at night.

Computer Manufacturing Systems

computer-aided design (CAD) the use of computers to aid in the development of products

computer-aided manufacturing (CAM) the use of computers to plan and control manufacturing processes

computer-integrated manufacturing (CIM) a computer system that not only helps design products but also controls the machinery needed to produce the finished product

People are quick to point out how computers have changed their everyday lives, but most people do not realize the impact computers have had on manufacturing. In simple terms, the factory of the future has already arrived. For most manufacturers, the changeover began with the use of computer-aided design and computer-aided manufacturing. **Computer-aided design (CAD)** is the use of computers to aid in the development of products. Using CAD, Ford speeds up car design, Canon designs new cameras and photocopiers, and American Greetings creates new birthday cards. **Computer-aided manufacturing (CAM)** is the use of computers to plan and control manufacturing processes. A well-designed CAM system allows manufacturers to become much more productive. Not only are a greater number of products produced, but speed and quality also increase. Toyota, Hasbro, Oneida, and Apple Computer have all used CAM to increase productivity.

If you are thinking that the next logical step is to combine the CAD and CAM computer systems, you are right. Today, the most successful manufacturers use CAD and CAM together to form a computer-integrated manufacturing system. Specifically, **computer-integrated manufacturing (CIM)** is a computer system that not only helps design products but also controls the machinery needed to produce the finished product. For example, Liz Claiborne, Inc., uses CIM to design clothing, to establish patterns for the new fashions, and then to cut the cloth needed to produce the finished product. Other advantages of using CIM include improved flexibility, more efficient scheduling, and higher product quality—all factors that make a production facility more competitive in today's global economy. Furthermore, specialized management software from firms like Maxager.com enables factory managers to optimize plant operations by providing information about manufacturing costs. Instead of simply guessing which product lines are most profitable, the software uses machinery performance data to analyze profits including the opportunity costs of the machinery used to produce the products. As a result, even though the cost is relative high, at one percent of revenues, client firms like Motorola believe that paybacks in improved production schedules and the product selection process are well worth the investment.[12]

A robot in every home? Sony Corporation sure hopes so! When Sony introduced AIBO—a small animal-like robot that can chase balls, bark for attention, and dance, it was an immediate success. AIBO's creator, Toshi Doi, and other product designers predict that future generations of home robots will be able to do the laundry, assist the handicapped, and serve as companions for the elderly who live alone.

Flexible Manufacturing Systems

Manufacturers have known for a number of years that the old-style, traditional assembly lines used to manufacture products present a number of problems. For example, although traditional assembly lines turn out extremely large numbers of identical products economically, the system requires expensive, time-consuming retooling of equipment whenever a new product is to be manufactured. Now it is possible to use flexible manufacturing systems to solve such problems. A **flexible manufacturing system (FMS)** combines robotics and computer-integrated manufacturing in a single production system. Instead of having to spend vast amounts of time and effort to retool the traditional mechanical equipment on an assembly line for each new product, an FMS is rearranged simply by reprogramming electronic machines. Because FMSs require less time and expense to reprogram, manufacturers can produce smaller batches of a variety of products without raising the production cost.

flexible manufacturing system (FMS) a single production system that combines robotics and computer-integrated manufacturing

Advanced software and a flexible manufacturing system have enabled Dell Computer to change to a more customer-driven manufacturing process. The process starts when a customer phones a sales representative on a toll-free line or accesses Dell's web site. Then the representative or the customer enters the specifications for the new product directly into a computer. The same computer processes the order to a nearby plant. Once the order is received, a team of employees with the help of a reprogrammable assembly line can build the product just the way the customer wants it. Products include desktops computers, notebook computers, and other Dell equipment.[13] Other firms that have used FMS include IBM, Levi Strauss, Motorola, and Andersen Windows.[14] Although the costs of designing and installing an FMS like this are high, the electronic equipment is used more frequently and efficiently than the machinery on a traditional assembly line.

Technological Displacement

Automation is increasing productivity by cutting manufacturing time, reducing error, and simplifying retooling procedures. Many of the robots being developed for use in manufacturing will not replace human employees. Rather, these robots will work with employees in making their jobs safer and easier, and help to prevent accidents. No one knows, however, what the effect will be on the work force. Some experts estimate that automation will bring changes to as many as 45 percent of all jobs by the end of the century. Total unemployment may not increase, but many workers will be faced with the choice of retraining for new jobs or seeking jobs in other sectors of the economy. Government, business, and education will have to cooperate to prepare workers for new roles in an automated workplace. According to the American Society of Travel Agents, the industry shift to Internet-based operations has been nothing short of catastrophic for small business travel operators. The number of agents has fallen from 33,000 in 1994 to 27,000 in 1999, and a Bear Stearns report suggests that as much as 25 percent of human agents are likely to be replaced by the online virtual services. Online operations are being transformed by firms like Travelocity.com and Expedia.com., motivated by customers and industry vendors seeking ways to cut their respective costs.[15]

LEARNING OBJECTIVE

7 Outline the reasons for recent trends in productivity.

The Management of Productivity

No coverage of production and operations management would be complete without a discussion of productivity. Productivity concerns all managers, but it is especially important to operations managers, the people who must oversee the creation of the firm's goods and services. We define **productivity** as a measure of output per unit of time per worker. Hence, if each worker at plant A produces 75 units per day, and each worker at plant B produces only 70 units per day, the workers at plant A are more productive. If one bank teller serves 25 customers per hour and another serves 28 per hour, the second teller is more productive.

productivity a measure of output per unit of time per worker

Productivity Trends

Although the United States has the highest level of productivity in the world, our *rate of productivity growth* is lagging behind the productivity growth rates of such countries as Japan, Italy, and Sweden.[16]

spotLight

Source: Copyright 2000, USA TODAY. Reprinted with permission.

Causes of Productivity Declines

Several factors have been cited as possible causes of the reduction in America's productivity growth rate. First, in recent years, the United States has experienced major changes in the composition of its work force. In particular, many inexperienced workers have entered the work force for the first time. The majority of these new entrants have relatively little work experience. Therefore, their productivity might be lower than average. As they develop new skills and experience, their downward influence on productivity trends should diminish.

During the last decade, businesses in some industries have slowed their rate of investment in new equipment and technology. As workers have had to use increasingly outdated equipment, their productivity has naturally declined.

Another important factor that has hurt U.S. productivity is the tremendous growth of the service sector in the United States. While this sector grew in the number of employees and economic importance, its productivity levels did not grow. Today, many economic experts agree that improving service-sector productivity is the next major hurdle facing U.S. business.

Finally, increased government regulation is frequently cited as a factor affecting productivity. Federal agencies such as the Occupational Safety and Health Administration (OSHA) and the Food and Drug Administration (FDA) are increasingly regulating business practices. The Goodyear Tire & Rubber Company generated 345,000 pages of computer printout weighing 3,200 pounds to comply with one new OSHA regulation! Furthermore, the company spends over $35 million each year solely to meet the requirements of six regulatory agencies.

Improving Productivity

Several techniques and strategies have been suggested as possible cures for downward productivity trends. For example, various government policies that may be hindering productivity could be eliminated or at least modified.

In addition, increased cooperation between management and labor could improve productivity. When unions and management work together, quite often the result is improved productivity. In a related area, many managers believe that increased employee motivation and participation can enhance productivity.

Still another potential solution to productivity problems is to change the incentives for work. Many firms simply pay employees for their time, regardless of how much or how little they produce. By changing the reward system so that people are paid for what they contribute, rather than for the time they put in, it may be possible to motivate employees to produce at higher levels.

Finally, business must invest more money in facilities, equipment, and employee training. While building a new factory or purchasing new equipment doesn't guarantee that a firm's productivity will increase, many companies like General Electric, Ford, and IBM have experienced dramatic increases in productivity when employees can use state-of-the-art equipment in a new or renovated manufacturing facility.[17] Once a business has made a commitment to invest in facilities and equipment, the next step is to train employees to use the new equipment. In turn, the employee's ability to use new equipment and new technology will increase productivity. To examine other methods that are used to increase productivity, read Adapting to Change.

Adapting to change

Sure-Fire Ways to Improve Productivity

PEOPLE WILL ALWAYS NEED "THINGS." And manufacturers will always make "things" and then sell their products in a competitive environment. Based on these facts of life, there is a real need for manufacturers to increase the productivity of their workers. At the same time, these manufacturers want to reduce costs and increase profits. After all, it is the workers who must produce the products that range from products as complicated as jet airliners to something as simple as pencils–all products that customers want.

Practical Applications of New Technology

Despite the fears of those who are afraid of change, the marriage of traditional manufacturing processes and emerging technologies is accomplishing the above goals and much, much more. There is hard evidence that technological innovations are linked to job growth, higher employee wages, new products, *and* increased productivity. Check out how the companies below have used technological innovations to improve their productivity.

- Ford Motor Company uses the Internet and online suppliers to lower purchasing costs and reduce delivery times of parts needed for its assembly lines.
- Honeywell International Inc. uses MyPlant.com software to help plant managers solve manufacturing problems online reducing production down times.
- Royal Dutch/Shell Group uses laser technology called "the light touch method" that senses hydrocarbon emissions to locate new oil reserves.
- Deere & Co. has boosted its sales by encouraging retailers and its other customers to use e-commerce and the Internet to sell Deere products.

Although these are just a few examples of how technology is changing the way employees work and the way companies do business, experts expect that technological change and the need to adapt to new methods of doing old jobs will only increase in the future. It is just as clear that companies that fail to adopt these "new" methods will fade away into oblivion.

The next chapter treats a very important aspect of management–human resource management. In Chapter 10 we discuss a number of major components of human resource management, and we see how managers use various reward systems to boost motivation, productivity, and morale.

RETURN TO Inside Business

WHILE THE FINANCIAL NUMBERS for sales, profits, and return on owners' equity are excellent for Campbell Soup, the company is more than just a profit-making machine. In fact, there are many other factors that can be used to measure the success of a company like Campbell Soup. Two such factors–the ability to produce a quality product and the ability to innovate must be considered when measuring this company.

Although Campbell Soup does have the ability to produce a quality product, the company didn't just stumble on to a manufacturing process that happened to work. In reality it took years to develop and refine the state-of-the-art manufacturing process that is used to manufacture soup and other products that most people consider "everyday items." Because most of the company's products are relatively inexpensive, every step of the manufacturing process must be carefully examined to insure that all waste has been eliminated. The steps that are involved in operations control–purchasing, inventory control, scheduling, and quality control–are especially important for a company like Campbell Soup that produces low-cost consumer items.

Another factor that can be used to measure Campbell Soup is the company's ability to innovate. Very few companies innovate better than Campbell Soup because innovation is at the heart of everything the company's employees do. Although Campbell Soup has been around for more than 130 years, the company is still looking for ways to increase the effectiveness of its manufacturing processes, improve existing products, and develop new products.

How does Campbell Soup Company get its new products? How does it develop products that will satisfy the taste buds of local customers around the globe? By first, focusing on the consumer's needs and listening to what customers say. This consumer feedback has changed the way the company does business. For example, many consumers in the United States live in what is termed an on-the-go society. To meet this need, Campbell Soup has developed ready-to-serve products that can be popped into a microwave at work or school. In other countries, customer feedback is also used to adapt or create products to meet the needs of local customers. For example, *Liebig Pur*, a thick vegetable soup, is sold in cartons with long-shelf-life in France. Australians enjoy Campbell's Pumpkin Soup. Condensed and dry soups have been specifically designed for the Hispanic consumer, like *Crema de Chile Poblano* and *Flor de Calabaza*. Germans can purchase *Erasco* canned soups and *Eintopf* hearty stews. Campbell Soup also develops products especially made for consumers in the Pacific Rim countries—soups like Watercress and Duck-Gizzard. Simply put, Campbell's research and taste tests result in new, locally pleasing products all over the globe.

Questions:

1. Most of Campbell Soup's products are relatively inexpensive. How does this factor affect the manufacturing process used to produce the company's soups and other products?
2. Given the fact that it was established in 1869 and has been around for over 130 years, how important is research and development to the success of the Campbell Soup Company? Explain your answer.

chapter Review

SUMMARY

1 Explain the nature of production.

Operations management consists of all the activities that managers engage in to create goods and services. Operations are as relevant to service organizations as to manufacturing firms. Generally, three major activities are involved in producing goods or services: product development, planning for production, and operations control. Today U.S. manufacturers are forced to compete in an ever-smaller world to meet the needs of more demanding customers. In an attempt to regain a competitive edge, they have taken another look at the importance of improving quality and meeting the needs of their customers. They have also reduced production costs, replaced outdated equipment, used computer-aided and flexible manufacturing systems, improved control procedures, and built new manufacturing facilities in foreign countries where labor costs are lower. Competing in the global economy is not only profitable; it is also an essential activity that requires the cooperation of everyone within the organization.

2 Outline how the conversion process transforms raw materials, labor, and other resources into finished products or services.

A business transforms resources into goods and services in order to provide utility to customers. Utility is the ability of a good or service to satisfy a human need. Form utility is created by converting raw materials, employees, finances, and information into finished products. Conversion processes vary in terms of the major resources used to produce goods and services (focus), the degree to which resources are changed (magnitude), and the number of production processes that a business uses. The application of the basic principles of operation management to the production of services has coincided with the growth of service businesses in the United States.

3 Describe how research and development lead to new products and services.

Operations management often begins with product research and development. The results of R&D may be entirely new products or extensions and refinements of existing products. Research and development activities are classified as basic research (aimed at uncovering new knowledge), applied research (discovering new knowledge with some potential use), and development and implementation (using new or existing knowledge to produce goods and services).

4 Discuss the components involved in planning the production process.

Planning for production involves three major phases: design planning, facilities planning and site selection, and operational planning. First, design planning is undertaken to address questions related to the product line, required production capacity, and the use of technology. Production facilities, site selection, and human resources must then be considered. Operational planning focuses on the use of production facilities and resources. The steps for operational planning include (a) selecting a planning horizon, (b) estimating market demand, (c) comparing market demand with capacity, and (d) adjusting production of products or services to meet demand.

5 Explain the four major areas of operations control: purchasing, inventory control, scheduling, and quality control.

The major areas of operations control are purchasing, inventory control, scheduling, and quality control. Purchasing involves selecting suppliers. The choice of suppliers should result from careful analysis of a number of factors, including price, quality, reliability, credit terms, and shipping costs. Inventory control is the management of stocks of raw materials, work in process, and finished goods to minimize the total inventory cost. Today most firms use a computerized system to maintain inventory records. In addition, many firms use a just-in-time inventory system, in which materials or supplies arrive at a facility just when they are needed so that storage and holding costs are minimized. Scheduling ensures that materials and other resources are at the right place at the right time—for use within the facility or for shipment to customers. Quality control guarantees that products meet the design specifications for the products.

6 Discuss the increasing role of computers, robotics, and flexible manufacturing in the production process.

Automation, the total or near-total use of machines to do work, has for some years been changing the way work is done in U.S. factories and offices. A growing number of industries are using programmable machines called robots to perform tasks that are tedious or hazardous to human beings. Computer-aided design, computer-aided manufacturing, and computer-integrated manufacturing use computers to help design and manufacture products. The flexible manufacturing system combines robotics and computer-integrated manufacturing to produce smaller batches of products more efficiently than on the traditional assembly line.

7 Outline the reasons for recent trends in productivity.

Although the U.S. has the highest level of productivity in the world, the productivity growth rate in this country has fallen behind the pace of growth in some of the other industrialized nations in recent years. Several factors have been cited as possible causes for this disturbing trend, and managers have begun to explore solutions for overcoming it. Possible solutions include less government regulation, increased cooperation between management and labor, increased employee motivation and participation, new incentives for work, and additional investment by business to fund new or renovated facilities, equipment, and employee training.

KEY TERMS

You should now be able to define and give an example relevant to each of the following terms:

operations management (239)
analytic process (241)
synthetic process (241)
utility (242)
form utility (242)
service economy (243)
research and development (R&D) (244)
design planning (246)
product line (246)
product design (246)
capacity (246)
labor-intensive technology (246)
capital-intensive technology (246)
plant layout (248)
planning horizon (250)
purchasing (251)
inventory control (253)
materials requirements planning (MRP) (253)
just-in-time inventory system (253)
scheduling (253)
Gantt chart (254)
PERT (Program Evaluation and Review Technique) (254)
critical path (254)
quality control (255)
statistical process control (SPC) (255)
statistical quality control (SQC) (255)
inspection (255)
quality circle (256)
robotics (257)
computer-aided design (CAD) (258)
computer-aided manufacturing (CAM) (258)
computer-integrated manufacturing (CIM) (258)
flexible manufacturing system (FMS) (259)
productivity (259)

REVIEW QUESTIONS

1. List all the activities involved in operations management.
2. What is the difference between an analytic and synthetic manufacturing process? Give an example of each type of process.
3. In terms of focus, magnitude, and number, characterize the production processes used by a local pizza parlor, a dry-cleaning establishment, and an auto repair shop.
4. Describe how research and development lead to new products.
5. What are the major elements of design planning?
6. What factors should be considered when selecting a site for a new manufacturing facility?
7. What is the objective of operational planning? What four steps are used to accomplish this objective?
8. If you were an operations manager, what would you do if market demand exceeds the production capacity of your manufacturing facility? What action would you take if the production capacity of your manufacturing facility exceeds market demand?
9. Why is selecting a supplier so important?
10. What costs must be balanced and minimized through inventory control?
11. How can materials requirements planning (MRP), manufacturing resource planning (MRP II), and enterprise resource planning (ERP) help control inventory and a company's production processes?
12. How does the just-in-time-inventory system help reduce inventory costs?
13. Explain in what sense scheduling is a *control* function of operations managers.
14. How can management and employees use statistical process control, statistical quality control, and inspection to improve a firm's products?
15. How can CAD, CAM, and CIM help a manufacturer produce products?
16. How might productivity be measured in a restaurant? In a department store? In a public school system?

DISCUSSION QUESTIONS

1. Why would Rubbermaid—a successful U.S. company—need to expand and sell its products to customers in foreign countries?
2. Do certain kinds of firms need to stress particular areas of operations management? Explain.
3. Is it really necessary for service firms to engage in research and development? In operations planning and control?
4. How are the four areas of operations control interrelated?
5. In what ways can employees help improve the quality of a firm's products?
6. Is operations management relevant to nonbusiness organizations such as colleges and hospitals? Why or why not?

VIDEO CASE

Saturn Listens to Its Customers

In the spring of 1990, people in the United States learned that "a different kind of company, a different kind of car" was about to burst forth in the American marketplace. At first, the creative, catchy ads focused on how management and the United Automobile Workers (UAW) union had set aside their long-standing adversarial positions to join together in a team effort to build and sell the best car they knew how to manufacture. After the first Saturn rolled off the assembly line on July 30, 1990, in Spring Hill, Tennessee, the ads switched to demonstrating how pleased owners were with the car and the service provided by the company that manufactured it.

Why was Saturn different from any other automobile produced that year? For one thing, it was manufactured in a production environment entirely different from the environments of other automobile assembly plants operating at the time. Initial planning started in 1982 when General Motors selected the code name *Saturn* for a new, innovative "small-car project." Two years later, GM joined forces with the UAW to create a new company—the Saturn Corporation—that would design and produce a quality, cost-competitive automobile. In a union-management cooperative effort unheard of until then, a separate contract was signed that made workers at Saturn partners with management and involved them in all decision-making aspects of the organization. A second, and equally important, reason Saturn automobiles were different was an increased emphasis on customer satisfaction. The people at Saturn Corporation vowed to use all means at their disposal to meet their customers' needs. It was the partnership between the UAW and management and the increased emphasis on customer satisfaction that made Saturn so successful in its early years.

Over the years, the company's philosophy hasn't changed. Today the Saturn Corporation is still "customer-driven." Employees listen very carefully to what customers want and expect in an automobile, and then they respond as quickly as possible to fill those needs. They constantly monitor the problems customers experience with their cars. Saturn's service facilities have online capabilities, so that whenever a car is brought in for service and a repair is performed, Saturn's production facilities know about it instantly. The company's salespeople are the "voice of the customer" because what they hear in the showrooms dictates what is changed in the automobiles or added to them.

Saturn has applied the science of operations management to every facet of its business, from planning and design to purchasing, inventory control, scheduling, and quality control. Using hi-tech information and state-of-the-art manufacturing equipment, the company adheres to the philosophy of "the right materials at the right time" to maximize the capacity of its production facility. By using improved technology, Saturn can now make changes in its product line in weeks or months rather than years. As a result, the downtime required to retool the assembly line is reduced, and new models reach the showroom that much faster.

Did cooperation between unions and management and the emphasis on customer satisfaction pay off? By any yardstick used to measure success at Saturn, its new and improved production methods are working. These methods have revolutionized the way cars are produced and sold in the United States. By 1993 the facility in Spring Hill could not keep up with the orders their dealers were receiving. In 1997 General Motors announced that another Saturn facility in Wilmington, Delaware would join the Spring Hill plant in continuing the production of "a different kind of company, a different kind of car!"[18]

Questions

1. A contract between Saturn and the UAW involved workers in all decision-making aspects of the organization. How could this type of cooperation change the traditional relationship between union employees and management?
2. Why is it important for a manufacturer of any product to listen to the "voice of the customer"?
3. In what ways does Saturn Corporation use planning, purchasing, inventory control, scheduling, and quality control to achieve a competitive edge?

Building skills for career success

1. Exploring the Internet

Improvements in the quality of products and services is an ever-popular theme in business management. Besides the obvious increase to profitability to be gained by such improvements, a company's demonstration of its continuous search for ways to improve operations can be a powerful statement to customers, suppliers, and investors. Two of the larger schools of thought in this field are Total Quality Management (TQM) and the European-based ISO 9000.

Assignment

1. After examining the related web links listed in the text web site for this chapter, use the Internet search engines to find more information. The W. Edward Demings Institute (http://deming.org/) and the International Standards Organization (http:www.iso.ch/) sites will be good places to begin.
2. From these web pages, can you tell whether there is any real difference between these two approaches?
3. Describe one success story of a firm that realized improvement by adopting either approach.

2. Developing Critical Thinking Skills

Plant layout—the arrangement of machinery, equipment, and personnel within a production facility—is a critical ingredient in a company's success. If the layout is inefficient, productivity will suffer, as will profits. The purpose of the business dictates the type of layout that will be most efficient. There are three general types: process layout, product layout, and fixed-position layout.

Assignment

1. For each of the following businesses, identify the best type of layout:
   - One-hour dry cleaner
   - Health club
   - Auto repair shop
   - Fast-food restaurant
   - Shipyard that builds supertankers
   - Automobile assembly plant
2. Prepare a two-page report explaining why you chose these layouts and why proper plant layout is important.

3. Building Team Skills

Suppose you are planning to build a house in the country. It will be a brick, one-story structure of approximately 2,490 square feet, centrally heated and cooled. It will have three bedrooms, two bathrooms, a family room, dining room, kitchen with breakfast nook, study, utility room, entry foyer, two-car garage, covered patio, and fireplace. Appliances will operate on electricity and propane fuel. You have received approval and can be connected to the cooperative water system at any time. Public sewerage services are not available; therefore, you must rely on a septic system. You want to know how long it will take to build the house.

Assignment

1. Identify the major activities involved in the project and sequence them in the proper order.
2. Estimate the time required for each activity and establish the critical path.
3. Working in a group, prepare a PERT diagram to show the steps involved in building your house.
4. In a two-page report, summarize what you learned about using PERT as a planning and control tool.

4. Researching Different Careers

Because service businesses are now such a dominant part of our economy, job seekers sometimes overlook the employment opportunities available in production plants. Three positions often found in these plants are production superintendent, quality assurance inspector, and purchasing agent.

Assignment

1. Using the *Dictionary of Occupational Titles (DOT)* and the *Occupational Outlook Handbook* at your local library, and/or the Occupational Informational Network (0*NET) on the Internet (www.doleta.gov/programs/onet) find the following information for the jobs of production superintendent, quality assurance inspector, and purchasing agent:
   - Job description, including main activities and responsibilities
   - Employment outlook
   - Earnings and working conditions
   - Skills, training, and education required

2. Look for other production jobs that may interest you and compile the same sort of information about them.
3. Summarize in a two-page report the key things you learned about jobs in production plants.

5. Improving Communication Skills

Total quality management (TQM) is a much broader concept than just controlling the quality of a single product. It is a philosophy that places quality at the center of everything a company does. In particular, TQM is aimed at improving customer satisfaction, increasing employee participation, strengthening supplier partnerships, and facilitating an organizational atmosphere of continuous quality improvement. For TQM to work successfully, it must start with a company's mission statement, be ingrained in the company's goals and objectives, and be implemented through the strategies that ultimately satisfy customer needs. Motorola and Hewlett-Packard are two companies in which a concern for total quality is the driving force. How have these companies successfully used TQM? How will TQM influence their operations as they move into the next century and compete on a more global basis?

Assignment

1. Read articles or use the Internet to find out how Motorola and Hewlett-Packard implement TQM.
2. Prepare a three-page report on your findings. The report should include answers to the following questions:
   a. Exactly how does each company focus on quality?
   b. How are the TQM programs of these two companies alike? How do they differ?
   c. How will TQM influence their operations in the twenty-first century?
   d. Using quality as a criterion, which company would you rather work for? Why?

E*Trade Trades on Smart Management, Organization, and Operations

Active military duty during the Vietnam war taught Christos M. Cotsakos the value of loyalty, teamwork, and trust. Now Cotsakos is applying those lessons as CEO of E*Trade, a fast-growing financial services firm offering electronic securities trading and banking. E*Trade, headquartered in Menlo Park, California, was an early Internet pioneer in discount securities trading. The company now holds nearly $5 billion in bank deposits and services more than 3.3 million customers in all 50 states as well as 119 countries worldwide.

Bytes and Bonds

Dr. Bill Porter, a physicist and prolific inventor, founded E*Trade in 1982 to provide online securities quotes and trading services to Fidelity, Charles Schwab, and Quick & Reilly. Looking ahead, Porter believed that individual investors would one day be able to use electronic services to trade stocks and bonds more efficiently—and at less cost—than the traditional method of trading through a stockbroker. Just ten years later, the growth of the Internet allowed Porter to bring his vision to life by starting an all-electronic securities brokerage firm. E*Trade was originally available online through America Online and CompuServe, but after the company launched its etrade.com web site (http://www.etrade.com) in 1996, demand for its low-price services skyrocketed.

Preparing for aggressive growth, Porter hired Cotsakos as CEO in 1996. Under Cotsakos, the company bought Telebanc—an all-electronic bank—and renamed it E*Trade Bank to complement the existing securities trading capabilities. The company also acquired the Card Capture Services network of 8,500 automated teller machines spread around the United States and set up E*Trade operations in the United Kingdom, Germany, Japan, and Scandinavia. Knowing that some investors prefer face-to-face contact, E*Trade is starting to open mini-branches in Target stores around the United States. It is also starting to offer online personalized financial planning tools and referrals to offline private money managers.

Growing Pains

The years of expansion have brought E*Trade millions of new customers and new operational and management challenges. The web site has suffered intermittently from service outages, including one week in early 1999 when customers could not place online trades for at least a few minutes on three different days. In 2000, a hacker attack on the web site caused more problems and delays. As more and more customers flocked to E*Trade's low-fee site, the company struggled to keep up. The volume of customer complaints briefly soared, causing regulators to fine E*Trade for its sluggish response. The company quickly boosted its staffing to bring the complaint rate down within a few months. E*Trade is still on the fast track. Its branchless E*Trade Bank recorded $1 billion in deposits during one recent three-month period—an impressive performance considering that Bank One, one of the largest U.S. banks, attracted $961 million through its branches during the same quarter.

This kind of rapid expansion is all in a day's work for CEO Cotsakos. Before joining E*Trade, Cotsakos logged more than twenty years of hands-on management time at A.C. Nielsen and FedEx. The stint at FedEx showed him how motivated teams can maintain a fast pace while meeting high standards. Now Cotsakos has transferred that experience to E*Trade, where he looks for employees with solid skills and provides coaching to create effective, high-performing teams. He also motivates employees by sharing his vision of building a worldwide financial services firm that will allow consumers to trade or bank via computer, telephone, pager, or just about any other electronic method. With strong top-level leadership and effective management and operational planning, E*Trade is poised to continue its growth anywhere and everywhere consumers want to do business.

Questions

1. How has the CEO's military and business experience affected E*Trade's corporate culture and organizational structure?
2. To what problem or opportunity was E*Trade responding with its plans to purchase the Card Capture Services' ATM network?
3. What kinds of issues might E*Trade's senior management consider when preparing contingency plans for the coming year?
4. Why is operational planning as important for a predominantly online business like E*Trade as it is for a manufacturer such as Ford?

Human Resources

This part of *Business* is concerned with the most important and least predictable of all resources—people. We begin by examining the human resource efforts that organizations use to hire, develop, and retain their best employees. Then, we discuss employee motivation and satisfaction. Finally, we look at organized labor and probe the sometimes controversial relationship between business management and labor unions.

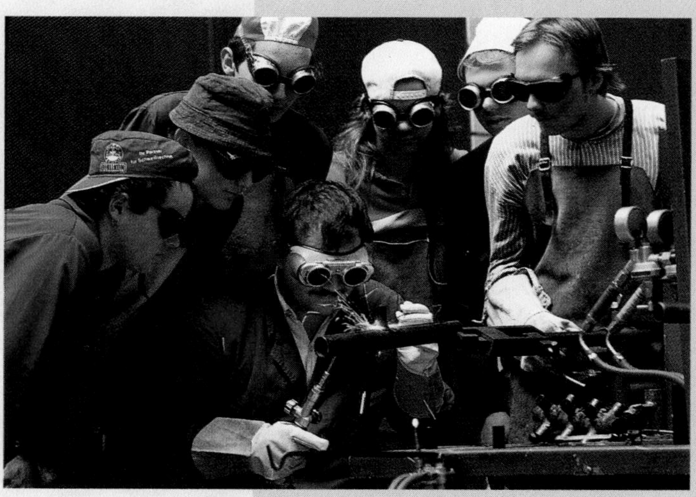

10 Attracting and Retaining the Best Employees

LEARNING OBJECTIVES

1. Describe the major components of human resources management.
2. Identify the steps in human resources planning.
3. Describe cultural diversity and understand some of the challenges and opportunities associated with it.
4. Explain the objectives and uses of job analysis.
5. Describe the processes of recruiting, employee selection, and orientation.
6. Discuss the primary elements of employee compensation and benefits.
7. Explain the purposes and techniques of employee training, development, and performance appraisal.
8. Outline the major legislation affecting human resources management.

At Dell, 100 recruiters fan out around the world in search of 8,000 recruits annually.

Rounding Up Recruits for Dell Computer

EVERYBODY IS A RECRUITER at Dell Computer. The fast-growing computer manufacturer, headquartered in Austin, Texas, is in a fierce fight for talent, competing with other high-tech firms as well as start-up web businesses. With Dell's computer sales growing as much as 40 percent annually, founder and CEO Michael Dell has put "people" on the top of his priority list for two years in a row.

Dell hires more than 8,000 employees each year—and during peak periods, as many as 200 per week go through orientation. Recruiting this many good employees isn't easy in a high-employment economy, where the brightest graduates and the most successful managers are pursued by numerous companies. So to keep up with the demand for employees to fill positions created by growth and to replace those who have been promoted, Dell has called "all hands on deck" for recruiting, in the words of Andy Esparza, Dell's vice president for staffing.

Esparza supervises the 100 recruiters in Dell's human resources department who fan out around the world in search of job candidates. The department mission statement he created summarizes Dell's aggressive approach: "Relentlessly recruit and hire world-class people." Esparza and his recruiters are always networking and scanning newspapers, industry publications, and web sites in search of people with potential. They have even aired television and radio commercials and put up billboards to bring in new recruits.

Although one-third of the new hires are drawn from candidates who apply to Dell through its web site (http://www.dell.com), the remainder come from leads attracted by recruiting campaigns or suggested by Dell recruiters, managers, and employees. Despite the unending need for employees, Esparza is particular about who Dell hires. Not everybody is cut out for the firm's dynamic work climate, he says. "It's a high-risk, high-reward environment. We have to screen for people who can thrive in that kind of culture. Short-term decisions or compromises you make today in the interests of getting something done will cost you later on." Based on research into who has and has not succeeded at Dell, Esparza knows to look for managers who can learn quickly, embrace change, achieve results, solve problems, and foster teamwork.

Esparza and his team are constantly on the prowl for top candidates—whether or not Dell has suitable openings. "Why would you choose not to hire a great person just because there's no job opening at the present time?" he asks. His recruiters assess the strengths of each candidate and, if no opening exists, create an appropriate position. When Esparza finds out that a key management candidate is weighing competing offers or wavering about joining Dell, he asks Michael Dell to call and talk up the company. This personal, top-level contact usually tips the balance in Dell's favor: "He's a great closer," says Esparza.[1]

In recruiting skilled employees and retaining them in a highly competitive industry, Dell Computer is able to recruit thousands of employees annually because of its aggressive recruiting efforts and its culture, management style, and employee benefits. For any company, these are very important factors in attracting, motivating, and retaining the appropriate mix of human resources.

We begin our study of human resources management, or HRM, with an overview of how businesses acquire, maintain, and develop their human resources. After listing the steps by which firms match their human resources needs with the supply available, we explore several dimensions of cultural diversity. Then we examine the concept of job analysis. Next we focus on a firm's recruiting, selection, and orientation procedures as the means of acquiring employees. We also describe forms of employee compensation that motivate employees to remain with the firm and to work effectively. Then we discuss methods of employee training, management development, and performance appraisal. Finally, we consider legislation that affects HRM practices.

LEARNING OBJECTIVE

1 Describe the major components of human resources management.

Human Resources Management: An Overview

The human resource is not only unique and valuable, it is also an organization's most important resource. It seems logical that an organization would expend a great deal of effort to acquire and make full use of such a resource, and most organizations do. That effort is known as human resources management, or HRM. It has also been called *staffing* and *personnel management.*

human resources management (HRM) all the activities involved in acquiring, maintaining, and developing an organization's human resources

Human resources management consists of all the activities involved in acquiring, maintaining, and developing an organization's human resources. As the definition implies, HRM begins with acquisition—getting people to work for the organization. Next, steps must be taken to keep these valuable resources. (This is important; after all, they are the only business resources that can leave the organization at will.) Finally, the human resources should be developed to their full capacity to contribute to the firm.

HRM Activities

Each of the three phases of HRM—acquiring, maintaining, and developing human resources—consists of a number of related activities. Acquisition, for example, includes planning, as well as the various activities that lead to hiring new personnel. Altogether, this phase of HRM includes five separate activities. They are

- *Human resources planning*—determining the firm's future human resources needs
- *Job analysis*—determining the exact nature of the positions to be filled
- *Recruiting*—attracting people to apply for positions in the firm
- *Selection*—choosing and hiring the most qualified applicants
- *Orientation*—acquainting new employees with the firm

Maintaining human resources consists primarily of encouraging employees to remain with the firm and to work effectively by using a variety of HRM programs including

- *Employee relations*—increasing employee job satisfaction through satisfaction surveys, employee communication programs, exit interviews, and fair treatment
- *Compensation*—rewarding employee effort through monetary payments
- *Benefits*—providing rewards to ensure employee well-being

The development phase of HRM is concerned with improving employees' skills and expanding their capabilities. The two important activities within this phase are

- *Training and development*—teaching employees new skills, new jobs, and more effective ways of doing their present jobs

- *Performance appraisal*—assessing employees' current and potential performance levels

These activities are discussed in more detail shortly, when we have completed this overview of human resources management.

HRM activities: an ongoing responsibility. HRM activities at Verizon begin with acquiring the right people, which includes giving these applicants at a job fair a data processing test. After selecting and hiring qualified people, Verizon will give them an orientation to the company, job-specific training, and an appropriate compensation and benefits package. Then the employees' performance will be evaluated on a regular basis.

Responsibility for HRM

In general, human resources management is a shared responsibility of line managers and staff HRM specialists.

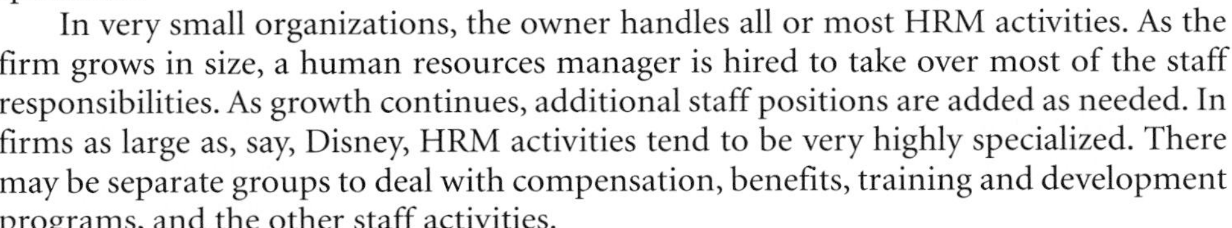

In very small organizations, the owner handles all or most HRM activities. As the firm grows in size, a human resources manager is hired to take over most of the staff responsibilities. As growth continues, additional staff positions are added as needed. In firms as large as, say, Disney, HRM activities tend to be very highly specialized. There may be separate groups to deal with compensation, benefits, training and development programs, and the other staff activities.

Specific HRM activities are assigned to those who are in the best position to perform them. Human resources planning and job analysis are usually done by staff specialists, with input from line managers. Similarly, recruiting and selection are generally handled by staff experts, although line managers are involved in the actual hiring decisions. Orientation programs are usually devised by staff specialists, and the orientation itself is carried out by both staff specialists and line managers. Compensation systems (including benefits) are most often developed and administered by the HRM staff. However, line managers recommend pay increases and promotions. Training and development activities are usually the joint responsibility of staff and line managers. Performance appraisal is the job of the line manager, although HRM staff personnel design the firm's appraisal system in many organizations.

LEARNING OBJECTIVE

2 Identify the steps in human resources planning.

Human Resources Planning

human resources planning the development of strategies to meet a firm's future human resources needs

Human resources planning is the development of strategies to meet the firm's future human resources needs. The starting point for this planning is the organization's overall strategic plan. From this, human resources planners can forecast the firm's future demand for human resources. Next, the planners must determine whether the needed human resources will be available; that is, they must anticipate the supply of human resources within the firm. Finally, they have to take steps to match supply with demand.

Forecasting Human Resources Demand

Planners should base forecasts of the demand for human resources on as much relevant information as they can gather. The firm's overall strategic plan will provide information about future business ventures, new products, and projected expansions or contractions of particular product lines. Information on past staffing levels, evolving technologies, industry staffing practices, and projected economic trends can also be very helpful.

spotLight

Source: Copyright 2000, USA TODAY. Reprinted with permission.

HRM staff use all this information to determine both the number of employees the firm will require and their qualifications—including skills, experience, and knowledge. Planners use a wide range of methods to forecast specific personnel needs. For example, with one simple method, personnel requirements are projected to increase or decrease in the same proportion as sales revenue. Thus, if a 30 percent increase in sales volume is projected over the next two years, then up to a 30 percent increase in personnel requirements might be expected for the same period. (This method can be applied to specific positions as well as to the work force in general. It is not, however, a very precise forecasting method.) At the other extreme are elaborate, computer-based personnel planning models used by some large firms such as Exxon Corporation.

Forecasting Human Resources Supply

The forecast of the supply of human resources must take into account both the present work force and any changes or movements that may occur within it. For example, suppose planners project that in five years a firm that currently employs 100 engineers will need to employ a total of 200 engineers. Planners cannot simply assume they will have to hire 100 engineers over the next five years; during that period, some of the firm's present engineers are likely to be promoted, leave the firm, or move to other jobs within the firm. Thus, planners might project the supply of engineers in five years at 87, which means that the firm will have to hire a total of 113 (or more) new engineers. When forecasting supply, planners should analyze the organization's existing employees to determine who can be retrained to perform the required tasks.

replacement chart a list of key personnel and their possible replacements within the firm

skills inventory a computerized data bank containing information on the skills and experience of all present employees

Two useful techniques for forecasting human resources supply are the replacement chart and the skills inventory. A **replacement chart** is a list of key personnel and their possible replacements within the firm. The chart is maintained to ensure that top management positions can be filled fairly quickly in the event of an unexpected death, resignation, or retirement. Some firms also provide additional training for employees who might eventually replace top managers.

A **skills inventory** is a computerized data bank containing information on the skills and experience of all present employees. It is used to search for candidates to fill new or newly available positions. For a special project a manager might be seeking a current employee with specific information technology skills, at least six years of experience, and fluency in French. The skills inventory can quickly identify employees who possess such qualifications. Skill assessment tests can be administered inside an organization or they can be provided by outside vendors. For example, SkillView Technologies Incorporated and Bookman Testing Services TeckChek are third party information technology skill assessment providers.[2] Furthermore, according to the Information Technology Association, the shortage of skilled knowledge workers is a driving force behind companies moving to outsourcing their computer system needs. By using Internet-based hosts that provide all software and technical services for a monthly fee firms can avoid staffing many highly specialized jobs. The association estimated that there are currently about 850,000 unfilled technology jobs, a problem exacerbated by the strong growth in e-business activities.[3]

Using the Internet

The Internet provides access to many excellent sources of both general information focusing on HR, such as the Society for Human Resource Management (**http://www.shrm.org/**), and more specialized areas such as the American Society for Training and Development (**http://www.astd.org/**).

Matching Supply with Demand

Once they have forecasts of both the demand for personnel and the firm's supply of personnel, planners can devise a course of action for matching the two. When demand is predicted to be greater than supply, plans must be made to recruit and select new employees. The timing of these actions depends on the types of positions to be filled. Suppose we expect to open another plant in five years. Along with other employees, a plant manager and twenty-five maintenance workers will be needed. We can probably wait quite a while before we begin to recruit maintenance personnel. However, because the job of plant manager is so critical, we may start searching for the right person for that position immediately.

When supply is predicted to be greater than demand, the firm must take steps to reduce the size of its work force. Several methods are available, although none of them is especially pleasant for managers or discharged employees. When the oversupply is expected to be temporary, some employees may be *laid off*—dismissed from the work force until they are needed again.

Perhaps the most humane method for making personnel cutbacks is through attrition. *Attrition* is the normal reduction in the work force that occurs when employees leave the firm. If these employees are not replaced, the work force eventually shrinks to the point where supply matches demand. Of course, attrition may be a very slow process—often too slow to really help the firm.

Early retirement is another option. Under early retirement, people who are within a few years of retirement are permitted (or encouraged) to retire early with full benefits. Depending on the age makeup of the work force, this may or may not reduce the staff enough.

As a last resort, unneeded employees are sometimes simply *fired*. However, because of its negative impact, this method is generally used only when absolutely necessary.

Cultural Diversity in Human Resources

LEARNING OBJECTIVE

3 Describe cultural diversity and understand some of the challenges and opportunities associated with it.

Today's work force is made up of many types of people. Firms can no longer safely assume that every employee walking in the door has similar beliefs or expectations. Whereas North American white males may believe in challenging authority, Asians tend to respect and defer to it. In Hispanic cultures, people often bring music, food, and family members to work, a custom that U.S. businesses have traditionally not allowed. A job applicant who won't make eye contact during an interview may be rejected for being unapproachable, when according to her culture, she was just being polite.

As a larger number of women, minorities, and immigrants enter the U.S. work force, the workplace is growing more diverse. It is estimated that by 2006 women will make up about 47 percent of the U.S. work force, and African Americans and Hispanics will each account for about 11 percent.[4] Hispanics will continue to be the fastest growing population in the United States.

Cultural (workplace) diversity differences among people in a work force due to race, ethnicity, and gender

Cultural, or **workplace**, **diversity** refers to the differences among people in a work force due to race, ethnicity, and gender. Increasing cultural diversity is forcing managers to learn to supervise and motivate people with a broader range of value systems. The flood of women into the work force, combined with a new emphasis on participative parenting by men, has brought many family-related issues to the workplace. Today's more educated employees also want greater independence and flexibility. In return for their efforts, they want both compensation and a better quality of life.

Although cultural diversity presents a challenge, managers should view it as an opportunity rather than a limitation. When properly managed, cultural diversity can provide competitive advantages for an organization. Table 10.1 shows several benefits that creative management of cultural diversity can offer. A firm that manages diversity properly can develop cost advantages over firms that do not manage diversity well.

table 10.1 Competitive Advantages of Cultural Diversity

Cost	As organizations become more diverse, the cost of a poor job in integrating workers will increase. Companies that handle this well can thus create cost advantages over those that do a poor job. In addition, companies also experience cost savings by hiring people with knowledge of various cultures as opposed to having to train Americans, for example, about how German people do business.
Resource acquisition	Companies develop reputations as being favorable or unfavorable prospective employers for women and ethnic minorities. Those with the best reputations for managing diversity will win the competition for the best personnel.
Marketing edge	For multinational organizations, the insight and cultural sensitivity that members with roots in other countries bring to the marketing effort should improve these efforts in important ways. The same rationale applies to marketing subpopulations domestically.
Flexibility	Culturally diverse employees often are open to a wider array of positions within a company and are more likely to move up the corporate ladder more rapidly, given excellent performance.
Creativity	Diversity of perspectives and less emphasis on conformity to norms of the past should improve the level of creativity.
Problem solving	Differences within decision-making and problem-solving groups potentially produce better decisions through a wider range of perspectives and more thorough critical analysis of issues.
Bilingual skills	Cultural diversity in the workplace brings with it bilingual and bicultural skills, which are very advantageous to the ever-growing global marketplace. Employees with knowledge about how other cultures work can not only speak to them in their language but prevent their company from making embarrassing moves due to lack of cultural sophistication. Thus, companies seek job applicants with perhaps a background in cultures in which the company does business.

Sources: Taylor H. Cox and Stacy Blake, "Managing Cultural Diversity: Implications for Organizational Competitiveness," *Academy of Management Executive*, Vol. 5, no.3, 1991, p. 46; Graciela Kenig, "Yo Soy Ingeniero: The Advantages of Being Bilingual in Technical Professions," *Diversity Monthly*, Feb 28, 1999, p. 13; and "Dialogue Skills in the Multicultural Workplace," *North American Post*, March 19, 1999, p.2.

Moreover, organizations that manage diversity creatively are in a much better position to attract the best personnel. A culturally diverse organization may gain a marketing edge because it understands different cultural groups. Proper guidance and management of diversity in an organization can also improve the level of creativity. Culturally diverse people frequently are more flexible in the types of positions they will accept. Workers who bring fresh viewpoints to problem solving and decision making may enliven these processes substantially. Bilingual skills bring numerous benefits to an organization.

Because cultural diversity creates challenges along with these advantages, it is important for an organization's employees to know how to cope with it. To accomplish that goal, numerous U.S. firms have taken action to train their managers to respect and manage diversity. Diversity training programs may include recruiting minorities, training minorities to be managers, training managers to view diversity positively, teaching English as a second language, providing mentoring programs, and facilitating support groups for immigrants. Due to the high quality of its cultural diversity program, Texas Instruments has received several awards for being one of the best places in America for minorities to work. Texas Instruments' cultural diversity program involves training and education, employee diversity groups, and corporate policies that support advancement of minorities in that organization. Thousands of managers, supervisors, and employees from all parts of the company have attended diversity training programs that have taught them to value the cultural differences in Texas Instruments. One of the reasons for this program's success is the strong commitment that senior management at Texas Instruments has made to this program.[5]

As is the case with many organizational goals, a diversity program will be successful only if it is systematic and ongoing and has a strong, sustained commitment from top leadership. Cultural diversity is here to stay. Its impact in organizations is widespread and will continue to grow within corporations. Management must learn to overcome the obstacles and capitalize on the advantages associated with the varying viewpoints and backgrounds of culturally diverse human resources.

LEARNING OBJECTIVE

4 Explain the objectives and uses of job analysis.

Job Analysis

There is no sense in trying to hire people unless we know what we are hiring them for. In other words, we need to know the exact nature of a job before we can find the right person to do it.

Job analysis is a systematic procedure for studying jobs to determine their various elements and requirements. Consider the position of clerk, for example. In a large corporation, there may be fifty kinds of clerk positions. They all may be called "clerks," but each position may differ from the others in the activities to be performed, the level of proficiency required for each activity, and the particular set of qualifications that the position demands. These distinctions are the focus of job analysis.

job analysis a systematic procedure for studying jobs to determine their various elements and requirements

The job analysis for a particular position typically consists of two parts—a job description and a job specification. A **job description** is a list of the elements that make up a particular job. It includes the duties the jobholder must perform, the working conditions under which the job must be performed, the jobholder's responsibilities (including number and types of subordinates, if any), and the tools and equipment that must be used on the job (see Figure 10.1).

job description a list of the elements that make up a particular job

A **job specification** is a list of the qualifications required to perform a particular job. Included are the skills, abilities, education, and experience the jobholder must have. When attempting to hire an RS-wireless engineer, Ericsson used the following job specification: "A BSEE or equivalent technical degree, two-plus years' experience in RS propagation, cellular planning, land mobile radio, and/or PCS systems is preferred."[6]

job specification a list of the qualifications required to perform a particular job

The job analysis is not only the basis for recruiting and selecting new employees, for either existing positions or new ones; it is also used in other areas of human resources management, including evaluation and the determination of equitable compensation levels.

LEARNING OBJECTIVE

5 Describe the processes of recruiting, employee selection, and orientation.

Recruiting, Selection, and Orientation

In an organization with jobs waiting to be filled, HRM personnel need to (1) find candidates for those jobs and (2) match the right candidate with each job. Three activities are involved: recruiting, selection, and (for new employees) orientation.

Recruiting

Recruiting is the process of attracting qualified job applicants. Because it is a vital link in a costly process (the cost of hiring an employee can be several thousand dollars), recruiting needs to be a systematic rather than haphazard process. One goal of recruiters is to attract the "right number" of applicants. The right number is enough to allow a good match between applicants and open positions, but not so many that matching them requires too much time and effort. For example, if there are five open

recruiting the process of attracting qualified job applicants

figure 10.1

Job Description and Job Specification

This job description explains the job of sales coordinator and lists the responsibilities of the position. The job specification is contained in the last paragraph.

HOUGHTON MIFFLIN COMPANY

JOB DESCRIPTION

TITLE:	Georgia Sales Coordinator	**DATE:**	3/25/98
DEPARTMENT:	College, Sales	**GRADE:**	12
REPORTS TO:	Regional Manager	**EXEMPT/NON-EXEMPT:**	Exempt

BRIEF SUMMARY:

Supervise one other Georgia-based sales representative to gain supervisory experience. Captain the 4 members of the outside sales rep team that are assigned to territories consisting of colleges and universities in Georgia. Oversee, coordinate, advise, and make decisions regarding Georgia sales activities. Based upon broad contact with customers across the state and communication with administrators of schools, the person will make recommendations regarding issues specific to the needs of higher education in the state of Georgia such as distance learning, conversion to the semester system, potential statewide adoptions, and faculty training.

PRINCIPLE ACCOUNTABILITIES:

1. Supervises/manages/trains one other Atlanta-based sales rep.
2. Advises two other sales reps regarding the Georgia schools in their territories.
3. Increases overall sales in Georgia as well as individual sales territory.
4. Assists regional manager in planning and coordinating regional meetings and Atlanta conferences.
5. Initiates a dialogue with campus administrators, particularly in the areas of the semester conversion, distance learning, and faculty development.

DIMENSIONS:

This position will have one direct report in addition to the leadership role played within the region. Revenue most directly impacted will be within the individually assigned territory, the supervised territory, and the overall sales for the state of Georgia.

KNOWLEDGE AND SKILLS:

Must have displayed a history of consistently outstanding sales in personal territory. Must demonstrate clear teamwork and leadership skills and be willing to extend beyond the individual territory goals. Should have a clear understanding of the company's systems and product offerings in order to train and lead other sales representatives. Must have the communication skills and presence to communicate articulately with higher education administrators and to serve as a bridge between the company and higher education in the state.

Source: Used with permission of Houghton Mifflin Company.

positions and five applicants, the firm essentially has no choice. It must hire those five applicants (qualified or not), or the positions will remain open. At the other extreme, if several hundred job seekers apply for the five positions, HRM personnel will have to spend weeks processing their applications.

Recruiters may seek applicants outside the firm, within the firm, or both. The source used depends on the nature of the position, the situation within the firm, and sometimes the firm's established or traditional recruitment policies. According to Michael Boyd, senior HR analyst at IDC, Internet-based sites such as Monster.com, CareerPath.com, and CareerMosaic, which hold millions of résumés for employers to choose from, are not the primary connections for successful high-tech job hunters. In fact, only 8.1 percent of those hired were recruited through web-based employment services. Boyd's studies suggest that it is still the complex social networks of human interaction such as word-of-mouth and employee referrals that account for more than a third of high-tech recruiting. Even job fairs, print and TV ads, and old-fashioned headhunters are better than online agencies.[7]

external recruiting the attempt to attract job applicants from outside the organization

External Recruiting

External recruiting is the attempt to attract job applicants from outside the organization. Among the means available for external recruiting are Internet web sites, newspaper advertising, recruiting on college campuses and in union

Adapting to change

Collegehire.Com's Approach to College Recruiting

Jeff Daniel, founder and CEO of collegehire.com (http://www.collegehire.com), wants to change the way companies recruit graduating seniors. Daniel was recruited by Trilogy Software after graduate school and quickly rose through the ranks to manage its recruiting department. So he knows the process inside and out. He is also aware that showing up on campus for a two-hour spring job fair isn't the way to attract the best recruits.

"Since few companies have buckets and buckets of money to throw at recruiting, you've got to create an A-to-Z strategy," he explains. He suggests companies first determine what kinds of students and schools would be a good match for the company and its job openings. This means investigating each school's degrees and reputation to narrow the list of colleges. Next, companies should meet with each school's career center staffers, find out what they need, and meet their requirements on time.

Now comes the heart of Daniel's process: Going beyond résumés to really learn about the students. "How can you decide to fly someone across the country for an on-site interview based only on a résumé and one short interview?" Daniel says. "You don't have enough to go on. It's pure guesswork." That's why Collegehire.com's recruiters are on campus every day, mingling with students and answering questions about job-hunting. Along the way, they learn about the academic standouts—and about the stars whose grades are less than stellar. "A lot of companies miss those people because they don't look deep enough," says Daniel. "But if you find out what gets someone jazzed and channel that energy into something that a company is doing, then that person would be awesome."

Collegehire.com recruits at Harvard, MIT, the University of Georgia, and more than thirty other schools for companies such as Trilogy, Amazon.com, and McKinsey & Company. Although Daniel's primary focus is high-tech positions, he plans to branch out into other industries to help companies improve their campus recruiting. "You need to stay ahead of the curve because hiring the wrong people is brutal," says Daniel. "You have to get it right."

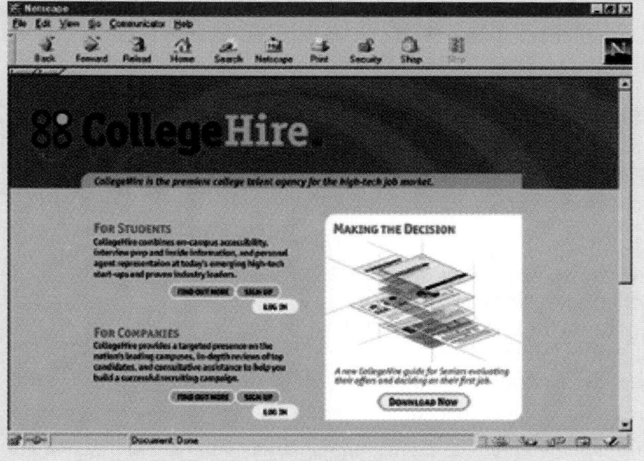

hiring halls, using employment agencies, soliciting the recommendations of present employees and conducting "open houses" in which potential employees are invited to visit the firm for a closer look. In addition, many people who are looking for work simply apply at the firm's employment office.

Clearly, it is best to match the recruiting means with the kind of applicant being sought. For example, private employment agencies most often handle professional people, whereas public employment agencies (operated by state or local governments) are usually more concerned with operations personnel. Hence, we might approach a private agency if we were looking for a vice president, but we would be more inclined to contact a public agency if we wanted to hire a machinist.

The primary advantage of external recruiting is that it enables the firm to bring in people with new perspectives and varied business backgrounds. It may also be the only way to attract applicants with the required skills and knowledge. A disadvantage of external recruiting is that it is often expensive, especially if private employment agencies must be used. External recruiting may also provoke resentment among present employees.

Internal Recruiting **Internal recruiting** means considering present employees as applicants for available positions. Generally, current employees are considered for *promotion* to higher-level positions. However, employees may also be considered for *transfer* from one position to another at the same level.

internal recruiting considering present employees as applicants for available positions

College job fairs. At CISCO Systems, recruiting at college job fairs is a part of its external recruiting efforts.

Promoting from within provides strong motivation for current employees and helps the firm retain quality personnel. General Electric, Exxon, and Eastman Kodak are companies dedicated to promoting from within. The practice of *job posting*, or informing current employees of upcoming openings, may be a company policy or be required by a union contract. The primary disadvantage of internal recruiting is that promoting a current employee leaves another position to be filled. Not only does the firm still incur recruiting and selection costs, but also it must now train two employees instead of one.

In many situations, it may be impossible to recruit internally. For example, a new position may be such that no current employee is qualified to fill it. Or the firm may be growing so rapidly there is no time to go through the reassigning of positions that promotion or transfer require.

selection the process of gathering information about applicants for a position and then using that information to choose the most appropriate applicant.

Selection

Selection is the process of gathering information about applicants for a position and then using that information to choose the most appropriate applicant. Note the use of the word *appropriate*. In selection, the idea is not to hire the person with the "most" qualifications but rather to choose the applicant with the qualifications that are most appropriate for the job. The actual selection of an applicant often is made by one or more line managers who have responsibility for the position being filled. However, HRM personnel usually help the selection process by developing a pool of applicants and expediting the assessment of these applicants. Common means of obtaining information about applicants' qualifications are employment applications, tests, interviews, references, and assessment centers.

Employment Applications Just about everyone who applies for anything must submit an application. You probably filled one out to apply for admission to your school. An employment application is useful in collecting factual information on a candidate's education, work experience, and personal history (see Figure 10.2). The data obtained from applications are usually used for two purposes: to identify applicants who are worthy of further scrutiny and to familiarize interviewers with their backgrounds.

Many job candidates submit résumés to prospective employers, and some firms require them. A *résumé* is a one-or two-page summary of the candidate's background and qualifications. It may include a description of the type of job the applicant is seeking. A résumé may be sent to a firm to request consideration for available jobs, or it may be submitted along with an employment application.

To improve the usefulness of information gathered HRM specialists ask current employees about the factors in their own backgrounds most strongly related to their

3M Employment Application
Form 14650 - D

3M Staffing Resource Center
3M Center, Building 224-1W-02
P.O. Box 33224
St. Paul, MN 55133-3224

Name (Print or Type)

Personal Data *(Print or Type)* **No.** 109060

Name	Last	First	MI	Social Security Number
Present Address	Street Address			Home Telephone (Include Area Code) ( )
	City, State and Zip			Work Telephone (Include Area Code) ( )
	Internet e-mail Address			
Permanent Address	*Leave blank if same as above*	Street Address		
		City, State and Zip		
Job Interest	Position applied for		Salary desired	
	Type of position applied for ☐ Regular ☐ Part-time ☐ Temporary ☐ Summer ☐			

Authorization to Work
It is unlawful for 3M to hire individuals that are not authorized to work in the Unite[d] citizens or aliens that are authorized to work in the United States. If you receive a[n] offer, before you will be placed on the payroll, you will be required to document th[at] that is authorized to work in the United States.
Are you a United States citizen or a lawful permanent resident? ☐ Yes ☐
If your answer is No, what type of Visa and employment authorization do you hav[e]

Education History

Schools Attended (Last School First)	Attendance Dates Mo./Yr. From - To	Grad. Date	Deg[ree] Ty[pe]
Name of School (City, State)	-		
	-		
	-		
	-		
High School or GED			

Additional Education Information
(If additional space is needed, attach separate page)
Faculty person who knows you best (name, telephone)
Memberships in professional or honorary societies and any other extracurricular activities
Post graduate research, title and description
Publications/Patents Issued

Please Open Folder and Complete Additional Informati[on]

Printed with soy inks on Torchglow Opaque (made of 50% recycled fiber, includi[ng]

General Information and Job Requirements
Are you willing to → Work Shifts ☐ Yes ☐ No; Work overtime ☐ Yes ☐ No; Work a schedule other than M/F ☐ Yes ☐ No; Work a rotation work schedule ☐ Yes ☐ No
Travel ☐ Yes ___% ☐ No; List any restrictions regarding relocation; Are you willing to relocate? ☐ Yes ☐ No
If you wish to indicate that you were referred to 3M by any of the following, please check appropriate box and specify
☐ Employment advertisement (Name of publication) ☐ Employment agency (Name of agency) ☐ 3M Employee (Name) ☐ Other
Are you under 18? ☐ Yes ☐ No
Have you ever ☐ been employed by 3M or any 3M Subsidiary ☐ previously applied to 3M or any 3M Subsidiary
If so, please check appropriate box and specify location, date, employee number - (include last two 3M performance reviews if appropriate and available.)
Date/Employee Number

Employment Record
List most current or recent employer first, include periods of unemployment, include U.S. Military Service (show rank/rate at discharge, but not type of discharge). Include previous 3M experience (summer/part time jobs and Cooperative Education assignments and any volunteer experience which relates to the position you are applying for).

Employer (company name) | Immediate supervisor's name | Your job title
Street Address | Employment dates (mo. and yr.) From To | Salary Begin End
City, State, Zip Code | Reason for leaving or why do you want to leave?
Company's Product or Service | Summarize your job duties

Employer (company name) | Immediate supervisor's name | Your job title
Street Address | Employment dates (mo. and yr.) From To | Salary Begin End
City, State, Zip Code | Reason for leaving
Company's Product or Service | Summarize your job duties

Employer (company name) | Immediate supervisor's name | Your job title
Street Address | Employment dates (mo. and yr.) From To | Salary Begin End
City, State, Zip Code | Reason for leaving
Company's Product or Service | Summarize your job duties

Employer (company name) | Immediate supervisor's name | Your job title
Street Address | Employment dates (mo. and yr.) From To | Salary Begin End
City, State, Zip Code | Reason for leaving
Company's Product or Service | Summarize your job duties

Additional Information
(Please include any additional information you think might be helpful to use in considering you for employment, such as additional work experience, activities, accomplishments, etc.)

figure 10.2

Typical Employment Application

Employers use applications to collect factual information on a candidate's education, work experience, and personal history.

Source: Courtesy 3M

current jobs. Then these factors are included on the applications and may be weighted more heavily when evaluating new applicants' qualifications.

Employment Tests Tests administered to job candidates usually focus on aptitudes, skills, abilities, or knowledge relevant to the jobs that are to be performed. Such tests (basic computer skills tests, for example) indicate how well the applicant will do on the job. Occasionally companies use general intelligence or personality tests, but these are seldom helpful in predicting specific job performance.

In order to evaluate the true value of an applicant's or employee's skills and knowledge, continuous assessment and certification are likely to become common in the future. This trend in assessing the firm's human resources is driven by the speed with which knowledge ages. For example, an employee's ten years of computer programming skills related to old and outdated software are of little value to a firm if they require Internet and e-commerce software programmers.[8] At one time, a number of companies were criticized for using tests that were biased against members of certain minority groups—in particular, African Americans. The test results were, to a great extent, unrelated to job performance. Today a firm must be able to prove that a test is not discriminatory by demonstrating that it accurately measures one's ability to perform on the job. Applicants who believe they have been discriminated against through an invalid test may file a complaint with the Equal Employment Opportunity Commission (EEOC).

Interviews The employment interview is perhaps the most widely used selection technique. Job candidates are usually interviewed by at least one member of the HRM staff and by the person for whom they will be working. Candidates for higher-level jobs may also meet with a department head or vice president and may have several additional interviews.

Interviews provide an opportunity for the applicant and the firm to learn more about each other. Interviewers can pose problems to test the candidate's abilities. They can probe employment history more deeply and learn something about the candidate's attitudes and motivation. The candidate, meanwhile, has a chance to find out more about the job and the people with whom he or she would be working.

Unfortunately, interviewing may be the stage at which discrimination enters the selection process. For example, suppose a female applicant mentions that she is the mother of small children. Her interviewer may assume she would not be available for job-related travel even though that may not be the case. In addition, interviewers may be unduly influenced by such factors as appearance. Or they may ask different questions of different applicants, so that it becomes impossible to compare candidates' qualifications.

Some of these problems can be solved through better interviewer training and the use of structured interviews. In a *structured interview*, the interviewer asks only a prepared set of job-related questions. The firm may also consider using several different interviewers for each applicant, but that solution is likely to be a costly one.

References A job candidate is generally asked to furnish the names of references—people who can verify background information and provide personal evaluations of the candidate. Naturally, applicants tend to list only references who are likely to say good things about them. Thus, personal evaluations obtained from references may not be of much value. However, references are often contacted to verify such information as previous job responsibilities and the reason an applicant chose to leave a former job.

Assessment Centers An assessment center is used primarily to select current employees for promotion to higher-level management positions. Typically, a group of employees is sent to the center for two or three days. While there, they participate in activities designed to simulate the management environment and to predict managerial effectiveness. Trained observers (usually managers) make recommendations regarding promotion possibilities. Although this technique is gaining popularity, the expense involved limits its use to larger organizations.

Orientation

Once all the available information about job candidates has been collected and analyzed, those involved in the selection decide which candidate they would like to hire. A job offer is extended to the candidate. If it is accepted, the candidate becomes an employee and starts to work for the firm.

Soon after a candidate joins the firm, he or she goes through the firm's orientation program. **Orientation** is the process of acquainting new employees with the organization. Orientation topics range from such basic items as the location of the company cafeteria to concerns about various career paths within the firm. The orientation itself may consist of a half-hour informal presentation by a human resources manager. Or it may be an elaborate program involving dozens of people and lasting several days or weeks.

orientation the process of acquainting new employees with an organization

Compensation and Benefits

LEARNING OBJECTIVE

6 Discuss the primary elements of employee compensation and benefits.

An effective employee reward system must (1) enable employees to satisfy their basic needs, (2) provide rewards comparable to those offered by other firms (3) be distributed fairly within the organization, and (4) recognize that different people have different needs.

The firm's compensation system can be structured to meet the first three of these requirements. The fourth is more difficult in that it must take into account many variables among many people. Most firms offer a number of benefits that, taken together, generally help provide for employees' varying needs.

Compensation Decisions

Compensation is the payment employees receive in return for their labor. Its importance to employees is obvious. And, because compensation may account for up to 80 percent of a firm's operating costs, it is equally important to management. The firm's **compensation system**—the policies and strategies that determine employee compensation—must therefore be carefully designed to provide for employee needs while keeping labor costs within reasonable limits. For most firms, designing an effective compensation system requires three separate management decisions—about wage level, wage structure, and individual wages.

compensation the payment employees receive in return for their labor

compensation system the policies and strategies that determine employee compensation

Wage Level

Management must first position the firm's general pay level relative to pay levels of comparable firms. In other words, will the firm pay its employees less than, more than, or about the same as similar organizations? Most firms choose a pay level near the industry average. A firm that is not in good financial shape may pay less than the going rate. Large, prosperous organizations, by contrast, may pay a little more than average to attract and retain the most capable employees.

To determine what the average is, the firm may use wage surveys. A **wage survey** is a collection of data on prevailing wage rates within an industry or a geographic area. Such surveys are compiled by industry associations, local governments, personnel associations, and (occasionally) individual firms.

wage survey a collection of data on prevailing wage rates within an industry or a geographic area

Wage Structure

Next management must decide on relative pay levels for all the positions within the firm. Will managers be paid more than secretaries? Will secretaries be paid more than custodians? The result of this set of decisions is often called the firm's *wage structure.*

The wage structure is almost always developed on the basis of a job evaluation. **Job evaluation** is the process of determining the relative worth of the various jobs within a firm. Most observers would probably agree that a secretary should make more money than a custodian, but how much more? Twice as much? One and one-half times as much? Job evaluation should provide the answers to such questions.

job evaluation the process of determining the relative worth of the various jobs within a firm

A number of techniques may be used to evaluate jobs. The simplest is to rank all the jobs within the firm according to their value to the firm. Of course, if there are more than a few jobs, this technique loses its simplicity very quickly. A more frequently used method is based on the job analysis. Points are allocated to each job for each of its elements and requirements, as set forth in the job analysis. For example, "college degree required" might be worth 50 points, whereas the need for a high school education might count for only 25 points. The more points a job is allocated, the more important it is presumed to be (and the higher its level in the firm's wage structure).

Individual Wages

Finally, the specific payments individual employees will receive must be determined. Consider the case of two secretaries working side by side. Job evaluation has been used to determine the relative level of secretarial pay within the firm's wage structure. However, suppose one secretary has fifteen years of experience and can accurately type 80 words per minute. The other has two years of experience and can type only 55 words per minute. In most firms, these people would not receive the same pay. Instead, a wage range would be established for the secretarial position. In this case, the range might be $7 to $9.50 per hour. The more experienced and proficient secretary would then be paid an amount near the top of the range (say, $8.90 per hour); the less experienced secretary would receive an amount that was lower but still within the range (say, $7.75 per hour).

Two wage decisions actually come into play here. First the employee's initial rate must be established. It is based on experience, other qualifications, and expected performance. Later the employee may be given pay increases based on seniority and performance.

Comparable Worth

comparable worth a concept that seeks equal compensation for jobs requiring about the same level of education, training, and skills

One reason women in the work force are paid less than men may be that a certain proportion of women occupy female-dominated jobs—nurses, secretaries, and medical records analysts, for example—that require education, skills, and training equal to higher-paid positions but that are undervalued by our economic system. **Comparable worth** is a concept that seeks equal compensation for jobs that require about the same level of education, training, and skills. Several states have enacted laws that require equal pay for comparable work in government positions. Critics of comparable worth argue that the market has determined the worth of these jobs and that laws should not be enacted to tamper with the pricing mechanism of the market. The Equal Pay Act, discussed later in this chapter, does not address the issue of comparable worth. Critics also argue that artificially inflating salaries for female-dominated occupations encourages women to keep these jobs rather than to seek out other higher-paying jobs.

EXPLORING BUSINESS

HR Secrets of the Container Store

THE FIRST YEAR THAT THE CONTAINER Store participated in *Fortune* magazine's annual survey of the best U.S. companies to work for, it came out on top–besting Southwest Airlines and other corporations renowned for their human resources practices. Ringing up $214 million in annual sales through twenty stores in eight states, the Dallas-based chain has built an enviable record of employee loyalty in an industry known for high turnover. Most retailers lose three-quarters of their salespeople every year. In contrast, the Container Store loses just over one-quarter. Industry-wide management turnover tops 33 percent. The Container Store's management turnover is a mere 5.3 percent.

Clearly, the Container Store is a breed apart from the typical retailer. "Frankly, most retailers decided a long time ago that it wasn't possible to get great people to work in a retail store," says president Kip Tindell. The Container Store, however, keeps positions open until they can find employees who are genuinely enthusiastic and interested in helping customers. The company pays above-average wages, with healthy raises for top performers. But compensation is only part of the attraction. Employees also enjoy considerable authority and are offered opportunities to develop their capabilities through new assignments and responsibilities.

The Container Store provides new employees with 185 hours of formal training during their first year, covering product knowledge as well as the company's six basic foundation principles. Instead of micromanaging or forcing slavish compliance with a detailed policy manual, managers trust employees to apply these basic principles when making decisions on the job. In another break with tradition, the company keeps no financial secrets: Employees are invited to look at its balance sheets and other records. Small wonder that employees feel like valuable assets–and agree with the *Fortune* ranking. "I knew I worked for what I thought was the best company in the world," says Debbie Crites, who works in a Dallas Container Store, "but to have it confirmed is fabulous."

Types of Compensation

Compensation can be paid in a variety of forms. Most forms of compensation fall into the following categories: hourly wage, weekly or monthly salary, commissions, incentive payments, lump-sum salary increases, and profit sharing.

Hourly Wage

An **hourly wage** is a specific amount of money paid for each hour of work. People who earn wages are paid their hourly wage for the first forty hours worked in any week. They are then paid one and one-half times their hourly wage for time worked in excess of forty hours. (That is, they are paid "time and a half" for overtime.) Workers in retailing and fast-food chains, on assembly lines, and in clerical positions are usually paid an hourly wage.

hourly wage a specific amount of money paid for each hour of work

Weekly or Monthly Salary

A **salary** is a specific amount of money paid for an employee's work during a set calendar period, regardless of the actual number of hours worked. Salaried employees receive no overtime pay, but they do not lose pay when they are absent from work (within reasonable limits). Most professional and managerial positions are salaried.

salary a specific amount of money paid for an employee's work during a set calendar period, regardless of the actual number of hours worked

Commissions

A **commission** is a payment that is a percentage of sales revenue. Sales representatives and sales managers are often paid entirely through commissions or through a combination of commissions and salary.

commission a payment that is a percentage of sales revenue

Incentive payments

An **incentive payment** is a payment in addition to wages, salary, or commissions. Incentive payments are really extra rewards for outstanding job performance. They may be distributed to all employees or only to certain employees within the organization. Some firms distribute incentive payments to all employees annually. The size of the payment depends on the firm's earnings and, at times, on the particular employee's length of service with the firm. Firms sometimes offer incentives to employees who exceed specific sales or production goals a practice called *gain sharing*.

To avoid yearly across-the-board salary increases, some organizations individually reward outstanding workers through merit pay. This pay-for-performance approach allows management to control labor costs while encouraging employees to work more efficiently. An employee's merit pay depends on his or her achievements relative to those of others.

incentive payment a payment in addition to wages, salary, or commissions

lump-sum salary increase an entire pay raise taken in one lump sum

profit sharing the distribution of a percentage of the firm's profit among its employees

Lump-Sum Salary Increases

In traditional reward systems, an employee who receives an annual pay increase is given part of the increase in each pay period. For example, suppose an employee on a monthly salary gets a 10 percent annual pay hike. He or she actually receives 10 percent of the former monthly salary added to each month's paycheck for a year. Companies that offer **lump-sum salary increases** give the employee the option of taking the entire pay raise in one lump sum at the beginning of the year. The employee then draws his or her "regular" pay for the rest of the year. The lump-sum payment is typically treated as an interest-free loan that must be repaid if the employee leaves the firm during the year. B. F. Goodrich, Aetna Life and Casualty, and Timex have all offered variations of this plan.

spotLight

Source: Copyright 2000, USA TODAY. Reprinted with permission.

Profit Sharing

Profit sharing is the distribution of a percentage of the firm's profit among its employees. The idea is to motivate employees to work effectively by giving them a stake in the company's financial success. Some firms—including Sears, Roebuck—have linked their profit-sharing plans to employee retirement programs; that is, employees receive their profit-sharing distributions, with interest, when they retire. The profit-sharing plan at Philip Morris, for example, results in a 13 to 15 percent contribution by the company to their employees' retirement programs.[9]

Employee Benefits

employee benefit a reward in addition to regular compensation that is provided indirectly to employees

An **employee benefit** is a reward in addition to regular compensation that is provided indirectly to employees. Employee benefits consist mainly of services (such as insurance) that are paid for partially or totally by employers, and employee expenses (such as college tuition) that are reimbursed by employers. Currently, the average cost of these benefits is 28 percent of an employee's total compensation, which includes wages plus benefits. Thus, a person who received total compensation (including benefits) of $40,000 a year earned $28,000 in wages and received an additional $11,200 in benefits.[10]

Types of Benefits Employee benefits take a variety of forms. *Pay for time not worked* covers such absences as vacation time, holidays, and sick leave. *Insurance packages* may include health, life, and dental insurance for employees and their families. Some firms pay the entire cost of the insurance package and others share the cost with the employee. The costs of *pension and retirement programs* may also be borne entirely by the firm or shared with the employee.

Some benefits are required by law. For example, employers must maintain *workers' compensation insurance*, which pays medical bills for injuries that occur on the job and provides income for employees who are disabled by job-related injuries. Employers must also pay for *unemployment insurance* and contribute to each employee's federal *Social Security* account.

Other benefits provided by employers include tuition-reimbursement plans, credit unions, child care, company cafeterias that sell reduced-price meals, exercise rooms and other recreational facilities, and broad stock option plans that are available to all employees, not just top management.

Some companies offer unusual benefits in order to attract and retain employees. At American Century, every employee gets a $650 ergonomic chair. At Capital One, vacation days are available on one-half hour notice. At Eli Lilly and Pfizer, all drugs made by these organizations are free to their employees. After being on the job for seven years at Intel, employees receive an eight-week sabbatical. At MBNA, employees get a limo on their wedding day plus $500 and a week's paid vacation. All employees at Micro Strategy go on a one-week Caribbean vacation in January. QUALCOM will donate $250.00 to support an employee's child's sports team. And finally, you can have your own gardening plot on company land if you work for Rodale.[11]

Daycare, an important employee benefit. A number of companies provide daycare facilities for employees' children as an employee benefit. Lotus Development Corporation in Cambridge, Massachusetts, is one such company.

Flexible Benefit Plans Through a **flexible benefit plan**, an employee receives a predetermined amount of benefit dollars and may allocate these dollars to various categories of benefits in the mix that best fits his or her needs. Some flexible benefit plans offer a broad array of benefit options including health care, dental care, life insurance, accidental death and dismemberment coverage for worker and dependents, long-term disability, vacation, retirement savings, and dependent care. Other firms offer limited options, primarily in health and life insurance and retirement plans.

Although the cost of administering flexible plans is high, a number of organizations, including Quaker Oats and Coca-Cola, have implemented this option for several reasons. Because employees' needs are so diverse, flexible plans help firms offer benefit packages that more specifically meet their employees' needs. Flexible plans can, in the long run, help a company contain costs because a specified amount is allocated to cover the benefits of each employee. Furthermore, organizations that offer flexible plans with many choices may be perceived as being employee-friendly. Thus, they are in a better position to attract and retain qualified employees.

flexible benefit plan compensation plan whereby an employee receives a predetermined amount of benefit dollars to spend on a package of benefits he or she has selected to meet individual needs

Training and Development

LEARNING OBJECTIVE

7 Explain the purposes and techniques of employee training, development, and performance appraisal.

Training and development is extremely important at the Container Store. Because great customer service is so important, every first-year full-time sales person receives about 185 hours of formal training as opposed to the industry standard which is approximately seven hours. Training and development continues throughout a person's career. Each store has a full-time trainer called the Super Sales Trainer (SST). This trainer provides product training, sales training, and employee development training. Top management believes that the financial and human resources invested in training and development are well worth it.[12]

Both training and development are aimed at improving employees' skills and abilities. However, the two are usually differentiated as either employee training or management development. **Employee training** is the process of teaching operations and technical employees how to do their present jobs more effectively and efficiently. **Management development** is the process of preparing managers and other professionals to assume increased responsibility in both present and future positions. Thus, training and development differ in who is being taught and the purpose of the teaching. Both are necessary for personal and organizational growth. Companies that hope to stay competitive typically make huge commitments to employee training and development. For example, Motorola spends about $120 million annually on such programs provided through Motorola University.[13] Motorola's substantial educational efforts are companywide and range from the basic three R's to technical training, problem solving, and even interpersonal skills. Interestingly, according to the American Society for Training and Development (ASTD), an industry association that monitors and also promotes employee learning strategies, Internet-based e-learning is growing at a rate greater than 90 percent per year and is expected to be worth $15 billion by 2002. Driven by cost, travel, and time-savings, online learning alone and in conjunction with face-to-face situations is a strong alternative strategy.[14] Development of a training program usually has three components: analysis of needs, determination of training and development methods, and creation of an evaluation system to assess the program's effectiveness.

employee training the process of teaching operations and technical employees how to do their present jobs more effectively and efficiently

management development the process of preparing managers and other professionals to assume increased responsibility in both present and future positions

Analysis of Training Needs

When thinking about developing a training program, managers must first determine if training is needed and, if so, what types of training needs exist. At times, what at first appears to be a need for training is actually, upon assessment, a need for motivation. Training needs can vary considerably. For example, some employees may need training to improve their technical skills, or they may need training about organizational procedures. Training might also focus on business ethics, product information, or customer service. Because training is expensive, it is critical that the correct training needs be identified.

Focus on training. At Sprint PCS, employees are given extensive training in the company's technology and systems so they have the skills they need to do their jobs and serve customers well.

Training and Development Methods

A variety of methods are available for employee training and management development. Some of these methods may be more suitable for one or the other, but most can be applied to both.

- *On-the-job methods*: The trainee learns by doing the work under the supervision of an experienced employee.
- *Simulations*: The work situation is simulated in a separate area so that learning takes place away from the day-to-day pressures of work.
- *Classroom teaching and lectures*: You probably already know these methods quite well.
- *Conferences and seminars*: Experts and learners meet to discuss problems and exchange ideas.
- *Role playing*: Participants act out the roles of others in the organization for better understanding of these roles (primarily a management development tool).

Evaluation of Training and Development

Training and development are very expensive. The training itself costs quite a bit, and employees are usually not working—or are working at a reduced load and pace—during training sessions. To ensure that training and development are cost effective, the managers responsible should evaluate the company's efforts periodically.

Talking Technology

Log On and Learn

TRAINING AND DEVELOPMENT ARE GOING high-tech as more companies improve employees' skills and abilities through web-based courses. Online training saves companies the expense and logistical headaches of gathering employees in one central location for classroom or seminar training. It also ensures consistency, because the information is presented in the same way every time students access the course. Employees also benefit: They can continue with their normal work activities while learning at their own pace.

Some employees have such hectic schedules that online training is the only way they can squeeze in the training they need. That's why Sun Microsystems is creating brief online learning modules–up to 15 minutes in length–that employees can access when they have time. "Work today is done in interrupt mode," explains John Ryan, group manager of field education for Sun's corporate university. "People can only handle little chunks of learning at their desks."

Companies of all sizes and types are also using online training to address key legal and ethical issues. For example, Akili Systems in Dallas, Texas, arranged for its 170 employees to take HighTechCampus.com's online course about identifying and preventing sexual harassment in the workplace. "It makes it very, very convenient for everyone to take a class and for the company to start complying with labor laws," says co-CEO Shiek Shah.

High-tech companies are especially concerned about keeping employees abreast of the latest trends and techniques. For example, Genzyme, a Massachusetts-based biotech company, offers its 3,700 employees online access to thousands of business and technical courses through TrainingNet, a web-based training firm. Employees in any of the company's twenty facilities across the United States are encouraged to sign up for these online courses. As a result, performance is up and turnover is down, because even employees far from headquarters have more training opportunities. "I can keep track of training plans and understand the relationships between training and company performance," says Russ Campanello, senior vice president of human resources. "This is the first time I've been able to do that."

A recent report prepared by the American Society for Training and Development (ASTD), an industry association that monitors and also promotes employee learning strategies, revealed the value of employee education programs. The report found that for an added $600 educational investment made by the firm in each employee, the firms surveyed experienced a 57 percent increase in sales per employee and 37 percent in gross profit. In dollar terms, the added investment returned $157,000 in net sales and $137,000 in gross profit per employee.[15] The starting point for this evaluation is a set of verifiable objectives that are developed *before* the training is undertaken. Suppose a training program is expected to improve the skills of machinists. The objective of the program might be stated as follows: "At the end of the training period, each machinist should be able to process thirty parts per hour with no more than one defective part per ninety parts completed." This objective clearly specifies what is expected and how training results may be measured or verified. Evaluation then consists of measuring machinists' output and the ratio of defective parts produced after the training.

The results of training evaluations should be made known to all those involved in the program—including trainees and upper management. For trainees, the results of evaluations can enhance motivation and learning. For upper management, the results may be the basis for making decisions about the training program itself.

Another form of evaluation—performance appraisal—is an equally important part of human resources management.

Performance Appraisal

Performance appraisal is the evaluation of employees' current and potential levels of performance to allow managers to make objective human resources decisions. The process has three main objectives. First, managers use performance appraisals to let workers know how well they are doing and how they can do better in the future. Second, a performance appraisal provides an effective basis for distributing rewards, such as pay raises and promotions. Third, performance appraisal helps the organization monitor its employee selection, training, and development activities. If large numbers of employees continually perform below expectations, the firm may need to revise its selection process or strengthen its training and development activities.

performance appraisal the evaluation of employees' current and potential levels of performance to allow managers to make objective human resources decisions

Common Evaluation Techniques

The various techniques and methods for appraising employee performance are either objective or judgmental in nature.

Objective Methods Objective appraisal methods use some measurable quantity as the basis for assessing performance. Units of output, dollar volume of sales, number of defective products, and number of insurance claims processed are all objective, measurable quantities. Thus, an employee who processes an average of twenty-six insurance claims per week is given a higher evaluation than one whose average is nineteen claims per week.

Such objective measures may require some adjustment for the work environment. Suppose the first of our insurance-claims processors works in New York City and the second works in rural Iowa. Both must visit each client because they are processing homeowners' insurance claims. The difference in their average weekly output may be due entirely to the long distances the Iowan must travel to visit clients. In this case, the two workers may very well be equally competent and motivated. Thus, a manager must take into account circumstances that may be hidden by a purely statistical measurement.

Judgmental Methods Judgmental appraisal methods are used much more frequently than objective methods. They require that the manager judge or estimate the employee's performance level. However, judgmental methods are not capricious. These methods are based on employee ranking or rating scales. When ranking is used, the manager ranks subordinates from best to worst. This approach has a number of drawbacks, including the lack of any absolute standard. Rating scales are the most popular judgmental appraisal technique. A *rating scale* consists of a number of statements; each employee is rated on the degree to which the statement applies (see Figure 10.3). For example, one statement might be, "This employee always does high-quality work." The supervisor would give the employee a rating, from 5 down to 1, corresponding to gradations ranging from "strongly agree" to "strongly disagree." The ratings on all the statements are added to obtain the employee's total evaluation.

3M **Contribution and Development Summary**
FORM 37450 - B

Employee Name	Employee Number	Job Title
Department		Location
Coach/Supervisor(s) Name(s)		Review Period From : To :

Major Job Responsibilities

Goals/Expectations	Contributions/Resu

Contribution (To be completed by coach/supervisor)

- ☐ **Good Level of Contribution for this year**
- ☐ **Unsatisfactory Level of Contribution for this year**
- ☐ **Exceptional Lev**

Development Summary

Areas of Strength	Development Priorities

Career Interests

Next job	Longer Range

Current Mobility

- ☐ 0 - Currently Unable to Relocate
- ☐ 1 - Position In Home Country Only (Use if Home Country is Outside U.S.)
- ☐ 2 - Position Within O.U.S. Region (e: Nordic, SEA...)
- ☐ 3 - Position Within O.U.S. Area (ex: Europe, Asia)
- ☐ 4 - Position In U.S.
- ☐ 5 - Position Anywhere In The World

Development

- ☐ **W** - Well placed. Development plans achievable in current role for at least the next year
- ☐ **C** - Ready now for a move to a different job for career broadening experience
- ☐ **I** - Ready now for a move to a different job involving increased responsibility
- ☐ **X** - Not well placed. Action required to resolve placement issues.

Comments on Development

Employee Comments

Coach/Supervisor Comments	**Other Supervisor (if applicable) and/or Reviewer**

Signatures

Coach/Supervisor	Date	Other Coach/Supervisor or Reviewer	Date
Employee			Date

figure 10.3

Performance Appraisal

Judgmental appraisal methods are used much more often than objective methods. Using judgmental methods requires that the manager estimate the employee's performance level, relative to some standard.

Source: Courtesy 3M

Avoiding Appraisal Errors Managers must be cautious if they are to avoid making mistakes when appraising employees. It is common to overuse one portion of an evaluation instrument, thus overemphasizing some issues and underemphasizing others. A manager must guard against allowing an employee's poor performance on one activity to influence his or her judgment of that subordinate's work on other activities. Similarly, putting too much weight on recent performance distorts an employee's evaluation. For example, if the employee is being rated on performance over the last year, a manager should not permit last month's disappointing performance to overshadow the quality of the work done in the first eleven months of the year. Finally, a manager must guard against discrimination on the basis of race, age, gender, religion, national origin, or sexual orientation.

Performance Feedback

No matter which appraisal technique is used, the results should be discussed with the employee soon after the evaluation is completed. The manager should explain the basis for present rewards and should let the employee know what he or she can do to be recognized as a better performer in the future. The information provided to an employee in such discussions is called a *performance feedback interview*.

There are three major approaches to performance feedback interviews: tell-and-sell, tell-and-listen, and problem-solving. In a *tell-and-sell* feedback interview, the superior tells the employee how good or bad the employee's performance has been and then attempts to persuade the employee to accept this evaluation. Since the employee has no input into the evaluation, the tell-and-sell interview can lead to defensiveness, resentment, and frustration on the part of the subordinate. The employee may not accept the results of the interview and may not be committed to achieving the goals that are set.

With the *tell-and-listen* approach, the supervisor tells the employee what has been right and wrong with the employee's performance and then gives the employee a chance to respond. The subordinate may simply be given an opportunity to react to the supervisor's statements or may be permitted to offer a full self-appraisal, challenging the supervisor's assessment.

In the *problem-solving approach*, employees evaluate their own performances and set their own goals for future performance. The supervisor is more a colleague than a judge and offers comments and advice in a noncritical manner. An active and open dialogue ensues, in which goals for improvement are mutually established. The problem-solving interview is more likely to result in the employee's commitment to the established goals.

To avoid some of the problems associated with the tell-and-sell interview, a mixed approach is sometimes used. The mixed interview uses the tell-and-sell approach to communicate administrative decisions and the problem-solving approach to discuss employee development issues and future performance goals.[16]

An appraisal approach which has become popular is called a *360-degree evaluation*. A 360-degree evaluation collects anonymous reviews about an employee from his or her peers, subordinates, and supervisors, and then compiles these reviews into a feedback report which is given to the employee. Companies that invest significant resources in employee development efforts are especially likely to use 360-degree evaluations. An employee should not be given a feedback report without first having a one-on-one meeting with his or her supervisor. The most appropriate way to introduce a 360-degree evaluation system in a company is to begin with upper-level management. Then managers should be trained on how to interpret feedback reports so that they can coach their employees on how to use the feedback to achieve higher level job-related skills and behaviors.[17]

Finally, we should note that many managers find it difficult to discuss the negative aspects of an appraisal. Unfortunately, they may ignore performance feedback altogether or provide it in a very weak and ineffectual manner. In truth, though, most employees have strengths that can be emphasized to soften the discussion of their weaknesses. An employee may not even be aware of weaknesses and their consequences. If they are not pointed out through performance feedback, they cannot possibly be eliminated. Only through tactful, honest communication can the results of an appraisal be fully utilized.

LEARNING OBJECTIVE

8 Outline the major legislation affecting human resources management.

The Legal Environment of HRM

Legislation regarding HRM practices has been passed mainly to protect the rights of employees, to promote job safety, and to eliminate discrimination in the workplace. The major federal laws affecting HRM are described in Table 10.2.

table 10.2 Federal Legislation Affecting Human Resources Management

Law	Purpose
National Labor Relations Act (1935)	Establishes a collective bargaining process in labor-management relations as well as the National Labor Relations Board (NLRB)
Fair Labor Standards Act (1938)	Establishes a minimum wage and an overtime pay rate for employees working more than forty hours per week
Labor-Management Relations Act (1947)	Provides a balance between union power and management power; also known as the Taft-Hartley Act
Equal Pay Act (1963)	Specifies that men and women who do equal jobs must be paid the same wage
Title VII of the Civil Rights Act (1964)	Outlaws discrimination in employment practices based on sex, race, color, religion, or national origin
Age Discrimination in Employment Act (1967/1986)	Outlaws personnel practices that discriminate against people aged 40 and older; the 1986 amendment eliminates a mandatory retirement age
Occupational Safety and Health Act (1970)	Regulates the degree to which employees can be exposed to hazardous substances and specifies the safety equipment that the employer must provide
Employment Retirement Income Security Act (1974)	Regulates company retirement programs and provides a federal insurance program for retirement plans that go bankrupt
Worker Adjustment and Retraining Notification (WARN) Act (1988)	Requires employer to give employees 60 days notice regarding plant closure or layoff of 50 or more employees
Americans with Disabilities Act (1990)	Prohibits discrimination against qualified individuals with disabilities in all employment practices, including job application procedures, hiring, firing, advancement, compensation, training, and other terms, conditions, and privileges of employment
Civil Rights Act (1991)	Facilitates employees' suing employers for sexual discrimination and collecting punitive damages
Family and Medical Leave Act (1993)	Requires an organization with 50 or more employees to provide up to 12 weeks of leave without pay upon the birth (or adoption) of an employee's child or if an employee or his or her spouse, child, or parent is seriously ill

National Labor Relations Act and Labor-Management Relations Act

These laws are concerned with dealings between business firms and labor unions. This general area is, in concept, a part of human resources management. However, because of its importance, it is often treated as a separate set of activities. We discuss both labor-management relations and these two acts in detail in Chapter 12.

Fair Labor Standards Act

This act, passed in 1938 and amended many times since, applies primarily to wages. It established minimum wages and overtime pay rates. Many managers and other professionals, however, are exempt from this law. Managers, for example, seldom get paid overtime when they work more than forty hours a week.

Equal Pay Act

Passed in 1963, this law overlaps somewhat with Title VII of the Civil Rights Act (see below). The Equal Pay Act specifies that men and women who are doing equal jobs must be paid the same wage. Equal jobs are jobs that demand equal effort, skill, and responsibility and that are performed under the same conditions. Differences in pay are legal if they can be attributed to differences in seniority, qualifications, or performance. But women cannot be paid less (or more) for the same work solely because they are women.

Civil Rights Acts

Title VII of the Civil Rights Act of 1964 applies directly to selection and promotion. It forbids organizations with fifteen or more employees to discriminate in those areas on the basis of sex, race, color, religion, or national origin. The purpose of Title VII is to ensure that employers make personnel decisions on the basis of employee qualifications only. As a result of this act, discrimination in employment (especially against African Americans) has been reduced in this country.

The Equal Employment Opportunity Commission (EEOC) is charged with enforcing Title VII. A person who believes he or she has been discriminated against can file a complaint with the EEOC. The EEOC investigates the complaint, and if it finds that the person has, in fact, been the victim of discrimination, the commission can take legal action on his or her behalf.

The Civil Rights Act of 1991 facilitates an employee's suing and collecting punitive damages for sexual discrimination. Discriminatory promotion and termination decisions as well as on-the-job issues, such as sexual harassment, are covered by this act.

Age Discrimination in Employment Act

The general purpose of this act, which was passed in 1967 and amended in 1986, is the same as that of Title VII—to eliminate discrimination. However, as the name implies, the Age Discrimination in Employment Act is concerned only with discrimination based on age. It applies to companies with twenty or more employees. In particular, it outlaws personnel practices that discriminate against people aged forty or older. (No federal law forbids discrimination against people younger than forty, but several states have adopted age-discrimination laws that apply to a variety of age groups.) Also outlawed are company policies that specify a mandatory retirement age. Employers must base employment decisions on ability and not on a number.

Occupational Safety and Health Act

Passed in 1970, this act is concerned mainly with issues of employee health and safety. For example, the act regulates the degree to which employees can be exposed to hazardous substances. It also specifies the safety equipment that the employer must provide.

The Occupational Safety and Health Administration (OSHA) was created to enforce this act. Inspectors from OSHA investigate employee complaints regarding unsafe working conditions. They also make spot checks on companies operating in particularly hazardous industries, such as chemicals and mining, to ensure compliance with the law. A firm found to be in violation of federal standards can be heavily fined or shut down.

Employee Retirement Income Security Act

This act was passed in 1974 to protect the retirement benefits of employees. It does not require that firms provide a retirement plan. However, it does specify that *if* a retirement plan is provided, it must be managed in such a way that the interests of employees are protected. It also provides federal insurance for retirement plans that go bankrupt.

Affirmative Action

Affirmative action is not one act but a series of executive orders, issued by the president of the United States. These orders established the requirement for affirmative action in personnel practices. This stipulation applies to all employers with fifty or more employees holding federal contracts in excess of $50,000. It prescribes that such employers (1) actively encourage job applications from members of minority groups and (2) hire qualified employees from minority groups not fully represented in their organizations. Many firms that do not hold government contracts voluntarily take part in this affirmative action program.

Occupational safety. OSHA, created by the Occupational Safety and Health Act, helps to protect workers' safety. Hardigg Industries—manufacturer of containers for transporting specialized equipment—is in the business of helping customers protect their goods during shipping. It is also in the business of obeying the law and protecting its own employees, such as this one wearing a face shield.

Americans with Disabilities Act

The Americans with Disabilities Act (ADA) prohibits discrimination against qualified individuals with disabilities in all employment practices—including job application procedures, hiring, firing, advancement, compensation, training, and other terms and conditions of employment. All private employers and government agencies with fifteen or more employees are covered by the ADA. Defining who is a qualified individual with a disability is, of course, difficult. Depending on how "qualified individual with a disability" is interpreted, up to 43 million Americans can be included under this law. This law also mandates that all businesses that serve the public must make their facilities accessible to people with disabilities.

Not only are individuals with obvious physical disabilities protected under the ADA, but also safeguarded are those with less visible conditions such as heart disease, diabetes, epilepsy, cancer, AIDS, and emotional illnesses. Because of this law, many organizations no longer require job applicants to pass physical examinations as a condition of employment. In 1998, there were about 42,000 civil complaints related to disability discrimination.[18]

Employers are required to provide disabled employees with reasonable accommodation. *Reasonable accommodation* is any modification or adjustment to a job or work environment that will enable a qualified employee with a disability to perform a central job function. Examples of reasonable accommodation include making existing facilities readily accessible to and usable by an individual confined to a wheelchair. Reasonable accommodation might also mean restructuring a job, modifying work schedules, acquiring or modifying equipment, providing qualified readers or interpreters, or changing training programs.

RETURN TO Inside Business

RECRUITING IS A NEVER-ENDING challenge for Dell Computer. To keep up with the demands of double-digit sales growth and worldwide expansion, the company has been forced to broaden its recruiting focus beyond technology firms. In addition, Dell supports its new hires with extensive training and a buddy system so new recruits can get advice and guidance during their early months. The company also sets specific performance goals for each new hire to achieve in the first thirty days. After they're hired, new employees fill out a questionnaire about their recruitment experience so Esparza, vice president of Dell Computer, and his team can learn how to be more effective, yet realistic, when describing Dell as an employer.

In the end, Dell's current employees–the people who really know what it's like to work at Dell–are the company's most powerful recruiting weapon. "You make decisions every day without 100 percent of the information, and you have to be comfortable doing that," comments Jay Martin, a Duke University MBA hired as a planning manager. "Every Sunday night, I look forward to Monday morning. I don't think there could be a stronger endorsement."

Questions

1. Why is orientation particularly vital for Dell employees hired from outside the computer industry?
2. Why would Dell set goals for new employees to achieve during their first month on the job?

chapter Review

SUMMARY

1 Describe the major components of human resources management.

Human resources management (HRM) is the set of activities involved in acquiring, maintaining, and developing an organization's human resources. Responsibility for HRM is shared by specialized staff and line managers. HRM activities include human resources planning, job analysis, recruiting, selection, orientation, compensation, benefits, training and development, and performance appraisal.

2 Identify the steps in human resources planning.

Human resources planning consists of forecasting the human resources that the firm will need and those that it will have available and then planning a course of action to match supply with demand. Layoffs, attrition, early retirement, and (as a last resort) firing are ways to reduce the size of the work force. Supply is increased through hiring.

3 Describe cultural diversity and understand some of the challenges and opportunities associated with it.

Cultural diversity refers to the differences among people in a work force due to race, ethnicity, and gender. With an increasing number of women, minorities, and immigrants entering the U.S. work force, management is faced with both challenges and competitive advantages. Some organizations are implementing diversity-related training programs and working to make the most of cultural diversity. With the proper guidance and management, a culturally diverse organization can prove beneficial to all involved.

4 Explain the objectives and uses of job analysis.

Job analysis provides a job description and a job specification for each position within the firm. A job description is a list of the elements that make up a particular job. A job specification is a list of qualifications required to perform a particular job. Job analysis is used in evaluation and determining compensation levels and serves as the basis for recruiting and selecting new employees.

5 Describe the processes of recruiting, employee selection, and orientation.

Recruiting is the process of attracting qualified job applicants. Candidates for open positions may be recruited from within or outside the firm. In the selection process, information about candidates is obtained from applications, résumés, tests, interviews, references, or assessment centers. This information is then used to select the most appropriate candidate for the job. Newly hired employees will then go through a formal or informal orientation program to acquaint them with the firm.

6 Discuss the primary elements of employee compensation and benefits.

Compensation is the payment employees receive in return for their labor. In developing a system for paying employees, management must decide on the firm's general wage level (relative to other firms), the wage structure within the firm, and individual wages. Wage surveys and job analyses are useful in making these decisions. Employees may be paid hourly wages, salaries, or commissions. They may also receive incentive payments, lump-sum salary increases, and profit-sharing payments. Employee benefits, which are nonmonetary rewards to employees, add about 28 percent to the cost of compensation.

7 Explain the purposes and techniques of employee training, development, and performance appraisal.

Employee training and management development programs enhance the ability of employees to contribute to the firm. When developing a training program, training needs should be analyzed. Then training methods should be selected. Because training is expensive, an organization should periodically evaluate the effectiveness of its training programs.

Performance appraisal, or evaluation, is used to provide employees with performance feedback, to serve as a basis for distributing rewards, and to monitor selection and training activities. Both objective and judgmental appraisal techniques are used. Their results are communicated to employees through three performance feedback approaches: tell-and-sell, tell-and-listen, and problem-solving.

8 Outline the major legislation affecting human resources management.

A number of laws have been passed that affect HRM practices and that protect the rights and safety of employees.

Some of these are the National Labor Relations Act of 1935; the Labor-Management Relations Act of 1947; the Fair Labor Standards Act of 1938; the Equal Pay Act of 1963; Title VII of the Civil Rights Act of 1964; the Age Discrimination in Employment Act of 1967/1986; the Occupational Safety and Health Act of 1970; the Employment Retirement Income Security Act of 1974; the Worker Adjustment and Retraining Notification Act of 1988; the Americans with Disabilities Act of 1990; the Civil Rights Act of 1991; and the Family and Medical Leave Act of 1993.

KEY TERMS

You should now be able to define and give an example relevant to each of the following terms:

human resources management (272)
human resources planning (273)
replacement chart (274)
skills inventory (274)
cultural (workplace) diversity (275)
job analysis (277)
job description (277)
job specification (277)
recruiting (277)
external recruiting (278)
internal recruiting (279)
selection (280)
orientation (282)
compensation (283)
compensation system (283)
wage survey (283)
job evaluation (283)
comparable worth (284)
hourly wage (285)
salary (285)
commission (285)
incentive payment (285)
lump-sum salary increase (285)
profit sharing (285)
employee benefit (286)
flexible benefit plan (287)
employee training (287)
management development (287)
performance appraisal (289)

REVIEW QUESTIONS

1. List the three main HRM activities and their objectives.
2. In general, on what basis is responsibility for HRM divided between line and staff managers?
3. How is a forecast of human resources demand related to the firm's organizational planning?
4. How do human resources managers go about matching the firm's supply of workers with its demand for workers?
5. What are the major challenges and benefits associated with a culturally diverse work force?
6. How are a job analysis, job description, and job specification related?
7. What are the advantages and disadvantages of external recruiting? Of internal recruiting?
8. In your opinion, what are the two best techniques for gathering information about job candidates?
9. Why is orientation an important HRM activity?
10. Explain how the three wage-related decisions result in a compensation system.
11. How is a job analysis used in the process of job evaluation?
12. Suppose you have just opened a new Ford auto sales showroom and repair shop. Which of your employees would be paid wages, which would receive salaries, and which would receive commissions?
13. What is the difference between the objective of employee training and the objective of management development?
14. Why is it so important to provide feedback after a performance appraisal?

DISCUSSION QUESTIONS

1. How accurately can managers plan for future human resources needs?
2. How might an organization's recruiting and selection practices be affected by the general level of employment?
3. Are employee benefits really necessary? Why?
4. As a manager, what actions would you take if an operations employee with six years of experience on the job refused ongoing training and ignored performance feedback?
5. Why are there so many laws relating to HRM practices? Which are the most important laws, in your opinion?

VIDEO CASE

Recruiting Goes High-Tech with Career Mosaic and Headhunter.net

So many jobs, so little time. Human resources professionals—especially those who work in giant multinational corporations—work hard to recruit candidates for a multitude of job openings throughout the organization. Typically, jobs open up when employees are promoted or switch employers, although companies undergoing expansion also create new jobs that must be filled. Once the job descriptions and job specifications have been written, HR personnel turn to the challenging task of finding qualified candidates. In the past, this meant placing newspaper advertisements, alerting employment agencies, scheduling job fairs, and then waiting days or even weeks for résumés to arrive.

These days, however, external recruiting runs at Internet speed, thanks to online job sites such as Career Mosaic (http://www.headhunter.net), which opened for business on July 4, 1994 and merged with Headhunter.net in 2000. One of the site's most attractive advantages is the thirty-day limit on job listings, which keeps the job database fresh. Another advantage is the frequency of updating, with new postings appearing every two hours or even more often. The résumés that job seekers submit electronically in response to job postings go directly to the employers rather than being posted for public viewing, which protects the confidentiality of the search process. And both employers and job seekers appreciate the convenience of the site's industry-specific web pages with job openings and employment news for health care, accounting, insurance, and other fields.

During its first year, an average of 10,000 job seekers visited the Career Mosaic site every day. Five years later, the site was drawing 500,000 job seekers per day, and the number continues to rise. Headhunter.net now features 250,000 open jobs posted by 10,000 employers. At any given point, its database contains data from one million job seekers searching for just the right position in technology, marketing, sales, engineering, accounting, health care, or another occupation. Job seekers can search the site for open positions by industry or use criteria such as geographic location to narrow the search. Headhunter.net is also linked to recruiting sites in Canada, India, Asia, and the United Kingdom, allowing easy online access to a world of jobs. Companies pay for job postings and, in addition, can buy colorful banner advertisements to draw more attention to their employment opportunities.

Wells Fargo Bank, Motorola, United Parcel Service, Walt Disney, and General Electric are among the many companies that have used Career Mosaic and Headhunter.net to publicize job openings and recruit applicants. "The Internet makes jobs available to a worldwide audience, and we can get a job posting out any time, any day," says GE's manager of staffing and quality initiatives. Of the 15,000 résumés GE receives every month, half come from Internet sources and are ready to be stored in the company's database, while the other half must be scanned to be stored in the database. Then the company's HR staff members use key words to electronically sort through the huge résumé database and identify candidates with the specific qualifications for open positions. Thanks to Career Mosaic and Headhunter.net, General Electric and thousands of other companies now spend much less time and money attracting suitable job applicants for jobs near and far—even halfway around the globe.[19]

Questions

1. What external recruiting costs would General Electric be likely to incur if it wanted to fill an open position in sales without using web sites such as Headhunter.net?
2. What are the disadvantages of a company such as General Electric using Headhunter.net or a similar web site for recruiting?
3. Should General Electric include both a job description and a job specification for each open position it posts on Headhunter.net? Why?

Building skills for career success

1. Exploring the Internet

Although students tend to believe that formal learning ends when they graduate and enter the working world, companies both large and small spend billions of dollars annually in training employees and updating their knowledge and skills. Besides supporting employees who attend accredited continuing-education programs, companies may also provide more specialized in-house course work on new technologies, products, and markets for strategic planning. The Internet is an excellent search tool to find out about course work offered by private training organizations as well as by traditional academic institutions. Learning online over the Internet is a fast-growing alternative especially for busy employees requiring updates to skills in the information technology (IT) field where software knowledge must be refreshed continuously. Visit the text web site for updates to this exercise.

Assignment

1. Visit the Web sites of several academic institutions and examine their course work offerings. Also examine the offerings of some of the following private consulting firms:

   Learning Tree: http://www.learningtree.com
   Andersen Consulting: http://www.ac.com
   KPMG Peat Marwick: http://www.kpmg.com
   Ernst and Young: http://www.ey.com
   Price Waterhouse: http://www.pw.com

2. What professional continuing-education training and services are provided by one of the academic institutions whose site you visited?
3. What sort of training is offered by one of the above consulting firms?
4. From the company's point of view, what is the total real cost of a day's worth of employee training? What is the money value of one day of study for a full-time college student? Can you explain why firms are willing to pay higher starting salaries for employees with higher levels of education?
5. The American Society for Training and Development (http://www.astd.org/) and the Society for Human Resource Management (http://www.shrm.org/) are two good sources for information about online training programs. Describe what you found out at these and other sites providing online learning solutions.

2. Developing Critical Thinking Skills

Suppose you are the manager of the six supervisors described in the following list. They have all just completed two years of service with you and are eligible for an annual raise. How will you determine who will receive a raise and how much each will receive?

- Joe Garcia has impressed you by his above-average performance on several difficult projects. Some of his subordinates, however, do not like the way he assigns jobs. You are aware that several family crises have left him short of cash.
- Sandy Vance meets her goals, but you feel she could do better. She is single, likes to socialize, and at times she arrives late for work. Several of her subordinates have low skill levels, but Sandy feels she has adequately explained their duties to them. You believe Sandy may care more about her friends than about coaching her subordinates. Her workers never complain and appear to be satisfied with their jobs.
- Paul Steiberg is not a good performer, and his work group does not feel he is an effective leader. You also know his group is the toughest one to manage. The work is hard and dirty. You realize it would be very difficult to replace him, and you therefore do not want to lose him.
- Anna Chen runs a tight ship. Her subordinates like her and feel she is an excellent leader. She listens to them and supports them. Recently, her group won the TOP (The Outstanding Performance) Award. Anna's husband is CEO of a consulting firm, and as far as you know, she is not in financial need.
- Jill Foster has successfully completed every assignment. You are impressed by this, particularly since she has a very difficult job. You recently learned that she spends several hours every week on her own taking classes to improve her skills. Jill seems to be motivated more by recognition than by money.
- Fred Hammer is a jolly person who gets along with everyone. His subordinates like him, but you don't think he is getting the job done to your expectations. He has missed a critical delivery date twice, and this cost the firm over $5,000 each time. He recently divorced his wife and is having an extremely difficult time meeting his financial obligations.

Assignment

1. You have $25,000 available for raises. As you think about how you will allot the money, consider the following:
   a. What criteria will you use in making a fair distribution?
   b. Will you distribute the entire $25,000? If not, what will you do with the remainder?
2. Prepare a four-column table in the following manner:
   a. In column 1, write the name of the employee.
   b. In column 2, write the amount of the raise.
   c. In column 3, write the percentage of the $25,000 the employee will receive.
   d. In column 4, list the reasons for your decision.

3. Building Team Skills

The New Therapy Company is soliciting a contract to provide five nursing homes with physical, occupational, speech, and respiratory therapy. The therapists will float among the five nursing homes. The therapists have not yet been hired, but the nursing homes expect them to be fully trained and ready to go to work in three months. The previous therapy company lost its contract because of high staff turnover due to "burnout" (a common problem in this type of work), high costs, and low-quality care. The nursing homes want a plan specifying how the New Therapy Company will meet staffing needs, keep costs low, and provide high-quality care.

Assignment

1. Working in a group, discuss how the New Therapy Company can meet the three-month deadline and still ensure that the care its therapists provide is of high quality. Also discuss the following:
   - How many of each type of therapist will the company need?
   - How will it prevent therapists from "burning out"?
   - How can it retain experienced staff and still limit costs?
   - Are promotions available for any of the staff? What is the career ladder?
   - How will the company manage therapists at five different locations? How will it keep in touch with them (computer, voice mail, monthly meetings)? Would it make more sense to have therapists work permanently at each location rather than rotate among them?
   - How will the company justify the travel costs? What other expenses might it expect?
2. Prepare a plan for the New Therapy Company to present to the nursing homes.

4. Researching Different Careers

A résumé provides a summary of your skills, abilities, and achievements. It may also include a description of the type of job you want. A well-prepared résumé indicates you know what your career objectives are, shows that you have given serious thought to your career, and tells a potential employer what you are qualified to do. The way a résumé is prepared can make a difference in whether you are considered for a job.

Assignment

1. Prepare a résumé for a job you want. (Use the information in Appendix A of this textbook.)
   - First, determine what your skills are and decide which skills are needed to do this particular job.

- Decide which type of format—chronological or functional—would be most effective in presenting your skills and experience.
- Keep the résumé to one page, if possible—definitely no more than two pages. (Portfolio items may be attached for certain types of jobs, such as artwork.)

2. Have several people review the résumé for accuracy.
3. Ask your instructor to comment on your résumé.

5. Improving Communication Skills

Workplaces in the United States are becoming more culturally diverse. Employees from other countries bring their customs, traditions, values, and language with them to the workplace. It can be difficult for some employees who have worked in a business for a long time to adjust to the changes that accompany cultural diversity. The work environment may become tense and full of distrust and hostility as conflicts erupt among employees. This appears to be the situation at the Zire Company, which manufactures fence posts from recycled plastic. As the company's human resources manager, you are faced with the job of changing this environment into one that encourages cooperation, trust, and mutual respect among employees.

Assignment

1. Putting yourself in the role of the Zire Company's human resources manager, address the following questions:
   a. What are the issues and problems associated with cultural diversity in your company?
   b. What benefits and opportunities could this diversity have for your company?
   c. How can you encourage employees to be more understanding and have greater empathy toward workers who are different from themselves?
2. On the basis of your answers to these questions, prepare a plan for creating an environment that will foster cooperation, trust, and mutual respect among the employees of the Zire Company.

Motivating and Satisfying Employees

11

LEARNING OBJECTIVES

1. Explain what motivation is.
2. Understand some major historical perspectives on motivation.
3. Describe three contemporary views of motivation: equity theory, expectancy theory, and goal-setting theory.
4. Explain several techniques for increasing employee motivation.

To encourage out-of-the-box innovation, Watson established a "think e-room," complete with lava lamps and inflatable chairs.

inside business

Motivated BMC Employees Mean Satisfied Customers

HOW MANY HIGH-TECH firms guarantee ontime installation—and then back up the promise with a money-back offer? BMC Software, based in Houston, is so confident of its employees' capabilities that it will give customers a 20 percent refund if it doesn't have certain software products up and running on schedule. But based on past performance, Chairman Max Watson knows his employees are motivated to do whatever it takes to satisfy their customers.

Founded in 1980, BMC originally developed software allowing giant corporate mainframe computers to communicate with each other. When Watson was hired as a sales manager in 1985, the company's annual revenues were just $8 million. Watson became Chairman in 1990, and soon began expanding the company through diversification into e-commerce software and acquisitions of specialized firms. Now annual revenues are approaching $2 billion as BMC motivates its more than 7,000 worldwide employees to work harder and smarter.

Watson prefers to keep organizational bureaucracy at a minimum so employees are empowered to use their own judgment and creativity. "I tend not to have a particularly structured environment, although we've had to do more as we've been growing," he explains. "I think a certain amount of ambiguity is important, so people can make independent decisions and try different things." To encourage out-of-the-box innovation, Watson established a "think e-room," complete with lava lamps and inflatable chairs, where employees can comfortably brainstorm ideas.

Empowerment, generous starting salaries, and comprehensive health insurance coverage are only some of the reasons people want to become BMCers (as employees are known). Other benefits include profit-sharing plans, stock purchase plans, tuition reimbursement, and plentiful vacation and holiday breaks. But that's not all. Some BMC facilities feature full health clubs, basketball courts, volleyball courts, putting greens, and horseshoe pits for employee use.

And there's more: BMCers have the convenience of a dry cleaner, a car wash and service station, a bank, a hair salon, and even a nail salon—all on the premises. Hungry employees can eat in the DOT. COMmissary cafeteria or stop by one of the office kitchens for free fruit, soft drinks, coffee, and popcorn. "You never have to leave the place," comments one employee about this full range of on-site amenities. "I know this is hard to believe, but you do feel like you can get away while you're here," says Roy Wilson, who heads BMC's human resources department. "It gives you a balanced life without having to leave."

Two years in a row, BMC's employee-friendly approach earned the company a spot on *Fortune* magazine's list of 100 Best Companies to Work for. More important, BMC's employees are so motivated that they complete well over 90 percent of their software installations on schedule. Now, with a money-back guarantee in place, the CEO is aiming for nearly 100 percent on-time performance, a level he feels "should be required by the customers of any vendor."[1]

To achieve its goals, any organization—whether it's BMC, Starbucks, IBM, or a local convenience store—must be sure its employees have more than the right raw materials, adequate facilities, and equipment that works. The organization must also ensure that its employees are *motivated*. To some extent, a high level of employee motivation derives from effective management practices.

In this chapter, after first explaining what motivation is, we present several views of motivation that have influenced management practices over the years: Taylor's ideas of scientific management, Mayo's Hawthorne Studies, Maslow's hierarchy of needs, Herzberg's motivation-hygiene theory, McGregor's Theory X and Theory Y, Ouchi's Theory Z, and reinforcement theory. Then, turning our attention to contemporary ideas, we examine equity theory, expectancy theory, and goal-setting theory. Finally, we discuss specific techniques managers can use to foster employee motivation and satisfaction.

LEARNING OBJECTIVE

1 Explain what motivation is.

What Is Motivation?

A motive is something that causes a person to act. A successful athlete is said to be "highly motivated." A student who avoids work is said to be "unmotivated." We define **motivation** as the individual, internal process that energizes, directs, and sustains behavior. It is the personal "force" that causes you or me to act in a particular way. For example, job rotation may increase your job satisfaction and your enthusiasm for your work so that you devote more energy to it, but perhaps job rotation would not have the same impact on me.

motivation the individual, internal process that energizes, directs, and sustains behavior; the personal "force" that causes us to behave in a particular way

morale an employee's feelings about his or her job and superiors and about the firm itself

Morale is an employee's attitude or feelings about the job, about superiors, and about the firm itself. To achieve organizational goals effectively, employees need more than the right raw materials, adequate facilities, and equipment that works. High morale results mainly from the satisfaction of needs on the job or as a result of the job. One need that might be satisfied on the job is the need *to be recognized* as an important contributor to the organization. A need satisfied as a result of the job is the need for *financial security*. High morale, in turn, leads to dedication and loyalty, as well as to the desire to do the job well. Low morale can lead to shoddy work, absenteeism, and high turnover rates as employees leave to seek more satisfying jobs with other firms. Sometimes, creative solutions are needed to motivate people and boost morale. This is especially true where barriers to change are deeply rooted in cultural stereotypes of the job and the industry. For example, to break down these barriers and enhance their creative development skills, clients of famed comedy house Second City, including Nortel Networks, AT&T, and Pricewaterhouse Coopers, provide corporate sessions using improvisation to change managers' behavior.[2]

What is motivation? Will taking your dog to work make you happy? Apparently management at Autodesk—a software company in San Rafael, California—thinks so. About 12% of the employees at Autodesk take their dogs to work every day.

Motivation, morale, and the satisfaction of employees' needs are thus intertwined. Along with productivity, they have been the subject of much study since the end of the nineteenth century. We continue our discussion of motivation by outlining some landmarks of that early research.

Going Global

Satisfying Employees Around the World

Motivating employees by satisfying their needs is a top priority for businesses all over the world. Money is not the only motivator, although companies must offer competitive salaries and benefits to attract and retain talented personnel. In the United States, companies are awarding smaller pay increases but boosting bonuses and stock options for top performers. They're also providing an ever-wider range of non-cash benefits such as on-site day-care centers and office concierges to help with personal tasks. How are companies in other countries satisfying employees?

Generous vacation periods are high on the list. Companies in the European Union must, by law, give employees at least 20 days of paid vacation every year, although many companies give much more. In France, where firms must provide at least 25 vacation days, most give up to 27 days. Companies in the Netherlands also give up to 27 days, even though they're only required to give 20 days. German firms must allow at least 20 vacation days, but they frequently give 30 days. Lengthy vacation periods "give people time to recharge their batteries and come back to work refreshed," explains Claudia Goldhammer, human resources vice president for TPS Labs AG, a software company in Munich, Germany.

Paid holidays and family leaves are increasingly common techniques for satisfying employees. For example, employees of Indian companies enjoy 20 paid holidays every year. South Korean employees get only one week of official vacation but are also entitled to several days off in succession, which makes for numerous long weekends during the year.

More companies are trying to meet employees' needs for resources and support in balancing work and home commitments. IBM Canada, for example, allows employees to work part-time, flexible hours, or at home when necessary. Toronto's Royal Bank offers flexible work schedules and gives time off for employees to take care of medical problems and other important personal issues. The result? "Our employees are happier and we have noticed that more customers are giving us their business–and that obviously has revenue implications," says one senior manager at Royal Bank.

Historical Perspectives on Motivation

LEARNING OBJECTIVE

2 Understand some major historical perspectives on motivation.

Researchers often begin a study with a fairly narrow goal in mind. But after they develop an understanding of their subject, they realize that both their goal and their research should be broadened. This is exactly what happened when early research into productivity blossomed into the more modern study of employee motivation.

Scientific Management

scientific management the application of scientific principles to management of work and workers

Toward the end of the nineteenth century, Frederick W. Taylor became interested in improving the efficiency of individual workers. This interest stemmed from his own experiences in manufacturing plants. It eventually led to **scientific management**, the application of scientific principles to management of work and workers.

One of Taylor's first jobs was with the Midvale Steel Company in Philadelphia, where he developed a strong distaste for waste and inefficiency. He also observed a practice he called "soldiering." Workers soldiered, or worked slowly, because they feared if they worked faster, they would run out of work and lose their jobs. Taylor realized managers were not aware of this practice because they had no idea what the workers' productivity levels *should* be.

Taylor later left Midvale and spent several years at Bethlehem Steel. It was there that he made his most significant contribution. In particular, he suggested that each job should be broken down into separate tasks. Then management should determine (1) the best way to perform these tasks and (2) the job output to expect when the tasks were performed properly. Next management should carefully choose the best person for each job and train that person to do the job properly. Finally, management should cooperate with workers to ensure that jobs were performed as planned.

Taylor also developed the idea that most people work only to earn money. He therefore reasoned that pay should be tied directly to output. The more a person produced, the more he or she should be paid. This gave rise to the **piece-rate system**, under which employees are paid a certain amount for each unit of output they produce. Under Taylor's piece-rate system, each employee was assigned an output quota. Those exceeding the quota were paid a higher per-unit rate for *all* units they produced (see Figure 11.1). Today the piece-rate system is still used by some manufacturers and by farmers who grow crops that are harvested by farm laborers.

piece-rate system a compensation system under which employees are paid a certain amount for each unit of output they produce

When Taylor's system was put into practice at Bethlehem Steel, the results were dramatic. Average earnings per day for steel handlers rose from $1.15 to $1.88. (Don't let the low wages that prevailed at the time obscure the fact that this was an increase of better than 60 percent!) The average amount of steel handled per day increased from 16 to 57 tons.

Taylor's revolutionary ideas had a profound impact on management practice. However, his view of motivation was soon recognized as overly simplistic and narrow. It is true that most people expect to be paid for their work. But it is also true that people work for a variety of reasons other than pay. Simply increasing a person's pay may not increase that person's motivation or productivity.

The father of scientific management. Frederick Taylor was one of the earliest researchers in motivation theory. His idea of tying worker pay to output had dramatic results when put into practice at Bethlehem Steel and is still used by some companies today.

The Hawthorne Studies

Between 1927 and 1932, Elton Mayo conducted two experiments at the Hawthorne plant of the Western Electric Company in Chicago. The original objective of these studies, now referred to as the Hawthorne Studies, was to determine the effects of the work environment on employee productivity.

In the first set of experiments, lighting in the workplace was varied for one group of workers but not for a second group. Then the productivity of both groups was measured to determine the effect of the light. To the amazement of the researchers, productivity increased for *both* groups. And for the group whose lighting was varied, productivity remained high until the light was reduced to the level of moonlight!

The second set of experiments focused on the effectiveness of the piece-rate system in increasing the output of *groups* of workers. Researchers expected that output

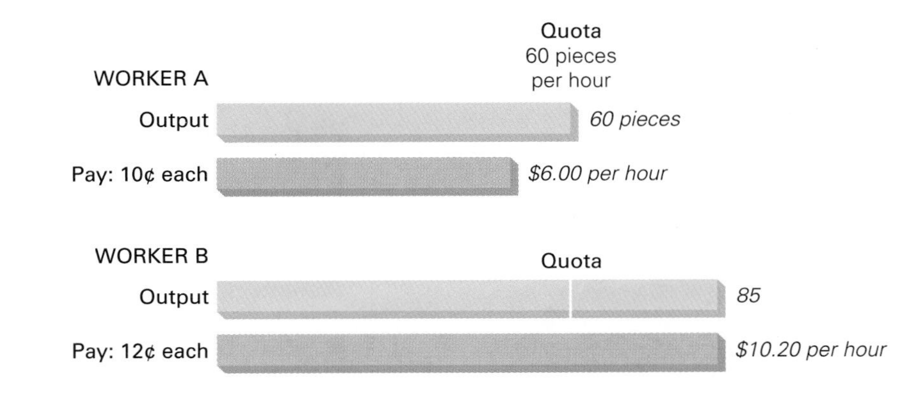

figure 11.1

Taylor's Piece-Rate System

Workers who exceeded their quota were rewarded by being paid at a higher rate per piece for all the pieces they produced.

would increase because faster workers would put pressure on slower workers to produce more. Again, the results were not as expected. Output remained constant, no matter what "standard" rates management set.

The researchers came to the conclusion that *human factors* were responsible for the results of the two experiments. In the lighting experiments, researchers had given both groups of workers a *sense of involvement* in their jobs merely by asking them to participate in the research. These workers—perhaps for the first time—felt as though they were an important part of the organization. In the piece-rate experiments, each group of workers informally set the acceptable rate of output for the group. To gain or retain the *social acceptance* of the group, each worker had to produce at that rate. Slower or faster workers were pressured to maintain the group's pace.

The Hawthorne Studies showed that such human factors are at least as important to motivation as pay rates. From these and other studies, the *human relations movement* in management was born. Its premise was simple: employees who are happy and satisfied with their work are motivated to perform better. Hence, management would do best to provide a work environment that maximizes employee satisfaction.

Maslow's Hierarchy of Needs

need a personal requirement

Maslow's hierarchy of needs a sequence of human needs in the order of their importance

physiological needs the things we require for survival

safety needs the things we require for physical and emotional security

social needs our requirements for love and affection and a sense of belonging

esteem needs our need for respect, recognition, and a sense of our own accomplishment and worth

Abraham Maslow, an American psychologist whose best-known works were published in the 1960s and 1970s, developed a theory of motivation based on a hierarchy of needs. A **need** is a personal requirement. Maslow assumed that humans are "wanting" beings who seek to fulfill a variety of needs. He observed that these needs can be arranged according to their importance in a sequence now known as **Maslow's hierarchy of needs** (see Figure 11.2).

At the most basic level are **physiological needs**, the things we require to survive. They include food and water, clothing, shelter, and sleep. In the employment context, these needs are usually satisfied through adequate wages.

At the next level are **safety needs**, the things we require for physical and emotional security. Safety needs may be satisfied through job security, health insurance, pension plans, and safe working conditions.

Next are the **social needs**, the human requirements for love and affection and a sense of belonging. To an extent, these needs can be satisfied through relationships in the work environment and the informal organization. But social networks beyond the workplace—with family and friends, for example—are usually needed too. Internet software solutions firms, like SAS Institute Inc. of Cary, N.C., compete hard to find and keep good high-technology workers. Interestingly, by promoting a normal workweek that takes into consideration the importance employees place on time spent with their families, relaxing, and participating in other things in life besides work has helped create a more content and motivated workforce. As a result, employee turnover is an astonishingly low 4 percent compared to a 20 percent industry rate.[3]

At the level of **esteem needs**, we require respect and recognition from others and a sense of our own accomplishment and worth (self-esteem). These needs may be satis-

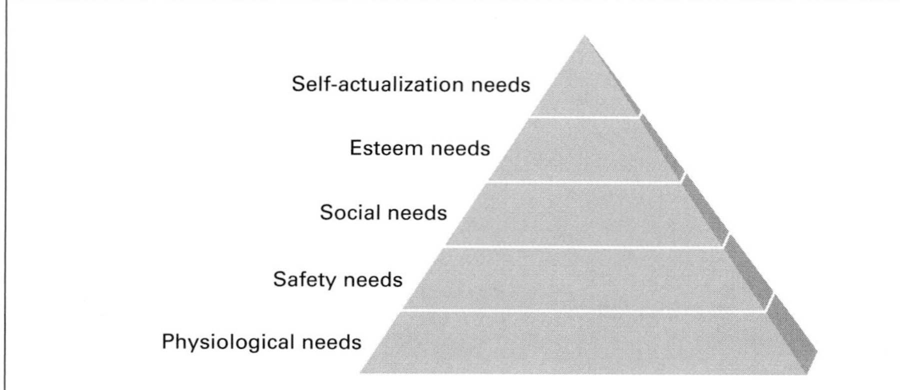

figure 11.2

Maslow's Hierarchy of Needs

Maslow believed that people act to fulfill five categories of needs.

fied through personal accomplishment, promotion to more responsible jobs, various honors and awards, and other forms of recognition.

At the top of the hierarchy are our **self-actualization needs**, the needs to grow and develop and to become all that we are capable of being. These are the most difficult needs to satisfy, and the means of satisfying them tend to vary with the individual. For some people, learning a new skill, starting a new career after retirement, or becoming "the best there is" at some endeavor may be the way to realize self-actualization.

self-actualization needs the need to grow and develop and to become all that we are capable of being

Maslow suggested that people work to satisfy their physiological needs first, then their safety needs, and so on up the "needs ladder." In general, they are motivated by the needs at the lowest level that remain unsatisfied. However, needs at one level do not have to be completely satisfied before needs at the next-highest level come into play. If the majority of a person's physiological and safety needs are satisfied, that person will be motivated primarily by social needs. But any physiological and safety needs that remain unsatisfied will also be important.

Maslow's hierarchy of needs provides a useful way of viewing employee motivation, as well as a guide for management. By and large, American business has been able to satisfy workers' basic needs, but the higher-order needs present more of a challenge. These needs are not satisfied in a simple manner, and the means of satisfaction vary from one employee to another.

Herzberg's Motivation-Hygiene Theory

In the late 1950s, Frederick Herzberg interviewed approximately two hundred accountants and engineers in Pittsburgh. During the interviews, he asked them to think of a time when they had felt especially good about their jobs and their work. Then he asked them to describe the factor or factors that had caused them to feel that way. Next he did the same regarding a time when they had felt especially bad about their work. He was surprised to find that feeling good and feeling bad resulted from entirely different sets of factors; that is, low pay might have made a particular person feel bad, but it was not high pay that had made that person feel good. Instead, it was some completely different factor.

Satisfaction and Dissatisfaction

Before Herzberg's interviews, the general assumption was that employee satisfaction and dissatisfaction lay at opposite ends of the same scale. People felt satisfied, dissatisfied, or somewhere in between. But Herzberg's interviews convinced him that satisfaction and dissatisfaction may be different dimensions altogether. One dimension might range from satisfaction to no satisfaction, and the other might range from dissatisfaction to no dissatisfaction. In other words, the opposite of satisfaction is not dissatisfaction. The idea that satisfaction and dissatisfaction are separate and distinct dimensions is referred to as the **motivation-hygiene theory** (see Figure 11.3).

motivation-hygiene theory the idea that satisfaction and dissatisfaction are separate and distinct dimensions

The job factors that Herzberg found most frequently associated with satisfaction are achievement, recognition, responsibility, advancement, growth, and the work itself.

MOTIVATION FACTORS
- Achievement
- Recognition
- Responsibility
- Advancement
- Growth
- The work itself

Satisfaction ⟷ No satisfaction

HYGIENE FACTORS
- Supervision
- Working conditions
- Interpersonal relationships
- Pay
- Job security
- Company policies and administration

Dissatisfaction ⟷ No dissatisfaction

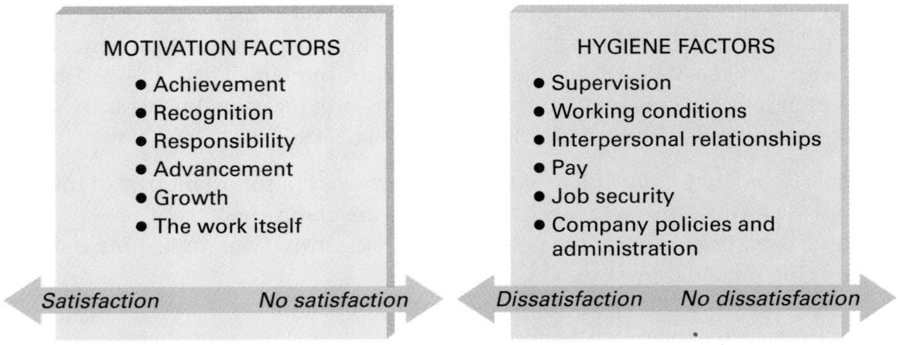

figure 11.3

Herzberg's Motivation-Hygiene Theory

Herzberg's theory takes into account that there are different dimensions to job satisfaction and dissatisfaction and that these factors do not overlap.

motivation factors job factors that increase motivation, but whose absence does not necessarily result in dissatisfaction

hygiene factors job factors that reduce dissatisfaction when present to an acceptable degree, but that do not necessarily result in high levels of motivation

These factors are generally referred to as **motivation factors** because their presence increases motivation. However, their absence does not necessarily result in feelings of dissatisfaction. When motivation factors are present, they act as *satisfiers*.

Job factors cited as causing dissatisfaction are supervision, working conditions, interpersonal relationships, pay, job security, and company policies and administration. These factors, called **hygiene factors**, reduce dissatisfaction when they are present to an acceptable degree. However, they do not necessarily result in high levels of motivation. When hygiene factors are absent, they act as *dissatisfiers*. For example, the level of dissatisfaction in Silicon Valley and especially among employees at dot-com start-ups is a growing reality as many people working long hours, often without much social contact outside of the workplace, have decided that career advancement is not offset by the absence of a personal life.[4]

Using Herzberg's Motivation-Hygiene Theory Herzberg provides explicit guidelines for using the motivation-hygiene theory of employee motivation. He suggests that the hygiene factors must be present to ensure that a worker can function comfortably. But he warns that a state of *no dissatisfaction* never exists. In any situation, people will always be dissatisfied with something.

According to Herzberg, managers should make hygiene as positive as possible, but should then expect only short-term, not long-term, improvement in motivation. Managers must instead focus on providing those motivation factors which *will* presumably enhance motivation and long-term effort.

We should note that employee pay has more effect than Herzberg's theory indicates. He suggests that pay provides only short-term change and not true motivation. Yet in many organizations, pay constitutes a form of recognition and reward for achievement—and recognition and achievement are both motivation factors. The effect of pay may depend on how it is distributed. If a pay increase does not depend on performance (as in across-the-board or cost-of-living raises), it may not motivate people. However, if pay is increased, as a form of recognition (as in bonuses or incentives), it may play a powerful role in motivating employees to higher performance.

Theory X and Theory Y

The concepts of Theory X and Theory Y were advanced by Douglas McGregor in his 1960 book *The Human Side of Enterprise*.[5] They are, in essence, sets of assumptions that underlie management's attitudes and beliefs regarding worker behavior.

Theory X a concept of employee motivation generally consistent with Taylor's scientific management; assumes that employees dislike work and will function only in a highly controlled work environment

Theory X is a concept of employee motivation generally consistent with Taylor's scientific management. Theory X assumes that employees dislike work and will function effectively only in a highly controlled work environment. According to Theory X,

1. People dislike work and try to avoid it.
2. Because people dislike work, managers must coerce, control, and frequently threaten employees to achieve organizational goals.
3. People generally must be led because they have little ambition and will not seek responsibility; they are concerned mainly with security.

The logical outcome of such assumptions will be a highly controlled work environment—one in which managers make all the decisions and employees take all the orders.

Theory Y a concept of employee motivation generally consistent with the ideas of the human relations movement; assumes that employees accept responsibility and work toward organizational goals if by so doing they also achieve personal rewards

On the other hand, **Theory Y** is a concept of employee motivation generally consistent with the ideas of the human relations movement. Theory Y assumes that employees accept responsibility and work toward organizational goals if by so doing they also achieve personal rewards. According to Theory Y,

1. People do not naturally dislike work; in fact, work is an important part of their lives.
2. People will work toward goals to which they are committed.
3. People become committed to goals when it is clear that accomplishing the goals will bring personal rewards.
4. People often seek out and willingly accept responsibility.
5. Employees have the potential to help accomplish organizational goals.
6. Organizations generally do not make full use of their human resources.

table 11.1 Theory X and Theory Y Contrasted

Area	Theory X	Theory Y
Attitude toward work	Dislike	Involvement
Control systems	External	Internal
Supervision	Direct	Indirect
Level of commitment	Low	High
Employee potential	Ignored	Identified
Use of human resources	Limited	Not limited

Obviously this view is quite different from—and much more positive than—that of Theory X. McGregor argued that most managers behave in accordance with Theory X. But he maintained that Theory Y is more appropriate and effective as a guide for managerial action (see Table 11.1).

The human relations movement and Theories X and Y increased managers' awareness of the importance of social factors in the workplace. However, human motivation is a complex and dynamic process to which there is no simple key. Neither money nor social factors alone can provide the answer. Rather, a variety of factors must be considered in any attempt to increase motivation.

Theory Z

William Ouchi, a management professor at UCLA, studied business practices in American and Japanese firms. He concluded that different types of management systems dominate in these two countries.[6] In Japan, Ouchi found what he calls *Type J* firms. They are characterized by lifetime employment for employees, collective (or group) decision making, collective responsibility for the outcomes of decisions, slow evaluation and promotion, implied control mechanisms, nonspecialized career paths, and a holistic concern for employees as people.

American industry is dominated by what Ouchi calls *Type A* firms, which follow a different pattern. They emphasize short-term employment, individual decision making, individual responsibility for the outcomes of decisions, rapid evaluation and promotion, explicit control mechanisms, specialized career paths, and a segmented concern for employees only as employees.

A few very successful American firms represent a blend of the Type J and Type A patterns. These firms, called *Type Z* organizations, emphasize long-term employment, collective decision making, individual responsibility for the outcomes of decisions, slow evaluation and promotion, informal control along with some formalized measures, moderately specialized career paths, and a holistic concern for employees.

Ouchi's **Theory Z** is the belief that some middle ground between his Type A and Type J practices is best for American business (see Figure 11.4). A major part of Theory Z is the emphasis on participative decision making. The focus is on "we" rather than on "us versus them." Theory Z employees and managers view the organization as a family. This participative spirit fosters cooperation and the dissemination of information and organizational values.

Theory Z the belief that some middle ground between Ouchi's Type A and Type J practices is best for American business

Reinforcement Theory

Reinforcement theory is based on the premise that behavior that is rewarded is likely to be repeated, whereas behavior that is punished is less likely to recur. A *reinforcement* is an action that follows directly from a particular behavior. It may be a pay raise following a particularly large sale to a new customer or a reprimand for coming to work late.

Reinforcements can take a variety of forms and can be used in a number of ways. A *positive reinforcement* is one that strengthens desired behavior by providing a reward. For example, many employees respond well to praise; recognition from their supervisors for a

reinforcement theory a theory of motivation based on the premise that behavior that is rewarded is likely to be repeated, whereas behavior that is punished is less likely to recur

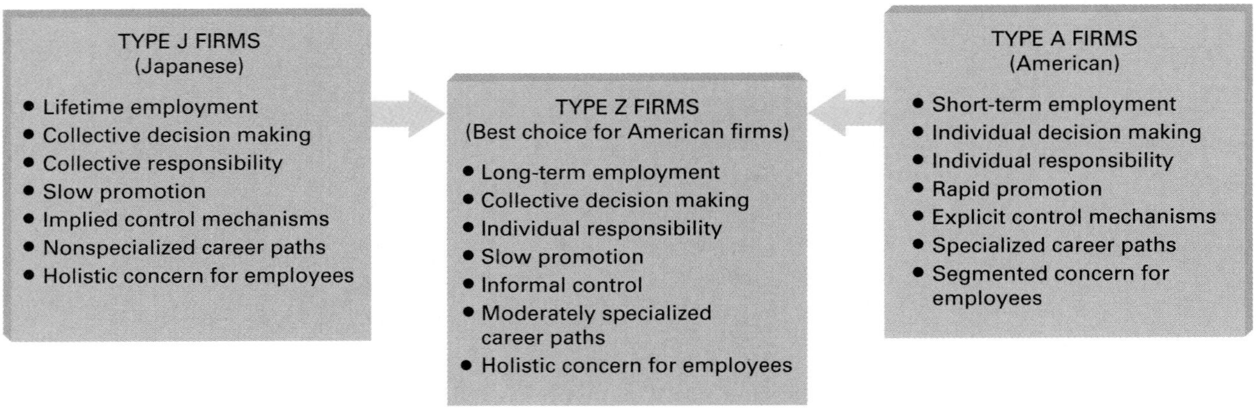

figure 11.4

The Features of Theory Z

The best aspects of Japanese and American management theories combine to form the nucleus of Theory Z.

job well done increases (strengthens) their willingness to perform well in the future. A *negative reinforcement* strengthens desired behavior by eliminating an undesirable task or situation. Suppose a machine shop must be cleaned thoroughly every month—a dirty, miserable task. During one particular month when the workers do a less-than-satisfactory job at their normal work assignments, the boss requires the workers to clean the factory rather than bringing in the usual private maintenance service. The employees will be motivated to work harder the next month to avoid the unpleasant cleanup duty again.

adapting to change

The Changing Roles of Men and Women in the Workplace

THE WORKPLACE ROLES OF MEN AND women are evolving as women continue to enter the work force in greater numbers, move higher into management, and start their own businesses. Women in top corporate jobs are still so rare that Carly Fiorina's promotion to CEO of Hewlett-Packard made headlines. Although the novelty of men and women working together has worn off in nearly every industry, research suggests that both genders have different perceptions of and reactions to workplace issues and interactions. Nonetheless, the roles of men and women in the workplace are definitely changing.

Today's collaborative business environment requires strong networking and interpersonal skills. Although these are skills which women, in particular, have traditionally emphasized, all managers and employees are now becoming more adept at dealing with people one-on-one. Similarly, as rigid hierarchies give way to more flexible organizations, the ability to build relationships rather than issue commands–often seen as one of women's strengths–is a skill that both men and women must have to succeed.

In the past, women–more than men–tended to take off from work to handle family crises such as tending a sick child or helping an elderly parent. These days, maternity and paternity leave policies are allowing both parents time to bond with a new baby. Family-friendly policies such as flextime are also giving mothers and fathers the freedom to juggle work and family obligations as needed so they can share care-giving responsibilities.

The changing roles of men and women at work can be especially challenging for firms active in global markets where gender roles are more narrowly defined. Despite these challenges, companies clearly benefit from the complementary insights and instincts of both genders. Says one corporate CEO: "I know that the mixture of male and female managers is good for a business."

Punishment is an undesired consequence of undesirable behavior. Common forms of punishment used in organizations include reprimands, reduced pay, disciplinary layoffs, and termination (firing). Punishment often does more harm than good. It tends to create an unpleasant environment, fosters hostility and resentment, and suppresses undesirable behavior only until the supervisor's back is turned.

Managers who rely on *extinction* hope to eliminate undesirable behavior by not responding to it. The idea is that the behavior will eventually become "extinct." Suppose, for example, that an employee has the habit of writing memo after memo to his or her manager about insignificant events. If the manager doesn't respond to any of these memos, the employee will probably stop writing them, and the behavior will have been squelched.

The effectiveness of reinforcement depends on which type is used and how it is timed. One approach may work best under certain conditions, but some situations lend themselves to the use of more than one approach. Generally, positive reinforcement is considered the most effective, and it is recommended when the manager has a choice.

Continual reinforcement can become tedious for both managers and employees, especially when the same behavior is being reinforced over and over in the same way. At the start, it may be necessary to reinforce a desired behavior every time it occurs. However, once a desired behavior has become more or less established, occasional reinforcement seems to be most effective.

Contemporary Views on Motivation

LEARNING OBJECTIVE

3 Describe three contemporary views of motivation: equity theory, expectancy theory, and goal-setting theory.

Maslow's hierarchy of needs and Herzberg's motivation-hygiene theory are popular and widely known theories of motivation. Each is also a significant step up from the relatively narrow views of scientific management and Theories X and Y. But they do have one weakness: each attempts to specify *what* motivates people, but neither explains *why* or *how* motivation develops or is sustained over time. In recent years, managers have begun to explore three other models that take a more dynamic view of motivation. These are equity theory, expectancy theory, and goal-setting theory.

Equity Theory

equity theory a theory of motivation based on the premise that people are motivated to obtain and preserve equitable treatment for themselves

The **equity theory** of motivation is based on the premise that people are motivated to obtain and preserve equitable treatment for themselves. As used here, *equity* is the distribution of rewards in direct proportion to the contribution of each employee to the organization. Everyone need not receive the *same* rewards, but the rewards should be in accordance with individual contributions.

According to the theory, we tend to implement the idea of equity in the following way. First, we develop our own input-to-outcome ratio. Inputs are the time, effort, skills, education, experience, and so on that we contribute to the organization. Outcomes are the rewards we get from the organization, such as pay, benefits, recognition, and promotions. Next, we compare this ratio with what we perceive as the input-to-outcome ratio for some other person. It might be a coworker, a friend who works for another firm, or even an average of all the people in our organization. This person is called the "comparison other." Note that our perception of this person's input-to-outcome ratio may be absolutely correct or completely wrong. However, we believe it is correct.

If the two ratios are roughly the same, we feel that the organization is treating us equitably. In this case we are motivated to leave things as they are. However, if our ratio is the higher of the two, we feel underrewarded and are motivated to make changes. We may (1) decrease our own inputs by not working so hard, (2) try to increase our total outcome by asking for a raise in pay, (3) try to get the comparison other to increase some inputs or receive decreased outcomes, (4) leave the work situation, or (5) do a new comparison with a different comparison other.

Equity theory is most relevant to pay as an outcome. Because pay is a very real measure of a person's worth to the organization, comparisons involving pay are a natural part of organizational life. Managers can try to avoid problems arising from inequity by making sure that rewards are distributed on the basis of performance and that everyone clearly understands the basis for his or her own pay.

Expectancy Theory

expectancy theory a model of motivation based on the assumption that motivation depends on how much we want something and on how likely we think we are to get it

Expectancy theory, developed by Victor Vroom, is a very complex model of motivation based on a deceptively simple assumption. According to expectancy theory, motivation depends on how much we want something and on how likely we think we are to get it (see Figure 11.5). Consider, for example, the case of three sales representatives who are candidates for promotion to one sales manager's job. Bill has had a very good sales year and always gets good performance evaluations. However, he isn't sure he wants the job because it involves a great deal of travel, long working hours, and much stress and pressure. Paul wants the job badly but doesn't think he has much chance of getting it. He has had a terrible sales year and gets only mediocre performance evaluations from his present boss. Susan wants the job as much as Paul, and she thinks she has a pretty good shot at it. Her sales have improved significantly this past year, and her evaluations are the best in the company.

Expectancy theory would predict that Bill and Paul are not very motivated to seek the promotion. Bill doesn't really want it, and Paul doesn't think he has much of a chance of getting it. Susan, however, is very motivated to seek the promotion because she wants it *and* thinks she can get it.

Expectancy theory is complex because each action we take is likely to lead to several different outcomes; some we may want and others we may not want. For example, a person who works hard and puts in many extra hours may get a pay raise, be promoted, and gain valuable new job skills. But that person may also be forced to spend less time with his or her family and be forced to cut back on social life.

For one person, the promotion may be paramount, the pay raise and new skills fairly important, and the loss of family and social life of negligible importance. For someone else, the family and social life may be the most important, the pay raise of moderate importance, the new skills unimportant, and the promotion undesirable because of the additional hours it would require. The first person would be motivated to work hard and put in the extra hours, whereas the second person would not be at all motivated to do so. In other words, it is the entire bundle of outcomes—and the individual's evaluation of the importance of each outcome—that determines motivation.

Expectancy theory is difficult to apply, but it does provide several useful guidelines for managers. It suggests that managers must recognize that (1) employees work for a variety of reasons; (2) these reasons, or expected outcomes, may change over time; and (3) it is necessary to clearly show employees how they can attain the outcomes they desire.

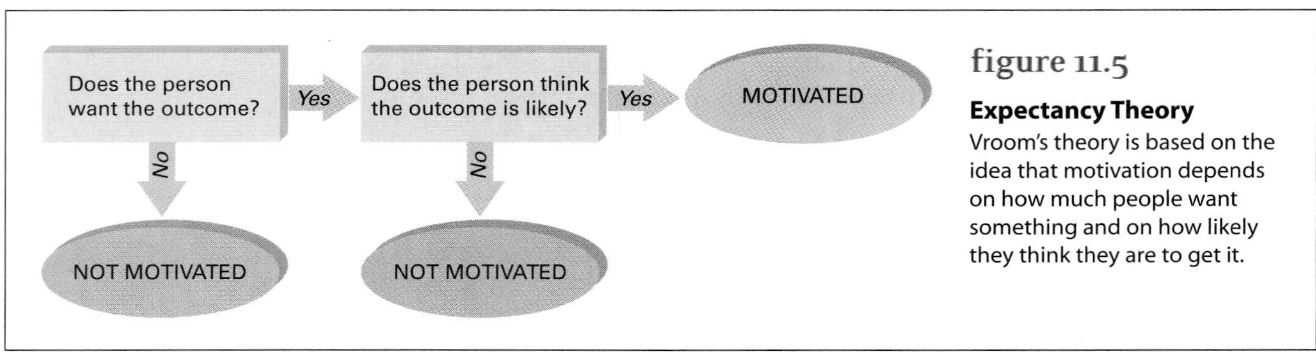

figure 11.5

Expectancy Theory

Vroom's theory is based on the idea that motivation depends on how much people want something and on how likely they think they are to get it.

Goal-Setting Theory

Goal-setting theory suggests that employees are motivated to achieve goals they and their managers establish together. The goal should be very specific, moderately difficult, and one the employee will be committed to achieve.[7] Rewards should be directly tied to goal achievement. Using goal-setting theory, a manager can design rewards that fit employee needs, clarify expectations, maintain equity, and provide reinforcement. A major benefit of this theory is that it provides a good understanding of the goal the employee is to achieve and the rewards that will accrue to the employee if the goal is accomplished.

goal-setting theory a theory of motivation suggesting that employees are motivated to achieve goals they and their managers establish together

Key Motivation Techniques

LEARNING OBJECTIVE

4 Explain several techniques for increasing employee motivation.

Today it takes more than a generous salary to motivate employees. Increasingly, companies are trying to provide motivation by satisfying employees' less tangible needs. For example, some major companies, such as AT&T, Discover Brokerage, Lucent Technologies, and Pitney Bowes, use corporate incentive programs provided by GiftCertificate.com. This organization provides gift certificates for a variety of restaurants, major retailers, and travel-related organizations. When an employee receives an incentive award, he or she can select a gift certificate, which is redeemable at hundreds of businesses, or a gift certificate for a specific company. Companies that use GiftCertificate.com's incentive program can meet the diverse needs of employees because recipients can redeem these gift certificates at one or more of hundreds of types of businesses.[8] In this section, we discuss several specific—and somewhat more orthodox—techniques that help managers boost employee motivation and job satisfaction.

Exploring Business

Dealing with Workplace Stress

Day in and day out, employees at all kinds of organizations face stress on the job. Many feel the pressure of unrelenting work deadlines, while others have the added worry of caring for sick family members or other personal problems. Technology also contributes to workplace stress, because employees with mobile phones, voice mail, and e-mail can be bombarded with questions and decisions at any hour.

Stress isn't just an employee problem–it affects company performance, as well. Lynn Fazio, director of work/life programs at Autodesk in California, says, "We are very attentive to work/life issues because when someone is close to the line and is going to burn out, he or she is not productive." When stress goes up, employee satisfaction goes down. But companies can–and should–break this vicious cycle. Sears, for example, found that a significant improvement in its employees' satisfaction levels translated into an even higher increase in customer satisfaction levels and, in turn, an increase in sales revenues.

Patrice Tanaka, CEO of the New York public relations firm Patrice Tanaka & Co., uses a variety of methods to help her forty-three employees keep stress under control. Workers can relax in the open-space office "living room" or close their eyes in the meditation room. One day a week, employees can stay home and telecommute if they choose, and the company shuts down entirely on four Fridays in the summer, the week between Christmas and New Year's, and on Valentine's Day.

Stress-busting pays off in performance and in loyalty for Tanaka. "A lot of agencies just let you fend for yourself," observes Beth Corwin, an account supervisor. "Here, there's a support network. This place has a soul, and it's a nice place to work." CEO Tanaka knows that employees can tell the difference between lip service and genuine caring. "If you say you are committed to your employees and to making your business a great place to work and yet your policies are bad, then it's just a lot of hot air. We don't want to be just a lot of hot air."

Management by Objectives

management by objectives (MBO) a motivation technique in which managers and employees collaborate in setting goals

Management by objectives (MBO) is a motivation technique in which managers and employees collaborate in setting goals. The primary purpose of MBO is to clarify the roles employees are expected to play in reaching the organization's goals. By allowing individuals to participate in goal setting and performance evaluation, MBO increases their motivation. Most MBO programs consist of a series of five steps, as shown in Figure 11.6.

The first step in setting up an MBO program is to secure the acceptance of top management. It is essential that top managers endorse and participate in the program if others in the firm are to accept it. The commitment of top management also provides a natural starting point for educating employees about the purposes and mechanics of MBO.

Next, preliminary goals must be established. Top management also plays a major role in this activity because the preliminary goals reflect the firm's mission and strategy. The intent of an MBO program is to have these goals filter down through the organization.

The third step, which actually consists of several smaller steps, is the heart of MBO:

1. The manager explains to each employee that he or she has accepted certain goals for the group (the manager as well as the employees) and asks the individual to think about how he or she can help achieve these goals.
2. The manager later meets with each employee individually. Together, they establish goals for the employee. Whenever possible, the goals should be measurable and should specify the time frame for completion (usually one year).
3. The manager and the employee decide what resources the employee will need to accomplish his or her goals.

As the fourth step, the manager and each employee meet periodically to review the employee's progress. They may agree to modify certain goals during these meetings if circumstances have changed. For example, a sales representative may have accepted a goal of increasing sales by 20 percent. However, an aggressive competitor may have entered the marketplace, making this goal unattainable. In light of this circumstance, the goal may be revised downward to 10 or 15 percent.

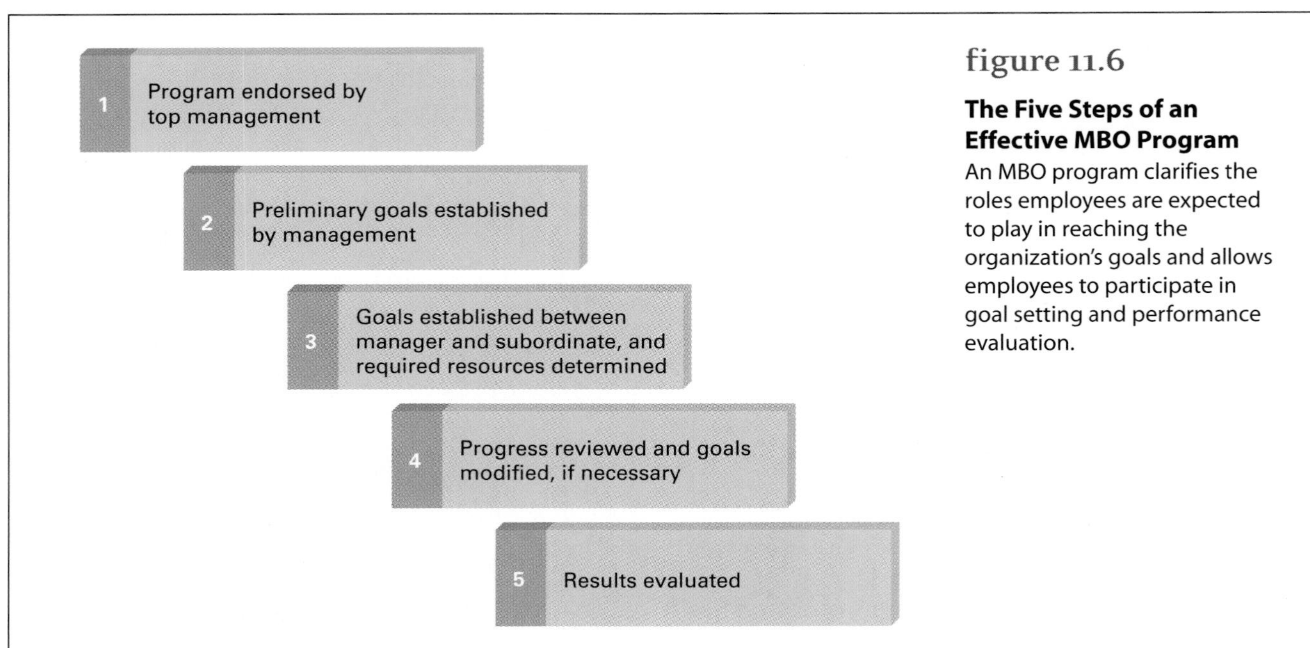

figure 11.6

The Five Steps of an Effective MBO Program

An MBO program clarifies the roles employees are expected to play in reaching the organization's goals and allows employees to participate in goal setting and performance evaluation.

The fifth step in the MBO process is evaluation. At the end of the designated time period, the manager and each employee meet again to determine which of the individual's goals were met, which were not met, and why. The employee's reward (in the form of a pay raise, praise, or promotion) is based primarily on the degree of goal attainment.

Like every other management method, MBO has advantages and disadvantages. MBO can motivate employees by involving them actively in the life of the firm. The collaboration on goal setting and performance appraisal improves communication and makes employees feel they are an important part of the organization. Periodic review of progress also enhances control within an organization. A major problem with MBO is that it does not work unless the process begins at the top of an organization. In some cases, MBO results in excessive paperwork. In addition, some managers have difficulty sitting down and working out goals with their employees and may instead just assign them goals.[9] Finally, MBO programs prove difficult to implement unless goals are quantifiable.

spotLight

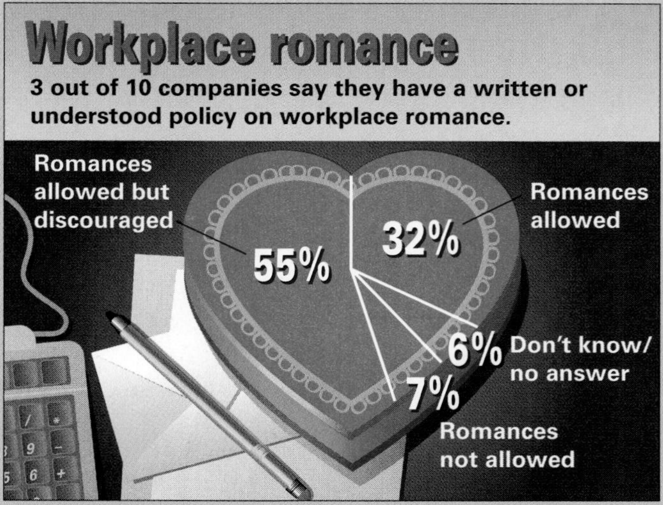

Workplace romance
3 out of 10 companies say they have a written or understood policy on workplace romance.
Romances allowed but discouraged
55%
32%
Romances allowed
6% Don't know/ no answer
7%
Romances not allowed

Source: Copyright 2000, USA TODAY. Reprinted with permission.

MBO has proved to be an effective motivational tool in many organizations. Tenneco, Black & Decker, Du Pont, General Foods, and General Motors have all reported success with MBO. Like any management technique, however, it must be applied with caution and in the right spirit if it is to work.

Job Enrichment

Job enrichment is a method of motivating employees by providing them with variety in their tasks while giving them some responsibility for, and control over, their jobs. At the same time, employees gain new skills and acquire a broader perspective about how their individual work contributes to the goals of the organization. Earlier in this chapter, we noted that Herzberg's motivation-hygiene theory is one rationale for the use of job enrichment; that is, the added responsibility and control that job enrichment confers on employees increases their satisfaction and motivation. At times, **job enlargement**—expanding a worker's assignments to include additional but similar tasks—can lead to job enrichment. Job enlargement might mean that a worker on an assembly line who used to connect three wires to components moving down the line now connects five wires. Unfortunately, the added tasks are often just as routine as those the worker performed before the change. In such cases, enlargement may not be effective. AT&T, IBM, and Maytag Corporation have all experimented with job enlargement.

job enrichment a motivation technique that provides employees with more variety and responsibility in their jobs

job enlargement expanding a worker's assignments to include additional but similar tasks

Whereas job enlargement does not really change the routine and monotonous nature of jobs, job enrichment does. Job enrichment requires that added tasks give an employee more responsibility for what he or she does. It provides workers with both more tasks to do and more control over how they perform them. In particular, job enrichment removes many controls from jobs, gives workers more authority, and assigns work in complete, natural units. Moreover, employees are frequently given fresh and challenging job assignments. By blending more planning and decision making into jobs, job enrichment gives work more depth and complexity.

Job redesign is a type of job enrichment in which work is restructured in ways that cultivate the worker-job match. Job redesign can be achieved by combining tasks, forming work groups, or establishing closer customer relationships. Employees are often more motivated when jobs are combined because the increased variety of tasks presents more challenge and therefore more reward. Work groups motivate employees

job redesign a type of job enrichment in which work is restructured to cultivate the worker-job match

spotLight

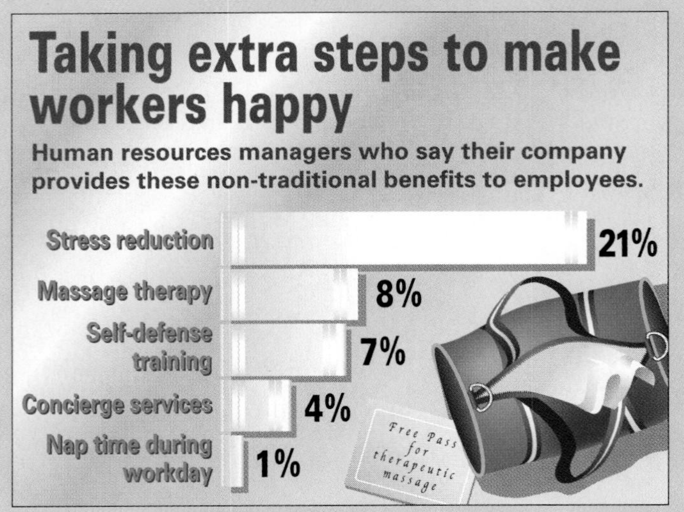

Source: Copyright 2000, USA TODAY. Reprinted with permission.

by showing them how their jobs fit within the organization as a whole and how they contribute to its success. Establishing client relationships allows employees to interact directly with customers. Not only does this type of redesign add a personal dimension to employment, but it also provides workers with immediate and relevant feedback about how they are doing their jobs.

Among the companies that have used job enrichment successfully are General Foods, Texas Instruments, and Chevron Corporation. Chevron's program focuses on employees' career development and on helping them enhance their effectiveness and job satisfaction. The company's career-enrichment process, now serving as a model for many other organizations, follows a step-by-step procedure that includes preparation, joint planning, plan review, implementation, and end-of-period review.

Job enrichment works best when employees seek more challenging work. Of course not all workers respond positively to job-enrichment programs. Employees must desire personal growth and have the skills and knowledge to perform enriched jobs. Lack of self-confidence, fear of failure, or distrust of management's intentions are likely to lead to ineffective performance on enriched jobs. In addition, some workers do not view their jobs as routine and boring, and others even prefer routine jobs because they find them satisfying and stress-free. Companies that use job enrichment as an alternative to specialization also face extra expenses, such as the cost of retraining.

Behavior Modification

behavior modification a systematic program of reinforcement to encourage desirable behavior

Behavior modification is a systematic program of reinforcement to encourage desirable behavior. Behavior modification involves both rewards to encourage desirable actions and punishments to discourage undesirable actions. However, studies have shown that rewards, such as compliments and expressions of appreciation, are much more effective behavior modifiers than punishments, such as reprimands and scorn.

When applied to management, behavior modification strives to encourage desirable organizational behavior. Use of this technique begins with the identification of a target behavior—the behavior that is to be changed. (It might be low production levels or a high rate of absenteeism, for example.) Existing levels of this behavior are then measured. Next, managers provide positive reinforcement in the form of a reward when employees exhibit the desired behavior (such as increased production or less absenteeism). The reward might be praise or a more tangible form of recognition, such as a gift, meal, or trip. Finally, the levels of the target behavior are measured again to determine whether the desired changes have been achieved. If they have, the reinforcement is maintained. However, if the target behavior has not changed significantly in the desired direction, the reward system must be changed to one that is likely to be more effective. The key is to devise effective rewards that will not only modify employees' behavior in desired ways but will also motivate them. To that end, experts suggest that management should reward quality, loyalty, and productivity.

Flextime

To most people, a work schedule means the standard 9-to-5, forty-hour workweek. In reality, though, many people have work schedules that are quite different from this. Police officers, firefighters, restaurant personnel, airline employees, and med-

Recognition and rewards help to modify behavior. Intangible recognition such as praise as well as tangible rewards are employed to modify behavior.

ical personnel usually have work schedules that are far from standard. Some manufacturers also rotate personnel from shift to shift. And many professional people—such as managers, artists, and lawyers—need more than forty hours each week to get their work done.

The needs and lifestyles of today's work force are changing. Dual-income families make up a much larger share of the work force than ever before, and women are its fastest-growing sector. In 1970, approximately one-third of U.S. women worked out the home. Today, about 60 percent are in the labor force.[10] And more employees are responsible for the care of elderly relatives. Recognizing that these changes increase the demand for family time, many employers are offering flexible work schedules that not only help employees manage their time better but also increase employee motivation and job satisfaction.

flextime a system in which employees set their own work hours within employer-determined limits

Flextime is a system in which employees set their own work hours within certain limits determined by employers. Typically the firm establishes two bands of time: the *core time*, when all employees must be at work, and the *flexible time*, when employees may choose whether to be at work. The only condition is that every employee must work a total of eight hours each day. For example, the hours between 9 and 11 A.M. and 1 and 3 P.M. might be core time, and the hours between 6 and 9 A.M., between 11 A.M. and 1 P.M., and between 3 and 6 P.M. might be flexible time. This would give employees the option of coming in early and getting off early, coming in later and leaving later, or taking an extra-long lunch break. But flextime also ensures that everyone is present at certain times, when conferences with supervisors and department meetings can be scheduled. Another type of flextime allows employees to work a forty-hour workweek in four days instead of five. Workers who put in ten hours a day instead of eight get an extra day off each week.

The sense of independence and autonomy employees gain from having a say in what hours they work can be a motivating factor. In addition, employees who have enough time to deal with nonwork issues often work more productively and with greater satisfaction when they are on the job. For example, at the Berndt Group, web professionals have intense, high-pressure jobs. Recognition of their hard work includes respecting each individual's best schedule for productivity. While employee turnover is common in the web industry, the Berndt Group experiences very little employee turnover. Flextime allows this organization to attract and hold super-creative, driven employees.[11] Two common problems associated with utilizing flextime are (1) supervisors sometimes find their jobs complicated by having employees who come and go at different times, and (2) employees without flextime sometimes resent coworkers who have it.

Part-Time Work and Job Sharing

part-time work permanent employment in which individuals work less than a standard workweek

Part-time work is permanent employment in which individuals work less than a standard workweek. The specific number of hours worked varies, but part-time jobs are structured so that all responsibilities can be completed in the number of hours an employee works. Part-time work is of special interest to parents who want more time with their children and people who simply desire more leisure time. One disadvantage of part-time work is that it often does not provide the benefits that come with a full-time position. This is not, however, the case at Starbucks, where approximately 80 percent of its employees work part-time. Starbucks doesn't treat its part-time employees any differently from its full-time employees; all receive the same benefits, which include health benefits and a stock option package.[12]

job sharing an arrangement whereby two people share one full-time position

Job sharing (sometimes referred to as work sharing) is an arrangement whereby two people share one full-time position. One job sharer may work from 8 A.M. to noon and the other from 1 to 5 P.M., or they may alternate workdays. For example, at a financial institution in Vancouver, two women share the same job. By communicating daily through computers, voice mail, and fax machines, these managers are able to handle challenging administrative positions and still have time for their families. Through their partnership at work, they have been able to share eight different positions during their careers.[13] Job sharing combines the security of a full-time position with the flexibility of a part-time job.

For firms, job sharing provides a unique opportunity to attract highly skilled employees who might not be available on a full-time basis. In addition, companies can save on expenses by reducing the cost of benefits and avoiding the disruptions of employee turnover. For employees, opting for the flexibility of job sharing may mean giving up some of the benefits received for full-time work. In addition, job sharing is difficult if tasks aren't easily divisible or if two people do not work or communicate well with one another.

Telecommuting

telecommuting working at home all of the time or for a portion of the workweek

A growing number of companies allow **telecommuting**—working at home all of the time or for a portion of the workweek. Personal computers, modems, fax machines, voice mail, cellular phones, and overnight couriers all facilitate the work-at-home trend. Working at home means individuals can set their own hours and have more time with their families. Companies that allow telecommuting experience several benefits including increased productivity, lower real estate and travel costs, reduced employee absenteeism and turnover, increased work/life balance and improved morale, and access to additional labor pools such as disabled workers.[14] Among the disadvantages to telecommuting are feelings of isolation, putting in longer hours, and being distracted by family or household responsibilities. In addition, some supervisors have difficulty monitoring productivity.

empowerment making employees more involved in their jobs by increasing their participation in decision making

Management at AlliedSignal believes that a critical issue in the success of a telecommuting program is that there be a thorough discussion between the supervisor and his or her employee regarding the goals and expectations for the employee who wants to telecommute. AlliedSignal uses a series of questionnaires that both employees and supervisors complete. The questions focus on the hours to be worked, the specific work activities, the child-care situation at home, the equipment and other support services that the company will provide, the expenses that will be reimbursed, and how the employee's performance will be measured.[15]

Using the Internet

Home offices, mobile offices, and telecommuting are growing in popularity. The Internet is a great source of personal and professional services the mobile worker can call on whenever assistance away from the office is needed. A few online service firms like Bungo.com, Nowonder.com, MyEvents.com, and Staples.com can provide calendar functions, printing, and secretarial services to mention just a few.

Employee Empowerment

Many companies are increasing employee motivation and satisfaction through the use of empowerment. **Empowerment** means making employees more involved in their jobs and in the operations of the organization by increasing their participation in decision making. With empowerment, control no longer flows exclusively from the top levels of the organization downward. Empowered employees have a voice in what they do, and how and when they do it. In some organizations, employees' input is restricted to individual choices, such as when to take breaks. In other companies, their responsibilities might encompass more far-reaching issues. At Ritz-Carlton Hotels, empowerment frequently requires people skills, such as conflict resolution. When a guest has a complaint, the employee who receives the complaint is considered to "own" it and must immediately and independently figure out how to address it. Employees empowered to solve such problems often become good candidates for promotion. Employee turnover at Ritz-Carlton is only one-fifth of the hotel industry average.[16]

For empowerment to work effectively, management must be involved. Managers should set expectations, communicate standards, institute periodic evaluations, and guarantee follow-up. Studies have shown that when effectively implemented, empowerment often leads to increased job satisfaction, improved job performance, higher-quality output, increased organizational commitment, lower turnover, and reduced sick leave.[17] Obstacles to empowerment include resistance on the part of management, distrust of management on the part of workers, insufficient training, and poor communication between management and employees.

Self-Managed Work Teams

self-managed work teams groups of employees with the authority and skills to manage themselves

Another method for increasing employee motivation is to introduce **self-managed work teams,** groups of employees with the authority and skills to manage themselves. Experts submit that workers on self-managed teams are more motivated and satisfied because they have more task variety and more job control. On many work teams, members rotate through all the jobs for which the team is responsible. Some organizations cross-train the entire team so that everyone can perform everyone else's job. In a traditional business structure, management is responsible for hiring and firing employees, establishing budgets, purchasing supplies, conducting performance reviews, and disciplining team members. When teams are in place, they take over some or all of these management functions.

To make the most effective use of teams, organizations must be committed to the team approach, team objectives must be clear, training and education must be ongoing, and there must be a system for compensating the accomplishment of team-based goals. One such compensation system is *gain sharing*, in which employee bonuses are tied to achievement of team goals, such as increased sales or productivity or improved customer satisfaction.[18]

When correctly implemented, use of work teams can lead to higher employee morale, increased productivity, and often innovation. Both Xerox and Procter & Gamble have successfully implemented the self-directed team strategy. Smaller organizations can also

Building team skills. Some organizations use exercises to develop team skills. These employees are participating in a corporate-sponsored workshop designed to help them use teamwork to handle stressful situations.

benefit. For example, Allina, a company that operates nonprofit hospitals in Minnesota, has had excellent results since creating management-union teams. One of these teams saved the company $200,000 annually by improving the procedure for equipment maintenance.

Although the work-team strategy is increasingly popular, it is not without its problems. Lack of support from managers and supervisors and insufficient training in the team approach can minimize or eliminate benefits. In addition, companies must be prepared for the initial costs of training and implementation.

Employee Ownership

employee ownership a situation in which employees own the company they work for by virtue of being stockholders

Some organizations are discovering that a highly effective technique for motivating employees is **employee ownership**—that is, employees own the company they work for by virtue of being stockholders. Employee-owned businesses directly reward employees for success. When the company enjoys increased sales or lower costs, employees benefit directly. The National Center for Employee Ownership, an organization that studies employee-owned American businesses, reports that employee stock ownership plans (ESOPs) provide considerable employee incentive and increase employee involvement and commitment. In the United States today, about 8.5 million employees participate in 11,500 ESOPs and stock bonus plans.[19] As a means to motivate top executives and, frequently, middle-ranking managers who are working long days for what are generally considered poor salaries, many Internet related firms provide stock options as part of the employee compensation package. The option is simply the right to buy shares of the firm within a prescribed time at a set price. If the firm does well, and its stock price rises past the set price (presumably because of all the work being done by the employee), the employee can exercise the option and immediately sell the stock to cash in on the company's success. For example, Joseph Galli was lured away from Black and Decker to take the president's post at Amazon.com. Along with an annual salary of $200,000, Galli was given 3.9 million options on Amazon.com stock. While Amazon stock soared, those options rose in theoretical value past $200 million but then fell to no value as the stock market turned on Amazon. Time will tell whether Galli's options turn out to be worthless for him or turn him into a fabulously rich man.[20]

Enjoying the benefit of employee ownership. When Continental/Midland Inc. was sold, CEO Robert Kaminsky handed out checks to more than 400 employees who shared in the profits from the sale.

RETURN TO inside business

BMC SOFTWARE'S SOPHISTICATED SOFTWARE systems include programs that let e-businesses such as Amazon.com anticipate and avert devastating power outages that can cripple their web sites. Other major clients include Continental Airlines and National Discount Brokers. Knowing that these customers depend on BMC for reliable, timely software installation and service, the company motivates its employees to make decisions and take actions on their own.

On-site amenities, generous compensation and benefits, and a policy of empowerment keep BMCers satisfied and challenged to do their best. Still, rapid advances in information technology and communications are forcing ongoing changes in the competitive climate for BMC and its customers. Keeping employees motivated to perform in this dynamic environment is critical if BMC is to keep pace with the changes. "The opportunity and the risk are so enormous that if you ever stop trying to change something, you're going to get behind," Watson says. "Catching up is almost impossible."

Questions

1. How does BMC help employees satisfy all five of the need categories in Maslow's hierarchy?
2. Does BMC follow Theory X or Theory Y for employee motivation? Explain your answer.

chapter Review

SUMMARY

1 Explain what motivation is.

Motivation is the individual, internal process that energizes, directs, and sustains behavior. Motivation is affected by employee morale—that is, the employee's feelings about the job, superiors, and the firm itself. Motivation, morale, and job satisfaction are closely related.

2 Understand some major historical perspectives on motivation.

One of the first approaches to employee motivation was Frederick Taylor's scientific management, the application of scientific principles to management of work and workers. Taylor believed that employees work only for money and that they must be closely supervised and managed. This thinking led to the piece-rate system, under which employees are paid a certain amount for each unit they produce. The Hawthorne Studies attempted to determine the effects of the work environment on productivity. Results of these studies indicated that human factors affect productivity more than do physical aspects of the workplace.

Maslow's hierarchy of needs suggests that people are motivated by five sets of needs. In ascending order of importance, these motivators are physiological, safety, social, esteem, and self-actualization needs. People are motivated by the lowest set of needs that remains unfulfilled. As needs at one level are satisfied, people try to satisfy needs at the next level.

Frederick Herzberg found that job satisfaction and dissatisfaction are influenced by two distinct sets of factors. Motivation factors, including recognition and responsibility, affect an employee's degree of satisfaction, but their absence does not necessarily cause dissatisfaction. Hygiene factors, including pay and working conditions, affect an employee's degree of dissatisfaction but do not affect satisfaction.

Theory X is a concept of motivation that assumes employees dislike work and will function effectively only in a highly controlled work environment. Thus, to achieve an organization's goals, managers must coerce, control, and threaten employees. This theory is generally consistent with Taylor's scientific management. Theory Y is more in keeping with the results of the Hawthorne Studies and the human relations movement. It suggests that employees can be motivated to behave as responsible members of the organization. Theory Z emphasizes long-term employment, collective decision making, individual responsibility for the outcome of decisions, informal control, and a holistic concern for employees. Reinforcement theory is based on the idea that people will repeat behavior that is rewarded and will avoid behavior that is punished.

3 Describe three contemporary views of motivation: equity theory, expectancy theory, and goal-setting theory.

Equity theory maintains that people are motivated to obtain and preserve equitable treatment for themselves. Expectancy theory suggests that our motivation depends on how much we want something and how likely we think we are to get it. Goal-setting theory suggests that employees are motivated to achieve a goal that they and their managers establish together.

4 Explain several techniques for increasing employee motivation.

Management by objectives is a motivation technique in which managers and employees collaborate in setting goals. MBO motivates employees by getting them more involved in their jobs and in the organization as a whole. Job enrichment seeks to motivate employees by varying their tasks and giving them more responsibility for, and control over, their jobs. Job enlargement, expanding a worker's assignments to include additional tasks, is one aspect of job enrichment. Job redesign is a type of job enrichment in which work is restructured to improve the worker-job match.

Behavior modification uses reinforcement to encourage desirable behavior. Rewards for productivity, quality, and loyalty change employees' behavior in desired ways and also increase motivation.

Allowing employees to work more flexible hours is another way to build motivation and job satisfaction. Flextime is a system of work scheduling that allows workers to set their own hours as long as they fall within limits established by employers. Part-time work is permanent employment in which individuals work less than a standard workweek. Job sharing is an arrangement whereby two people share one full-time position. Telecommuting allows employees to work at home all or part of the workweek. All these types of work arrangements give employees more time outside the workplace to deal with family responsibilities or to enjoy free time.

Employee empowerment, self-managed work teams, and employee ownership are also techniques that boost employee motivation. Empowerment increases employees' involvement in their jobs by increasing their decision-making authority. Self-managed work teams are groups of employees with the authority and skills to manage themselves. When employees participate in ownership programs such as employee stock ownership plans (ESOPs), they have more incentive to make the company succeed, and therefore work more effectively.

KEY TERMS

You should now be able to define and give an example relevant to each of the following terms:

motivation (303)
morale (303)
scientific management (304)
piece-rate system (305)
need (306)
Maslow's hierarchy of needs (306)
physiological needs (306)
safety needs (306)
social needs (306)
esteem needs (306)
self-actualization needs (307)
motivation-hygiene theory (307)
motivation factors (308)
hygiene factors (308)
Theory X (308)
Theory Y (308)
Theory Z (309)
reinforcement theory (309)
equity theory (311)
expectancy theory (312)
goal-setting theory (313)
management by objectives (MBO) (314)
job enrichment (315)
job enlargement (315)
job redesign (315)
behavior modification (316)
flextime (317)
part-time work (318)
job sharing (318)
telecommuting (318)
empowerment (318)
self-managed work teams (319)
employee ownership (320)

REVIEW QUESTIONS

1. How do scientific management and Theory X differ from the human relations movement and Theory Y?
2. How did the results of the Hawthorne Studies influence researchers' thinking about employee motivation?
3. What are the five sets of needs in Maslow's hierarchy? How are a person's needs related to motivation?
4. What are the two dimensions in Herzberg's theory? What kinds of elements affect each dimension?
5. What is the fundamental premise of reinforcement theory?
6. According to equity theory, how does an employee determine whether he or she is being treated equitably?
7. According to expectancy theory, what two variables determine motivation?
8. Identify and describe the major techniques for motivating employees.
9. Describe the steps involved in the MBO process.
10. What are the objectives of MBO? What do you think might be its disadvantages?
11. How does employee participation increase motivation?
12. Describe the steps in the process of behavior modification.
13. What are the major benefits and most common problems associated with the use of self-managed work teams?

DISCUSSION QUESTIONS

1. How might managers make use of Maslow's hierarchy of needs in motivating employees? What problems would they encounter?

2. Do the various theories of motivation contradict each other or complement each other? Explain.
3. What combination of motivational techniques do you think would result in the best overall motivation and reward system?
4. Reinforcement theory and behavior modification have been called demeaning because they tend to treat people "like mice in a maze." Do you agree?

VIDEO CASE

Motivation Is the Recipe for Success at Harbor Sweets

Fine chocolate started as Ben Strohecker's hobby. By day, he was marketing director of Schrafft's Candy in Boston, looking for ways to boost the company's candy sales. By night, he stood in his home kitchen in Marblehead, Massachusetts, cooking up batch after batch of chocolate in his quest for the world's richest, best-quality confection. When he made an almond butter crunch chocolate triangle and dipped the point into white chocolate, his son remarked that the candy looked like a sailboat, and his wife called it a "sweet sloop." The name stuck, and the Sweet Sloop became Strohecker's first chocolate product—the product that launched his new business, dubbed Harbor Sweets after the nautical atmosphere of his harbor town.

At first, the entrepreneur ran Harbor Sweets part-time from his basement, retaining his job in Boston and relying on neighbors in Marblehead to cook the candy and ship it to customers as ordered. When Strohecker lost his job, he decided to put his marketing skills to use in building a special kind of company. "I longed to run a business in which people of all ages, races, and colors, including the physically and mentally handicapped, would be welcome to work," he remembers. "Hours would be flexible to suit individual needs. There would be no secrets. Employees would share in profits, and the financial books would be open for all to see."

Strohecker's first step was to locate a facility where he could make chocolate in larger batches. He refurbished a run-down warehouse a few miles down the road in Salem, Massachusetts, then obtained loans to buy the kitchen equipment he needed. He hired a small core of full-time employees and began adding more part-time employees to help during peak periods such as Christmas and Valentine's Day.

One of those part-timers was Phyllis LeBlanc, a college student who dipped chocolate at Harbor Sweets starting in 1977 to help pay her way through Salem State College. By the time she graduated, she had been promoted to marketing manager of the company's wholesale division. With Strohecker as her mentor, LeBlanc worked her way up to executive vice president and chief operating officer, and she was named president in 1993. By 1998, Harbor Sweets was sailing along at $3 million in annual sales, and Strohecker was ready to sell. LeBlanc bought the business and continued to follow the founder's management philosophy.

Now Sweet Sloops, Marblehead Mints, and Dark Horse Chocolates are just three of the luscious hand-dipped candies made by the firm's 150 employees, who range in age from sixteen to over sixty-five. Employees can choose from two different four-hour work shifts, but they must work at least twenty hours per week. Because they are cross-trained, employees can handle a variety of tasks, and they are encouraged to contribute new product ideas and to help solve problems. Most important, LeBlanc, like Strohecker, believes in trusting employees. "Trust is the most powerful management tool that I've ever known," the founder says. "If I trust you and you know that I trust you, I've put a burden on your shoulders, and you're not going to violate that trust." This foundation of trust has put Harbor Sweets on course for smooth sailing in the candy industry.[21]

Questions

1. Which motivation theory or theories explains how trust motivates employees at Harbor Sweets?
2. Which of the needs in Maslow's hierarchy is fulfilled by mentoring?
3. Are trust and mentoring motivation factors or hygiene factors? Why?

Building skills for career success

1. Exploring the Internet

There are few employee incentives as motivating as owning "a piece of the action." Either through profit sharing or equity, many firms realize that the opportunity to share in the wealth generated by their effort is a primary force to drive employees towards better performance and sense of ownership. The Foundation for Enterprise Development (http://www.fed.org/) is a nonprofit organization dedicated to helping entrepreneurs and executives use employee ownership and equity compensation as a fair and effective means of motivating the work force and improving corporate performance. You can learn more about this approach at their site. Visit the text web site for updates to this exercise.

Assignment

1. Describe the content and services provided by the Foundation for Enterprise Development through their web site.
2. Do you agree with this orientation towards motivation of employees/owners or does it seem contrived to you? Discuss.
3. How else might employees be motivated to improve their performance?

2. Developing Critical Thinking Skills

This chapter has described several theories managers can use as guidelines in motivating employees to do the best job possible for the company. Among these theories are Maslow's hierarchy of needs, equity theory, expectancy theory, and goal-setting theory. How effective would each of these theories be in motivating you to be a more productive employee?

Assignment

1. Identify five job needs that are important to you.
2. Determine which of the theories mentioned above would work best to satisfy your job needs.
3. Prepare a two-page report explaining how you reached these conclusions.

3. Building Team Skills

By increasing employees' participation in decision making, empowerment makes workers feel more involved in their jobs and the operations of the organization. While empowerment may seem like a common-sense idea, it is a concept not universally found in the workplace. If you had empowerment in your job, how would you describe it?

Assignment

1. Use brainstorming to explore the concept of empowerment.
   a. Write each letter of the word *empowerment* in a vertical column on a sheet of paper or on the classroom chalkboard.
   b. Think of several words that begin with each letter.
   c. Write the words next to the appropriate letter.
2. Formulate a statement by choosing one word from each letter that best describes what empowerment means to you.
3. Analyze the statement.
   a. How relevant is the statement for you in terms of empowerment? Or empowerment in your workplace?
   b. What changes must occur in your workplace for you to have empowerment?
   c. How would you describe yourself as an empowered employee?
   d. What opportunities would empowerment give you in your workplace?
4. Prepare a report of your findings.

4. Researching Different Careers

Because a manager's job varies from department to department within firms, as well as among firms, it is virtually impossible to write a generic description of a manager's job. If you are contemplating becoming a manager, you may find it very helpful to spend time on the job with several managers learning firsthand what they do.

Assignment

1. Make an appointment with managers in three firms, preferably firms of different sizes. When you make the appointments, request a tour of the facilities.
2. Ask the managers the following questions:
   a. What do you do in your job?
   b. What do you like most and least about your job? Why?
   c. What skills do you need in your job?
   d. How much education does your job require?
   e. What advice do you have for someone thinking about pursuing a career in management?
3. Summarize your findings in a two-page report. Include answers to questions:
   a. Is management a realistic field of study for you? Why?
   b. What might be a better career choice? Why?

5. Improving Communication Skills

Suppose you and a friend went into the auto repair business some years ago. You had the technical expertise, and he had the business knowledge. Although funds were tight for the first three years, your customer base grew, and you were able to hire extra help and expand business hours. Your business is now six years old and very successful. You have five people working under you. Henry, your most productive employee, wants to be promoted to a supervisory position. However, two other employees, Jack and Fred, have seniority over Henry, and you anticipate much dissension and poor morale if you go ahead and promote Henry. Henry clearly deserves the supervisory position because of his hard work and superior skills, but you stand to lose the other two employees if you promote him.

Assignment

1. Analyze the scenario, and answer these questions:
   a. Will you promote Henry? If so, why?
   b. How can you motivate Jack and Fred to stay with you if you promote Henry?
2. Refer to specific motivational techniques or theories to explain your reasoning in resolving the situation with Henry, Jack, and Fred.
3. Prepare a three-page report outlining and justifying your decision.

Enhancing Union-Management Relations

12

LEARNING OBJECTIVES

1 Explain how and why labor unions came into being.

2 Discuss the sources of unions' negotiating power and trends in union membership.

3 Identify the main focus of several major pieces of labor-management legislation.

4 Enumerate the steps involved in forming a union, and show how the National Labor Relations Board is involved in the process.

5 Describe the basic elements in the collective bargaining process.

6 Identify the major issues covered in a union-management contract.

7 Explain the primary bargaining tools available to unions and management.

The NLRB decided to allow the meat-cutters to vote, and a majority voted to unionize.

inside business

Union-Management Tug of War at Wal-Mart

WAL-MART'S 885,000 U.S. employees are an attractive target for union organizers. However, the world's largest retailer is resolutely nonunion, saying its benefits and profit-sharing plan make union representation unnecessary. "We're not saying unions aren't good for some companies," comments a company spokesperson, "we're saying they have no place at Wal-Mart."

Nearly thirty years ago, the Teamsters tried to organize Wal-Mart warehouse workers in Arkansas. The company fought back by setting up a bulletin board with dozens of newspaper clippings describing allegedly illegal Teamster activities. Founder Sam Walton also came down to talk with employees. That organizing attempt, like so many that followed, failed. Now a union has won its battle for recognition in some company stores—with an unforeseen outcome.

The United Food and Commercial Workers union (UFCW) had tried, unsuccessfully, to organize Wal-Mart employees since the chain began selling groceries in its Supercenters a decade ago. Then a Wal-Mart butcher working in Jacksonville, Texas, contacted the union, seeking help in getting higher pay. The UFCW organizer showed the butcher that unionized meat-cutters working for another chain in a nearby town earned almost $5 more in hourly pay. They also enjoyed employer-paid medical insurance coverage and a retirement plan. The butcher immediately signed a union card and began telling his coworkers about the union.

Eleven of the Jacksonville meat-cutters filed papers with the National Labor Relations Board, seeking the right to vote on union representation. Wal-Mart objected, stating that all the employees in the store should vote in the election, not just the meat-cutters. According to published reports, management also began meeting with small groups of store employees, telling them that union representation could mean lower wages and benefits.

The NLRB decided to allow the meat-cutters to vote, and a majority voted to unionize. One week later, Wal-Mart raised objections to a union-vote petition by meat-cutters in another Texas store. Then it made an announcement that changed the entire situation.

In an effort to improve meat sales, Wal-Mart said it planned to switch from cutting meat in its Supercenter stores to buying prepackaged meat from outside suppliers. A Wal-Mart spokesperson insisted, "This decision was in no way related to the Jacksonville situation This is the way the whole industry is going." The union disagreed, intensifying its tug of war with Wal-Mart management.[1]

Wal-Mart management strives to avoid unionization. Some companies have been unionized for years and have experienced ups and downs for both management and the unions. Many businesses today have highly cooperative relationships with labor unions. A **labor union** is an organization of workers acting together to negotiate their wages and working conditions with employers. In the United States, nonmanagement employees have the legal right to form unions and to bargain, as a group, with management. The result of the bargaining process is a *labor contract*, a written agreement that is in force for a set period of time (usually one to three years). The dealings between labor unions and business management, both in the bargaining process and beyond it, are called **union-management relations** or, more simply, **labor relations**.

labor union an organization of workers acting together to negotiate their wages and working conditions with employers

union-management (labor) relations the dealings between labor unions and business management, both in the bargaining process and beyond it

Because labor and management have different goals, they tend to be at odds with each other. But these goals must be attained by the same means—through the production of goods and services. At contract bargaining sessions, the two groups must work together to attain their goals. Perhaps mainly for this reason, antagonism now seems to be giving way to cooperation in union-management relations.

We open this chapter by reviewing the history of labor unions in this country. Then we turn our attention to organized labor today, noting current membership trends and union-management partnerships and summarizing important labor-relations laws. We discuss the unionization process, why employees join unions, how a union is formed, and what the National Labor Relations Board does. Collective bargaining procedures are then explained. Next we consider issues in union-management contracts, including employee pay, working hours, security, management rights, and grievance procedures. We close with a discussion of various labor and management negotiating techniques: strikes, slowdowns and boycotts, lockouts, mediation, and arbitration.

LEARNING OBJECTIVE

1 Explain how and why labor unions came into being.

The Historical Development of Unions

Until the middle of the nineteenth century, there was very little organization of labor in this country. Groups of workers did occasionally form a **craft union**, an organization of skilled workers in a single craft or trade. These alliances were usually limited to a single city, and they often lasted only a short time. In 1786, the first known strike in the United States involved a group of Philadelphia printers who stopped working over demands for higher wages. When the employers granted the printers a pay increase, the group disbanded.

craft union an organization of skilled workers in a single craft or trade

Early History

In the mid-1800s, improved transportation opened new markets for manufactured goods. Improved manufacturing methods made it possible to supply those markets, and American industry began to grow. The Civil War and the continued growth of the railroads after the war led to further industrial expansion.

Large-scale production required more and more skilled industrial workers. As the skilled labor force grew, craft unions emerged in the more industrialized areas. From these craft unions, three significant labor organizations evolved. (See Figure 12.1 for a historical overview of unions and their patterns of membership.)

Knights of Labor

The first significant national labor organization to emerge was the Knights of Labor, which was formed as a secret society in 1869 by Uriah Stephens, a utopian reformer and abolitionist from Philadelphia. Membership reached approximately 700,000 by 1886. One major goal of the Knights was to eliminate the depersonalization of the worker that resulted from mass-production technology. Another was to improve the moral standards of both employees and society. To the detriment of the group, its leaders concentrated so intently on social and economic change that they did not recognize the effects of technological change. Moreover, they assumed that all employees had the same goals as the Knights' leaders—social and moral reform. The major reason for the demise

The Haymarket riot of 1886. The Haymarket riot, one of the most violent in labor history, was one of the main reasons for the decline of the Knights of Labor.

of the Knights was the Haymarket riot of 1886. At a rally (called to demand a reduction in the length of a workday from ten to eight hours) in Chicago's Haymarket Square, a bomb exploded. Several police officers and civilians were killed or wounded. The Knights were not directly implicated, but they quickly lost public favor.

American Federation of Labor In 1886 several leaders of the Knights joined with independent craft unions to form the *American Federation of Labor (AFL).* Samuel Gompers, one of the AFL's founders, became its first president. Gompers believed that the goals of the union should be those of its members rather than those of its leaders. The AFL did not seek to change the existing business system, as the Knights of Labor had. Instead, its goal was to improve its members' living standards within that system.

strike a temporary work stoppage by employees, calculated to add force to their demands

Another major difference between the Knights of Labor and the AFL was in their positions regarding strikes. A **strike** is a temporary work stoppage by employees, calcu-

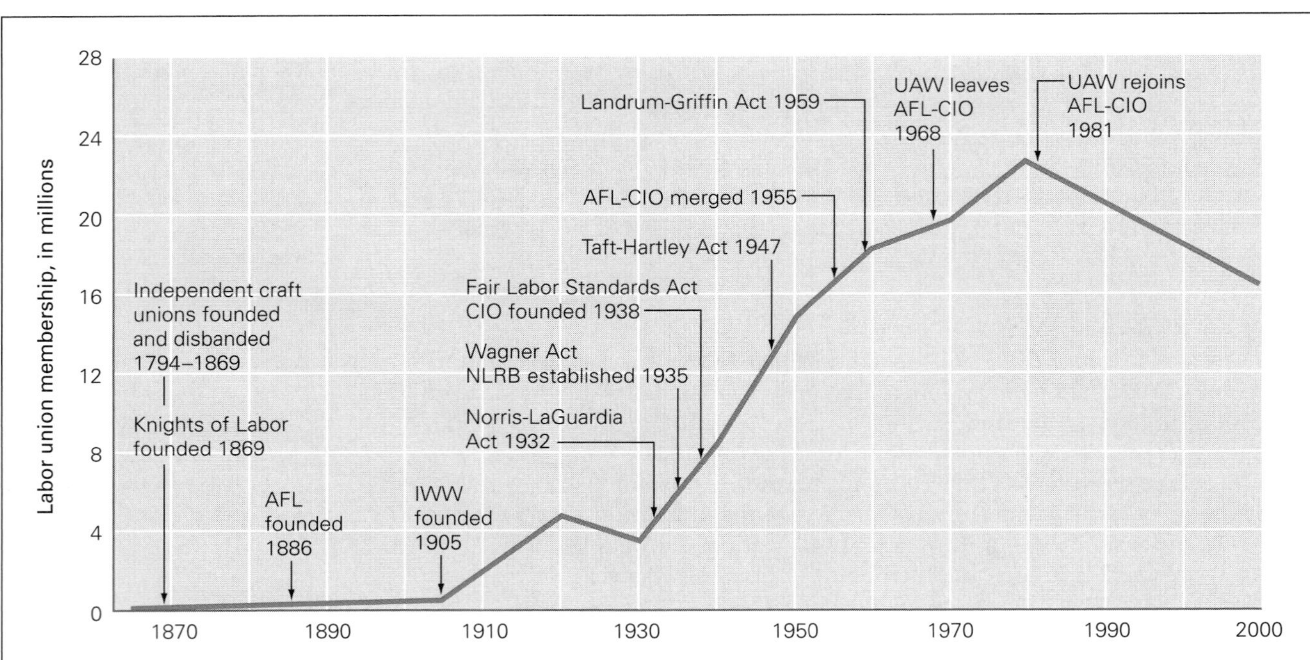

figure 12.1

Historical Overview of Unions

The total number of members for all unions has risen dramatically since 1869, when the first truly national union was organized. The dates of major events in the history of labor unions are singled out along the line of membership change.

Sources: U.S. Bureau of Labor Statistics, *Dictionary of U.S. Labor Organizations*, 1986–1987; Aaron Bernstein, "Why America Needs Unions," *Business Week*, May 23, 1994, p. 70; www.aflcio.org/publ/press2000.

lated to add force to their demands. The Knights did not favor the use of strikes, whereas the AFL strongly believed that striking was an effective labor weapon. The AFL also believed that organized labor should play a major role in politics. As we will see, the AFL is still very much a part of the American labor scene.

Industrial Workers of the World The *Industrial Workers of the World (IWW)* was created in 1905 as a radical alternative to the AFL. Among its goals was the overthrow of capitalism. This revolutionary stance prevented the IWW from gaining much of a foothold. Perhaps its major accomplishment was to make the AFL seem, by comparison, less threatening to the general public and to business leaders.

Evolution of Contemporary Labor Organizations

Between 1900 and 1920 both business and government attempted to keep labor unions from growing. This period was plagued by strikes and violent confrontations between management and unions. In steelworks, garment factories, and auto plants, clashes took place in which striking union members fought bitterly against nonunion workers, police, and private security guards.

The AFL continued to be the major force in organized labor. By 1920 its membership included 75 percent of all those who had joined unions. Throughout its existence, however, the AFL had been unsure of the best way to deal with unskilled and semiskilled workers. Most of its members were skilled workers in specific crafts or trades. But technological changes during World War I had brought about a significant increase in the number of unskilled and semiskilled employees in the work force. These people sought to join the AFL, but they were not well received by its established membership.

Some unions within the AFL did recognize the need to organize unskilled and semiskilled workers, and they began to penetrate the automotive and steel industries. The type of union they formed was an **industrial union**, an organization of both skilled and unskilled workers in a single industry. Soon workers in the rubber, mining, newspaper, and communications industries were also organized into unions. Eventually, these unions left the AFL and formed the *Congress of Industrial Organizations (CIO)*.

industrial union an organization of both skilled and unskilled workers in a single industry

During this same time (the late 1930s), there was a major upswing in rank-and-file membership—in the AFL, CIO, and independent unions. Strong union leadership, the development of effective negotiating tactics, and favorable legislation combined to increase total union membership to 9 million in 1940. At this point, the CIO began to rival the AFL in size and influence. There was another bitter rivalry: the AFL and CIO often clashed over which of them had the right to organize and represent particular groups of employees.

Since World War II, the labor scene has gone through a number of changes. For one thing, during and after the war years there was a downturn in public opinion regarding unions. A few isolated but very visible strikes during the war caused public sentiment to shift against unionism. Perhaps the most significant occurrence, however, was the merger of the AFL and the CIO. After years of bickering, the two groups recognized that they were wasting effort and resources by fighting each other and that a merger would greatly increase the strength of both. The merger took place on December 5, 1955. The resulting organization, called the *AFL-CIO*, had a membership of as many as 16 million workers, which made it the largest labor organization of its kind in the world. Its first president was George Meany, who served until 1979.

Organized Labor Today

LEARNING OBJECTIVE

2 Discuss the sources of unions' negotiating power and trends in union membership.

The power of unions to negotiate effectively with management is derived from two sources. The first is their membership. The more workers a union represents within an industry, the greater its clout in dealing with firms operating in that industry. The second source of union power is the group of laws that guarantee unions the right to negotiate and, at the same time, regulate the negotiating process.

Union Membership

At present, union members account for a relatively small portion of the American work force: approximately 14.5 percent of the nation's workers belong to unions. Union membership is concentrated in a few industries and job categories. Within these industries, though, unions wield considerable power.

The AFL-CIO is still the largest union organization in this country, boasting approximately 13.1 million members. Those represented by the AFL-CIO include actors, barbers, construction workers, carpenters, retail clerks, musicians, teachers, postal workers, painters, steel and iron workers, firefighters, bricklayers, and newspaper reporters. Figure 12.2 shows the organization of the AFL-CIO.

One of the largest unions not associated directly with the AFL-CIO is the Teamsters Union. The *Teamsters* were originally part of the AFL-CIO, but in 1957 they were expelled for corrupt and illegal practices. The union started out as an organization of professional drivers, but it has recently begun to recruit employees in a wide variety of jobs. Current membership is about 1.3 million workers.

The *United Auto Workers* represents employees in the auto industry. The UAW, too, was originally part of the AFL-CIO, but it left the parent union—of its own accord—in 1968. Currently, the UAW has about 748,000 members. For a while, the Teamsters and the UAW formed a semistructured partnership called the Alliance for Labor Action. This partnership was eventually dissolved, and the UAW again became part of the AFL-CIO in 1981.

Membership Trends

The proportion of union members, relative to the size of the nation's work force, has declined over the last thirty years. Moreover, total union membership has dropped since 1980, despite steadily increasing membership in earlier years (see Figure 12.1). To a great extent, this decline in membership is caused by changing trends in business, like the following:

- Heavily unionized industries have either been decreasing in size or have not been growing as fast as nonunionized industries. For example, recent cutbacks in the steel industry have tended to reduce union membership. At the same time, the growth of high-tech industries has increased the ranks of nonunion workers.
- Many firms have moved from the heavily unionized Northeast and Great Lakes regions to the less unionized Southeast and Southwest—the so-called Sunbelt. At the relocated plants, formerly unionized firms tend to hire nonunion workers.
- The largest growth in employment is occurring in the service industries, and these industries are typically not unionized.
- Some U.S. companies have moved their manufacturing operations to other countries where less unionized labor is employed.
- Management is providing benefits that tend to reduce employees' need for unionization. Increased employee participation and better wages and working conditions are goals of unions. When these benefits are already supplied by management, workers are less likely to join existing unions or start new ones. The number of elections to vote on forming new unions was 3,229 in 1998, down from 7,000 per year during the 1970s. The unions usually win about half of the elections.[2]

spotlight

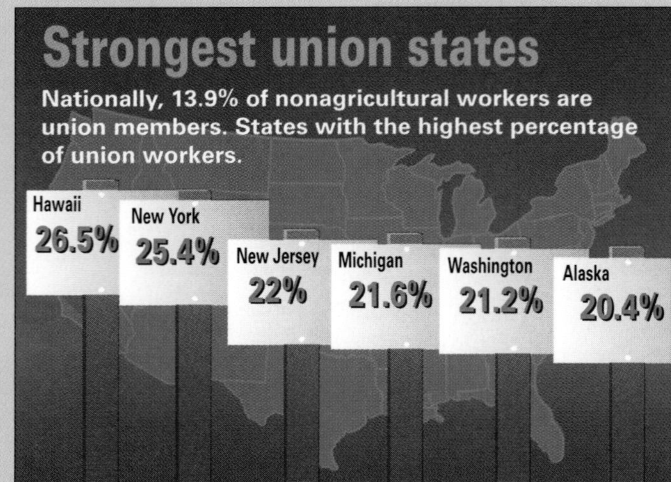

Source: Copyright 2000, USA TODAY. Reprinted with permission.

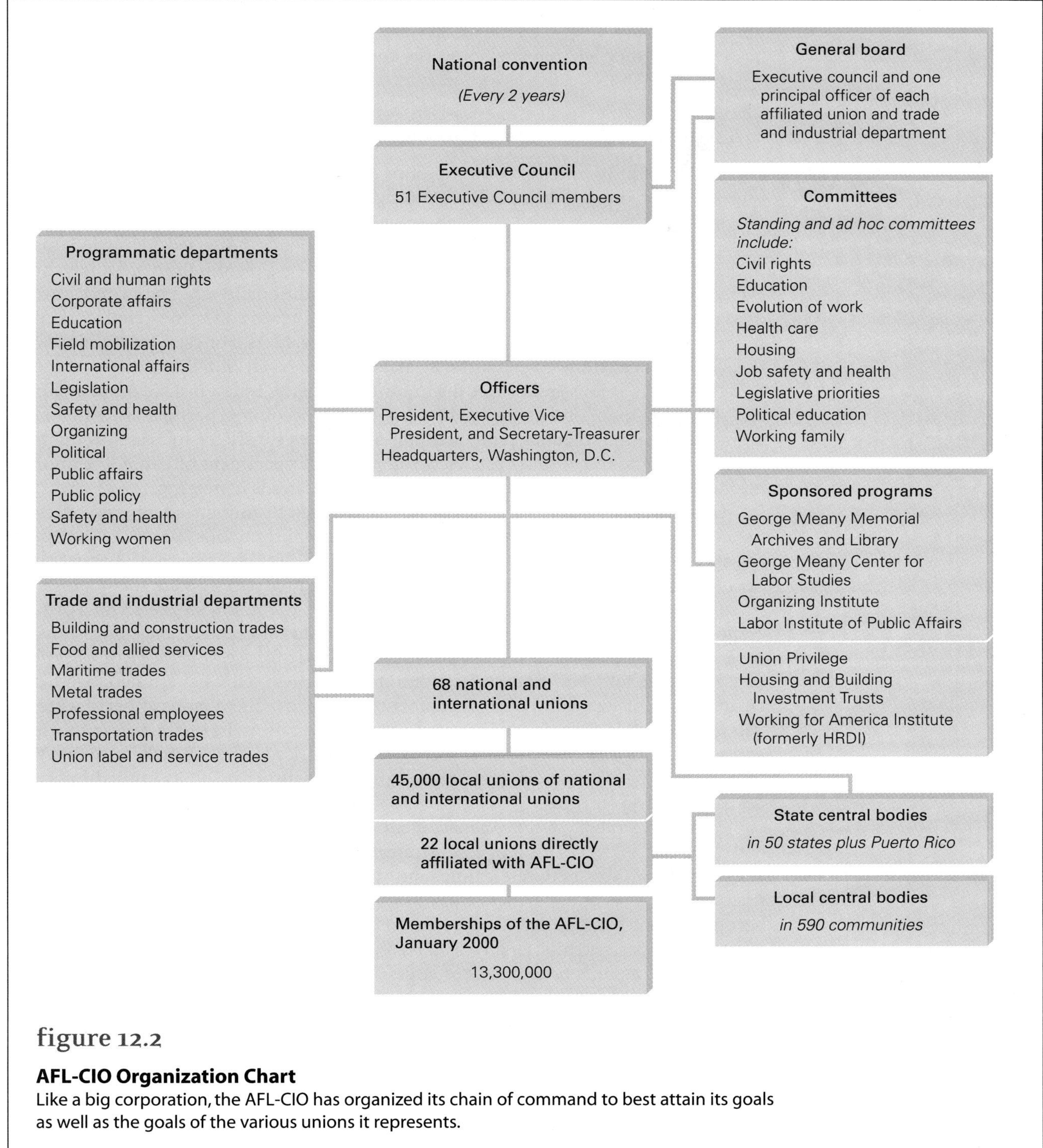

figure 12.2

AFL-CIO Organization Chart
Like a big corporation, the AFL-CIO has organized its chain of command to best attain its goals as well as the goals of the various unions it represents.

Source: Adapted from American Federation of Labor and Congress of Industrial Organizations, "How the AFL-CIO Works," www.aflcio.org, April 10, 2000.

- According to Allan Greenspan, chairman of the Federal Reserve, American labor laws and culture allow for the quicker displacement of unneeded workers and their replacement with those that are in demand, whereas labor laws in other countries tend to take longer for the change to take place. As a result the Internet and high-technology in general are contributing to a greater increase in worker productivity in the United States in comparison to Asia and Europe.[3]

It remains to be seen whether unions will be able to regain the prominence and power they enjoyed between the world wars and during the 1950s. There is little doubt, however, that they will remain a powerful force in particular industries.

Union-Management Partnerships

For most of the twentieth century, unions have represented workers with respect to wages and working conditions. To obtain rights for workers and recognition for themselves, unions have engaged in often-antagonistic collective-bargaining sessions and strikes. At the same time, management has traditionally protected its own rights of decision making, workplace organization, and strategic planning. Increasingly, however, management has become aware that this traditionally adversarial relationship does not result in the kind of high-performance workplace and empowered work force necessary to succeed in today's highly competitive markets. For their part, unions and their members acknowledge that most major strikes result in failures that cost members thousands of jobs and reduce the union's credibility. Today, instead of maintaining an "us-versus-them" mentality, many unions are becoming partners with management, cooperating to enhance the workplace, empower workers, increase production, improve quality, and reduce costs. According to the Department of Labor, the number of union-management partnerships in the United States is increasing.

Union-management partnerships can be initiated by union leaders, employees, or management. *Limited* partnerships center on accomplishing one specific task or project, such as the introduction of teams or the design of training programs. For example, Levi Strauss formed a limited partnership with its employees who are members of the Amalgamated Clothing and Textile Workers Union; the union workers will assist the company in setting up team operations in its nonunion plants.[4] *Long-range strategic* partnerships focus on sharing decision-making power for a whole range of workplace and business issues. For example, eight unions in the AFL-CIO have joined together to create a partnership with Kaiser Permanente to improve the quality of health care. At two new hospitals, they have designed the way the work is to be organized on the floor, and how nurses and ancillary staff members will work together to make sure that they provide quality care.[5] Long-range partnerships sometimes begin as limited ones and develop slowly over time.

Although strategic union-management partnerships vary, most of them have several characteristics in common. First, strategic partnerships focus on developing cooperative relationships between unions and management instead of arguing over contractual rights. Second, partners work toward mutual gain, in which the organization becomes more competitive, employees are better off, and unions are stronger as a result of the partnership. Finally, as already noted, strategic partners engage in joint decision making on a broad array of issues.[6] These issues include performance expectations, organizational structure, strategic alliances, new technology, pay and benefits, employee security and involvement, union-management roles, product development, and education and training.

Good labor management relations can help everyone deal with new and difficult labor issues as they develop. For example, according to the U.S. Bureau of Labor Statistics, the highest median number of work days lost among all work-related ailments is from carpal tunnel syndrome, a muscular affliction often associated with computer keyboard workers. Like back pain, this ailment is not detectable by medical testing and is only known through self-reporting. Although carpal tunnel syndrome accounts for less than 2 percent of work-related conditions, almost half of all cases result in thirty-one days or more of work loss.[7]

Union-management partnerships have many potential benefits for management, workers, and unions. For management, partnerships can result in lower costs, increased revenue, improved product quality, and greater customer satisfaction. For workers, benefits may include increased response to their needs, more decision-making opportunities, less supervision, more responsibility, and increased job security. Unions can gain credibility, strength, and increased membership.

Among the many organizations that have found union-management partnerships beneficial is Saturn. The labor-management partnership between the Saturn Corporation and the United Auto Workers (UAW) is one of the boldest experiments in U.S. industrial relations today. It was created through a joint design effort that included the UAW as a full partner in decisions regarding product, technology, suppliers, retailers, site selection, business planning, training, quality systems, job design, and manufacturing systems. This partnership has resulted in a dense communications network throughout the company's management system as well as improvement in quality performance.[8]

Labor-Management Legislation

LEARNING OBJECTIVE

3 Identify the main focus of several major pieces of labor-management legislation.

As we have noted, business opposed early efforts to organize labor. The federal government generally supported anti-union efforts through the court system, and in some cases federal troops were used to end strikes. Gradually, however, the government began to correct this imbalance through the legislative process.

Norris-LaGuardia Act

The first major piece of legislation to secure rights for unions, the *Norris-LaGuardia Act* of 1932, was considered a landmark in labor-management relations. This act made it difficult for businesses to obtain court orders that banned strikes, picketing, or union membership drives. Previously, courts had issued such orders readily as a means of curbing these activities.

National Labor Relations Act

The *National Labor Relations Act*, also known as the *Wagner Act*, was passed by Congress in 1935. It established procedures by which employees decide whether they want to be represented by a union. If workers choose to be represented, the Wagner Act requires management to negotiate with union representatives. Before this law was passed, union efforts were sometimes interpreted as violating the Sherman Act (1890) because they were viewed as attempts to monopolize. The Wagner Act also forbids certain unfair labor practices on the part of management, such as firing or punishing workers because they are pro-union, spying on union meetings, and bribing employees to vote against unionization.

Finally, the Wagner Act established the **National Labor Relations Board (NLRB)** to enforce the provisions of the law. The NLRB is primarily concerned with (1) overseeing the elections in which employees decide whether they will be represented by a union and (2) investigating complaints lodged by unions or employees. For example, approximately twelve unionized hospital workers at Battle Creek Health Systems were ejected from the hospital cafeteria by hospital administrators when the workers attempted to meet on their time off. The workers were meeting, in part, to discuss improving relations between hospital management and the workers. Unfair labor practice charges were filed with the National Labor Relations Board (NLRB) against the hospital on behalf of the employees. The union asserts that under the NLRB Labor Relations Act, the employees had every right to hold their meeting.[9]

National Labor Relations Board (NLRB) the federal agency that enforces the provisions of the Wagner Act

Using the Internet

The U.S. Department of Labor web site (**http://www.dol.gov/**) provides a good overview of the major issues concerning labor news, legislation, and statistics. There are also links to other web sites focusing on labor issues.

Fair Labor Standards Act

In 1938 Congress enacted the *Fair Labor Standards Act*. One major provision of this act permits the federal government to set a minimum wage. The first minimum wage, which was set in the late

1930s and did not include farm workers and retail employees, was $0.25 an hour. Today the minimum wage is $5.15 an hour. Some employees, such as farm workers, are still exempt from the minimum wage provisions. The act also requires that employees be paid overtime rates for work in excess of forty hours a week. Finally, it prohibits the use of child labor.

Labor-Management Relations Act

The legislation of the 1930s sought to discourage unfair practices on the part of employers. Recall from Figure 12.1 that union membership grew from approximately 2 million in 1910 to almost 12 million by 1945. Unions represented over 35 percent of all nonagricultural employees in 1945. As union membership and power grew, however, the federal government began to examine the practices of labor. Several long and bitter strikes, mainly in the coal mining and trucking industries in the early 1940s, led to a demand for legislative restraint on unions. As a result, in 1947 Congress passed the *Labor-Management Relations Act*, also known as the *Taft-Hartley Act*, over President Harry Truman's veto.

The objective of the Taft-Hartley Act is to provide a balance between union power and management authority. It lists unfair labor practices that unions are forbidden to use. These include refusal to bargain with management in good faith, charging excessive membership dues, harassing nonunion workers, and using various means of coercion against employers.

The Taft-Hartley Act also gives management more rights during union organizing campaigns. For example, management may outline for employees the advantages and disadvantages of union membership, as long as the information it presents is accurate. The act gives the president of the United States the power to obtain a temporary injunction to prevent or stop a strike that endangers national health and safety. An **injunction** is a court order requiring a person or group either to perform some act or to refrain from performing some act. Finally, the Taft-Hartley Act authorized states to enact laws to allow employees to work in a unionized firm without joining the union. About twenty states (many in the South) have passed such *right-to-work laws.*

injunction a court order requiring a person or group either to perform some act or to refrain from performing some act

Landrum-Griffin Act

In the 1950s, Senate investigations and hearings exposed racketeering in unions and uncovered cases of bribery, extortion, and embezzlement among union leaders. It was discovered that a few union leaders had taken union funds for personal use and accepted payoffs from employers for union protection. Some were involved in arson, blackmail, and murder. Public pressure for reform resulted in the 1959 *Landrum-Griffin Act.*

This law was designed to regulate the internal functioning of labor unions. Provisions of the law require unions to file annual reports with the U.S. Department of Labor regarding their finances, elections, and various decisions made by union officers. The Landrum-Griffin Act also ensures each union member the right to seek, nominate, and vote

Opposition to the Taft-Hartley Act. Union leaders and members, along with President Harry Truman, opposed the passage of the Taft-Hartley Act.

for each elected position in his or her union. It provides safeguards governing union funds, and it requires management and unions to report the lending of management funds to union officers, union members, or local unions.

The various pieces of legislation we have reviewed here effectively regulate much of the relationship between labor and management after a union has been established. The next section demonstrates that forming a union is also a carefully regulated process.

The Unionization Process

LEARNING OBJECTIVE

4 Enumerate the steps involved in forming a union, and show how the National Labor Relations Board is involved in the process.

For a union to be formed at a particular firm, some employees of the firm must first be interested in being represented by a union. They must then take a number of steps to formally declare their desire for a union. To ensure fairness, most of the steps in this unionization process are supervised by the NLRB.

Why Some Employees Join Unions

Obviously, employees start or join a union for a variety of reasons. One commonly cited reason is to combat alienation. Some employees—especially those whose jobs are dull and repetitive—may perceive themselves as merely parts of a machine. They may feel they lose their individual or social identity at work. Union membership is one way to establish contact with others in the firm.

Another common reason for joining a union is the perception that union membership increases job security. No one wants to live in fear of arbitrary or capricious dismissal from a job. Unions actually have only limited ability to guarantee a member's job, but they can help increase job security by enforcing seniority rules.

Employees may also join a union because of dissatisfaction with one or more elements of their jobs. If they are unhappy with their pay, benefits, or working conditions, they may look to a union to correct the perceived deficiencies.

Some people join unions because of their personal backgrounds. For example, a person whose parents are strong believers in unions might be inclined to feel just as positive about union membership.

In some situations, employees *must* join a union to keep their jobs. Many unions try, through their labor contracts, to require that a firm's new employees join the union after a specified probationary period. Under the Taft-Hartley Act, states may pass right-to-work laws prohibiting this practice.

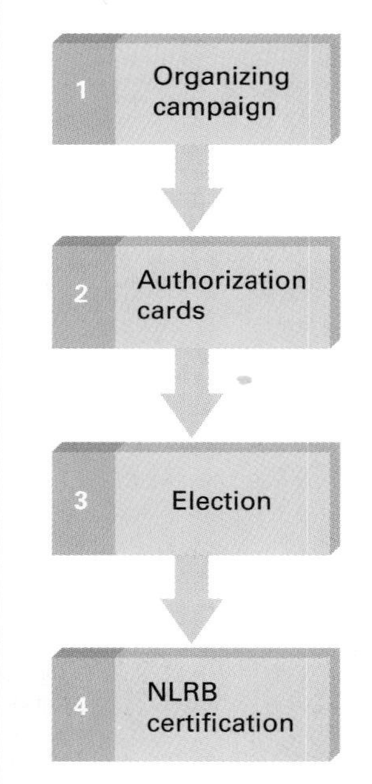

figure 12.3

Steps in Forming a Union

The unionization process consists of a campaign, signing of authorization cards, a formal election, and certification of the election by the National Labor Relations Board.

Steps in Forming a Union

The first step in forming a union is the *organizing campaign* (see Figure 12.3). Its primary objective is to develop widespread employee interest in having a union. To kick off the campaign, a national union may send organizers to the firm to stir this interest. Alternatively, the employees themselves may decide they want a union. Then they contact the appropriate national union and ask for organizing assistance.

The organizing campaign can be quite emotional, and it may lead to conflict between employees and management. On the one hand, the employees who want the union will be dedicated to its creation. On the other hand, management will be extremely sensitive to what it sees as a potential threat to its power and control.

At some point during the organizing campaign, employees are asked to sign *authorization cards* (see Figure 12.4) to indicate—in writing—their support for the union. Because of various NLRB rules and regulations, both union organizers and company management must be very careful in their behavior during this authorization drive. For example, employees cannot be asked to sign the cards when they are supposed to be working. And management may not indicate in any way that employees' jobs or job security will be in jeopardy if they *do* sign the cards.

figure 12.4

Sample Authorization Card

Unions must have written authorization to represent employees.

OBLIGATION OF

"I, ..., in the
(PLEASE PRINT NAME)

presence of members of the

promise and agree to conform to and abide by the Constitution and laws of the and its Local Unions. I will further the purposes for which the is instituted. I will bear true allegiance to it and will not sacrifice its interest in any manner."

FORM 107 REV. 9-94 125

TO BE SIGNED BY APPLICANT — PLEASE DO NOT PRINT

PRINT OR TYPE IN BLACK INK ONLY — SEX—MALE ☐ FEMALE ☐

LAST NAME	FIRST	INITIAL	SOCIAL SECURITY NO.
ADDRESS (STREET & NUMBER)			DATE OF BIRTH
CITY & STATE (OR PROVINCE)		POSTAL CODE	TELEPHONE NO.
PRESENT EMPLOYER			DATE HIRED
CLASSIFICATION			DATE OF THIS APPLICATION

HAVE YOU EVER BEEN A MEMBER OF ?	YES ☐ NO ☐	IF SO, WHERE?	LOCAL NO.	STATE

PORTION BELOW TO BE FILLED IN BY L.U. SECRETARY

LOCAL UNION NO.	DATE OF INITIATION	TYPE OF MEMBERSHIP	CARD NO.

If at least 30 percent of the eligible employees sign authorization cards, the organizers generally request that the firm recognize the union as the employees' bargaining representative. Usually the firm rejects this request, and a *formal election* is held to decide whether to have a union. This election usually involves secret ballots and is conducted by the NLRB. The outcome of the election is determined by a simple majority of eligible employees who choose to vote.

If the union obtains a majority, it becomes the official bargaining agent for its members and the final step, *NLRB certification*, takes place. The union may immediately begin the process of negotiating a labor contract with management. If the union is voted down, the NLRB will not allow another election for one year.

bargaining unit the specific group of employees represented by a union

Several factors can complicate the unionization process. For example, the **bargaining unit**, which is the specific group of employees that the union is to represent, must be defined. Union organizers may want to represent all hourly employees at a particular site (such as all workers at a manufacturing plant). Or they may wish to represent only a specific group of employees (such as all electricians in a large manufacturing plant).

jurisdiction the right of a particular union to organize particular workers

Another issue that may have to be resolved is that of **jurisdiction**, which is the right of a particular union to organize particular groups of workers (such as nurses). When jurisdictions overlap or are unclear, the employees themselves may decide who will represent them. In some cases, two or more unions may be trying to organize some or all of the employees of a firm. Then the election choices may be union A, union B, or no union at all.

The Role of The NLRB

As we have demonstrated, the NLRB is heavily involved in the unionization process. Generally, the NLRB is responsible for overseeing the organizing campaign, conducting the election (if one is warranted), and certifying the election results.

During the organizing campaign, both employers and union organizers can take steps to educate employees regarding the advantages and disadvantages of having a union. However, neither is allowed to use underhanded tactics or to distort the truth. If violations occur, the NLRB can stop the questionable behavior, postpone the election, or set aside the results of an election that has already taken place.

The NLRB usually conducts the election within forty-five days of receiving the required number of signed authorization cards from the organizers. A very high percentage of the eligible voters generally participates in the election, and it is held at the workplace during normal working hours. In certain cases, however, a mail ballot or other form of election may be called for.

Certification of the election involves counting the votes and considering challenges to the election. After the election results are announced, management and the union organizers have five days in which to challenge the election. The basis for a challenge might be improper conduct prior to the election or participation by an ineligible voter. After considering any challenges, the NLRB passes final judgment on the election results.

When union representation is established, union and management get down to the serious business of contract negotiations.

Collective Bargaining

LEARNING OBJECTIVE

5 Describe the basic elements in the collective bargaining process.

Once certified by the NLRB, a new union's first task is to establish its own identity and structure. It immediately signs up as many members as possible. Then, in an internal election, members choose officers and representatives. A negotiating committee is also chosen to begin **collective bargaining**, the process of negotiating a labor contract with management.

collective bargaining the process of negotiating a labor contract with management

The First Contract

To prepare for its first contract session with management, the negotiating committee decides on its position on the various contract issues and determines the issues that are most important to the union's members. For example, the two most pressing concerns might be a general wage increase and an improved benefits package.

The union then informs management it is ready to begin negotiations, and the two parties agree on a time and location. Both sides continue to prepare for the session up until the actual date of the negotiations.

Negotiations are occasionally held on company premises, but it is more common for the parties to meet away from the workplace—perhaps in a local hotel. The union is typically represented by the negotiating committee and one or more officials from the regional or national union office. The firm is normally represented by managers from the industrial-relations, operations, HRM, and legal departments. Each side is required by law to negotiate in good faith and not to stall or attempt to extend the bargaining proceedings unnecessarily.

The union normally presents its contract demands first. Management then responds to the demands, often with a counterproposal. The bargaining may move back and forth, from proposal to counterproposal, over a number of meetings. Throughout the process, union representatives constantly keep their members informed of what is going on and how the negotiating committee feels about the various proposals and counterproposals.

Each side clearly tries to "get its own way" as much as possible, but each also recognizes the need for compromise. For example, the union may begin the negotiations by demanding a wage increase of $1 per hour but may be willing to accept 60 cents per hour. Management may initially offer 40 cents but may be willing to pay 75 cents. Eventually, the two sides will agree on a wage increase of between 60 and 75 cents per hour.

If an agreement cannot be reached, the union may strike. Strikes are rare during a union's first contract negotiations. In most cases, the negotiating teams are able to agree on an initial contract without recourse to a strike.

ratification approval of a labor contract by a vote of the union membership

The final step in collective bargaining is **ratification**, which is approval of the contract by a vote of the union membership. If the membership accepts the terms of the contract, it is signed and becomes a legally binding agreement. If the contract is not ratified, the negotiators must go back and try to iron out a more acceptable agreement.

Later Contracts

A labor contract may cover a period of one to three years or more, but every contract has an expiration date. As that date approaches, both management and the union begin to prepare for new contract negotiations. Now, however, the entire process is likely to be much thornier than the first negotiation.

For one thing, the union and the firm have "lived with each other" for several years, during which some difficulties may have emerged. Each side may see certain issues as being of critical importance—issues that provoke a great deal of emotion at the bargaining table and are often difficult to resolve. For another thing, each side has learned from the earlier negotiations. Each may take a harder line on certain issues and be less willing to compromise.

The contract deadline itself also produces tension. As the expiration date of the existing contract draws near, each side feels pressure—real or imagined—to reach an agreement. This pressure may nudge the negotiators toward agreement, but it can also have the opposite effect, making an accord more difficult to reach. Moreover, at some point during the negotiations, union leaders are likely to take a *strike vote*. This vote reveals whether union members are willing to strike in the event that a new contract is not negotiated before the old one expires. In almost all cases, this vote supports a strike. So the threat of a strike may add to the pressure mounting on both sides as they go about the business of negotiating.

Union-Management Contract Issues

LEARNING OBJECTIVE

6 Identify the major issues covered in a union-management contract.

As you might expect, many diverse issues are negotiated by unions and management and are incorporated into a labor contract. Unions tend to emphasize issues related to members' income, their standard of living, and the strength of the union. Management's primary goals are to retain as much control as possible over the firm's operations and to maximize its strength relative to that of the union. The balance of power between union and management varies from firm to firm.

Employee Pay

An area of bargaining central to union-management relations is employee pay. Three separate issues are usually involved: the forms of pay, the magnitude of pay, and the means by which the magnitude of pay will be determined.

Forms of Pay The primary form of pay is direct compensation—the wage or salary and benefits an employee receives in exchange for his or her contribution to the organization. Because direct compensation is a fairly straightforward issue, negotiators often spend much more of their time developing a benefits package for employees. And, as the range of benefits and their costs have escalated over the years, this element of pay has become increasingly important and complex.

Exploring Business

White-Collar Contract Issues at Boeing

When thousands of unionized engineers and technical workers went out on strike against Boeing in 2000, they were seeking more than better pay and benefits—they also wanted more respect. The 15,000 white-collar strikers worked on new aircraft design, not on the assembly line. Some never thought they'd join a union, let alone walk a picket line. But after negotiations toward a new three-year contract stalled, the Society of Professional Engineering Employees in Aerospace (SPEEA) called a strike, and union members began picketing Boeing facilities.

One major issue was pay. The union wanted a guaranteed package of yearly raises, inflation adjustments, and bonuses similar to the pay package negotiated by the machinists union for Boeing's production workers. The company offered selective pay increases based on merit, and said it lacked the money to pay bonuses to professional and technical employees.

Another major issue was benefits. The union wanted to maintain the current life and health insurance coverage and payments. Boeing wanted to lower the life insurance benefits and raise the health insurance premiums and co-payments.

Yet another issue was where the engineers and technical employees fit within Boeing. As the company refocused on new financial targets, the workers felt they were not as highly prized as in the past. This issue complicated the negotiations over the more tangible issues.

The white-collar strike dragged on while management and union officials held talks. Meanwhile, because the striking workers were responsible for approving changes to airplane designs, production and deliveries slowed considerably. The situation became even more tense when some striking engineers publicly questioned Boeing's ability to ensure the safety of its jets during the walkout.

During the sixth week of the strike, federal mediators brought Boeing and SPEEA negotiators together for more intense bargaining. The two sides reached an agreement that gave the union's members nearly everything they wanted. Boeing's CEO also announced a new task force to monitor workplace issues, saying that management had gained a greater appreciation for the concerns of its employees.

We discussed the various employee benefits in Chapter 10. Of these, health, life, disability, and dental insurance are important benefits that unions try to obtain for their members. Deferred compensation, in the form of pension or retirement programs, is also a common focal point.

Other benefits commonly dealt with in the bargaining process include paid vacation time, holidays, and a policy on paid sick leave. Obviously, unions argue for as much paid vacation and holiday time as possible and for liberal sick-leave policies. Management naturally takes the opposite position.

Magnitude of Pay Of considerable importance is the *magnitude*, or amount, of pay that employees receive as both direct and indirect compensation. The union attempts to ensure that pay is on par with that received by other employees in the same or similar industries, both locally and nationally. The union also attempts to include in the contract clauses that provide pay increases over the life of the agreement. The most common is the *cost-of-living clause*, which ties periodic pay increases to increases in the cost of living, as defined by various economic statistics or indicators.

Of course, the magnitude of pay is also affected by the organization's ability to pay. If the firm has recently posted large profits, the union may expect large pay increases for its members. If the firm has not been very profitable, the union may agree to

spotLight

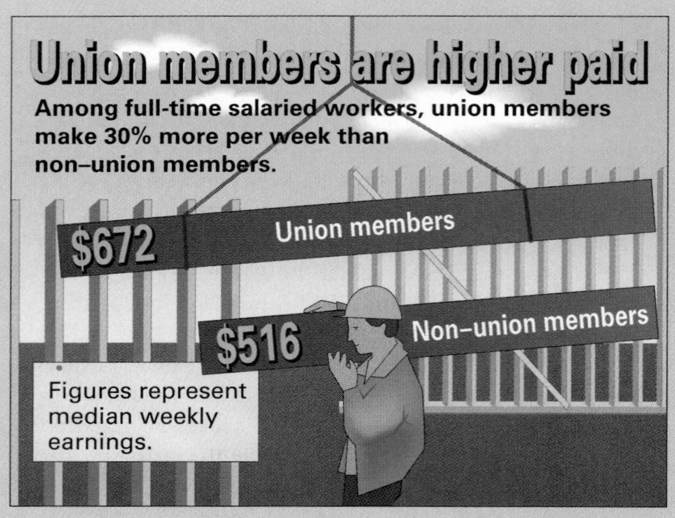

Source: U.S. Dept. of Labor, Bureau of Labor Statistics, *Union Membership* (Annual), Table 2.

smaller pay hikes or even to a pay freeze. In an extreme situation (for example, when the firm is bordering on bankruptcy), the union may agree to pay cuts. Very stringent conditions are usually included in any agreement to a pay cut.

A by-product of the boon in Internet and information technology employment is the high demand for highly skilled workers in a fast-changing work environment. Interestingly, many high-technology workers fear losing their jobs and with it, access to learning about new knowledge and skills. The result is somewhat of a counterbalance to the salary and wage demands in this sector of the economy.[10]

Bargaining with regard to magnitude also revolves around employee benefits. At one extreme, unions seek a wide range of benefits, entirely or largely paid for by the firm. At the other extreme, management may be willing to offer the benefits package but may want its employees to bear most of the cost. Again, factors such as equity (with similar firms and jobs) and ability to pay enter into the final agreement.

Pay Determinants Negotiators also address the question of how individual pay will be determined. For management, the ideal arrangement is to tie wages to each employee's productivity. As we saw, this method of payment tends to motivate and reward effort. Unions, on the other hand, feel this arrangement can create unnecessary competition among employees. They generally argue that employees should be paid—at least in part—according to seniority. **Seniority** is the length of time an employee has worked for the organization.

seniority the length of time an employee has worked for the organization

Determinants regarding benefits are also negotiated. For example, management may want to provide profit-sharing benefits only to employees who have worked for the firm for a specified number of years. The union may want these benefits provided to all employees.

Working Hours

Working hours are another important issue in contract negotiations. The matter of overtime is of special interest. Federal law defines **overtime** as time worked in excess of forty hours in one week. And it specifies that overtime pay must be at least one and one-half times the normal hourly wage. Unions may attempt to negotiate overtime rates for all hours worked beyond eight hours in a single day. Similarly, the union may attempt to obtain higher overtime rates (say, twice the normal hourly wage) for weekend or holiday work. Still another issue is an upper limit to overtime, beyond which employees can refuse to work.

overtime time worked in excess of forty hours in one week; under some union contracts, time worked in excess of eight hours in a single day

In firms with two or more work shifts, workers on less desirable shifts are paid a premium for their time. Both the amount of the premium and the manner in which workers are chosen for (or choose) particular shifts are negotiable issues. Other issues related to working hours are the work starting times and the length of lunch periods and coffee breaks.

Security

Security actually covers two issues. One is the job security of the individual worker; the other is the security of the union as the bargaining representative of the firm's employees.

Going Global

Manufacturing Moves Out of Bloomington, Indiana

Bloomington, Indiana, was once a booming industrial center. Thomson Consumer Electronics, Otis Elevator, Asea Brown Boveri (ABB), and General Electric (GE) all operated factories in the area. But by the end of the 1990s, the Thomson plant was closed, with production moved to Mexico. Otis was cutting jobs through attrition, and employment at the ABB plant was winding down. The General Electric plant was still turning out side-by-side refrigerators, but its future was in doubt.

To comply with more stringent energy efficiency regulations and environmental standards, GE knew it had to entirely change its refrigerator models. GE was also feeling the heat from global competitors with production facilities in other countries. In response, management planned a new line of refrigerators to be produced through a joint venture in Mexico. GE still had to decide what to do with the Bloomington plant and its 3,000-plus workers.

Officials of the International Brotherhood of Electrical Workers Local 2249 opened talks with GE management about reducing costs through lower absenteeism and other techniques, with the aim of saving the Bloomington plant. "The Indiana plant has already adopted 'lean' manufacturing techniques that emphasize deploying workers in teams where they do a variety of tasks," noted Steve Norman, the president of the local.

For its part, GE said changes were necessary if the Bloomington plant was to remain competitive. "Two years ago, a side-by-side refrigerator sold for $1,099, as advertised in the Bloomington *Herald-Times*," said Terry Dunn, a GE spokesperson. "Earlier this spring, the same refrigerator with premium water filtration features sold for $999. Comparable competitive products have been advertised for about $749. That's the face of the beast. This is about a plant that is rapidly becoming noncompetitive."

After several months of discussion, GE decided to invest $100 million in a new line of high-end refrigerators to be made at the Bloomington plant. This decision saved 1,800 jobs. However, GE also decided to shift some refrigerator production to its Mexican operations, cutting more than 1,000 jobs at Bloomington. In the end, Bloomington was able to keep some of its manufacturing jobs—for now.

Job security is protection against the loss of employment. It is a major concern of individuals. As we noted earlier, the desire for increased job security is a major reason for joining unions in the first place. In the typical labor contract, job security is based on seniority. If employees must be laid off or dismissed, those with the least seniority are the first to go. Some of the more senior employees may have to move to lower-level jobs, but they remain employed.

job security protection against the loss of employment

The Internet is a contributing factor. For example, more government services are moving onto the Internet and the likely loss of bureaucratic and labor-intensive jobs of the past will undoubtedly create labor issues in the future. Less than 1 percent of the more than $1 trillion of government transactions currently takes place over the Internet. IBM put Arizona's vehicle-registration program online and turned the average wait time from forty-five minutes to only three. Furthermore, the cost of registration to the state fell from $6.60 to $1.60, saving the motor bureau about $1.25 each year. In exchange, IBM earned $1 on each transaction.[11]

Union security is protection of the union's position as the employees' bargaining agent. Union security is frequently a more volatile issue than job security. Unions strive for as much security as possible, but management tends to see an increase in union security as an erosion of its control.

union security protection of the union's position as the employees' bargaining agent

Union security arises directly from its membership. The greater the ratio of union employees to nonunion employees, the more secure the union is. In contract negotiations, unions thus attempt to establish various union-membership conditions. The most restrictive of these is the **closed shop**, in which workers must join the union before they are hired. This condition was outlawed by the Taft-Hartley Act, but several other arrangements, including the following, are subject to negotiation:

closed shop a workplace in which workers must join the union before they are hired; outlawed by the Taft-Hartley Act

- The **union shop**, in which new employees must join the union after a specified probationary period.

union shop a workplace in which new employees must join the union after a specified probationary period

agency shop a workplace in which employees can choose not to join the union but must pay dues to the union anyway

maintenance shop a workplace in which an employee who joins the union must remain a union member as long as he or she is employed by the firm

- The **agency shop**, in which employees can choose not to join the union but must pay dues to the union anyway. (The idea is that nonunion employees benefit from union activities and should help support them.)
- The **maintenance shop**, in which an employee who joins the union must remain a union member as long as he or she is employed by the firm.

Management Rights

Of particular interest to the firm are those rights and privileges that are to be retained by management. For example, the firm wants as much control as possible over whom it hires, how work is scheduled, and how discipline is handled. The union, in contrast, would like some control over these and other matters affecting its members. It is interesting that some unions are making progress toward their goal of playing a more direct role in corporate governance. Some union executives have, in fact, been given seats on corporate boards of directors.

Grievance Procedures

grievance procedure a formally established course of action for resolving employee complaints against management

A **grievance procedure** is a formally established course of action for resolving employee complaints against management. Virtually every labor contract contains a grievance procedure. Procedures vary in scope and detail, but they may involve all four steps described below (see Figure 12.5).

shop steward an employee elected by union members to serve as their representative

Original Grievance The process begins with an employee who believes he or she has been treated unfairly, in violation of the labor contract. For example, an employee may be entitled to a formal performance review after six months on the job. If no such review is conducted, the employee may file a grievance. To do so, the employee explains the grievance to a **shop steward**, an employee elected by union members to serve as

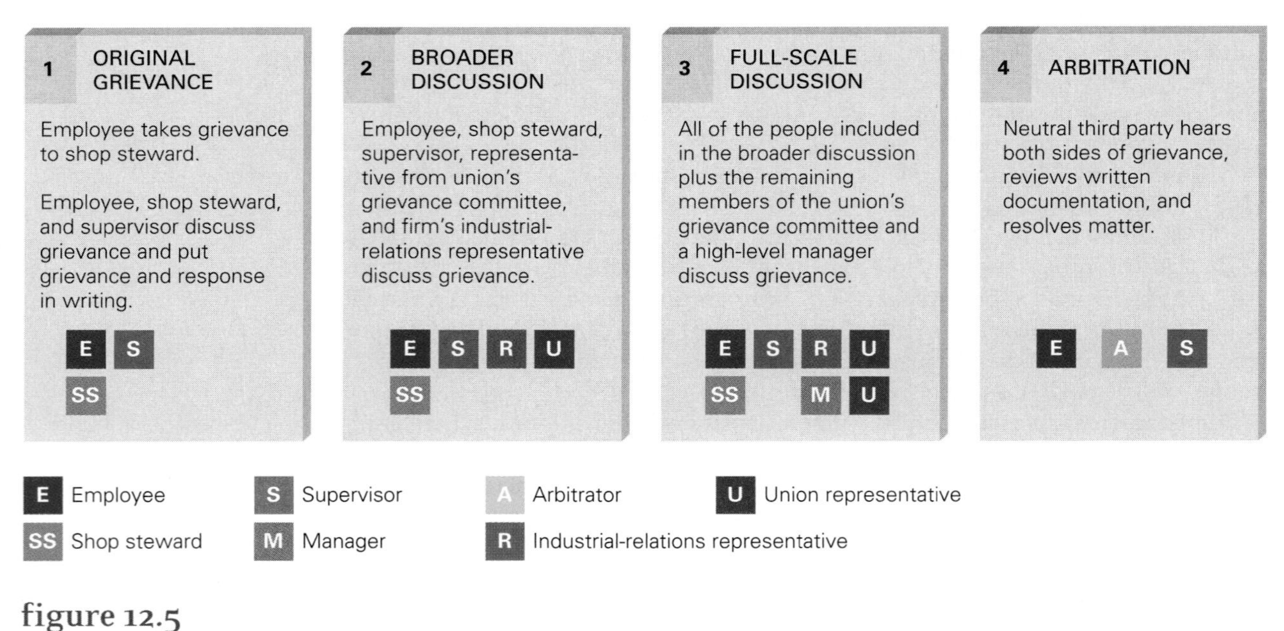

figure 12.5

Steps in Resolving a Grievance
The employee grievance procedure for most organizations consists of four steps. Each ensuing step involves all the personnel from the preceding step plus at least one higher-level person. The final step is to go to a neutral third party, the arbitrator.

their representative. The employee and the steward then discuss the grievance with the employee's immediate supervisor. Both the grievance and the supervisor's response are put in writing.

Broader Discussion In most cases, the problem is resolved during the initial discussion with the supervisor. If it is not, a second discussion is held. Now the participants include the original parties (employee, supervisor, and steward), a representative from the union's grievance committee, and the firm's industrial-relations representative. Again, a record is kept of the discussion and its results.

Full-Scale Discussion If the grievance is still not resolved, a full-scale discussion is arranged. This discussion includes everyone involved in the broadened discussion, as well as all remaining members of the union's grievance committee and another high-level manager. As usual, all proceedings are put in writing. All participants are careful not to violate the labor contract during this attempt to resolve the complaint.

Arbitration The final step in a grievance procedure is **arbitration**, in which a neutral third party hears the grievance and renders a binding decision. As in a court hearing, each side presents its case and has the right to cross-examine witnesses. In addition, the arbitrator reviews the written documentation of all previous steps in the grievance procedure. Both sides may then give summary arguments and/or present briefs. The arbitrator then decides whether a provision of the labor contract has been violated and proposes a remedy. The arbitrator cannot make any decision that would add to, detract from, or modify the terms of the contract. If it can be proved that the arbitrator exceeded the scope of his or her authority, either party may appeal the decision to the courts.

arbitration the step in a grievance procedure in which a neutral third party hears the two sides of a dispute and renders a decision

What actually happens when union and management "lock horns" over all the issues we have mentioned? We can answer this question by looking now at the negotiating tools each side can wield.

Union and Management Negotiating Tools

Management and unions can draw on certain tools to influence one another during contract negotiations. Both sides may use advertising and publicity to gain support for their respective positions. The most extreme tools are strikes and lockouts, but there are other, milder techniques as well.

LEARNING OBJECTIVE

7 Explain the primary bargaining tools available to unions and management.

Strikes

Unions go out on strike only in a very few instances and almost always only after an existing labor contract has expired. (In 1996, there were only 17 major strikes—"major" meaning those involving over 1,000 workers.[12]) Even then, if new contract negotiations seem to be proceeding smoothly, a union does not actually start a strike. The union does take a strike vote, but the vote may be used primarily to show members' commitment to a strike if negotiations fail.

The main objective of a strike is to put financial pressure on the company to encourage management to meet unions' demands. When union members do go out on strike, it is usually because negotiations seem to be stalled. A strike is simply a work stoppage: the employees do not report for work. In addition, striking workers engage in **picketing**, marching back and forth in front of their place of employment with signs informing the public that a strike is in progress. In doing so, they hope that (1) the public will be sympathetic to the strikers and will not patronize the struck firm; (2) nonstriking employees of the firm will honor the picket line and not report to work

picketing marching back and forth in front of the place of employment with signs informing the public that a strike is in progress

Using a strike to negotiate. A strike can summon public support for the union's cause and decrease the firm's ability to operate effectively. Employees at Caterpillar have used strikes as negotiating tools on several occasions.

either; and (3) members of other unions will not cross the picket line (for example, to make deliveries) and will thereby further restrict the operations of the struck firm.

Obviously, strikes are expensive to both the firm and the strikers. The firm loses business and earnings during the strike, and the striking workers lose the wages they would have earned if they had been at their jobs. The engineers' strike at Boeing is viewed as a "white-collar" strike. This strike has resulted in lower earnings for Boeing and a slowing of the delivery of new aircraft. Since the strikers have no strike fund to use, they must rely on their savings and pensions during the strike. The major reason for the strike by the engineers is compensation.[13]

During a strike, unions try to provide their members with as much support as possible. Larger unions are able to put a portion of their members' dues into a *strike fund*. The fund is used to provide financial support for striking union members.

wildcat strike a strike not approved by the strikers' union

At times, workers may go out on a **wildcat strike**, which is a strike that has not been approved by the union. In this situation, union leaders typically work with management to convince the strikers to return to work.

Slowdowns and Boycotts

slowdown a technique whereby workers report to their jobs but work at a slower pace than normal

boycott a refusal to do business with a particular firm

Almost every labor contract contains a clause that prohibits strikes during the life of the contract. (This is why strikes, if they occur, usually take place after a contract has expired.) However, a union may strike a firm while the contract is in force if members believe management has violated its terms. Workers may also engage in a **slowdown**, a technique whereby workers report to their jobs but work at a pace slower than normal. Recently, for example, employees at three airlines, including Conair, American Airlines, and Northwest Airlines, have been involved in work slowdowns that cause some flights to be delayed or cancelled.[14]

A **boycott** is a refusal to do business with a particular firm. Unions occasionally bring this strategy to bear by urging members (and sympathizers) not to purchase the products of a firm with which they are having a dispute. A *primary boycott*, aimed at the employer directly involved in the dispute, can be a powerful weapon. A *secondary boycott*, aimed at a firm doing business with the employer, is prohibited by the Taft-Hartley Act. Cesar Chavez, a migrant worker who founded the United Farm Workers Union, used boycotts to draw attention to the low pay and awful conditions endured by produce pickers.

Lockouts and Strikebreakers

lockout a firm's refusal to allow employees to enter the workplace

Management's most potent weapon is the lockout. In a **lockout**, the firm refuses to allow employees to enter the workplace. Like strikes, lockouts are expensive for both the firm and its employees. For this reason, they are rarely used, and then only in certain circumstances. A firm that produces perishable goods, for example, may use a lockout if management believes its employees will soon go on strike. The idea is to stop production in time to ensure minimal spoilage of finished goods or work in process. Baltimore-based Crown Central Petroleum has staged one of the longest lockouts in U.S. labor history. The lockout of 252 union workers began at the company's main refinery in Pasadena, Texas, on February 5, 1996. Since the lockout, Crown has suffered repeated financial losses and a rash of civil rights, environmental, and shareholder losses.[15]

Protesting lockouts. After three dozen members of a steel workers union demonstrated to call for a new contract, AK Steel in Mansfield, Ohio, locked out about 620 employees. A worker dressed as Darth Vader helps fellow workers protest the lockout by standing at the entrance to the company's annual meeting.

Management may also attempt to hire strikebreakers. A **strikebreaker** is a nonunion employee who performs the job of a striking union member. Hiring strikebreakers can result in violence when picketing employees confront the nonunion workers at the entrance to the struck facility. The firm also faces the problem of finding qualified replacements for the striking workers. Sometimes management personnel take over the jobs of strikers. Managers at telephone companies have handled the switchboards on more than one occasion.

Mediation and Arbitration

Strikes and strikebreaking, lockouts and boycotts, all pit one side against the other. Ultimately one side "wins" and the other "loses." Unfortunately, the negative effects of such actions—including resentment, fear, and distrust—may linger for months or years after a dispute has been resolved.

More productive techniques that are being increasingly used are mediation and arbitration. Either one may come into play before a labor contract expires or after some other strategy, such as a strike, has proved ineffective.

Mediation is the use of a neutral third party to assist management and the union during their negotiations. This third party (the mediator) listens to both sides, trying to find common ground for agreement. The mediator also tries to facilitate communication between the two sides, to promote compromise, and generally to keep the negotiations moving. At first the mediator may meet privately with each side. Eventually, however, his or her goal is to get the two to settle their differences at the bargaining table.

strikebreaker a nonunion employee who performs the job of a striking union member

mediation the use of a neutral third party to assist management and the union during their negotiations

Unlike mediation, the *arbitration* step is a formal hearing. Just as it may be the final step in a grievance procedure, it may also be used in contract negotiations (perhaps after mediation attempts) when the two sides cannot agree on one or more issues. Here, the arbitrator hears the formal positions of both parties on outstanding, unresolved issues. The arbitrator then analyzes these positions and makes a decision on the possible resolution of the issues. If both sides have agreed in advance that the arbitration will be binding, they must accept the arbitrator's decision.

If mediation and arbitration are unsuccessful, then, under the provisions of the Taft-Hartley Act, the president of the United States can obtain a temporary injunction to prevent or stop a strike if it would jeopardize national health or security.

This chapter ends our discussion of human resources. Next we examine the marketing function of business. We begin, in Chapter 13, by discussing the meaning of the term *marketing* and the various markets for products and services.

Adapting to change

Forging Labor Peace in the Auto Industry

LABOR PEACE IS STARTING TO SETTLE over the auto industry. In the past, relations between the Big Three Detroit automakers and the United Auto Workers union were strained, to say the least. UAW locals called eighteen strikes against General Motors in one recent five-year period. Ford and DaimlerChrysler also felt union pressure over issues such as pay and job security. During the most recent round of national negotiations, however, both sides got much of what they wanted.

UAW president Stephen Yokich wanted more money for his members. He successfully bargained for a 25 percent raise in worker pay and benefits plus bonuses over the four years of the contract. He also wanted a more open door for organizing at nonunion plants. DaimlerChrysler agreed to allow UAW recruiters to meet with workers in plants during nonwork hours, but it refused to officially recognize the union without elections at nonunion plants. Finally, Yokich wanted to protect jobs, so he got the Big Three to agree to hire new workers if employment falls below set levels—except if the job losses are caused by lower sales.

In exchange for higher pay and benefits, General Motors gained more flexibility to reorganize and boost productivity. Just as important, GM benefited from the contract clause on hiring new workers. Because its market share has been slipping, GM will be able to cut its workforce by almost 20 percent through attrition, a move that will lower its overall costs. GM also agreed to build a new factory in Lansing, Michigan, a key win for the union.

Although Ford also agreed to higher pay and benefits, it faced another situation. Ford was thinking about making its Visteon parts division into a separate company. UAW officials feared this would put the 23,500 UAW members who work for Visteon beyond the protection of the automaker's union contract. To avoid problems, Ford agreed to give Visteon workers the same wages and benefits as the automaker's employees receive. Visteon workers will enjoy this parity until they retire, whether or not the division is spun off. With these agreements, the auto industry hopes to maintain labor peace for some time.

RETURN TO Inside Business

WAL-MART HAS LONG RESISTED efforts to unionize its employees, arguing that it already offers employees such valuable benefits as profit sharing. The United Food and Commercial Workers union believes Wal-Mart's grocery workers would do better with union representation. When the meat-cutters in Wal-Mart's Jacksonville, Texas, store held an official election to decide the question, a majority voted to join the UFCW.

Within two weeks, however, Wal-Mart announced a switch from fresh-cut meat to prepackaged meat. After the changeover, the stores would no longer need meat-cutters, who would be offered other positions. The chain said this plan had been in the works for months, unrelated to the unionizing effort. The union said that Wal-Mart could not make such changes without bargaining with the newly unionized workers. Even as the prepackaged meat began appearing on Wal-Mart shelves, the union prepared to battle on.

Questions

1. What did the meat-cutters, the union, and Wal-Mart stand to gain or lose from the union vote in Jacksonville?
2. Do you agree with Wal-Mart's decision to eliminate meat-cutters by selling prepackaged meats? Explain your answer.

chapter Review

SUMMARY

1 Explain how and why labor unions came into being.

A labor union is an organization of workers who act together to negotiate wages and working conditions with their employers. Labor relations are the dealings between labor unions and business management.

The first major union in the United States was the Knights of Labor, formed in 1869 to eliminate the depersonalization of workers. The Knights were followed in 1886 by the American Federation of Labor (AFL). The goal of the AFL was to improve its members' living standards without changing the business system. In 1905 the radical Industrial Workers of the World was formed; its goal was the overthrow of capitalism. Of these three, only the AFL remained when the Congress of Industrial Organizations (CIO) was founded as a body of industrial unions between World War I and World War II. After years of competing, the AFL and CIO merged in 1955. The largest union not affiliated with the AFL-CIO is the Teamsters Union.

2 Discuss the sources of unions negotiating power and trends in union membership.

The power of unions to negotiate with management comes from two sources. The first is the size of their membership. The second source is the groups of laws that guarantee unions the right to negotiate and that regulate the negotiation process. At present, union membership accounts for less than 15 percent of the American work force, and it seems to be decreasing for various reasons. Nonetheless, unions wield considerable power in many industries—those in which their members comprise a large proportion of the work force.

Many unions today are entering into partnerships with management rather than maintaining their traditional adversarial position. Unions and management cooperate to increase production, improve quality, lower costs, empower workers, and enhance the workplace. Limited partnerships center on accomplishing one specific task or project. Long-range strategic partnerships focus on sharing decision-making power for a range of workplace and business matters.

3 Identify the main focus of several major pieces of labor-management legislation.

Important laws that affect union power are the Norris-LaGuardia Act (limits management's ability to obtain injunctions against unions), the Wagner Act (forbids certain unfair labor practices by management), the Fair Labor Standards Act (allows the federal government to set the minimum wage and to mandate overtime rates), the Taft-Hartley Act (forbids certain unfair practices by unions), and the Landrum-Griffin Act (regulates the internal functioning of labor unions). The National Labor Relations Board, a federal agency that oversees union-management relations, was created by the Wagner Act.

4 Enumerate the steps involved in forming a union, and show how the National Labor Relations Board is involved in the process.

Attempts to form a union within a firm begin with an organizing campaign to develop widespread employee interest in having a union. Next employees sign authorization cards indicating in writing their support for the union. The third step is to hold a formal election to decide whether to have a union. Finally, if the union obtains a majority, it receives NLRB certification, making it the official bargaining agent for its members. The entire process is supervised by the NLRB, which oversees the organizing campaign, conducts the election, and certifies the election results.

5 Describe the basic elements in the collective bargaining process.

Once a union is established, it may negotiate a labor contract with management through the process of collective bargaining. First, the negotiating committee decides on its position on the various contract issues. The union informs the management that it is ready to begin negotiations and a time and place are set. The union is represented by the negotiating committee, and the organization is represented by managers from several departments in the company. Each side is required to negotiate in good faith and not to stall or attempt to extend the bargaining unnecessarily. The final step is ratification, which is the approval of the contract by a vote of the union membership.

6 Identify the major issues covered in a union-management contract.

As the expiration date of an existing contract approaches, management and the union begin to negotiate a new contract. Contract issues include employee pay and benefits, working hours, job and union security, management rights, and grievance procedures.

7 Explain the primary bargaining tools available to unions and management.

Management and unions can use certain tools to sway one another—and public opinion—during contract negotiations. Advertising and publicity help each side gain support. When contract negotiations do not run smoothly, unions may apply pressure on management through strikes, slowdowns, or boycotts. Management may counter by imposing lockouts or hiring strikebreakers. Less drastic techniques for breaking contract deadlocks are mediation and arbitration. In both, a neutral third party is involved in the negotiations.

KEY TERMS

You should now be able to define and give an example relevant to each of the following terms:

labor union (327)
union-management (labor) relations (327)
craft union (327)
strike (328)
industrial union (329)
National Labor Relations Board (NLRB) (333)
injunction (334)
bargaining unit (336)
jurisdiction (336)
collective bargaining (337)
ratification (338)
seniority (340)
overtime (340)
job security (341)
union security (341)
closed shop (341)
union shop (341)
agency shop (342)
maintenance shop (342)
grievance procedure (342)
shop steward (342)
arbitration (343)
picketing (343)
wildcat strike (344)
slowdown (344)
boycott (344)
lockout (344)
strikebreaker (345)
mediation (345)

REVIEW QUESTIONS

1. Briefly describe the history of unions in the United States.
2. Describe the three characteristics common to most union-management partnerships. Discuss the benefits of union-management partnerships to management, unions, and workers.
3. How has government regulation of union-management relations evolved during this century?
4. For what reasons do employees start or join unions?
5. Describe the process of forming a union, and explain the role of the NLRB in that process.
6. List the major areas that are negotiated in a labor contract.
7. Explain the three issues involved in negotiations concerning employee pay.
8. What is the difference between job security and union security? How do unions attempt to enhance union security?
9. What is a grievance? Describe the typical grievance procedure.
10. What steps are involved in collective bargaining?
11. For what reasons are strikes and lockouts relatively rare nowadays?
12. What are the objectives of picketing?
13. In what ways do the techniques of mediation and arbitration differ?

DISCUSSION QUESTIONS

1. Do unions really derive their power mainly from their membership and labor legislation? What are some other sources of union power?
2. Which labor-contract issues are likely to be the easiest to resolve? Which are likely to be the most difficult?
3. Discuss the following statement: Union security means job security for union members.
4. How would you prepare for labor contract negotiations as a member of management? As head of the union negotiating committee?
5. Under what circumstances are strikes and lockouts justified in place of mediation or arbitration?

VIDEO CASE

Management and Unions Team Up at Xerox

In Xerox Corporation's motto, "Be the Best of the Best Together," *together* is the operative word. Xerox has welded a remarkable partnership with the Union of Needletrades, Industrial and Textile Employees (UNITE). Thousands of Xerox manufacturing employees belong to UNITE, which cooperates with management to cut costs, increase revenues, improve quality, respond to workers' needs, and keep Xerox competitive. The partnerships are working out well for both sides. Xerox and the union ratified a contract in which workers agreed to forgo raises in exchange for a seven-year job guarantee. In turn, management gets workers' commitment to increase efforts to raise profits and productivity. This kind of relationship has helped earn Xerox a Malcolm Baldrige Quality Award and *Personnel Journal*'s Optimas Award, which honored the partnership between Xerox and the union.

For some time, Xerox reigned supreme in the plain-paper copier market. During the 1970s, however, Japanese competitors like Sharp and Canon and U.S. manufacturer IBM grabbed a substantial chunk of Xerox's market share, reducing it from 90 to 43 percent. Inefficient operations and lost business were costing the company about $2 billion a year. In addition, a two-week strike in 1973 alerted the company and its workers to the need for a genuine partnership that would help avoid such conflict in the future.

Instead of saving money by closing plants, subcontracting the production of component parts, and laying off workers, Xerox joined forces with UNITE to solve its problems and keep its employees. Since then, Xerox and its union employees have worked together to make Xerox production facilities among the most modern, efficient, and quality-oriented in the world. The company established "Leadership through Quality," a program in which union workers receive extensive training in problem solving and effective team skills, and "Employee Involvement," a program that focuses on trust, communication, and training. Any group of employees can form a team to solve a problem and are given up to two hours a week to work on it. Union leadership knows that workers can suggest changes and voice ideas without fear of reprisal, and the company knows that the unions will cooperate with changes designed to increase productivity and reduce costs.

Xerox's contract with the union states that if management concludes the company is not manufacturing a product cost-effectively, it will work with the unions to establish a study team composed of union officers, hourly workers, and management personnel. The study team explores ways of restructuring the department to cut costs. Only if the team cannot find a way to make a competitive, high-quality product is Xerox free to subcontract.

Xerox had a chance to put its partnership to a dramatic test. To save about $3 million, the company considered subcontracting its wire-harness manufacturing operations, a plan that would have eliminated 180 jobs. As mandated in Xerox's labor agreement, a study team proposed alternatives. When implemented, the alternatives not only reduced costs and saved jobs but also improved the quality of the wire harnesses, raised worker morale, and intensified worker commitment to Xerox.

At Xerox, whenever a manufacturing glitch or a faulty part threatens product quality, workers are authorized to stop production until they find a remedy. Management is committed to the concept that its employees are human beings who have more to offer than repetitive, circumscribed, unthinking performance. The unions are committed to work jointly with the company to improve quality, as well. This cooperation has helped Xerox cut production costs by 30 percent, slash the time for new-product development in half, increase return on investment from 8 to 14 percent, and become the first U.S. company to win back market share from the Japanese without government intervention.

By mid-2000, however, competitive pressure had Xerox in a terrible jam. The company's share of the lucrative market for black-and-white copiers had plummeted from 75 to 45 percent during the previous three years. At the upper end of the market, customers seeking high-speed copiers were snapping up sophisticated new models from savvy rivals such as Canon, IBM, and Heidelberger. Caught in the middle, Xerox reported its first quarterly loss in sixteen years and cut costs by selling assets and eliminating more than 3,000 jobs. As part of this restructuring, the company moved production of some equipment to its Mexican plants, which meant the loss of several hundred union jobs in the United States. In search of new sales opportunities, Xerox also signed a $310 million deal to supply the entire Kinko's chain with copiers, printers, and other equipment. Still, no matter what challenges are ahead, management and the union are continuing to work together so Xerox can remain competitive in the global marketplace.[16]

Questions

1. What benefits does the Xerox Corporation receive from its commitment to partnerships with unions?
2. What are the advantages and disadvantages for union members of participating in the partnerships?
3. In your judgment, do union-management partnerships like those at Xerox strengthen or weaken the power of American labor unions? Defend your answer.

Building skills for career success

1. Exploring the Internet

Union web sites provide a wealth of information about union activity and concerns. Just as a corporate home page gives a firm the opportunity to describe its mission and goals and present its image to the world, so too does a web site allow a union to speak to its membership as well as the public at large. Visit the text web site for updates to this exercise.

Assignment

1. Visit the following web sites: AFL-CIO: http://www.aflcio.com; United Auto Workers: http://www.uaw.org
2. What are the mission statements of these unions?
3. Briefly describe your impression of the areas of interest to union members.
4. What is your impression of the tone of these web sites? Do they differ in any way from a typical business web site?

2. Developing Critical Thinking Skills

Recently, while on its final approach to an airport in Lubbock, Texas, a commercial airliner encountered a flock of ducks. The flight crew believed one or more of the ducks hit the aircraft and were ingested into the plane's main engine. The aircraft landed safely and taxied to the terminal. The flight crew advised the maintenance and operations crews of the incident. Operations grounded the plane until it could be inspected, but because of the time of day, maintenance personnel available to perform the inspection were in short supply. The airline had to call in two off-duty mechanics. A supervisor, calling from an overtime list, made calls until contacting two available mechanics. They worked on overtime pay to perform the inspection and return the aircraft to a safe flying status. Several days after the inspection, a mechanic on the overtime list who was not home when the supervisor called complained that she had been denied overtime. This union member believed the company owed her overtime pay for the same number of hours worked by a mechanic who performed the actual inspection. The company disagreed. What options are available to resolve this conflict?

Assignment

1. Using the following questions as guidelines, determine how this dispute can be resolved:
   a. What options are available to the unhappy mechanic? What process must she pursue? How does this process work?
   b. Do you believe the mechanic should receive pay for time she did not work? Justify your answer.
   c. What do you think was the final outcome of this conflict?
2. Prepare a report describing how you would resolve this situation.

3. Building Team Skills

For more than a century, American unions have played an important role in the workplace, striving to improve the working conditions and quality of life of employees. Today, federal laws cover many of the workers' rights that unions first championed. For that reason, some people believe unions are no longer necessary. But, according to some experts, as technology changes the workplace and as cultural diversity and the number of part-time workers increase, unions will increase their memberships and become stronger as we enter the next century. What do you think?

Assignment

1. Form a "pro" group and a "con" group and join one of them.
2. Debate whether unions will be stronger or weaker in the next century.
3. Record the key points for each side.
4. Summarize in a report what you learned about unions and their usefulness, and state your position on the debated issue.

4. Researching Different Careers

When applying for a job, whether mailing or faxing in your résumé, you should always include a letter of application, or a cover letter as it is often called. A well-prepared cover letter should convince the prospective employer to read your résumé and to phone you for an interview. The letter should describe the job you want and your qualifications for the job. It should also let the firm know where you can be reached to set up an appointment for an interview.

Assignment

1. Prepare a letter of application to use with the résumé you prepared in Chapter 10. (An example appears in Appendix A.)
2. After having several friends review your letter, edit it carefully.
3. Ask your instructor to comment on your letter.

5. Improving Communication Skills

A union contract is an agreement between a company and its employees who are union members. The contract sets forth the procedures that both parties must use to resolve disputes. Sometimes, however, the disputed issues become so complex they cannot be easily resolved by union and management. At that point, mediators usually step in to help move both sides closer to resolving their issues. At times, even that measure is not enough, and the union calls a strike.

Assignment

1. Read recent newspaper articles about issues that divide a firm's management and its union employees.
2. Find answers to the following questions:
   a. What are the disputed issues?
   b. Which issues are the most difficult to resolve? Why?
   c. Where does each party stand on the issues?
   d. How are the issues being resolved, or if already resolved, how were they resolved?
   e. What might be the effect of this dispute on union-management relations?
3. Summarize your findings and what you learned about unions in a report.

The Challenge of Human Resources Management at Motorola

Motorola is the world's number one supplier of equipment for cellular telephones, pagers, and two-way radios. It is also a leading manufacturer of semiconductors and the first company ever to win the Malcolm Baldrige Quality Award, a national award for quality presented by the U.S. Department of Commerce. What is the role of human resources management in helping to create an organization that can deliver this kind of quality? Motorola's HRM department recruits the right employees, administers a motivating and lifestyle-enhancing benefits program, and provides extensive and ongoing training. Everyone at Motorola, notes one industry analyst, seems "enrolled in a crusade for quality and customer satisfaction."

From Galvin Manufacturing to Motorola

Founded in Chicago in 1928 as Galvin Manufacturing, the company introduced the first practical car radio in the early 1930s. During the 1940s, when it changed its name to Motorola, it developed the first handheld two-way radio, introduced its first television, and invested increasingly in research and development. As the decades passed, Motorola's investment led to technological advances and continued growth.

The 1950s saw Motorola launch its first color television and pager and create its semiconductor division. During the 1960s, Motorola went international, and during the 1970s and 1980s, the company went into space with the Lunar Rover and Voyagers I and II. During the 1990s, Motorola ventured into global communications. Today Motorola is organized into three major divisions covering its worldwide operations. The Integrated Electronic Systems Sector focuses on electronic components, products, and systems for cars, computers, transportation, and energy uses in industrial and consumer markets. The Semiconductor Products Sector makes chips for use in consumer products, networking systems, transportation systems, and wireless communications. The Communications Enterprise brings together various high-volume business units that account for 70 percent of the company's global sales, including consumer communications; broadband communications; commercial, industrial, and government communications; global telecommunications; and Internet and networking solutions. Motorola owes its success in part to its HRM department, which brings together and keeps the kind of people who support the company's goals and who work to achieve them.

Managing an Empowered Workforce

One of the most challenging responsibilities of Motorola's HRM personnel is recruiting. What makes the process particularly challenging is finding people who have not only the required education and skills but also the ability and willingness to think creatively, to make decisions, and to continue learning. In the past, Motorola allowed the divisions to handle their own external recruiting and hiring, which created problems. "We would have product managers looking at the same candidate for different positions, and they might have been using different techniques for recruiting the same person," says one of the company's executive search managers. As a result, Motorola created a centralized staffing organization known as Global Talent Supply (GTS) to manage external recruiting, university relations, diversity initiatives, executive search, and online recruiting (http://www.motorolacareer.com). Managers within the different businesses still make the final hiring decisions, based on candidates that have been brought into the selection process by GTS.

Once people come to work at Motorola, they must choose from among a sometimes confusing array of employee benefits, and it is the job of HRM to help them. Industry experts report that Motorola's menu of flexible and personalized benefits is setting industry standards. The company's "Essentials" program includes a variety of medical plans and its "Lifesteps" program offers benefits in numerous other areas. "Balance" provides tools for managing daily life, such as child and dependent care, family leave, and prenatal and adoption assistance. "Milestones," designed to help Motorola's employees attain personal goals, provides help with home buying, continuing education, and legal problems. "Horizons" helps employees build financial security through pension plans, profit sharing, and investment advice. Educating employees about all these benefits, helping them select the ones that are best for them, and administering benefits makes HRM at Motorola especially challenging.

Motorola's president insists that "you can't empower people and drive decision making down to the individual level unless you give people the tools. It's great to say, 'You're empowered to stop the line.' But you have to teach people when and why to stop the line." To make sure its employees are educated, Motorola requires each one to take at least five days of training each year. Because products and processes vary from one division to another, each Motorola division has its own training organization. HRM personnel within each division make sure employees receive training that meets that division's unique requirements. Augmenting the training employees receive within their divisions is

Motorola University. Launched in 1981, the university's mission is to serve as a catalyst for change and continuous improvement by providing training and education to all Motorola employees. Quality training, cycle time reduction, and cross-functional process mapping are just three of the hundreds of courses offered at the year-round Motorola University. In all, Motorola spends $200 million every year on classroom and online training programs for its global workforce.

As Motorola has expanded around the globe, the company has not lost sight of HRM's vital contribution. To ensure it will have the right people to lead Motorola's HRM into the next century, the company launched a Leadership Development Program. Participants in this international program receive intensive training in company goals and culture, HRM information systems, compensation and benefits, employee communication and relations, and staffing and training. After gaining experience by rotating through three six-month stints in HR departments in selected business units, graduates are ready to put their skills to work all over the world as HRM professionals who help the people who make Motorola succeed. Despite its acknowledged position as a leader in global communications, Motorola has not been immune to the competitive and financial pressures that have gripped so many high-tech companies. To cut costs, the company has begun consolidating production facilities, outsourcing the manufacturing of some products, and laying off workers—creating even more challenges for its human resources managers.

Questions

1. Which of the needs in Maslow's hierarchy does Motorola's empowerment policy seek to fulfill?
2. Why does Motorola provide such a big menu of employee benefits?
3. What is the role of training at Motorola?
4. How might Motorola's Leadership Development Program affect the motivation of program participants?

13 **Building Customer Relationships Through Effective Marketing**

14 **Creating and Pricing Products that Satisfy Customers**

15 **Wholesaling, Retailing, and Physical Distribution**

16 **Developing Integrated Marketing Communications**

marketing

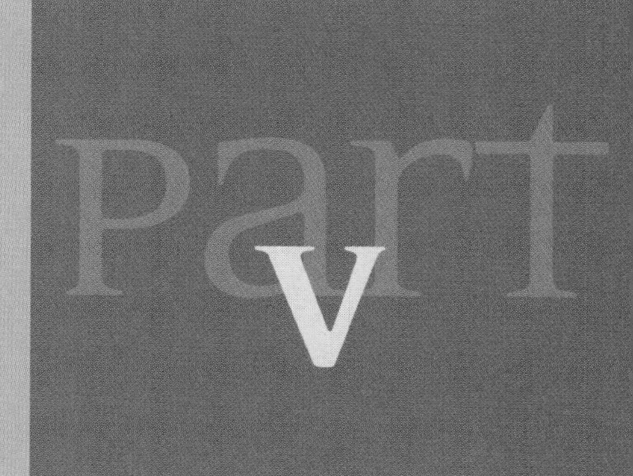

part V

The business activities that make up a firm's marketing efforts are those most directly concerned with satisfying customers' needs. In this part, we explore these activities in some detail. Initially, we discuss markets, marketing mix and environment, marketing plans, and buying behavior. Then, in turn, we discuss the four elements that together make up a marketing mix: product, price, distribution, and promotion.

13 Building Customer Relationships Through Effective Marketing

LEARNING OBJECTIVES

1 Understand the meaning of *marketing*, and explain how it creates utility for purchasers of products.

2 Trace the development of the marketing concept and understand how it is implemented.

3 Understand what markets are and how they are classified.

4 Identify the four elements of the marketing mix, and be aware of their importance in developing a marketing strategy.

5 Explain how the marketing environment affects strategic market planning.

6 Understand the major components of a marketing plan.

7 Describe how market measurement and sales forecasting are used.

8 Distinguish between a marketing information system and marketing research.

9 Identify the major steps in the consumer buying decision process and the sets of factors that may influence this process.

10 Describe three ways of measuring consumer income.

USAA constantly monitors customer satisfaction.

inside business

USAA's Personalized Service Keeps Customers Loyal

How does a company build a legendary reputation for personalized service without seeing any of its customers in person? The answer, for Texas-based USAA, is to use sophisticated information technology to better serve customers. Founded in 1922, USAA offers insurance, banking, and investment services to more than 3 million customers around the world, mainly current or former military personnel and their families. During wartime, when other insurers refused to sell life insurance to people in the military, USAA continued to sell policies. But that's not the only reason for its extraordinary customer loyalty. Over the years, USAA has developed a number of specialized systems to help employees understand customer needs and customize appropriate solutions.

Because it serves customers located in many states and countries, USAA handles most requests, claims, and complaints by mail, phone, and Internet. Its computerized call distribution system routes 500,000 customer calls daily to USAA representatives in different call centers. Every representative can tap into USAA's comprehensive database to examine customer profiles, see what products customers have purchased, and look at the history of customer contacts. For example, when a customer writes in with a question or claim, the letter is scanned and stored in the database. Well over 200 million such documents are already in USAA's system, ready to be accessed by representatives handling customer inquiries.

USAA's technology forms the foundation for its ECHO (Every Contact Has Opportunity) program. Although the company's aim is to resolve problems when customers first complain, more complex issues occasionally require special handling. That's where ECHO comes in. Representatives use the ECHO system to pass along service ideas, comments, and complaints to a team of employees who are dedicated to handling that customer feedback as quickly as possible.

USAA constantly monitors customer satisfaction, using marketing research tools such as focus groups and mail and phone surveys. The company also uses research to gauge customer reaction to new offerings and to solicit additional ideas for new services. To keep its customer database updated—and to identify future needs—USAA periodically surveys its customers about changes in status, such as marriage, children, and retirement plans. Based on the results of these surveys, the company can individualize its marketing approach for each customer's needs and circumstances. For example, if a customer has a child entering college, USAA sends the student literature about the wise use of credit cards.

USAA has won many awards for its emphasis on superior service. However, the most important measure of its success is customer loyalty. The company retains an astounding 98 percent of its customers. Small wonder that USAA has been named a "customer-care superstar."[1]

marketing the process of planning and executing the conception, pricing, promotion, and distribution of ideas, goods, and services to create exchanges that satisfy individual and organizational objectives

At USAA, marketing efforts are directed at providing customer satisfaction. Although marketing encompasses a diverse set of decisions and activities performed by individuals and by both business and nonbusiness organizations, marketing always begins and ends with the customer. The American Marketing Association defines **marketing** as "the process of planning and executing the conception, pricing, promotion, and distribution of ideas, goods, and services to create exchanges that satisfy individual and organizational objectives." The marketing process involves eight major functions and numerous related activities (see Table 13.1). All these functions are essential if the marketing process is to be effective.

In this chapter, we examine marketing activities that add value to products. We trace the evolution of the marketing concept and describe how organizations practice it. Next our focus shifts to market classifications and marketing strategy. We analyze the four elements of a marketing mix and also discuss uncontrollable factors in the marketing environment. Then we examine the major components of a marketing plan. We consider tools for strategic market planning, including market measurement, sales forecasts, marketing information systems, and marketing research. Last, we look at the forces that influence consumer and organizational buying behavior.

LEARNING OBJECTIVE

1 Understand the meaning of *marketing*, and explain how it creates utility for purchasers of products.

Utility: The Value Added by Marketing

utility the ability of a good or service to satisfy a human need

form utility utility created by converting production inputs into finished products

As defined in Chapter 9; **utility** is the ability of a good or service to satisfy a human need. A lunch at a Pizza Hut, an overnight stay at a Holiday Inn, and a Mercedes S 500 L all satisfy human needs. Thus, each possesses utility. There are four kinds of utility.

Form utility is created by converting production inputs into finished products. Marketing efforts may indirectly influence form utility because the data gathered as

table 13.1 Major Marketing Functions

Exchange Functions: All companies—manufacturers, wholesalers, and retailers—buy and sell to market their merchandise.

1. **Buying** includes obtaining raw materials to make products, knowing how much merchandise to keep on hand, and selecting suppliers.
2. **Selling** creates possession utility by transferring the title of a product from seller to customer.

Physical Distribution Functions: These functions involve the flow of goods from producers to customers. Transportation and storage provide time utility and place utility, and require careful management of inventory.

3. **Transporting** involves selecting a mode of transport that provides an acceptable delivery schedule at an acceptable price.
4. **Storing** goods is often necessary to sell them at the best selling time.

Facilitating Functions: These functions help the other functions take place.

5. **Financing** helps at all stages of marketing. To buy raw materials, manufacturers often borrow from banks or receive credit from suppliers. Wholesalers may be financed by manufacturers, and retailers may receive financing from the wholesaler or manufacturer. Finally, retailers often provide financing to customers.
6. **Standardizing** sets uniform specifications for products or services. **Grading** classifies products by size and quality, usually through a sorting process. Together, standardization and grading facilitate production, transportation, storage, and selling.
7. **Risk taking**—even though competent management and insurance can minimize risks—is a constant reality of marketing because of such losses as bad-debt expense, obsolescence of products, theft by employees, and product-liability lawsuits.
8. **Gathering market information** is necessary for making all marketing decisions.

part of marketing research are frequently used to determine the size, shape, and features of a product.

The three kinds of utility that are directly created by marketing are place, time, and possession utility. **Place utility** is created by making a product available at a location where customers wish to purchase it. A pair of shoes is given place utility when it is shipped from a factory to a department store.

place utility utility created by making a product available at a location where customers wish to purchase it

Time utility is created by making a product available when customers wish to purchase it. For example, Halloween costumes might be manufactured in April but not displayed until late September, when consumers start buying them. By storing the costumes until they are wanted, the manufacturer or retailer provides time utility.

time utility utility created by making a product available when customers wish to purchase it

Possession utility is created by transferring title (or ownership) of a product to the buyer. For a product as simple as a pair of shoes, ownership is usually transferred by means of a sales slip or receipt. For such products as automobiles and homes, the transfer of title is a more complex process. Along with the title to its products, the seller transfers the right to use that product to satisfy a need (see Figure 13.1).

possession utility utility created by transferring title (or ownership) of a product to the buyer

Place, time, and possession utility have real value in terms of both money and convenience. This value is created and added to goods and services through a wide variety of marketing activities—from research indicating what customers want to product warranties ensuring that customers get what they pay for. Overall, these marketing activities account for about half of every dollar spent by consumers. When they are part of an integrated marketing program that delivers maximum utility to the customer, many would agree that they are worth the cost.

Place, time, and possession utility are only the most fundamental applications of marketing activities. In recent years, marketing activities have been influenced by a broad business philosophy known as *the marketing concept.*

The Marketing Concept

LEARNING OBJECTIVE

2 Trace the development of the marketing concept and understand how it is implemented.

The process that leads any business to success seems simple. First, the firm must talk to its potential customers to assess their needs for its goods or services. Then the firm must develop a good or service to satisfy those needs. Finally, the firm must continue to seek ways to provide customer satisfaction. This process is an application of the marketing concept, or marketing orientation. As reasonable and logical as it appears to be, American business has been slow to accept it, but it is making some progress. An example of an organization that is implementing the marketing concept is Commerce Bancorp, located in New Jersey, Delaware, and Pennsylvania. Commerce Bancorp has

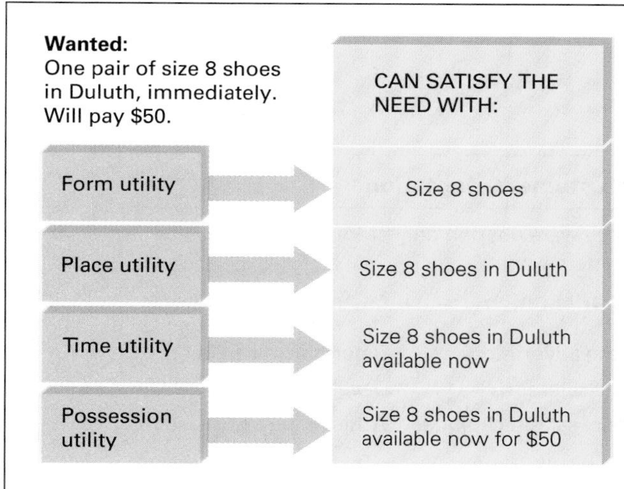

figure 13.1

Types of Utility

Form utility is created by the production process, but marketing creates place, time, and possession utility.

ascertained what retail banking customers want—good service and low fees. Commerce offers its customers free checking, free money orders, weekday teller service from 7:30 A.M. to 8:00 P.M., and weekend teller hours. By providing customers with what they want, Commerce Bancorp is also able to achieve its objectives. Its earnings are growing almost twice as fast as the average bank, and its stock price has surged 278 percent over the last five years compared with 118 percent for the average bank stock.[2]

Evolution of the Marketing Concept

From the start of the Industrial Revolution until the early twentieth century, business effort was directed mainly toward the production of goods. Consumer demand for manufactured products was so great that manufacturers could almost bank on selling everything they produced. Business had a strong *production orientation*, in which emphasis was placed on increased output and production efficiency. Marketing was limited to taking orders and distributing finished goods.

In the 1920s, production caught up with and began to exceed demand. Now producers had to direct their efforts toward selling goods rather than just producing goods that consumers readily bought. This new *sales orientation* was characterized by increased advertising, enlarged sales forces, and, occasionally, high-pressure selling techniques. Manufacturers produced the goods they expected consumers to want, and marketing consisted primarily of promoting products through personal selling and advertising, taking orders, and delivering goods.

During the 1950s, however, businesspeople started to realize that even enormous advertising expenditures and the most thoroughly proven sales techniques were not enough. Something else was needed if products were to sell as well as expected. It was then that business managers recognized they were not primarily producers or sellers but rather were in the business of satisfying customers' needs. Marketers realized that the best approach was to adopt a customer orientation—in other words, the organization had to first determine what customers need and then develop goods and services to fill those particular needs (see Table 13.2).

marketing concept a business philosophy that involves the entire organization in the process of satisfying customers' needs while achieving the organization's goals

relationship marketing developing mutually beneficial long-term partnerships with customers to enhance customer satisfaction and to stimulate long-term customer loyalty

This **marketing concept** is a business philosophy that involves the entire organization in the process of satisfying customers' needs while achieving the organization's goals. All functional areas—research and development, production, finance, human resources, and, of course, marketing—are viewed as playing a role in providing customer satisfaction. Based on the marketing concept, some organizations today are employing **relationship marketing**, which involves developing mutually beneficial, long-term partnerships with customers to enhance customer satisfaction and to stimulate long-term customer loyalty. Frequency programs that reward customer loyalty are one way of fostering long-term customer relationships. For example, Marriott Rewards gives its members three frequent flyer miles per dollar spent at Marriott, Renaissance, Marriott Vacation Club International, and Marriott Conference Centers. This program also awards one mile per dollar spent at Courtyard, Fairfield Inn, and Residence Inn.[3]

table 13.2 Evolution of Customer Orientation

Business managers recognized they were not primarily producers or sellers but rather were in the business of satisfying customers' wants.

Production Orientation	Sales Orientation	Customer Orientation
Take orders	Increase advertising	Determine customer needs
Distribute goods	Enlarge sales force	Develop products to fill these needs
	Intensify sales techniques	Achieve the organization's goals

Implementing the Marketing Concept

The marketing concept has been adopted by many of the most successful business firms. Some firms, such as Ford Motor Company and Apple Computer, have gone through minor or major reorganizations in the process. Because the marketing concept is essentially a business philosophy, anyone can say, "I believe in it." But to make it work, management must fully adopt and then implement it.

As the 84-year-old William Rosenberg, founder of the five-thousand-unit Dunkin' Donuts organization, puts it: "If you have a philosophy that you work for the customer and that starts to permeate, the organization finds a way to give them what they want in the form of quality, service, and value."[4]

To implement the marketing concept, a firm must first obtain information about its present and potential customers. The firm must determine not only what customers' needs are but also how well those needs are being satisfied by products currently on the market—both its own products and those of competitors. It must ascertain how its products might be improved and what opinions customers have of the firm and its marketing efforts.

The firm must then use this information to pinpoint the specific needs and potential customers toward which it will direct its marketing activities and resources. (Obviously, no firm can expect to satisfy all needs. And not every individual or firm can be considered a potential customer for every product manufactured or sold by a firm.) Next, the firm must mobilize its marketing resources to (1) provide a product that will satisfy its customers, (2) price the product at a level that is acceptable to buyers and that will yield an acceptable profit, (3) promote the product so that potential customers will be aware of its existence and its ability to satisfy their needs, and (4) ensure that the product is distributed so that it is available to customers where and when needed.

Finally, the firm must again obtain marketing information—this time, regarding the effectiveness of its efforts. Can the product be improved? Is it being promoted properly? Is it being distributed efficiently? Is the price too high or too low? The firm must be ready to modify any or all of its marketing activities based on information about its customers and competitors.

Satisfying customers' needs. Part of implementing the marketing concept is providing a product that satisfies customers. Northwest Airlines tries to increase traveler satisfaction by making flight check-in more convenient.

LEARNING OBJECTIVE

3 Understand what markets are and how they are classified.

Markets and Their Classification

A **market** is a group of individuals or organizations, or both, that need products in a given category and that have the ability, willingness, and authority to purchase such products. The people or organizations must want the product. They must be able to purchase the product by exchanging money, goods, or services for it. They must be willing to use their buying power. Finally, they must be socially and legally authorized to purchase the product.

market a group of individuals or organizations, or both, that need products in a given category and that have the ability, willingness, and authority to purchase such products

Markets are broadly classified as consumer or business-to-business markets. These classifications are based on the characteristics of the individuals and organizations within each market. Because marketing efforts vary depending on the intended market, marketers should understand the general characteristics of these two groups.

Business-to-business markets. Staples.com primarily aims at business customers.

Consumer markets consist of purchasers and/or household members who intend to consume or benefit from the purchased products and who do not buy products to make profits.

Business-to-business markets, also called *industrial markets*, are grouped broadly into producer, reseller, governmental, and institutional categories. These markets purchase specific kinds of products for use in making other products, for resale, or for day-to-day operations. *Producer markets* consist of individuals and business organizations that buy certain products to use in the manufacturing of other products. *Reseller markets* consist of intermediaries such as wholesalers and retailers that buy finished products and sell them for a profit. *Governmental markets* consist of federal, state, county, and local governments. They buy goods and services to maintain internal operations and to provide citizens with such products as highways, education, water, energy, and national defense. Governmental purchases total billions of dollars each year. *Institutional markets* include churches, not-for-profit private schools and hospitals, civic clubs, fraternities and sororities, charitable organizations, and foundations. Their goals are different from such typical business goals as profit, market share, or return on investment.

Developing Marketing Strategies

marketing strategy a plan that will enable an organization to make the best use of its resources and advantages to meet its objectives

marketing mix a combination of product, price, distribution, and promotion developed to satisfy a particular target market

A **marketing strategy** is a plan that will enable an organization to make the best use of its resources and advantages to meet its objectives. A marketing strategy consists of (1) the selection and analysis of a target market and (2) the creation and maintenance of an appropriate **marketing mix**, a combination of product, price, distribution, and promotion developed to satisfy a particular target market.

spotLight

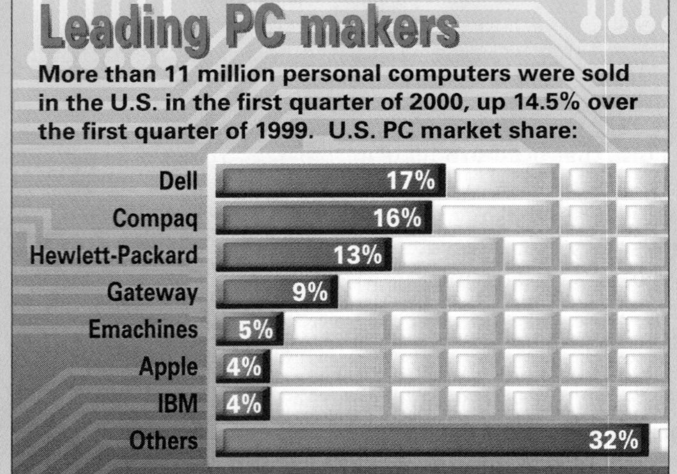

Source: Copyright 2000, USA TODAY. Reprinted with permission.

Target Market Selection and Evaluation

A **target market** is a group of individuals, organizations, or both, for which a firm develops and maintains a marketing mix suitable for the specific needs and preferences of that group. In selecting a target market, marketing managers examine potential markets for their possible effects on the firm's sales, costs, and profits. The managers attempt to determine whether the organization has the resources to produce a marketing mix that meets the needs of a particular target market and whether satisfying those needs is consistent with the firm's overall objectives. They also analyze the strengths and numbers of competitors already marketing to people in this target market. When selecting a target market, marketing managers generally take either the undifferentiated approach or the market segmentation approach.

Examining Ethics

Marketing Tobacco Products Around the World

SHOULD TOBACCO MANUFACTURERS BE allowed to market their products around the world? Slow growth plus legal and regulatory fights have made the U.S. market less profitable in recent years. So major tobacco companies are seeking more lucrative opportunities by targeting overseas markets.

Philip Morris, which markets Marlboro, holds 17 percent of the world cigarette market. British American Tobacco, which markets Lucky Strike, holds 16 percent of the world cigarette market. Winston's maker, R.J. Reynolds, is also a major player in international tobacco markets. Japan and Europe are the largest international markets for U.S. tobacco products, although developing countries, where Western brands are particularly desirable, are also being targeted.

Critics charge that the tobacco makers are using slick advertising to glamorize an unhealthy product. Although tobacco product-makers are not allowed to air television commercials in the United States and Europe, they face fewer advertising restrictions in many developing countries. The tobacco companies argue that their products are entirely legal, and that they use advertising to encourage adult smokers to switch brands, not to attract new or underage smokers.

Clearly, the tobacco companies face more legal pressure in the United States than abroad. Some tobacco manufacturers have been successfully sued under U.S. product-liability laws. In contrast, few product-liability cases are filed in Japan or Europe—and in Europe, people who sue and lose must pay the legal fees of the defendants. This concerns experts, who fear that consumers in other countries have little legal recourse against unhealthy products such as cigarettes.

Citing the health hazards of smoking, the World Health Organization has called for a global ban on tobacco advertising and an international tobacco control treaty. Meanwhile, the tobacco makers continue moving aggressively into international markets. Thus, the ethical issue remains: Should cigarette makers be allowed to target global markets?

Issues to Consider

1. Should U.S.-based cigarette makers be required to follow U.S. laws and regulations when marketing in other countries?
2. Should countries be able to restrict or ban advertising for legal but unhealthy products?

Undifferentiated Approach A company that designs a single marketing mix and directs it at the entire market for a particular product is using an **undifferentiated approach** (see Figure 13.2). This approach assumes that individual customers in the target market for a specific kind of product have similar needs and that the organization therefore can satisfy most customers with a single marketing mix. This single marketing mix consists of one type of product with little or no variation, one price, one promotional program aimed at everyone, and one distribution system to reach all customers in the total market. Products that can be marketed successfully with the undifferentiated approach include staple food items, such as sugar and salt, and certain kinds of farm produce. An undifferentiated approach is useful in only a limited number of situations because for most product categories, buyers have different needs. When customers' needs vary, a company should use the market segmentation approach.

target market a group of individuals or organizations, or both, for which a firm develops and maintains a marketing mix suitable for the specific needs and preferences of that group

undifferentiated approach directing a single marketing mix at the entire market for a particular product

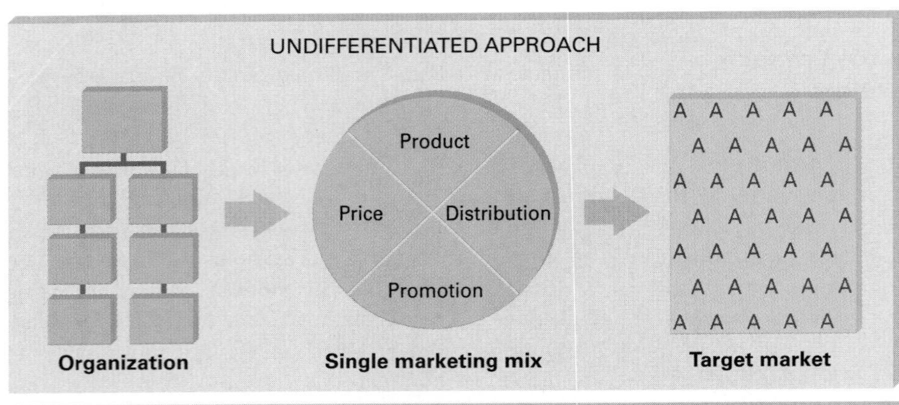

CONCENTRATED MARKET SEGMENTATION APPROACH

Organization

Product

Price

Distribution

Promotion

Single marketing mix

A A A A A
A A A A A
A A A A A
B B B B B
B B B B B
B B B B B
C C C C C
C C C C C
C C C C C

Target market

DIFFERENTIATED MARKET SEGMENTATION APPROACH

Organization

Product

Price

Distribution

Promotion

Marketing mix I

Product

Price

Distribution

Promotion

Marketing mix II

A A A A A
A A A A A
A A A A A
B B B B B
B B B B B
B B B B B
C C C C C
C C C C C
C C C C C

Target markets

NOTE: The letters in each target market represent potential customers. Customers that have the same letters have similar characteristics and similar product needs.

figure 13.2

General Approaches for Selecting Target Markets
The undifferentiated approach assumes that individual customers have similar needs and that most customers can be satisfied with a single marketing mix. When customers' needs vary, the market segmentation—either concentrated or differentiated—approach should be used.

Source: W[illegible]n M. Pride and O. C. Ferrell, *Marketing: Concepts and Strategies*, Eleventh Edition. Copyright © 2000 by Houghton Mifflin Company. Adapted with

Market Segmentation Approach A firm that is marketing 40-foot yachts would not direct its marketing effort toward every person in the total boat market. Some might want a sailboat or a canoe. Others might want a speedboat or an outboard-powered fishing boat. Still others might be looking for something resembling a small ocean liner. Marketing efforts directed toward these boat buyers would be wasted.

Instead, the firm would direct its attention toward a particular portion, or *segment*, of the total market for boats. A **market segment** is a group of individuals or organizations within a market that share one or more common characteristics. The process of dividing a market into segments is called **market segmentation.** As shown in Figure 13.2, there are two types of market segmentation approaches: concentrated and differentiated. When an organization uses *concentrated* market segmentation, a single marketing mix is directed at a single market segment. If *differentiated* market segmentation is employed, multiple marketing mixes are focused on multiple market segments.

market segment a group of individuals or organizations within a market that share one or more common characteristics

market segmentation the process of dividing a market into segments and directing a marketing mix at a particular segment or segments rather than at the total market

In our boat example, one common characteristic, or *basis*, for segmentation might be "end use" of a boat. The firm would be interested primarily in that market segment whose uses for a boat could lead to the purchase of a 40-foot yacht. Another basis for segmentation might be income; still another might be geographic location. Each of these variables can affect the type of boat an individual might purchase. When choosing a basis for segmentation, it is important to select a characteristic that relates to differences in people's needs for a product. The yacht producer, for example, would not use religion to segment the boat market because people's needs for boats do not vary based on religion.

Marketers use a wide variety of segmentation bases. Those bases most commonly applied to consumer markets are shown in Table 13.3. Each may be used as a single basis for market segmentation or in combination with other bases. For example, Taco Bell uses the combination of age and gender, aiming at 18 to 34-year-old males.[5]

Creating a Marketing Mix

LEARNING OBJECTIVE

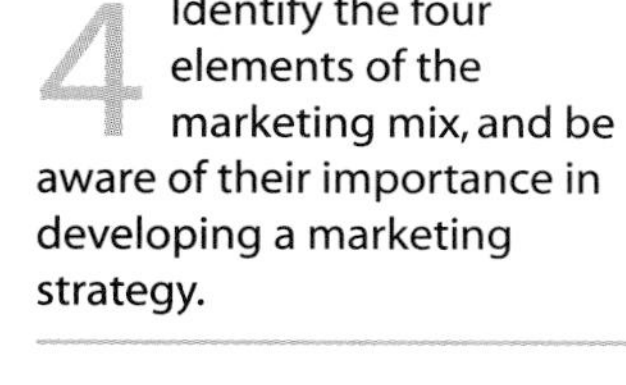

4 Identify the four elements of the marketing mix, and be aware of their importance in developing a marketing strategy.

A business firm controls four important elements of marketing that it combines in a way that reaches the firm's target market. These are the *product* itself, the *price* of the product, the means chosen for its *distribution*, and the *promotion* of the product. When combined, these four elements form a marketing mix (see Figure 13.3).

A firm can vary its marketing mix by changing any one or more of these ingredients. Thus, a firm may use one marketing mix to reach one target market and a second, somewhat different marketing mix to reach another target market. For example, most automakers produce several different types and models of vehicles and aim them at different market segments based on age, income, and other factors.

Kids are target markets, too. Many firms develop marketing mixes aimed at satisfying the needs and preferences of children. Here a ten-year-old girl examines an electronically locked diary in a toy store. She is a "tween"—the eight- to twelve-year-old age group that is being targeted by toy manufacturers looking for a new market for electronic toys.

table 13.3 Common Bases of Market Segmentation

Demographic	Psychographic	Geographic	Behavioristic
Age	Personality attributes	Region	Volume usage
Gender	Motives	Urban, suburban, rural	End use
Race	Lifestyles	Market density	Benefit expectations
Ethnicity		Climate	Brand loyalty
Income		Terrain	Price sensitivity
Education		City size	
Occupation		County size	
Family size		State size	
Family life cycle			
Religion			
Social class			

Source: William M. Pride and O. C. Ferrell, *Marketing: Concepts and Strategies*, Eleventh Edition. Copyright © 2000 by Houghton Mifflin Company. Adapted with permission.

The *product* ingredient of the marketing mix includes decisions about the product's design, brand name, packaging, warranties, and the like. When McDonald's decides on brand names, package designs, sizes of orders, flavors of sauces, and recipes, these choices are all part of the product ingredient.

The *pricing* ingredient is concerned with both base prices and discounts of various kinds. Pricing decisions are intended to achieve particular goals, such as to maximize profit or even to make room for new models. The rebates offered by automobile manufacturers are a pricing strategy developed to boost low auto sales. Product and pricing are discussed in detail in Chapter 14.

The *distribution* ingredient involves not only transportation and storage but also the selection of intermediaries. How many levels of intermediaries should be used in

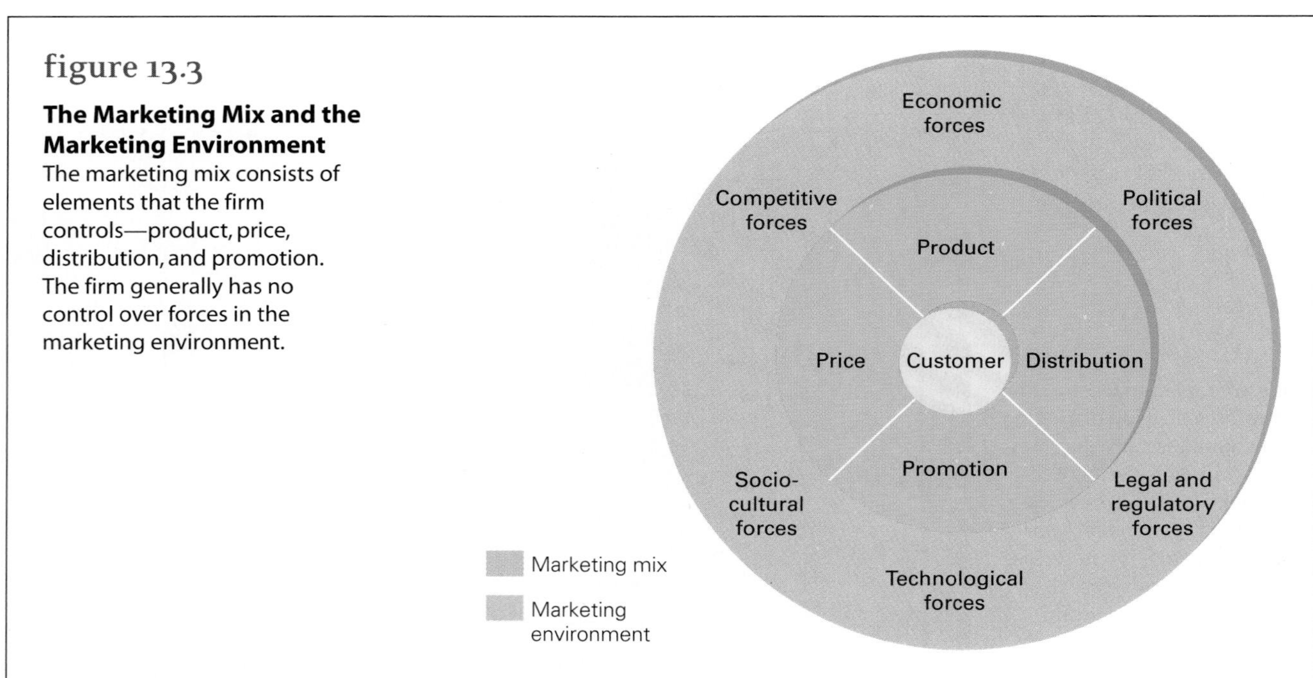

figure 13.3

The Marketing Mix and the Marketing Environment

The marketing mix consists of elements that the firm controls—product, price, distribution, and promotion. The firm generally has no control over forces in the marketing environment.

Source: William M. Pride and O. C. Ferrell, *Marketing: Concepts and Strategies*, Eleventh Edition. Copyright © 2000 by Houghton Mifflin Company. Adapted with permission.

EXPLORING BUSINESS

South Beach Markets Healthy and Hip

JOHN BELLO DOESN'T JUST MARKET BEVerages–he markets drinks that "uplift the mind, body, and spirit." Bello is cofounder of Connecticut-based South Beach Beverage, maker of the popular SoBe line of healthy refreshment drinks. Before founding South Beach, the entrepreneur worked at PepsiCo, the National Football League, and Arizona Beverages. Now he's putting all this marketing background to the test as he brews up new drinks for New Age consumers.

Bello launched his first line of South Beach flavored teas in the mid-1990s, when similar beverages from Snapple and other competitors were already crowding store shelves. Yet his Orange Elixir, enhanced with beta carotene, was selling well. So Bello dropped the other teas and added a variety of herb-enriched drinks. For example, 3G Black Tea contains ginseng, ginkgo, and guarana, and 3C Elixirs contain calcium, chromium picolinate, and carnitine. "Even more so now than ever, there has been a wellness cultural shift, and there is a demand for healthy refreshment and excitement," he says. "Our products are consistent with that."

To catch the eye of his target market, health-minded consumers aged 18 to 34, Bello designed distinctive bottles featuring lizards with attitude. Then he wove the lizard theme through other marketing mix activities. He built a buzz around the brand by sponsoring sports events, sending "lizard fun buses" out to festivals, and signing athletes such as track star Anna Norgren to Team Lizard.

To get SoBe drinks into supermarket chains and convenience stores, Bello signed up a number of distributors that had formerly handled competing products and understood the market. In turn, these distributors were able to get SoBe into refrigerated cases at Safeway, 7-Eleven, and other chains. With SoBe's annual sales soaring over $100 million, Bello remains alert to signs of change in consumer tastes and trends. "We have the ability to react and get to the market quickly," he notes. "Flexibility is one of our strategies."

the distribution of a particular product? Should the product be distributed as widely as possible? Or should distribution be restricted to a few specialized outlets in each area? These and other questions related to distribution are considered in Chapter 15.

The *promotion* ingredient focuses on providing information to target markets. The major forms of promotion are advertising, personal selling, sales promotion, and public relations. These four forms are discussed in Chapter 16.

These ingredients of the marketing mix are controllable elements. A firm can vary each of them to suit its organizational goals, marketing goals, and target markets. As we extend our discussion of marketing strategy, we will see that the marketing environment includes a number of *uncontrollable* elements.

Marketing Strategy and the Marketing Environment

LEARNING OBJECTIVE

5 Explain how the marketing environment affects strategic market planning.

The marketing mix consists of elements that a firm controls and uses to reach its target market. In addition, the firm has control over such organizational resources as finances and information. These resources, too, may be used to accomplish marketing goals. However, the firm's marketing activities are also affected by a number of external—and generally uncontrollable—forces. As Figure 13.3 illustrates, the forces that make up the external *marketing environment* are

- *Economic forces*—the effects of economic conditions on customers' ability and willingness to buy
- *Sociocultural forces*—influences in a society and its culture that result in changes in attitudes, beliefs, norms, customs, and lifestyles
- *Political forces*—influences that arise through the actions of elected and appointed officials
- *Competitive forces*—the actions of competitors, who are in the process of implementing their own marketing plans
- *Legal and regulatory forces*—laws that protect consumers and competition, and government regulations that affect marketing

- *Technological forces*—technological changes that, on the one hand, can create new marketing opportunities, or on the other, can cause products to become obsolete almost overnight

These forces influence decisions about marketing mix ingredients. Changes in the environment can have a major impact on existing marketing strategies. In addition, changes in environmental forces may lead to abrupt shifts in customers' needs. New opportunities will continue to emerge due to changes in technology. For example, according to research analysts IDC, Inc., as more and more customers around the world connect to the Internet, any product that can be digitized and thereby delivered on the Internet will contribute to an explosion in e-commerce sales projected to reach $1.5 trillion by 2003. Products like music, e-books, interactive TV, and online auction items are only a few of the first products that will find their way onto the Internet as access speed increases and the number of users grows.[6]

LEARNING OBJECTIVE

6 Understand the major components of a marketing plan.

Developing a Marketing Plan

marketing plan a written document that specifies an organization's resources, objectives, strategy, and implementation and control efforts to be used in marketing a specific product or product group

A **marketing plan** is a written document that specifies an organization's resources, objectives, marketing strategy, and implementation and control efforts to be used in marketing a specific product or product group. The marketing plan describes the firm's current position or situation, establishes marketing objectives for the product, and specifies how the organization will attempt to achieve these objectives. Marketing plans vary with respect to the time period involved. Short-range plans are for one year or less, medium-range plans cover from over one year and up to five years, and long-range plans cover periods of more than five years.

Though time-consuming, developing a clear, well-written marketing plan is important. The plan will be used for communication among the firm's employees. It covers the assignment of responsibilities, tasks, and schedules for implementation. It specifies how resources are to be allocated to achieve marketing objectives. It helps marketing managers monitor and evaluate the performance of the marketing strategy. Because the forces of the marketing environment are subject to change, marketing plans have to be updated frequently. The major components of a marketing plan are shown in Table 13.4.

LEARNING OBJECTIVE

7 Describe how market measurement and sales forecasting are used.

Market Measurement and Sales Forecasting

Using the Internet

An excellent online resource for marketing information is the American Marketing Association's web site (**http://www.ama.org/**). The site also provides access to a host of specialized marketing publications such as *Marketing News, Marketing Management, Marketing Research,* and the *Journal of Marketing* (**http://www.ama.org/pubs/index.asp**), to list but a few.

Measuring the sales potential of specific types of market segments helps an organization make some important decisions. It can evaluate the feasibility of entering new segments. The organization can also decide how best to allocate its marketing resources and activities among market segments in which it is already active. All such estimates should identify the relevant time frame. Like marketing plans, these estimates may be short-range, covering periods of less than one year; medium-range, covering one to five years; and long-range, covering more than five years. The estimates should also define the geographic boundaries of the forecast. For example, sales potential can be estimated for a city, county, state, or group of nations. Finally, analysts should indicate whether their estimates are for a specific product item, a product line, or an entire product category.

table 13.4 Components of a Marketing Plan

Executive Summary

This short statement summarizing the entire report is sometimes easier to write *after* the marketing plan has been developed.

Environmental Analysis

This consists of current information about the environment in which a company will market its product, the target market, and performance objectives.

Assessing the *marketing environment* includes

1. Looking at forces affecting marketing—competitive, legal, political, economic, technological, and sociocultural.
2. Assessing the organization's marketing resources—availability of human resources, capacity of equipment, and financial resources.

Assessing the *target market* includes asking

1. What are the current needs of each target market?
2. What changes in these needs are anticipated?
3. How well are the company's products meeting these needs?
4. What are the relevant aspects of consumer behavior and product use?

Evaluating the firm's *current marketing objectives and performance* includes

1. Making sure the firm's objectives are consistent with the marketing environment.
2. Analyzing the company's sales volume, market share, and profitability.

Strengths and Weaknesses

Here the focus is on the advantages and disadvantages that an organization has in meeting the target market's needs.

- *Example of a strength*: The company has a highly trained and capable sales force.
- *Example of a weakness*: The company's products have a low-quality image even though the actual quality is equal to or exceeds the quality of the major competitor's products.

Opportunities and Threats

This section covers factors that exist outside and independent of the company but that nonetheless can affect operations.

- *Opportunity*: Favorable conditions in the environment that could produce rewards for the company if acted on—for example, consumers have less leisure time and demand more convenience products.
- *Threat*: Conditions that may prevent the company from achieving its objectives unless acted on—for example, more women are working outside the home, which means that the company's door-to-door sales are suffering.

Marketing Objectives

This section states what the marketing activities are designed to accomplish. Forms of marketing objectives include

- Product introduction, improvement, or innovation
- Sales or market share
- Profitability
- Pricing
- Distribution
- Advertising

Marketing objectives must

- Be expressed in clear, simple terms.
- Be written so that they can be accurately measured.
- Give a time frame for achieving objectives.
- Be consistent with the company's overall marketing strategy.

Marketing Strategies

Marketing strategy includes selecting the target market and developing the marketing mix.

- *Selecting a target market*: Describe the target market in terms of demographic, geographic, psychographic, and product usage characteristics.
- *Determining the marketing mix*: Decide how product distribution, promotion, and price will satisfy customer needs.

Marketing Implementation

This section describes the process of putting the marketing strategies into action and answers

- What specific actions will we take?
- How will we perform these activities?
- Who is responsible for completing the activities?
- How much will these activities cost?

Evaluation and Control

How will the results of the marketing plan be measured and evaluated? Factors to be considered include

- *Performance standards*: How will the product's performance be judged?
- *Financial controls*: How will the company assess whether the marketing plan is working?
- *Monitoring procedures*: How will the cause of any problems be pinpointed?

Source: William M. Pride and O. C. Ferrell, *Marketing: Concepts and Strategies*, Eleventh Edition. Copyright © 2000 by Houghton Mifflin Company. Reprinted with permission.

sales forecast an estimate of the amount of a product that an organization expects to sell during a certain period of time, based on a specified level of marketing effort

A **sales forecast** is an estimate of the amount of a product that an organization expects to sell during a certain period of time, based on a specified level of marketing effort. Managers in different divisions of the organization rely on sales forecasts when they purchase raw materials, schedule production, secure financial resources, consider plant or equipment purchases, hire personnel, and plan inventory levels. Because the accuracy of a sales forecast is so important, organizations often use several forecasting methods, including executive judgments, surveys of buyers or sales personnel, time series analyses, correlation analyses, and market tests. The specific methods used depend on the costs involved, type of product, characteristics of the market, time span of the forecast, purposes for which the forecast is used, stability of historical sales data, availability of the required information, and expertise and experience of forecasters.

LEARNING OBJECTIVE

8 Distinguish between a marketing information system and marketing research.

Marketing Information

marketing information system a system for managing marketing information that is gathered continually from internal and external sources

The availability and use of accurate and timely information are critical to making effective marketing decisions. A wealth of marketing information is obtainable. There are two general ways to obtain it: through a marketing information system and through marketing research.

Marketing Information Systems

A **marketing information system** is a framework for managing marketing information that is gathered continually from internal and external sources. Most such systems are computer-based because of the amount of data the system must accept, store, sort, and retrieve. *Continual* collection of data is essential if the system is to incorporate the most up-to-date information.

In concept, the operation of a marketing information system is not complex. Data from a variety of sources are fed into the system. Data from *internal* sources include sales figures, product and marketing costs, inventory levels, and activities of the sales force. Data from *external* sources relate to the organization's suppliers, intermediaries, and customers; competitors' marketing activities; and economic conditions. All these data are stored and processed within the marketing information system. Its output is a flow of information in the form that is most useful for making marketing decisions. This information might include daily sales reports by territory and product, forecasts of sales or buying trends, and reports on changes in market share for the major brands in a specific industry. Both the information outputs and their form depend on the requirements of the personnel in the organization.

Marketing information provider. Many organizations, such as PricewaterhouseCoopers, provide information to help marketers develop, implement, and manage marketing strategies effectively.

Marketing Research

Marketing research is the process of systematically gathering, recording, and analyzing data concerning a particular marketing problem. Thus, marketing research is used in specific situations to obtain information not otherwise available to decision makers. It is an intermittent, rather than a continual, source of marketing information.

Table 13.5 outlines a six-step procedure for conducting marketing research. This procedure is particularly well suited to testing new products, determining various characteristics of consumer markets, and evaluating promo-

table 13.5 The Six Steps of Marketing Research

1. Define the problem	In this step, the problem is clearly and accurately stated to determine what issues are involved in the research, what questions to ask, and what types of solutions are needed. This is a crucial step that should not be rushed.
2. Make a preliminary investigation	The objective of preliminary investigation is to develop both a sharper definition of the problem and a set of tentative answers. The tentative answers are developed by examining internal information and published data and by talking with persons who have some experience with the problem. These answers will be tested by further research.
3. Plan the research	At this stage, researchers know what facts are needed to resolve the identified problem and what facts are available. They make plans on how to gather needed but missing data.
4. Gather factual information	Once the basic research plan has been completed, the needed information can be collected by mail, telephone, or personal interviews; by observation; or from commercial or government data sources. The choice depends on the plan and the available sources of information.
5. Interpret the information	Facts by themselves do not always provide a sound solution to a marketing problem. They must be interpreted and analyzed to determine the choices available to management.
6. Reach a conclusion	Sometimes the conclusion or recommendation becomes obvious when the facts are interpreted. However, in other cases, reaching a conclusion may not be so easy because of gaps in the information or intangible factors that are difficult to evaluate. If and when the evidence is less than complete, it is important to say so.

Source: Adapted from Small Business Administration, *Small Business Bibliography No. 9* (Washington, D.C.).

tional activities. Food processing companies, like Kraft General Foods and Kelloggs, use a variety of marketing research methods to avoid costly mistakes in introducing the wrong products or products in the wrong way or at the wrong time. They have been particularly interested in using marketing research to learn more about the African-American and Hispanic markets. Understanding of the food preferences, loyalties, and purchase motivators of these groups enables these companies to serve them better.

marketing research the process of systematically gathering, recording, and analyzing data concerning a particular marketing problem

Using Technology to Gather and Analyze Marketing Information

Technology is making information for marketing decisions increasingly accessible. The ability of firms to electronically track the purchase behavior of customers and to better determine what they want is changing the nature of marketing. The integration of telecommunications with computing technology provides marketers with access to accurate information not only about customers and competitors but also about industry forecasts and business trends. Among the communication tools that are radically changing the way marketers obtain and use information are databases, online information services, and the Internet. Lack of expertise is not a barrier to firms wishing to use the Internet for marketing activities. According to research by IDC, Inc., hosting a firm's web site and providing product information on a host's computer system on behalf of their client for a monthly fee is expected to grow from $1.8 in 2000 to $18.9 billion in 2004.[7]

A *database* is a collection of information arranged for easy access and retrieval. Using databases, marketers tap into internal sales reports, newspaper articles, company news releases, government economic reports, bibliographies, and more. Many marketers use commercial databases, such as LEXIS-NEXIS, to obtain useful information for marketing decisions. Many of these commercial databases are available (for a fee) in printed form, online for a fee, or on CD-ROMs. Others develop their own databases in-house. Some firms sell their databases to other organizations. *Reader's Digest*, for example, markets a database that provides information on 100 million households. Dunn & Bradstreet markets a database that includes information on the addresses, phone numbers, and contacts of businesses located in specific areas.

Information provided by a single firm on household demographics, purchases, television viewing behavior, and responses to promotions such as coupons and free samples is called *single-source data*. For example, Behavior Scan, offered by Information Resources, Inc., screens about 60,000 households in twenty-six U.S. markets. This single-source information service monitors household televisions and records the programs and commercials viewed. When buyers from these households shop in stores equipped with scanning registers, they present Hotline cards (similar to credit cards) to cashiers. This enables each customer's identification to be electronically coded so that the firm can track each product purchased and store the information in a database.

Online information services offer subscribers access to e-mail, web sites, files for downloading (such as with Acrobat Reader), news, databases, and research materials. By subscribing to "mailing lists," marketers can receive electronic newsletters and participate in online discussions with other network users. This ability to communicate online with customers, suppliers, and employees improves the capability of a firm's marketing information system and helps the company track its customers' changing desires and buying habits.

The *Internet* has evolved as a powerful communication medium, linking customers and companies around the world via computer networks with e-mail, forums, web pages, and more. Growth in Internet use, and especially the World Wide Web, has given rise to an entire industry that makes marketing information easily accessible to both companies and customers. The web organizes a great deal of the information available on the Internet into a series of interconnected "pages." Among the many web pages useful for marketing research are the home pages of Nielsen marketing research and *Advertising Age*. While most web home pages are open to all Internet users, some companies, like U.S. West and Turner Broadcasting System, also maintain internal web pages, called *intranets,* that allow employees to access internal data and facilitate communication among departments.

Table 13.6 lists a number of web sites that may serve as valuable resources for marketing research. The Bureau of the Census, for example, uses the World Wide Web to disseminate information that may be useful to marketing researchers, particularly through the *Statistical Abstract of the United States* and data from the most recent census. The Census Lookup option allows marketing researchers to create their own customized information. With this online tool, researchers can select tables by clicking boxes to select a state and then, within the state, the county, place, and urbanized area or metropolitan statistical area to be examined.

Types of Buying Behavior

buying behavior the decisions and actions of people involved in buying and using products

consumer buying behavior the purchasing of products for personal or household use, not for business purposes

business buying behavior the purchasing of products by producers, resellers, governmental units, and institutions

Buying behavior may be defined as the decisions and actions of people involved in buying and using products.[8] **Consumer buying behavior** refers to the purchasing of products for personal or household use, not for business purposes. **Business buying behavior** is the purchasing of products by producers, resellers, governmental units, and institutions. Since a firm's success depends greatly on buyers' reactions to a particular marketing strategy, it is important to understand buying behavior. Marketing managers are better able to predict customer responses to marketing strategies and to develop a satisfying marketing mix if they are aware of the factors that affect buying behavior.

table 13.6 Internet Sources of Marketing Information

Government Sources	
U.S. Bureau of the Census	**www.census.gov**
U.S. Department of State	**www.state.gov**
FedWorld	**www.fedworld.gov**
Chamber of Commerce	**chamber-of-commerce.com**
Commercial Sources	
A. C. Nielsen	**www.acnielsen.com**
Information Resources, Inc.	**www.infores.com**
Gallup	**www.gallup.com**
Arbitron	**www.arbitron.com**
Periodicals and Books	
American Demographics	**www.americandemographics.com**
Advertising Age	**www.adage.com**
Sales & Marketing Management	**www.salesandmarketing.com**
Fortune	**www.pathfinder.com/fortune**
Inc.	**www.inc.com**
Business Week	**www.businessweek.com**
Bloomberg Report	**www.bloomberg.com**

Source: William M. Pride and O. C. Ferrell, *Marketing: Concepts and Strategies*, Eleventh Edition. Copyright © 2000 by Houghton Mifflin Company. Reprinted with permission.

Consumer Buying Behavior

LEARNING OBJECTIVE

9 Identify the major steps in the consumer buying decision process and the sets of factors that may influence this process.

Consumers' buying behaviors differ when they buy different types of products. For frequently purchased, low-cost items, a consumer employs routine response behavior, involving very little search or decision-making effort. The buyer uses limited decision making for purchases made occasionally or when more information is needed about an unknown product in a well-known product category. When buying an unfamiliar, expensive item or one that is seldom purchased, the consumer engages in extensive decision making.

A person deciding on a purchase goes through some or all of the steps shown in Figure 13.4. First, the consumer acknowledges that a problem exists. A problem is usually the lack of a product or service that is desired or needed. Then the buyer looks for information, which may include brand names, product characteristics, warranties, and other features. Next, the buyer weighs the various alternatives he or she has discovered and then finally makes a choice and acquires the item. In the after-purchase stage, the consumer evaluates the suitability of the product. This judgment will affect future purchases. As Figure 13.4 shows, the buying process is influenced by situational factors (physical surroundings, social surroundings, time, purchase reason, and buyer's mood and condition), psychological factors (perception, motives, learning, attitudes, personality, lifestyles), and social factors (family, roles, peer groups, social class, culture and subculture). Many marketers use the Internet to expand channels of communication with buyers. Research suggests that consumers will not just visit a consumer product site without a motivating reason. Understanding why consumers visit sites drives their design and use by marketers. For example, Unilever Inc., makers of Wisk laundry detergent, has integrated consumer information about stain removal with the product's label and web site. Consumers can check the web site for the extra information that is a value-added utility in the marketing mix.[9]

Talking Technology

Digging Deeper into Buying Behavior

WHO, WHAT, WHEN, WHERE, WHY, AND how—marketers are looking for new ways to track and analyze consumer and business buying behavior. One approach is to use collaborative filtering software to gather and analyze buying information about many customers. By segmenting customers according to similarities and preferences in purchasing, this software can predict the buying behavior of other customers with comparable preferences. One online retailer used collaborative filtering when a customer wanted to buy a $28 shirt. Knowing that other people who had bought that type of shirt also bought cigar humidors, the retailer offered the customer a $130 humidor—and made the sale.

Another way to meet customer needs is by digging deeper to analyze their online behavior. Net-Temps, an online recruiting service, used to count how many hits each of its web pages received. The firm quickly decided that it needed "to know more—the frequency of hits, page population, repeat visitors," says vice president Kevin Strange. Using special software, Net-Temps was able to analyze what types of jobs visitors were searching for and create channels with appropriate job groupings. It also used the software to test different placements of a "submit résumé" button and see which attracted the highest response.

Customer-management software is helping Honeywell International come up with ideas for new business services by better understanding its customers' buying headaches. The company uses a sophisticated program to track interaction with the airlines who buy jet engines and other products from its air-transport division. Studying the data, Honeywell found that some airlines were complaining about problems with parts inventories. In response to this need, the company began offering customers a new inventory-management service.

Marriott International is using customer-management software to store the preferences of its hotel guests so it can anticipate their needs during future stays. The hotel chain has generated millions of dollars in additional revenue by selling services based on its customers' buying behavior. Marriott's chairman explains, "It's a big competitive advantage to be able to greet a customer with: 'Mr. Jones, welcome back to Marriott. We know you like a king-size bed. We know you need a rental car.' "

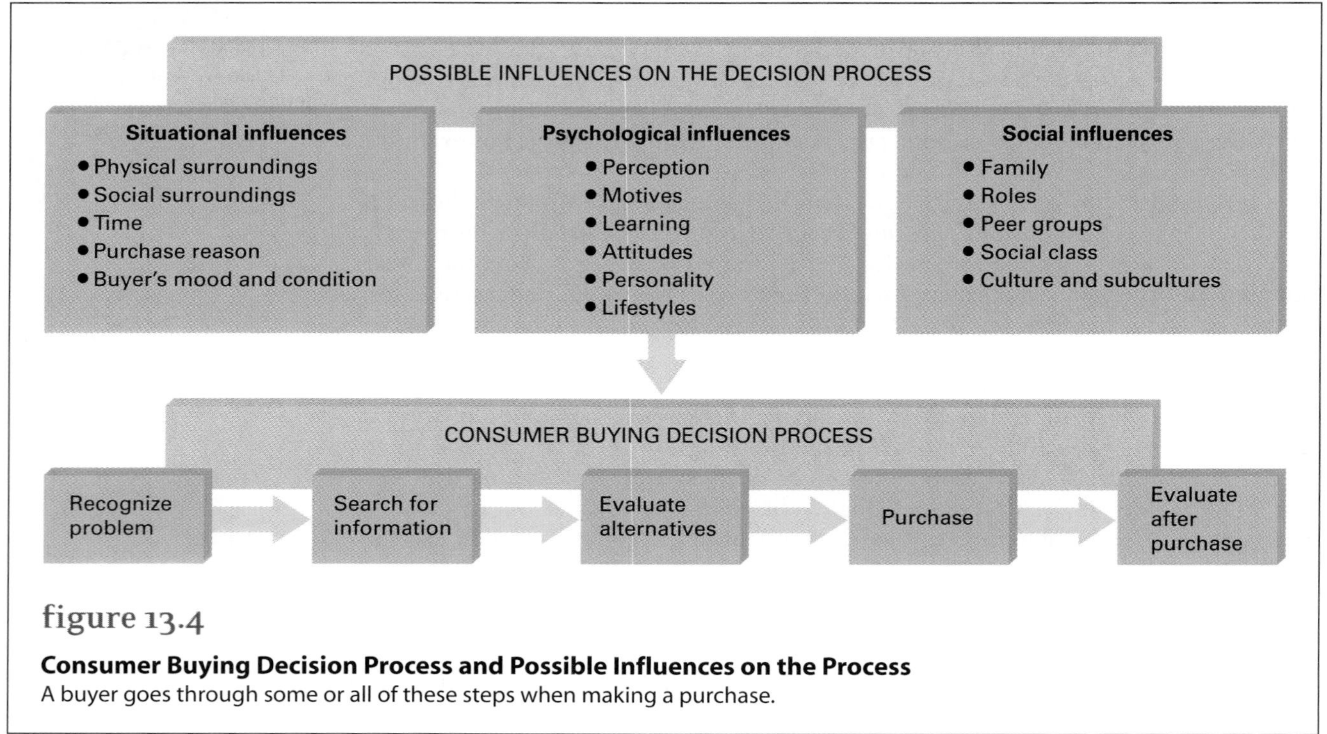

figure 13.4

Consumer Buying Decision Process and Possible Influences on the Process

A buyer goes through some or all of these steps when making a purchase.

Source: William M. Pride and O. C. Ferrell, *Marketing: Concepts and Strategies*, Eleventh Edition. Copyright © 2000 by Houghton Mifflin Company. Reprinted with permission.

Business Buying Behavior

Business buyers consider a product's quality, its price, and the service provided by suppliers. Marketers at GraniteRock Company understand the value of customer service and thus concentrate their efforts on on-time delivery to distinguish GraniteRock from its competitors.[10] They are usually better informed than consumers about products and generally buy in larger quantities. In a business, a committee or group of people, rather than single individuals, often decides on purchases. Committee members must consider the organization's objectives, purchasing policies, resources, and personnel. Business buying occurs through description, inspection, sampling, or negotiation. A number of organizations buy a variety of products online. School districts save 10 to 20 percent on school supplies and receive their orders in two days instead of seven days.[11]

Buying behavior. Buying behavior involves both the decisions and actions associated with buying and using products. Before this consumer actually purchases a tennis racket, she will make up her mind that she wants one, and then will learn more about the different brands and features that are available.

The American Consumer

In this section, we examine several measures of consumer income, a major source of buying power. By looking at why, what, where, and when consumers buy, we gain a better understanding of how this income is spent.

Consumer Income

Purchasing power is created by income. However, as every taxpayer knows, not all income is available for spending. For this reason, marketers consider income in three different ways. **Personal income** is the income an individual receives from all sources *less* the Social Security taxes the individual must pay. **Disposable income** is personal income *less* all additional personal taxes. These taxes include income, estate, gift, and property taxes levied by local, state, and federal governments. About 3 percent of all disposable income is saved. **Discretionary income** is disposable income *less* savings and expenditures on food, clothing, and housing. Discretionary income is of particular interest to marketers because consumers have the most choice in spending it. Consumers use their discretionary income to purchase items ranging from automobiles and vacations to movies and pet food.

LEARNING OBJECTIVE

10 Describe three ways of measuring consumer income.

Why Do Consumers Buy?

Consumers buy with the hope of getting a large amount of current and future satisfaction relative to their buying power. They buy because they would rather have a particular good or service than the money they have to spend to buy it. Here are major reasons why consumers choose to buy some specific products.

1. *They have a use for the product.* Many items fill an immediate "use" need. A family needs pots and pans; a student needs books.
2. *They like the convenience a product offers.* Such items as electric can openers and cordless telephones are not essential, but they offer convenience and thus satisfaction.
3. *They believe the purchase will enhance their wealth.* People collect antiques or gold coins as investments as well as for enjoyment. Homeowners buy paint, landscape services, and ornamental fences to add to the value of their property.

personal income the income an individual receives from all sources *less* the Social Security taxes the individual must pay

disposable income personal income *less* all additional personal taxes

discretionary income disposable income *less* savings and expenditures on food, clothing, and housing

spotLight

Source: Copyright 2000, USA TODAY. Reprinted with permission.

4. *They take pride in ownership.* Many consumers purchase items like Rolex watches because such products provide status and pride of ownership, as well as utility.
5. *They buy for safety.* Consumers buy health, life, and fire insurance to protect themselves and their families. Smoke detectors, burglar alarms, traveler's checks, and similar products also provide safety and protection.

What Do Consumers Buy?

Figure 13.5 shows how consumer spending is divided among various categories of goods and services. The average American household spent $35,535 in 1998, according to the latest available data from the Bureau of Labor Statistics. The greatest proportion of disposable income was spent on food, clothing, and shelter. The largest share—$11,713—went toward housing and related expenses, such as supplies, utilities, and furnishings. The second-largest expense was transportation, with families spending an average of $6,616 on cars and other vehicles, insurance, repairs, and public transportation. The average household spent $4,810 on food, including $2,780 to eat at home. Clothing and related services, such as dry cleaning, used up $1,674. Another $1,746 went toward entertainment, and slightly more than $1,903 was spent on health care.[12]

Consumers are changing their spending patterns. They are spending more money on goods and services that they think will keep them healthy, mobile, and informed. Over the last year, participation in selected sport and fitness activities has changed. Participation increased for kickboxing, skateboarding, muzzle-loading, martial arts, and bow hunting, while participation declined in windsurfing, sailing, mountain biking, volleyball, inline skating, and racketball.[13] Engaged couples are showing a preference for experiences and activities over possessions; many skip registering at stores that sell traditional wedding gifts like china and silver and instead request gifts such as sporting goods, camping equipment, and tools. Spending on computers and educational toys is also on the rise. Parents may scrimp in other areas but buy educational toys because they believe those toys are "an investment" in their children's future. Working parents also place high value on scarce family time, thus spending more of their budgets on family vacations and outings. The top 1 percent of the wealthier Americans shun luxury items, like furs and jewelry, in favor of spending money on their children or investing for retirement.[14]

Why do consumers buy? Consumers buy products for a variety of reasons. Some might use Tropicana Pure Premium Orange Juice because of its taste and nutritional value.

Where Do Consumers Buy?

Probably the most important influence on a consumer's decision about where to buy a particular product is his or her perception of the store. Consumers' general impressions of an establishment's products, prices, and sales personnel can mean the difference between repeat sales and lost business. Consumers distinguish among various types of retail outlets (such as specialty shops, department stores,

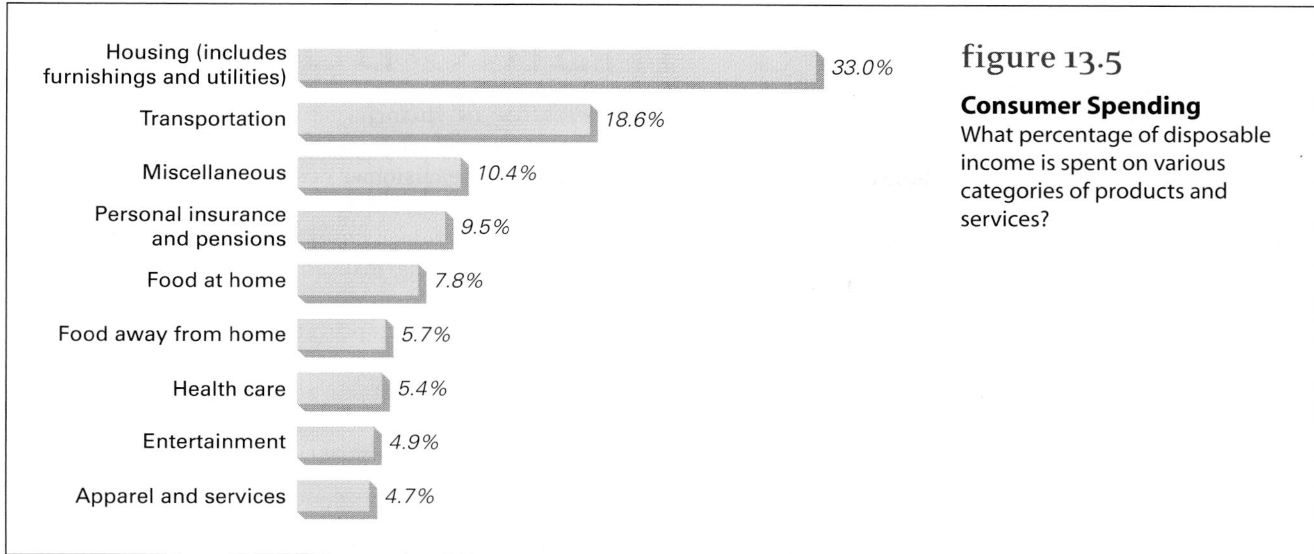

figure 13.5

Consumer Spending
What percentage of disposable income is spent on various categories of products and services?

Source: Bureau of Labor Statistics, Office of Pricing and Living Conditions, ftp://ftp.bls.gov/pub/specialrequests, March 2000.

and discount outlets), and they choose particular types of stores for specific purchases. Many retail outlets go to a great deal of trouble to build and maintain a particular image, and they carry only those products that fit the image. Consumers also select the businesses they patronize on the basis of location, product assortment, and such services as credit terms, return privileges, and free delivery.

People buy online, too. A recent survey shows that the top three sites for both men and women are Amazon.com, Barnes&Noble.com, and CD.now. For women, the most often purchased products bought online are books, CDs, computers, health and beauty products, toys, and clothing. Men's online purchases focus on computers, CDs, books, small consumer electronics, videos, and air travel. Due to convenience, speed, and efficiency, men prefer to shop at online malls. However, women prefer to shop at brick and mortar malls.[15] More and more consumers are choosing to shop on the Internet or seek information to enable a purchase at a later time. According to Nielsen/NetRatings there are an estimated 15 million web sites today. However, people tend to visit their favorite top ten sites repeatedly. When they do venture onto a new site for the first time they usually don't stay very long. According to NetSmart America, 87 percent of viewers quickly abandon a new site due to the frustration they experience navigating unfamiliar content. If building web traffic is a serious goal, the message for site designers is clear: keep it simple.[16]

When Do Consumers Buy?

In general, consumers buy when buying is most convenient. Certain business hours have long been standard for establishments that sell consumer products. However, many of these establishments have stretched their hours to include evenings, holidays, and Sundays. Also, many catalog and online companies are accessible twenty-four hours a day, seven days a week. Ultimately, customers control when they do their buying. Ironically, the very power of the Internet to allow convenient shopping online anytime and anywhere the consumer has access to the web is also a great concern for marketers who fear losing control of sales and distribution of products. The recorded music industry, for instance, has felt particularly threatened by software like MP3 and Napster that allowed users to share their recorded files of music. Others argue that the film industry cried the same song when television and later videotape technology entered the marketplace.[17]

In the next chapter, we discuss two elements of the marketing mix: product and price. Our emphasis will be on product development and pricing within a marketing strategy.

RETURN TO Inside Business

DESPITE INCREASED COMPETITION IN financial services, USAA is thriving because of its devotion to personalized customer service. Using cutting-edge computer systems, USAA employees can analyze customer needs and suggest specific services to meet those needs. They can also respond to customer claims and complaints more quickly and track changes in customer status that signal future needs.

Already one of the largest auto and home insurance firms in the United States, USAA expects to double its customer base over the next decade. As part of its ongoing commitment to customer service improvements, the company is expanding its Internet operations so customers can log on from anywhere in the world, enter a password, and check the status of their accounts or handle other transactions. Even though these customers will never actually meet a USAA representative, they can still enjoy customized customer service at the click of a mouse.

Questions

1. Is USAA practicing the marketing concept and relationship marketing? Explain.
2. Which forces in the marketing environment are most likely to affect USAA? Why?

chapter Review

SUMMARY

1 Understand the meaning of *marketing*, and explain how it creates utility for purchasers of products.

Marketing is the process of planning and executing the conception, pricing, promotion, and distribution of ideas, goods, and services to create exchanges that satisfy individual and organizational objectives. Marketing adds value in the form of utility, or the power of a product or service to satisfy a need. It creates place utility by making products available where customers want them, time utility by making products available when customers want them, and possession utility by transferring the ownership of products to buyers.

2 Trace the development of the marketing concept and understand how it is implemented.

From the Industrial Revolution until the early twentieth century, businesspeople focused on the production of goods; from the 1920s to the 1950s, the emphasis moved to the selling of goods. During the 1950s, however, businesspeople recognized that their enterprises involved not only producing and selling products but also satisfying customers' needs. They began to implement the marketing concept, a business philosophy that involves the entire organization in the dual processes of meeting the customers' needs and achieving the organization's goals.

Implementation of the marketing concept begins and ends with customers—first to determine what customers' needs are and later to evaluate how well the firm is meeting those needs.

3 Understand what markets are and how they are classified.

A market consists of people with needs, the ability to buy, and the desire and authority to purchase. Markets are classified as consumer and industrial (producer, reseller, governmental, and institutional) markets.

4 Identify the four elements of the marketing mix, and be aware of their importance in developing a marketing strategy.

A marketing strategy is a plan for the best use of an organization's resources to meet its objectives. Developing a marketing strategy involves selecting and analyzing a target market and creating and maintaining a marketing mix that will satisfy that target market. A target market is chosen through either the undifferentiated approach or the market segmentation approach. A market segment is a group of individuals or organizations within a market that have similar characteristics and needs. Businesses that use an undifferentiated approach design a single marketing mix and direct it at the entire market for a particular product. The market segmentation approach directs a marketing mix at a segment of a market.

The four elements of a firm's marketing mix are product, price, distribution, and promotion. The product ingredient includes decisions about the product's design, brand name, packaging, and warranties. The pricing ingredient is concerned with both base prices and various types of discounts. Distribution involves not only transportation and storage but also the selection of intermediaries. Promotion focuses on providing information to target markets. The elements of the marketing mix can be varied to suit broad organizational goals, marketing objectives, and target markets.

5 Explain how the marketing environment affects strategic market planning.

To achieve a firm's marketing objectives, marketing mix strategies must begin with an assessment of the marketing environment, which in turn will influence decisions about marketing mix ingredients. Marketing activities are affected by a number of external forces that make up the marketing environment. These forces include economic forces, sociocultural forces, political forces, competitive forces, legal and regulatory forces, and technological forces. Economic forces affect customers' ability and willingness to buy. Sociocultural forces are societal and cultural factors, such as attitudes, beliefs, and lifestyles, that affect customers' buying choices. Political forces and legal and regulatory forces influence marketing planning through laws that protect consumers and regulate competition. Competitive forces are the actions of competitors who are implementing their own marketing plans. Technological forces can create new marketing opportunities or quickly cause a product to become obsolete.

6 Understand the major components of a marketing plan.

A marketing plan is a written document that specifies an organization's resources, objectives, strategy, and implementation and control efforts to be used in marketing a specific product or product group. The marketing plan describes a firm's current position, establishes marketing objectives, and specifies the methods the organization will use to achieve these objectives. Marketing plans can be short-range, covering one year or less; medium-range, covering two to five years; and long-range, covering periods of more than five years.

7 Describe how market measurement and sales forecasting are used.

Market measurement and sales forecasting are used to estimate sales potential and predict product sales in specific market segments.

8 Distinguish between a marketing information system and marketing research.

Strategies are monitored and evaluated through marketing research and the marketing information system, which stores and processes internal and external data in a form that aids marketing decision making. A marketing information system is a system for managing marketing information that is gathered continually from internal and external sources. Marketing research is the process of systematically gathering, recording, and analyzing data concerning a particular marketing problem. It is an intermittent, rather than a continual, source of marketing information. Technology is making information for marketing decisions more accessible. Electronic communication tools can be very useful for accumulating accurate information with minimal customer interaction. Information technologies that are changing the way marketers obtain and use information are databases, online information services, and the Internet.

9 Identify the major steps in the consumer buying decision process and the sets of factors that may influence this process.

Buying behavior consists of the decisions and actions of people involved in buying and using products. Consumer buying behavior refers to the purchase of products for personal or household use. Organizational buying behavior is the purchase of products by producers, resellers, governments, and institutions. Understanding buying behavior helps marketers predict how buyers will respond to marketing strategies. The consumer buying decision process consists of five steps, including recognizing the problem, searching for information, evaluating alternatives, purchasing and evaluating after purchase. Factors affecting the consumer buying decision process fall into three categories: situational influences, psychological influences, and social influences.

10 Describe three ways of measuring consumer income.

Personal income is the income an individual receives, less the Social Security taxes he or she must pay. Disposable income is personal income minus all other taxes. Discretionary income is what remains of disposable income after savings and expenditures for necessities. Consumers use discretionary income to buy goods and services that best satisfy their needs.

KEY TERMS

You should now be able to define and give an example relevant to each of the following terms:

marketing (356)
utility (356)
form utility (356)
place utility (357)
time utility (357)
possession utility (357)
marketing concept (358)
relationship marketing (358)
market (359)
marketing strategy (360)
marketing mix (360)

target market (361)
undifferentiated approach (361)
market segment (363)
market segmentation (363)
marketing plan (366)
sales forecast (368)
marketing information system (368)
marketing research (369)
buying behavior (370)
consumer buying behavior (370)
business buying behavior (370)
personal income (373)
disposable income (373)
discretionary income (373)

REVIEW QUESTIONS

1. How, specifically, does marketing create place, time, and possession utility?
2. How is a marketing-oriented firm different from a production-oriented firm or a sales-oriented firm?
3. What are the major requirements for a group of individuals and organizations to be a market? How does a consumer market differ from a business-to-business market?
4. What are the major components of a marketing strategy?
5. What is the purpose of market segmentation? What is the relationship between market segmentation and the selection of target markets?
6. What are the four elements of the marketing mix? In what sense are they "controllable"?
7. Describe the forces in the marketing environment that affect an organization's marketing decisions.
8. What is a marketing plan and what are its major components?
9. What major issues should be specified before conducting a sales forecast?
10. What is the difference between a marketing information system and a marketing research project? How might the two be related?
11. What new information technologies are changing the ways that marketers keep track of business trends and customers?
12. Why do marketers need to understand buying behavior?
13. How are personal income, disposable income, and discretionary income related? Which is the best indicator of consumer purchasing power?
14. List five reasons why consumers make purchases. What need is satisfied in each case?

DISCUSSION QUESTIONS

1. In what way is each of the following a marketing activity?
   a. The provision of sufficient parking space for customers at a suburban shopping mall
   b. The purchase by a clothing store of seven dozen sweaters in assorted sizes and colors
   c. The inclusion of a longer and more comprehensive warranty on an automobile
2. How might adoption of the marketing concept benefit a firm? How might it benefit the firm's customers?
3. Is marketing information as important to small firms as it is to larger firms? Explain.
4. How does the marketing environment affect a firm's marketing strategy?

VIDEO CASE

1-800-Flowers Keeps Its Business in Bloom

Call toll-free to send a bouquet anywhere for any reason—that's the simple, customer-friendly idea that transformed a small Manhattan flower shop into the world's largest flower seller. In the mid-1980s, Jim McCann added a toll-free phone line to his shop, then called Flora Plenty. He chose the phone number 1-800-356-9377 to spell 1-800-Flowers, a number that would be easy for people to remember. Right away, McCann noticed that more customers were calling in flower orders for family and friends, rather than visiting the store. By 1986, he had operators taking phone orders 24 hours a day, seven days a week. The phone operation generated so much business that McCann changed the name of his company to 1-800-Flowers and began looking for more ways to make buying as fast and convenient as possible for customers.

As Internet technology emerged in the early 1990s, McCann saw another opportunity to expand by allowing customers to order bouquets with a click of the mouse. He negotiated to get 1-800-Flowers a spot on CompuServe in 1992, making it the first online store. In 1994, he arranged to put 1-800-Flowers in a prominent position on the America Online screen. Then he opened a separate web site called 1-800-Flowers.com in 1995 and partnered with Microsoft Network, Yahoo!, and thousands of other sites to draw visitors there. Although the company's phone sales remain strong, online flower sales are growing even more rapidly, already topping $30 million per year.

McCann knows that many of his customers buy flowers as gifts for different occasions. Mother's Day remains the busiest day of the year for flower sales, but customers also send bouquets for all kinds of reasons: to celebrate a birthday, to cheer someone who is ill, or to apologize. When a customer orders flowers by phone or on the web, the bouquet is prepared and delivered by one of 1,500 participating florists (including 120 company-owned or franchised shops), depending on the location of the recipient. The company has also added specialty gifts and collectibles plus fine jewelry, candy, and gourmet food to give customers a wider range of choices and bring them back again and again for different gift-giving occasions.

After years of handling flower and gift orders, the database at 1-800-Flowers is filled with details about the buying behavior of the company's 8 million customers. Marketing experts use special software to analyze these details and, by adding demographic and psychographic data purchased from external sources, get a well-rounded picture of their customer base. With this background, the company can develop as many as 100 different marketing campaigns to acquire and retain customers in targeted segments. For example, one prime segment being targeted is 18 to 35 year-old men with $60,000-plus in annual income.

1-800-Flowers.com is pioneering online customer service techniques, just as 1-800-Flowers pioneered telephone ordering in the flower industry. Originally, the company handled online customer inquiries by e-mail or phone. But management quickly realized that customers asking for help wanted answers immediately, not the next day or even a few hours later. So in 1998, management introduced live online customer-service chat technology. Now customers can type in their questions and receive typed responses instantly from customer service representatives. This encourages customers to complete their purchases rather than going to competitors, and it reinforces the quality service image of 1-800-Flowers. Just as important, this chat system has sliced the company's customer service e-mail volume in half, saving time and money.

Despite the success of the phone operation and web site, McCann knows that some 1-800-Flowers customers really enjoy seeing and smelling the flowers they are buying. That's why McCann started Happy Hour on Friday afternoons. During these special events, the company invites local customers to stop in to a nearby 1-800-Flowers shop, see some new or unusual flowers, get a special price on featured items—and be inspired to visit, phone, or click on 1-800-Flowers again.[18]

Questions

1. How does 1-800-Flowers create time and place utility for its customers?
2. Which market segmentation approach is 1-800-Flowers using?
3. How has 1-800-Flowers used its knowledge of consumer buying behavior to attract and retain customers?

Building skills for career success

1. Exploring the Internet

Consumer products companies with a variety of famous brand names known around the world are making their presence known on the Internet through web sites and online banner advertising. The giants in consumer products include U.S.-based Procter & Gamble (http://www.pg.com/), Swiss-based Nestlé (http://www.nestle.com/), and British-based Unilever (http://www.unilever.com/).

According to Tony Romeo, cofounder and chairman of the Unilever Interactive Brand Center in New York, the firm is committed to making the Internet part of its marketing strategy. The center carries out research and development and serves as a model for others now in operation in the Netherlands and Singapore. Information uncovered is shared with interactive marketers assigned to specific business units. Eventually, centers will be established globally, reflecting the fact that most of Unilever's $34 billion of sales takes place in Europe and in 88 countries around the world.

Unilever's view that online consumer product sales are the way of the future was indicated by online alliances established with Microsoft Network, America Online, and NetGrocer.com. Creating an online dialogue with consumers on a global scale is no simple task. Cultural differences are often subtle and difficult to explain but nonetheless, are perceived by the viewers interacting with a site. Unilever's web site, which is its connection to customers all over the world, has a global feel to it. The question is whether or not it is satisfactory to each target audience.[19] Visit the text web site for updates to this exercise.

Assignment

1. Examine the Unilever, Procter & Gamble, and Nestlé sites and describe the features you think would be most interesting to consumers.
2. Describe those features you do not like and explain why.
3. Do you think the sites can contribute to better consumer buyer behavior? Explain your thinking.

2. Developing Critical Thinking Skills

Market segmentation is the process of breaking down a larger target market into smaller segments. One common base of market segmentation is demographics. Demographics for the consumer market, which consists of individuals and household members who buy goods for their own use, include such criteria as age, gender, race, religion, income, family size, occupation, education, social class, and marital status. Liz Claiborne, Inc., retailer of women's apparel, uses demographics to target a market it calls *Liz Lady*. The company knows Liz Lady's age, income range, professional status, and family status, and it uses this profile to make marketing decisions.

Assignment

1. Identify a company that markets to the consumer.
2. Identify the company's major product.
3. Determine the demographics of one of their markets.
   a. From the list on the next page, choose the demographics that apply to this market. (Remember that the demographics chosen must relate to the interest, need, and ability of the customer to purchase the product.)
   b. Briefly describe each demographic.

Consumer Market	*Description*
Age ___	____________
Income ___	____________
Gender ___	____________
Race ___	____________
Ethnicity ___	____________
Income ___	____________
Occupation ___	____________
Family size ___	____________
Education ___	____________
Religion ___	____________
Homeowner ___	____________
Marital Status ___	____________
Social class ___	____________

4. Summarize your findings in a statement that describes the target market for the company's product.

3. Building Team Skills

Review the text definitions of *market* and *target market.* Markets can be classified as consumer or industrial. Buyer behavior consists of the decisions and actions of those involved in buying and using products or services. By examining aspects of a company's products you can usually determine the company's target market and the characteristics important to members of that target market.

Assignment

1. Working in teams of three to five, identify a company and its major products.
2. List and discuss characteristics that customers might find important. These factors might include price, quality, brand name, variety of services, salespeople, customer service, special offers, promotional campaign, packaging, convenience of use, convenience of purchase, location, guarantees, store/office decor, payment terms.
3. Write a description of the company's primary customer (target market).

4. Researching Different Careers

Before interviewing for a job, you should learn all you can about the company. With this information, you will be prepared to ask meaningful questions about the firm during the interview, and the interviewer will no doubt be impressed with your knowledge of the business and your interest in it. To find out about a company, you can conduct some market research.

Assignment

1. Choose at least two local companies for which you might like to work.
2. Contact your local Chamber of Commerce. (The Chamber of Commerce collects information about local businesses, and most of its services are free.) Ask for information about the companies.
3. Call the Better Business Bureau in your community and ask if there are any complaints against the companies.
4. Prepare a report summarizing your findings.

5. Improving Communication Skills

Each year, *Sales and Marketing Management* magazine publishes an issue called "Survey of Buying Power." It contains data on every county in the United States and cities with populations over 10,000. Included are:

- Total population
- Number of households
- Median cash income per household
- Population percentage breakdown by income
- Total retail sales for each of the following businesses: automotive, drug, food, furniture, general merchandise, and household appliances

Assignment

1. Choose one of the businesses whose total retail sales are given in *Sales and Marketing Management* magazine's annual "Survey of Buying Power."
2. Use the magazine to evaluate trends in the industry. Is demand for the product increasing or decreasing?
4. Report to the class on total retail sales and potential demand.
5. Summarize your findings in a report.

creating and pricing products that satisfy customers

14

LEARNING OBJECTIVES

1 Explain what a product is and how products are classified.

2 Discuss the product life cycle and how it leads to new-product development.

3 Define *product line* and *product mix*, and distinguish between the two.

4 Identify the methods available for changing a product mix.

5 Explain the uses and importance of branding, packaging, and labeling.

6 Describe the economic basis of pricing and the means by which sellers can control prices and buyers' perceptions of prices.

7 Identify the major pricing objectives used by businesses.

8 Examine the three major pricing methods that firms employ.

9 Explain the different strategies available to companies for setting prices.

10 Describe three major types of pricing associated with business products.

their first product, a football, was received so well, they moved quickly to introduce new designs of basketballs, volley balls, soccer balls, and baseballs.

inside Business

Classic Sport Scores a New Product Touchdown

Kicking footballs and dribbling basketballs are just part of the daily work routine for Randy Jones and Mike Oister. As cofounders of Classic Sport, based in Denver, Jones and Oister are in business to make a better ball. Their entrepreneurial spirit was ignited in 1992, when the two former high school and college buddies were tossing a football around on a windy November afternoon. Watching the ball drift in the breeze, they hatched the idea of developing a higher-quality football that would stay on course during a pass.

If they were going to sell footballs and become major players in the sporting-goods industry, Jones and Oister had to be prepared to compete with well-established, deep-pocketed giants such as Wilson, Nike, and Spalding. That's why their first step was to carefully analyze the market. Visiting sporting-goods retailers, the entrepreneurs talked with sales staff about what customers were buying. They also asked what store managers wanted from their suppliers. In more conversations at the Super Show, a yearly industry convention, Jones and Oister learned that retail chains were looking for new, exclusive brands rather than carrying the same old brands that are available everywhere.

Now they needed to find a unique new twist on the standard football. Oister dissected a 1950s football and found that the rubber bladder inside was the key to keeping the ball spinning in a tight spiral. After months of experimentation, Oister and Jones created a prototype football with a heavyweight rubber bladder for stability, a durable exterior for longer life, and cotton laces that players can more easily grip. Then, using their knowledge of the product and the market, the partners developed a detailed business plan showing estimated levels of sales and profits.

Convinced they could score a touchdown in sporting goods, the two registered their business as R.A.M. Sports (for "Randy and Mike"). Then they began taking cash advances on their credit cards and raising money from friends and family to put their football into production. With prototypes in hand, Jones and Oister traveled the Northeast, selling the Classic Sport football to retail chains. Part of their marketing strategy was to train store salespeople in how to explain the features and benefits of their footballs.

Their first product was received so well that the two went on to design new basketballs, volleyballs, soccer balls, and baseballs. During the first year, their company generated $201,000 in sales. Within a few years, the company—renamed Classic Sport, after its top brand—was ringing up more than $10 million in annual sales. Just as important, an intense focus on the needs of consumers and retailers has helped Jones and Oister score a critical touchdown. Their share of the football market is now higher than Nike's share.[1]

A **product** is everything one receives in an exchange, including all tangible and intangible attributes and expected benefits. A Classic Sport football for example, includes not only the ball itself but also instructions, an inflation needle, and a warranty. A car includes a warranty, owner's manual, and perhaps free emergency road service for a year. Some of the intangibles that may go with an automobile include the status associated with ownership and the memories generated from past rides. Developing and managing products effectively is crucial to an organization's ability to maintain successful marketing mixes.

product everything one receives in an exchange, including all tangible and intangible attributes and expected benefits; it may be a good, service, or idea

A product may be a good, service, or idea. A *good* is a real, physical thing that we can touch, such as a Classic Sport football. A *service* is the result of applying human or mechanical effort to a person or thing. Basically, a service is a change we pay others to make for us. A real estate agent's services result in a change in the ownership of real property. A barber's services result in a change in your appearance. An *idea* may take the form of philosophies, lessons, concepts, or advice. Often, ideas are included with a good or service. Thus, we might buy a book (a good) that provides ideas on how to lose weight. Or we might join Weight Watchers for ideas on how to lose weight and for help (services) in doing so.

Our definition of the term *product* is based on the concept of an exchange. In a purchase, the product is exchanged for money—an amount of money equal to the *price* of the product. When the product is a good, the price may include such services as delivery, installation, warranties, and training. A good *with* such services is not the same product as the good *without* such services. In other words, sellers set a price for a particular "package" of goods, services, and ideas. When the makeup of that package changes, the price should change as well.

We look first in this chapter at products. We examine product classifications and describe the four stages, or life cycle, through which every product moves. Next we illustrate how firms manage products effectively by modifying or deleting existing products and by developing new products. We also discuss branding, packaging, and labeling of products. Then our focus shifts to pricing. We explain competitive factors that influence sellers' pricing decisions and also explore buyers' perceptions of prices. After considering organizational objectives that can be accomplished through pricing, we outline several methods for setting prices. Finally, we describe pricing strategies by which sellers can reach target markets successfully.

Classification of Products

LEARNING OBJECTIVE

1 Explain what a product is and how products are classified.

Different classes of products are directed at particular target markets. A product's classification largely determines what kinds of distribution, promotion, and pricing are appropriate in marketing the product.

Products can be grouped into two general categories: consumer and business (also called *business-to-business* or *industrial products*). A product purchased to satisfy personal and family needs is a **consumer product**. A product bought for resale, for making other products, or for use in a firm's operations is a **business product**. The buyer's use of the product determines the classification of an item. Note that a single item can be both a consumer and a business product. A broom is a consumer product if you use it in your home. However, the same broom is a business product if you use it in the maintenance of your business. After a product is classified as a consumer or business product, it can be further categorized as a particular type of consumer or business product.

consumer product a product purchased to satisfy personal and family needs

business product a product bought for resale, for making other products, or for use in a firm's operations

Consumer Product Classifications

The traditional and most widely accepted system of classifying consumer products consists of three categories: convenience, shopping, and specialty products. These groupings are based primarily on characteristics of buyers' purchasing behavior.

Convenience products. Most products available at grocery stores are convenience products.

A **convenience product** is a relatively inexpensive, frequently purchased item for which buyers want to exert only minimal effort. Examples include bread, gasoline, newspapers, soft drinks, and chewing gum. The buyer spends little time in planning the purchase of a convenience item or in comparing available brands or sellers.

A **shopping product** is an item for which buyers are willing to expend considerable effort on planning and making the purchase. Buyers allocate ample time for comparing stores and brands with respect to prices, product features, qualities, services, and perhaps warranties. Appliances, upholstered furniture, men's suits, bicycles, and cellular phones are examples of shopping products. These products are expected to last for a fairly long time and thus are purchased less frequently than convenience items.

A **specialty product** possesses one or more unique characteristics for which a group of buyers is willing to expend considerable purchasing effort. Buyers actually plan the purchase of a specialty product; they know exactly what they want and will not accept a substitute. In searching for specialty products, purchasers do not compare alternatives. Examples include unique sports cars, a specific type of antique dining table, a rare imported beer, or perhaps special handcrafted stereo speakers.

One problem with this approach to classification is that buyers may behave differently when purchasing a specific type of product. Thus, a single product can fit into more than one category. To minimize this problem, marketers think in terms of how buyers are most likely to behave when purchasing a specific item.

convenience product a relatively inexpensive, frequently purchased item for which buyers want to exert only minimal effort

shopping product an item for which buyers are willing to expend considerable effort on planning and making the purchase

specialty product an item that possesses one or more unique characteristics for which a significant group of buyers is willing to expend considerable purchasing effort

raw material a basic material that actually becomes part of a physical product; usually comes from mines, forests, oceans, or recycled solid wastes

major equipment large tools and machines used for production purposes

accessory equipment standardized equipment used in a firm's production or office activities

component part an item that becomes part of a physical product and is either a finished item ready for assembly or a product that needs little processing before assembly

Business Product Classifications

Based on their characteristics and intended uses, business products can be classified into the following categories: raw materials, major equipment, accessory equipment, component parts, process materials, supplies, and services.

A **raw material** is a basic material that actually becomes part of a physical product. It usually comes from mines, forests, oceans, or recycled solid wastes. Raw materials are usually bought and sold according to grades and specifications.

Major equipment includes large tools and machines used for production purposes. Examples of major equipment are lathes, cranes, and stamping machines. Some major equipment is custom-made for a particular organization, but other items are standardized products that perform one or several tasks for many types of organizations.

Accessory equipment is standardized equipment used in a firm's production or office activities. Examples include hand tools, typewriters, fractional-horsepower motors, and calculators. Compared with major equipment, accessory items are usually much less expensive and are purchased routinely with less negotiation.

A **component part** becomes part of a physical product and is either a finished item ready for assembly or a product that needs little processing before assembly. Although it becomes part of a larger product, a component part can often be identified easily. Clocks, tires, computer chips, and switches are examples of component parts.

A **process material** is used directly in the production of another product. Unlike a component part, however, a process material is not readily identifiable in the finished product. Like component parts, process materials are purchased according to industry standards or to the specifications of the individual purchaser. Examples include industrial glue and food preservatives.

A **supply** facilitates production and operations, but it does not become part of the finished product. Paper, pencils, oils, and cleaning agents are examples.

A **business service** is an intangible product that an organization uses in its operations. Examples include financial, legal, online, janitorial, and marketing research services. Purchasers must decide whether to provide their own services internally or to hire them from outside the organization.

Major equipment. Large pieces of machinery, such as the one shown here, are business products and are classified as major equipment.

The Product Life Cycle

LEARNING OBJECTIVE

2 Discuss the product life cycle and how it leads to new-product development.

In a way, products are like people. They are born, they live, and they die. Every product progresses through a **product life cycle,** a series of stages in which its sales revenue and profit increase, reach a peak, and then decline. A firm must be able to launch, modify, and delete products from its offering of products in response to changes in product life cycles. Otherwise, the firm's profits will disappear and the firm will fail. Depending on the product, life-cycle stages will vary in length. In this section, we discuss the stages of the life cycle and how marketers can use this information.

Stages of the Product Life Cycle

Generally, the product life cycle is assumed to be composed of four stages—introduction, growth, maturity, and decline—as shown in Figure 14.1. Some products progress through these stages rapidly, in a few weeks or months. Others may take years to go through each stage. The Rubik's Cube had a relatively short life cycle. Parker Brothers' Monopoly game, which was introduced over sixty years ago, is still going strong.

Introduction In the *introduction stage*, customer awareness and acceptance of the product are low. Sales rise gradually as a result of promotion and distribution activities, but, initially, high development and marketing costs result in low profit, or even in a loss. There are relatively few competitors. The price is sometimes high, and purchasers are primarily people who want to be "the first" to own the new product. The marketing challenge at this stage is to make potential customers aware of the product's existence and its features, benefits, and uses.

A new product is seldom an immediate success. Marketers must watch early buying patterns carefully and be prepared to modify the new product promptly if necessary. The product should be priced to attract the particular market segment that has

process material a material that is used directly in the production of another product but is not readily identifiable in the finished product

supply an item that facilitates production and operations but does not become part of the finished product

business service an intangible product that an organization uses in its operations

product life cycle a series of stages in which a product's sales revenue and profit increase, reach a peak, and then decline

figure 14.1

Product Life Cycle
The graph shows sales volume and profits during the life cycle of a product.

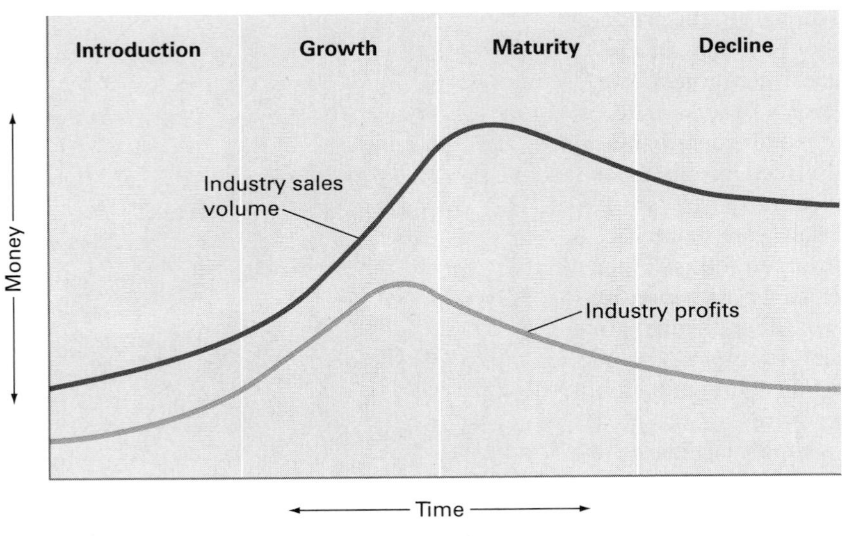

Source: William M. Pride and O.C. Ferrell, *Marketing: Concepts and Strategies*, Eleventh Edition. Copyright © 2000 by Houghton Mifflin Company. Adapted with permission.

the greatest desire and ability to buy the product. Plans for distribution and promotion should suit the targeted market segment. As with the product itself, the initial price, distribution channels, and promotional efforts may need to be adjusted quickly to maintain sales growth during the introduction stage.

British children's author J.K. Rowling made good use of the Internet to help launch her international marketing effort of *Harry Potter and the Goblet of Fire*. The book launch became an event with an unheard-of-before record advanced sales of 5.3 million copies in the first international print run. Many of these sales were facilitated through Amazon.com and Barnesandnoble.com as customers took advantage of ordering online and shipping the books as gifts to children for their summertime reading enjoyment.[2]

Growth stage. Digital cameras are in the growth stage of the product life cycle. Several firms, such as Sony, Casio, and Tomy, are introducing digital cameras with new features. When Sony unveiled this Cybershot camera, it was the smallest of its kind.

Growth In the *growth stage*, sales increase rapidly as the product becomes well known. Other firms have probably begun to market competing products. The competition and lower unit costs (due to mass production) result in a lower price, which reduces the profit per unit. Note that industry profits reach a peak and begin to decline during this stage. To meet the needs of the growing market, the originating firm offers modified versions of its product and expands its distribution. The 3M Company, the maker of Post-it Notes, has developed a variety of sizes, colors, and designs.

Management's goal in the growth stage is to stabilize and strengthen the product's position by encouraging brand loyalty. To beat the competition, the company may further improve the product or expand the product line to appeal to specialized market segments. Management may also compete by lowering prices if increased production efficiency has resulted in savings for the company. As the product becomes more widely accepted, marketers may be able to broaden the network of distributors. Marketers can also emphasize customer service and prompt credit for defective products. During this period, promotional efforts attempt to build brand loyalty among customers.

The Internet has been a boon for the growth of digital photography. According to Info Trends Research Group of Boston, consumers currently spend about $1.2 billion on digital cameras partly because of photo dot-coms like Zing.com. Zing allows digital photographers to upload their pictures to free personal web sites. Within their reserved area, users can edit, create albums, and e-mail images over the Internet.[3]

Maturity Sales are still increasing at the beginning of the *maturity stage*, but the rate of increase has slowed. Later in this stage, the sales curve peaks and begins to decline. Industry profits decline throughout this stage. Product lines are simplified, markets are segmented more carefully, and price competition increases. The increased competition forces weaker competitors to leave the industry. Refinements and extensions of the original product continue to appear on the market.

During a product's maturity stage, its market share may be strengthened by redesigned packaging or style changes. Also, consumers may be encouraged to use the product more often or in new ways. Pricing strategies are flexible during this stage. Markdowns and price incentives are not uncommon, although price increases may work to offset production and distribution costs. Marketers may offer incentives and assistance of various kinds to dealers to encourage them to support mature products, especially in the face of competition from private-label brands. New promotional efforts and aggressive personal selling may be necessary during this period of intense competition.

Decline During the *decline stage*, sales volume decreases sharply. Profits continue to fall. The number of competing firms declines, and the only survivors in the marketplace are those firms that specialize in marketing the product. Production and marketing costs become the most important determinant of profit.

When a product adds to the success of the overall product line, the company may retain it; otherwise, management must determine when to eliminate the product. A product usually declines because of technological advances or environmental factors, or because consumers have switched to competing brands. Therefore, few changes are made in the product itself during this stage. Instead, management may raise the price to cover costs, reprice to maintain market share, or lower the price to reduce inventory. Similarly, management will narrow distribution of the declining product to the most profitable existing markets. During this period, the company will probably not spend heavily on promotion, although it may use some advertising and sales incentives to slow the product's decline. The company may choose to eliminate less profitable versions of the product from the product line or may decide to drop the product entirely.

Using the Product Life Cycle

Marketers should be aware of the life-cycle stage of each product they are responsible for. And they should try to estimate how long the product is expected to remain in that stage. Both must be taken into account in making decisions about the marketing strategy for a product. If a product is expected to remain in the maturity stage for a long time, a replacement product might be introduced later in the maturity stage. If the maturity stage is expected to be short, however, a new product should be introduced much earlier. In some cases, a firm may be willing to take the chance of speeding up the decline of existing products. In other situations, a company will attempt to extend a product's life cycle. For example, General Mills has extended the life of Bisquick baking mix (launched in the mid-1930s) by significantly improving the product's formulation, and creating and promoting a variety of uses.

Another example is that the convergence of television with the Internet is taking place at a fast pace, as the necessary cable and satellites providing larger bandwidth find their way into more and more communities. According to Jupiter Communications, about 20 percent of U.S. homes will have some form of interactivity by 2004. This will provide new ways for consumers to interact with programs, advertising, and other online content. New technology will allow marketers to market, once again, many older content products that can be redesigned with interactivity features. For example, Disney's old animations could be relaunched as interactive games.[4]

LEARNING OBJECTIVE

3 Define *product line* and *product mix,* and distinguish between the two.

Product Line and Product Mix

product line a group of similar products that differ only in relatively minor characteristics

product mix all the products a firm offers for sale

A **product line** is a group of similar products that differ only in relatively minor characteristics. Generally, the products within a product line are related to each other in the way they are produced, marketed, or used. Procter & Gamble, for example, manufactures and markets several shampoos, including Prell, Head & Shoulders, Pert Plus, and Ivory.

Many organizations tend to introduce new products within existing product lines. This permits them to apply the experience and knowledge they have acquired to the production and marketing of new products. Other firms develop entirely new product lines.

An organization's **product mix** consists of all the products the firm offers for sale. Two "dimensions" are often applied to a firm's product mix. The *width* of the mix is the number of product lines it contains. The *depth* of the mix is the average number of individual products within each line. These are general measures; we speak of a *broad* or a *narrow* mix, rather than a mix of exactly three or five product lines. Some organizations provide broad product mixes to be competitive. For example, GE Financial Network (GEFN), a comprehensive Internet-based consumer-friendly financial services resource, provides an extensive product mix of financial services including home mortgages, mutual funds, stock price quotes, annuities, life insurance, auto insurance, long-term care insurance, credit cards, and auto warranty plans.[5]

Many firms seek new products to broaden their product mix, just as Eastman Kodak has done with digital cameras. By developing new product lines, firms gain additional experience and expertise. Moreover, they achieve stability by operating within several different markets. Problems in one particular market do not affect a multiline firm nearly as much as they would affect a firm that depended entirely on a single product line.

LEARNING OBJECTIVE

4 Identify the methods available for changing a product mix.

Managing the Product Mix

To provide products that satisfy people in a firm's target market or markets and that also achieve the organization's objectives, a marketer must develop, adjust, and maintain an effective product mix. Seldom can the same product mix be effective for long. Because customers' product preferences and attitudes change, their desire for a prod-

Product line. The soft drink products at the Coca-Cola Company represent a product line. The Coca-Cola Company also produces several other lines of products, such as juice (Minute Maid), sports drinks (POWERaDE), and water (DASANI).

Managing the product mix. Marketers at Arm & Hammer have engaged in highly effective product management by finding and promoting new uses for its products.

uct may diminish or grow. In some cases, a firm needs to alter its product mix to adapt to competition. A marketer may have to eliminate a product from the mix because one or more competitors dominate that product's specific market segment. Similarly, an organization may have to introduce a new product or modify an existing one to compete more effectively. A marketer may expand the firm's product mix to take advantage of excess marketing and production capacity. For whatever reason a product mix is altered, the product mix must be managed to bring about improvements in the mix. There are three major ways to improve a product mix: change an existing product, delete a product, or develop a new product.

Changing Existing Products

product modification the process of changing one or more of a product's characteristics

Product modification refers to changing one or more of a product's characteristics. For this approach to be effective, several conditions must be met. First, the product must be modifiable. Second, existing customers must be able to perceive that a modification has been made, assuming that the modified item is still directed at the same target market. Third, the modification should make the product more consistent with customers' desires so that it provides greater satisfaction.

Existing products can be altered in three primary ways: in quality, function, and aesthetics. *Quality modifications* are changes that relate to a product's dependability and durability and are usually achieved by alterations in the materials or production process. *Functional modifications* affect a product's versatility, effectiveness, convenience, or safety; they usually require redesign of the product. Typical product categories that have undergone extensive functional modifications include home appliances, office and farm equipment, and consumer electronics. *Aesthetic modifications* are directed at changing the sensory appeal of a product by altering its taste, texture, sound, smell, or visual characteristics. Because a buyer's purchasing decision is affected by how a product looks, smells, tastes, feels, or sounds, an aesthetic modification may have a definite impact on purchases. Through aesthetic modifications, a firm can differentiate its product from competing brands and perhaps gain a sizable market share if customers find the modified product more appealing.

Deleting Products

product deletion the elimination of one or more products from a product line

To maintain an effective product mix, an organization often has to eliminate some products. This is called **product deletion**. A weak product costs a firm time, money, and resources that could be used to modify other products or develop new ones. Also, when a weak product generates an unfavorable image among customers, the negative image may rub off on other products sold by the firm.

Most organizations find it difficult to delete a product. Some firms drop weak products only after they have become severe financial burdens. A better approach is some form of systematic review of the product's impact on the overall effectiveness of

Going Global

Swatch Watches Its Product Mix

BASED IN SWITZERLAND, A COUNTRY renowned for timepiece quality, Swatch has made its mark by selling watches as fashionable accessories. Until Swatch, many good watches were designed and marketed as status symbols to be handled carefully and preserved for the next generation. Then Swatch revolutionized the industry with its diverse line of eye-catching watches for nearly every taste, occasion, and wallet, including limited-edition collectible watches and artsy watches designed by Kiki Picasso and other artists. Swatch reinforces its fashion positioning by regularly introducing a number of new watches while dropping some existing watches. This constant change keeps the overall product mix of 30,000 items fresh and timely. It also brings customers back again and again in search of the latest watch styles.

However, the firm's drive to stay ahead of competitors by developing ever more fashionable watches with popular appeal has resulted in some misfires. For example, Swatch's first working models of a wristphone turned out too large for comfort. As another example, one of its early web-access watches required the use of a computer and a specially-designed mousepad.

Despite such setbacks, Swatch's relentless release of new products has proven to be a powerful competitive weapon. In recent years, Swatch has been opening dedicated retail stores all over the world to get even more exposure for its extensive product mix. Other manufacturers have used this approach, but not with Swatch's special twist. Instead of offering every watch in every store, some watches will be sold only in one store. Now Swatch fans in search of unique watches will have yet another reason to stop into Swatch stores wherever they go.

a firm's product mix. Such a review should analyze a product's contribution to a company's sales for a given period. It should include estimates of future sales, costs, and profits associated with the product and a consideration of whether changes in the marketing strategy could improve the product's performance.

A product deletion program can definitely improve a firm's performance. For example, Unilever recently launched a program to delete niche, marginal, and nonstrategic brands to provide more room and resources for its core brands. Prior to the deletion program, Unilever had 1,800 products in 67 product categories. After implementing the deletion program, Unilever now participates in 14 product categories. Unilever is putting more energy into its big brands because these have the highest growth potential.[6]

Spotlight

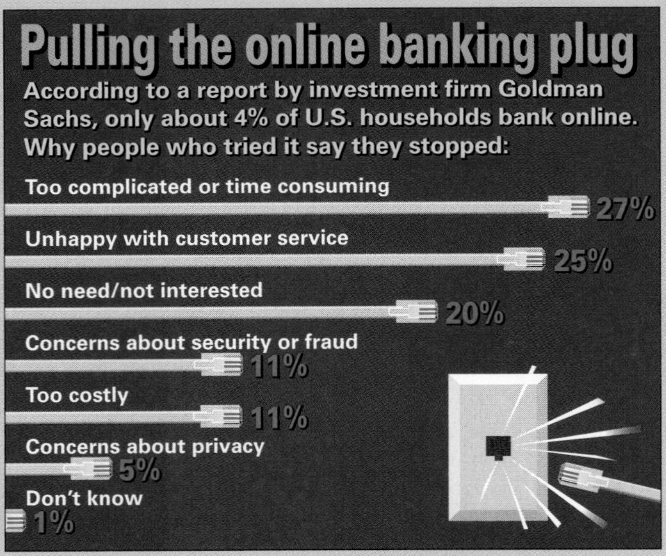

Pulling the online banking plug

According to a report by investment firm Goldman Sachs, only about 4% of U.S. households bank online. Why people who tried it say they stopped:

Reason	Percent
Too complicated or time consuming	27%
Unhappy with customer service	25%
No need/not interested	20%
Concerns about security or fraud	11%
Too costly	11%
Concerns about privacy	5%
Don't know	1%

Source: Copyright 2000, USA TODAY. Reprinted with permission.

Developing New Products

Developing and introducing new products is frequently time-consuming, expensive, and risky. Thousands of new products are introduced annually. Depending on how we define it, the failure rate for new products ranges between 60 to 75 percent. Although developing new products is risky, failing to introduce new products can be just as hazardous. Kellogg, for example, was slow to introduce new products during the 1990s. By 2000, General Mills had become the number one cereal producer in the United States, putting Kellogg in second place.[7] New products are generally grouped into three categories on the basis of their degree of similarity to existing products. *Imitations* are products designed to be similar to—and to compete with—existing products of other firms. Examples are the various brands of whitening toothpastes that were developed to compete with Rembrandt. *Adaptations* are variations of existing products that are intended for an established market. Caffeine-free, diet soft drinks are product adaptations. Product refinements and extensions are most often considered adaptations, although imitative products may also include some refinement and extension. Polaroid, for example, has introduced inexpensive digital cameras for the mass market and has become the number one digital camera seller in the United States.[8] *Innovations* are entirely new products. They may give rise to a new industry or revolutionize an existing one. The introduction of compact discs, for example, has brought major changes to the recording industry. Innovative products take considerable time, effort, and money to develop. They are therefore less common than adaptations and imitations. As shown in Figure 14.2, the process of developing a new product consists of seven phases.

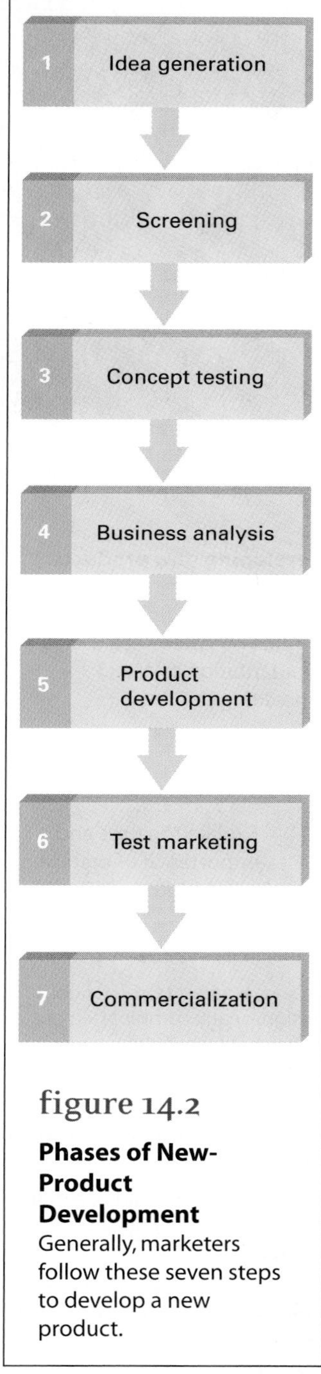

figure 14.2

Phases of New-Product Development
Generally, marketers follow these seven steps to develop a new product.

Source: William M. Pride and O.C. Ferrell, *Marketing: Concepts and Strategies*. Eleventh Edition. Copyright © 2000 by Houghton Mifflin Company. Adapted with permission.

Idea Generation Idea generation involves looking for product ideas that will help a firm achieve its objectives. Although some organizations get their ideas almost by chance, firms trying to maximize product-mix effectiveness usually develop systematic approaches for generating new-product ideas. Ideas may come from managers, researchers, engineers, competitors, advertising agencies, management consultants, private research organizations, customers, salespersons, or top executives.

Screening During screening, ideas that do not match organizational resources and objectives are rejected. In this phase, a firm's managers consider whether their organization has personnel with the expertise to develop and market the proposed product. Management may reject a good idea because the company lacks the necessary skills and abilities. The largest number of product ideas are rejected during the screening phase.

Concept Testing Concept testing is a phase in which a product idea is presented to a small sample of potential buyers through a written or oral description (and perhaps a few drawings) to determine their attitudes and initial buying intentions regarding the product. For a single product idea, an organization can test one or several concepts of the same product. Concept testing is a low-cost means for an organization to determine consumers' initial reactions to a product idea before investing considerable resources in product research and development. Product development personnel can use the results of concept testing to improve product attributes and product benefits that are most important to potential customers. The types of questions asked vary considerably depending on the type of product idea being tested. The following are typical questions:

- Which benefits of the proposed product are especially attractive to you?
- Which features are of little or no interest to you?
- What are the primary advantages of the proposed product over the one you currently use?
- If this product were available at an appropriate price, how often would you buy it?
- How could this proposed product be improved?

Business Analysis Business analysis provides tentative ideas about a potential product's financial performance, including its probable profitability. During this stage, the firm considers how the new product, if it were introduced, would affect the firm's sales, costs, and profits. Marketing personnel usually work up preliminary sales and cost projections at this point, with the help of R&D and production managers.

Product Development In the product development phase, the company must find out first if it is technically feasible to produce the product and then if the product can be made at costs low enough to justify a reasonable price. If a product idea makes it to this point, it is transformed into a working model, or *prototype*.

Test Marketing Test marketing is the limited introduction of a product in several towns or cities chosen to be representative of the intended target market. Its aim is to determine buyers' probable reactions. The product is left in the test markets long

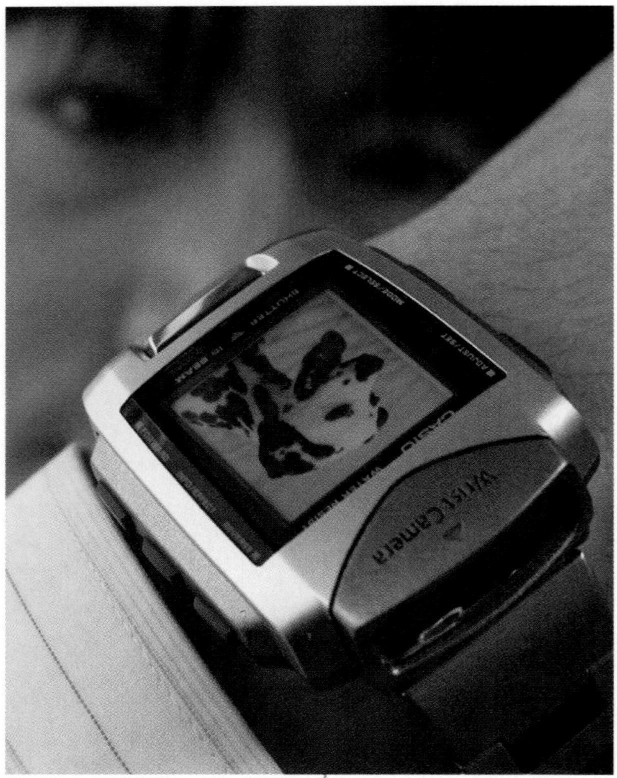

Developing new products. Casio has developed a wrist-type wearable digital camera. Would you categorize this as an adaptation or an innovation?

enough to give buyers a chance to repurchase the product if they are so inclined. Marketers can experiment with advertising, pricing, and packaging in different test areas and can measure the extent of brand awareness, brand switching, and repeat purchases that result from alterations in the marketing mix.

Commercialization During commercialization, plans for full-scale manufacturing and marketing must be refined and completed, and budgets for the project must be prepared. In the early part of the commercialization phase, marketing management analyzes the results of test marketing to find out what changes in the marketing mix are needed before the product is introduced. The results of test marketing may tell the marketers, for example, to change one or more of the product's physical attributes, to modify the distribution plans to include more retail outlets, to alter promotional efforts, or to change the product's price. Products are not usually introduced nationwide overnight. Most new products are marketed in stages, beginning in selected geographic areas and expanding into adjacent areas over a period of time.

Why Do Products Fail? In spite of this rigorous process for developing product ideas, the majority of new products end up as failures. In fact, many well-known companies have produced market failures (see Table 14.1).

Why does a new product fail? Mainly because the product and its marketing program are not planned and tested as completely as they should be. For example, to save on development costs, a firm may market-test its product but not its entire marketing mix. Or a firm may market a new product before all the "bugs" have been worked out. Or, when problems show up in the testing stage, a firm may try to recover its product development costs by pushing ahead with full-scale marketing anyway. Finally, some firms try to market new products with inadequate financing.

LEARNING OBJECTIVE

5 Explain the uses and importance of branding, packaging, and labeling.

Branding, Packaging, and Labeling

Three important features of a product (particularly a consumer product) are its brand, package, and label. These features may be used to associate a product with a successful product line or to distinguish it from existing products. They may be designed to attract customers at the point of sale or to provide information to potential purchasers. Because the brand, package, and label are very real parts of the product, they deserve careful attention during product planning.

brand a name, term, symbol, design, or any combination of these that identifies a seller's products as distinct from those of other sellers

brand name the part of a brand that can be spoken

brand mark the part of a brand that is a symbol or distinctive design

trademark a brand name or brand mark that is registered with the U.S. Patent and Trademark Office and is thus legally protected from use by anyone except its owner

trade name the complete and legal name of an organization

What Is a Brand?

A **brand** is a name, term, symbol, design, or any combination of these that identifies a seller's products as distinct from those of other sellers.[9] A **brand name** is the part of a brand that can be spoken. It may include letters, words, numbers, or pronounceable symbols, like the ampersand in *Procter & Gamble*. A **brand mark,** on the other hand, is the part of a brand that is a symbol or distinctive design, like the Nike "swoosh." A **trademark** is a brand name or brand mark that is registered with the U.S. Patent and Trademark Office and is thus legally protected from use by anyone except its owner. A **trade name** is the complete and legal name of an organization, such as Pizza Hut or Houghton Mifflin Company (the publisher of this text).

table 14.1 Examples of Product Failures

Company	Product
3M	Floptical storage disk
AT&T	Personal Digital Assistant
Time Warner Inc.	*TV-Cable Week*
General Mills	Betty Crocker MicroRave Singles
NeXT Inc.	Optical drive personal computer
General Motors Corp.	Cadillac Allante luxury sedan
BIC Corp.	$5 glass flask perfume
Anheuser-Busch Companies	Bud Dry and Michelob Dry beer
Colgate-Palmolive Co.	Fab 1-Shot laundry detergent
PepsiCo, Inc.	Pepsi A.M. cola
Heinz	Ketchup Salsa
NutraSweet	Simplesse fat substitute
RJR Nabisco, Inc.	Premier smokeless cigarettes

Sources: Ted Anthony, "Where's Farrah Shampoo?" *Marketing News*, March 6, 1996, p. 13: Jeffrey D. Swaddling and Mark W. Zobel, "Beating the Odds," *Marketing Management*, winter/spring 1996, pp. 20–33; Robert M. McMath, "Copycat Cupcakes Don't Cut It," *American Demographics*, January 1997, p. 60., and Eric Berggren and Thomas Nacher, "Why Good Ideas Go Bust," *Management Review*, February 2000, p. 32–36.

Types of Brands

Brands are often classified according to who owns them: manufacturers or stores. A **manufacturer** (or **producer**) **brand**, as the name implies, is a brand that is owned by a manufacturer. Many foods (Frosted Flakes), major appliances (Whirlpool), gasolines (Exxon), automobiles (Honda), and clothing (Levis) are sold as manufacturers' brands. Some consumers prefer producer brands because they usually are nationally known, offer consistent quality, and are widely available.

manufacturer (or producer) brand a brand that is owned by a manufacturer

store (or private) brand a brand that is owned by an individual wholesaler or retailer

A **store** (or **private**) **brand** is one that is owned by an individual wholesaler or retailer. Among the better-known store brands are Kenmore and Craftsman, both owned by Sears, Roebuck. Owners of store brands claim that they can offer lower prices, earn greater profits, and improve customer loyalty with their own brands. Some companies that manufacture private brands also produce their own manufacturer brands. They often find such operations profitable because they can use excess capacity and at the same time avoid most marketing costs. Many private-branded grocery products are produced by companies that specialize in making private-label products. About 20 percent of products sold in supermarkets are private-branded items.[10]

spotLight

Source: Adapted from William M. Pride and O.C. Ferrell, *Marketing: Concepts and Strategies*, Eleventh Edition. Copyright © 2000 by Houghton Mifflin Company. Reprinted with permission.

Consumer confidence is the most important element in the success of a branded product, whether the brand is owned by a producer or a retailer. Because branding identifies each product completely, customers can easily repurchase products that provide satisfaction, performance, and quality. And they can just as easily avoid or ignore

generic product (or **brand**) a product with no brand at all

products that do not. In supermarkets, the products most likely to keep their shelf space are the brands with large market shares and strong customer loyalty.

A **generic product** (sometimes called a **generic brand**) is a product with no brand at all. Its plain package carries only the name of the product—applesauce, peanut butter, potato chips, or whatever. Generic products, available in supermarkets since 1977, sometimes are made by the major producers that manufacture name brands. Even though generic brands may have accounted for as much as 10 percent of all grocery sales several years ago, they currently represent less than one-half of 1 percent.

Benefits of Branding

Both buyers and sellers benefit from branding. Because brands are easily recognizable, they reduce the amount of time buyers must spend shopping; buyers can quickly identify the brands they prefer. Choosing particular brands, such as Tommy Hilfiger, Polo, Nautica, and Nike, can be a way of expressing oneself. When buyers are unable to evaluate a product's characteristics, brands can help them judge the quality of the product. For example, most buyers aren't able to judge the quality of stereo components but may be guided by a well-respected brand name. Brands can symbolize a certain quality level to a customer, allowing that perception of quality to represent the actual quality of the item. Brands thus help reduce a buyer's perceived risk of purchase. Finally, customers may receive a psychological reward that comes from owning a brand that symbolizes status. The Lexus brand is an example.

Because buyers are already familiar with a firm's existing brands, branding helps a firm introduce a new product that carries the same brand name. Branding aids sellers in their promotional efforts because promotion of each branded product indirectly promotes other products of the same brand. H.G. Heinz, for example, markets many products with the Heinz brand name, such as ketchup, vinegar, vegetarian beans, gravies, barbecue sauce, and steak sauce. Promotion of one Heinz product indirectly promotes the others.

brand loyalty extent to which a customer is favorable toward buying a specific brand

One chief benefit of branding is the creation of **brand loyalty,** the extent to which a customer is favorable toward buying a specific brand. The stronger the brand loyalty, the greater the likelihood that buyers will consistently choose the brand. There are three levels of brand loyalty: recognition, preference, and insistence. Brand recognition is the level of loyalty at which customers are aware that the brand exists and will purchase it if their preferred brands are unavailable or if they are unfamiliar with available brands. This is the weakest form of brand loyalty. Brand preference is the level of brand loyalty at which a customer prefers one brand over competing brands. However, if the preferred brand is unavailable, the customer is willing to substitute another brand. Brand insistence is the strongest level of brand loyalty. Brand-insistent customers strongly prefer a specific brand and will not buy substitutes. Brand insistence is the least common type of brand loyalty. Partly due to marketers' increased dependence on discounted prices, coupons, and other short-term promotions, and partly because of the enormous array of new products with similar characteristics, brand loyalty in general seems to be declining.

brand equity marketing and financial value associated with a brand's strength in a market

Brand equity is the marketing and financial value associated with a brand's strength in a market. Although difficult to measure, brand equity represents the value of a brand to an organization. Some of the world's most valuable brands include Coca-Cola, Microsoft, IBM, General Electric, and Ford.[11] The four major factors that contribute to brand equity are brand-name awareness, brand associations, perceived brand quality, and brand loyalty. Brand awareness leads to brand familiarity, and buyers are more likely to select a familiar brand than an unfamiliar one. The associations linked to a brand can connect a personality type or lifestyle with a particular brand. For example, consumers may associate De Beers diamonds with loving, long-lasting relation-

Using the Internet

The U.S. government gateways to consumer information about products, safety, pricing, fraud, and many other issues of interest are available through a variety of online publications and links at **http://www.pueblo.gsa.gov/** and **http://www.consumer.gov/**.

Exploring Business

Nike Swings Away from the Swoosh

Few trademarks are as distinctive and recognizable as the Nike swoosh. In years past, the Oregon-based maker of athletic footwear and clothing plastered its swoosh across every product, advertisement, and sponsorship. With top athletes such as Michael Jordan wearing the swoosh, audiences all over the world grew accustomed to the Nike brand and the products it represents.

Then the fashion world changed, as did the sports world. Michael Jordan retired from basketball. Extreme sports such as snowboarding and mountain biking became more popular. Women's soccer and basketball teams drew ever-larger crowds. Suddenly, a new mix of products was in demand—and Nike was caught flat-footed. Faster than a speeding swoosh, its brand cooled off while competing brands, sporting up-to-the-minute styling and features, became red-hot.

Battling back, Nike moved quickly to boost its brand. The company signed rising-star endorsers such as soccer player Brandi Chastain to wear its products. It also assigned a team of specialists to create shoes, boots, and clothing for skateboarding and other fast-growing sports.

In a radical break from tradition, Nike has also reduced its use of the swoosh, hoping to recapture the brand's cachet. The swoosh still appears on many Nike items, but it's often smaller and subtler. Some new products are even being introduced with different logos rather than the once-ubiquitous swoosh. As Nike CEO Philip Knight explains, "If you blast it on every T-shirt, every sign in the soccer match, you dilute it." Now, he says, "There's more thought given to how we use it."

ships. When consumers are unable to judge for themselves the quality of a product, they may rely on their perception of the quality of the product's brand. Finally, brand loyalty is a valued element of brand equity because it reduces both a brand's vulnerability to competitors and the need to spend tremendous resources to attract new customers; it also provides brand visibility and encourages retailers to carry the brand.

Marketing on the Internet sometimes is best done in collaboration with a better-known web brand. For instance, Unilever's joint effort with web portal Excite@Home, a better known web brand than Unilever or any of its 1,000 individual brands, scored results that Unilever's site would never have been able to achieve independently. By distributing Recipe Secrets on Excite@Home's site, consumers were able to see practical demonstrations of Unilever products and effectively view cooking lessons online. The Recipe Secrets banner advertisement prompted 8 percent of consumers who saw it to visit the site; of those consumers, 62 percent obtained a recipe. Given that about 11 percent of visitors to the site were further motivated to actually buy a Recipe Secrets product at their grocery store is testimony to the success of the joint effort.[12]

Choosing and Protecting a Brand

A number of issues should be considered when selecting a brand name. The name should be easy for customers to say, spell, and recall. Short, one-syllable names such as *Tide* often satisfy this requirement. The brand name should suggest, in a positive way, the product's uses, special characteristics, and major benefits and should be distinctive enough to set it apart from competing brands. Choosing the right brand name has become a challenge because many obvious product names have already been used. In 1999, the U.S. Patent and Trademark Office registered an estimated 138,600 new trademarks.[13]

It is important that a firm select a brand that can be protected through registration, reserving it for exclusive use by that firm. Some brands, because of their designs, are more easily infringed on than others. Although registration protects trademarks domestically for ten years and can be renewed indefinitely, a firm should develop a system for ensuring that its trademarks will be renewed as needed. To protect its exclusive right to the brand, the company must ensure that the selected brand will not be considered an infringement on any existing brand already registered with the U.S. Patent and Trademark Office. This task may be complicated by the fact that infringement is determined by the courts, which base their decisions on whether a brand causes consumers to be confused, mistaken, or deceived about the source of the product.

individual branding the strategy in which a firm uses a different brand for each of its products

A firm must guard against a brand name's becoming a generic term that refers to a general product category. Generic terms cannot be legally protected as exclusive brand names. For example, names such as *yo-yo, aspirin, escalator*, and *thermos*—all exclusively brand names at one time—were eventually declared generic terms that refer to product categories. As such, they could no longer be protected. To ensure that a brand name does not become a generic term, the firm should spell the name with a capital letter and use it as an adjective to modify the name of the general product class, as in Jell-O Brand Gelatin. An organization can deal directly with this problem by advertising that its brand is a trademark and should not be used generically. Firms can also use the registered trademark symbol ® to indicate that the brand is trademarked.

Is this a good brand name? Yes, because V8 is easy to say, spell, and remember. This brand name is short and relates directly to the characteristics of the product.

GOT THAT DAILY VEGETABLE THING DOWN YET?

100% JUICE

V8

100% VEGETABLE JUICE

Take a shortcut on the road to better eating. Each 12-ounce bottle of V8 has more than a full serving of vegetables and good things like potassium and the antioxidant vitamins A & C. Now, if they could just bottle that daily exercise thing.

Branding Strategies

The basic branding decision for any firm is whether to brand its products. A producer may market its products under its own brands, private brands, or both. A retail store may carry only producer brands, its own brands, or both. Once either type of firm decides to brand, it chooses one of two branding strategies: individual branding or family branding.

Individual branding is the strategy in which a firm uses a different brand for each of its products. For example, Procter & Gamble uses individual branding for its line of bar soaps, which includes Ivory, Camay, Zest, Safeguard, Coast, and Oil of Olay. Individual branding offers two major advantages. A problem with one product will not affect the good name of the firm's other products. And the different brands can be directed toward different market segments. For example, Marriotts' Fairfield Inns are directed toward budget-minded travelers and Marriott Hotels toward upscale customers.

Family branding is the strategy in which a firm uses the same brand for all or most of its products. Sony, Dell, IBM, and Xerox use family branding for their entire product mixes. A major advantage of family branding is that the promotion of any one item that carries the family brand tends to help all other products with the same brand name. In addition, a new product has a head start when its brand name is already known and accepted by customers.

family branding the strategy in which a firm uses the same brand for all or most of its products

Packaging

Packaging consists of all the activities involved in developing and providing a container with graphics for a product. The package is a vital part of the product. It can make the product more versatile, safer, or easier to use. Through its shape, appearance, and printed message, a package can influence purchasing decisions.

packaging all the activities involved in developing and providing a container with graphics for a product

Packaging Functions

Effective packaging means more than simply putting products in containers and covering them with wrappers. The basic function of packaging materials is to protect the product and maintain its functional form. Fluids such as milk, orange juice, and hair spray need packages that preserve and protect them; the packaging should prevent damage that could affect the product's usefulness and increase costs. Since product tampering has become a problem for marketers of many types of goods, several packaging techniques have been developed to counter this danger. Some packages are also designed to foil shoplifting.

Another function of packaging is to offer consumer convenience. For example, small aseptic packages—individual-serving boxes or plastic bags that contain liquids and do not require refrigeration—appeal strongly to children and to young adults with active lifestyles. The size or shape of a package may relate to the product's storage, convenience of use, or replacement rate. Small, single-serving cans of vegetables, for instance, may prevent waste and make storage easier. A third function of packaging is to promote a product by communicating its features, uses, benefits, and image. Sometimes, a firm develops a reusable package to make the product more desirable. For example, the Cool Whip package doubles as a food-storage container.

Packaging design. This package design is very compatible with the brand name Toilet Duck. Also, the package design makes the product easy to use.

Package Design Considerations

Many factors must be weighed when developing packages. Obviously, one major consideration is cost. Although a variety of packaging materials, processes, and designs are available, some are rather expensive. While U.S. buyers have shown a willingness to pay more for improved packaging, there are limits.

Marketers must also decide whether to package the product in single or multiple units. Multiple-unit packaging can increase demand by increasing the amount of the product available at the point of consumption (in the home, for example). However, multiple-unit packaging does not work for infrequently used products because buyers do not like to tie up their dollars in an excess supply or to store these products for a long time. Multiple-unit packaging can, however, make storage and handling easier (as in the case of six-packs used for soft drinks); it can also facilitate special price offers, such as two-for-one sales. In addition, multiple-unit packaging may increase consumer acceptance of a product by encouraging the buyer to try it several times. On the other hand, customers may hesitate to try the product at all if they do not have the option to buy just one.

Marketers should consider how much consistency is desirable among an organization's package designs. To promote an overall company image, a firm may decide that all packages must be similar or include one major element of the design. This approach, called *family packaging*, is sometimes used only for lines of products, as with Campbell's soups, Weight Watchers entrees, and Planters nuts. The best policy is sometimes no consistency, especially if a firm's products are unrelated or aimed at vastly different target markets.

Packages also play an important promotional role. Through verbal and non-verbal symbols, the package can inform potential buyers about the product's content, uses, features, advantages, and hazards. Firms can create desirable images and associations by choosing particular colors, designs, shapes, and textures. Many cosmetics manufacturers, for example, design their packages to create impressions of richness, luxury, and exclusiveness. The package performs another promotional function when it is designed to be safer or more convenient to use, if such features help stimulate demand.

Packaging must also meet the needs of intermediaries. Wholesalers and retailers consider whether a package facilitates transportation, handling, and storage. Resellers may refuse to carry certain products if their packages are cumbersome.

Finally, firms must consider the issue of environmental responsibility when developing packages. Companies must balance consumers' desires for convenience against the need to preserve the environment. About one-half of all garbage consists of discarded plastic packaging, such as plastic soft-drink bottles and carryout bags. Plastic packaging material is not biodegradable, and paper necessitates destruction of valuable forest lands. Consequently, many companies are exploring packaging alternatives and recycling more materials.

Labeling

labeling the presentation of information on a product or its package

Labeling is the presentation of information on a product or its package. The *label* is the part that contains the information. This information may include the brand name and mark, the registered trademark symbol ®, the package size and contents, product claims, directions for use and safety precautions, a list of ingredients, the name and address of the manufacturer, and the Universal Product Code symbol, which is used for automated checkout and inventory control.

A number of federal regulations specify information that *must* be included in the labeling for certain products. For example,

- Garments must be labeled with the name of the manufacturer, country of manufacture, fabric content, and cleaning instructions;
- Any food product for which a nutritional claim is made must have nutrition labeling that follows a standard format;
- Food product labels must state the number of servings per container, the serving size, the number of calories per serving, the number of calories derived from fat, and amounts of specific nutrients;
- Nonedible items such as shampoos and detergents must carry safety precautions as well as instructions for their use.

Such regulations are aimed at protecting customers from both misleading product claims and the improper (and thus unsafe) use of products.

express warranty a written explanation of the responsibilities of the producer in the event that the product is found to be defective or otherwise unsatisfactory

Labels may also carry the details of written or express warranties. An **express warranty** is a written explanation of the responsibilities of the producer in the event that the product is found to be defective or otherwise unsatisfactory. As a result of consumer discontent (along with some federal legislation), firms have begun to simplify the wording of warranties and to extend their duration. The L.L. Bean warranty states, "Our products are guaranteed to give 100% satisfaction in every way. Return anything purchased from us at any time if it proves otherwise. We will replace it, refund your purchase price or credit your credit card, as you wish."

Pricing Products

LEARNING OBJECTIVE

6 Describe the economic basis of pricing and the means by which sellers can control prices and buyers' perceptions of prices.

A product is a set of attributes and benefits that has been carefully designed to satisfy its market while earning a profit for its seller. But no matter how well a product is designed, it cannot help an organization achieve its goals if it is priced incorrectly. Few people will purchase a product with too high a price, and a product with too low a price will earn little or no profit. Somewhere between too high and too low there is a "proper," effective price for each product. Let's take a closer look at how businesses go about determining a product's right price.

The Meaning and Use of Price

The **price** of a product is the amount of money a seller is willing to accept in exchange for the product, at a given time and under given circumstances. At times, the price results from negotiations between buyer and seller. But in many business situations, the price is fixed by the seller. Suppose a seller sets a price of $10 for a particular product. In essence, the seller is saying, "Anyone who wants this product can have it here and now, in exchange for $10."

price the amount of money a seller is willing to accept in exchange for a product at a given time and under given circumstances

Each interested buyer then makes a personal judgment regarding the utility of the product, often in terms of some dollar value. A particular person who feels that he or she will get at least $10 worth of want satisfaction (or value) from the product is likely to buy it. But if that person can get more want satisfaction by spending $10 in some other way, he or she will not buy it.

Price thus serves the function of *allocator*. First, it allocates goods and services among those who are willing and able to buy them. (As we noted in Chapter 1, the answer to the economic question "For whom to produce?" depends primarily on prices.) Second, price allocates financial resources (sales revenue) among producers according to how well they satisfy customers' needs. And third, price helps customers to allocate their own financial resources among various want-satisfying products.

Can Firms Control Their Prices?

To focus on the extent to which firms can control their prices, we must take another look at the forces of supply and demand and the actions of firms in a real economy.

Supply and Demand—Once Again

In Chapter 1, we defined the **supply** of a product as the quantity of the product that producers are willing to sell at each of various prices. We can draw a graph of the supply relationship for a particular product, say, jeans (see the left graph of Figure 14.3). Note that the quantity supplied by producers *increases* as the price increases along this *supply curve.*

supply the quantity of a product that producers are willing to sell at each of various prices

As defined in Chapter 1, the **demand** for a product is the quantity that buyers are willing to purchase at each of various prices. We can also draw a graph of the demand relationship (see the middle graph of Figure 14.3). Note that the quantity demanded by purchasers *increases* as the price decreases along the *demand curve.* The buyers and sellers of a product interact in the marketplace. We can show this interaction by superimposing the supply curve onto the demand curve for our product, as shown in the right graph of Figure 14.3. The two curves intersect at point *E*, which represents a quantity of 15 million pairs of jeans and a price of $30 per pair. Point *E* is on the supply curve; thus, producers are willing to supply 15 million pairs at $30 each. Point *E* is also on the demand curve; thus, buyers are willing to purchase 15 million pairs at $30 each. Point *E* represents *equilibrium.* If 15 million pairs are produced and priced at $30, they will all be sold. And everyone who is willing to pay $30 will be able to buy a pair of jeans.

demand the quantity of a product that buyers are willing to purchase at each of various prices

Prices in the Real Economy

In a (largely theoretical) system of pure competition, no producer has control over the price of its product. All producers must accept the equilibrium price. If they charge a higher price, they will not sell their products. If

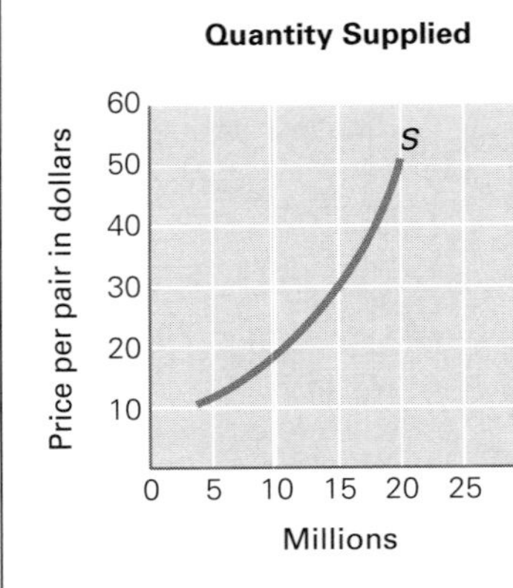

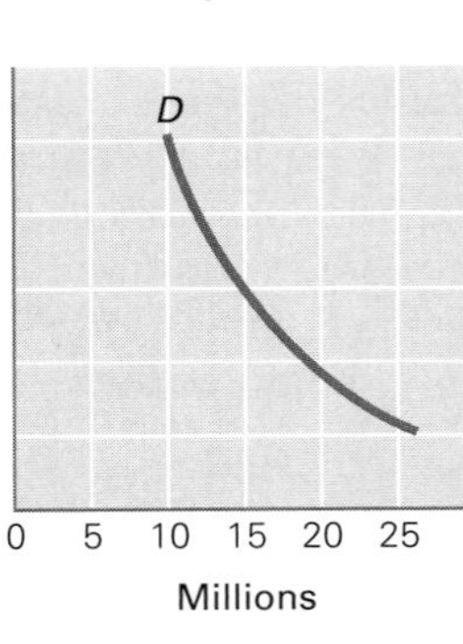

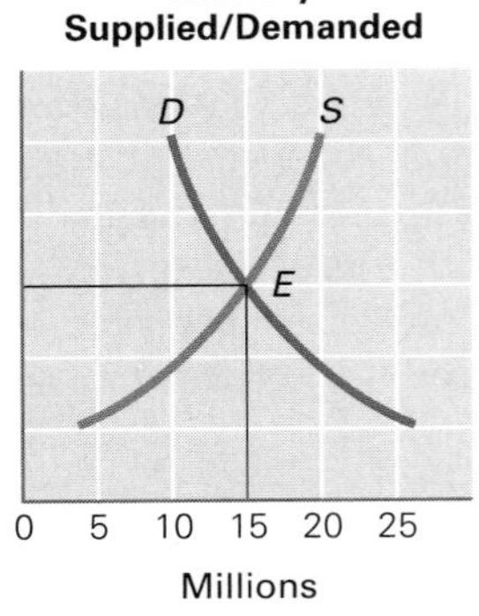

figure 14.3

Supply and Demand Curves

Supply curve *(left):* The upward slope means that producers will supply more jeans at higher prices. **Demand curve** *(middle):* The downward slope (to the right) means that buyers will purchase fewer jeans at higher prices. **Supply and demand curves together** *(right):* Point *E* indicates equilibrium in quantity and price for both sellers and buyers.

they charge a lower price, they will lose sales revenue and profits. In addition, the products of the various producers are indistinguishable from each other when a system of pure competition exists. Every bushel of wheat, for example, is exactly like every other bushel of wheat.

product differentiation the process of developing and promoting differences between one's product and all similar products

In the real economy, however, producers try to gain some control over price by differentiating their products from similar products. **Product differentiation** is the process of developing and promoting differences between one's product and all similar products. The idea behind product differentiation is to create a specific demand for the firm's product—to take the product out of competition with all similar products. Then, in its own little "submarket," the firm can control price to some degree. Jeans with certain designer labels are a result of product differentiation.

Firms also attempt to gain some control over price through advertising. If the advertising is effective, it will increase the quantity demanded. This may permit a firm to increase the price at which it sells its particular output.

In a real market, firms may reduce prices to obtain a competitive edge. A firm may hope to sell more units at a lower price, thereby increasing its total sales revenue. Although each unit earns less profit, total profit may rise.

Finally, the few large sellers in an oligopoly (an industry in which there are few sellers) have considerable control over price, mainly because each controls a large proportion of the total supply of its product. However, as we pointed out in Chapter 1, this control of price is diluted by each firm's wariness of its competitors.

Overall, then, firms in the real economy do exert some control over prices. How they use this control depends on their pricing goals and their production and marketing costs, as well as on the workings of supply and demand in competitive markets.

Price and Nonprice Competition

Before the price of a product can be set, an organization must decide on the basis on which it will compete—on the basis of price alone or some combination of factors. The choice influences pricing decisions as well as other marketing mix variables.

price competition an emphasis on setting a price equal to or lower than competitors' prices to gain sales or market share

Price competition occurs when a seller emphasizes the low price of a product and sets a price that equals or beats competitors' prices. To use this approach most effectively, a seller must have the flexibility to change prices often and must do so rapidly and aggressively whenever competitors change their prices. Price competition allows a marketer to set prices based on demand for the product or in response to changes in the firm's finances. Competitors can do likewise, however, which is a major drawback of price competition. They, too, can quickly match or outdo an organization's price cuts. In addition, if circumstances force a seller to raise prices, competing firms may be able to maintain their lower prices.

The Internet makes price comparison relatively easy for users. Perhaps not surprisingly, the biggest-selling consumer product on the Internet is computer hardware. However, if trends continue, online airline transactions will fly right by to an estimated $17 billion by 2004, more than $1 billion higher than computer hardware. In 1999 about 5 percent of transactions were conducted over the Internet, but this figure is expected to grow to 18 percent by 2004 as customers seek lower prices and convenient shopping for what is fast becoming a commodity item.[14]

Nonprice competition is based on factors other than price. It is used most effectively when a seller can make its product stand out from the competition by distinctive product quality, customer service, promotion, packaging, or other features. Buyers must be able to perceive these distinguishing characteristics and consider them desirable. Once customers have chosen a brand for nonprice reasons, they may not be as easily attracted to competing firms and brands. In this way, a seller can build customer loyalty to its brand. For example, Petsmart competes on value rather than price. The store has variety, 12,000 items in stock and another 80,000 available for order. And it offers service right in the store, including pet grooming, a veterinary clinic, and a pet adoption center. All these features add to the total experience of shopping at Petsmart and are part of its nonprice competition with other pet supply stores.[15]

nonprice competition competition based on factors other than price

Buyers' Perceptions of Price

In setting prices, managers should consider the price sensitivity of people in the target market. How important is price to them? Is it always "very important"? Members of one market segment may be more influenced by price than members of another. For a particular product, the price may be a bigger factor to some buyers than to others. For example, buyers may be more sensitive to price when purchasing gasoline than when purchasing running shoes.

Buyers will accept different ranges of prices for different products; that is, they will tolerate a narrow range for certain items and a wider range for others. Consider the wide range of prices that consumers pay for soft drinks—from 10 cents per ounce at the movies down to 1.5 cents per ounce on sale at the grocery store. Management should be aware of these limits of acceptability and the products to which they apply. The firm should also

Talking Technology

Customers Set Their Own Prices at Priceline

FROM AIRLINE TICKETS AND HOTEL ROOMS to cars, long-distance telephone service, and even cruise vacations–Priceline.com lets online customers set their own prices on an ever-wider range of goods and services. Customers have the opportunity to pay less than they would if buying from traditional sources. Manufacturers and service providers also benefit, because they can sell products that might otherwise go unsold, such as empty seats on particular flights. Priceline's web-based pricing technology is so original that the company has been granted a patent on the process.

Here's how the pricing system works for airline tickets. The customer logs onto the Priceline web site (http://www.priceline.com), and selects a specific product category–in this case, airline tickets. The next screen prompts the customer to enter departure and arrival cities, return dates, and the number of tickets to be purchased. Next, the customer selects the departure and arrival airports, the form of ticket, and enters the price bid. When Priceline accepts a bid, it charges the customer's credit card right away.

Although Priceline lets customers set their own prices, it allows them much less control over other aspects of the transaction, such as which brand they actually buy. Jay Walker, Priceline's founder, likes to stress that "the price you get is based on your own flexibility." Customers with strong brand preferences may not like having to accept alternate brands in order to save money. Similarly, travelers who pay less for airline tickets must be willing to fly at odd hours or put up with other inconveniences. Still, 10 million bidders annually use Priceline's technology to name their own prices on an ever-expanding array of items. Coming soon will be the chance to set a price for life insurance, car insurance, and credit cards, among other new offerings.

take note of buyers' perceptions of a given product in relation to competing products. A premium price may be appropriate if a product is considered superior to others in that category or if the product has inspired strong brand loyalty. On the other hand, if buyers have even a hint of a negative view of a product, a lower price may be necessary.

Sometimes buyers relate price to quality. They may consider a higher price to be an indicator of higher quality. Managers involved in pricing decisions should determine whether this outlook is widespread in the target market. If it is, a higher price may improve the image of a product and, in turn, make the product more desirable.

Pricing Objectives

LEARNING OBJECTIVE

7 Identify the major pricing objectives used by businesses.

Before setting prices for a firm's products, management must decide what it expects to accomplish through pricing. That is, management must set pricing objectives that are in line with both organizational and marketing objectives. Of course, one objective of pricing is to make a profit, but this may not be a firm's primary objective. One or more of the following factors may be just as important.

Survival

A firm may have to price its products to survive—either as an organization or as a player in a particular market. This usually means that the firm will cut its price to attract customers, even if it then must operate at a loss. Obviously, such a goal can hardly be pursued on a long-term basis, for consistent losses would cause the business to fail.

Profit Maximization

Many firms may state that their goal is to maximize profit, but this goal is impossible to define (and thus impossible to achieve). What, exactly, is the "maximum" profit? How does a firm know when it has been reached? Firms that wish to set profit goals should express them as either specific dollar amounts or percentage increases over previous profits.

Target Return on Investment

The *return on investment (ROI)* is the amount earned as a result of that investment. Some firms set an annual-percentage ROI as their pricing goal. ConAgra, the company that produces Healthy Choice meals and a multitude of other products, has a target after-tax ROI of 20 percent.

Market Share Goals

A firm's *market share* is its proportion of total industry sales. Some firms attempt, through pricing, to maintain or increase their share of the market. To gain market share, Toyota prices its Echo subcompact starting at $10,000. AOL priced five hours of service for $9.95 in order to increase its market share.[16]

Status Quo Pricing

In pricing their products, some firms are guided by a desire to avoid "making waves," or to maintain the status quo. This is especially true in industries that depend on price stability. If such a firm can maintain its profit or market share simply by meeting the competition—charging about the same price as competitors for similar products—then it will do so.

Pricing Methods

LEARNING OBJECTIVE

8 Examine the three major pricing methods that firms employ.

Once a firm has developed its pricing objectives, it must select a pricing method to reach that goal. Two factors are important to every firm engaged in setting prices. The first is recognition that the market, and not the firm's costs, ultimately determines the price at which a product will sell. The second is awareness that costs and expected sales can be used only to establish some sort of *price floor*, the minimum price at which the firm can sell its product without incurring a loss. In this section, we look at three kinds of pricing methods: cost-based, demand-based, and competition-based pricing.

Cost-Based Pricing

Using the simplest method of pricing, cost-based pricing, the seller first determines the total cost of producing (or purchasing) one unit of the product. The seller then adds an amount to cover additional costs (such as insurance or interest) and profit. The amount that is added is called the **markup**. The total of the cost plus the markup is the selling price of the product.

markup the amount a seller adds to the cost of a product to determine its basic selling price

A firm's management can calculate markup as a percentage of its total costs. Suppose, for example, that the total cost of manufacturing and marketing 1,000 portable stereos is \$100,000, or \$100 per unit. If the manufacturer wants a markup that is 20 percent above its costs, the selling price will be \$100 plus 20 percent of \$100, or \$120 per unit.

Markup pricing is easy to apply, and it is used by many businesses (mostly retailers and wholesalers). However, it has two major flaws. The first is the difficulty of determining an effective markup percentage. If this percentage is too high, the product may be overpriced for its market; then too few units may be sold to return the total cost of producing and marketing the product. In contrast, if the markup percentage is too low, the seller is "giving away" profit it could have earned simply by assigning a higher price. In other words, the markup percentage needs to be set to account for the workings of the market, and that is very difficult to do.

The second problem with markup pricing is that it separates pricing from other business functions. The product is priced *after* production quantities are determined, *after* costs are incurred, and almost without regard for the market or the marketing mix. To be most effective, the various business functions should be integrated. *Each* should have an impact on *all* marketing decisions.

Cost-based pricing can also be facilitated through the use of breakeven analysis. For any product, the **breakeven quantity** is the number of units that must be sold for the total revenue (from all units sold) to equal the total cost (of all units sold). **Total revenue** is the total amount received from the sales of a product. We can estimate projected total revenue as the selling price multiplied by the number of units sold.

breakeven quantity the number of units that must be sold for the total revenue (from all units sold) to equal the total cost (of all units sold)

total revenue the total amount received from sales of a product

The costs involved in operating a business can be broadly classified as either fixed or variable costs. A **fixed cost** is a cost incurred no matter how many units of a product are produced or sold. Rent, for example, is a fixed cost; it remains the same whether 1 unit or 1,000 are produced. A **variable cost** is a cost that depends on the number of units produced. The cost of fabricating parts for a stereo receiver is a variable cost. The more units produced, the higher the cost of parts. The **total cost** of producing a certain number of units is the sum of the fixed costs and the variable costs attributed to those units.

fixed cost a cost incurred no matter how many units of a product are produced or sold

variable cost a cost that depends on the number of units produced

total cost the sum of the fixed costs and the variable costs attributed to a product

If we assume a particular selling price, we can find the breakeven quantity either graphically or by using a formula. Figure 14.4 graphs the total revenue earned and the total cost incurred by the sale of various quantities of a hypothetical product. With fixed costs of \$40,000, variable costs of \$60 per unit, and a selling price of \$120, the breakeven quantity is 667 units. To find the breakeven quantity, first deduct the variable cost from the selling price to determine how much money the sale of one unit contributes to offsetting fixed costs. Then divide that contribution into the total fixed costs to arrive at the breakeven quantity. (The breakeven quantity in Figure 14.4 is the quantity represented by the intersection of the total revenue and total cost axes.) If the firm sells more than 667 units at \$120 each, it will earn a profit. If it sells fewer units, it will suffer a loss.

figure 14.4

Breakeven Analysis

Breakeven analysis answers the question, What is the lowest level of production and sales at which a company can break even on a particular product?

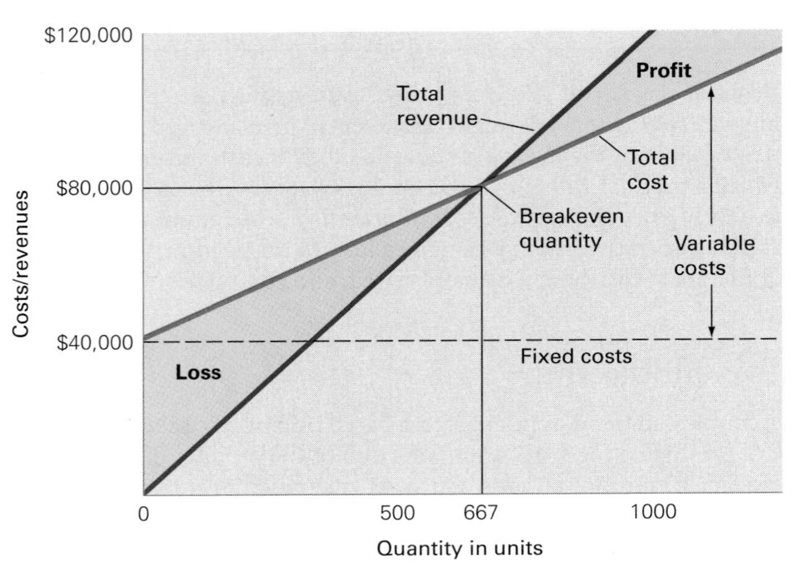

Demand-Based Pricing

Rather than basing the price of a product on its cost, companies sometimes use a pricing method based on the level of demand for the product: *demand-based pricing*. This method results in a high price when product demand is strong and a low price when demand is weak. Some long-distance telephone companies use demand-based pricing. Buyers of new cars that are in high demand such as the Honda Odyssey, Mercedes S500, Chrysler PT Cruiser, Toyota MR2 Spider, and BMW X5, paid sticker prices and in some cases sticker prices plus a premium.[17] To use this method, a marketer estimates the amount of a product that customers will demand at different prices and then chooses the price that generates the highest total revenue. Obviously, the effectiveness of this method depends on the firm's ability to estimate demand accurately.

A firm may favor a demand-based pricing method called *price differentiation* if it wants to use more than one price in the marketing of a specific product. Price differentiation can be based on such considerations as time of the purchase, type of customer, or type of distribution channel. For example, Florida hotel accommodations are more expensive in winter than in summer; a homeowner pays more for air-conditioner filters than does an apartment complex owner purchasing the same size filters in greater quantity; and Christmas tree ornaments are usually cheaper on December 26 than on December 16. For price differentiation to work correctly, the company must first be able to segment a market on the basis of different strengths of demand and then to keep the segments separate enough so that segment members who buy at lower prices cannot sell to buyers in segments that are charged a higher price. This isolation could be accomplished, for example, by selling to geographically separated segments.

Compared with cost-based pricing, demand-based pricing places a firm in a better position to attain higher profit levels, assuming that buyers value the product at levels sufficiently above the product's cost. To use demand-based pricing, however, management must be able to estimate demand at different price levels, which may be difficult to do accurately.

Competition-Based Pricing

In using *competition-based pricing*, an organization considers costs and revenue secondary to competitors' prices. The importance of this method increases if competing products are quite similar and the organization is serving markets in which price is the crucial variable of the marketing strategy. A firm that uses competition-based pricing may choose to be below competitors' prices, slightly above competitors' prices, or at the same level. The price that your bookstore paid to the publishing company of this text was determined using competition-based pricing. Competition-based pricing can help attain a pricing objective to increase sales or market share. Competition-based pricing may be combined with other cost approaches to arrive at profitable levels.

Pricing Strategies

LEARNING OBJECTIVE

9 Explain the different strategies available to companies for setting prices.

A pricing strategy is a course of action designed to achieve pricing objectives. Generally, pricing strategies help marketers solve the practical problems of setting prices. The extent to which a business uses any of the following strategies depends on its pricing and marketing objectives, the markets for its products, the degree of product differentiation, the life-cycle stage of the product, and other factors. Figure 14.5 contains a list of the major types of pricing strategies. We discuss these strategies in the remainder of this section.

New-Product Strategies

The two primary types of new-product pricing strategies are price skimming and penetration pricing. An organization can use either one or even both over a period of time.

price skimming the strategy of charging the highest-possible price for a product during the introduction stage of its life cycle

Price Skimming

Some consumers are willing to pay a high price for an innovative product, either because of its novelty or because of the prestige or status that ownership confers. **Price skimming** is the strategy of charging the highest-possible price for a product during the introduction stage of its life cycle. The seller essentially "skims the cream" off the market, which helps to recover the high costs of research and development more quickly. Also, a skimming policy may hold down demand for the product, which is helpful if the firm's production capacity is limited during the introduction stage. The greatest disadvantage is that a skimming price may make the product appear lucrative to potential competitors, who may then attempt to enter that market.

figure 14.5

Types of Pricing Strategies

Companies have a variety of pricing strategies available to them.

penetration pricing the strategy of setting a low price for a new product

Penetration Pricing At the opposite extreme, **penetration pricing** is the strategy of setting a low price for a new product. The main purpose of setting a low price is to build market share for the product quickly. The seller hopes that the building of a large market share quickly will discourage competitors from entering the market. If the low price stimulates sales, the firm may also be able to order longer production runs, which result in lower production costs per unit. A disadvantage of penetration pricing is that it places a firm in a less flexible position. It is more difficult to raise prices significantly than it is to lower them.

Differential Pricing

An important issue in pricing decisions is whether to use a single price or different prices for the same product. A single price is easily understood by both employees and customers, and since many salespeople and customers do not like having to negotiate a price, it reduces the chance of a marketer developing an adversarial relationship with a customer.

Differential pricing means charging different prices to different buyers for the same quality and quantity of product. For differential pricing to be effective, the market must consist of multiple segments with different price sensitivities. When this method is employed caution should be used to avoid confusing or antagonizing customers. Differential pricing can occur in several ways, including negotiated pricing, secondary-market pricing, periodic discounting, and random discounting.

negotiated pricing establishing a final price through bargaining

secondary-market pricing setting one price for the primary target market and a different price for another market

periodic discounting temporary reduction of prices on a patterned or systematic basis

Negotiated Pricing **Negotiated pricing** occurs when the final price is established through bargaining between the seller and the customer. Negotiated pricing occurs in a number of industries and at all levels of distribution. Even when there is a predetermined stated price or a price list, manufacturers, wholesalers, and retailers may still negotiate to establish the final sales price. Consumers commonly negotiate prices for houses, cars, and used equipment.

Secondary-Market Pricing **Secondary-market pricing** means setting one price for the primary target market and a different price for another market. Often, the price charged in the secondary market is lower. However, when the costs of serving a secondary market are higher than normal, secondary-market customers may have to pay a higher price. Examples of secondary markets include a geographically isolated domestic market, a market in a foreign country, and a segment willing to purchase a product during off-peak times (such as "early bird" diners at restaurants and off-peak users of cellular phones).

Random discounting. This sale at a shoe store is an example of random discounting.

Periodic Discounting **Periodic discounting** is the temporary reduction of prices on a patterned or systematic basis. For example, many retailers have annual holiday sales, and some women's apparel stores have two seasonal sales each year: a winter sale in the last two weeks of January, and a summer sale in the first two weeks of

July. From the marketer's point of view, a major problem with periodic discounting is that customers can predict when the reductions will occur and may delay their purchases until they can take advantage of the lower prices.

Random Discounting To alleviate the problem of customers' knowing when discounting will occur, some organizations employ **random discounting**. That is, they temporarily reduce their prices on an unsystematic basis. When price reductions of a product occur randomly, current users of that brand are not likely to be able to predict when the reductions will occur and so will not delay their purchases in anticipation of buying the product at a lower price. Marketers also use random discounting to attract new customers.

random discounting temporary reduction of prices on an unsystematic basis

Psychological Pricing Strategies

Psychological pricing strategies encourage purchases based on emotional responses rather than on economically rational responses. These strategies are used primarily for consumer products rather than business products.

Odd-Number Pricing Many retailers believe that consumers respond more positively to odd-number prices like $4.99 than to whole-dollar prices like $5. **Odd-number pricing** is the strategy of setting prices using odd numbers that are slightly below whole dollar amounts. Nine and five are the most popular ending figures for odd-number prices.

odd-number pricing the strategy of setting prices using odd numbers that are slightly below whole dollar amounts

Sellers who use this strategy believe that odd-number prices increase sales. The strategy is not limited to low-priced items. Auto manufacturers may set the price of a car at $11,999 rather than $12,000. Odd-number pricing has been the subject of various psychological studies, but the results have been inconclusive.

Multiple-Unit Pricing Many retailers (and especially supermarkets) practice **multiple-unit pricing**, setting a single price for two or more units, such as two cans for 99 cents rather than 50 cents per can. Especially for frequently purchased products, this strategy can increase sales. Customers who see the single price, and who expect eventually to use more than one unit of the product, regularly purchase multiple units to save money.

multiple-unit pricing the strategy of setting a single price for two or more units

Reference Pricing **Reference pricing** means pricing a product at a moderate level and positioning it next to a more expensive model or brand in the hope that the customer will use the higher price as a reference price (i.e., a comparison price). Because of the comparison, the customer is expected to view the moderate price favorably. When you go to Sears to buy a VCR, a moderately priced VCR may appear especially attractive because it offers most of the important attributes of the more expensive alternatives on display and at a lower price.

reference pricing pricing a product at a moderate level and positioning it next to a more expensive model or brand

Bundle Pricing **Bundle pricing** is the packaging together of two or more products, usually of a complementary nature, to be sold for a single price. To be attractive to customers, the single price is usually considerably less than the sum of the prices of the individual products. Being able to buy the bundled combination of products in a single transaction may be of value to the customer as well. Bundle pricing is commonly used for banking and travel services, computers, and automobiles with option packages. Bundle pricing can help to increase customer satisfaction. Bundling slow-moving products with ones with higher turnover, an organization can stimulate sales and increase its revenues. Selling products as a package rather than individually may also result in cost savings.

bundle pricing packaging together two or more complementary products and selling them for a single price

Everyday Low Prices (EDLP) To reduce or eliminate the use of frequent short-term price reductions, some organizations use an approach referred to as **everyday low prices (EDLP)**. When EDLP is used, a marketer sets a low price for its products on a consistent basis rather than setting higher prices and frequently discounting

everyday low prices (EDLP) setting a low price for products on a consistent basis

Everyday low prices. Wal-Mart employs the everyday low price strategy, as indicated by the sign above this display.

them. Everyday low prices, though not deeply discounted, are set far enough below competitors' prices to make customers feel confident they are receiving a fair price. EDLP is employed by retailers like Wal-Mart and by manufacturers like Procter & Gamble. A company that uses EDLP benefits from reduced promotional costs, reduced losses from frequent mark-downs, and more stability in its sales. A major problem with this approach is that customers have mixed responses to it. In some instances, customers simply don't believe that everyday low prices are what they say they are, but are instead a marketing gimmick.

customary pricing pricing on the basis of tradition

Customary Pricing

In **customary pricing**, certain goods are priced primarily on the basis of tradition. Examples of customary, or traditional, prices would be those set for candy bars and chewing gum.

Product-Line Pricing

Rather than considering products on an item-by-item basis when determining pricing strategies, some marketers employ product-line pricing. *Product-line pricing* means establishing and adjusting the prices of multiple products within a product line. Product-line pricing can provide marketers with flexibility in price setting. For example, marketers can set prices so that one product is quite profitable while another increases market share by virtue of having a lower price than competing products.

When marketers employ product-line pricing, they have several strategies from which to choose. These include captive pricing, premium pricing, and price lining.

captive pricing pricing the basic product in a product line low, but pricing related items at a higher level

Captive Pricing

When **captive pricing** is used, the basic product in a product line is priced low, but the price on the items required to operate or enhance it can be at a higher level. For example, a manufacturer of cameras and film may price a camera at a low level to attract customers, but price the film at a relatively high price because customers must continue to purchase film in order to use their cameras.

premium pricing pricing the highest-quality or most versatile products higher than other models in the product line

Premium Pricing

Premium pricing occurs when the highest-quality product or the most versatile version of similar products in a product line is given the highest price. Other products in the line are priced to appeal to price-sensitive shoppers or to those who seek product-specific features. Marketers that use premium pricing often realize a significant portion of their profits from premium-priced products. Examples of product categories in which premium pricing is common are small kitchen appliances, beer, ice cream, and television cable service.

Price Lining

Price lining is the strategy of selling goods only at certain predetermined prices that reflect definite price breaks. For example, a shop may sell men's ties only at $22 and $37. This strategy is widely used in clothing and accessory stores. It eliminates minor price differences from the buying decision—both for customers and for managers who buy merchandise to sell in these stores.

price lining setting a limited number of prices for selected groups or lines of merchandise

Promotional Pricing

Price, as an ingredient in the marketing mix, is often coordinated with promotion. The two variables sometimes are so interrelated that the pricing policy is promotion-oriented. Examples of promotional pricing include price leaders, special-event pricing, and comparison discounting.

Price Leaders

Sometimes a firm prices a few products below the usual markup, near cost, or below cost, which results in prices known as **price leaders**. This type of pricing is used most often in supermarkets and restaurants to attract customers by giving them especially low prices on a few items. Management hopes that sales of regularly priced products will more than offset the reduced revenues from the price leaders.

price leaders products priced below the usual markup, near cost, or below cost

Special-Event Pricing

To increase sales volume, many organizations coordinate price with advertising or sales promotions for seasonal or special situations. **Special-event pricing** involves advertised sales or price cutting linked to a holiday, season, or event. If the pricing objective is survival, then special sales events may be designed to generate the necessary operating capital.

special-event pricing advertised sales or price cutting linked to a holiday, season, or event

Comparison Discounting

Comparison discounting sets the price of a product at a specific level and simultaneously compares it with a higher price. The higher price may be the product's previous price, the price of a competing brand, the product's price at another retail outlet, or a manufacturer's suggested retail price. Customers may find comparative discounting informative, and it can have a significant impact on them. However, because this pricing strategy has on occasion led to deceptive pricing practices, the Federal Trade Commission has established guidelines for comparison discounting. If the higher price against which the comparison is made is the price formerly charged for the product, sellers must have made the previous price available to customers for a reasonable period of time. If sellers present the higher price as the one charged by other retailers in the same trade area, they must be able to demonstrate that this claim is true. When they present the higher price as the manufacturer's suggested retail price, then the higher price must be similar to the price at which a reasonable proportion of the product was sold. Some manufacturers' suggested retail prices are so high that very few products are actually sold at those prices. In such cases, it would be deceptive to use comparison discounting.

comparison discounting setting a price at a specific level and comparing it with a higher price

Pricing Business Products

LEARNING OBJECTIVE

10 Describe three major types of pricing associated with business products.

Many of the pricing issues discussed thus far in this chapter deal with pricing in general. Setting prices for business products can be different from setting prices for consumer products due to several factors such as size of purchases, transportation considerations, and geographic issues. We examine three types of pricing associated with business products including geographic pricing, transfer pricing, and discounting.

Geographic Pricing

Geographic pricing strategies deal with delivery costs. The pricing strategy that requires the buyer to pay the delivery costs is called *FOB origin pricing*. It stands for "free on board at the point of origin," which means that the price does not include freight charges and thus the buyer must pay the transportation costs from the seller's warehouse to the buyer's place of business. *FOB destination* indicates that the price does include freight charges and thus the seller pays these charges.

Transfer Pricing

transfer pricing prices charged in sales between an organization's units

When one unit in an organization sells a product to another unit, **transfer pricing** occurs. The price is determined by calculating the cost of the product. A transfer price can vary depending on the types of costs included in the calculations. The choice of the costs to include when calculating the transfer price depends on the company's management strategy and the nature of the units' interaction. An organization must also ensure that transfer pricing is fair to all units involved in the purchases.

Discounting

discount a deduction from the price of an item

A **discount** is a deduction from the price of an item. Producers and sellers offer a wide variety of discounts to their customers, including the following:

- *Trade discounts* are discounts from the list prices that are offered to marketing intermediaries, or middlemen. A furniture retailer, for example, may receive a 40 percent discount from the manufacturer. The retailer would then pay $60 for a lamp carrying a list price of $100. Intermediaries, discussed in Chapter 15, perform various marketing activities in return for trade discounts.
- *Quantity discounts* are discounts given to customers who buy in large quantities. The seller's per-unit selling cost is lower for larger purchases. The quantity discount is a way of passing part of these savings on to the buyer.
- *Cash discounts* are discounts offered for prompt payment. A seller may offer a discount of "2/10, net 30," meaning that the buyer may take a 2 percent discount if the bill is paid within ten days and that the bill must be paid in full within thirty days.
- A *seasonal discount* is a price reduction to buyers who purchase out of season. This discount lets the seller maintain steadier production during the year. For example, automobile rental agencies offer seasonal discounts in winter and early spring to encourage firms to use automobiles during the slow months of the automobile rental business.
- An *allowance* is a reduction in price to achieve a desired goal. Trade-in allowances, for example are price reductions granted for turning in used equipment when purchasing new equipment. This type of discount is popular in the aircraft industry. Another example is a promotional allowance, which is a price reduction granted to dealers for participating in advertising and sales support programs intended to increase sales of a particular item.

In this chapter, we discussed two ingredients of the marketing mix—product and pricing. Chapter 15 is devoted to a third marketing mix element—distribution. As that chapter shows, distribution includes not only the physical movement of products but also the organizations that facilitate exchanges among the producers and users of products.

RETURN TO inside business

RANDY JONES AND MIKE OISTER WERE ONLY playing around when they stumbled on a new product idea for a better-quality football. They carefully researched the market and, over the course of two years, applied their knowledge of customer and retailer needs to bring their product from idea generation to commercialization. Their company has since expanded into other sporting goods and added a variety of product lines geared toward different types of retailers. For discount stores such as Target, for example, Classic Sport offers the lower-priced CBC line of balls.

Classic Sport started life in a business incubator, but it quickly outgrew that space and had to move to a larger facility. Although the address has changed, what hasn't changed is the founders' intense focus on the customer. To keep growing, says Oister, "we're going to listen to our customers–not just the retailers but our end customers. We're all about innovation, and this business is evolving very fast."

Questions

1. After more than six years of sales, do you think the Classic Sport football is in the introduction, growth, maturity, or decline stage of its life cycle? Explain.
2. Does Classic Sport's CBC line of balls appear to be competing on the basis of price or on factors other than price?

chapter Review

SUMMARY

1 Explain what a product is and how products are classified.

A product is everything one receives in an exchange, including all attributes and expected benefits. The product may be a manufactured item, a service, an idea, or some combination of these.

Products are classified according to their ultimate use. Classification affects a product's distribution, promotion, and pricing. Consumer products, which include convenience, shopping, and specialty products, are purchased to satisfy personal and family needs. Business products are purchased for resale, for making other products, or for use in a firm's operations. Business products can be classified as raw materials, major equipment, accessory equipment, component parts, process materials, supplies, and services.

2 Discuss the product life cycle and how it leads to new-product development.

Every product moves through a series of four stages—introduction, growth, maturity, and decline—which together form the product life cycle. As the product progresses through these stages, its sales and profitability increase, peak, and then decline. Marketers keep track of the life-cycle stage of products in order to estimate when a new product should be introduced to replace a declining one.

3 Define *product line* and *product mix*, and distinguish between the two.

A product line is a group of similar products marketed by a firm. The products in a product line are related to each other in the way they are produced, marketed, and used. The firm's product mix includes all the products it offers for sale. The width of a mix is the number of product lines it contains. The depth of the mix is the average number of individual products within each line.

4 Identify the methods available for changing a product mix.

Customer satisfaction and organizational objectives require marketers to develop, adjust, and maintain an effective product mix. Marketers may improve a product mix by changing existing products, deleting products, and developing new products.

New products are developed through a series of seven steps. The first step, idea generation, involves the accumulation of a pool of possible product ideas. Screening, the second step, removes from consideration those product ideas that do not mesh with organizational goals or resources. Concept testing, the third step, is a phase in which a small sample of potential buyers is exposed to a proposed product through a written or oral description in order to determine their initial reaction and buying intentions. The fourth step, business analysis, generates information about the potential sales, costs, and profits. During the development step, the product idea is transformed into mock-ups and actual prototypes to determine if the product is technically feasible to build and can be produced at reasonable costs. Test marketing is an actual launch of the product in several selected cities. Finally, during commercialization, plans for full-scale production and marketing are refined and implemented. Most product failures result from inadequate product planning and development.

5 Explain the uses and importance of branding, packaging, and labeling.

A brand is a name, term, symbol, design, or any combination of these that identifies a seller's products as distinct from those of other sellers. Brands can be classified as manufacturer brands, store brands, or generic brands. A firm can choose between two branding strategies—individual branding or family branding. Branding strategies are used to associate (or *not* associate) particular products with existing products, producers, or intermediaries. Packaging protects goods, offers consumer convenience, and enhances marketing efforts by communicating product features, uses, benefits, and image. Labeling provides customers with product information, some of which is required by law.

6 Describe the economic basis of pricing and the means by which sellers can control prices and buyers' perceptions of prices.

Under the ideal conditions of pure competition, an individual seller has no control over the price of its products. Prices are determined by the workings of supply and demand. In our real economy, however, sellers do exert some control, primarily through product differentiation. Product differentiation is the process of developing and promoting differences between one's product and all similar products. Firms also attempt to gain some control over pricing through advertising. A few large sellers have considerable control over prices because each controls a large proportion of the total supply of the product. Firms must consider the relative importance of price to buyers in the target market before setting prices. Buyers' perceptions of prices are affected by the importance of the product to them, the range of prices they consider acceptable, their perceptions of competing products, and their association of quality with price.

7 Identify the major pricing objectives used by businesses.

Objectives of pricing include survival, profit maximization, target return on investment, achieving market goals, and maintaining the status quo. Firms sometimes have to price products to survive, which usually requires cutting prices to attract customers. Return on investment (ROI) is the amount earned as a result of the investment in developing and marketing the product. The firm sets an annual-percentage ROI as the pricing goal. Some firms use pricing to maintain or increase their market share. And in industries in which price stability is important, firms often price their products by charging about the same as competitors.

8 Examine the three major pricing methods that firms employ.

The three major pricing methods are cost-based pricing, demand-based pricing, and competition-based pricing. When cost-based pricing is employed, a proportion of the cost is added to the total cost to determine the selling price. When demand-based pricing is used, the price will be higher when demand is higher, and the price will be lower when demand is lower. A firm that uses competition-based pricing may choose to price below competitors' prices, at the same level as competitors' prices, or slightly above competitors' prices.

9 Explain the different strategies available to companies for setting prices.

Pricing strategies fall into five categories: new-product pricing, differential pricing, psychological pricing, product-line pricing, and promotional pricing. Price skimming and penetration pricing are two strategies used for pricing new products. Differential pricing can be accomplished through negotiated pricing, secondary-market pricing, periodic discounting, and random discounting. The types of psychological pricing strategies are odd-number pricing, multiple-unit pricing, reference-pricing, bundle pricing, everyday low prices, and customary pricing. Product-line pricing can be achieved through captive pricing, premium pricing, and price lining. The major types of promotional pricing are: price leader pricing, special-event pricing, and comparison discounting.

10 Describe three major types of pricing associated with business products.

Setting prices for business products can be different from setting prices for consumer products due to several factors such as size of purchases, transportation considerations, and geographic issues. The three types of pricing associated with the pricing of business products are: geographic pricing, transfer pricing, and discounting.

KEY TERMS

You should now be able to define and give an example relevant to each of the following terms:

product (383)
consumer product (383)

business product (383)
convenience product (384)
shopping product (384)
specialty product (384)
raw material (384)
major equipment (384)
accessory equipment (384)
component part (384)
process material (385)
supply (385)
business service (385)
product life cycle (385)
product line (388)
product mix (388)
product modification (389)
product deletion (389)
brand (392)
brand name (392)
brand mark (392)
trademark (392)
trade name (392)
manufacturer (or producer) brand (393)
store (or private) brand (393)
generic product (or brand) (394)
brand loyalty (394)
brand equity (394)
individual branding (396)
family branding (397)
packaging (397)
labeling (398)
express warranty (398)
price (399)
supply (399)
demand (399)
product differentiation (400)
price competition (400)
nonprice competition (401)
markup (403)
breakeven quantity (403)
total revenue (403)
fixed cost (403)
variable cost (403)
total cost (403)
price skimming (405)
penetration pricing (406)
negotiated pricing (406)
secondary-market pricing (406)
periodic discounting (406)
random discounting (407)
odd-number pricing (407)
multiple-unit pricing (407)
reference pricing (407)
bundle pricing (407)
everyday low prices (EDLP) (407)
customary pricing (408)
captive pricing (408)
premium pricing (408)
price lining (409)
price leaders (409)
special-event pricing (409)
comparison discounting (409)
transfer pricing (410)
discount (410)

REVIEW QUESTIONS

1. What does the purchaser of a product obtain besides the good, service, or idea itself?
2. What are the products of (a) a bank, (b) an insurance company, and (c) a university?
3. What major factor determines whether a product is a consumer or a business product?
4. Describe each of the classifications of business products.
5. What are the four stages of the product life cycle? How can a firm determine which stage a particular product is in?
6. What is the difference between a product line and a product mix? Give an example of each.
7. Under what conditions does product modification work best?
8. Why do products have to be deleted from a product mix?
9. Why must firms introduce new products?
10. Briefly describe the seven new-product development stages.
11. What is the difference between manufacturer brands and store brands? between family branding and individual branding?
12. How can packaging be used to enhance marketing activities?
13. For what purposes is labeling used?
14. What is the primary function of prices in our economy?
15. Compare and contrast the characteristics of price and nonprice competition.
16. How might buyers' perceptions of price influence pricing decisions?
17. List and briefly describe the five major pricing objectives.
18. What are the differences among markup pricing, pricing by breakeven analysis, and competition-based pricing?
19. In what way is demand-based pricing more realistic than markup pricing?
20. Why would a firm use competition-based pricing?
21. What are the five major categories of pricing strategies? Give at least two examples of specific strategies that fall into each category.
22. Identify and describe the main types of discounts that are used in the pricing of business products.

DISCUSSION QUESTIONS

1. Why is it important to understand how products are classified?
2. What factors might determine how long a product remains in each stage of the product life cycle? What can a firm do to prolong each stage?
3. Some firms do not delete products until they become financially threatening. What problems may result from relying on this practice?
4. Which steps in the evolution of new products are most important? Which are least important? Defend your choices.
5. Do branding, packaging, and labeling really benefit consumers? Explain.

6. To what extent can a firm control its prices in our market economy? What factors limit such control?
7. Under what conditions would a firm be most likely to use nonprice competition?
8. Can a firm have more than one pricing objective? Can it use more than one of the pricing methods discussed in this chapter? Explain.
9. What are the major disadvantages of price skimming?
10. What is an "effective" price?
11. Under what conditions would a business most likely decide to employ one of the differential pricing strategies?
12. For what type of products are psychological pricing strategies most likely to be used?

VIDEO CASE

Product Development Keeps Gillette on the Cutting Edge

Humorist Dave Barry predicts that someday soon, Gillette will announce a new razor so advanced it can travel forward in time and shave beards that don't yet exist. Although Gillette has thus far not developed products suitable for science fiction, the $10-billion consumer product company does generate enough cutting-edge products every year to make it a Wall Street superstar. Selling everything from Right Guard deodorants and shaving systems to Duracell flashlight batteries, Gillette bases its strategy on aggressively rolling out new products.

The company traces its origins to 1895, when King C. Gillette came up with the idea of disposable razor blades. After six years of searching for interested investors and toolmakers to back him, he found machinist William Nickerson, and together they perfected the safety razor and formed the American Safety Razor Company. In its first year of operation, the company sold just fifty-one safety razors. The next year, it sold over 90,000, and a little more than a decade later, during World War I, it sold 3.5 million shaving kits to the U.S. government. In 1948 the American Safety Razor Company began to diversify, and in the 1950s, after buying Paper Mate Pens, it changed its name to Gillette.

Over time, the flow of new products evolved from a steady stream into a torrent, as Gillette sought to boost U.S. market share and sales by introducing one innovative new product after another. Today, the company dominates its markets in the United States. In dollar terms, Gillette's shaving products account for more than 70 percent of razor sales and 80 percent of blade sales; its Duracell products account for 50 percent of all battery sales; and its Oral-B products account for more than 32 percent of all toothbrush sales.

Gillette will not even put a prototype into production until a model for the product's next generation is ready to test. Unlike most consumer product companies, however, Gillette releases new products only if they represent significant improvements. Just one out of three product ideas makes it to the development stage, and many prototypes are not further developed into commercialized products. A large annual research and development budget facilitates the kind of technological breakthroughs that make Gillette's new products truly new. For example, Gillette invested $300 million to develop the ergonomic handle, cushion-edged blade, and special storage unit for its Venus women's razor, based in part on technology created for its Mach3 men's razor.

While Gillette's research and development staff work in the lab, its marketing research staff is out in the field talking to potential customers. For example, when the company was developing its line of men's toiletries, marketing staff spoke to 70,000 men about what they like in shaving creams, antiperspirants, and deodorants. And, as a matter of routine, over 300 Gillette employees come to work unshaven every day and test shaving products in the company's on-site "Shaving Test Lab."

Gillette gives its new products a running start by providing extensive promotional support. For the launch of the Venus razor, the company spent $150 million on television, print, outdoor, and Internet advertising. Similarly, the company spent $100 million launching a new line of Braun Oral-B electric toothbrushes for children and adults, aiming to capture a commanding share of this fast-growing market segment. Backed by such strong promotional campaigns, new product sales have become the cornerstone of Gillette's performance, contributing nearly half of the firm's yearly revenue. Yet overall sales have been flat, due to sluggish results in foreign markets, leading management to bring costs into line by downsizing and closing selected facilities. The financial pressure has made new product development even more important to Gillette's future, fueling hopes for renewed growth in the coming years.[18]

Questions

1. Into which category would most of Gillette's products be classified: convenience, shopping, or specialty?
2. At Gillette, many prototypes never reach the commercialization phase of the new-product development process. In what phase of this process are prototypes developed?
3. Gillette does not put a prototype into production until a model for the product's next generation is ready for testing. Evaluate this practice.

Building skills for career success

1. Exploring the Internet

The Internet has been a boon to any marketer with a product that can be digitized. Music, photographic images, and video streaming now deliver a wide range of entertaining content to consumers for free. However, firms that wish to control the sale of their product and limit distribution over the Internet are having a hard time. Consumers are naturally motivated whenever something of value to them, like a hit song, is available free of charge. MP3 (http://www.mp3.com) and Napster (http://www.napster.com) are two of the better-known software programs that allow users to share recorded files of music, but there are others and more will likely emerge. Visit the text web site for updates to this exercise.

Assignment

1. Examine the MP3.com and Napster.com web sites and explain what their services are all about.
2. What were the ethical issues raised by consumers who downloaded music for free?
3. Did you support the free distribution of content on MP3 and Napster? Explain your thinking.
4. What strategic advice would you give to the music industry?

2. Developing Critical Thinking Skills

A feature is a characteristic of a product or service that enables it to perform its function. Benefits are the results a person receives from using the product or service. For example, a toothpaste's stain-removing formula is a feature; the benefit to the user is whiter teeth. While features are valuable and enhance a product, benefits motivate people to buy. The customer is more interested in how the product can help (the benefits) than in the details of the product (the features).

Assignment

1. Choose a product and identify its features and benefits.
2. Divide a sheet of paper into two columns.
   - In one column, list the features of the product.
   - In the other column, list the benefits each feature yields to the buyer.
3. Prepare a statement that would motivate you to buy this product.

3. Building Team Skills

In his book, *The Post-Industrial Society*, Peter Drucker wrote:

> Society, community, and family are all conserving institutions. They try to maintain stability and to prevent, or at least slow down, change. But the organization of the post-capitalist society of organizations is a destabilizer. Because its function is to put knowledge to work—on tools, processes, and products; on work; on knowledge itself—it must be organized for constant change. It must be organized for innovation.

New-product development is important in this process of systematically abandoning the past and building a future. Current customers can be sources of ideas for new products and services and ways of improving existing ones.

Assignment

1. Working in teams of five to seven, brainstorm ideas for new products or services for your college.
2. Construct questions to ask currently enrolled students (your customers). Sample questions might include
   a. Why did you choose this college?
   b. How can this college be improved?
   c. What products or services do you wish were available?
3. Conduct the survey and review the results.
4. Prepare a list of improvements and/or new products or services for your college.

4. Researching Different Careers

Standard & Poor's Industry Surveys, designed for investors, provides insight into various industries and the companies that compete within those industries. The "Basic Analysis" section gives overviews of industry trends and issues. The other sections define some basic industry terms, report the latest revenues and earnings of more than 1,000 companies, and occasionally list major reference books and trade associations.

Assignment

1. Identify an industry in which you might like to work.
2. Find the industry in *Standard & Poor's, (Note: Standard & Poor's* uses broad categories of industry. For example, an apparel or home furnishings store would be included under "Retail" or "Textiles").
3. Identify the following:
   a. Trends and issues in the industry.
   b. Opportunities and/or problems that might arise in the industry in the next five years.
   c. Major competitors within the industry. (These companies are your potential employers.)
4. Prepare a report of your findings.

5. Improving Communication Skills

One often-overlooked source of business information is the Yellow Pages of the local telephone directory. The Yellow Pages can give you insight into the nature and scope of local companies.

Assignment

1. Choose a product and look it up in the Yellow Pages.
2. Telephone three companies that provide the product and ask for directions from your campus.
3. Evaluate the quality of the directions given and your impression of each company's service.
4. Report on your findings.

Wholesaling, Retailing, and Physical Distribution

15

LEARNING OBJECTIVES

1. Identify the various channels of distribution that are used for consumer and industrial products.
2. Explain the concept of market coverage.
3. Understand how supply chain management facilitates partnering among channel members.
4. Describe what a vertical marketing system is, and identify the types of vertical marketing systems.
5. Discuss the need for wholesalers, and describe the services they provide to retailers and manufacturers.
6. Identify and describe the major types of wholesalers.
7. Distinguish among the major types of retailers.
8. Explain the wheel of retailing hypothesis.
9. Identify the categories of shopping centers and the factors that determine how shopping centers are classified.
10. Explain the five most important physical distribution activities.

Barnes and Noble has forged close relationships with book publishers, wholesalers, and other supply chain partners.

inside business

At Barnes and Noble, Size Matters

BARNES AND NOBLE has built its retail empire on the premise that size matters. The largest U.S. book store operator made retailing history when it opened the first category-killer book store in the late 1980s. At 15,000 square feet, the store was five times the size of a typical book store. Today, Barnes and Noble routinely opens massive 100,000-square-foot stores while managing hundreds of smaller mall-based stores, a fast-growing Internet business (http://www.bn.com), and a network of gigantic warehouses. This multi-pronged distribution strategy has helped the chain boost annual sales to $3.5 billion.

For years, Barnes and Noble managed inventory by having suppliers and wholesalers send book and music orders directly to individual stores. However, as the company opened larger book stores, it needed a new system to ensure that the right items would be available in the right quantities at the right time and in the right place. To accomplish this, Barnes and Noble built three warehouses totaling one million square feet to receive and store products until they are shipped out to the stores. Once the web site came online, just a few years after the warehouses were built, even this huge expanse of warehouse space proved too small to accommodate the amount of merchandise needed to keep up with the surge in sales. Now, after a round of expansion, the warehouses can hold an inventory of 20 million items at any one time, ready to go out to Barnes and Noble stores and to web customers in more than 200 countries.

To effectively manage all the intricate details of store and Internet sales, orders, and shipments, Barnes and Noble has forged close relationships with book publishers, wholesalers, and other supply chain partners. A sophisticated Internet-based system helps the retailer capture and communicate customer demand data to help suppliers plan ahead for production. The system also gathers and communicates supplier information about product availability to help Barnes and Noble's buyers plan ahead for ordering. Finally, the system analyzes location-by-location inventory levels to help managers plan ahead for shipments to stores and online customers.

Even with the retailer's high inventory levels, however, some customers are bound to be disappointed now and then because the books they want aren't in stock. "To live up to our promise to the consumer, we want to have everything that's in print available from our facilities," says William F. Duffy, Barnes and Noble's vice president of operations. "The trick is in the appropriate quantities. That's the balancing we're going through right now in our demand model. We can't be in stock 100 percent of the time."[1]

More than 2 million firms in the United States help move products from producers to consumers. Of all marketers, retail firms that sell directly to consumers are the most visible. Store chains like Barnes and Noble, Starbucks, Sears, and Wal-Mart operate retail outlets where consumers make purchases. Some retailers, like Avon Products and Amway, send their salespeople to the homes of customers. Other retailers, like Lands' End and L.L. Bean, sell through catalogs or through both catalogs and stores. Still others like Amazon sell online to customers.

In addition, there are more than half a million wholesalers that sell merchandise to other firms. Most consumers know little about these firms, which work "behind the scenes" and rarely sell directly to consumers. These and other intermediaries are concerned with the transfer of both products and ownership. They thus help create the time, place, and possession utilities that are critical to marketing. As we will see, they also perform a number of services for their suppliers and their customers.

In this chapter, we initially examine various channels of distribution that products follow as they move from producer to ultimate user. Then we discuss wholesalers and retailers within these channels. Next we examine the types of shopping centers. Finally, we explore the physical distribution function and the major modes of transportation that are used to move goods.

Channels of Distribution

channel of distribution (or **marketing channel**) a sequence of marketing organizations that directs a product from the producer to the ultimate user

middleman (or **marketing intermediary**) a marketing organization that links a producer and user within a marketing channel

merchant middleman a middleman that actually takes title to products by buying them

functional middleman a middleman that helps in the transfer of ownership of products but does not take title to the products

A **channel of distribution**, or **marketing channel**, is a sequence of marketing organizations that directs a product from the producer to the ultimate user. Every marketing channel begins with the producer and ends with either the consumer or the business user.

A marketing organization that links a producer and user within a marketing channel is called a **middleman**, or **marketing intermediary.** For the most part, middlemen are concerned with the transfer of *ownership* of products. A **merchant middleman** (or, more simply, a *merchant*) is a middleman that actually takes title to products by buying them. A **functional middleman**, on the other hand, helps in the transfer of ownership of products but does not take title to the products.

Different channels of distribution are generally used to move consumer and business products. The six most commonly used channels are illustrated in Figure 15.1.

Channels for Consumer Products

LEARNING OBJECTIVE

1 Identify the various channels of distribution that are used for consumer and industrial products.

Producer to Consumer This channel, often called the *direct channel*, includes no marketing intermediaries. Practically all services, and a few consumer goods, are distributed through a direct channel. Examples of marketers that sell goods directly to consumers include Dell Computer, Mary Kay Cosmetics, Spiegel, and Avon Products.

Producers sell directly to consumers for several reasons. They can better control the quality and price of their products. They don't have to pay (through discounts) for the services of intermediaries. And they can maintain closer ties with customers.

retailer a middleman that buys from producers or other middlemen and sells to consumers

Producer to Retailer to Consumer A **retailer** is a middleman that buys from producers or other middlemen and sells to consumers. Producers sell directly to retailers when retailers (such as Wal-Mart) can buy in large quantities. This channel is most often used for products that are bulky, such as furniture and automobiles, for which additional handling would increase selling costs. It is also the usual channel for perishable products, such as fruits and vegetables, and for high-fashion products that must reach the consumer in the shortest possible time.

wholesaler a middleman that sells products to other firms

Producer to Wholesaler to Retailer to Consumer This channel is known as the *traditional channel* because many consumer goods (especially convenience goods) pass through wholesalers to retailers. A **wholesaler** is a middleman that sells products

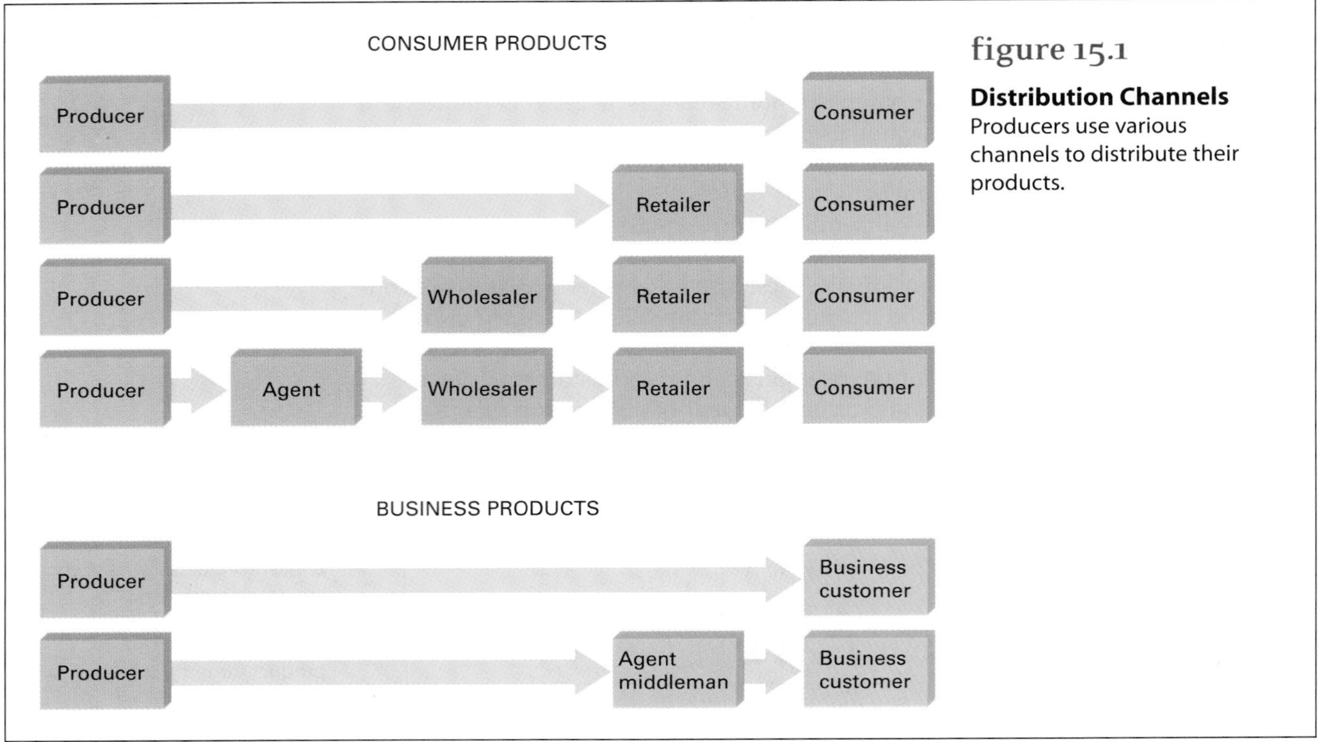

figure 15.1

Distribution Channels
Producers use various channels to distribute their products.

to other firms. These firms may be retailers, industrial users, or other wholesalers. A producer uses wholesalers when its products are carried by so many retailers that the producer cannot deal with all of them. For example, the maker of Wrigley's gum uses this type of channel.

Producer to Agent to Wholesaler to Retailer to Consumer Producers may use agents to reach wholesalers. Agents are functional middlemen that do not take title to products and that are compensated by commissions paid by producers. Often, these products are inexpensive, frequently purchased items. For example, to reach a large number of potential customers, a small manufacturer of gas-powered lawn-edgers might choose to use agents to market its product to wholesalers, which in turn sell the lawn-edgers to a large number of retailers. This channel is also used for highly seasonal products (such as Christmas tree ornaments) and by producers that do not have their own sales forces.

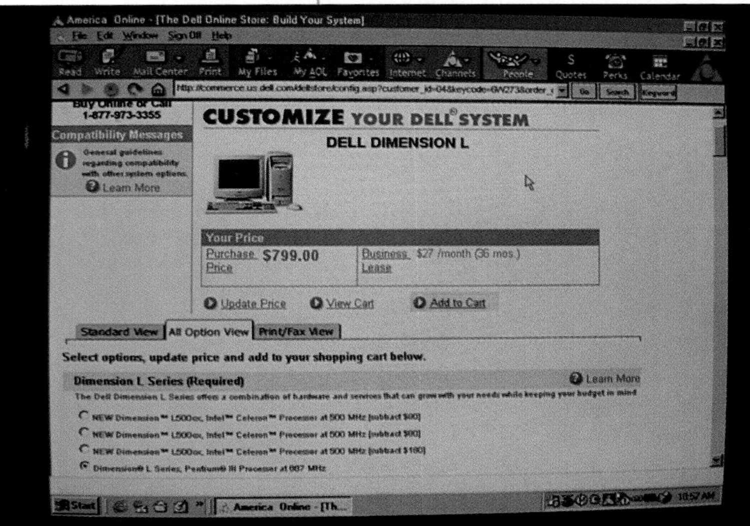

Direct distribution channels. Dell Computer Corporation uses direct distribution channels. Dell employs the producer-to-consumer channel and the producer-to-business user channel.

Multiple Channels for Consumer Products Often a manufacturer uses different distribution channels to reach different market segments. A manufacturer uses multiple channels, for example, when the same product is sold to consumers and business customers. Multiple channels are also used to increase sales or to capture a larger share of the market. With the goal of selling as much merchandise as possible, Firestone markets its tires through its own retail outlets as well as through independent dealers.

Channels for Business Products

Producers of business products generally tend to use short channels. We will outline the two that are most commonly used.

Producer to Business User In this direct channel, the manufacturer's own sales force sells directly to business users. Heavy machinery, airplanes, and major equipment are usually distributed in this way. The very short channel allows the producer to provide customers with expert and timely services, such as delivery, machinery installation, and repairs.

Producer to Agent Middleman to Business User Manufacturers use this channel to distribute such items as operating supplies, accessory equipment, small tools, and standardized parts. The agent is an independent intermediary between the producer and the user. Generally, agents represent sellers.

Market Coverage

LEARNING OBJECTIVE

2 Explain the concept of market coverage.

How does a producer decide which distribution channels (and which particular intermediaries) to use? Like every other marketing decision, this one should be based on all relevant factors. These include the firm's production capabilities and marketing resources, the target market and buying patterns of potential customers, and the product itself. After evaluating these factors, the producer can choose a particular *intensity of market coverage*. Then the producer selects channels and intermediaries to implement that coverage (see Figure 15.2).

intensive distribution the use of all available outlets for a product

Intensive distribution is the use of all available outlets for a product. The producer that wants to give its product the widest possible exposure in the marketplace chooses intensive distribution. The manufacturer saturates the market by selling to any intermediary of good financial standing that is willing to stock and sell the product. For the consumer, intensive distribution means being able to shop at a convenient store and spend minimum time buying the product. Many convenience goods, including candy, gum, and soft drinks, are distributed intensively.

selective distribution the use of only a portion of the available outlets for a product in each geographic area

Selective distribution is the use of only a portion of the available outlets for a product in each geographic area. Manufacturers of goods such as furniture, major home appliances, and clothing typically prefer selective distribution. Franchisors also

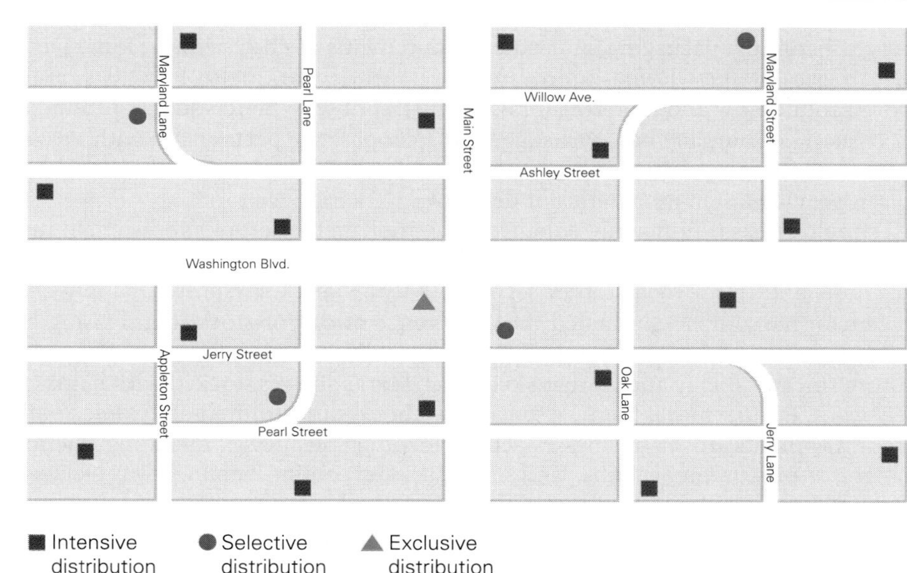

figure 15.2

Market Coverage

The number of outlets a producer chooses for a product depends on the type of product. Batteries, for example, are distributed intensively in this area; sports equipment is selectively distributed; and Steubenglass is exclusively distributed.

Exclusive distribution. In the United States, Mercedes-Benz automobiles are sold through exclusive distribution.

use selective distribution in granting franchises for the sale of their goods and services in a specific geographic area.

exclusive distribution the use of only a single retail outlet for a product in a large geographic area

Exclusive distribution is the use of only a single retail outlet for a product in a large geographic area. Exclusive distribution is usually limited to very prestigious products. It is appropriate, for instance, for specialty goods such as upscale pianos, fine china, and expensive jewelry. The producer usually places many requirements (inventory levels, sales training, service quality, warranty procedures) on exclusive dealers.

Partnering Through Supply Chain Management

LEARNING OBJECTIVE

3 Understand how supply chain management facilitates partnering among channel members.

supply chain management long-term partnership among channel members working together to create a distribution system that reduces inefficiencies, costs, and redundancies while creating a competitive advantage and satisfying customers

Supply chain management is a long-term partnership among channel members working together to create a distribution system that reduces inefficiencies, costs, and redundancies while creating a competitive advantage and satisfying customers. Supply chain management requires cooperation throughout the entire marketing channel, including manufacturing, research, sales, advertising, and shipping. Supply chains focus not only on producers, wholesalers, retailers, and customers but also on component-parts suppliers, shipping companies, communication companies, and other organizations that participate in product distribution.

Traditionally, buyers and sellers have been adversarial when negotiating purchases. Supply chain management, however, encourages cooperation in reducing the costs of inventory, transportation, administration, and handling; in speeding order-cycle times; and in increasing profits for all channel members. When buyers, sellers, marketing intermediaries, and facilitating agencies work together, customers' needs regarding delivery, scheduling, packaging, and other requirements are better met. Home Depot, North America's largest home-improvement retailer, is working to help its suppliers improve productivity and thereby supply Home Depot with better-quality products at lower costs. The company has even suggested a cooperative partnership with its competitors so that regional trucking companies making deliveries to all these organizations can provide faster, more efficient delivery.

Technology has significantly enhanced the implementation of supply chain management. Through computerized integrated information sharing, channel members reduce costs and improve customer service. At Wal-Mart, for example, supply chain management has almost eliminated the occurrence of out-of-stock items. Using barcode and electronic data interchange (EDI) technology, stores, warehouses, and suppliers communicate quickly and easily to keep Wal-Mart's shelves stocked with items customers want. Furthermore, there are currently about four hundred electronic trading communities made up of businesses selling to other businesses including auctions, exchanges, e-procurement hubs, and multisupplier online catalogs. According to investment bank Goldman Sachs, online business-to-business selling will grow from \$114 billion in 1999 to \$1.5 trillion in 2004, as all major industries transform their processes over the next 5 to 10 years. The result will be increased productivity by reducing inventory, shortening cycle time, and removing wasted human effort.[2]

Vertical Marketing Systems

LEARNING OBJECTIVE

4 Describe what a vertical marketing system is, and identify the types of vertical marketing systems.

Vertical channel integration occurs when two or more stages of a distribution channel are combined and managed by one firm. A **vertical marketing system (VMS)** is a centrally managed distribution channel resulting from vertical channel integration. This merging eliminates the need for certain intermediaries. One member of a marketing channel may assume the responsibilities of another member, or it may actually purchase the operations of that member. For example, a large-volume discount retailer that ships and warehouses its own stock directly from manufacturers does not need a wholesaler. Total vertical integration occurs when a single management controls all operations from production to final sale. Oil companies that own wells, transportation facilities, refineries, terminals, and service stations exemplify total vertical integration.

vertical channel integration the combining of two or more stages of a distribution channel under a single firm's management

vertical marketing system (VMS) a centrally managed distribution channel resulting from vertical channel integration

There are three types of VMSs: administered, contractual, and corporate. In an *administered VMS*, one of the channel members dominates the other members, perhaps because of its large size. Under its influence, the channel members collaborate on production and distribution. A powerful manufacturer, such as Procter & Gamble, receives a great deal of cooperation from intermediaries that carry its brands. Although the goals of the entire system are considered when decisions are made, control rests with individual channel members, as in conventional marketing channels. Under a *contractual VMS*, cooperative arrangements and the rights and obligations of channel members are defined by contracts or other legal measures. In a *corporate VMS*, actual ownership is the vehicle by which production and distribution are joined. For example, Benetton manufactures clothing, which it then ships to its own retail outlets. Most vertical marketing systems are organized to improve distribution by combining individual operations.

Marketing Intermediaries: Wholesalers

LEARNING OBJECTIVE

5 Discuss the need for wholesalers, and describe the services they provide to retailers and manufacturers.

Wholesalers may be the most misunderstood of marketing intermediaries. Producers sometimes try to eliminate them from distribution channels by dealing directly with retailers or consumers. Yet wholesalers provide a variety of essential marketing services. Although wholesalers can be eliminated, their functions cannot be eliminated; these functions *must* be performed by other channel members or by the consumer or ultimate user. Eliminating a wholesaler may or may not cut distribution costs.

Justifications for Marketing Intermediaries

The press, consumers, public officials, and other marketers often charge wholesalers, at least in principle, with inefficiency and parasitism. Consumers in particular feel strongly that the distribution channel should be made as short as possible. They assume that the fewer the intermediaries in a distribution channel, the lower the price of the product will be.

Those who believe that the elimination of wholesalers would bring about lower prices, however, do not recognize that the services wholesalers perform would still be needed. Those services would simply be provided by other means, and consumers would still bear the costs. Moreover, all manufacturers would have to keep extensive records and employ enough personnel to deal with a multitude of retailers individually. Even with direct distribution, products might be considerably more expensive because prices would reflect the costs of producers' inefficiencies. Figure 15.3 shows that sixteen contacts could result from the efforts of four buyers purchasing the products of four producers. With the assistance of an intermediary, only eight contacts would be necessary.

To illustrate further the useful role of wholesalers in the marketing system, assume that all wholesalers in the candy industry were abolished. With thousands of candy

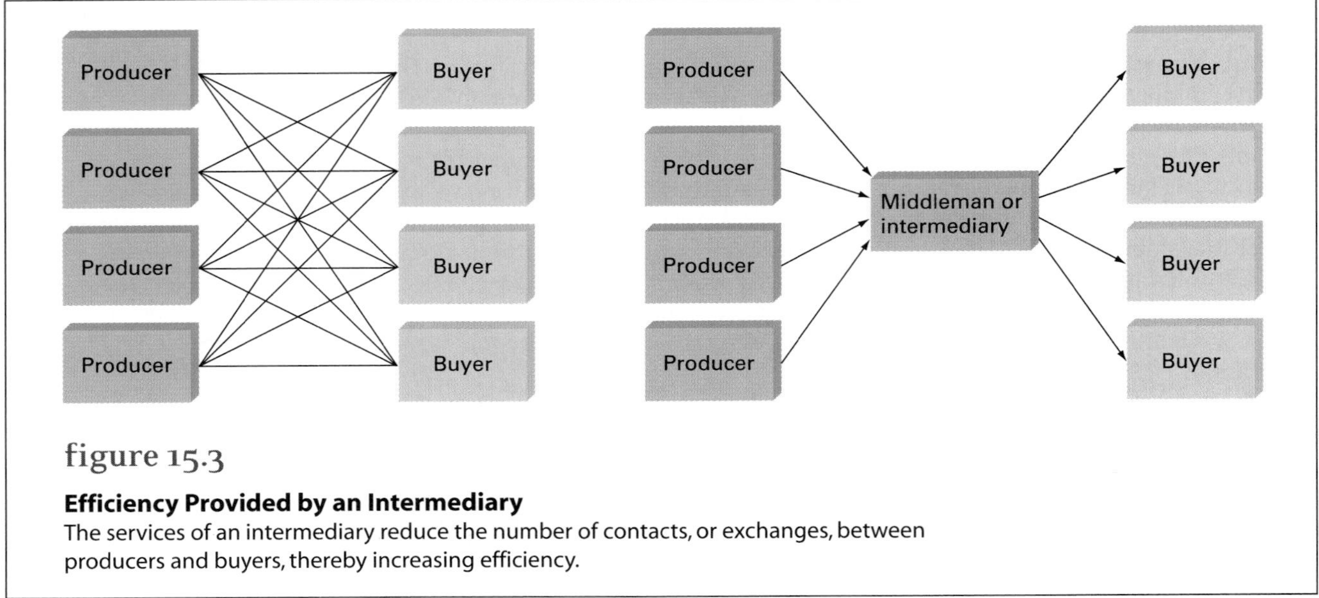

figure 15.3

Efficiency Provided by an Intermediary

The services of an intermediary reduce the number of contacts, or exchanges, between producers and buyers, thereby increasing efficiency.

Source: William M. Pride and O. C. Ferrell, *Marketing: Concepts and Strategies*, Eleventh Edition. Copyright © 2000 by Houghton Mifflin Company. Adapted with permission.

retailers to contact, candy manufacturers would be making an extremely large number of sales calls just to maintain the present level of product visibility. Hershey Foods, for example, would have to set up warehouses all over the country, organize a fleet of trucks, purchase and maintain thousands of vending machines, and deliver all of its own candy. Sales and distribution costs for candy would soar. Candy producers would be contacting and shipping products to thousands of small businesses, instead of to a limited number of large wholesalers and retailers. The outrageous costs of this inefficiency would be passed on to consumers. Candy bars would be more expensive and likely available through fewer retailers.

Wholesalers often are more efficient and economical not only for manufacturers but also for consumers. Because pressure to eliminate them comes from both ends of the marketing channel, wholesalers should perform only those functions that are genuinely in demand. To stay in business, wholesalers should also take care to be efficient and productive and to provide high-quality services to other channel members. Given the variety of Internet-based products and services to choose from, it is interesting to note that the conventional concept of a wholesaler who bundles together a mix of products for a customer is already well under way. For example, Redmond, Washington-based InfoSpace Inc. works with all sorts of Internet content providers, from weather services to news and information sites, to package together specific product mixes for customers looking for specific content mixes for their sites.[3]

Wholesalers' Services to Retailers

Wholesalers help retailers by buying in large quantities and then selling to retailers in smaller quantities and by delivering goods to retailers. They also stock—in one place—the variety of goods that retailers would otherwise have to buy from many producers. And wholesalers provide assistance in three other vital areas: promotion, market information, and financial aid.

Promotion Some wholesalers help promote the products they sell to retailers. These services are usually either free or performed at cost. Wholesalers, for example, are major sources of display materials designed to stimulate impulse buying. They may also help retailers build effective window, counter, and shelf displays; they may even assign their own employees to work on the retail sales floor during special promotions.

Market Information Wholesalers are a constant source of market information. Wholesalers have numerous contacts with local businesses and distant suppliers. In the course of these dealings, they accumulate information about consumer demand, prices, supply conditions, new developments within the trade, and even industry personnel. This information may be relayed to retailers informally, through the wholesaler's sales force. Some wholesalers provide information to their customers through web sites.

Information regarding industry sales and competitive prices is especially important to all firms. Dealing with a number of suppliers and many retailers, a wholesaler is a natural clearinghouse for such information. And most wholesalers are willing to pass information on to their customers.

Financial Aid Most wholesalers provide a type of financial aid that retailers often take for granted. By making prompt and frequent deliveries, wholesalers enable retailers to keep their own inventory investments small in relation to sales. Such indirect financial aid reduces the amount of operating capital that retailers need.

In some industries, wholesalers extend direct financial assistance through long-term loans. Most wholesalers also provide help through delayed billing, giving customers thirty to ninety days *after delivery* to pay for merchandise. Wholesalers of seasonal merchandise may offer even longer payment periods. For example, a wholesaler of lawn and garden supplies may deliver seed to retailers in January but not bill them for it until May.

Wholesalers' Services to Manufacturers

Some of the services that wholesalers perform for producers are similar to those they provide to retailers. Others are quite different.

Providing an Instant Sales Force A wholesaler provides its producers with an instant sales force so that producers' sales representatives need not call on retailers. This can result in enormous savings for producers. For example, Lever Brothers and General Foods would have to spend millions of dollars each year to field a sales force large enough to call on all the retailers that sell their numerous products. Instead, these producers rely on wholesalers to sell and distribute their products to many retailers. These producers do have sales forces that call on wholesalers and large retailers.

Reducing Inventory Costs Wholesalers purchase goods in sizable quantities from manufacturers and store these goods for resale. By doing so, they reduce the amount of finished-goods inventory that producers must hold and, thereby, reduce the cost of carrying inventories.

Assuming Credit Risks When producers sell through wholesalers, it is the wholesalers who extend credit to retailers, make collections from retailers, and assume the risks of nonpayment. These services reduce the producers' cost of extending credit to customers and the resulting bad-debt expense.

Furnishing Market Information Just as they do for retailers, wholesalers supply market information to the producers they serve. Valuable information accumulated by wholesalers may concern consumer demand, the producers' competition, and buying trends.

Types of Wholesalers

LEARNING OBJECTIVE

6 Identify and describe the major types of wholesalers.

Wholesalers generally fall into three categories: merchant wholesalers; commission merchants, agents, and brokers; and manufacturers' sales branches and sales offices. Of these, merchant wholesalers constitute the largest portion. They account for about 57 percent of wholesale sales and about four-fifths of all wholesale employees and wholesale establishments.[4]

merchant wholesaler a middleman that purchases goods in large quantities and then sells them to other wholesalers or retailers and to institutional, farm, government, professional, or industrial users

full-service wholesaler a middleman that performs the entire range of wholesaler functions

general merchandise wholesaler a middleman that deals in a wide variety of products

limited-line wholesaler a middleman that stocks only a few product lines, but carries numerous product items within each line

specialty-line wholesaler a middleman that carries a select group of products within a single line

limited-service wholesaler a middleman that assumes responsibility for a few wholesale services only

commission merchant a middleman that carries merchandise and negotiates sales for manufacturers

agent a middleman that expedites exchanges, represents a buyer or a seller, and often is hired permanently on a commission basis

broker a middleman that specializes in a particular commodity, represents either a buyer or a seller, and is likely to be hired on a temporary basis

manufacturer's sales branch essentially a merchant wholesaler that is owned by a manufacturer

Merchant Wholesalers

A **merchant wholesaler** is a middleman that purchases goods in large quantities and then sells them to other wholesalers or retailers and to institutional, farm, government, professional, or industrial users. Merchant wholesalers usually operate one or more warehouses at which they receive, take title to, and store goods. These wholesalers are sometimes called *distributors* or *jobbers*.

Most merchant wholesalers are businesses composed of salespeople, order takers, receiving and shipping clerks, inventory managers, and office personnel. The successful merchant wholesaler must analyze available products and market needs. It must be able to adapt the type, variety, and quality of its products to changing market conditions.

Merchant wholesalers may be classified as full-service or limited-service wholesalers, depending on the number of services they provide. A **full-service wholesaler** performs the entire range of wholesaler functions described earlier in this section. These functions include delivering goods, supplying warehousing, arranging for credit, supporting promotional activities, and providing general customer assistance.

Under this broad heading are the general merchandise wholesaler, limited-line wholesaler, and specialty-line wholesaler. A **general merchandise wholesaler** deals in a wide variety of products, such as drugs, hardware, nonperishable foods, cosmetics, detergents, and tobacco. A **limited-line wholesaler** stocks only a few product lines, but carries numerous product items within each line. A **specialty-line wholesaler** carries a select group of products within a single line. Food delicacies such as shellfish represent the kind of product handled by this wholesaler.

In contrast to a full-service wholesaler, a **limited-service wholesaler** assumes responsibility for a few wholesale services only. Other marketing tasks are left to other channel members or consumers. This category includes cash-and-carry wholesalers, truck wholesalers, drop shippers, and mail-order wholesalers.

Commission Merchants, Agents, and Brokers

Commission merchants, agents, and brokers are functional middlemen. Functional middlemen do not take title to products. They perform a small number of marketing activities and are paid a commission that is a percentage of the sales price.

A **commission merchant** usually carries merchandise and negotiates sales for manufacturers. In most cases, commission merchants have the power to set the prices and terms of sales. After a sale is made, they either arrange for delivery or provide transportation services.

An **agent** is a middleman that expedites exchanges, represents a buyer or a seller, and often is hired permanently on a commision basis. When agents represent producers, they are known as *sales agents* or *manufacturer's agents*. As long as the products represented do not compete, a sales agent may represent one or several manufacturers on a commission basis. The agent solicits orders for the manufacturers within a specific territory. As a rule, the manufacturers ship the merchandise and bill the customers directly. The manufacturers also set the prices and other conditions of the sales. What do the manufacturers gain by using a sales agent? The sales agent provides immediate entry into a territory, regular calls on customers, selling experience, and a known, predetermined selling expense (a commission that is a percentage of sales revenue).

A **broker** is a middleman that specializes in a particular commodity, represents either a buyer *or* a seller, and is likely to be hired on a temporary basis. However, food brokers, which sell grocery products to resellers, generally have long-term relationships with their clients. Brokers may perform only the selling function or both buying and selling, using established contacts or special knowledge of their fields.

Manufacturers' Sales Branches and Sales Offices

A **manufacturer's sales branch** is, in essence, a merchant wholesaler that is owned by a manufacturer. Sales branches carry inventory, extend credit, deliver goods, and offer help in promoting products. Their customers are retailers, other wholesalers, and industrial purchasers.

Because sales branches are owned by producers, they stock primarily the goods manufactured by their own firms. Selling policies and terms are usually established centrally and then transmitted to branch managers for implementation.

A **manufacturer's sales office** is essentially a sales agent owned by a manufacturer. Sales offices may sell goods manufactured by their own firms and also certain products of other manufacturers that complement their own product lines. For example, Hiram Walker & Sons imports wine from Spain to increase the number of products its sales offices can offer to customers.

manufacturer's sales office essentially a sales agent owned by a manufacturer

Marketing Intermediaries: Retailers

LEARNING OBJECTIVE

7 Distinguish among the major types of retailers.

Retailers are the final link between producers and consumers. Retailers may buy from either wholesalers or producers. They sell not only goods but also such services as auto repairs, haircuts, and dry cleaning. Some retailers sell both. Sears, Roebuck sells consumer goods, financial services, and repair services for home appliances bought at Sears.

Of the more than 2.67 million retail firms in the United States, about 90 percent have annual sales of less than $1 million.[5] On the other hand, some large retail organizations realize well over $1 million in sales revenue per day. Table 15.1 lists the twenty largest retail organizations and their approximate sales revenues and yearly profits. Figure 15.4 shows retail sales categorized by major merchandise type and the percentage of total sales for each type.

table 15.1 **The Twenty Largest Retail Firms in the United States**

Rank	Company	Annual Sales (in millions)	Annual Profits (in millions)	Number of Stores
1	Wal-Mart, Inc.	$165,013,000	$5,377,000	3,989
2	The Kroger Co.	45,352,000	628,000	3,473
3	Sears, Roebuck and Co.	41,071,000	1,453,000	3,011
4	The Home Depot	38,434,000	2,320,000	930
5	Albertson's	37,478,079	404,000	2,492
6	K mart Corp.	35,925,000	403,000	2,171
7	Target Corp.	33,702,000	1,144,000	1,243
8	J.C. Penney	32,510,000	336,000	4,076
9	Safeway	28,859,900	970,900	1,659
10	Costco	27,456,031	397,298	302
11	Dell Computer	25,265,000	1,860,000	NA
12	Ahold USA**	20,340,000	1,001,000	1,063
13	CVS Corp.	18,098,300	635,100	4,098
14	Walgreen	17,838,800	624,100	2,821
15	Federated Department Stores	17,716,000	795,000	403
16	Lowe's Cos.	15,905,595	672,795	576
17	Winn-Dixie	14,136,503	182,335	1,188
18	May Department Stores	13,869,000	927,000	408
19	Rite Aid	14,681,442	(1,143,056)	3,802
20	Publix Super Market	13,205,561	462,409	614

** U.S. retail operations only; operating income reported + continuing operations.
Source: *Chain Store Age* (August 2000). Reprinted with permission from Lebhar-Friedman, Inc.

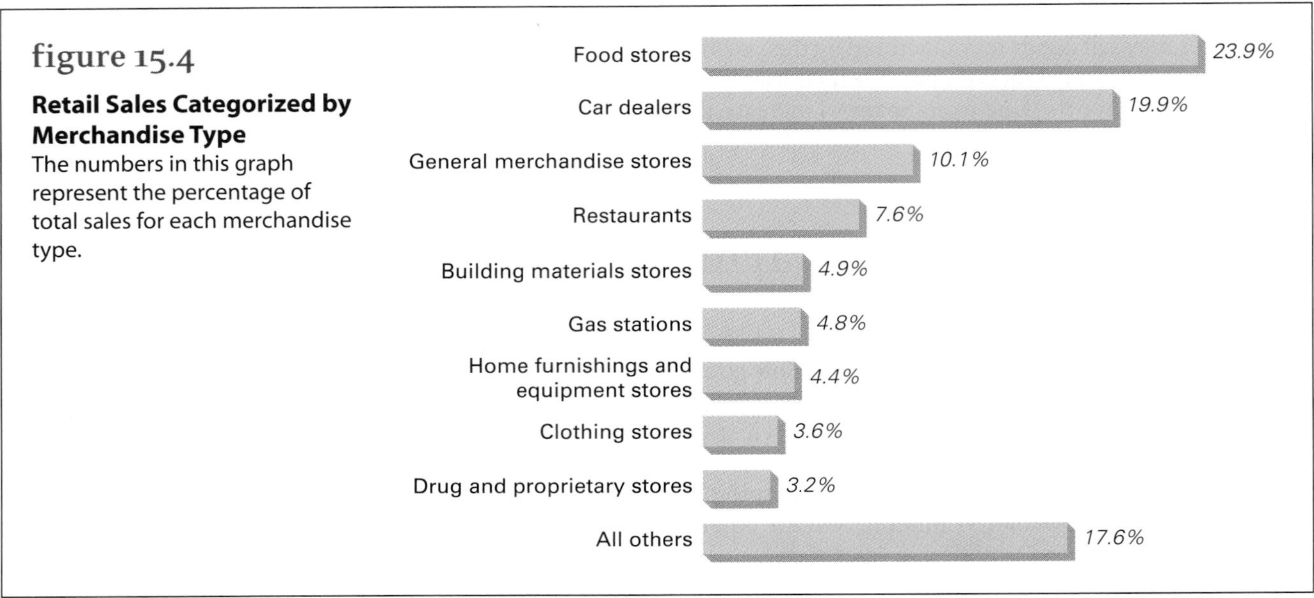

figure 15.4

Retail Sales Categorized by Merchandise Type

The numbers in this graph represent the percentage of total sales for each merchandise type.

Source: U.S. Bureau of the Census, *Monthly Retail Trade: Sales and Inventories*, Jan. 2000, www.census.gov.

independent retailer a firm that operates only one retail outlet

chain retailer a company that operates more than one retail outlet

department store a retail store that (1) employs twenty-five or more persons and (2) sells at least home furnishings, appliances, family apparel, and household linens and dry goods, each in a different part of the store

Classes of In-Store Retailers

One way to classify retailers is by the number of stores owned and operated by the firm. An **independent retailer** is a firm that operates only one retail outlet. Approximately 75 percent of retailers are independent.[6] One-store operators, like all small businesses, generally provide personal service and a convenient location.

A **chain retailer** is a company that operates more than one retail outlet. By adding outlets, chain retailers attempt to reach new geographic markets. As sales increase, chains may buy merchandise in larger quantities and thus take advantage of quantity discounts. They also wield more power in their dealings with suppliers. About 25 percent of retail organizations operate chains.[7]

Another way to classify in-store retailers is by store size and the kind and number of products carried. Let's take a closer look at store types based on these dimensions.

spotlight

Source: "What's in Store at Retail," *American Demographics*, May 2000, p.9.

Department Stores These large retail establishments consist of several sections, or departments, that sell a wide assortment of products. According to the U.S. Bureau of the Census, a **department store** is a retail store that (1) employs twenty-five or more persons and (2) sells at least home furnishings, appliances, family apparel, and household linens and dry goods, each in a different part of the store. Marshall Field's in Chicago (and several other cities), Harrods in London, and Au Printemps in Paris are examples of large department stores. Sears, Roebuck and J.C. Penney are also department stores. Traditionally department stores have been service-oriented. Along with the goods they sell, these retailers provide credit, delivery, personal assistance, liberal return policies, and pleasant shopping atmospheres.

Talking Technology

How Stores Are Battling Online Rivals

BRICKS-AND-MORTAR RETAILERS ARE harnessing technology to fend off the onslaught of competition from online retailers. In book retailing, where web pioneer Amazon.com is challenging the big store chains with low prices, wide assortment, and fast delivery, Borders Books & Music is fighting back using a high-tech enhancement: computerized in-store kiosks. Through these kiosks, called Title Sleuths, customers can browse and order from the company's entire online inventory, instead of being limited to the books on hand in any individual store.

Like Borders, the Ohio-based Stambaugh Hardware chain is using technology to enhance the retail experience by electronically expanding in-store access to merchandise. Rather than build gigantic stores and force customers to hunt through aisles and aisles of items, the company has kept its stores relatively compact. Customers who want something other than the 18,000 items in stock can use computers in each store to search through 54,000 additional items on Stambaugh's web site. For added convenience, Stambaugh offers a choice of having purchases sent directly home or to the store for pickup when customers order from online inventory.

The technology revolution in retailing is also reaching into car dealerships. Knowing that customers are surfing the web in search of details about cars such as special features and pricing, the MotorQuest Automotive Group has outfitted its dealerships in Michigan and Massachusetts with computer stations and high-speed Internet access. Car shoppers are invited to spend time browsing car-related Internet sites and using special software to calculate the value of their current vehicles. "The goal is to give the consumer everything on the Net along with all the sources of information that we have at our disposal," says Renny Coe, general manager of one MotorQuest dealership.

Although competition between physical stores and Internet retailers has intensified in recent years, analysts expect a shakeout to thin the ranks of online retailers. As traditional retailers face fewer but stronger web rivals, they will continue to use technology to streamline their businesses and improve customer service.

Discount Stores A **discount store** is a self-service, general merchandise outlet that sells products at lower-than-usual prices. These stores can offer lower prices by operating on smaller markups, by locating large retail showrooms in low-rent areas, and by offering minimal customer services. To keep prices low, discount stores operate on the basic principle of high turnover of such items as appliances, toys, clothing, automotive products, and sports equipment. To attract customers, many discount stores also offer some food and household items at low prices. Popular discount stores include Kmart, Wal-Mart, Dollar General, and Target.

discount store a self-service, general merchandise outlet that sells products at lower-than-usual prices

As competition among discount stores has increased, some discounters have improved their services, store environments, and locations. As a consequence, many of the better-known discount stores have assumed the characteristics of department stores. This upgrading has boosted their prices and blurred the distinction between some discount stores and department stores.[8]

Catalog and Warehouse Showrooms A **catalog showroom** is a retail outlet that displays well-known brands and sells them at discount prices through catalogs within the store. Colorful catalogs are available in the showroom (and sometimes by mail). The customer selects the merchandise, either from the catalog or from the showroom display. The customer fills out an order form provided by the store and hands the form to a clerk. The clerk retrieves the merchandise from a warehouse room that is adjacent to the selling area. Service Merchandise is a catalog showroom.

catalog showroom a retail outlet that displays well-known brands and sells them at discount prices through catalogs within the store

Warehouse showrooms are retail facilities with five basic characteristics: (1) large, low-cost buildings, (2) warehouse materials-handling technology, (3) vertical merchandise displays, (4) large on-premises inventories, and (5) minimal service. Some of the best-known showrooms are operated by big furniture retailers. These operations employ few personnel and offer few services. Most customers carry away purchases in the manufacturer's carton, although some warehouse showrooms will deliver for a fee.

warehouse showroom a retail facility in a large, low-cost building with large on-premises inventories and minimal service

convenience store a small food store that sells a limited variety of products but remains open well beyond normal business hours

Convenience Stores A **convenience store** is a small food store that sells a limited variety of products but remains open well beyond normal business hours. Almost 70 percent of convenience store customers live within a mile of the store. White Hen Pantry, 7-Eleven, Circle K, and Open Pantry stores, for example, are found in some areas, as are independent convenience stores. Their limited product mixes and higher prices keep convenience stores from becoming a threat to other grocery retailers.

supermarket a large self-service store that sells primarily food and household products

Supermarkets A **supermarket** is a large self-service store that sells primarily food and household products. It stocks canned, fresh, frozen, and processed foods, paper products, and cleaning supplies. Supermarkets may also sell such items as housewares, toiletries, toys and games, drugs, stationery, books and magazines, plants and flowers, and a few clothing items.

Supermarkets are large-scale operations that emphasize low prices and one-stop shopping for household needs. The first self-service food market opened over sixty years ago; it grossed only $5,000 per week, with an average sale of just $1.31.[9] Today a supermarket has annual sales of at least $2 million. Current top-ranking supermarkets include Food Lion, Von's, Safeway, Kroger, Winn-Dixie Stores, Albertson's, and A & P.

superstore a large retail store that carries not only food and nonfood products ordinarily found in supermarkets but also additional product lines

Superstores A **superstore** is a large retail store that carries not only food and non-food products ordinarily found in supermarkets but also additional product lines—housewares, hardware, small appliances, clothing, personal-care products, garden products, and automotive merchandise. Superstores also provide a number of services to entice customers. Typically these include automotive repair, snack bars and restaurants, film developing, and banking.

warehouse club a large-scale, members-only establishment that combines features of cash-and-carry wholesaling with discount retailing

Warehouse Clubs The **warehouse club** is a large-scale, members-only establishment that combines cash-and-carry wholesaling features with discount retailing. For a nominal annual fee (about $25), small retailers may purchase products at wholesale prices for business use or for resale. Warehouse clubs also sell to ultimate consumers. Instead of paying a membership fee, individual consumers pay about 5 percent more on each item than do small-business owners. Individual purchasers can usually choose to pay yearly dues for membership cards that allow them to avoid the 5 percent additional charge.

Going Global

Making Convenience Stores More Convenient in Japan

7-ELEVEN JAPAN, THE LARGEST CONVENIENCE-store chain in the country, wants to make it even more convenient for shoppers to buy all kinds of goods and services in any of its 8,200 outlets. The chain has forged several e-commerce ventures to sell books, travel packages, concert tickets, CDs, photos, sporting goods, and hundreds of other items on the Internet and through multimedia web terminals in 7-Eleven stores. Each of the chain's stores serves an average of 950 customers daily, which means that more than 2.5 billion customers will have the chance to use the terminals every year—a sizable market by any standard.

Now music lovers can stop in at the local 7-Eleven branch and use the store's terminals to examine seating diagrams and buy tickets to see the Tokyo Symphony Orchestra or other concerts. Fashion-conscious shoppers can also use the terminals to view and order the latest clothing and jewelry styles. When ordering at the store, customers can have their purchases sent to their homes or to the store for pickup. Customers can also access the web site from home, place orders, and then go to a nearby store to pay and pick up their purchases. However, because phone connections are expensive, consumers in Japan spend relatively little time surfing the Internet from home. For this reason, 7-Eleven believes its terminals will be popular—and profitable.

In addition, 7-Eleven Japan is setting up its own bank and planning to install automated teller machines in all of its branches, allowing customers to make deposits and withdrawals at any hour. In contrast, most ATMs in Japan operate only during specified days and hours, so 7-Eleven's ATMs will be extremely convenient for people who need to complete banking transactions during off-hours. And convenience is what 7-Eleven Japan is all about.

Warehouse clubs offer the same types of products offered by discount stores but in a limited range of sizes and styles. Because their product lines are shallow and sales volumes are high, warehouse clubs can offer a broad range of merchandise, including perishable and nonperishable foods, beverages, books, appliances, housewares, automotive parts, hardware, furniture, and sundries. The sales volume of most warehouse clubs is four to five times that of a typical department store. With stock turning over at an average rate of eighteen times each year, warehouse clubs sell their goods before manufacturers' payment periods are up, thus reducing their need for capital.

Warehouse clubs. Sam's Club is an example of a warehouse club. To make purchases at Sam's Club, customers must be members and pay annual membership fees.

To keep their prices 20 to 40 percent lower than those of supermarkets and discount stores, warehouse clubs provide few services. They generally advertise only through direct mail. Their facilities often have concrete floors and aisles wide enough for forklifts. Merchandise is stacked on pallets or displayed on pipe racks. Usually customers must transport purchases themselves. Although at one time there were about twenty competing warehouse clubs, only two major competitors remain: Sam's Club and Costco.

traditional specialty store a store that carries a narrow product mix with deep product lines

off-price retailer a store that buys manufacturers' seconds, overruns, returns, and off-season merchandise for resale to consumers at deep discounts

Traditional Specialty Stores

A **traditional specialty store** carries a narrow product mix with deep product lines. Traditional specialty stores are sometimes called *limited-line retailers*. If they carry depth in one particular product category, they may be called *single-line retailers*. Specialty stores usually sell such products as clothing, jewelry, sporting goods, fabrics, computers, flowers, baked goods, books, and pet supplies. Examples of specialty stores include the Gap, Radio Shack, Bath and Body Works, and Foot Locker.

Specialty stores usually offer deeper product mixes than department stores. They attract customers by emphasizing service, atmosphere, and location. Consumers who are dissatisfied with the impersonal atmosphere of large retailers often find the attention offered by small specialty stores appealing.

Traditional specialty store. Crate & Barrel is a traditional specialty store.

Off-Price Retailers

Off-price retailers are stores that buy manufacturers' seconds, overruns, returns, and off-season merchandise at below-wholesale prices and sell them to consumers at deep discounts. Off-price retailers sell limited lines of national-brand and designer merchandise, usually clothing, shoes, or housewares. Examples of off-price retailers include T.J. Maxx, Burlington Coat Factory, and Marshalls. Off-price stores charge up to 50 percent less than department stores do for comparable merchandise but offer few customer services. They often include community dressing rooms and central checkout counters, and some off-price retailers have a no-returns, no-exchanges policy.

category killer a very large specialty store that concentrates on a single product line and competes on the basis of low prices and product availability

Category Killers A **category killer** is a very large specialty store that concentrates on a single product line and competes by offering low prices and an enormous number of products. These stores are called category killers because they take business away from smaller, high-cost retail stores. Examples of category killers include The Home Depot (building materials), Office Depot (office supplies and equipment), and Toys "R" Us. Category killers, due to the size of their product offerings and low prices, may attract large numbers of customers. For example, IKEA, the Swedish furniture retailer, attracted over 265,000 customers to its new store just outside of Moscow during the first two weeks it was opened. IKEA management estimated that approximately 30 percent of these customers made purchases.[10]

Kinds of Nonstore Retailing

nonstore retailing a type of retailing whereby consumers purchase products without visiting a store

Nonstore retailing is selling that does not take place in conventional store facilities; consumers purchase products without visiting a store. Nonstore retailers use direct selling, direct marketing, and vending machines.

direct selling the marketing of products to ultimate consumers through face-to-face sales presentations at home or in the workplace

Direct Selling **Direct selling** is the marketing of products to customers through face-to-face sales presentations at home or in the workplace. Traditionally called door-to-door selling, direct selling generates about $85 billion in sales annually worldwide.[11] Instead of the door-to-door approach, many companies today—such as Mary Kay, Amway, and Avon—identify customers by mail, telephone, or at shopping malls and then make appointments. The "party-plan" method of direct selling takes place in homes or in the workplace. Customers act as hosts and invite friends or coworkers to view products. A salesperson conducts the "party" and demonstrates products. Companies that rely on the party plan are Tupperware, Stanley Home Products, and Sarah Coventry.

Benefits of direct selling include product demonstration, personal attention, and convenience. In fact, personal attention is the foundation on which some direct sellers base their companies. The primary disadvantage of direct selling is that it is the most expensive form of retailing. Overall costs of direct selling are high because of high salesperson commissions and efforts required to locate prospects. In addition, some people view direct selling negatively, and some communities have enacted local ordinances regulating or even banning direct selling.

direct marketing the use of computers, telephones, and nonpersonal media to show products to customers, who can then purchase them by mail, telephone, or online

Direct Marketing **Direct marketing** is the use of computers, telephones, and nonpersonal media to communicate product and organizational information to customers, who can then buy products by mail, telephone, or online. Catalog marketing, direct-response marketing, telemarketing, television home shopping, and online marketing are all types of direct marketing.

catalog marketing marketing in which an organization provides a catalog from which customers make selections and place orders by mail or telephone

With **catalog marketing**, an organization provides a catalog from which customers make selections and place orders by mail or telephone. Some companies, such as Spiegel and J. C. Penney, offer a wide range of products. Other catalog companies, such as L.L. Bean and Lands' End, offer one major line of products. Certain catalog companies specialize in only a few products, such as educational toys or specialty foods. Many customers find catalog marketing efficient and convenient. Retailers do not have to invest in expensive store fixtures, and personal selling and operating expenses are significantly reduced. However, catalog marketing provides limited service and is most effective for only certain types of products. Some catalog retailers have reputations for excellent service. However, some catalog customers complain about product quality, delivery times, and shipment errors. Sears, Roebuck & Company is building its well-known catalog brands online, especially Kenmore appliances and Craftsman tools, through partnerships with AOL.[12]

direct-response marketing marketing that occurs when a retailer advertises a product and makes it available through mail or telephone orders

Direct-response marketing occurs when a retailer advertises a product and makes it available through mail or telephone orders. Customers usually use a credit card to make purchases. Examples of direct-response marketing are a television commercial promoting a set of knives available through a toll-free number and a magazine ad for a series of cookbooks available by completing and mailing an order form. Sending letters, samples, brochures, or booklets to prospects on a mailing list are also forms of direct-response marketing.

Telemarketing is using the telephone to perform marketing-related activities. Companies that use telemarketing to supplement other marketing methods include Merrill Lynch, Allstate Insurance, Avis, General Motors, MCI, and American Express. Some organizations use a prepared list of customers, and others rely on names from telephone directories and data banks. Advantages of telemarketing include generating sales leads, improving customer service, speeding up payment on past-due accounts, raising funds for nonprofit organizations, and gathering marketing information.

Online retailing. This individual is a picker at Amazon.com, which is an online retailer. Quick and accurate order fulfillment is an essential component of an online retailer's marketing strategy.

One problem with telemarketing is employee turnover. To attract and retain employees at its call center, Boston Communications Group designed the physical environment so that people would perceive this organization to be a good place to work. The company invested heavily to make the facility very comfortable for workers. The pay scale for these workers is on the upper end. Boston Communications is developing a child-care center adjacent to its facility so that employees' children can be in day care in close proximity to their parents. In addition, this company provides workers with highly flexible hours. Boston Communications' employee turnover rate is considerably lower than the average for call centers.[13]

telemarketing the performance of marketing-related activities by telephone

television home shopping selling in which products are displayed to television viewers, who can then order them by calling a toll-free number and paying by credit card

online retailing presenting and selling products through computer connections

Television home shopping displays products to television viewers, who can then order them by calling a toll-free number and paying by credit card. There are several home shopping cable channels. The most common products sold through television home shopping are electronics, clothing, housewares, and jewelry. Benefits of home shopping include time for thorough product demonstration and customer convenience.

Online retailing makes the presentation and sale of products possible through computer connections. Customers purchase products by ordering them through their terminals or by telephone. The phenomenal growth of the World Wide Web and of online information service providers, such as America Online, has created new retailing opportunities. Although some retailers with web sites are currently using them primarily to promote products, a number of companies sell their goods online. Some online retailers such as Amazon.com and AOL began as online sellers and have remained exclusively as online sellers, while others began as traditional retail stores and later became online retailers as well. Examples include Barnes and Noble, Office Max, and Toys "R" Us. Consumers can purchase hard-to-find items like Pez candy dispensers and Elvis memorabilia at e-Bay, an Internet auction company that brings buyers and sellers together and charges a commission. Banks and brokerage firms have established web sites to give their customers direct access to manage their accounts and to enable them to trade online. California-based Encirq.com has developed a new approach to gathering customer information and guarding the privacy of online customers at the same time. In association with a bank credit card program, online banking customers can choose to opt in or out of the Encirq's Illuminated Statement function at any time—free of charge. For those who participate there are benefits. To begin with, their bank's customer service site presents a colorful, easy-to-read version of their credit card statement that may include logos of the companies on

spotLight

Source: Copyright 2000, USA TODAY. Reprinted with permission.

their statement, links to merchants' web sites, and special promotions. By clicking on an item in the statement, consumers can also see more detailed information about the transaction. Encirq generates its revenues by selling advertising on the statement. Personal information remains secure on the customer's computer and will only be engaged to help direct their purchasing if they want it to. Those links are with merchants the customer has already bought from and so, logically, the customer should feel more relaxed about associating in this manner.[14] With advances such as this in computer technology and consumers continuing to be pressed for time, online retailing will only escalate.

automatic vending the use of machines to dispense products

Automatic Vending **Automatic vending** is the use of machines to dispense products. Although vending machines only account for 2 percent of all retail sales, they are widely popular, with about 1,000 different types. They sell items that require little or no thought before making the decision to buy, such as candy, cigarettes, newspapers, postage stamps, chewing gum, soft drinks, and coffee. These are goods that people will purchase at the nearest possible location. This category of vending also includes such machines as video game machines and automatic teller machines, which satisfy needs other than tangible products. Machines in areas of heavy traffic provide efficient and continuous services to consumers. Such high-volume areas may have more diverse product availability—for example, hot and cold sandwiches, as well as soups.

Automatic vending is one of the most impersonal forms of retailing. Machines do not require sales personnel, they permit twenty-four-hour service, and they do not require much space. Thus, they can be placed in convenient locations in office buildings, educational institutions, motels and hotels, shopping malls, and service stations. But these advantages are partly offset, however, by the high costs of equipment and frequent servicing and repairs.

LEARNING OBJECTIVE

8 Explain the wheel of retailing hypothesis.

The Wheel of Retailing

wheel of retailing a hypothesis that suggests that new retail operations usually begin at the bottom—in price, profits, and prestige—and gradually move up the cost/price scale, competing with newer businesses that are evolving in the same way

Newly developing retail businesses strive for a secure position in the ever-changing retailing environment. One theory attempts to explain how types of retail stores originate and develop. The **wheel of retailing** hypothesis (see Figure 15.5) suggests that new retail operations usually begin at the bottom—in price, profits, and prestige. In time, their facilities become more elaborate, their investments increase, and their operating costs go up. Finally, the retailers emerge at the top of the cost/price scale, competing with newer businesses that are evolving in the same way.[15]

In Figure 15.5, the wheel of retailing illustrates the development of department and discount stores. Department stores such as Sears were originally high-volume, low-cost retailers competing with general stores and other small businesses. As the costs of services rose in department stores, discount stores began to fill the low-price retailing niche. Now many discount stores, in turn, are following the pattern by expanding services, improving locations, upgrading inventories, and raising prices.

Like most hypotheses, the wheel of retailing may not be universally applicable. The theory cannot predict what new retailing developments will occur, or when, for example. In industrialized, expanding economies, however, the hypothesis does help explain retailing patterns.

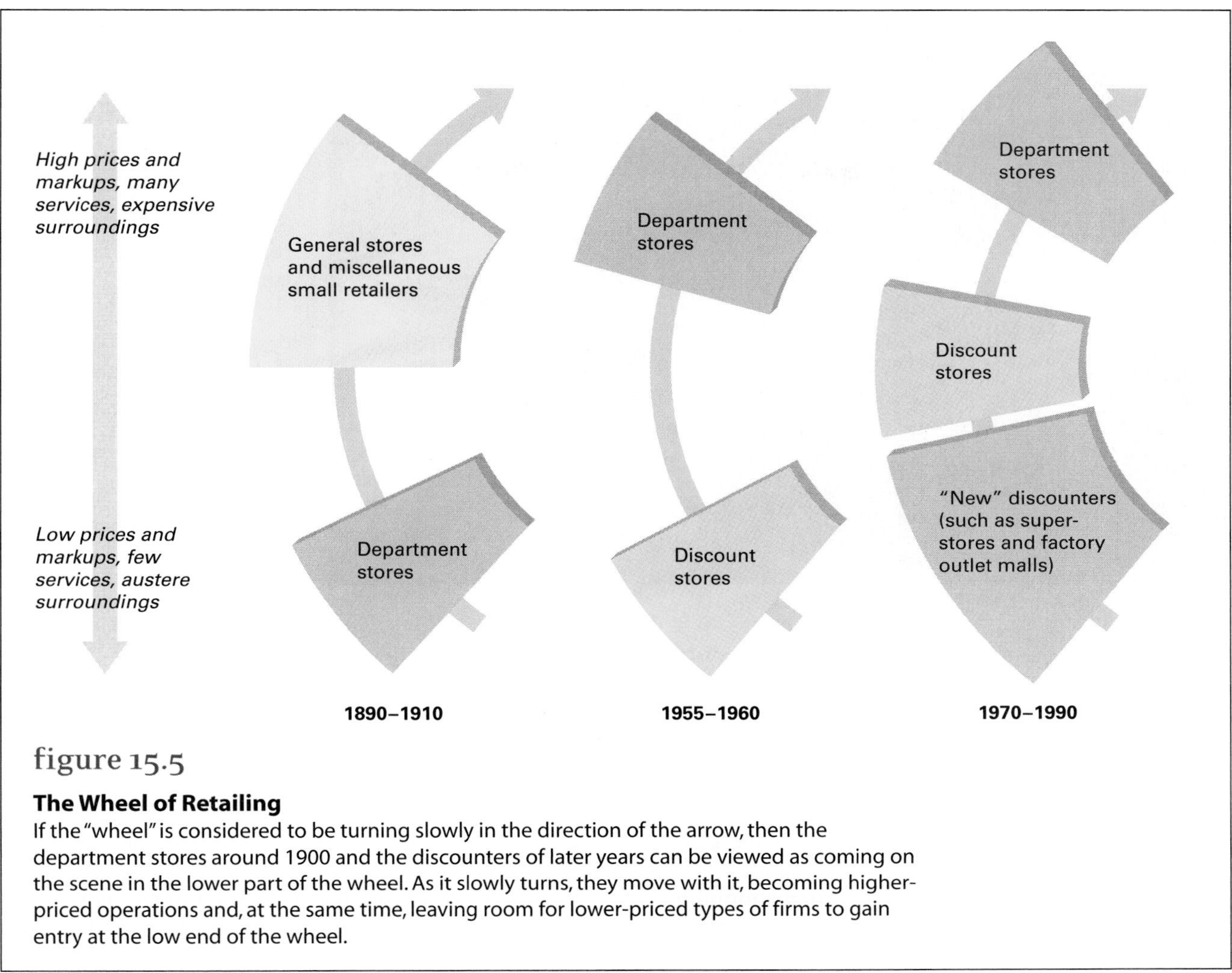

figure 15.5

The Wheel of Retailing

If the "wheel" is considered to be turning slowly in the direction of the arrow, then the department stores around 1900 and the discounters of later years can be viewed as coming on the scene in the lower part of the wheel. As it slowly turns, they move with it, becoming higher-priced operations and, at the same time, leaving room for lower-priced types of firms to gain entry at the low end of the wheel.

Source: Adapted from Robert F. Hartley, *Retailing: Challenge and Opportunity*, 3rd ed., p. 42. Copyright © 1984 by Houghton Mifflin Company. Used by permission.

Planned Shopping Centers

LEARNING OBJECTIVE

9 Identify the categories of shopping centers and the factors that determine how shopping centers are classified.

The planned shopping center is a self-contained retail facility, constructed by independent owners, consisting of various stores. Shopping centers are designed and promoted to serve diverse groups of customers with widely differing needs. The management of a shopping center strives for a coordinated mix of stores, a comfortable atmosphere, adequate parking, pleasant landscaping, and special events to attract customers. The convenience of shopping for most family and household needs in a single location is an important part of shopping-center appeal.

A planned shopping center is one of three types: neighborhood, community, or regional. Although shopping centers vary, each offers a complementary mix of stores for the purpose of generating consumer traffic.

Neighborhood Shopping Centers

A **neighborhood shopping center** typically consists of several small convenience and specialty stores. Businesses in neighborhood shopping centers might include small grocery stores, drugstores, gas stations, and fast-food restaurants. These retailers serve consumers who live less than ten minutes away, usually within a two- to three-mile radius of

neighborhood shopping center a planned shopping center consisting of several small convenience and specialty stores

Planned shopping center. The mix of retailers in a planned shopping center is managed in such a way as to attract numerous shoppers and to effectively satisfy their needs with respect to the products offered by these retailers. This shopping center, Horton Plaza, is located in downtown San Diego.

the stores. Because most purchases in the neighborhood shopping center are based on convenience or personal contact, these retailers generally make only limited efforts to coordinate promotional activities among stores in the shopping center.

Community Shopping Centers

A **community shopping center** includes one or two department stores and some specialty stores, along with convenience stores. It attracts consumers from a wider geographic area who will drive longer distances to find products and specialty items unavailable in neighborhood shopping centers. Community shopping centers, which are carefully planned and coordinated, generate traffic with special events such as art exhibits, automobile shows, and sidewalk sales. The management of a community shopping center maintains a balance of tenants so that the center can offer wide product mixes and deep product lines.

community shopping center a planned shopping center that includes one or two department stores and some specialty stores, along with convenience stores

regional shopping center a planned shopping center containing large department stores, numerous specialty stores, restaurants, movie theaters, and sometimes even hotels

Regional Shopping Centers

A **regional shopping center** usually has large department stores, numerous specialty stores, restaurants, movie theaters, and sometimes even hotels. It carries most of the merchandise offered by a downtown shopping district. Downtown merchants, in fact, have often renovated their stores and enlarged their parking facilities to meet the competition of successful regional shopping centers. Urban expressways and improved public transportation have also helped many downtown shopping areas to remain vigorous.

Regional shopping centers carefully coordinate management and marketing activities to reach the 150,000 or more customers in their target market. These large centers usually advertise, hold special events, and provide transportation to certain groups of customers. They also maintain a suitable mix of stores. National chain stores can gain leases in regional shopping centers more easily than small independent stores because they are better able to meet the centers' financial requirements.

LEARNING OBJECTIVE

10 Explain the five most important physical distribution activities.

Physical Distribution

physical distribution all those activities concerned with the efficient movement of products from the producer to the ultimate user

Physical distribution is all those activities concerned with the efficient movement of products from the producer to the ultimate user. Physical distribution is thus the movement of the products themselves—both goods and services—through their channels of distribution. It is a combination of several interrelated business functions. The most important of these are inventory management, order processing, warehousing, materials handling, and transportation.

Not too long ago, each of these functions was considered distinct from all the others. In a fairly large firm, one group or department would handle each function. Each of these groups would work to minimize its own costs and to maximize its own effectiveness, but the result was usually high physical distribution costs.

Various studies of the problem emphasized both the interrelationships among the physical distribution functions *and* the relationships between physical distribution and other marketing functions. Long production runs may reduce per-unit product costs, but they can cause inventory-control and warehousing costs to skyrocket. A new automated warehouse may reduce materials-handling costs, but if the warehouse is not located properly, transportation time and costs may increase substantially. Because of such interrelationships, marketers now view physical distribution as an integrated effort that provides important marketing functions: getting the right product to the right place at the right time and at minimal *overall* cost.

Using the Internet

The National Retail Federation (**http://www.nrf.com/**) and the American Wholesale Marketers Association (**http://www.awmanet.org/**) are two industry gateways for information about their respective distribution channels. Each site provides access to online journals and links to related web sites of interest to retailers and wholesalers.

Inventory Management

In Chapter 9 we discussed inventory management from the standpoint of operations. We defined **inventory management** as the process of managing inventories in such a way as to minimize inventory costs, including both holding costs and potential stock-out costs. Both the definition and the objective of inventory control apply here as well.

inventory management the process of managing inventories in such a way as to minimize inventory costs, including both holding costs and potential stock-out costs

Holding costs are the costs of storing products until they are purchased or shipped to customers. *Stock-out costs* are the costs of sales lost when items are not in inventory. Of course, holding costs can be reduced by minimizing inventories, but then stock-out costs could be financially threatening to the organization. And stock-out costs can be minimized by carrying very large inventories, but then holding costs would be enormous.

Inventory management is thus a sort of balancing act between stock-out costs and holding costs. The latter include the cost of money invested in inventory, the cost of storage space, insurance costs, and inventory taxes. Often, even a relatively small reduction in inventory investment can provide a relatively large increase in working capital. And sometimes this reduction can best be accomplished through a willingness to incur a reasonable level of stock-out costs.

Order Processing

Order processing consists of activities involved in receiving and filling customers' purchase orders. It may include not only the means by which customers order products but also procedures for billing and for granting credit.

order processing activities involved in receiving and filling customers' purchase orders

Fast, efficient order processing is an important marketing service—one that can provide a dramatic competitive edge. The people who purchase goods for intermediaries are especially concerned with their suppliers' promptness and reliability in order processing. To them, promptness and reliability mean minimal inventory costs as well as the ability to order goods when they are needed rather than weeks in advance. The Internet is adding a new service opportunity in this area. According to Yankee Group Research Inc., increased Internet hosting services, such as taking e-commerce orders and routing delivery instructions to clients' warehouses, is expected to grow from $5 billion in 1999 to $46 billion in 2003.[16]

Warehousing

Warehousing is the set of activities involved in receiving and storing goods and preparing them for reshipment. Goods are stored to create time utility; that is, they are held until they are needed for use or sale. Warehousing includes the following activities:

warehousing the set of activities involved in receiving and storing goods and preparing them for reshipment

- *Receiving goods*—The warehouse accepts delivered goods and assumes responsibility for them.
- *Identifying goods*—Records are made of the quantity of each item received. Items may be marked, coded, or tagged for identification.

Warehousing. This warehouse for Ralph's Grocery Company is highly automated. Ralphs uses private warehouses to keep goods flowing smoothly and efficiently to its 450 supermarkets in the western United States.

- *Sorting goods*—Delivered goods may have to be sorted before being stored.
- *Dispatching goods to storage*—Items must be moved to specific storage areas, where they can be found later.
- *Holding goods*—The goods are kept in storage under proper protection until needed.
- *Recalling, picking, and assembling goods*—Items that are to leave the warehouse must be efficiently selected from storage and assembled.
- *Dispatching shipments*—Each shipment is packaged suitably and directed to the proper transport vehicle. Shipping and accounting documents are prepared.

A firm may use its own warehouses or rent space in public warehouses. A *private warehouse*, owned and operated by a particular firm, can be designed to serve the firm's specific needs. However, the organization must take on the task of financing the facility, determining the best location for it, and ensuring that it is used fully. Generally, only companies that deal in large quantities of goods can justify private warehouses.

Public warehouses offer their services to all individuals and firms. Most are huge, one-story structures on the outskirts of cities, where rail and truck transportation are easily available. They provide storage facilities, areas for sorting and assembling shipments, and office and display spaces for wholesalers and retailers. Public warehouses will also hold—and issue receipts for—goods used as collateral for borrowed funds.

Many organizations locate and design their warehouses not only to be cost efficient but also to provide excellent customer service. Fast delivery is a particularly important competitive requirement for Internet-based companies. Hewlett-Packard's online marketing division (www.hpshopping.com), for example, maintains a warehouse close to the FedEx facility in Memphis. This allows the firm to take customer orders later in the evening and still guarantee next-day delivery.[17]

Materials Handling

materials handling the actual physical handling of goods, in warehousing as well as during transportation

Materials handling is the actual physical handling of goods, in warehouses as well as during transportation. Proper materials-handling procedures and techniques can increase the usable capacity of a warehouse or that of any means of transportation. Proper handling can reduce breakage and spoilage as well.

Modern materials handling attempts to reduce the number of times a product is handled. One method is called *unit loading*. Several smaller cartons, barrels, or boxes are combined into a single standard-size load that can be handled efficiently by forklift, conveyer, or truck.

Transportation

transportation the shipment of products to customers

carrier a firm that offers transportation services

As a part of physical distribution, **transportation** is simply the shipment of products to customers. The greater the distance between seller and purchaser, the more important is the choice of the means of transportation and the particular carrier.

A firm that offers transportation services is called a **carrier.** A *common carrier* is a transportation firm whose services are available to all shippers. Railroads, airlines, and most long-distance trucking firms are common carriers. A *contract carrier* is available for hire by one or several shippers. Contract carriers do not serve the general public. Moreover, the number of firms they can handle at any one time is limited by law. A *private carrier* is owned and operated by the shipper.

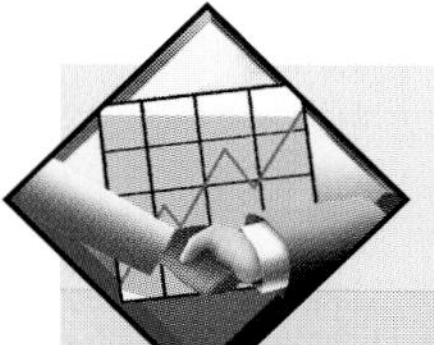

EXPLORING BUSINESS

FedEx Custom Critical Coddles Customers

WHEN ROBERTS EXPRESS RECENTLY changed its name to FedEx Custom Critical, the company was not only acknowledging its ownership, it was highlighting its most important benefit: meeting critical delivery deadlines. All kinds of customers depend on this FedEx truck and air freight firm to get precious cargo to its destination on time—guaranteed. Oprah Winfrey, for example, once hired the company to ship special lighting equipment to Texas on short notice for a live telecast. PPG Ohio, which manufactures glass for building construction, has seen only one shipment delivered late during a decade of sending urgent shipments via FedEx Custom Critical.

Weekdays and weekends, at any hour, in any weather, FedEx Custom Critical is ready to pick up a shipment within 90 minutes of a customer's call. Even more important, once the company sets a delivery time, it guarantees to have the cargo at its destination within 15 minutes of that time. If a delivery is two hours late, the customer gets a 25 percent discount; four hours late, and the customer gets a 50 percent discount. But the company rarely has to give discounts, because it delivers on schedule 96 percent of the time. Still, with profits—and customer satisfaction—hanging in the balance, FedEx Custom Critical uses technology to keep everything running smoothly. Trucks are equipped with satellite dishes and computers so the company can track every shipment through every mile of its journey.

For especially dangerous or delicate freight, such as hazardous materials or temperature-sensitive commodities, the company rolls out its White Glove Services. Trained operators using specially-equipped trucks and tools know exactly how to load, transport, and unload such shipments without damage. For customers who must get a shipment out immediately, regardless of cost, FedEx Custom Critical offers chartered airplanes and dedicated ground transportation. The company's transportation rates are not cheap, but customers find its superior service and record of on-time performance well worth the price.

In addition, a shipper can hire agents called *freight forwarders* to handle its transportation. Freight forwarders pick up shipments from the shipper, ensure that the goods are loaded on selected carriers, and assume responsibility for the safe delivery of the shipments to their destinations. Freight forwarders can often group a number of small shipments into one large load (which is carried at a lower rate). This, of course, saves money for shippers.

The U.S. Postal Service offers *parcel post* delivery, which is widely used by mail-order houses. The post office provides complete geographic coverage at the lowest rates, but it limits the size and weight of the shipments it will accept. United Parcel Service, a privately owned firm, also provides small-parcel services for shippers. Other privately owned carriers, such as Federal Express, DHL, and Airborne, offer fast—often overnight—parcel delivery, both within and outside the United States. There are also many local parcel carriers, including specialized delivery services for various time-sensitive industries, such as publishing.

The six major criteria used for selecting transportation modes are compared in Table 15.2. Obviously, the cost of a transportation mode is important to marketers. At times, marketers choose higher-cost modes of transportation because of the benefits they provide. Speed is measured by the total time that a carrier possesses the products, including time required for pickup and delivery, handling, and movement between point of origin and destination. Usually there is a direct relationship between cost and speed; that is, faster modes of transportation are more expensive. A transportation mode's dependability is determined by the consistency of service provided by that mode. Load flexibility is

table 15.2 Relative Ratings of Transportation Modes by Selection Criteria

Mode	Selection Criteria					
	Cost	**Speed**	**Dependability**	**Load Flexibility**	**Accessibility**	**Frequency**
Railroads	Moderate	Average	Average	High	High	Low
Trucks	High	Fast	High	Average	Very high	High
Airplanes	Very high	Very fast	High	Low	Average	Average
Waterways	Very low	Very slow	Average	Very high	Limited	Very low
Pipelines	Low	Slow	High	Very low	Very limited	Very high

the degree to which a transportation mode can provide appropriate equipment and conditions for moving specific kinds of products and can be adapted for moving other kinds of products. For example, certain types of products may need controlled temperatures or humidity levels. Accessibility refers to a transportation mode's ability to move goods over a specific route or network. Frequency refers to how often a marketer can ship products by a specific transportation mode. Whereas pipelines provide continuous shipments, railroads and waterways follow specific schedules for moving products from one location to another. In Table 15.2, each transportation mode is rated on a relative basis for these six selection criteria. Figure 15.6 shows recent trends and a breakdown by use of the five different modes of transportation.

Railroads In terms of total freight carried, railroads are America's most important mode of transportation. They are also the least expensive for many products. Almost all railroads are common carriers, although a few coal-mining companies operate their own lines.

Many commodities carried by railroads could not be transported easily by any other means. They include a wide range of foodstuffs, raw materials, and manufactured goods. Coal ranks first by a considerable margin. Other major commodities carried by railroads include grain, paper and pulp products, liquids in tank-car loads, heavy equipment, and lumber.

Rail tranportation. Relative to other transportation modes, railroads rank high on load flexibility, high on accessibility, and moderate with respect to cost.

Trucks The trucking industry consists of common, contract, and private carriers. It has undergone tremendous expansion since the creation of a national highway system in the 1920s. Trucks can move goods to suburban and rural areas not served by railroads. They can handle freight quickly and economically, and they carry a wide range of shipments. Many shippers favor this mode of transportation because it offers door-to-door service, less stringent packaging requirements than ships and airplanes, and flexible delivery schedules.

Railroad and truck carriers have teamed up to provide a form of transportation called *piggyback*. Truck trailers are carried from city to city on specially equipped railroad flatcars. Within each city, the trailers are then pulled in the usual way by truck tractors.

Airplanes Air transport is the fastest but most expensive means of transportation. All certified airlines are common carriers. Supplemental or charter lines are contract carriers.

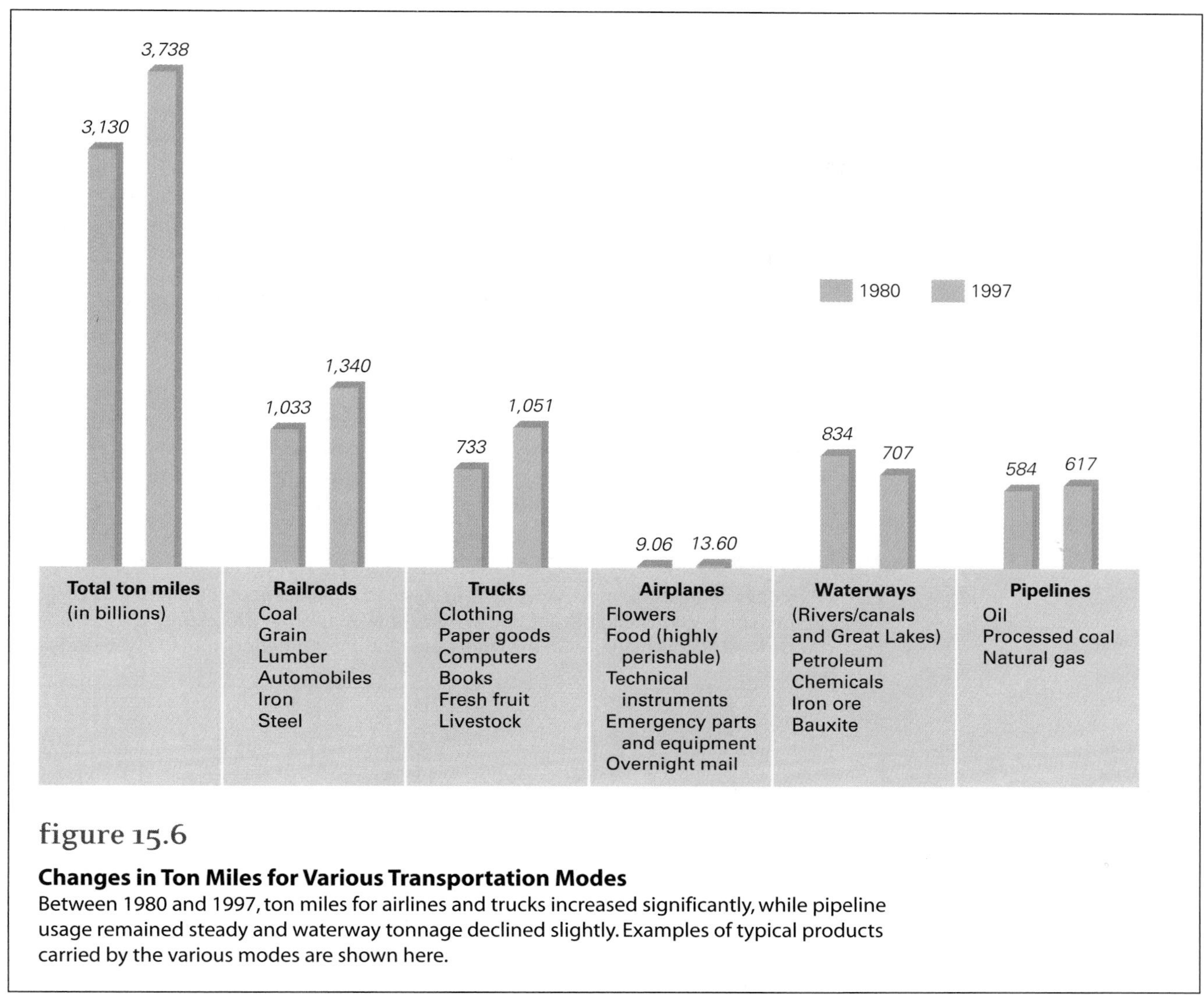

figure 15.6

Changes in Ton Miles for Various Transportation Modes

Between 1980 and 1997, ton miles for airlines and trucks increased significantly, while pipeline usage remained steady and waterway tonnage declined slightly. Examples of typical products carried by the various modes are shown here.

Source: U.S. Department of Transportation, Bureau of Transportation Statistics, *National Transportation Statistics 1999.*

Because of the high cost, lack of airport facilities in many areas, and reliance on weather conditions, airlines carry less than 1 percent of all intercity freight. Only high-value or perishable items, such as flowers, aircraft parts, and pharmaceuticals, or goods that are needed immediately are usually shipped by air.

Waterways Cargo ships and barges offer the least expensive but slowest form of transportation. They are used mainly for bulky, nonperishable goods such as iron ore, bulk wheat, motor vehicles, and agricultural implements. Of course, shipment by water is limited to cities located on navigable waterways. But ships and barges account for about 19 percent of all intercity freight hauling.

Pipelines Pipelines are a highly specialized mode of transportation. They are used primarily to carry petroleum and natural gas. Pipelines have become more important as the nation's need for petroleum products has increased. Such products as semiliquid coal and wood chips can also be shipped through pipelines continuously, reliably, and with minimal handling.

In the next chapter, we discuss the fourth element of the marketing mix—promotion.

RETURN TO Inside Business

MANAGING MULTIPLE CHANNELS OF distribution is all in a day's work for Barnes and Noble personnel. In the course of operating more than 1,000 stores spread across the United States plus a popular web site featuring four million book titles, the company has become an expert at supply chain management and at physical distribution. A growing share of the company's sales comes from its web site, but its book stores sales are not suffering. Quite the opposite: Barnes and Noble's store-by-store sales are going up at the same time that its web sales are rising. Vice Chairman Steve Riggio says the web site is "like having a free TV station for the retail stores," serving as a promotional device to bring online customers into nearby stores.

Despite fierce competition from Amazon.com and other Internet-based book retailers, Riggio sees a bright future for store sales, thanks to Barnes and Noble's distribution strategy. Through a combination of carefully-planned stores and an aggressive online retailing presence, Barnes and Noble is prepared to defend its leadership position in book retailing against all comers.

Questions

1. Why does Barnes and Noble say it "can't be in stock 100 percent of the time"?
2. In the Barnes and Noble distribution system, how does order processing at the warehouse level affect customers in the stores and customers ordering from the web site?

chapter Review

SUMMARY

1 Identify the various channels of distribution that are used for consumer and industrial products.

A marketing channel is a sequence of marketing organizations that directs a product from producer to ultimate user. The marketing channel for a particular product is concerned with the transfer of ownership of that product. Merchant middlemen (merchants) actually take title to products, whereas functional middlemen simply aid in the transfer of title.

The channels used for consumer products include the direct channel from producer to consumer; the channel from producer to retailer to consumer; the channel from producer to wholesaler to retailer to consumer; and the channel from producer to agent to wholesaler to retailer to consumer. There are two major channels of industrial products: (a) producer to user and (b) producer to agent middleman to user.

2 Explain the concept of market coverage.

Channels and intermediaries are chosen to implement a given level of market coverage. Intensive distribution is the use of all available outlets for a product, providing the widest market coverage. Selective distribution uses only a portion of the available outlets in an area. Exclusive distribution uses only a single retail outlet for a product in a large geographical area.

3 Understand how supply chain management facilitates partnering among channel members.

Supply chain management is a long-term partnership among channel members working together to create a distribution system that reduces inefficiencies, costs, and redundancies while creating a competitive advantage and satisfying customers. Cooperation is required among all channel members including manufacturing, research, sales, advertising, and shipping. When all channel partners work together, delivery, scheduling, packaging, and other customer requirements are better met. Technology, such as barcoding and electronic data exchange (EDI), makes supply chain management easier to implement.

4 Describe what a vertical marketing system is, and identify the types of vertical marketing systems.

A vertical marketing system (VMS) is a centrally managed system. It results when two or more channel members from different levels combine under one management. Administered, contractual, and corporate systems represent the three major types of VMSs.

5 Discuss the need for wholesalers, and describe the services they provide to retailers and manufacturers.

Wholesalers are intermediaries that purchase from producers or other intermediaries and sell to industrial users, retailers, or other wholesalers. Wholesalers perform many functions in a distribution channel. If they are eliminated, other channel members—such as the producer or retailers—must perform these functions. Wholesalers provide retailers with help in promoting products, collecting information, and financing. They provide manufacturers with sales help, reduce their inventory costs, furnish market information, and extend credit to retailers.

6 Identify and describe the major types of wholesalers.

Merchant wholesalers buy and then sell products. Commission merchants and brokers are essentially agents and do not take title to the goods they distribute. Sales branches and offices are owned by the manufacturers they represent and resemble merchant wholesalers and agents, respectively.

7 Distinguish among the major types of retailers.

Retailers are intermediaries that buy from producers or wholesalers and sell to consumers. In-store retailers include department stores, discount stores, catalog and warehouse showrooms, convenience stores, supermarkets, superstores, warehouse clubs, traditional specialty stores, off-price retailers, and category killers. Nonstore retailers do not sell in conventional store facilities. Instead, they use direct selling, direct marketing, and automatic vending. Types of direct marketing include catalog marketing, direct-response marketing, telemarketing, television home shopping, and online retailing.

8 Explain the wheel of retailing hypothesis.

The wheel of retailing hypothesis states that retailers begin as low-status, low-margin, low-priced stores and over time evolve into high-cost, high-priced operations.

9 Identify the categories of shopping centers and the factors that determine how shopping centers are classified.

There are three major types of shopping centers: neighborhood, community, and regional. A center fits one of these categories based on its mix of stores and the size of the geographic area it serves.

10 Explain the five most important physical distribution activities.

Physical distribution consists of activities designed to move products from producers to ultimate users. Its five major functions are inventory management, order processing, warehousing, materials handling, and transportation. These interrelated functions are integrated into the marketing effort.

KEY TERMS

You should now be able to define and give an example relevant to each of the following terms:

channel of distribution (or marketing channel) (419)
middleman (or marketing intermediary) (419)
merchant middleman (419)
functional middleman (419)
retailer (419)
wholesaler (419)
intensive distribution (421)
selective distribution (421)
exclusive distribution (422)
supply chain management (422)
vertical channel integration (423)
vertical marketing system (VMS) (423)
merchant wholesaler (426)
full-service wholesaler (426)
general merchandise wholesaler (426)
limited-line wholesaler (426)
specialty-line wholesaler (426)
limited-service wholesaler (426)
commission merchant (426)
agent (426)
broker (426)
manufacturer's sales branch (426)
manufacturer's sales office (427)
independent retailer (428)
chain retailer (428)
department store (428)
discount store (429)
catalog showroom (429)
warehouse showroom (429)
convenience store (430)
supermarket (430)
superstore (430)
warehouse club (430)
traditional specialty store (431)
off-price retailer (431)
category killer (432)
nonstore retailing (432)
direct selling (432)
direct marketing (432)
catalog marketing (432)
direct-response marketing (432)
telemarketing (433)
television home shopping (433)
online retailing (433)
automatic vending (434)
wheel of retailing (434)

neighborhood shopping center (435)
community shopping center (436)
regional shopping center (436)
physical distribution (436)
inventory management (437)
order processing (437)
warehousing (437)
materials handling (438)
transportation (438)
carrier (438)

REVIEW QUESTIONS

1. In what ways is a channel of distribution different from the path taken by a product during physical distribution?
2. What are the most common marketing channels for consumer products? for industrial products?
3. What are the three general approaches to market coverage? What types of products is each used for?
4. What is a vertical marketing system? Identify examples of the three types of VMSs.
5. List the services performed by wholesalers. For whom is each service performed?
6. What is the basic difference between a merchant wholesaler and an agent?
7. Identify three kinds of full-service wholesalers. What factors are used to classify wholesalers into one of these categories?
8. Distinguish between (a) commission merchants and agents and (b) manufacturers' sales branches and manufacturers' sales offices.
9. What is the basic difference between wholesalers and retailers?
10. What is the difference between a department store and a discount store with regard to selling orientation and philosophy?
11. How do (a) convenience stores, (b) traditional specialty stores, and (c) category killers compete with other retail outlets?
12. What can nonstore retailers offer their customers that in-store retailers cannot?
13. What does the wheel of retailing hypothesis suggest about new retail operations?
14. Compare and contrast community shopping centers and regional shopping centers.
15. What is physical distribution? Which major functions does it include?
16. What activities besides storage are included in warehousing?
17. List the primary modes of transportation, and cite at least one advantage of each.

DISCUSSION QUESTIONS

1. Which distribution channels would producers of services be most likely to use? Why?
2. Many producers sell to consumers both directly and through middlemen. How can such a producer justify competing with its own middlemen?
3. In what situations might a producer use agents or commission merchants rather than its own sales offices or branches?
4. If a middleman is eliminated from a marketing channel, under what conditions will costs decrease? Under what conditions will costs increase? Will the middleman's functions be eliminated? Explain.
5. Which types of retail outlets are best suited to intensive distribution? to selective distribution? to exclusive distribution? Explain your answer in each case.
6. How are the various physical distribution functions related to each other? to the other elements of the marketing mix?

VIDEO CASE

Dash.com Rewards Loyal Online Shoppers

All online retailers, like their brick-and-mortar counterparts, face the day-in, day-out challenge of attracting and retaining customers. Now they can dash their customers. Dash.com, on the Internet since November 1999, helps web stores get targeted messages to online shoppers at the time of purchase. Consumers have to take the first step by downloading Dash.com's free software, which puts a special dashBar on the bottom of each user's Internet browser. The dashBar tracks the user's web browsing patterns and sends the data back to Dash.com's system. When the system notices a user surfing a web site that sells products also available at one of Dash.com's participating web stores, it transmits a banner ad promoting the Dash.com merchant. If the user clicks to buy from the Dash.com merchant, he or she will receive a rebate ranging from as little as 1 percent of the purchase to as much as 20 percent or more.

The amount of the rebate depends on the deal negotiated with the web store, and it can vary from month to month. Not long ago, for example, users who shopped at apparel e-tailer Jos. A. Bank received a 5 percent rebate during the summer months but received 8 percent during January. Cooking.com customers received a 20 percent rebate during that summer but received only 10 percent if they shopped in January. A wide variety of online retailers have signed with Dash.com, including Barnesandnoble.com, L.L. Bean, Wine.com, Avon, 1–800–Flowers.com, Patagonia, Expedia.com, KBKids.com, REI.com, Dell, OfficeMax.com, and Walmart.com. Even United Airlines has begun using Dash.com to reinforce traveler loyalty by providing members of its frequent flyer program with bonus miles when they shop at participating web stores.

Dash.com was founded by CEO Daniel Kaufman with Jason Priest, Chris Dowhan, and Joshua Abram. Their goal was to provide a shopper-friendly service that would help web retailers get and keep customers at less cost. The company's concept was so intriguing that it quickly attracted funding from telecommunications giant AT&T, ad agency group Omnicom, and other investors. Dash.com has been enthusiastically received by both Internet retailers and consumers. Before the company celebrated its one-year anniversary, it had signed 135 web stores and registered more than 900,000 consumer users.

Knowing that consumers are increasingly concerned about their privacy when surfing the Internet, Dash.com allows users to view everything that the company has on file about their browsing habits and purchases. Then users can delete any or all of the information, at their discretion. Few Internet businesses allow users access to their data, let alone invite them to edit their files. But Kaufman feels strongly about respecting the privacy of Dash.com users. "Many consumers hesitate to participate in e-commerce opportunities because they fear they will leave a trail of personal information that's beyond their control," states Kaufman. By providing customers with the opportunity to see and modify their information, he says, business can lessen this concern. Dash.com's combination of privacy protection, targeted promotions, and shopping rebates have made the company a powerful partner for retailers doing business on the web.[18]

Questions

1. Why would a category killer such as OfficeMax.com, which relies on low prices to build high sales volume, arrange for Dash.com to offer a rebate on top of its discount pricing?
2. How can Dash.com work with its participating retailers to sign up more users?
3. What do you think of Dash.com's approach to privacy?

Building skills for career success

1. Exploring the Internet

One reason the Internet has generated so much excitement and interest among both buyers and distributors of products is that it is a highly effective method of direct marketing. Already a multibillion dollar industry, electronic commerce is growing exponentially as more businesses recognize the power of the Internet to reach customers twenty-four hours a day anywhere in the world. In addition to using the Internet to provide product information to potential customers, businesses can use it to process orders and accept payment from customers. Quick delivery from warehouses or stores by couriers like UPS and Federal Express adds to the convenience of Internet shopping.

Businesses whose products have traditionally sold well through printed catalogs are clear leaders in the electronic marketplace. Books, CDs, clothing, and other frequently purchased, relatively low-cost items sell well through both the Internet and catalogs. As a result, many successful catalog companies are including the Internet in their market coverage. And many of their customers are finding that they prefer the more dynamic online versions of the catalogs. Visit the text web site for updates to this exercise.

Assignment

1. Explore the web sites listed below, or just enter "shopping" on one of the web search engines ... then stand back!

   http://www.llbean.com
   http://www.jcpenney.com
   http://www.sears.com
   http://www.landsend.com
   http://www.barnesandnoble.com
   http://www.amazon.com

2. Which web site does the best job of selling merchandise? Explain your answer.
3. Find a product you would be willing to buy over the Internet, and explain why you would buy it. Name the web site and describe the product.
4. Find a product you would be unwilling to buy over the Internet and, again, explain your reasoning. Name the web site and describe the product.

2. Developing Critical Thinking Skills

According to the wheel of retailing hypothesis, retail businesses begin as low-margin, low-priced, low-status operations. As they successfully challenge established retailers for market share, they upgrade their facilities and offer more services. This raises their costs and forces them to increase their prices so that eventually they become like the conventional retailers they replaced. As they move up from the low end of the wheel, new firms with lower costs and prices move in to take their place. For example, Kmart started as a low-priced operation that competed with department stores. Over time, it upgraded its facilities and products; big Kmart stores now offer such exclusive merchandise as Martha Stewart's bed-and-bath collection, full-service pharmacies, café areas, and "Pantry" areas stocked with frequently bought grocery items including milk, eggs, and bread. In consequence, Kmart has become a higher-cost, higher-priced operation and, as such, is vulnerable to lower-priced firms entering at the low end of the wheel.

Assignment

1. Investigate the operations of a local retailer.
2. Use Figure 15.15 to explain how this retailer is evolving on the wheel of retailing.
3. Prepare a report on your findings.

3. Building Team Skills

Surveys are a commonly used tool in marketing research. The information they provide can reduce business risk and facilitate decision making. Retail outlets often survey their customers' wants and needs by distributing comment cards or questionnaires. The customer survey below is an example of a survey that a local photography shop might distribute to its customers.

Assignment

1. Working in teams of three to five, choose a local retailer.
2. Classify the retailer according to the major types of retailers.
3. Design a survey to help the retailer improve customer service. (You may find it beneficial to work with the retailer and actually administer the survey to the retailer's customers. Prepare a report of the survey results for the retailer.)
4. Present your findings to the class.

4. Researching Different Careers

When you are looking for a job, the people closest to you can be extremely helpful. Family members and friends may be able to answer your questions directly or put you in touch with someone else who can. This type of "networking" can lead to an "informational interview," in which you can meet with someone who will answer your questions about a career or a company and who can also provide inside information on related fields and other helpful hints.

Assignment

1. Choose a retailer or wholesaler and a position within the company that interests you.
2. Call the company and ask to speak to the person in a particular position. Explain that you are a college student interested in the position and ask to set up an "informational interview."
3. Prepare a list of questions to ask in the interview. The questions should focus on:
   a. the type of training recommended for the position
   b. how the person entered the position and advanced in it
   c. what he or she likes and dislikes about the work
4. Present your findings to the class.

5. Improving Communication Skills

As the first step in finding a home, an increasing number of people are turning to the Internet rather than a realtor. The National Association of Realtors (NAR) lists over 1 million homes each month. However, over the past five years, the NAR has lost 100,000 members, a 12.2 percent decline. In addition, the total value of mortgages initiated online is expected to rise from $217 million at the end of 1996 to $25.5 billion by 2001. Home buyers can search the Internet for demographic information about a particular town or region, including school quality, crime rates, and income level, and can use relocation calculators, which estimate how much the cost of living differs from one region to another.

Assignment

1. Compare shopping for a home over the Internet with the traditional experience of shopping for a home with a realtor. (Be sure to consider the time required to gather information on housing, prices, order processing, and payment methods.)
2. Prepare a brief position paper, "A Perspective: Nonstore Retailers Are/Are Not a Threat to Traditional Retailers."

Customer Survey

To help us serve you better please take a few minutes while your photographs are being developed to answer the following questions. Your opinions are important to us.

1. Do you live/work in the area? (Circle one or both if they apply.)
2. Why did you choose us? (Circle all that apply.)
   Close to home
   Close to work
   Convenience
   Good service
   Quality
   Full-service photography shop
   Other
3. How did you learn about us? (Circle one.)
   Newspaper
   Flyer/coupon
   Passing by
   Recommended by someone
   Other
4. How frequently do you have film developed? (Please estimate.)
   ________ Times per month
   ________ Times per year
5. Which aspects of our photography shop do you think need improvement?
6. Our operating hours are from 8:00 A.M. to 7:00 P.M. weekdays and Saturdays from 9:30 A.M. to 6:00 P.M. We are closed on Sundays and legal holidays. If changes in our operating hours would serve you better please specify how you would like them changed.
7. Age (Circle one.)
   Under 25
   26–89
   40–59
   Over 60
   Comments:

Developing Integrated Marketing Communications

16

LEARNING OBJECTIVES

1 Describe integrated marketing communications.

2 Understand the role of promotion.

3 Explain the purposes of the three types of advertising.

4 Describe the advantages and disadvantages of the major advertising media.

5 Identify the major steps in developing an advertising campaign.

6 Recognize the various kinds of salespersons, the steps in the personal-selling process, and the major sales management tasks.

7 Describe sales promotion objectives and methods.

8 Understand the types and uses of public relations.

9 Identify the factors that influence the selection of promotion mix ingredients.

McDonald's spent $30 million on Disney's "Toy Story 2" promotional tie-ins while Burger King spent $22 million on "Pokemon: The First Movie" tie-ins.

inside business

McDonald's Maintains Market Share Through Promotion

Buy a burger, get a toy. Toy giveaways are a major promotional weapon in McDonald's global battle for fast-food market share. McDonald's has 13,000 U.S. restaurants, and its national market share is approaching 43 percent. However, rival Burger King, with 8,000 U.S. restaurants and nearly 22 percent of the market, is working hard to narrow the gap. So to maintain market leadership in this high-stakes food fight, McDonald's is turning up the heat on its promotional efforts by using a variety of promotional tools to target families as well as African-American and Latino consumers.

Fast-food restaurants have long put toys in kiddie meals to build traffic and encourage repeat visits from families. In recent years, however, the competition has gotten fiercer—and the budgets bigger—as the top chains develop promotional offers linked to new movies and hit television shows. Knowing that Disney films are generally big box-office draws for families, McDonald's preempted other chains by signing a ten-year, multimillion-dollar agreement to be the only fast-food restaurant promoting Disney movies.

Although movie and television tie-ins are costly, they generate a great deal of excitement and, while the promotional offers last, give families an incentive to return to McDonald's again and again. McDonald's spent $30 million on promotional tie-ins for Disney's *Toy Story 2*, for example, while Burger King fought back by spending $22 million on promotional tie-ins for *Pokemon: The First Movie.* Then McDonald's invested nearly $75 million on Disney *Dinosaurs* tie-in promotional activities, including store displays, free toys, and a sweepstakes. Next, the chain created displays and tray liners to promote a traveling dinosaur exhibit, followed by a variety of promotional efforts linked to the Power Rangers television series. Meanwhile, Burger King planned its own promotional attack, budgeting $20 million for toys and in-store displays related to the Flintstones in *Viva Rock Vegas.*

The family segment is just one of several market segments that McDonald's has been targeting. Through research, the chain learned that African-American consumers and Hispanic consumers each account for 15 percent of its customer base. As a result, McDonald's has developed special promotional offers geared to these two segments. "McDonald's is doing bigger and better things to reach both African Americans and Hispanics with campaigns designed to be very specific to them," explains Mary Kay Eschbach, McDonald's U.S. media director. "Both communities are incredibly important to us."

One January, for example, McDonald's mounted a chainwide salute to Martin Luther King, Jr., followed by a February sweepstakes in which the top prize was a family vacation. In June, the chain's promotional activities highlighted Black Music Month. Then, in early fall, McDonald's promotional efforts carried an African-American heritage theme. McDonald's has also been promoting its annual in-store Monopoly game and other promotions on the BET cable channel and web site to heighten interest and build restaurant traffic. To reach out to Latino consumers, McDonald's is airing a Spanish-language advertising campaign and spotlighting its in-store promotions on Galavision. The burger wars are far from over, so watch for more promotional activities ahead as McDonald's and the other chains keep battling over market share.[1]

Gert Boyle gives Columbia Sportswear both a business style and personality that are communicated through multiple promotional methods, creating very favorable company and product images in the minds of customers. Her skillful use of promotion is of great benefit to Columbia Sportswear.

Promotion is communication about an organization and its products that is intended to inform, persuade, or remind target market members. The promotion with which we are most familiar—advertising—is intended to inform, persuade, or remind us to buy particular products. But there is more to promotion than advertising, and it is used for other purposes as well. Charities use promotion to inform us of their need for donations, to persuade us to give, and to remind us to do so in case we have forgotten. Even the Internal Revenue Service uses promotion (in the form of publicity) to remind us of its April 15 deadline for filing tax returns.

promotion communication about an organization and its products that is intended to inform, persuade, or remind target market members

A **promotion mix** (sometimes called a *marketing communications mix*) is the particular combination of promotional methods a firm uses to reach a target market. The makeup of a mix depends on many factors, including the firm's promotional resources and objectives, the nature of the target market, the product characteristics, and the feasibility of various promotional methods.

promotion mix the particular combination of promotion methods a firm uses to reach a target market

In this chapter, we introduce four promotional methods and describe how they are used in an organization's marketing plans. First, we examine the role of advertising in the promotion mix. We discuss different types of advertising, the process of developing an advertising campaign, and social and legal concerns in advertising. Next we consider several categories of personal selling, noting the importance of effective sales management. We also look at sales promotion—why firms use it and which sales promotion techniques are most effective. Then we explain how public relations can be used to promote an organization and its products. Finally, we illustrate how these four promotional methods are combined in an effective promotion mix.

What Is Integrated Marketing Communications?

LEARNING OBJECTIVE

1 Describe integrated marketing communications.

Integrated marketing communications is the coordination of promotion efforts to ensure the maximum informational and persuasive impact on customers. A major goal of integrated marketing communications is to send a consistent message to customers. Integrated marketing communications provides an organization with a way to coordinate and manage its promotional efforts to ensure that customers do receive consistent messages. This approach fosters not only long-term customer relationships, but also the efficient use of promotional resources.

integrated marketing communications coordination of promotion efforts for maximum informational and persuasive impact on customers

The concept of integrated marketing communications has been increasingly accepted for several reasons. Mass media advertising, a very popular promotional method in the past, is used less today because of its high costs and less predictable audience sizes. Marketers can now take advantage of more precisely targeted promotional tools, such as cable TV, direct mail, CD ROMs, the Internet, special interest magazines, and voice broadcasts. Database marketing is also allowing marketers to be more precise in targeting individual customers. Until recently, suppliers of marketing communications were specialists. Advertising agencies provided advertising campaigns, sales promotion companies provided sales promotion activities and materials, and public relations organizations engaged in public relations efforts. Today, a number of promotion-related companies provide one-stop shopping to the client seeking advertising, sales promotion, and public relations, thus reducing coordination problems for the sponsoring company. Because the overall cost of marketing communications has risen significantly, upper management demands systematic evaluations of communication efforts to ensure that promotional resources are being used efficiently.[2] Although the fundamental role of promotion is not changing, the specific communication vehicles employed and the precision with which they are used are changing.

Promotion comes in many shapes. Oscar Mayer's Hot Dog vehicle helps create customer awareness and reminds customers of this well-established brand. It may influence customers to think of the Oscar Mayer brand when they are grocery shopping.

The Role of Promotion

LEARNING OBJECTIVE

2 Understand the role of promotion.

Promotion is commonly the object of two misconceptions. Often, people take note of highly visible promotional activities, such as advertising and personal selling, and conclude that these make up the entire field of marketing. People also sometimes consider promotional activities to be unnecessary, expensive, and the cause of higher prices. Neither view is accurate.

The role of promotion is to facilitate exchanges directly or indirectly by informing individuals, groups, or organizations and influencing them to accept a firm's products or to have more positive feelings about the firm. To expedite changes directly, marketers convey information about a firm's goods, services, and ideas to particular market segments. To bring about exchanges indirectly, marketers address interest groups (such as environmental and consumer groups), regulatory agencies, investors, and the general public concerning a company and its products. The broader role of promotion, therefore, is to maintain positive relationships between a company and various groups in the marketing environment.

Marketers frequently design promotional communications, such as advertisements, for specific groups, although some may be directed at wider audiences. Several different messages may be communicated simultaneously to different market segments. For example, Exxon Corporation may address customers about a new motor oil, inform investors about the firm's financial performance, and update the general public on the firm's environmental efforts.

Marketers must carefully plan, implement, and coordinate promotional communications to make the best use of them. The effectiveness of promotional activities depends greatly on the quality and quantity of information available to marketers about the organization's marketing environment (see Figure 16.1). If a marketer wants to influence customers to buy a certain product, for example, the firm must know who these customers are and how they make purchase decisions for that type of product. Marketers must gather and use information about particular audiences to communicate successfully with them.

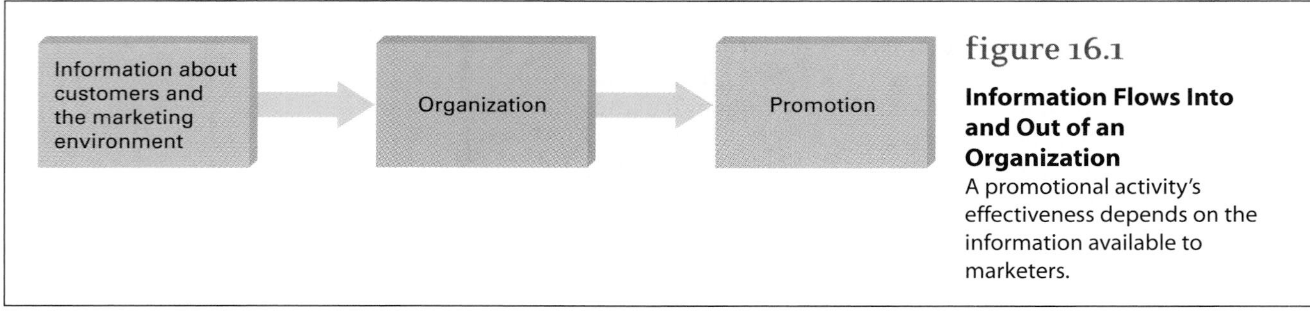

figure 16.1

Information Flows Into and Out of an Organization

A promotional activity's effectiveness depends on the information available to marketers.

Source: William M. Pride and O. C. Ferrell, *Marketing: Concepts and Strategies*, Eleventh Edition. Copyright © 2000 by Houghton Mifflin Company. Adapted with permission.

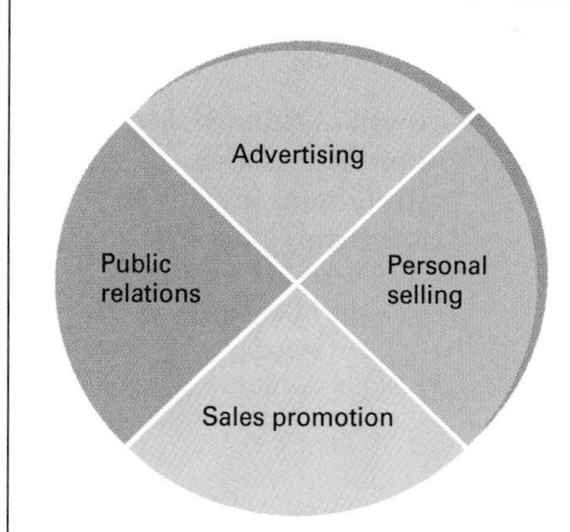

figure 16.2

Possible Ingredients for an Organization's Promotion Mix

Depending on the type of product and target market involved, two or more of these ingredients are used in a promotion mix.

Source: William M. Pride and O. C. Ferrell, *Marketing: Concepts and Strategies*, Eleventh Edition. Copyright © 2000 by Houghton Mifflin Company. Adapted with permission.

The Promotion Mix: An Overview

Marketers can use several promotional methods to communicate with individuals, groups, and organizations. The methods that are combined to promote a particular product make up the promotion mix for that item.

Advertising, personal selling, sales promotion, and public relations are the four major elements in an organization's promotion mix (see Figure 16.2). Two, three, or four of these ingredients are used in a promotion mix, depending on the type of product and target market involved.

Advertising is a paid, nonpersonal message communicated to a select audience through a mass medium. Advertising is flexible enough that it can reach a very large target group or a small, carefully chosen one. **Personal selling** is personal communication aimed at informing customers and persuading them to buy a firm's products. It is more expensive to reach a consumer through personal selling than through advertising, but this method provides immediate feedback and is often more persuasive than advertising. **Sales promotion** is the use of activities or materials as direct inducements to customers or salespersons. It adds extra value to the product or increases the customer's incentive to buy the product. **Public relations** is a broad set of communication activities used to create and maintain favorable relationships between an organization and various public groups, both internal and external. Public relations activities are numerous and varied and can be a very effective form of promotion.

advertising a paid, nonpersonal message communicated to a select audience through a mass medium

personal selling personal communication aimed at informing customers and persuading them to buy a firm's products

sales promotion the use of activities or materials as direct inducements to customers or salespersons

public relations communication activities used to create and maintain favorable relations between an organization and various public groups, both internal and external

Advertising

In 1999 organizations spent $215 billion on advertising in the United States.[3] Figure 16.3 shows how advertising expenditures and employment in advertising have increased since 1972. In recent years, the growth of advertising has subsided to some extent.

LEARNING OBJECTIVE

3 Explain the purposes of the three types of advertising.

Types of Advertising by Purpose

Depending on its purpose and message, advertising may be classified into one of three groups: primary-demand, selective demand, or institutional.

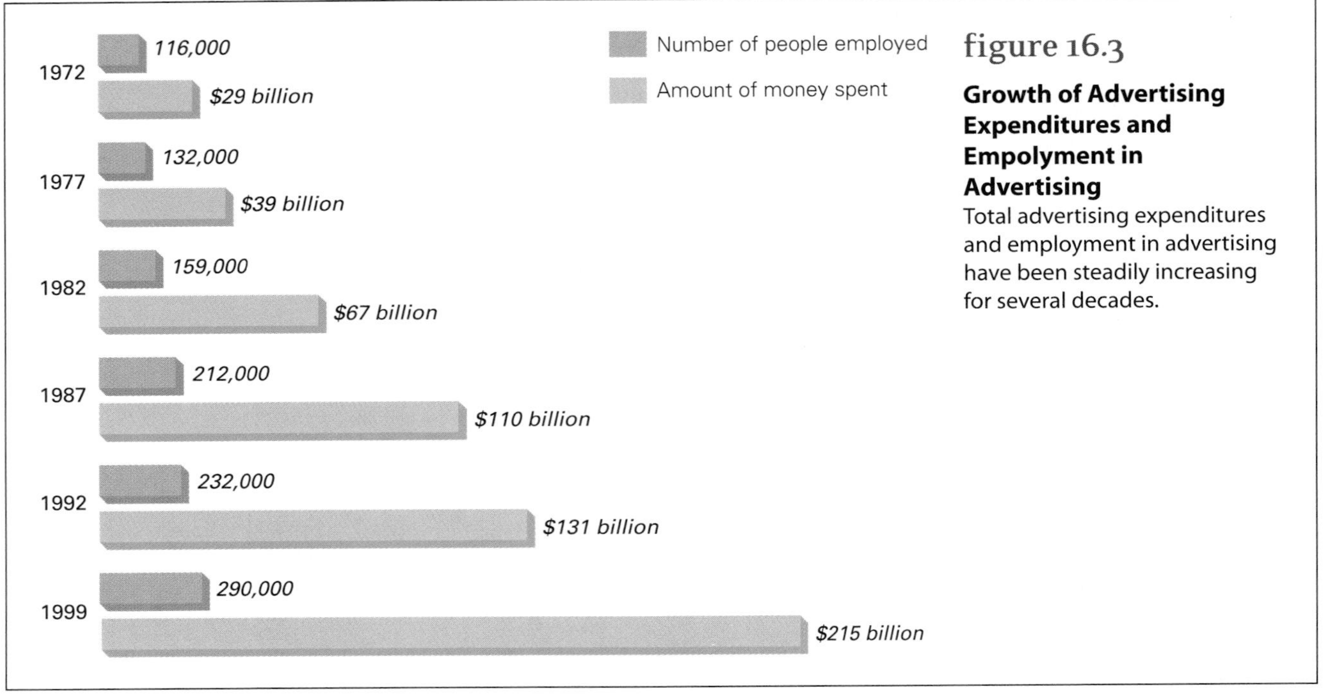

figure 16.3

Growth of Advertising Expenditures and Empolyment in Advertising
Total advertising expenditures and employment in advertising have been steadily increasing for several decades.

Source: Reprinted with permission from the May 22, 2000, issue of *Advertising Age*. Copyright © Crain Communications, Inc., 2000; and U.S. Department of Labor Bureau of Labor Statistics, *Employment and Earnings*, April 2000, p. 74.

primary-demand advertising advertising whose purpose is to increase the demand for *all* brands of a product within a specific industry

Primary-Demand Advertising **Primary-demand advertising** is advertising aimed at increasing the demand for *all* brands of a product within a specific industry. Trade and industry associations, such as the California Milk Processor Board ("Got Milk?"), are the major users of primary-demand advertising. Their advertisements promote broad product categories, such as beef, milk, pork, potatoes, and prunes, without mentioning specific brands.

selective demand (or brand) advertising advertising that is used to sell a particular brand of product

Selective Demand Advertising **Selective demand** (or **brand**) **advertising** is advertising that is used to sell a particular brand of product. It is by far the most common type of advertising, and it accounts for the lion's share of advertising expenditures. Producers use brand-oriented advertising to convince us to buy everything from Bubble Yum to Buicks.

Selective advertising that aims at persuading consumers to make purchases within a short time is called *immediate-response advertising*. Most local advertising is of this type. Often, local advertisers promote products with immediate appeal. Selective advertising aimed at keeping a firm's name or product before the public is called *reminder advertising*.

Comparative advertising, which has become more popular over the last two decades, compares specific characteristics of two or more identified brands. Of course, the comparison shows the advertiser's brand to be as good as or better than the other identified competing brands. Comparisons are often based on the outcome of surveys or research studies. Though competing firms act as effective watchdogs against each other's advertising claims, consumers themselves would do well to cultivate a certain sophistication concerning claims based on "scientific studies" and various statistical manipulations. Comparative advertising is unacceptable or illegal in a number of other countries.

institutional advertising advertising designed to enhance a firm's image or reputation

Institutional Advertising **Institutional advertising** is advertising designed to enhance a firm's image or reputation. Many public utilities and larger firms, such as AT&T and the major oil companies, use part of their advertising dollars to build goodwill rather than to stimulate sales directly. A positive public image helps an organization attract not only customers but also employees and investors.

Advertising Media

LEARNING OBJECTIVE

4 Describe the advantages and disadvantages of the major advertising media.

The **advertising media** are the various forms of communication through which advertising reaches its audience. The major media are newspapers, magazines, direct mail, outdoor displays, television, radio, and the Internet. Figure 16.4 shows how organizations allocate their advertising expenditures among the various media. Note that *electronic media*—television and radio—account for less than one-third of all media expenditures. Online advertising is growing rapidly. It is estimated that annual spending by U.S. advertisers will hit $21 billion by 2004.

advertising media the various forms of communication through which advertising reaches its audience

Newspapers

Newspaper advertising accounts for about 22 percent of all advertising expenditures. Approximately 86 percent is purchased by local retailers. Retailers extensively use newspaper advertising because it is relatively inexpensive compared with other media. Moreover, since most newspapers provide local coverage, advertising dollars are not wasted in reaching people outside the organization's market area. It is also timely. Ads can usually be placed just a few days before they are to appear.

There are some drawbacks, however, to newspaper advertising. It has a short life span; newspapers are generally read through once and then discarded. Color reproduction in newspapers is usually not high quality; thus most ads must be run in black and white. Finally, marketers cannot target specific demographic groups through newspaper ads because newspapers are read by such a broad spectrum of people.

direct-mail advertising promotional material mailed directly to individuals

Magazines

The advertising revenues of magazines have been climbing steadily since 1976. In 1999 they reached $11.4 billion, or about 5.3 percent of all advertising expenditures.

Advertisers can reach very specific market segments through ads in special-interest magazines. A boat manufacturer has a ready-made consumer audience in subscribers to *Yachting* or *Sail*. Producers of photographic equipment advertise in *Travel & Leisure* or *Popular Photography*. A number of magazines like *Time* and *Cosmopolitan* publish regional editions, which provide advertisers with geographic flexibility as well.

Magazine advertising is more prestigious than newspaper advertising, and it allows for high-quality color reproduction. In addition, magazine advertisements have a longer life span than those in other media. Issues of *National Geographic*, for example, may be kept for months or years, and the ads they contain may be viewed repeatedly.

The major disadvantages of magazine advertising are high cost and lack of timeliness. Because magazine ads must normally be prepared two to three months in advance, they cannot be adjusted to reflect the latest market conditions. Magazine ads—especially full-color ads—are also expensive. Although the cost of reaching a thousand people may compare favorably with that of other media, the cost of a full-page, four-color ad can be very high—$183,000 in *Time*.

Direct Mail

Direct-mail advertising is promotional material mailed directly to individuals. Direct mail is the most selective medium: mailing lists are available (or can be compiled) to reach almost any target audience, from airplane enthusiasts to zoologists. The effectiveness of direct-mail advertising can be measured because the advertiser has a record of who received the advertisement and can track who responds to the ads.

Some organizations are using direct e-mail. To avoid customers' receiving un-wanted e-mail, a firm should ask customers to complete a request form in order to receive promotional e-mail from the company. For example, Lands' End's weekly e-mail newsletter, "What's New," goes to over 200,000 subscribers. Each has completed a subscription form on the company web site.[4]

Brand-building advertising. Coca-Cola gave unprecedented permission to the American Advertising Federation (AAF) to modify their logo for use in the "Great Brands" campaign. This integrated communications program was launched by AAF to reinforce the essential strategic importance of advertising to CEOs, COOs, and CFOs. Ad space was donated by numerous national newspapers, and trade and consumer magazines. To date, other participating brands are Sunkist, Energizer, and Budweiser.

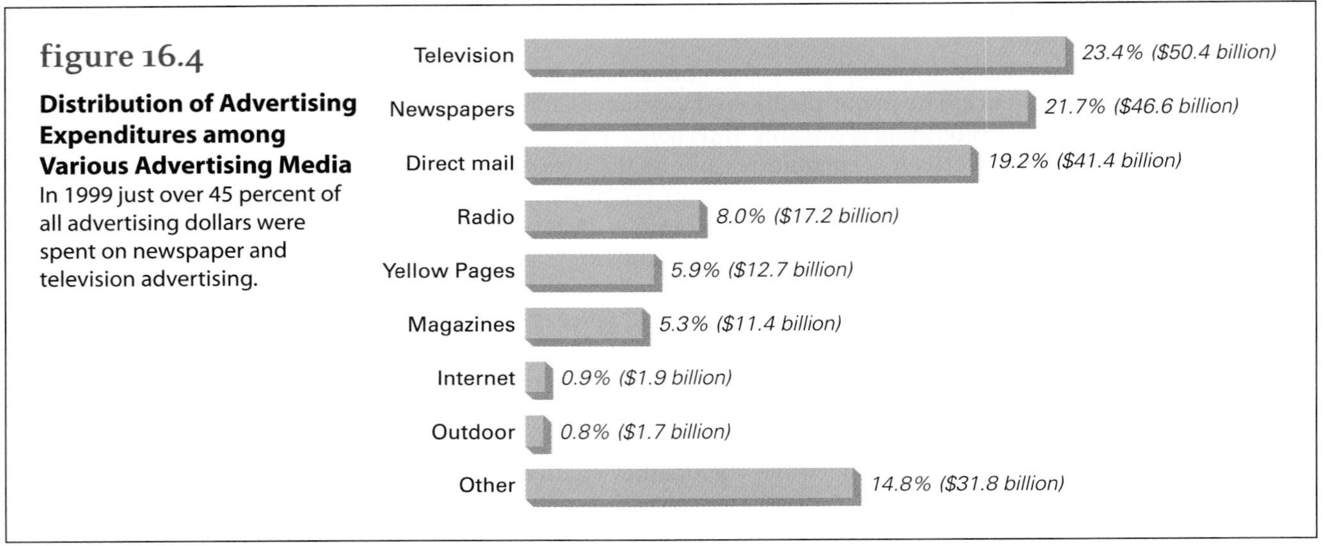

figure 16.4

Distribution of Advertising Expenditures among Various Advertising Media
In 1999 just over 45 percent of all advertising dollars were spent on newspaper and television advertising.

Source: Reprinted with permission from the May 22, 2000, issue of *Advertising Age*. Copyright © Crain Communications, Inc., 2000.

The success of direct-mail advertising depends to some extent on appropriate and current mailing lists. A direct-mail campaign may fail if the mailing list is outdated and the mailing does not reach the right people. In addition, this medium is relatively costly. Direct-mail advertising expenditures in 1999 amounted to more than $41 billion, almost 20 percent of the total.

outdoor advertising short promotional messages on billboards, posters, and signs

Outdoor Advertising **Outdoor advertising** consists of short promotional messages on billboards, posters, and signs. In 1999 outdoor advertisers spent $1.7 billion, or slightly less than 1 percent of total advertising expenditures, on outdoor advertising.

Sign and billboard advertising allows the marketer to focus on a particular geographic area; it is fairly inexpensive. However, because most outdoor promotion is directed toward a mobile audience, the message must be limited to a few words. The medium is especially suitable for products that lend themselves to pictorial display.

Outdoor advertising. Outdoor advertising is relatively inexpensive and allows the advertiser to provide short messages to customers in targeted geographic locations.

Television Television ranks number one in total advertising revenue. In 1999 almost one-fourth of all advertising expenditures, about $50 billion, went to television. Approximately 99 percent of American homes have at least one television set which is watched an average of seven and one-half hours each day. The average U.S. household can receive twenty-eight TV channels, including cable and pay stations, according to Nielson Media Research, and 75 percent of households receive basic cable/satellite television.[5] Television obviously provides advertisers with considerable access to consumers.

Television advertising is the primary medium for larger firms whose objective is to reach national or regional markets. A national advertiser may buy *network time*, which means that its message usually will be broadcast by hundreds of local stations affiliated with the network. However, the opportunity to reach extremely large television audiences has been reduced by the increased availability and popularity of cable channels and home videos. Both national and local firms may buy *local time* on a single station that covers a particular geographic area.

spotLight

Source: Copyright 2000, USA TODAY. Reprinted with permission.

Advertisers may *sponsor* an entire show, participate with other sponsors of a show, or buy *spot time* for a single 10-, 20-, 30-, or 60-second commercial during or between programs. To an extent, they may select their audience by choosing the day of the week and the approximate time of day their ads will be shown. Anheuser-Busch advertises Budweiser Beer during TV football games because the majority of viewers are men, who are likely to buy beer.

Another option available to television advertisers is the infomercial. An **infomercial** is a program-length (usually a half-hour) televised commercial message resembling an entertainment or consumer affairs program. Infomercials for products such as exercise equipment tell customers why they need the product, what benefits it provides, in what ways it out-performs its competitors, and how much it costs. Infomercials, together with other promotional methods, resulted in the Billy Blanks Tae-Bo fitness videos becoming the best selling fitness videos last year.[6] Although infomercials were initially aired primarily over cable television, today they are becoming more common on other types of television. Currently, infomercials are responsible for marketing over $1 billion worth of products annually. Even some Fortune 500 companies are now using them.

infomercial a program-length televised commercial message resembling an entertainment or consumer affairs program

Television advertising rates are based on the number of people expected to be watching when the commercial is aired. In 2000, the average cost of a 30-second Superbowl commercial was $2.2 million.[7] Advertisers spend over $500,000 for a 30-second television commercial during a top-rated prime-time program.

Unlike magazine advertising, television advertising has a short life. If a viewer misses a commercial, it is missed forever. Viewers may also become indifferent to commercial messages. Or they may use the commercial time as a break from viewing, thus missing the message altogether. Remote-control devices make it especially easy to avoid television commercials.

Radio Advertisers spent over $17.2 billion, or 8 percent of total expenditures, on radio advertising in 1996. Like magazine advertising, radio advertising offers selectivity. Radio stations develop programming for—and are tuned in by—specific groups of listeners. There are almost half a billion radios in the United States (about six per household), which makes radio the most accessible medium.

Radio can be less expensive than other media. Actual rates depend on geographic coverage, the number of commercials contracted for, the time period specified, and whether the station broadcasts on AM, FM, or both. Even small retailers are able to afford radio advertising. A radio advertiser can schedule and change ads on short notice. The disadvantages of using radio are the absence of visual images and (because there are so many stations) the small audience size.

Internet The newest advertising medium, and one that is increasing in popularity, is the Internet. In 1999 U.S. advertisers spent $1.9 billion on Internet advertising, approximately 85 percent more than during the previous year.[8] Although the top three advertisers on the Internet, Microsoft, IBM, and Compaq, are technology-related organizations, many other companies advertise there as well. Some of the biggest Internet advertising spenders include General Motors, AT&T, Ford Motor and Barnes and Noble.[9] By 2004, according to Forrester Research Inc., Yahoo!, MSN, and AOL, the so-called Big Three, along with specialized niche sites such as those focusing on weddings and pets, will dominate the Internet and account for 64 percent of all traffic and 72 percent of advertising revenues.[10]

Internet advertising can take various forms. The most common type of Internet ad is the banner ad, rectangular graphics that appear at the top of most consumer web sites. Advertisers can use animation and interactive capabilities in their banner ads. Another type of Internet advertisement is the button ad, a small squarish ad containing only a corporate or brand name and usually appearing at the bottom of a web page. By clicking on the button, viewers go directly to a corporate web site. For example, by clicking on a Netscape button, Internet users are taken directly to the Netscape web site where they can download Navigator browser software. The third type of Internet advertisement is sponsorship (or co-branded) ads. These ads integrate a company's brand with editorial content. The goal of this type of advertisement is to get users to strongly identify the advertiser with the site's mission. Keyword ads are another type of Internet advertisement. Featured primarily on web search engines such as Yahoo! and Excite, advertisers can link a specific ad to text or subject matter that an information seeker may enter. For example, Miller Brewing bought the word "beer" on Yahoo! so that every time someone conducts a search using that word, an ad for "Miller Genuine Draft Beer" pops up. Finally, there are interstitial ads, also known as "In-Your-Face-Ads." When viewers click on a web site, a window pops up to display a product ad. For example, when web users click on a nutrition site, Phys.com, a full-screen animated ad for Procter & Gamble's Sunny Delight drink appears first. According to Erick Hachenburg, president and CEO of pogo.com, an advertising-sponsored free Internet multiplayer gaming site, sites like pogo.com draw an audience that regards the placed advertising differently than most web users. Instead of wanting to move on as quickly as possible, advertisements displayed between sets in the player's game are welcomed as a reprieve. Players do not rush off to another site. Pogo.com players spend an average of 45 minutes at a time playing a variety of Java versions of word puzzles, checkers, and card games like hearts. Given the 300 million impressions (exposures to a viewer) per game per month, served on the web site, and advertising revenue doubling every quarter in 1999, pogo.com and other game sites appear to be offering a marketable content site interesting to advertisers. As a result, CPM rates (the cost of reaching 1000 people) range from $15 to $30. With above average industry click rates (players clicking on an advertisement) of about 1 percent, they suggest game sites will likely find niches of viewers.[11]

Although the CPM of Internet advertising is higher than that of advertising on television, there are benefits of Internet advertising that experts say outweigh the expense. First, the number of people using the Internet continues to rise, which increases the potential size of the advertising audience. Second, online advertising can be more precise in targeting specific customers than most other media. In addition to expense, however, there are other problems associated with advertising on the Internet. First, many web ads are crude by comparison with television commercials. Second, there is no hard evidence that Net browsers pay more attention to the ads they see there than they do to ads anywhere else. One way one might draw an international audience is with a perfectly created internationalist cyber-persona. The question of whether global teens and young Internet savvy internationalists would find Ananova, the hybrid British/American accented female virtual newscaster, attractive enough to create a successful web site has already been answered. Modeled after Spice girl Victoria "Posh" Beckman, Australian pop singer Kyle Minogue, and British news announcer Carol Vorderman, according to her cyber-creators, Ananova.com was bought for $143 million by Orange PLC from the British Press Association after less than four months on the web.[12]

Major Steps in Developing an Advertising Campaign

LEARNING OBJECTIVE

5 Identify the major steps in developing an advertising campaign.

An advertising campaign is developed in several stages. These stages may vary in number and the order in which they are implemented, depending on the company's resources, products, and audiences. A campaign in any organization, however, will include the following steps in some form.

1. Identify and Analyze the Advertising Target Audience The target audience is the group of people toward which a firm's advertisements are directed. To pinpoint the organization's target audience and develop an effective campaign, marketers must analyze such information as the geographic distribution of potential customers; their age, sex, race, income, and education; and their attitudes toward both the advertiser's product and competing products. How marketers use this information will be influenced by the features of the product to be advertised and the nature of the competition. Precise identification of the target audience is crucial to the proper development of subsequent stages and, ultimately, to the success of the campaign itself.

2. Define the Advertising Objectives The goals of an advertising campaign should be stated precisely and in measurable terms. The objectives should include the current position of the firm, indicate how far and in what direction from that original reference point the company wishes to move, and specify a definite period of time for the achievement of the goals. Advertising objectives that focus on sales will stress increasing sales by a certain percentage or dollar amount, or expanding the firm's market share. Communication objectives will emphasize increasing product or brand awareness, improving consumer attitudes, or conveying product information.

Target audience. Generally, advertisements are not aimed at everyone. Who is the target for this Liz Claiborne advertisement?

3. Create the Advertising Platform An advertising platform includes the important selling points or features that an advertiser wishes to incorporate into the advertising campaign. These features should be important to customers in their selection and use of a product and, if possible, they should be features that competing products lack. Although research into what consumers view as important issues is expensive, it is the most productive way to determine which issues to include in an advertising platform.

4. Determine the Advertising Appropriation The advertising appropriation is the total amount of money designated for advertising in a given period. This stage is critical to the success of the campaign because advertising efforts based on an inadequate budget will understimulate customer demand, and a budget too large will waste a company's resources. Advertising appropriations may be based on last year's (or next year's forecasted) sales, on what competitors spend on advertising, or on executive judgment.

5. Develop the Media Plan A media plan specifies exactly which media will be used in the campaign and when advertisements will appear. Though cost-effectiveness is not easy to measure, the primary concern of the media planner is to reach the largest possible number of persons in the target audience for each dollar spent. In addition to cost, media planners must consider the location and demographics of people in the advertising target, the content of the message, and the characteristics of the audiences reached by various media. The media planner begins with general media decisions, selects subclasses within each medium, and finally chooses particular media vehicles for the campaign.

6. Create the Advertising Message The content and form of a message are influenced by the product's features, the characteristics of people in the advertising target, the objectives of the campaign, and the choice of media. An advertiser must consider these factors to choose words and illustrations that will be meaningful and appealing to persons in the advertising target. The copy, or

Using the Internet

Advertising Age (**http://www.adage.com/**) is the industry's preeminent source of marketing, advertising and media news, information, and analysis. The web site provides a variety of information about the advertising industry and online advertising in particular. Articles from various trade publications as well as links to advertising agencies and samples of advertising are among the many useful features presented.

words, of an advertisement will vary depending on the media choice but should attempt to move the audience through attention, interest, desire, and action. Artwork and visuals should complement copy by attracting the audience's attention and communicating an idea quickly.

7. Execute the Campaign Execution of an advertising campaign requires extensive planning, scheduling, and coordination because many tasks must be completed on time and the efforts of many people and firms must be coordinated. Production companies, research organizations, media firms, printers, photoengravers, and commercial artists are just a few of the people and firms that may contribute to a campaign. Advertising managers must constantly assess the quality of the work and take corrective action when necessary. In some instances, advertisers make changes during the campaign to meet objectives more effectively.

8. Evaluate Advertising Effectiveness A campaign's success should be measured, in terms of its original objectives, before, during, and/or after the campaign. An advertiser should at least be able to estimate whether sales or market share went up because of the campaign or whether any change occurred in customer attitudes or brand awareness. Data from past and current sales, responses to coupon offers, and customer surveys administered by research organizations are some of the ways in which advertising effectiveness can be evaluated.

Advertising Agencies

advertising agency an independent firm that plans, produces, and places advertising for its clients

Advertisers can plan and produce their own advertising with help from media personnel, or they can hire advertising agencies. An **advertising agency** is an independent firm that plans, produces, and places advertising for its clients. Many large ad agencies offer help with sales promotion and public relations as well. The media usually pay a commission of 15 percent to advertising agencies. Thus, the cost to the agency's client can be quite moderate. The client may be asked to pay for selected services that the agency performs. Other methods for compensating agencies are also used.

Firms that do a lot of advertising may use both an in-house advertising department and an independent agency. This approach gives the firm the advantage of being able to call on the agency's expertise in particular areas of advertising. An agency can also bring a fresh viewpoint to the firm's products and advertising plans.

Table 16.1 lists the nation's twenty leading advertisers in all media. In 1999 the number one spot went to General Motors.

Social and Legal Considerations in Advertising

Critics of U.S. advertising have two main complaints—that it is wasteful and that it can be deceptive. Although advertising (like any other activity) can be performed inefficiently, it is far from wasteful. Let's look at the evidence:

- Advertising is the most effective and least expensive means of communicating product information to a large number of individuals and organizations.
- Advertising encourages competition and is, in fact, a means of competition. It thus leads to the development of new and improved products, wider product choices, and lower prices.
- Advertising revenues support our mass communications media—newspapers, magazines, radio, and television. This means that advertising pays for much of our news coverage and entertainment programming.
- Advertising provides job opportunities in fields ranging from sales to film production.

Along with pure fact, advertising tends to include some exaggeration and occasional deception. Consumers usually spot such distortion in short order. Also, various government and private agencies scrutinize advertising for false or misleading claims or offers. At the national level, the Federal Trade Commission, the Food and Drug

table 16.1 Advertising Expenditures and Sales Volume for the Top Twenty National Advertisers

Rank	Company	Advertising Expenditures (in millions)	Sales (in millions)	Advertising Expenditures as Percentage of Sales
1	General Motors Corp.	$4,040.4	$130,073.0	3.12
2	Procter & Gamble Co.	2,611.8	20,038.0	13.03
3	Philip Morris Cos.	2,201.6	40,287.0	5.46
4	Pfizer	2,142.4	9,896.0	21.65
5	AT&T Corp.	1,950.9	62,391.0	3.13
6	DaimlerChrysler	1,804.1	82,699.1	2.18
7	Ford Motor Co.	1,639.8	112,420.0	1.46
8	Sears, Roebuck & Co.	1,505.2	36,938.0	4.07
9	PepsiCo	1,315.7	11,772.0	11.18
10	Verizon Communications	1,312.7	58,759.0	2.23
11	Walt Disney Co.	1,304.0	18,657.0	6.99
12	Time Warner, Inc.	1,202.9	21,654.0	5.56
13	Diageo	1,198.4	9,160.6	13.08
14	McDonald's Corp.	1,134.8	5,093.0	22.28
15	IBM Corp.	1,128.5	37,171.0	3.04
16	Intel Corp.	1,119.3	12,740.0	8.79
17	WorldCom	1,108.4	31,718.0	3.49
18	Viacom	1,064.5	10,207.0	10.43
19	Toyota Motor Corp.	1,025.2	39,131.9	2.62
20	Johnson & Johnson	1,004.5	15,385.0	6.53

Source: Reprinted with permission from the September 25, 2000, issue of *Advertising Age*. Copyright © Crain Communications, Inc., 2000.

Administration, and the Federal Communications Commission oversee advertising practices. Advertising may also be monitored by state and local agencies, Better Business Bureaus, and industry associations. These organizations have varying degrees of control over advertising, but their overall effect has been a positive one.

Personal Selling

Personal selling is the most adaptable of all promotional methods because the person who is presenting the message can modify it to suit the individual buyer. However, personal selling is also the most expensive method of promotion.

Most successful salespeople are able to communicate with others on a one-to-one basis and are strongly motivated. They strive to have a thorough knowledge of the products they offer for sale. And they are willing and able to deal with the details involved in handling and processing orders. Sales managers tend to emphasize these qualities when recruiting and hiring.

Many selling situations demand the face-to-face contact and adaptability of personal selling. This is especially true of industrial sales, in which a single purchase may amount to millions of dollars. Obviously, sales of that size must be based on carefully planned sales presentations, personal contact with customers, and thorough negotiations.

LEARNING OBJECTIVE

6 Recognize the various kinds of salespersons, the steps in the personal-selling process, and the major sales management tasks.

Kinds of Salespersons

Because most businesses employ different salespersons to perform different functions, marketing managers must select the kinds of sales personnel that will be most effective in selling the firm's products. Salespersons may be identified as order getters, order takers, and support personnel. A single individual can, and often does, perform all three functions.

order getter a salesperson who is responsible for selling the firm's products to new customers and increasing sales to present customers

creative selling selling products to new customers and increasing sales to present customers

order taker a salesperson who handles repeat sales in ways that maintain positive relationships with customers

sales support personnel employees who aid in selling but are more involved in locating prospects, educating customers, building goodwill for the firm, and providing follow-up service

Order Getters

An **order getter** is responsible for what is sometimes called **creative selling:** selling the firm's products to new customers and increasing sales to present customers. An order getter must perceive buyers' needs, supply customers with information about the firm's product, and persuade them to buy the product. Order-getting activities may be separated into two groups. In current-customer sales, salespeople concentrate on obtaining additional sales, or leads for prospective sales, from customers who have purchased the firm's products at least once. In new-business sales, sales personnel seek out new prospects and convince them to make an initial purchase of the firm's product. The real estate, insurance, appliance, heavy industrial machinery, and automobile industries in particular depend on new-business sales.

Order Takers

An **order taker** handles repeat sales in ways that maintain positive relationships with customers. An order taker sees that customers have products when and where they are needed and in the proper amounts. *Inside order takers* receive incoming mail and telephone orders in some businesses; salespersons in retail stores are also inside order takers. *Outside* (or *field*) *order takers* travel to customers. Often the buyer and the field salesperson develop a mutually beneficial relationship of placing, receiving, and delivering orders. Both inside and outside order takers are active salespersons and often produce most of their companies' sales.

Support Personnel

Sales support personnel aid in selling but are more involved in locating *prospects* (likely first-time customers), educating customers, building goodwill for the firm, and providing follow-up service. The most common categories of support personnel are missionary, trade, and technical salespersons.

A **missionary salesperson,** who usually works for a manufacturer, visits retailers to persuade them to buy the manufacturer's products. If the retailers agree, they buy the products from wholesalers, who are the manufacturer's actual customers. Missionary salespersons are often employed by producers of medical supplies and pharmaceuticals to promote these products to retail druggists, physicians, and hospitals.

Personal selling still works. CDW successfully competes in the desktop and laptop computer reseller market through personal selling on the telephone. President Greg Zeman believes that this personal touch—as opposed to web-based sales used by companies such as Dell—will lead to greater success.

A **trade salesperson,** who generally works for a food producer or processor, assists customers in promoting products, especially in retail stores. A trade salesperson may obtain additional shelf space for the products, restock shelves, set up displays, and distribute samples. Because trade salespersons are usually order takers as well, they are not strictly support personnel.

A **technical salesperson** assists the company's current customers in technical matters. He or she may explain how to use a product, how it is made, how to install it, or how a system is designed. A technical salesperson should be formally educated in science or engineering. Computers, steel, and chemicals are some of the products handled by technical salespeople.

Marketers usually need sales personnel from several of these categories. Factors that affect hiring and other personnel decisions include the number of customers and their characteristics; the product's attributes, complexity, and price; the distribution channels used by the company; and the company's approach to advertising.

Adapting to change

"Real Whirled" Sales Training

How can a multinational company train retail salespeople in the subtleties of selling dozens of different products to different customer segments? For global appliance maker Whirlpool, the key is Real Whirled, an unusual training program for the trainers who work with store salespeople at Sears, Home Depot, and other retailers. This program puts a cadre of trainers together in a home equipped with Whirlpool appliances, where they live and work for eight weeks. Every day, the trainers do laundry, cook, clean, and bake with Whirlpool appliances. In between, they analyze product features and benefits, swap product-use tips and frustrations, and critique each other's sales-training talks.

Because the Real Whirled home is located close to Whirlpool's headquarters in Benton Harbor, Michigan, the trainers sometimes have to show off their knowledge of company products by cooking impromptu dinners for senior managers who arrive without warning. Training directors are also apt to stop by to see how the trainers are progressing. After eight weeks of actually using the different appliances, the trainers sound more knowledgeable–and more credible–when they go on the road to train store salespeople.

The purpose of Real Whirled is to keep Whirlpool's trainers and their retail sales trainees focused squarely on how the appliances satisfy consumer needs. "It seems like such a no-brainer, but we tend to get away from spending time with the consumer," comments Jackie Seib, the company's national manager of training for sales and operations. "The biggest challenge in changing the retail culture is teaching salespeople what the consumer wants." Real Whirled gives the trainers first-hand experience in solving everyday problems using Whirlpool products, so they have real anecdotes and solutions–not just product facts and specifications–to share with the salespeople they train.

The Personal-Selling Process

No two selling situations are exactly alike, and no two salespeople perform their jobs in exactly the same way. Most salespeople, however, follow the six-step procedure illustrated in Figure 16.5.

Prospecting The first step in personal selling is to research potential buyers and choose the most likely customers, or prospects. Sources of prospects include business associates and customers, public records, telephone and trade-association directories, and company files. The salesperson concentrates on those prospects who have the financial resources, willingness, and authority to buy the product.

Approaching the Prospect First impressions are often lasting impressions. Thus, the salesperson's first contact with the prospect is crucial to successful selling. The best approach is one based on knowledge of the product, of the prospect's needs, and of how the product can meet those needs. Salespeople who understand each customer's particular situation are likely to make a good first impression—and to make a sale.

Making the Presentation The next step is the actual delivery of the sales presentation. In many cases, this includes demonstrating the product. The salesperson points out the product's features, its benefits, and how it is superior to competitors' merchandise. If the product has been used successfully by other firms, the salesperson may mention this as part of the presentation.

missionary salesperson a salesperson—generally employed by a manufacturer—who visits retailers to persuade them to buy the manufacturer's products

trade salesperson a salesperson—generally employed by a food producer or processor—who assists customers in promoting products, especially in retail stores

technical salesperson a salesperson who assists the company's current customers in technical matters

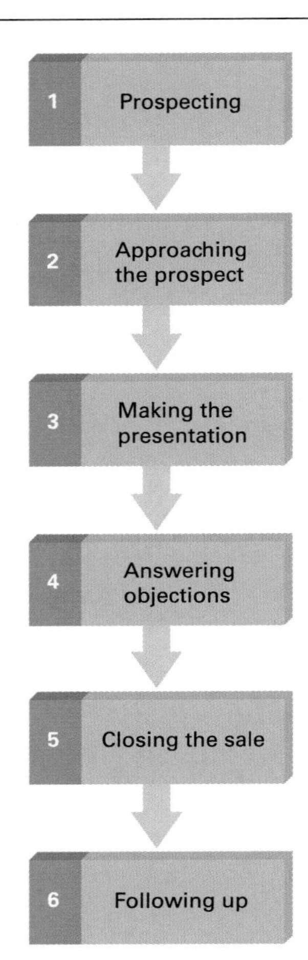

figure 16.5

The Six Steps of the Personal-Selling Process
Personal selling is not only the most adaptable of all promotional methods but also the most expensive.

Source: William M. Pride and O. C. Ferrell, *Marketing: Concepts and Strategies,* Eleventh Edition. Copyright © 2000 by Houghton Mifflin Company. Adapted with permission.

LEARNING OBJECTIVE

7 Describe sales promotion objectives and methods.

During a demonstration, the salesperson may suggest that the prospect try out the product personally. The demonstration and product trial should underscore specific points made during the presentation.

Answering Objections The prospect is likely to raise objections or ask questions at any time. This gives the salesperson a chance to eliminate objections that might prevent a sale, to point out additional features, or to mention special services the company offers.

Closing the Sale To close the sale, the salesperson asks the prospect to buy the product. This is considered the critical point in the selling process. Many experienced salespeople make use of a *trial closing,* in which they ask questions based on the assumption that the customer is going to buy the product. The questions "When would you want delivery?" and "Do you want the standard model or the one with the special options package?" are typical of trial closings. They allow the reluctant prospect to make a purchase without having to say, "I'll take it."

Following Up The salesperson must follow up after the sale to ensure that the product is delivered on time, in the right quantity, and in proper operating condition. During follow-up, the salesperson also makes it clear that he or she is available in case problems develop. Follow-up leaves a good impression and eases the way toward future sales. Hence, it is essential to the selling process. The salesperson's job does not end with a sale. It continues as long as the seller and the customer maintain a working relationship.

Managing Personal Selling

A firm's success often hinges on the competent management of its sales force. Although some companies operate efficiently without a sales force, most firms rely on a strong sales force—and the sales revenue it brings in—for their success.

Sales managers have responsibilities in a number of areas. They must set sales objectives in concrete, quantifiable terms, specifying a certain period of time and a certain geographic area. They must adjust the size of the sales force to meet changes in the firm's marketing plan and the marketing environment. Some sales forces, such as those of The Hartford, Conseco, and Primerica exceed 150,000 people.[13] Sales managers must attract and hire effective salespersons. They must develop a training program and decide where, when, how, and for whom to conduct the training. They must formulate a fair and adequate compensation plan to keep qualified employees. They must motivate salespersons to boost their productivity. They must define sales territories and determine scheduling and routing of the sales force. Finally, sales managers must evaluate the operation as a whole through sales reports, communications with customers, and invoices.

Sales Promotion

Sales promotion consists of activities or materials that are direct inducements to customers or salespersons. Are you a member of an airline frequent flyer program? Did you recently receive a free sample in the mail or at a supermarket? Did you or someone that you know get a Beanie Baby at McDonald's? Have you recently received a rebate from a manufacturer? Do you use coupons? All of these are examples of sales promotion efforts. Sales promotion techniques often are used to enhance and supplement other promotional methods. They can have a significant impact on sales.

The dramatic increase in spending for sales promotion shows that marketers have recognized the potential of this promotional method. Many firms now include numerous sales promotion efforts as part of their overall promotion mix.

Sales Promotion Objectives

Sales promotion activities may be used singly or in combination, both offensively and defensively, to achieve one goal or a set of goals. Marketers use sales promotion activities and materials for a number of purposes, including

Following up the sale. Saying thanks to a customer is a part of the following up step in the personal selling process. A handwritten note such as this one leaves the customer feeling good, which means they are inclined to become a repeat customer.

Linda,
I want to thank you for your recent visit To my store, I trust your experience was a pleasant one. I appreciate the trust you put in my staff and I. Please call me anytime I can be of help. I would be grateful if you would recommend us to family and friends.

Best Regards,
Richard Basler

For Good Vibrations Call Sound Installations

Richard Basler
President

411 Lynnway • Lynn, MA 01905
Email: soundrich@aol.com
781-598-1770
FAX-781-595-5110

- Car Stereo Systems
- Viper Alarms
- Remote Car Starters
- Smart Beep
- Radar Detectors
- Voicestream PCS

- Quality Products
- Professional Installs
- We Finance
- Open Mon-Sat

1. to draw new customers
2. to encourage trial purchases of a new product
3. to invigorate the sales of a mature brand
4. to boost sales to current customers
5. to reinforce advertising
6. to increase traffic in retail stores
7. to steady irregular sales patterns
8. to build up reseller inventories
9. to neutralize competitive promotional efforts
10. to improve shelf space and displays[14]

Any sales promotion objectives should be consistent with the organization's general goals and with its marketing and promotional objectives.

Sales Promotion Methods

Most sales promotion methods can be classified as promotional techniques for either consumer sales or trade sales. A **consumer sales promotion method** attracts consumers to particular retail stores and motivates them to purchase certain new or established products. A **trade sales promotion method** encourages wholesalers and retailers to stock and actively promote a manufacturer's product. Incentives such as money, merchandise, marketing assistance, or gifts are commonly awarded to resellers who buy products or respond positively in other ways. Of the combined dollars spent on sales promotion and advertising in 1998, 50 percent was spent on trade promotions, 24 percent on consumer promotions, and 26 percent on advertising.[15]

consumer sales promotion method a sales promotion method designed to attract consumers to particular retail stores and to motivate them to purchase certain new or established products

trade sales promotion method a sales promotion method designed to encourage wholesalers and retailers to stock and actively promote a manufacturer's product

A number of factors enter into marketing decisions about which and how many sales promotion methods to use. Of greatest importance are the objectives of the promotional effort. Product characteristics—size, weight, cost, durability, uses, features, and hazards—and target market profiles—age, gender, income, location, density, usage rate, and buying patterns—must likewise be considered. Distribution channels and availability of appropriate resellers also influence the choice of sales promotion methods, as do the competitive and regulatory forces in the environment. Let's now discuss a few important sales promotion methods.

Rebates A **rebate** is a return of part of the purchase price of a product. Usually the refund is offered by the producer to consumers who send in a coupon along with a specific proof of purchase. Rebating is a relatively low-cost promotional method. Once used mainly to help launch new product items, it is now applied to a wide variety of products.

rebate a return of part of the purchase price of a product

Talking Technology

Sampling Builds Online Beauty Business

SELLING PRIVATE-BRAND PRODUCTS CAN be extremely challenging for a start-up Internet retailer because people in the target market are not familiar with the new brand and can't see or handle the products in local stores. So when Katherine Legatos and Amy Ryberg started Ingredients.com (http://www.ingredients.com), they decided to use samples to get their line of herb-infused beauty and personal care products into the hands of potential customers.

Leading up the site's launch, the kickoff campaign invited women to sign up for free samples of bath and body products. Once the site opened for business, web surfers registered through the Ingredients.com home page to receive their free samples. During the first two months of operation, Legatos and Ryberg spent $1.2 million sending samples to more than 100,000 people. Deals with complementary Internet retailers, such as women's clothing stores, also helped the company get its samples to the target audience. The result? About 75 percent of the orders received were from people who tried samples. Each shipment included at least one more sample, rewarding customers and encouraging them to try and then buy more products.

Now the company is taking its sampling promotion in another direction by placing samples of selected products, such as body lotion, in hotel rooms so noncustomers can try them out. In addition, the company is providing samples of its foot scrubs for distribution to participants in marathon races. To build brand recognition and widen distribution, Ingredients.com has also arranged to promote and sell its products through America Online, Microsoft Network, and other high-profile portals. As online sales grow and Ingredients.com expands, the cofounders plan to continue their sampling promotions as a way of gauging customer response to new products and bringing customers back to their site again and again.

coupon reduces the retail price of a particular item by a stated amount at the time of purchase

Coupons A **coupon** reduces the retail price of a particular item by a stated amount at the time of purchase. Coupons may be worth anywhere from a few cents to a few dollars. They are made available to customers through newspapers, magazines, direct mail, online, and shelf dispensers in stores. Billions of coupons are distributed annually. Of these, just under 2 percent are redeemed by consumers. The average value of a coupon increased from 54 cents in 1993 to 83 cents in 1998. About 58 percent of consumers use at least one coupon per month.[16] The largest single category of coupons is health and beauty aids, followed by prepared foods, frozen and refrigerated foods, cereals, and household products. Stores in some areas even deduct double or triple the value of manufacturers' coupons from the purchase price as a sales promotion technique of their own. Coupons may also offer free merchandise, either with or without an additional purchase of the product.

sample a free product given to customers to encourage trial

Samples A **sample** is a free product given to customers to encourage trial. Samples may be offered via online coupons, direct mail, or in stores. It is the most expensive sales promotion technique and while often used to promote new products, it can be used to promote established brands, too. The Almond Board of California supported its "Who's Your Nut?" promotion in Indianapolis, Indiana, with sampling in grocery stores.[17]

premium a gift that a producer offers the customer in return for buying its product

Premiums A **premium** is a gift that a producer offers the customer in return for buying its product. A producer of packaged foods may, for instance, offer consumers a cookbook as a premium. Premiums can be attached to or enclosed inside packages. Clearly Canadian attached free sample packs of sugarless Trident Advantage Gum with Baking Soda to the necks of its Clearly Canadian bottles.[18]

frequent-user incentive a program developed to reward customers who engage in repeat (frequent) purchases

Frequent-User Incentives A **frequent-user incentive** is a program developed to reward customers who engage in repeat (frequent) purchases. Such programs are commonly used by service businesses like hotels and auto rental agencies. Frequent-user incentives build customer loyalty. Examples of successful frequent-user incentives include airline frequent-flyer programs and Subway's Sub Club Cards. Subway gives customers card stamps with each purchase and free sandwiches when they turn in cards with the requisite number of stamps. There are several online organizations such as Netcentives,

MyPoints, RealTime Media, and Cybergold, that provide businesses with customer-loyalty incentive programs. Customers of businesses that use these programs are rewarded in several ways including cash, points for prizes, and airline miles.[19]

Trade show. The International Boat Show in Florida is an example of a trade show. Some trade shows are open to dealers only, while others are open to the general public.

Point-of-Purchase Displays A **point-of-purchase display** is promotional material placed within a retail store. The display is usually located near the product being promoted. It may actually hold merchandise (as do L'eggs hosiery displays) or inform customers about what the product offers and encourage them to buy it. Most point-of-purchase displays are prepared and set up by manufacturers and wholesalers. Kellogg recently created point of purchase materials for supermarkets to transform traditional cereal aisles into Breakfastland, which included attention getting overhead signs, shelving and interactive displays, and special counter signage.[20]

Trade Shows A **trade show** is an industrywide exhibit at which many sellers display their products. Some trade shows are organized exclusively for dealers—to permit manufacturers and wholesalers to show their latest lines to retailers. Others are promotions designed to stimulate consumer awareness and interest. Among the latter are boat shows, home shows, and flower shows put on each year in large cities. About 14 percent of total promotional dollars is spent on trade shows.[21]

point-of-purchase display promotional material placed within a retail store

trade show an industrywide exhibit at which many sellers display their products

buying allowance a temporary price reduction to resellers for purchasing specified quantities of a product

cooperative advertising an arrangement whereby a manufacturer agrees to pay a certain amount of the retailer's media cost for advertising the manufacturer's product

Buying Allowances A **buying allowance** is a temporary price reduction to resellers for purchasing specified quantities of a product. For example, a laundry detergent manufacturer might give retailers $1 for each case of detergent purchased. A buying allowance may serve as an incentive to resellers to handle new products and may stimulate purchase of items in large quantities. While the buying allowance is simple, straightforward, and easily administered, competitors can respond quickly by offering a better buying allowance.

Cooperative Advertising **Cooperative advertising** is an arrangement whereby a manufacturer agrees to pay a certain amount of the retailer's media cost for advertising the manufacturer's products. To be reimbursed, a retailer must show proof that the advertisements actually did appear. A large percentage of all cooperative advertising dollars are spent on newspaper advertisements. Not all retailers take advantage of available cooperative advertising offers because they cannot afford to advertise or do not choose to do so.

Public Relations

LEARNING OBJECTIVE

8 Understand the types and uses of public relations.

As noted earlier, public relations is a broad set of communication activities used to create and maintain favorable relationships between an organization and various public groups, both internal and external. These groups can include customers, employees, stockholders, suppliers, educators, the media, government officials, and society in general.

EXPLORING BUSINESS

Microsoft Reshapes Its Public Image

IS MICROSOFT AN OVER-AGGRESSIVE monopoly or a consumer-friendly, high-tech innovator? The government holds the first view, as shown during a recent U.S. Department of Justice antitrust trial. Although Microsoft is continuing its legal battle against the trial's guilty verdict and the subsequent ruling to break the company in half, repairing Microsoft's severely damaged reputation is a major challenge for its public relations experts.

One priority has been to spotlight Microsoft's software innovations and stress the benefits for customers. To do this, the company used a series of low-key television and print advertisements featuring Bill Gates, Microsoft's chairman, and Steve Ballmer, the CEO, talking about how Microsoft products help people get things done at work and at home. "We view [the ads] as an opportunity to talk directly to our customers and policy makers," says the public affairs director.

The company's post-trial public relations strategy also builds on public interest in Bill Gates as the richest man in the world. Gates has devoted more time to public appearances at industry conferences and schools, where he can personally represent the company's views. In addition, he broke with the past by giving media interviews about nonbusiness topics such as his charitable contributions. This higher visibility shows off Gates's human side while polishing his image as a technology visionary.

Microsoft is particularly adept at using public relations to build excitement and advance demand for new products. Starting with a barrage of media coverage in the weeks leading up to an introduction, the blitz culminates with a series of launch-day events that create a buzz for weeks afterward. In contrast, Microsoft used to make charitable donations to causes such as Guide Dogs for the Blind with a lot less fanfare. Now the company has named a community affairs manager to build closer relations with charities and community groups and, in the process, call attention to Microsoft's socially-responsible activities. No matter what the future holds for Microsoft, its public relations strategy is proving to be a powerful tool in reshaping the company's public image.

Types of Public Relations Tools

Organizations use a variety of public relations tools to convey messages and to create images. Public relations professionals prepare written materials such as brochures, newsletters, company magazines, annual reports, and news releases. They also create corporate-identity materials such as logos, business cards, signs, and stationery. Speeches are another public relations tool. Speeches can affect an organization's image and must therefore convey the desired message clearly.

Source: Copyright 2000, USA TODAY. Reprinted with permission.

Another public relations tool is event sponsorship, in which a company pays for all or part of a special event such as a concert, sports competition, festival, or play. Sponsoring special events is an effective way for organizations to increase brand recognition and receive media coverage with comparatively little investment. Eastman Kodak's sponsorship of the Olympic games and Evian's sponsorship of a convention for gourmet food lovers are examples of event sponsorship, as is Best Buy's three-year sponsorship of RIF (Reading Is Fundamental) programs in Maryland, Massachusetts, Virginia, and California at a cost of $300,000. Last year, Best Buy provided 35,700 books to approximately 3,000 children in four states.[22]

Some public relations tools have traditionally been associated specifically with publicity, which is a part of public relations. **Publicity** is communication in news-story form about an organization, its products, or both. Publicity is transmitted through a mass medium, such as newspapers or radio, at no charge. Organizations use publicity to provide information about products; to announce new-product launches, expansions, or research; and to strengthen the company's image. Public relations personnel sometimes organize events, such as grand openings with prizes and celebrities, to create news stories about the company.

The most widely used type of publicity is the **news release.** It is generally one typed page of about 300 words provided by an organization to the media. The release includes the firm's name, address, phone number, and contact person. Table 16.2 lists some of the issues news releases can address. There are also several other kinds of publicity-based public relations tools. A **feature article,** which may run as long as 3,000 words, is usually written for inclusion in a particular publication. For example, a software firm might send an article about its new product to a computer magazine. A **captioned photograph,** a picture accompanied by a brief explanation, is an effective way to illustrate a new or improved product. A **press conference** allows invited media personnel to hear important news announcements and to receive supplementary textual materials and photographs. Finally, letters to the editor, special newspaper or magazine editorials, films, and tapes may be prepared and distributed to appropriate media for possible use.

publicity communication in news-story form about an organization, its products, or both

news release a typed page of about 300 words provided by an organization to the media as a form of publicity

feature article a piece (of up to 3,000 words) prepared by an organization for inclusion in a particular publication

captioned photograph a picture accompanied by a brief explanation

press conference a meeting at which invited media personnel hear important news announcements and receive supplementary textual materials and photographs

At times, a single type of public relations tool will be adequate for a promotion mix. At other times, one public relations tool will predominate in a mix. The specific types of public relations tools chosen depend on the composition of the target audience, the response of media personnel, the significance of the news item, and the nature and quantity of information to be communicated.

The Uses of Public Relations

Public relations can be used to promote people, places, activities, ideas, and even countries. Public relations focuses on enhancing the reputation of the total organization by making people aware of a company's products, brands, or activities and by creating specific company images such as innovativeness or dependability. For example, ice-cream maker Ben and Jerry's uses news stories and other public relations efforts to

table 16.2 Possible Issues for News Releases

Use of new information technology	Packaging changes
Support of a social cause	New products
Improved warranties	Creation of new software
Reports on industry conditions	Research developments
New uses for established products	Company's history and development
Product endorsements	Employment, production, and sales records
Winning of quality awards	Award of contracts
Company name changes	Opening of new markets
Interviews with company officials	Improvements in financial position
Improved distribution policies	Opening of an exhibit
Global business initiatives	History of a brand
Sponsorship of athletic events	Winners of company contests
Visits by celebrities	Logo changes
Reports of new discoveries	Speeches of top management
Innovative marketing activities	Merit awards to the organization
Economic forecasts	Anniversaries of inventions

reinforce its reputation as a socially responsible company. By getting the media to report on a firm's accomplishments, public relations helps a company maintain positive public visibility. Effective management of public relations efforts can also reduce the unfavorable effects of negative events.

Promotion Planning

LEARNING OBJECTIVE

9 Identify the factors that influence the selection of promotion mix ingredients.

promotional campaign a plan for combining and using the four promotional methods—advertising, personal selling, sales promotion, and publicity—in a particular promotion mix to achieve one or more marketing goals

A **promotional campaign** is a plan for combining and using the four promotional methods—advertising, personal selling, sales promotion, and public relations—in a particular promotion mix to achieve one or more marketing goals. When selecting promotional methods to include in promotion mixes, it is important to coordinate promotional elements to maximize total informational and promotional impact on customers. Integrated marketing communication requires a marketer to look at the broad perspective when planning promotional programs and coordinating the total set of communication functions.

In planning a promotional campaign, marketers must answer these two questions:

- What will be the role of promotion in the overall marketing mix?
- To what extent will each promotional method be used in the promotion mix?

The answer to the first question depends on the firm's marketing objectives, since the role of each element of the marketing mix—product, price, distribution, and promotion—depends on these detailed versions of the firm's marketing goals. The answer to the second question depends on the answer to the first, as well as on the target market.

Promotion and Marketing Objectives

Promotion is naturally better suited to certain marketing objectives than to others. For example, promotion can do little to further a marketing objective such as "reduce delivery time by one-third." It can, however, be used to inform customers that delivery is faster. Let's consider some objectives that *would* require the use of promotion as a primary ingredient of the marketing mix.

Providing Information This is, of course, the main function of promotion. It may be used to communicate to target markets the availability of new products or product features. It may alert them to special offers or give the locations of retailers that carry the firm's products. In other words, promotion can be used to enhance the effectiveness of each of the other ingredients of the marketing mix.

Increasing Market Share Promotion can be used to convince new customers to try a product, while maintaining the product loyalty of established customers. Comparative advertising, for example, is directed mainly at those who might—but presently do not—use a particular product. Advertising that emphasizes the product's features also assures those who *do* use the product that they have made a smart choice.

Positioning the Product The sales of a product depend, to a great extent, on its competition. The stronger the competition, the more difficult it is to maintain or increase sales. For this reason, many firms go to great lengths to position their products in the marketplace. **Positioning** is the development of a product image in buyers' minds relative to the images they have of competing products.

positioning the development of a product image in buyers' minds relative to the images they have of competing products

Promotion is the prime positioning tool. A marketer can use promotion to position a brand away from competitors to avoid competition. Promotion may also be used to position one product directly against another product. For example, Coca-Cola and Pepsi position their products to compete head-to-head against each other.

Stabilizing Sales Special promotional efforts can be used to increase sales during slack periods, such as the "off season" for certain sports equipment. By stabilizing sales in this way, a firm can use its production facilities more effectively and reduce both capital costs and inventory costs. Promotion is also often used to increase the sales of products that are in the declining stage of their life cycle. The objective is to keep them going for a little while longer.

Developing the Promotion Mix

Once the role of promotion is established, the various methods of promotion may be combined in a promotional campaign. As in so many other areas of business, promotion planning begins with a set of specific objectives. The promotion mix is then designed to accomplish these objectives.

Marketers often use several promotion mixes simultaneously if a firm sells multiple products. The selection of promotion mix ingredients and the degree to which they are used depend on the organization's resources and objectives, the nature of the target market, the characteristics of the product, and the feasibility of various promotional methods.

The amount of promotional resources available in an organization influences the number and intensity of promotional methods that marketers can use. A firm with a limited budget for promotion will probably rely on personal selling, because the effectiveness of personal selling can be measured more easily than that of advertising. An organization's objectives also have an effect on its promotional activities. A company wishing to make a wide audience familiar with a new convenience item will probably depend heavily on advertising and sales promotion. If a company's objective is to communicate information to consumers—on the features of countertop appliances, for example—then the company may develop a promotion mix that includes some advertising, some sales promotion to attract consumers to stores, and much personal selling. The Internet is fast becoming an important promotional strategy. For example, best-selling author, spiritualist, and pioneer of alternative medicine Deepak Chopra has leveraged an Internet site called HowToKnowGod.com as a companion to help promote his book by the same name. People without access to the book but a connection to the Internet could read about the seven stages of God consciousness free. Chat rooms on Yahoo.com, Amazon.com, CNN.com, Borders.com, iVillage.com, and barnesandnoble.com with links to his site have helped launch the book onto the best-seller list.[23]

The size, geographic distribution, and socioeconomic characteristics of the target market play a part in the composition of a product's promotion mix. If the market is small, personal selling will probably be the most important element in the promotion mix. This is true of organizations that sell to small industrial markets and businesses that use only a few wholesalers to market their products. Companies that need to contact millions of potential customers, however, will emphasize sales promotion and advertising because these methods are relatively inexpensive. The age, income, and education of the target market will also influence the choice of promotion techniques. For example, with less-educated consumers, personal selling may be more effective than ads in newspapers or magazines.

In general, industrial products require a considerable amount of personal selling, whereas consumer goods depend on advertising. This is not true in every case, however. The price of the product also influences the composition of the promotion mix. Because consumers often want the advice of a salesperson on an expensive product, high-priced consumer goods may call for more personal selling. Similarly, advertising and sales promotion may be more crucial to marketers of seasonal items because having a year-round sales force is not always appropriate.

The cost and availability of promotional methods are important factors in the development of a promotion mix. Although national advertising and sales promotion activities are expensive, the cost per customer may be quite small if the campaign succeeds in reaching large numbers of people. In addition, local advertising outlets—newspapers, magazines, radio and television stations, and outdoor displays—may not be that costly for a small, local business. In some situations, a firm may find that no available advertising medium reaches the target market effectively.

This chapter concludes our discussion of marketing. In the next chapter, we begin our examination of information for business by discussing management information and computers.

RETURN TO Inside Business

BIG-BUDGET ADVERTISING CAMPAIGNS and high-profile sales promotion efforts, such as games and free toys, are helping McDonald's defend its market share in the United States and other countries. However, on rare occasions, a promotional offer can get out of hand, creating too much excitement and generating unwanted publicity because of fights and other problems. When McDonald's offered a limited number of miniature McTeddy Bears in Singapore, for instance, adults lined up for hours. But the crowds became unruly, and—as newspapers later reported—McDonald's had to hire security guards to maintain order after customers broke windows and traded punches over the toys.

The following year, when crowds again gathered in response to a promotion of Hello Kitty toy cats in Singapore, McDonald's changed the rules to prevent further problems. Instead of restricting the offer to one week per limited-edition toy, the chain allowed two weeks per toy. The stores also issued vouchers to be redeemed at larger, centrally located public sites where crowd control was easier, rather than offering the toys in McDonald's outlets. Finally, the chain showed its sensitivity to public opinion—and its promotional savvy—by apologizing in newspaper ads that included a coupon good for a discount on any McDonald's purchase.

Questions

1. What are the major components of McDonald's promotion mix?
2. What objectives might McDonald's have set for its teddy bear and cat toy promotions in Singapore? How did the resulting publicity affect the chain's ability to reach these objectives?

chapter Review

SUMMARY

1 Describe integrated marketing communications.

Integrated marketing communications is the coordination of promotion efforts to achieve maximum informational and persuasive impact on customers.

2 Understand the role of promotion.

Promotion is communication about an organization and its products that is intended to inform, persuade, or remind target market members. The major ingredients of a promotion mix are advertising, personal selling, sales promotion, and public relations. The role of promotion is to facilitate exchanges directly or indirectly and to help an organization maintain favorable relationships with groups in the marketing environment.

3 Explain the purposes of the three types of advertising.

Advertising is a paid, nonpersonal message communicated to a specific audience through a mass medium. Primary-demand advertising promotes the products of an entire industry rather than just a single brand. Selective demand advertising promotes a particular brand of product. Institutional advertising is image-building advertising for a firm.

4 Describe the advantages and disadvantages of the major advertising media.

The major advertising media are newspapers, magazines, direct mail, outdoor displays, television, radio, and the Internet. Television accounts for the largest share of advertising expenditures, with newspapers running a close second. Newspapers are relatively inexpensive compared with other media, reach only people in the market area, and are timely. Disadvantages include a short life span, poor color reproduction, and inability to target specific demographic groups. Magazine advertising can be quite prestigious. In addition, it can reach very specific market segments, can provide high-quality color reproduction, and has a relatively long life span. Major disadvantages are high cost and lack of timeliness. Direct mail is the most selective medium, and its effectiveness is easily measured. The disadvantage of direct mail is that if the mailing list is outdated and the advertisement does not reach the right people, then the campaign cannot be successful. Outdoor advertising allows marketers to focus on a particular geographic area and is relatively inexpensive. Messages, though, must be limited to a few words because the audience is usually moving. Television offers marketers the opportunity to broadcast a firm's message nationwide. However, television advertising can be very expensive, has a short life span, and the advent of cable channels and home videos has reduced the likelihood of reaching extremely large audiences. Radio advertising offers selectivity, can be less expensive than other media, and is flexible for scheduling purposes. Radio's limitations include no visual presentation and fragmented, small audiences. Benefits of using the Internet as an advertising medium include the growing number of people using the Internet, which means a growing audience, and the ability to precisely target specific customers. Disadvantages include the relatively simplistic nature of the ads that can be produced, especially in comparison with television, and the lack of evidence that Net browsers actually pay attention to the ads.

5 Identify the major steps in developing an advertising campaign.

An advertising campaign is developed in several stages. A firm's first task is to identify and analyze its advertising target. The goals of the campaign must also be clearly defined. Then the firm must develop the advertising platform, or statement of important selling points, and determine the size of the advertising budget. The next steps are to develop a media plan, to create the advertising message, and to execute the campaign. Finally, promotion managers must evaluate the effectiveness of the advertising efforts before, during, and/or after the campaign.

6 Recognize the various kinds of salespersons, the steps in the personal-selling process, and the major sales management tasks.

Personal selling is personal communication aimed at informing customers and persuading them to buy a firm's products. It is the most adaptable promotional method because the salesperson can modify the message to fit each buyer. Three major kinds of salepersons are order getters, order takers, and support personnel. The six steps in the personal-selling process are prospecting, approaching the prospect, making the presentation, answering objections, closing the sale, and following up. Sales managers are directly involved in setting sales force objectives; recruiting, selecting, and training salespersons; compensating and motivating sales personnel; creating sales territories; and evaluating sales performance.

7 Describe sales promotion objectives and methods.

Sales promotion is the use of activities and materials as direct inducements to customers and salespersons. The primary objective of sales promotion methods is to enhance and supplement other promotional methods. Methods of sales promotion include rebates, coupons, samples, premiums, frequent-user incentives, point-of-purchase displays, trade shows, buying allowances, and cooperative advertising.

8 Understand the types and uses of public relations.

Public relations is a broad set of communication activities used to create and maintain favorable relationships between an organization and various public groups, both internal and external. Organizations use a variety of public relations tools to convey messages and create images. Brochures, newsletters, company magazines, and annual reports are written public relations tools. Speeches, event sponsorship, and publicity are other public relations tools. Publicity is communication in news-story form about an organization, its products, or both. Types of publicity include news releases, feature articles, captioned photographs, and press conferences. Public relations can be used to promote people, places, activities, ideas, and even countries. It can be used to enhance the reputation of an organization and also to reduce the unfavorable effects of negative events.

9 Identify the factors that influence the selection of promotion mix ingredients.

A promotional campaign is a plan for combining and using advertising, personal selling, sales promotion, and publicity to achieve one or more marketing goals. Campaign objectives are developed from marketing objectives. Then the promotion mix is developed based on the organization's promotional resources and objectives, the nature of the target market, the product characteristics, and the feasibility of various promotional methods.

KEY TERMS

You should now be able to define and give an example relevant to each of the following terms:

promotion (449)
promotion mix (449)

integrated marketing communications (449)
advertising (451)
personal selling (451)
sales promotion (451)
public relations (451)
primary-demand advertising (452)
selective demand (or brand) advertising (452)
institutional advertising (452)
advertising media (453)
direct-mail advertising (453)
outdoor advertising (454)
infomercial (455)
advertising agency (458)
order getter (460)
creative selling (460)
order taker (460)
sales support personnel (460)
missionary salesperson (461)
trade salesperson (461)
technical salesperson (461)
consumer sales promotion method (463)
trade sales promotion method (463)
rebate (463)
coupon (464)
sample (464)
premium (464)
frequent-user incentive (464)
point-of-purchase display (465)
trade show (465)
buying allowance (465)
cooperative advertising (465)
publicity (467)
news release (467)
feature article (467)
captioned photograph (467)
press conference (467)
promotional campaign (468)
positioning (468)

REVIEW QUESTIONS

1. What is integrated marketing communications and why is it becoming increasingly accepted?
2. Identify and describe the major ingredients of a promotion mix.
3. What is the major role of promotion?
4. How are selective, institutional, and primary-demand advertising different from one another? Give an example of each.
5. List the four major print media and give an advantage and a disadvantage of each.
6. What types of firms use each of the two electronic media?
7. Outline the main steps involved in developing an advertising campaign.
8. Why would a firm with its own advertising department use an ad agency?
9. Identify and give examples of the three major types of salespersons.
10. Explain how each step in the personal-selling process leads to the next step.
11. What are the major tasks involved in managing a sales force?
12. What are the major differences between consumer and trade sales promotion methods? Give examples of each.
13. What is cooperative advertising? What sorts of firms use it?
14. What is the difference between publicity and public relations? What is the purpose of each?
15. Why is promotion particularly effective in positioning a product? In stabilizing or increasing sales?
16. What factors determine the specific promotion mix that a firm should use?

DISCUSSION QUESTIONS

1. Discuss the pros and cons of comparative advertising from the viewpoint of (a) the advertiser, (b) the advertiser's competitors, and (c) the target market.
2. Which kinds of advertising—in which media—influence you most? Why?
3. Which kinds of retail outlets or products require mainly order taking by salespeople?
4. A number of companies have shifted a portion of their promotion dollars from advertising to trade sales promotion methods? Why?
5. Why would a producer offer refunds or cents-off coupons rather than simply lowering the price of its products?
6. How can public relations efforts aimed at the general public help an organization?
7. Why do firms use event sponsorship?
8. What kind of promotion mix might be used to extend the life of a product that has entered the declining stage of its product life cycle?

VIDEO CASE

The Ups and Downs of Dot-Com Advertising

The adage, "What goes up must come down," is an appropriate description of the short but volatile history of dot-com spending on advertising. At the height of the dot-com advertising boom—1999 into 2000—Internet businesses flush with cash from investors spent lavishly on television advertising, in particular, to build their brands and attract web surfers. During the Super Bowl game in January, 2000, seventeen e-commerce companies vied for viewer attention with television commercials. Netpliance.com, maker of the i-opener web appliance, paid more than $3 million—the highest-ever Super Bowl ad price—for just one commercial during that game. Other dot-com Super Bowl advertisers that year included the recruitment web sites Monster.com and HotJobs.

Other media benefited from the influx of e-commerce ads as well. In the first half of 1999 alone, dot-com advertising in television, radio, print, and outdoor media totaled $775 million. That year, Priceline.com's high-profile television and radio ads featuring William Shatner made the name-your-own price web site a household name. Pet.com's sock puppet starred in a series of tongue-in-cheek television ads that made the puppet popular even though the site went out of business. So many dot-coms were crowding the airwaves that Amazon.com tripled its advertising spending during the crucial holiday shopping season at year-end 1999 to rise above the uproar.

By early 2001, the situation had changed dramatically. Only three e-commerce companies (the online brokerage firm E*Trade and the recruiting sites HotJobs and Monster.com) aired television commercials during the Super Bowl game in January 2001, amid a general fall-off in advertising spending among Internet businesses. The major reason for this downturn in advertising was money. Internet businesses were out of favor with investors during much of 2000, and they were spending heavily on technology and staffing. This left less cash for advertising, especially pricey television spots.

Another reason for the downturn in major media advertising was the increased clutter. "Two years ago, Yahoo! could advertise on TV and it would stand out," observed one analyst. "Now you watch a half-hour show and you'll see five or six [Internet] ads." Although dot-coms generally cut back on advertising spending to conserve cash, many sought out less traditional promotional techniques to keep their brands in front of target audiences.

For example, to stand out from the Internet crowd, the Ask Jeeves search site put its best foot forward in the Macy's Thanksgiving Day parade in New York, entering its 16-foot-tall float of the site's butler surrounded by books. Ask Jeeves also arranged to put stickers with questions on apples in New York City grocery stores, directing consumers to find the answers on the company's web site. Such unusual advertising is generally less costly than television advertising, but it can be risky. "Consumers are getting a little tired of ad messages," said a spokesperson for Ask Jeeves. "The point is not to inundate them every place they are, it's to surprise them but to do it in a way that isn't annoying."

Some dot-coms still see advertising as a vital expenditure for fueling ongoing sales. When HotJobs doubled its advertising spending, it saw revenue rise 66 percent. Charles Schwab, a major brokerage firm, also experienced a significant jump in revenue when it boosted advertising spending for its web operation. On the other hand, BizRate.com, which rates online businesses, started with a $10 million advertising campaign to build brand awareness and then switched to online advertising to build usage, because of its cost efficiency and the ability to track results. With advertising costs on the rise and online competition fiercer than ever, watch for more ups and downs in dot-com advertising.[24]

Questions

1. Is the Ask Jeeves campaign an example of selective-demand, institutional, or primary-demand advertising?
2. How might Ask Jeeves evaluate the effectiveness of its non-traditional promotion efforts?
3. What objectives would you suggest that BizRate.com set for its online advertising campaign?

Building Skills for Career Success

1. Exploring the Internet

As a promotional tool, the Internet stands alone among all media for cost-effectiveness and variety. A well-designed company web site can employ all the promotional strategies discussed in this chapter. It can provide consumers with advertising copy and sales representatives with personal-selling support services and information anytime on demand. A company can also use its web site to disseminate publicity about its products and activities.

In addition, many companies use the Internet for sales promotion. For instance, most newspapers and magazines provide sample articles in the hope that interested readers will eventually become subscribers. And virtually all software companies present demonstration editions of their products for potential customers to explore and test. Visit the text web site for updates to this exercise.

Assignment

1. Visit two of the following sites and examine the promotional activity taking place there. Note the sort of promotion being used and its location within the site.

   http://www.wsj.com
   http://www.businessweek.com
   http://www.forbes.com

2. Describe the promotional strategies exhibited on one of these sites.
3. What would you recommend the company do to improve the site?

2. Developing Critical Thinking Skills

Obviously, salespeople must know the products they are selling, but to give successful sales presentations, they must also know their competition. Armed with information about competing products, they are better able to field prospective customers' questions and objectives regarding their own products.

Assignment

1. Choose a product or service offered by one company and gather samples of the competitors' sales literature.
2. After examining the competitors' sales literature, answer the following questions:
   a. What type of literature do the competitors use to advertise their product or service? Do they use full-color brochures?

b. Do they use videotapes?
c. Do they offer giveaways or special discounts?

3. Compare the product or service you chose with what the competition is selling.
4. Compile a list of all the strengths and weaknesses you have discovered.

3. Building Team Skills

The cost of promotional methods is an important factor in a promotional campaign. Representatives who sell advertising space for magazines, newspapers, radio stations, and television stations can quote the price of the medium to the advertiser. The advertiser can then use cost per thousand (CPM) to compare the cost efficiency of vehicles in the same medium.

Assignment

1. Working in teams of five to seven, choose one of these media: local television stations, newspapers, or radio stations. You can choose magazines if your library has a copy of *Standard Rate and Data Service*.
2. Using the following equation, compare the cost per thousand of advertising in whatever local medium you chose:

$$\text{CPM} = \frac{\text{Price of the medium to the advertiser} \times 1000}{\text{Circulation}}$$

3. To compare different newspapers' rates, use the milline rate (the cost of a unit of advertising copy):

$$\text{Milline} = \frac{1{,}000{,}000}{\text{Circulation} \times \text{Line rate}}$$

4. Report your team's findings to the class.

4. Researching Different Careers

Most public libraries maintain relatively up-to-date collections of occupational or career materials. Begin your library search by looking at the computer listings under "vocations" or "careers" and then under specific fields. Check the library's periodicals section, where you will find trade and professional magazines and journals about specific occupations and industries. (*Business Periodicals Index*, published by H.W. Wilson, is an index to articles in major business publications. Arranged alphabetically, it is easy to use.) Familiarize yourself with the concerns and activities of potential employers by skimming their annual reports and other information they distribute to the public. You can also find occupational information on videocassettes, in kits, and through computerized information systems.

Assignment

1. Choose a specific occupation.
2. Conduct a library search of the occupation.
3. Prepare an annotated bibliography for the occupation.

5. Improving Communication Skills

The basis for a sales presentation is the prospect's needs. Successful salespeople divide their presentations into components, each of which is an important element in making the sale. Sales presentations typically include an introduction, definition of the need, benefits of the product or service, and the cost of the product or service. One of the most important components of the sales presentation is the demonstration. Commonly used presentation aids include the product itself, videotapes, slides, overheads, flip charts, and computers. A well-planned presentation turns prospects into customers.

Assignment

1. Choose a product that you can demonstrate.
2. Select the audiovisuals most appropriate for the demonstration.
3. Acting the part of a salesperson, explain step-by-step how the product works. Ask a classmate to play a skeptical customer who questions the reliability of the product. (This presentation may be videotaped or conducted before your classmates.)
4. Summarize what you learned about being a salesperson.

K'NEX Connects with Its Target Market

Walk into the lobby of the Pennsylvania headquarters of K'NEX Industries, Inc., and you will see a full-size motorcycle and a model of the Empire State Building, both made from colorful plastic parts. The people you'll see throughout the building making Ferris wheels, spaceships, and roller coasters with rods, connectors, pulleys, and tires are really researchers and engineers at work. In the highly competitive toy industry, where everyone dreams of launching the next Barbie and where today's Pokemon card is tomorrow's dust collector, K'NEX—the maker of innovative plastic construction toys for children five and older—has found a niche. With annual sales of over $120 million in forty-four countries, it is the world's number two construction-toy company. According to K'NEX's founder Joel Glickman, his company's focus on customers has been its key to success.

Inventing Inventive Toys

In 1988 Glickman was sitting at a table at a wedding reception bending colored plastic drinking straws and connecting them to make geometric shapes. Out of this preoccupation came K'NEX. Relying on his background in the plastics industry, Glickman perfected his designs, creating sturdy, brightly colored plastic components. After trying to sell the idea to established toy marketers like Mattel and Hasbro, and receiving only rejections, Glickman and his associates decided to get into the toy business themselves. In less than two years, what had begun as a way to avoid dancing at a wedding turned into K'NEX. Instead of showing drawings or prototypes to toy retailers, K'NEX created and packaged actual products. Toys "R" Us, K Mart, and Target all signed up to test market K'NEX toys in Philadelphia and Detroit.

Having started with just one set of twenty-two multifunctional pieces, K'NEX now markets dozens of products. With names like "Fun Park Rides," "K'NEXosaurus," and "Wild Wheelies," K'NEX toys range in price from $1.99 to over $100. Knowing that construction toys that move are more exciting than immobile ones, K'NEX always builds motion into its designs. The earliest sets were powered by rubber bands, cranks, and gears. Later sets featured plug-in electric motors, battery power, and solar power.

K'NEX recognizes that it must continually modify its toys to keep them engaging. By monitoring its competitors and identifying what its customers like, the toy maker learns what to change and what to add. K'NEX always knows what competitors, such as Lego and Mattel, are doing—where they are advertising, what new products they are launching, what tie-ins they have—and then adjusts its own products and strategies. For example, K'NEX asked itself what Lego, the world's number one construction-toy maker, had that K'NEX didn't. The answer was themed sets and human figures, so K'NEX introduced products such as "Planetary Rovers," "Crater Runner," and "Ultrabots," outer space sets with alien invaders and vehicles.

Marketing to Children and Gift-Givers

K'NEX customers are children aged five to twelve and the parents, grandparents, and friends who give the construction toys as gifts. To learn what these customers want, K'NEX conducts focus groups, each comprised of five to ten children who experiment with pieces and finished toys. A moderator guides participants through professionally developed questionnaires, and the information that results helps K'NEX revise and enhance its toys. The focus groups assess building instructions for age-appropriateness, readability, and errors and test the effectiveness of packaging and advertising. K'NEX also uses an online panel of customers to evaluate new product ideas. From this research have come such product ideas as smaller, more modestly priced kits, toys for children older than ten, more detailed and color-coded instructions, and many other product and marketing innovations.

Glickman tells people that inventing K'NEX toys was the easy part of starting his business and that building a company around it was the hardest. He acknowledges that K'NEX's multimillion dollar media budget, sales promotion, and intensive public relations efforts have contributed to his company's success. For example, K'NEX has been successful in stimulating impulse purchases through the use of point-of-purchase displays. A gigantic display of 3,500 K'NEX pieces with colorful, rolling balls has "stopped pedestrians in their tracks," according to the marketing director of a major British toy chain. The company has also arranged to have its products serve as premiums for Shell Oil, Pizza Hut, Tetley Group, and other companies. In Belgium, Shell gas stations gave away packages of K'NEX construction pieces with each fill-up. "Getting 1.5 million packs into the hands of existing and new consumers is far more effective than 30 seconds on the telly," observes the head of K'NEX International. Still, commercials play an important role in the firm's strategy to build its brand and combat competition from computer games and other toys by showing the fun of building.

Distribution is a pivotal part of the K'NEX marketing strategy. In the United States and Canada, K'NEX works so closely with the major toy chains that it has won awards, such as being chosen as the Toys "R" Us Vendor of the Year. To reach other markets, K'NEX set up a joint venture with Hasbro for international distribution. The company also posts a full product catalog on its web site and encourages online customer interaction through an e-mail club and periodic surveys. With many construction toys under development, K'NEX has also begun making Lincoln Logs toys under a brand license from Hasbro, allowing the company to expand its target market to youngsters aged three to five. But it is K'NEX's commitment to bringing a child's perspective to the marketing process that is making venerable construction toys such as Tinker Toys, Erector Sets, and Legos move over and make room on the shelf for those produced by K'NEX.

Questions

1. To what extent does K'NEX use the marketing concept? What are some specific examples of this use?
2. Why would K'NEX put more emphasis on selling through category killers rather than selling directly to customers through its web site?
3. While all the marketing environment forces could have an impact on K'NEX toys, which are likely to have the strongest effects and thus are most likely to be monitored by K'NEX management?
4. Why does the head of K'NEX International prefer sales promotion over television advertising?

Information for Business Strategy and Decision Making

Part VI

In this part of the book, we focus on information, one of the four essential resources on which all businesses rely. First, we discuss the different kinds of information necessary for effective decision making, where it can be found, how it is organized, and how it can be used throughout an organization by those who need it. We then examine the role of accounting and how financial information is collected, stored, processed and presented, and used to better control managerial decision making.

17 Acquiring, organizing, and using information

LEARNING OBJECTIVES

1. Understand how information is organized to help people make decisions.
2. Discuss management's information requirements.
3. Describe the four functions of a management information system.
4. Describe how business research is conducted.
5. Explain how the Internet, intranet, standards for communications, and web pages affect business today.
6. Discuss how managers and employees can use the Internet to communicate, assist the firm's sales force, train and recruit employees, and conduct financial activities.
7. Understand how to use applications software and the Internet to collect and distribute information.

want to have some fun the next time you explore the internet? well, just log on to iwon.com.

iWon.com Rewards Its Users

WANT TO HAVE SOME fun the next time you explore the Internet? Well, just log on to iWon.com! For every click an Internet user makes while checking their e-mail, obtaining current news, weather, or sports' scores, tracking the value of their investments, scanning horoscopes, using a search engine, or shopping online, users qualify to win big bucks. The more you use iWon.com, the more chances you collect—up to 100 per day, and the greater your chances of winning. Entries are free, and you can even track your chances of winning using iWon.com's real-time tally that appears at the top of each screen.

The iWon.com web site is capitalizing on the public's passion for lotteries, sweepstakes, and high-stake game shows by luring their visitors with cash prizes. This web site is basically a portal or gateway to the Internet like Yahoo!, Excite, and AOL, but with a gimmick. It gives away a lot of money—$10,000 a day to one lucky Internet user. Internet users can also qualify for a monthly prize of $1 million, and a yearly grand prize of $10 million paid to a lucky winner on April 15—income tax day. In addition, Internet users can also win noncash prizes with the iWon Prize Machine. It is even possible to win prizes by using iWon.com's three-tiered "Refer-A-Friend" program which gives a bonus if a major cash prize is awarded to someone in the user's referral network. Through September, 2000, more than $25 million had been given away in prizes.

On April 17, 2000 (income tax day), the first iWon.com Annual $10 Million Giveaway was broadcast live on the CBS television network. Four iWon.com finalists appeared on the program. Three major prizes were awarded to runners-up—the March monthly $1 million prize, a Mercedes-Benz SLK-Class convertible, and a seven-day trip for four to Hawaii plus $25,000 in spending money. The winner of the $10 million grand prize, Lee Truong, a first-generation Vietnamese-American, of San Jose, California, said through tears of joy, "I am stunned that I won $10 million for doing something I would have been doing anyway."

But iWon.com is more than just a business that gives away money and prizes. After all, this firm must generate revenues to not only finance its give-away promotions, but also pay the typical expenses that all business firms incur in day-to-day operations and hopefully earn a profit for investors. IWon.com, like many high-tech companies, generates revenues by selling advertising space that is then viewed by its users. Simply put, the more users, the more a company can charge for its advertising. While a simple concept, iWon.com must compete in a very competitive market. It does so by offering Internet users a quick and efficient method to access up-to-date information. The factors of improved customer satisfaction, ease of access, reliability, and security features also help guarantee that users will continue to return to the iWon.com web site. And, the firms that pay for advertising on Internet sites like iWon.com know that in order to increase their chances of winning, web surfers will click, click, and click again on those ad banners. They also know surfers spend more time at a site if the ad-bearing page is also linked to giveaways, contests, and games of chance. This approach to Internet advertising has become the fastest-growing segment of the consumer Internet.

The idea for iWon.com was created when William Daugherty, then a senior vice president for the National Basketball Association, and Jonas Steinman, then a general partner at Chase Capital Partners, a globally diversified, multibillion dollar private equity mutual fund, got together over a lunch which became a brainstorming session to develop ideas for new high-tech businesses. After raising more than $100 million in initial capital, these two executives left their jobs and launched the iWon.com web site on October 5, 1999. Four months later they secured an additional $100 million from private investors. More importantly, in just six months, iWon.com went from zero visitors to more than 11 million a month, and it became the fastest-growing web site in the history of the Internet. Today, iWon.com attracts one out of every nine people who visit the web from work, and one out of every ten people who visit the web from home. In June of 2000, the cofounders and co-CEO's were awarded the Ernst & Young Entrepreneur of the Year Award for their ability to grow their company from a concept to a business far surpassing others in the industry. *For more information on how to win prizes, sweepstakes rules, or to access all the services provided by this Internet company, go to iWon.com.*[1]

Internet users are enthralled with the idea of winning a bundle of money for staying online at iWon.com. And because of rapid increases in its number of users, iWon.com has been able to attract advertisers who are willing to spend more money on advertising. Major advertisers know that more users and increased user time translate into increased sales. But to survive in this very competitive industry, companies like iWon.com have to be good at what they do. With so much competition, can iWon.com keep up with or surpass the larger and more recognized Internet search engines? One of its chief competitors, Yahoo!, has links to sixteen news organizations and provides access to thousands of newspapers and magazines *and* has a loyal customer base. Excite.com provides users with links to five major automobile sites while iWon.com has one link to Autoweb.com. In the personal finance area, iWon has some of the same tools as AOL and Yahoo!, but according to many Internet users, it lacks the range and depth of investment research. And yet, iWon.com knows that it must continue to offer new services and provide better access to information if it is to continue its unheard of growth.

In this chapter, we examine the nature of information, how it is related to decision making and risk, and how it is organized and distributed within the firm. Next we look at business research and methods used to acquire information. Finally we will examine the way the Internet and communication technologies allow the firm to both acquire and distribute information globally to both employees and outsiders interested in the company.

The Nature of Information

As we noted in Chapter 1, information is one of the four major resources (along with material, human, and financial resources) managers must have to operate a business. While a successful business uses all four resources efficiently, it is information that helps managers reduce risk when making a decision.

Information and Risk

The more information a manager has, the less risk there is that a decision will be incorrect; theoretically, with accurate and complete information, there is no risk whatsoever. On the other hand, a decision made without any information is a gamble. These two extreme situations are rare in business. For the most part, business decision makers see themselves located some place between either extreme. As illustrated in Figure 17.1, when the amount of available information is high, there is less risk; when the amount of available information is low, there is more risk.

For example, suppose a marketing manager for Procter & Gamble responsible for the promotion of a well-known shampoo like Pantene Pro-V has called a meeting of her department team to consider the selection of a new magazine advertisement to

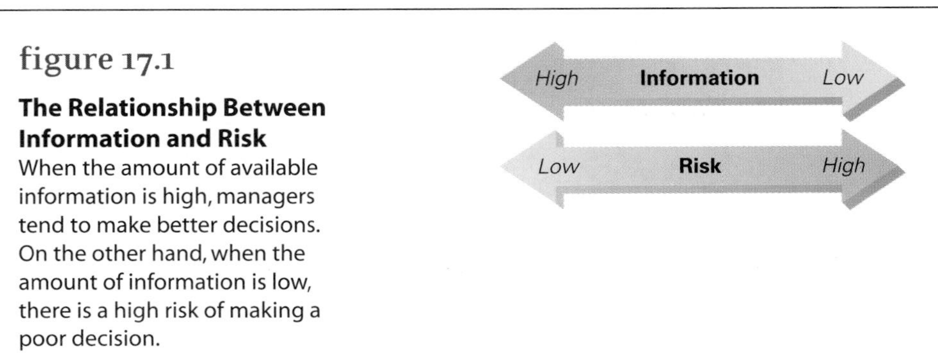

figure 17.1

The Relationship Between Information and Risk

When the amount of available information is high, managers tend to make better decisions. On the other hand, when the amount of information is low, there is a high risk of making a poor decision.

replace a current one. The company's advertising agency has submitted two new advertisements in sealed envelopes. Neither the manager nor any of her team has seen them before. Only one selection will be made for the new advertising campaign. Which advertisement should be chosen?

Without any further information available to the group, any selection is equally risky, and the team might as well make the decision by flipping a coin. If, however, team members were allowed to open the envelopes and examine the advertisements, they would have more information with which to form an opinion and thereby make an informed recommendation. If in addition to allowing them to examine the advertisements, the marketing manager circulated a report detailing the options and general reaction of a group of target consumers toward each of the two advertisements, the team would have even more information to work with.

Information, when understood properly, produces knowledge and empowers managers and employees to make better decisions. To know what to do in a particular situation, people need information to guide their behavior. Without correct and timely information, individual performance will be undermined and, consequently, so will the performance of the entire organization.

If having more information reduces risk and increases the chance of making a good decision then having all the information available changes everything. According to Forrester Research Inc., the Internet auction giant e-Bay controls about 85 percent of what is estimated to be a $3.3 billion market for trade between individual buyers and sellers. Given the size of e-Bay, many individuals would not even bother to check around other auction sites for what might be a better deal on the item they are interested in buying. To provide individuals with a method of comparing prices on different auction web sites, Bidder's Edge Inc. of Burlington, Massachusetts, has developed software that will search sites and report back to the user. To protect its competitive advantage in the market, e-Bay first tried to buy Bidder's Edge and after failing took court action to prevent its software from scanning e-Bay's site. The more important basic issue is whether a web site owner can arbitrarily deny access to someone or charge them for leaving with information of value to someone else.[2]

Information Rules

LEARNING OBJECTIVE

1 Understand how information is organized to help people make decisions.

Business research continues to show that discounts influence almost all car buyers. Simply put, if dealers lower their prices, they'll sell more cars. This relationship between buyer behavior and price can be thought of as a general *information rule*, which will usually correctly guide marketing decision makers. A rule like this emerges when business research confirms the same results each time it studies the same or a similar set of circumstances. The experienced businessperson often makes decisions using information rules to quicken and simplify all kinds of tasks. Because of the volume of information they receive each day and their need to make decisions on a daily basis, businesspeople try to accumulate information rules to shorten the time spent analyzing choices.

Similarly, consumers use information rules to help them make purchasing decisions. Research on consumer behavior suggests that buyers will attempt to simplify a complex decision-making process by considering only a few critical determining factors, such as the brand name of the product, the warranty, or perhaps the price.

Information rules are the highest order of information organization and structure. They are the "great simplifiers" for all decision makers. Business research is continuously on the lookout for new rules that can be put to good use and discrediting old ones that are no longer valid. This ongoing process is necessary because business conditions rarely stay the same for very long.

Information Organization and Structure

Many people use the terms *data* and *information* interchangeably, but the two differ in important ways. **Data** are numerical or verbal descriptions that usually result from some sort of measurement. (The word *data* is plural; the singular form is *datum*.) Your

data numerical or verbal descriptions that usually result from some sort of measurement

current wage level, the amount of last year's after-tax profit for Compaq Computers, and the current retail prices of Honda automobiles are all data. Most people think of data as being numerical only, but they can be nonnumerical as well. A description of an individual as a "tall, athletic person with short, dark hair" would certainly qualify as data.

Information is data presented in a form useful for a specific purpose. Suppose a human resources manager wants to compare the wages paid to male and female employees over a period of seven years. The manager might begin with a stack of computer printouts listing every person employed by the firm, along with each employee's current and past wages. The manager would be hard-pressed to make any sense of all the names and numbers. Such printouts consist of data rather than information.

Now suppose the manager uses a computer to graph the average wages paid to men and to women in each of the seven years. As Figure 17.2 on page 483 shows, the result is information because the manager can use it for the purpose at hand—to compare wages paid to men with those paid to women over the seven-year period. When summarized in the graph, the wage data from the printouts become information.

Large sets of data often must be summarized if they are to be useful, but this is not always the case. If the manager in our example had wanted to know only the wage history of a specific employee, that information would be contained in the original computer printout. That is, the data (the employee's name and wage history) would already be in the most useful form for the manager's purpose; they would need no further processing.

She reads customers' minds. Each month, Alissa Kozuh, editor of Nordstrom.com, analyzes *data* consisting of more than 45,000 words that customers enter into the firm's search engine. The resulting *information* enables Kozuh to tweak the search engine so that customers are more effectively guided to the merchandise they are seeking. These improvements have helped to increase the firm's online sales.

The average company maintains a great deal of data that can be transformed into information. Among these data are records pertaining to personnel, inventory, sales, and accounting. Often, each type of data is stored in individual departments within an organization. In a large organization, the data can be more effectively used when it is organized into a **database**. A database is a single collection of data stored in one place that can be used by people throughout an organization to make decisions. In addition to just storing data, the organization must establish procedures for gathering, updating, and processing facts in the database. Today, most companies have several databases which form the foundation for a management information system.

The Management Information System

information data presented in a form useful for a specific purpose

database a single collection of data stored in one place that can be used by people throughout an organization to make decisions

management information system (MIS) a system that provides managers with the information they need to perform their jobs as effectively as possible

Where do managers get the information they need? In many organizations, the answer lies in a **management information system (MIS)**. An MIS is a system that provides managers with the information they need to perform their jobs as effectively as possible (see Figure 17.3). The purpose of an MIS is to distribute timely and useful information from both internal and external sources to the decision makers who need it. From simple e-mail to large, well-structured, user-friendly, and easily queried databases, today's typical management information system (MIS) is built around a computerized system of recordkeeping and communications software. (For a look at the kinds of problems that can develop with computerized systems of communication, read Examining Ethics.)

In many firms, the MIS is combined with a marketing information system (discussed in Chapter 13) so that it can provide information based on a wide variety of data. In fact, it makes little sense to have separate information systems for the various functional areas within a business. After all, the goal is to provide needed information to all managers.

Female Employees	Jan	Feb	March	April	May	June	July	Aug	Sept	Oct	Nov	Dec	Totals
Employee 1	1,150	1,150	1,150	1,150	1,150	1,150	1,200	1,200	1,200	1,200	1,200	1,300	$14,200
Employee 2	1,400	1,400	1,400	1,400	1,400	1,400	1,400	1,400	1,400	1,400	1,400	1,400	$16,800
Employee 3	1,600	1,600	1,600	1,600	1,800	1,800	1,800	1,800	1,800	1,900	1,900	1,900	$21,100
Employee 4	1,200	1,200	1,200	1,200	1,200	1,200	1,250	1,250	1,250	1,250	1,250	1,250	$14,700
Male Employees													
Employee 5	1,800	1,800	1,800	1,800	1,800	1,800	1,800	1,800	1,800	1,800	1,800	1,800	$21,600
Employee 6	2,000	2,000	2,000	2,000	2,000	2,000	2,100	2,100	2,100	2,100	2,100	2,100	$24,600
Employee 7	1,900	1,900	1,900	1,900	1,900	1,900	1,950	1,950	1,950	1,950	2,000	2,000	$23,200
Employee 8	2,400	2,400	2,400	2,400	2,400	2,400	2,500	2,500	2,500	2,500	2,500	2,500	$29,400

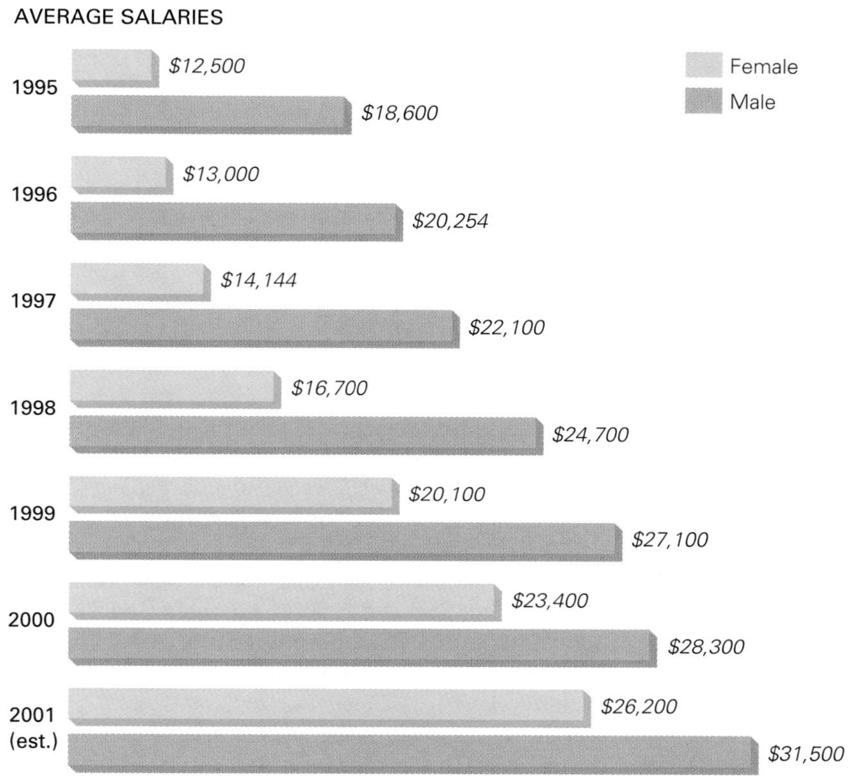

AVERAGE SALARIES

Female
Male

1995 $12,500 $18,600
1996 $13,000 $20,254
1997 $14,144 $22,100
1998 $16,700 $24,700
1999 $20,100 $27,100
2000 $23,400 $28,300
2001 (est.) $26,200 $31,500

figure 17.2

Data versus Information
Data are numerical or verbal descriptions that usually result from measurements; information is data presented in a form useful for a specific purpose. Thus, the computer printout of every employee's wages is data, whereas the graph that compares average wages year by year is information.

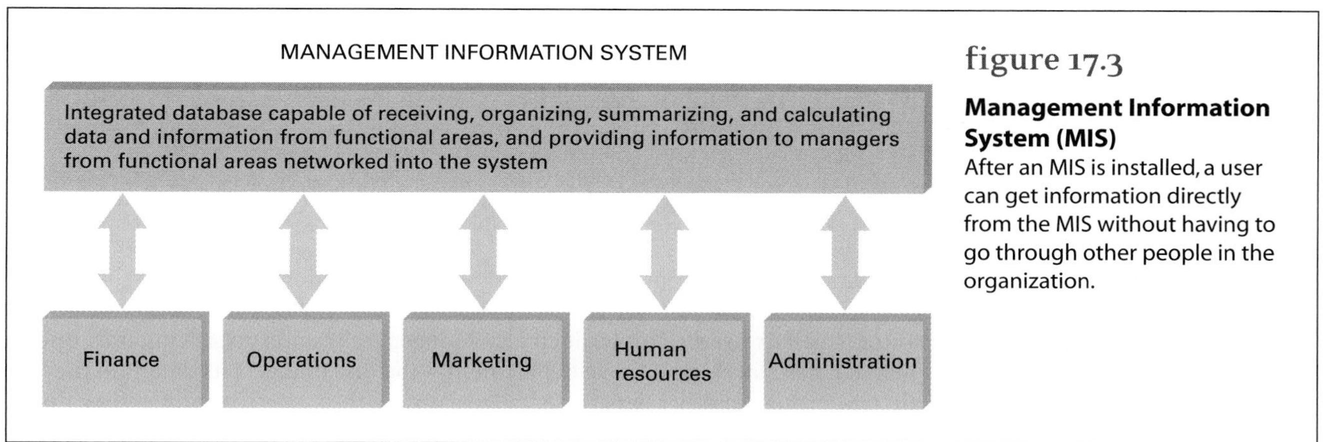

figure 17.3

Management Information System (MIS)
After an MIS is installed, a user can get information directly from the MIS without having to go through other people in the organization.

Source: *Management*, Sixth Edition, by Ricky W. Griffin. Copyright © 1999 by Houghton Mifflin Company. Adapted with permission.

For Carrier Corp., the web is pretty cool. According to Jonathan Ayers, president of Carrier Corp., after the firm encouraged suppliers to use its web-based procurement system last year, Carrier saved more than $100 million. What's more impressive is that during the same time period, Carrier generated more than $1 billion through its web-based sales efforts while improving customer satisfaction and profitability.

LEARNING OBJECTIVE

2 Discuss management's information requirements.

Managers' Information Requirements

Managers have to plan for the future, implement their plans in the present, and evaluate results against what has been accomplished in the past. Thus, they need access to information that summarizes future possibilities, the present situation, and past performance. Of course, the specific types of information they need depend on their area of management and on their level within the firm.

In Chapter 7, we identified five areas of management: finance, operations, marketing, human resources, and administration. Financial managers are obviously most concerned with their firm's finances. They study its debts and receivables, cash flow, future capitalization needs, financial ratios, and other accounting information. Of equal importance to financial managers is information about the present state of the economy, interest rates, and predictions of business conditions in the future.

Operations managers are concerned with present and future sales levels and with the availability and cost of the resources required to produce products and services. And they are involved with new-product planning. They must also keep abreast of any innovative production technology that might be useful to their firm.

Marketing managers need to have detailed information about their firm's product mix and the products offered by competitors. Such information includes prices and pricing strategies, new promotional campaigns, and products that competitors are test marketing. Information concerning target markets, current and projected market share, new and pending product legislation, and developments within channels of distribution is also important to marketing managers.

Human resources managers must be aware of anything that pertains to their firm's employees. Key examples include current wage levels and benefits packages both within their firm and in firms that compete for valuable employees, current legislation and court decisions that affect employment practices; union activities; and their firm's plans for growth, expansion, or mergers.

Administrative managers are responsible for the overall management of their organization. Thus, they are concerned with the coordination of information—just as they are concerned with the coordination of material, human, and financial resources. First, administrators must ensure that all employees have access to the information they need to do their jobs. And, second, they must ensure that the information is used in a consistent manner. Suppose, for example, that the operations group at General Electric is designing a plant that will open in five years and be devoted to manufacturing consumer electronic products. GE's management will want answers to many questions: Is the capacity of the plant consistent with marketing plans based on sales projections? Will human resources managers be able to staff the plant on the basis of employement forecasts? And do sales projections indicate enough income to cover the expected cost of the plant?

Size and Complexity of the System

A management information system (MIS) must be tailored to the needs of the organization it serves. In some firms, a tendency to save on initial costs may result in a system that is too small or overly simple. Such a system generally ends up serving only one or two management levels or a single department—the one that gets its data into the system first. Managers in other departments "give up" on the system as soon as they find it cannot accept or process their data. They either look elsewhere for information or do without.

Examining Ethics

Who Is Reading Your E-Mail?

8:00 A.M. IT'S THE BEGINNING OF another day at the office. You quickly read your e-mail. Reply to the routine messages. Click. Forward messages to others. Click. Delete *all* unwanted e-mails. Clic . . . Wait! What's this message? A personalized request from a well-known executive search firm? According to the e-mail message, "They have a prospective employer looking for someone with your expertise." Maybe, this is your big chance. OOPS! You bite and respond to their inquiry only to find yourself in the middle of a "cyber sting" set up by your own employer to test your integrity and loyalty to the company.

Think Before You Use Your Computer

This example may be extreme, but according to the American Management Association, more and more firms are monitoring electronic mail (often referred to as e-mail), computer files, and even telephone conversations. Although employees often feel that such monitoring is an invasion of privacy, employers feel they must identify disloyal employees and ensure that company equipment is not used for illegal purposes, visits to porn sites, or sexual harassment activities.

For years, a number of business firms have prohibited personal phone calls or personal e-mail messages during the regular workday. But as the average workweek for more and more employees has extended beyond 40 hours, many employers are more tolerant of employees using their Internet connections at work for personal use. But, before *you* use your office computer for personal communication, *always* check with your employer on company policies.

Guidelines for Sending E-Mail

E-mail is an easy, informal way to send messages to others and a convenient way to surf the Internet. But, before striking those keys remember the following:

- E-mail often creates misunderstandings because it does not reflect body language and visual contact that accompanies verbal communication.
- The convenience of communicating with "everyone" may cause your messages to be misdirected to people you never intended to receive it. You never know how many people will read them before they reach their destination.
- Keep your messages brief and to the point. The subject line should be descriptive of the message, so it doesn't get lost among the dozens of messages people receive every day.
- Send messages only when necessary and only to those who need to see them. Never discuss bad news, never criticize, and never discuss coworkers or personal issues. Censor your language. Remember that your words could come back and haunt you.

Issues to Consider

1. Should employers have the right to monitor their employee's e-mail? Why or why not?
2. How can you protect yourself from being caught in a "cyber sting"?

Almost as bad is an MIS that is too large or too complex for the organization. Unused capacity and complexity do nothing but increase the cost of owning and operating the system. In addition, a system that is difficult to use will probably not be used at all. Managers may find that it is easier to maintain their own system of gathering information. Or, again, they may try to operate without information that could be helpful in their decision making.

Obviously, much is expected of an effective MIS. Let's examine the functions an MIS must perform to provide the information managers need.

Functions of the Management Information System

LEARNING OBJECTIVE

3 Describe the four functions of a management information system.

To provide information, a management information system must perform four specific functions. It must collect data, store and then update the data, process the data into information, and present information to users (see Figure 17.4).

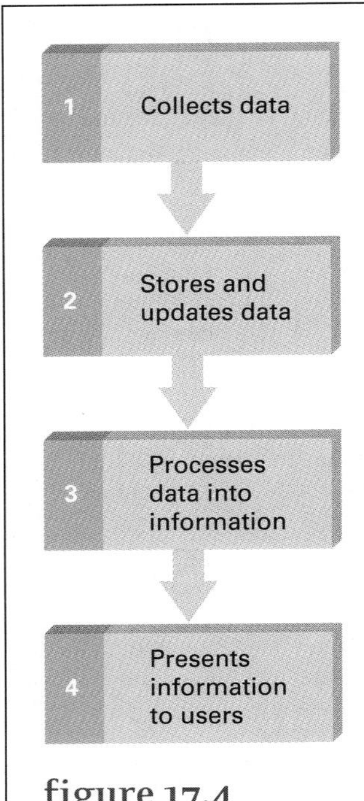

figure 17.4

Four MIS Functions
Every MIS must be tailored to the organization it serves and must perform four functions.

Collecting Data

An MIS must gather the data needed to establish the firm's *data bank*. The data bank should include all past and current data that may be useful in managing the firm. The data entered into the system must be *relevant* to the needs of the firm's managers. And, perhaps most important, the data must be *accurate*. Irrelevant data are simply useless; inaccurate data can be disastrous. The data can be obtained from within the firm and from outside sources.

Internal Sources of Data Typically, most of the data gathered for an MIS comes from internal sources. The most common internal sources of information are the managers themselves, company records, reports, and minutes of meetings.

Past and present accounting data can provide information about the firm's customers, creditors, and suppliers. Sales reports are a source of data on sales, pricing strategies, and the effectiveness of promotional campaigns. Human resources records are useful as a source of data on wage and benefits levels, hiring patterns, employee turnover, and other personnel variables.

Present and past production forecasts should also be included in the MIS, with data indicating how well these forecasts predicted actual events. Similarly, specific plans and management decisions—regarding capital expansion and new-product development, for example—should be incorporated into the system.

External Sources of Data External sources of management data include customers, suppliers, bankers, trade and financial publications, industry conferences, online computer services, and firms that specialize in gathering data for organizations. Like internal data, data from external sources take various forms, depending on the requirements of the firm and its managers.

A marketing research company may be used to acquire forecasts pertaining to product demand, consumer tastes, and other marketing variables. Suppliers are an excellent source of information about the future availability and costs of raw materials and component parts. Bankers can often provide valuable economic insights and projections. And the information furnished by trade publications and industry conferences is usually concerned as much with future projections as with present conditions.

Legal issues and court decisions that may affect a firm are occasionally discussed in local newspapers and, more often, in specialized publications such as the *Wall Street Journal, Fortune*, and *Business Week*. Government publications like the *Monthly Labor Review* and the *Federal Reserve Bulletin* are also quite useful as sources of external data, as are a number of online computer services.

Cautions in Collecting Data Three cautions should be observed in collecting data for an MIS. First, the cost of obtaining data from some external sources, such as marketing research firms, can be quite high. In all cases—whether the data come from internal or external sources—the cost of obtaining data should be weighed against the potential benefits that having the data will confer on the firm.

Second, although computers do not make mistakes, the people who use them can make or cause errors. Simply by pushing the wrong key on a computer keyboard, you can change an entire set of data, along with the information it contains. When data (or information) and your judgment disagree, always check the data.

Third, outdated or incomplete data usually yield inaccurate information. Data collection is an ongoing process. New data must be added to the data bank, either as they are obtained or in regularly scheduled updates.

Storing and Updating Data

A management information system must be capable of storing data until they are needed. An MIS must also be able to update stored data regularly to ensure that the information presented to managers is accurate, complete, and timely. Operations managers at Goodyear Tire & Rubber Company, for instance, cannot produce finished goods with last week's work-in-process inventory. They need to know what is available today.

Manual Updating To update stored data manually, an employee inserts the proper computer disk into a computer, locates the data to be changed, and inputs the new data. The computer automatically replaces the old data with the new.

The frequency with which data are updated depends on how fast they change and how often they are used. When it is vital to have current data, updating may occur daily. Otherwise, new data may be collected and held for updating at a certain time each week or perhaps each month.

Automatic Updating In automatic updating, the system itself updates the existing data bank as new data become available. The data bank, usually in the form of hard disks, is a permanent part of the computer. The computer automatically finds the proper disk and replaces the existing data with the new.

For example, Giant Food, a Maryland-based grocery-store chain, has cash registers that automatically transmit data on each item sold to a central computer. The computer adjusts the store's inventory records accordingly. At any time of the day, a manager can get precise, up-to-the-minute information on the inventory of every item the store sells. In some systems, the computer may even be programmed to reorder items whose inventories fall below some specified level.

A house of cards could be toppled by poor inventory records. For retailers like Hallmark, inventory records must be updated continually. Without this information, a store manager would not be able to determine how much merchandise to order, when to place new orders, or the value of a store's current inventory.

Processing Data

Data are collected, stored in an MIS, and updated under the assumption that they will be of use to managers. Some data are used in the form in which they are stored. This is especially true of verbal data—a legal opinion, for example. Other data require processing to extract, highlight, or summarize the information they contain. **Data processing** is the transformation of data into a form useful for a specific purpose. For verbal data, this processing consists mainly of extracting the pertinent material from storage and combining it into a report. For information on how MP3.com and Napster.com process and distribute a special type of information—music—read Adapting to Change.

data processing the transformation of data into a form useful for a specific purpose

Most business data, however, are in the form of numbers—large groups of numbers, such as daily sales volumes or annual earnings of workers in a particular city. Such groups of numbers are difficult to handle and to comprehend, but their contents can be summarized through the use of statistics.

Statistics as Summaries A **statistic** is a measure that summarizes a particular characteristic of an entire group of numbers. In this section, we discuss the most commonly used statistics, using the data given in Figure 17.5. Figure 17.5 contains only eleven items of data, which simplifies our discussion, but most business situations involve hundreds or even thousands of items. Fortunately, computers can be programmed to process such large volumes of numbers quickly. Managers are free to concern themselves mainly with the information that results.

statistic a measure that summarizes a particular characteristic of an entire group of numbers

frequency distribution a listing of the number of times each value appears in a set of data

The number of items in a set of data can be reduced by developing a frequency distribution. A **frequency distribution** is a listing of the number of times each value appears in the set of data. For the data in Figure 17.5, the frequency distribution is as follows:

Monthly salary	Frequency
$3,500	2
3,000	3
2,800	1
2,500	1
2,400	1
2,000	2
1,800	1

It is also possible to obtain a grouped frequency distribution:

Salary range	Frequency
$3,000—$3,500	5
2,500—2,999	2
2,000—2,499	3
1,500—1,999	1

Note that summarizing the data into a grouped frequency distribution has reduced the number of data items by approximately 65 percent.

Measures of Size and Dispersion The arithmetic mean, median, and mode are statistical measures used to describe the size of numerical values in a set of data. Perhaps the most familiar statistic is the arithmetic mean, commonly called the *average.*

arithmetic mean the sum of all the values of a set of data, divided by the number of items in the set

The **arithmetic mean** of a set of data is the sum of all the data values, divided by the number of items in the set. The sum of employee salaries given in Figure 17.5 is $29,500. The average (arithmetic mean) of employee salaries is $2,681.82 ($29,500 ÷ 11 = $2,681.82).

median the value at the exact middle of a set of data when the data are arranged in order

The **median** of a set of data is the value at the exact middle of the data when they are arranged in order. The data in Figure 17.5 are already arranged from the highest value to the lowest value. Their median is thus $2,800, which is exactly halfway between the top and bottom values.

figure 17.5

Statistics

A statistic is a measure that summarizes a particular characteristic for an entire group of numbers.

Rondex Corporation

Employee Salaries for April 2001

Employee	Monthly Salary
Thomas P. Ouimet	$ 3,500
Marina Ruiz	3,500
Ronald F. Washington	3,000
Sarah H. Abrams	3,000
Kathleen L. Norton	3,000
Martin C. Hess	2,800
Jane Chang	2,500
Margaret S. Fernandez	2,400
John F. O'Malley	2,000
Robert Miller	2,000
William G. Dorfmann	1,800
Total	$29,500

Adapting to change

Copyright Laws vs. the Internet

THROUGHOUT HISTORY, COPYRIGHT laws have protected "intellectual property" usually defined as text material, musical recordings, artwork, photographs, software, videos, films, and interactive multimedia programs. And while numerous copyright laws have been enacted, the Internet has created new problems for the authors, artists, and companies that sell products protected by copyright laws. As a result, artists that include Metallica and Dr. Dre along with companies that produce and distribute music and videos have filed lawsuits to protect copyrighted material against such web sites as MP3.com and Napster.com. While each web site works a little differently, users can obtain high-quality music from either site without paying for it in traditional retail outlets.

The MP3 System of Storing Music

Here's how the MP3 web site works. Customers purchase CDs from MP3. Then MP3 immediately downloads the music to the customers' computers and sends the actual CDs to customers by regular mail. MP3 also allows users to store music on its computer server. After opening an account, users must prove that they have purchased original CDs by inserting them into their computer's CD player. Once MP3 detects the disk, it places a digital version of the CD into the users' account that can be accessed by any computer from any location. When sued by Universal Music Group, MP3 argued that its business practices were legal because users had already paid for CDs and were simply making copies for personal use. Eventually, a U.S. federal judge disagreed stating that MP3 had willfully violated the copyright of Universal Music Group. Penalties could exceed $250 million.

The Napster System of Sharing Music

Similar copyright lawsuits were brought against Napster. In court testimony, Napster argued that it is an Internet CD-swapping group of 22 million members. Napster's technique is different from MP3's. Instead of storing music files on its servers, it only retains catalogs of music titles. A member registers with Napster by sending a list of music files available on his or her computer for others to download. A user wanting music files logs on, requests a title, Napster locates a user that registered the song, and the computers that belong to the two members connect. Napster also argued that its members have a constitutional right to trade music on a one-to-one basis. Although Napster lost its first round in federal court, it continues to operate while its appeal to the federal appellate court is considered.

Copyright Law: What's Next?

Is there an easy answer to the questions of who owns intellectual property and when does transfer of ownership occur? Probably not. Internet advocates don't condone piracy, but they are concerned about individuals' rights. On the other hand, the individuals and companies that own copyrights feel they should be compensated when someone uses their materials. Balancing copyright protection and freedom of information is a complex issue. Both sides do suggest that because of the vast reach of the Internet, changes in copyright laws are inevitable.

The **mode** of a set of data is the value that appears most frequently in the set. In Figure 17.5, the $3,000 monthly salary appears three times, more often than any other salary amount appears. Thus, $3,000 is the mode for this set of data.

mode the value that appears most frequently in a set of data

Although the arithmetic mean, or average, is the most commonly used statistical measure of size, it may be distorted by a few extremely small or large values in the set of data. In this case, a manager may want to rely on the median or mode, or both, to describe the values in the data set. Managers often use the median to describe dollar values or income levels when the arithmetic mean for the same numbers is distorted. In a similar fashion, marketers often use the mode to describe a firm's most successful or popular product when average sales amounts for a group of products would be inaccurate or misleading.

Another characteristic of the items within a set of values is the dispersion, or spread. The simplest measure of dispersion is the **range,** which is the difference between the highest value and the lowest value in a set of data. The range of the data in Figure 17.5 is $3,500 − $1,800 = $1,700.

range the difference between the highest value and the lowest value in a set of data

The smaller the range of the numbers in a set of data, the closer the values are to the mean—and, thus, the more effective the mean is as a measure of those values.

Other measures of dispersion used to describe business data are the *variance* and the *standard deviation*. These are somewhat more complicated than the range, and we shall not define or calculate them here. However, you should remember that larger values of both the variance and the standard deviation indicate a greater spread among the values of the data.

With the proper software, a computer can provide these and other statistical measures almost as fast as a user can ask for them. How they are used is then up to the manager. Although statistics provide information in a more manageable form than raw data, they can be interpreted incorrectly. Note, for example, that the average of the employee salaries given in Figure 17.5 is $2,681.82, yet not one of the employee salaries is exactly equal to that amount. This distinction between actual data and the statistics that describe them is an important one that you should never disregard.

Presenting Information

A management information system must be capable of presenting the information in a usable form. That is, the method of presentation—reports, tables, graphs, or charts, for example—must be appropriate for the information itself and for the uses to which it will be put.

Verbal information may be presented in list or paragraph form. Employees are often asked to prepare formal business reports. A typical business report includes (1) an introduction, (2) the body of the report, (3) the conclusions, and (4) the recommendations.

The *introduction*, which sets the stage for the remainder of the report, describes the problem to be studied in the report, identifies the research techniques that were used, and previews the material that will be presented in the report. The *body of the report* should objectively describe the facts that were discovered in the process of completing the report. The body should also provide a foundation for the conclusions and the recommendations. The *conclusions* are statements of fact that describe the findings contained in the report. They should be specific, practical, and based on the evidence contained in the report. The *recommendations* section presents suggestions on how the problem might be solved. Like the conclusions, recommendations should be specific, practical, and based on the evidence.

Visual and tabular displays may be necessary in a formal business report. For example, numerical information and combinations of numerical and verbal information may be easier to understand if presented in charts and tables.

Visual Displays

A visual display is a diagram that represents several items of information in a manner that makes comparison easier. The most accurate visual display is a *graph*, in which values are plotted to scale on a set of axes. Graphs are most effective for presenting information about one variable that changes with time (such as variations in sales figures for a business over a five- or ten-year period). Graphs tend to emphasize trends as well as peaks and low points in the value of the variable. Figure 17.6 illustrates examples of visual displays generated by a computer.

In a *bar chart*, each value is represented as a vertical or horizontal bar. The longer the bar, the greater the value. This type of display is useful for presenting values that are to be compared. The eye can quickly pick out the longest or shortest bar, or even those that seem to be of average size.

A *pie chart* is a circle ("pie") divided into "slices," each of which represents a different item. The circle represents the whole—for example, total sales. The size of each slice shows the contribution of that item to the whole. The larger the slice, the larger the contribution. By their nature, pie charts are most effective in displaying the relative size or importance of various items of information.

Tabular Displays

A tabular display is used to present verbal or numerical information in columns and rows. It is most useful in presenting information about two or more related variables (for example, variations in both sales volume and size of sales force by territory).

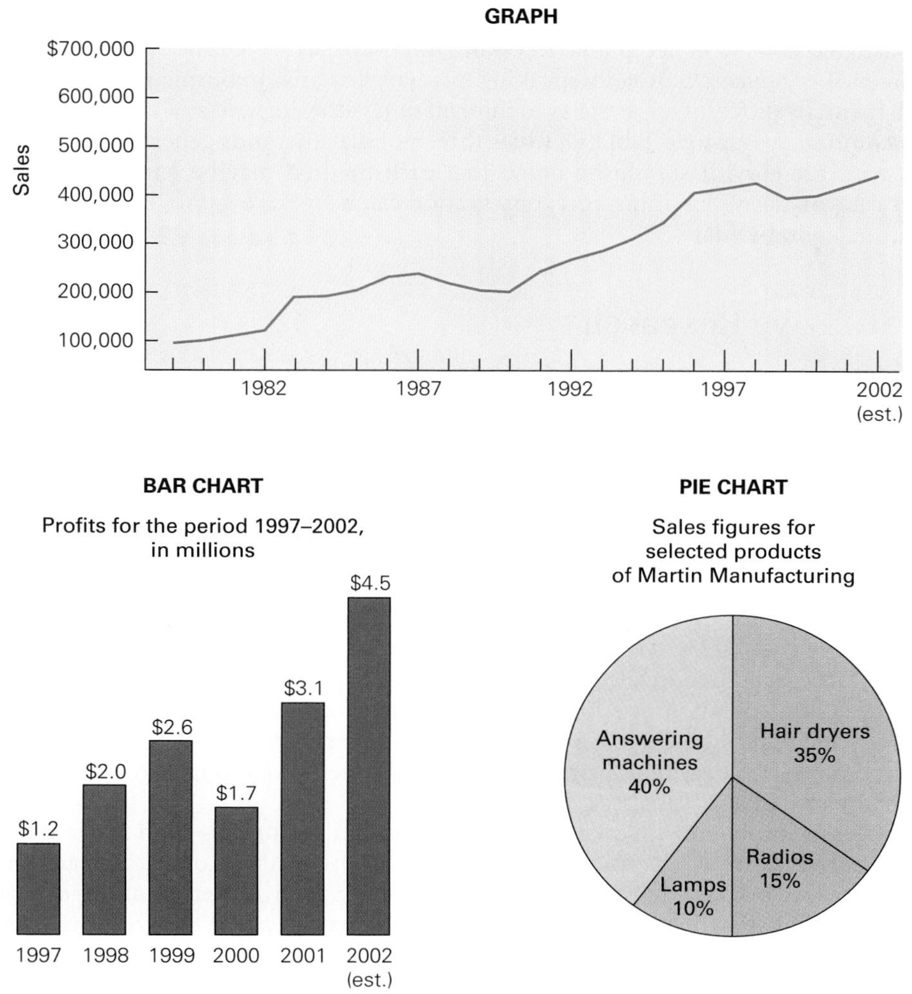

GRAPH

Sales

$700,000
600,000
500,000
400,000
300,000
200,000
100,000

1982 1987 1992 1997 2002 (est.)

BAR CHART

Profits for the period 1997–2002, in millions

1997	1998	1999	2000	2001	2002 (est.)
$1.2	$2.0	$2.6	$1.7	$3.1	$4.5

PIE CHART

Sales figures for selected products of Martin Manufacturing

Answering machines 40%
Hair dryers 35%
Radios 15%
Lamps 10%

figure 17.6

Typical Visual Displays Used in Business Presentations

Visual displays help businesspeople present information in a form that can be easily understood.

Tabular displays generally have less impact than visual displays. Moreover, the data contained in most two-column tables (like Figure 17.5) can be displayed visually. However, displaying the information that could be contained in a three-column table would require several bar or pie charts. In such cases, the items of information are easier to compare when they are presented in a table. Information that is to be manipulated—for example, to calculate loan payments—is also usually displayed in tabular form.

To better understand how a business finds all of the information it needs to establish an effective management information system, lets take a look at how business research is conducted.

Business Research

LEARNING OBJECTIVE

Describe how business research is conducted.

For information about important issues that affect their ability to make decisions, businesspeople read trade journals and professional publications, attend conferences, and talk to experts both inside and outside their firms. Gathering information in this way is referred to as *secondary research*, since the original research was done by someone else. For example, a business decision maker may read articles published in *Fortune* magazine, the *Wall Street Journal, Business Week*, or one of the academic publications from the American Marketing Association or the Academy of Management. When secondary sources do not provide businesspeople with sufficient information to make decisions with acceptable levels of risk, they may weigh the value of undertaking *primary research*. Broadly speaking, primary research in business employs two fundamentally different approaches to information gathering and analysis: *qualitative* and *quantitative research*. Table 17.1 lists three popular methods generally associated with each category. It should be noted that each method may be employed in the other category as well. For instance, observation can be used to gather both quantitative and qualitative data.

Qualitative Research

qualitative research a process that involves the descriptive or subjective reporting of information discovered by a researcher

Qualitative research involves the descriptive or subjective reporting of information discovered by a researcher. Generally, qualitative research is conducted in one of three ways: observation, interviews, or focus groups. For example, *observation* may be used to better understand retail shoppers' levels of satisfaction. The researcher might simply walk around a J.C. Penncy department store observing the facial expressions and mannerisms of shoppers. Several researchers may also study the behavior of the same group of subjects so that a consensus of opinion can develop. The researchers then create a formal report detailing each researcher's observations.

Business researchers also conduct *interviews* with individual subjects as well as group interviews. The latter, which usually involve six to ten subjects, are called *focus groups*. These methods involve discussion of questions or statements posed by the researcher or members of the focus group. The researcher observes the subjects and records their responses. Often, valuable information emerges from the group interaction and dialogue. Ideas that the researcher would never have thought to ask about in the first place can also arise.

The basic problem with qualitative research is that it is only as good as the ability of the analysts to "read" the situation under study. These methods of research are generally criticized because they rely on the researcher's subjective interpretations of reality. Given that two people observing the same event may interpret the event quite differently, it is little wonder that some researchers are hesitant to place too great a value on qualitative research without knowing the credentials of the researchers involved. Even then, many are reluctant to place too much confidence in the "reading" of behavior.

table 17.1 Methods Used by Business Researchers

A number of different methods can be used to conduct qualitative and quantitative research.

Qualitative Research Methods	Quantitative Research Methods
1. *Observation* The act of noting or recording something, such as the facial expressions of shoppers in a retail store	1. *Survey* A research method that relies on asking the same questions to a large number of people to elicit responses and information
2. *Interview* A conversation conducted by a researcher with an individual to elicit responses and information	2. *Experiment* A research method that involves the use of two or more groups of people to determine how people in each group react to different research variables
3. *Focus group* A conversation conducted by a researcher with a small group of people to elicit responses and information	3. *Content analysis* A research method that involves measuring particular items in a written publication, television program, or radio program

Quantitative Research

quantitative research a process that involves the collection of numerical data for analysis through a survey, experiment, or content analysis

Quantitative research involves the collection of numerical data for analysis through a *survey, experiment*, or *content analysis*. Many researchers believe that the statistical information that results from analysis of numerical data represents a more objective and unbiased picture than the subjective interpretation used in qualitative research. To gather numerical data through a *survey*, a researcher might approach shoppers in a Target discount store with a list of questions to determine their degree of satisfaction with store service, personnel, and atmosphere. A response scale is often used to simplify this process. For example, the researcher might ask customers to rank the following statements on a scale of 1 to 5, 5 indicating strong agreement with the statement; 4 indicating agreement; 3, indecision; 2, disagreement; and 1, strong disagreement:

1. The store personnel are friendly toward me when I shop.
2. The store personnel are informed about their merchandise.
3. The store's prices are competitive with prices charged by other retailers in the same area.

A trained researcher walking around with a clipboard can easily ask such questions and record customers' responses. But validity is a concern with this method, too. Some people might not want to speak to a stranger walking about with a clipboard; this may be especially true of customers who are strongly dissatisfied with store personnel. If that is the case, the data will be heavily biased. To avoid bias, researchers should use several different methods to test the validity of their data. Consistency among the test results can help alleviate management's concerns about the accuracy and validity of the research.

Experiments in business research typically involve comparison studies of two or more groups of people. Suppose managers at American Airlines want to know which of three television advertisements is the best choice for the company's target market. Researchers might select three groups of people believed to be representative of the target market. Each group would be shown a film of only one advertisement, and a variety of measurements would be taken after they finished watching it. If the managers were interested in knowing the level of "brand awareness" among the target market, and the level of brand awareness was significantly higher among one group than among the other two, they would likely select the advertisement that was shown to that group. Researchers might also measure brand preferences *before* each group watched the advertisement and then immediately *after*. In this way, the effect of watching the advertisement would be more clearly evident.

Content analysis is a simple technique that involves measuring particular items in a written publication, television program, or radio program. For instance, suppose footwear manufacturer Adidas wants to know the extent to which its competitors use a specific sports magazine to advertise their products. If the magazine is a popular choice among competitors, a marketing manager at Adidas might think it is appropriate to use the same magazine to reach the same type of customer. To determine how much competing manufacturers use the magazine, researchers would examine back issues of the magazine over the last twelve months and count the number and size of advertisements bought by competitors. Based on how much competitors are using the magazine, Adidas might decide to begin an advertising campaign in the same magazine.

Which Research Method to Choose

The decision about which research method or methods to use is often based on a combination of factors, including limitations on time and money, and the need or concern for accuracy and validity. In general, managers rely on the results of proven research methods until those methods no longer work well.

Nielsen Media Research has traditionally led the research industry in measuring the viewing behavior of television audiences. The firm uses a variety of techniques, including "smart boxes" placed on top of television sets in the households of paid participants. The boxes record not only the channels being viewed but also, through the use of sensors, the number of people in the room, whether they leave the room, and when they return. All these data are relayed through phone lines to a central computer that summarizes the data. Nielsen then sells the information to advertisers who want to know when their target audience watches television and, in particular, which programs they watch.

This costly technique is a relatively recent response to the problems associated with earlier methods, such as the diary reports written by people paid to record their television viewing habits. Because the smart-box technology can also determine when viewers are watching videotaped, prerecorded programs and are speeding ahead through advertisements, they solve a variety of research problems for advertisers who buy television time based on estimated audience numbers.

LEARNING OBJECTIVE

5 Explain how the Internet, intranet, standards for communications, and web pages affect business today.

The Internet and New Telecommunication Technologies

information society a society in which large groups of employees generate or depend on information to perform their jobs

We live in a rapidly changing **information society**—that is, a society in which large groups of employees generate or depend on information to perform their jobs. The need for more and better information will only continue to grow. Most experts predict that in the future computers will affect every aspect of our lives. Computers are already installed in cars, toys, and appliances. They are used by musicians and engineers, artists and bank tellers, students and teachers. In fact, it would be very difficult to find a person not affected in some way by a computer or the information generated by a computer.

Internet a worldwide network of computers linked through telecommunications

telecommunications the merger of computer and telephone technologies

Today, businesses are using the Internet to find and distribute information to global users. Currently, the primary business use of the Internet is gathering information about competitors' products, prices, and other business strategies readily available on corporate web sites and through online publications such as Bloomberg.com. And business use of the Internet is expected to increase dramatically in the next five to ten years. According to Jupiter Communications Research, expenditures for creating the building blocks for the information infrastructure on which the Internet will depend for web-based software and communications is estimated to grow from a $150 billion a year in 1999 to over $350 billion a year by the year 2003.[3] Clearly, the Internet is here to stay.

spotLight

Source: Copyright 2000, USA TODAY. Reprinted with permission.

The Internet and the Intranet

The **Internet** is a worldwide network of computers linked through **telecommunications**—that is, the merger of computer and telephone technologies. Enabling users around the world to talk with each other electronically, the Internet provides access to a huge array of information sources. It connects all kinds of networks, including small local area networks (LANs) as well as much larger ones. The Internet's most commonly used network for finding information is the *World Wide Web*. The web contains numerous *sites*—documents whose pages include text, graphics, and sound. To get on the Internet, you need a computer, modem, and *Internet service provider* (ISP), such as America Online, AT&T, or other telecommunications companies. As tools like cellular telephones, pagers, and fax machines have converged with computer technology, inexpensive telecommunications services have become the norm in business.

Consider the tools a salesperson for a clothing manufacturer might use during a typical sales call to a nationwide retailer like the Gap. After discussing the customer's needs, the salesperson opens her portable laptop computer and, using her own personal cellular phone or a convenient phone jack in the office, dials the local phone number of her Internet service provider. Once she is on the Internet, her *Web browser*—software that helps users navigate and move around the World Wide Web—automatically connects her to her firm's own web site.

The screen on the site's *home page* (first page) offers her several choices, including access to the firm's MIS. By clicking on the appropriate icons, or graphic symbols, she is able to see invoicing records, the present status of outstanding orders, inventory at warehouses located around the globe, and photographs of all available products. Although she brought a few samples with her to show her client the quality of the workmanship and fabrics, she can generate images on her computer screen showing the color, pattern, and fabric of any of the firm's products. Furthermore, slow-selling items are flashed on the side of the screen for the sales representative to consider.

As she enters the items and quantities of the order into the computer, a new icon appears on her screen indicating that the volume of buying entered thus far requires a credit check before the sale can be closed. While she completes her sales presentation, the firm's *decision-support system* (DSS), automatically calculates the allowable credit limit for the customer and provides credit authorization. It also displays her commission bonus for helping move "slow inventory."

SiteMerlin: The wizard that can help add an "e" to your business. Verio, the world's leading web hosting company, makes it fast and easy for any business to create a professionally designed web site by using its SiteMerlin service.

Scenarios like this are rapidly becoming commonplace, as are various other Internet applications. Because the Internet provides a relatively inexpensive way to advertise their products, take orders, and obtain information about customers for research purposes, companies have taken to the web in droves. Traditional catalog shoppers at L.L. Bean and J.C. Penney can browse through photographs of an array of consumer products on these companies' web sites, place their orders, and select delivery dates. Federal Express distributes communications software to customers that allows them to schedule their own pickups and trace their shipments. And Dell Computer provides a user-friendly screen on which customers can select the configuration specifications for their computer. After completing the order, Dell's MIS automatically transfers the order to the manufacturing plant where production of the computer is begun.

In addition to corporate sites, the World Wide Web has a wide array of government and institutional sites that provide information to the public. See Table 17.2 for a listing of favorite web sites for business.

An **intranet** is a smaller version of the Internet for use within a firm. Using a series of customized web pages, employees can quickly find information about their firm as well as connect to external sources. For instance, an employee might use the intranet to access the firm's policy documents on customer warranties or even take a company-designed course on new products and how to introduce them to customers.

intranet a smaller version of the Internet for use only within a firm

Internet Standards for Communications

To permit communication between different components of the Internet, a common standard language or protocol has emerged which is called *TCP/IP*. TCP/IP stands

table 17.2 Favorite Web Sites Used by Managers and Employees to Obtain Information about Business and the Economy

Sponsor and Description	Web Address
1. ***Department of Commerce*** The Department of Commerce is the primary source of government-generated business information.	**www.doc.gov**
2. ***Federal Reserve Bank of New York*** The Federal Reserve Bank of New York provides information about banking and the economy. In addition, it provides material on how the Federal Reserve monitors economic growth.	**www.ny.frb.org**
3. ***American Marketing Association*** The association uses its site to provide marketing information and services useful both to its professional and academic members and to the general public.	**www.ama.org**
4. ***Business Week Online*** This site provides articles about business, finance, and economic issues that affect both businesses and investors. In addition, you can search the magazine's archives.	**www.businessweek.com**
5. ***Fortune Magazine Online*** This site provides articles about business, finance, and economic issues that affect both individual businesses and investors. In addition, you can search the magazine's archives.	**www.fortune.com**

for Transport Control Protocols and Internet Protocols. These protocols allow computers from all over the world to communicate with each other. Because the protocols are used by all Internet users, they have allowed the Internet to grow rapidly and provide access to all. Without a standard set of protocols, one company could have dominated and controlled access to the Internet. To see how important standardization is and how it applies to the computer industry, read Talking Technology.

The fact that no single company controls the Internet is significant. Students of history may recall that when the railroads of Europe were built, different-sized rail widths were installed to prevent unwanted foreign use. In essence, anyone wishing to travel the rails within a country was required to use trains that "fit" on the tracks. A similar situation could have developed with the Internet. For a moment, consider what could have happened if Microsoft, Sun Systems, Oracle, or some other large technology company were allowed to establish "their" protocol as the standard. Anyone who wanted to use the Internet would have had to use the company's protocol and the company would be in a very powerful position to control the Internet.

Web Site Addresses Every web site on the Internet is identified by its *Uniform Resource Locator (URL)*, which acts as its address. To connect to a site, you enter its URL in your web browser. The URLs of most corporate sites are similar to the organizations' real names. For instance, you can reach Lotus Development Corporation by entering http://www.lotus.com. The first part of the entry, "http," sets the software protocols for proper transfer of information between your computer and the one at the site to which you are connecting. *Http* stands for *hypertext transfer protocol. Hypertext* refers to words or phrases highlighted or underlined on a web page; when you select these, they link you to other web sites.

Talking Technology

The Importance of Standardization

IMAGINE WALKING INTO A GAP CLOTHING store to buy a pair of Levis and the jeans are not labeled with a size. Because there are no standardized sizes, shopping takes longer because you have to try on pair after pair until you find jeans that fit. To make matters worse, buying jeans as a gift for a friend is impossible. Can you guess which pair of jeans will fit your friend's "dimensions"? And without size standards, ordering clothing online, by mail, or by telephone is virtually impossible. Without standardization, shopping becomes a nightmare.

What Is Standardization?

Standardization is defined as the guidelines that let products, services, materials, and processes perform their purpose. On the personal level, standardization allows a car mechanic to choose the correct air filter for your car, the power company to channel the necessary voltage into your home, and the grocer to sell toilet paper that fits on the holder in your bathroom.

On the business level, standardization is just as important. For example, standardization allows computers to interact with other computers. Establishing standards is vital to ensure that an IBM computer in McPherson, Kansas can "talk" with a Dell computer in San Francisco, California. It is just as important for software to be standardized if computers are going to communicate and conduct business activities through the Internet.

Who Establishes International Standards?

Generally, various international organizations decide the standards that manufacturers use to produce the products and services that people use throughout the globe. The three international organizations described below have developed standards that impact people and how they use their computers and the Internet.

- The International Organization for Standardization, referred to as ISO, has worked to improve quality standards since 1947. The term *ISO* is derived from the Greek word meaning *equal.* An international federation representing 130 different countries, the ISO has determined standards varying from establishing film speeds that are internationally accepted to refining the way computers use bar-code technology. ISO certification is especially important for international firms in the technology industry.
- The International Electrotechnical Commission (IEC), established in 1906, publishes standards for all electrical, electronic, and related technologies. With a membership of over fifty countries, the IEC's goal is to make sure that one nation's product or technology can be used in all other countries.
- The International Telecommunications Union (ITU) began as the International Telegraph Union in 1865. It aimed to facilitate the connection of telegraph lines used in the United States with those used in European nations. Today the ITU works to provide standards for different vendors that manufacture and sell wireless communication devices around the globe to an estimated 10 billion customers.

Organizations like the three described above know that global standardization is more important today than ever before. In order to keep individual countries from issuing their own specifications, these organizations are working together to keep the global marketplace connected. To discover more about these organizations, visit www.iso.ch, www.iec.ch, and www.itu.ch.

Web Search Engines To find a particular web site, you can take advantage of several free search programs available on the web, such as iWon.com, Yahoo!, Alta Vista, and Infoseek. These programs are free of charge because advertisers buy space on their screens, so the services are paid for in much the same way advertisements pay for television and radio broadcasts. To locate a search engine, enter its URL in your browser. Some URLs for very popular search engines are:

Using the Internet

From arts and humanities to health to society and culture, it's all at **www.yahoo.com**. Along with many other "hot buttons," Yahoo! allows users to obtain information with just a click of a mouse. Your topic not included? No problem—users can enter a name, location, or just about any imaginable topic in the Yahoo! search box, and this search engine will provide links to information available on the web.

http://iWon.com
http://home.netscape.com
http://www.altavista.com
http://www.yahoo.com
http://www.lycos.com

The home page for each search engine provides a short list of primary topic divisions, such as *business and economics, news and media*, and *reference*, as well as a search window where you can enter the particular topic you are looking for. Each site provides instructions and suggestions for finding what you want. With practice you will get a general sense of how search engines function.

Software for Creating Web Pages

Although it is possible to write a computer program to develop a web page, it is often easier to use a commercially available program like Microsoft's FrontPage (http://www.microsoft.com/frontpage/) that requires a minimal amount of user programming knowledge. Generally, once a *template* or structure for the web page has been created, content such as text or images can be readily changed, allowing the site to remain current.

The design of the firm's web site should be carefully thought out. The web page is, after all, the global image distributed to customers, suppliers, and other parties interested in knowing more about the firm and possibly doing business with the firm. What the web site says about a company is important and should be carefully developed to portray the "right" image. Therefore, it is understandable that a firm without the internal human resources to design, launch, and manage its web site will turn to the talents of creative experts available through web consulting firms. Once a web site is established, firms may then choose to manage their sites with their own personnel or continue to secure the services provided by firms that specialize in web page design, updating, e-commerce and other web activities.

Although most companies prefer to manage their web sites on their own computers, many have opted for hosting services provided by firms that often furnish guaranteed user accessibility, e-commerce shopping software, site updating services, and other specialized operational products and services. The company can often benefit by outsourcing these specialized web activities to firms that have the expertise to provide faster access to customers while maintaining a higher degree of security and lower operational costs.

Managing Internet Activities

LEARNING OBJECTIVE

6 Discuss how managers and employees can use the Internet to communicate, assist the firm's sales force, train and recruit employees, and conduct financial activities.

Today, many managers and executives supervise employees who conduct day-to-day business activities with the help of the Internet. In these situations, employees use the Internet to conduct research, improve productivity and performance, and communicate with other employees while at the office or away from the office. In this section, we examine several solutions to problems created when a firm or its employees uses the Internet. In each case, a solution is always evaluated in terms of its costs and compared to the benefits a firm receives, generally referred to as a *cost/benefit analysis*. Typical areas of concern for a business using the Internet include communications, sales, training and recruiting, and accounting and finance.

Helping Employees Communicate

One of the first business applications of computer technology was e-mail. Once software was chosen and employees trained, communications could be carried out globally within and outside the firm at any time, twenty-four hours a day, seven days a week. The firm's cost for software, training, and Internet connection services were small when compared to the benefits of being able to communicate with all the firm's employees without having to use traditional pencil and paper methods or the telephone.

Because e-mail provides an efficient means for people in various locations to work on a common project, there is less need for meetings and travel expenses can be reduced while still providing an effective method of communication.

Groupware is the latest type of software that facilitates the management of large projects among geographically dispersed employees, as well as such group activities as problem-solving and brainstorming. This software promises to revolutionize the manner in which work and information are organized and distributed. Groupware, such as Lotus Notes, is built on the client-server structure. This means that a portion of the software is run on the firm's main computer, called the server, and another portion operates on an employee's personal computer. A company that purchases this sort of software pays a licensing fee based on the number of users.

groupware one of the latest types of software that facilitates the management of large projects among geographically dispersed employees as well as such group activities as problem solving and brainstorming

A firm with thousands of employees linked together through its server can be thought of as a large-scale "thinking unit" with expertise and information available to anyone connected to the system. For example, suppose the home office of a software development firm in a major city has been hired to prepare customized software for a client in another city. Using groupware, the project team leader sets up a "work-template," a modified version of a design for a similar project. The software allows the team leader to check availability of employees around the world, give individuals specific work assignments, and set up a schedule for work completion, testing, and final installation on the client's computer. As work progresses, the program automatically signals team members for their input. The team leader is able to monitor work progress and may intervene if asked or if problems develop. Questions or details required by design engineers may be routed electronically to others in the group as well. When needed, people from various locations, possessing an array of knowledge and skills, can be called to the "workspace" created on the server for their contribution. When the work is finally completed, it can be forwarded to the client's server and installed.

Besides being useful in project management, groupware provides an opportunity for "knowledge engineering." In fact, the total knowledge of the organization can be orchestrated to produce the needed output. Firms can also use groupware to nurture a **collaborative learning system,** a work environment that allows problem-solving participation by all team members. By posting a question or problem on the groupware's conference site, the team leader invites members, who may be located anywhere in the world, to submit messages that can help move the group toward a solution. If the conference site lists both successful and unsuccessful solutions to problems, members can learn from each other and presumably improve their performance in the future. Firms are rapidly recognizing the training and educational opportunities available through groupware and collaborative learning systems.

collaborative learning system a work environment that allows problem-solving participation by all team members

Today, e-mail solutions are available to firms of all sizes and provide a major source of sales revenue for companies that provide communications software programs. Products like Microsoft's NetMeeting and MSN's Messenger Service and AOL's ICQ and Instant Messenger are only a few of the available Internet-based communications programs. Recent developments suggest visual e-mail and real-time conference calls will soon be commonplace in both the consumer and business market.

Assisting the Firm's Sales Force

In addition to general purpose communication tools that may be used by all of a firm's employees, there are also Internet-based software application programs that focus on the special informational needs of sales personnel. For example, sales force automation programs support sales representatives with organized databases of information such as names of clients, status of pending orders, sales leads and opportunities, as well as any related advice or recommendations from other company personnel. Consider what happens when a sales representative for a pharmaceutical company like Johnson & Johnson is planning to visit doctors, health-care providers, and hospitals in the Chicago area. A sales force automation software program can help map out which clients should be visited by providing useful information such as how long it has been since they were last contacted. The software can also provide information about how clients were approached, what the results were of the last contacts, who else in the pharmaceutical firm has interacted with the client, and previous purchases the client has made.

In large organizations like pharmaceutical firms, it is not uncommon to have several sales representatives dealing with different individuals in various departments of a hospital or a large medical clinic. Sales force automation systems can prevent embarrassment for sales representatives who work in their own specialized areas and may not be aware of the bigger picture with respect to their firm's total sales efforts with the prospective client. As sales representatives complete their visits, information about what was learned should be entered into the sales force automation system as soon as possible so that everyone can use the latest information. For instance, a sales representative might learn from an individual within the client's organization that another department is seeking information about a product that could provide a sales opportunity. Although the sales representative may not directly be involved in that field, the information can be entered into the firm's database of information. At the same time, a message can be sent to the sales manager or sales representative in the appropriate department that a new opportunity has been identified. Once notified of the sales opportunity, a sales representative in the appropriate department can provide information to the potential customer and ultimately increase sales of the firm's products or services.

A sales force automation program can automatically transfer files and notes to appropriate personnel. In this way, decisions about which employees should actually be notified about a new sales opportunity do not have to be made by the sales representative that uncovered the opportunity. Instead, the system can intelligently notify people who might use the information. An alternative design is simply to let an individual at the firm's office make the decision about who to notify. The industry leading sales force automation software program is distributed by Siebel Systems (http://www.siebel.com). Many others computer programs such as OverQuota from Relavis Corporation (http://www.relavis.com) also compete in this growing sector of the software industry.

Training Employees

Large and mid-sized companies spend a great deal of money on educational and training programs for employees. By distributing information about the firm, the organization, products and services, new procedures, and general information to employees through the Internet for reading and study at convenient times and places, firms can dramatically reduce training costs. For example, new employees are generally required to attend an intensive training program where a wide variety of information about the firm is presented in a classroom setting. Online training may then be used on a variety of topics to provide additional information and keep both new and experienced employees up-to-date on the latest information about the firm and its products and services.

Information on a wide range of topics ranging from ethical behavior to sexual harassment to discrimination can also be distributed to a firm's employees. Often, these sites may only be needed on rare occasions, However, it is important that employees know that the information exists and where it is. Furthermore, revision and distribution of important changes to this type of information are much easier if it is provided on the company's web site. Important announcements about changes to policies and procedures can be e-mailed and linked to the appropriate document that is maintained on the web site. This sort of Internet-based information system is provided by Lotus Notes (http://www.lotus.com) and other software vendors.

Recruiting Employees

Jump start your job search by using the Internet. According to Baraka Dorsey, now an executive recruiter with Silicon Alley Connections in New York, using the Internet to find out about a potential employer's job openings, benefit packages, and corporate culture enabled him to identify companies that offered challenging employment opportunities.

A common icon on most corporate web sites is a link to the human resources department. Firms looking for people with specialized skills can post their employee needs on their web sites and reach potential candidates from around the globe. This is an extremely important method of recruiting employees for positions in the information technology job market where labor shortages are common and individuals with the *right* skills are in high demand.

Furthermore, software programs can help large firms like IBM or Microsoft establish a database of potential employees. This is an especially important function for a firm that receives thousands of unsolicited employment applications from people all over the world. The cost of organizing and processing this information is high, but software can reduce this expense when compared to a paper-based system. As a bonus, the software can organize data in a way most useful to the firm. Critical data such as an applicant's knowledge about IBM's AS400 computer, for example, may be quickly identified by managers using the database. Finally, a firm using this type of software can save money by making would-be employees input application data.

In addition to individual corporate web sites, would-be employees can also access online recruiting web sites that can help match up job seekers with businesses seeking to hire additional employees. Perhaps the best known of these is Monster.com which recognized the advantages of providing a clearinghouse for job seekers and employers. This type of online service helps resolve the problems that a person living in one city encounters when searching for employment in another city. On the other hand, this type of online service can also help employers attract job applicants who presently reside in other cities or countries.

Conducting Financial Activities

The banking and financial services industries were quick to recognize the advantages of using the Internet. Now other businesses are using the Internet to process e-business transactions, bank online, and track employee expenses. Each of these activities is important for a business that wants to compete in today's technological world.

Completing E-Business Transactions.

Today, theft of credit card information is a common concern for online shoppers. And to avoid losing potential online sales, businesses must make it easy for customers to pay for purchases online while insuring that transactions are secure. To provide a sense of security, many businesses use the *secure electronic transaction*, or *SET* encryption process, which prevents merchants from actually seeing transaction data, including the customer's credit card number. (More information on this topic can be found at

spotLight

Top three high-tech regions

Nine states and Washington, D.C., have about 70% of the fastest-growing technology companies.

21% CA

16% NJ, NY, CT

15% MD, VA, DC

Source: Copyright 2000, USA TODAY. Reprinted with permission.

http://www.setco.org.) Other options include offering shoppers the choice of calling in their orders over the phone and speaking to an operator. Still another option is the use of a separate online-use credit card, such as Visa's "NextCard." Finally, it is possible for a customer to bill their purchase through third parties. Acting like a bank, they process credit card transactions for merchants and assume the responsibility for collection.

Online Banking Services Today, online banking and financial services are available to businesses as well as consumers. Financial institutions can provide direct access to both checking and savings accounts, allow clients to make payments, transfer funds between accounts, apply for loans, and obtain financial information. For both businesses and consumers, online banking is fast and easy with many transactions completed with a click of the mouse any time of the day or night, seven days a week. For the financial institution, online banking is often cheaper than traditional banking activities because of the savings that occur when processing large numbers of transactions online. For both customer and financial institution, these systems provide an added measure of security. Many transactions can be handled without human intermediaries and paper documents thus reducing potential mistakes and the risk of theft.

Tracking Employee Expenses The use of expense-tracking software provides an opportunity for firms to improve the way they process employee expense requests. One such software package, Boomerang, allows employees such as sales representatives, who regularly pay for many expenses that are part of their job, to report their expenses. Expenses are then charged to the appropriate accounts in the firm's accounting system and sales representatives are issued a refund. Because the Boomerang software package makes use of the Lotus Notes platform, sales representatives can input data whenever they want and wherever they happen to be in the world as long as they can access the Internet. The information they input will be securely transferred to appropriate company personnel and once expenses are approved, reimbursement checks may be issued quickly. Clients, such as Procter & Gamble, simplify recording and reduce internal financial management costs by using Boomerang. (More information on this topic can be found at www.momentum.com.)

Using Computers to Obtain and Process Information

LEARNING OBJECTIVE

7 Understand how to use applications software and the Internet to collect and distribute information.

Until businesses began using computers twenty-five or thirty years ago, management information systems were manual affairs. Clerical personnel were responsible for typing the company's records, storing them in file cabinets, and retrieving the data when needed. Any manipulation to transform the data contained in each file folder into useful information was done manually—usually by the manager who needed the information.

In the early computerized MIS systems, a large mainframe computer served a network of users. Mainframes are still in place in many firms that do large-scale data processing. However, they have been joined over the years by progressively smaller, faster, and less expensive desktop and laptop computers. Once a specialized staff function providing service to individuals in need of information, the management information system is now wholly decentralized so that individuals, using software designed to analyze, prepare, and distribute business information, are free to carry on their work independently.

Early software typically performed a single function. Today, however, *integrated software* combines many functions in a single package. Integrated packages allow for the easy *linking* of text, numerical data, graphs, photos, and even audiovisual clips. A business report prepared using either the Lotus SmartSuites or Microsoft Office package can include all these components, and the report may then be disseminated electronically through the firm's MIS or externally through the Internet.

Current Business Applications Software

Software has been developed to satisfy almost every business need. Today the most common types of software for business applications include

- Database management
- Graphics
- Spreadsheets
- Word processing
- Desktop publishing
- Accounting
- Communications

From a career standpoint, you should realize that firms will assume you possess, or will possess after training, a high degree of working comfort with several of these programs, particularly word processing, communications, spreadsheets, and graphics.

database management program software that allows users to electronically store large amounts of data and to transform the data into information

graphics program software that enables users to display and print pictures, drawings, charts, and diagrams

spreadsheet program a software package that allows the user to organize numerical data into a grid of rows and columns

Database Management Programs

As noted earlier, a database is a single collection of data stored in one place and used by people throughout an organization to make decisions. A **database management program** allows users to electronically store large amounts of data and to transform the data into information. Data can be sorted by different criteria. For example, a firm's personnel department might sort by each worker's gender, salary, and years of service. If management needs to know the names of workers who have at least fifteen years of experience, an employee using database management software can print a list of such employees in a matter of minutes. The same type of manipulation of data for other departments within a business is possible with database management software. In addition to building its own database, a company can subscribe to online computer services that enable users to access large external databases.

Graphics Programs

Whether you are playing a video game or watching the computerized scoreboard at a football stadium, you are viewing computer-generated graphics. A **graphics program** enables users to display and print pictures, drawings, charts, and diagrams. In business, graphics are used for oral or written presentations of financial analyses, budgets, sales projections, and the like.

Although visual aids have always been available, their use was restricted because someone had to take the time to draw them. With the aid of a graphics program, the computer can generate drawings in seconds. Typically, graphics software allows the user to select a type of visual aid from a menu of options. The user enters the numerical data, such as sales figures, to be illustrated. The computer program then converts the data into a graph, bar chart, or pie chart.

Spreadsheet Programs

A **spreadsheet program** is a software package that allows the user to organize numerical data into a grid of rows and columns. Among the popular spreadsheet programs are Microsoft

A peach of a solution. For over 20 years, Peachtree Software, Inc. has provided accounting solutions for small business. Today, it continues to develop state-of-the-art software programs that provide information that enables business owners to solve financial problems, reduce expenses, and increase profits.

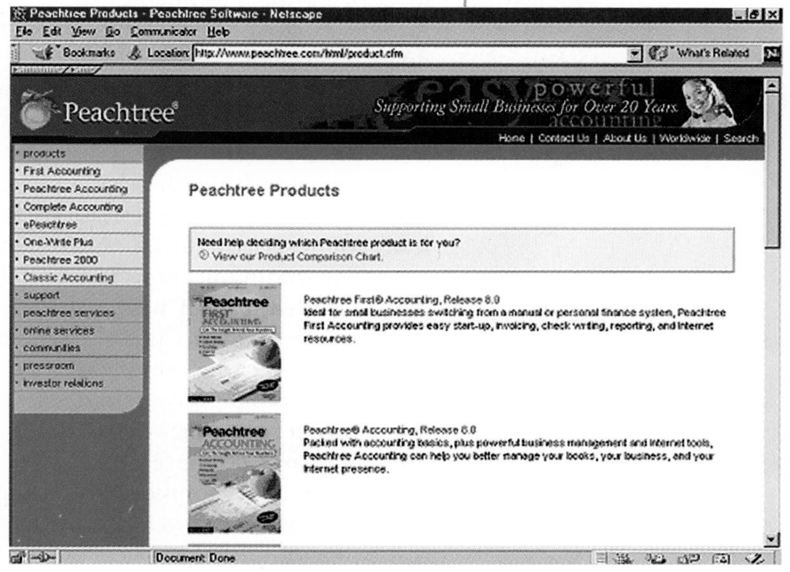

Excel and Lotus 1-2-3. With a spreadsheet, the computer performs mathematical calculations automatically. For example, a manager at Dallas-based Malone's Cost-Plus Grocery Stores may want to project sales and expenses for the next three-month period. The manager enters numerical data for both sales and expenses, and the spreadsheet software calculates the dollar amount of profit or loss based on the data. Spreadsheet software can also be used to answer "what if" questions. By changing data to match new assumptions, the manager can see how the change will affect other data in the spreadsheet. If the manager wanted to calculate the firm's profits based on projections that sales will increase 5, 10, and 15 percent, three additional spreadsheets could be prepared, based on each set of assumptions. In fact, a spreadsheet user can change any variable and, within seconds, have new information to aid in the decision-making process.

word processing program software that allows a user to prepare and edit written documents and to store them in the computer or on a disk

Word Processing Programs A **word processing program** allows the user to prepare and edit letters, memos, reports, and other written documents and to store them in the computer or on a disk. Text revision is greatly simplified because the user can make changes where necessary without having to retype the entire document. In addition, the sort and merge features of word processing software enable users to send personalized copies of form letters. For example, most firms use a standard collection letter to urge prompt payment of past-due amounts. With a word processing program, they can send a personalized letter to all overdue accounts. To appeal to customers, mail-order firms and direct-mail marketing firms make extensive use of sort and merge features. Thousands of letters—each addressed to a particular individual—can be prepared from one master document.

desktop publishing program a software package that enables users to combine text and graphics in reports, newsletters, and pamphlets

Desktop Publishing Programs A **desktop publishing program** is a software package that enables users to combine text and graphics in reports, newsletters, and pamphlets. Most desktop publishing programs go beyond word processing programs to give the user more control over complex designs and page layout. With the aid of a state-of-the-art printer, the user can prepare documents almost as professional-looking as those produced by a printing company.

accounting program a software package that enables the user to record and report financial information

Accounting Programs An **accounting program** is a software package that enables the user to record and report financial information. Almost all commercially available accounting packages contain three basic modules: general ledger and financial reporting, accounts receivable, and accounts payable. The general ledger and financial reporting module processes routine, daily accounting entries. This module should also prepare financial statements at the end of each accounting period. The accounts receivable module prepares customer invoices, maintains customer balances, allows different payment terms to different customers, and generates past-due notices to slow-paying customers. The accounts payable module records and monitors invoices from vendors or suppliers. It should also take advantage of cash discounts offered by suppliers and vendors for prompt payment. The better accounting packages prepare checks to pay suppliers, vendors, and employees.

communications program software that allows computers to communicate with each other

Communications Programs A **communications program** allows computers to communicate with each other. Practically all business computers today are equipped with some type of communications program. Networking software is one type. It typically connects users within the firm and also people outside of the firm. For example, a popular communications function is sending electronic mail (e-mail) by computer. Once received, e-mail messages are stored at their destination until the recipients choose to "open them." It is also possible to use facsimile (fax) software to send a document or image to a remote location. Most communications programs today enable the computer to perform multiple functions.

Today, it seems that everyone has e-mail and wants to "talk." For some computer users, this may be more difficult than it seems if they have older, slower computer hardware. A clever solution for putting slower performing computers back to productive work has been developed by NewDeal, Inc. The Somerville, Massachusetts firm makes operating and application software that looks and feels like Windows 98 and

Microsoft's Office suite of software, but runs on older pre-Pentium equipped computers. The number of obsolete computers is expected to grow to more than half a billion by 2007 providing NewDeal with a large potential market.[4]

Other Business Applications Programs Although it is impossible to describe all the software business firms use today, three programs described in Chapter 9 deserve special mention here. Computer-aided design (CAD) programs use computers to aid in the development of products. Computer-aided manufacturing (CAM) programs use computers to plan and control manufacturing processes. And computer-integrated manufacturing (CIM) not only helps design products but also controls the machinery needed to produce finished products. Each of these programs streamlines the manufacturing process and ultimately makes a manufacturer more productive. As a result, programs like these have become an integral part of business firms involved in manufacturing. In this chapter, we have explored some of the functions and requirements of a business firm's MIS and how a computer can help people obtain the information they need to be effective employees. In Chapter 18, we examine the accounting process, which is a major source of information for business.

RETURN TO Inside Business

TODAY, IWON.COM IS OFFERING A SERVICE that customers want—the ability to access information quickly while at the same time providing a site that is entertaining. Not content to relax and rest on past performance, iWon.com continues to improve the services it offers Internet users. To accomplish this goal, it has forged alliances and links that make the iWon search function one of the most comprehensive and easy-to-navigate search engines on the Internet. Users can access information by simply entering a keyword and clicking on iWon's search button. At the same time iWon provides a relevant index of related documents, a professionally edited directory of information sources, and access to web sites for major companies and products, music files, and news stories.

Although it has already acquired a reputation as one of the Internet's most innovative search engines, iWon.com continues to improve the services it offers its users. In September 2000, iWon.com introduced a new link to Fact Finder—the Internet's first comprehensive fact-finding search service. Fact Finder is an Internet platform sponsored by Fact City that accumulates and distributes more than 10 million facts and statistics. What's neat about Fact Finder and what makes it a real asset for iWon.com is that Internet users access the information by simply asking questions in plain English.

According to the experts, it takes this type of innovation to stay competitive in this ever-changing technology industry. And iWon.com is committed to innovation. It is this commitment that will enable iWon.com to increase its user base while attracting sponsors willing to pay more for advertising space on its web site. And the bottom line: Move over Yahoo!. Watch out Excite and Lycos. iWon.com is here to stay!

Questions

1. iWon.com lures users to their web site by a chance to win big bucks. Would you log on just for the opportunity to gain entries?
2. According to the experts, a firm like iWon.com must innovate to increase both its number of users and its advertising revenues. Explain the relationship between innovation, number of users, and advertising revenues.
3. It is said that Yahoo! has a loyal customer base. What attributes does a web site need in order to attract and keep users? Explain your answer.

chapter Review

SUMMARY

1 Understand how information is organized to help people make decisions.

The more information a manager has, the less risk there is that a decision will be incorrect. Information produces knowledge and empowers managers and employees to make better decisions. Without correct and timely information, individual performance will be undermined and, consequently, so will the performance of the entire organization. Because of the volume of information they receive each day and their need to make decisions on a daily basis, businesspeople use information rules to shorten the time spent analyzing choices. Information rules emerge when business research confirms the same results each time it studies the same or a similar set of circumstances. Although many people use the terms *data* and *information* interchangeably, there is a difference. Data are numerical or verbal descriptions that usually result from some sort of measurement. Information is data presented in a form useful for a specific purpose. A database is a single collection of data stored in one place that can be used by people throughout an organization to make decisions.

2 Discuss management's information requirements.

A management information system (MIS) is a means of providing managers with the information they need to perform their jobs as effectively as possible. The purpose of an MIS is to distribute timely and useful information from both internal and external sources to the decision makers who need it. The specific types of information managers need depend on their area of management and level within the firm. An MIS must be tailored to the information needs of the organization it serves.

3 Describe the four functions of a management information system.

The four functions performed by an MIS are collecting data, storing and updating data, processing data into information, and presenting information to users. Data may be collected from such internal sources as company records, reports, and minutes of meetings, as well as from the firm's managers. External sources include customers, suppliers, bankers, trade and financial publications, industry conferences, online computer services, and information-gathering organizations. An MIS must be able to store data until they are needed and to update them regularly to ensure that the information presented to managers is accurate, complete, and timely. Data processing is the MIS function that transforms stored data into a form useful for a specific purpose. Large groups of numerical data are usually processed into summary numbers called statistics. The most commonly used statistics are the arithmetic mean, median, and mode. Other statistics are the frequency distribution and the range, which is a measure of the dispersion, or spread, of data values. Finally, the processed data (which can now be called information) must be presented for use. Verbal information is generally presented in the form of a report. Numerical information is most often displayed in graphs, charts, or tables.

4 Describe how business research is conducted.

When secondary sources do not provide businesspeople with sufficient information to make decisions with acceptable levels of risk, they may undertake primary research. Primary research in business employs two fundamentally different approaches to information gathering and analysis. Qualitative research involves the descriptive or subjective reporting of information discovered by research. Generally, qualitative research is conducted in one of three ways: observation, interviews, or focus groups. Quantitative research involves the collection of numerical data for analysis through a survey, experiment, or content analysis. The decision about which research method to use is often based on a combination of factors, including limitations on time and money, and the need or concern for accuracy and validity. In general, managers rely on the results of proven research methods until those methods no longer work well.

5 Explain how the Internet, intranet, standards for communications, and web pages affect business today.

We live in an information society—one in which large groups of employees generate or depend on information to perform their jobs. To find needed information, many businesses and individuals use the Internet. The Internet is a worldwide network of computers linked through telecommunications. Firms can also use an intranet to distribute information within a firm. To permit communication, a common standard language or protocol has emerged which allows computers to communicate with other computers. Because the same protocols are used by all Internet users, the Internet has grown rapidly and provides access to all users. By using the Internet to access web sites, search engines, and web pages, users can obtain a wealth of information with the click of a computer's mouse.

6 Discuss how managers and employees can use the Internet to communicate, assist the firm's sales force, train and recruit employees, and conduct financial activities.

Today, many managers and executives supervise employees who conduct day-to-day business activities on the Internet to improve communications, increase sales, train and recruit employees, and conduct financial activities. One of the first computer applications in the workplace was electronic mail or simply e-mail which provides for communication within and outside the firm at any time, twenty-four hours a day, seven days a week. An extension of e-mail is called *groupware*. Groupware is software that facilitates the management of large projects among geographically dispersed employees as well as such group activities as problem solving and brainstorming. The Internet and a sales-force automation software program can provide a database of information that can be used to assist a sales representative. The Internet can also be used to improve employee training and recruitment while lowering costs. Finally, the Internet can help firms complete e-business transactions, bank online, and track employee expenses.

7 Understand how to use applications software and the Internet to collect and distribute information.

In the early computerized MISs, a large mainframe computer served a network of users. Mainframes are still in place in many firms that do large-scale data processing. However, they have been joined over the years by progressively smaller, faster and less expensive desktop and laptop computers. In addition, software has been developed to satisfy almost every business need. The most common programs for business applications include database management, graphics, spreadsheets, word processing, desktop publishing, accounting, and communications. Although it is impossible to describe all the software business firms use today, computer-aided design (CAD), computer-aided manufacturing (CAM), and computer-integrated manufacturing (CIM) should be mentioned because they are used to help manufacture the products a firm sells in the marketplace. Each of these programs streamlines the manufacturing process and ultimately makes a manufacturer more productive. As a result, programs like these have become an integral part of business.

KEY TERMS

You should now be able to define and give an example relevant to each of the following terms:

data (481)
information (482)
database (482)
management information system (MIS) (482)
data processing (487)
statistic (487)
frequency distribution (488)
arithmetic mean (488)
median (488)
mode (489)
range (489)
qualitative research (492)
quantitative research (493)
information society (494)
Internet (494)
telecommunications (494)
intranet (495)
groupware (499)
collaborative learning system (499)
database management program (503)
graphics program (503)
spreadsheet program (503)
word processing program (504)
desktop publishing program (504)
accounting program (504)
communications program (504)

REVIEW QUESTIONS

1. In your own words, describe how information reduces risk when you make a personal or work-related decision.
2. What are information rules? How do they simplify the process of making decisions?
3. What is the difference between data and information? Give one example of accounting data and one example of accounting information.
4. How do the information requirements of managers differ by management area?
5. Why must a management information system (MIS) be tailored to the needs of the organization it serves?
6. List four functions of an MIS.
7. What are the differences among the mean, median, and mode of a set of data? How can a few extremely small or large numbers affect the mean?
8. What are the components of a typical business report?
9. What is the difference between qualitative research and quantitative research?
10. Describe the methods used to conduct qualitative research and quantitative research.
11. Explain the differences between the Internet and an intranet. What types of information does each of these networks provide?
12. Why is a common language or protocols necessary for the Internet to operate properly?
13. How can a web search engine like Yahoo!, Alta Vista, or iWon.com help you find information on a business topic like interest rates or the consumer price index?
14. What factors should be considered when a firm is developing a web page?
15. How do business firms use groupware to encourage collaborative learning systems?
16. Describe how the Internet and software can help a firm assist sales representatives, train and recruit employees, and track expenses.
17. Describe how businesses use database management programs, graphics programs, spreadsheet programs, word processing programs, desktop publishing programs, accounting programs, and communication programs.

DISCUSSION QUESTIONS

1. Assume you have been out of college for ten years, are unemployed, and your computer skills are seriously outdated. How would you go about updating your computer skills?

2. How can confidential data (such as the wages of individual employees) be kept confidential and yet still be available to managers who need them?
3. Do managers really need all the kinds of information discussed in this chapter? If not, which kinds can they do without?
4. Why are computers so well suited to management information systems? What are some things computers *cannot* do in dealing with data and information?
5. How could the Internet help you find information about employement opportunities at Coca-Cola, Johnson & Johnson, or Microsoft? Describe the process you would use to access this information.

VIDEO CASE

CSX Transportation: From "Iron Horse" to High Technology

Chances are that any product you purchase at your local supermarket, department store, or automobile showroom began its journey to the marketplace on a CSX Transportation rail car. CSXT is one of the largest railroad systems in the United States. Operating over a network of 23,000 miles, it transports raw materials and finished goods—metals, automobiles, chemicals, minerals, coal, phosphates, fertilizers, agricultural, and forest products—to major markets in twenty-three states east of the Mississippi, the District of Columbia, and the Canadian provinces of Quebec and Ontario. Nearly 1,300 trains are dispatched, tracked, and traced every single day out of CSXT's computerized Kenneth C. Dufford Transportation Center in Jacksonville, Florida.

CSXT has a colorful history in rail transportation dating as far back as the "iron horse" days of over a century and a half ago. In recent years, it became the *first* U.S. railroad to control its operations from one central location. In 1984 CSXT began studies aimed at merging its eighteen divisions, 20,000 miles of track, and thirty-three dispatch locations into regional sites. What came out of years of planning and going back to the drawing board over and over again was one central facility that houses the Operations and Crew Management Centers. Did the new computerized facility responsible for tracking both operations and crew make a difference? It did indeed. By 1994 CSXT showed record earnings and its highest-ever efficiency rating.

Information on the precise location, condition, and destination of each shipment on CSXT's rail lines is recorded at the Operations Center—a staggering three levels in a circular room 150 feet in diameter. Giant screens project a panoramic view of CSXT's rail network to all personnel. The employees responsible for managing the trains work on the second level. On the third level are the managers responsible for deciding about train cancellations, rerouting, and detouring work, as well as a passenger coordinator who oversees the performance of all Amtrak trains on CSXT's tracks. On both the first and third levels are the thirty-two dispatchers who actually control the trains. Each dispatcher has a color monitor that can display close-ups of the big screens. They also have touch screens for communications and computers to input the latest train and engineering information. This information is forwarded to the center by a state-of-the-art computer signaling system based on satellites and transponders located throughout the eastern part of the United States and Canada.

What's ahead for CSXT? Its Dufford Transportation Center will be even more important in the future. The company's recent merger with Conrail will enable it to offer shippers an even larger distribution system in the East, South, and Midwest. It will provide more direct lines to ports on the Atlantic, the Gulf of Mexico, and the Great Lakes, as well as expand its connections to western railroads. CSXT predicts that the single-line service created by its consolidation with Conrail will reduce transit times and result in more efficient service, which will in turn lower transportation fees. So, as their locomotives and rail cars continue to move across the face of America with the aid of computerized management information technology, CSX Transportation is ready to roll through the twenty-first century.[5]

Questions

1. In 1984 CSX Transporation began to explore new ways to utilize information technology. What was the result of these efforts?
2. How has management used the Kenneth C. Dufford Transportation Center to improve productivity and profitability?

Building skills for career success

1. Exploring the Internet

Computer technology is a fast-paced, highly competitive industry in which product life cycles are sometimes measured in months or even weeks. To keep up with changes and trends in hardware and software, MIS managers must routinely scan computer publications and web sites that discuss new products.

A major topic of interest among MIS managers is "groupware," software that facilitates the management of large projects among geographically dispersed employees as well as group activities like problem solving and brainstorming. Both Lotus and Microsoft have groupware products, as do other software development firms. Visit the text web site for updates to this exercise.

Assignment

1. Examine the web sites whose addresses appear below, as well as the sites of any other groupware producers you can find using one of the web search engines (enter the keyword *groupware*). Try the demonstration edition of the groupware, if it is available.

   http://www.microsoft.com
   http://www.lotus.com
   http://www.oracle.com

2. Why do you think groupware is growing in popularity?
3. Describe the structure of one of the groupware programs you examined as well as your impressions of its value to users.

2. Developing Critical Thinking Skills

To stay competitive in the marketplace, businesses must process data into information and make it readily available to decision makers. For this, many businesses rely on a management information system. The purpose of an MIS is to provide managers with accurate, complete, and timely information so that they can perform their jobs as effectively as possible. Because a MIS must fit the needs of the firm it serves, these systems vary in the way they collect, store, update, and process data and present information to users.

Assignment

1. Select a local company large enough to have a management information system. Set up an interview with the person responsible for managing the flow of information within the company.
2. Prepare a list of questions you will ask during the interview. Structure the questions around the four basic functions of an MIS. Some sample questions follow.
   a. *Collecting data*: What type of data are needed? How often are data collected? What sources produce the data? How do you ensure that the data are accurate?
   b. *Storing and updating data*: How are data stored and updated? What is the process for updating?
   c. *Processing data*: Can you show me some examples of the types of data that will be processed into information? How is the processing done?
   d. *Presenting information*: Would you show me some examples (reports, tables, graphs, charts) of how the information is presented to various decision makers and tell me why that particular format is used?
3. At the end of the interview, ask the interviewee to predict how the system will change in the next three years.
4. In a report, describe what you believe the strengths and weaknesses of this firm's MIS are and make recommendations for improving the system. Also describe the most important thing you learned from the interview.

3. Building Team Skills

To provide marketing managers with information about consumers' reactions to a particular product or service, business researchers often conduct focus groups. The participants in these groups are representative of the target market for the product or service under study. The leader poses questions and lets members of the group express their feelings and ideas about the product or service. The ideas are recorded, transcribed, and analyzed.

Assignment

1. Working in a small team, select a product or service to research—for example, you college's food service or bookstore, or a new item you would like to see stocked in your local grocery store.
2. Form a focus group of five to seven people representative of the market for the product or service your team has selected. To help control group bias, it is best to use several focus groups.
3. During the group sessions, record the input. Later, transcribe it into printed form, analyze it, and process it into information. On the basis of this information, make recommendations for improving the product or service.
4. In a report, describe your team's experiences in forming the focus groups and the value of focus groups in collecting data. Use the report as the basis for a ten-minute class presentation.

4. Researching Different Careers

Firms today expect employees to be proficient in using computer software, particularly word processing, communications, spreadsheet, and graphics software. By improving your skills in these areas, you can increase your chances not only of being employed but of being promoted once you are employed.

Assignment

1. Assess your computer skills by placing a check in the appropriate column in the following table:

	Skill Level			
Software	**None**	**Low**	**Average**	**High**
Database management				
Graphics				
Spreadsheet				
Word processing				
Desktop publishing				
Accounting				
Communications				
Groupware				

2. Describe your self-assessment in a written report. Specify the programs in which you need to become more proficient, and outline a plan for doing this.

5. Improving Communication Skills

Over the past decade, computers have changed the way we do business and conduct our daily lives. As computer technology continues to improve over the next decade, it will affect our lives in new and very different ways.

Assignment

1. Research articles that predict how computers will be used in the next decade and how their use will change the way we live.
2. Write a paper focusing on the future use of computers in two or more of the following areas: health care, genetics, travel, communications, manufacturing, transportation, management, farming, or meal preparation. Conclude your paper with a discussion of how you think computers will affect your life over the next ten years.

Using Accounting Information

18

LEARNING OBJECTIVES

1. Understand why accounting information is important and what accountants do.
2. Discuss the accounting process.
3. Read and interpret a balance sheet.
4. Read and interpret an income statement.
5. Describe business activities that affect a firm's cash flow.
6. Summarize how managers evaluate the financial health of a business.

Although accountants are sometimes referred to as "bean counters," the people at Andersen are much more than just highly paid employees who concentrate on increasing revenues and earning profits.

Inside Business

Arthur Andersen—Not "Just Another Accounting Firm"!

For decades, Arthur Andersen, a major business division of Andersen Worldwide, was recognized as the number 1 accounting firm in the world. But in 1998, with the merger of Price Waterhouse and Coopers & Lybrand that formed the accounting firm of PricewaterhouseCoopers, Andersen dropped to the number 2 spot on the list of Big Five accounting firms in the world. Undaunted by its number 2 ranking, Andersen, a Chicago-based partnership, attributes its past and present success to its founder's philosophy of teaching and implementing a business-oriented approach to accounting, auditing, and consulting services.

As an educator and head of the Department of Accounting at Northwestern University, Arthur Andersen recruited the brightest students for his accounting classes and turned them into thoroughly trained accountants. In 1913, he formed a public accounting firm, Andersen, DeLany & Company, with Clarence DeLany. After DeLany left in 1918, the firm was renamed Arthur Andersen & Co. As an innovator, Andersen didn't create just another accounting firm. He taught his employees to use knowledge, information, and education to provide excellent service to the firm's growing list of clients. Simply put: Andersen's employees were told to think straight, talk straight, probe deeply into a client's operations, and then have the courage to tell the client what changes were needed to improve overall performance and achieve success. Now almost ninety years later, this very same commitment to excellence is the driving force for all partners and employees of the Andersen worldwide organization. Today, Arthur Andersen provides audit, tax, and financial consulting services and has more than 70,000 employees in 385 offices in 83 countries. In 1999, the last year that complete financial results are available, Andersen generated $3.4 billion in revenues in North America alone, and more than $13 billion worldwide.

To maintain its eighty-eight-year history of uninterrupted revenue growth, Andersen recruits only the best and the brightest prospective employees. Those applicants that are chosen are then expected to continue training throughout their career at Andersen University—a 150-acre center for professional education outside of Chicago. This state-of-the-art facility is staffed by 500 of the best professional educators in the accounting industry and offers more than 400 technical, business, industry, and management development courses to help ensure that both new and experienced Andersen employees have the knowledge to provide only the highest standard of client service.

Although accountants are sometimes referred to as "bean counters," the people at Andersen are much more than just highly paid employees who concentrate on increasing revenues and earning profits. The firm is well known for its excellent social responsibility programs. For example, Andersen has established the GROW (Growth and Retention of Women) program that encourages the advancement of women partners and employees in the United States. As a result, *Working Mother* magazine recognized Arthur Andersen as one of the "100 Best Companies for Working Mothers" in 1999. Programs to help people and charitable organizations are funded through the Arthur Andersen Foundation. Each year, the Andersen foundation provides more than $3 million in support of scholarships and fellowships to students and teachers. And during the summer of 1999, over 1,200 partners and employees participated in the Arthur Andersen Habitat for Humanity Build. This project helped house thirty-five families in nearly twenty cities. As we begin the twenty-first century, it's comforting to know that organizations like Arthur Andersen are making dreams come true for not only their business clients, but also people in the communities that they serve.[1]

What is an average day in the life of an accountant like? Many people have the idea that accountants spend their day working with endless columns of numbers in a small office locked away from other people. In fact, accountants do spend a lot of time at their desks, but their job entails far more than just adding or subtracting numbers. Accountants are expected to share their ideas and the information they possess with people who need the information. Accounting is serious business, but it can also be an exciting and rewarding career—one that offers higher than average starting salaries. Today many accounting firms are, like Arthur Andersen, eager to hire both women and men to help them in their task of providing accounting information to individuals and businesses.

We begin this chapter by looking at the importance of accounting information both to a firm's managers and to individuals and groups outside a firm. We also identify different types of accountants. Then we focus on the accounting process and the basics of an accounting system: the accounting equation, double-entry bookkeeping, and the process by which raw data are organized into financial statements. Next we examine the three most important financial statements: the balance sheet, the income statement, and the statement of cash flows. Finally, we show how ratios are used to measure specific aspects of a firm's financial health.

LEARNING OBJECTIVE

1 Understand why accounting information is important and what accountants do.

accounting the process of systematically collecting, analyzing, and reporting financial information

Why Accounting Information Is Important

You can bet the 800,000 pound gorilla has sound financial and accounting strategies. Without an accurate accounting system, it is impossible to manage even a small business let alone a large corporation. Thus, accounting information is, first and foremost, management information.

Accounting is the process of systematically collecting, analyzing, and reporting financial information. Some people would even go so far as to say that accounting is the language of business. Today it is impossible to manage a business without accurate and up-to-date information supplied by the firm's accountants. Managers and employees, lenders, suppliers, stockholders, and government agencies all rely on the information contained in three financial statements, each no more than one page in length. These three reports—the balance sheet, the income statement, and the statement of cash flows—are concise summaries of a firm's activities during a specific time period. Together, they represent the results of perhaps tens of thousands of transactions that have occurred during the accounting period. Moreover, the form of the financial statements is pretty much the same for all businesses, from a neighborhood video store or small dry cleaner to giant conglomerates like the Home Depot, Boeing, and BankAmerica. This information has a variety of uses, both within the firm and outside it. However, first and foremost, accounting information is management information. As such, it is of most use to those who manage the business.

The People Who Use Accounting Information

The primary users of accounting information are *managers*. The firm's accounting system provides information that can be compiled for the entire firm; for each product; for each sales territory, store, or salesperson; for each division or department; and generally in any way that will help those who manage the organization. At a company like Kraft Foods, for example, financial information is gathered for all of its hundreds of food products: Maxwell House Coffee, Tombstone Pizza, Post Cereals, Jell-O Desserts, Kool Aid, and so on. The president of the company would be interested in total sales for all these products. The vice president for marketing would be interested in national sales for Tombstone Pizza and Jell-O Desserts. The northeastern sales manager might want to look at sales figures for Kool Aid in New England. For a large, complex organization like Kraft, the accounting system must be complete and yet flexible because managers at different levels must be able to get the information they need.

Much of this accounting information is *proprietary*; it is not divulged to anyone outside the firm. This type of information is used by a firm's managers and employees to plan and set goals, organize, lead and motivate, and control all of the management functions that were described in Chapter 7. To see how important this type of information is, just think about what happens when an employee or manager asks a supervisor for a new piece of equipment or a salary increase. Immediately, all involved in the decision begin discussing how much it will cost and what effect it will have on the firm's profits. It is the firm's accounting system that provides the answers to these and many more questions that affect the firm's financial future. In addition to proprietary information used inside the firm, certain financial information must be supplied to particular individuals and organizations outside the firm (see Table 18.1).

- *Lenders* require information contained in the firm's financial statements before they will commit themselves to either short- or long-term loans. *Suppliers* who provide the raw materials, component parts, or finished goods a firm needs also generally ask for financial information before they will extend credit to a firm.
- *Stockholders* are provided with a summary of the firm's financial position in quarterly and annual reports. In addition, *potential investors* must be provided with financial information about each new securities issue that the firm sells to the public.
- *Government agencies* require a variety of information about the firm's tax liabilities, payroll deductions for employees, and new issues of stocks and bonds.

An important function of accountants is to ensure that such information is accurate and thorough enough to satisfy these outside groups. To see what can happen when accounting records are questionable, read Examining Ethics.

Careers in Accounting

Wanted: An individual with at least two years of college accounting courses. Must be honest, dependable, and willing to complete all routine accounting activities for a manufacturing business. Salary dependent on experience.

Want a job? Positions like the one described in this newspaper advertisement are becoming increasingly available to those with the required training. According to the *Occupational Outlook Quarterly*, published by the Department of Labor, job opportu-

table 18.1 Users of Accounting Information

The primary users of accounting information are a company's managers, but individuals and organizations outside the company also require information on its finances.

Management	Lenders and Suppliers	Stockholders and Potential Investors	Government Agencies
Plan and set goals Organize Lead and motivate Control	Evaluate credit risks before committing to short-term or long-term financing	Evaluate the financial health of the firm before purchasing stocks or bonds	Confirm tax liabilities Confirm payroll deductions Approve new issues of stocks and bonds

Examining Ethics

Do Big Corporations "Cook the Books"?

A WARNING FROM THE SECURITIES AND Exchange Commission to corporate America: "Don't even try to 'cook the books'!" Today creative methods of reporting earnings and other important financial information are not only unethical, but there is a high probability that these same methods could land you in jail. And although high-level executives are supposed to "manage earnings" to make a firm's finances appear positive, they often step over ethical and possibly legal boundaries when they manipulate figures to overstate profits or carefully craft deliberate misstatements in financial reports.

Pressure from Wall Street and Investors

Today much of the pressure on corporate executives to "cook the books" is driven by the desire to look good to Wall Street analysts and investors. Every three months, companies report their revenues, expenses, profits, and projections for the future. If a company meets or exceeds "the street's" expectations everything is usually fine. But if a company reports financial numbers that are lower than expected, the company's stock value can drop dramatically. An earnings report that is lower by even a few pennies per share than what it is expected can cause a company's stock value to immediately drop as much as 30 to 40 percent.

So Who Cares if Executives "Cook the Books"?

Everyone! Wall Street analysts need accurate financial information to make buy and sell recommendations to investors. In turn, investors use the analysts' recommendations to make their decisions to buy or sell a particular company's stock. In addition to Wall Street analysts and investors, the federal agency in charge of policing the securities industry–the Securities and Exchange Commission or SEC–requires that all financial information reported by a company be accurate. Although the SEC has no power to prosecute, it has aligned itself with the U.S. Attorney General and the attorney generals for individual states who do have the power to prosecute. According to Arthur Levitt, current chairman of the SEC, prison time, fines, and other drastic actions are necessary to retain the credibility and respect of the U.S. financial-reporting system. The people at the SEC in cooperation with attorney generals across the nation are conducting an aggressive campaign against this type of fraud and use every opportunity to indict wrong-doers, no matter the size of the crime. For example, a 71-year-old former CEO of a New York insurance brokerage firm, recently received a 12-year sentence for the most basic of accounting offenses: he reported higher than real revenues and lower than actual expenses for his company.

Questions

1. What type of pressures would lead a corporate executive to "cook the books"?
2. As a corporate executive, you know that your company is not going to meet its Wall Street expectations for the first quarter of the year. You also know that your continued employment could depend on how you report your firm's revenues, expenses, and profits. How do you resist the temptation to report fraudulent financial numbers?

nities for accountants, auditors, and managers in the accounting area are expected to experience average growth between now and the year 2008.[2] Both private and public accountants will be in demand.

A **private accountant** is employed by a specific organization. A medium-sized or large firm may employ one or more private accountants to design its accounting information system, manage its accounting department, and provide managers with advice and assistance. Private accountants also perform the following services for their employers:

private accountant an accountant employed by a specific organization

1. *General accounting*—Recording business transactions and preparing financial statements
2. *Budgeting*—Helping managers develop budgets for sales and operating expenses
3. *Cost accounting*—Determining the cost of producing specific products or services
4. *Tax accounting*—Planning tax strategy and preparing tax returns for the firm
5. *Internal auditing*—Reviewing the company's finances and operations to determine whether goals and objectives are being achieved.

Individuals, self-employed business owners, and smaller firms that don't require their own full-time accountants can hire the services of public accountants. A **public accountant** works on a fee basis for clients and may be self-employed or be the

public accountant an accountant who provides services to clients on a fee basis

spotLight

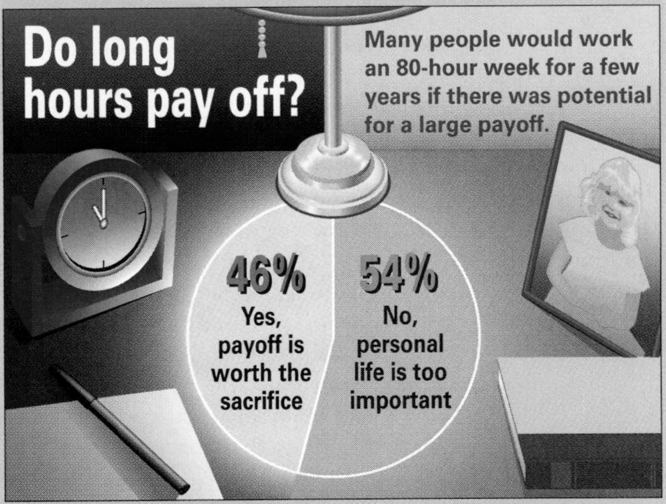

Source: Copyright 2000, USA TODAY. Reprinted with permission.

employee of an accounting firm. Accounting firms range in size from one-person operations to huge, international firms with hundreds of accounting partners and thousands of employees. Table 18.2 lists the largest public accounting firms in the world and some of their clients. Today, accounting firms do more than just accounting work. They provide clients with consulting services and advice on how to develop management information systems. And because of these activities, today's accounting firms hire not only accountants, but also people with educational training and experience in management, finance, and management information.

Typically, public accounting firms include on their staffs at least one **certified public accountant (CPA),** an individual who has met state requirements for accounting education and experience and has passed a rigorous two-day accounting examination. The uniform CPA examination is prepared by the American Institute of Certified Public Accountants (AICPA) and covers accounting practice, accounting theory, auditing, taxation, and business law. More information about general requirements and the CPA profession can be obtained by contacting the AICPA at www.aicpa.org. State requirements usually include a college degree in accounting and from one to three years of on-the-job experience. Details regarding specific state requirements for practice as a CPA can be obtained by contacting the state's board of accountancy. Once an individual becomes a CPA, he or she must participate in continuing-education programs to maintain state certification. These specialized programs are designed to provide the current training needed in today's changing business environment. CPAs must also take an ethics course to satisfy the continuing-education requirement.

certified public accountant (CPA) an individual who has met state requirements for accounting education and experience and has passed a rigorous two-day accounting examination

table 18.2 **The Big Five Accounting Firms**

Firm	Worldwide Revenues (in billions of dollars)	Major Clients
PricewaterhouseCoopers	$15.0	Allied Signal, AT&T, Avon, Compaq, Exxon IBM, Johnson & Johnson, Nike, Shell Oil
Andersen Worldwide	13.9	Enron, GTE, Sara Lee, Texaco, United Airlines
Ernst & Young International	10.9	Bank America, Coca-Cola, Eli Lilly, Lockheed, McDonald's, Time Warner, Wal-Mart
KPMG International	10.6	Aetna, Apple Computer, City of New York, Motorola, NBC, PepsiCo, Wells Fargo
Deloitte Touche Tohmatsu	9.0	Allstate, General Motors, Merrill Lynch, MetLife, Procter & Gamble, Sears

Source: Gary Hoover, *Hoover's Handbook of American Business 2000* (Austin, Texas: Hoover's Business Press 1999).

Certification as a CPA brings both status and responsibility. Only an independent CPA can audit the financial statements contained in a corporation's annual report and express an opinion—as required by law—regarding the acceptability of the corporation's accounting practices. And because CPAs have a great deal of experience, they are often asked to consult with business firms troubled by financial and/or management difficulties. In addition to auditing a corporation's financial statements and consulting, typical services performed by CPAs include planning and preparing tax returns, determining the true cost of producing and marketing a firm's goods or services, and compiling the financial information needed to make major management decisions. Fees for the services provided by CPAs generally range from $50 to $300 an hour.

Using the Internet

The American Institute of Certified Public Accountants is the preeminent professional body governing the profession. The organization's web site (**http://www.aicpa.org/**) provides users with a wide variety of information related to the accounting profession including a host of online publications, articles, guidelines, forums for discussion, employment opportunities, and links to other sites important to the field of accountancy.

The Accounting Process

LEARNING OBJECTIVE

2 Discuss the accounting process.

In the last chapter, information was defined as data presented in a form useful for a specific purpose. In this section, we examine accounting as the system for transforming raw financial *data* into useful financial *information*. We begin by looking at how a typical accounting system operates. Then, in the next sections, we describe the three most important financial statements provided by the accounting process.

The Accounting Equation

The accounting equation is a simple statement that forms the basis for the accounting process. This important equation shows the relationship between the firm's assets, liabilities, and owners' equity.

- **Assets** are the resources a business owns—cash, inventory, equipment, and real estate.
- **Liabilities** are the firm's debts—what it owes to others.
- **Owners' equity** is the difference between total assets and total liabilities—what would be left for the owners if the firm's assets were sold and the money used to pay off its liabilities.

assets the resources that a business owns

liabilities a firm's debts and obligations

owners' equity the difference between a firm's assets and its liabilities—what would be left for the owners if assets were used to pay off its liabilities

The relationship between assets, liabilities, and owners' equity is shown by the following **accounting equation:**

assets = liabilities + owners' equity

accounting equation the basis for the accounting process: *assets = liabilities + owners' equity*

Whether a business is a small corner grocery store or a giant corporation like General Motors, its assets must equal the sum of its liabilities and owners' equity. To use this equation, a firm's accountants must record raw data—that is, the firm's day-to-day financial transactions—using the double-entry system of bookkeeping.

The Double-Entry Bookkeeping System

Double-entry bookkeeping is a system in which each financial transaction is recorded as two separate accounting entries to maintain the balance shown in the accounting equation (assets = liabilities + owners' equity). By offsetting one side of the accounting equation with a change on the other side, the equation always remains in balance. For example, suppose an entrepreneur named Maria Martin invests $50,000 in cash to start a new business called Maple Tree Software. Before she makes this investment, both sides of the accounting equation equal zero. The firm has no assets, no liabilities, and no owners' equity. After Maria makes her original investment, the firm's cash account (an asset) would be increased by $50,000, and the owners' equity account

double-entry bookkeeping a system in which each financial transaction is recorded as two separate accounting entries to maintain the balance shown in the accounting equation

Imagine if SMALL companies had the power of a BIG accounting system! A state-of-the-art accounting system like the one provided by NetLedger can leverage the power of the Internet to turn your accounting system into an e-business rocket that increases both efficiency and speed.

would be increased by $50,000. The accounting equation would now look like this:

assets	=	**liabilities**	+	**owners' equity**
$50,000	=	$0	+	$50,000

Thus, the books are still balanced. Assets ($50,000) are equal to liabilities plus owners' equity ($50,000). Once established, the accounting system for Maple Tree Software must be able to process the accounting transactions that accurately reflect the financial decisions that are necessary to operate the business. For example, if Martin obtains a $10,000 bank loan to purchase computer equipment, two different accounts—liabilities and equipment—are affected. Liabilities are increased by the amount of the $10,000 loan. Equipment—an asset—is also increased by $10,000. After this transaction is recorded the accounting equation would look like this:

assets	=	**liabilities**	+	**owners' equity**
$60,000	=	$10,000	+	$50,000

After the first two transactions, assets total $60,000, and liabilities and owners' equity total $60,000. That is, assets are indeed equal to liabilities plus owners' equity. Additional transactions are recorded in much the same way using the five steps described below.

The Accounting Cycle

In the typical accounting system, raw data are transformed into financial statements in five steps. The first three—analyzing, recording, and posting—are performed on a regular basis throughout the accounting period. The last two—preparation of the trial balance and of the financial statements—are performed at the end of the accounting period.

Analyzing Source Documents

Basic accounting data are contained in *source documents*, the receipts, invoices, sales slips, and other documents that show the dollar amounts for day-to-day business transactions. The accounting cycle begins with the analysis of each of these documents. The purpose of the analysis is to determine which accounts are affected by the documents and how they are affected.

Recording Transactions

general journal a book of original entry in which typical transactions are recorded in order of their occurrence

Every financial transaction is then recorded in a journal—a process called *journalizing*. Transactions must be recorded in the firm's general journal or in specialized journals. The **general journal** is a book of original entry in which typical transactions are recorded in order of their occurrence. An accounting system may also include *specialized journals* for specific types of transactions that occur frequently. Thus, a retail store might have journals for cash receipts, cash disbursements, purchases, and sales in addition to its general journal.

Posting Transactions

general ledger a book of accounts containing a separate sheet or section for each account

posting the process of transferring journal entries to the general ledger

After the information is recorded in the general journal and specialized journals, it is transferred to the general ledger. The **general ledger** is a book of accounts containing a separate sheet or section for each account. The process of transferring journal entries to the general ledger is called **posting.** Today most businesses use a computer and software to journalize and post accounting entries.

Preparing the Trial Balance

trial balance a summary of the balances of all general ledger accounts at the end of the accounting period

A **trial balance** is a summary of the balances of all general ledger accounts at the end of the accounting period. To prepare a trial balance, the accountant determines and lists the balances for all ledger accounts. If the trial balance totals are correct and the accounting equation is still in balance, the accountant can prepare the financial statements. If not, a mistake has occurred somewhere, and the accountant must find it and correct it before proceeding.

Preparing Financial Statements and Closing the Books The firm's financial statements are prepared from the information contained in the trial balance. This information is presented in a standardized format to make the statements as accessible as possible to the various people who may be interested in the firm's financial affairs—managers, employees, lenders, suppliers, stockholders, potential investors, and government agencies. A firm's financial statements are prepared at least once a year. Most firms also have financial statements prepared semiannually, quarterly, or monthly.

Once these statements have been prepared and checked, the firm's books are "closed" for the accounting period, and a *post-closing* trial balance is prepared. Although like the trial balance described above, the *post-closing* trial balance is generally prepared after *all* accounting work is completed for one accounting period. If the post-closing trial balance totals agree, the accounting equation is still in balance at the end of the cycle. Only then can a new accounting cycle begin for the next accounting period.

With this brief information about the steps of the accounting cycle in mind, let's now examine the three most important financial statements generated by the accounting process: the balance sheet, the income statement, and the statement of cash flows.

The Balance Sheet

LEARNING OBJECTIVE

3 Read and interpret a balance sheet.

Question: Where could you find the total amount of assets, liabilities, or owners' equity for Hershey Foods Corporation?
Answer: The firm's balance sheet.

A **balance sheet** (sometimes referred to as a **statement of financial position**) is a summary of the dollar amounts of a firm's assets, liabilities, and owners' equity accounts at the end of a specific accounting period. The balance sheet must demonstrate that the accounting equation does indeed balance; that is, it must show that assets are equal to liabilities plus owners' equity. Most people think of a balance sheet as a statement that reports the financial condition of a business firm like Hershey Foods Corporation, but balance sheets apply to individuals, too. Let's begin our discussion with an example of a personal balance sheet for a recent college graduate named Marty Campbell. Three years ago, Marty graduated from college and obtained a full-time position as a sales representative for an office supply firm. After going to work, he established a checking and savings account, purchased an automobile, stereo, television, and a few pieces of furniture. Marty paid cash for some purchases, but he had to borrow money to pay for the larger ones. Figure 18.1 shows Marty's current personal balance sheet.

balance sheet (or statement of financial position) a summary of the dollar amounts of a firm's assets, liabilities, and owners' equity accounts at a particular time

Marty Campbell's assets total $26,500, and his liabilities amount to $10,000. While the difference between total assets and total liabilities is referred to as *owners' equity* or *stockholders' equity* for a business, it is normally called *net worth* for an individual. As reported on Marty's personal balance sheet, net worth is $16,500. The total assets ($26,500) and the total liabilities *plus* net worth ($26,500) are equal.

A balance sheet for a business reports the same type of financial information as a personal balance sheet. Although the dollar amounts for a business are likely to be larger, the total dollar value of assets must still equal the total value of liabilities plus owners' equity. Figure 18.2 shows the balance sheet for Northeast Art Supply, a small corporation that sells picture frames, paints, canvases, and other artists' supplies to retailers in New England. Note that assets are reported at the top of the statement, followed by liabilities and stockholders' equity. Let's work through the different accounts in Figure 18.2 on page 521, from top to bottom.

Assets

On a balance sheet, assets are listed in order, from the *most liquid* to the *least liquid*. The **liquidity** of an asset is the ease with which it can be converted into cash.

liquidity the ease with which an asset can be converted into cash

figure 18.1

Personal Balance Sheet

Even individuals can determine their net worth, or owner's equity, by subtracting the value of their debts from the value of their assets.

Marty Campbell
Personal Balance Sheet
December 31, 20XX

ASSETS		
Cash	$ 2,500	
Savings account	5,000	
Automobile	15,000	
Stereo	1,000	
Television	500	
Furniture	2,500	
TOTAL ASSETS		$26,500
LIABILITIES		
Automobile loan	$ 9,500	
Credit card balance	500	
TOTAL LIABILITIES		$10,000
NET WORTH (Owner's Equity)		16,500
TOTAL LIABILITIES AND NET WORTH		$26,500

Current Assets **Current assets** are assets that can quickly be converted into cash or that will be used in one year or less. Because cash is the most liquid asset, it is listed first. Next are *marketable securities*—stocks, bonds, and other investments—that can be converted into cash in a matter of days. These are short-term investments of excess cash that Northeast Art Supply doesn't need immediately.

Next are the firm's receivables. Its *accounts receivables*, which result from allowing customers to make credit purchases, are generally paid within thirty to sixty days. However, the firm expects that some of these debts will not be collected. Thus, it has reduced its accounts receivables by a 5 percent *allowance for doubtful accounts*. The firm's *notes receivables* are receivables for which customers have signed promissory notes. They are generally repaid over a longer period of time than the firm's accounts receivables.

Beautiful botanical assets. Typical current assets include cash, marketable securities, receivables, inventory, and prepaid expenses. However, for growers in Holland, tulips represent not simply an asset sold worldwide, but a beautiful one at that.

Northeast's *merchandise inventory* represents the value of goods on hand for sale to customers. These goods are listed as current assets because they will be sold in one year or less. Since Northeast Art Supply is a wholesale operation, the inventory listed in Figure 18.2 represents finished goods ready for sale to retailers. For a manufacturing firm, merchan-

NORTHEAST ART SUPPLY, INC.

Balance Sheet
December 31, 20XX

ASSETS			
Current assets			
Cash		$ 59,000	
Marketable securities		10,000	
Accounts receivable	$ 40,000		
Less allowance for doubtful accounts	2,000	38,000	
Notes receivable		32,000	
Merchandise inventory		41,000	
Prepaid expenses		2,000	
Total current assets			$182,000
Fixed assets			
Delivery equipment	$110,000		
Less accumulated depreciation	20,000	$ 90,000	
Furniture and store equipment	62,000		
Less accumulated depreciation	15,000	47,000	
Total fixed assets			137,000
Intangible assets			
Patents		$ 6,000	
Goodwill		15,000	
Total intangible assets			21,000
TOTAL ASSETS			$340,000
LIABILITIES AND STOCKHOLDERS' EQUITY			
Current liabilities			
Accounts payable	$ 35,000		
Notes payable	25,675		
Salaries payable	4,000		
Taxes payable	5,325		
Total current liabilities		$ 70,000	
Long-term liabilities			
Mortgage payable on store equipment	$ 40,000		
Total long-term liabilities		$ 40,000	
TOTAL LIABILITIES			$110,00
Stockholders's equity			
Common stock		$150,000	
Retained earnings		80,000	
TOTAL OWNERS'S EQUITY			$230,000
TOTAL LIABILITIES AND OWNERS' EQUITY			$340,000

figure 18.2

Business Balance Sheet

A balance sheet summarizes a firm's accounts at the end of an accounting period, showing the various dollar amounts that enter into the accounting equation. Note that assets ($340,000) equal liabilities plus owners' equity ($340,000).

dise inventory may represent raw materials that will become part of a finished product or work that has been partially completed but requires further processing. For information on the methods used to determine the dollar value of inventory, read Exploring Business on page 522.

Northeast's last current asset is **prepaid expenses**, which are assets that have been paid for in advance but have not yet been used. An example is insurance premiums. They are usually paid at the beginning of the policy year. The unused portion (say, for the last four months of the time period covered by the policy) is a prepaid expense. For Northeast Art, all current assets total $182,000.

current assets assets that can quickly be converted into cash or that will be used in one year or less

prepaid expenses assets that have been paid for in advance but have not yet been used

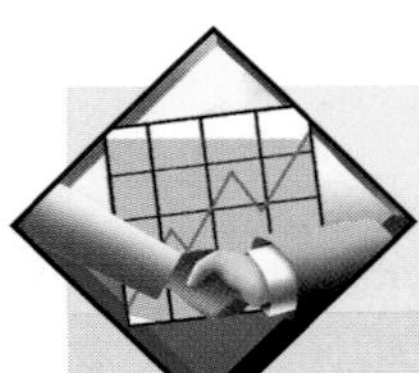

Exploring Business

Evaluating Inventory

WHAT DO GOODYEAR AND J.C. PENNEY have in common?

Like many other large firms, both companies have millions of dollars invested in inventory. At the end of 1999, Goodyear–an international manufacturer of tires and other rubber products for the transportation industry–reported inventory valued at $2.3 billion. J.C. Penney–a major retailer, with department stores in all fifty states and Puerto Rico–reported inventory valued at $5.9 billion. Both corporations have invested vast sums of money in inventory for one simple reason: they must have merchandise to sell when their customers want it. For each firm, the dollar value of inventory represents a large part of its total assets. These dollar values must be accurately reported to investors, lenders, suppliers, and government regulatory agencies.

Methods Used to Evaluate Inventories

Reporting the dollar value of inventory on a firm's financial statement can be complicated because the prices a firm pays for the goods it sells or the materials it uses in manufacturing are likely to change during an accounting period. To determine the dollar value of inventory, one of four methods can be used. When the *specific identification method* is used, each inventory item is marked, tagged, or coded with its "specific" unit cost. The *average-cost method* assumes that each inventory item carries an equal, or average, cost. To arrive at the average cost, the total cost of all items available for sale is divided by the number of items. When the *first-in, first-out (FIFO) method* is used, the accountant assumes that the merchandise purchased at the beginning of the accounting period is sold first. With FIFO, the costs for the items purchased at the end of the accounting period are used to determine the value of the remaining inventory. Finally, the *last-in, first-out (LIFO) method* assumes that the merchandise purchased at the end of the accounting period is sold first. With LIFO, the costs for the items purchased at the beginning of the accounting period are used to determine the value of the remaining inventory.

Which Inventory Method Is Best?

Although none of these four methods of evaluating inventory is considered perfect, each method is acceptable for use in published financial statements. When choosing an inventory method, a firm should consider the effect each method will have on its balance sheet, income statement, taxes, and management decisions.

fixed assets assets that will be held or used for a period longer than one year

depreciation the process of apportioning the cost of a fixed asset over the period during which it will be used

Fixed Assets **Fixed assets** are assets that will be held or used for a period longer than one year. They generally include land, buildings, and equipment. Although Northeast owns no land or buildings because like a lot of businesses it rents or leases the space it needs to operate, it does own *delivery equipment* that originally cost $110,000. It also owns *furniture and store equipment* that originally cost $62,000.

Note that the values of both fixed assets are decreased by their *accumulated depreciation*. **Depreciation** is the process of apportioning the cost of a fixed asset over its useful life. The depreciation amount allotted to each year is an expense for that year, and the value of the asset must be reduced by that expense amount. Although the actual method used to calculate the dollar amounts for depreciation expense and accumulated depreciation reported on a firm's financial statements are beyond the scope of this text, you should know that there are a number of different methods that can be used. You should also know that one method may increase or decrease the dollar amounts reported on a firm's financial statements when compared with another method of calculating depreciation expense and accumulated depreciation. In the case of Northeast's delivery equipment, $20,000 of its value has been depreciated (or used up) since it was purchased. Its value at this time is thus $110,000 less $20,000, or $90,000. In a similar fashion, the original value of furniture and store equipment ($62,000) has been reduced by accumulated depreciation of $15,000. Furniture and store equipment now has a reported value of $47,000. For Northeast Art, all fixed assets total $137,000.

Intangible Assets

Intangible assets are assets that do not exist physically but that have a value based on the rights or privileges they confer on a firm. They include patents, copyrights, trademarks, franchises, and goodwill. By their nature, intangible assets are long-term assets—they are of value to the firm for a number of years. According to Baruch Lev, professor of Accounting and Finance at New York University's Stern School of Management and a director of the Project for Research on Intangibles, current accounting methods used to evaluate and measure Internet-related firms are inadequate. He suggests accounting and finance need to apply new principles that are better equipped to communicate value in a world of intangibles. Most accountants fail to properly value the most valuable corporate assets: intangibles such as brand, market power, business processes, and research and development and instead focus on hard assets and current revenues as though online business was no different than any other.[3]

intangible assets assets that do not exist physically but that have a value based on the rights or privileges they confer on a firm

Northeast Art Supply lists two intangible assets. The first is a *patent* for an oil paint that the company has developed. The firm's accountants estimate the patent has a current market value of $6,000. The second intangible asset, **goodwill,** is the value of a firm's reputation, location, earning capacity, and other intangibles that make the business a profitable concern. Goodwill is not normally listed on a balance sheet unless the firm has been purchased from previous owners. In this case, the new owners have actually paid an additional amount over and above the value of the firm's assets for goodwill. Goodwill exists because most businesses are worth more as going concerns than as a collection of assets. Northeast Art's accountants included a $15,000 amount for goodwill. The firm's intangible assets total $21,000. Now it is possible to total all three types of assets for Northeast Art. As calculated in Figure 18.2, total assets are $340,000.

goodwill the value of a firm's reputation, location, earning capacity, and other intangibles that make the business a profitbale concern

Liabilities and Owners' Equity

The liabilities and the owners' equity accounts complete the balance sheet. The firm's liabilities are separated into two categories—current and long-term.

Current Liabilities

A firm's **current liabilities** are debts that will be repaid in one year or less. Northeast Art Supply purchased merchandise from its suppliers on credit. Thus, its balance sheet includes an entry for accounts payable. **Accounts payable** are short-term obligations that arise as a result of making credit purchases.

Notes payable are obligations that have been secured with promissory notes. They are usually short-term obligations, but they may extend beyond one year. Only those that must be paid within the year are listed under current liabilities.

Northeast also lists *salaries payable* and *taxes payable* as current liabilities. These are both expenses that have been incurred during the current accounting period but will be paid in the next accounting period. For Northeast Art, current liabilities total $70,000.

current liabilities debts that will be repaid in one year or less

accounts payable short-term obligations that arise as a result of making credit purchases

notes payable obligations that have been secured with promissory notes

Long-Term Liabilities

Long-term liabilities are debts that need not be repaid for at least one year. Northeast lists only one long-term liability—a $40,000 *mortgage payable* for store equipment. Bonds and other long-term loans would be included here as well, if they existed. As you see in Figure 18.2, Northeast's current and long-term liabilities total $110,000.

long-term liabilities debts that need not be repaid for at least one year

retained earnings the portion of a business's profits not distributed to stockholders

Owners' or Stockholders' Equity For a sole proprietorship or partnership, the owners' equity is shown as the difference between assets and liabilities. In a partnership, each partner's share of the ownership is reported separately in each owner's name. For a corporation, the owners' equity is usually referred to as *stockholders' equity*. The dollar amount reported on the balance sheet is the total value of stock, plus retained earnings that have accumulated to date. **Retained earnings** are the portion of a business's profits not distributed to stockholders.

The original investment by the owners of Northeast Art Supply was $150,000. In addition, $80,000 of Northeast's earnings have been reinvested in the business since it was founded. Thus, owners' equity totals $230,000.

As the two grand totals in Figure 18.2 show, Northeast's assets and the sum of its liabilities and owners' equity are equal—at $340,000.

LEARNING OBJECTIVE

4 Read and interpret an income statement.

The Income Statement

Question: Where can you find the profit or loss amount for The Gap, Inc.?
Answer: The firm's income statement

income statement a summary of a firm's revenues and expenses during a specified accounting period

An **income statement** is a summary of a firm's revenues and expenses during a specified accounting period. The income statement is sometimes called the *earnings statement* or the *statement of income and expenses*. Let's begin our discussion by constructing a personal income statement for Marty Campbell. Having worked as a sales representative for an office supply firm for the past three years, Marty now earns $33,600 a year, or $2,800 a month. After income tax withholding and deductions for Social Security and Medicare, his take-home pay is $1,900 a month. As illustrated in Figure 18.3, Marty's typical monthly expenses include payments for an automobile loan, credit card purchases, apartment rent, utilities, food, clothing, and recreation and entertainment.

While the difference between income and expenses is referred to as *profit* or *loss* for a business, it is normally referred to as a cash *surplus* or cash *deficit* for an individual.

figure 18.3

Personal Income Statement

By subtracting expenses from income, you can determine if you have a surplus or deficit at the end of a specific calendar month.

Marty Campbell
Personal Income Statement
For the month ended December 31, 20XX

INCOME (Take-home pay)		$1,900
LESS MONTHLY EXPENSES		
Automobile loan	$ 250	
Credit card payment	100	
Apartment rent	500	
Utilities	200	
Food	250	
Clothing	100	
Recreation & entertainment	250	
TOTAL MONTHLY EXPENSES		1,650
CASH SURPLUS (or profit)		$ 250

Fortunately for Marty, he has a surplus of $250 at the end of each month. He can use this surplus for savings, investing, or paying off debts.

The typical income statement for a business reports the same type of information as Marty Campbell's personal income statement. Although the dollar amounts for most businesses are larger, the total income minus expenses still equals profit or loss. Figure 18.4 shows the income statement for Northeast Art Supply. Note that it consists of four sections: revenues, costs of goods sold, operating expenses, and net income. Generally, revenues *less* cost of goods sold *less* operating expenses equals net income.

Revenues

Revenues are the dollar amounts earned by a firm from selling goods, providing services, or performing business activities. Thus, revenues includes all the money received from all sources. For most businesses, sales are the primary source of rev-

revenues the dollar amounts earned by a firm from selling goods, providing services, or performing business activities

NORTHEAST ART SUPPLY, INC.		Income Statement For the Year Ended December 31, 20XX	
Revenues			
Gross sales		$465,000	
Less sales returns and allowances	$ 9,500		
Less sales discounts	4,500	14,000	
Net sales			$451,000
Cost of goods sold			
Beginning inventory, January 1, 20XX		$ 40,000	
Purchases	$346,000		
Less purchase discounts	11,000		
Net purchases		335,000	
Cost of goods available for sale		$375,000	
Less ending inventory December 31, 20XX		41,000	
Cost of goods sold			334,000
Gross profit			$117,000
Operating expenses			
Selling expenses			
Sales salaries	$ 22,000		
Advertising	4,000		
Sales promotion	2,500		
Depreciation—store equipment	3,000		
Depreciation—delivery equipment	4,000		
Miscellaneous selling expenses	1,500		
Total selling expenses		$ 37,000	
General expenses			
Office salaries	$ 28,500		
Rent	8,500		
Depreciation—office furniture	1,500		
Utilities expense	2,500		
Insurance expense	1,000		
Miscellaneous expense	500		
Total general expense		42,500	
Total operating expenses			$ 79,500
Net income from operations			$ 37,500
Less interest expense			2,000
NET INCOME BEFORE TAXES			$ 35,500
Less federal income taxes			5,325
NET INCOME AFTER TAXES			$ 30,175

figure 18.4

Business Income Statement

An income statement summarizes a firm's revenues and expenses during a specified accounting period—one month, three months, six months, or a year.

Sales make the business world go 'round. Sales is often a team effort involving all of a firm's employees—not just the person who makes a sales presentation to a prospective customer. Here, employees must accurately select the merchandise needed to fill an order before it can be shipped to the customer.

enues. However, some businesses have other sources of revenues that may include money from renting property or equipment, allowing other businesses to use the firm's patents and copyrights, and receiving interest and dividends on investments. Northeast obtains its revenues solely from the sale of its products to retailers in New England. The revenues section of its income statement begins with gross sales. **Gross sales** are the total dollar amount of all goods and services sold during the accounting period. From this amount are deducted the dollar amounts of

- *Sales returns*—merchandise returned to the firm by its customers
- *Sales allowances*—price reductions offered to customers who accept slightly damaged or soiled merchandise
- *Sales discounts*—price reductions offered to customers who pay their bills promptly

The remainder is the firm's net sales. **Net sales** are the actual dollar amounts received by the firm for the goods and services it has sold, after adjustment for returns, allowances, and discounts. For Northeast Art, net sales are $451,000.

Cost of Goods Sold

The standard method of determining the **cost of goods sold** by a retailing or wholesaling firm can be summarized as follows:

$$\textbf{costs of goods sold} = \textbf{beginning inventory} + \textbf{net purchases} - \textbf{ending inventory}$$

A manufacturer must include raw materials inventories, work in progress, and direct manufacturing costs in this computation.

According to Figure 18.4, Northeast began its accounting period on January 1 with a merchandise inventory that cost $40,000. During the next twelve months, the firm purchased merchandise valued at $346,000. But after taking advantage of *purchase discounts*, it paid only $335,000 for this merchandise. Thus, during the year, Northeast had total *goods available for sale* valued at $40,000 plus $335,000, or $375,000.

At the end of the accounting period on December 31, Northeast had sold all but $41,000 worth of the available goods. The cost of goods sold by Northeast was therefore $375,000 less ending inventory of $41,000, or $334,000. A firm's **gross profit** is its net sales *less* the cost of goods sold. For Northeast, gross profit was therefore $117,000.

Operating Expenses

A firm's **operating expenses** are all business costs other than the cost of goods sold. They are generally classed as either selling expenses or general expenses.

Selling expenses are costs related to the firm's marketing activities. For Northeast Art, selling expenses total $37,000. General expenses are costs incurred in managing a business. For Northeast Art, general expenses total $42,500. Now it is possible to total both selling and general expenses. As Figure 18.4 shows, total operating expenses for the accounting period are $79,500.

gross sales the total dollar amount of all goods and services sold during the accounting period.

net sales the actual dollar amounts received by a firm for the goods and services it has sold, after adjustment for returns, allowances, and discounts

cost of goods sold the dollar amount equal to beginning inventory *plus* net purchases *less* ending inventory

gross profit a firm's net sales *less* the cost of goods sold

operating expenses all business costs other than the cost of goods sold

Net Income

Net income is the profit earned (or the loss suffered) by a firm during an accounting period, after all expenses have been deducted from revenues. As Figure 18.4 shows, Northeast's *net income* is computed as gross profit ($117,000) *less* total operating expenses ($79,500). For Northeast Art, net income from operations is $37,500. From this amount, *interest expense* of $2,000 is deducted to obtain a *net income before taxes* of $35,500. The interest expense is deducted in this section of the income statement because it is not an operating expense. Rather, it is an expense that results from financing the business. Also, note the difference between gross profit and net income before taxes. *Gross profit* is the amount that results from subtracting the cost of goods sold from net sales. A firm's gross profit amount *does not* include any operating expenses. *Net income before taxes*, on the other hand, is what remains after cost of goods sold *and* all expenses are deducted from net sales.

Northeast's *federal income taxes* are $5,325. Although these taxes may or may not be payable immediately, they are definitely an expense that must be deducted from income. This leaves Northeast with a *net income after taxes* of $30,175. This amount may be used to pay a dividend to stockholders, retained or reinvested in the firm, used to reduce the firm's debts, or all three.

Both technical and managerial skills lead to profitability. While this construction worker knows how to provide a service to customers, it would all be useless if his business didn't increase sales, control expenses, and ultimately earn a profit—all amounts that are reported on a firm's income statement.

net income the profit earned (or the loss suffered) by a firm during an accounting period, after all expenses have been deducted from revenues

The Statement of Cash Flows

LEARNING OBJECTIVE

5 Describe business activities that affect a firm's cash flow.

Cash is the lifeblood of any business. In 1987 the Securities and Exchange Commission (SEC) and the Financial Accounting Standards Board (FASB) required all publicly traded companies to include a statement of cash flows, along with their balance sheet and income statement, in their annual report. The **statement of cash flows** illustrates how the operating, investing, and financing activities of a company affect cash during an accounting period. A statement of cash flows for Northeast Art Supply is illustrated in Figure 18.5. It provides information concerning the company's cash receipts and cash payments and is organized around three different activities: operations, investing, and financing.

statement of cash flows a statement that illustrates how the operating, investing, and financing activities of a company affect cash during an accounting period

- *Cash flows from operating activities.* This is the first section of a statement of cash flows. It addresses the firm's primary revenue source—providing goods and services. The amounts paid to suppliers, employees, interest, taxes, and expenses are deducted from the amount received from customers. Finally the interest and dividends received by the firm are added to determine the total. After all adjustments are made, the total represents a true picture of cash flows from operating activities.
- *Cash flows from investing activities.* The second section of the statement is concerned with cash flow from investments. This includes the purchase and sale of land, equipment, and other long-term assets, and investments.

figure 18.5

Statement of Cash Flows

A statement of cash flows summarizes how a firm's operating, investing, and financing activities affect its cash during a specified period—one month, three months, six months, or a year.

NORTHEAST ART SUPPLY, INC.

Statement of Cash Flows
For the Year Ended
December 31, 20XX

Cash flows from operating activities		
Cash received from customers	$ 451,000	
Cash paid to suppliers and employees	(384,500)	
Interest paid	(2,000)	
Income taxes paid	(5,325)	
Interest and dividends received	500	
Net cash provided by operating activities		$ 59,675
Cash flows from investing activities		
Purchase of equipment	$(4,250)	
Purchase of short-term investments	(10,000)	
Sale of short-term investments	11,500	
Net cash provided by investing activities		$(2,750)
Cash flows from financing activities		
Payment of short-term debt	$(4,000)	
Payment of long-term debt	(7,000)	
Payment of dividends	(15,000)	
Net cash provided by financing activities		$(26,000)
NET INCREASE (DECREASE) IN CASH		$ 30,925
Cash at beginning of year		28,075
CASH AT END OF YEAR		$ 59,000

- *Cash flows from financing activities.* The third and final section deals with the cash flow from all financing activities. It reports changes in debt obligation and owners' equity accounts. This includes loans and repayments, the sale and repurchase of the company's own stock, and cash dividends.

The totals of all three activities are added to the beginning cash balance to determine the ending cash balance. For Northeast Art Supply the ending cash balance is $59,000. Note that this is the same amount reported on the firm's balance sheet. Together, the cash flow statement, balance sheet, and income statement illustrate the results of past business decisions and reflect the firm's ability to pay debts and dividends and to finance new growth.

Evaluating Financial Statements

LEARNING OBJECTIVE

6 Summarize how managers evaluate the financial health of a business.

All three financial statements—the balance sheet, the income statement, and the statement of cash flows—can provide answers to a variety of questions about the firm's ability to do business and stay in business, its profitability, its value as an investment, and its ability to repay its debts. Even more information can be obtained by comparing present financial statements with those prepared for past accounting periods. Such comparisons permit managers, lenders, suppliers, and investors to (1) identify trends in growth, borrowing, and other business variables and (2) determine whether the firm is on track in terms of meeting its long-term goals.

Why Audited Financial Statements Are Important

Many managers wish they could forget about audits. But audits are a necessary part of the accounting process. In fact, audits are so important that many companies turn to professional firms like RHI Management Resources and their staff of business solutions specialists for help when preparing for an audit.

Assume you are a bank officer responsible for evaluating loan applications. A business has applied for a loan. How do you make a decision to approve or reject the loan request? In this situation, most bank officers rely on the information contained in the firm's balance sheet, income statement, and statement of cash flows along with other information provided by the prospective borrower. In fact, most lenders insist that these financial statements be audited by a CPA. An **audit** is an examination of a company's financial statements and the accounting practices that produced them. The purpose of an audit is to make sure that the financial statements have been prepared in accordance with *generally accepted accounting principles*. Today, generally accepted accounting principles, commonly referred to as *GAAP*, have been developed to provide guidelines for companies reporting financial information and for the accounting profession. If an accountant determines that a firm's financial statements present financial information fairly and conform to GAAP, then she or he will issue the following statement:

> In our opinion, the financial statements . . . present fairly, in all material respects . . . in conformity with generally accepted accounting principles.

While an audit and the resulting report do not *guarantee* that a company hasn't "cooked the books," it does imply that on the whole, the company has followed generally accepted accounting principles. Because of the historically ethical reputation and independence of auditors, banks, creditors, investors, and government agencies are willing to rely on an auditor's opinion when deciding to invest in a company or to make loans to a firm that has been audited. Finally, it should be noted that without the audit function and GAAP, there would be very little oversight or supervision. The validity of a firm's financial statements and its accounting records would quickly drop and firms would find it difficult to obtain debt financing, acquire goods and services from suppliers, find investor financing, or prepare documents requested by government agencies.

audit an examination of a company's financial statements and accounting practices that produced them

Comparing Data for Previous Accounting Periods

Most corporations include in their annual reports comparisons of the important elements of their financial statements for recent years. Figure 18.6 shows such comparisons—of sales, long-term debt, earnings per share, and other important financial measures—for the Boeing Corporation, a world leader in the aerospace industry. By examining these data, a marketing manager for Boeing can judge how fast annual sales are increasing. An operating manager can tell whether R&D expenditures are decreasing. And the vice president of finance can determine if the dollar amount of debt is changing. Stockholders and potential investors, on the other hand, may be more concerned with increases or decreases in Boeing's earnings per share.

spotLight

Following their money

Among students with investments, 52% of males and 41% of females say they follow the ups and downs. Students who follow their investments, by grade level:

7th–9th: 35%
10th–12th: 44%
College: 59%

Source: Copyright 2000, USA TODAY. Reprinted with permission.

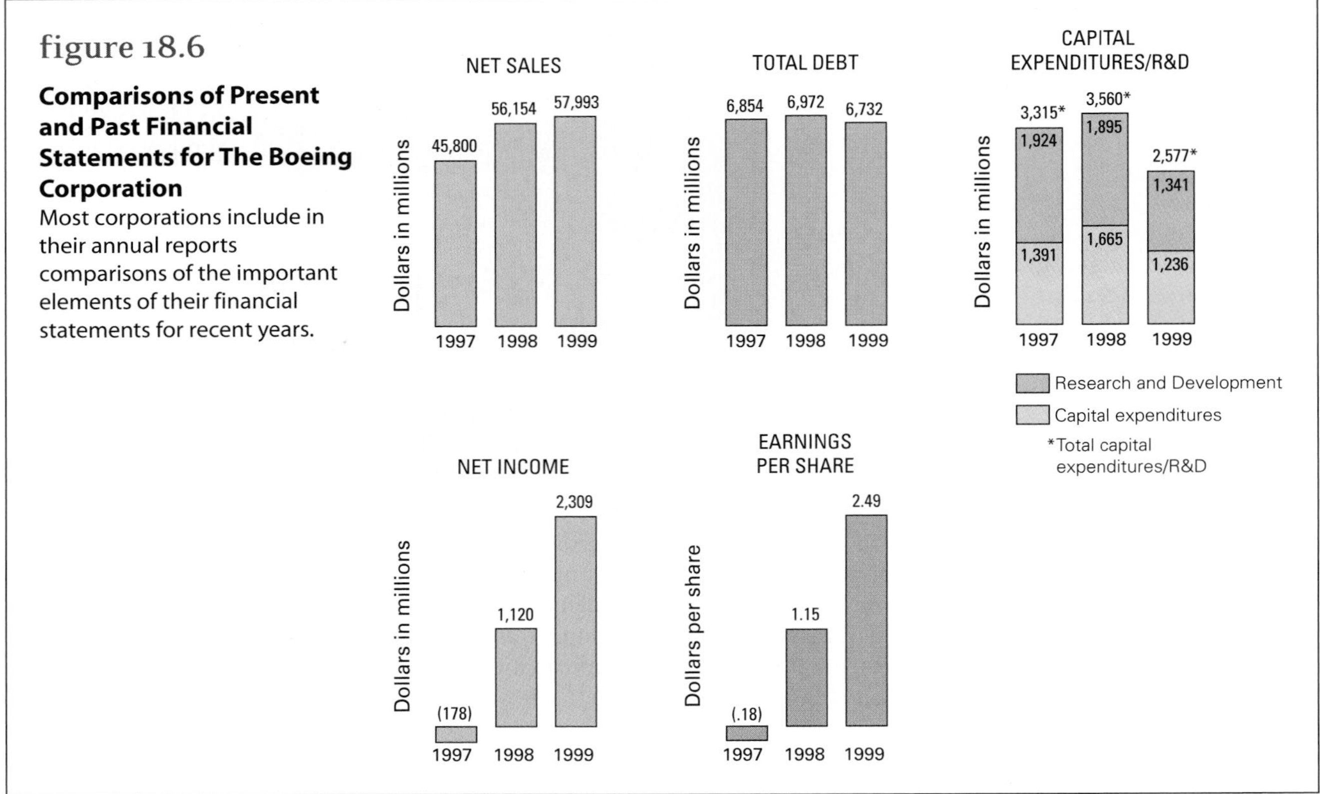

figure 18.6

Comparisons of Present and Past Financial Statements for The Boeing Corporation
Most corporations include in their annual reports comparisons of the important elements of their financial statements for recent years.

Source: Adapted from the Boeing Corporation, 1999 Annual Report, p. 3.

Comparing Data with Other Firms' Data

Many firms also compare their financial results with those of competing firms and with industry averages. Comparisons are possible as long as accountants follow the generally accepted accounting principles. Except for minor differences in format and terms, the balance sheet and income statement of Procter & Gamble, for example, will be similar to those of other large corporations, such as Alberto-Culver, Clorox, Colgate-Palmolive, and Unilever in the consumer goods industry. Comparisons among firms give managers a general idea of a firm's relative effectiveness and its standing within the industry. Competitors' financial statements can be obtained from their annual reports—if they are public corporations. Industry averages are published by reporting services like Dun & Bradstreet and Standard & Poor's, as well as by some industry trade associations. (For information on the importance of accounting standards for foreign firms, read Going Global.)

financial ratio a number that shows the relationship between two elements of a firm's financial statements

Still another type of analysis of a firm's financial health involves computation of financial ratios. A **financial ratio** is a number that shows the relationship between two elements of a firm's financial statements. Among the most useful ratios are profitability ratios, short-term financial ratios, activity ratios, and the debt-to-owners' equity ratio. Like the individual elements in financial statements, these ratios can be compared with the firm's past ratios, with those of competitors, and with industry averages. The information required to form these ratios is found in the balance sheet and the income statement (in our examples, Figures 18.2 and 18.4).

Profitability Ratios

A firm's net income after taxes indicates whether the firm is profitable. It does not, however, indicate how effectively the firm's resources are being used. For this latter purpose, three ratios can be computed.

Going Global

International Accounting Standards

ASSUME YOU ARE TRYING TO DETERMINE which of two companies is the better investment. One company is located in the United States; the other is located in Germany. You obtain an annual report from both companies, but are concerned that the reports may be prepared by using different accounting standards.

Your concern is justified. Today there are at two standards for accounting: one standard used in the United States and a different standard used throughout the remainder of the world. In the United States, accountants use what is referred to as generally accepted accounting principles or *GAAP*. In the rest of the world, accountants use international accounting standards or *IAS*.

How Different Are GAAP and IAS?

While GAAP and IAS agree on how accountants report many financial items, there are important differences. One major difference is that generally accepted accounting principles or GAAP are usually thought to be more stringent on how a company reports important financial information. As a result, when compared to foreign firms, U.S. companies provide more disclosure of important financial information to lenders, suppliers, investors, and government agencies.

International accounting standards or IAS, on the other hand, are more lenient and allow accountants some flexibility when choosing how to document financial information. The IAS have been constructed over the last twenty-six years by the International Accounting Standards Committee. This committee, based in London, consists of accountants representing 104 countries.

The Problem for Foreign Firms Listed on the U.S. Stock Exchanges

The Securities and Exchange Commission (SEC) requires that both U.S. and foreign firms listed on U.S. stock exchanges use generally accepted accounting principles. According to the SEC, it has a responsibility to maintain the integrity and strength of the U.S. stock market. And the SEC believes that international accounting standards deliberately permit inconsistencies that will likely confuse and mislead investors.

But those firms using IAS refuse to accept GAAP. They reason that the added expense of complying with GAAP is simply not worth it. They argue that GAAP is too time consuming and out-of-date. And many smaller foreign companies simply don't have the resources to deal with the type of complex accounting required by GAAP.

Is There a Solution?

Although more and more firms are involved in global business, a common set of accounting guidelines that everyone accepts does not exist at the present time. Proponents of GAAP and IAS must reach a compromise that will guarantee all accounting and financial information is prepared in the same way and is based on the same assumptions. Although the need for one set of accounting standards is obvious, experts predict that it will be at least ten years before U.S. regulators will accept anything other than generally accepted accounting principles.

Return on Sales **Return on sales** is a financial ratio calculated by dividing net income after taxes by net sales. For Northeast Art Supply,

return on sales a financial ratio calculated by dividing net income after taxes by net sales

$$\textbf{return on sales} = \frac{\textbf{net income after taxes}}{\textbf{net sales}} = \frac{\$30{,}175}{\$451{,}000}$$

$$= 0.067, \text{ or } 6.7\%$$

The return on sales indicates how effectively the firm is transforming sales into profits. A higher return on sales is better than a low one. Today, the average return on sales for all business firms is between 4 and 5 percent. With a return on sales of 6.7 percent, Northeast Art Supply is above average. A low return on sales can be increased by reducing expenses, by increasing sales, or both.

Return on Owners' Equity **Return on owners' equity** is a financial ratio calculated by dividing net income after taxes by owners' equity. For Northeast Art Supply,

return on owners' equity a financial ratio calculated by dividing net income after taxes by owners' equity

$$\textbf{return on owners' equity} = \frac{\textbf{net income after taxes}}{\textbf{owners' equity}} = \frac{\$30{,}175}{\$230{,}000}$$

$$= 0.13, \text{ or } 13\%$$

Return on owners' equity indicates how much income is generated by each dollar of equity. Northeast is providing income of 13 cents per dollar invested in the business; the average for all businesses is between 12 and 15 cents. A higher return on owners' equity is better than a low one, and the only practical way to increase return on owners' equity is to reduce expenses, increase sales, or both.

earnings per share a financial ratio calculated by dividing net income after taxes by the number of shares of common stock outstanding

Earnings per Share From the point of view of stockholders, **earnings per share** is one of the best indicators of a corporation's success. It is calculated by dividing net income after taxes by the number of shares of common stock outstanding. If we assume that Northeast Art Supply has issued 25,000 shares of stock, then its earnings per share are:

$$\textbf{earnings per share} = \frac{\textbf{net income after taxes}}{\textbf{common-stock shares outstanding}} = \frac{\$30{,}175}{25{,}000}$$
$$= \$1.21 \text{ per share}$$

There is no meaningful average for this ratio, mainly because the number of outstanding shares of a firm's stock is subject to change as a result of stock splits and stock dividends. As a general rule, however, an increase in earnings per share is a healthy sign for any corporation. Critics of current accounting practice point to the way firms measure their earnings. Given that investors in stocks are willing to pay a certain amount of money for every dollar of earnings generated by a firm, they argue it is misleading when companies do not distinguish between the different sources of total earnings in their firm's reports. Real performance they argue is best reflected by cash flows from operations of the business. Critics suggest that IBM has inflated earnings reports because actual earnings are linked to pension fund accounts, which in turn are linked to the firm's stock market value. As long as IBM continues to ride the wave of higher stock market values, its earnings reports will continue to attract critics.[4]

Short-Term Financial Ratios

Two short-term financial ratios permit managers (and lenders) to evaluate the ability of a firm to pay its current liabilities.

current ratio a financial ratio computed by dividing current assets by current liabilities

Current Ratio A firm's **current ratio** is computed by dividing current assets by current liabilities. For Northeast Art Supply,

$$\textbf{current ratio} = \frac{\textbf{current assets}}{\textbf{current liabilities}} = \frac{\$182{,}000}{\$70{,}000} = 2.6$$

This means that Northeast Art Supply has \$2.60 of current assets for every \$1 of current liabilities. The average current ratio for all industries is 2.0, but it varies greatly from industry to industry. Each firm should compare its current ratio with those of its own industry to determine whether it is high or low. A high current ratio indicates that a firm can pay its current liabilities. A low current ratio can be improved by repaying current liabilities or by reducing dividend payments to increase the firm's cash balance.

acid-test ratio a financial ratio calculated by subtracting the value of inventory from the current asset amount and dividing the total by current liabilities

Acid-Test Ratio This ratio, sometimes called the *quick ratio*, is a measure of the firm's ability to pay current liabilities *quickly*—with its cash, marketable securities, and receivables. The **acid-test ratio** is calculated by subtracting the value of inventory from the current asset amount and dividing the total by current liabilities. The value of inventory is "removed" from current assets because merchandise inventory is not converted into cash as easily as other current assets. For Northeast Art Supply,

$$\textbf{acid-test ratio} = \frac{\textbf{current assets} - \textbf{inventory}}{\textbf{current liabilities}}$$
$$= \frac{\$182{,}000 - \$41{,}000}{\$70{,}000} = \frac{\$141{,}000}{\$70{,}000} = 2.01$$

For all businesses, the desired acid-test ratio is 1.0. Northeast Art Supply is above average with a ratio of 2.01, and the firm should be well able to pay its current liabilities. To increase a low ratio, a firm would have to repay current liabilities or obtain additional cash from investors.

Activity Ratios

Two activity ratios permit managers to measure how many times each year a company collects its accounts receivable or sells its inventory. Both activity ratios are described below.

Accounts Receivable Turnover

A firm's **accounts receivable turnover** is the number of times the firm collects its accounts receivable in one year. If the data are available, this ratio should be calculated using a firm's net credit sales. Since data for Northeast Art Supply's credit sales are unavailable, this ratio can be calculated by dividing net sales by accounts receivable:

accounts receivable turnover a financial ratio calculated by dividing net sales by accounts receivable

$$\textbf{accounts receivable turnover} = \frac{\textbf{net sales}}{\textbf{accounts receivable}} = \frac{\$451{,}000}{38{,}000}$$
$$= 11.9 \text{ times each year}$$

Northeast Art Supply collects its accounts receivable 11.9 times each year, or about every thirty days. If a firm's credit terms require customers to pay in twenty-five days, a collection period of thirty days is considered acceptable. There is no meaningful average for this measure, mainly because credit terms differ among companies. A high accounts receivable turnover is better than a low one. As a general rule, a low accounts receivable turnover ratio can be improved by pressing for payment of past due accounts and by tightening requirements for prospective credit customers.

Inventory Turnover

A firm's **inventory turnover** is the number of times the firm sells its merchandise inventory in one year. It is approximated by dividing the cost of goods sold in one year by the average value of the inventory.

inventory turnover a financial ratio calculated by dividing the cost of goods sold in one year by the average value of the inventory

The average value of the inventory can be found by adding the beginning inventory value and the ending inventory value (given on the income statement) and dividing the sum by 2. For Northeast Art Supply, this comes out to $40,500. Thus,

$$\textbf{inventory turnover} = \frac{\textbf{cost of goods sold}}{\textbf{average inventory}} = \frac{\$334{,}000}{\$40{,}500}$$
$$= 8.2 \text{ times each year}$$

Northeast Art Supply sells its merchandise inventory 8.2 times each year, or about once every forty-five days.

The average inventory turnover for all firms is about 9 times per year, but turnover rates vary widely from industry to industry. For example, supermarkets may have turnover rates of 20 or higher, whereas turnover rates for furniture stores are generally well below the national average. The quickest way to improve inventory turnover is to order merchandise in smaller quantities at more frequent intervals.

Debt-to-Owners' Equity Ratio

Our final category of financial ratios indicates the degree to which a firm's operations are financed through borrowing. Although other ratios can be calculated, the debt-to-owners' equity ratio is often used to determine whether a firm has too much debt. The **debt-to-owners' equity ratio** is calculated by dividing total liabilities by owners' equity. For Northeast Art Supply,

debt-to-owners' equity ratio a financial ratio calculated by dividing total liabilities by owners' equity

$$\textbf{debt-to-owners' equity ratio} = \frac{\textbf{total liabilities}}{\textbf{owners' equity}} = \frac{\$110{,}000}{\$230{,}000} = 0.48, \text{ or } 48\%$$

A debt-to-owners' equity ratio of 48 percent means that creditors have provided about 48 cents of financing for every dollar provided by owners.

The debt-to-owners' equity ratio for business in general ranges between 33 and 50 percent. The higher this ratio, the riskier the situation is for lenders. A high debt-to-owners' equity ratio may make borrowing additional money from lenders difficult. It can be reduced by paying off debts or by increasing the owners' investment in the firm.

Northeast's Financial Ratios: A Summary

Table 18.3 compares the financial ratios of Northeast Art Supply with the average financial ratios for all businesses. It also lists the formulas we used to calculate Northeast's ratios. Northeast seems to be in good financial shape. Its return on sales, current ratio, and acid-test ratio are all above average. Its other ratios are about average, although its inventory turnover debt-to-equity ratio could be improved.

Accounting Software and Systems

Recent developments suggest that software, including accounting systems, will increasingly be sold by monthly subscription through Internet service centers rather than as a complete accounting system purchase. The popularity of outsourcing complicated technical work to specialists is likely to grow in popularity as a means to control related computer services costs and software upgrades. For example, Chief Information Officer Al Herak of Talbert Medical Group in Costa Mesa, California, chose to pay Trizetto Group in Newport Beach, California, about $100,000 a month to provide all accounting software and computer services instead of setting up his own million dollar system at the firm's offices.[5]

Problems arise when organizations still using one of many different older-generation accounting computer applications that were never designed to communicate with other systems wish to enter Internet-based business-to-business exchanges. Hospitals typically use accounting systems for handling billing and order management from providers such as McKessonHBOC, Lawson Software, PeopleSoft, or Meditech. Med-

table 18.3 Financial Ratios of Northeast Art Supply Compared with Average Ratios for All Businesses

Ratio	Formula	Northeast Ratio	Average Business Ratio	Direction for Improvement
Profitability Ratios				
Return on sales	$\frac{\text{net income after taxes}}{\text{net sales}}$	6.7%	4%–5%	Higher
Return on owners' equity	$\frac{\text{net income after taxes}}{\text{owners' equity}}$	13%	12%–15%	Higher
Earnings per share	$\frac{\text{net income after taxes}}{\text{common-stock shares outstanding}}$	$1.21 per share	—	Higher
Short-Term Financial Ratios				
Current ratio	$\frac{\text{current assets}}{\text{current liabilities}}$	2.6	2.0	Higher
Acid-test ratio	$\frac{\text{current assets} - \text{inventory}}{\text{current liabilities}}$	2.01	1.0	Higher
Activity Ratios				
Accounts receivable turnover	$\frac{\text{net sales}}{\text{accounts receivable}}$	11.9	—	Higher
Inventory turnover	$\frac{\text{cost of goods sold}}{\text{average inventory}}$	8.2	9	Higher
Debt-to-owners' equity ratio	$\frac{\text{total liabilities}}{\text{owners' equity}}$	48%	33%–50%	Lower

ical equipment sellers on the other hand tend to use incompatible SAP, Oracle, or J.D. Edwards's systems.

Traditional methods for allowing two systems to communicate with each other would cost thousands of dollars in consulting and computer coding changes. By some estimates, classical integration methods cost the *Fortune* 1000 more than $100 billion per year. However, firms like Neoforma.com of Santa Clara, California, have set up exchange hubs that act as information transfer points for incompatible software communication. By acting as a translator for the software, messaging can be exchanged. The average hospital places between 50,000 to 70,000 purchase orders a year to its suppliers and the online market for medical products and pharmaceuticals is expected to surge from $4.3 billion in 2000 to $124 billion in 2004, according to Forrester Research. About a fourth of those revenues are expected to be generated by Internet trading exchanges, suggesting firms like Neoforma.com will continue to play a vital role in bridging the technology gap.[6]

This chapter ends our discussion of accounting information. In Chapter 19, we begin our examination of business finances by discussing money, banking, and credit.

RETURN TO Inside Business

ACCORDING TO THE PEOPLE at Arthur Andersen, it isn't how big you are or if you're ranked number 1 according to revenues, but how well you serve your clients' needs. And although this philosophy applies to all businesses, it is especially apt for an accounting firm. The basic product an accounting firm sells is information—information that must serve clients' needs. This same philosophy has also enabled a very large firm with more than 70,000 employees to become a respected leader in the accounting industry.

Today, Arthur Andersen derives about a fourth of its revenues from its U.S. operations, but attracting new business in North America has never been more difficult. As a result of corporate mergers, the number of companies needing auditing has diminished. To keep current U.S. clients or attract new ones most accounting firms have had to cut their fees. In response, Arthur Andersen is focusing on increasing the value of its services to clients and is initiating a wide range of financial consulting services that are generating revenue growth. At the same time, Arthur Andersen is continuing to concentrate on global operations. Because we live in a global economy, today's multinational corporations face "special" accounting problems relating to financial reporting, operations, mergers, acquisitions, and strategic alliances that the people at Arthur Andersen can help solve. To meet this need Arthur Andersen has consolidated its worldwide operations into three geographic areas: Europe, India, Africa, and the Middle East; Asia Pacific; and the Americas, and the firm is committed to developing accounting systems that cut across national boundaries.

To help accomplish these goals, Arthur Andersen continues to recruit only the brightest and best new employees. Once a part of the Arthur Andersen team, new employees are expected to take advantage of extensive training and professional development programs. In fact, there is so much training that many in the accounting field refer to the firm's employees as "Arthur Androids." However, it is this philosophy and way of management that has kept Arthur Andersen at the top of the accounting profession for many decades. If you're interested in learning more about Arthur Andersen, log on to their web site at www.arthurandersen.com.

Questions

1. Because of the competition in the accounting industry, many firms have had to cut their fees for auditing and other services. How has Arthur Andersen continued to increase annual revenues in this very competitive environment?
2. Arthur Andersen expects a lot from its new professionals. At the same time, it provides extensive training and professional development programs to train employees to become "Arthur Androids." Would this type of career appeal to you? Explain your answer.

chapter Review

SUMMARY

1 Understand why accounting information is important and what accountants do.

Accounting is the process of systematically collecting, analyzing, and reporting financial information. Accounting information is used primarily by management, but it is also demanded by lenders, suppliers, stockholders, potential investors, and government agencies. Typical services performed by accountants for their clients include general accounting, budgeting, cost accounting, tax accounting, and internal auditing. A private accountant is employed by a specific organization to operate its accounting system. A public accountant performs these functions for various individuals or firms on a fee basis. Most accounting firms include on their staffs at least one certified public accountant (CPA).

2 Discuss the accounting process.

The accounting process is based on the accounting equation: *assets = liabilities + owners' equity*. Double-entry bookkeeping ensures that the balances shown by the accounting equation is maintained. The accounting process involves five steps: (a) Source documents are analyzed. (b) Each transaction is recorded in a journal. (c) Each journal entry is posted in the appropriate general ledger accounts. (d) At the end of each accounting period, a trial balance is prepared to make sure that the accounting equation is in balance. (e) Financial statements are prepared from the trial balance. Once statements are prepared, the books are closed. A new accounting cycle is then begun for the next accounting period.

3 Read and interpret a balance sheet.

A balance sheet is a summary of a firm's assets, liabilities, and owners' equity accounts at the end of an accounting period. This statement must demonstrate that the accounting equation is in balance. On the balance sheet, assets are categorized as current, fixed, or intangible. Similarly, liabilities can be divided into current liabilities and long-term ones. For a sole proprietorship or partnership, owners' equity is shown as the difference between assets and liabilities. For corporations, the owners' equity section reports the values of stock and retained earnings.

4 Read and interpret an income statement.

An income statement is a summary of a firm's financial operations during the specified accounting period. On the income statement, the company's gross profit is computed by subtracting the cost of goods sold from net sales. Operating expenses and interest expense are then deducted to compute net income before taxes. Finally, income taxes are deducted to obtain the firm's net income after taxes.

5 Describe business activities that affect a firm's cash flow.

Since 1987, the Securities and Exchange Commission (SEC) and the Financial Accounting Standards Board (FASB) have required all publicly traded companies to include a statement of cash flows in their annual reports. This statement illustrates how the operating, investing, and financing activities of a company affect cash during an accounting period. Together, the cash flow statement, balance sheet, and income statement illustrate the results of past decisions and the business's ability to pay debts and dividends and to finance new growth.

6 Summarize how managers evaluate the financial health of a business.

The information in a firm's financial statements becomes more meaningful when compared with corresponding information for previous years, for competitors, and for the industry in which the firm operates. Such comparisons permit managers and other interested people to pick out trends in growth, borrowing, income, and other business variables and to determine whether the firm is on the way to accomplishing its long-term goals. Comparisons are possible as long as accountants follow the basic rules of accounting, often referred to as *generally accepted accounting principles (GAAP)*. A number of financial ratios can be computed from the information in a firm's financial statements. These ratios provide a picture of the firm's profitability, its short-term financial position, its activity in the area of accounts receivable and inventory, and its long-term debt financing. Like the information on the firm's financial statements, these ratios can and should be compared with those of past accounting periods, those of competitors, and those representing the average of the industry as a whole.

KEY TERMS

You should now be able to define and give an example relevant to each of the following terms:

accounting (513)
private accountant (515)
public accountant (515)
certified public accountant (CPA) (516)
assets (517)
liabilities (517)
owners' equity (517)

accounting equation (517)
double-entry bookkeeping (517)
general journal (518)
general ledger (518)
posting (518)
trial balance (518)
balance sheet (or statement of financial position) (519)
liquidity (519)
current assets (521)
prepaid expenses (521)
fixed assets (522)
depreciation (522)
intangible assets (523)
goodwill (523)
current liabilities (523)
accounts payable (523)
notes payable (523)
long-term liabilities (523)
retained earnings (524)
income statement (524)
revenues (525)
gross sales (526)
net sales (526)
cost of goods sold (526)
gross profit (526)
operating expenses (526)
net income (527)
statement of cash flows (527)
audit (529)
financial ratio (530)
return on sales (531)
return on owners' equity (531)
earnings per share (532)
current ratio (532)
acid-test ratio (532)
accounts receivable turnover (533)
inventory turnover (533)
debt-to-owners' equity ratio (533)

REVIEW QUESTIONS

1. List four groups that use accounting information, and briefly explain why each group has an interest in this information.
2. What is the difference between a private accountant and a public accountant? What are certified public accountants?
3. State the accounting equation, and list two specific examples of each term in the equation.
4. How is double-entry bookkeeping related to the accounting equation? Briefly, how does it work?
5. Briefly describe the five steps of the accounting cycle, in order.
6. What is the principal difference between a balance sheet and an income statement?
7. How are current assets distinguished from fixed assets? Why are fixed assets depreciated on a balance sheet?
8. Explain how a retailing firm would determine the cost of goods sold during an accounting period.
9. How does a firm determine its net income after taxes?
10. What is the purpose of a statement of cash flows?
11. For each of the accounts listed below, indicate if the account should be included on a firm's balance sheet, income statement, or statement of cash flows.

Type of Account	Statement Where Reported
Assets	____________
Income	____________
Expenses	____________
Operating Activities	____________
Liabilities	____________
Investing Activities	____________
Owners' Equity	____________

12. Explain the calculation procedure for and the significance of each of the following:
    a. One of the profitability ratios
    b. A short-term financial ratio
    c. An activity ratio
    d. Debt-to-owners' equity ratio

DISCUSSION QUESTIONS

1. Bankers usually insist that prospective borrowers submit audited financial statements along with a loan application. Why should financial statements be audited by a CPA?
2. What can be said about a firm whose owners' equity is a negative amount? How could such a situation come about?
3. Do the balance sheet, the income statement, and the statement of cash flows contain all the information you might want as a potential lender or stockholder? What other information would you like to examine?
4. Why is it so important to compare a firm's current financial statements with those of previous years, those of competitors, and the average of all firms in the industry in which the firm operates?
5. Which do you think are the two or three most important financial ratios? Why?

VIDEO CASE

Office Depot, Inc.

Taking care of business! Those four words describe Office Depot's approach to doing business in the new millennium. Founded in 1986, with headquarters in Delray Beach, Florida, Office Depot is a merchandising firm that has already opened over 850 office supply retail stores in the United States and Canada and operates in 17 other countries. In addition to retail stores, it also sells office supplies by telephone, direct mail, and e-commerce transactions over the Internet. Is this fast-growing company satisfied? Not at all! It wants to be the most successful office products retailer in the world. And it may very well obtain its goal with the help of its accounting system.

Too often retailers concentrate on just selling merchandise and assume that profitability will follow. Unfortunately, they don't think about controlling inventory costs and managing cash flow—two very important concerns for a merchandising firm. But that is not the case with Office Depot. Management realized early on that it was essential to control inventory costs, reduce theft, and manage cash flow if the firm were to earn the profit it needed to continue to expand and open new stores.

Consider, for example, how Office Depot manages merchandise inventory. If a retailer like Office Depot is going to generate sales revenues, it must have merchandise to sell. In fact, the dollar value of merchandise inventory is one of the firm's largest assets. With this fact in mind, managers at Office Depot knew from the start that they would have to maintain a large inventory of every conceivable brand and variety of office product that its customers would want. At the same time, it also realized that it would be necessary to protect each of its stores from merchandise theft. To accomplish both goals, Office Depot keeps accurate records and uses proven internal accounting control procedures for receiving, storing, and delivering the products it sells to its customers.

In addition to controlling merchandise inventory and reducing theft, Office Depot's accounting systems must also manage the firm's cash flow carefully during its operating cycle—the time required to buy products, sell them, and collect payment for them. Often referred to as the lifeblood of a business, cash flow enables a firm like Office Depot to buy new goods and pay its bills. While some of the firm's purchases are paid for with cash, most of its purchases are made on credit. This gives the firm a margin of time between when it is able to sell the goods and receive payment for them and when it must pay its suppliers. Since most of Office Depot's sales are to retail customers who either pay with cash or credit cards, the company receives cash as quickly as it can sell its merchandise. This helps reduce the length of Office Depot's operating cycle, and therefore its need for cash. But because Office Depot also sells to some businesses on credit, the company must also wait for a period of time before it receives payment.

While procedures to account for merchandise inventory, reduce theft, and manage cash flow don't necessarily guarantee profits, they do provide a solid foundation to build a profitable business. And Office Depot is very profitable. For the first nine months of 2000, Office Depot reported net income of $217.6 million. Three key factors explain the firm's ability to earn a profit. First, it sells merchandise at a price that produces a high gross margin. Gross margin is often defined by accountants as the difference between the proceeds from the sales of merchandise and the amount the firm pays for the merchandise that was sold. Office Depot's gross margin not only exceeds its costs, but is also large enough to provide an excellent income or profit after paying its operating expenses. Second, Office Depot has developed strategies to ensure that it sells large quantities of merchandise. Third, Office Depot operates very efficiently so that it can keep operating expenses low in relation to sales.

What does the future hold for Office Depot? According to their accountants, the future looks bright because this is one retailer that really is *taking care of business!*[7]

Questions

1. Management at Office Depot would like to become the largest office products retailer in the world. In what ways can the information provided by the firm's accounting system help fulfill this goal?
2. How can a firm's accounting system manage merchandise inventory and at the same time reduce merchandise theft?
3. Accountants often refer to cash flow as the lifeblood of any business. Why must a retailer like Office Depot manage its cash flow?
4. Based on what you read in the chapter, describe the typical types of assets, liabilities, and owners' equity that Office Depot would include on its balance sheet. What are the typical types of revenues and expenses it would list on its income statement?

Building skills for career success

1. Exploring the Internet

To those unacquainted with current activities and practices in larger accounting firms, there is often some surprise at just how varied the accounting work involved actually is. Although setting up and maintaining accounting software for clients is standard, accounting firms can also provide a wide range of specialized services. For example, research into mergers or acquisitions of other firms, investment advice, and studies on specific issues important to clients are now common strategies for revenue growth within accounting firms.

One area gaining in popularity is the demand for information about e-business practices. On a simple level, clients may request an industry study to better understand what competitors are doing or planning to do. If the consulting advice received suggests opportunities exist for the firm, a cost-benefit analysis may be undertaken by the accounting firm to assess the value of entering e-business. More importantly the study might show the loss to future revenue if the firm does not take advantage of e-business opportunities. Visit the text web site for updates to this exercise.

Assignment

1. Visit the web site of a major accounting firm such as Deloitte & Touche (http://www.dttus.com/), KPMG (http://www.kpmg.com/), or one of the other firms listed in the student resource web site associated with this chapter. Describe in general terms how the web site is used to communicate with clients and prospective clients.
2. What are some of the content items presented on the site? What do these tell you about the firm and their clients?
3. Search the site for activity in the e-business area. Often the firm will post descriptions of clients they have already served in this area and present their success stories for promotional purposes. Describe what you find.

2. Developing Critical Thinking Skills

According to the experts, you must evaluate your existing financial condition before establishing an investment plan. As pointed out in this chapter, a personal balance sheet provides a picture of your assets, liabilities and net worth. A personal income statement will tell you whether you have a cash surplus or cash deficit at the end of a specific period.

Assignment

1. Using your own financial information from last month, construct a personal balance sheet and personal income statement.
2. Based on the information contained in your financial statements, answer the following:
   a. What is your current net worth?
   b. Do you have a cash surplus or a cash deficit?
   c. What specific steps can you take to improve your financial condition?
3. Based on your findings, prepare a plan for improving your financial condition over the next six months.

3. Building Team Skills

This has been a bad year for Miami-based Park Avenue Furniture. The firm increased sales revenues to $1,400,000, but total expenses ballooned to $1,750,000. Although management realized that some of the firm's expenses were out of control, including cost of goods sold ($700,000), salaries ($450,000), and advertising costs ($140,000), it could not contain expenses. As a result, the furniture retailer lost $350,000. To make matters worse, the retailer applied for a $350,000 loan at Fidelity National Bank and was turned down. The bank officer, Mike Nettles, said that the firm already had too much debt. At that time, liabilities totaled $420,000; owners' equity was $600,000.

Assignment

1. In a group of four, analyze the financial condition of Park Avenue Furniture.
2. Discuss why you think the bank officer turned down Park Avenue's loan request.
3. Prepare a detailed plan of action to improve the financial health of Park Avenue Furniture over the next twelve months.

4. Researching Different Careers

As pointed out in this chapter, job opportunities for accountants and managers in the accounting area are expected to experience average growth between now and the year 2008. Employment opportunities range from entry-level positions for clerical workers and technicians to professional positions that require a college degree in accounting, management consulting, or computer technology. Typical job titles in the accounting field include bookkeeper, corporate accountant, public accountant, auditor, managerial accountant, and controller.

Assignment

1. Answer the following questions based on information obtained from interviews with people employed in accounting, from library research, or from your college's career center:
   a. What types of activities would a person employed in one of the accounting positions listed above perform on a daily basis?
   b. Would you choose this career? Why, or why not?
2. Summarize your findings in a report.

5. Improving Communication Skills

One of the best resources for determining the soundness of an investment opportunity is a corporation's annual report. An annual report will tell you about a company's management, its past performance, and its future goals. Most annual reports contain a letter from the chairman of the board, as well as photographs of smiling employees. While these are nice to look at, it is the financial statements and footnotes in an annual report that give the true picture of a corporation's financial health.

Assignment

1. Obtain a printed copy of an annual report or use the Internet to access a corporation's annual report for a company that you consider a "promising investment."
2. Use the report to answer the following questions:
   a. What does the CEO/president say about the company's past performance and future projections?
   b. Is the firm profitable? Are profits increasing or decreasing?
   c. Most annual reports contain graphs or illustrations that show trends for sales, profits, earnings per share, and other important financial measures over a five-year or ten-year period. What significant trends for this company are illustrated in its annual report?
3. On the basis of your examination of its annual report, would you invest in this company? Prepare a brief report justifying your decision.

United Parcel Service

You've seen them because they're everywhere. Big, brown, boxy trucks with the UPS logo wind their way through your neighborhood every day. These trucks, owned by United Parcel Service, one of the largest package distribution companies in the world, are just one link in the chain that helps UPS meet the needs of its customers in the global marketplace. Started back in 1907 by two teenagers, Jim Casey and Claude Ryan of Seattle, Washington, UPS quickly developed a strict policy that centered on customer courtesy, reliability, round-the-clock service, and low rates. These same principles still guide UPS. Now almost 100 years later, UPS processes more than 12 million packages and documents every single day to any street address in the United States as well as customers in more than 200 foreign countries. Today, this corporate giant employs over 340,000 people, operates more than 150,000 delivery vehicles and over 500 airplanes, and generates more than $23 billion in sales revenues each year.

Success Is in the Details

What makes UPS different from other package delivery services? While there are many reasons why UPS is successful, two very important reasons are the firm's attention to detail and its management information system. To appreciate the firm's attention to detail, consider what happens when a package is shipped via UPS. Whether a shipment is bound for the other side of town or the other side of the world, each letter or package is tracked at all times by UPS as it passes through a network of packaging and sorting centers called hubs. Each distribution hub has been carefully designed to provide speed, reliability, and efficiency. But the cost of information is not cheap. UPS has invested billions of dollars in its global management information system.

To help justify the cost, managers use the UPS management information system not only to track packages, but also to make decisions that ensure the firm is using its resources wisely, operating profitably, paying debts, and abiding by laws and regulations. Every decision, regardless of how small or large, is backed by information. This quest for the information needed to make important decisions often begins with questions. For example, typical questions include:

- What should the company charge to ship a next-day air letter from Chicago to San Francisco?
- What will it cost to expand services to another country in Asia?
- How much will it cost to build a new super hub in Latin America?

The answers to these and similar questions can be found by using the firm's managerial accounting information system — an extension of the firm's management information system. For UPS, management accounting is a process within the organization that measures, accumulates, analyzes, prepares, interprets, and communicates both financial and non-financial information in a timely and useful manner to the people who need it. Like the accounting systems used in most businesses, the UPS system was also designed to allow managers to plan, execute, review, and report important information to the people who need it. For example,

- In the *planning stage,* UPS managers must develop strategic plans and operating plans and identify what resources will be needed and when they will be available.
- In the *executing stage,* managers implement the firm's plans. At UPS, management accounting provides information such as the revenues and costs for the service provided, the actual time spent in providing the service, and the actual miles traveled.
- In the *reviewing stage,* UPS managers compare the results to the original plan. This information can help managers evaluate the performance of individuals, teams, and super distribution hubs.
- In the *reporting stage,* managers receive relevant, timely information every day. The information provided in the reporting stage helps managers to evaluate how past performance affects planning for the future.

Without the ability to plan, execute, review, and report accounting information, a problem related to a firm's revenues or expenses could develop and go undetected. If not corrected, this problem could cause profits to be lower than expected. In the worst case scenario, the firm could experience an operating loss. But with a state-of-the-art accounting system, problems can be identified and corrective actions taken to improve the firm's operations. Even small changes in operating procedures can amount to substantial savings for a large company like UPS. For instance, adjustments to truck engines to reduce the truck's idle time were made based on a specialized information system. The result: the company saved over 1.5 million gallons of fuel.

UPS operates in a very competitive environment and information can make the difference between success and failure. And while information technology along with a well-engineered network of operations and highly-trained employees have made the firm highly profitable, UPS is not content to sit back and rest on past success. The firm continues to research new and better ways to improve the way it does business and provide its customers with even better service. UPS really has come a long way from the days of two teenagers delivering packages and messages by bicycle.

Questions

1. Critics often ask what makes UPS different from other package distribution services. Why do you think this firm has become a corporate giant in the package-distribution business?
2. How has the firm's management information system enabled UPS to become one of the most competitive firms in the package-distribution industry?
3. The accounting system at UPS allows managers to plan, execute, review, and report important information. How do each of these activities affect the way a firm like UPS is managed? How are each of these activities related?
4. The management information and accounting systems at UPS generate a lot of information. Do you feel all this information is needed? Justify your answer.

Finance and Investment

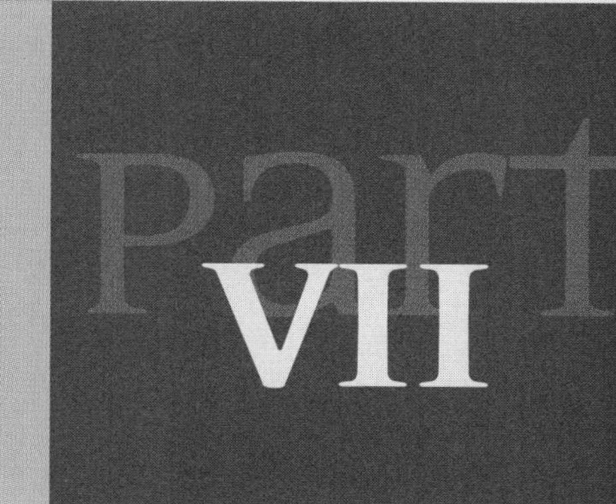

In this part, we look at another business resource—money. First we discuss the functions of money and the financial institutions that are part of our banking system. Then we examine the concept of financial management and investing, for both firms and individuals.

19 Understanding Money, Banking, and Credit

LEARNING OBJECTIVES

1. Identify the functions and characteristics of money.
2. Summarize how the Federal Reserve System regulates the money supply.
3. Describe the differences between commercial banks and other financial institutions in the banking industry.
4. Identify the services provided by financial institutions.
5. Understand how financial institutions are changing to meet the needs of domestic and international customers.
6. Explain the function of the Federal Deposit Insurance Corporation, Savings Association Insurance Fund, Bank Insurance Fund, and National Credit Union Association.
7. Discuss the importance of credit and credit management.

Wingspan.com had to do more than just offer traditional banking services. It had to give people a reason to change.

inside business

Wingspan.com: Internet Banking

NOT LONG AGO, IF YOU wanted to go to a bank, savings and loan association, or credit union, you had to get there between the hours of nine and five on a weekday. Many customers felt hampered by "bankers' hours." But now these same financial institutions realize that to remain competitive, customer service is essential. At the same time, they have also developed new services to meet customer needs. Drive-through banking, Saturday operating hours, off-site automated teller machines (ATMs), and online banking are now common. Some banks like Wingspan.com have taken the next step. Wingspan.com is a virtual bank that operates only through the Internet. Because it is an Internet-only facility, it doesn't have doors that close at 5:00 P.M. on a Friday afternoon.

Wingspan.com, a division of First USA Bank, N.A., was founded in mid-1999. A year later, it had almost 110,000 customer accounts. From the beginning, Wingspan wanted to be different from more "stuffy" traditional banks. Although it conducts business over the Internet, it realized early on that it had to provide traditional services that people expect a bank to offer. For that reason, a customer can open checking and savings accounts, purchase certificates of deposit, apply for credit cards, locate automated teller machines, apply for a loan, and pay bills online.

But Wingspan had to do more than just offer traditional banking services. It had to give people a reason to change. The reasons behind Wingspan's phenomenal growth are more apparent when a customer accesses the Wingspan.com web site. At Wingspan.com, you can manage your financial life with electronic speed. It takes only thirty seconds to learn if your credit card application has been accepted. The loan approval process also takes less time than the process used by more traditional financial institutions. And Wingspan offers customers higher interest rates on savings accounts and certificates of deposit and lower interest rates on loans because its operating costs are low; it has no elaborate, expensive buildings to maintain.

In addition to speed and attractive interest rates, management and employees at Wingspan.com. have increased the amount of service that customers receive. As a customer, you can go online any time—day or night—to access your accounts. For anyone wanting to speak to a human teller, personal contact is possible through e-mail or telephone calls twenty-four hours a day, seven days a week. It is also possible to learn about money management and financial planning by accessing Wingspan's web page and clicking on an icon labeled "Plan." Here you can access various financial calculators and tools complete with graphics, animation, and links to additional financial resources that enable you to evaluate different investment and insurance alternatives—all with the click of your computer's mouse.

According to material posted on the Wingspan.com web site, the bank's mission is to become more than an online bank. Simply put, Wingspan wants to become a versatile one-stop financial resource. Is it accomplishing its mission? Even through Wingspan is "the new kid on the block," there are enough statistics to indicate a high level of customer satisfaction at Wingspan.com. And according to *Kiplinger's Personal Finance Magazine*, all banking and financial operations at Wingspan are "seamless." Users can conduct all of their financial business through one easy-to-access Internet location. As further proof, Gomez.com, a company that evaluates Internet web sites, also rates Wingspan as one of the top three Internet banking firms in the United States. To learn more about Wingspan and other Internet banking opportunities, visit www.wingspan.com or www.gomez.com.[1]

In Chapter 1, we defined a business as the organized effort of individuals to produce and sell for a profit the goods and services that satisfy society's needs. Wingspan.com fulfills the last part of this definition by accepting deposits, making loans, and providing other financial services to its customers. But Wingspan does more than just provide traditional banking services. It has developed a loyal base of customers that want to bank online—twenty-four hours a day, seven days a week. As a result, Wingspan.com has experienced phenomenal growth since it was created in mid-1999. Although the bank is the "new kid on the block," it shows every sign of continuing to increase its customer base and the amount of profit it earns from its Internet banking services. But how does Wingspan.com—or for that matter any bank—earn profits? To answer that question, you must understand the basic "bread and butter" operations of a bank or similar financial institution.

Most people regard a bank, savings and loan association, or similar financial institution as a place to deposit or borrow money. When you deposit money, you *receive* interest. When you borrow money, you must *pay* interest. You may borrow to buy a home, a car, or some other high-cost item. In this case, the resource that will be transformed into money to repay the loan is the salary you receive for your labor.

Businesses also transform resources into money. A business firm (even a new one) may have a valuable asset in the form of an idea for a product or service. If the firm (or its founder) has a good credit history and the idea is a good one, a bank or other lender will probably lend it the money to develop, produce, and market the product or service. The loan—with interest—will be repaid out of future sales revenue. In this way, both the firm and the lender will earn a reasonable profit.

LEARNING OBJECTIVE

1 Identify the functions and characteristics of money.

In each of these situations, the borrower needs the money now and will have the ability to repay it later. But also, in each situation, the money will be used to *purchase something* and will be repaid through the use of *resources.*

In this chapter, we take a good look at money and the financial institutions that create and handle it. We begin by outlining the functions and characteristics of money that make it an acceptable means of payment for products, services, and resources. Then we consider the role of the Federal Reserve System in maintaining a healthy economy. Next we describe the banking industry—commercial banks, savings and loan associations, credit unions, and other institutions that offer banking services. Then we turn our attention to how banking practices are changing to meet the needs of customers. We also describe the safeguards established by the federal government to protect depositors against losses. In closing, we examine credit transactions, sources of credit information, and effective collection procedures.

barter system a system of exchange in which goods or services are traded directly for other goods or services

What Is Money?

The members of some societies still exchange goods and services through barter, without using money. A **barter system** is a system of exchange in which goods or services are traded directly for other goods or services. One family may raise vegetables and herbs, and another may weave cloth. To obtain food, the family of weavers trades cloth for vegetables, provided that the farming family is in need of cloth.

The trouble with the barter system is that the two parties in an exchange must need each other's

One new euro equals a lot of German marks. Europe's dream of a monetary union became a reality when 11 nations locked their currencies together to form the euro. Beginning in 2002, the euro will become the measure of exchange, the measure of value, and the store of value for European nations that extend from the Arctic Circle to the shores of the Mediterranean Sea.

products at the same time, and the two products must be roughly equal in value. So even very isolated societies soon develop some sort of money to eliminate the inconvenience of trading by barter.

Money is anything a society uses to purchase products, services, or resources. Different groups of people have used all sorts of objects as money—whales' teeth, stones, beads, copper crosses, clam shells, and gold and silver, for example. Today, the most commonly used objects are metal coins and paper bills, which together are called *currency*.

money anything a society uses to purchase products, services, or resources

The Functions of Money

Money aids in the exchange of goods and services. But that is a rather general (and somewhat theoretical) way of stating money's function. Let's look instead at three *specific* functions money serves in any society.

Money as a Medium of Exchange

A **medium of exchange** is anything accepted as payment for products, services, and resources. This definition looks very much like the definition of money. It is meant to, because the primary function of money is to serve as a medium of exchange. The key word here is *accepted*. As long as the owners of products, services, and resources accept money in an exchange, it is performing this function. For example, if you want to purchase a Hewlett-Packard Desk Jet printer that is priced at $229 in a Circuit City store, you must give the store the correct amount of money. In return, the store gives you the product. Of course, the folks at Circuit City accept your money because they know it is acceptable to the owners of other products, services, and resources, which *they* may wish to purchase. The family in our earlier example can sell their vegetables and use the money to purchase cloth from the weavers. This eliminates the problems associated with the barter system.

medium of exchange anything accepted as payment for products, services, and resources

Money as a Measure of Value

A **measure of value** is a single standard or "yardstick" used to assign values to, and compare the values of, products, services, and resources. Money serves as a measure of value because the prices of all products, services, and resources are stated in terms of money. It is thus the "common denominator" we use to compare products and decide which we will buy. Imagine the difficulty you would have in deciding whether you could afford new Nike running shoes if they were priced in terms of yards of cloth or pounds of vegetables—especially if your employer happened to pay you in toothbrushes.

measure of value a single standard or "yardstick" used to assign values to, and compare the values of, products, services, and resources

Money as a Store of Value

Money received by an individual or firm need not be used immediately. It may be held and spent later. Hence, money serves as a **store of value,** or a means of retaining and accumulating wealth. This function of money comes into play whenever we hold on to money—in a pocket, a cookie jar, a savings account, or whatever.

store of value a means of retaining and accumulating wealth

Value that is stored as money is affected by *inflation*. Remember from Chapter 1; inflation is a general rise in the level of prices. As prices go up in an inflationary period, money loses purchasing power. Suppose you can buy a Sony stereo system for $1,000. Your $1,000 has a value equal to the value of that stereo system. But suppose you wait and don't buy the stereo immediately. If the price goes up to $1,050 in the meantime because of inflation, you can no longer buy the stereo with your $1,000. Your money has *lost* purchasing power because it is now worth less than the stereo. To determine the effect of inflation on the purchasing power of a dollar, economists often refer to a consumer price index like the one illustrated in Figure 19.1 on page 548. The consumer price index measures prices of a fixed amount of goods bought by a typical consumer, including food, transportation, shelter, utilities, clothing, and medical care. The base amount for the consumer price index is 100 and was established by averaging the cost of the items included in the consumer price index over the 1982 to 1984 time period.

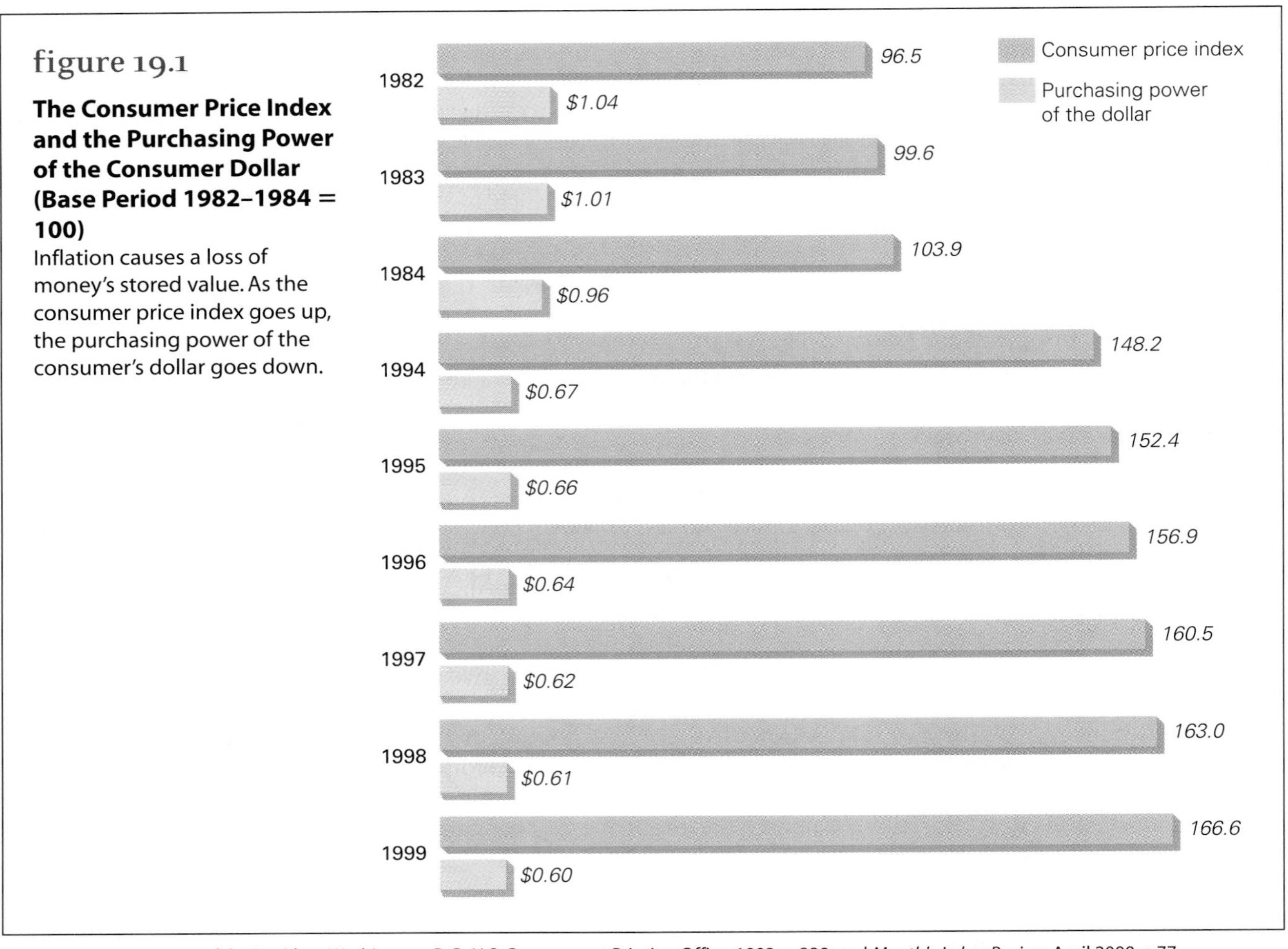

figure 19.1

The Consumer Price Index and the Purchasing Power of the Consumer Dollar (Base Period 1982–1984 = 100)
Inflation causes a loss of money's stored value. As the consumer price index goes up, the purchasing power of the consumer's dollar goes down.

Source: *Economic Report of the President*, Washington, D.C., U.S. Government Printing Office, 1993, p. 339; and *Monthly Labor Review*, April 2000, p. 77.

Important Characteristics of Money

To be acceptable as a medium of exchange, money must be easy to use, trusted, and capable of performing the three functions just mentioned. To meet these requirements, money must possess the following five characteristics.

Divisibility The standard unit of money must be divisible into smaller units to accommodate small purchases as well as large ones. In the United States, our standard is the dollar, and it is divided into pennies, nickels, dimes, quarters, and half-dollars. These coins allow us to make purchases of less than a dollar and of odd amounts greater than a dollar. Other nations have their own divisible currencies: the franc in France, the mark in Germany, and the yen in Japan, to mention a few.

Portability Money must be small enough and light enough to be carried easily. For this reason, paper currency is issued in larger *denominations*—multiples of the standard dollar unit. Five-, ten-, twenty-, fifty-, and hundred-dollar bills make our money convenient for almost any purchase.

Stability Money should retain its value over time. When it does not, people tend to lose faith in their money. On October 27, 1997, when stock markets around the world took a deep plunge, the New York Stock Exchange lost approximately 8 percent of its total dollar value in one day. Although there were many reasons for the decline, one important reason heard time and again was the instability of foreign currencies in

Hong Kong, Japan, and other nations in the Pacific Rim. When money becomes extremely unstable, people may turn to other means of storing value, such as gold and jewels, works of art, and real estate. They may even use such items as a medium of exchange in a barter system. During upheavals in Eastern Europe including Russia in the 1990s, farmers traded farm products for cigarettes because the value of cigarettes was more stable than each nation's money.

Durability The objects that serve as money should be strong enough to last through reasonable usage. No one would appreciate (or use) dollar bills that disintegrated as they were handled or coins that melted in the sun. To increase the life expectancy of paper currency, most nations use special paper with a high fiber content.

Difficulty of Counterfeiting If a nation's currency were easy to counterfeit—that is, to imitate or fake—its citizens would be uneasy about accepting it as payment. Thus, countries do their best to ensure that it is very hard to reproduce their currency. In an attempt to make paper currency more difficult to counterfeit, the U.S. government redesigned hundred-, fifty-, twenty-, ten-, and five-dollar bills. Typically, countries use special paper and watermarks and print intricate designs on the currency to discourage counterfeiting.

The Supply of Money: M_1, M_2, and M_3

How much money is there in the United States? Before we can answer that question, we need to define a couple of concepts. A **demand deposit** is an amount on deposit in a checking account. It is called a *demand* deposit because it can be claimed immediately—on demand—by presenting a properly made-out check, withdrawing cash from an automated teller machine (ATM), or transferring money between accounts.

demand deposit an amount on deposit in a checking account

A **time deposit** is an amount on deposit in an interest-bearing savings account. Financial institutions generally permit immediate withdrawal of money from savings accounts. However, they can require written notice prior to withdrawal. The time between notice and withdrawal is what leads to the name *time* deposits. Although time deposits are not immediately available to their owners, they can be converted to cash easily. For this reason, they are called *near-monies.* Other near-monies include short-term government securities, government bonds, money-market mutual fund shares, and the cash surrender values of insurance policies.

time deposit an amount on deposit in an interest-bearing savings account

Now we can discuss the question of how much money there is in the United States. There are three main measures of the supply of money: M_1, M_2, and M_3.

The *M_1 supply of money* is a narrow definition and consists only of currency and demand deposits. By law, currency must be accepted as payment for products, services, and resources. Checks (demand deposits) are accepted as payment because they are convenient, convertible to cash, and generally safe.

The *M_2 supply of money* consists of M_1 (currency and demand deposits) plus certain money-market securities and small-denomination time deposits or certificates of deposit of less than $100,000. Another common definition of money—*M_3*—consists of M_1 and M_2 plus time deposits or certificates of deposit of $100,000 or more. The definitions of money that include the M_2 and M_3 supplies of money are based on the assumption that time deposits can be converted to cash for spending. Figure 19.2 shows the elements of the M_1, M_2, and M_3 supplies. About 17 percent are coins, paper currency, and demand deposits; the remaining 83 percent are time deposits and certain securities.

We have, then, at least three measures of the supply of money. (Actually, there are other measures as well, which may be broader or narrower than M_1, M_2, and M_3.) So the answer to our original question is that the amount of money in the United States depends very much on how we measure it. Generally, economists, politicians, and bankers tend to focus on M_1 or some variation of M_1.

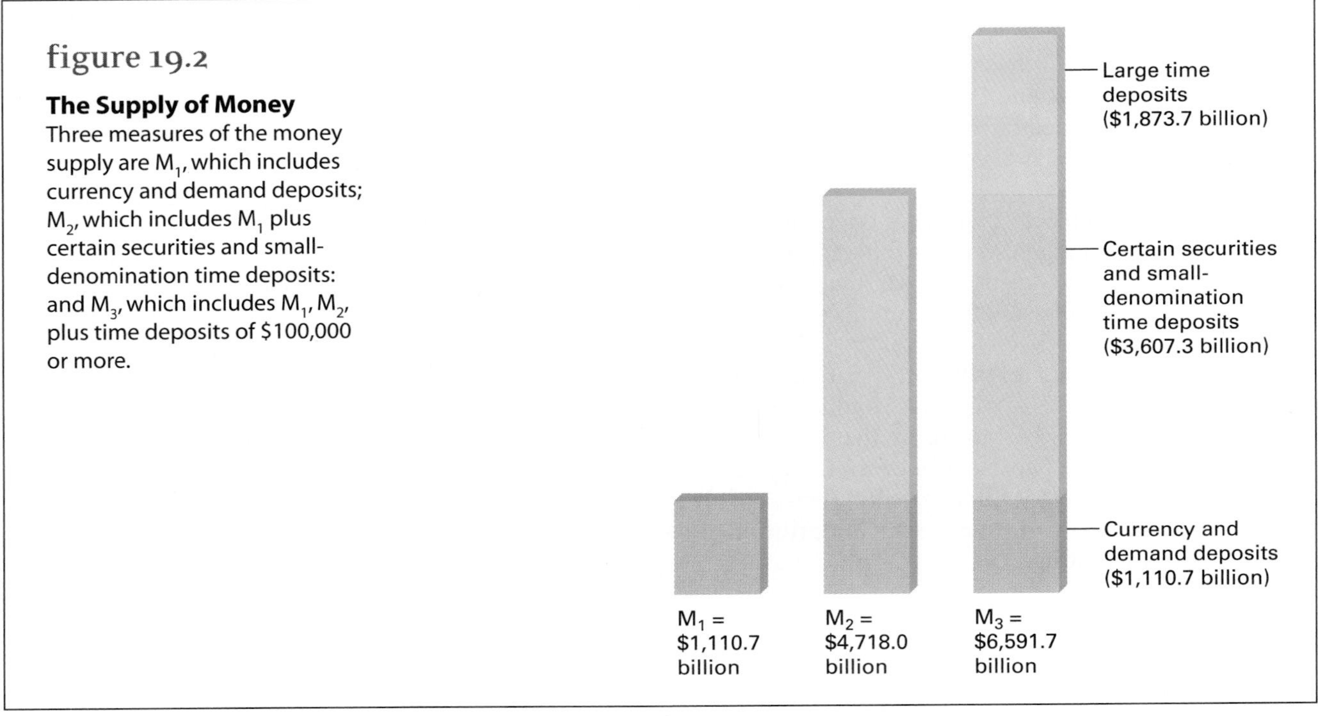

figure 19.2

The Supply of Money
Three measures of the money supply are M_1, which includes currency and demand deposits; M_2, which includes M_1 plus certain securities and small-denomination time deposits: and M_3, which includes M_1, M_2, plus time deposits of $100,000 or more.

Source: *Federal Reserve Bulletin*, June 2000, p. A12.

The Federal Reserve System

LEARNING OBJECTIVE

2 Summarize how the Federal Reserve System regulates the money supply.

Federal Reserve System the central bank of the United States responsible for regulating the banking industry

What is the Federal Reserve System? How much power does the Federal Reserve have? And how does it affect you and me? The **Federal Reserve System** (or simply "the Fed") is the central bank of the United States and is responsible for regulating the banking industry. It was created by Congress on December 23, 1913. Its mission is to maintain an economically healthy and financially sound business environment in which banks can operate. Today the Federal Reserve has tremendous power to regulate the money supply, control inflation, and regulate financial institutions. Its decisions can, for example, increase or decrease the interest rates homeowners pay for home mortgages. And comments by its current board chairman, Alan Greenspan, about interest rates or inflation can send the stock and bond markets into a tailspin or provide support for sagging financial markets.

The Federal Reserve System is controlled by the seven members of its board of governors, who meet in Washington, D.C. Each governor is appointed by the president and confirmed by the Senate for a fourteen-year term. The president also selects the chairman and vice chairman of the board from among the board members for four-year terms. These terms may be renewed.

The Federal Reserve System comprises twelve district banks located in major cities throughout the United States, as well as twenty-five branch banks (see Figure 19.3). Each Federal Reserve District Bank is actually owned—but not controlled—by the commercial banks that are members of the Federal Reserve System. All national (federally chartered) banks must be members of the Fed. State banks may join if they choose to and if they meet membership requirements. For more information about the Federal Reserve System, visit their web site at www.federalreserve.gov.

The most important function of the Fed is to regulate the nation's supply of money in such a way as to maintain a healthy economy. It does so by controlling bank reserve requirements, regulating the discount rate, and running open-market operations.

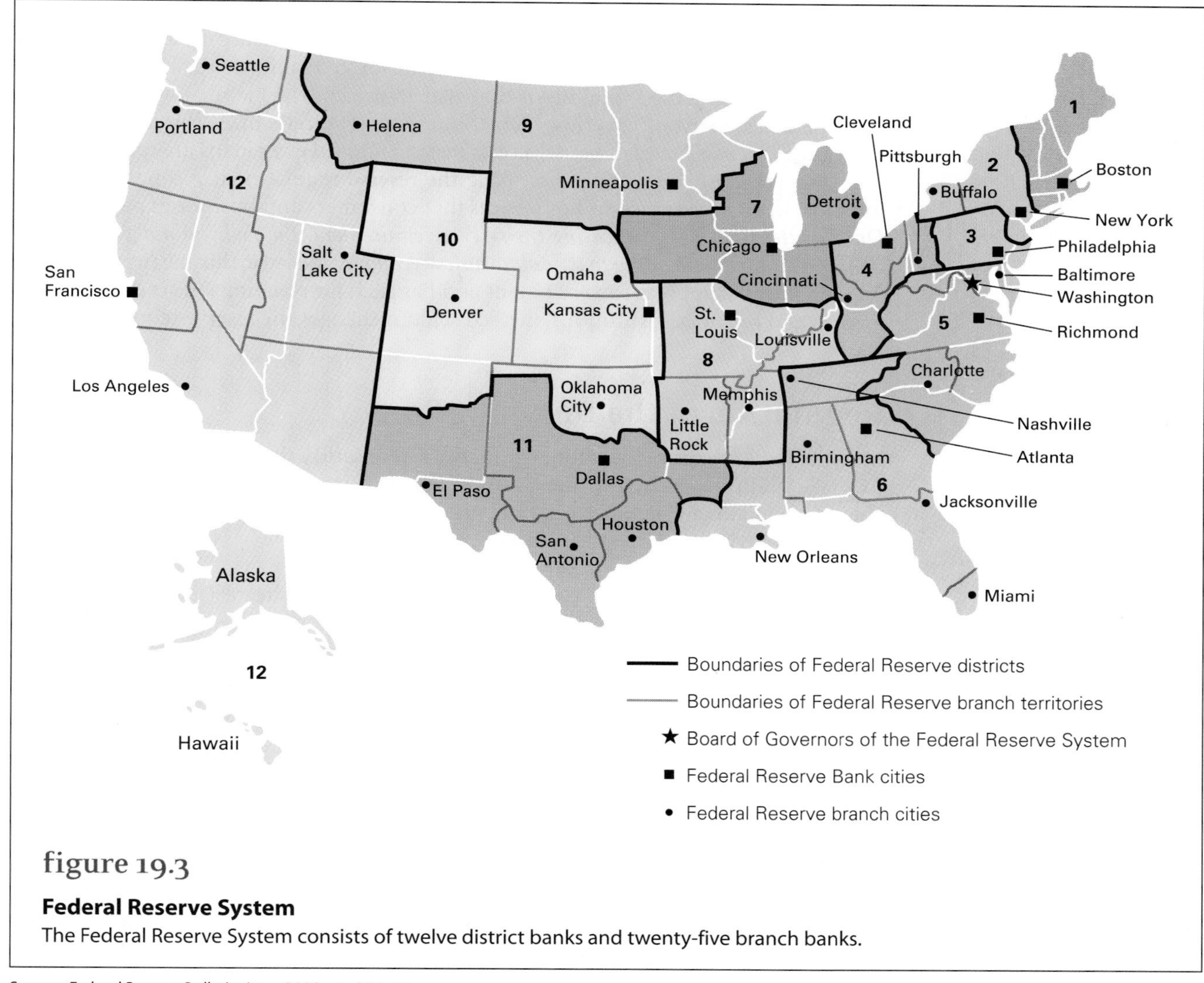

figure 19.3

Federal Reserve System

The Federal Reserve System consists of twelve district banks and twenty-five branch banks.

Source: *Federal Reserve Bulletin*, June 2000, pp. A74–75.

Regulation of Reserve Requirements

When money is deposited in a bank, the bank must retain a portion of it to satisfy customers who may want to withdraw money from their accounts. The remainder is available to fund loans. The **reserve requirement** is the percentage of its deposits a bank *must* retain, either in its own vault or on deposit with its Federal Reserve District Bank. For example, if a bank has deposits of $20 million and the reserve requirement is 10 percent, the bank must retain $2 million. The present reserve requirements range from 3 to 10 percent, depending on such factors as the total amount individual banks have on deposit, average daily deposits, and the location of the particular member bank.[2]

reserve requirement the percentage of its deposits a bank *must* retain, either in its own vault or on deposit with its Federal Reserve District Bank

Once reserve requirements are met, banks can use remaining funds to create more money and make more loans through a process called *deposit expansion.* Here's how deposit expansion works. In the above example, the bank must retain $2 million in a reserve account. It can use the remaining $18 million to fund consumer and business loans. Assume that the bank lends all $18 million to different borrowers. Also assume that before using any of the borrowed funds, all borrowers deposit the $18 million in their bank accounts at the lending institution. Now, the bank's deposits have increased by an additional $18 million. Since these deposits are subject to the same reserve requirement described above, the bank must maintain $1.8 million in a reserve account, and the bank can lend the additional $16.2 million to other bank customers.

Of course, the bank's lending potential becomes steadily smaller and smaller as it makes more loans. And we should point out that since bankers are usually very conservative by nature, they will not use deposit expansion to maximize their lending activities; they will take a more middle-of-the-road approach.

The Fed's board of governors sets the reserve requirement. *When it increases the requirement, banks have less money available for lending.* Fewer loans are made, and the economy tends to slow. Thus, increasing the reserve requirement is a powerful anti-inflation weapon designed to hold prices that consumers and businesses pay in check. *On the other hand, by decreasing the reserve requirement, the Fed can make additional money available for lending to stimulate a slow economy.* Because this means of controlling the money supply is so very potent and has such far reaching effects on both consumers and financial institutions, the Fed seldom changes the reserve requirement.

Regulation of the Discount Rate

discount rate the interest rate the Federal Reserve System charges for loans to member banks

Member banks may borrow money from the Fed to satisfy the reserve requirement and to make additional loans to their customers. The interest rate the Federal Reserve charges for loans to member banks is called the **discount rate.** It is set by the Fed's board of governors. In the past twenty years, the discount rate has been as low as 3 percent and as high as 14 percent.[3]

When the Fed *lowers* the discount rate, it is easier and cheaper for banks to obtain money. Member banks feel free to make more loans and to charge lower interest rates. This increases the amount of money available to both consumers and businesses and generally stimulates the nation's economy. When the Fed *raises* the discount rate, banks begin to restrict loans. They increase the interest rates they charge and tighten their own loan requirements. The overall effect is to slow the economy—to check inflation—by making money more difficult and more expensive to obtain.

In the summer of 2000, Federal Reserve Board Chairman Alan Greenspan acknowledged for the first time that the current expanding business cycle was being driven by noninflationary improvements in worker productivity derived by the expanding use of the Internet and information technology in American industry. That workers were more productive because of new technologies being introduced into the work environment remains a debated issue among many analysts. Nonetheless, on that day, the stock and bond markets reacted favorably to Mr. Greenspan in the belief that the Federal Reserve would not be raising interest rates soon out of fear of an inflationary drive in the economy.[4]

Open-Market Operations

open-market operations the buying and selling of U.S. government securities by the Federal Reserve System for the purpose of controlling the supply of money

The federal government finances its activities partly by selling U.S. government securities. These securities, which pay interest, may be purchased by any individual, firm, or organization—including the Fed. **Open-market operations** are the buying and selling of U.S. government securities by the Federal Reserve System for the purpose of controlling the supply of money. They are the Fed's most frequently used tool to control the nation's economy.

To reduce the nation's money supply, the Fed simply *sells* government securities on the open market. The money it receives from purchasers is taken out of circulation. Thus, less money is available for investment, purchases, or lending. To increase the money supply, the Fed *buys* government securities. The money the Fed pays for securities goes back into circulation, making more money available to individuals and firms.

Because the major purchasers of government securities are financial institutions, open-market operations tend to have an immediate effect on lending and investment. Moreover, the Fed can control and adjust this effect by varying the amount of securities it sells or buys at any given time and the amount of interest paid on these securities. Table 19.1 summarizes the effects of open-market operations and the other tools used by the Fed to regulate the money supply and control the economy.

table 19.1 Methods Used by the Federal Reserve System to Control the Money Supply and the Economy

Method Used	Immediate Result	End Result
Regulating reserve requirement		
1. Fed **increases** reserve requirement	Less money for banks to lend to customers—reduction in overall money supply	Economic slowdown
2. Fed **decreases** reserve requirement	More money for banks to lend to customers—increase in overall money supply	Increased economic activity
Regulating the discount rate		
1. Fed **increases** the discount rate	Less money for banks to lend to customers—reduction in overall money supply	Economic slowdown
2. Fed **decreases** the discount rate	More money for banks to lend to customers—increase in overall money supply	Increased economic activity
Open-market operations		
1. Fed **sells** government securities	Reduction in overall money supply	Economic slowdown
2. Fed **buys** government securities	Increase in overall money supply	Increased economic activity

Other Fed Responsibilities

In addition to its regulation of the money supply, the Fed is also responsible for serving as the government's bank, clearing checks and electronic transfers, inspecting currency, and applying selective credit controls.

Serving as Government Bank The Federal Reserve is the bank for the U.S. government. As the government's bank, it processes a variety of financial transactions involving trillions of dollars each year. For example, the U.S. Treasury keeps a checking account with the Federal Reserve through which incoming tax deposits and outgoing government payments are handled.

Clearing Checks and Electronic Transfers Today people use checks to pay for nearly everything they buy. A check written by a customer of one bank and presented for payment to another bank in the same town may be processed through a local clearinghouse. But the procedure becomes more complicated when the banks are not in the same town. That's where the Federal Reserve System comes in. The Fed is responsible for the prompt and accurate collection of more than 18 billion checks each year.[5]

The steps involved in clearing a check through the Federal Reserve System are outlined in Figure 19.4. About one-fourth of all the checks written in the United States are cleared in this way. Banks that use the Fed to clear checks are charged a fee for this service. The remainder are either presented directly to the paying bank or processed through local clearinghouses. Through the use of electronic equipment, most checks can be cleared within two or three days.

Inspection of Currency As paper currency is handled, it becomes worn or dirty. The typical one-dollar bill has a life expectancy of less than one year (larger denominations usually last longer because they are handled less). When member banks deposit their surplus cash in a Federal Reserve Bank, the currency is inspected. Bills unfit for further use are separated and destroyed.

Selective Credit Controls The Federal Reserve System has the responsibility for enforcing the Truth-in-Lending Act, which Congress passed in 1968. This act requires lenders to state clearly the annual percentage rate and total finance charge for a consumer loan. It also prohibits discrimination in lending based on race, color, sex, marital status, religion, or national origin. To see what happens when lenders take advantage of borrowers, read Examining Ethics.

figure 19.4

Clearing a Check Through the Federal Reserve System

Approximately one-fourth of all U.S. checks are cleared this way, a process that usually takes two to three days.

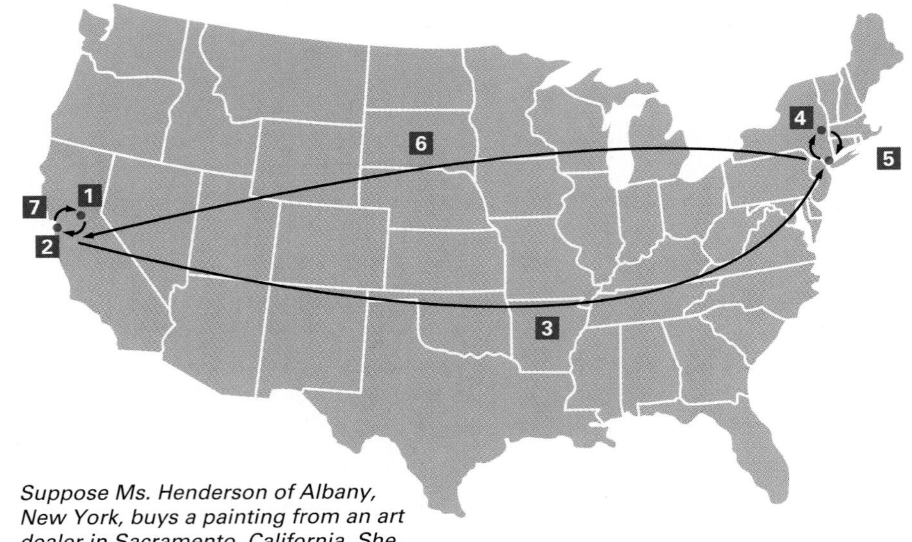

Suppose Ms. Henderson of Albany, New York, buys a painting from an art dealer in Sacramento, California. She sends her check to the art dealer.

1 The dealer deposits the check in his account at a Sacramento bank.

2 The Sacramento bank deposits the check for credit in its account with the Federal Reserve Bank of San Francisco.

3 The Federal Reserve Bank of San Francisco sends the check to the Federal Reserve Bank of New York for collection.

4 The Federal Reserve Bank of New York forwards the check to the Albany bank, which deducts the amount of the check from Ms. Henderson's account.

5 The Albany bank authorizes the Federal Reserve Bank of New York to deduct the amount of the check from its deposit account with the Federal Reserve Bank.

6 The Federal Reserve Bank of New York pays the Federal Reserve Bank of San Francisco.

7 The Federal Reserve Bank of San Francisco credits the Sacramento bank's deposit account, and the Sacramento bank credits the art dealer's account.

Source: Federal Reserve Bank of New York, The *Story of Checks*, 7th ed., 1995, p. 11.

The Federal Reserve System is also responsible for setting the margin requirements for stock transactions. The *margin* is the minimum portion of the purchase price that must be paid in cash. (The investor may borrow the remainder.) The current margin requirement is $2,000, or 50 percent, whichever is greater. Thus, if an investor purchases $4,000 worth of stock, he or she must pay at least $2,000 in cash. The remaining $2,000 may be borrowed from the brokerage firm. Although margin rules are regulated by the Federal Reserve, margin requirements and the interest charged on the loans used to fund margin transactions may vary among brokerage firms. And investors may choose to use more of their money and to borrow less than the amount permitted by the Federal Reserve.

The American Banking Industry

LEARNING OBJECTIVE

3 Describe the differences between commercial banks and other financial institutions in the banking industry.

Any banker you ask will tell you that for the American banking industry, the last ten years have been exciting, to say the least. Competition among banks, savings and loan associations, credit unions, and other business firms that want to perform banking activities has never been greater. In addition, banks from Japan, Canada, France, and other foreign nations have thrown their hat into U.S. banking circles. As a result, major banks like BankAmerica, Chase Manhattan, and Bank One have begun to provide

Examining Ethics

What Is a Predatory Lender?

HOW DO YOU DEFINE THE WORD *PREDator*? Most of us picture an animal in the jungle preying on another animal in order to plunder or rob its victim. Well, in today's world of financing, people who have blemished credit histories, who are members of a minority, or who have moderate to low income, don't have to go on a jungle safari to find a predator. All they have to do is start looking for a way to purchase a new home or automobile, avoid foreclosure on their home, or try to get a credit card. The "financial" predators are everywhere in human form, dressed in tailored business suits, ready to "help" the most vulnerable people–those who often don't understand money or personal financial management.

Methods Used by Predatory Lenders

Although most financial predators operate just inside the law, their business practices are similar to those used by the old-fashioned loan sharks–the gangsters who wore striped suits and loaned money at exorbitant interest rates. Today's financial predators won't break your legs if you don't pay on time, but they often grant loans that they know a borrower can't repay. And when the borrower defaults on a loan, the predator is there just waiting to repossess the property that was pledged as collateral for the loan. Another common practice used by predators is to "trick" borrowers into paying higher interest rates than they should pay. Usually the predator talks fast and gets the borrower so confused that they don't know what the real interest rate is. If all else fails, predators sometimes convince unsuspecting borrowers that they need longer repayment terms or credit life insurance. In reality, these two conditions increase the cost of borrowing for unsuspecting borrowers and increase the amount of profit the lender makes on a loan.

How to Avoid a Predator?

Fact of Life: Financial predators are for real. They are out there just waiting to take advantage of the unsuspecting borrower. Realize that they have no conscience and are more than happy to charge higher than usual interest rates to separate you from your money. The following suggestions will help protect you from falling prey to a financial predator:

- Learn all you can about financing and the loan application process.
- Check your credit report before applying for a loan. If you have poor credit, work to improve it.
- Compare interest rates and repayment terms for a loan with different lenders. You may be surprised and find a lender who offers lower interest rates or better repayment terms.
- Above all, know the lender you are dealing with.

Issues to Consider

1. Assume that you are interviewing a loan applicant with a poor credit history, low income, and no apparent knowledge of money management who wants to borrow $3,000. Would you charge this individual a higher interest rate than the usual rate charged for this type of loan? Is your decision ethical or unethical?
2. Suppose you have a poor credit history. Would you turn to a predatory lender, knowing he or she may take advantage of your circumstances? Why or why not?

innovative services for their customers. Even smaller banks have adopted the full-service banking philosophy and compete aggressively for customers, who expect more services than ever before. As you read the material in this section, keep in mind that banking will become even more competitive as bankers offer more services to attract new customers. Let's begin this section with some information about one of the major players in the banking industry—the commercial bank.

Commercial Banks

A **commercial bank** is a profit-making organization that accepts deposits, makes loans, and provides related services to its customers. As is the case in other businesses, the bank's primary goal—its mission—is to meet the need of its customers while earning a profit. In a nutshell, here's how a bank earns its profit. It accepts money in the form of deposits, for which it pays interest. Once money is deposited in a bank, the bank lends it to qualified individuals and businesses that pay interest for the use of borrowed money. If the bank is successful, its income is greater than its expenses, and it will show a profit.

commercial bank a profit-making organization that accepts deposits, makes loans, and provides related services to its customers

The key word in this photo may be *security*. Like most commercial banks, Security Pacific National Bank is concerned with providing its depositors not only with innovative banking services, but also with a safe place to deposit their money.

Because they deal with money belonging to individuals and other business firms, banks are carefully regulated. They must also meet certain requirements before they receive a charter, or permission to operate, from either federal or state banking authorities. A **national bank** is a commercial bank chartered by the U.S. Comptroller of the Currency. There are approximately 2,500 national banks, accounting for about 42 percent of all bank deposits.[6] These banks must conform to federal banking regulations and are subject to unannounced inspections by federal auditors.

A **state bank** is a commercial bank chartered by the banking authorities in the state in which it operates. State banks outnumber national banks by about two to one, but they tend to be smaller than national banks. They are subject to unannounced inspections by both state and federal auditors.

Table 19.2 lists the seven largest banks in the United States. All of these are classified as national banks.

Other Financial Institutions

In addition to commercial banks, at least eight other types of financial institutions perform either full or limited banking services for their customers. Included in this group are savings and loan associations, mutual savings banks, credit unions, insurance companies, pension funds, brokerage firms, finance companies, and investment banking firms.

national bank a commercial bank chartered by the U.S. Comptroller of the Currency

state bank a commercial bank chartered by the banking authorities in the state in which it operates

savings and loan association (S&L) a financial institution that offers checking and savings accounts and certificates of deposit and that invests most of its assets in home-mortgage loans and other consumer loans

NOW account an interest-bearing checking account: *NOW* stands for Negotiable Order of Withdrawal

Savings and Loan Associations

A **savings and loan association (S&L)** is a financial institution that offers checking and savings accounts and certificates of deposit and that invests most of its assets in home-mortgage loans and other consumer loans. Originally, S&Ls were permitted to offer their depositors *only* savings accounts. But since Congress passed the Depository Institutions Deregulation and Monetary Control Act in 1980, they have been able to offer NOW accounts to attract depositors. A **NOW account** is an interest-bearing checking account. (*NOW* stands for Negotiable Order of Withdrawal.)

table 19.2 The Seven Largest U.S. Banks, Ranked by Total Revenues

Rank	Commercial Bank	Revenues (in millions)	Number of Employees
1	Bank of America Corp.	51,392	155,906
2	Chase Manhattan Corp.	33,710	74,801
3	Bank One Corp.	25,986	86,198
4	First Union Corp.	22,084	71,659
5	Wells Fargo	21,795	89,355
6	FleetBoston	20,000	59,157
7	J.P. Morgan & Co.	18,110	15,512

Source: *Fortune* 500, April 17, 2000, p. F57.

Today there are approximately 1,700 savings and loan associations in the United States.[7] Federal associations are chartered under provisions of the Home Owners' Loan Act of 1933 and are supervised by the Office of Thrift Supervision, a branch of the U.S. Treasury. Savings and loan associations can also be chartered by state banking authorities in the state in which they operate. State-chartered S&Ls are subject to unannounced audits by state authorities.

During the 1980s and first part of the 1990s, high interest rates, along with a reduced demand for homes, an increase in nonperforming loans and foreclosures, fraud and corruption, and mergers and acquisitions led to a decrease in the number of S&Ls. In fact, over 1,000 S&Ls failed during the 1980s and early 1990s. However, the number of failed S&Ls had decreased dramatically by the end of the 1990s. In fact, for the eighteen-month period from January 1999 to June 2000, only two savings and loan associations failed.[8] Reasons for the reduced number of failures include better regulation, much less corruption, and a strong economy that led to an increased demand for loans to purchase homes, automobiles, and other major consumer items. Experts still believe the future of the industry will be determined by the ability of savings and loan associations to provide home mortgages, consumer loans, and other financial services that their customers need.

Mutual Savings Banks Approximately 400 mutual savings banks are in operation, primarily in the Northeast.[9] **Mutual savings banks** are financial institutions that are owned by their depositors and offer many of the same services offered by savings and loan associations, including checking accounts, savings accounts, and certificates of deposit. Like S&Ls, they also fund home mortgages, commercial loans, and consumer loans. Generally, mutual savings banks have state charters and are controlled by state banking authorities. Unlike the profits of other types of financial institutions, the profits of a mutual savings bank go to the depositors, usually in the form of slightly higher interest rates on savings.

mutual savings banks financial organizations that are owned by their depositors and offer many of the same services offered by savings and loan associations

Credit Unions Today there are approximately 11,000 credit unions in the United States.[10] A **credit union** is a financial institution that accepts deposits from, and lends money to, only those people who are its members. Usually the membership is composed of employees of a particular firm, people in a particular profession, or those who live in a community served by a local credit union. Some credit unions require that members purchase at least one share of ownership, at a cost of about $5 to $10. Credit unions generally pay higher interest on deposits than commercial banks and S&Ls, and they may provide loans at lower cost. Federally chartered credit unions are regulated by the National Credit Union Administration. Credit unions with state charters are regulated by state authorities.

credit union a financial institution that accepts deposits from, and lends money to, only those people who are its members

Organizations That Perform Banking Functions Five other types of financial institutions are involved in limited banking activities. Though not actually banks, they offer customers limited banking services.

- *Insurance companies* provide long-term financing for office buildings, shopping centers, and other commercial real estate projects throughout the United States. The funds used for this type of financing are obtained from policyholders' insurance premiums.
- *Pension funds* are established by employers to guarantee their employees a regular monthly income on retirement. Contributions to the fund may come from the employer, the employee, or both. Pension funds earn additional income through generally conservative investments in corporate stocks, corporate bonds, and government securities, and through financing real estate developments.
- *Brokerage firms* offer combination savings and checking accounts that pay higher-than-usual interest rates (so-called

Using the Internet

The American Bankers Association (**http://www.aba.com**), the long-established organization representing the banking industry's interests, provides a window into the world of banking through its web site. Users can view articles on banking issues and concerns as well as statistics on the industry, personal financial advice, and links to related sites of interest.

money-market rates). Many people have switched to these accounts to get the higher rates, but banks have instituted similar types of accounts, hoping to lure their depositors back.

- *Finance companies* provide financing to individuals and business firms that may not be able to get financing from banks, savings and loan associations, or credit unions. Lenders like Beneficial Finance or Household Finance provide short-term loans to individuals. Firms like Ford Motor Credit, GE Capital Credit, and General Motors Acceptance Corporation provide loans to both individuals and business firms. The interest rates charged by these lenders may be higher than the interest rates charged by other financial institutions.
- *Investment banking firms* are organizations that assist corporations in raising funds, usually by helping sell new issues of stocks, bonds, or other financial securities. Although these firms do not make loans like traditional banking firms, they do help companies raise millions of dollars that can be used to finance initial business startups, mergers and acquisitions, expansion, and new product development. More information about investment banking firms and the role they play in American business is provided in Chapters 20 and 21.

Careers in the Banking Industry

Take a second look at Table 19.2. The seven largest banks in the United States employ approximately 550,000 people. If you add to this amount the people employed by smaller banks not listed in Table 19.2 and those employed by savings and loan associations and credit unions, the number of employees grows dramatically. And according to the *Occupational Outlook Quarterly*, published by the Department of Labor, the number of people employed in the banking industry is expected to increase over the next ten years.

To be successful in the banking industry, you need a number of different skills. For starters, employees for a bank, savings and loan association, or credit union must possess the following traits.

1. *You must be honest.* Because you are handling other people's money, many financial institutions go to great lengths to discover dishonest employees. In fact, some employees are warned when they are hired that they may be asked to take a polygraph test which detects employees who steal.
2. *You must be able to interact with people.* A number of positions in the banking industry require that you possess the interpersonal skills needed to interact not only with other employees, but also with customers.
3. *You need a strong background in accounting.* Many of the routine tasks performed by employees in the banking industry are basic accounting functions. For example, a teller must post deposits or withdrawals to a customer's account and then balance out at the end of the day to insure accuracy.
4. *You need to appreciate the relationship between banking and finance.* Bank officers must interview loan applicants and determine if their request for money is based on sound financial principles. Above all, loan officers must be able to evaluate applicants and their loan requests to determine if the borrower will be able to repay a loan.
5. *You should possess basic computer skills.* Almost all employees in the banking industry use a computer for some aspect of their work on a daily basis.

Typical job titles in the banking industry include teller, receptionist, computer specialist, supervisor, loan officer, and bank officer. Depending on qualifications, work experience, and education, starting salaries generally are between $15,000 and $25,000 a year, but it is not uncommon for college graduates to earn $30,000 a year or more.

If banking seems like an area you might be interested in, why not do more career exploration? You could take a banking course if your college or university offers one, or you could obtain a part-time job during the school year or a summer job in a bank, savings and loan association, or credit union.

Services Provided by Financial Institutions

LEARNING OBJECTIVE

4 Identify the services provided by financial institutions.

If it seems to you that banks and other financial institutions are competing for your business, you're right. Never before have so many different financial institutions offered such a tempting array of services to attract customers. Most individuals and business firms would find it impossible to operate without at least some of these services. To determine how important banking services are to you, ask yourself the following questions:

- How many checks did you write last month?
- Do you have a major credit card? If so, how often do you use it?
- Do you have a savings account or a certificate of deposit?
- Have you ever financed the purchase of a new or used automobile?
- How many times did you visit an ATM last month?

check a written order for a bank or other financial institution to pay a stated dollar amount to the business or person indicated on the face of the check.

If you're like most people, you'd find it hard to live a normal life without the services provided by banks and other financial institutions. These services include the following:

- Checking accounts
- Savings accounts
- Loans
- Credit and debit cards
- Automatic teller machines
- Online banking
- Electronic transfer of funds
- Financial advice
- Payroll service
- Certified checks
- Trust services
- Safe-deposit boxes

The most important traditional banking services for both individuals and businesses are described in this section. Online banking, electronic transfer of funds, along with other significant, and future developments, are discussed in the next section.

Unique services for unique people. Today, many financial institutions like Wilmington Trust offer unique services to meet the needs of their customers. Services include typical banking services plus online banking, trust services, and personalized financial and investment advice.

Checking Accounts

Imagine what it would be like living in today's world without a checking account. Although a few people don't have one, most of us like the convenience a checking account offers. Firms and individuals deposit money in checking accounts (demand deposits) so that they can write checks to pay for purchases. A **check** is a written order for a bank or other financial institution to pay a stated dollar amount to the business or person indicated on the face of the check. Many financial institutions charge an activity fee (or service charge) for checking accounts. It is generally somewhere between \$10 and \$20 per month for individuals. For businesses, monthly charges are based on the average daily balance in the checking account and/or the number of checks written. Typically, charges for business checking accounts are higher than those for individual accounts.

Today most financial institutions offer interest-paying checking accounts, often called *NOW* accounts. For these accounts, the usual interest rate is between 1.5 and 4 percent. However, individual banks may impose certain restrictions on their *NOW* accounts, including the following:

- A minimum balance before any interest is paid
- Monthly fees for accounts whose balances fall below a set minimum amount
- Restrictions on the number of checks that may be written each month

When opening a checking account at a bank or financial institution, it pays to shop around for the highest interest rates. Although banks and other financial institutions may pay low interest rates on checking accounts, even small earnings are better than no earnings. In addition to interest rates, be sure to compare monthly fees before opening a checking account.

Savings Accounts

Savings accounts (time deposits) provide a safe place to store money and a very conservative means of investing. The usual *passbook savings account* earns between 2 and 4 percent in commerical banks and S&Ls, and slightly more in credit unions.

certificate of deposit (CD) a document stating that the bank will pay the depositor a guaranteed interest rate for money left on deposit for a specified period of time.

A depositor who is willing to leave money on deposit with a bank for a set period of time can earn a higher rate of interest. To do so, the depositor buys a certificate of deposit. A **certificate of deposit (CD)** is a document stating that the bank will pay the depositor a guaranteed interest rate for money left on deposit for a specified period of time. The interest rates paid on CDs change weekly; they once briefly exceeded 11 percent in 1980. Recently, interest rates have ranged from 4 to 7 percent. The rate always depends on how much is invested and for how long. Depositors are penalized for early withdrawal of funds invested in CDs.

Short- and Long-Term Loans

Banks, savings and loan associations, credit unions, and other financial institutions provide short- and long-term loans to both individuals and businesses. *Short-term business loans* must be repaid within one year or less. Businesses generally use short-term loans to provide working capital that will be repaid with future sales revenues. Typical uses for the money obtained through short-term loans include solving cash-flow problems, purchasing inventory, financing promotional needs, and meeting unexpected emergencies.

line of credit a loan that is approved before the money is actually needed

revolving credit agreement a guaranteed line of credit

To ensure that short-term money will be available when needed, many firms establish a line of credit. A **line of credit** is a loan that is approved before the money is actually needed. Because all the necessary paperwork is already completed and the loan is preapproved, the business can later obtain the money without delay, as soon as it is required. Even with a line of credit, a firm may not be able to borrow money if the bank does not have sufficient funds available. For this reason, some firms prefer a **revolving credit agreement**, which is a guaranteed line of credit.

Long-term business loans are repaid over a period of years. The average length of a long-term business loan is generally three to seven years but sometimes as long as fifteen years. Long-term loans are most often used to finance the expansion of buildings and retail facilities, replacement of equipment, or development of the firm's product mix.

collateral real estate or property pledged as security for a loan

Most lenders require some type of collateral for long-term loans. **Collateral** is real estate or property (stocks, bonds, land, equipment, or any other asset of value) pledged as security for a loan. For example, when an individual obtains a loan to pay for a new Chevrolet Camaro, the automobile is the collateral for the loan. If the borrower fails to repay the loan according to the terms specified in the loan agreement, the lender can repossess the car.

Repayment terms and interest rates for both short- and long-term loans are arranged between the lender and the borrower. For businesses, repayment terms may include monthly, quarterly, semiannual, or annual payments. Repayment terms (and interest rates) for personal loans vary, depending on how the money will be used and what type of collateral, if any, is pledged. However, individuals typically make monthly payments to repay personal loans. Borrowers should always "shop" for a loan, comparing the repayment terms and interest rates offered by competing financial institutions.

Credit Card and Debit Card Transactions

"Charge it!" If those two words sound familiar, it is no wonder. Over 155 million Americans use credit cards to pay for everything from tickets on American Airlines to Zebco fishing gear.[11] And the number of cardholders increases every month. In fact, most Americans receive at least two or three credit card applications in the mail every month. Why have credit cards become so popular?

EXPLORING BUSINESS

A Case of "Too Much" Consumer Credit

JACK AND JILL WENT TO THE STORE TO make a credit purchase. Jack went broke because of finance charges and Jill came tumbling after.

Unfortunately the nursery rhyme you're familiar with has taken on new meaning when it comes to credit purchases. But like Jack and Jill, many people are set up for a fall when they get their first credit card and begin to use consumer credit. Take the case of Jack and Jill Lambert. It all began so innocently. When they graduated from college, they responded to numerous letters offering preapproved credit cards. At first, they were cautious about how often they used their cards, and they paid off their credit card debt each month. But, as the years went by, and after they purchased a home, and their children were born, it became easier and easier to whip out a credit card to obtain whatever they thought they needed and to acquire cash advances for emergencies. Eventually all eleven of their cards were "maxed out," and the mounting interest, finance charges, and late fees became too much for the Lamberts. Their creditors began calling and demanding immediate payment.

According to Jill Lambert, they knew they had to find a way out of debt, but the Lamberts both felt helpless. Jack had read in a local newspaper that over one million Americans file personal bankruptcy each year, so the Lamberts thought this might be a way out of debt. But then they found out that personal bankruptcy would remain on their credit report for ten years. They also felt a "responsibility" to repay their debts. So they turned to their local chapter of the Consumer Credit Counseling Service.

Consumer Credit Counseling Service, usually referred to as CCCS, is a national network of nonprofit groups that help clients assess their current financial situation and create a plan for repaying outstanding debts. Often the people at CCCS negotiate with creditors for new repayment terms that lower monthly payments and finance charges. Some chapters offer free repayment programs, while others charge a fee based on what the consumer owes, with a maximum charge of $25 a month. Clients make all of their payments to the Consumer Credit Counseling Service and then CCCS pays the creditors. By following this type of program, most people climb out of debt within two to three years. And for the Lamberts, the best part was that the creditors stopped calling on the phone.

If you find yourself getting deeper into debt, the first step for you to take is to "stop shopping." Next, cut up those credit cards! Then, contact your creditors and discuss options for repaying your debts with lower payments. If you do need assistance, organizations like a local chapter of the Consumer Credit Counseling Service (800-783-5018 or www.cccs.net), Debt Counselors of America (800-680-3328 or www.dca.org), or a local support group like Debtors Anonymous are there to help you.

For a merchant, the answer is obvious. By depositing charge slips in a bank or other financial institution, the merchant can convert credit card sales into cash. In return for processing the merchant's credit card transactions, the bank charges a fee that ranges between 1.5 and 5 percent. Typically, small, independent businesses pay more than larger stores or chain stores. Let's assume that you use a Visa credit card to purchase a microwave oven for $400 from Richardson Appliance, a small retailer in Richardson, Texas. At the end of the day, the retailer deposits your charge slip, along with other charge slips, checks, and currency collected during the day, at its bank. If the bank charges Richardson Appliance 5 percent to process each credit card transaction, the bank deducts a processing fee of $20 ($400 × .05 = $20) for your credit card transaction and immediately deposits the remainder ($380) in Richardson Appliance's account. Actual bank fees are determined by the number of credit card transactions, total dollar amount of credit sales, and how well the merchant can negotiate the fees the bank charges.

For the consumer, credit cards permit the purchase of goods and services even when funds are low. Today most major credit cards are issued by banks or other financial institutions in cooperation with Visa International or MasterCard International. The unique feature of bank credit cards is that they extend a line of credit to the cardholder, much as a bank's consumer loan department does. Thus, credit cards provide immediate access to short-term credit for the cardholder. Of course, the ability to obtain merchandise immediately and pay for it later can lead to credit card misuse. Today the average American cardholder has a credit card balance in excess of $2,000. And with typical finance charges ranging from 1 percent to 1.5 percent a month (that's 12 to 18 percent a year), you can end up paying large finance charges. For example, if you carry a $4,000 balance on your credit card and your credit card company charges 1.5 percent a month, your monthly finance charge will be $60 ($4,000 × .015 = $60). And the monthly finance charges continue until you manage to pay off your credit card debt. (See Exploring Business for some helpful hints on using credit cards wisely.)

Don't confuse debit cards with credit cards. Although they may look alike, there are important differences. A **debit card** electronically subtracts the amount of your purchase from your bank account at the moment the purchase is made. (By contrast, when you use your credit card, the credit card company extends short-term financing, and you do not make payment until you receive your next statement.) Debit cards are most commonly used to obtain cash at automatic teller machines and to purchase products and services from retailers. The use of debit cards is expected to increase because many people feel they are more convenient than writing checks.

debit card a card that electronically subtracts the amount of your purchase from your bank account at the moment the purchase is made

Fraudulent use of credit cards is a growing concern especially with expansion of Internet-based e-commerce. According to Meridian Research, online credit card fraud is expected to cost merchants $9 billion annually in 2001. Only about 1 percent of credit card purchases at brick-and-mortar stores is fraudulent but nearly 10 percent of all Internet transactions are suspect, suggesting costs to banks will boost charges to merchants and ultimately, consumers.[12]

The Future of Banking

LEARNING OBJECTIVE

5 Understand how financial institutions are changing to meet the needs of domestic and international customers.

Stanley Wood used an automatic teller machine (ATM) three times this week. Why? He needed cash and didn't have time to make a trip to the bank and wait in line. Like Stanley, many Americans are finding it convenient to do their banking electronically. By going online or using a touch-tone phone, many people can do most of the banking activities that used to require a trip to the bank. Experts predict that the use of technology in banking will only increase in the next ten years. For example, according to a report by research firm Cyber Dialogue's Internet strategies group, in the second quarter of 1999, there were 6.3 million people using some form of Internet banking with 10.2 million expected to be active by the start of 2001.[13] Let's begin by looking at how banking has changed over the last twenty years. Then we'll discuss how those changes may provide a foundation for the future.

Recent Changes in the Banking Industry

During the last thirty years, Congress has enacted a number of laws designed to deregulate the banking industry. Probably the most important of these is the Financial Services Modernization Banking Act of 1999. This act allowed banks to establish one-stop financial supermarkets where customers can bank, buy and sell securities, and purchase insurance coverage. Because of this act, competition between banks, brokerage firms, and insurance companies increased and consumers have more choices on where to perform needed financial activities. This act also repealed the Glass Steagall Act of 1933 which prohibited banks from owning full-service brokerage firms and engaging in investment banking activities. As mentioned earlier, investment banking activities include helping corporations raise capital by selling stocks and bonds. To understand the significance of the Glass Steagall Act, you must realize that a large number of commercial banks lost money on their investment banking activities and collapsed during the first part of the depression. By eliminating these high-risk activities, Congress helped protect depositors from the risk of bank failures.

Another significant congressional act designed to increase competition was the Depository Institutions Deregulation and Monetary Control Act of 1980. Specifically, this act

- Allowed savings and loan associations to offer NOW (interest-bearing) checking accounts.
- Began a phaseout of interest-rate ceilings on deposits.
- Eliminated state interest-rate ceilings on home mortgages.
- Raised the deposit insurance ceiling to $100,000.

The result was more competition between commercial banks and savings and loan associations. Unfortunately, increased competition, coupled with bad loans, fraud, and financial mismanagement, increased the failure rate of banks, savings and loan associations, and credit unions. For the 1992–1993 period, more than 150 banks with approximately $30 billion in assets went broke.[14] In addition to actual bank failures, the number of banks on the government's "problem list" reached almost 1,000 during this same period. Fortunately, the last part of the 1990s and the year 2000 have been relatively calm. The best evidence that things are improving is that less than ten banks a year have failed since 1999.[15]

The failure of any financial institution is an especially serious problem because of its effect on individuals, businesses, and other financial institutions. Yet, it is comforting to note three important facts. First, the majority of banks and financial institutions that perform banking functions are operating at a profit. Second, the government still provides deposit insurance to protect depositors. Finally, the banking crisis of the early 1990s is a strong reminder that without a sound banking system, the nation and our economy would grind to a screeching halt.

spotLight

Where the ATMs are

The Asia/Pacific region has 34.4% of the world's automated teller machines.

275,007 Asia/Pacific

218,394 Western Europe

214,832 North America

Source: Copyright 2000, USA TODAY. Reprinted with permission.

What's Ahead for the Banking Industry?

Will banking change in the future? The answer to that question is a definite "yes," because of an increasing use of technology and the need for bankers to help American businesses compete in the global marketplace.

Online Banking and the Use of Technology

Today many banks, savings and loan associations, and credit unions offer online and telephone banking services. Online banking allows you to access your bank's computer system from home or even while you are traveling. For the customer, online banking offers a number of advantages which include the following:

- The convenience of electronic deposits
- The ability to obtain current account balances
- The convenience of the transfer of funds from one account to another
- The ability to pay bills
- The convenience of seeing which checks have cleared
- Easy access to current interest rates
- Simplified loan application procedures

Internet-based banking services are a well-established part of the banking industry today. Banks like Citibank.com, Americanexpress.com, and Commerceonline.com are a few good examples to examine for insight into the sector. Most banks have expanded their telephone and automatic teller machines (ATMs) customer access to the web-based customer. Some specialized web sites focus on specific areas of banking or lending instruments like mortgages, such as Quickenloans.quicken.com. and Bankrate.com.

For people who bank online, the largest disadvantage is not being able to discuss financial matters with their "personal banker." Even so, with more and more people using online banking, the day may come when very few people will actually step inside a bank.

There are also a number of advantages for the financial institution. Probably the most important advantage is the lower cost of processing large numbers of transactions. As you learned in the accounting chapter, lower costs often lead to larger profits. In addition to lower costs and increased profits, financial institutions believe that online banking offers increased security because fewer people handle less paper documents.

electronic funds transfer (EFT) system a means of performing financial transactions through a computer terminal or telephone hookup

Although electronic funds transfer systems have been used for years, their use will increase dramatically as we continue through the twenty-first century. An **electronic funds transfer (EFT) system** is a means of performing financial transactions through a computer terminal or telephone hookup. The following three EFT applications are changing how banks do business:

1. *Automatic teller machines (ATMs)*. An ATM is an electronic bank teller—a machine that provides almost any service a human teller can provide. Once the customer is properly identified, the machine dispenses cash from the customer's checking or savings account or makes a cash advance charged to a credit card. ATMs are located in bank parking lots, supermarkets, drugstores, and even gas stations. Customers have access to them at all times of the day or night. Generally, there is a fee for each transaction.
2. *Automated clearinghouses (ACHs)*. Large companies use ACHs to transfer wages and salaries directly into their employees' bank accounts, thus eliminating the need to make out individual paychecks. The ACH system saves time and effort for both employers and employees, and adds a measure of security to the transfer of these payments.

The world of banking is getting smaller. To meet the needs of its customers, the Bank of Canton opened a branch in the Chinatown section of San Francisco, California.

3. *Point-of-sale (POS) terminals.* A POS terminal is a computerized cash register located in a retail store and connected to a bank's computer. At the cash register, you pull your bank debit card through a magnetic card reader and enter your personal identification number (PIN). A central processing center notifies a computer at your bank that you want to make a purchase. The bank's computer immediately deducts the amount of the purchase from your bank account and adds the amount of the purchase to the store's account. The store is then notified that the transaction is complete, and the cash register prints out your receipt.

Bankers and business owners are generally pleased with online banking and EFT systems. Both online banking and EFT are fast, and they eliminate the costly processing of checks. However, many customers are reluctant to use online banking or EFT systems. Some simply don't like "the technology," whereas others fear the computer will garble their accounts. Early on, in 1978, Congress responded to such fears by passing the Electronic Funds Transfer Act, which protects the customer in case the bank makes an error or the customer's personal identification number is stolen.

International Banking Services For international businesses, banking services are extremely important. Depending on the needs of an international firm, a bank can help by providing a letter of credit or a banker's acceptance.

- A **letter of credit** is a legal document issued by a bank or other financial institution guaranteeing to pay a seller a stated amount for a specified period of time—usually 30 to 60 days. (With a letter of credit, certain conditions like delivery of the merchandise may be specified before payment is made.)
- A **banker's acceptance** is a written order for the bank to pay a third party a stated amount of money on a specific date. (With a banker's acceptance, no conditions are specified. It is simply an order to pay without any strings attached.)

letter of credit a legal document issued by a financial institution guaranteeing to pay a seller a stated amount for a specified period of time

banker's acceptance a written order for the bank to pay a third party a stated amount of money on a specific date

Both a letter of credit and a banker acceptance are popular methods of paying for import and export transactions. For example, imagine you are a business owner in the United States who wants to purchase some leather products from a small business in Florence, Italy. You offer to pay for the merchandise with your company's check drawn on an American bank, but the Italian business owner is worried. After all, you've only talked over the phone and have never met this person. To solve the problem, your bank can issue either a letter of credit or a banker's acceptance to guarantee that payment will be made.

One other international banking service should be noted. Banks and other financial institutions provide for currency exchange. If you place an order for Japanese merchandise valued at $50,000, how do you pay for the order? Do you use U.S. dollars or Japanese yen? If you take advantage of a bank's currency exchange service, it doesn't matter. You can use either currency, and if necessary, the bank will exchange one currency for the other to complete your transaction.

The FDIC, SAIF, BIF, and NCUA

LEARNING OBJECTIVE

6 Explain the function of the Federal Deposit Insurance Corporation, Savings Association Insurance Fund, Bank Insurance Fund, and National Credit Union Association.

During the Depression, a number of banks failed and their depositors lost all their savings. To make sure that such a disaster does not happen again and to restore public confidence in the banking industry, Congress passed the Banking Act of 1933 to protect depositors from the risk of bank failures. This act also organized the *Federal Deposit Insurance Corporation (FDIC)*. The primary purpose of the FDIC is to insure deposits against bank failures. As a result of Congress enacting the Financial Institutions Reform, Recovery, and Enforcement Act (FIREA) in 1989, the FDIC now provides similar protection to depositors at savings and loan associations. The FIREA act was enacted to reform, recapitalize, and consolidate the federal deposit insurance system. To accomplish this goal, the Bank Insurance Fund (BIF) and the Savings Association Insurance Fund (SAIF) were created. BIF members are predominantly

FDIC coverage: A necessity? You bet! Deposit insurance provides protection for up to $100,000 per individual at one financial institution and is considered a necessity by most depositors.

commercial and savings banks supervised by the FDIC, the Office of the Comptroller of the Currency, or the Federal Reserve System. SAIF members are predominantly savings and loan associations and are supervised by the Office of Thrift Supervision.

Today, The FDIC insures all accounts in each member financial institution for up to $100,000 per individual at one bank or savings and loan association. A depositor may obtain additional coverage by opening separate accounts in different banks or savings and loan associations.

All banks that are members of the Federal Reserve System are required to belong to the FDIC. Nonmember banks and savings and loan associations are allowed to join if they qualify. To obtain coverage, member banks and savings and loan associations must pay insurance premiums to the FDIC. In a similar manner, the National Credit Union Association (NCUA) insures deposits in member credit unions for up to $100,000 per individual at one credit union. Like the FDIC, the NCUA charges member credit unions for deposit insurance.

The FDIC and NCUA have improved banking in the United States. When either of these organizations insures a financial institution's deposits, they reserve the right to examine that institution's operations periodically. If a bank, S&L, savings bank, or credit union is found to be poorly managed, it is reported to the proper banking authority. In extreme cases, the FDIC or NCUA may cancel its insurance coverage. This is a particularly unwelcome action. It causes many depositors to withdraw their money from the institution and discourages most prospective depositors from opening an account.

Lending to individuals and firms is a vital function of banks. And deciding wisely to whom it will extend credit is one of the most important activities of any financial institution or business. The material in the next section explains the different factors used to evaluate credit applicants.

credit immediate purchasing power that is exchanged for a promise to repay borrowed money, with or without interest, at a later date

spotLight

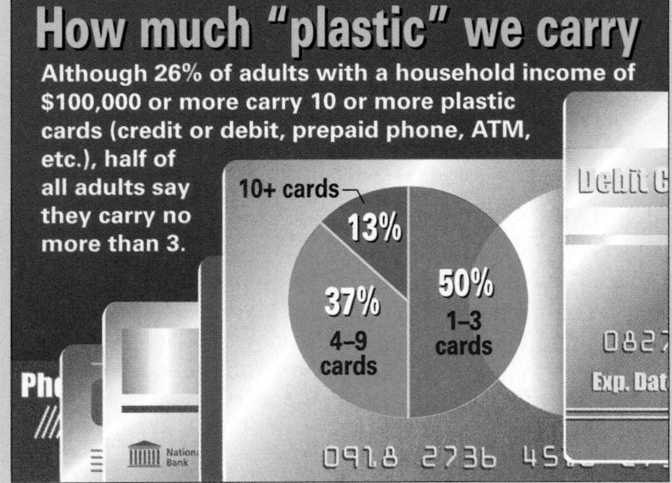

Source: Copyright 2000, USA TODAY. Reprinted with permission.

Effective Credit Management

Credit is immediate purchasing power that is exchanged for a promise to repay borrowed money, with or without interest, at a later date. A credit transaction is a two-sided business activity that involves both a borrower and a lender. The borrower is most often a person or business that wishes to make a purchase. The lender may be a bank, some other lending institution, or a business firm selling merchandise or services on credit.

For example, suppose you obtain a bank loan to buy a $60,000 Porsche automobile. You, as the borrower, obtain immediate purchasing power. In return, you agree to certain terms imposed by the bank. As the lender, the bank requires that you make a down payment, make monthly payments, pay interest, and purchase insurance to protect the car until the loan is paid in full.

LEARNING OBJECTIVE

7 Discuss the importance of credit and credit management.

Banks and other financial institutions lend money because they are in business for that purpose. The interest they charge is what provides their profit. Other businesses extend credit to their customers for at least three reasons. First, some customers simply cannot afford to pay the entire amount of their purchase immediately, but they *can* repay credit in a number of smaller payments, stretched out over some period of time. Second, some firms are forced to sell goods or services on credit to compete effectively when other firms offer credit to their customers. Finally, firms can realize a profit from interest charges that a borrower pays on some credit arrangements.

How Do You Get Money From a Bank or Lender?

Many individuals and business owners are nervous when applying for a loan. They're not sure what information they need. And what happens if they are turned down? Let's begin with the basics. Interest is what keeps a bank, savings and loan association, or credit union in business. While lenders need interest from loans to help pay their business expenses, they also want to make sure the loans they make will be repaid. Your job is to convince the lender that you are able and willing to repay the loan.

For individuals, the following suggestions may be helpful when applying for a loan:

- Although it may pay to shop around for lower interest rates, you usually have a better chance of obtaining a loan at a bank, savings and loan association, or credit union where you already have an account.
- Obtain a loan application and complete it at home. At home, you have the information needed to answer *all* the questions on the loan application.
- Be prepared to describe how you will use the money and how the loan will be repaid.
- For most loans, an interview with a loan officer is required. Here again, preparation is the key. Think about how you would respond to questions a loan officer might ask.
- If your loan request is rejected, try to analyze what went wrong. Ask the loan officer why you were rejected. If the rejection is based on incorrect information, supply the correct information and reapply.

Business owners in need of financing may find the following additional tips helpful:

- It is usually best to develop a relationship with your banker before you need financing. Help the banker understand what your business is and how you may need future financing for expansion, cash-flow problems, or unexpected emergencies.
- Apply for a preapproved line of credit or revolving credit agreement even if you don't need the money. View the application as another way to showcase your company and its products or services.
- In addition to the application, supply CPA-prepared financial statements and business tax returns for the last three years and your own personal financial statements and tax returns for the same period.
- Write a cover letter describing how much experience you have, whether you are operating in an expanding market, or any other information that would help convince the banker to provide financing.

From the lender's viewpoint, the major pitfall in granting credit is the possibility of nonpayment. However, if a lender follows the five Cs of credit management, it can minimize this possibility.

Banks want to make good loans. Bank of America, like many financial institutions, offers free loan seminars to prospective homeowners. Here a loan officer describes the different types of loans and loan features that a borrower should understand before applying for a loan.

The Five Cs of Credit Management

When a business extends credit to its customers, it must face the fact that some customers will be unable or unwilling to pay for their credit purchases. With this in mind, lenders must establish policies for determining who will receive credit and who will not. Most lenders build their credit policies around the five Cs of credit: character, capacity, capital, collateral, and conditions.

Character *Character* means the borrower's attitude toward credit obligations. Experienced lenders often see this as the most important factor in predicting whether a borrower will make regular payments and ultimately repay a credit obligation. Typical questions to consider in judging a borrower's character include the following:

1. Is the borrower prompt in paying bills?
2. Have other lenders had to dun the borrower with overdue notices before receiving payment?
3. Have lenders been forced to take the borrower to court to obtain payment?
4. Has the customer ever filed for bankruptcy? If so, did the customer make an attempt to repay debts voluntarily?

Although it is illegal to discriminate, personal factors such as marital status and drinking or gambling habits may affect a lender's decision to loan money or extend credit to an individual.

Capacity *Capacity* means the borrower's financial ability to meet credit obligations—that is, to make regular loan payments as scheduled in the credit or loan agreement. If the customer is a business, the lender looks at the firm's income statement. For individuals, the lender checks salary statements and other sources of income, such as dividends and interest. The borrower's other financial obligations and monthly expenses are also taken into consideration before credit is approved.

Capital The term *capital* as used here refers to the borrower's assets or net worth. In general, the greater the capital, the greater the borrower's ability to repay a loan. The capital position of a business can be determined by examining its balance sheet. For individuals, information on net worth can be obtained by requiring that the borrower complete a credit application like the one illustrated in Figure 19.5. The borrower must also authorize employers and financial institutions to release information to confirm the claims made in the credit application.

Collateral For large amounts of credit—and especially for long-term loans—the lender may require some type of collateral. As mentioned earlier, collateral is real estate or property pledged as security for a loan. If the borrower fails to live up to the terms of the credit agreement, the lender can repossess the collateral and then sell it to satisfy the debt.

Conditions *Conditions* refers to the general economic conditions that can affect a borrower's ability to repay a loan or other credit obligation. How well a business firm can withstand an economic storm may depend on the particular industry the firm is in, its relative strength within that industry, the type of products it sells, its earnings history, and its earnings potential. For individuals, the basic question focuses on security—of both the applicant's job and the firm she or he works for.

Apply today! Just complete this application or call 1-800-438-9222.

Citizens Bank Customer Credit Card Application

Branch # ___________

This offer is for existing Citizens Bank Customers applying for a new credit card account

Existing Citizens Bank cardholders should call 1-800-438-9222 for special cardholder rate information.

Citizens Bank VISA® (Code: BVCFNU)

Please tell us about yourself

First Name Middle Initial Last Name

Address (street)

(City, state, zip)

Date of Birth Social Security Number

❑ Own ❑ Rent ❑ Live with Parents

Years/Months at Present Address

$ ( )

Monthly Housing Payment Home Telephone

Previous Address Years/Months There

(if less than 2 years at present address)

Mother's Maiden Name

Citizens Bank Account Information

❑ Checking ❑ Savings ❑ Loan ❑ Citizens Circle[SM] Checking

account # ___________________________

Please tell us about your employment

Present Employer Position

( )

Years/Months Employed There Business Telephone

Previous Employer Years/Months There

(if less than 2 years at present employer)

$ $

Gross Monthly Household Income Other Monthly Income*

*Alimony, child support, or separate maintenance income need not be revealed if you do not wish it to be considered as a basis for repaying this obligation.

24-hour banking convenience

Your card(s) can be encoded with a four-digit personal identification number (PIN) to obtain cash advances at automated teller machines. This four-digit PIN will be known only to you. So that we may properly encode your card(s), please select the four digits of your choice and enter them in the spaces below:

____ ____ ____ ____

Please send a second card at no cost for

First Name Middle Initial Last Name

Please read and sign

Your Signature Date

All information on this application is true and complete, and Citizens Bank of Rhode Island, the card issuer, is authorized to obtain further credit and employment information from any source. I understand that you will retain this application whether or not it is approved. You may share with others, only for valid business reasons, any information relating to me, this application, and any of my banking relationships with you. I request issuance of a Citizens credit card and agree to be bound by the terms and conditions of the Agreement received with the card(s). I understand that Citizens Bank of Rhode Island will assign a credit line based on information provided and information obtained from any other source; and the issuance of a Gold card is subject to a minimum annual income of $35,000 and qualification for a minimum $5,000 credit line.

Transfer balances and save

Citizens will transfer your high interest rate balances to your new Citizens Bank VISA Card at no extra charge. Use the form below to indicate the amount(s) to be transferred in order of priority. (Citizens Bank will not transfer balances from existing Citizens Bank accounts.) (see reverse side for balance transfer disclosure)

Creditor Name	Account Number	$ Amount
Creditor Name	Account Number	$ Amount
Creditor Name	Account Number	$ Amount

Bank Use Only Bank Code: ❒ CBMA ❒ CBRI ❒ CBCT Sales ID# ______________ Application code: 1122

figure 19.5

Credit Application Form

Lenders use the information on credit application forms to help determine which customers should be granted credit.

Source: Courtesy of Citizens Financial Group, Inc., Providence, Rhode Island.

Checking Credit Information

The five Cs of credit are concerned mainly with information supplied by the applicant. But how can the lender determine whether this information is accurate? That depends on whether the potential borrower is a business or an individual consumer.

Credit information concerning businesses can be obtained from the following four sources:

- *Global credit-reporting agencies.* Dun & Bradstreet is the most widely used credit-reporting agency in the world. Dun & Bradstreet Reports present detailed credit information about specific companies. The company's reference books include credit ratings for more than 57 million businesses in more than 200 countries.[16]
- *Local credit-reporting agencies*, which may require a monthly or yearly fee for providing information on a continual basis.
- *Industry associations*, which may charge a service fee.
- *Other firms* that have given the applicant credit.

Various credit bureaus provide credit information concerning individuals. The following are the three major consumer credit bureaus:

- Experian—Allen, Texas (888-397-3742)
- Trans Union—Springfield, Pennsylvania (800-888-4213)
- Equifax Credit Information Services—Atlanta, Georgia (800-685-1111)

Consumer credit bureaus are subject to the provisions of the Fair Credit Reporting Act, which became effective in 1971. This act safeguards consumers' rights in two ways. First, every consumer has the right to know what information is contained in his or her credit bureau file. In most cases, a consumer who has been denied credit on the basis of information provided by a credit bureau can also obtain a credit report without charge. In other situations, the consumer may obtain the information for a fee that is usually about $8.50.

Second, a consumer who feels that some information in the file is inaccurate, misleading, or vague has the right to request that the credit bureau verify it. If the disputed information is found to be correct, the consumer can provide an explanation of up to one hundred words, giving his or her side of the dispute. This explanation must become part of the consumer's credit file. If the disputed information is found to be inaccurate, it must be deleted or corrected. Furthermore, any lender that has been supplied an inaccurate credit report within the past six months must be sent a corrected credit report. For information on how credit bureaus are polishing their image, read Adapting to Change.

Sound Collection Procedures

The vast majority of borrowers follow the lender's repayment terms exactly. However, some accounts inevitably become overdue for a variety of reasons. Experience shows that such accounts should receive immediate attention.

Some firms handle their own delinquent accounts; others prefer to use a professional collection agency. (Charges for a collection agency's services are usually high—up to half of the amount collected.) Both tend to use the following techniques, generally in the order in which they are listed:

1. Subtle reminders, such as duplicate statements marked "Past Due"
2. Telephone calls to urge prompt payment

Adapting to change

Credit Bureaus Polish Their Image

TODAY, VOLUMES OF CREDIT INFORMATION are reported by banks, finance companies, credit card companies, retail merchants, the Internal Revenue System, and even courts in the legal system. Unfortunately, when so much information is obtained from so many different sources, mistakes are made. And invariably those mistakes can cause problems for individuals. To avoid these potentially serious problems, experts recommend that you obtain a copy of your credit report from a national credit bureau before applying for credit cards, loans to purchase a home or automobile, a job, or even insurance coverage.

The Fair Credit Reporting Act—a federal regulation—allows you to obtain a copy of the information contained in your credit report. But until recently, the process required to obtain a credit report from a national credit bureau had been both lengthy and cumbersome. Now the three national credit bureaus—Experian, Equifax, and Trans Union—have begun a public relations campaign to polish their image. For a small fee, usually about $8.50, each bureau will send you a copy of your credit report. And reports are free under the following conditions:

- You've been turned down for credit within the last sixty days. By law, you'll receive notification of the rejection from the prospective lender, and it will state which credit bureau supplied the information on which the rejection was based.
- You've been placed on a "fraud alert." If you have any reason to suspect that you may be a victim of credit fraud, notify the national credit bureaus and have your credit file marked "on alert." You will immediately receive a free credit report. Something as simple as giving your social security number to a stranger can cause problems. With just your social security number, it is possible for the crooks to obtain credit cards and make purchases that could ultimately ruin your credit. Once a fraud alert is reported to a credit bureau, it's a good idea to obtain additional credit reports every six months to make sure that no unauthorized credit entries or false information appears.
- You're verifiably unemployed, receiving public assistance, or both.
- You're a resident of Colorado, Georgia, Massachusetts, Maryland, New Jersey, or Vermont. The laws in these states require that credit bureaus provide you with one free credit report per calendar year.

Request for credit reports can be made by phone or mail, but using the Internet often provides a quicker response. To obtain a credit report, contact Experian at www.experian.com or 888-397-3742, Equifax at www.equifax.com or 888-685-1111, and Trans Union at www.transunion.com or 800-888-4213. To find out more about your rights as a consumer and the provisions of the Fair Credit Reporting Act, contact the Federal Trade Commission Consumer Response Center at www.ftc.gov or 202-326-2222.

3. Personal visits to business customers to stress the necessity of paying overdue amounts immediately
4. Legal action, although the time, expense, and uncertain outcome of a lawsuit make this action a last resort

Good collection procedures should be firm, but they should also allow for compromise. Harassment is both illegal and bad business. Ideally, the customer will be convinced to make up missed payments, and the firm will retain the customer's goodwill.

In the next chapter, you will see why firms need financing, how they obtain the money they need, and how they ensure that funds are utilized efficiently, in keeping with their organizational objectives.

RETURN TO Inside Business

A SURVEY BY NCR CORPORATION found that 73 percent of banking customers prefer to complete financial transactions with a human teller at a traditional bank. These same customers cite concerns over security and privacy as the two main reasons for not using an online bank.[17] To ease these concerns, Wingspan.com and other Internet-only banks go to great lengths to make sure that their customer's transactions are not only secure, but also private.

Today, there are at least four different safeguards that protect people who bank online. First, most customers use either Microsoft Explorer or Netscape to process their banking transactions. With each of these Internet browsers, encryption software is used to guard against an unauthorized person stealing account numbers and other financial information. Second, Internet banks have strict rules on who can process online transactions. Only employees with proper authorization can add or subtract amounts from a customer's account. Third, Internet banks can now require an "electronic signature" to validate transactions. Beginning in July, 2000, a federal law was enacted that makes an electronic signature valid for business and consumer transactions. When used with banking transactions, an electronic signature provides a special code that resides inside your computer and "stamps" your online transmissions as uniquely yours. Finally, deposits at most online banks are insured, even if the bank is "cyberrobbed." Internet banks with FDIC coverage have to meet the same criteria and are monitored just as closely as traditional banks. In return, customers at Internet banks with FDIC coverage are insured for up to $100,000 per individual at one bank. Most customers assume that an Internet or traditional banks have FDIC coverage, but you can verify coverage by calling the FDIC at 800-934-3342 or go to its web site at www.fdic.gov.

Questions

1. After just eighteen months, Wingspan.com has over 110,000 customer accounts and continues to open new accounts every day. Why do you think customers have chosen Wingspan.com?
2. Both Internet banks and their customers are concerned with security and privacy. What actions do Internet banks take to safeguard their customers?

chapter Review

SUMMARY

1 Identity the functions and characteristics of money.

Money is anything a society uses to purchase products, services, or resources. Money must serve as a medium of exchange, a measure of value, and a store of value. To perform its functions effectively, money must be divisible into units of convenient size, light and sturdy enough to be carried and used on a daily basis, stable in value, and difficult to counterfeit.

The M_1 supply of money is made up of coins and bills (currency) and deposits in checking accounts (demand deposits). The M_2 supply includes M_1 plus certain money-market securities and small-denomination time deposits. Another common definition of the money supply—M_3—consists of M_1 and M_2 plus time deposits of $100,000 or more.

2 Summarize how the Federal Reserve System regulates the money supply.

The Federal Reserve System is responsible for regulating the U.S. banking industry and maintaining a sound economic environment. Banks with federal charters (national banks) must be members of the Fed. State banks may join if they choose to and if they can meet the requirements for membership. Twelve district banks and twenty-five branch banks compose the Federal Reserve System, whose seven-member Board of Governors is headquartered in Washington, D.C.

To control the supply of money, the Federal Reserve System regulates the reserve requirement, or the percentage of deposits a bank must keep on hand. It also regulates the discount rate, or the interest rate the Fed charges member banks for loans. And it engages in open-market operations, in which it buys and sells government securities. The Fed serves as the government's bank and is also responsible for clearing checks and electronic transfers, inspecting currency, enforcing the Truth-in-Lending Act, and setting margin requirements for stock transactions.

3 Describe the differences between commercial banks and other financial institutions in the banking industry.

A commercial bank is a profit-making organization that accepts deposits, makes loans, and provides related services to customers. Commercial banks are chartered by the federal government or state governments. Savings and loan associations, mutual savings banks, and credit unions offer the same basic services that commercial banks provide. Insurance companies, pension funds, brokerage firms, finance companies, and investment banking firms provide some limited banking services. A large number of people work in the banking industry because of the number of banks and other financial institutions. To be successful in the banking industry, you must be honest, be able to interact with people, have a strong background in accounting, appreciate the relationship between banking and finance, and possess basic computer skills.

4 Identify the services provided by financial institutions.

Banks and other financial institutions offer today's customers a tempting array of services. Among the most important and attractive banking services for both individuals and businesses are checking accounts, savings accounts, short- and long-term loans, and credit card and debit card transactions. Other services include online banking, electronic transfer of funds, financial advice, payroll services, certified checks, trust services, and safe-deposit boxes.

5 Understand how financial institutions are changing to meet the needs of domestic and international customers.

Among the laws enacted during the last thirty years to deregulate the banking industry, probably the most important is the Financial Services Modernization Banking Act of 1999. This act allowed banks to establish one-stop financial supermarkets where customers can bank, buy and sell securities, and purchase insurance coverage. Because of this act, competition between banks, brokerage firms, and insurance companies has increased. Another important piece of legislation that increased competition in the banking industry is the Depository Institutions Deregulation and Monetary Control Act of 1980. This act promoted more competition between commercial banks and savings and loan associations. Unfortunately, increased competition, coupled with bad loans, fraud, and financial mismanagement, increased the failure rate of financial institutions. The last part of the 1990s and the year 2000 have, however, witnessed fewer bank failures.

As we enter the twenty-first century, an increasing use of technology and the need for bankers to help American businesses compete in the global marketplace will change the way banks and other financial institutions do business. The use of technology will increase as financial institutions continue to offer online banking and touch-tone telephone banking. Increased use of electronic funds transfer systems (automated teller machines, automated clearinghouses, and point-of-sale terminals) will also change the way people bank. For firms in the global marketplace, a bank can provide letters of credit and bank acceptances that will reduce the risk of nonpayment for sellers. Banks and financial institutions can also provide currency exchange to reduce payment problems for import or export transactions.

6 Explain the function of the Federal Deposit Insurance Corporation, Savings Association Insurance Fund, Bank Insurance Fund, and National Credit Union Association.

The Federal Deposit Insurance Corporation (FDIC), Savings Association Insurance Fund (SAIF), Bank Insurance Fund (BIF), and National Credit Union Association (NCUA) insure accounts in member commercial banks, S&Ls, savings banks, and credit unions, respectively, for up to $100,000 per individual at one financial institution. The FDIC and NCUA have improved banking in the United States. When either of these organizations insures a financial institution's deposits, they reserve the right to examine that institution's operations periodically. If a bank, savings and loan, or credit union is found to be poorly managed, it is reported to the proper banking authority.

7 Discuss the importance of credit and credit management.

Credit is immediate purchasing power that is exchanged for a promise to repay borrowed money, with or without interest, at a later date. Banks lend money because they are in business for that purpose. Businesses sell goods and services on credit because some customers cannot afford to pay cash and because they must keep pace with competitors who offer credit. Businesses may also realize a profit from interest charges.

Decisions on whether to grant credit to businesses and individuals are usually based on the five Cs of credit: character, capacity, capital, collateral, and conditions. Credit information can be obtained from various credit reporting agencies, credit bureaus, industry associations, and other firms. The techniques used to collect past-due accounts should be firm enough to prompt payment but flexible enough to maintain the borrower's goodwill.

KEY TERMS

You should now be able to define and give an example relevant to each of the following terms:

barter system (546)
money (547)
medium of exchange (547)
measure of value (547)
store of value (547)
demand deposit (549)
time deposit (549)
Federal Reserve System (550)
reserve requirement (551)
discount rate (552)
open-market operations (552)
commercial bank (555)
national bank (556)
state bank (556)
savings and loan association (S&L) (556)
NOW account (556)
mutual savings banks (557)
credit union (557)
check (559)
certificate of deposit (CD) (560)
line of credit (560)
revolving credit agreement (560)
collateral (560)
debit card (562)
electronic funds transfer (EFT) system (564)
letter of credit (565)
banker's acceptance (565)
credit (566)

REVIEW QUESTIONS

1. How does the use of money solve the problems associated with a barter system of exchange?
2. What are three functions money must perform in a sound monetary system?
3. Explain why money must have each of the following characteristics:
   a. Divisibility
   b. Portability
   c. Stability
   d. Durability
   e. Difficulty of counterfeiting
4. What is included in the definition of the M_1 supply of money? Of the M_2 supply? Of the M_3 supply?
5. What is the Federal Reserve System? How is it organized?
6. Explain how the Federal Reserve System uses each of the following to control the money supply.
   a. Reserve requirements
   b. The discount rate
   c. Open-market operations
7. The Federal Reserve is responsible for enforcing the Truth-in-Lending Act. How does this act affect you?
8. What is the difference between a national bank and a state bank? What other financial institutions compete with national and state banks?
9. Describe the major banking services provided by financial institutions today.
10. What are the major advantages of online banking? What is its major disadvantage?
11. How can a bank or other financial institution help American businesses compete in the global marketplace?
12. What is the basic function of the FDIC, SAIF, BIF, and NCUA? How do they perform this function?
13. Assume you want to borrow $10,000. What can you do to convince the loan officer that you are a good credit risk?
14. List and explain the five Cs of credit management.
15. How would you check the information provided by an applicant for credit at a department store? By a business applicant at a heavy-equipment manufacturer's sales office?

DISCUSSION QUESTIONS

1. It is said that financial institutions "create" money when they make loans to firms and individuals. Explain what this means.
2. Is competition among financial institutions good or bad for the following:
   a. The institutions themselves
   b. Their customers
   c. The economy in general
3. Why would banks pay higher interest on money left on deposit for longer periods of time (for example, on CDs)?
4. How could an individual get in financial trouble by using a credit card?
5. Why does the Fed use indirect means of controlling the money supply, instead of simply printing more money or removing money from circulation when necessary?
6. Lenders are generally reluctant to extend credit to individuals with no previous credit history (and no outstanding debts). Yet they willingly extend credit to individuals who are in the process of repaying debts. Is this reasonable? Is it fair? Explain your answer.

VIDEO CASE

Why Stokes Interactive Needs Bank Financing

How much money does a small, rapidly growing high-tech company need? According to John J. Carey, the president of Stokes Interactive, the answer is simple: a lot. The more important question is, Where does the money come from? Before answering that question, let's take a look at the type of products and services Stokes Interactive offers its clients, which include Cinemark USA, American Airlines, Mary Kay Cosmetics, Fujitsu America, and IBM Interactive Media.

Stokes Interactive is a multimedia company that develops advanced computer and video technology for marketing, employee training, sales presentations, trade shows, and information kiosks. Through its sister company, the Stokes Group—a winner of more than 100 film and graphic animation awards—it also offers a full range of video and animation production services for television.

The goal of the people at Stokes Interactive is "not to just meet their client's expectations, but to exceed them."

The process begins with an evaluation of customer needs. Then, the talented employees at Stokes create interactive video in a cost-effective manner. Among their products are the following:

- **Web Page Development**: A turnkey solution for companies that need consultation, page design, graphics, employee training, and maintenance of marketing materials for the World Wide Web
- **CD-Roms**: Electronic storage systems that deliver a large amount of information through a multimedia computer system
- **Video CDs**: Video systems that play video material from a compact disc with fast forward, rewind, pause, and play features similar to VHS tapes
- **Pitchman TM**: An interactive package of broadcast-quality video for high-level business applications

(For more information about Stokes Interactive's products, visit the company's web site at http://www.stokesfx.com)

The facilities and equipment required to create the type of marketing and employee-training tools produced by Stokes Interactive are expensive to purchase and to maintain. But state-of-the-art, high-tech equipment is essential to attract large corporate clients. From the start, the company's founders—John Carey, Bill Stokes, and Don Stokes—realized it was crucial to establish a sound financial partnership with a bank that could provide needed financing. To develop this financial partnership, they created a business plan that convinced their bankers to provide loans for equipment and a line of credit for financing production costs, salaries, and ongoing expenses until major projects were completed and customers paid for Stokes Interactive's products and services.

Through the years, Stokes Interactive has maintained a working relationship with its bankers. This relationship has enabled Stokes Interactive to grow and provide the best possible service to its clients. Management at Stokes Interactive also realizes it has a responsibility to its bankers. Making loan payments on time and keeping bankers informed about the firm's financial needs enhances this relationship. It all boils down to trust. John Carey summarizes it like this: "You just need to stick with the agreement you have with your bankers."[18]

Questions

1. Like most multimedia firms, Stokes Interactive needs cash to pay production costs, salaries, and ongoing expenses until major projects are completed and its customers pay their bills. What type of financial assistance can a banker provide to a firm like Stokes Interactive?
2. From the start, the founders of Stokes Interactive knew they had to develop a sound financial partnership with a bank that could provide financing. How did the company's founders develop this relationship?
3. The relationship between a business firm and a bank is often built on trust. Why is it important to "stick with an agreement" when you borrow money? How could failure to make loan payments to bankers or suppliers hurt a firm like Stokes Interactive?

Building skills for career success

1. Exploring the Internet

Internet-based banking is no longer a new concept. With the explosive growth in e-commerce, online credit and debit cards are fast becoming specialized financial tools for facilitating transactions over the Internet. Designed to minimize consumer resistance to providing important personal information to "virtual strangers" over the Internet, these cards transfer much of the financial risk of their theft or unauthorized use to the company who has issued the card.

Consumers have good reason to be concerned with credit card and banking fraud in general. Unauthorized use of someone's credit can be costly and destroy good credit histories in no time. How then, can consumers be made to feel more confident that they won't be penalized by fraud? Both Master Card and Visa have specialized products to combat fraud, and other bankcards are following their example to satisfy the growing demand for secure virtual money. Visit the text web site for updates to this exercise.

Assignment

1. Examine the web sites for several major banks you are familiar with. Describe their online banking services. Are they worthwhile in your opinion?
2. Describe the special features associated with their specialized Internet cards.
3. How are the banks marketing these new financial instruments to customers? to merchants?
4. What fee structures are offered for use of these online cards? In your opinion, are they worth having? Explain your answer.

2. Developing Critical Thinking Skills

Every year your grandmother in Seattle, Washington, sends you a personal check for $100 for your birthday. You live in Monticello, Georgia, seventy-five miles southeast of Atlanta. You either cash the check or deposit it in your savings account at a local bank. Your banker does not directly return the canceled check to your grandmother, but somehow it ends up back in your grandmother's hands in Seattle. How does this happen?

Assignment

1. Research the process for returning canceled checks to their owners.
2. Prepare a diagram showing the various steps in the process and explain what happens in each step.
3. Summarize what you learned and how this information might be helpful to you in the future.

3. Building Team Skills

Three years ago, Ron and Ginger were happy to learn that upon graduation, Ron would be teaching history in a large high school, making $30,000 a year, and Ginger would be working in a public accounting firm, starting at $34,000. They married immediately after graduation and bought a new home for $110,000. Since Ron had no personal savings, Ginger used her savings for the down payment. They soon began furnishing their home, charging their purchases to three separate credit cards, and that is when their debt began to mount. When the three credit cards reached their $10,000 limits, Ron and Ginger signed up for four additional credit cards with $10,000 limits that were offered through the mail, and they started using them. Soon their monthly payments were more than their combined take-home pay. To make their monthly payments, Ron and Ginger began to obtain cash advances on their credit cards. When they reached the credit ceilings on their seven credit cards, they could no longer get the cash advances they needed to exist. Stress began to mount as creditors called and demanded payment. Ron and Ginger began to argue over money and just about everything else. Finally, things got so bad they considered filing for personal bankruptcy, but ironically they could not afford the legal fees. What options are available to this couple?

Assignment

1. Working in teams of three or four, use your local library, the Internet, and personal interviews to investigate the following:
   a. Filling for personal bankruptcy
      - What is involved in filing for personal bankruptcy?
      - How much does it cost?
      - How does bankruptcy affect individuals?

   b. The Consumer Credit Counseling Service (800-783-5018) or Debt Counselors of America (800-680-3328).
      - What services do these organizations provide?
      - How could they help Ron and Ginger?
      - What will it cost?
2. Prepare a specific plan for repaying Ron and Ginger's debt.
3. Outline the advantages and disadvantages of credit cards, and make the appropriate recommendations for Ron and Ginger concerning their future use of credit cards.
4. Summarize what you have learned about credit card misuse.

4. Researching Different Careers

It has long been known that maintaining a good credit record is essential to obtaining loans from financial institutions, but did you know that employers often check credit records before offering an applicant a position? This is especially true of firms that handle financial accounts for others. Information contained in your credit report can tell an employer a lot about how responsible you are with money and how well you manage it. Individuals have the right to know what is in their credit bureau files and to have the credit bureau verify any inaccurate, misleading, or vague information. Before you apply for a job or a loan, you should check with a credit bureau to learn what is in your file.

Assignment

1. Using information in the chapter, call a credit bureau and ask for a copy of your credit report. A small fee may be required, depending on the bureau and circumstances.
2. Review the information.
3. Have the bureau verify any information you feel is inaccurate, misleading, or vague.
4. If the verification shows the information is correct, prepare a brief statement explaining your side of the dispute and send it to the bureau.
5. Prepare a statement summarizing what the credit report says about you. Based on your credit report, would a firm hire you as its financial manager?

5. Improving Communication Skills

Technology has changed the way we conduct our banking transactions. Most people no long carry their paychecks to the bank to be deposited; instead, the money is directly deposited into their accounts. An increasing number of individuals and businesses are using computers and the Internet to handle their finances and pay their bills. Banking from a home computer is continually being made easier, giving you access to your account at any time and more control over your money. *Kiplinger's Personal Finance Magazine* projected that by the end of 2002, 18 million U.S. households will use online banking.

Assignment

1. In the past three years, how has technology changed the way you handle your money and conduct your banking transactions, such as depositing your paychecks, paying your monthly bills, obtaining cash, paying for purchases, and applying for loans?
2. In the next five to ten years, what will the banking industry be like? How will these changes affect you and the way you do your banking? How readily will you adapt to change? The Internet and the library can help you learn what is in the forefront of banking technology.
3. Prepare a report covering your answers to these questions.

Mastering Financial Management

20

LEARNING OBJECTIVES

1 Explain the need for financing and financial management in business.

2 Summarize the process of planning for financial management.

3 Describe the advantages and disadvantages of different methods of short-term debt financing.

4 Evaluate the advantages and disadvantages of equity financing.

5 Evaluate the advantages and disadvantages of long-term debt financing.

6 Discuss the importance of using funds effectively.

Like a lot of dot.com companies, PriceLine was an immediate success and needed money – a lot of money.

inside business

Priceline.com: The Anatomy of an IPO

HARDLY A DAY GOES BY when you don't hear of a new dot-com company selling stock. Usually, these Internet-based businesses are started by an entrepreneur or a group of entrepreneurs with a marketable idea. One such company—Priceline.com—was started by Jay Walker. In 1997, his company became the first to offer what he calls *buyer-driven commerce* over the Internet. In simple terms, Priceline matches a customer's travel destination with an airline. Then the customer pays by credit card and Priceline books the transaction at a cost that is lower than a more traditional travel agency can provide for the same service.

Based on customer acceptance, Priceline was an immediate success and needed money—a lot of money—to fund corporate growth. Specifically, financing was needed to expand the services it provided its customers, hire more employees, purchase the latest technological equipment, and pay for advertising to build a customer base that would continue to purchase the firm's products and services. To obtain the needed financing, Mr. Walker decided to use an IPO. An IPO—which stands for initial public offering—is the first time a corporation sells common stock to the general public. As he soon discovered, preparing to sell stock for the first time is a road full of potholes.

For Priceline.com, the process began by selecting an investment banking firm. An investment banking firm is an organization that assists corporations in raising funds, usually by helping sell new issues of stocks, bonds, or other financial securities. Generally, an investment banking firm is chosen because it can help a company gain regulatory approval, find customers for new securities, and the amount of commissions that the investment banker will charge the company. The investment banking firm is concerned about how hard it will be to find customers for the company's new securities. Because the investment banking firm generally purchases the securities from the company and then resells them to its customers, the quality of the company, management, products and services, and investment potential are extremely important factors when deciding if the firm will help the company sell its new securities. After much time and deliberation, Priceline.com chose the investment banking firm of Morgan Stanley.

For Priceline.com, the next step was to obtain the approval of the Securities and Exchange Commission, often referred to as the *SEC*. In order to comply with current SEC requirements, a company must draft a prospectus—a detailed, written description of a new security, the issuing corporation, and the corporation's top management. In some ways, a prospectus is like a road map starting with the company's past experience and moving through various financial analyses stressing growth plans for the future. Creating a prospectus is vital because it is the only "document" that the company can use to attract investors. In addition to the prospectus, the SEC often requires additional information about the company and its proposed security offerings. If the SEC approves the new securities issue, then the company, with the help of its investment banker, can begin the process of selling the new security issue.

The actual date of the initial public offering is chosen by executives of the company and the investment banking firm. All people involved want "just the right" economic environment so the company gets top dollar for its stock and the investment banking firm sells the new securities quickly. It is not at all uncommon for an initial public offering to be postponed for a variety of reasons that include actions by the Federal Reserve to raise interest rates, rumors that a competitor is going to offer a competing product or service, a prolonged downturn in the stock market, or even the unexpected illness of a company executive.

In addition to timing, executives for the company and the investment banking firm must determine the price for the new security. Every dollar that increases or decreases the price per share means millions in total investments. When the haggling is finished and the price is set, the process of selling the securities begins. Invariably, there's always more orders for the new securities than what are available, so the company ends up wondering why it didn't get a higher price.

Was all the effort worth it? Well consider the results. On March 30, 1999, the Priceline IPO opened selling 10 million shares, at $16 a share. By the end of the trading day, all the company's shares were sold, and Priceline.com received over $150 million that it could use to fund corporate growth.[1]

A dot-com company like Priceline is no different than more traditional businesses—they all need money. Typical business activities like hiring employees, replacing outdated equipment, paying suppliers, and funding expansion all require financial resources. To raise the money needed to satisfy these needs, Priceline.com decided to sell stock to the general public. The process began with choosing an investment banker—Morgan Stanley. Then approval for its initial public offering was obtained from the Securities and Exchange Commission. Next a date was chosen to sell the stock, Finally, executives for Priceline and Morgan Stanley determined the price for the new shares. When the big day arrived, investors were waiting and 10 million shares were sold. More importantly, Priceline.com received over $150 million that it could use to fund corporate growth.

In this chapter, we focus on two needs of business organizations like Priceline.com: first, the need for money to start a business and keep it going, and second, the need to manage that money effectively. We also look at how firms develop financial plans and evaluate financial performance. Then we compare various methods of obtaining short-term financing—money that will be used one year or less. We also examine sources of long-term financing, which a firm may require for expansion, new-product development, or replacement of equipment.

LEARNING OBJECTIVE

1 Explain the need for financing and financial management in business.

What Is Financial Management?

Financial management consists of all the activities concerned with obtaining money and using it effectively. Within a business organization, the financial manager must not only determine the best way (or ways) to raise money. She or he must also ensure that projected uses are in keeping with the organization's goals. Effective financial management thus involves careful planning. That planning begins with a determination of the firm's financing needs.

financial management all the activities concerned with obtaining money and using it effectively

The Need for Financing

Money is needed both to start a business and to keep it going. The original investment of the owners, along with money they may have borrowed, should be enough to open the doors. After that, it would seem that sales revenues could be used to pay the firm's expenses and to provide a profit as well.

This is exactly what happens in a successful firm—over the long run. But income and expenses may vary from month to month or from year to year. Temporary financing may be needed when expenses are high or sales are low. Then, too, situations such as the opportunity to purchase a new facility or expand an existing plant may require more money than is currently available within a firm. In either case, the firm must look for outside sources of financing.

Short-Term Financing

Short-term financing is money that will be used for one year or less. Many financial managers define short-term financing as money that will be used for one year *or* one operating cycle of the business, whichever is longer. The *operating cycle of the business* may be longer than one year and is the amount of time between the purchase of raw materials and the sale of finished products to wholesalers, retailers, or consumers.

short-term financing money that will be used for one year or less

As illustrated in Table 20.1, there are many short-term financing needs, but two deserve special attention. First, certain business practices may affect a firm's cash flow and create a need for short-term financing. **Cash flow** is the movement of money into and out of an organization. The ideal is to have sufficient money coming into the firm in any period to cover the firm's expenses during that period. But the ideal is not always achieved. For example, California-based Callaway Golf offers credit to retailers and wholesalers that carry the firm's golf clubs and balls. For Callaway, this extension of credit often creates cash-flow problems. Credit purchases are generally not paid until thirty to sixty days (or more) after the transaction. Callaway may therefore need short-term

cash flow the movement of money into and out of an organization

A high-flying deal. American Airlines agreed to acquire most of the assets of financially troubled Trans World Airlines (TWA). The deal, which will merge two of the largest airline carriers in the world, is valued at approximately $750 million and required careful financial planning to raise the capital needed to complete the acquisition.

financing to pay its bills until retailers and wholesalers have paid theirs.

A second major need for short-term financing that is related to a firm's cash-flow problem is inventory. For most manufacturers, wholesalers, and retailers, inventory requires considerable investment. Moreover, most goods are manufactured four to nine months before they are actually sold to the ultimate customer. Consider what happens when a firm like Black & Decker begins to manufacture small appliances for sale during the Christmas season. Manufacturing begins in February, March, and April, and Black & Decker negotiates short-term financing to buy materials and supplies, to pay wages and rent, and to cover inventory costs until the appliances are eventually sold to wholesalers and retailers later in the year. Take a look at Figure 20.1. Although Black & Decker manufactures and sells finished products all during the year, expenses peak during the first part of the year. During this same period, sales revenues are low. When manufacturing is completed, finished products are shipped to retailers. Then sales revenues begin to increase. Once payment is received, usually thirty to sixty days after the merchandise is shipped, Black & Decker can use these sales revenues to repay its short-term financing.

Retailers that range in size from Wal-Mart to the neighborhood drugstore also need short-term financing to build up their inventories before peak selling periods. For example, Dallas-based Bruce Miller Nurseries must increase the amount of shrubs, trees, and flowering plants that it makes available for sale during the spring and summer growing seasons. To obtain this merchandise from growers or wholesalers, it uses short-term financing and repays the loan when the merchandise is sold.

long-term financing money that will be used for longer than one year

Long-Term Financing

Long-term financing is money that will be used for longer than one year. Long-term financing is obviously needed to start a new business. As Table 20.1 shows, it is also needed for business expansions and mergers, product development and marketing, and replacement of equipment that has become obsolete.

table 20.1 Comparison of Short- and Long-Term Financing

Whether a business seeks short- or long-term financing depends on what the money will be used for.

Corporate Cash Needs

Short-term financing needs	Long-term financing needs
Cash-flow problems	Business start-up costs
Current inventory needs	New-product development
Monthly expenses	Long-term marketing activities
Speculative production	Expansion of facilities
Short-term promotional needs	Replacement of equipment
Unexpected emergencies	Mergers and acquisitions

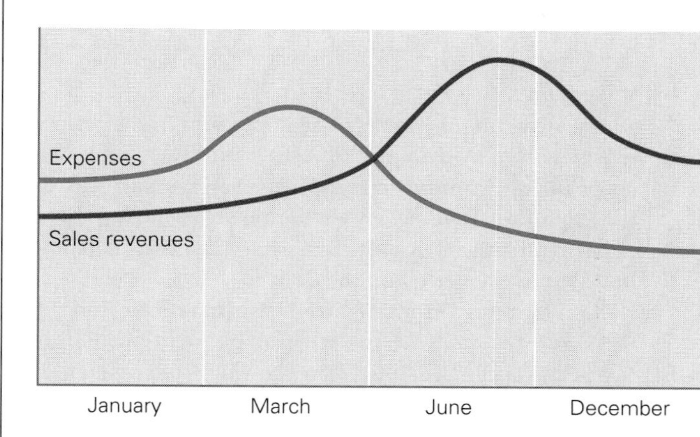

figure 20.1

Cash Flow for a Manufacturing Business
Manufacturers often use short-term financing to pay expenses during the production process. Once goods are shipped to retailers and payment is received, sales revenues are used to repay short-term financing.

The amounts of long-term financing needed by large firms can seem almost unreal. Exxon spends about $10 million to drill an exploratory offshore oil well—without knowing for sure whether oil will be found. Toyota spent millions to develop, manufacture, and market the Lexus automobile. And according to the Pharmaceutical Research and Manufacturers of America, a Washington, D.C. trade group, pharmaceutical companies spend $500 million and 12 to 15 years to develop and market a new prescription drug.[2]

The Need for Financial Management

Without financing, there would be very little business. Financing gets a business started in the first place. Then it supports the firm's production and marketing activities; pays its bills; and, when carefully managed, produces a reasonable profit.

Many firms have failed because their managers did not pay enough attention to finances. In fact, poor financial management was one of the major reasons why over 72,000 businesses filed for bankruptcy in 1998 (the most recent year for which complete statistics are available). To see what happens when businesses in a foreign country can't get the financing they need, read Going Global. In addition, many fairly successful firms could be highly successful if they managed their finances more carefully. But many people often take finances for granted. Their first focus may be on production or marketing. As long as there is sufficient financing today, they don't worry about how well it is used or whether it will be there tomorrow.

Proper financial management can ensure that

- Financing priorities are established in line with organizational goals and objectives.
- Spending is planned and controlled in accordance with established priorities.
- Sufficient financing is available when it is needed, both now and in the future.
- Excess cash is invested in certificates of deposit (CDs), government securities, or conservative, marketable securities.

These functions define effective management as applied to a particular resource: money. And, like all effective management, financial management begins with people who must set goals and plan for the future.

Careers in Finance

When you hear the word *finance*, you may think of highly paid executives who determine what a corporation can afford to do and what it can't. While some people in finance do make $300,000 a year or more, many entry-level and lower-level positions that pay quite a bit less are available. Banks, insurance companies, and investment firms obviously have a need for workers who can manage and analyze financial data. So do businesses involved in manufacturing, services, and marketing. Colleges and

Going Global

Just Say the Word "Russia" to Investors and They Shudder!

When communism fell in the early 1990s, Russia began to endorse a limited form of capitalism. This new era started when government officials began to return government-owned businesses and industries to the private sector. By 1995, investment bankers from the United States and Europe were successfully convincing investors from all over the globe to purchase Russian stocks. Proceeds were used to modernize production facilities that would allow Russian businesses to compete in the world marketplace.

What Went Wrong?

But six years later in 2001, just say the word *Russia* to private investors or in corporate boardrooms and a silence pervades the atmosphere and people begin to shudder. Why? For many people, Russian investments have turned into a nightmare that many would like to forget. It all began with political upheaval and the devaluation of the ruble in 1998. These two events caused a financial crisis for both Russian businesses and a struggling country trying to compete in a very competitive global environment. Russian stocks and bonds that were once chosen for their investment potential became nearly worthless.

What Does the Future Hold?

Today, investment bankers are struggling to negotiate terms with government officials and Russian businesses in an attempt to recapture even a small part of the $12 billion invested by their clients. While anything is better than nothing, the eventual payoff may result in less than five cents on the dollar.

On March 26, 2000, Vladimir Putin was elected the Russian president. At the time of publication of this text, Russia remains mired in the worst depression of modern history. Only time will tell if Putin can pull off economic recovery, restore the faith of investors, and open the door of opportunity for both investors and Russian businesses.

A Word of Caution

It is essential that you evaluate foreign stocks or international mutual funds. Don't just read advertising and marketing brochures, but dig deeper into the financial statements for a foreign company before purchasing its stock. If the foreign investment is an international fund, look at the fund's prospectus and annual report. Realize that accounting rules different from those generally accepted in the United States may affect the profit or loss amounts reported on financial statements of a company or a mutual fund. Above all, consider political and economic conditions in a foreign country that may affect the value of your investment.

universities, not-for-profit organizations, and government entities at all levels also need finance workers.

Whether they are high-level managers or entry-level employees, people in finance must have certain traits and skills. They must

1. Be responsible and honest because they are working with other people's money.
2. Have a strong background in accounting or mathematics.
3. Know how to use a computer to analyze data.
4. Be an expert at both written and oral communication.

Typical job titles in finance include bank officer, consumer credit officer, financial analyst, financial planner, loan officer, insurance analyst, and investment account executive. Depending on qualifications, work experience, and education, starting salaries generally begin at $25,000 a year, but it is not uncommon for college graduates to earn $30,000 a year or more.

LEARNING OBJECTIVE

2 Summarize the process of planning for financial management

Planning—The Basis of Sound Financial Management

financial plan a plan for obtaining and using the money needed to implement an organization's goals

In Chapter 7, we defined a plan as an outline of the actions by which an organization intends to accomplish its goals. A **financial plan**, then, is a plan for obtaining and using the money needed to implement an organization's goals.

Developing the Financial Plan

It takes a lot of money to start a movie studio. To *raise capital*, Joe Roth sold 25 percent of his new startup—Revolution Studios—for $250 million to investors. To *generate revenues*, he signed Julia Roberts, Bruce Willis, Adam Sandler, Catherine Zeta-Jones and other big-name stars to act in movies produced by Revolution.

Financial planning (like all planning) begins with the establishment of a set of valid goals and objectives. Financial managers must next determine how much money is needed to accomplish each goal and objective. Finally, financial managers must identify available sources of financing and decide which to use. In the process, they must make sure that financing needs are realistic and that sufficient funding is available to meet those needs. The three steps involved in financial planning are illustrated in Figure 20.2.

Establishing Organizational Goals and Objectives As pointed out in Chapter 7, a goal is an end state that the organization expects to achieve. Objectives are *specific* statements detailing what the organization intends to accomplish within a certain period of time. If goals and objectives are not specific and measurable, they cannot be translated into dollar costs, and financial planning cannot proceed. Goals and objectives must also be realistic. Otherwise, they may be impossible to finance or achieve. One objective for the Levi Strauss Company in 2000 was to develop an advertising campaign to increase sales of its traditional jeans and a new line of corduroy products. To fulfill this objective, management spent over $70 million on nationwide advertising.[3]

Although there are many Internet-based business success stories, critics suggest that companies whose business plans cannot produce profits—the primary goal—will be doomed in the near future. Of particular concern are firms like online retailers and content-oriented web sites that need to spend huge amounts of money to generate brand awareness through costly advertising campaigns. For example, search engine AltaVista.com that is 83 percent owned by CMGI Inc, cut back its marketing and advertising budget by one-third to $100 million and reduced the number of people employed in an attempt to improve the firm's bottom-line profit amount.[4]

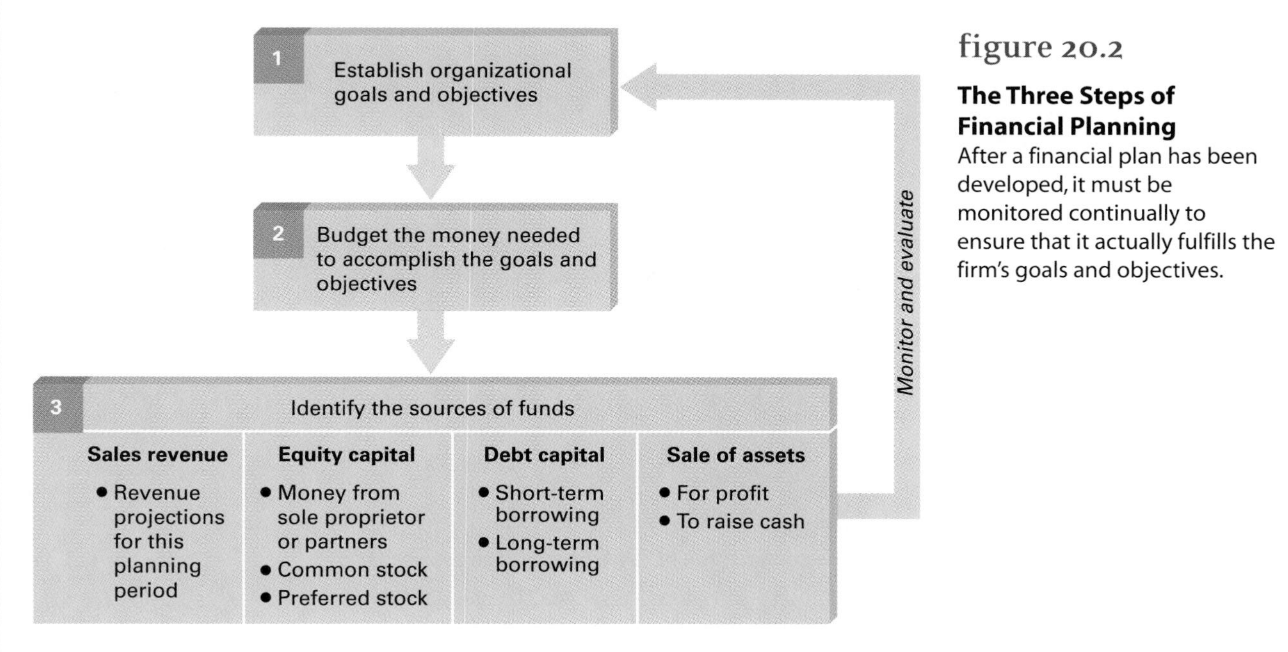

figure 20.2

The Three Steps of Financial Planning

After a financial plan has been developed, it must be monitored continually to ensure that it actually fulfills the firm's goals and objectives.

spotLight

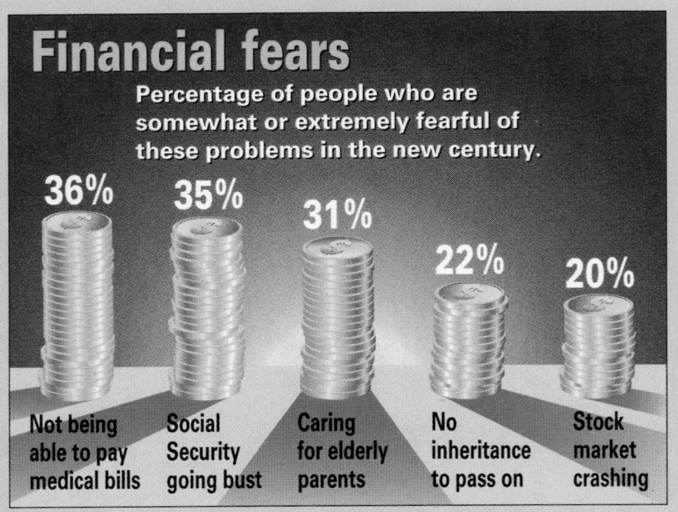

Source: Copyright 2000, USA TODAY. Reprinted with permission.

Budgeting for Financial Needs A **budget** is a financial statement that projects income and/or expenditures over a specified future period. Once planners know what the firm's goals and objectives are for a specific period—say, the next calendar year—they can forecast the costs the firm will incur and the sales revenues it will receive. By combining these items into a companywide budget, financial planners can determine whether they must seek additional funding from sources outside the firm.

Usually the budgeting process begins with the construction of budgets for sales and various types of expenses for individual departments—production, human resources, promotion, administration, and so on. (A typical sales budget—for Stars and Stripes Clothing, a California-based retailer—is shown in Figure 20.3.) Budgeting accuracy is improved when budgets are first constructed for separate departments and for shorter periods of time.

Financial managers can easily combine each department's budget for sales and expenses into a companywide cash budget. A **cash budget** estimates cash receipts and cash expenditures over a specified period. Notice in the cash budget for Stars and Stripes Clothing, shown in Figure 20.4, that cash sales and collections are listed at the top for each calendar quarter. Payments for purchases and routine expenses are listed in the middle section. Using this information, it is possible to calculate the anticipated cash gain or loss at the end of each quarter.

budget a financial statement that projects income and/or expenditures over a specified future period

cash budget a financial statement that projects cash receipts and expenditures over a specified period

Most firms today use one of two approaches to budgeting. In the *traditional* approach, each new budget is based on the dollar amounts contained in the budget for the preceding year. These amounts are modified to reflect any revised goals, and managers are required to justify only new expenditures. The problem with this approach is that it leaves room for padding budget items to protect the (sometimes selfish) interests of the manager or his or her department.

STARS AND STRIPES CLOTHING

Sales Budget For January 1, 2002 to December 31, 2002

Department	First quarter	Second quarter	Third quarter	Fourth quarter	Totals
Infants'	$ 50,000	$ 55,000	$ 60,000	$ 70,000	$235,000
Children's	45,000	45,000	40,000	40,000	170,000
Women's	35,000	40,000	35,000	50,000	160,000
Men's	20,000	20,000	15,000	25,000	80,000
Totals	$150,000	$160,000	$150,000	$185,000	$645,000

figure 20.3

Sales Budget for Stars and Stripes Clothing

Usually the budgeting process begins with the construction of departmental budgets for sales and various expenses.

STARS AND STRIPES CLOTHING
Cash Budget   For January 1, 2002 to December 31, 2002

	First quarter	Second quarter	Third quarter	Fourth quarter	Totals
Cash sales and collections	$150,000	$160,000	$150,000	$185,000	$645,000
Less payments					
Purchases	$110,000	$ 80,000	$ 90,000	$ 60,000	$340,000
Wages/salaries	25,000	20,000	25,000	30,000	100,000
Rent	10,000	10,000	12,000	12,000	44,000
Other expenses	4,000	4,000	5,000	6,000	19,000
Taxes	8,000	8,000	10,000	10,000	36,000
Total payments	$157,000	$122,000	$142,000	$118,000	$539,000
Cash gain or (loss)	$ (7,000)	$ 38,000	$ 8,000	$ 67,000	$106,000

figure 20.4

Cash Budget for Stars and Stripes Clothing

A companywide cash budget projects sales, collections, purchases, and expenses over a specified period to anticipate cash surpluses and deficits.

This problem is essentially eliminated through zero-base budgeting. **Zero-base budgeting** is a budgeting approach in which every expense in every budget must be justified. It can dramatically reduce unnecessary spending because every budget item must stand on its own merits. However, some managers oppose zero-base budgeting on the grounds that it requires entirely too much time-consuming paperwork.

zero-base budgeting a budgeting approach in which every expense in every budget must be justified

Because they focus on income and expenditures within a calendar year, departmental and cash budgets emphasize short-term financing needs. To develop a plan for long-term financing needs, managers often construct a capital budget. A **capital budget** estimates a firm's expenditures for major assets, including new-product development, expansion of facilities, replacement of obsolete equipment, and mergers and acquisitions. For example, AT&T constructed a capital budget to determine the best way to finance its $48 billion purchase of TCI Cable. It also used a capital budget to determine the best way to raise the millions needed to pay for renovation and improvement of its existing cable systems so that it could deliver telephone calls, video, and data on a single line.

capital budget a financial statement that estimates a firm's expenditures for major assets and its long-term financing needs

Identifying Sources of Funds

The four primary sources of funds, listed in Figure 20.2, are sales revenue, equity capital, debt capital, and proceeds from the sale of assets. Future sales revenue generally provides the greatest part of a firm's financing. Figure 20.4 shows that, for Stars and Stripes Clothing, sales for the year are expected to cover all expenses and to provide a cash gain of about 16 percent of sales. However, Stars and Stripes has a problem in the first quarter, when sales are expected to fall short of expenses by $7,000. In fact, one of the primary reasons for financial planning is to provide management with adequate lead time to solve this type of cash-flow problem.

A second type of funding is **equity capital.** For a sole proprietorship or partnership, equity capital is provided by the owner or owners of the business. For a corporation, equity capital is money obtained from the sale of shares of ownership in the business. Equity capital is used almost exclusively for long-term financing. Thus, it might be used to start a business and to fund expansions or mergers. It would not be considered for short-term financing needs, such as Stars and Stripes' first-quarter $7,000 shortfall.

equity capital money received from the owners or from the sale of shares of ownership in the business

debt capital borrowed money obtained through loans of various types

A third type of funding is **debt capital**, which is borrowed money obtained through loans. Debt capital may be borrowed for either short- or long-term use—and a short-term loan seems made to order for Stars and Stripes Clothing's short-fall problem. The firm would probably borrow the needed $7,000 (or perhaps a bit more) at some point during the first quarter and repay it from second-quarter sales revenue. Stars and Stripes Clothing might already have established a line of credit—discussed in Chapter 19—at a local bank to cover just such periodic short-term needs.

Proceeds from the sale of assets is the fourth type of funding. A firm generally acquires assets because it needs them for its business operations. Therefore, selling assets is a drastic step. However, it may be a reasonable last resort when neither equity capital nor debt capital can be found.

Assets may also be sold when they are no longer needed or don't "fit" with the company's core business. To concentrate on its core defense business, Raytheon Company sold its D.C. Heath publishing unit to Houghton Mifflin for $455 million. To raise capital, Kellogg Company sold its Lender's Bagel business to Aurora Foods, Inc. for $275 million.[5] For the same reason Atlantic Richfield Corporation sold its Ecuadorian assets and exploration properties in Columbia and Peru to Burlington Resources for $214 million.[6]

Monitoring and Evaluating Financial Performance

It is important to ensure that financial plans are being properly implemented and to catch minor problems before they become major ones. Accordingly, the financial manager should establish a means of monitoring financial performance. Interim budgets (weekly, monthly, or quarterly) may be prepared for comparison purposes. These comparisons point up areas that require additional or revised planning—or at least those areas calling for a more careful investigation. Pets.com is an example of a dot-com start-up that lost control of its finances. In 1999, backed by Disney and Amazon, the firm spent $27 million on television and other media advertising to generate awareness and sales. The funny advertisements presented by the famous talking dog sock-puppet could not create the critical mass of buyers quickly enough to offset the advertising and other operational costs. As a result, the firm lost five dollars for every dollar of pet supplies revenue received. This quickly created a cash crisis.[7]

Figure 20.5 shows a quarterly comparison of budgeted and actual sales for Stars and Stripes Clothing. Sales of children's wear are about 7 percent over budget, and sales of infants' wear are about 9 percent below budget. Although neither discrepancy is a cause for immediate concern, the sales for both departments should be watched, and such comparisons should be routinely reported to department heads and upper-level managers. They may be used as the basis for budgeting for the next accounting period, and they may reveal a need to take corrective action (such as promoting infants' wear more vigorously).

figure 20.5

Budget Comparison for Stars and Stripes Clothing
Budget comparisons can point out areas that require additional planning or careful investigation.

STARS AND STRIPES CLOTHING
Sales Budget Update — First Quarter, 2002

Department	First-quarter estimate	Actual sales	Dollar difference
Infants'	$ 50,000	$ 45,600	$-4,400
Children's	45,000	48,200	+3,200
Women's	35,000	36,300	+1,300
Men's	20,000	21,100	+1,100
Totals	$150,000	$151,200	$+1,200

Sources of Short-Term Debt Financing

LEARNING OBJECTIVE

3 Describe the advantages and disadvantages of different methods of short-term debt financing.

The decision to borrow money does not necessarily mean that a firm is in financial trouble. On the contrary, astute financial management often means regular, responsible borrowing of many different kinds to meet different needs. In this section, we examine the sources of short-term debt financing available to businesses. In the next two sections, we look at long-term financing options: equity capital and debt capital.

Sources of Unsecured Short-Term Financing

unsecured financing financing that is not backed by collateral

trade credit a type of short-term financing extended by a seller who does not require immediate payment after delivery of merchandise

Short-term debt financing (money repaid in one year or less) is usually easier to obtain than long-term debt financing for three reasons:

1. For the lender, the shorter repayment period means less risk of nonpayment.
2. The dollar amounts of short-term loans are usually smaller than those of long-term loans.
3. A close working relationship normally exists between the short-term borrower and the lender.

Most lenders do not require collateral for short-term financing. When they do, it is usually because they are concerned about the size of a particular loan, the borrowing firm's poor credit rating, or the general prospects of repayment.

Unsecured financing is financing that is not backed by collateral. A company seeking unsecured short-term financing has several options. They include trade credit, promissory notes, bank loans, and commercial paper.

Trade Credit Manufacturers and wholesalers often provide financial aid to retailers by allowing them thirty to sixty days (or more) in which to pay for merchandise. This delayed payment, known as **trade credit**, is a type of short-term financing extended by a seller who does not require immediate payment after delivery of merchandise. It is the most popular form of short-term financing; 80 to 90 percent of all transactions between businesses involve some trade credit.

When trade credit is used, the purchased goods are delivered along with an invoice that states the credit terms. Let's assume that a Barnes & Noble bookstore receives a shipment of books from a publisher. Along with the merchandise, the publisher sends an invoice that states the terms of payment. Barnes & Noble now has two options for payment. First, the book retailer may pay the invoice promptly and take advantage of any cash discount the publisher offers. Cash discount terms are specified on the invoice. For instance, "2/10, net 30" means that the customer—Barnes & Noble—may take a 2 percent discount if it pays the invoice within ten days of the invoice date. Cash discounts can generate substantial savings and lower the cost of purchasing merchandise for a retailer like Barnes & Noble. Let's assume that the dollar amount of the above invoice is $140,000. In this case, the cash discount is $2,800 ($140,000 × 0.02 = $2,800). A second option is to wait until the end of the credit period before making payment. If Barnes & Noble does not have the cash available to take advantage of

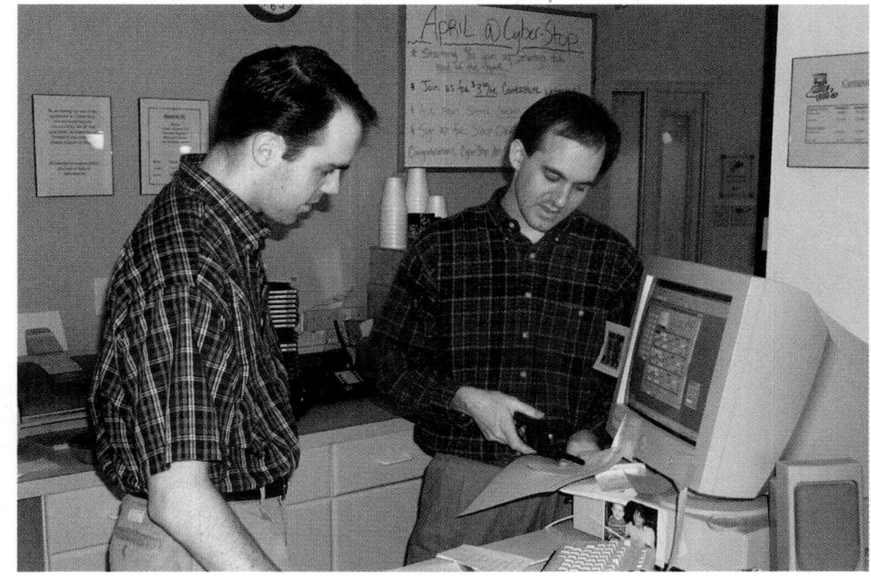

It's nice to have short-term financing when you need it! Brian and Jonathan Bentrim pooled personal savings and obtained a short-term loan from a local bank to start Cyber-Stop, Inc.—a computer resource center. Then, after only four months, these two entrepreneurs acquired the adjoining sandwich shop and are now in the process of expanding the café aspect of their high-tech business. To merge the two ideas, the Bentrims are seeking additional financing through a second short-term loan.

the cash discount, payment within the first ten days is out of the question. And if payment is made between eleven and thirty days, the customer must pay the entire (net) amount. As long as payment is made before the end of the credit period, the customer maintains the ability to purchase additional merchandise using the trade credit arrangement.

promissory note a written pledge by a borrower to pay a certain sum of money to a creditor at a specified future date

Promissory Notes Issued to Suppliers A **promissory note** is a written pledge by a borrower to pay a certain sum of money to a creditor at a specified future date. Suppliers uneasy about extending trade credit may be less reluctant to offer credit to customers who sign promissory notes. Unlike trade credit, however, promissory notes usually require the borrower to pay interest. Although repayment periods may extend to one year, most promissory notes are repaid in 60 to 180 days. A typical promissory note is shown in Figure 20.6. Note that the customer buying on credit (Richland Company) is called the *maker* and is the party that issues the note. The business selling the merchandise on credit (Shelton Company) is called the *payee.*

A promissory note offers two important advantages to the firm extending the credit. First, a promissory note is a legally binding and enforceable document that has been signed by the individual or business borrowing the money. Second, most promissory notes are negotiable instruments that can be sold when the money is needed immediately. If it chose, the Shelton Company could discount, or sell, the note to its own bank. The maturity value is $820 ($800 principal + $20, interest = $820 maturity value). If the note is discounted, the price would be slightly less than the $820 maturity value, because the bank charges a fee for the service. Shelton would recoup most of its money immediately, and the bank would collect the $820 when the note matured.

figure 20.6

An Interest-Bearing Promissory Note

A promissory note is a borrower's written pledge to pay a certain sum of money to a creditor at a specified date.

$ 800.00 (1) Abilene, Texas. June 6 (4) A.D. 20 02

Sixty days (3) *after date, without grace, for value received, I, we, or either of us, promise to pay to the order of* The Shelton Company (7)

(1) Eight hundred and no/100 --------------------- *Dollars*

at First Bank *with interest from* June 6 *to maturity at the rate of* 15 (2) *per cent, per annum.*

AND FROM MATURITY AT THE RATE OF FIFTEEN PER CENT PER ANNUM, WE THE MAKERS, SURETIES, ENDORSERS, AND GUARANTORS OF THIS NOTE HEREBY SEVERALLY WAIVE PRESENTATION FOR PAYMENT, NOTICE OF NONPAYMENT, PROTEST, AND NOTICE OF PROTEST AND DILIGENCE IN BRINGING SUIT AGAINST ANY PARTY HERETO AND CONSENT THAT THE TIME OF PAYMENT MAY BE EXTENDED BY RENEWAL NOTE OR OTHERWISE ONE OR MORE TIMES FOR PERIODS DISCRETIONARY WITH THE HOLDER WITHOUT NOTICE THEREOF TO ANY OF THE SURETIES, ENDORSERS, AND/OR GUARANTORS ON THIS NOTE. IT IS FURTHER EXPRESSLY AGREED THAT IF THIS NOTE IS PLACED IN THE HANDS OF AN ATTORNEY FOR COLLECTION OR IS COLLECTED THROUGH THE PROBATE OF BANKRUPTCY COURT, OR THROUGH OTHER LEGAL PROCEEDINGS, THEN IN ANY OF SAID EVENTS, A REASONABLE AMOUNT SHALL BE ADDED AND COLLECTED AS ATTORNEY AND COLLECTION FEES.

Due August 5, 2002 (5) — Paul Robertson (6)

Address 326 East Main Street — Financial Vice President

Phone (972) 555-1732 — The Richland Company

1. The principal ($800.00) is the original amount of the debt.
2. The rate (15 percent) expresses the annual interest rate paid for use of the borrowed money.
3. The time (60 days) is the period for which the money is borrowed.
4. The date (June 6) is the date the note was issued.
5. The maturity date (August 5) is the day the principal and interest are due ($800 principal + $20 interest = $820 maturity value).
6. The maker (The Richland Company) is the individual or company borrowing the money.
7. The payee (The Shelton Company) is the individual or company extending the credit.

Unsecured Bank Loans Banks and other financial institutions offer unsecured short-term loans to businesses at interest rates that vary with each borrower's credit rating. The **prime interest rate** (sometimes called the *reference rate*) is the lowest rate charged by a bank for a short-term loan. Figure 20.7 traces the fluctuations in the average prime rate charged by U.S. banks from 1990 to 1998. This lowest rate is generally reserved for large corporations with excellent credit ratings. Organizations with good to high credit ratings may pay the prime rate plus 2 percent. Firms with questionable credit ratings may have to pay the prime rate plus 4 percent. Of course, if the banker believes loan repayment may be a problem, the borrower's loan application may well be rejected.

prime interest rate the lowest rate charged by a bank for a short-term loan

Banks generally offer unsecured short-term loans through promissory notes, a line of credit, or a revolving credit agreement. The *line of credit*—in essence, a prearranged short-term loan—was discussed in Chapter 19. A bank that offers a line of credit may require that a *compensating balance* be kept on deposit at the bank. This balance may be as much as 20 percent of the line-of-credit amount. Assume that Bank of America requires a 20 percent compensating balance on short-term loans. If you borrow \$50,000, at least \$10,000 ($\$50,000 \times 0.20 = \$10,000$) of the loan amount must be kept on deposit at the bank. In this situation, the actual interest rate you must pay on the original \$50,000 loan increases because you have the use of only \$40,000. The bank may also require that every commercial borrower *clean up* (pay off completely) its line of credit at least once each year and not use it again for a period of thirty to sixty days. This second requirement ensures that the money obtained through a line of credit is used only to meet short-term needs and that it doesn't gradually become a source of long-term financing.

Even with a line of credit, a firm may not be able to borrow on short notice if the bank does not have sufficient funds available. For this reason, some firms prefer a **revolving credit agreement**, which is a *guaranteed* line of credit. Under this type of agreement, the bank guarantees that the money will be available when the borrower needs it. In return for the guarantee, the bank charges a commitment fee ranging from 0.25 to 1.0 percent of the *unused* portion of the revolving credit agreement. The usual interest is charged for the portion that *is* borrowed.

revolving credit agreement a guaranteed line of credit

Commercial Paper **Commercial paper** is a short-term promissory note issued by a large corporation. Commercial paper is secured only by the reputation of the issuing firm; no collateral is involved. It is usually issued in large denominations, ranging from \$5,000 to \$100,000. Corporations issuing commercial paper pay interest rates slightly below the interest rates charged by banks for short-term loans. Thus, issuing commercial paper is cheaper than getting short-term financing from a bank. The interest rate a corporation pays when it issues commercial paper is tied to its credit rating and its

commercial paper a short-term promissory note issued by a large corporation

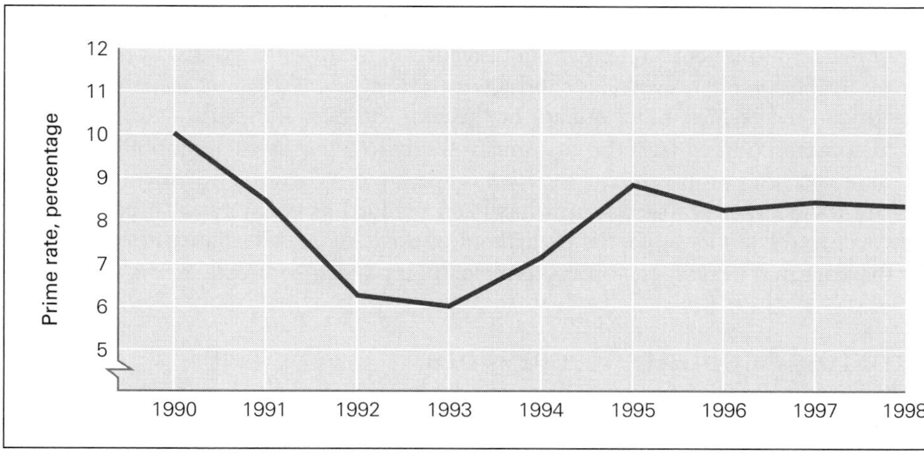

figure 20.7

Average Prime Interest Rate Paid by U.S. Businesses, 1990–1998
The prime rate is the interest rate charged by U.S. banks when businesses with the 'best' credit ratings borrow money. All other businesses pay interest rates higher than the prime rate.

Source: *Statistical Abstract of the United States*, Washington, D.C., 2000 U.S. Government Printing Office, p. 530.

ability to repay the commercial paper. For example, when the major U.S. credit reporting agencies lowered the credit ratings of Rite-Aid[8] and Reebok[9] these firms had to pay higher interest rates on commercial paper issues.

Large firms with excellent credit reputations can quickly raise large sums of money by issuing commercial paper. General Motors Acceptance Corporation (GMAC), and GE Capital for example, may issue commercial paper totaling millions of dollars. However, commercial paper is not without risks. If a corporation has severe financial problems, it may not be able to repay commercial paper. Recently, Illinois-based Mercury Finance Company—one of the largest used-car finance companies in the nation—defaulted on commercial paper valued at over $40 million.[10]

Sources of Secured Short-Term Financing

Financially secure firms prefer to reserve collateral for long-term borrowing needs. Yet if a business cannot obtain enough capital through unsecured financing, it must put up collateral to obtain additional short-term financing. Almost any asset can serve as collateral. However, *inventories* and *accounts receivable* are the assets most commonly pledged for short-term financing. Even when it is willing to pledge collateral to back up a loan, a firm that is financially weak may have difficulty obtaining short-term financing.

Loans Secured by Inventory

Normally, manufacturers, wholesalers, and retailers have large amounts of money invested in finished goods. In addition, manufacturers carry raw materials and work-in-process inventories. All three types of inventory may be pledged as collateral for short-term loans. However, lenders prefer the much more salable finished merchandise to raw materials or work-in-process inventories.

A lender may insist that inventory used as collateral be stored in a public warehouse. In such a case, the receipt issued by the warehouse is retained by the lender. Without this receipt, the public warehouse will not release the merchandise. The lender releases the warehouse receipt—and the merchandise—to the borrower when the borrowed money is repaid. In addition to paying the interest on the loan, the borrower must pay for storage in the public warehouse. As a result, this type of loan is more expensive than an unsecured short-term loan.

floor planning method of financing in which title to merchandise is given to lenders in return for short-term financing

A special type of financing called floor planning is used by automobile, furniture, and appliance dealers. **Floor planning** is a method of financing in which title to merchandise is given to lenders in return for short-term financing. The major difference between floor planning and other types of secured short-term financing is that the borrower maintains control of the inventory. As merchandise is sold, the borrower repays the lender a portion of the loan. To ensure that the borrower is doing so, the lender periodically checks to see whether the collateral is still in the borrower's possession.

accounts receivable amounts owed to a firm by its customers

Loans Secured by Receivables

Accounts receivable are amounts owed to a firm by its customers. They are created when trade credit is given to customers and are usually due within thirty to sixty days. A firm can pledge its accounts receivable as collateral to obtain short-term financing. A lender may advance 70 to 80 percent of the dollar amount of the receivables. First, however, it conducts a thorough investigation to determine the *quality* of the receivables. (The quality of the receivables is the credit standing of the firm's customers, coupled with the customers' ability to repay their credit obligations.) If a favorable determination is made, the loan is approved. When the borrowing firm collects from a customer whose account has been pledged as collateral, it must turn the money over to the lender as partial repayment of the loan. An alternative approach is to notify the borrower's credit customers to make their payments directly to the lender.

Factoring Accounts Receivable

factor a firm that specializes in buying other firms' accounts receivable

Accounts receivable may be used in one other way to help raise short-term financing: they can be sold to a factoring company (or factor). A **factor** is a firm that specializes in buying other firms' accounts receivable. The factor buys the accounts receivable for less than their face value, but it collects the full dollar amount when each account is due. The factor's profit is thus the difference between the face value of the accounts receivable and the amount the factor has paid for them. Generally, the amount of profit the factor receives is based on the risk the factor assumes. Risk, in this case, is the probability that the accounts receivable will not be repaid when they mature.

Even though the firm selling its accounts receivable gets less than face value, it does receive needed cash immediately. Moreover, it has shifted both the task of collecting and the risk of nonpayment to the factor, which now owns the accounts receivable. In many cases, the factor may purchase only selected accounts receivable—usually those with the highest potential of repayment. In other cases, the firm selling its accounts receivable must obtain approval from the factor *before* selling merchandise to a credit customer. Thus, the firm receives instant feedback on whether the factor will purchase the credit customer's account. Generally, customers whose accounts receivable have been factored are given instructions to make their payments directly to the factor.

Cost Comparisons

Table 20.2 compares the various types of short-term financing. As you can see, trade credit is the least expensive. Generally, the less favorable a firm's credit rating, the more likely the firm will have to use a higher-cost means of financing. Factoring of accounts receivable is the highest-cost method shown.

For many purposes, short-term financing suits a firm's needs perfectly. At other times, however, long-term financing may be more appropriate. In this case, a business may try to raise equity capital or debt capital.

Sources of Equity Financing

LEARNING OBJECTIVE

4 Evaluate the advantages and disadvantages of equity financing.

Sources of long-term financing vary with the size and type of business. As mentioned earlier, a sole proprietorship or partnership acquires equity capital (sometimes referred to as owner's equity) when the owner or owners invest money in the business. For corporations, equity-financing options include the sale of stock and the use of profits not distributed to owners, and obtaining venture capital.

table 20.2 Comparison of Short-Term Financing Methods

Type of Financing	Cost	Repayment Period	Businesses That May Use It	Comments
Trade credit	Low, if any	30 to 60 days	All businesses	Usually no finance charge
Promissory note issued to suppliers	Moderate	1 year or less	All businesses	Usually unsecured but requires legal document
Unsecured bank loan	Moderate	1 year or less	All businesses	Promissory note, a line of credit, or revolving credit agreement generally required
Commercial paper	Moderate	1 year or less	Large corporations with high credit ratings	Available only to large firms
Secured loan	High	1 year or less	Firms with questionable credit ratings	Inventory or accounts receivable often used as collateral
Factoring	Highest	None	Firms that have large numbers of credit customers	Accounts receivable sold to a factor

spotlight

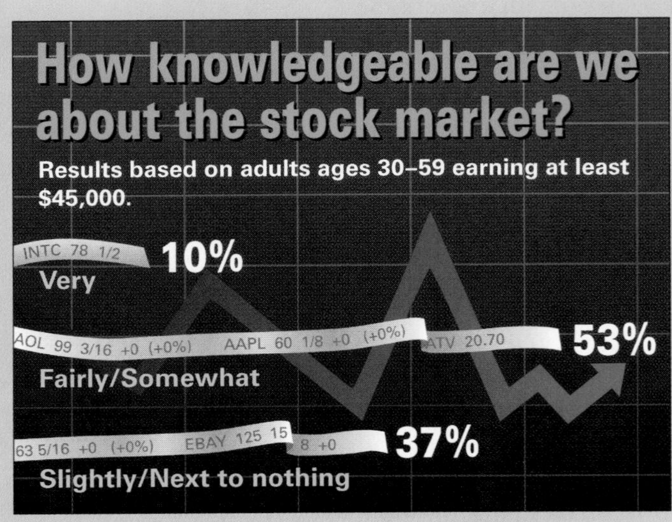

Source: Copyright 2000, USA TODAY. Reprinted with permission.

Selling Stock

Some equity capital is used to start every business—sole proprietorship, partnership, or corporation. In the case of corporations, equity capital is provided by stockholders who buy shares in the company. To raise money, Priceline.com—the company profiled in the Inside Business opening case for this chapter—used an initial public offering and raised over $150 million that it could use to fund expansion and other business activities. An **initial public offering (IPO)** occurs when a corporation sells common stock to the general public for the first time. Although a corporation can have only one IPO, it can sell additional stock after the IPO assuming that there is a market for the company's stock. Whether an IPO or a later sale of stock, selling stock is the most logical way for a corporation to raise capital.

There are at least two reasons why large corporations sell stock, First, the corporation doesn't have to repay money obtained from the sale of stock. While many investors assume the corporation will repay the money it obtains from selling stock, the company is under no legal obligation to do so. If you purchase corporate stock and later decide to sell your stock, you may sell it to another investor—not the corporation.

initial public offering (IPO) when a corporation sells common stock to the general public for the first time

A second advantage of selling stock is that a corporation is under no legal obligation to pay dividends to stockholders. As noted in Chapter 5, a *dividend* is a distribution of earnings to the stockholders of a corporation. An investor often purchases the stock of a corporation because she or he expects to receive dividends. Recall from Chapter 5 that one of the basic rights of shareholders is the right to share in earnings through the receipt of dividends. However, for any reason (if a company has a bad year, for example), the board of directors can vote to omit dividend payments. Earnings are then retained for use in funding business operations. Of course, the corporate management may hear from unhappy stockholders if expected dividends are omitted too frequently.

There are two types of stock: common and preferred. Each type has advantages and drawbacks as a means of long-term financing.

Corporations, brokerage firms, and investors: A match made in heaven. For corporations, selling stock is the most logical way to raise capital. And yet, investors won't purchase the stock if they can't sell it to other investors at a later date. That's where CharlesSchwab enters the picture. Schwab, like other brokerage firms, enables investors to sell their stock to other investors.

Common Stock

A share of **common stock** represents the most basic form of corporate ownership. A common-stock certificate for Houghton Mifflin Company is shown in Figure 20.8. In return for the financing provided by selling common stock, management must make certain concessions to stockholders that may restrict or change corporate policies. By law, every corporation must hold an annual meeting, at which the holders of common stock may vote for the board of directors and approve or disapprove major corporate actions. Among such actions are

1. Amendments to the corporate charter or bylaws
2. Sale of certain assets

figure 20.8

A Common-Stock Certificate

Stockholders provide a company with capital when they purchase shares of stock (equity) in the company.

Source: Used with permission of Houghton Mifflin Company.

3. Mergers and acquisitions
4. Issue of preferred stock or bonds
5. Changes in the amount of common stock issued

Money acquired through the sale of common stock is essentially cost-free, but few investors will buy common stock if they cannot foresee some return on their investment. Information on how stockholders can evaluate stock investments is provided in Chapter 21. To see what happens when investors don't evaluate stock investments, read Examining Ethics.

common stock stock whose owners may vote on corporate matters, but whose claims on profits and assets are subordinate to the claims of others

preferred stock stock whose owners usually do not have voting rights, but whose claims on dividends and assets are paid before those of common-stock owners

par value an assigned (and often arbitrary) dollar value printed on the stock certificate

Preferred Stock As noted in Chapter 5, the owners of **preferred stock** must receive their dividends before holders of common stock receive theirs. And preferred stockholders have first claim (after creditors) on assets if the corporation is dissolved or declares bankruptcy. Even so, like common stock, dividends on preferred stock must be approved by the board of directors, and this type of financing does not represent a debt that must be legally repaid. In return for preferential treatment, preferred stockholders generally give up the right to vote at a corporation's annual meeting and on corporate actions. (Remember from the previous section, that the right to vote is usually reserved for common stockholders.)

The dividend to be paid on a share of preferred stock is known before the stock is purchased. It is stated on the stock certificate either as a percent of the par value of the stock or as a specified dollar amount. The **par value** of a stock is an assigned (and often arbitrary) dollar value printed on the stock certificate. For example, Pitney Bowes—a U.S. manufacturer of office and business equipment—issued 4 percent preferred stock with a par value of $50. The annual dividend amount is $2 per share ($50 par value × .04 = $2 annual dividend).

Although a corporation usually issues only one type of common stock, it may issue many types of preferred stock with varying dividends or dividend rates. For example, Ohio Edison has one common-stock issue but ten preferred-stock issues with different dividend amounts for each type of preferred stock.

Using the Internet

The New York Stock Exchange (**http://www.nyse.com**) and the NASDAQ (**http://www.nasdaq.com**) are the two most cited equity markets. Each provides financial information about the companies they list and news that might influence their stock values.

Examining Ethics

An Investment Too Good to Be True!

One evening as Barbara and Bill Thomas browsed the Internet, they stumbled across several message-board sites discussing Uniprime Capital—a company that was involved in developing a cure for AIDS. The comments about a new prescription medicine were glowing. And based on the early research and the desperate need for an AIDS cure, the company's stock was increasing in value. The next day, the Thomases decided to take a chance, and against the advice of their broker, purchased 1,000 shares of Uniprime Capital at $5 a share. They weren't alone. That same day, a buying frenzy took place and 5.2 million shares changed hands.

Without researching the stock and based on information posted on several message boards, Barbara and Bill had invested $5,000 in Uniprime Capital. Although they had both shared a dream of "cashing in" on Uniprime's new prescription medicine, their dream quickly turned to a nightmare. Promising new products were never developed, tested, approved, and marketed—a very long process for a pharmaceutical company. Eventually, the company was charged with issuing a series of false press releases in order to pump up the price of its stock. Civil and criminal cases were filed against both the company and its officers while the company's stock became virtually worthless. Today, if Barbara and Bill sold their stock, they would receive $30 or about 3 cents per share.

Investment Scams on the Increase

Everyday you hear stories of people making a fortune in the stock market. And like Barbara and Bill Thomas, many people think they can "cash in" on a stock investment and pick the next new company that will become the darling of Wall street. Unfortunately, there are more losers than winners. In the United States, investors of all ages, geographical locations, occupations, and net worth are being caught up in the search for "a piece of the pie." To make matters worse, there are promoters and con artists out there just waiting to take advantage of unsuspecting investors. The experts estimate that investors lose $10 billion a year in fraudulent investment schemes. And the amount investors lose increases each year.

Part of the reason for the increase is that more and more investors are using the Internet to obtain information about companies. Unethical investors with a large number of shares of a company's stock or corporate officials know they can post messages on message boards or chat rooms without having to disclose their true identity. These "experts" using an alias can report artificial stock-price moves, false corporate earnings, increases in new sales, or just about any other news item to increase interest in a company's stock.

What You Can Do to Protect Yourself

Begin with the realization that investment fraud is a real problem. The SEC's Internet complaint hotline gets nearly 300 messages a day. Then protect yourself! Read the financial documents published by the company and learn about the people behind the company. Answer the following questions: (1) Are you being pressured to act? (2) Does the investment match your goals and objectives? (3) Can you afford to lose the money you invest? And if you are caught up in a scheme, alert the security police at the Securities and Exchange Commission (www.sec.gov), the New York Stock Exchange (www.nyse.com), or the National Association of Securities Dealers (www.nasdaq.com). For more information on evaluating investments, read Chapter 21—Understanding Securities Markets and Investments.

Issues to Consider

1. Why do you think Barbara and Bill Thomas invested $5,000 in Uniprime Capital?
2. What type of pressures would lead a corporate official, brokerage firm employee, or investor to post false information about a company or its stock on the Internet?

When a corporation believes it can issue new preferred stock at a lower dividend rate (or common stock with no specified dividend) it may decide to "call in" or buy back, an earlier stock issue. In this case, management has two options. First, it can buy shares in the market—just like any other investor. Second, it can buy back the stock, since practically all preferred stock is *callable* at the option of the corporation. When the corporation exercises a call provision, the investor may receive a call premium. A **call premium** is a dollar amount over par value that the corporation has to pay an investor when it redeems either preferred stock or a corporate bond. (Corporate bonds are discussed later in this chapter.) When considering the two options, management will naturally obtain the preferred stock in the less costly way.

call premium a dollar amount over par value that the corporation has to pay an investor when it redeems either preferred stock or a corporate bond

To make preferred stock more attractive to investors, some corporations include a conversion feature in various issues. **Convertible preferred stock** is preferred stock that the owner may exchange for a specified number of shares of common stock. The Textron Corporation—a manufacturer of component parts for the automotive and aerospace industries—has issued convertible preferred stock. Each share of Textron preferred stock is convertible to 2.2 shares of the firm's common stock. This conversion feature provides the investor with the safety of preferred stock and the hope of greater speculative gain through conversion to common stock.

convertible preferred stock preferred stock that the owner may exchange for a specified number of shares of common stock

Retained Earnings

Most large corporations distribute only a portion of their after-tax earnings to stockholders. The portion of a corporation's profits not distributed to stockholders is called **retained earnings.** Because they are undistributed profits, retained earnings are considered a form of equity financing.

retained earnings the portion of a business's profits not distributed to stockholders

The amount of retained earnings in any year is determined by corporate management and approved by the board of directors. Most small and growing corporations pay no cash dividend—or a very small dividend—to their stockholders. All or most earnings are reinvested in the business for research and development, expansion, or the funding of major projects. Reinvestment tends to increase the value of their stock while it provides essentially cost-free financing for the business. More mature corporations may distribute 40 to 60 percent of their after-tax profits as dividends. Utility companies and other corporations with very stable earnings often pay out as much as 80 to 90 percent of what they earn. For a large corporation, retained earnings can amount to a hefty bit of financing. For example, in 1999 the total amount of retained earnings for General Electric was in excess of $54 billion.[11] And for Exxon/Mobil Corporation, in 1999 retained earnings totaled more than $75 billion.[12]

Venture Capital

To establish a new business or expand an existing one, an entrepreneur may try to obtain venture capital. In Chapter 6, we defined venture capital as money invested in small (and sometimes struggling) firms that have the potential to become very successful. The key word here is *successful.* Most venture capital firms do not invest in the typical small business—a neighborhood convenience store or a local dry cleaner—but in firms that have the potential for rapid increases in sales and profits. It is not out of the ordinary for Internet-based firms to have no currently generated revenues at all. What makes them attractive to investors is the race to develop new products which results in corporate valuations often getting well ahead of any current positive cash flow.[13] A concern among many financial analysts is whether investments into many of the current and future Internet-related firms will ever produce sufficient profits for investors. For the time being, it appears investment dollars will continue to find their way to businesses with ideas but

Financial boot camp. These would-be entrepreneurs are learning how to apply for the venture capital needed to finance their business. Eighty percent of all requests for venture capital are dropped after less than a day's study because the applicant doesn't have a carefully developed, written business plan.

with little chance of profits in the short run.[14] Generally, a venture capital firm consists of a pool of investors, a traditional partnership established by a wealthy family, or an insurance company. In return for financing, these investors receive an equity position in the business and share in its profits.

Venture capital firms vary in size and scope of interest. Some offer financing for start-up businesses, while others finance only established businesses. Whether the firm requesting the money is a start-up or an established business, a business plan is essential. Eighty percent of requests for venture capital are dropped after less than a day's study; most of these lack a business plan. Of the remaining requests, 10 percent are dropped within a week, and 8 percent are dropped within a month. Only 2 percent are finally accepted.[15]

Many factors are considered in the selection process. For example, the Denver-Boulder area is emerging as a telecommunications and high-tech hub, drawing on the region's roots in the telecom and cable-television industries, an educated labor pool, plenty of amenities, and a lifestyle that doesn't require the same outrageous sums demanded in California's Silicon Valley. As a result, venture capital is flowing into start-up and expansion projects that once were more likely to be found in traditional high-tech centers.[16]

Sources of Long-Term Debt Financing

LEARNING OBJECTIVE

5 Evaluate the advantages and disadvantages of long-term debt financing.

financial leverage the use of borrowed funds to increase the return on owners' equity

Many people think that when a business borrows money, it signifies weakness. To be sure, borrowing may be a sign of financial weakness, but as we pointed out earlier in this chapter, businesses borrow money on a short-term basis for many valid reasons other than desperation. There are equally valid reasons for long-term borrowing. In addition to using borrowed money to meet the long-term needs listed in Table 20.1, successful businesses often use the financial leverage it creates to improve their financial performance. **Financial leverage** is the use of borrowed funds to increase the return on owners' equity. The principle of financial leverage works as long as a firm's earnings are larger than the interest charged for the borrowed money. Of course, if the firm's earnings should drop below the interest cost of borrowed money, the return on owners' equity will decrease.

To understand how financial leverage can increase a firm's return on owners' equity, study the financial information for Texas-based Cypress Springs Plastics presented in Table 20.3. Pete Johnston, the owner of the firm, is trying to decide how best

table 20.3 **Analysis of the Effect of Additional Capital from Debt or Equity for Cypress Springs Plastics, Inc.**

Additional Debt		**Additional Equity**	
Owners' equity	$500,000	Owners' equity	$500,000
Additional equity	+ -0-	Additional equity	+ 100,000
Total equity	$500,000	Total equity	$600,000
Loan (@ 9 percent)	+ 100,000	No loan	+ -0-
Total Capital	$600,000	Total capital	$600,000
	Year-end Earnings		
Gross profit	$95,000	Gross Profit	$95,000
Less loan interest	− 9,000	No interest	− -0-
Operating profit	$86,000	Operating profit	$95,000
Return on owners' equity	17.2%	Return on owners' equity	15.8%
($86,000 ÷ $500,000 = 17.2%)		($95,000 ÷ $600,000 = 15.8%)	

to finance a $100,000 purchase of new high-tech manufacturing equipment. He could borrow the money and pay 9 percent annual interest. As a second option, Johnston could invest additional money in the firm. Assuming that the firm earns $95,000 a year and annual interest for this loan totals $9,000 ($100,000 × 0.09 = $9,000), the return on owners' equity for Cypress Springs Plastics would be higher if the firm borrowed the additional financing. Return on owners' equity—a topic covered in Chapter 18—is determined by dividing a firm's net income by the dollar amount of owners' equity. For Cypress Springs Plastics, return on owners' equity equals 17.2 percent ($86,000 ÷ $500,000 = .172, or 17.2 percent) if Johnston borrows the additional $100,000. The firm's return on owners' equity would decrease to 15.8 percent ($95,000 ÷ $600,000 = .158, or 15.8 percent) if Johnston invests an additional $100,000 in the business.

The most obvious danger when using financial leverage is that the firm's earnings may be less than expected. If this situation occurs, the fixed interest charge actually works to reduce or eliminate the return on owners' equity. Of course, borrowed money must eventually be repaid. Periodic payments for interest and debt reduction may be hard to manage for some businesses, especially if the firm has a bad year. Finally, because lenders always have the option to turn down a loan request, many managers are reluctant to rely on borrowed money.

A big man with big financial challenges. Former Baltimore Colts defensive guard, Charlie Johnson, is now manager and part owner of Active Transportation and Automotive Carrier Services—the largest black-owned business in the United States. Although the company has enjoyed steady growth, shipping is a very cyclical industry. In 2000, the company was forced to borrow $80 million from its bankers.

A company that cannot obtain a long-term loan to acquire property, buildings, and equipment may be able to lease these assets. A **lease** is an agreement by which the right to use real estate, equipment, or other assets is temporarily transferred from the owner to the user. The owner of the leased item is called the *lessor*; the user is called the *lessee*. With the typical lease agreement, the lessee makes regular payments on a monthly, quarterly, or yearly basis. Even when a firm is able to obtain long-term debt financing, it may choose to lease assets because under the right circumstances, a lease can have tax advantages.

lease an agreement by which the right to use real estate, equipment, or other assets is temporarily transferred from the owner to the user

For a small business, long-term debt financing is generally limited to loans. Large corporations have the additional option of issuing corporate bonds. Before reading the material in the remainder of this section, read Exploring Business for specific methods business owners use to obtain financing.

Long-Term Loans

Many businesses finance their long-range activities with loans from commercial banks, insurance companies, pension funds, and other financial institutions. Business start-up costs, new-product development, long-term marketing activities, expansion of facilities, replacement of equipment, and mergers and acquisitions are likely to be partially or fully funded by long-term loans. Manufacturers and suppliers of heavy machinery may also provide long-term financing by granting extended credit terms to their customers.

When the loan repayment period is longer than one year, the borrower must sign a term-loan agreement. A **term-loan agreement** is a promissory note that requires a borrower to repay a loan in monthly, quarterly, semiannual, or annual installments.

term-loan agreement a promissory note that requires a borrower to repay a loan in monthly, quarterly, semiannual, or annual installments

Long-term business loans are normally repaid in three to seven years.

Assume that Pete Johnson, the owner of Cypress Springs Plastics, decides to borrow $100,000 and take advantage of the principle of financial leverage illustrated in Table 20.3. Although the firm's return on owners' equity does increase, interest must be paid each year and eventually the loan must be repaid. Before accepting the loan, the owners or managers of a firm must determine if a company can pay interest and the

Exploring Business

Finance 101: The Basics of How To Get Financing for a Business

One of the biggest mistakes a small- or medium-size business makes when faced with a need for financing is not being prepared. Raising money for a business is like building a home. You don't order a lot of bricks and mortar and just start putting it together. You need to draw up plans, make time projections for each stage of the project, and get acquainted with your contractor. The steps are the same when raising money for a business. And if you are prepared and you are *credit-worthy*, the task may be easier than you think.

Preparation Is a Key Ingredient

To begin your search for money, write out a business plan including a two-page executive summary. Explain exactly what your business is and how much funding you require to accomplish your goals. Then have your CPA prepare financial statements. Most lenders and investors insist that you submit current financial statements that have been prepared by an independent CPA along with a business plan. Finally compile a list of references that includes your suppliers, potential partners, or the professionals you associate with.

What Type of Financing?

There are two basic types of funding available for small- to medium-size companies—debt financing and equity financing. If you use debt financing, you are asking a lender to loan you money. A loan requires that you sign a legal document and requires you to repay the borrowed money plus interest. Typically, you will be asked to fill out a loan application. Then the loan application will be examined by a loan officer or a loan committee. Before submitting your loan application, request a credit report from a national credit bureau. If you have previous credit problems, you may be turned down. For help with "cleaning up your credit report" read the Exploring Business feature in Chapter 19. Some lenders also require collateral to secure a loan. *Be Warned*: Using your home as collateral is risky. If you can't repay the loan, you could lose your home *and* your business.

If you use equity funding, you have two choices. First, you can invest your own money. Many small- and medium-size business owners use their own personal funds to start a business. But when personal funds are exhausted, business owners often sell partial ownership in the company to private investors, venture capital firms, or friends and relatives. In return for the needed financing, you must give up a portion of the ownership of the business, part of the profits the business earns, and often some control of the business.

Professional Assistance You Can Use

The U.S. Small Business Administration (SBA), a federal agency, helps established businesses grow and helps new businesses get started. By law, the SBA is permitted to guarantee a loan at a commercial bank. The ceiling or upper limit for guaranteed loans is $750,000 for qualified loan applicants. Many financial institutions like Bank of America, Citibank, Wells Fargo, and many smaller banks also assist businesspeople in completing loan applications and provide financing to qualified loan applicants. Finally, you can go online to the web sites for any major bank to access information or to begin the process of filling out applications.

payments required to pay off the loan as scheduled. To pay off a $100,000 loan over a three-year period with annual payments, Cypress Springs Plastics must pay $33,333 on the loan balance plus $9,000 annual interest or a total of $42,333 the first year. While the amount of interest decreases each year because of the previous year's payment on the loan balance, annual payments of this amount are still a large commitment for a small firm like Cypress Springs Plastics.

The interest rate and other specific terms are often based on such factors as the reasons for borrowing, the borrowing firm's credit rating, and the value of collateral.

Although long-term loans may occasionally be unsecured, the lender usually requires some type of collateral. Acceptable collateral includes real estate, machinery, and equipment. Lenders may also require that borrowers maintain a minimum amount of working capital.

Corporate Bonds

Large corporations issue bonds in denominations of $1,000 to $50,000; the total face value of all the bonds in an issue usually amounts to millions of dollars. In fact, one of the reasons why corporations sell bonds is that they can borrow a lot of money from a lot of different bondholders and raise larger amounts of money than could be borrowed from one lender. A **corporate bond** is a corporation's written pledge that it will repay a specified amount of money with interest. Figure 20.9 shows a corporate bond for the American & Foreign Power Company. Note that it includes the interest rate (5 percent) and the maturity date. The **maturity date** is the date on which the corporation is to repay the borrowed money. The bond also has spaces for the amount of its face value, the registration number, and the bond owner's name.

corporate bond a corporation's written pledge that it will repay a specified amount of money with interest

maturity date the date on which the corporation is to repay the borrowed money

An individual or firm generally buys a corporate bond through a securities broker. After the purchase, the corporation pays interest to the bond owner—usually every six months—at the stated rate. Owners of the American & Foreign Power Company bond receive 5 percent a year for each bond. Because interest for corporate bonds is usually paid semiannually, bond owners receive a payment every six months for each bond they own.

Types of Bonds

Today most corporate bonds are registered bonds. A **registered bond**—like the American & Foreign Power Company bond—is a bond registered in the owner's name by the issuing company. When the owner of a registered bond sells it, he or she must endorse it before ownership can be transferred on the company books. At the maturity date, the owner returns a registered bond to the corporation and receives cash equaling the face value.

registered bond a bond registered in the owner's name by the issuing company

figure 20.9

A Corporate Bond

A corporate bond is a corporation's written pledge that it will repay on the date of maturity a specified amount of money with interest.

debenture bond a bond backed only by the reputation of the issuing corporation

mortgage bond a corporate bond secured by various assets of the issuing firm

convertible bond a bond that can be exchanged, at the owner's option, for a specified number of shares of the corporation's common stock

Corporate bonds are generally classified as debentures, mortgage bonds, or convertible bonds. Most corporate bonds are debenture bonds. A **debenture bond** is a bond backed only by the reputation of the issuing corporation. To make its bonds more appealing to investors, a corporation may issue mortgage bonds. A **mortgage bond** is a corporate bond secured by various assets of the issuing firm. The corporation can also issue convertible bonds. A **convertible bond** can be exchanged, at the owner's option, for a specified number of shares of the corporation's common stock. Westinghouse Electric's bond that matures in 2007 is convertible: each bond can be converted to 64.5 shares of Westinghouse common stock. A corporation can gain in two ways by issuing convertible bonds. Convertibles usually carry a lower interest rate than nonconvertible bonds. And once an owner converts a bond to common stock, the corporation no longer has to redeem it.

bond indenture a legal document that details all the conditions relating to a bond issue

Repayment Provisions for Corporate Bonds Maturity dates for bonds generally range from ten to thirty years after the date of issue. If the interest is not paid or the firm becomes insolvent, bond owners' claims on the assets of the corporation take precedence over the claims of both common and preferred stockholders. Some bonds are callable before the maturity date; that is, a corporation can buy back, or redeem, them. For these bonds, the corporation usually pays the bond owner a call premium. The amount of the call premium is specified, along with other provisions, in the bond indenture. The **bond indenture** is a legal document that details all the conditions relating to a bond issue.

From the corporation's standpoint, financing through a bond issue differs considerably from equity financing. Bond interest must be paid periodically, usually every six months, but because interest expense lowers corporate profits, the corporation pays less taxes.

As mentioned earlier, the total face value for a corporate bond issue usually amounts to millions of dollars. Before deciding if bonds are the best way to obtain corporate financing, managers must determine if the company can afford to pay the interest on the corporate bonds. It should be obvious that the larger the bond issue, the higher the interest will be. For example, assume that AMR—the parent company of American Airlines—issues bonds with a face value of $80 million. If the interest rate is 8.5 percent, the interest on this bond issue is $6.8 million ($80 million × 0.085 = $6.8 million) each year until the bonds are repaid.

serial bonds bonds of a single issue that mature on different dates

In addition, corporate bonds must be redeemed for their face value at maturity. If the corporation defaults on (does not pay) either of these interest or redemption payments, owners of bonds can force the firm into bankruptcy.

sinking fund a sum of money to which deposits are made each year for the purpose of redeeming a bond issue

A corporation may use one of three methods to ensure that it has sufficient funds available to redeem a bond issue. First, it can issue the bonds as **serial bonds**, which are bonds of a single issue that mature on different dates. For example, a company might use a twenty-five-year, $50-million bond issue to finance its expansion. None of the bonds mature during the first fifteen years. Thereafter, 10 percent of the bonds mature each year, until all the bonds are retired at the end of the twenty-fifth year. Second, the corporation can establish a sinking fund. A **sinking fund** is a sum of money to which deposits are made each year for the purpose of redeeming a bond issue. When H.J. Heinz sold a $50-million bond issue, the company agreed to contribute $3 million to a sinking fund every year until the bond's maturity in the year 2007. Third, a corporation can pay off an old bond issue by selling new bonds. Although this may appear to perpetuate the corporation's long-term debt, a number of utility companies and railroads use this repayment method.

trustee an individual or an independent firm that acts as the bond owners' representative

A corporation that issues bonds must also appoint a **trustee**, an individual, or an independent firm that acts as the bond owners' representative. A trustee's duties are most often handled by a commercial bank or other large financial institution. The corporation must report to the trustee periodically regarding its ability to make interest payments and eventually redeem the bonds. In turn, the trustee transmits this information to the bond owners, along with its own evaluation of the corporation's ability to pay.

table 20.4 Comparison of Long-Term Financing Methods

Type of Financing	Repayment	Repayment Period	Interest/Cost Dividends	Businesses That May Use It
Equity				
Common stock	No	None	Dividends not required	All corporations that sell stock to investors
Preferred stock	No	None	Dividends not required but must be paid before common stockholders receive any dividends	Large corporations that have an established investor base of common stockholders
Debt				
Long-term loan	Yes	Usually 3 to 7 years	Interest rates between 8% and 14%, depending on economic conditions and the financial stability of the company requesting the loan	All firms that can meet the lender's repayment and collateral requirements
Corporate bond	Yes	Usually 10 to 30 years	Interest rates between 8% and 12%, depending on economic conditions and the financial stability of the company issuing the bonds	Large corporations that investors trust

Cost Comparisons

Table 20.4 compares some of the methods of long-term equity and debt financing. Obviously, the least expensive type of financing is through an issue of common stock. Generally, selling common stock is also the first choice for most financial managers. The most expensive is a long-term loan.

A Word About the Uses of Funds

LEARNING OBJECTIVE

6 Discuss the importance of using funds effectively.

In this chapter, we have mentioned a variety of ways in which businesses use funds. These uses range from the payment of recurring expenses, such as rent, wages, and the cost of raw materials, to the payment of one-time costs like plant expansions and mergers. In general, a business uses funds to pay for the resources it needs to produce and market its products.

The effective use of finances, as we have noted, is an important function of financial management. To some extent, financial management can be viewed as a two-sided problem. On one side, the uses of funds often dictate the type or types of financing needed by a business. On the other side, the activities a business can undertake are determined by the types of financing available. Financial managers must ensure that funds are available when needed, that they are obtained at the lowest possible cost, and that they are used as efficiently as possible. And, finally, financial managers must ensure that funds are available for the repayment of debts in accordance with lenders' financing terms. Prompt repayment is essential to protect the firm's credit rating and its ability to obtain financing in the future.

To a great extent, firms are financed through the investments of individuals—money that people have deposited in banks or have used to purchase stocks, mutual funds, and bonds. In Chapter 21, we look at securities markets and how they help people invest their money in business.

RETURN TO Inside Business

WOULD YOU INVEST IN AN INITIAL PUBLIC OFFERING (IPO) from a company that experienced a $115 million loss in one year? Well, a lot of investors did invest in such a company just one year later. The company was Priceline.com and it sold 10 million shares in its initial public offering. As a result, it received over $150 million that it could use to fund corporate growth. And Priceline.com was not alone. Many companies that were operating at a loss sold stock to investors during the last part of the 1990s and the first part of the twenty-first century.

For investors, the lure of quick profits is the driving force behind an investment in an initial public offering. It seems that most everyone has heard the success stories of how someone invested $5,000 to $10,000 in a small company and became a millionaire almost overnight when the company's stock value increased. Based on these stories and the desire to be the world's next millionaire, there is no shortage of investors for IPOs—especially for high-tech firms. And yet, IPOs are for people willing to take chances—not conservative investors. Priceline.com promises to become a profitable company that provides a unique service—a new way of buying airline tickets, hotel rooms, long-distance phone service and other consumer items. *Be warned*: Not all companies that issue stock for the first time offer as much potential for profits as Priceline.com. Therefore, it's more important than ever before to fully evaluate any IPO to determine the true risk. In fact, you may want to read the material in the next chapter on evaluating a company's stock before investing your money.

For the company selling a new stock issue, the process can be long and complicated. Yet, the results can be financially rewarding. While a new company like Priceline.com may want to avail itself of an initial public offering by selling stocks, bonds, or other securities, it may be put off by the expense of doing so. An investment banker's fees range from 2 to 20 percent of the total money raised. In addition, even a small company that goes public can expect to pay $100,000 to lawyers, accountants, and printers; the sum is closer to $500,000 or more for larger companies that want to sell more stock.

Another pitfall for a company selling stock for the first time is the feeling of "being watched" when it sells a new issue of stocks, bonds, or other securities. Making the company's finances public can be especially traumatic. To many company executives, the most disturbing part of getting a new issue approved is that they themselves become public figures.

Questions

1. Although corporate executives complain about the cost and hassle of selling stocks, bonds, and other financial securities, they continue to sell securities to raise capital. Why?
2. A large number of dot-com companies raised millions of dollars through IPOs during the last five years. Now five years later, some of these dot-com companies are beginning to fail. What is the difference between a firm that uses money from an IPO to grow and succeed and one that fails?

chapter Review

SUMMARY

1 Explain the need for financing and financial management in business.

Financial management consists of all activities concerned with obtaining money and using it effectively. Short-term financing is money that will be used for one year or less and then repaid. There are many short-term needs, but cash flow and inventory are two for which financing is often required. Long-term financing is money that will be used for more than one year. Such financing may be required for a business start-up or expansion, for a merger or acquisition, for new-product development, or for replacement of production facilities. Proper financial management can ensure that money is available when it is needed and that it is used efficiently, in keeping with organizational goals.

2 Summarize the process of planning for financial management.

A financial plan begins with the organization's goals and objectives. Next these goals and objectives are "translated" into departmental budgets that detail expected income and expenses. From these budgets, which may be combined into an overall cash budget, the financial manager determines what funding will be needed and where it may be obtained. Whereas departmental and cash budgets emphasize short-term financing needs, a capital budget can be used to estimate a firm's expenditures for major assets and its long-term financing needs. The four principal sources of financing are sales revenues, equity capital, debt capital, and proceeds from the sale of assets. Once the needed funds have been obtained, the financial manager is responsible for ensuring that they are properly used. This is accomplished through a system of monitoring and evaluating the firm's financial activities.

3 Describe the advantages and disadvantages of different methods of short-term debt financing.

Most short-term financing is unsecured; that is, no collateral is required. Sources of unsecured short-term financing include trade credit, promissory notes issued to suppliers, unsecured bank loans, and commercial paper. Sources of secured short-term financing include loans secured by inventory and accounts receivable. A firm may also sell receivables to factors. Trade credit is the least expensive source of short-term financing. The cost of financing through other sources generally depends on the source and on the credit rating of the firm that requires the financing. Factoring is generally the most expensive approach.

4 Evaluate the advantages and disadvantages of equity financing.

Long-term financing may be obtained as equity capital or debt capital. A corporation can raise equity capital by selling either common or preferred stock. Common stock is voting stock; holders of common stock elect the corporation's directors and must approve changes to the corporate charter. Holders of preferred stock must be paid dividends before holders of common stock are paid any dividends. Another source of equity funding is retained earnings, which is the portion of a business's profits not distributed to stockholders. Venture capital—money invested in small (and sometimes struggling) firms that have the potential to become very successful—is yet another source of equity funding. Generally, the venture capital is provided by investors, partnerships established by wealthy families, or insurance companies. In return, they share in the profits of the business.

5 Evaluate the advantages and disadvantages of long-term debt financing.

Financial leverage is the use of borrowed funds to increase the return on owners' equity. Sources of long-term debt financing are long-term loans and sales of corporate bonds. The rate of interest for long-term loans usually depends on the financial status of the borrower, the reason for borrowing, and the kind of collateral pledged to back up the loan. Long-term loans are normally repaid in three to seven years. Money realized from the sale of corporate bonds must be repaid when the bonds mature. In addition, the corporation must pay interest on that money from the time the bonds are sold until maturity. Maturity dates for bonds generally range from ten to thirty years after the date of issue. The least expensive type of long-term financing is through an issue of common stock. The most expensive is a long-term loan.

6 Discuss the importance of using funds effectively.

Financial management can be viewed as a two-sided problem. On one side, the uses of funds often dictate the type or types of financing needed by a business. On the other side, the activities a business can undertake are determined by the types of financing available. Financial managers must ensure that funds are available when needed, that they are obtained at the lowest possible cost, and that they are available for the repayment of debts.

KEY TERMS

You should now be able to define and give an example relevant to each of the following terms:

financial management (579)
short-term financing (579)

cash flow (579)
long-term financing (580)
financial plan (582)
budget (584)
cash budget (584)
zero-base budgeting (585)
capital budget (585)
equity capital (585)
debt capital (586)
unsecured financing (587)
trade credit (587)
promissory note (588)
prime interest rate (589)
revolving credit agreement (589)
commercial paper (589)
floor planning (590)
accounts receivable (590)
factor (590)
initial public offering (IPO) (592)
common stock (593)
preferred stock (593)
par value (593)
call premium (594)
convertible preferred stock (595)
retained earnings (595)
financial leverage (596)
lease (597)
term-loan agreement (597)
corporate bond (599)
maturity date (599)
registered bond (599)
debenture bond (600)
mortgage bond (600)
convertible bond (600)
bond indenture (600)
serial bonds (600)
sinking fund (600)
trustee (600)

REVIEW QUESTIONS

1. How does short-term financing differ from long-term financing? Give two business uses for each type of financing.
2. What is the function of a cash budget? A capital budget?
3. What is zero-base budgeting? How does it differ from the traditional concept of budgeting?
4. What are four general sources of funds?
5. How does a financial manager monitor and evaluate a firm's financing?
6. How important is trade credit as a source of short-term financing?
7. What is the prime rate? Who gets the prime rate?
8. What is the difference between a line of credit and a revolving credit agreement?
9. Why would a supplier require a customer to sign a promissory note?
10. Explain how factoring works. Of what benefit is factoring to a firm that sells its receivables?
11. What are the advantages of financing through the sale of stock?
12. From a corporation's point of view, how does preferred stock differ from common stock?
13. Where do a corporation's retained earnings come from? What are the advantages of this type of financing?
14. What is venture capital?
15. Describe how financial leverage can increase return on owners' equity.
16. For the corporation, what are the advantages of corporate bonds over long-term loans?
17. Describe the three methods used to ensure that funds are available to redeem corporate bonds at maturity.

DISCUSSION QUESTIONS

1. What does a financial manager do? How can she or he monitor a firm's financial success?
2. If you were the financial manager of Stars and Stripes Clothing, what would you do with the excess cash that the firm expects in the second and fourth quarters? (See Figure 20.4.)
3. Develop a personal cash budget for the next six months. Explain what you would do if there are budget shortfalls or excess cash amounts at the end of any month during the six-month period.
4. Why would a supplier offer both trade credit and cash discounts to its customers?
5. Why would a lender offer unsecured loans when it could demand collateral?
6. How can a small-business owner or corporate manager use financial leverage to improve a firm's profits and return on owners' equity?
7. In what circumstances might a large corporation sell stock rather than bonds to obtain long-term financing? In what circumstances would it sell bonds rather than stock?

VIDEO CASE

Physician Sales & Service Sets Long-Term Goals

In the sales of pharmaceuticals, equipment, and medical supplies to physicians, Physician Sales & Service (PSS) leads the industry. The Florida-based corporation, which operates 101 service centers throughout the United States, guarantees more than 200,000 physicians next-day delivery service, thus eliminating their need to keep a large stock of medical supplies on hand. Quite possibly, your physician may be one of PSS's customers.

Patrick Kelly, chairman and CEO, and two partners founded PSS in 1983. With one warehouse and a couple of sales representatives, they could only promise a service their competitors could not match. Just four years later, PSS had five branch offices in Florida, a fleet of its own delivery trucks, the latest in computer technology, and $13 million in annual sales revenue. It was then that Kelly set a long-term goal for PSS. He wanted the company to become the first physician-supply company in the United States to go nationwide.

From the beginning, Kelly recruited aggressive employees, promising to make them part of an organization with a future and putting no barriers in the way of their success.

He rewarded their hard work with a share of the profits, opportunities for extensive training programs, and all the tools they needed to be successful. With the help of his employees, Kelly accomplished his first long-term goal for PSS. He then set two new ones: to serve every physician in every U.S. zip code by 1997, and to be a billion-dollar company by the end of the year 2000.

Although PSS was growing rapidly, it needed capital to continue its growth and expansion into new markets. The company initially sold common stock valued at nearly $16 million in 1994, but it still need additional financing. So in 1995, Kelly and his partners turned to Alex Brown & Sons, an investment banking firm. Through Alex Brown's efforts, PSS was able to sell common stock valued at $170 million. This much-needed capital allowed the company to double in size, equip its sales staff with lap-top computers that link into an "Instant Customer Order Network," acquire an exclusive distribution agreement with Abbott Laboratories, merge with the fourth largest medical supply distributor in the United States, and purchase an imaging-products business.

What role did the investment banking firm of Alex Brown & Sons play in helping PSS achieve financial success? To begin with, it calculated how many shares of PSS common stock to offer as an initial public offering (IPO) and determined the initial selling price. To do this, it examined PSS's historical and projected financial statements and financial goals. On this basis, it developed a series of projections that estimate what the company may be worth in the future. Alex Brown & Sons also prepared a marketing strategy for selling the stock and communicated information about PSS to investors to generate interest in the company.

Would your account executive recommend PSS common stock for your investment portfolio? Before your account executive could make any recommendation, he or she would want information about you and your investment philosophy. The first step would be to analyze your investment objectives and your plans for the future. Next you and your account executive would determine the rate of return you need to meet your goals. Then you would have to decide how much risk you are willing to assume to attain your investment goals. Once these important questions are answered, you could decide if you were ready to purchase a high-risk investment like the PSS stock issue. If you had purchased the Physician Sales & Services IPO when it was first offered, you could have realized more than five times your original investment. Even investors who purchased PSS stock after the IPO have more than doubled or tripled their investment.[17]

Questions

1. Patrick Kelly set goals for Physician Sales & Service. How did his goal-setting affect the company's financial performance? How did it affect employees?
2. What role did the investment banking firm of Alex Brown & Sons play in helping PSS sell stock for the first time?
3. Investors who purchased PSS stock when it was first offered to the general public have realized gains totaling more than five times their original investment. Would this type of investment appeal to you? Explain your answer.

Building skills for career success

1. Exploring the Internet

Finding capital for new business start-ups is never an easy task. Besides a good business plan, those seeking investor funds must be convincing and clear about how their business activities will provide sufficient revenue to payback investors that help get them going in the first place. To find out what others have done, it is useful to read histories of successful launches as well as failures in journals that specialize in this area. Visit the text web site for updates to this exercise.

Assignment

1. Examine articles that profile successes and failures in the following publications and highlight the main points that led to either result.

   American Venture magazine (http://www.avce.com)
   Business 2.0 (http://www.business2.com)
   Red Herring (http://www.redherring.com)
   Fast Company (http://www.fastcompany.com)

2. What are the shared similarities?
3. What advice would you give to a start-up venture after reading these stories?

2. Developing Critical Thinking Skills

Financial management involves preparing a plan for obtaining and using the money needed to accomplish a firm's goals and objectives. After a financial plan has been developed, it must be monitored continually to ensure that it actually fulfills these goals and objectives. To accomplish your own goals, you should prepare a personal financial plan. Determine what is important in your life and what you want to accomplish, budget the amount of money required to get it, and identify sources for acquiring the funds. You should regularly monitor and evaluate the results and make changes when necessary.

Assignment

1. Using the three steps shown in Figure 20.2, prepare a personal financial plan.
2. Prepare a three-column table to display it.
   a. In column 1, list at least two objectives under each of the following areas:
      - Financial (savings, investments, retirement)
      - Education (training, degrees, certificates)
      - Career (position, industry, location)
      - Family (children, house, education, trips, entertainment)

b. In column 2, list the amount of money it will take to accomplish your objectives.
c. In column 3, identify the sources of funds for each objective.

3. Describe what you learned from doing this exercise in a comments section at the bottom of the table.

3. Building Team Skills

Suppose that for the past three years, you have been repairing lawn mowers in your garage. Your business has grown steadily, and recently you hired two part-time workers. Your garage is no longer adequate for your business; it is also in violation of the city code, and you have been fined twice for noncompliance. You have decided it's time to find another location for your shop and that it would also be a good time to expand your business. If the business continues to grow in the new location, you plan to hire a full-time employee to repair washing machines. You are concerned, however, about how you will get the money to move your shop and get it established in a new location.

Assignment

1. With all class members participating, use brainstorming to identify the following:
   a. The funds you will need to accomplish your business goals
   b. The sources of short-term financing available to you
   c. Problems that might prevent you from getting a short-term loan
   d. How you will repay the money if you get it
2. Have a classmate write the ideas on the board.
3. Discuss how you can overcome any problems that might hamper your current chances of getting a loan and how your business can improve its chances of securing short-term loans in the future.
4. Summarize what you learned from participating in this exercise.

4. Researching Different Careers

Financial managers are responsible for determining the best way to raise funds, for ensuring that the funds are used to accomplish their firm's goals, and for developing and implementing their firm's financial plan. Their decisions have a direct impact on the firm's level of success. When managers do not pay enough attention to finances, a firm is likely to fail. The challenge for financial managers is to balance the risks in money management with the opportunities for growth and profits.

Assignment

1. Investigate the job of financial manager by searching the library or Internet, and/or by interviewing a financial manager.
2. Find answers to the following questions:
   a. What skills do financial managers need?
   b. How much education is required?
   c. What is the starting salary? Top salary?
   d. What will the job of financial manager be like in the future?
   e. What opportunities are available?
   f. What types of firms are most likely to hire financial managers? What is the employment potential?
3. Prepare a report on your findings.

5. Improving Communication Skills

Trade credit is a source of short-term financing extended by a seller who does not require immediate payment upon delivery of merchandise. The bill, or invoice, states the credit terms, often offering a cash discount for prompt payment. Many managers and owners, however, fail to take advantage of these discounts, which can save a business hundreds and even thousands of dollars each year.

Assignment

1. Prepare an invoice that offers the buyer a 2 percent cash discount if the bill is paid within ten days.
2. Using the data in the following table, calculate how much a business would save per transaction and in the course of a year, based on six transactions, if it took advantage of trade credit that offered a 2 percent cash discount.

Invoice Amount	**Amount Saved per Transaction**	**Amount Saved Annually** (Based on six transactions)
$1,000		
$2,300		
$5,600		
$11,000		
$22,500		
Totals		

3. Discuss why you think businesses fail to take advantage of cash discounts.
4. Summarize what you have learned about trade credit from this exercise.

understanding securities markets and investments

21

LEARNING OBJECTIVES

1 Describe how securities are bought and sold.

2 Develop a personal investment plan.

3 Explain how the factors of safety, risk, income, growth, and liquidity affect your investment decisions.

4 Identify the advantages and disadvantages of savings accounts, bonds, stocks, mutual funds, and real estate.

5 Describe high-risk investment techniques.

6 Use financial information to evaluate investment alternatives.

7 Explain how federal and state authorities regulate trading in securities.

Qualcomm is a real company that happens to be very profitable because it produces a product that its customers need.

inside Business

Qualcomm: What an Investment!

For Rosario Maiolino, Qualcomm, Inc. was a dream come true. He had never made a large financial investment on anything other than his own home. Then one day he got a tip on a hot stock from "a friend of a friend." While many people would have invested their money without doing any research, Mr. Maiolino researched Qualcomm by studying analysts' reports, visiting the library, reading wireless-technology literature, and testing products that contained Qualcomm technology. He even checked out Qualcomm's competitors to see how they were doing in the ever-changing high-tech industry. Then and only then, did he decide to purchase stock in a little known, high-tech company named *Qualcomm.* He took his life savings—$350,000—and purchased Qualcomm stock. Although friends thought he was insane, he had the last laugh. In 1999, the market value of the company's stock sky rocketed, and he sold his investment for $17 million.

Not many people have $350,000, or the courage to sink their life savings into a single investment. But let's suppose you had bought just 100 shares of Qualcomm stock on April 1, 1992 when the company sold stock to the public for the first time. Your initial investment would have cost $2,187.50. At the time of publication, you would now own 1,600 shares because of a number Qualcomm stock splits—a topic we discuss later in this chapter. More importantly, your 1,600 shares of Qualcomm would be worth $122,800, and you would have experienced a 5,514 percent increase in just eight years. No wonder analysts describe this company with superlatives such as "a best performer" and "the hottest," or simply as a company that has "IT."

Based on past performance, it's easy to see why Qualcomm was named the top-performing stock of the Standard & Poor stock index in 1999. It's also easy to understand why so many investors want to purchase the company's stock. And yet, Qualcomm is a real company that happens to be very profitable because it produces a product that its customers need. It all began in 1985 when two professors—Irwin Mark Jacobs and Andrew Viterbi—initially provided research and development services for telecommunications businesses in the defense industry. At that time, Jacobs concentrated his research efforts on transforming a communications code that was used for wireless radio transmissions on the World War II battlefield into a product that could be sold commercially. The resulting product was called *Code Division Multiple Access (CDMA)* technology and was adopted as the North American standard for digital wireless transmissions in 1993. Today, many products including cell phones, digital pagers, and even portable computers manufactured by Nokia, Lucent Technologies, Motorola, and Ericsson use the CDMA technology. And for each piece of equipment sold that uses this technology, Qualcomm receives royalties and licensing fees. The fact that these products have become increasingly popular accounts for Qualcomm's success in just a sixteen-year period of time.

Although Qualcomm has enjoyed tremendous past success, not everyone is convinced that the company's stock is such a great buy today. Many analysts wonder if the company can continue to introduce new, state-of-the-art products needed to remain competitive in the ever-changing high-tech industry. For a company like Qualcomm, this type of innovation is essential to sustain continued growth in sales and profits, and to support an increase in the market value of the company's stock. Naysayers believe that no company can maintain this type of innovation and growth. These same experts believe that the uncertainty about Qualcomm's ability to innovate and its ability to generate even larger annual sales and profit amounts is one reason why the stock's market value dropped by 50 percent during a recent four-month period. If Rosario Maiolino had invested his $350,000 in December, 1999, he would have lost $175,000 by April 2000.[1]

Too often, people try to build an investment program around risky investments that yield quick profits. But Rosario Maiolino resisted the temptation to just invest money in Qualcomm stock without researching the corporation. Only after he had learned about the company, its products, and had a "feel" for what the future might hold, did he invest his life savings of $350,000. Fortunately his investment paid off when he sold his stock for $17 million. While not everyone can expect the type of returns that Mr. Maiolino experienced, the fact is that there is no substitute for researching potential investments.

Today a lot of people invest money. Why? The most obvious reason is simple: they want a return on their investment. While all investments may promise to deliver "big" returns, not all perform as well as investors would like. For example, between 1926 and 1999, common stocks included in the Standard & Poor's Stock Index provided a 10.7 percent annual return before adjusting for inflation and a 7.4 percent return after adjustment. During the same period, corporate bonds returned only 5.6 percent before adjusting for inflation and 2.4 percent after adjustment for inflation, and U.S. Treasury bills returned only 3.7 percent before adjustment and 0.6 percent after adjustment.[2] Clearly stocks outperformed the more conservative investment alternatives. But there are reasons why investors would choose corporate bonds, U.S. treasury bills, and the other investment alternatives discussed later in this chapter. And yet, choosing the right investment is only part of a successful investment program. It also takes discipline and the knowledge of where to find the information needed to evaluate an investment. That's what this chapter is all about.

We begin by examining the process of buying and selling securities, noting the functions of securities exchanges and stock brokerage firms. After outlining the reasons for developing a personal investment plan and pointing out several factors that should be considered before investing any money, we discuss both traditional investments, and high-risk ones—that is, investments that can lead to large gains but that are also quite speculative. We also explain how to obtain and interpret financial information from the Internet, newspapers, brokerage firms, corporate reports, and periodicals. Finally, we discuss the evolution of state and federal laws governing the sale of financial securities.

How Securities Are Bought and Sold

LEARNING OBJECTIVE

1 Describe how securities are bought and sold.

To purchase a Geoffrey Beene sweater, you simply walk into a store that sells these sweaters, choose one, and pay for it. To purchase stocks, bonds, mutual funds, and many other investments, you often work through a representative—your account executive or stockbroker. In turn, your account executive must buy or sell for you in either the primary or secondary market.

The Primary Market

primary market a market in which an investor purchases financial securities (via an investment bank) directly from the issuer of those securities

investment banking firm an organization that assists corporations in raising funds, usually by helping sell new issues of stocks, bonds, or other financial securities

The **primary market** is a market in which an investor purchases financial securities (via an investment bank) directly from the issuer of those securities. An **investment banking firm** is an organization that assists corporations in raising funds, usually by helping sell new issues of stocks, bonds, or other financial securities. Typically, this type of stock offering is referred to as an initial public offering (IPO). An initial public offering (*IPO*) occurs when a corporation sells common stock to the general public for the first time. An example of an initial public offering sold through the primary market is the common stock issue sold by the Internet service provider America Online (AOL). In March 1992, investors bought those shares through the investment banking firm Goldman Sachs and paid $0.09 per share when adjusted for stock splits. At the beginning of 2000, those shares were worth $83 a share.[3] Because this was an IPO, the money investors paid for the stock went to America Online. (Although stock can be sold again and again in the secondary market—as you will see later in this section, the company only receives money from the IPO for the first time it is sold to the public.) Another IPO that received a lot of attention occurred in November, 1999, when United Parcel Service (UPS) raised over $5 billion. In fact, UPS currently holds the record as the largest American IPO ever. Other highly visible companies that have sold stock to raise capital include Home Depot, Microsoft, Lucent Technologies, and E-bay. The promise of quick profits often lures investors to purchase an IPO. Investors should be aware, however, that an IPO is generally classified as a **high-risk investment**—one made in the uncertain hope of earning a relatively large profit in a short time. Depending on the corporation selling the new security, IPOs may be too risky for most people.

high-risk investment an investment made in the uncertain hope of earning a relatively large profit in a short time

According to the Corporate Venturing Report, there are currently more than 200 corporations making investments into Internet-related start-ups. An estimated $10 billion was invested in 1999, five times the amount invested in 1998. Investments of $10 million in start-ups can easily turn into $100 million if and when the firm goes public with an IPO. For example, Oracle Venture Fund was up 504 percent in its first year of operation after successful IPOs by both C-bridge Internet Solutions and Red Hat.[4]

For a large corporation, the decision to sell securities is often complicated, time-consuming, and expensive. Such companies usually choose one of two basic methods. Large firms that need a lot of financing often use an investment banking firm to sell and distribute the new security issue. Analysts for the investment bank examine the corporation's financial condition to determine whether the company is financially sound and how difficult it will be to sell the new stock issue. If the analysts for the investment banking firm are satisfied that the new security issue is a good risk, the bank will buy the securities and then resell them to its customers—institutional investors or individuals. **Institutional investors** are pension funds, insurance companies, mutual funds, banks, and other organizations that trade large quantities of securities. The investment banking firm generally charges a fee of 2 to 20 percent of the proceeds received by the corporation issuing the securities. The size of the commission depends on the financial health of the corporation issuing the new securities and the size of the new security issue.

institutional investors pension funds, insurance companies, mutual funds, banks, and other organizations that trade large quantities of securities

The second method used by a corporation trying to obtain financing through the primary market is to sell directly to current stockholders. Usually, promotional materials describing the new security issue are mailed to current stockholders. These stockholders may then purchase securities directly from the corporation. Why would a corporation try to sell securities on its own? The most obvious reason is to avoid the investment bank's commission.

The Secondary Market

After securities are originally sold through the primary market, shares of open corporations are traded on a regular basis through the secondary market. Remember from Chapter 5, an open corporation—sometimes referred to as a *publicly-traded corporation*—is one whose stock can be purchased by any individual. The **secondary market** is a market for existing financial securities that are traded between investors. Usually, secondary-market transactions are completed through a securities exchange or the over-the-counter market.

secondary market a market for existing financial securities that are traded between investors

Securities Exchanges

A **securities exchange** is a marketplace where member brokers meet to buy and sell securities. The securities sold at a particular exchange must first be *listed*, or accepted for trading, at that exchange. Generally, securities issued by larger, nationwide corporations are traded at the New York Stock Exchange, the American Stock Exchange, or at *regional exchanges*, located in Chicago, San Francisco, Philadelphia, Boston, and several other cities. The securities of very large corporations may be traded at more than one of these exchanges. Securities of firms may also be listed on foreign securities exchanges—in Tokyo, London, or Paris, for example.

securities exchange a marketplace where member brokers meet to buy and sell securities

One of the largest and best-known securities exchange in the world is the New York Stock Exchange (NYSE). The NYSE lists stocks for over 3,000 corporations, with a total market value of $12 trillion.[5] The actual trading floor of the NYSE, where listed securities are bought and sold, is approximately the size of a football field. A glass-enclosed visitors' gallery lets people watch the proceedings below; on a busy day, the floor of the NYSE can best be described as organized confusion. Yet, the system does work and enables brokers to trade in excess of 1 billion shares per day. Before a corporation's stock is approved for listing on the New York Stock Exchange, the firm must usually meet four criteria (see Figure 21.1).

A picture is worth a thousand words. What looks like confusion is actually an orderly system that allows investors to buy and sell over 3,000 different stocks listed on the New York Stock Exchange.

The American Stock Exchange handles about 5 percent of U.S. stock transactions. Regional exchanges and the over-the-counter market account for the remainder. The American and regional exchanges and the over-the-counter market have generally less stringent listing requirements than the NYSE.

The Over-the-Counter Market

Not all securities are traded on organized exchanges. Stocks issued by several thousand companies are traded in the over-the-counter market. The **over-the-counter (OTC) market** is a network of dealers who buy and sell the stocks of corporations that are not listed on a securities exchange. The term *over-the-counter* was coined more than 100 years ago when securities were actually sold "over the counter" in stores and banks.

over-the-counter (OTC) market a network of dealers who buy and sell the stocks of corporations that are not listed on a securities exchange

Nasdaq computerized electronic exchange system through which most over-the-counter securities are traded

Most OTC securities today are traded through an electronic exchange called **Nasdaq** (pronounced nazzdack). The Nasdaq quotation system provides price information on over 6,000 different stocks. Begun in 1971 and regulated by The National Association of Securities Dealers, Nasdaq is now one of the largest securities markets in the world. Today, Nasdaq is known for its forward-looking, innovative, growth companies. Although most companies that trade on Nasdaq are small, it is also used by some large firms, including Intel, Microsoft, MCI, Cisco Systems, and Dell Computer.

When you want to sell shares of a company that trades on Nasdaq—for example, Apple Computer—your account executive sends your order into the Nasdaq computer system, where it shows up on the screen, together with all the other orders from people who want to buy or sell Apple Computer. A Nasdaq dealer (sometimes referred to as a *marketmaker*) sits at a computer terminal, putting together these buy and sell orders for Apple Computer. Once a match is found, your order is completed. In 1998, the national association of Securities Dealers and the American Stock Exchange merged to create the Nasdaq-Amex Market Group.

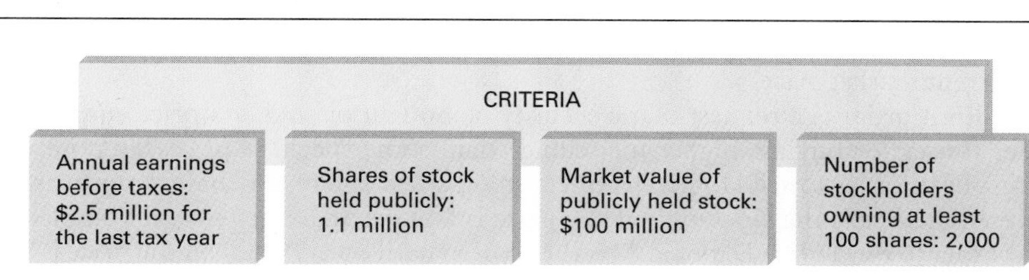

figure 21.1

Criteria a Firm Must Meet before Being Listed on the New York Stock Exchange

Over 3,000 corporations are currently listed on the New York Stock Exchange.

Source: New York Stock Exchange, at www.nyse.com on June 20, 2000.

The Role of an Account Executive

account executive an individual, sometimes called a *stock-broker* or *registered representative,* who buys and sells securities for clients

An **account executive**—sometimes called a *stockbroker* or *registered representative*—is an individual who buys and sells securities for clients. Actually, *account executive* is the more descriptive title because account executives handle all securities—not only stocks. Choosing an account executive can be difficult for at least three reasons. First, you must exercise a shrewd combination of trust and mistrust when you approach an account executive. Remember that you are interested in the broker's recommendations to increase your wealth, but the account executive is interested in your investment trading as a means to swell commissions. Unfortunately, some account executives are guilty of *churning*—a practice that generates commissions by excessive buying and selling of securities.

Second, you must decide whether you need a *full-service* broker or a *discount* broker. A full-service broker usually charges higher commissions but gives you personal investment advice. He or she can provide you with research reports from Moody's Investors Service, Standard & Poor's, and Value Line Inc.—all companies that specialize in providing investment information to investors. A full-service broker should also provide additional reports prepared by the brokerage firm's financial analysts. A discount broker simply executes buy and sell orders, usually over the phone. Most discount brokers offer no or very little free investment advice; you must make your own investment decisions. Some discount brokers will supply research reports for a nominal fee—usually \$5 to \$10. Before deciding if you should use a full-service or a discount brokerage firm, you should consider how much help you need when making an investment decision. Many full-service brokerage firms argue that you need a professional to help you make important investment decisions. While this may be true for some investors, most account executives employed by full-service brokerage firms are too busy to spend unlimited time with you on a one-on-one basis, especially if you are investing a small amount. Still, the full-service account executive is there to answer questions and make investment recommendations. On the other side, many discount brokerage firms argue that you alone are responsible for making your investment decisions. They are quick to point out that the most successful investors are the ones involved in their investment programs. And they argue that discount brokerage firms have both the personnel and research materials that can help you become a better investor.

Finally, you must consider the factor of compatibility. It is always wise to interview several potential account executives. During each interview, ask some questions to determine if you and the account executive understand each other. You must be able to communicate the types of investments that interest you, your expected rate of return, and the amount of risk you are willing to take to achieve your goals. If you become dissatisfied with your investment program, do not hesitate to discuss your dissatisfaction with the account executive. If your dissatisfaction continues, you may find it necessary to choose another account executive.

Account executives are employed by stock brokerage firms, such as Merrill Lynch, Dean Witter Reynolds, and Charles Schwab & Company. To trade at a particular exchange, a brokerage firm must be a member of that exchange.

The Mechanics of a Transaction

Once investors have decided on a particular security, most simply telephone their account executive and place a market, limit, or discretionary order. A **market order** is a request that a security be purchased or sold at the current market price.

market order a request that a security be purchased or sold at the current market price

limit order a request that a security be bought or sold at a price that is equal to or better than some specified price

A **limit order** is a request that a security be bought or sold at a price equal to or better (lower for buying, higher for selling) than some specified price. Suppose you place a limit order to *sell* Home Depot common stock at \$49 per share. Your broker's representative sells the stock only if the price is \$49 per share or *more.* If you place a limit order to *buy* Home Depot at \$49, the representative buys it only if the price is \$49 per share or *less.* Limit orders may or may not be transacted quickly, depending on how close the limit price is to the current market price. Usually, a limit order is good for one day, one week, one month, or good until canceled (GTC).

Investors can also choose to place a discretionary order. A **discretionary order** is an order to buy or sell a security that lets the broker decide when to execute the transaction and at what price. *Caution*: financial planners advise against using a discretionary order for two reasons. First, a discretionary order gives the account executive a great deal of authority. If the account executive makes a mistake, it is the investor who suffers the loss. Second, financial planners argue that only investors (with the help of their account executives) should make investment decisions.

discretionary order an order to buy or sell a security that lets the broker decide when to execute the transaction and at what price

A typical stock transaction includes the five steps shown in Figure 21.2. The entire process, from receipt of the selling order to confirmation of the completed transaction, takes about twenty minutes. It is also possible for a brokerage firm to match a buy order for a security for one of its customers with a sell order for the same security from another of its customers. Let's say you want to purchase 100 shares of Cisco Systems at the market price. You call your account executive at Charles Schwab and place a market order to purchase Cisco Systems. Your order is then "matched" with an order to sell 100 shares of Cisco placed by another Charles Schwab customer. Matched orders are not completed through a security exchange or the over-the-counter market. Payment for stocks, bonds, and other financial securities is generally required within three business days of the transaction.

Online Security Transactions Although most people still prefer to use the telephone to place orders for buying and selling stock, a growing number of investors are using computers to complete security transactions. A good investment software package can help you evaluate potential investments, manage your investments, monitor their value more closely *and* place buy and sell orders online. While a computer and software can help you make decisions about buying and selling stocks, bonds, and other financial securities, you are still the one who has to analyze the information and make the final decision; all the software does is provide more information and in most cases complete transactions more quickly and economically. As a rule of thumb, the more active an investor is the more it makes sense to use computers. Other reasons that justify using a computer and software include:

1. The size of your investment portfolio
2. The ability to manage your investments closely
3. The capability of your computer and the software package

For more information on investing online, read Talking Technology.

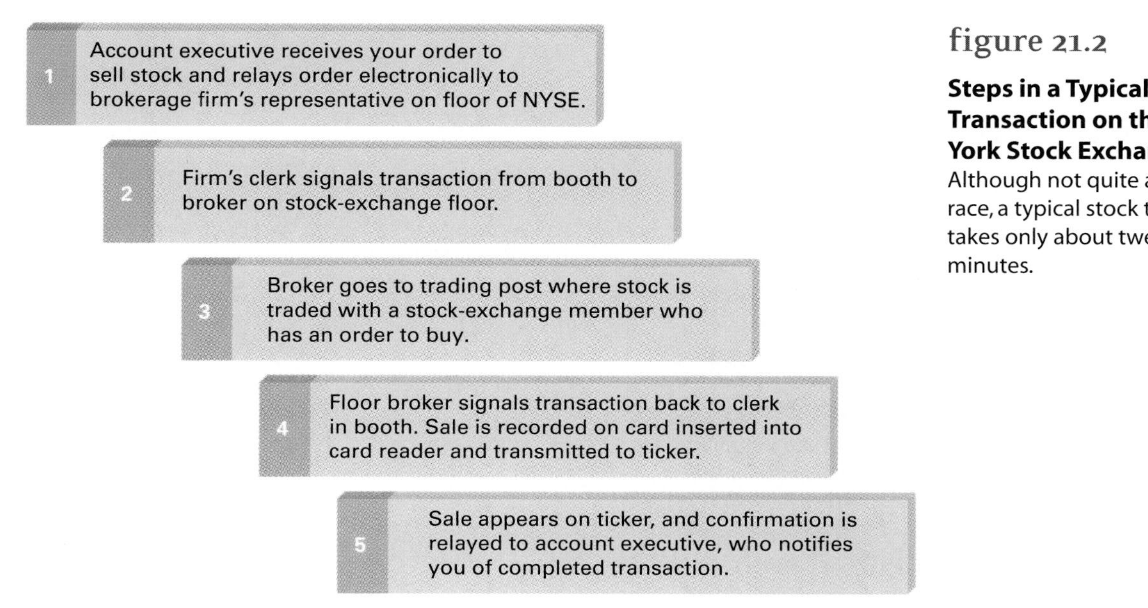

figure 21.2

Steps in a Typical Stock Transaction on the New York Stock Exchange

Although not quite a horse race, a typical stock transaction takes only about twenty minutes.

spotLight

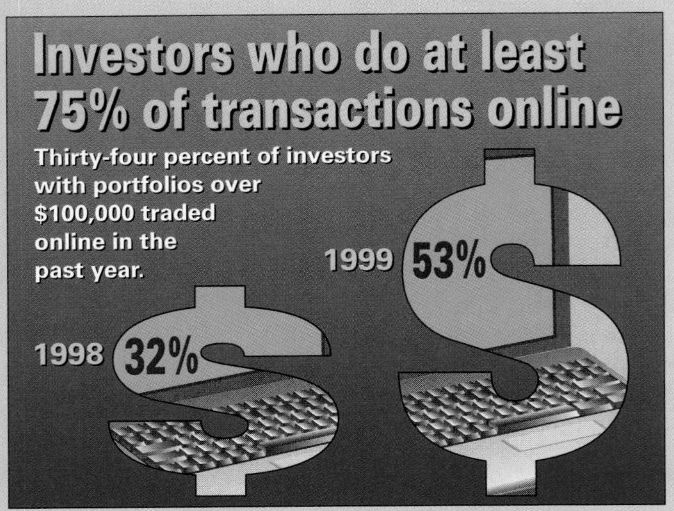

Source: Copyright 2000, USA TODAY. Reprinted with permission.

Another kind of computerized transaction is called program trading. **Program trading** is a computer-driven program to buy or sell selected stocks. When program trading is used, a computer monitors the market value of stocks and other securities. If security prices increase or decrease to a specified amount, the computer enters an order to buy or sell. Generally, institutional investors like pension funds, mutual funds, banks, and insurance companies use program trading to monitor the value of their securities.

Commissions Brokerage firms are free to set their own commission charges. Like other businesses, however, they must be concerned with the fees charged by competing firms.

On the trading floor, stocks are traded in round lots. A **round lot** is a unit of 100 shares of a particular stock. An **odd lot** is fewer than 100 shares of a particular stock. Brokerage firms generally charge more for odd-lot transactions. Table 21.1 shows typical charges and services provided by online bro-

table 21.1 Typical Commission Charges and Services Provided by Online Brokerage Firms

Firm	Cost of trades	Research	Extras
Datek Online	Online trade: $9.99 for up to 5,000 shares. No automated phone trading available. Broker: $25	Free BigCharts, NewsAlert, and Thomson reports.	Market orders that take more than 60 seconds to execute are free.
DLJdirect	$20 for up to 1,000 shares and 2 cents per share thereafter.	With $100,000 in an account you get free DLJ research.	With $100,000 you get in on DLJ-underwritten IPOs.
Discover Brokerage	$14.95 for up to 5,000 shares. Broker: $34 minimum	Research reports are free for clients with over $100,000.	Recognized for its excellent options-trading capacities.
E*Trade	$14.95. Automated phone: Connect fees are 27 cents per minute, but call is free if it takes less than 12 minutes per trade. Broker: $29.95	$9.95 for reports from securities analysts.	Free unlimited real-time quotes.
Fidelity Investments	$25 for up to 1,000 shares. Clients with $100,000 in mutual funds or those who have made 12 trades per year can pay $14.95 for up to 1,000 shares.	Subscriptions for quality reports cost $50 a month.	It's hard to beat the mutual-fund screening tools.
National Discount Brokers	Online: $14.75. Automated phone: $19.95. Broker: $24.95	Free articles from investment newsletters.	Fast page loads and real-time balance updates.
Charles Schwab	$29.95 for up to 1,000 shares and then 3 cents per share. Automated phone: 10 percent off broker prices. Broker: maximum $55 for 100 shares or fewer	Reports cost $29.95 a month.	Custom financial plans and personalized advice.
Suretrade	Online: $7.95 for up to 5,000 shares. Automated phone: $11.95 for up to 5,000 shares. Broker: $32.95	Free BigCharts, First Call, Reuters, and Zacks.	Low margin rates: 5.75 percent on loans under $100,000.
A.B. Watley	$9.95 for up to 5,000 shares. Phone $11.95. Broker: $24.95	Charges a minimum of $1.50 per report.	Simple web site and fast execution of trades.

Source: "Typical Commission Charges and Services Provided by Online Brokerage Firms," from "Can't Beat 'Em," by Fred Vogelstein. Copyright June 14, 2000, *U.S. News & World Report*. (Additional information at www.usnews.com.)

Talking Technology

Investing Online

THE NUMBER OF PEOPLE WHO OWN stocks, mutual funds, or other investments in their own investment portfolio or as part of an individual retirement account, 401 (k) retirement account, or 403 (b) retirement account has increased from 20 percent in 1983 to almost 50 percent today. And most experts expect that the number of people with investments will continue to grow in the next five years. Why the increase? Although there are many reasons, two of the causes of this growth deserve a closer look.

Online Information You Can Use

One reason why investments have become so popular is the ability to access the information needed to evaluate investments. Whether you're a rookie who wants to learn investing basics or an investment-savvy researcher looking for potential buys, your best bet is to access one of the many available web sites that are geared toward personal financial planning. Why not take a look at the investing information provided by *Business Week* at www.businessweek.com? You can also use the investing link found on the home page of most Internet service providers or search engines. For example, the Yahoo! finance page (http://finance.yahoo.com) provides a wealth of information about various investments and links that allow you to access more detailed information. You can also take advantage of the free memberships at sites dedicated to investment planning, such as Intuit's Quicken (www.quicken.com).

Once at a site, you can retrieve charts, graphs, and a variety of historical data about potential investments. You can read analysts reports, study trends, use calculators to examine "what if" scenarios, and practice with mock portfolios before you invest a dime. Some sites will even e-mail daily reports that monitor the value of your portfolio—whether real or imaginary.

Now's the Time to Go Online

A second reason for the increased popularity of investments is the number of brokerage firms—more than 160 different firms—that provide online investment services. Once you've decided to invest online, the next step is to choose an online broker. Many of the same factors you would consider when choosing a full-service broker or a discount broker apply to online brokers. Generally, the more service you want, the higher the cost of investing. After choosing an online brokerage firm, you must have $1,000 to $2,000 to open an account. Once your account is open, you will receive an identification number, password, and instructions on how to access your online broker. Although most brokerage firms compete on cost, many do offer additional services to attract new clients. For example, many firms have a technical advisor—a real live human being—standing by waiting to answer the telephone in case your computer goes on the fritz. If you're interested in online brokerage services and want more information, check out Charles Schwab (www.schwab.com), Ameritrade (www.ameritrade.com), E*Trade (www.etrade.com), or Datek Online (www.datek.com).

A Word of Caution

Experts have compiled statistics comparing the success of investors who trade online with more traditional methods of buying and selling stocks, mutual funds, and other investments. They've concluded that there's a direct correlation between individuals who make a large number of online trades and lower financial returns. *The reason*: Heavy trading incurs more commissions and transaction fees. And because buying and selling investments online is so easy, investors may not evaluate investment alternatives as thoroughly as they should.

kerage firms. Notice that many of the online brokerage firms listed in Table 21.1 charge for research information and other investor services. As a rule of thumb, full-service brokerage firms charge as much as 1 1/2 to 2 percent of the transaction amount. For example, if you use a full-service brokerage firm like Dean Witter Reynolds to purchase Exxon/Mobil stock valued at $10,000, and the brokerage firm charges 1 1/2 percent, you will pay commissions totaling $150 ($10,000 × 0.015 = $150). Discount brokerage firms, on the other hand, would charge commissions ranging between $55 to $85.

program trading a computer-driven program to buy or sell selected stocks

round lot a unit of 100 shares of a particular stock

odd lot fewer than 100 shares of a particular stock

Commissions for trading bonds, commodities, and options are usually lower than those for trading stocks. The charge for buying or selling a $1,000 corporate bond is typically $10. With the exception of some mutual funds, the investor generally pays a commission when buying *and* when selling securities.

Most brokerage firms charge a minimum commission ranging from $25 to $55 per transaction. If you purchase one share of Johnson & Johnson for $64 and you have to pay a minimum commission of $40, the commission is almost as expensive as the stock. No successful investor is going to pay $104 for a $64 stock. To avoid this problem and get the most for your commission dollars, most financial experts recommend that you not invest until you can purchase at least $1,000 of stock. In the next section, we discuss methods you can use to establish an investment program and accumulate the money you need to start investing.

LEARNING OBJECTIVE

2 Develop a personal investment plan.

Developing an Investment Plan

personal investment the use of your personal funds to earn a financial return

Personal investment is the use of your personal funds to earn a financial return. Thus, in the most general sense, the goal of investing is to earn money with money. But that goal is completely useless for the individual, because it is so vague and so easily attained. If you place $100 in a savings account paying 4 percent annual interest, your money will earn 33 cents in one month. If your goal is simply to earn money with your $100, you will have attained that goal at the end of the month. If your goals are somewhat more ambitious, you'll find Exploring Business of considerable interest. After reading it, you should realize that the sooner you establish your financial goals and start an investment program, the more time your investment dollars will have to work for you.

Investment Goals

To be useful, an investment goal must be specific and measurable. It must be tailored to you so that it takes into account your particular financial needs. It must also be oriented toward the future because investing is usually a long-term undertaking. Finally, an investment goal must be realistic in terms of the economic conditions that prevail and the investment opportunities that are available.

Some financial planners suggest that investment goals be stated in terms of money: "By January 1, 2007, I will have total assets of $80,000." Others believe that people are more motivated to work toward goals that are stated in terms of the particular things they desire: "By May 1, 2007, I will have accumulated enough money so that I can take a year off from work to travel around the world." Like the goals themselves, the way they are stated depends on you.

The following questions can be helpful in establishing valid investment goals:

1. What financial goals do you want to achieve?
2. How much money will you need, and when?
3. What will you use the money for?
4. Is it reasonable to assume that you can obtain the amount of money you will need to meet your investment goals?
5. Do you expect your personal situation to change in a way that will affect your investment goals?
6. What economic conditions could alter your investment goals?
7. Are you willing to make the necessary sacrifices to ensure that your investment goals are met?
8. What are the consequences of not obtaining your investment goals?

Managing wealth often takes the help of an expert. The professionals at Phoenix Home Life Mutual Insurance Company know different investors have different needs and goals. They cater to helping entrepreneurs—who know how to make money—preserve it by managing it wisely.

A Personal Investment Plan

Once you have formulated specific goals, investment planning is similar to planning for a business. It begins with the assessment of different investment opportunities—including the potential return and risk involved in each. At the very least,

Exploring Business

Do You Want to Be a Millionaire?

Today, it seems like everyone wants to be a millionaire. Each week over 32 million people tune in to get-rich-quick game shows such as ABC's "Who Wants to Be a Millionaire" and Fox's "Greed." The increasing popularity of this type of programming illustrates the public's fascination with getting money fast. The contestants that sit in the "hot seat" can walk away with thousands of dollars in as little as thirty minutes. Ben Stein, who has his own game show, "Win Ben Stein's Money," explained, America doesn't want to wait years to get rich anymore. What many viewers don't realize is that becoming a participant in these game shows is not a quick and easy process; it may take months of phone calls, e-mails, and preliminary quizzes just to get a chance to become a televised player. And if you are one of the lucky contestants to get on television, the odds are that you won't become the world's next millionaire. In fact, there is only one sure-fire method to acquire that kind of money: create a long-term investment plan.

The Value of Long-Term Investments

Financial planners often tell clients that there is no substitute for a long-term investment plan. As pointed out at the beginning of this chapter, the stocks listed in the Standard & Poor's 500 Stock Index have provided investors with a 10.7 percent average annual return since 1926. And because stocks are generally part of a mutual fund's investment portfolio that is professionally managed and diversified, mutual funds should provide about the same or an even better return than stock investments over a long period of time. As a result, most financial planners suggest you make stocks and mutual funds the centerpiece of your long-term investment plan.

How You Can Become a Millionaire

If you start an investment program when you are young, make quality investments in individual stocks or mutual funds, and let your investment earnings accumulate, you won't have to worry about money when you reach retirement age. For example, if you begin an investment program when you are 25 and invest $150 a month, or $1,800 a year, and choose investments that earn 11 percent a year, your investments will be worth $1,047,294 when you reach age 65. However, if you wait until you are 35 to start your investment program and invest in the same investments over a 30 year period, the value of your investments when you reach age 65 will be just $358,236. By waiting 10 years before starting to invest, you would lose almost $700,000. *The bottom line*: Regardless of your age, it's time to start investing.

this process requires some expert advice and careful study. Investors should beware of people who call themselves "financial planners" but who are in reality nothing more than salespersons for various financial investments, tax shelters, or insurance plans.

A true **financial planner** has had at least two years of training in securities, insurance, taxation, real estate, and estate planning and has passed a rigorous examination. As evidence of training and successful completion of the qualifying examination, the Institute of Certified Financial Planners in Denver allows individuals to use the designation Certified Financial Planner (CFP). Similarly, the American College in Bryn Mawr, Pennsylvania, allows individuals who have completed the necessary requirements to use the designation Chartered Financial Consultant (ChFC). Most CFPs and ChFCs don't sell a particular investment product or charge commissions for their investment recommendations. Instead, they charge consulting fees that range from $100 to $250 an hour.

financial planner an individual who has had at least two years of training in securities, insurance, taxation, real estate, and estate planning and has passed a rigorous examination

Many financial planners suggest that you begin an investment program by accumulating an "emergency fund"—a certain amount of money that can be obtained quickly in case of immediate need. This money should be deposited in a savings account at the highest available interest rate. The amount of money that should be salted away in the emergency fund varies from person to person. However, most financial planners agree that an amount equal to three months' living expenses is reasonable.

After the emergency account is established, you may invest additional funds according to your investment plan. Some additional funds may already be available, or money for further investing may be saved out of earnings. For suggestions to help you obtain the money needed to fund your investment plan, see Table 21.2.

Once a plan has been put into operation, you must monitor it and, if necessary, modify it. Your circumstances and economic conditions are both subject to change. Hence, all investment programs should be re-evaluated regularly.

Important Factors in Personal Investment

LEARNING OBJECTIVE

3 Explain how the factors of safety, risk, income, growth, and liquidity affect your investment decisions.

How can you (or a financial planner) tell which investments are "right" for an investment plan and which are not? One way to start is to match potential investments with investment goals in terms of safety, risk, income, growth, and liquidity.

blue-chip stock a safe investment that generally attracts conservative investors

Safety and Risk

Safety and risk are two sides of the same coin. Safety in an investment means minimal risk of loss; risk in an investment means a measure of uncertainty about the outcome. If you want a steady increase in value over an extended period of time, choose safe investements, such as certificates of deposit, highly rated corporate and municipal bonds, and the stocks of highly regarded corporations—sometimes called *blue-chip stocks*. A **blue-chip stock** is a safe investment that generally attracts conservative investors. Corporations that are generally industry leaders and have provided their stockholders with stable earnings and dividends over a number of years include Johnson & Johnson, Kellogg, General Electric, and Sara Lee Corporation. Mutual funds and real estate may also be very safe investments.

To implement goals that stress higher dollar returns on your investments, you must generally give up some safety. How much risk should you take in exchange for how much return? The answer depends very much on your investment goals and your age. In general, however, *the potential return should be directly related to the assumed risk*. That is, the greater the risk assumed by the investor, the greater the potential monetary reward should be. As you will see shortly, there are a number of risky—and

table 21.2 Suggestions to Help You Accumulate the Money Needed to Fund an Investment Plan

1. *Learn to balance your budget.* Many people regularly spend more than they make. It makes no sense to begin an investment program while you have large balances and high interest charges on credit card accounts
2. *Pay yourself first.* Many financial experts recommend that you (1) pay your monthly bills, (2) save a reasonable amount of money, and (3) use whatever money is left over for personal expenses.
3. *Take advantage of employer-sponsored retirement programs.* Many employers will match part or all of the contributions you make to a 401 (k) or 403 (b) retirement account. (*Hint*: when looking for a new job, check out the retirement plan offered by the employer.)
4. *Participate in an elective savings program.* You can elect to have money withheld from your paycheck each payday and automatically deposited in a savings account.
5. *Make a special savings effort one or two months each year.* By cutting back to the basics, you can obtain money for investment purposes.
6. *Take advantage of gifts, inheritances, and windfalls.* During your lifetime, you will likely receive gifts, inheritances, salary increases, year-end bonuses, or federal income tax returns. Instead of spending these windfalls, invest these funds.

Source: Jack R. Kapoor, Les R. Dlabay, and Robert J. Hughes, *Personal Finance*, 6th ed. (Burr Ridge, IL: Irwin-McGraw Hill, 2001), pp. 410–411.

potentially profitable—investments. They include some stocks and bonds, commodities, and stock options. The securities issued by new and growing corporations usually fall in this category.

Creating good publicity and reducing risk for investors in a start-up dot-com is a rare achievement. Justin Dangel, the founder and CEO of Voter.com, did just that when he brought Carl Bernstein, the reporter who uncovered President Nixon's Watergate scandal for *The Washington Post* in 1972, in as executive vice president and executive editor. Voter.com is one of several new political portals on the Internet that directly connects voters with candidates, issues, and advocacy groups. Voter.com has a working relationship with the Center for Responsive Politics and runs political stories from the National Journal, MSN, Slate, and MSNBC.[6]

Investment Income Certificates of deposit, corporate and government bonds, and certain stocks pay a predictable amount of interest or dividends each year. Such investments are generally used to implement investment goals that stress income.

Investors in certificates of deposit and bonds know exactly how much income they will receive each year. The dividends paid to stockholders can and do vary, even for the largest and most stable corporations. However, a number of corporations have built their reputations on a policy of paying dividends every three months. (The firms listed in Table 21.3 have paid dividends to their owners for at least ninety-five years.) Some mutual funds also offer steady income potential.

Investment Growth To investors, *growth* means that their investments will increase in value. For example, a growing corporation like Wal-Mart usually pays a small cash dividend or no dividend at all. Instead, profits are reinvested in the business (as retained earnings) to finance additional expansion. In this case, the value of their stock increases as the corporation expands.

For investors who carefully choose their investments, both mutual funds and real estate may offer substantial growth possibilities. More speculative investments like precious metals, gemstones, and collectibles (antiques and paintings) offer less predictable growth possibilities. Investments in commodities and stock options usually stress immediate returns as opposed to continued growth. Generally, corporate and government bonds are not purchased for growth.

Investment Liquidity **Liquidity** is the ease with which an investment can be converted into cash. Investments range from cash or cash equivalents (like investments in government securities or money-market accounts) to the other extreme of frozen investments, which you cannot convert into cash like some real estate investments.

liquidity the ease with which an investment can be converted into cash

Although you may be able to sell other investments quickly, you might not regain the amount of money you originally invested because of market conditions, economic

table 21.3 Corporations That Have Made Consecutive Dividend Payments for at Least Ninety-Five Years

Corporation	Dividends Since	Type of Business
AT&T	1881	Telephone utility
E.I. du Pont de Nemours	1904	Chemicals
Exxon/Mobil	1882	Chemical & petroleum products
General Electric	1899	Electrical equipment
Procter & Gamble	1891	Soap products
Union Pacific	1900	Railroad

Source: *Standard & Poor's Stock Guide*, June 1997 (New York: Standard & Poor's, a division of McGraw-Hill, May, 2000).

conditions, or many other reasons. For example, the owner of real estate may have to lower the asking price to find a buyer for a property. Finding a buyer for investments in certain types of collectibles may also be difficult.

Traditional Investment Alternatives

LEARNING OBJECTIVE

4 Identify the advantages and disadvantages of savings accounts, bonds, stocks, mutual funds, and real estate.

In this section, we look at traditional investments; in the next, we explore high-risk ones. A number of the investments listed in Table 21.4 have already been discussed. Others have only been mentioned and will be examined in more detail.

Bank Accounts

Bank accounts that pay interest—and are therefore investments—include passbook savings accounts, certificates of deposit, and interest-bearing accounts. These were discussed in Chapter 19. They are the most conservative of all investments, and they provide safety and either income or growth. That is, the interest paid on bank accounts can be withdrawn to serve as income, or it can be left on deposit to earn additional interest and increase the size of the bank account.

Corporate And Government Bonds

In Chapter 20, we discussed the issuing of bonds by corporations to obtain financing. The U.S. government and state and local governments also issue bonds, for the same reason.

Corporate Bonds Because they are a form of long-term debt financing that must be repaid, bonds are generally considered a more conservative investment than either stocks or mutual funds. One of the principal advantages of corporate bonds is that they are primarily long-term, income-producing investments. Between the time of purchase and the maturity date, the bondholder will receive interest payments—usually semiannually, or every six months—at the stated interest rate. For example, assume you purchase a $1,000 bond issued by Atlantic Richfield and the interest rate for this bond is 8.5 percent. In this situation, you receive interest of $85 ($1,000 × .085 = $85) a year from the corporation. Atlantic Richfield pays the interest every six months in $42.50 installments.

Most beginning investors think that a $1,000 bond is always worth $1,000. In reality, the price of a bond may fluctuate until its maturity date. Changes in the overall

table 21.4 Investment Alternatives

Traditional investments involve less risk than high-risk investments.

Traditional	High Risk
Bank accounts	Margin transactions
Corporate and government bonds	Short transactions
Common stock	Stock options
Preferred stock	Commodities
Mutual funds	Precious metals
Real estate	Gemstones
	Coins
	Antiques/collectibles

interest rates in the economy are the primary cause of most bond price fluctuations. For example, when overall interest rates in the economy are rising, the market value of existing bonds with a fixed interest rate typically declines. They may then be purchased for less than their face value. By holding such bonds until maturity or until overall interest rates decline (causing the bond's market value to increase), bond owners can realize increased profit in addition to interest income.

A typical corporate bond transaction is illustrated in Table 21.5. Assume that on October 21, 1992, you purchased an 8.125 percent corporate bond issued by AT&T Corporation. Your cost for the bond was $910 plus a $10 commission, for a total investment of $920. Also assume that you held the bond until October 21, 2000, and then sold it at its current market value of $1,020. As illustrated in Table 21.5, your total return for this bond transaction, including interest, is $740. Even though this AT&T bond increased in value, one of the principal disadvantages of corporate bond investments is that they lack the growth potential offered by stock, mutual fund, and real estate investments.

We should point out that everything in the bond investment illustrated in Table 21.5 went "as planned." But remember that the price of a corporate bond can decrease and that interest payments and eventual repayment may be a problem for a corporation that encounters financial difficulty. When the LTV Corporation filed for reorganization under the provisions of the U.S. Bankruptcy Act, LTV bonds immediately dropped in value because of questions concerning the prospects of repayment.

The investing world doesn't have to be a jungle.
Beginning investors often feel that the investment world is a jungle because of the number of different investment alternatives. With the aid of a financial advisor and the mutual funds offered by companies like Dreyfus, it is possible to obtain your financial goals.

Convertible Bonds Some corporations prefer to issue convertible bonds because they carry a lower interest rate than nonconvertible bonds—by about 1 to 2 percent. In return for accepting a lower interest rate, owners of convertible bonds have the opportunity for increased investment growth. For example, assume you purchase Westinghouse Electric's $1,000 corporate bond that is convertible to 64.5 shares of the company's common stock. This means you could convert the bond to common stock whenever the price of the company's stock is $15.50 (1,000 ÷ 64.5 = $15.50) or higher.

table 21.5 Sample Corporate Bond Transaction for AT&T Corporation

Assumptions: face value, $1,000; annual interest, 8.125 percent; maturity date, 2022; purchased October 21, 1992, for $910; sold October 21, 2000, for $1,020

Costs When Purchased		Return When Sold	
1 bond @ $910	$910	1 bond @ $1,020	$1,020
Plus commission	+ 10	Minus commission	− 10
Total investment	$920	Total return	$1,010

Transaction Summary

Total return when sold	$1,010
Minus total investment	− 920
Profit from bond sale	$ 90
Plus interest (8 years)	+ 650
Total return for this transaction	$ 740

However, owners may opt not to convert their bonds to common stock even if the market value of the common stock does increase to $15.50 or more. The reason for not exercising the conversion feature is quite simple. As the market value of the common stock increases, the price of the convertible bond also increases. By not converting to common stock, bondholders enjoy interest income from the bond, in addition to the increased bond value caused by the price movement of the common stock.

Government Bonds The federal government sells bonds and securities to finance both the national debt and the government's ongoing activities. Generally, investors choose from four different types of U.S. government bonds:

1. *Treasury bills*—A treasury bill, sometimes called a "T-bill," is sold in a minimum unit of $1,000 and has maturities that range from thirteen weeks to fifty-two weeks.
2. *Treasury notes*—A treasury note is issued in $1,000 units with a maturity of more than one year but not more than ten years.
3. *Treasury bonds*—A treasury bond is issued in minimum units of $1,000 and has maturities ranging from ten to thirty years.
4. *Savings bonds*—Series EE bonds, often called U.S. savings bonds, are purchased for one-half of their maturity value. Thus, a $100 bond costs $50 when purchased. *Note:* If the income derived from savings bonds is used to pay college tuition, it is exempt from federal taxation.

The main reason investors choose U.S. government bonds is that they consider them risk-free. The other side of the coin is that these bonds pay a lower interest than most other investments.

municipal bond a debt security issued by a state or local government

general obligation bond a bond backed by the full faith, credit, and unlimited taxing power of the government unit that issued it

revenue bond a bond repaid from the income generated by the government-sponsored project it is designed to finance

Like the federal government, state and local governments sell bonds to obtain financing. A **municipal bond**, sometimes called a "muni," is a debt security issued by a state or local government. These bonds are classified as either general obligation bonds or revenue bonds. A **general obligation bond** is backed by the full faith, credit, and unlimited taxing power of the government unit that issued it. A **revenue bond** is repaid from the income generated by the government-sponsored project it is designed to finance. One of the most important features of municipal bonds is that the interest on them may be exempt from federal taxes. Whether or not the interest on municipal bonds is tax exempt often depends on how the funds obtained from their sale are used. *It is your responsibility, as an investor, to determine whether or not the interest paid by municipal bonds is taxable.*

Although both general obligation and revenue bonds are relatively safe, defaults have occurred in recent years. The largest municipal bond default in recent history occurred when Washington Public Power Supply was unable to pay off its debt on municipal bonds worth more than $2 billion, and thousands of investors lost money. Thus, municipal bonds, like all other investments, must be carefully evaluated.

Common Stock

How do you make money by buying common stock? Basically, there are three ways: through dividend payments, through an increase in the value of the stock, or through stock splits.

Dividend Payments One of the reasons why many stockholders invest in common stock is *dividend income.* Although corporations are under no legal obligation to pay dividends, most corporate board members like to keep stockholders happy (and prosperous). Therefore, board members usually declare dividends if the corporation's after-tax profits are sufficient to do so. A corporation may pay stock dividends in place of—or in addition to—cash dividends. A **stock dividend** is a dividend in the form of additional stock. It is paid to shareholders just as cash dividends are paid: in proportion to the number of shares owned. An individual stockholder may sell the additional stock to obtain income or retain it to increase the total value of her or his stock holdings.

stock dividend a dividend in the form of additional stock

Increase in Dollar Value Another way to make money on stock investments is through capital gains. A **capital gain** is the difference between a security's purchase price and selling price. To earn a capital gain, you must sell when the market value of the stock is higher than the original purchase price. The **market value** is the price of one share of the stock at a particular time. It is determined solely by the interaction of buyers and sellers in the various stock markets. If the market value of a stock increases, you must decide whether to sell the stock at the higher price or to continue to hold it. Let's assume that on June 18, 1997, you purchase 100 shares of General Mills at a cost of $29 a share and that you pay $55 in commission charges, for a total investment of $2,955. Let's also assume that you hold your 100 shares until June 18, 2000, and then sell the General Mills stock for $40 a share. Your total return on investment is shown in Table 21.6. You realized a profit of $1,085 because you received dividends totaling $1.10 a share and because the stock's market value increased by $11 a share. Of course, if the stock's market value had decreased, or if the firm's board of directors had voted to reduce or omit dividends, your return would have been less than the total dollar return illustrated in Table 21.6.

capital gain the difference between a security's purchase price and selling price

market value the price of one share of a stock at a particular time

Generally, the stock market is described as either a bull market or a bear market. A **bull market** is a market in which average stock prices are increasing. A **bear market** is a market in which average stock prices are declining. Similarly, a *bull* is an investor who expects prices to go up; a *bear* is an investor who expects prices to go down.

bull market a market in which average stock prices are increasing

bear market a market in which average stock prices are declining

Stock Splits Directors of many corporations feel there is an optimal price range within which their firm's stock is most attractive to investors. When the market value increases beyond that range, they may declare a *stock split* to bring the price down. A **stock split** is the division of each outstanding share of a corporation's stock into a greater number of shares.

stock split the division of each outstanding share of a corporation's stock into a greater number of shares

The most common stock splits result in one, two, or three new shares for each original share. For example, in 2000 the board of directors of Cisco Systems approved a two-for-one stock split. After this split, a stockholder who originally owned 100 shares owned 200 shares. The value of an original share was proportionally reduced. In the case of Cisco Systems, the market value per share was reduced to approximately half of the stock's value before the two-for-one stock split. Every shareholder retained his or her proportional ownership of the firm. Although there are no guarantees, the stock is more attractive to the investing public because of the potential for a rapid increase in dollar value. This attraction is based on the belief that most corporations split their stock only when their financial future is improving and on the upswing.

table 21.6 Sample Common-Stock Transaction for General Mills

Assumptions: 100 shares of common stock purchased on June 18, 1997 for $29 a share; 100 shares sold on June 18, 2000, for $40 a share; total dividends of $1.10 a share

Costs When Purchased		Return When Sold	
100 shares @ $29	$2,900	100 shares @ $40	$4,000
Plus commission	+ 55	Minus commission	− 70
Total investment	$2,955	Total return	$3,930

Transaction Summary

Total return	$3,930
Minus total investment	− 2,955
Profit from stock sale	$ 975
Plus total dividends (3 years)	+ 110
Total return for this transaction	$1,085

Preferred Stock

As we noted in Chapter 20, a firm's preferred stockholders must receive their dividends before common stockholders are paid any dividend. Moreover, the terms of payment of a preferred-stock dividend are specified on the stock certificate. And the owners of preferred stock have first claim, after bond owners and general creditors, on corporate assets if the firm is dissolved or enters bankruptcy. These features tend to provide the holders of preferred stocks with an added degree of safety and a more predictable income than the holders of common stock.

In addition, owners of preferred stock may gain through special features offered with certain stock issues. Owners of *cumulative* preferred stocks are assured that omitted dividends will be paid to them before common stockholders receive any dividends. Owners of *convertible* preferred stock may profit through growth as well as dividends. When the value of a firm's common stock increases, the market value of its convertible preferred stock also grows. Convertible preferred stock thus combines the lower risk of preferred stock with the possibility of greater speculative gain through conversion to common stock.

Mutual Funds

mutual fund a professionally managed investment vehicle that combines and invests the funds of many individual investors

Today investors *love* their mutual fund investments. In 1970 there were only about 400 mutual funds. In mid-2000, there were over 7,500 mutual funds and the number of funds continues to grow. A **mutual fund** combines and invests the funds of many investors under the guidance of a professional manager. The major advantages of a mutual fund are its professional management and its diversification, or investment in a wide variety of securities. Diversification spells safety, because an occasional loss incurred with one security is usually offset by gains from other investments.

Mutual Fund Shares and Fees

A *closed-end* mutual fund sells shares in the fund to investors only when the fund is originally organized. And only a specified number of shares are made available at that time. Once all the shares are sold, an investor must purchase shares from some other investor who is willing to sell them. The mutual fund itself is under no obligation to buy back shares from investors. Shares of closed-end mutual funds are traded on the floor of stock exchanges like the NYSE or in the over-the-counter market. The investment company sponsoring an *open-end* mutual fund issues and sells new shares to any investor who requests them. It also buys back shares from investors who wish to sell all or part of their holdings.

net asset value (NAV) current market value of the mutual fund's portfolio minus the mutual fund's liabilities, divided by the number of outstanding shares

The share value for any mutual fund is determined by calculating net asset value. **Net asset value (NAV)** per share is equal to the current market value of the mutual fund's portfolio minus the mutual fund's liabilities, divided by the number of outstanding shares. The following formula can be used to calculate NAV.

$$\text{Net asset value} = \frac{\text{Value of the fund's portfolio} - \text{Liabilities}}{\text{Number of shares outstanding}}$$

For example, assume the portfolio of all investments contained in the Hawthorne Global Mutual Fund has a current market value of \$33 million. The fund also has liabilities of \$3 million. If this mutual fund has 2 million shares outstanding, the net asset value is \$15

$$\text{Net asset value} = \frac{\text{Value of the fund's portfolio} - \text{Liabilities}}{\text{Number of shares outstanding}}$$

$$\text{Net asset value} = \frac{\$33\text{ million} - \$3\text{ million}}{2\text{ million shares}}$$

$$\text{Net asset value} = \$15$$

For most mutual funds, NAV is calculated at least once a day and is reported in newspapers, financial publications, and the Internet.

With regard to costs, there are two types of mutual funds: load and no-load funds. An individual who invests in a *load fund* pays a sales charge every time he or she purchases shares. This charge may be as high as 8.5 percent for investments under $10,000. The purchaser of shares in a *no-load fund* pays no sales charges at all. No-load funds offer the same type of investment opportunities as load funds. Because they do, you should investigate them further before deciding which type of mutual fund is right for you.

Mutual funds also collect a yearly management fee of about 0.5 to 1 percent of the total dollar amount of assets in the fund. In addition, some funds charge a redemption fee (sometimes called a "contingent deferred sales fee") of 1 to 5 percent of the total amount withdrawn from a mutual fund. Finally, some mutual funds charge a 12b-1 fee (sometimes referred to as a *distribution fee*) to defray the costs of advertising and marketing a mutual fund. Approved by the Securities and Exchange Commission in 1980, annual 12b-1 fees are calculated on the value of a fund's assets and are approximately 1 percent of the fund's assets per year.

Today, mutual funds can also be classified as A, B, or C shares. With A shares, investors pay commissions when they purchase shares in the mutual fund. With B shares, investors pay commissions when money is withdrawn or shares are sold during the first five to seven years. With C shares, investors pay no commissions to buy or sell shares, but must pay higher ongoing 12b-1 fees.

spotLight

Mutual fund owners

Mutual fund shareholders by age.

Age	Share
18–33	22%
34–52	51%
53 or older	27%

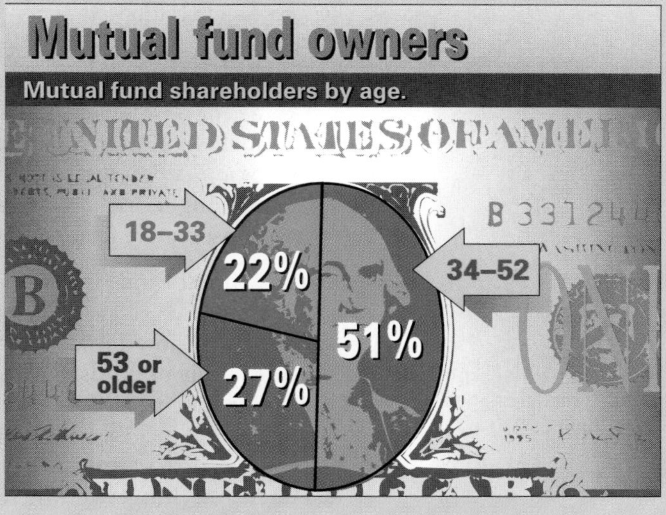

Source: Copyright 2000, USA TODAY. Reprinted with permission.

Mutual Fund Investments It would take a whole book to describe all the mutual funds available today. In summary, however, mutual fund managers tailor their investment portfolios to provide growth, income, or a combination of both. The following list describes the major categories of mutual funds in terms of the types of securities they invest in:

- *Aggressive growth funds* invest in stocks whose prices are expected to increase dramatically in a short period of time.
- *Balanced funds* apportion their investments among common stocks, preferred stock, and bonds.
- *Bond funds* invest in federal, municipal, and/or corporate bonds that provide investors with interest income.
- *Global funds* invest in stocks, bonds, and other securities issued by firms throughout the world, including the United States.
- *Growth funds* invest in the common stock of well-managed, rapidly growing corporations.
- *Growth-income funds* invest in common and preferred stocks that pay good dividends *and* are expected to increase in market value.
- *Income funds* invest in stocks and bonds that pay high dividends and interest.
- *Index funds* invest in common stocks that react in the same way as the overall stock market.

Using the Internet

Looking for an investment? Today, more and more investors are using the Internet to access information provided by brokerage firms like Charles Schwab Investments. These same online web sites allow investors to buy and sell stocks, bonds, and mutual funds. You can connect to the Charles Schwab web site at http://www. schwab. com. There you can

- open an account
- get free quotes and charts
- create your own home page
- demo customer research
- evaluate stocks
- discuss the market on message boards

and much more.

- *International funds* invest in foreign stocks sold in securities markets throughout the world. Unlike global funds, which invest in stocks issued by companies in both foreign nations and the United States, a true international fund invests outside the United States.
- *Money-market funds* invest in short-term corporate obligations and government securities that pay interest.
- *Sector funds* invest in companies within the same industry. Examples of sectors include Biotech, Science, and Technology and Computers.
- *Small-cap funds* invest in smaller companies that offer higher growth potential and higher risk when compared with funds that invest in larger, more conservative funds.

Mutual funds designed to meet just about any conceivable investment objective are available. To help investors obtain their investment objectives, most investment companies now allow shareholders to switch from one fund to another fund within the same family of funds. A **family of funds** exists when one investment company manages a group of mutual funds. For example, shareholders, at their option, can change from an AIM Global Aggressive Growth fund to the AIM Value fund. Generally investors may give instructions to switch from one fund to another fund within the same family either in writing, over the telephone, or via the Internet. Charges for exchanges, if any, are small for each transaction. For funds that do charge, the fee may be as low as $5 per transaction.

family of funds a group of mutual funds managed by one investment company

Generally speaking, the decision-making of a mutual fund manager is somewhat secretive and limited to public display. However, Internet-based MetaMarket.com, believes providing continuous information about what its fund managers are thinking and how they are making their decisions will differentiate their product. Therefore, uncharacteristically, the firm posts volumes of notes on its site describing the fund's strategy and even presents an online camera-shot of traders working in the office to create the sense of an open-door policy with clients.[7]

Real Estate

Real estate ownership represents one of the best hedges against inflation, but it, too, has its risks. A piece of property in a poor location, for example, can actually decrease in value—as a number of people who bought land in the Florida Everglades from unscrupulous promoters learned to their dismay. Table 21.7 cites some of the many factors you should consider before investing in real estate.

table 21.7 Real Estate Checklist

Although real estate offers one of the best hedges against inflation, not all property increases in value. Many factors should be considered before investing in real estate.

Evaluation of property	Inspection of the surrounding neighborhood	Other factors
Is the property priced competitively with similar property?	What are the present zoning requirements?	Why are the present owners selling the property?
What type of financing, if any, is available?	Is the neighborhood's population increasing or decreasing?	How long will you have to hold the property before selling it to someone else?
How much are the taxes?	What is the average income of people in the area?	How much profit can you reasonably expect to obtain?
	What is the state of repair of surrounding property? Do most of the buildings and houses need repair?	Is there a chance that the property value will decrease?

There are, of course, disadvantages to any investment, and real estate is no exception. If you want to sell your property, you must find an interested buyer with the ability to obtain enough money to complete the transaction. Finding such a buyer can be difficult if loan money is scarce, the real estate market is in a decline, or you overpaid for a piece of property. If you are forced to hold your investment longer than you originally planned, taxes, interest, and installment payments can be a heavy burden. As a rule, real estate increases in value and eventually sells at a profit, but there are no guarantees. The degree of your success depends on how well you evaluate different alternatives.

High-Risk Investment Techniques

LEARNING OBJECTIVE 5 Describe high-risk investment techniques.

As defined earlier in the chapter, a high-risk investment is one made in the uncertain hope of earning a relatively large profit in a short time. (See the high-risk investment category in Table 21.4.) Most high-risk investments become so because of the methods used by investors to earn a quick profit. These methods can lead to large losses as well as to impressive gains. They should not be used by anyone who does not fully understand the risks involved.

Buying Stock on Margin

An investor buys stock *on margin* by borrowing part of the purchase price, usually from a stock brokerage firm. The **margin requirement** is the portion of the price of a stock that cannot be borrowed. This requirement is set by the Federal Reserve Board.

margin requirement the portion of the price of a stock that cannot be borrowed

Today investors can borrow up to half the cost of a stock purchase. But why would they want to do so? Simply because they can buy twice as much stock by buying on margin. Suppose an investor expects the market price of Abbott Lab's common stock to increase in the next month or two. Let's say this investor has enough money to purchase 500 shares of the stock. But if she buys on margin, she can purchase an additional 500 shares. If the price of the Abbott Lab's stock increases by $5 per share, her profit will be $5 × 500, or $2,500, if she pays cash. But it will be $5 × 1,000, or $5,000, if she buys on margin. That is, by buying more shares on margin, she will earn double the profit (less the interest she pays on the borrowed money and customary commission charges).

Financial leverage—a topic covered in Chapter 20—is the use of borrowed funds to increase the return on an investment. When margin is used as leverage, the investor's profit is earned by both the borrowed money and the investor's own money. The investor retains all the profit and pays interest only for the temporary use of the borrowed funds. Note that the stock purchased on margin serves as collateral for the borrowed funds. Before you become a margin investor, you should consider two factors. First, if the market price of the purchased stock does not increase as quickly as expected, interest costs mount and eventually drain your profit. Second, if the price of the margined stock falls, the leverage works against you. That is, because you have purchased twice as much stock, you lose twice as much money.

If the value of a stock you bought on margin decreases to approximately half its original price, you will receive a *margin call* from the brokerage firm. You must then provide additional cash or securities to serve as collateral for the borrowed money. If you cannot provide additional collateral, the stock is sold and the proceeds are used to pay off the loan. Any funds remaining after the loan is paid off are returned to you.

Selling Short

Normally, you buy stocks expecting that they will increase in value and can then be sold at a profit. This procedure is referred to as **buying long.** However, many securities decrease in value, for various reasons. You can use a procedure called *selling short* to

buying long buying stock with the expectation that it will increase in value and can then be sold at a profit

selling short the process of selling stock that an investor does not actually own but has borrowed from a brokerage firm and will repay at a later date

make a profit when the price of an individual stock is falling. **Selling short** is the process of selling stock that an investor does not actually own but has borrowed from a brokerage firm and will repay at a later date. The idea is to sell at today's higher price and then buy later at a lower price.

To make a profit from a short transaction, you must proceed as follows:

1. Arrange to borrow a certain number of shares of a particular stock from a brokerage firm.
2. Sell the borrowed stock immediately, assuming that the price of the stock will drop in a reasonably short time.
3. After the price drops, buy the same number of shares that were sold in step 2.
4. Give the newly purchased stock to the brokerage firm in return for the stock borrowed in step 1.

Your profit is the difference between the amount received when the stock is sold in step 2 and the amount paid for the stock in step 3. For example, assume that you think that Sony Corporation's stock is overvalued at $84 a share. You also believe the stock will decrease in value over the next three to four months. You call your broker and arrange to borrow 100 shares of Sony stock (step 1). The broker then sells your borrowed Sony stock for you at the current market price of $84 a share (step 2). Also assume that three months later, the Sony stock has dropped to $72 a share. You instruct your broker to purchase 100 shares of Sony stock at the current lower price (step 3). The newly purchased Sony stock is given to the brokerage firm to repay the borrowed stock (step 4). In this example, you made $1,200 by selling short ($8,400 selling price − $7,200 purchase price = $1,200 profit). Naturally, the $1,200 profit must be reduced by the commissions you paid to the broker for buying and selling the Sony stock.

People often ask where the broker obtains the stock for a short transaction. The broker probably borrows the stock from other investors who have purchased Sony stock through a margin arrangement or from investors who have left stock certificates on deposit with the brokerage firm. As a result, the person who is selling short must pay any dividends declared on the borrowed stock. The most obvious danger when selling short, of course, is that a loss can result if the stock's market value increases instead of decreases. If the market value of the stock increases after the investor has sold it in step 2, he or she loses money.

A great opportunity to sell short, for those who were willing to take the risk, was during March 2000, when stock values of many recently formed dot-coms fell dramatically in a short time. For example, after losing more than $100 million due to start-up advertising and other operational costs Pets.com, a supplier of pet products, failed to generate the sales revenue to sustain the firm for the long run. As a result, investors lost confidence in the firm's value and their shares fell 85 percent from their high in just a few months.[8]

Other High-Risk Investments

We have already discussed two high-risk investments—margin transactions and selling short. Other high-risk investments include the following:

Stock options	Gemstones
Commodities	Coins
Precious metals	Antiques and collectibles

Without exception, investments of this kind are normally referred to as high-risk investments for one reason or another. For example, the gold market has many unscrupulous dealers who sell worthless gold-plated lead coins to unsuspecting, uninformed investors. With each of the investments in this last category, it is extremely important that you deal with reputable dealers and recognized investment firms. It pays to be careful. *Although investments in this category can lead to large dollar gains, they should not be used by anyone who does not fully understand all the potential risks involved.*

Diversification to Reduce Risk

diversification the process of spreading assets among several types of investments to lessen risk

Diversification is the process of spreading assets among several types of investments to lessen risk. Many financial planners suggest grouping investments into four categories. The following list ranks these categories according to level of risk and notes the type of investments that might be included in each level:

- *Level 1.* This level stresses *financial security*. It includes certificates of deposits, savings accounts, and money-market funds.
- *Level 2.* This level stresses *safety and income*. Typical investments include government bonds, high-grade corporate bonds, selected mutual funds, and utility stocks.
- *Level 3.* This level stresses *growth*. Blue-chip stocks, growth-oriented mutual funds, rental property, and certain growth stocks are included in this category.
- *Level 4.* This level stresses *high-risk investments*. Stock options, commodities, very speculative stocks, margin transactions, selling short, and other high-risk investments are usually found at this level.

While people who are ultraconservative may never progress pass level 1, more aggressive investors may invest in the securities listed in level 2 and level 3. The investments in level 4 are often considered too speculative for the average investor. Above all, the principal of diversification avoids the problem of putting all your eggs in one basket—a common mistake among investors.

Sources of Financial Information

LEARNING OBJECTIVE

6 Use financial information to evaluate investment alternatives.

A wealth of information is available to investors. Sources include the Internet, newspapers, brokerage firm reports, business periodicals, corporate reports, and investors' services.

The Internet

Today, more people have access to information provided by computers located in their homes or at libraries, universities, or businesses than ever before. And this number is growing. More important, a wealth of information is available on most investment and personal finance topics. For example, you can obtain interest rates for certificates of deposits, current price information for stocks, bonds, and mutual funds, and experts' recommendation to buy, hold, or sell an investment. You can even trade securities online just by pushing the right button on your computer keyboard.

Because the Internet makes so much information available, you need to use it selectively. One of the web search engines like Yahoo! (www.yahoo.com), Alta Vista (www.altavista.com), or Infoseek (www.infoseek.com) can help you locate the information you really need. These search engines allow you to do a word search for the personal finance or investment alternative you want to explore.

Corporations, investment companies that sponsor mutual funds, and federal, state, and local governments also have a home page where you can obtain valuable information. You may want to explore these web sites for two reasons. First, they are easily accessible. All you have to do is type in the web address or use one of the above search engines to locate the site. Second, the information on these sites may be more up to date than printed material obtained from published sources. Especially useful is the information provided on the home page of the Securities and Exchange Commission (www.sec.gov).

In addition, you can access professional advisory services—a topic discussed later in this section—for information on stocks, bonds, mutual funds, and other investment alternatives. While some

Using the Internet

Online brokerage firms like American Express (**http://www.americanexpress.com/direct**), Charles Schwab (**http://www.schwab.com**), Datek (**http://www.datek.com**), and CSFBdirect (**http://www.csfbdirect.com**) are among the top online trading sites and, of course, offer information about online stock trading.

Financial news you can use. Because the Internet makes so much information available, you need to use it selectively. A web site like CNBC.com can help you evaluate potential stocks, bonds, and mutual funds, track the investments in your portfolio, and access a wealth of information about personal finance topics.

of the information provided by these services is free, there is a charge for the more detailed information you may need to evaluate an investment. Although it is impossible to list all the Internet sites related to investments, those listed in Table 21.8 will get you started.

Newspaper Coverage of Securities Transactions

Most local newspapers carry several pages of business news, including reports of securities transactions. The *Wall Street Journal* (published on weekdays) and *Barron's* (published once a week) are devoted almost entirely to financial and economic news. Both include complete coverage of transactions on all major securities exchanges.

Securities transactions are reported as long tables of figures that tend to look somewhat forbidding. However, they are easy to decipher when you know how to read them. Because transactions involving stocks, bonds, and mutual funds are reported differently, we shall examine each type of report separately.

Common and Preferred Stocks

Transactions involving common and preferred stocks are reported together in the same table. This table usually looks like the top section of Figure 21.3. Stocks are listed alphabetically. Your first task is to move down the table to find the stock you're interested in. To read the *stock quotation*, you read across the table. The highlighted line in Figure 21.3 gives detailed information about common stock issued by Eastman Kodak Corporation.

table 21.8 Internet Sites that Provide Useful Information for Evaluating Investments

The following five Internet sites provide information that you can use to establish a financial plan and begin an investment program.

Sponsor and Description	Web Address
1. The **Business Week Online** web site provides financial news and tutorials that can help both beginning and experienced investors.	**www.businessweek.com**
2. The **Quicken** web site provides information about investments, home mortgages, insurance, taxes, banking and credit, and different types of retirement programs.	**www.quicken.com**
3. **The Financial Center, Inc.** web site helps individuals calculate the cost of purchasing investments, homes, and autos. The site can also help you establish an investment program.	**www.financecenter.com**
4. **The Motley Fool** web site provides lighthearted but excellent investment advice. It also provides educational materials for beginning investors.	**www.fool.com**
5. The **Invest-O-Rama** web site contains a useful web directory of more than 11,500 links to investment information. It also provides articles and research tools that can help you become a better investor.	**www.investorama.com**

52 WEEKS HI	LO	STOCK	SYM	DIV	YLD %	PE	VOL 100s	HI	LO	CLOSE	NET CHG
24	18^{19}	Eastgroup	EGP	1.64	7.1	21	398	23^{50}	23^{13}	23^{19}	– 0^{31}
23^{25}	18^{75}	Eastgroup	pfA	2.25	9.9	...	34	22^{75}	22^{50}	22^{75}	+ 0^{31}
54^{75}	33^{63}	EastmanChm	EMN	1.76	3.7	18	5342	48^{38}	46^{44}	47^{69}	+ 0^{69}
66^{63}	35^{31}	EKodak	EK	1.76	4.3	8	21123	42^{19}	39^{75}	40^{63}	– 1^{38}

1. Highest price paid for one share of Eastman Kodak during the past 52 weeks: $66.63
2. Lowest price paid for one share of Eastman Kodak during the past 52 weeks: $35.31
3. Name (often abbreviated) of the corporation: Eastman Kodak
4. Ticker symbol or letters that identify a stock for trading: EK
5. Total dividends paid per share during the last 12 months: $1.76
6. Yield percentage, or the percentage of return based on the current dividend and current price of the stock: $1.76 ÷ $40.63 = 0.043 = 4.3%
7. Price earnings (PE) ratio—the price of a share of stock divided by the corporation's earnings per share of stock outstanding over the last 12 months: 8
8. Number of shares of Eastman Kodak traded during the day, expressed in hundreds of shares: 2,112,300
9. Highest price paid for one share of Eastman Kodak during the day: $42.19
10. Lowest price paid for one share of Eastman Kodak during the day: $39.75
11. Price paid in the last transaction of the day: $40.63
12. Difference between the price paid for the last share sold today and the price paid for the last share sold on the previous day: $1.38 (in Wall Street terms, Eastman Kodak "closed down $1.38" on this day).

1	2	3	4	5	6	7	8	9	10	11	12
52 WEEKS HI	LO	STOCK	SYM	DIV	YLD %	PE	VOL 100s	HI	LO	CLOSE	NET CHG
24	1819	Eastgroup	EGP	1.64	7.1	21	398	2350	2313	2319	– 031
2325	1875	Eastgroup	pfA	2.25	9.9	...	34	2275	2250	2275	+ 031
5475	3363	EastmanChm	EMN	1.76	3.7	18	5342	4838	4644	4769	+ 069
6663	3531	EKodak	EK	1.76	4.3	8	21123	4219	3975	4063	– 138

figure 21.3

Reading Stock Quotations

Reproduced at the top of the figure is a portion of the stock quotations listed on the New York Stock Exchange. At the bottom is an enlargement of the same information. The numbers above each of the enlarged columns correspond to the numbered entries in the list of explanations that appears in the middle of the figure.

Source: *Wall Street Journal*, January 9, 2001, p. C6.

If a corporation has more than one stock issue, the common stock is listed first. A preferred stock issue is indicated by the letters *pf* that follow the company's name in the symbol column and is listed below the firm's common-stock issue.

Bonds Purchases and sales of bonds are reported in tables like that shown at the top of Figure 21.4. In bond quotations, prices are given as a percentage of the face value, which is usually $1,000. Thus, to find the actual price paid, you must multiply the face value ($1,000) by the quotation listed in the newspaper. For example, a price quoted as 84 translates to a selling price of $840 ($1,000 × 84 percent, or .84, = $840). The second row of Figure 21.4 gives detailed information for the Lucent Technologies $1,000 bond, which pays 7¼ percent interest and matures in 2006.

Mutual Funds Purchases and sales of shares of mutual funds are reported in tables like the one shown in Figure 21.5. As in reading stock and bond quotations, your first task is to move down the table to find the mutual fund you're interested in. Then, to

figure 21.4

Reading Bond Quotations

Reproduced at the top of the figure is a portion of the bond quotations as reported by the *Wall Street Journal*. At the bottom is an enlargement of the same information. The numbers above each of the enlarged columns correspond to numbered entries in the list of explanations that appears in the middle of the figure.

BONDS	CUR YLD	VOL	CLOSE	NET CHG
Lucent 6.9s01	7.0	60	99	– 1/4
Lucent 7 1/4 06	7.5	546	97 3/8	+ 1
MSC Sf 7 7/8 04	cv	4	87	– 1
Malan 9 1/2 04	cv	3	85	+ 1/2

1. Abbreviated name of the corporation (Lucent for Lucent Technologies), the bond's interest rate (7 1/4% of its face value, or \$1,000 x .0725 = \$72.50, and the year of maturity (2006)
2. Current yield, determined by dividing the dollar amount of annual interest by the current price of the bond (\$72.50 ÷ \$973.75 = 7.5%)
3. Number (volume) of bonds traded during the day: 546
4. Price paid in the last transaction of the day: \$1,000 x 97.375% = \$973.75
5. Difference between the price paid for the last bond today and the price paid for the last bond on the previous day: \$10 (\$10 more than the day before). In Wall Street terms, the Lucent Technologies bond "closed up 1" on this day.

1	2	3	4	5
BONDS	CUR YLD	VOL	CLOSE	NET CHG
Lucent 6.9s01	7.0	60	99	– 1/4
Lucent 7 1/4 06	7.5	546	97 3/8	+ 1
MSC Sf 7 7/8 04	cv	4	87	– 1
Malan 9 1/2 04	cv	3	85	+ 1/2

Source: *Wall Street Journal*, January 9, 2001, p. C17.

figure 21.5

Reading Mutual Fund Quotations

Reproduced at the top of the figure is a portion of the mutual fund quotations as reported by the *Wall Street Journal*. At the bottom is an enlargement of the same information. The numbers above each of the enlarged columns correspond to numbered entries in the list of explanations that appears in the middle of the figure.

NAME	NAV	NET CHG	YTD %RET
TxFSI	10.49	+0.01	+ 1.1
US Eq	11.66	+0.12	+ 1.0
First American Cl A			
Balance p	11.39	+0.10	+ 0.2
EqIdx	24.60	+0.23	– 0.5

1. The name of the mutual fund: First American Balance Fund. The "p" after the fund name indicates that a 12b-1 distribution fee is charged by the company sponsoring this fund.
2. The net asset value (NAV) is the value of one share of First American Balance Fund: \$11.39.
3. The difference between the net asset value today and the net asset value on the previous trading day: \$0.10 (in Wall Street terms, First American Balance Fund closed up \$0.10 on this day).
4. The last column (YTD % RET) gives the total return for First American Balance Fund for the year to date: +0.2 percent.

1	2	3	4
NAME	NAV	NET CHG	YTD %RET
TxFSI	10.49	+0.01	+ 1.1
US Eq	11.66	+0.12	+ 1.0
First American Cl A			
Balance p	11.39	+0.10	+ 0.2
EqIdx	24.60	+0.23	– 0.5

Source: *Wall Street Journal*, January 11, 2001, p. C23.

find the mutual fund price quotation, read across the table. Figure 21.5 gives detailed information for the First American Balanced mutual fund.

Other Sources of Financial Information

In addition to the Internet and newspaper coverage, other sources, which include brokerage firm reports, business periodicals, corporate reports, and investors' services, offer detailed and varied information about investment alternatives.

Brokerage Firm Reports

Brokerage firms employ financial analysts to prepare detailed reports on individual corporations and their securities. Such reports are based on the corporation's sales, profits or losses, management, and planning, plus other information on the company, its industry, demand for its products, and its efforts to develop new products. The reports, which may include buy or sell recommendations, are usually provided free to the clients of full-service brokerage firms. Firms offering this service include Paine Webber, Solomon Smith Barney, Merrill Lynch, and most other full-service brokerage firms. Brokerage firm reports may also be available from discount brokerage firms for a fee.

Would you make investment decisions based on information provided by a couple of fools? Well, it depends on who the fools are. David and Tom Gardner started the Motley Fool web site, which is recognized as one of the best sources of financial and investment information available today.

Business Periodicals

Business magazines like *Business Week, Fortune, Forbes*, and *Harvard Business Review* provide not only general economic news but also detailed financial information about individual corporations. Trade or industry publications like *Advertising Age* and *Business Insurance* include information about firms in a specific industry. News magazines like *U.S. News & World Report, Time*, and *Newsweek* feature financial news regularly. *Money, Kiplinger's Personal Finance Magazine, Consumer Reports*, and similar magazines provide information and advice designed to improve your investment skills. These periodicals are available at libraries and are sold at newsstands and by subscription.

Corporate Reports

Publicly held corporations must send their stockholders annual and quarterly reports. These reports include a description of the company's performance provided by the corporation's top management, information about the firm's products or services, and detailed financial statements that readers can use to evaluate the firm's actual performance. In addition, a corporation issuing a new security must—by law—prepare a prospectus and ensure that copies are distributed to potential investors. A **prospectus** is a detailed, written description of a new security, the issuing corporation, and the corporation's top management. A corporation's prospectus and its annual and quarterly reports are available to the general public. For more information on using annual reports to research a stock investment, read Adapting to Change.

prospectus a detailed written description of a new security, the issuing corporation, and the corporation's top management

Investors' Services

For annual fees ranging from $30 to $500 or more, various investors' services provide information about investments to subscribers. Information from investors' services may also be available at university and public libraries. Four of the most widely accepted investors' services are Standard & Poor's, Value Line, Mergent FIS, Inc., and Moody's Investors Service.

Moody's and Standard & Poor's provide information that can be used to determine the quality and risk associated with bond issues. The bond ratings used by Moody's range from Aaa to C. Standard & Poor's ratings range from AAA to D. Quality bonds are rated A or higher by both companies and are considered investment grade securities. Bonds with a B rating are considered speculative in nature and may not be suitable for all investors. Bonds with C and D ratings may be in default because of poor prospects of repayment or even continued payment of interest.

Adapting to change

Annual Reports and the Bottom Line!

YOU DID ALL THE RIGHT THINGS! YOU did the research. Based on the research, you decided to purchase 100 shares of a blue-chip corporation. Now you are looking forward to long-term growth, safety, stability, and receiving quarterly dividends. When the first dividend check arrives, you smile, and feel proud that you have reached the status of being "a stockholder."

Then, one day the Annual Report arrives in the mail. You thumb through it and decide that it really is a beautiful publication. Why it must contain 100 pages or more. Look at those glossy pictures: pictures of the key people in the organization and the corporation's products and facilities. There are messages from the CEO and the chairman of the board about the corporation's operations, prospects for the future, and financial strengths. *But*, the really important part of this report is the financial statements and the footnotes contained in the back!

According to the experts, the best investors use an annual report as a research tool to decide if a company's stock is a good investment. An annual report can also be used to help you decide if you want to sell a stock you own. The following four suggestions can help you get to the "bottom line" of a corporation's annual report.

1. *Look at the firm's income statement to determine whether a company is profitable or not.* For many investors, this may be the most important number in a firm's annual report.
2. *Compare the corporation's current income statement and balance sheet with previous accounting statements.* Look at trends for sales, expenses, and profits or losses—all information contained on a firm's income statement. Look at trends for current assets, current liabilities, inventory, total liabilities, and owners' equity—all information contained on a corporation's balance sheet.
3. *Learn how to calculate the following financial ratios and determine how they may change a firm's financial condition.* (Remember that each of these ratios was discussed in Chapter 18—Using Accounting Information.)
   - *Net profit margin*—a measure of how effectively the firm is transforming sales into profits.
   - *Earnings per share*—a measure of the amount the firm earned for each share of stock owned by investors.
   - *Return on equity*—a measure of how successfully the firm invested the owners' money.
   - *Current ratio*—a measure of a firm's ability to pay its current liabilities.
   - *Debt-to-assets ratio*—a measure of whether a company has too much debt.
   - *Inventory turnover*—a measure of how many times each year a firm sells its merchandise inventory.
4. *Examine the footnotes closely and look for red flags that may be in the fine print.* Often the footnotes contain (and sometimes hide) important information.

Based on the information in an annual report, you may decide to buy shares in a corporation or keep the shares you already own. But above all, don't forget to examine each year's annual report. You may be surprised at the information it provides.

Standard & Poor's, Mergent FIS, Inc., and Value Line also rate the companies that issue common and preferred stock. Each investor service provides detailed financial reports. Take a look at the Mergent's research report for General Motors illustrated in Figure 21.6. Notice that there are six main sections. The top section provides information about stock prices, earnings, and dividends. The business, recent developments, and prospects sections describe the company's major operations in detail and provide information about what may happen in the future. The annual financial data section provides important financial data on the company for the past ten years. The final section of the report states where and when the company was incorporated, where its principal office is located, who its transfer agent is, and who it main corporate officers are. Research reports published by Standard & Poor's and Value Line are like Mergent's report and provide similar information.

A number of investors' services provide detailed information on mutual funds. Morningstar, Inc., Standard & Poor's, Lipper Analytical Services, and the Wiesenberger Investment Companies are four widely tapped sources of such information. A portion of a research report for the AIM Value mutual fund is illustrated in Figure 21.7. In addition, various mutual fund newsletters supply financial information to subscribers for a fee.

GENERAL MOTORS CORP.

EXCHANGE	SYM.	REC. PRICE	P/E RATIO	YIELD	MARKET CAP.	RANGE (52-WK.)
NYSE	GM	72 11/16 (12/31/99)	7.8	2.8%	$55.33 bill.	94 7/8 - 59 3/4

INVESTMENT GRADE. GM'S 2000 MODEL YEAR FULL-SIZED SPORT UTILITY VEHICLES ARE EXPECTED TO PROVIDE IMPROVED FUEL ECONOMY OF ONE MILE FOR EVERY GALLON OF FUEL USED.

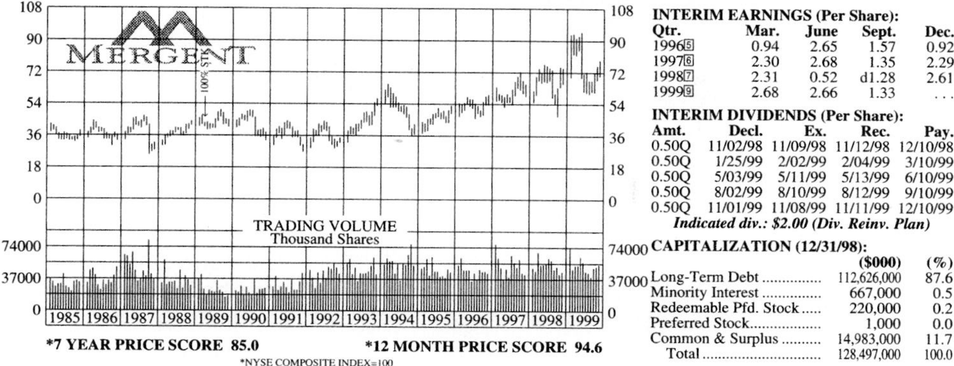

INTERIM EARNINGS (Per Share):

Qtr.	Mar.	June	Sept.	Dec.
1996 [5]	0.94	2.65	1.57	0.92
1997 [6]	2.30	2.68	1.35	2.29
1998 [7]	2.31	0.52	d1.28	2.61
1999 [9]	2.68	2.66	1.33	...

INTERIM DIVIDENDS (Per Share):

Amt.	Decl.	Ex.	Rec.	Pay.
0.50Q	11/02/98	11/09/98	11/12/98	12/10/98
0.50Q	1/25/99	2/02/99	2/04/99	3/10/99
0.50Q	5/03/99	5/11/99	5/13/99	6/10/99
0.50Q	8/02/99	8/10/99	8/12/99	9/10/99
0.50Q	11/01/99	11/08/99	11/11/99	12/10/99

Indicated div.: $2.00 (Div. Reinv. Plan)

CAPITALIZATION (12/31/98):

	($000)	(%)
Long-Term Debt	112,626,000	87.6
Minority Interest	667,000	0.5
Redeemable Pfd. Stock	220,000	0.2
Preferred Stock	1,000	0.0
Common & Surplus	14,983,000	11.7
Total	128,497,000	100.0

BUSINESS:

General Motors is the world's largest auto maker, operating through Chevrolet, Pontiac, Cadillac, Buick, Oldsmobile, GMC Truck and internationally via Holder, OPEL and Vauxhall. GMAC operates the financial and insurance segment of the Company, which includes vehicle leasing and financing. Other product segments include: Hughes Electronics Review, a telecommunications company; Allison Transmission Review, which produces medium and heavy duty automatic transmissions for commercial-duty trucks and buses; and GM Locomotive Group Review, which produces diesel-electric locomotives, diesel engines and locomotive components. GM completed the spin-off of Delphi Automotive Systems in May 1999.

RECENT DEVELOPMENTS:

For the quarter ended 9/30/99, net income climbed sharply to $877.0 million compared with a loss from continuing operations of $309.0 million in the corresponding quarter of the prior year. Results of 1998 excluded income of $500.0 million from discontinued operations. Total net sales and revenues increased 27.6% to $42.79 billion versus $33.53 billion a year ago. Manufactured products sales and revenues increased 29.1% to $36.75 billion from $28.46 billion, while financing revenues grew 10.9% to $3.73 billion versus $3.36 billion in the comparable 1998 period. The increase in income was attributed to continued improvement in the profitability of new vehicles.

PROSPECTS:

On 12/10/99, GM and Fuji Heavy Industries formed a broad stategic alliance that will allow the automakers to collaborate in the design, development and manufacture of cars, trucks and related technology. The Company also outlined a proposal to purchase South Korea's Motor Co. assets, but dosen't wants to pay off the 18.4 trillion won debt. The bid is a part of GM's aggressive strategy to bolster the Company's position in the Asia-Pacific region, which has explosive potential in auto sales in the coming years. Meanwhile, GM's 2000 model year full-size SUVs are expected to provide improved fuel economy of one mile for every gallon of fuel used.

ANNUAL FINANCIAL DATA:

FISCAL YEAR	TOT. REVS. ($mill.)	NET INC. ($mill.)	TOT. ASSETS ($mill.)	OPER. PROFIT %	NET PROFIT %	RET. ON EQUITY %	RET. ON ASSETS %	CURR. RATIO	EARN. PER SH. $	CASH FL. PER SH. $	TANG. BK. VAL. $	DIV. PER SH. $	PRICE RANGE	AVG. P/E RATIO	AVG. YIELD %
12/31/98	**161,315.0**	**[9] 2,956.0**	**257,389.0**	**8.6**	**1.8**	**19.7**	**1.1**	**1.0**	**[9] 4.18**	**19.28**	**6.25**	**2.00**	**76 11/16 - 47 1/16**	**14.8**	**3.2**
12/31/97	178,174.0	[7] 6,698.0	228,888.0	8.6	3.8	38.3	2.9	4.1	[7] 8.62	27.90	6.73	2.00	72 7/16 - 52 1/4	7.2	3.2
12/31/96	164,013.0	[6] 4,953.0	222,142.0	8.8	3.0	21.2	2.2	4.1	[6] 6.06	22.11	8.25	1.60	59 3/8 - 45 3/4	8.7	3.0
12/31/95	168,828.6	[5] 6,932.5	217,123.4	9.9	4.1	29.7	3.2	4.5	[5] 7.28	24.90	15.20	1.10	53 1/8 - 37 1/4	6.2	2.4
12/31/94	154,951.2	[5] 5,658.7	198,598.7	9.8	3.7	42.6	2.8	4.0	[5] 6.20	21.13	1.20	0.80	65 3/8 - 36 1/8	8.2	1.6
12/31/93	138,219.5	[4] 2,465.8	188,202.0	7.1	1.8	40.8	1.3	3.8	[4] 2.13	16.39	...	0.80	57 1/8 - 32	20.9	1.8
12/31/92	132,430.0	[3] d2,621.0	191,014.0	4.2	...	...	...	3.5	[3] d4.85	9.17	...	1.40	44 3/8 - 28 5/8	...	3.8
12/31/91	123,056.0	[2] d4,992.0	184,331.0	3.2	...	...	...	2.6	[2] d8.85	4.96	27.23	1.60	44 3/8 - 26 3/4	...	4.5
12/31/90	124,705.0	[1] d1,986.0	180,237.0	6.3	...	...	...	2.4	[1] d4.09	9.35	31.28	3.00	50 1/2 - 33 1/8	...	7.2
12/31/89	126,932.0	4,224.0	173,298.0	13.0	3.3	11.5	2.4	2.3	6.33	19.24	45.58	3.00	50 1/2 - 39 1/8	7.1	6.7

Statistics are as originally reported. [1] Incl. extraord. chrg. $2.10 bill. [2] Bef. acctg. change chrg. $1.10 bill. [3] Bef. acctg. change, chrg. $20.88 bill & Incl non-recurr chrg. $749.0 mill. fr restruc. [4] Incl. non-recurr chrg. $478.0 mill. [5] Bef. acctg. change chrg. $758.0 mill., 1994; $51.8 mill. ($0.07/sh.), 1995 [6] Bef. disc. opers. gain $10.0 mill. & Incl. non-recurr. chrg. $938,000 [7] Incl. non-recurr. credit $4.30 bill.; chrg. $4.00 bill. [8] Includes long-term debt from GMAC [9] Bef. disc. opers. chrg. $500.0 mill.

OFFICERS:
J. F. Smith Jr., Chmn., C.E.O.
H. J. Pearce, Vice-Chmn.
G. R. Wagoner Jr., Pres., C.O.O.
J. M. Losh, Exec. V.P., C.F.O.

INVESTOR CONTACT: GM Investor Relations, (212) 418-6270

PRINCIPAL OFFICE: 100 Renaissance Center, Detroit, MI 48265-1000

TELEPHONE NUMBER: (313) 556-5000
WEB: www.gm.com

NO. OF EMPLOYEES: 594,000 (avg.)

SHAREHOLDERS: 731,487 ($1 2/3 par - 525,583; class H - 205,904)

ANNUAL MEETING: In Jun.

INCORPORATED: DE, Oct., 1916

INSTITUTIONAL HOLDINGS:
No. of Institutions: 636
Shares Held: 402,470,120
% Held: 62.5

INDUSTRY: Motor vehicles and car bodies (SIC: 3711)

TRANSFER AGENT(S): BankBoston c/o Boston EquiServe Trust Co., Boston, MA

figure 21.6

Mergent's Research Report for the General Motors Corporation

A research report from Mergent is divided into six main parts that describe not only the financial condition of a company, but also its history and the outlook for the future.

Source: *Handbook of Common Stocks*, Winter 1999/2000 (New York: Mergent, Inc., 2000).

Snapshot
AIM Value A

How Has This Fund Performed?
Growth of $10,000
Fund: AIM Value A
Category: Large Value
Index: S&P 500

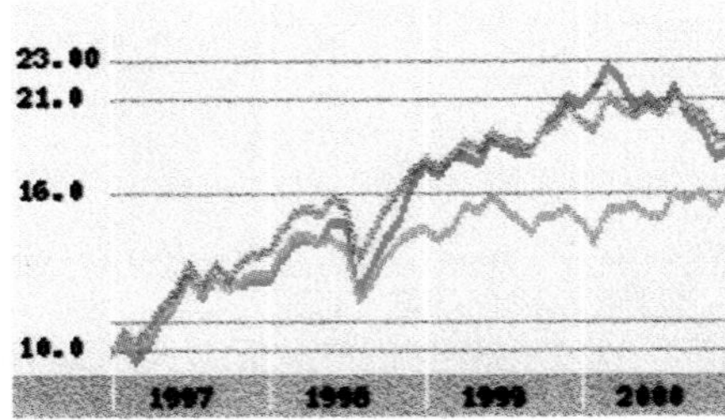

Annual Returns

	1998	1999	2000	12-00
Fund	32.8	29.9	-15.0	-15.0
+/- Cat	19.7	23.0	-20.4	-20.4
+/- Index	4.2	8.9	-5.9	-5.9

Data through 12-31-00

View additional performance information

Category Rating What is this?

Return
Above Avg

Risk
Above Avg

Data through 12-31-00

Fund Details
Sales Charge %

Front:	5.50
Deferred:	None
Expense Ratio %	1.00

Manager Name: Joel E. Dobberpuhl
Manager Start Date: 07-01-92
Manager Name: Evan Harrel
Manager Start Date: 07-01-98

View additional fund details

Quick Stats

NAV (01-25-01)	$13.08
Day Change	$-0.05
YTD Return	4.56%
Morningstar Rating	★★★★
Morningstar Category	Large Value
Net Assets ($mil)	11,260

View ratings details

Inside Scoop
This fund is more aggressive than your typical value offering. It invests in stocks that are cheap relative to their growth rates. That growth slant has helped returns. Investors looking for a pure value play won't find it here, but it's a fine choice for a core holding. Read full analysis

What Does This Fund Own?
Style Box What is this?
Compare investment-style returns

Size: Large, Medium, Small
Investment Valuation: Value, Blend, Growth

Style Box as of 12-31-00
View Style Box details

Asset Allocation %		Top 3 Stock Sectors %	
Cash	6.9	Technology	31.5
Stocks	93.1	Services	19.6
Bonds	0.0	Financials	16.5
Other	0.0		

Asset data through 12-31-00
Sector data through 12-31-00

View complete asset breakdown

figure 21.7

Morningstar Research Report for the AIM Value Mutual Fund
Morningstar research reports provide detailed financial information about a mutual fund's past financial performance, the investments in the fund's portfolio, the fund manager(s), and additional information that can be used to evaluate a mutual fund.

Source: "Morningstar Research Report for the AIM Value Mutual Fund," from morningstar.com. Chicago-based Morningstar, Inc. is a leading provider of investment information, research, and analysis. Its extensive line of Internet, software, and print products provides unbiased data and commentary on mutual funds, U.S. and international equities, closed-end funds, and variable annuities. Established in 1984, Morningstar continues to be the industry's most trusted source on key investment issues of the day. For more information about Morningstar, visit www.morningstar.com or call 800-735-0700.

table 21.9 **The Thirty Corporations Whose Common-Stock Prices Make Up the Dow Jones Industrial Average**

AT&T	Exxon/Mobil	McDonald's
Alcoa	General Electric	Merck
American Express	General Motors	Microsoft
Boeing	Hewlett Packard	Minnesota Mining & Mfg.
Caterpillar	Home Depot	Morgan (J.P.)
Citigroup	Honeywell	Philip Morris
Coca-Cola	IBM	Procter & Gamble
Disney	Intel	SBC Communications
Du Pont	International Paper	United Technologies
Eastman Kodak	Johnson & Johnson	Wal-Mart

Source: www.yahoo.com, June 15, 2000.

Security Averages

Investors often gauge the stock market through the security averages reported in newspapers and on television news programs. A **security average** (or **security index**) is an average of the current market prices of selected securities. Over a period of time, these averages indicate price trends, but they cannot predict the performance of individual investments. At best, they can give the investor a "feel" for what is happening to investment prices generally.

security average (or security index) an average of the current market prices of selected securities

The *Dow Jones Industrial Average*, established in 1897, is the oldest security index in use today. This average is composed of the prices of the common stocks of thirty leading industrial corporations. (These firms are listed in Table 21.9.) In addition, Dow Jones publishes the following averages:

- A *transportation average*, computed from the prices of twenty transportation stocks
- A *utility average*, computed from the prices of fifteen utility stocks
- A *composite average*, computed from the prices of the sixty-five stocks included in the industrial, transportation, and utility averages

The Standard & Poor's 500 Stock Index and the New York Stock Exchange Composite Index include more stocks than the Dow Jones averages. Thus, they tend to reflect the stock market more fully. The *Standard & Poor's 500 Stock Index* is an average of the prices of 400 industrial, 60 transportation and utility, and 40 financial stocks. The *New York Stock Exchange Composite Index* is computed from the prices of all stocks listed on the NYSE, weighted to reflect the number and value of outstanding shares. The *American Stock Exchange (AMEX) Index* is an average of more than 1,300 stocks listed on the American Stock Exchange. Finally, the *Nasdaq Composite Index* includes the prices of 6,000 stocks that are traded over the counter. The Philadelphia semiconductor index, the computer chip-maker's industry top index, is extremely cyclical, following the sales pattern set by manufacturers that use chips to produce everything from computers to washing machines. From October 1998 to March 2000 an investor in the index would have seen their money increase 602 percent as the global demand for chips soared and 365 percent over two years ending in June 2000.[9] In addition to stock averages, there are averages for bonds, mutual funds, real estate, commodities, precious metals, and most collectibles.

It should be apparent that vast sums of money are involved in securities trading. In an effort to protect investors from unfair treatment, both federal and state governments have acted to regulate securities trading.

Regulation of Securities Trading

LEARNING OBJECTIVE

7 Explain how federal and state authorities regulate trading in securities.

Government regulation of securities began as a response to abusive and fraudulent practices in the sale of stocks, bonds, and other financial securities. The states were the first to react, early in this century. Later, federal legislation was passed to regulate the interstate sale of securities.

State Regulation

blue-sky laws state laws that regulate securities trading

The first state law regulating the sale of securities was enacted in Kansas in 1911. Within a few years, several other states had passed similar laws. Today most states require that new issues be registered with a state agency and that brokers and securities dealers operating within the state be licensed. The states also provide for the prosecution of individuals accused of the fraudulent sale of stocks, bonds, and other securities.

The state laws that regulate securities trading are often called **blue-sky laws.** They are designed to protect investors from purchasing securities backed up by nothing but the "clear blue sky."

Federal Regulation

Securities and Exchange Commission (SEC) the agency that enforces federal securities regulations

National Association of Securities Dealers (NASD) the organization responsible for the self-regulation of the over-the-counter securities market

The *Securities Act of 1933*, sometimes referred to as the *Truth in Securities Act*, provides for full disclosure of important facts about corporations issuing new securities. Such corporations are required to file a *registration statement* containing specific information about the corporation's earnings, assets, and liabilities; its products or services; and the qualifications of its top management. Publication of a prospectus that can be given to prospective investors is also a requirement.

The *Securities Exchange Act of 1934* created the **Securities and Exchange Commission (SEC)**, which is the agency that enforces federal securities regulations. The 1934 act gave the SEC the power to regulate trading on all national securities exchanges. It also requires that corporations' registration statements be brought up-to-date periodically. Finally, this act requires brokers and securities dealers to register with the SEC.

Nine other federal acts have been passed primarily to protect investors:

- The *Maloney Act of 1938* made it possible to establish the **National Association of Securities Dealers (NASD)** to oversee the self-regulation of the over-the-counter securities market.
- The *Investment Company Act of 1940* placed investment companies that sell mutual funds under the jurisdiction of the SEC.
- The *Investment Advisers Act of 1940* required financial advisers with more than fifteen clients to register with the SEC.
- The *Federal Securities Act of 1964* extended the SEC's jurisdiction to include companies whose stock is sold over the counter, if they have total assets of at least $1 million or have more than 500 stockholders of any one class of stock.
- The *Securities Investor Protection Act of 1970* created the *Securities Investor Protection Corporation (SIPC)*. The SIPC provides insurance of up to $500,000 per customer, including $100,000 for cash left on deposit with a brokerage firm that later fails.
- The *Securities Amendments Act of 1975* prohibited fixed commissions. As a result, commissions now vary from one brokerage firm to another.
- The *Insider Trading Sanctions Act of 1984* strengthened the penalty provisions of the Securities Exchange Act of 1934. Under the 1984 act, people are guilty of

insider trading if they use information that should be available only to account executives or other brokerage firm employees.

- The *Insider Trading and Securities Fraud Enforcement Act of 1988* made the top management of brokerage firms responsible for reporting to the SEC any transaction based on inside information. In addition, this act empowered the SEC to levy fines of up to $1 million for failure to report such trading violations.
- The *Financial Services Modernization Banking Act of 1999* repealed the Glass Steagall Act of 1933 and portions of the Bank Holding Company Act of 1956. This act allows banks to establish one-stop financial supermarkets where customers can bank, buy and sell securities, and purchase insurance coverage.

Before they can start investing, most people have to decide on a career and obtain a job that will provide the money needed to finance an investment program. In Appendix A—Careers in Business, we provide information that can help you explore different career options.

RETURN TO Inside Business

MAKING ANY INVESTMENT SHOULD be based on research and knowledge. Before Rosario Maiolino invested even one dollar in Qualcomm stock, he did his homework. Although friends thought he was insane to invest his life savings–$350,000–in one investment, he had the last laugh when he sold his stock for $17 million. While researching an investment doesn't guarantee success, it is the most logical first step for both beginning and experienced investors.

To be a successful investor, you have to start an investment program. The fact is that most people put off starting a program until tomorrow, and tomorrow can be too late. As you learned in the Exploring Business feature on page 617, the best time to start an investment program is NOW. You'll also have to engage in many of the activities we discussed in this chapter. You'll need to not only develop an investment program but establish an emergency fund and find enough money to fund your program. To make wise investment decisions, you'll have to know how to evaluate different investment alternatives. By studying the sources of information that were described in this chapter, you can separate quality investments that will increase in value from investments that are destined to decrease in value. Above all, keep in mind that a long-term investment program requires discipline, research, and a little bit of luck. Why not accept the challenge? After all, an investment program is something that can help you obtain your investment goals and ensure your financial future. Good luck!

Questions

1. Assume that you are thirty years old and, your take-home pay totals $2,400 a month, and you have monthly living expenses of $1,800. Using the information presented in this chapter, develop a three-part plan to (a) establish long-term investment goals, (b) establish an emergency fund, and (c) save $5,000 to start an investment program.
2. Assume that you now have $5,000 to start an investment program. Would you invest in Qualcomm stock? Explain your answer.
3. Using *The Wall Street Journal* or the Internet, determine the current market value for a share of Qualcomm stock. On Monday, June 26, 2000, a share of Qualcomm stock was selling for $64. Based on this information, would your Qualcomm investment have been profitable had you purchased the stock for $64 a share on June 26, 2000?

chapter Review

SUMMARY

1 Describe how securities are bought and sold.

Securities may be purchased in either the primary or the secondary market. The primary market is a market in which an investor purchases financial securities (via an investment bank) directly from the issuer of those securities. A corporation can also obtain financing by selling securities directly to current stockholders. The secondary market involves transactions for existing securities that are currently traded between investors and that are usually bought and sold through a securities exchange or the over-the-counter market.

If you invest in securities, chances are that you will use the services of an account executive who works for a brokerage firm. An investor should choose an account executive who is ethical, compatible, and able to provide the desired level of service. It is also possible to use a discount broker or trade securities online with a computer.

2 Develop a personal investment plan.

Personal investment planning begins with formulating measurable and realistic investment goals. A personal investment plan is then designed to implement those goals. Many financial planners suggest that as a first step, the investor establish an emergency fund equivalent to three months' living expenses. Then additional funds may be invested according to the investment plan. Finally, all investments should be carefully monitored and, if necessary, the investment plan should be modified.

3 Explain how the factors of safety, risk, income, growth, and liquidity affect your investment decisions.

Depending on their particular investment goals, investors seek varying degrees of safety, risk, income, growth, and liquidity from their investments. Safety is, in essence, freedom from the risk of loss. Generally, the greater the risk, the greater should be the potential return on an investment. *Income* is the periodic return from an investment. *Growth* is an increase in the value of the investment. *Liquidity* is defined as the ease with which an asset can be converted to cash.

4 Identify the advantages and disadvantages of savings accounts, bonds, stocks, mutual funds, and real estate.

In this section, we examined traditional investments that include bank accounts, corporate bonds, government bonds, common stock, preferred stock, mutual funds, and real estate. Although bank accounts and bonds can provide investment growth, they are generally purchased by investors who seek a predictable source of income. Both corporate and government bonds are a form of debt financing. As a result, bonds are generally considered a more conservative investment than stocks or mutual funds. With stock investments, investors can make money through dividend payments, an increase in the value of the stock, or stock splits. The major advantages of mutual fund investments are professional management and diversification. Today, there are mutual funds to meet just about any conceivable investment objective. The success of real estate investments is often tied to how well each investment alternative is evaluated.

5 Describe high-risk investment techniques.

High-risk investment techniques can provide greater returns, but they also entail greater risk of loss. An investor buys stock on margin by borrowing part of the purchase price, usually from a stock brokerage firm. Because you can purchase up to twice as much stock by using margin, you can increase your return on investment as long as the stock's market value increases. You can also make money by selling short when the market value of a financial security is decreasing. Selling short is the process of selling stock that an investor does not actually own but has borrowed from a brokerage firm and will repay at a later date. Other high-risk investments include stock options, commodities, precious metals, gemstones, coins, and antiques and collectibles.

6 Use financial information to evaluate investment alternatives.

Information on securities and the firms that issue them can be obtained from the Internet, newspapers, brokerage firm reports, business periodicals, corporate reports, and investors' services. The Internet and most local newspapers report daily securities transactions and security indexes, or averages. These averages indicate price trends but reveal nothing about the performance of individual securities. In addition to the Internet and newspaper coverage, other sources of information about investments include brokerage firm reports, business periodicals, corporate reports, and investors' services.

7 Explain how federal and state authorities regulate trading in securities.

State and federal regulations protect investors from unscrupulous securities trading practices. Federal laws, which are enforced by the Securities and Exchange Commission, require the registration of new securities, the publication and distribution of prospectuses, and the registration of brokers and securities dealers. These laws apply to securities listed on the national security exchanges, to mutual funds, and to some OTC stocks.

KEY TERMS

You should now be able to define and give an example relevant to each of the following terms:

primary market (609)
investment banking firm (609)
high-risk investment (610)
institutional investors (610)
secondary market (610)
securities exchange (610)
over-the-counter (OTC) market (611)
Nasdaq (611)
account executive (612)
market order (612)
limit order (612)
discretionary order (613)
program trading (615)
round lot (615)
odd lot (615)
personal investment (616)
financial planner (617)
blue-chip stock (618)
liquidity (619)
municipal bond (622)
general obligation bond (622)
revenue bond (622)
stock dividend (622)
capital gain (623)
market value (623)
bull market (623)
bear market (623)
stock split (623)
mutual fund (624)
net asset value (NAV) (624)
family of funds (626)
margin requirement (627)
buying long (627)
selling short (628)
diversification (629)
prospectus (633)
security average (or security index) (637)
blue-sky laws (638)
Securities and Exchange Commission (SEC) (638)
National Association of Securities Dealers (NASD) (638)

REVIEW QUESTIONS

1. What is the difference between the primary market and the secondary market?
2. When a corporation decides to sell stock, what is the role of an investment banking firm?
3. What is the difference between a securities exchange and the over-the-counter market?
4. In what ways could a computer help you invest?
5. How would you go about developing a personal investment plan?
6. What is an "emergency fund," and why is it recommended?
7. What is meant by the safety of an investment? What is the tradeoff between safety and return on the investment?
8. In general, what kinds of investments provide income? What kinds provide growth?
9. Characterize the purchase of corporate bonds as an investment in terms of safety, risk, income, growth, and liquidity.
10. Describe the three methods by which investors can make money with stock investments.
11. An individual may invest in stocks either directly or through a mutual fund. How are the two investment methods different?
12. What are the risks and rewards of purchasing stocks on margin?
13. When would a speculator sell short?
14. How could the Internet help you research an investment?
15. In what ways are newspaper stock quotations useful to investors? In what ways are security averages useful?
16. In addition to the Internet and newspapers, what other sources of financial information could help you obtain your investment goals?
17. What is the Securities and Exchange Commission? What are its principal functions?

DISCUSSION QUESTIONS

1. Many financial planners recommend that you begin an investment program by accumulating an "emergency fund" equal to three months' living expenses. How could you accumulate enough money to fund your emergency fund?
2. What personal circumstances might lead investors to emphasize income rather than growth in their investment planning? What might lead them to emphasize growth rather than income?
3. Suppose you have just inherited 500 shares of IBM common stock. What would you do with it, if anything?
4. What type of individual would invest in government bonds? In global mutual funds? In real estate?
5. What kinds of information would you like to have before you invest in a particular common stock or mutual fund? From what sources can you get that information?
6. Take another look at Figure 21.6 (Mergent's Research Report for General Motors) and Figure 21.7 (Morningstar Research Report for the AIM Value Mutual Fund). Based on the research provided by Mergent's and Morningstar would you buy either of these two investments? Justify your decision by providing specific examples from Figure 21.6 and Figure 21.7.
7. Federal laws prohibit corporate managers from making investments that are based on "inside information"—that is, special knowledge about their firms that is not available to the general public. Why are such laws needed?

VIDEO CASE

DLJdirect: A Firm that Knows the Value of Customer Service

Service is the name of the game at online brokerage firm DLJdirect. Started back in 1988 when the Internet was in its infancy, this online brokerage firm now has more than 600,000 investor accounts and $11 billion in customer assets. More importantly, DLJdirect is ranked the No. 1 online brokerage firm by *Barron's, Kiplinger's Personal Finance Magazine*, and Internet news provider Street.com. The company also received Forbes' "Best of the Web" award last year. How does DLJdirect do it?

To answer that question, you have to understand DLJdirect's commitment to helping individuals become better investors. To begin investing at DLJdirect, you must open an account. For most non-retirement individual accounts, there is no minimum to open an account. All you have to do is complete an online application. After the firm has verified the information on the application and obtained a credit check, you can begin investing and pick from more than 10,000 stocks and 9,000 mutual funds.

To help you make informed decisions, DLJdirect, a branch of the investment banking firm Donaldson, Lufkin & Jenrette, Inc., provides some of the best research in the industry. Even small investors have access to the same research that the firm provides to its institutional clients that have $1 billion or more in assets. Investors can obtain highly-respected research reports prepared by the firm's own staff of 300 market analysts that cover 3,000 different companies. And the DLJdirect web site has links to some of the most respected financial news and research web sites available today including Standard & Poor's, Zacks, and Thomson Insider. Clients can also receive non-stop market coverage from online publications such as *TheStreet* and *RealMoney*. DLJdirect was also the first online brokerage web site to offer Dow Jones Newswire—a web site recognized for its ability to report breaking stories around the world.

Once you make a decision to buy stocks or mutual funds, your order is sent to the market and executed within minutes. Investors are then required to deposit funds to pay for their purchase within three business days—the standard SEC time requirement for settling security transactions. DLJdirect charges investors the same fee whether the transaction is handled over the Internet, by a touch-tone telephone, or directly through one of the firm's 600 investor service representatives. A commission rate comparison table at their web site shows that they charge $20 for a limit order of 1,000 shares of an over-the-counter stock priced at $20 a share—one of the lowest commission charges in the online securities industry.

While many competitors cater to small investors and day traders, DLJdirect caters to people who know how to take advantage of the unique research products and services the firm offers. Although the amount of service a client receives is determined by the amount of assets on deposit with DLJdirect, all account holders are entitled to 24-hour customer support; the ability to place pre- and post-market buy and sell orders; access to real-time quotes, portfolio balances, and wireless stock alerts through pagers, cell phones, and Palm Pilots; and the use of the firm's award-winning MarketSpeed™ software for reliable, secure, and efficient trading. Preferred clients (those with $100,000 or more invested) have access to initial public offerings (IPOs) and opportunities to have portfolios handled by professional money managers.

In November, 2000, Donaldson, Lufkin & Jenrette was acquired by one of Switzerland's giant financial firms and is now operated by Credit Suisse First Boston, an investment bank operating in more than thirty-seven countries. As a result, DLJdirect was renamed CSFBdirect on January 15, 2001. The new CSFBdirect is aggressively marketing to clients across the globe while maintaining the same quality services that the original DLJdirect was known for. Recently, it has opened sites in the United Kingdom, Hong Kong, Japan, and the Middle East (which also serves North Africa). According to Blake Darcy, CSFBdirect's CEO, "Even though we have a lead time as far as being in this business a long time, we know we have to fight every single day to provide a quality experience for our customers."[10]

Questions

1. Today, investors have opened more than seven million online brokerage accounts. And that number is expected to double within the next two years. Why do you think investors are choosing online accounts instead of traditional full-service brokerage accounts?
2. CSFBdirect (formerly DLJdirect) has received numerous awards and is often referred to as the No. 1 online brokerage firm. What factors have led to the firm's success?
3. Too often investors think that being successful when investing in stocks and mutual funds is more luck than skill. And yet, CSFBdirect caters to people who know how to take advantage of the unique research products and services the firm offers. How important are research and information when choosing an investment? Explain your answer.

Building skills for career success

1. Exploring the Internet

For investors seeking information about individual companies and the industry to which they belong, the Internet is an excellent source of analysis and opinion. It provides the investor with sales and revenue histories, graphs of recent trading on stock and bond markets, and discussions of anticipated changes within a firm or industry. The interested investor can also look at Internet business reports of stock and bond market activity. Among the many companies that issue these reports are Dow Jones, Standard & Poors, Moody's, and Dun & Bradstreet—all firms that provide, for a fee, analysis and private research services. Visit the text web site for updates to this exercise.

Assignment

1. Suppose you are interested in investing within a particular industry, such as the semiconductor or computer industry. Explore some of the web sites listed below, gathering information about the industry and a few related stocks that are of interest to the "experts."

   Wall Street Journal: http://www.wsj.com
   Business Week: http://www.businessweek.com
   Dow Jones: http://www.dowjones.com
   Moody's: http://www.moodys.com
   Dun & Bradstreet: http://www.dnb.com
   New York Stock Exchange: http://www.nyse.com
   Morgan Stanley: http://www.ms.com

2. List the stocks the experts recommend and their current trading value. (You can use one of the web search engines to check the price.) Also list several stocks the experts do not like and their current selling prices. Then list your own choices of "good" and "bad" stocks.
3. Explain why you and the experts believe these stocks are good or poor buys today. (You might want to monitor these same web sites over the next six months to see how well your "good" stocks are performing.)

2. Developing Critical Thinking Skills

One way to achieve financial security is to invest a stated amount of money on a systematic basis. This investment strategy is called "dollar-cost-averaging." When the cost is lower, your investment buys more shares. When the cost is higher, your investment buys fewer shares. A good way to begin investing is to select a mutual fund that meets your financial objectives and to invest the same amount each month.

Assignment

1. Select several mutual funds from the financial pages of the *Wall Street Journal* or a business periodical that provides information about mutual funds. Call the toll-free number for each fund and ask about its objectives. Also request that the company send you a prospectus and an annual report.
2. Select a fund that meets your financial objectives.
3. Prepare a table that includes the following data:
   a. An initial investment of $2,000 in the mutual fund you have selected
   b. The NAV (net asset value)
   c. The number of shares purchased.
4. Record the investment information on a weekly basis. Look in the *Wall Street Journal* to find the NAV for each week.
5. Determine the value of your investments until the end of the semester.
6. Write a report describing the results. Include a summary of what you learned about investments.

3. Building Team Skills

Investing in stocks can be a way to beat inflation and accumulate money. Traditionally, stocks have returned an average of 10 percent or more per year. Fixed-rate investments, on the other hand, often earn little more than the inflation rate, making it very difficult to accumulate enough money for retirement. For a better understanding of how investing in stocks works, complete this exercise through the end of the semester.

Assignment

1. Form teams of three people. The teams will compete against each other, striving for the largest gain in investments.
2. Assume you are buying stock in three companies; some should be listed on the NYSE, and some should be traded in the over-the-counter market.
   a. Divide your investment amount of $25,000 into three budgets.
   b. Determine the number of shares of stock you can purchase from each company by dividing the budgeted amount by the price of the stock. Allow enough money to pay for the commission. To find the cost of the stock, multiply the number of shares you are going to purchase by the closing price of the stock.
   c. Assume the commission is 2 percent. Calculate it by multiplying the cost of the stock by .02. Add the dollar amount of commission to the cost of the stock to determine the total purchase price.
3. Set up a table to reflect the following information:
   a. Name of the company
   b. Closing price per share
   c. Number of shares purchased
   d. Amount of the commission
   e. Cost of the stock
4. Record the closing price of the stock on a weekly basis. Prepare a chart to use for this step.
5. Before the end of the semester, assume you sell the stock.
   a. Take the closing price and multiply it by the number of shares; then calculate the commission at 2 percent.

b. Deduct the amount of commission from the selling price of the stock. This is the total return on your investment.

6. Calculate your profit or loss. Subtract the total purchase price of the stock from the total return. If the total return is less than the total purchase price, you have a loss.
7. Prepare a report summarizing the results of the project. Include the table and individual stock charts, as well as a statement describing what you learned about investing in stocks.

4. Researching Different Careers

Stockbrokers (sometimes referred to as "account executives") are agents who buy and sell stock for clients. After completing this exercise, you will have a better understanding of what stockbrokers do on a daily basis.

Assignment

1. Look in the telephone directory for the names and numbers of financial companies or securities firms that sell stock.
2. Contact a stockbroker at one of these firms and explain that you would like to set up an interview so that you can learn firsthand about a stockbroker's job.
4. Summarize the results of your interview in a report. Include a statement about whether the job of stockbroker appeals to you, and explain your thoughts.

5. Improving Communication Skills

Assessment involves determining the amount of progress relative to a standard. It is a critical part of evaluating results in the workplace, as well as determining what you have learned in a course. Since you are nearing the end of this course, it is time to assess what you have learned about business and business operations. Learning often takes place in bits and pieces, and when you take the time for review and assessment as you complete a course, you may be surprised at how much you have learned.

Assignment

If you have been writing in a journal as suggested in Exercise 5 in Chapter 1, you should refer to your journal notes to complete this exercise. Otherwise, use your class or study notes. Prepare a report reflecting your thoughts on the following questions:

1. What are three things you learned about business that impressed you the most? Or what was the greatest surprise to you?
2. How will you use the information you learned? Give several examples applicable to your personal life, your career, and your job.
3. Has this course helped you make a decision on a career in business? If so, how did it make a difference?
4. What have you learned about systematically writing your thoughts in a journal? How important is this exercise for personal growth and development?

Worldlyinvestor.com: The One Source for Global Information

Who needs investment information? You do! Now the more important question: Where do you get the information you need to make informed investment decisions? Today, there are literally hundreds of web sites that offer financial and investment advice. But one web site—worldlyinvestor.com—provides a wealth of information to help individuals become better investors. Logging on to worldlyinvestor.com can be a truly educational experience with its award-winning concise content and easy-to-use organization. Best of all, it's free.

The Mission

The mission of the worldlyinvestor.com web site, which was launched on August 31, 1998, is to provide quality information to a savvy, upscale investor who wants to take advantage of events that are affecting not only the U.S. financial markets, but the global markets as well. The site's editors focus on what's going on in the world, what it means to individual investors, and how investors can use this information to increase their profits. According to Lewis Gersh, Chairman and CEO, the ultimate goal is to help an individual become a smarter and more worldly investor by educating and presenting ideas so people can make smarter investment decisions. Apparently, their mission is fulfilling the needs of a growing number of investors. More than a million users a month access the worldlyinvestor.com web site. And for two years in a row, it has been included in the 50 Best Financial Sites by *Money* magazine.

Covering the World

When the editors at the worldlyinvestor.com web site say they cover the financial world, they really mean it. What happens in the London and Tokyo exchanges is just as important as the ups and downs on the Nasdaq and the Big Board. Once at the worldlyinvestor.com web site, with just a click of your mouse you can access a world of information to help you manage your money, learn more about financial management and how to invest in the global markets around the world. For example, every morning the site's front page summarizes the overnight action in markets abroad as well as what's going on with American business. And there are twenty newsletters devoted to stock and industry sectors including biotech, blue chip, emerging markets, and the Internet. A separate group of weekly newsletters focuses on business trends and developments in Asia, Latin America, Canada, Europe, and emerging markets. There is even a glossary of investment terms. All information is written by a staff of forty-five journalists, professional analysts, and money managers.

According to many users, the site's most unique feature is its resource center. Here you will find top-performing U.S. and global stock recommendations, lists of currency values from around the world, an ADR* screener, and a list of foreign stocks that trade on U.S. exchanges. You can even buy and sell international securities on the web site and create and track your own investment portfolio through a partnership between worldlyinvestor.com and INTL-TRADER.COM.

Worldlyinvestor.com is not trying to break news. It's trying to break ideas, according to Jeremy Pink, worldlyinvestor.com's editor in chief. At a time when the world seems to be shrinking and one nation's economy is dependent on another nation's economy, it seems a web site like worldlyinvestor.com can provide information that just about everyone can use.

Questions

1. According to the editors at worldlyinvestor.com, the focus of this web site is to determine what's going on around the world, what it means to individual investors, and how to make money on that information. Can accessing a web site like worldlyinvestor.com really make you a better investor? Explain your answer.
2. More than a million users a month access the web site of worldlyinvestor.com. Why do you think so many people are interested in foreign stocks or mutual funds that invest in foreign companies?
3. Assume you have accumulated $5,000 that can be invested in stocks and mutual funds. Visit the worldlyinvestor.com web site at www.worldlyinvestor.com and research at least two different investments. Based on the available information, which investment would you choose? Summarize in a two-page report why you think this investment is the right one for you.

*American Depositary Receipts, or ADRs, are receipts for the shares of foreign-based corporations held in the vaults of U.S. banks. They entitle shareholders to all dividends and capital gains. ADRs are traded in U.S. dollars in the U.S. markets and dividends are paid to receipt holders in U.S. dollars. ADRs are available for hundreds of stocks from numerous countries.

careers in Business

Words like *excited, challenged, scared,* and *frustrated* have been used to describe someone involved in a job search. But the reality is that everyone who is employed must have looked for a job at one time or another, and survived. Although first-time employees often think they will work for the same company for their entire career, most people change jobs and even careers during their lifetime. In fact, according to the Bureau of Labor Statistics, today's job applicants will change jobs over ten times. Therefore, the employment information that follows will be of lasting value. Let's begin our discussion with a look at the factors affecting an individual's career choices.

The Importance of Career Choices

Most people think that career planning begins with an up-to-date résumé and a job interview. In reality, it begins long before you prepare your résumé. It starts with *you* and what you want to become. In some ways, you have been preparing for a career ever since you started first grade. Everything you have experienced during your lifetime you can now use as a resource to help define your career goals. Let's start with a basic assumption: it's likely that you will spend more time at work than at any other single place during your lifetime. It therefore makes sense to spend those hours doing something you enjoy. Unfortunately, some people just work at a *job* because they need money to survive. Other people choose a *career* because there is a commitment not only to a profession but also to their own interests and talents. Whether you are looking for a job or a career, you should examine your own priorities. Before reading the next section, you may want to evaluate your priorities by completing the exercise in Figure A.1.

Personal Factors Influencing Career Choices

Before you choose your career or job, you need to have a pretty good idea of what motivates you and what skills you can offer an employer. The following four questions may help you further refine what you consider important in life.

1. *What types of activities do you enjoy?* Although most people know what they enjoy in a general way, a number of interest inventories exist that can help you determine specific interests and activities that can help you land a job that will lead to a satisfying career. In some cases, it may help just to list the interests or activities you enjoy, along with those you dislike. Watch for patterns that may influence your career choices.
2. *What do you do best?* All jobs in all careers require employees to be able to "do something." It is extremely important to assess what you do best. Be honest with yourself about your ability to succeed in a specific job. It may help to make a list of your strongest job-related skills. Also try looking at your skills from an employer's perspective. What can you do that an employer would be willing to pay for?

figure A.1

Which Priorities Are Important to You?

Look over the list of job and personal variables. In the left-hand column, number them in order of current priority to you. Then renumber them in the right-hand column based on the priorities you anticipate having five or ten years down the road.

Priorities Now	Job and Personal Variables	Priorities in 5–10 years
____	Salary	____
____	Family (children/spouse/parents)	____
____	Personal time	____
____	Job location	____
____	Work-related travel	____
____	Potential for advancement	____
____	Commuting time	____
____	Friendly coworkers/boss	____
____	Job responsibilities	____
____	Personal hobbies	____
____	Prestige	____
____	Benefits	____
____	Vacation time	____
____	Retirement plan	____
____	Security/stability	____
____	Personal growth/fulfillment	____
____	Exposure to new skills	____

Source: Susan D. Greene and Melanie C. L Martel, *The Ultimate Job Hunter's Guidebook*, Third Edition, p.14. Copyright © 2001 by Houghton Mifflin Company. Reprinted with permission.

3. *What kind of education will you need?* The amount of education you need is determined by the type of career you choose. In some careers, it is impossible to get an entry-level position without at least a college degree. In other careers, technical or hands-on skills are more important than formal education. Generally, more education increases your potential earning power, as illustrated in Figure A.2.
4. *Where do you want to live?* When you enter the job market, you may want to move to a different part of the country. According to the *Occupational Outlook Handbook*, the western and southern sections of the United States will experience the greatest population increase between now and the year 2008. The population in the Midwest will stay about the same, whereas the Northeast will decrease slightly in population. These population changes will affect job prospects in each of those areas.

Before entering the job market, most people think they are free to move any place they want. In reality, job applicants may be forced to move to a town, city, or metropolitan area that has jobs available.

Trends in Employment

The new millennium brings change in employment opportunities to the U.S. labor market. Employment in 2008 is expected to reach 160.8 million, an increase of 20.3 million or 14 percent above the 1998 level. For the latest information, visit the Office of Employment Projections web site at http://stats.bls.gov/emphome.htm. (See Figure A.3)

As you look ahead to your own career, you should consider the effects that the trends described below will have on employment and employment opportunities.

- Jobs in service industries will account for a larger proportion of total employment.

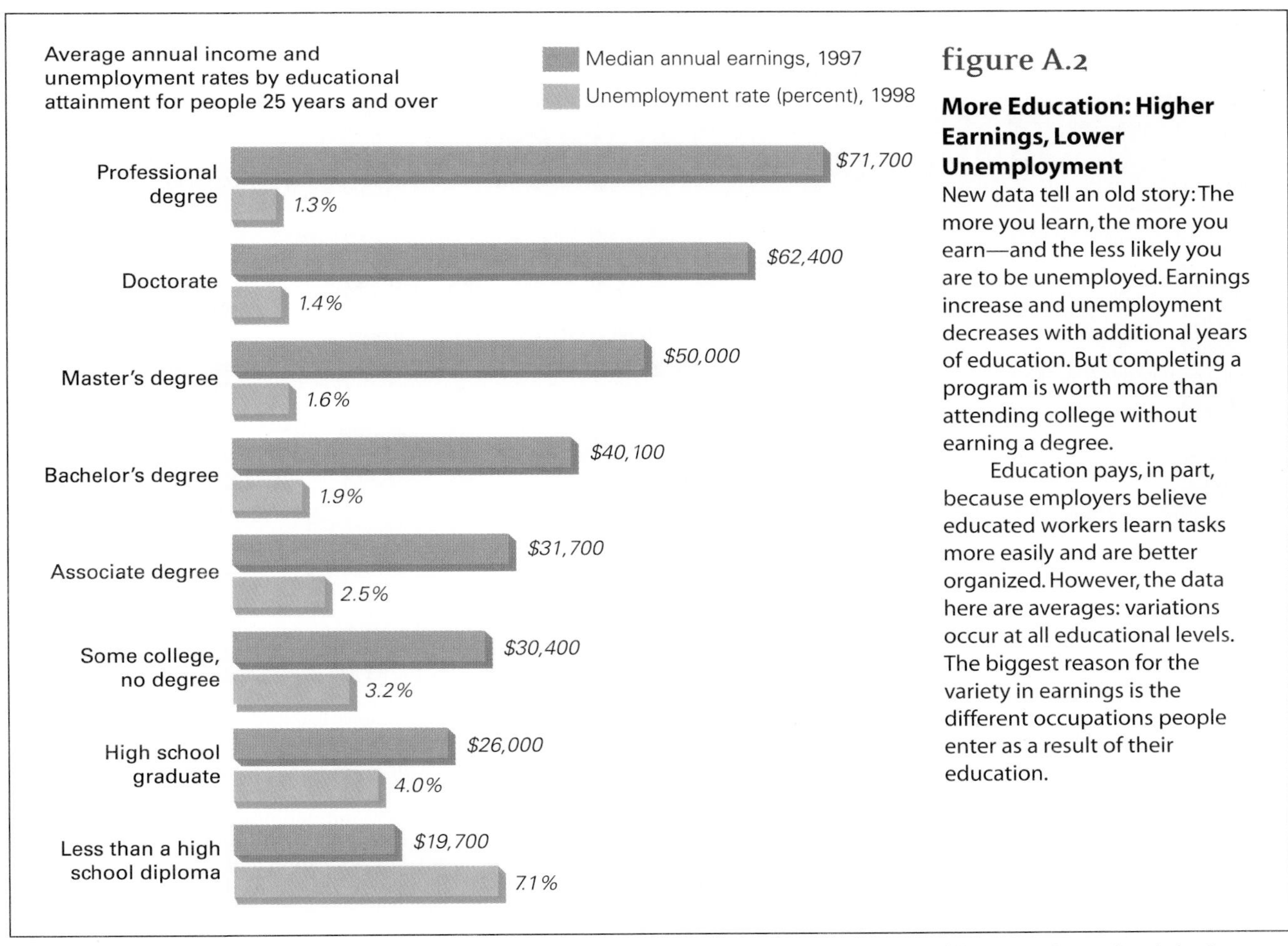

figure A.2

More Education: Higher Earnings, Lower Unemployment

New data tell an old story: The more you learn, the more you earn—and the less likely you are to be unemployed. Earnings increase and unemployment decreases with additional years of education. But completing a program is worth more than attending college without earning a degree.

Education pays, in part, because employers believe educated workers learn tasks more easily and are better organized. However, the data here are averages: variations occur at all educational levels. The biggest reason for the variety in earnings is the different occupations people enter as a result of their education.

Source: Bureau of Labor Statistics, unpublished data from the Current Population Survey (unemployment): Bureau of the Census, Current Population Survey, *PPL-99, Educational Attainment in the United States: March 1998*, table 9 (unpublished data), and *Current Population Reports*, P20–513, October 1998, "Educational Attainment in the United States: March 1998 (Update)" (earnings), and *Occupational Outlook Quarterly*, Fall 1999, p. 40.

- Training—and retraining—will become increasingly important as firms require their employees to use the latest technology. Good jobs will require strong educational qualifications.
- Automation of factories and offices will create new types of jobs. Many of these will be computer-related.
- The number of women, Hispanics, Asians, two-income families, and older workers in the work force will increase.
- There will be a greater emphasis on job sharing, flexible hours, and other innovative work practices to accommodate employees. In some cases, employees will be able to complete assignments at home on remote computer terminals.

College graduates with majors in business and management, computer science, education, engineering, and health professions will be in high demand, according to human resources experts. There will be fewer manufacturing jobs, and those that remain will require high-tech skills.

Figure A.4 shows the twenty occupations that the Bureau of Labor Statistics projects will grow faster or much faster than average between now and the year 2008. And Figure A.5 shows the twenty occupations that are projected to add about 8 million jobs, 39 percent of all projected growth. The jobs also have a great deal of variety with regard to the skills and aptitudes of workers, working conditions, and the nature of the work.

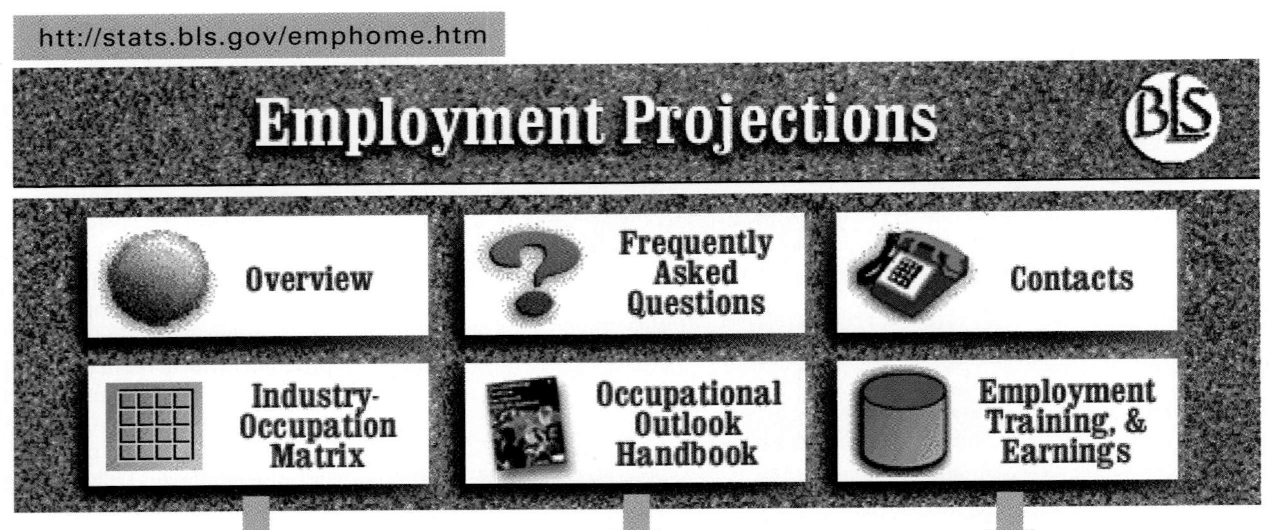

Online database. Helps you identify industries in which job growth for a given occupation may be greatest. Also shows how employment growth differs for occupations within a particular industry. Includes data on current and projected employment for over 500 detailed occupations within more than 240 detailed industries. It also provides data on self-employed and unpaid family workers. Searchable by occupation and by industry.

Full text of the *Occupational Outlook Handbook*. Gives you detailed statements on 250 occupations for in-depth career exploration. Each statement addresses employment outlook for the next decade, job duties, employment and earnings, working conditions, training, education, qualifications, and career advancement. Offers clickable occupational index and key word search.

Online database. Allows you to compare over 500 detailed occupations in terms of employment size, projected employment growth, earnings, education and training requirements, opportunities for self-employment and part-time work, and unemployment. Searchable by occupation or by education and training category.

figure A.3

Easy Online Access to Job Outlook Information

The U.S. Bureau of Labor Statistics web site offers a wealth of employment-related information. Even the full text of the *Occupational Outlook Handbook* is accessible on this web site.

Source: U.S. Bureau of Labor Statistics, *Occupational Outlook Quarterly*, Summer 2000.

Occupational Search Activities

When most people begin to search for a job they immediately think of the classified ads in the local newspaper. Those ads are an important source of information about jobs in your particular area, but they are only one source. Many other sources can lead to employment and a satisfying career. As illustrated in Figure A.6 (see page A7), there is a wealth of information about career planning. Therefore, you must be selective in both the type and the amount of information you use to guide your job search.

The library, a traditional job-hunting tool, has been joined in recent years by the Internet. Both the library and the Internet are sources of everything from classified newspaper ads and government job listings to detailed information on individual companies and industries. You can use either of them to research an area of employment that interests you or a particular company. In addition, the Internet allows you to

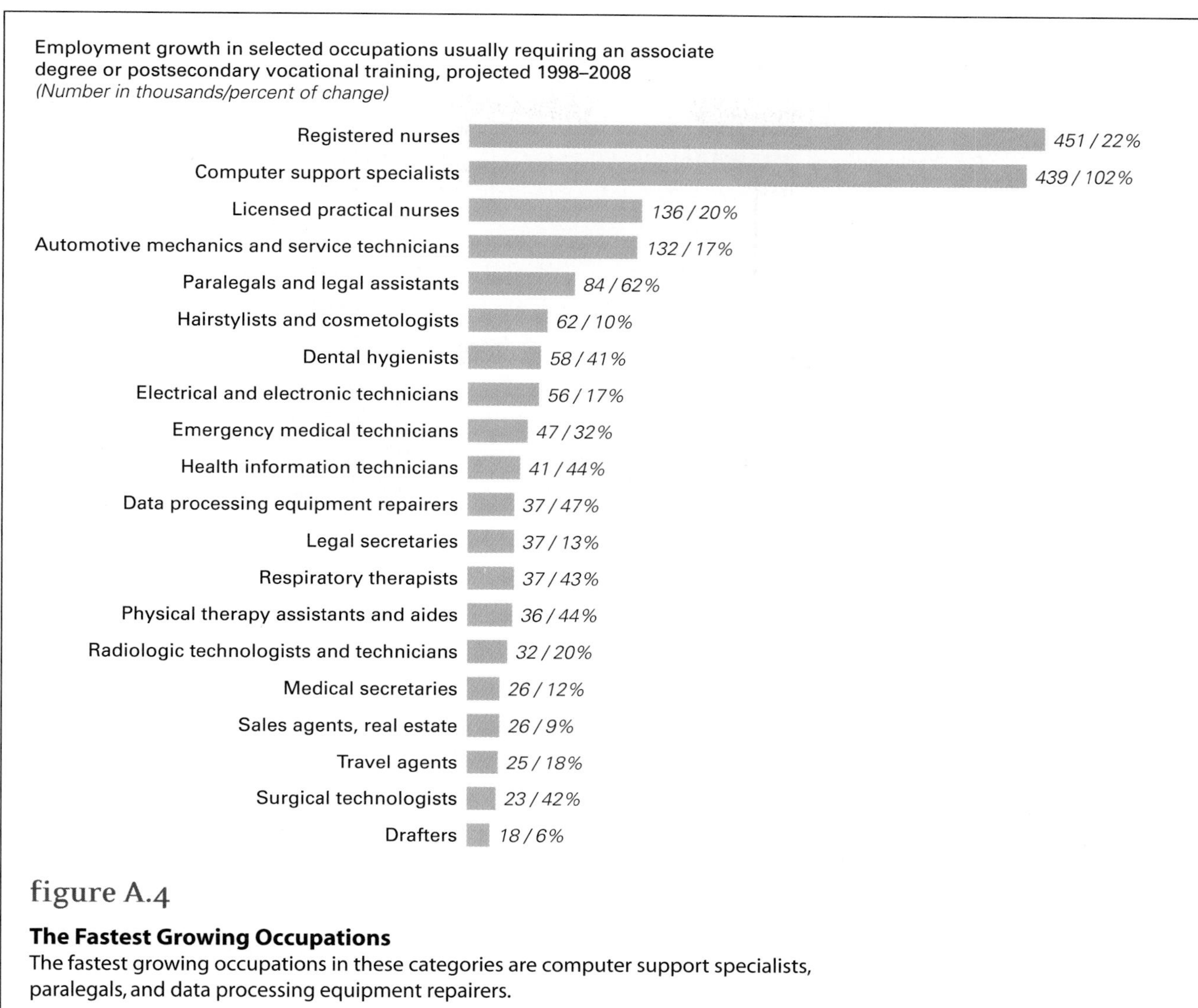

figure A.4

The Fastest Growing Occupations
The fastest growing occupations in these categories are computer support specialists, paralegals, and data processing equipment repairers.

Source: U.S. Bureau of Labor Statistics, *Occupational Outlook Quarterly*, winter 1999–2000, p. 17.

check electronic bulletin boards for current job information, exchange ideas with other job seekers through online discussion groups or e-mail, and get career advice from professional counselors. You can also create your own web page to inform prospective employers of your qualifications. And you may even have a job interview online. Many prominent companies are now using their web sites to post job openings, accept applications, and interview candidates. In fact, the Internet has been called the future of recruiting.

As you start a job search, you may find web sites helpful. In addition to the library and the Internet, the following sources can be of great help when you are trying to find the "perfect job":

1. *Campus placement offices.* Colleges and universities have placement offices staffed by trained personnel specialists. In most cases, these offices serve as clearinghouses for career information. The staff may also be able to guide you in creating your résumé and preparing for a job interview.
2. *Professional sources and networks.* A network is a group of people—friends, relatives, and professionals—who are in a position to exchange information (including information about job openings) in your field of business. And according to

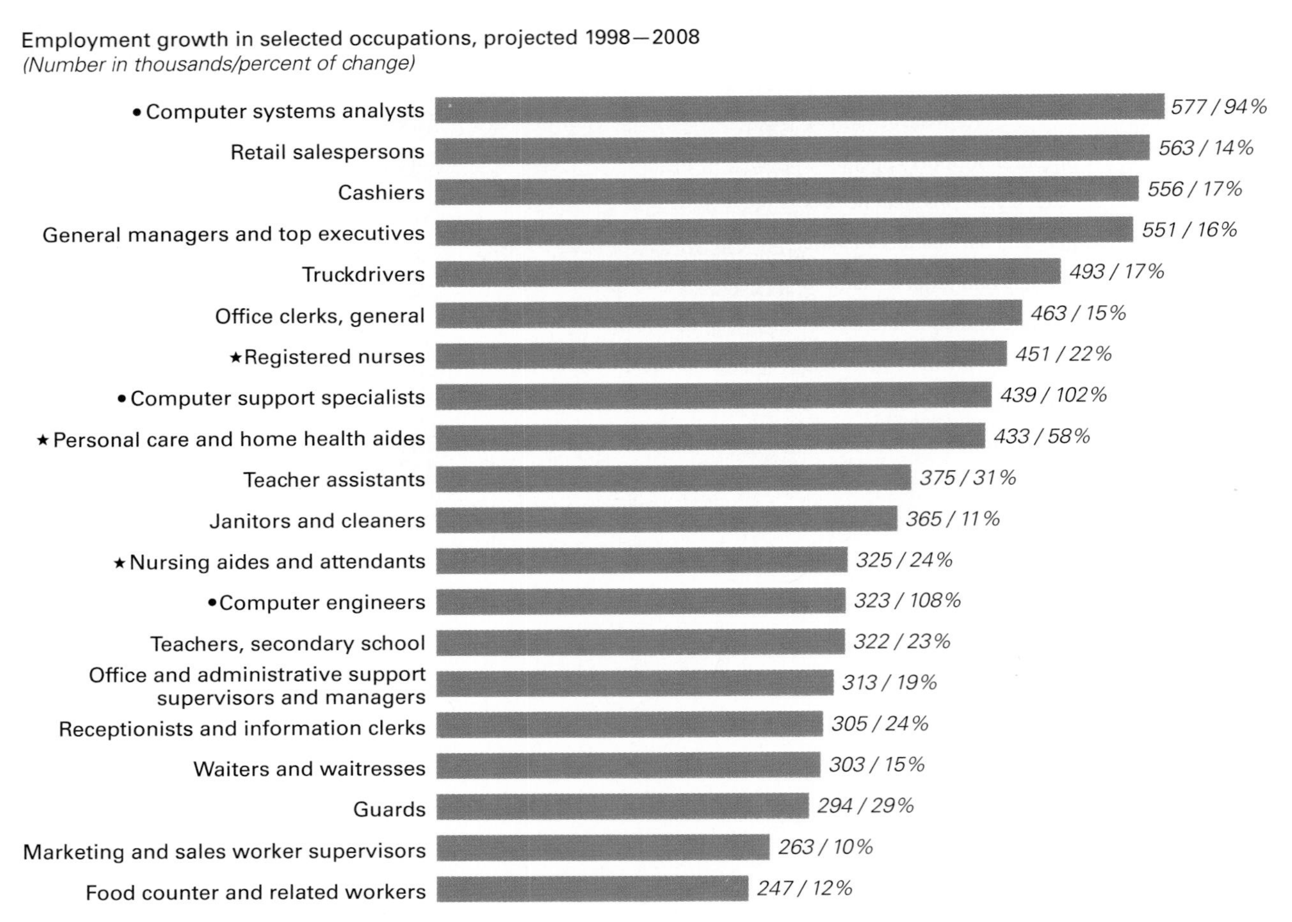

figure A.5

Occupations Gaining the Largest Number of Jobs

These 20 occupations—out of about 500—are projected to add about 8 million jobs, 39 percent of all projected growth. Three are health-related occupations (designated by ★), and three are computer related (•). Three have below average growth rates. Nine are in the upper two of four earnings quartiles. Twelve require short-term on-the-job training, and four require a bachelor's degree or more education.

Four occupations also appear in the chart of fastest growing occupations: computer systems analysts, computer support specialists, personal care and home health aides, and computer engineers.

Source: U.S. Bureau of Labor Statistics, *Occupational Outlook Quarterly*, winter 1999–2000, p. 20.

many job applicants, networking is one of the best sources of career information and job leads. Start with as many people as you can think of to establish your initial network. (The Internet can be very useful in this regard.) Contact these individuals and ask specific questions about job opportunities that they may be aware of. Also, ask each of these individuals to introduce or refer you to someone else who may be able to help you continue your job search. For networking to work, you must continue this process. Remember that you must follow all leads. Even if you have referrals and introductions, *you* must still "get" the job. Finally, remember to thank the people who have helped you.

3. *Private employment agencies.* Private employment agencies charge a fee for helping people find jobs. Typical fees can be as high as 15 to 20 percent of an employee's first-year salary. The fee may be paid by the employer or the employee.

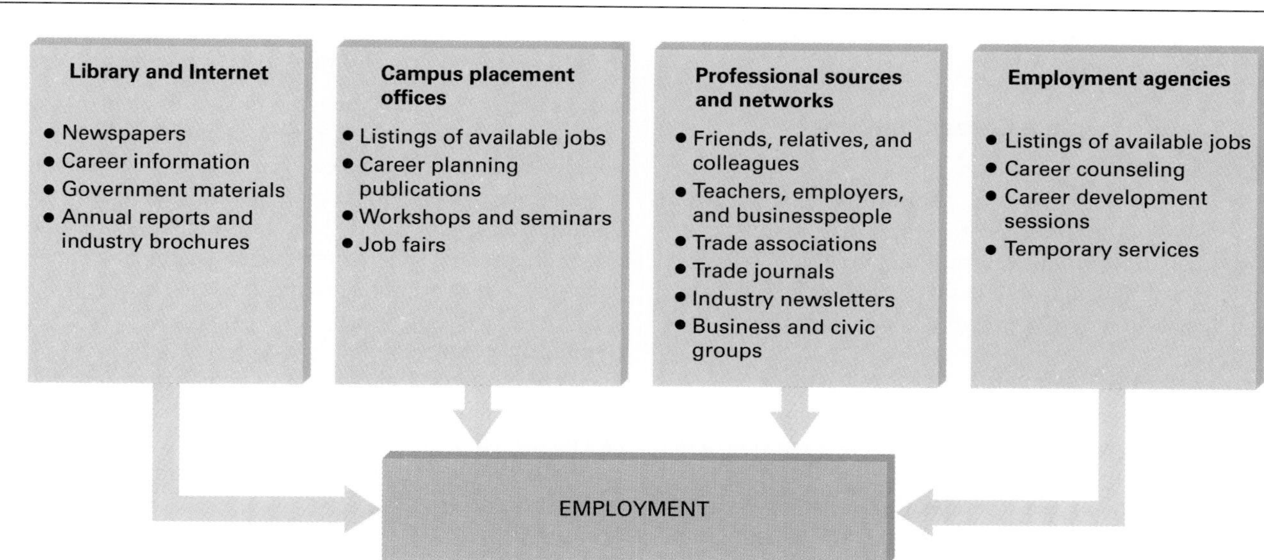

figure A.6

Career Information Sources

Career information is available from the library, campus placement offices, professional sources, and employment agencies.

Like college placement offices, private employment agencies provide career counseling, help create résumés, and provide preparation for job interviews. Before you use a private employment agency, be sure you understand the terms of any contract or agreement you sign. Above all, make sure you know who is responsible for paying the agency's fee.

4. *State employment agencies.* Another source of information about job openings in your immediate area is the local office of your state employment agency. Some job applicants are reluctant to use state agencies because the majority of jobs available through these agencies are for semiskilled or unskilled workers. From a practical standpoint, it can't hurt to consult state employment agencies. They will have information about some professional and managerial positions available in your area, and you will not be charged a fee if you obtain a job through a state employment agency.

Many people want a job immediately and are discouraged at the thought of an occupational search taking months. But in fact people seeking entry-level jobs should expect that their job search will take three to six months. Job applicants who want higher-paying positions can expect to be looking for work for as long as a year, eighteen months, or more. Of course, the state of the economy and whether employers are hiring or not can shorten or extend a job search for anyone.

Regardless of how long it takes, most people will tell you that a job search always takes too long. During a job search, you should use the same work habits that effective employees use on the job. When searching for a job, resist the temptation to "take the day off." Instead, make a master list of activities that you want to accomplish each day. If necessary, force yourself to make contacts, do job research, or schedule interviews that might lead to job opportunities. (Actually, many job applicants look at the job hunt as their job and work from eight to five, five days a week until they find the job they want.) Above all, realize that an occupational search requires patience and perseverance. And according to many individuals who have been through the process of trying to find a job, perseverance may be the most important trait that successful job-hunters need.

Talking Technology

Online Career Planning

EACH DAY, MORE AND MORE PEOPLE ARE using the Internet for their career planning activities. Obtaining information, making contacts, and upgrading employment skills are just a few of the web-based career tasks growing in popularity.

Career Planning Assistance

For tips on preparing a résumé and dressing for an interview, go to www.hotjobs.com, www.careers.wsj.com, and www.careerpath.com. The Career Path site features classified employment ads from twenty-one major newspapers, including the *New York Times*, the *Washington Post*, the *Chicago Tribune*, the *Los Angeles Times*, and the *Boston Globe*, as well as from some smaller newspapers. America's Job Bank: www.ajb.dni.us is a massive site containing information on nearly 250,000 jobs. Listings come from 1,800 state employment offices around the country and represent every line of work, from professional and technical to blue-collar, and from entry-level on up.

Identifying Employment Opportunities

To research career trends and employment opportunities, go to web sites such as www.ajb.dni.us, campus.monster.com, and www.careerbuilder.com. Hoover's Online: www.hoovers.com offers a variety of job-search tools, including information on potential employers and links to sites that post job openings.

Posting Your Résumé on the Web

When creating a résumé for online distribution, keep the format simple and avoid e-mail attachments that some computer systems may be unable to open. Many web sites exist for posting résumés; some of the most popular ones include www.careerpath.com, www.careermosaic.com, www.hotjobs.com, and www.monster.com. The Monster Board carries hundreds of job listings and offers links to related sites, such as company home pages and sites with information about job fairs.

Cyber-Interviews

A preliminary interview may take place via e-mail. You may be asked to respond online about your background and experience. Additional information about online interviews is available at www.headhunter.net and www.jobtrak.com.

Online Career Advancement

Online courses to expand your career skills, along with information from professional organizations, may be accessed at www.ama.org (the American Marketing Association) and with a web search for "online courses."

Career Resource Centers

Several web sites and search engines offer a variety of career information, such as www.aol.com, www.excite.com, www.yahoo.com, www.lycos.com, www.webcrawler.com, and www.hotbot.com/jobs. Federal jobs: www.fedworld.gov/jobs/jobsearch.html is a good choice for those interested in working for a government agency. This site lists positions all across the country. You can limit your search to specific states or do a general cross-country search for job openings.

Planning and Preparation

It is generally agreed that competition for the better jobs will get tougher and tougher. The key to landing the job you want is planning and preparation—and planning begins with goals. In particular, it is important to determine your *personal* goals, to decide on the role your career will play in reaching those goals, and then to develop your career goals. Once you know where you are going, you can devise a reasonable plan for getting there.

The time to begin planning is as early as possible. You must, of course, satisfy the educational requirements for the occupational area you wish to enter. Early planning will give you the opportunity to do so. But those people with whom you will be competing for the better jobs will also be fully prepared. Can you do more?

The answer is yes. Corporate recruiters say that the following factors give job candidates a definite advantage.

- *Work experience*—You can get valuable work experience in cooperative work/school programs, during summer vacations, or in part-time jobs during the school year. Experience in your chosen occupational area carries the most weight, but even unrelated work experience is important.
- *The ability to communicate well*—Verbal and written communication skills are increasingly important in all aspects of business. Yours will be tested in your letters to recruiters, in your résumé, and in interviews. You will use these same communication skills throughout your career.
- *Clear and realistic job and career goals*—Recruiters feel most comfortable with candidates who know where they are headed and why they are applying for a specific job.

Again, early planning can make all the difference in defining your goals; in sharpening your communication skills (through elective courses, if necessary); and in obtaining solid work experience.

Letter and Résumé

Preparation is also important when it is time to apply for a position. Your college placement office and various publications available in your library (including such directories as *Standard & Poor's Register of Corporations* and *Thomas Register*) can help you find firms to apply to for jobs. As already mentioned, help-wanted ads, the Internet, networking, and employment agencies may also provide leads.

Your first contact with a prospective employer will probably be through the mail—in a letter in which you express your interest in working for that firm. This letter should be clear and straightforward, and it should follow proper business-letter form—see Figure A.7. It (and any other letters you write to potential employers) will be considered part of your employment credentials.

This first letter should be addressed to the personnel or human resources manager—by name if possible. You may include in this letter, very briefly, some information regarding your qualifications and your reason for writing to that particular firm. If your source of information (newspaper advertisement, employment agency, current employee of the firm, and so on) indicates that this employer is looking for specific job skills, you may also want to state and describe in the cover letter the skills you possess. You should request an interview and, if the firm requires it, an employment application.

You should include a copy of your résumé with your first letter. (Most applicants do.) In any case, you should already have prepared the résumé, which is a summary of all your attention-getting employment achievements and capabilities. Your goal in preparing both the cover letter and the résumé is to give the potential employer the impression that you are someone who deserves an interview.

A résumé should highlight and summarize your abilities and work achievements. The résumé should fit on a single sheet of white, high-quality, bond letter paper. It should be carefully thought out—rework it as many times as necessary to get it right and put your best foot forward. Make your résumé concise, but be sure to note everything important. You need not include explanations or details; you will have an opportunity to discuss your qualifications during the interviews. It should be written to grab a potential employer's interest. The employer reading your résumé should want to meet you to find out more. Your résumé needs to show that despite your current job title, you are qualified for the higher-level position you seek.

Remember that you are writing a résumé that will sell you to a potential employer. If necessary, ask former supervisors and colleagues to tell you what happened to projects or work that you produced. Then use action verbs to describe your major contributions. Words such as *managed, created, developed,* or *coordinated* sound high-powered. Passive words or phrases such as *was responsible for* or *performed* are not attention-getting. Highlight your work achievements by using percentages, numbers, or dollar amounts. Such concrete details demonstrate just how important your contributions were. In some cases, personal traits or the ability to "do something" may be

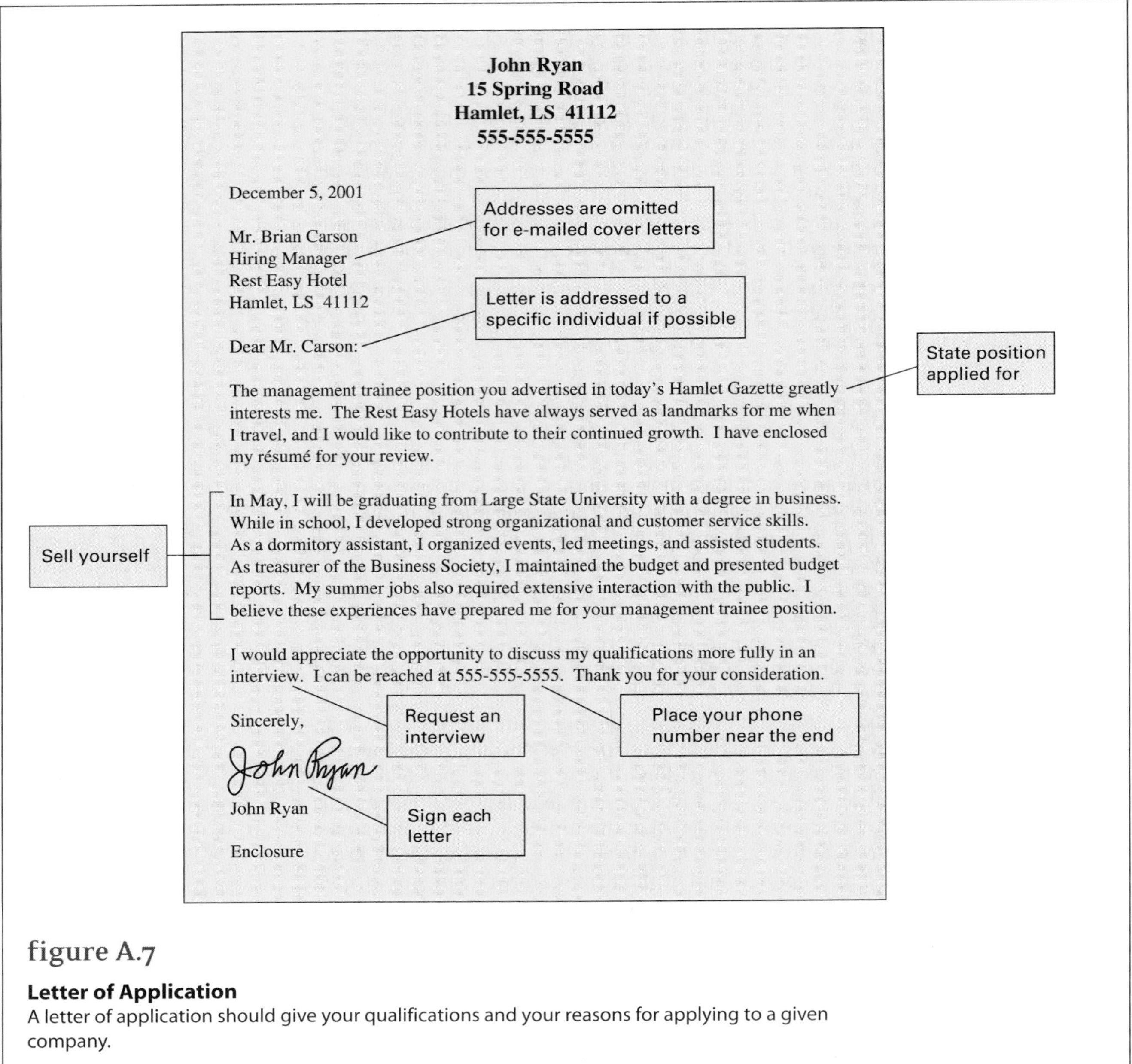

John Ryan
15 Spring Road
Hamlet, LS 41112
555-555-5555

December 5, 2001

Mr. Brian Carson
Hiring Manager
Rest Easy Hotel
Hamlet, LS 41112

Dear Mr. Carson:

The management trainee position you advertised in today's Hamlet Gazette greatly interests me. The Rest Easy Hotels have always served as landmarks for me when I travel, and I would like to contribute to their continued growth. I have enclosed my résumé for your review.

In May, I will be graduating from Large State University with a degree in business. While in school, I developed strong organizational and customer service skills. As a dormitory assistant, I organized events, led meetings, and assisted students. As treasurer of the Business Society, I maintained the budget and presented budget reports. My summer jobs also required extensive interaction with the public. I believe these experiences have prepared me for your management trainee position.

I would appreciate the opportunity to discuss my qualifications more fully in an interview. I can be reached at 555-555-5555. Thank you for your consideration.

Sincerely,

John Ryan

John Ryan

Enclosure

figure A.7

Letter of Application
A letter of application should give your qualifications and your reasons for applying to a given company.

Source: U.S. Bureau of Labor Statistics, *Occupational Outlook Quarterly*, summer 1999, p. 13.

more important than technical skills. Employers may be looking for someone who has the ability to

1. Prepare letters, memos, and other written communications.
2. Answer the telephone and talk with customers.
3. Analyze and solve problems related to a specific job.
4. Work independently and make decisions.
5. Be flexible and get the job done.
6. Get along with others and be a team player.

These traits may be extremely important to some employers. And a job applicant who doesn't have a lot of occupational experience can use these traits to "beef up" a slim résumé.

Figures A.8, A.9, and A.10 show a chronological résumé, a functional résumé, and a new database résumé. The chronological résumé presents your education, work experience, and other information in a reverse-time sequence (the most recent item first). The functional résumé emphasizes your abilities and skills in categories such as communication, supervision, project planning, human relations, and research. The database résumé, also called *plain text* or *e-mailed resume*, includes the same basic information, except that the database résumé is written without columns, bullets, or bold or italic styles. Regardless of the form used, a résumé should include the following: your name, address, and telephone number; your work experience and major accomplishments on the job; your educational background; and any awards you have won. Avoid all extraneous information (such as weight, age, marital status, and the names and addresses of references) that could be supplied during an interview. Reserve your employment and/or career objectives for mention in the one-page cover letters you send to potential employers with copies of your résumé.

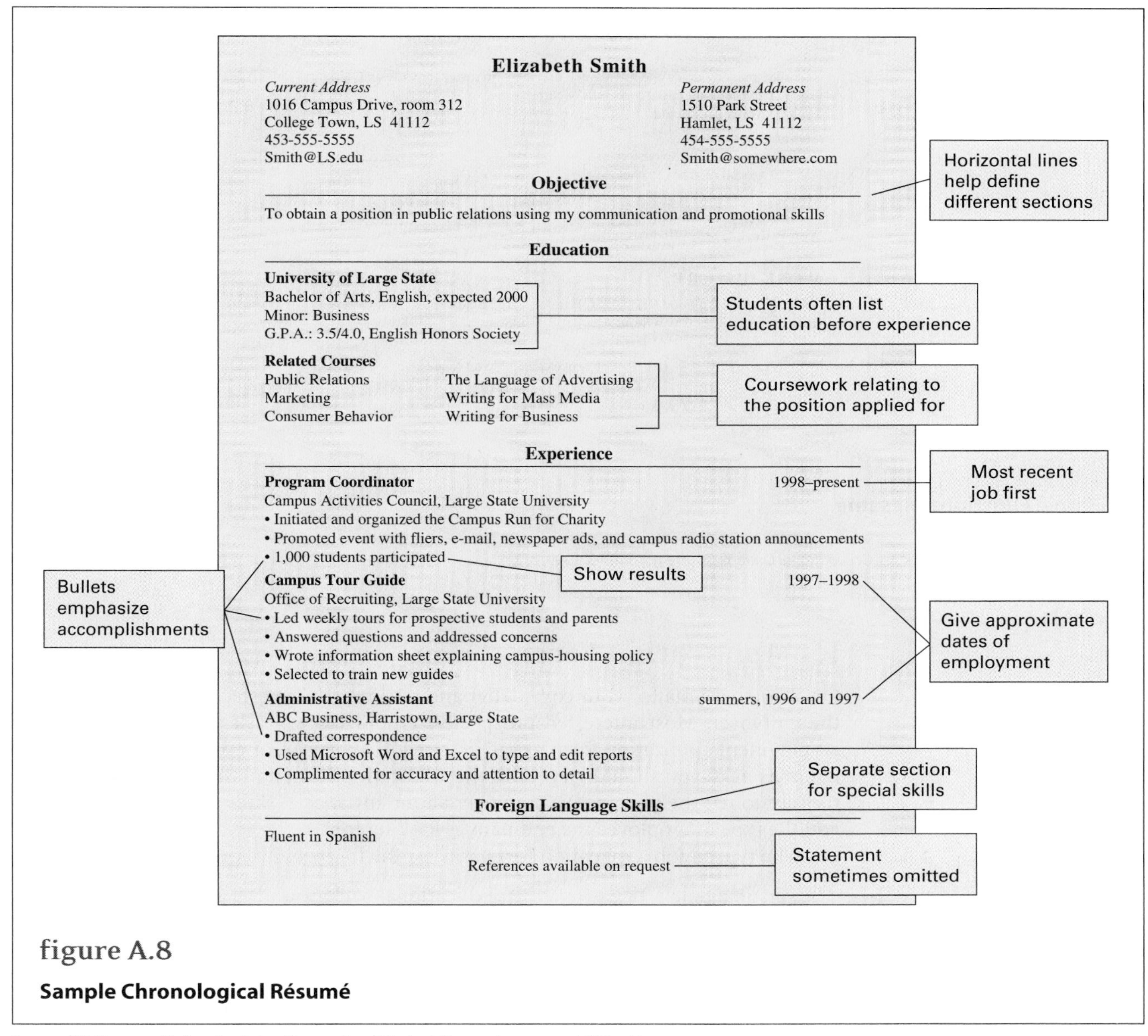

Elizabeth Smith

Current Address
1016 Campus Drive, room 312
College Town, LS 41112
453-555-5555
Smith@LS.edu

Permanent Address
1510 Park Street
Hamlet, LS 41112
454-555-5555
Smith@somewhere.com

Objective

To obtain a position in public relations using my communication and promotional skills

Education

University of Large State
Bachelor of Arts, English, expected 2000
Minor: Business
G.P.A.: 3.5/4.0, English Honors Society

Related Courses

Public Relations	The Language of Advertising
Marketing	Writing for Mass Media
Consumer Behavior	Writing for Business

Experience

Program Coordinator 1998–present
Campus Activities Council, Large State University
- Initiated and organized the Campus Run for Charity
- Promoted event with fliers, e-mail, newspaper ads, and campus radio station announcements
- 1,000 students participated

Campus Tour Guide 1997–1998
Office of Recruiting, Large State University
- Led weekly tours for prospective students and parents
- Answered questions and addressed concerns
- Wrote information sheet explaining campus-housing policy
- Selected to train new guides

Administrative Assistant summers, 1996 and 1997
ABC Business, Harristown, Large State
- Drafted correspondence
- Used Microsoft Word and Excel to type and edit reports
- Complimented for accuracy and attention to detail

Foreign Language Skills

Fluent in Spanish

References available on request

figure A.8

Sample Chronological Résumé

Source: U.S. Bureau of Labor Statistics, *Occupational Outlook Quarterly*, summer 1999, p. 7.

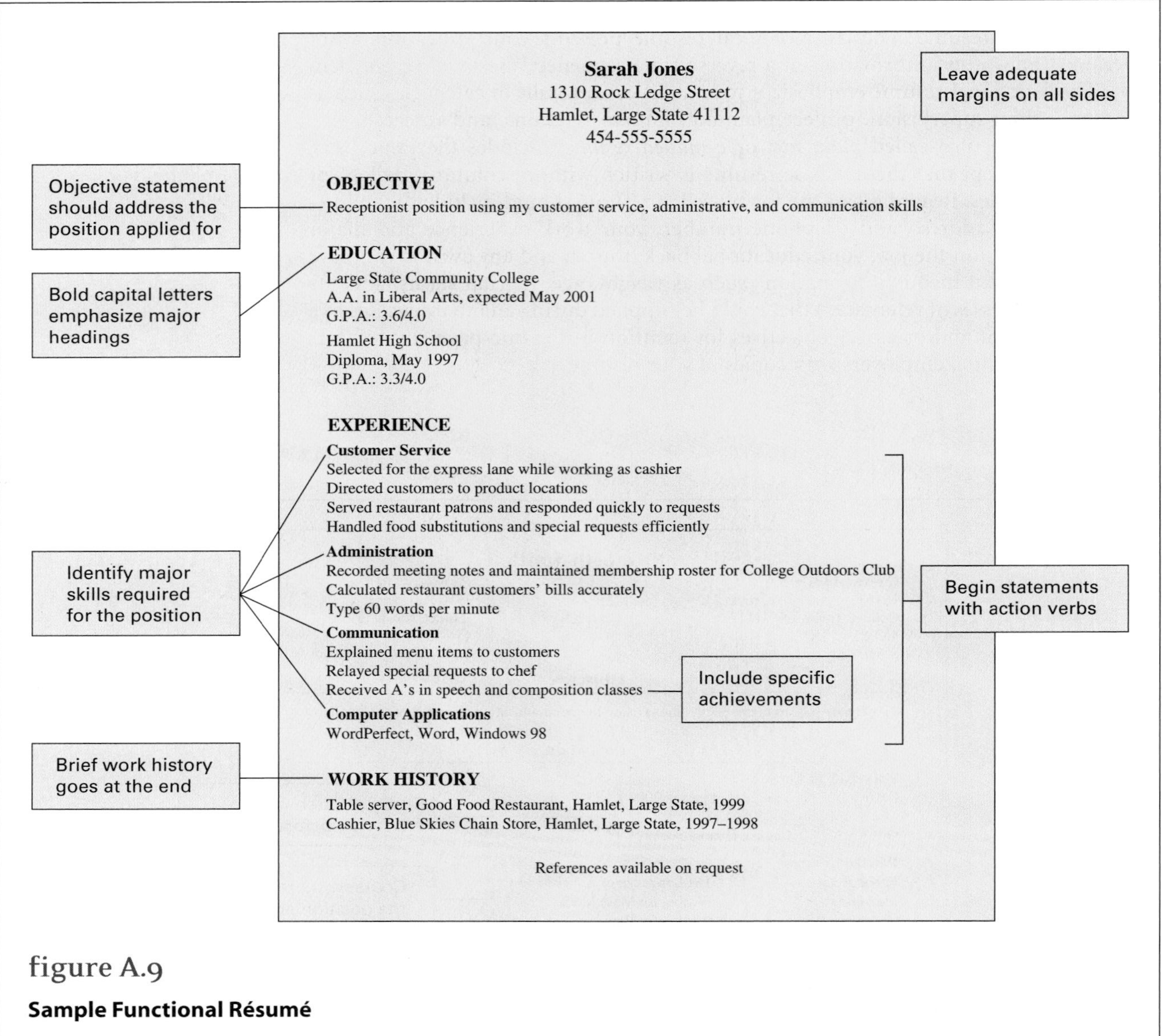

figure A.9

Sample Functional Résumé

Source: U.S. Bureau of Labor Statistics, *Occupational Outlook Quarterly*, summer 1999, p. 9.

Job Application Forms

Once you have mailed your cover letter and résumé, the next step generally depends on the employer. Most interested prospective employers will ask that you complete an employment application form, come in for a job interview, or both. Regardless of what happens next, you should view both the application form and the interview as opportunities to tell the prospective employer about any special skills and talents that make you the type of employee the company is looking for.

The typical job application form asks for the following information;

- Personal data
- Military record
- Criminal record
- Educational background
- Employment history
- Character references

Do the best job you can when answering questions in each of these areas. The way you complete an application form demonstrates your ability to follow directions and to communicate effectively. The suggestions listed in Table A.1 can help you avoid some of the most common mistakes applicants make.

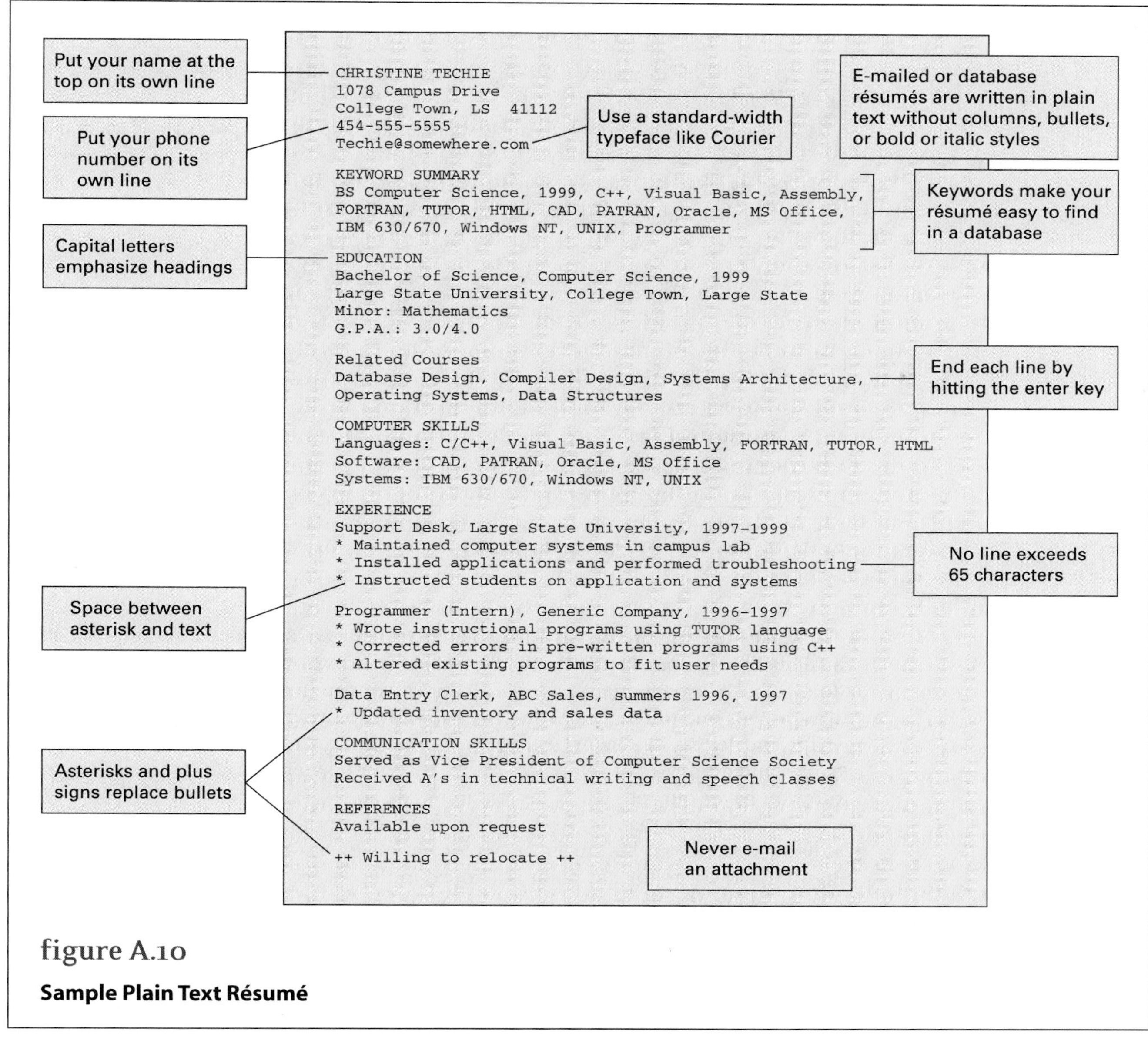

figure A.10

Sample Plain Text Résumé

Source: U.S. Bureau of Labor Statistics, *Occupational Outlook Quarterly*, summer 1999, p. 11.

The Job Interview

Your résumé and cover letter are, in essence, an introduction. The deciding factor in the hiring process is the interview (or several interviews) with representatives of the firm. It is through the interview that the firm gets to know you and your qualifications. At the same time, the interview provides a chance for you to learn about the firm.

Here, again, preparation is the key to success. Research the firm before your first interview. Learn all you can about its products, its subsidiaries, the markets it operates in, its history, the locations of its facilities, and so on. If possible, obtain and read the firm's most recent annual report. Be prepared to ask questions about the firm and the opportunities it offers. Interviewers welcome such questions. They expect you to be interested enough to spend some time thinking about your potential relationship with their firm.

Prepare also to respond to questions the interviewer may ask. Table A.2 is a list of typical interviewer questions that job applicants often find difficult to answer. But don't expect interviewers to stick to the list given in the table or to the items appearing in your résumé. They will be interested in anything that helps them decide what kind of person and worker you are.

table A.1 Tips for Completing Employment Application Forms

1. Do a "dry run" to practice answering the questions on a typical employment application.
2. If it is not possible to take the application home, complete the application in ink. Print clearly. Use one lettering style.
3. Follow the directions on the employment application.
4. Read all questions before you begin answering them.
5. Judge the amount of space that you have to answer each question.
6. Fill in every blank even if you must write *not applicable* (N/A) or *none*.
7. Read over the completed application, and look for grammatical or spelling errors.
8. Answer all questions honestly.
9. Choose references carefully.
10. Be careful when writing salary requirements.
11. Be neat. Proofread.
12. Know your work history.

Source: Adapted from Susan D. Greene and Melanie C. L. Martel, *The Ultimate Job Hunter's Guidebook*, Third Edition, pp. 116–117. Copyright © 2001 by Houghton Mifflin Company. Adapted with permission.

Make sure you are on time for your interview and are dressed and groomed in a businesslike manner. Interviewers take note of punctuality and appearance, just as they do of other personal qualities. Have a copy of your résumé with you, even if you have already sent one to the firm. You may also want to bring a copy of your course transcript and letters of recommendation. If you plan to furnish interviewers with the names and addresses of references rather than with letters of recommendation, make sure you have your references' permission to do so.

Consider the interview itself as a two-way conversation, rather than as a question-and-answer session. Volunteer any information that is relevant to the interviewer's questions. If an important point is skipped in the discussion, don't hesitate to bring it up. Be yourself, but emphasize your strengths. Good eye contact and posture are important, too. They should come naturally if you take an active part in the interview.

At the conclusion of the interview, thank the recruiter for taking the time to see you. Then, a day or two later, follow up by sending a short letter of thanks. (See Figure A.11.) In this letter, you can ask a question or two that may have occurred to you after the interview or add pertinent information that may have been overlooked.

In most cases, the first interview is used to *screen* applicants, or choose those who are best qualified. These applicants are then given a second interview, and perhaps a third—usually with one or more department heads. If the job requires relocation to a different area, applicants may be invited there for these later interviews. After the interviewing process is complete, applicants are told when to expect a hiring decision.

Accepting an Offer

"We'd like to offer you the job" may be the best news a job applicant can hear. To accept the job, you should send the firm a letter in which you express your appreciation, accept the offer, and restate the conditions of employment as you understand them. These conditions should include the starting salary, employee benefits, and a general description of the job (responsibilities, training, the immediate supervisor's name, and such). If you have any concerns regarding the job, make sure they are cleared up before you send your letter of acceptance: the job offer and your acceptance constitute a contract between you and the firm.

Less exciting is the news that begins "We thank you for your interest in our firm, *but*. . . ." The fact is, there are many more applicants for jobs than there are jobs. (This

figure A.11

Sample Thank You Letter

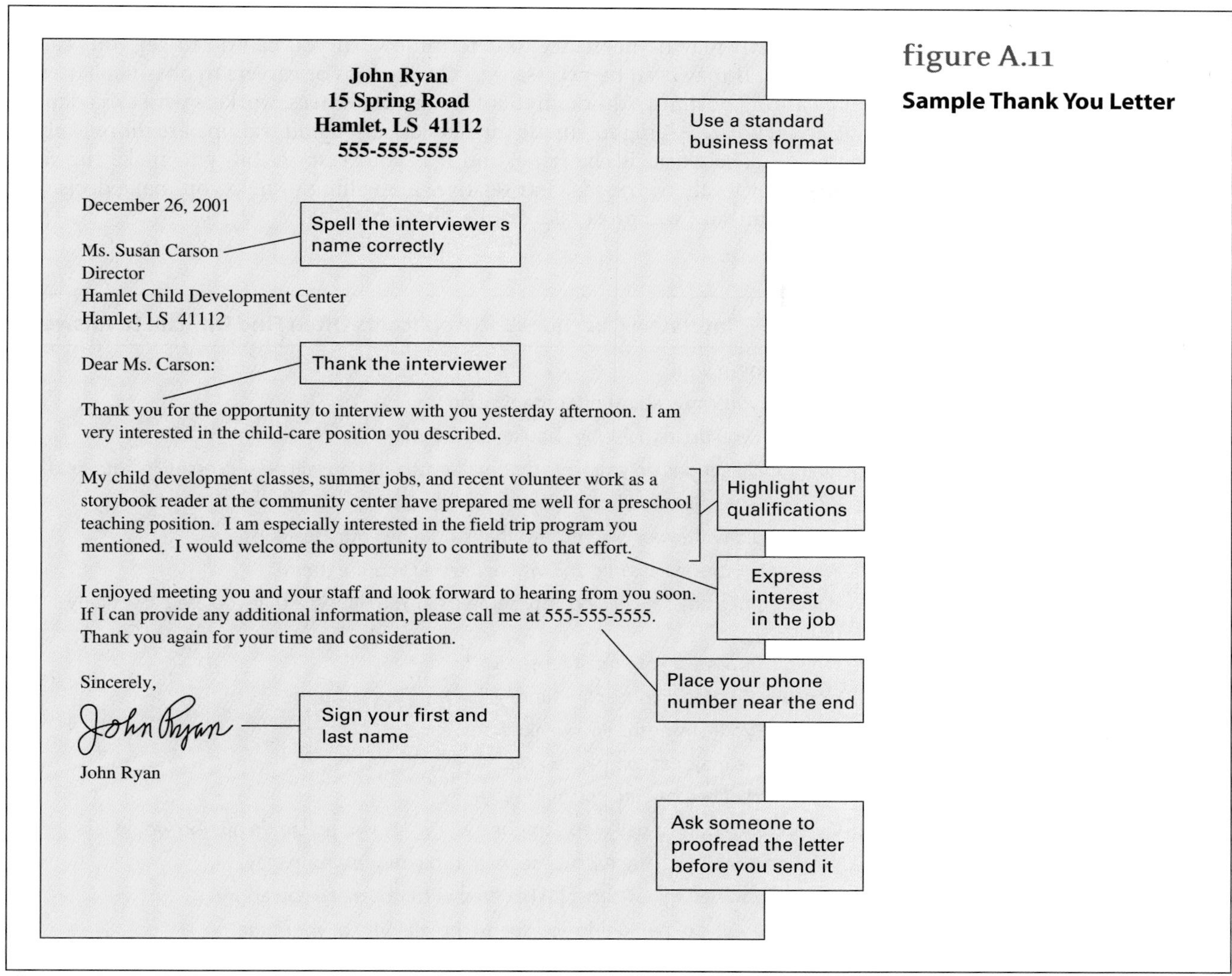

John Ryan
15 Spring Road
Hamlet, LS 41112
555-555-5555

December 26, 2001

Ms. Susan Carson
Director
Hamlet Child Development Center
Hamlet, LS 41112

Dear Ms. Carson:

Thank you for the opportunity to interview with you yesterday afternoon. I am very interested in the child-care position you described.

My child development classes, summer jobs, and recent volunteer work as a storybook reader at the community center have prepared me well for a preschool teaching position. I am especially interested in the field trip program you mentioned. I would welcome the opportunity to contribute to that effort.

I enjoyed meeting you and your staff and look forward to hearing from you soon. If I can provide any additional information, please call me at 555-555-5555. Thank you again for your time and consideration.

Sincerely,

John Ryan

John Ryan

Source: U.S. Bureau of Labor Statistics, *Occupational Outlook Quarterly*, summer 2000, p. 21.

is because most people apply for several positions at the same time.) As a result, most people are turned down for some jobs during their careers. Don't be discouraged if you don't get the first position you apply for. Instead, think back over the application process, analyze it, and try to determine what you might improve. In other words, learn from your experience—and keep trying. Success will come if you persevere.

A Final Note About Careers

A job is for today, but a career can last a lifetime. Although most applicants are excited when they get their first job, the employment process doesn't stop with your first job—it continues throughout your career. Additional training and education, promotions and advancement, and even changing jobs or careers are all part of a continuing process.

Although different people measure success in different ways, success in a career means more than just knowing how to do a job. You must combine technical skills and managerial skills with the ability to get along with people. A number of traits that successful people usually possess are presented in Table A.3. Generally, people who are promoted know how to make decisions, communicate well, and handle stress. These same people can also manage another valuable asset—their time.

In any career, there will be times when you need to re-evaluate your decisions and opportunities. It may be necessary to determine what you can do to get your career back on track. It may even be necessary to change jobs or careers to obtain a better or more rewarding position. Although there are no guarantees, workers who can adapt to change and who are willing to pursue further education and training are more likely to be successful. The world is changing, and it is your responsibility to make the right decisions. Your teachers, friends, and relatives are willing to help you make decisions, but it is your life and you must take charge. Good luck!

table A.2 Interview Questions Job Applicants Often Find Difficult to Answer

1. Tell me about yourself.
2. What do you know about our organization?
3. What can you do for us? Why should we hire you?
4. What qualifications do you have that make you feel you will be successful in your field?
5. What have you learned from the jobs you've held?
6. If you could write your own ticket, what would be your ideal job?
7. What are your special skills, and where did you acquire them?
8. Have you had any special accomplishments in your lifetime that you are particularly proud of?
9. Why did you leave your most recent job?
10. How do you spend your spare time? What are your hobbies?
11. What are your strengths and weaknesses?
12. Discuss five major accomplishments.
13. What kind of boss would you like? Why?
14. If you could spend a day with someone you've known or known of, who would it be?
15. What personality characteristics seem to rub you the wrong way?
16. How do you show your anger? What type of things make you angry?
17. With what type of person do you spend the majority of your time?
18. What activities have you ever quit?
19. Define cooperation.

Source: Adapted from Susan D. Greene and Melanie C.L. Martel, *The Ultimate Job Hunter's Guidebook*, Third Edition, pp. 135–137. Copyright © 2001 by Houghton Mifflin Company. Adapted with permission.

table A.3 Traits That Successful People Usually Possess

1. An ability to work well with others in a variety of settings
2. A desire to do tasks better than they have to be done
3. An interest in reading a wide variety and large quantity of materials
4. A willingness to cope with conflict and adapt to change
5. An ability to anticipate problems
6. A knowledge of technology and computer software such as word processing, spreadsheet, and database programs
7. An ability to solve problems creatively
8. A knowledge of research techniques and library resources
9. Well-developed written and oral communication skills
10. An understanding of both their own motivations and the motivations of others

Source: Jack R. Kapoor, Les Dlabay, and Robert J. Hughes, *Personal Finance*, Sixth Edition, p. 38. Copyright © 2001 by McGraw-Hill/Irwin, Inc. Reprinted by permission of the McGraw-Hill Companies.

Risk Management and Insurance

We begin this appendix by defining two broad categories of risk: pure risk and speculative risk. We then examine several methods of risk management available to individuals and businesses and consider situations in which each method is appropriate. Next we turn our attention to insurance companies—organizations that for a fee, assume financial responsibility for losses resulting from certain kinds of risks. We see how insurance companies determine which risks they will cover and what prices they will charge for coverage. Then we list the major types of insurance against loss of property and loss due to accidents and discuss workers' compensation and healthcare insurance. We close the appendix with a comparison of several kinds of life insurance.

The Element of Risk

Risk is the possibility that a loss or injury will occur. It is impossible to escape all types of risk in today's world. For individuals, driving an automobile, investing in stocks or bonds, and even jogging along a country road are situations that involve some risk. For businesses, risk is a part of every decision. In fact, the essence of business decision making is weighing the potential risks and gains involved in various courses of action.

risk the possibility that a loss or injury will occur

There is obviously a difference between, say, the risk of losing money one has invested and the risk of being hit by a car while jogging. This difference leads to the classification of risks as either speculative or pure risks.

A **speculative risk** is a risk that accompanies the possibility of earning a profit. Most business decisions, such as the decision to market a new product, involve speculative risks. If the new product succeeds in the marketplace, there are profits; if it fails, there are losses. For example, PepsiCo repeatedly gambles on the introduction of new products to compete with Coca-Cola and reach the elusive top spot. But the gamble doesn't pay off when the product fizzles.

speculative risk a risk that accompanies the possibility of earning a profit

A **pure risk** is a risk that involves only the possibility of loss, with no potential for gain. The possibility of damage due to hurricane, fire, or auto accident is a pure risk because there is no gain if such damage does not occur. Another pure risk is the risk of large medical bills resulting from a serious illness. Again, if there is no illness, there is no monetary gain.

pure risk a risk that involves only the possibility of loss, with no potential for gain

Let us now look at the various techniques available for managing risk.

Risk Management

Risk management is the process of evaluating the risks faced by a firm or an individual and then minimizing the costs involved with those risks. Any risk entails two types of costs. The first is the cost that will be incurred if a *potential* loss becomes an *actual* loss.

risk management the process of evaluating the risks faced by a firm or an individual and then minimizing the costs involved with those risks

An example is the cost of rebuilding and re-equipping an assembly plant that burns to the ground. The second type consists of the costs of reducing or eliminating the risk of potential loss. Here we would include the cost of purchasing insurance against loss by fire or the cost of not building the plant at all (this cost is equal to the profit that the plant might have earned). These two types of costs must be balanced, one against the other, if risk management is to be effective.

Most people think of risk management as simply buying insurance. But insurance, although an important part of risk management, is not the only means of dealing with risk. Other methods may be less costly in specific situations. And some kinds of risks are uninsurable—not even an insurance company will issue a policy to protect against them. In this section, we examine the four general risk-management techniques. Then, in the following sections, we look more closely at insurance.

Risk Avoidance

An individual can avoid the risk of an automobile accident by not riding in a car. A manufacturer can avoid the risk of product failure by refusing to introduce new products. Both would be practicing risk avoidance—but at a very high cost. The person who avoids automobile accidents by foregoing cars may have to give up his or her job to do so. The business that does not take a chance on new products will probably fail when the product life cycle, discussed in Chapter 14, catches up with existing products.

There are, however, situations in which risk avoidance is a practical technique. At the personal level, individuals who stop smoking or refuse to walk through a dark city park late at night are avoiding risks. Jewelry stores lock their merchandise in vaults at the end of the business day to avoid losses through robbery. And, to avoid the risk of a holdup, many gasoline stations accept only credit cards or the exact amount of the purchase for sales made after dark.

Obviously, no person or business can eliminate all risks. But, by the same token, no one should assume that all risks are unavoidable.

Risk Reduction

If a risk cannot be avoided, perhaps it can be reduced. An automobile passenger can reduce the risk of injury in an auto accident by wearing a seat belt. A manufacturer can reduce the risk of product failure through careful product planning and market testing. In both situations, the cost of reducing risk seems to be well worth the potential saving.

Businesses face risks as a result of their operating procedures and management decision making. An analysis of operating procedures—by company personnel or outside consultants—can often point out areas in which risk can be reduced. Among the techniques that can be used are

- The establishment of an employee safety program to encourage employees' awareness of safety
- The purchase *and* use of proper safety equipment, from hand guards on machinery to goggles and safety shoes for individuals
- Burglar alarms, security guards, and even guard dogs to protect warehouses from burglary
- Fire alarms, smoke alarms, and sprinkler systems to reduce the risk of fire and the losses due to fire
- Accurate and effective accounting and financial controls to protect the firm's inventories and cash from pilfering

The risks involved in management decisions can be reduced only through effective decision making. These risks *increase* when a decision is made hastily or is based on less than sufficient information. However, the cost of reducing these risks goes up when managers take too long to make decisions. Costs also increase when managers require an overabundance of information before they are willing to decide.

Risk Assumption

An individual or firm will—and probably must—take on certain risks as part of living or doing business. Individuals who drive to work *assume* the risk of having an accident, but they wear a seat belt to reduce the risk of injury in the event of an accident. The firm that markets a new product *assumes* the risk of product failure—after first reducing that risk through market testing.

Risk assumption, then, is the act of taking responsibility for the loss or injury that may result from a risk. Generally, it makes sense to assume a risk when one or more of the following conditions exist:

1. The potential loss is too small to worry about.
2. Effective risk management has reduced the risk.
3. Insurance coverage, if available, is too expensive.
4. There is no other way of protecting against the loss.

Large firms with many facilities often find a particular kind of risk assumption, called self-insurance, a practical way to avoid high insurance costs. **Self-insurance** is the process of establishing a monetary fund that can be used to cover the cost of a loss. For instance, suppose approximately 16,000 7-Eleven convenience stores, each worth $400,000, are scattered around the country. A logical approach to self-insurance against fire losses would be to collect a certain sum—say, $600—from each store every year. The funds are placed in an interest-bearing reserve fund and used as necessary to repair any fire damage that occurs to 7-Eleven stores. Money not used remains the property of the firm. Eventually, if the fund grows, the yearly contribution from each store can be reduced.

self-insurance the process of establishing a monetary fund that can be used to cover the cost of a loss

Self-insurance does not eliminate risks; it merely provides a means for covering losses. And it is, itself, a risky practice—at least in the beginning. For example, 7-Eleven would suffer a considerable financial loss if more than twenty-four stores were destroyed by fire in the first year the self-insurance program was in effect.

Shifting Risks

Perhaps the most common method of dealing with risk is to shift, or transfer, the risk to an insurance company. An **insurer** (or **insurance company**) is a firm that agrees, for a fee, to assume financial responsibility for losses that may result from a specific risk. The fee charged by an insurance company is called a **premium**. A contract between an insurer and the person or firm whose risk is assumed is known as an **insurance policy**. Generally, an insurance policy is written for a period of one year. Then, if both parties are willing, it is renewed each year. It specifies exactly which risks are covered by the agreement, the dollar amounts the insurer will pay in case of a loss, and the amount of the premium.

Insurance is thus the protection against loss that the purchase of an insurance policy affords. Insurance companies will not, however, assume every kind of risk. A risk that insurance companies will assume is called an **insurable risk**. Insurable risks include the risk of loss by fire and theft, the risk of loss by automobile accident, and the risks of sickness and death. A risk that insurance companies will not assume is called an **uninsurable risk.**

In general, pure risks are insurable, whereas speculative risks are uninsurable (see Figure B.1). An insurance company will protect a Ford Motor Company assembly plant against losses due to fire or tornadoes. It will not, however, protect Ford against losses resulting from a lack of sales orders for automobiles.

The next section provides an overview of the basic principles of insurance and the kinds of companies that provide insurance.

insurer (or insurance company) a firm that agrees, for a fee, to assume financial responsibility for losses that may result from a specific risk

premium the fee charged by an insurance company

insurance policy the contract between an insurer and the person or firm whose risk is assumed

insurance the protection against loss that the purchase of an insurance policy affords

insurable risk a risk that insurance companies will assume

uninsurable risk a risk that insurance companies will not assume

figure B.1

Insurable and Uninsurable Risk for Businesses and Individuals
Generally, an insurance company will not protect against speculative risks such as lack of sales.

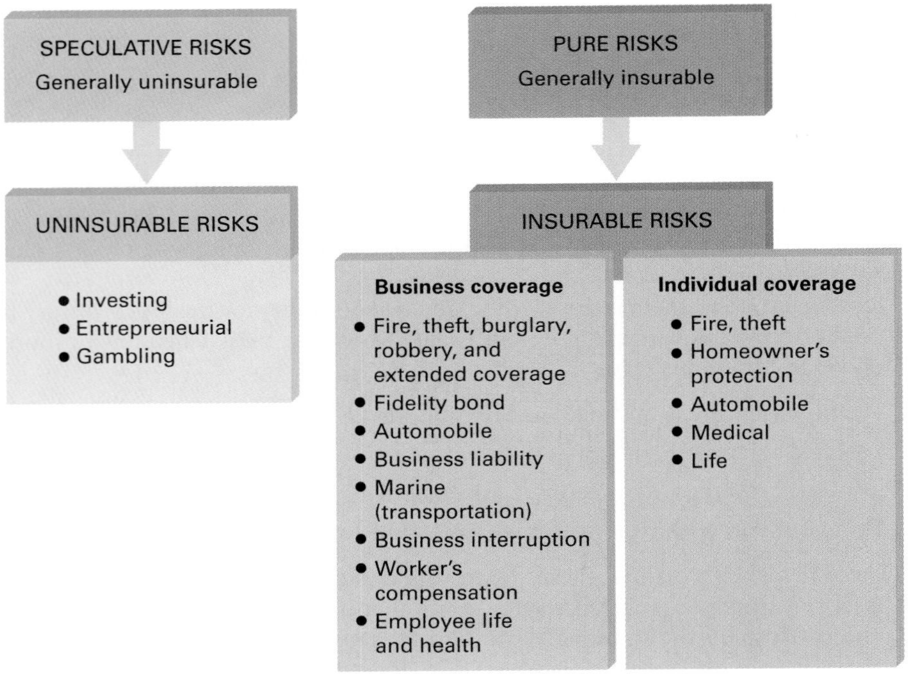

Insurance and Insurance Companies

An insurance company is a business. Like other businesses, an insurer provides a product—protection from loss—in return for a reasonable fee. Its sales revenues are the premiums it collects from the individuals and firms it insures. (Insurance companies typically invest the money they have on hand; thus, we should include interest and dividend income as part of their revenues.) Its expenses are the costs of the various resources—salaries, rent, utilities, and so on—*plus* the amounts the insurance company pays out to cover its clients' losses.

Pricing and product are very important and exacting issues to an insurance company, primarily because it must set its price (its premiums) before knowing the specific cost of its product (the amount of money it will have to pay out in claims). For this reason, insurance companies employ mathematicians called *actuaries* to predict the likelihood of losses and to determine the premiums that should be charged. Let us look at some of the more important concepts on which insurance (and the work of actuaries) is based.

Basic Insurance Concepts

Insurance is based on several principles, including the principle of indemnity, insurability of the risk, and low-cost, affordable coverage.

principle of indemnity in the event of a loss, an insured firm or individual cannot collect from the insurer an amount greater than the actual dollar amount of the loss

The Principle of Indemnity The purpose of insurance is to provide protection against loss; it is neither speculation nor gambling. This concept is expressed in the **principle of indemnity**: in the event of a loss, an insured firm or individual cannot collect from the insurer an amount greater than the actual dollar amount of the loss. Suppose you own a home valued at $150,000. However, you purchase $200,000 worth of fire insurance on your home. Even if it is destroyed by fire, the insurer will pay you only $150,000, the actual amount of your loss.

The premiums set by actuaries are based on the amount of risk involved and the amount to be paid in case of a loss. Generally, the greater the risk and the amount to be paid, the higher the premium.

Insurability of the Risk Insurers will accept responsibility for risks that meet at least the following conditions:

1. *Losses must not be under the control of the insured.* Losses caused by fire, wind, or accident are generally insurable, but gambling losses are not. Nor will an insurer pay a claim for damage intentionally caused by the insured person. For example, a person who sets fire to an insured building cannot collect on a fire insurance policy.
2. *The insured hazard must be geographically widespread.* That is, the insurance company must be able to write many policies covering the same specific hazard throughout a wide geographic area. This condition allows the insurer to minimize its own risk: the risk that it will have to pay huge sums of money to clients within a particular geographic area in the event of a catastrophe caused, for example, by a tornado.
3. *The probability of a loss should be predictable.* Insurance companies cannot tell which particular clients will suffer losses. However, their actuaries must be able to determine, statistically, what *fraction* of their clients will suffer each type of loss. They can do so, for insurable risks, by examining records of losses for past years. They can then base their premiums, at least in part, on the number and value of the losses that are expected to occur.
4. *Losses must be measurable.* Insured property must have a value that is measurable in dollars because insurance firms reimburse losses with money. Moreover, premiums are based partly on the measured value of the insured property. As a result of this condition, insurers will not insure an item for its emotional or sentimental value, but only for its actual monetary value.
5. *The policyholder must have an insurable interest.* That is, the individual or firm that purchases an insurance policy must be the one that would suffer from a loss. You can purchase insurance on your own home, but you cannot insure your neighbor's home in the hope of making a profit if it should burn down! Generally, individuals are considered to have an insurable interest in their family members. Therefore, a person can insure the life of a spouse, a child, or a parent. Corporations may purchase "key executive" insurance covering certain corporate officers. The proceeds from this insurance help offset the loss of the services of these key people if they die or become incapacitated.

Low-Cost, Affordable Coverage Price is usually a marketing issue rather than a technical concept. However, the price of insurance is intimately tied to the risks and potential losses involved in a particular type of coverage. Insurers would like to "produce" insurance at a very low cost to their policyholders, but they must charge enough in premiums to cover their expected payouts.

Customers purchase insurance when they believe premiums are low in relation to the possible dollar loss. For certain risks, premiums can soar so high that insurance is simply not cost-effective. A $1,000 life insurance policy for a ninety-nine-year-old man would cost about $950 per year. Clearly, a man of that age would be better off if he invested the premium amount in a bank. He would thus be using self-insurance rather than shifting the risk. Although this is an extreme example, it illustrates that insurers must compete, through their prices, with alternative methods of managing risk.

Ownership of Insurance Companies

Insurance companies are owned either by stockholders or by policyholders. A **stock insurance company** is owned by stockholders and is operated to earn a profit. Like other profit-making corporations, stock insurance companies pay dividends to stock-

stock insurance company an insurance company owned by stockholders and operated to earn a profit

mutual insurance company an insurance company that is collectively owned by its policyholders and is thus a cooperative

holders from surplus of income (left over after benefit payments, operating expenses, and taxes have been paid). Most of the approximately 6,000 insurance companies in the United States are stock insurance companies.

A **mutual insurance company** is collectively owned by its policyholders and is thus a cooperative. Because a mutual insurance company has no stockholders, its policyholders elect the board of directors. The members of the board, in turn, choose the executives who manage the firm. Any surplus of income over expenses is distributed to policyholders as a return of part of their premiums. (This return may take the form of a reduced premium at the start of the policy year or of a "dividend" at the end of the policy year.)

Both stock and mutual insurance companies must maintain cash reserves to cover future obligations and policyholders' claims. Cash reserves are typically invested in certificates of deposit, stocks, bonds, and real estate.

Careers in Insurance

Insurance companies form one of the largest industries in the United States. The industry ranks in importance with banking and finance, manufacturing, building, and electronics. Careers in insurance generally fall into two categories: sales and administration.

In the sales category, individuals can work as employees of insurance companies or as independent agents representing more than one insurance company. Recently, the insurance industry has placed more emphasis on advanced training for sales personnel. Life insurance salespeople who pass examinations and meet other requirements are awarded the Chartered Life Underwriter (CLU) designation. The Chartered Property Casualty Underwriter (CPCU) designation is awarded to individuals who pass examinations and meet the requirements in all areas *except* life insurance.

Administrative employees work to meet the needs of the firm's customers. They must process policies and claims and handle an amazing amount of paper-work. Jobs in this category include actuary, claims adjuster, claims clerk, underwriter, and a number of other essential positions. In addition to meeting the needs of customers, administrative employees are responsible for investing funds for an insurance company.

Property and Casualty Insurance

Businesses and individuals insure their property, such as buildings, against losses, and purchase casualty insurance to cover financial losses resulting from injuries or damages caused by automobile accidents.

Insurance is available to cover most pure risks, but specialized or customized policies can be expensive. A part of effective risk management is to ensure that, when insurance is purchased, the coverage is proper for the individual situation. Three questions can be used as guidelines in this regard.

- What hazards must be insured against?
- Is the cost of insurance coverage reasonable in this situation?
- What other risk-management techniques can be used to reduce insurance costs?

Fire Insurance

fire insurance insurance that covers losses due to fire

Fire insurance covers losses due to fire. The standard fire insurance policy provides protection against partial or complete loss of a building and/or its contents when that loss is caused by fire or lighting. Premiums depend on the construction of the building, its use and contents, whether risk-reduction devices (such as smoke and fire alarms) are installed in the building, and other factors. If a fire occurs, the insurance company reimburses the policyholder for either the actual dollar loss or the maximum amount stated in the policy, whichever is lower.

Coinsurance Clause To reduce their insurance premiums, individuals and businesses sometimes insure property for less than its actual cash value. Their theory is that fire rarely destroys a building completely—thus they need not buy full insurance. However, if the building is partially destroyed, they expect their insurance to cover all the damage. This places an unfair burden on the insurance company, which receives less than the full premium but must cover the full loss. To avoid this problem, insurance companies include a coinsurance clause in most fire insurance policies.

A **coinsurance clause** is a part of a fire insurance policy that requires the policyholder to purchase coverage at least equal to a specified percentage of the replacement cost of the property to obtain full reimbursement for losses. In most cases, the requirement is 80 percent of the replacement cost. Suppose the owners of a $600,000 building decide to purchase only $300,000 worth of fire insurance. If the building is totally destroyed, the insurance company must pay the policy's face value of $300,000. However, if the building is only partially destroyed, and the damage amounts to $200,000, the insurance company will pay only $125,000. This dollar amount is calculated in the following manner:

coinsurance clause a part of a fire insurance policy that requires the policyholder to purchase coverage at least equal to a specified percentage of the replacement cost of the property to obtain full reimbursement for losses

1. The coinsurance clause requires coverage of at least 80 percent of $600,000, or $480,000.
2. The owners have purchased only $300,000 of insurance. Thus, they have insured themselves for only a portion of any loss. That portion is $300,000 ÷ $480,000 = 0.625, or 62.5 percent.
3. The insurance company will therefore reimburse the owner for only 62.5 percent of any loss. In the case of a $200,000 loss, the insurance company will pay 62.5 percent of $200,000, or $125,000.

If the owners of the building had insured it for $480,000, the insurance company would have covered the entire $200,000 loss.

Extended Coverage **Extended coverage** is insurance protection against damage caused by wind, hail, explosion, vandalism, riots or civil commotion, falling aircraft, and smoke. Extended coverage is available as an *endorsement*, or addition, to some other insurance policy—usually a fire insurance policy. The premium for extended coverage is generally quite low (much lower than the total cost of separate policies covering each individual hazard). Normally, losses caused by war, nuclear radiation or contamination, and water (other than in storms and floods) are excluded from extended-coverage endorsements.

extended coverage insurance protection against damage caused by wind, hail, explosion, vandalism, riots or civil commotion, falling aircraft, and smoke

Burglary, Robbery, and Theft Insurance

Burglary is the illegal taking of property through forcible entry. A kicked-in door, a broken window pane, or pry marks on a windowsill are evidence of a burglary or attempted burglary. *Robbery* is the unlawful taking of property from an individual by force or threat of violence. A thief who uses a gun to rob a gas station is committing robbery. *Theft* (or *larceny*) is a general term that means the wrongful taking of property that belongs to another. Insurance policies are available to cover burglary only, robbery only, theft only, or all three. Premiums vary with the type and value of the property covered by the policy.

Business owners must also be concerned about crimes that employees may commit. A **fidelity bond** is an insurance policy that protects a business from theft, forgery, or embezzlement by its employees. If such a crime does occur, the insurance company reimburses the business for financial losses up to the dollar amount specified in the policy. Individual employees or specific positions within an organization may be bonded. It is also possible to purchase a "blanket" policy that covers the entire work force. Fidelity bonds are most commonly purchased by banks, savings and loan associations, finance companies, and other firms whose employees handle cash on a regular basis.

fidelity bond an insurance policy that protects a business from theft, forgery, or embezzlement by its employees

Although business owners are concerned about shoplifting, they often find that insurance coverage, if available, is too expensive. And it is often difficult to collect on losses resulting from shoplifting because such losses are difficult to prove.

Motor Vehicle Insurance

Individuals and businesses purchase automobile insurance because it is required by state law, because it is required by the firm financing the purchase of the vehicle, and/or because they want to protect their investment. Most types of automobile coverage can be broadly classified as either liability or physical damage insurance. Table B.1 shows the distinction.

automobile liability insurance insurance that covers financial losses resulting from injuries or damages caused by the insured vehicle

Automobile Liability Insurance **Automobile liability insurance** is insurance that covers financial losses resulting from injuries or damages caused by the insured vehicle. Most automobile policies have a liability limit that contains three numbers. For example, the liability limits stated on a policy might be 100/300/50. The first two numbers indicate the maximum amounts, in thousands of dollars, the insurance company will pay for bodily injury. *Bodily injury liability coverage* pays medical bills and other costs in the event that an injury or death results from an automobile accident in which the policyholder is at fault. Bodily injury liability coverage protects the person in the other car and is usually specified as a pair of dollar amounts. In the above example, the policy limits are $100,000 for each person and $300,000 for each occurrence. This means the insurance company will pay up to $100,000 to each person injured in an accident and up to a total of $300,000 to all those injured in a single accident. Coverage limits can be as low as the state requires and as high as $500,000 per person and $1 million per accident. Payment for additional damages above the policy limits is the responsibility of the insured. In view of the cost of medical care today, and considering the size of legal settlements resulting from automobile accidents, insurance companies recommend coverage of at least $100,000 per person and $300,000 per occurrence.

Property damage liability coverage pays for the repair of damage that the insured vehicle does to the property of another person. Such damage is covered up to the amount specified in the policy. In the above example, the third number (50) indicates that the insurance company will pay up to $50,000 to repair property damage. Insurance companies generally recommend at least $100,000 worth of property damage liability.

Along with other automobile liability insurance, most car owners also purchase protection for the passengers in their own cars. A *medical payments endorsement* can be included in automobile coverage for a small additional premium. This endorsement provides for the payment of medical bills, up to a specified amount, for passengers (including the policyholder) injured in the policyholder's vehicle. Most insurers sell this coverage in increments of $1,000 or $5,000, up to $25,000. There is no deductible.

automobile physical damage insurance insurance that covers damage to the insured vehicle

Automobile Physical Damage Insurance Liability insurance does not pay for the repair of the insured vehicle. **Automobile physical damage insurance** is insurance that covers damage to the insured vehicle. *Collision insurance* pays for the repair of damage to the insured vehicle as a result of an accident. Most collision coverages include a *deductible amount*—anywhere from $100 up—that the policyholder must pay. The insurance company then pays either the remaining cost of the repairs or the actual cash value of the vehicle (when the vehicle is "totaled"), whichever is less. For most automobiles, collision insurance is the most costly coverage. Premiums can, however, be reduced by increasing the deductible amount.

table B.1 Automobile Insurance Coverage

Liability insurance covers financial losses resulting from injuries or damages caused *by* the insured vehicle; physical damage insurance covers damage *to* the insured vehicle.

Liability Insurance	Physical Damage Insurance
Bodily injury	Collision
Property damage	Comprehensive
Medical payments	Uninsured motorists

Comprehensive insurance covers damage to the insured vehicle caused by fire, theft, hail, dust storm, vandalism, and almost anything else that could damage a car, except collision and normal wear and tear. With the possible exception of CB radios and tape decks that are installed by the owner of the car, even the contents of the car are insured. For example, comprehensive coverage will pay for a broken windshield, stolen hubcaps, or small dents caused by a hailstorm. Like collision coverage, comprehensive coverage includes a deductible amount, usually up to $1,000.

Uninsured motorists insurance covers the insured driver and passengers from bodily injury losses (and, in some states, property damage losses) resulting from an accident caused by a driver with no liability insurance. It also covers damages caused by a hit-and-run driver. In some states and with some insurance companies, uninsured motorists coverage is not automatically included in a typical policy. And yet it is important coverage that is quite reasonable. Often, annual premiums are about $50.

No-Fault Auto Insurance **No-fault auto insurance** is a method of paying for losses suffered in an automobile accident. It is enacted by state law and requires that those suffering injury or loss be reimbursed by their own insurance companies, without regard to who was at fault in the accident. Although there are numerous exceptions, most no-fault laws also limit the rights of involved parties to sue each other.

no-fault auto insurance a method of paying for losses suffered in an automobile accident; enacted by state law, requires that those suffering injury or loss be reimbursed by their own insurance companies, without regard to who was at fault in the accident

Massachusetts enacted the first no-fault law in 1971 in an effort to reduce both auto insurance premiums and the crushing caseload in its court system. Since then, at least twenty-seven states have followed suit. Every state with a no-fault law requires coverage for all vehicles registered in the state.

Business Liability Insurance

Business liability coverage protects the policyholder from financial losses resulting from an injury to another person or damage to another person's property. During the past fifteen years or so, both the number of liability claims and the size of settlements have increased dramatically. The result has been heightened awareness of the need for liability coverage—along with quickly rising premiums for this coverage.

Public liability insurance protects the policyholder from financial losses due to injuries suffered by others as a result of negligence on the part of a business owner or employee. It covers injury or death resulting from hazards at the place of business or from the actions of employees. For example, liability claims totaling more than $2 billion were filed on behalf of the victims of the 1981 skybridge collapse at the Hyatt Regency Hotel in Kansas City, Missouri. More recent examples in which damage claims totaled more than a billion dollars include the chemical accident at Union Carbide's plant in Bhopal, India, the 1987 Du Pont Hotel fire in San Juan, Puerto Rico, and the proposed $368 billion tobacco industry settlement in 1997. *Malpractice insurance*, which is purchased by physicians, lawyers, accountants, engineers, and other professionals, is a form of public liability insurance.

public liability insurance insurance that protects the policyholder from financial losses due to injuries suffered by others as a result of negligence on the part of a business owner or employee

Product liability insurance protects the policyholder from financial losses due to injuries suffered by others as a result of using the policyholder's products. Recent court settlements for individuals injured by defective products have been extremely large. A classic product liability case involved the Ford Motor Company and Richard Grimshaw. Grimshaw was injured when he was a passenger in a Ford compact automobile that was hit from behind and burst into flames. He was so severely burned that more than fifty operations were required to treat him. He sued Ford and was awarded $128.5 million by a jury, which decided that his injuries resulted from poor design on the part of Ford. (Later, on appeal, the award was reduced to $6 million.)

product liability insurance insurance that protects the policyholder from financial losses due to injuries suffered by others as a result of using the policyholder's products

Some juries have found manufacturers and retailers guilty of negligence even when the consumer used the product incorrectly. This develpment and the very large awards given to injured consumers have caused management to take a hard look at potential product hazards. As part of their risk-management efforts, most manufacturers now take the following precautions:

1. Include thorough and explicit directions with products.
2. Warn customers about the hazards of using products incorrectly.
3. Remove from the market those products that are considered hazardous.
4. Test products in-house to determine whether safety problems can arise from either proper *or* improper use.

Such precautions can reduce both the risk of product liability losses and the cost of liability insurance. When the risk of death, injury, or lawsuits cannot be eliminated or at least reduced, some manufacturers have simply discontinued the product.

Marine (Transportation) Insurance

Marine, or transportation, insurance provides protection against the loss of goods that are being shipped from one place to another. It is the oldest type of insurance, having originated with the ancient Greeks and Romans. The term *marine insurance* was coined at a time when only goods transported by ship were insured.

Today marine insurance is available for goods shipped over water or land. **Ocean marine insurance** protects the policyholder against loss or damage to a ship or its cargo on the high seas. **Inland marine insurance** protects against loss or damage to goods shipped by rail, truck, airplane, or inland barge. Both types cover losses from fire, theft, and most other hazards.

ocean marine insurance insurance that protects the policyholder against loss or damage to a ship or its cargo on the high seas

inland marine insurance insurance that protects against loss or damage to goods shipped by rail, truck, airplane, or inland barge

business interruption insurance insurance protection for a business whose operations are interrupted because of a fire, storm, or other natural disaster

Business Interruption Insurance

Business interruption insurance provides protection for a business whose operations are interrupted because of a fire, storm, or other natural disaster. It is even possible to purchase coverage to protect a firm if its employees should go out on strike. For most businesses, interruption coverage is available as an endorsement to a fire insurance policy. Premiums are determined by the amount of coverage and the risks that are covered.

The standard business interruption policy reimburses the policyholder for both loss of profit and fixed costs in the event that it cannot operate. Profit payments are based on profits earned by the firm during some specified period. Fixed-cost payments cover expenses the firm incurs even when it is not operating. Employee salaries are normally not covered by the standard policy. However, they may be included for an increased premium.

Public and Employee-Sponsored Insurance for Individuals

Both the government and private insurance companies offer a number of different types of coverage for individuals in the United States. In this section, we discuss Social Security, unemployment insurance, workers' compensation, and medical insurance.

Public Insurance

Federal and state governments offer insurance programs to meet the specific needs of individuals who are eligible for coverage. The Social Security program, established by the Social Security Act of 1935, today, provides benefits for more than 44 million people, almost one out of every six Americans. The Social Security program—financed by taxes paid by both employees and employers—actually consists of four programs. First, *retirement* benefits are paid to eligible employees and self-employed individuals when they reach age sixty-five. They can obtain reduced benefits at age sixty-two. Second, *survivor* benefits are paid to a worker's spouse, dependent children, or in some cases dependent parents when a covered worker dies before retirement. Third, *disability* benefits are paid to workers who are severely disabled and unable to work. Benefits continue until it is determined that the individual is no longer disabled. When a disabled worker reaches age 65, the worker is then eligible for retirement benefits. Fourth, the *Medicare* program provides both hospital and medical coverage. Workers are eligible for coverage when they reach age 65. Persons who have received disability benefits for a period of at least twenty-four months are also eligible for Medicare coverage.

Unlike the federal Social Security program, *unemployment insurance* is a joint program between the federal and state governments. The purpose of the program is to provide benefits (employment services and money) to unemployed workers. The dollar amount and the duration of benefits are determined by state laws. The program is funded by a tax paid by employers.

Workers' Compensation

Workers' compensation insurance covers medical expenses and provides salary continuation for employees who are injured while at work. This insurance also pays benefits to the dependents of workers killed on the job. Every state now requires employers to provide some form of workers' compensation insurance; specific benefits are established by the state. Employers may purchase this type of insurance from insurance companies or, in some cases, from the state. Self-insurance can also be used to meet requirements in a few states. State laws do vary; some are more stringent than others. In fact, the low cost of workers' compensation in some states is one of many reasons businesses might choose to locate or move there.

workers' compensation insurance insurance that covers medical expenses and provides salary continuation for employees who are injured while at work

Salary continuation payments to employees unable to work because of injuries sustained on the job normally range from 60 to 75 percent of an employee's usual wage. They may, however, be limited to a specified number of payments. In all cases, they stop when the employee is able to return to work.

Workers' compensation premiums, paid by the employer, are generally computed as a small percentage of each employee's wages. The percentage varies with the type of job and is, in general, higher for jobs that involve greater risk of injury.

Healthcare Insurance

Today most employers pay, as an employee benefit, part or all of the cost of healthcare insurance for employees. When the employer doesn't pay for coverage, most individuals purchase their own healthcare insurance—when they can afford the coverage. **Healthcare insurance** covers the cost of medical attention, including hospital care, physicians' and surgeons' fees, prescription medicines, and related services. In addition, some firms also provide employees with dental and life insurance. *Major medical insurance* can also be purchased to extend medical coverage beyond the dollar limits of the standard healthcare insurance policy. In all cases, the types of coverage and the premiums vary according to the provisions of the specific healthcare policy, whether it is paid for by the employer or the individual.

healthcare insurance insurance that covers the cost of medical attention, including hospital care, physicians' and surgeons' fees, prescription medicines, and related services

The cost of medical care has been increasing over the last thirty-five years. National expenditures for health care in 1999 were more than $1.2 trillion, or $4,340 per individual, according to the Health Care Financing Administration. Thus, about 13.6 percent of our gross domestic product is spent on health care.[1] In an attempt to keep medical insurance premiums down, insurers have developed a variety of insurance plans that are less expensive than full-coverage plans. Some plans have deductibles of $500 to $1,000. Some require that the policyholder pay 20 to 30 percent of the first $1,000 to $3,000 in medical bills. And some pay the entire hospital bill but only a percentage of other medical expenses. One additional method that can reduce the cost of healthcare coverage is the use of a health maintenance organization. A **health maintenance organization (HMO)** is an insurance plan that directly employs or contracts with selected physicians and hospitals to provide healthcare services in

health maintenance organization (HMO) an insurance plan that directly employs or contracts with selected physicians and hospitals to provide healthcare services in exchange for a fixed, prepaid monthly premium

exchange for a fixed, prepaid monthly premium. Although there have been concerns about the quality of care provided by some health maintenance organizations, they are expected to grow in the next century because they offer a lower-cost alternative to traditional healthcare plans.

preferred provider organization (PPO) an insurance plan that offers the services of doctors and hospitals at discount rates or gives breaks in copayments and deductibles

Preferred provider organizations (PPOs) offer the services of doctors and hospitals at discount rates or give breaks in copayments (the portion of the bill the insured must pay each time services are used) and deductibles. An insurance company or an employer contracts with a PPO to provide specified services at predetermined fees to PPO members.

Life Insurance

life insurance insurance that pays a stated amount of money on the death of the insured individual

beneficiary person or organization named in a life insurance policy as a recipient of the proceeds of that policy on the death of the insured

Life insurance pays a stated amount of money on the death of the insured individual. The money is paid to one or more beneficiaries. A **beneficiary** is a person or organization named in a life insurance policy as a recipient of the proceeds of that policy on the death of the insured.

Life insurance thus provides protection for the beneficiaries of the insured. The amount of insurance needed depends very much on *their* situation. A wage earner with three small children generally needs more life insurance than someone who is single. Moreover, the need for life insurance changes as a person's situation changes. When the wage earner's children are grown and on their own, they need less protection (through their parent's life insurance) than they did when they were young.

For a particular dollar amount of life insurance, premiums depend primarily on the age of the insured and on the type of insurance. The older a person is, the higher the premium. (On the average, older people are less likely to survive each year than younger people.) Finally, insurers offer several types of life insurance for customers with varying insurance needs. The price of each type depends on the benefits it provides.

Term Life Insurance

term life insurance life insurance that provides protection to beneficiaries for a stated period of time

Term life insurance provides protection to beneficiaries for a stated period of time. Because term life insurance includes no other benefits, it is the least expensive form of life insurance. It is especially attractive to young married couples who want as much protection as possible but cannot afford the higher premiums charged for other types of life insurance.

Most term life policies are in force for a period of one year. At the end of each policy year, a term life policy can be renewed at a slightly higher cost—to take into account the fact that the insured individual has aged one year. In addition, some term policies can be converted into other forms of life insurance at the option of the policyholder. This feature permits policyholders to modify their insurance protection to keep pace with changes in their personal circumstances.

Whole Life Insurance

whole life insurance life insurance that provides both protection and savings

Whole life insurance, also called ordinary life insurance, provides both protection and savings. In the beginning, premiums are generally higher than those for term life insurance. However, premiums for whole life insurance remain constant for as long as the policy is in force.

cash surrender value the amount payable to the holder of a whole life insurance policy if the policy is canceled

A whole life policy builds up savings over the years. These savings are in the form of a **cash surrender value,** which is the amount payable to the holder of a whole life insurance policy if the policy is canceled. In addition, the policyholder may borrow from the insurance company, at a relatively low interest rate, amounts up to the policy's cash surrender value.

Whole life insurance policies are sold in these three forms:

- *Straight life insurance*, for which the policyholder must pay premiums as long as the insured is alive
- *Limited-payment life insurance*, for which premiums are paid for only a stated number of years
- *Single-payment life insurance*, for which one lump-sum premium is paid at the time the insurance is purchased.

Which of these is best for a given individual depends, as usual, on that individual's particular situation and insurance needs.

Endowment Life Insurance

Endowment life insurance provides protection and guarantees the payment of a stated amount to the policyholder after a specified number of years. Endowment policies are generally in force for twenty years or until the insured person reaches age 65. If the insured dies while the policy is in force, the beneficiaries are paid the face amount of the policy. However, if the insured survives through the policy period, the stated amount is paid to the policyholder.

endowment life insurance life insurance that provides protection and guarantees the payment of a stated amount to the policyholder after a specified number of years

The premiums for endowment policies are generally higher than those for whole life policies. In return, the policyholder is guaranteed a future payment. Thus, the endowment policy includes a sort of "enforced savings" feature. In addition, the cash surrender values of endowment policies are usually higher than those of whole life policies.

Universal Life Insurance

Universal life insurance combines insurance protection with an investment plan that offers a potentially greater return than that guaranteed by a whole life insurance policy. Universal life insurance is the newest product available from life insurance companies. It offers policyholders several options unavailable with other types of policies. For example, policyholders may choose to make larger or smaller premium payments, to increase or decrease their insurance coverage, or even to withdraw the policy's cash value without canceling the policy. Essentially, the purchase of universal life insurance combines the purchase of annual term insurance with the buying and selling of investments.

universal life insurance life insurance that combines insurance protection with an investment plan that offers a potentially greater return than that guaranteed by a whole life insurance policy

Universal life insurance generally offers lower premiums than whole life insurance. In fact, the premium is often called a "contribution." However, companies that offer universal life insurance may charge a fee when the policy is first purchased, each time an annual premium is paid, and when funds are withdrawn from the policy's cash value. Such fees tend to decrease the return on the savings account part of the policy.

Business Law, Regulation, and Taxation

Our initial task in this appendix is to examine the sources of laws and the functions of federal and state court systems. Next, we discuss the major categories of laws that apply to business activities: contract law, property law, and laws relating to negotiable instruments, the agent-principal relationship, and bankruptcy. Then, we describe federal laws that encourage competition, and we look at the issue of deregulation of business. We conclude with a discussion of federal, state, and local taxes—the primary means by which all governments finance their activities.

Laws and the Courts

A **law** is a rule developed by a society to govern the conduct of, and relationships among, its members. Laws set standards of behavior for both businesses and individuals. They establish the rights of parties in exchanges and various types of agreements. Laws provide remedies in the event that one business (or individual) believes it has been injured by another. In the United States, the supreme law of the land is the U.S. Constitution. The federal, state, and local governments enact and administer laws, but no law is valid if it violates the Constitution.

law a rule developed by a society to govern the conduct of, and relationships among, its members

Sources of Laws

Each level of government derives its laws from two major sources: (1) judges' decisions, which make up common law, and (2) legislative bodies, which enact statutory laws.

Common Law **Common law,** also known as *case law* or *judicial law*, is the body of law created by court decisions rendered by judges. Common law began as custom and tradition in England. It was then transported to America during the colonial period and, since then, has been further enlarged by the decisions of American judges.

common law the body of law created by court decisions rendered by judges; also known as *case law or judicial law*

The growth of common law is founded on the doctrine of *stare decisis,* a Latin term meaning "to stand by a previous decision." The doctrine of *stare decisis* is a practical source of law for two reasons. First, a judge's decision in a case may be used by other judges as the basis for later decisions. The earlier decision thus has the strength of law and is, in effect, a source of law. Second, the doctrine of *stare decisis* makes law more stable and predictable. If someone brings a case to court *and* the facts are the same as those in a case that has already been decided, the court will make a decision based on the previous legal decision. The court may depart from the doctrine of *stare decisis* if the facts in the current case differ from those in an earlier case or if business practices, technology, or the attitudes of society have changed.

Statutory Law A **statute** is a law passed by the U.S. Congress, a state legislature, or a local government. **Statutory law,** then, consists of all the laws that have been enacted by legislative bodies. For businesses, one very important part of statutory law is the

statute a law passed by the U.S. Congress, a state legislature, or a local government

statutory law all the laws that have been enacted by legislative bodies

Uniform Commercial Code (UCC) a set of laws designed to eliminate differences among state regulations affecting business and to simplify interstate commerce

administrative law the regulations created by government agencies established by legislative bodies

Uniform Commercial Code. The **Uniform Commercial Code (UCC)** is a set of laws designed to eliminate differences among state regulations affecting business and to simplify interstate commerce. The UCC consists of eleven articles, or chapters, that cover sales, commercial paper, bank deposits and collections, letters of credit, transfers of title, securities, and transactions that involve collateral. It has been adopted with variations in all fifty states. The state statutes that the UCC replaced varied from state to state and caused problems for firms that did business in more than one state.

Today most legal experts have expanded the concept of statutory law to include administrative law. **Administrative law** consists entirely of the regulations created by government agencies established by legislative bodies. The Nuclear Regulatory Commission, for example, has the power to set specific requirements for nuclear power plants. It can even halt the construction or operation of plants that do not meet such requirements. These requirements thus have the force and effect of law.

Most regulatory agencies hold hearings that are similar to court trials. Evidence is introduced, and the parties are represented by legal counsel. Moreover, the decisions of these agencies may be appealed in state or federal courts.

Public Law and Private Law: Crimes and Torts

public law the body of law that deals with the relationships between individuals or businesses and society

crime a violation of a public law

Public law is the body of law that deals with the relationships between individuals or businesses and society. A violation of a public law is called a **crime.** Among the crimes that can affect a business are the following:

- Burglary, robbery, and theft
- Embezzlement, or the unauthorized taking of money or property by an employee, agent, or trustee
- Forgery, or the false signing or changing of a legal document with the intent to alter the liability of another person
- The use of inaccurate weights, measures, or labels
- The use of the mails to defraud, or cheat, an individual or business
- The receipt of stolen property
- The filing of a false and fraudulent income tax return

Those accused of violating public laws—or committing crimes—are prosecuted by a federal, state, or local government.

private law the body of law that governs the relationships between two or more individuals or businesses

tort a violation of a private law

negligence a failure to exercise reasonable care, resulting in injury to another

Private law is the body of law that governs the relationships between two or more individuals or businesses. A violation of a private law is called a **tort.** In some cases, a single illegal act—such as embezzlement—can be both a crime and a tort.

Torts may result either from intentional acts or from negligence. Such acts as shoplifting and embezzlement are intentional torts. **Negligence,** on the other hand, is a failure to exercise reasonable care, resulting in injury to another. Suppose the driver of a delivery truck loses control at the wheel and rams into a building. A tort has been committed, and the owner of the building may sue both the driver and the driver's employer to recover the cost of repairing the damages. Among the torts that can affect a business are the following:

- *Slander*—A false oral statement that injures a person's or business's reputation
- *Libel*—A false written statement that injures a person's or business's reputation
- *Fraud*—A misrepresentation of facts designed to take advantage of another individual or business
- *Product liability*—A manufacturer's responsibility for negligence in designing, manufacturing, or providing operating instructions for its products
- *Personal injury*—Damages caused by accidents, intentional acts, or defective products
- *Unfair competitive practices*—Behavior of an entity that unfairly lessens another organization's ability to compete

The purpose of private law is to provide a remedy for the party injured by a tort. In most cases, the injured party must bring a legal action and present the facts in a court of law. Either a judge or jury will then render a decision. In most cases, the remedy consists of monetary damages to compensate the injured party and punish the person committing the tort. For example, the courts ruled that Eastman Kodak committed a tort by infringing on certain patent rights owned by Polaroid. Eastman Kodak was forced to pay Polaroid almost $900 million in damages. Because large dollar settlements have become commonplace, many business owners and politicians insist there is a need for tort reform.

The Court System

The United States has two separate and distinct court systems. The federal court system consists of the Supreme Court of the United States, which was established by the Constitution, and other federal courts that were created by Congress. In addition, each of the fifty states has established its own court system. Figure C.1 shows both the federal court system and a typical state court system.

The Federal Court System Federal courts generally hear cases that involve

- Questions of constitutional law
- Federal crimes or violations of federal statutes
- Property valued at $50,000 or more in dispute between citizens of different states, or between a U.S. citizen and a foreign nation
- Bankruptcy; the Internal Revenue Service; the postal laws; or copyright, patent, and trademark laws
- Admiralty and maritime cases

The United States is divided into federal judicial districts. Each state includes at least one district court, and more populous states have two or more. A district court is a **court of original jurisdiction,** which is the first court to recognize and hear testimony in a legal action. In many cases, the decision reached in the district court may be appealed to a higher court. A court that hears cases appealed from lower courts is called an **appellate court.** If the appellate court finds the lower court's ruling to be in error, it may reverse that ruling, modify the decision, or return the case to the lower court for a new trial. Currently, there are thirteen U.S. courts of appeal.

court of original jurisdiction the first court to recognize and hear testimony in a legal action

appellate court a court that hears cases appealed from lower courts

The U.S. Supreme Court—the highest court in the land—consists of nine justices (the chief justice and eight associate justices). The Supreme Court has original jurisdiction in cases that involve ambassadors and consuls and in certain cases involving one or more states. However, its main function is to review decisions made by the U.S. courts of appeal and, in some cases, by state supreme courts.

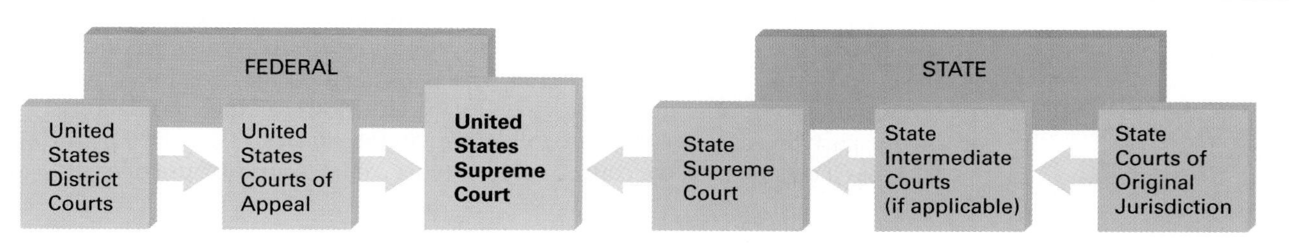

figure C.1

The Court System

The United States has two separate and distinct court systems, as illustrated here by the federal court system and a typical state court system.

The State Court Systems The state court systems are quite similar to the federal system in structure. All have courts of original jurisdiction and supreme courts, and most have intermediate appellate courts as well. The decision of a state supreme court may be appealed to the U.S. Supreme Court if it involves a question of constitutional or federal law.

court of limited jurisdiction a court that hears only specific types of cases

Other Types of Courts Other courts have been created to meet special needs at both the federal and state levels. A **court of limited jurisdiction** hears only specific types of cases. At the federal level, for example, Congress has created courts to hear cases that involve international trade, taxes and disputes with the IRS, and bankruptcy. At the state level, there are small-claims courts, which hear cases involving claims for less than a specified dollar amount (usually $500 or $5,000, depending on the state), traffic courts, divorce courts, juvenile courts, and probate courts.

Contract Law

Contract law is perhaps the most important area of business law because contracts are so much a part of doing business. Every businessperson should understand what a valid contract is and how a contract is fulfilled or violated.

contract a legally enforceable agreement between two or more competent parties who promise to do, or not to do, a particular thing

A **contract** is a legally enforceable agreement between two or more competent parties who promise to do, or not to do, a particular thing. An *implied contract* is an agreement that results from the actions of the parties. For example, a person who orders dinner at a local Chili's restaurant assumes that the food will be served within a reasonable time and will be fit to eat. The restaurant owner, for his or her part, assumes that the customer will pay for the meal.

Most contracts are more explicit and formal than that between a restaurant and its customers. An *expressed contract* is one in which the parties involved have made oral or written promises about the terms of their agreement.

Requirements for a Valid Contract

To be valid and legally enforceable, a contract must meet five specific requirements, as follows: (1) voluntary agreement, (2) consideration, (3) legal competence of all parties, (4) lawful subject matter, and (5) proper form.

voluntary agreement a contract requirement consisting of an *offer* by one party to enter into a contract with a second party and *acceptance* by the second party of all the terms and conditions of the offer

Voluntary Agreement **Voluntary agreement** consists of both an *offer* by one party to enter into a contract with a second party and *acceptance* by the second party of all the terms and conditions of the offer. If any part of the offer is not accepted, there is no contract. And if it can be proved that coercion, undue pressure, or fraud was used to obtain a contract, it may be voided by the injured party.

consideration the value or benefit that one party to a contract furnishes to the other party

Consideration A contract is a binding agreement only when each party provides something of value to the other party. The value or benefit that one party furnishes to the other party is called **consideration**. This consideration may be money, property, a service, or the promise not to exercise a legal right. However, the consideration given by one party need not be equal in dollar value to the consideration given by the other party. As a general rule, the courts will not void a contract just because one party got a bargain.

Legal Competence All parties to a contract must be legally competent to manage their own affairs *and* must have the authority to enter into binding agreements. The intent of the legal competence requirement is to protect individuals who may not have been able to protect themselves. The courts generally will not require minors, persons of unsound mind, or those who entered into contracts while they were intoxicated to comply with the terms of their contracts.

Lawful Subject Matter A contract is not legally enforceable if it involves an unlawful act. Certainly, a person who contracts with an arsonist to burn down a building cannot go to court to obtain enforcement of the contract. Equally unenforceable is a contract that involves **usury**, which is the practice of charging interest in excess of the maximum legal rate. Other contracts that may be unlawful include promissory notes resulting from illegal gambling activities, contracts to bribe public officials, agreements to perform services without required licenses, and contracts that restrain trade or eliminate competition.

usury the practice of charging interest in excess of the maximum legal rate

Proper Form of Contract Businesses generally draw up all contractual agreements in writing so that differences can be resolved readily if a dispute develops. Figure C.2 shows that a contract need not be complicated to be legally enforceable.

A written contract must contain the names of the parties involved, their signatures, the purpose of the contract, and all terms and conditions to which the parties have agreed. Any changes to a written contract should be made in writing, initialed by all parties, and attached to the original contract.

The *Statute of Frauds*, which has been passed in some form by all states, requires that certain types of contracts be in writing to be enforceable. These include contracts dealing with

- The exchange of land or real estate
- The sale of goods, merchandise, or personal property valued at $500 or more
- The sale of securities, regardless of the dollar amount
- Acts that will not be completed within one year after the agreement is made
- A promise to assume someone else's financial obligation
- A promise made in contemplation of marriage

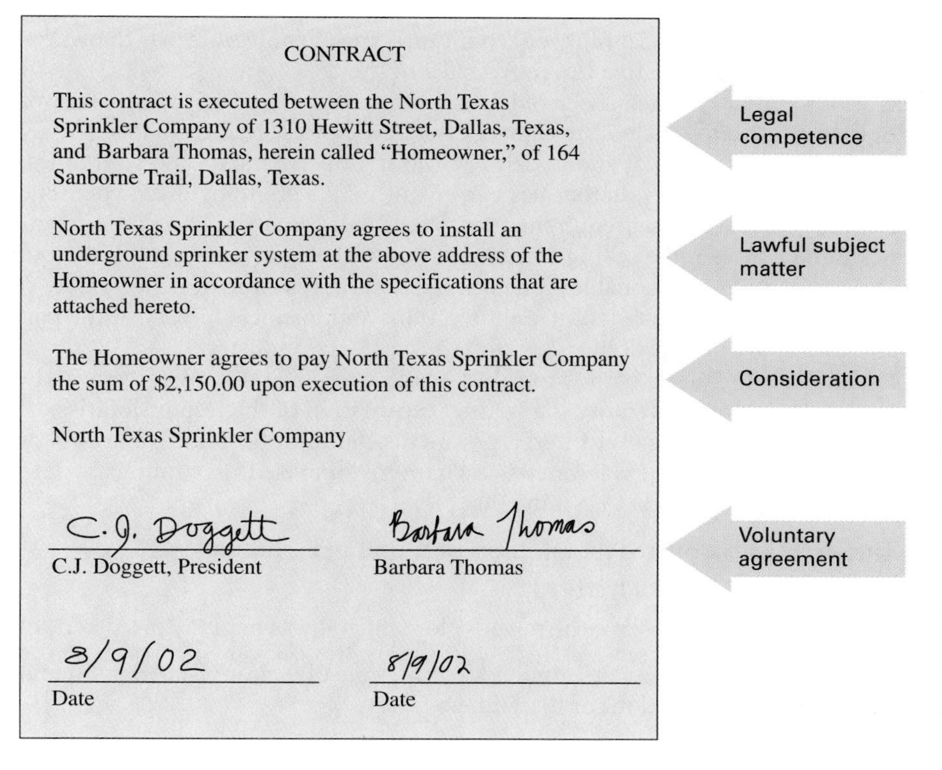

CONTRACT

This contract is executed between the North Texas Sprinkler Company of 1310 Hewitt Street, Dallas, Texas, and Barbara Thomas, herein called "Homeowner," of 164 Sanborne Trail, Dallas, Texas.

North Texas Sprinkler Company agrees to install an underground sprinker system at the above address of the Homeowner in accordance with the specifications that are attached hereto.

The Homeowner agrees to pay North Texas Sprinkler Company the sum of $2,150.00 upon execution of this contract.

North Texas Sprinkler Company

C.J. Doggett ——— Barbara Thomas

C.J. Doggett, President ——— Barbara Thomas

8/9/02 ——— 8/9/02

Date ——— Date

figure C.2

Contract Between a Business and a Customer
Notice that the requirements for a valid contract are satisfied and that the contract takes the proper form by containing the names of the parties involved, their signatures, the purpose of the contract, and all terms and conditions.

Performance and Nonperformance

performance the fulfillment of all obligations by all parties to the contract

breach of contract the failure of one party to fulfill the terms of a contract when there is no legal reason for that failure

discharge by mutual assent termination of a contract by mutual agreement of all parties

damages a monetary settlement awarded to a party injured through a breach of contract

specific performance the legal requirement that the parties to a contract fulfill their obligations according to the contract

Ordinarily, a contract is terminated by **performance**, which is the fulfillment of all obligations by all parties to the contract. Occasionally, however, performance may become impossible. Death, disability, or bankruptcy for example may legally excuse one party from a contractual obligation. But what happens when one party simply does not perform according to a legal contract? A **breach of contract** is the failure of one party to fulfill the terms of a contract when there is no legal reason for that failure. In such a case, it may be necessary for the other parties to the contract to bring legal action to discharge the contract, obtain monetary damages, or require specific performance.

Discharge by mutual assent is the termination of a contract when all parties agree to void a contract. Any consideration received by the parties must be returned when a contract is discharged by mutual assent.

Damages are a monetary settlement awarded to a party injured through a breach of contract. When damages are awarded, an attempt is made to place the injured party in the position it would be in if the contract had been performed.

Specific performance is the legal requirement that the parties to a contract fulfill their obligations according to the contract. Generally, the courts require specific performance if a contract calls for a unique service or product unobtainable from another source.

Most individuals and firms enter into a contract expecting to live up to its terms. Very few end up in court. When they do, it is usually because one or more of the parties did not understand all the conditions of the agreement. Thus, it is imperative to know what you are signing before you sign it. If you have any doubt, get legal help! A signed contract is very difficult—and often very costly—to void.

Sales Agreements

sales agreement a type of contract by which ownership is transferred from a seller to a buyer

A **sales agreement** is a special (but very common) type of contract by which ownership is transferred from a seller to a buyer. Article 2 of the UCC (entitled "Sales") provides much of our sales law, which is derived from both common and statutory law. Among the topics included in Article 2 are rights of the buyer and seller, acceptance and rejection of an offer, inspection of goods, delivery, transfer of ownership, and warranties.

Article 2 also provides that a sales agreement may be binding even when one or more of the general contract requirements are omitted. For example, a sales agreement is legally binding when the selling price is left out of the agreement. Article 2 requires that the buyer pay the reasonable value of the goods at the time of delivery. Key considerations in resolving such issues are the actions and business history of the parties and any customary sales procedures within the particular industry.

express warranty a written explanation of the responsibilities of the producer (or seller) in the event that a product is found to be defective or otherwise unsatisfactory

implied warranty a guarantee imposed or required by law

Finally, Article 2 deals with warranties—both express and implied. As we saw in Chapter 14, an **express warranty** is a written explanation of the responsibilities of the producer (or seller) in the event that a product is found to be defective or otherwise unsatisfactory. An **implied warranty** is a guarantee imposed or required by law. In general, the buyer is entitled to assume that

1. The merchandise offered for sale has a clear title and is not stolen.
2. The merchandise is as advertised.
3. The merchandise will serve the purpose for which it was manufactured and sold.

Any limitation to an express or implied warranty must be clearly stated so the buyer can understand any exceptions or disclaimers.

Other Laws That Affect Business

In addition to contract law, many other kinds of law affect the way a firm does business. In this section, we describe the impact of laws relating to property, negotiable instruments, the agent-principal relationship, and bankruptcy on the day-to-day operations of a business firm.

Property Law

Property is anything that can be owned. The concept of private ownership of property is fundamental to the free-enterprise system. Our Constitution guarantees to individuals and businesses the right to own property and to use it in their own best interests.

property anything that can be owned

Kinds of Property Property is legally classified as either real property or personal property. **Real property** is land and anything permanently attached to it. The term also applies to water on the ground and minerals and natural resources beneath the surface. Thus, a house, a factory, a garage, and a well are all considered real property.

real property land and anything permanently attached to it

The degree to which a business is concerned with real-property law depends on its size and the kind of business it is. The owner of a small convenience store needs only a limited knowledge of real-property law. But a national grocery-store chain like Albertson's might employ several real estate experts with extensive knowledge of real-property law, property values, and real estate zoning ordinances throughout the country.

Personal property is all property other than real property. Personal property that has physical or material value—such as inventories, equipment, store fixtures, an automobile, or a book—is referred to as *tangible personal property* because it is movable and can be felt, tasted, or seen. Property that derives its value from a legal right or claim is called *intangible personal property*. Examples include stocks and bonds, receivables, trademarks, patents, and copyrights.

personal property all property other than real property

A trademark is a brand that is registered with the U.S. Patent and Trademark Office. Registration guarantees the owner the exclusive use of the trademark for ten years. At the end of that time, the registration can be renewed for additional ten-year periods. The owner may at times have to defend the trademark from unauthorized use—usually through legal action. McDonald's was forced to do exactly that, when the trademark "Big Mac" was used by another fast-food outlet in a foreign country.

A **patent** is the exclusive right to make, use, or sell, or to license others to make and sell, a newly invented product or process. Patents are granted by the U.S. Patent and Trademark Office for a period of seventeen years. After that period has elapsed, the invention becomes available for general use.

patent the exclusive right to make, use, or sell a newly invented product or process

A **copyright** is the exclusive right to publish, perform, copy, or sell an original work. Copyright laws cover fiction and nonfiction, plays, poetry, musical works, photographs, films, and computer programs. For example, the copyright on this textbook is held by the publisher, Houghton Mifflin Company. The copyright on the movie *The Lion King* is held by Walt Disney. A copyright is usually held by the creator or the owner of the work and is generally in effect for the lifetime of the creator or owner plus fifty years.

copyright the exclusive right to publish, perform, copy, or sell an original work

Transfer of Ownership The transfer of ownership for both real property and personal property usually involves either a purchase, a gift, or an inheritance. As we noted earlier, the Statute of Frauds requires that exchanges of real estate be in writing. A **deed** is a written document by which the ownership of real property is transferred from one person or organization to another. The deed must contain the names of the previous owner and the new owner, as well as a legally acceptable description of the property being transferred. A **lease** is an agreement by which the right to use real property is temporarily transferred from its owner, the landlord, to a tenant. In return for the use of the property, the tenant generally pays rent on a weekly, monthly, or yearly basis. A lease is granted for a specific period of time, after which a new lease may be negotiated. If the lease is terminated, the right to use the real property reverts to the landlord.

deed a written document by which the ownership of real property is transferred from one person or organization to another

lease an agreement by which the right to use real estate, equipment, or other assets is temporarily transferred from its owner to the user

Transfer of ownership for personal property depends on how payment is made. When the buyer pays the *full cash price* at the time of purchase, the title to personal property passes to the buyer immediately. When the buyer purchases goods on an *installment plan*, the title passes to the buyer when he or she takes possession of the goods. Although the full cash price has not been paid, the buyer has made a legally enforceable promise to pay it. This is sufficient consideration for the transfer of ownership. Moreover, if the purchased goods are stolen from the buyer, the buyer must still pay the full purchase price.

negotiable instrument a written document that (1) is a promise to pay a stated sum of money and (2) can be transferred from one person or firm to another

Laws Relating to Negotiable Instruments

A **negotiable instrument** is a written document that (1) is a promise to pay a stated sum of money and (2) can be transferred from one person or firm to another. In effect, a negotiable instrument is a substitute for money. Checks are the most familiar form of negotiable instruments. However, promissory notes, drafts, certificates of deposit, and commercial paper are also negotiable. Even a warehouse receipt can qualify as a negotiable instrument if certain conditions are met.

Requirements for Negotiability The UCC establishes the following conditions for negotiability:

- The credit instrument must be in writing and signed.
- The instrument must contain an unconditional promise or order to pay a stated sum of money.
- The instrument must be payable on demand or at a definite future date.
- The instrument must be payable to a specified person or firm or to the bearer.

A financial document that does not meet all these requirements is not negotiable. It may still be valid and legally enforceable, but it cannot be transferred to another business or individual.

endorsement the payee's signature on the back of a negotiable instrument

Endorsements To transfer a negotiable instrument, the payee (the person named on the face of the document) must sign it on the back. The payee's signature on the back of a negotiable instrument is called an **endorsement.** There are three types of endorsements, as shown at the bottom of Figure C.3.

A *blank endorsement* consists only of the payee's signature. It is quick, easy, and dangerous because it makes the instrument payable to anyone who gets possession of it—legally or otherwise. A *restrictive endorsement* states the purpose for which the instrument is to be used. For example, the words "for deposit only" mean that this check *must* be deposited in the specified account.

figure C.3

Endorsements

The names of both the payee (Charles Hall) and the payor (Maria Martinez) are included on the front of the check. The payee's signature on the back of a negotiable instrument is called an *endorsement*. There are three types of endorsements.

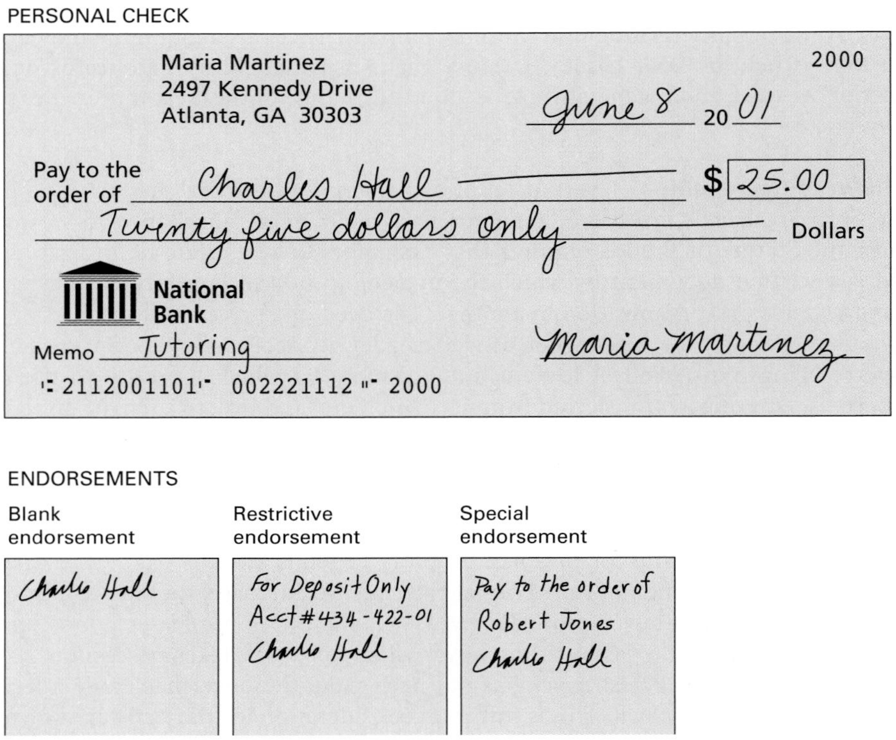

A *special endorsement* identifies the person or firm to whom the instrument is payable. The words "Pay to the order of Robert Jones" means that the only person who can cash, deposit, or negotiate this check is Robert Jones.

Agency Law

An **agency** is a business relationship in which one party, called the *principal*, appoints a second party, called the *agent*, to act on its behalf. Most agents are independent businesspeople or firms and are paid for their services with either set fees or commissions. They are hired to use their special knowledge for a specific purpose. For example, real estate agents are hired to sell or buy real property, insurance agents are hired to sell insurance, and theatrical agents are hired to obtain engagements for entertainers. The officers of a corporation, lawyers, accountants, and stockbrokers also act as agents.

agency a business relationship in which one party, called the *principal*, appoints a second party, called the *agent*, to act on its behalf

Almost any legal activity that can be accomplished by an individual can also be accomplished through an agent. (The exceptions are voting, giving sworn testimony in court, and making a will.) Moreover, under the law, the principal is bound by the actions of the agent. However, the principal may sue an agent who performs an unauthorized act and may collect damages. For this reason, a written contract describing the conditions and limits of the agency relationship is extremely important to both parties.

A **power of attorney** is a legal document that serves as evidence that an agent has been appointed to act on behalf of a principal. In the majority of states in the United States, a power of attorney is required in agency relationships involving the transfer of real estate, as well as in other specific situations.

power of attorney a legal document that serves as evidence that an agent has been appointed to act on behalf of a principal

An agent is responsible for carrying out the principal's instructions in a professional manner, for acting reasonably and with good judgment, and for keeping the principal informed of progress according to their agreement. The agent must also be careful to avoid a conflict involving the interests of two or more principals. The agency relationship is terminated when its objective is accomplished, at the end of a specified time period, or, in some cases, when either party renounces the agency relationship.

Bankruptcy Law

Bankruptcy is a legal procedure designed both to protect an individual or business that cannot meet its financial obligations and to protect the creditors involved. The Bankruptcy Reform Act was enacted in 1978 and was subsequently amended in July 1984. Under the act, bankruptcy proceedings may be initiated by either the person or the business in financial difficulty or by the creditors.

bankruptcy a legal procedure designed both to protect an individual or business that cannot meet its financial obligations and to protect the creditors involved

Initiating Bankruptcy Proceedings **Voluntary bankruptcy** is a bankruptcy procedure initiated by an individual or business that can no longer meet its financial obligations. Individuals, partnerships, and most corporations may file for voluntary bankruptcy. **Involuntary bankruptcy** is a bankruptcy procedure initiated by creditors. The creditors must be able to prove that the individual or business has debts in excess of $5,000 and cannot pay its debts as they come due.

voluntary bankruptcy a bankruptcy procedure initiated by an individual or business that can no longer meet its financial obligations

involuntary bankruptcy a bankruptcy procedure initiated by creditors

Today most bankruptcies are voluntary. Creditors are wary of initiating bankruptcy proceedings because they usually end up losing most of the money they are owed. They usually prefer to wait and to hope the debtor will eventually be able to pay.

Resolving a Bankruptcy Case A petition for bankruptcy is filed in a bankruptcy court. If the court declares the individual or business bankrupt, three means of resolution are available: liquidation, reorganization, and repayment.

Chapter 7 of the Bankruptcy Reform Act concerns *liquidation*, the sale of assets of a bankrupt individual or business to pay its debts (see Figure C.4). In principle, the assets of the individual or business are sold to satisfy the claims of creditors. The

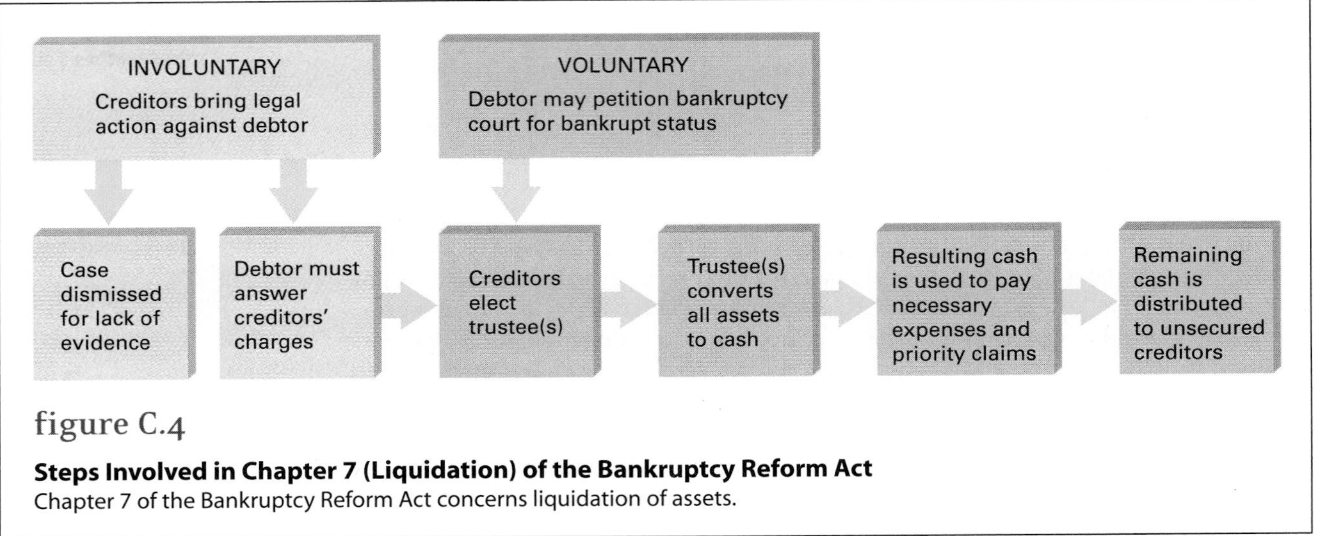

figure C.4

Steps Involved in Chapter 7 (Liquidation) of the Bankruptcy Reform Act
Chapter 7 of the Bankruptcy Reform Act concerns liquidation of assets.

debtor is then relieved of all remaining debts. Liquidation pursuant to Chapter 7 does not apply to railroads, banks, savings and loan associations, insurance companies, or government units. Chapter 7 also specifies the order in which claims are to be paid. First, creditors with secured claims are allowed to repossess (or assume ownership of) the collateral for their claims. Then, the remaining cash and assets—if any—are paid to unsecured creditors in the order prescribed by the bankruptcy act.

Chapter 11 of the Bankruptcy Reform Act outlines the procedure for *reorganizing* a bankrupt business. The idea is simple. The distressed business will be preserved by correcting or eliminating the factors that got the firm into financial trouble. To implement this idea, a plan to reorganize the business is developed. Only a debtor may file a reorganization plan for the first 120 days, unless a trustee has been appointed by the court. After 120 days, any interested party may file a reorganization plan. After the plan has been filed with the court, both the plan and a written disclosure statement are distributed to all individuals and businesses with claims against the bankrupt firm. These people and firms may testify at a hearing held for the purpose of confirming the plan. If the plan is confirmed by the court, the reorganized business emerges from bankruptcy with only the financial obligations imposed on it by the plan. This is exactly what occurred when Colt's Manufacturing Company, Federated Department Stores, Trans World Airlines, and Texaco filed for protection under Chapter 11.

Chapter 13 of the Bankruptcy Reform Act permits a bankrupt individual to file, with the courts, a plan for *repaying* specific debts. (Only individuals with a regular income, less than $100,000 in unsecured debts, and less than $350,000 in secured debts are eligible to file for repayment under Chapter 13.) The plan must provide for the repayment of specified amounts in up to three years. (In unusual circumstances, the court may extend the repayment period to five years.) If the plan is approved by the court, the individual usually pays the money to a court-appointed trustee in monthly installments. The trustee, in turn, pays the individual's creditors.

Government Regulation of Business

Government helps to ensure that there is an even playing field for businesses and consumers. In this section, we examine laws designed to promote competition and other areas of regulation in which government oversight is needed to reduce or eliminate abuses.

Federal Regulations to Encourage Competition

Most states have laws to encourage competition, but for the most part, these laws duplicate federal laws. Therefore, we discuss only federal legislation designed to encourage competition. Federal laws protect consumers by ensuring that they have a choice in the marketplace. The same laws protect businesses by ensuring that they are free to compete.

The need for such laws became apparent in the late 1800s, when trusts, or monopolies, developed in the sugar, whiskey, tobacco, shoe, and oil industries, among others. A **trust** is created when one firm gains control of an entire industry and can set prices and manipulate trade to suit its own interests.

trust a business combination created when one firm obtains control of an entire industry and can set prices and manipulate trade to suit its own interest

One of the most successful trusts was the Standard Oil Trust, created by John D. Rockefeller in 1882. Until 1911, the Standard Oil Trust controlled between 80 and 90 percent of the petroleum industry. The firm earned extremely high profits primarily because it had obtained secret price concessions from the railroads that shipped its products. Very low shipping costs, in turn, enabled the firm systematically to eliminate most of its competition by deliberately holding prices down. Once this was accomplished, Standard Oil quickly raised its prices.

In response to public outcry against such practices—and high prices—Congress passed the Sherman Antitrust Act in 1890. Since then, Congress has enacted a number of other laws designed to protect American businesses and consumers from monopolies.

The Sherman Antitrust Act (1890) The objectives of the *Sherman Antitrust Act* are to encourage competition and to prevent monopolies. The act specifically prohibits any contract or agreement entered into for the purpose of restraining trade. Specific business practices prohibited by the Sherman Antitrust Act include price fixing, allocation of markets among competitors, and boycotts in restraint of trade. **Price fixing** is an agreement between two businesses about the prices to be charged for goods. A **market allocation** is an agreement to divide a market among potential competitors. A **boycott in restraint of trade** is an agreement between businesses not to sell to or buy from a particular entity. Power to enforce the Sherman Antitrust Act was given to the Department of Justice.

price fixing an agreement between two businesses about the prices to be charged for goods

market allocation an agreement to divide a market among potential competitors

boycott in restraint of trade an agreement between businesses not to sell or buy from a particular entity

Today the Sherman Act is still the cornerstone of the federal government's commitment to encourage competition and to break up large businesses that monopolize trade. An amendment to the Sherman Antitrust Act, the *Antitrust Procedures and Penalties Act of 1974*, made violation of the Sherman Act a felony rather than a misdemeanor. It provides for fines of up to $100,000 and prison terms of up to three years for individuals convicted of antitrust violations. The act also provides that a guilty corporation may be fined up to $1 million and may be sued by competitors or customers for treble monetary damages plus attorneys' fees.

The Clayton Act (1914) Because the wording of the Sherman Antitrust Act is somewhat vague, it could not be used to halt specific monopolistic tactics. Congress therefore enacted the *Clayton Act* in 1914. This legislation identifies and prohibits five distinct practices that had been used to weaken trade competition:

- **Price discrimination**—The practice in which producers and wholesalers charge larger firms a lower price for goods than they charge smaller firms. The Clayton Act does, however, allow quantity discounts.
- **Tying agreement**—A contract that forces an intermediary to purchase unwanted products along with the products it actually wants to buy. This practice was used to "move" a producer's slow-selling merchandise along with its more desirable merchandise.
- **Binding contract**—An agreement that requires an intermediary to purchase products from a particular supplier, not from the supplier's competitors. In return for signing a binding contract, the intermediary was generally given a price discount.

price discrimination the practice in which producers and wholesalers charge larger firms a lower price for goods than they charge smaller firms

tying agreement a contract that forces an intermediary to purchase unwanted products along with the products it actually wants to buy

binding contract an agreement that requires an intermediary to purchase products from a particular supplier, not from the supplier's competitors

interlocking directorate an arrangement in which members of the board of directors of one firm are also directors of a competing firm

community of interests a situation in which one firm buys the stock of a competing firm to reduce competition between the two

Federal Trade Commission (FTC) a five-member committee charged with the responsibility of investigating illegal trade practices and enforcing antitrust laws

- **Interlocking directorate**—An arrangement in which members of the board of directors of one firm are also directors of a competing firm. Thus, for example, a person may not sit on the board of American Airlines and Delta Air Lines at the same time.
- **Community of interests**—A situation in which one firm buys the stock of a competing firm. If this type of merger substantially lessens competition or tends to create a monopoly, it is unlawful.

The Federal Trade Commission Act (1914) In 1914 Congress also passed the *Federal Trade Commission Act*, which states, "Unfair methods of competition in commerce are hereby declared unlawful." This act also created the **Federal Trade Commission (FTC)**, a five-member committee charged with the responsibility of investigating illegal trade practices and enforcing antitrust laws.

At first, the FTC was limited to enforcement of the Sherman Antitrust, Clayton, and FTC Acts. However, in the 1938 *Wheeler-Lea Amendment* to the FTC Act, Congress gave the FTC the power to eliminate deceptive business practices—including those aimed at consumers rather than competitors. This early "consumer legislation" empowered the FTC to deal with a variety of unfair business tactics without having to prove that they endangered competition.

The Robinson-Patman Act (1936) Although the Clayton Act prohibits price discrimination, it does permit quantity discounts. This provision turned out to be a major loophole in the law. It was used by large chain retailers to obtain sizable price concessions that gave them a strong competitive edge over independent stores. To correct this imbalance, Congress passed the *Robinson-Patman Act* in 1936. This law specifically prohibits

- Price differentials that "substantially" weaken competition, unless they can be justified by the actual lower selling costs associated with larger orders
- Advertising and promotional allowances, unless they are offered to small retailers as well as large retailers

The Robinson-Patman Act is more controversial than most antitrust legislation. Many economists believe the act tends to discourage price competition rather than to eliminate monopolies.

The Celler-Kefauver Act (1950) The Clayton Act prohibited building a trust by purchasing the stock of competing firms. To get around that prohibition, however, a firm could still purchase the *assets* of its competitors. The result was the same: the elimination of competition. This gigantic loophole was closed by the *Celler-Kefauver Act*, which prohibits mergers through the purchase of assets if these mergers will tend to reduce competition. The act also requires all proposed mergers to be approved by both the FTC and the Justice Department.

The Antitrust Improvements Act (1976) In 1976 Congress passed the *Antitrust Improvements Act* to strengthen previous legislation. This law provided additional time for the FTC and the Justice Department to evaluate proposed mergers, and it expanded the investigative powers of the Justice Department. It also authorized the attorneys general of individual states to prosecute firms accused of price fixing and to recover monetary damages for *consumers*.

The Present Antitrust Environment The problem with antitrust legislation and its enforcement is that it is hard to define exactly what an appropriate level of competition is. For example, a particular merger may be in the public interest because it increases the efficiency of an industry. But at the same time it may be harmful because it reduces competition. There is really no rule of law (or of economics) that can be used to determine which of these two considerations is more important in a given case.

Three factors tend to influence the enforcement and effectiveness of antitrust legislation at the present time. The first is the growing presence of foreign firms in American markets. Foreign firms have increased competition in America and thus have made it more difficult for any firm to monopolize an industry. Second, most antitrust legislation must be interpreted by the courts because the laws are often vague and open-ended. Thus, the attitude of the courts has a lot to do with the effectiveness of these laws. And third, political considerations often determine how actively the FTC and the Justice Department pursue antitrust cases.

Other Areas of Regulation

It is impossible to manage even a small business without being affected by local, state, and federal regulations. And it is just as impossible to describe all the government regulations that affect business. In addition to the regulations that affect competition just discussed, we have examined a variety of regulations in this text. Chapter 2 discussed laws and regulations dealing with the environment, consumerism, and discrimination; Chapter 3, international trade; Chapter 4, organization of business entities; Chapter 10, human resources and employee relations; Chapter 12 union-management relations; and Chapter 21, securities.

By now, you may think that there must be a government regulation to govern any possible situation. Actually, government regulations increased from the 1930s through the 1970s, but the country then entered a deregulation period that lasted over twenty years. Today the deregulation drive continues, but there is a question as to how far it should go. Many experts now suggest that any evaluation of government regulations should determine which regulations make sense, which should be modified, and which should be eliminated. Above all, they believe, any reworking of the regulatory environment should create a "livable" environment for consumers, workers, and businesses. We look at the current status of the deregulation movement in the next section.

The Deregulation Movement

Deregulation is the process of removing existing government regulations, forgoing proposed regulations, or reducing the rate at which new regulations are enacted. The primary aim of the deregulation movement is to minimize the complexity of regulations that affect business and the cost of compliance.

deregulation the process of removing existing government regulations, forgoing proposed regulations, or reducing the rate at which new regulations are enacted

Today many Americans believe the federal government is out of control and out of touch with the needs of average citizens. These same people often complain that the federal government has too many employees and spends too much money. At the time of publication, the U.S. government

- Employed approximately 2.8 million civilian workers (in addition to 1.1 million military personnel).
- Spent more than $1.7 trillion a year, which is approximately $6,300 for every person in the United States.

Critics also complain that too many government agencies regulate business activities. More than one hundred federal agencies are currently responsible for enforcing a staggering array of regulations. And at least fifteen federal agencies now have a direct impact on business firms. These agencies and the activities they regulate are listed in Table C.1 on page A44.

Advocates of deregulation are quick to point out that every business—both large and small—must obey a large number of government restrictions and directives and that doing so is costly. Large corporations can cope with government regulation. They have been doing so for some time. In essence, coping means passing the cost of regulation along to stockholders in the form of lower dividends and to consumers in the form of higher prices. Smaller firms bear a smaller regulatory burden, but they may find it harder to cope with that burden. Some may not have the staff necessary to comply with the various documentation requirements. And for many small businesses, stiff

table C.1 Government Agencies and What They Regulate

Government Agency or Commission	Regulates
Consumer Product Safety Commission	Consumer protection
Environmental Protection Agency	Pollution control
Equal Employment Opportunity Commission	Discrimination in employment practices
Federal Aviation Administration	Airline industry
Federal Communications Commission	Radio, television, telephone, and telegraph communications
Federal Energy Regulatory Commission	Electric power and natural gas
Federal Highway Administration	Vehicle safety
Federal Maritime Commission	Ocean shipping
Federal Mine Safety and Health Review Commission	Worker safety and health in the mining industry
Federal Trade Commission	Antitrust, consumer protection
Food and Drug Administration	Consumer protection
Interstate Commerce Commission	Railroads, bus lines, trucking, pipelines, and waterways
Nuclear Regulatory Commission	Nuclear power and nuclear industry
Occupational Safety and Health Review Commission	Worker safety and health
Securities and Exchange Commission	Corporate securities

competition for customers requires that they pass the cost of compliance directly to their owners.

In every presidential election since the 1970s, the candidates elected to office were sincere when they promised the American people they were prepared to declare war on the bureaucracy in Washington and cut unnecessary government spending from the federal budget. Presidents Nixon, Carter, Reagan, Bush, and Clinton all had their own ideas on how government should be reorganized. But each president found that government reform is often stymied by overwhelming red tape in federal regulations, duplication of services, rigid civil service rules, and opposition from senators and representatives who seek to protect their favorite agencies or "pork barrel." Each president found that decades of growth and power in government cannot be swept away overnight.

Government Taxation

Whether you believe there is too much government or too little, you are required to help pay for it. In one way or another, each of us pays for everything government does—from regulating business to funding research into the causes and cures of cancer. We pay taxes to our local, state, and federal governments on the basis of what we earn, what we own, and even what we purchase.

Federal Taxes

It takes a lot of money to run something as big as the U.S. government. Each year, vast sums are spent for human services, national defense, and interest on the national debt. In addition, the federal government must pay the salaries of its employees, cover its operating expenses, and purchase equipment and supplies that range from typewriter ribbons to aircraft carriers. Most of the money comes from taxes. Figure C.5 shows that the federal government had revenues of $1,418.3 billion in 1996. About 95 percent of that sum was obtained through taxation.

Individual Income Taxes An individual's income tax liability is computed from his or her taxable income, which is gross income less various authorized deductions from income. In 1914, the federal government collected an average of 28 cents per taxpayer. Today that average is more than $2,100 per person.

The federal income tax is a progressive tax. A **progressive tax** requires the payment of an increasing proportion of income as the individual's income increases. For example, a single individual with a taxable income of $20,000 must currently pay a federal income tax of $3,000, or 15 percent of that taxable income. A single taxpayer with a taxable income of $40,000 must pay $7,905, or about 20 percent of that income.

progressive tax a tax that requires the payment of an increasing proportion of income as the individual's income increases

Taxpayers must file an annual tax return by April 15 of each year, for the previous calendar year. The return shows the income, deductions, and computations on which the taxpayer's tax liability is based.

Corporate Income Taxes Corporate income taxes provide approximately 12 percent of total federal revenues. Corporations pay federal income tax only on their taxable income, which is what remains after deducting *all* legal business expenses from net sales. Currently, the federal corporate tax rate is

Taxable income:	Tax is:
Not over $50,000	15%
Over $50,000 but not over $75,000	$7,500 + 25% of excess over $50,000
$75,000 but not over $100,000	$13,750 + 34% of excess over $75,000
$100,000 but not over $330,000	$22,250 + 39% of excess over $100,000
$330,000 but not over $10,000,000	$113,900 + 34% of excess over $330,000
$10,000,000 but not over $15,000,000	$3,400,000 + 35% of excess over $10,000,000
$15,000,000 but not over $18,333,333	$5,150,000 + 38% of excess over $15,000,000
$18,333,333 and over	35%

As Table C.2 shows, a corporation with a taxable income of $330,000 must pay a total of $111,950 to the federal government.

Other Federal Taxes Additional sources of federal revenue include Social Security, unemployment, and excise taxes, as well as customs duties. An objective of all taxes is to raise money, but excise taxes and customs duties are also designed to regulate the use of specific goods and services.

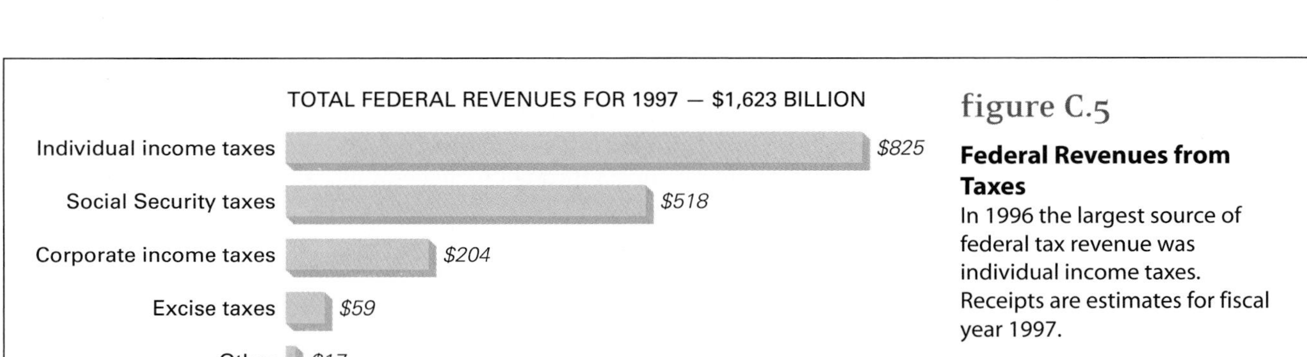

figure C.5

Federal Revenues from Taxes

In 1996 the largest source of federal tax revenue was individual income taxes. Receipts are estimates for fiscal year 1997.

Source: U.S. Bureau of the Census, *Statistical Abstract of the United States*, 119th ed., 1999, p.357.

table C.2 Federal Corporate Income Tax on an Income of $330,000

According to the tax rate table, the tax is $22,250 + 39% of the excess over $100,000.

Step 1 Determine the excess over $100,000.

$330,000
− 100,000
$230,000

Step 2 Multiply the excess amount (step 1) by the tax rate (39%).

$230,000 × 0.39 = $89,700

Step 3 To determine the total tax, add the base amount to the additional tax determined in step 2.

$ 22,250
+ 89,700
111,950

As Figure C.5 shows, the second largest source of federal revenue is the *Social Security tax*, which is collected under the Federal Insurance Contributions Act (FICA). This tax provides funding for retirement, disability, and death benefits for contributing employees. FICA taxes are paid by both the employer and the employee. The employee's share is withheld from his or her salary by the employer and sent to the federal government with the employer's share. The Social Security tax is broken into two components: (1) old age, survivors, and disability insurance and (2) Medicare. For old age, survivors, and disability insurance, the annual tax in 1998 was 12.4 percent of the first $68,400 earned. For Medicare, the annual tax was 2.9 percent of *all* wages.

Under the provisions of the Federal Unemployment Tax Act (FUTA), employers must pay an *unemployment tax* equal to 6.2 percent of the first $7,000 of each employee's annual wages. Because employers are allowed credits against the 6.2 percent through participation in state unemployment programs, the actual unemployment rate paid by most employers is 0.8 percent. The tax is paid to the federal government to fund benefits for unemployed workers. Unlike the Social Security tax, the FUTA tax is levied only on employers.

excise tax a tax on the manufacture or sale of a particular domestic product

An **excise tax** is a tax on the manufacture or sale of a particular domestic product. Excise taxes are used to help pay for government services directed toward the users of these products and, in some cases, to limit the use of potentially harmful products. Alcohol and tobacco products are potentially harmful to consumers. They are taxed to raise the prices of these goods and thus discourage consumption. The federal excise tax on gasoline is a source of income that can be used to build and repair highways. Although manufacturers and retailers are responsible for paying excise taxes, these taxes are usually passed on to the consumer in the form of higher retail prices.

customs (or import) duty a tax on a foreign product entering a country

A **customs** (or **import**) **duty** is a tax on a foreign product entering a country. Import duties are designed to protect specific domestic industries by raising the prices of competing imported products. They are first paid by the importer, but the added costs are passed on to consumers through higher—and less competitive—prices.

State and Local Taxes

Like the federal government, state and local governments are financed primarily through taxes. As illustrated in Figure C.6, sales taxes provide about 35 percent of state and local tax revenues. Most states and some cities also levy taxes on the incomes of individuals and businesses. Finally, many local and county governments also tax consumer sales, real estate, and some forms of personal property.

Sales Taxes Sales taxes are levied by both states and cities and are paid by the purchasers of consumer products. Retailers collect sales taxes as a specified percentage of the price of each taxed product and then forward them to the taxing authority. A sales tax is a regressive tax. A **regressive tax** is one that takes a greater percentage of a lower income than of a higher income. The regressiveness of the sales tax stems from the fact that lower-income households generally spend a greater proportion of their income on taxable products such as food, clothing, and other essentials. Consider the impact of a 5 percent sales tax on food items purchased by a low-income family. A family that earns $10,000 a year and spends $3,000 on food will pay sales taxes of $150, or 1.5 percent of their total earnings. By comparison, a family that earns $40,000 a year and spends $3,000 on food will pay the same amount of sales tax, but the amount represents only 0.38 percent of their total earnings. Not all states collect a sales tax on all items. In fact, many states exempt food from their sales tax.

regressive tax a tax that takes a greater percentage of a lower income than of a higher income

Property Taxes Many local governments rely on the property taxes they levy on real estate and personal property owned by businesses and individuals to finance their ongoing activities. *Real estate taxes* are usually computed as a percentage of the assessed value of the real property. (The assessed value is determined by the local tax assessor as the fair market value of the property, a portion of its fair market value, or its replacement cost.) For example, suppose the city council has established a real estate tax rate of $2.10 per $100 of assessed valuation. Then the property tax bill for an office building with an assessed value of $200,000 will be $4,200 ($200,000 × $2.10/$100 = $4,200). This type of tax is called a proportional tax. A **proportional tax** is one whose percentage rate remains constant as the tax base increases. Therefore, if the tax rate remains constant at $2.10 per $100, a taxpayer who owns real estate valued at $10,000 pays $210 in taxes; a taxpayer who owns real estate valued at $100,000 pays $2,100 in taxes.

proportional tax a tax whose percentage rate remains constant as the tax base increases

Certain personal property owned by businesses and individuals is also subject to local taxation. For businesses, taxable personal property normally includes machinery, equipment, raw materials, and finished inventory. In some cases, local authorities also tax the value of stocks, bonds, mortgages, and promissory notes held by businesses. For individuals, such items as trucks, automobiles, and boats may be classified as personal property and taxed by local authorities.

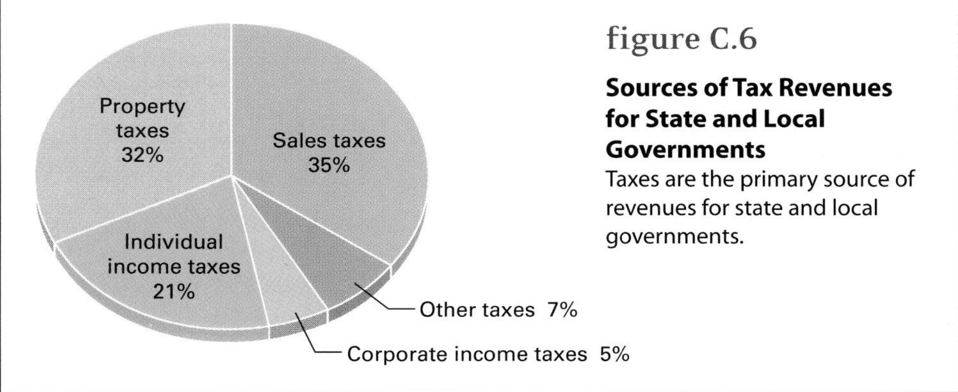

figure C.6

Sources of Tax Revenues for State and Local Governments

Taxes are the primary source of revenues for state and local governments.

Source: U.S. Bureau of the Census, *Statistical Abstract of the United States*, 119th ed., 1999, p.316.

Glossary

absolute advantage the ability to produce a specific product more efficiently than any other nation (3)

accessory equipment standardized equipment used in a firm's production or office activities (14)

account executive (or **stock broker**) an individual—sometimes called a *stock broker* or *registered representative*—who buys and sells securities for clients (21)

accountability the obligation of a worker to accomplish an assigned job or task (8)

accounting the process of systematically collecting, analyzing, and reporting financial information (18)

accounting equation the basis for the accounting process: *assets = liabilities + owners' equity* (18)

accounting program a software package that enables users to record and report financial information (17)

accounts payable short-term obligations that arise as a result of making credit purchases (18)

accounts receivable turnover a financial ratio calculated by dividing net sales by accounts receivable (18)

accounts receivables amounts that are owed to a firm by its customers (20)

acid-test ratio a financial ratio calculated by subtracting the value of inventory from the current asset amount and dividing the total by current liabilities (18)

Active Corps of Executives (ACE) a group of active managers who counsel small-business owners on a volunteer basis (6)

ad hoc committee a committee created for a specific short-term purpose (8)

administrative law the regulations created by government agencies that have been established by legislative bodies (Appendix C)

administrative manager a manager who is not associated with any specific functional area but who provides overall administrative guidance and leadership (7)

advertising a paid, nonpersonal message communicated to a select audience through a mass medium (16)

advertising agency an independent firm that plans, produces, and places advertising for its clients (16)

advertising media the various forms of communication through which advertising reaches its audience (16)

affirmative action program a plan designed to increase the number of minority employees at all levels within an organization (2)

agency a business relationship in which one party, called the principal, appoints a second party, called the agent, to act on its behalf (Appendix C)

agency shop a workplace in which employees can choose not to join the union but must pay dues to the union anyway (12)

agent a middleman that facilitates exchanges, represents a buyer or a seller, and often is hired permanently on a commission basis (15)

alien corporation a corporation chartered by a foreign government and conducting business in the United States (5)

analytic process a process in operations management in which raw materials are broken into different component parts (9)

appellate court a court that hears cases appealed from lower courts (Appendix C)

arbitration the step in a grievance procedure in which a neutral third party hears the two sides of a dispute and renders a decision (12)

arithmetic mean the sum of all the values of a set of data, divided by the number of items in the set (17)

assets the resources that a firm owns (18)

audit an examination of a company's financial statements and accounting practices that produced them (18)

authoritarian leader one who holds all authority and responsibility, with communication usually moving from top to bottom (7)

authority the power, within the organization, to accomplish an assigned job or task (8)

automatic vending the use of machines to dispense convenience goods automatically when customers deposit money (15)

automobile liability insurance insurance that covers financial losses resulting from injuries or damages caused by the insured vehicle (Appendix B)

automobile physical damage insurance insurance that covers damage to the insured vehicle (Appendix B)

balance of payments the total flow of money into the country minus the total flow of money out of the country, over some period of time (3)

balance of trade the total value of a nation's exports minus the total value of its imports, over some period of time (3)

balance sheet (or **statement of financial position**) a summary of the dollar amounts of a firm's assets, liabilities, and owners' equity accounts at the end of an accounting period (18)

banker's acceptance a written order for the bank to pay a third party a stated amount of money on a specific date (19)

bankruptcy a legal procedure designed both to protect an individual or business that cannot meet its financial obligations and to protect the creditors involved (Appendix C)

bargaining unit the specific group of employees represented by a union (12)

barter a system of exchange in which goods or services are traded directly for other goods and/or services—without using money (1, 19)

bear market a market in which average stock prices are declining (21)
behavior modification a systematic program of reinforcement to encourage desirable behavior (11)
beneficiary person or organization named in a life insurance policy as recipient of the proceeds of that policy on the death of the insured (Appendix B)
bill of lading issued by the transport carrier to the exporter to prove merchandise has been shipped (3)
binding contract an agreement that requires an intermediary to purchase products from a particular supplier, not from the supplier's competitors (Appendix C)
blue-chip stock a stock that is a safe investment that generally attracts conservative investors (21)
blue-sky laws state laws that regulate securities trading (21)
board of directors the top governing body of a corporation, the members of which are elected by the stockholders (5)
bond indenture a legal document that details all the conditions relating to a bond issue (20)
boycott a refusal to do business with a particular firm (12)
boycott in restraint of trade an agreement between businesses not to sell to or buy from a particular entity (Appendix C)
brand a name, term, symbol, design, or any combination of these that identifies a seller's products and distinguishes them from competitors' products (14)
brand (or **selective demand) advertising** advertising that is used to sell a particular brand of product (16)
brand equity the marketing and financial value associated with a brand's strength in a market (14)
brand loyalty extent to which a customer is favorable toward buying a specific brand (14)
brand mark the part of a brand that is a symbol or distinctive design (14)
brand name the part of a brand that can be spoken (14)
breach of contract the failure of one party to fulfill the terms of a contract when there is no legal reason for that failure (Appendix C)
breakeven quantity the number of units that must be sold for the total revenue (from all units sold) to equal the total cost (of all units sold) (14)
broker a middleman that specializes in a particular commodity, represents either a buyer or a seller, and is likely to be hired on a temporary basis (15)
budget a financial statement that projects income and/or expenditures over a specified future period (20)
bull market a market in which average stock prices are increasing (21)
bundle pricing the packaging together of two or more products, usually of a complementary nature, to be sold for a single price (14)
bureaucratic structure a management system based on a formal framework of authority that is carefully outlined and precisely followed (8)
business the organized effort of individuals to produce and sell, for a profit, the goods and services that satisfy society's needs (1)
business buying behavior the purchasing of products by producers, governmental units, and institutions (13)
business cycle the recurrence of periods of growth and recession in a nation's economic activity (1)
business ethics the application of moral standards to business situations (2)
business interruption insurance insurance protection for a business whose operations are interrupted because of a fire, storm, or other natural disaster (Appendix B)
business model a group of shared characteristics and behavior in a business situation (4)
business plan a carefully constructed guide for the person starting a business (6)
business product a product bought for resale, for making other products, or for use in a firm's operations (14)
business service an intangible product that an organization uses in its operations (14)
business-to-business (B2B) model firms that conduct business with other businesses (4)
business-to-consumer (B2C) model firms that focus on conducting business with individual buyers (4)
buying allowance a temporary price reduction to resellers for purchasing specified quantities of a product (16)
buying behavior the decisions and actions of people involved in buying and using products (13)
buying long buying stock with the expectation that it will increase in value and can then be sold at a profit (21)

call premium the dollar amount over par value that the corporation has to pay an investor when it redeems either preferred stock or a corporate bond (20)
capacity the amount of products or services that an organization can produce in a given time (9)
capital all the financial resources, buildings, machinery, tools, and equipment that are used in an organization's operations (1)
capital budget a financial statement that estimates a firm's expenditures for major assets and its long-term financing needs (20)
capital gain the difference between a security's purchase price and selling price (21)
capital-intensive technology a process in which machines and equipment do most of the work (9)
capitalism an economic system in which individuals own and operate the majority of businesses that provide goods and services (1)
captioned photograph a picture accompanied by a brief explanation (16)
captive pricing the pricing of a basic product in a product line at a low price, but pricing related items at a higher level (14)
carrier a firm that offers transporation services (15)
cash budget a financial statement that projects cash receipts and expenditures over a specified period (20)
cash flow the movement of money into and out of an organization (20)
cash surrender value the amount payable to the holder of a whole life insurance policy if the policy is canceled (Appendix B)
catalog marketing marketing in which an organization provides a catalog from which customers make selections and place orders by mail or telephone (15)
catalog showroom a retail outlet that displays well-known brands and sells them at discount prices through catalogs within the store (15)
category killer a very large specialty store that concentrates on a single product line and competes on the basis of low prices and product availability (15)
caveat emptor a Latin phrase meaning "let the buyer beware" (2)
centralized organization an organization that systematically works to concentrate authority at the upper levels of the organization (8)
certificate of deposit (CD) a document stating that the bank will pay the depositor a guaranteed interest rate for money left on deposit for a specified period of time (19)

certified public accountant (CPA) an individual who has met state requirements for accounting education and experience and has passed a rigorous two-day accounting examination (18)
chain of command the line of authority that extends from the highest to the lowest levels of an organization (8)
chain retailer a firm that operates more than one retail outlet (15)
channel of distribution (or **marketing channel**) a sequence of marketing organizations that directs a product from the producer to the ultimate user (15)
check a written order for a bank or other financial institution to pay a stated dollar amount to the business or person indicated on the face of the check (19)
close corporation a corporation whose stock is owned by relatively few people and is not sold to the general public (5)
closed shop a workplace in which workers must join the union before they are hired, outlawed by the Taft-Hartley Act (12)
cluster structure an organization that consists primarily of teams with no or very few underlying departments (8)
code of ethics a guide to acceptable and ethical behavior as defined by an organization (2)
coinsurance clause a part of a fire insurance policy that requires the policyholder to purchase coverage at least equal to a specified percentage of the replacement cost of the property to obtain full reimbursement for losses (Appendix B)
collaborative learning system a work environment that allows problem-solving participation by all team members (17)
collateral real estate or personal property pledged as security for a loan (19)
collective bargaining the process of negotiating a labor contract with management (12)
command economy an economic system in which the government decides what will be produced, how it will be produced, who gets what is produced, and the prices of what is produced (1)
commercial bank a profit-making organization that accepts deposits, makes loans, and provides related services to its customers (19)
commercial paper a short-term promissory note issued by a large corporation (20)
commission a payment that is a percentage of sales revenue (10)
commission merchant a middleman that carries merchandise and negotiates sales for manufacturers (15)
common law the body of law created by court decisions rendered by judges; also known as case law or judicial law (Appendix C)
common stock stock owned by individuals or firms who may vote on corporate matters, but whose claims on profit and assets are subordinate to the claims of others (5, 20)
communications program software that allows computers to communicate with each other (17)
community of interests a situation in which one firm buys the stock of a competing firm to reduce competition between the two (Appendix C)
community shopping center a planned shopping center that includes one or two department stores and some specialty stores, along with convenience stores (15)
comparable worth a concept that seeks equal compensation for jobs requiring about the same level of education, training, and skills (10)
comparative advantage within a nation, the ability to produce a specific product more efficiently than any other product (3)
comparison discounting sets the price of a product at a specific level and simultaneously compares it with a higher price (14)
compensation the payment that employees receive in return for their labor (10)
compensation system the policies and strategies that determine employee compensation (10)
competition a rivalry among businesses for sales to potential customers (1)
component part an item that becomes part of a physical product and is either a finished item ready for assembly or a product that needs little processing before assembly (14)
computer-aided design (CAD) the use of computers to aid in the development of products (9)
computer-aided manufacturing (CAM) the use of computers to plan and control manufacturing processes (9)
computer-integrated manufacturing (CIM) a computer system that not only helps design products but also controls the machinery needed to produce the finished product (9)
computer viruses software codes that are designed to disrupt normal computer operations (4)
conceptual skill the ability to think in abstract terms (7)
consideration the value or benefit that one party to a contract furnishes to the other party (Appendix C)
consumer buying behavior the purchasing of products for personal or household use, not for business purposes (13)
consumer products goods and services purchased by individuals for personal consumption (1)
consumer product a product purchased to satisfy personal and family needs (14)
consumer sales promotion method a sales promotion method designed to attract consumers to particular retail stores and motivate them to purchase certain new or established products (16)
consumerism all activities undertaken to protect the rights of consumers (2)
consumers individuals who purchase goods or services for their own personal use (1)
contingency plan a plan that outlines alternative courses of action that may be taken if the organization's other plans are disrupted or become ineffective (7)
contract a legally enforceable agreement between two or more competent parties who promise to do, or not to do, a particular thing (Appendix C)
controlling the process of evaluating and regulating ongoing activities to ensure that goals are achieved (7)
convenience product a relatively inexpensive, frequently purchased item for which buyers want to exert only minimal effort (14)
convenience store a small retail store that sells a limited variety of products but remains open well beyond the normal business hours (15)
convergence of technologies the overlapping capabilities and the merging of products and services into one fully integrated interactive system (4)
convertible preferred stock preferred stock that the owner may exchange for a specified number of shares of common stock (20)
cookie a small piece of software sent by a web site that tracks an individual's Internet use (4)
cooperative an association of individuals or firms whose purpose it is to perform some business function for its members (5)
cooperative advertising an arrangement whereby a manufacturer agrees to pay a certain amount of the retailer's media cost for advertising the manufacturer's product (16)
copyright control of content ownership (4, Appendix B)

corporate bond a corporation's written pledge that it will repay a specified amount of money, with interest (20)
corporate charter a contract between the corporation and the state, in which the state recognizes the formation of the artifical person that is the corporation (5)
corporate culture the inner rites, rituals, heroes, and values of a firm (8)
corporate officers the chairman of the board, president, executive vice presidents, corporate secretary and treasurer, or any other top executive appointed by the board of directors (5)
corporation an artifical person created by law, with most of the legal rights of a real person, including the rights to start and operate a business, to buy or sell property, to borrow money, to sue or be sued, and to enter into binding contracts (5)
cost of goods sold the dollar amount equal to beginning inventory *plus* net purchases *less* ending inventory (18)
countertrade an international barter transaction (3)
coupon reduces the retail price of a particular item by a stated amount at the time of purchase (16)
court of limited jurisdiction a court that hears only specific types of cases (Appendix C)
court of original jurisdiction the first court to recognize and hear testimony in a legal action (Appendix C)
craft union an organization of skilled workers in a single craft or trade (12)
creative selling selling products to new customers and increasing sales to present customers (16)
credit immediate purchasing power that is exchanged for a promise to repay borrowed money, with or without interest, at a later date (19)
credit union a financial institution that accepts deposits from, and lends money to, only those people who are its members (19)
crime a violation of a public law (Appendix C)
critical path the sequence of production activities that takes the longest time from start to finish (9)
cross-functional team a group of employees from different departments who work together on a specific team (8)
cultural diversity differences among people in a work force due to race, ethnicity, and gender (10)
currency devaluation the reduction of the value of a nation's currency relative to the currencies of other countries (3)
current assets assets that can be quickly converted into cash or that will be used in one year or less (18)
current liabilities debts that will be repaid in one year or less (18)
current ratio a financial ratio computed by dividing current assets by current liabilities (18)
customary pricing certain goods priced primarily on the basis of tradition (14)
customs (or import) duty a tax on a foreign product entering a country (Appendix C)

damages a monetary settlement awarded to a party that is injured through a breach of contract (Appendix C)
data numerical or verbal descriptions that usually result from some sort of measurement (17)
data processing the transformation of data into a form useful for a specific purpose (17)
database a single collection of data stored in one place that can be used by people throughout an organization to make decisions (17)
database management program software that allows users to electronically store large amounts of data and to transform the data into information (17)
debenture bond a bond backed only by the reputation of the issuing corporation (20)
debit card a card that electronically subtracts the amount of your purchase from your bank account at the moment the purchase is made (19)
debt capital borrowed money obtained through loans of various types (20)
debt-to-owners' equity a financial ratio calculated by dividing total liabilities by owners' equity (18)
decentralized organization an organization in which management consciously attempts to spread authority widely in the lower levels of the organization (8)
decision making the act of choosing one alternative from among a set of alternatives (7)
decisional role a role that involves various aspects of management decision making (7)
deed a written document by which the ownership of real property is transferred from one person or organization to another (Appendix C)
delegation assigning part of a manager's work and power to other workers (8)
demand the quantity of a product that buyers are willing to purchase at each of various prices (1, 14)
demand deposit an amount on deposit in a checking account (19)
democratic leader one who holds final responsibility but also delegates authority to others, who help determine work assignments; communication is active upward and downward (7)
department store a retail store that (1) employs twenty-five or more persons and (2) sells at least home furnishings, appliances, family apparel, and household linens and dry goods, each in a different part of the store (15)
departmentalization the process of grouping jobs into manageable units (8)
departmentalization by customer grouping activities according to the needs of the various customer populations (8)
departmentalization by function grouping jobs that relate to the same organizational activity (8)
departmentalization by location grouping activities according to a defined geographic area in which they are performed (8)
departmentalization by product grouping activities related to a particular product or service (8)
depreciation the process of apportioning the cost of a fixed asset over its useful life (18)
depression a severe recession that lasts longer than a recession (1)
design planning the development of a plan for converting a product idea into an actual product (9)
desktop publishing program a software package that enables users to combine text and graphics in reports, newsletters, and pamphlets (17)
digitized data that has been converted to a type of signal that the computers and telecommunications equipment that make up the Internet can understand (4)
direct-mail advertising promotional material that is mailed directly to individuals (16)
direct marketing the use of the telephone and nonpersonal media to introduce products to consumers, who can then purchase them by mail or telephone (15)
direct-response marketing a type of marketing that occurs when a retailer advertises a product and makes it available through mail or telephone orders (15)
direct selling the marketing of products to ultimate consumers through face-to-face sales presentations at home or in the workplace (15)

directing the combined processes of leading and motivating (7)

discharge by mutual assent termination of a contract by mutual agreement of all parties (Appendix C)

discount a deduction from the price of an item (14)

discount rate the interest rate that the Federal Reserve System charges for loans to member banks (19)

discount store a self-service, general-merchandise outlet that sells goods at lower-than-usual prices (15)

discretionary income disposable income less savings and expenditures on food, clothing, and housing (13)

discretionary order an order to buy or sell a security that lets the broker decide when to execute the transaction and at what price (21)

disposable income personal income less all additional personal taxes (13)

diversification the process of spreading assets among several types of investments to lessen risk (21)

divestiture the process of dismantling a company and selling off different parts (5)

dividend a distribution of earnings to the stockholders of a corporation (5)

domestic corporation a corporation in the state in which it is incorporated (5)

domestic system a method of manufacturing in which an entrepreneur distributed raw materials to various homes, where families would process them into finished goods to be offered for sale by the merchant entrepreneur (1)

double-entry bookkeeping a system in which each financial transaction is recorded as two separate accounting entries to maintain the balance shown in the accounting equation (18)

draft issued by the exporter's bank, ordering the importer's bank to pay for the merchandise, thus guaranteeing payment once accepted by the importer's bank (3)

dumping exportation of large quantities of a product at a price lower than that of the same product in the home market (3)

earnings per share a financial ratio calculated by dividing net income after taxes by the number of shares of common stock outstanding (18)

e-business the organized effort of individuals to produce and sell, for a profit, the products and services that satisfy society's needs through the facilities available on the Internet (4)

e-commerce buying and selling activities conducted online (1, 4)

economic community an organization of nations formed to promote the free movement of resources and products among its members and to create common economic policies (3)

economic model of social responsibility the view that society will benefit most when business is left alone to produce and market profitable products that society needs (2)

economics the study of how wealth is created and distributed (1)

economy the system through which a society answers the two economic questions—how wealth is created and distributed (1)

electronic funds transfer (EFT) system a means of performing financial transactions through a computer terminal or telephone hookup (19)

embargo a complete halt to trading with a particular nation or in a particular product (3)

employee benefit a reward in addition to regular compensation that is provided indirectly to employees (10)

employee ownership a situation in which employees own the company they work for by virtue of being stockholders (11)

employee training the process of teaching operations and technical employees how to do their present jobs more effectively and efficiently (10)

empowerment making employees more involved in their jobs by increasing their participation in decision making (11)

endorsement the payee's signature on the back of a negotiable instrument (Appendix C)

endowment life insurance life insurance that provides protection and guarantees the payment of a stated amount to the policyholder after a specified number of years (Appendix B)

entrepreneur a person who risks time, effort, and money to start and operate a business (1)

Environmental Protection Agency (EPA) the federal agency charged with enforcing laws designed to protect the environment (2)

Equal Employment Opportunity Commission (EEOC) a government agency with power to investigate complaints of employment discrimination and power to sue firms that practice it (2)

equity capital money received from the owners or from the sale of shares of ownership in the business (20)

equity theory a theory of motivation based on the premise that people are motivated to obtain and preserve equitable treatment for themselves (11)

esteem needs our need for respect, recognition, and a sense of our own accomplishment and worth (11)

ethics the study of right and wrong and of the morality of the choices individuals make (2)

everyday low prices (EDLP) setting low prices for products on a consistent basis rather than setting higher prices and frequently discounting them (14)

excise tax a tax on the manufacture or sale of a particular domestic product (Appendix C)

exclusive distribution the use of only a single retail outlet for a product in each geographic area (15)

expectancy theory a model of motivation based on the assumption that motivation depends on how much we want something and on how likely we think we are to get it (11)

expenses the costs incurred in operating a business (18)

Export-Import Bank of the United States an independent agency of the U.S. government whose function it is to assist in financing the exports of American firms (3)

exporting selling and shipping raw materials or products to other nations (3)

express warranty a written explanation of the responsibilities of the producer (or seller) in the event that a product is found to be defective or otherwise unsatisfactory (14, Appendix C)

extended coverage insurance protection against damage caused by wind, hail, explosion, vandalism, riots or civil commotion, falling aircraft, and smoke (Appendix B)

external recruiting the attempt to attract job applicants from outside the organization (10)

e-zines small online magazines (4)

factor a firm that specializes in buying other firms' accounts receivables (20)

factors of production the resources used to produce goods and services—natural resources, labor, capital, and entrepreneurship (1)

factory system a system of manufacturing in which all of the materials, machinery, and workers required to manufacture a product are assembled in one place (1)

family branding the strategy in which a firm uses the same brand for all or most of its products (14)
family of funds exists when one investment company manages a group of mutual funds (21)
feature article a piece of up to 3,000 words prepared by an organization for inclusion in a particular publication (16)
federal deficit a shortfall created when the federal government spends more in a fiscal year than it receives (1)
Federal Reserve System the central bank of the United States that is responsible for regulation of the banking industry (19)
Federal Trade Commission (FTC) a five-member committee charged with the responsibility of investigating illegal trade practices and enforcing antitrust laws (Appendix C)
fidelity bond an insurance policy that protects a business from theft, forgery, or embezzlement by its employees (Appendix B)
financial leverage the use of borrowed funds to increase the return on owners' equity (20)
financial management all the activities concerned with obtaining money and using it effectively (20)
financial manager a manager who is primarily responsible for the organization's financial resources (7)
financial plan a plan for obtaining and using the money needed to implement an organization's goals (20)
financial planner an individual who has had at least two years of training in securities, insurance, taxation, real estate, and estate planning and has passed a rigorous examination (21)
financial ratio a number that shows the relationship between two elements of a firm's financial statements (18)
fire insurance insurance that covers losses due to fire (Appendix B)
first-line manager a manager who coordinates and supervises the activities of operating employees (7)
fiscal policy government influence on the amount of savings and expenditures; accomplished by altering the tax structure and by changing the levels of government spending (1)
fixed assets assets that will be held or used for a period longer than one year (18)
fixed cost a cost that is incurred no matter how many units of a product are produced or sold (14)
flexible benefit plan compensation plan whereby an employee receives a predetermined amount of benefit dollars to spend on a package of benefits selected to meet individual needs (10)
flexible manufacturing system (FMS) a single production system that combines robotics and computer-aided manufacturing (9)
flextime a system in which employees set their own hours within employer-determined limits (11)
floor planning a method of financing where the title to merchandise is given to lenders in return for short-term financing (20)
foreign corporation a corporation in any state in which it does business except the one in which it is incorporated (5)
foreign-exchange control a restriction on the amount of a particular foreign currency that can be purchased or sold (3)
form utility utility created by converting raw materials, people, finances, and information into finished products (9, 12)
franchise a license to operate an individually owned business as though it were part of a chain of outlets or stores (6)
franchisee a person or organization purchasing a franchise (6)
franchising the actual granting of a franchise (6)
franchisor an individual or organization granting a franchise (6)
free enterprise the system of business in which individuals are free to decide what to produce, how to produce it, and at what price to sell it (1)
frequency distribution a listing of the number of times each value appears in a set of data (17)
frequent user incentive a program developed to reward customers who engage in repeat (frequent) purchases (16)
full-service wholesaler a middleman that performs the entire range of wholesaler functions (15)
functional middleman a middleman that helps in the transfer of ownership of products but does not take title to the products (15)

Gantt chart a graphic scheduling device that displays the tasks to be performed on the vertical axis and the time required for each task on the horizontal axis (9)
General Agreement on Tariffs and Trade (GATT) an international organization of nations dedicated to reducing or eliminating tariffs and other barriers to world trade (3)
general journal a book of original entry in which typical transactions are recorded in order of their occurrence (18)
general ledger a book of accounts that contains a separate sheet or section for each account (18)
general merchandise wholesaler a middleman that deals in a wide variety of products (15)
general obligation bond a bond backed by the full faith, credit, and unlimited taxing power of the government unit that issued it (21)
general partner a person who assumes full or shared responsibility for operating a business (5)
general partnership a business co-owned by two or more general partners who are liable for everything the business does (5)
generic product (or **brand**) a product with no brand at all (14)
goal an end result that the organization is expected to achieve over a one-to-ten year period (7)
goal-setting theory a theory of motivation suggesting that employees are motivated to achieve goals they and their managers establish together (11)
goodwill the value of a firm's reputation, location, earning capacity, and other intangibles that make the business a profitable concern (18)
government-owned corporation a corporation owned and operated by a local, state, or federal government (5)
grapevine the informal communications network within an organization (8)
graphics program software that enables users to display and print pictures, drawings, charts, and diagrams (17)
grievance procedure a formally established course of action for resolving employee complaints against management (12)
gross domestic product (GDP) the total dollar value of all goods and services produced by all people within the boundaries of a country during a one-year period (1)
gross profit a firm's net sales *less* the cost of goods sold (18)
gross sales the total dollar amount of all goods and services sold during the accounting period (18)
groupware one of the latest types of software that facilitates the management of large projects among geographically dispersed employees as well as such group activities as problem solving and brainstorming (17)

hard-core unemployed workers with little education or vocational training and a long history of unemployment (2)
health maintenance organization (HMO) an insurance plan that directly employs or contracts with selected physicians and hospitals to provide healthcare services in exchange for a fixed, prepaid monthly premium (Appendix B)

healthcare insurance insurance that covers the cost of medical attention, including hospital care, physicians' and surgeons' fees, prescription medicines, and related services (Appendix B)
high-risk investment an investment made in the uncertain hope of earning a relatively large profit in a short time (21)
hostile takeover a situation in which the management and board of directors of the firm targeted for acquisition disapprove of the merger (5)
hourly wage a specific amount of money paid for each hour of work (10)
human resources management all the activities involved in acquiring, maintaining, and developing an organization's human resources (10)
human resources manager a person charged with managing the organization's human resources programs (7)
human resources planning the development of strategies to meet a firm's human resources needs (10)
hygiene factors job factors that reduce dissatisfaction when present to an acceptable degree, but do not necessarily result in high levels of motivation, according to the motivation-hygiene theory (11)

implied warranty a guarantee imposed or required by law (Appendix C)
import (or **customs**) **duty** (or **tariff**) a tax that is levied on a particular foreign product entering a country (3, Appendix C)
import quota a limit on the amount of a particular good that may be imported into a country during a given period of time (3)
importing purchasing raw materials or products in other nations and bringing them into one's own country (3)
incentive payment a payment in addition to wages, salary, or commissions (10)
income statement a summary of a firm's revenues and expenses during a specified accounting period (18)
incorporation the process of forming a corporation (5)
independent retailer a firm that operates only one retail outlet (15)
individual branding the strategy in which a firm uses a different brand for each of its products (14)
industrial union an organization of both skilled and unskilled workers in a single industry (12)
inflation a general rise in the level of prices (1)
infomercial a program-length televised commercial message resembling an entertainment or consumer affairs program (16)
informal group a group created by the members themselves to accomplish goals that may or may not be relevant to the organization (8)
informal organization the pattern of behavior and interaction that stems from personal rather than offical relationships (8)
information data that are presented in a form useful for a specific purpose (17)
information society a society in which large groups of employees generate or depend on information to perform their jobs (17)
informational role a role in which the manager either gathers or provides information (7)
initial public offering (IPO) the first time a corporation sells common stock to the general public (20, 21)
injunction a court order requiring a person or group either to perform some act or to refrain from performing some act (12)
inland marine insurance insurance that protects against loss or damage to goods shipped by rail, truck, airplane, or inland barge (Appendix B)

inspection the examination of the quality of work in process (9)
institutional advertising advertising designed to enhance a firm's image or reputation (16)
institutional investors pension funds, insurance companies, mutual funds, banks, and other organizations that trade large quantities of securities (21)
insurable risk a risk that insurance companies will assume (Appendix B)
insurance the protection against loss the purchase of an insurance policy affords (Appendix B)
insurance company (or **insurer**) a firm that agrees, for a fee, to assume financial responsibility for losses that may result from a specific risk (Appendix B)
insurance policy the contract between an insurer and the person or firm whose risk is assumed (Appendix B)
insurer (or **insurance company**) a firm that agrees, for a fee, to assume financial responsibility for losses that may result from a specific risk (Appendix B)
intangible assets assets that do not exist physically but that have a value based on the rights or privileges they confer on a firm (18)
integrated marketing communications coordination of promotional elements to maximize total informational and persuasive impact on customers (16)
intensive distribution the use of all available outlets for a product (15)
interlocking directorate an arrangement in which members of the board of directors of one firm are also directors of a competing firm (Appendix B)
internal recruiting considering present employees as applicants for available positions (10)
international business all business activities that involve exchanges across national boundaries (3)
International Monetary Fund (IMF) an international bank with more than 150 member nations that makes short-term loans to countries experiencing balance-of-payment deficits (3)
Internet a worldwide network of computers linked through telecommunications (17)
interpersonal role a role in which the manager deals with people (7)
interpersonal skill the ability to deal effectively with other people (7)
intranet a smaller version of the Internet for use only with a firm (17)
intrapreneur an employee who pushes an innovative idea, product, or process through the organization (8)
inventory control the process of managing inventories in such a way as to minimize inventory costs, including both holding costs and potential stock-out costs (9, 15)
inventory management see **inventory control**
inventory turnover a financial ratio calculated by dividing the cost of goods sold in one year by the average value of the inventory (18)
investment banking firm an organization that assists corporations in raising funds, usually by helping sell new issues of stocks, bonds, or other financial securities (19)

job analysis a systematic procedure for studying jobs to determine their various elements and requirements (10)
job description a list of the elements that make up a particular job (10)
job enlargement expanding a worker's assignments to include additional but similar tasks (11)

job enrichment a motivation technique that provides employees with more variety and responsibility in their jobs (11)
job evaluation the process of determining the relative worth of the various jobs within a firm (10)
job redesign a type of job enrichment in which work is restructured to cultivate the worker-job match (11)
job rotation the systematic shifting of employees from one job to another (8)
job security protection against the loss of employment (12)
job sharing an arrangement whereby two people share one full-time position (11)
job specialization the separation of all organizational activities into distinct tasks and the assignment of different tasks to different people (8)
job specification a list of the qualifications required to perform a particular job (10)
joint venture an agreement between two or more groups to form a business entity in order to achieve a specific goal or to operate for a specific period of time (5)
jurisdiction the right of a particular union to organize particular workers (12)
just-in-time inventory system a system designed to ensure that materials or supplies arrive at a facility just when they are needed so that storage and handling costs are minimized (9)

labeling the presentation of information on a product or its package (14)
labor (or **union-management**) **relations** the dealings between labor unions and business management, both in the bargaining process and beyond it (12)
labor union an organization or workers acting together to negotiate their wages and working conditions with employers (12)
labor-intensive technology a process in which people must do most of the work (9)
laissez-faire leader one who gives authority to employees and allows subordinates to work as they choose with a minimum of interference; communication flows horizontally among group members (7)
law a rule developed by a society to govern the conduct of, and relationship among, its members (Appendix C)
leadership the ability to influence others (7)
leading the process of influencing people to work toward a common goal (7)
lease an agreement by which the right to use real estate, equipment, or other assets is temporarily transferred from the owner to the user (20, Appendix C)
letter of credit a legal document issued by a financial institution guaranteeing to pay a seller a stated amount for a specified period of time (3, 19)
leveraged buyout (LBO) a purchase arrangement that allows a firm's managers and employees or a group of investors to purchase the company (5)
liabilities a firm's debts and obligations (18)
licensing a contractual agreement in which one firm permits another to produce and market its product and use its brand name in return for a royalty or other compensation (3)
life insurance insurance that pays a stated amount of money on the death of the insured individual (Appendix B)
limit order a request that a stock be bought or sold at a price that is equal to or better than some specified price (21)
limited liability a feature of corporate ownership that limits each owner's financial liability to the amount of money she or he has paid for the corporation's stock (5)
limited liability company a form of business ownership that provides limited liability protection and is taxed like a partnership (5)
limited partner a person who contributes capital to a business but has no management responsibility or liability for losses beyond the amount he or she invested in the partnership (3)
limited partnership a business co-owned by one or more general partners who manage the business and limited partners who invest money in it (5)
limited-line wholesaler a middleman that stocks only a few product lines but carries numerous product items within each line (15)
limited-service wholesaler a middleman that assumes responsibility for a few wholesale services only (15)
line management position a position that is part of the chain of command and that includes direct responsibility for achieving the goals of the organization (8)
line of credit a loan that is approved before the money is actually needed (19)
liquidity the ease with which an asset can be converted into cash (18, 21)
lockout a firm's refusal to allow employees to enter the workplace (12)
long-term financing money that will be used for longer than one year (20)
long-term liabilities debts that need not be repaid for at least one year (18)
lump-sum salary increase an entire pay raise taken in one lump sum (10)

maintenance shop a workplace in which an employee who joins the union must remain a union member as long as he or she is employed by the firm (12)
major equipment large tools and machines used for production purposes (14)
management the process of coordinating people and other resources to achieve the goals of the organization (7)
management by objectives (MBO) a motivation technique in which managers and subordinates collaborate in setting goals (11)
management development the process of preparing managers and other professionals to assume increased responsibility in both present and future positions (10)
management information system (MIS) a system that provides managers with the information they need to perform their jobs as effectively as possible (17)
managerial hierarchy the arrangement that provides increasing authority at higher levels of management (8)
manufacturer (or **producer**) **brand** a brand that is owned by a manufacturer (14)
manufacturer's sales branch essentially a merchant wholesaler that is owned by a manufacturer (15)
manufacturer's sales office essentially a sales agent that is owned by a manufacturer (15)
margin requirement the portion of the price of a stock that cannot be borrowed (21)
market a group of individuals or organizations, or both, that need products in a given category and have the ability, willingness, and authority to purchase such products (13)

market allocation an agreement to divide a market among potential competitors (Appendix B)
market economy an economic system in which individuals and businesses decide what to produce and buy, and the market determines prices and quantities sold (1)
market order a request that a stock be purchased or sold at the current market price (21)
market price the price at which the quantity demanded is exactly equal to the quantity supplied (1)
market segment a group of individuals or organizations within a market that share one or more common characteristics (13)
market segmentation the process of dividing a market into segments and directing a marketing mix at a particular segment or segments rather than at the total market (13)
market value the price of one share of a stock at a particular time (21)
marketing the process of planning and executing the conception, pricing, promotion, and distribution of ideas, goods, and services to create exchanges that satisfy individual and organizational objectives (13)
marketing channel (or **channel of distribution**) a sequence of marketing organizations that directs a product from the producer to the ultimate user (15)
marketing concept the business philosophy that involves the entire organization in the process of satisfying customers' needs while achieving the organization's goals (13)
marketing information system a system for managing marketing information that is gathered continually from internal and external sources (13)
marketing intermediary (or **middleman**) a marketing organization that links a producer and user within a marketing channel (15)
marketing manager a manager who is responsible for facilitating the exchange of products between the organization and its customers or clients (7)
marketing mix a combination of product, price, distribution, and promotion developed to satisfy a particular target market (13)
marketing plan a written document that specifies an organization's resources, objectives, strategy, and implementation and control efforts to be used in marketing a specific product or product group (13)
marketing research the process of systematically gathering, recording, and analyzing data concerning a particular marketing problem (13)
marketing strategy a plan that will enable an organization to make the best use of its resources and advantages to meet its objectives (13)
markup the amount a seller adds to the cost of a product to determine its basic selling price (14)
Maslow's hierarchy of needs a sequence of human needs in order of their importance (11)
master limited partnership (MLP) a business partnership that is owned and managed like a corporation but taxed like a partnership (5)
materials handling the actual physical handling of goods, in warehousing as well as during transportation (15)
materials requirements planning (MRP) a computerized system that integrates production planning and inventory control (9)
matrix structure an organizational structure that combines vertical and horizontal lines of authority usually by superimposing product departmentalization on a functionally departmentalized organization (8)
maturity date the date on which the corporation is to repay the borrowed money (20)
measure of value a single standard or "yardstick" used to assign values to, and compare the values of, products, services, and resources (19)
median the value at the exact middle of a set of data when the data are arranged in order (17)
mediation the use of a neutral third party to assist management and the union during their negotiations (12)
medium of exchange anything accepted as payment for products, services, and resources (19)
merchant middleman a middleman that actually takes title to products by buying them (15)
merchant wholesaler a middleman that purchases goods in large quantities and then sells them to other wholesalers or retailers and to institutional, farm, government, professional, or industrial users (15)
merger the purchase of one corporation by another (5)
middle manager a manager who implements the strategy and major policies developed by top management (7)
middleman (or **marketing intermediary**) a marketing organization that links a producer and user within a marketing channel (15)
minority a racial, religious, political, national, or other group regarded as different from the larger group of which it is a part, and that is often singled out for unfavorable treatment (2)
mission a statement of the basic purpose that makes an organization different from others (7)
missionary salesperson a salesperson—generally employed by a manufacturer—who visits retailers to persuade them to buy the manufacturer's products (16)
mixed economy an economy that exhibits elements of both capitalism and socialism (1)
mode the value that appears most frequently in a set of data (17)
money anything a society uses to purchase products, services, or resources (19)
monetary policies Federal Reserve's decisions that determine the size of the supply of money in the nation and the level of interest rates (1)
monopolistic competition a market situation in which there are many buyers along with a relatively large number of sellers who differentiate their products from the products of competitors (1)
monopoly a market (or industry) with only one seller (1)
morale a person's attitude about his or her job, superiors, and about the firm itself (11)
mortgage bond a corporate bond that is secured by various assets of the issuing firm (20)
motivating the process of providing reasons for people to work in the best interests of the organization (7)
motivation the individual, internal process that energizes, directs, and sustains behavior; the personal "force" that causes us to behave in a particular way (11)
motivation factors job factors that increase motivation, but whose absence does not necessarily result in dissatisfaction according to the motivation-hygiene theory (11)
motivation-hygiene theory the idea that satisfaction and dissatisfaction are distinct and separate dimensions (11)
multilateral development bank (MDB) an internationally supported bank that provides loans to developing countries to help them grow (3)
multinational enterprise a firm that operates on a worldwide scale, without ties to any specific nation or region (3)

multiple-unit pricing the strategy of setting a single price for two or more units (14)
municipal bond a debt security issued by a state or local government (21)
mutual fund a professionally managed investment vehicle that combines and invests the funds of many individual investors (21)
mutual insurance company an insurance company that is collectively owned by its policyholders and is thus a cooperative (Appendix B)
mutual savings bank financial institutions that are owned by their depositors and offer many of the same services offered by savings and loan associations (19)

NASDAQ a computerized electronic exchange through which most over-the-counter securities are traded (21)
National Alliance of Business (NAB) a joint business-government program to train the hard-core unemployed (2)
National Association of Securities Dealers (NASD) the organization responsible for the self-regulation of the over-the-counter securities market (21)
national bank a commercial bank chartered by the U.S. Comptroller of the Currency (19)
national debt the total of all federal deficits (1)
National Labor Relations Board (NLRB) the federal agency that enforces the provisions of the Wagner Act (12)
natural monopoly an industry requiring huge investments in capital and within which duplication of facilities would be wasteful and thus not in the public interest (1)
need a personal requirement (11)
negligence a failure to exercise reasonable care, resulting in injury to another (Appendix C)
negotiable instrument a written document that (1) is a promise to pay a stated sum of money and (2) can be transferred from one person or firm to another (Appendix C)
negotiated pricing occurs when the final price is established through bargaining between the seller and the customer (14)
neighborhood shopping center a planned shopping center consisting of several small convenience and specialty stores (15)
net asset value (NAV) current market value of a mutual fund's portfolio minus the mutual fund's liabilities, divided by the number of outstanding shares (21)
net income the profit earned (or the loss suffered) by a firm during an accounting period after all expenses have been deducted from revenues (18)
net sales the actual dollar amounts received by a firm for the goods and services it has sold, after adjustment for returns, allowances, and discounts (18)
network structure an organization in which administration is the primary function and most other functions are contracted out to other firms (8)
news release a typed page of about 300 words provided by an organization to the media as a form of publicity (16)
no-fault auto insurance a method of paying for losses suffered in an automobile accident; enacted by state law, requires that those suffering injury or loss be reimbursed by their own insurance companies, without regard to who was at fault in the accident (Appendix B)
nonprice competition competition that is based on factors other than price (14)
nonstore retailing a type of retailing whereby consumers purchase products without visiting a store (15)
nontariff barrier a nontax measure imposed by a government to favor domestic over foreign suppliers (3)
not-for-profit corporation a corporation that is organized to provide a social, educational, religious, or other service, rather than to earn a profit (3)
notes payable obligations that have been secured with promissory notes (18)
NOW account an interest-bearing checking account; NOW stands for Negotiable Order of Withdrawal (19)

objective a specific statement detailing what the organization intends to accomplish over a shorter period of time (7)
ocean marine insurance insurance that protects the policyholder against loss or damage to a ship or its cargo on the high seas (Appendix B)
odd lot fewer than 100 shares of a particular stock (21)
odd-number pricing the strategy of setting prices using odd numbers that are slightly below whole dollar amounts (14)
off-price retailer a store that buys manufacturers' seconds, overruns, returns, and off-season merchandise for resale to consumers at deep discounts (15)
oligopoly a market situation (or industry) in which there are few sellers (1)
online communities groups of individuals or firms that want to exchange information, products, or services over the Internet (4)
online retailing presents products on customers' computer screens, customers place orders through their terminals or by telephone (15)
open corporation a corporation whose stock is bought and sold on security exchanges and can be purchased by any individual (5)
open-market operations the buying and selling of U.S. government securities by the Federal Reserve System for the purpose of controlling the supply of money (19)
operating expenses all business costs other than the cost of goods sold (18)
operational plan a type of plan designed to implement tactical plans (7)
operations management all activities that managers engage in to produce goods and services (9)
operations manager a manager who manages the systems that convert resources into goods and services (7)
order getter a salesperson who is responsible for selling the firm's products to new customers and increasing sales to present customers (16)
order processing those activities that are involved in receiving and filling customers' purchase orders (15)
order taker a salesperson who handles repeat sales in ways that maintain positive relationships with customers (16)
organization a group of two or more people working together to achieve a common set of goals (8)
organization chart a diagram that represents the positions and relationships within an organization (8)
organizational height the number of layers, or levels, of management in a firm (8)
organizing the grouping of resources and activities to accomplish some end result in an efficient and effective manner (7)
orientation the process of acquainting new employees with an organization (10)
outdoor advertising short promotional messages on billboards, posters, and signs (16)

over-the-counter (OTC) market a network of dealers who buy and sell the stocks of corporations that are not listed on securities exchange (21)

overtime time worked in excess of forty hours in one week; under some union contracts, it can be time worked in excess of eight hours in a single day (12)

owners' equity the difference between a firm's assets and its liabilities—what would be left for the owners if assets were used to pay off its liabilities (18)

packaging all the activities involved in developing and providing a container for a product (14)

par value an assigned (and often arbitrary) dollar value printed on the face of a stock certificate (20)

part-time work permanent employment in which individuals work less than a standard workweek (11)

partnership a voluntary association of two or more persons to act as co-owners of a business for profit (5)

patent the exclusive right to make, use, or sell, or license others to make or sell a newly invented product or process (Appendix C)

penetration pricing the strategy of setting a low price for a new product (14)

performance the fulfillment of all obligations by all parties to the contract (Appendix C)

performance appraisal the evaluation of employees' current and potential levels of performance to allow managers to make objective human resource decisions (10)

periodic discounting the temporary reduction of prices on a patterned or systematic basis (14)

personal income the income an individual receives from all sources less the Social Security taxes that the individual must pay (13)

personal investment the use of your personal funds to earn a financial return (21)

personal property all property other than real property (Appendix C)

personal selling personal communication aimed at informing customers and persuading them to buy a firm's products (16)

PERT (Program Evaluation and Review Technique) a scheduling technique that identifies the major activities necessary to complete a project and sequences them based on the time required to perform each one (9)

physical distribution all those activities concerned with the efficient movement of products from the producer to the ultimate user (15)

physiological needs the things we require for survival (11)

picketing marching back and forth in front of the place of employment with signs informing the public that a strike is in progress (12)

piece-rate system a compensation system under which employees are paid a certain amount for each unit of output they produce (11)

place utility utility that is created by making a product available at a location where customers wish to purchase it (13)

plan an outline of the actions by which an organization intends to accomplish its goals and objectives (7)

planning establishing organizational goals and deciding how to accomplish them (7)

planning horizon the period during which a plan will be in effect (9)

plant layout the arrangement of machinery, equipment, and personnel within a production facility (9)

point-of-purchase display promotional material that is placed within a retail store (16)

pollution the contamination of water, air, or land through the actions of people in an industrialized society (2)

positioning the development of a product image in buyers' minds relative to the images they have of competing products (16)

possession utility utility that is created by transferring title (or ownership) of a product to the buyer (13)

posting the process of transferring journal entries to the general ledger (18)

power of attorney a legal document that serves as evidence that an agent has been appointed to act on behalf of a principal (Appendix C)

preferred provider organizations (PPOs) offer the services of doctors and hospitals at discount rates or give breaks in copayments and deductibles (Appendix B)

preferred stock stock owned by individuals or firms who usually do not have voting rights, but whose claims on dividends are paid before those of common stock owners (5, 20)

premium (promotion) a gift that a producer offers the customer in return for buying its product (16)

premium the fee charged by an insurance company (21)

premium pricing occurs when the highest-quality product or the most versatile version of similar products in a product line is given the highest price (14)

prepaid expenses assets that have been paid for in advance but have not yet been used (18)

press conference a meeting at which invited media personnel hear important news announcements and receive supplementary textual materials and photographs (16)

price the amount of money a seller is willing to accept in exchange for a product, at a given time and under given circumstances (14)

price competition an emphasis on setting a price equal to or lower than competitors' prices to gain sales or market share (14)

price discrimination the practice in which producers and wholesalers charge larger firms a lower price for goods than they charge smaller firms (Appendix C)

price fixing an agreement between two businesses about the prices to be charged for goods (Appendix C)

price leaders when a firm prices a few products below the usual markup, near cost, or below cost in hopes that sales of regularly priced products will more than offset the reduced revenues from the lower-priced products (14)

price lining the strategy of selling goods only at certain predetermined prices that reflect definite price breaks (14)

price skimming the strategy of charging the highest-possible price for a product during the introduction stage of its life cycle (14)

primary market a market in which an investor purchases financial securities (via an investment bank) directly from the issuer of those securities (21)

primary-demand advertising advertising whose purpose is to increase the demand for all brands of a product within a specific industry (16)

prime interest rate the lowest rate charged by a bank for a short-term loan (20)

principle of indemnity in the event of a loss, an insured firm or individual cannot collect from the insurer an amount greater than the actual dollar amount of the loss (Appendix B)

private accountant an accountant employed by a specific organization (18)

private (or **store**) **brand** a brand that is owned by an individual wholesaler or retailer (14)

private law the body of law that governs the relationships between two or more individuals or businesses (Appendix C)

problem the discrepancy between an actual condition and a desired condition (7)

process material a material that is used directly in the production of another product but is not readily identifiable in the finished product (14)

producer (or **manufacturer**) **brand** a brand that is owned by a manufacturer (14)

product everything one receives in an exchange, including all tangible and intangible attributes and expected benefits; it may be a good, service, or idea (14)

product deletion the elimination of one or more products from a product line (14)

product design the process of creating a set of specifications from which a product can be produced (9)

product differentiation the process of developing and promoting differences between one's product and all similar products (1, 14)

product liability insurance insurance that protects the policyholder from financial losses due to injuries suffered by others as a result of using the policyholder's products (Appendix B)

product life cycle a series of stages in which a product's sales revenue and profit increase, reach a peak, and then decline (14)

product line a group of similar products that differ only in relatively minor characteristics (14)

product mix all the products that a firm offers for sale (14)

product modification the process of changing one or more of a product's characteristics (14)

production the process of converting resources into goods, services, or ideas (9)

productivity the average level of output per worker per hour (1, 9)

profit what remains after all business expenses have been deducted from sales revenue (1)

profit sharing the distribution of a percentage of the firm's profit among its employees (10)

program trading a computer-driven program to buy or sell a group of stocks (21)

progressive tax a tax that requires the payment of an increasing proportion of income as the individual's income increases (Appendix C)

promissory note a written pledge by a borrower to pay a certain sum of money to a creditor at a specified future date (19)

promotion communication about an organization and its product that is intended to inform, persuade, or remind target market members (16)

promotion mix the particular combination of promotion methods that a firm uses to reach a target market (16)

promotional campaign a plan for combining and using the four promotional methods—advertising, personal selling, sales promotion, and publicity—in a particular promotion mix to achieve one or more marketing goals (16)

property anything that can be owned (Appendix C)

proportional tax a tax whose percentage rate remains constant as the tax base increases (Appendix C)

prospectus a detailed written description of a new security, the issuing corporation, and the corporation's top management (21)

proxy a legal form that lists issues to be decided at a stockholders' meeting; enables stockholders to transfer their voting rights to some other individual or individuals (5)

proxy fight a technique used to gather enough stockholder votes to control the targeted company (5)

public accountant an accountant who provides services to clients on a fee basis (18)

public law the body of law that deals with the relationships between individuals or businesses and society (Appendix C)

public liability insurance insurance that protects the policyholder from financial losses due to injuries suffered by others as a result of negligence on the part of a business owner or employee (Appendix B)

public relations communication activities used to create and maintain favorable relations between an organization and various public groups, both internal and external (16)

publicity communication in news-story form about an organization, its products, or both (16)

purchasing all the activities involved in obtaining required materials, supplies, and parts from other firms (9)

pure competition the market situation in which there are many buyers and sellers of a product, and no single buyer or seller is powerful enough to affect the price of that product (1)

pure risk a risk that involves only the possibility of loss, with no potential for gain (Appendix B)

qualitative research a process that involves the descriptive or subjective reporting of information discovered by a researcher (17)

quality circle a group of employees who meet on company time to solve problems of product quality (9)

quality control the process of ensuring that goods and services are produced in accordance with design specifications (9)

quantitative research a process that involves the collection of numerical data for analysis through a survey, experiment, or content analysis (17)

quasi-government corporation a business owned partly by the government and partly by private citizens or firms (5)

random discounting temporarily reducing prices on an unsystematic basis (14)

range the difference between the highest value and the lowest value in a set of data (17)

ratification approval of a labor contract by a vote of the union membership (12)

raw material a basic material that actually becomes part of a physical product; usually comes from mines, forests, oceans, or recycled solid wastes (14)

real property land and anything that is permanently attached to it (Appendix C)

rebate a return of part of the purchase price of a product (16)

recession two consecutive three-month periods of decline in a country's gross domestic product (1)

recruiting the process of attracting qualified job applicants (10)

reference pricing pricing a product at a moderate level and positioning it next to a more expensive model or brand in the hope that the customer will use the higher price as a reference price (i.e., a comparison price) (14)

regional shopping center a planned shopping center containing large department stores, numerous specialty stores, restaurants, movie theaters, and sometimes even hotels (15)

registered bond a bond that is registered in the owner's name by the issuing company (20)

regressive tax a tax that takes a greater percentage of a lower income than of a higher income (Appendix C)

reinforcement theory a theory of motivation based on the premise that behavior that is rewarded is likely to be repeated, whereas behavior that is punished is less likely to recur (11)

relationship marketing developing mutually beneficial, long-term partnerships with customers to enhance customer satisfaction and to stimulate long-term customer loyalty (13)

replacement chart a list of key personnel and their possible replacements within the firm (10)

research and development (R&D) a set of activities intended to identify new ideas that have the potential to result in new goods and services (9)

reserve requirement the percentage of its deposits a bank *must* retain, either in its own vault or on deposit with its Federal Reserve District Bank (19)

responsibility the duty to do a job or perform a task (8)

retailer a middleman that buys from producers or other middlemen and sells to consumers (15)

retained earnings the portion of a business's profits not distributed to stockholders (18, 20)

return on owner's equity a financial ratio calculated by dividing net income after taxes by owners' equity (18)

return on sales a financial ratio that is calculated by dividing net income after taxes by net sales (18)

revenue bond a bond repaid from the income generated by the government-sponsored project it is designed to finance (21)

revenue stream a source of revenue flowing into a firm (4)

revenues the dollar amounts earned by a firm (18)

revolving credit agreement a guaranteed line of credit (19, 20)

risk the possibility that a loss or injury will occur (Appendix B)

risk management the process of evaluating the risks faced by a firm or an individual and then minimizing the costs involved with those risks (Appendix B)

robotics the use of programmable machines to perform a variety of tasks by manipulating materials and tools (9)

round lot a unit of 100 shares of a particular stock (21)

safety needs the things we require for physical and emotional security (11)

salary a specific amount of money paid for an employee's work during a set calendar period, regardless of the actual number of hours worked (10)

sales agreement a type of contract by which ownership is transferred from a seller to a buyer (Appendix C)

sales forecast an estimate of the amount of a product that an organization expects to sell during a certain period of time, based on a specified level of marketing effort (13)

sales promotion the use of activities or materials as direct inducements to customers or salespersons (16)

sales support personnel employees who aid in selling but are more involved in locating prospects, educating customers, building goodwill for the firm, and providing follow-up service (16)

sample a free package or container of a product (16)

savings and loan association (S&L) a financial institution that offers checking and savings accounts and certificates of deposit and provides home-mortgage loans and other consumer loans (19)

scheduling the process of ensuring that materials and other resources are at the right place at the right time (9)

scientific management the application of scientific principles to management of work and workers (11)

S-corporation a corporation that is taxed as though it were a partnership (5)

secondary market a market for existing financial securities that are currently traded between investors (21)

secondary-market pricing setting one price for the primary target market and a different price for another market (14)

Securities and Exchange Commission (SEC) the agency that enforces federal securities regulations (21)

securities exchange a marketplace where member brokers meet to buy and sell securities (21)

security average (or **security index**) an average of the current market prices of selected securities (21)

selection the process of gathering information about applicants for a position and then using that information to choose the most appropriate applicant (10)

selective demand (or **brand**) **advertising** advertising that is used to sell a particular brand of product (16)

selective distribution the use of only a portion of the available outlets for a product in each geographic area (15)

self-actualization needs the needs to grow and develop and to become all that we are capable of being (11)

self-insurance the process of establishing a monetary fund that can be used to cover the cost of a loss (Appendix B)

self-managed work teams groups of employees with the authority and skills to manage themselves (11)

selling short the process of selling stock that an investor does not actually own but has borrowed from a stockbroker and will repay at a later date (21)

seniority the length of time an employee has worked for the organization (12)

serial bonds bonds of a single issue that mature on different dates (20)

Service Corps of Retired Executives (SCORE) a group of retired businesspeople who volunteer their services to small businesses through the SBA (6)

service economy an economy in which more effort is devoted to the production of services than to the production of goods (9)

shop steward an employee elected by union members to serve as their representative (12)

shopping product an item for which buyers are willing to expend considerable effort on planning and making the purchase (14)

short-term financing money that will be used for one year or less and then repaid (20)

sinking fund a sum of money to which deposits are made each year for the purpose of redeeming a bond issue (20)

skills inventory a computerized data bank containing information on the skills and experience of all present employees (10)

slowdown a technique whereby workers report to their jobs but work at a slower pace than normal (12)

small business one that is independently owned and operated for profit and is not dominant in its field (6)

Small Business Administration (SBA) a governmental agency that assists, counsels, and protects the interests of small businesses in the United States (6)

Small Business Development Center (SBDC) a university-based group that provides individual counseling and practical training to owners of small businesses (6)

Small Business Institute (SBI) a group of senior and graduate students in business administration who provide management counseling to small businesses (6)

Small Business Investment Company (SBIC) a privately owned firm that provides venture capital to small enterprises that meet its investment standards (6)

social audit a comprehensive report of what an organization has done, and is doing, with regard to social issues that affect it (2)

social needs our requirements for love and affection and a sense of belonging (11)

social responsibility the recognition that business activities have an impact on society and the consideration of that impact in business decision making (2)

socioeconomic model of social responsibility the concept that business should emphasize not only profits but also the impact of its decisions on society (2)

sole proprietorship a business that is owned (and usually operated) by one person (5)

span of management (or **span of control**) the number of workers who report directly to one manager (8)

special-event pricing involves advertised sales or price-cutting linked to a holiday, season, or event (14)

specialization the separation of a manufacturing process into distinct tasks and the assignment of different tasks to different individuals (1)

specialty product an item that possesses one or more unique characteristics for which a significant group of buyers is willing to expend considerable purchasing effort (14)

specialty-line wholesaler a middleman that carries a select group of products within a single line (15)

specific performance the legal requirement that the parties to a contract fulfill their obligations according to the contract (Appendix C)

speculative risk a risk that accompanies the possibility of earning a profit (Appendix B)

spreadsheet program a software package that allows the user to organize numerical data into a grid of rows and columns (17)

staff management position a position created to provide support, advice, and expertise within an organization (8)

standard of living a loose, subjective measure of how well-off an individual or a society is, mainly in terms of want-satisfaction through goods and services (1)

standing committee a relatively permanent committee charged with performing some recurring task (8)

state bank a commercial bank chartered by the banking authorities in the state in which it operates (19)

statement of cash flows a statement that illustrates how the operating, investing, and financing activities of a company affect cash during an accounting period (18)

statement of financial position (or **balance sheet**) a summary of the dollar amounts of a firm's assets, liabilities, and owners' equity accounts at the end of an accounting period (18)

statistic a measure that summarizes a particular characteristic of an entire group of numbers (17)

statistical process control (SPC) an information-gathering system that plots data on control charts and graphs to identify and pinpoint problems in product quality (9)

statistical quality control (SQC) a set of specific statistical techniques used to sample both work in progress and finished products to find problems in the production process and improve product quality (9)

statute a law that is passed by the U.S. Congress, a state legislature, or a local government (Appendix C)

statutory law all the laws that have been enacted by legislative bodies (Appendix C)

stock the shares of ownership of a corporation (5)

stock broker an individual—sometimes called an *account executive* or *registered representative*—who buys and sells securities for clients (21)

stock dividend a dividend in the form of additional stock (21)

stock insurance company an insurance company owned by stockholders and operated to earn a profit (Appendix B)

stock split the division of each outstanding share of a corporation's stock into a greater number of shares (21)

stockholder a person who owns a corporation's stock (5)

store (or **private**) **brand** a brand that is owned by an individual wholesaler or retailer (14)

store of value a means of retaining and accumulating wealth (19)

strategic alliance partnership formed to create competitive advantage on a worldwide basis (3)

strategic planning the process of establishing an organizations' major goals and objectives and allocating the resources to achieve them (7)

strategy an organization's broadest set of plans, developed as a guide for major policy setting and decision making (7)

strike a temporary work stoppage by employees, calculated to add force to their demands (12)

strikebreaker a nonunion employee who performs the job of a striking union member (12)

supermarket a large, self-service store that sells primarily food and household products (15)

superstore a large retail store that carries not only food and nonfood products ordinarily found in supermarkets but also additional product lines (15)

supply (product) an item that facilitates production and operations but does not become part of the finished product (14)

supply (economics) the quantity of a product that producers are willing to sell at each of various prices (1, 14)

supply chain management long term partnership among channel members working together to create a distribution system that reduces inefficiencies, costs, and redundancies while creating a competitive advantage and satisfying customers (15)

syndicate a temporary association of individuals or firms, organized to perform a specific task that requires a large amount of capital (5)

synthetic process a process in operations management in which raw materials are combined to create a finished product (9)

tactical plan a smaller-scale plan developed to implement a strategy (7)

target market a group of individuals or organizations, or both, for which a firm develops and maintains a marketing mix suitable for the specific needs and preferences of that group (13)

tariff (or **import duty** or **customs duty**) a tax that is levied on a particular foreign product entering a country (3, Appendix C)

task force a committee established to investigate a major problem or pending decision (8)

technical salesperson a salesperson who assists the company's current customers in technical matters (16)

technical skill a specific skill needed to accomplish a specialized activity (7)

telecommunications the merger of computer and telephone technologies (17)

telecommuting working at home all of the time or for a portion of the workweek (11)

telemarketing the performance of marketing-related activities by telephone (15)

television home shopping selling in which products are displayed to television viewers, who can then order them by calling a toll-free number and paying by credit card (15)

tender offer an offer to purchase the stock of a firm targeted for acquisition at a price just high enough to tempt stockholders to sell their shares (5)

term life insurance life insurance that provides protection to beneficiaries for a stated period of time (Appendix B)

term-loan agreement a promissory note that requires a borrower to repay a loan in monthly, quarterly, semiannual, or annual installments (20)

Theory X a concept of employee motivation generally consistent with Taylor's scientific management; assumes that employees dislike work and will function only in a highly controlled work environment (11)

Theory Y a concept of employee motivation generally consistent with the ideas of the human relations movement; assumes that employees accept responsibility and work toward organizational goals if by so doing they also achieve personal rewards (11)

Theory Z the belief that some middle ground between Ouchi's Type A and Type J practices is best for American business (11)

time deposit an amount on deposit in an interest-bearing savings account (19)

time utility utility that is created by making a product available when customers wish to purchase it (13)

top manager an upper-level executive who guides and controls the overall fortunes of the organization (7)

tort a violation of a private law (Appendix C)

total cost the sum of the fixed costs and the variable costs attributed to a product (14)

total quality management (TQM) the coordination of efforts directed at improving customer satisfaction, increasing employee participation, strengthening supplier partnerships, and facilitating an organizational atmosphere of continuous quality improvement (7)

total revenue the total amount received from sales of a product (14)

trade credit a type of short-term financing extended by a seller who does not require immediate payment after delivery of merchandise (20)

trade deficit a negative balance of trade (3)

trade name the complete and legal name of an organization (14)

trade sales promotion method a sales promotion method designed to encourage wholesalers and retailers to stock and actively promote a manufacturer's product (16)

trade salesperson a salesperson—generally employed by a food producer or processor—who assists customers in promoting products, especially in retail stores (16)

trade show an industrywide exhibit at which many sellers display their products (16)

trademark a brand that is registered with the U.S. Patent and Trademark Office and is thus legally protected from use by anyone except its owner (14)

trading company provides a link between buyers and sellers in different countries (3)

traditional specialty store a store that carries a narrow product mix with deep product lines (15)

transfer pricing when one unit in an organization sells a product to another unit (14)

transportation the shipment of products to customers (15)

trial balance a summary of the balances of all general ledger accounts at the end of the accounting period (18)

trust when one firm gains control of an entire industry and can set prices and maintain trade to suit its own interests (Appendix C)

trustee an individual or an independent firm that acts as the bond owners' representative (20)

tying agreement a contract that forces an intermediary to purchase unwanted products along with the products it actually wants to buy (Appendix C)

undifferentiated approach an approach directing a single marketing mix at the entire market for a particular product (13)

Uniform Commercial Code (UCC) a set of laws designed to eliminate differences among state regulations affecting business and to simplify interestate commerce (Appendix C)

uninsurable risk a risk that insurance firms will not assume (Appendix B)

union security protection of the union's position as the employees' bargaining agent (12)

union shop a workplace in which new employees must join the union after a specified probationary period (12)

union-management (or **labor**) **relations** the dealings between labor unions and business management, both in the bargaining process and beyond it (12)

universal life insurance life insurance that combines insurance protection with an investment plan that offers a potentially greater return than that guaranteed by a whole life insurance policy (Appendix B)

unlimited liability a legal concept that holds a business owner personally responsible for all the debts of the business (5)

unsecured financing financing that is not backed by collateral (20)

usury the practice of charging interest in excess of the maximum legal rate (Appendix C)

utility the ability of a good or service to satisfy a human need (9, 13)

variable cost a cost that depends on the number of units produced (14)

venture capital money that is invested in small (and sometimes struggling) firms that have the potential to become very successful (6)

vertical channel integration the combining of two or more stages of a distribution channel under a single firm's management (15)

vertical marketing system (VMS) a centrally managed distribution channel resulting from vertical channel integration (15)

voluntary agreement a contract requirement consisting of an offer by one party to enter into a contract with a second party and acceptance by the second party of all the terms and conditions of the offer (Appendix C)

voluntary bankruptcy a bankruptcy procedure initiated by an individual or business that can no longer meet its financial obligations (Appendix C)

wage survey a collection of data on prevailing wage rates within an industry or a geographic area (10)

warehouse club a large-scale, members-only establishment that combines features of cash-and-carry wholesaling with discount retailing (15)

warehouse showroom a retail facility in a large, low-cost building with large on-premises inventories and minimal service (15)

warehousing the set of activities that are involved in receiving and storing goods and preparing them for reshipment (15)

wheel of retailing a hypothesis that suggests that new retail operations usually begin at the bottom—in price, profits, and prestige—and gradually evolve up the cost/price scale, competing with newer businesses that are evolving in the same way (15)
whistle blowing informing the press or government officials about unethical practices within one's organization (2)
whole life insurance life insurance that provides both protection and savings (Appendix B)
wholesaler a middleman that sells products to other firms (15)
wildcat strike a strike not approved by the strikers' union (12)
word processing program software that allows the user to prepare and edit written documents and to store them in the computer memory or on a disk (17)
workers' compensation insurance insurance that covers medical expenses and provides salary continuation for employees who are injured while they are at work (Appendix B)
workplace diversity see **cultural diversity**
World Trade Organization (WTO) an organization established by GATT to enforce the provisions of the Uruguay Round and to resolve any disputes arising therefrom (3)
world wide web (the web) the Internet's multimedia environment of audio, visual, and text data (4)

zero-based budgeting a budgeting approach in which every expense in every budget must be justified (20)

Notes

CHAPTER 1

1. Based on information from "FORTUNE 5 Hundred Largest U.S. Corporations," *Fortune*, April 17, 2000, pp. F-1+; Geoffrey Colvin, "American's Most Admired Companies," *Fortune*, February 21, 2000, pp. 108+; John A. Byrne, "The Best & Worst Boards," *Business Week*, January 24, 2000, pp. 142+; Jennifer Reingold and Marcia Stepanek, with Diane Brady, "Why the Productivity Revolution Will Spread," *Business Week*, February 14, 2000, pp. 112+; Aaron Bernstein, "Welch's March to the South," *Business Week*, December 6, 1999, p. 74; and General Electric, http://www.ge.com, (April 11, 2000).
2. Information taken from The Dudley Products, Inc. web site, www.dudleyq.com on April 29, 2000.
3. Dave Ellis, *Becoming a Master Student*, 8th ed. (Boston: Houghton Mifflin, 1997), p. 20.
4. Alan Goldstein, "Most Dot.Coms Doomed to Fail, Cuban Tells Entrepreneurs," *The Dallas Morning News*, April 7, 2000, p. 1D.
5. Julie Landry, "Ford's Internet Efforts Encounter Roadblocks," http://www.redherring.com/insider/1999/1214/news-ford.html (December 14, 1999).
6. David Akin, "Amazon.com Plummets on Talk of Cash Crunch," *Financial Post*, June 24, 2000, pp. C1, C2.
7. Board of Governors of the Federal Reserve System, *Federal Reserve Bulletin*, April, 2000, p. A48.
8. "Microsoft Rushes to Judgment," http://www.redherring.com/insider/2000/0327/techmicrosoft032700.html (March 27, 2000).
9. Based on information from the Motorola web site (www.motorola.com) on May 7, 2000; Motorola Corporation, 1999 Annual Report; Rick Tetzeh, "And Now for Motorola's Next Trick," *Fortune*, April 28, 1997, pp. 122–123+; and Peter Elstrom, "Does This Galvin Have the Right Stuff?" *Business Week*, March 17, 1997, pp. 102–105.

CHAPTER 2

1. Based on information from Susan J. Wells, "Turn Employees Into Saints?" HRMagazine, December 1999, pp. 49+; Texas Instruments, "Ethics at TI," http://www.ti.com/ (May 17, 2000).
2. Lynna Goch, "Lawyers, Guns and Money," *Best Reviews*, January 2000, p. 55.
3. "State Court Cuts Punitive Award in BMW Car Case," *Wall Street Journal*, May 12, 1997, p. B5.
4. Betsy Stevens, "Persuasion, Probity and Paltering: The Prudential Crisis," *The Journal of Business Communication*, October 1999, p. 319.
5. James Underwood, "Should You Watch Them on the Web," *CIO*, http://www.cio.com/archive/051500_face.html (May 15, 2000).
6. "Community," www.unioncarbide.com/ (May 12, 2000).
7. AT&T, 1999 Annual Report, p. 57: "AT&T Foundation," http://www.att.com/foundation, May 14, 2000.
8. The Dow Chemical Company, 1999 Annual Report, p. 16.
9. "United States of America," www.arthurandersen.com (May 12, 2000).
10. "Feeding the Children," www.conagra.com (May 13, 2000).
11. "The Shell Oil Foundation," www.shelloil.com/community (May 12, 2000).
12. "GE in the Community," http://www.ge.com/community (May 12, 2000).
13. Ilan Greenberg, "The PC Crowd," *Red Herring*, http://www.redherring.com/mag/issue51/rd.html (May 18, 2000).
14. Paul Kapustka, "Big Fish: Clinton pushes to close digital divide," *Red Herring*, http://www.redherring.com/companies/2000/0419/com-bigfish041900.html (April 19, 2000).
15. U.S. House Committee on Government Operations, "Water Pollution: Stronger Efforts Needed by EPA to Control Toxic Water Pollution," in *Report to the Chairman, Environment, Energy, and Natural Resources Subcommittee* (Washington, D.C.: General Accounting Office, July 1999), p. 8.
16. *Month in Review: February 1999*, "Aviation and the Environment: Aviation's Effects on Global Atmosphere Are Potentially Significant and Expected to Grow," (Washington, D.C.: General Accounting Office, February 18, 2000).
17. Seth Godin, ed., 1997 *Information Please Business Almanac* (Boston: Houghton Mifflin, 1997), p. 489.
18. Jeffrey L. Seglin, "Should Your Eco-Ethics Follow You Online?" *Business 2.0*, http://www.business2.com/content/insights/getalife/2000/06/13/12866?page=1 (June 2000).
19. *Month in Review: February 2000*, "Superfund: Analysis of Costs at Five Superfund Sites," GAO/RCED-00-22, (Washington, D.C.: General Accounting Office, February 2000), pp. 13–14.
20. Jeffrey L. Seglin, "Should Your Eco-Ethics Follow You Online?" *Business2.0*, http://www.business2.com/content/insights/getalife/2000/06/13/12866?page=1 (June 2000).
21. Based on information from Patti Bond, "Lowe's to Quit Selling Products Made with Wood from Endangered Forests," *Atlanta Journal and Constitution*, August 7, 2000; "The Home Depot 'Saves the Trees' with Reusable Wood Pallets," *Chain Store Age Executive*, August 2000, p. 101; Cora Daniels, "To Hire a Lumber Expert, Click Here," *Fortune*, April 3, 2000, pp. 267+; Patti Bond, "Oregon Lawsuit Accuses Home Depot of Age Bias," *Atlanta Journal and Constitution*, November 7, 2000; "Michigan Employees File Discrimination Suit Against Home Depot," *Do-It-Yourself Retailing*, February 2000, p. 33; Home Depot, www.homedepot.com (November 3, 1997); "Home Depot to Open 10 Stores in Virginia in 1998," http://www.prnewswire.com (November 3, 1997); Kirstin Downey Grimsley, "Home Depot Settles Gender Bias Lawsuit," *Washington Post*, September 20, 1997, p. D1; "Kmart Completes Builders Square Sale," September 26, 1997, http://www.foxnews.co/business (November 3, 1997) and Susan Jackson and Tim Smart, "Mom and Pop Fight Back," *Business Week*, April 14, 1997, p. 46.

CHAPTER 3

1. Based on information from "JLG Selected as a Regional Finalist for Exporter of the Year Award," JLG news release, March 1, 2000, http://www.jlg.com/products/showcase/EXPORT_AWARD.pdf (May 22, 2000); Mike Brezonick, "How Rental Has Changed Lift Equipment," *Diesel Progress North American Edition*, January 2000, p. 14; "Fuel Cell Boom Lift," *Design News*, December 20, 1999, p. 29; Philip Siekman, "The Secret of U.S. Exports: Great Products," *Fortune*, January 10, 2000, pp. 154B+.
2. The White House, Office of the Press Secretary. Press Release, April 19, 2000.

3. Clay Shirky, "Go Global or Bust," *Business2.0*, http://www.business2.com/content/magazine/breakthrough/2000/03/01/11018 (March 2000).
4. U.S. Department of Commerce, International Trade Administration, http://www.ita.doc.gov/td/industry/ostea (May 16, 2000).
5. Matthew R. Sanders and Bruce D. Temkin, "Global E-Commerce Approaches Hypergrowth," *The Forrester Brief*, http://www.forrester.com/ (April 18, 2000).
6. "U.S. Pencil Makers Point to Thai, Chinese Imports," *Wall Street Journal*, January 24, 1993, p. A2.
7. Nancy E. Kelly, "Plate Duties High: U.S. Hits Imports from China, Russia," *American Metal Market*, June 5, 1997.
8. William M. Pride and O.C. Ferrell, *Marketing*, 2000e (Boston: Houghton Mifflin, 2000), p. 111.
9. Mohanbir Sawhney and Sumant Mandal, "Go Global," *Business 2.0*, http://www.business2.com/content/magazine/indepth/2000/05/01/11057 (May 2000).
10. David Gould, "The Benefits of GATT for the U.S. and World Economies," *Southwest Economy*, (Federal Reserve Bank of Dallas, May 1994), p. 2.
11. "American Free Trade Policy: Rhetoric or Reality?" *Imprimis*, August 1989, p. 2.
12. Mohanbir Sawhney and Sumant Mandal, "Go Global," *Business 2.0*, http://www.business2.com/content/magazine/indepth/2000/05/01/11057 (May 2000).
13. All trade and growth statistics from the "World Economic Outlook," The International Monetary Fund, April 2000.
14. Renato Ruggiero, "The High Stakes of World Trade," *Wall Street Journal*, April 28, 1997, p. A18.
15. Pride and Ferrell, *Marketing*, p. 116.
16. Ibid., p. 123.
17. Archer Daniels Midland Company, 1997 Annual Report, p. 11.
18. Kim Cross, "The Ultimate Enablers: Business Partners," *Business 2.0*, http://www.business2.com/content/magazine/indepth/2000/02/01/10441 (February 2000).
19. Colgate-Palmolive Company, 1991 Third Quarter Report, pp. 3–4.
20. Peter G. Peterson, "Japan's 'Invasion': A Matter of 'Fairness,' " *Wall Street Journal*, November 3, 1989, p. A12.
21. Pride and Ferrell, *Marketing*, p. 124.
22. *Ibid.*, p. 122.
23. Quoted in Carl A. Gerstacker, *A Look at Business in 1990* (Washington, D.C.: Government Printing Office, November 1990), pp. 274–275.
24. Based on information from http://www.datldoit.com (January 15, 2001); Susanna P. Barton, "Chip Selling Tough, and That's No Bull," *Jacksonville Business Journal*, September 27, 1996, p. 1; "Florida Company Cashing In on Hot Pepper Craze," *Chattanooga Free Press*, June 18, 1995; Jan Norris, "The Pepper Cult," *Palm Beach Post*, July 28, 1994; Steven Wolcott, "Hotter Is Better at Dat'l Do-It in St. Augustine," *Jacksonville Business Journal*, January 21, 1994, p. 1–1.

CHAPTER 4

1. "America Online and Time Warner Announce New Content and Promotional Agreements," http://media.web.aol.com/media/search.cfm (Feb. 16, 2000); "AOL and Time Warner Will Merge to Create World's First Internet-Age Media and Communications Company," http://media.web.aol.com/media/search.cfm (Jan. 10, 2000).
2. For more information about e-business definitions, terminology, and strategies, visit IBM's web site at http://www.ibm.com/ebusiness.
3. Forrester Research, Inc., online glossary, http://www.forrester.com.
4. "U.S. Q4 E-commerce Sales at $5.3B," http://www.usatoday.com/money/ (March 2, 2000).
5. "Small Business Buy, but Shy to Sell, Online," http://cyberatlas.internet.com/markets/professional/article/0,1323,5971_365281,00.html (May 17, 2000).
6. *Business Week*, special supplement, Feb. 28, 2000, p. 74.
7. Don Tapscott, "Online Parts Exchange Heralds New Era," *Financial Post*, May 5, 2000, p.C7.
8. "Global E-Commerce Approaches Hypergrowth," http://www.forrester.com/ (Apr. 18, 2000).
9. "Daily Web Surfing Now the Norm," http://www.usatoday.com/life/cyber/tech/cth591.htm (March 22, 2000).
10. "U.S. Q4 E-Commerce Sales at $5.3B," http://www.usatoday.com/money/ (Mar. 2, 2000), .
11. "April 2000 Internet Usage Stats," http://cyberatlas.internet.com/ (May 16, 2000).
12. "Media Metrix Releases Worldwide Internet Measurement Results for Australia, Canada, France, Germany & United Kingdom," http://www.mediametrix.com/ (May 10, 2000).
13. Ibid.; "Media Metrix Releases U.S. Top 50 Web and Digital Media Properties for March 2000," http://www.mediametrix.com/ (April 24, 2000).
14. Based on information from Blackboard Corporate Video, November 2000, Blackboard, Inc., 1899 L Street, NW, 5th Floor, Washington, D.C. 20036 and the Blackboard.com web site at www.blackboard.com on December 18, 2000.

CHAPTER 5

1. Based on information from by Martin Wolk, MSNBC, with contribution by Reuters (May 2, 2000 and April 21, 2000); Feliciano Garcia, "The Lists," *Fortune*, April 17, 2000, p. 294; *Hoover's Handbook of American Business 2000, A Profile of 750 Major U.S. Companies*," Copyright 1999 by Hoover's Inc. (Austin, Texas 2000) pp. 724–725; Quentin Hardy, "The Cult of Carly," *Forbes*, December 13, 1999, pp. 138+; Peter Burrows, "The Hottest Property in the Valley?" *Business Week*, August 30, 1999, pp. 69+.
2. "Emerging Company of the Year Award," *Black Enterprise*, May, 2000, p. 47.
3. Jerry Useem, "Partners on the Edge," *Inc.*, August, 1998, p. 57.
4. Karen Witham Lynch, "Taxation Vexation", *Web Business* Magazine, http://webbusiness.cio.com/archive/062800_etax.html (June 2000).
5. Patricia Guadalupe, "A Heritage of Success," *Hispanic Business*, March, 2000, p. 18.
6. Emily Thornton and Dexter Roberts, "Beijing Gives Foreign Auto Makers the Green Light," *Business Week Online*, www.businessweek.com (July 19, 1999).
7. Based on information at Oracle Corporation's corporate information web site, http://www.oracle.com/corporate/.
8. Based on a press release available at the Lucent Technologies web site entitled "Lucent Technologies acquires Herrmann Technology, a leading supplier of optical devices for next-generation DWDM networks," http://www.lucent.com/press/0600/000619.coa.html (June 19, 2000).
9. Based on information from "IMCO Recycling, Inc., Company Snapshot," http://www.marketguide.com (June 3, 2000); "IMCO Recycling, Inc., http://www.hoovers.com (June 3, 2000); "IMCO Recycling, Inc., http://yahoo.finance (June 5, 2000); and IMCO Recycling, Inc., 1999 Annual Report.

CHAPTER 6

1. Based on information from Evantheia Schibsted, "Americas Online," *Business 2.0*, January 2000, pp. 70–74; "She's So Savvy: Meet Lavonne Luquis, President, LatinoLink Enterprises, Inc.," *Cybergrrl*, n.d., http://www.cybergrrls.com/tech/savvy/art1701/ (June 2, 2000); "Latino.com Ramps Up New York Office With Appointment of Three New Staffers," LatinoLink press release, November 22, 1999, http://www.latino.com/ (June 2, 2000); Dianne See, "Building Community on the Web," *thestandard.com*, September 28, 1998, http://www.thestandard.com/article/display/0,1151,1793,00.html (June 2, 2000); Soledad O'Brien, "Lavonne Luquis," *Women.com*, n.d., http://www.women.com/tech/spotlight/luquis.html (June 2, 2000); "Latino.com To Be Launched From LatinoLink.com Following Successful Funding Efforts," LatinoLink press release, October 19, 1999, http://www.latinolink.com/company/press/1019rele.php3 (June 2, 2000).
2. U.S. Small Business Administration, SBA Size Standards. Frequently Asked Questions, http://www.sba.gov/size/Main-faq.html (May 25, 2000).
3. U.S. Small Business Administration, *Small Business's Vital Statistics*, (Washington, D.C., April 28, 2000), p. 2.
4. *Ibid.*
5. *Ibid.*

6. Online Women Business Center, SBA Success Stories, "Business Was Always Her Passion," http://www.onlinewbc.org/docs/success_stories/ss_innovativetech. html, June 3, 2000.
7. U.S. Small Business Administration, *Small Business's Vital Statistics.*
8. U.S. Small Business Administration, 1992 Annual Report, p. 70.
9. Sheila Robbins, "Let's Play to Win," *Marketwise*, Federal Reserve Bank of Richmond, Issue 2, 1999, pp. 3–4.
10. Kim Girard and Sean Donahue, "Crash and Learn: A Field Manual for e-Business Survival," *Business2.0*, http://www.business2.com/content/magazine/indepth/2000/06/28/13700 (June 11, 2000).
11. Carlye Adler and other staff writers, "The FSB 25," *Fortune's Small Business Online* Magazine, http://fortunesb.com/articles/0,2227,565,00. html (February 8, 2000).
12. U.S. Small Business Administration, *Small Business Vital Statistics*, (Washington, D.C., April 28, 2000), p. 2.
13. U.S. Small Business Administration, *Facts About Small Business.*
14. Alan Joch, "E-Business Without the E-Cost," *Fortune's Small Business Online* Magazine, http://www.fsb.com/fortunesb/articles/0,2227,320,00. html (July 16, 1999).
15. "Challenges to Small Businesses on the Net," *Business 2.0*, http://www. business2.com/content/research/numbers/2000/06/26/13389 (June 26, 2000).
16. Marc Leepsonn, "Building a Business: A Matter of Course," *Nation's Business*, April 1988, pp. 42–43.
17. U.S. Small Business Administration, *Did You Know the SBA*? (Washington, D.C. March 1997), Form 959.
18. U.S. Small Business Administration, 1992 Annual Report, p. 53.
19. U.S. Small Business Administration, 1997 Annual Report, www.sba. gov (May 28, 2000).
20. John Oleck, "Franchise Finds: Buying a He-Man Franchise," *Executive Female*, July/August, 1994, p. 30.
21. *Wall Street Journal*, March 4, 1997, p. B2.
22. Doctor's Associates, Inc., *SUBWAY: A Business You Can Be Proud to Own*, 1997.
23. "7-Eleven Franchises File for Lack of Support," *National Petroleum News*, May 1994, p. 17.
24. Rick Romell, "Dunkin' Donuts Sues Three Milwaukee Franchisees," *Milwaukee Journal Sentinel*, March 24, 1997, p. 324B.
25. Janean Chun, "Franchise Frenzy," *Entrepreneur*, January 1997, p. 163.
26. Barry M. Heller and Elaine A. Panagakos, "Territorial Encroachment: The Burger King and Taco Bell Cases," *Franchise Law Journal*, summer 1994, p. 3.
27. *Ibid.*
28. "Challenges to Small Businesses on the Net," *Business 2.0*, http://www. business2.com/content/research/numbers/2000/06/26/13389 (June 26, 2000).
29. Based on information from Debbie Hiott, "The Right Stuff at the Airport: City Inspectors Aim to Keep Project from Taking a Nosedive," *Austin American-Statesman*, November 6, 1997; Daryl Janes, "Pelzel Builds Company from Ground Up," *Austin Business Journal*, July 26, 1996, p. 4; "Austin's Top Woman-Owned Businesses Cover the Spectrum," *Austin Business Journal*, July 26, 1996, p. B6; Debbie Hiott and Nina Reyes, "Why Your Airport May Become Mary Guerrero-Pelzel's $100 Million Job," *Austin American-Statesman*, January 25, 1996, p. 1; and "Hispanic Magazine and NationsBank Present the 1997 Adelante Awards," http://www.prnewswire.com, June 18, 1997 (October 13, 1997).

CHAPTER 7

1. Based on information from Steve Rosenbush, "How Can Tim Koogle Stay So Cool in the Face of AOL's Assault?" *Business Week*, May 15, 2000, pp. EB26–EB27; Kristi Heim, "Yahoo! Inc. Succeeds on Internet with Unique Business Methods, Philosophy," *San Jose Mercury News*, April 3, 2000, http://www.lexis-nexis.com (April 18, 2000); Brent Schlender, "How a Virtuoso Plays the Web," *Fortune*, March 6, 2000, pp. F 79–F 83; "The Customer Is the Decision-Maker,"*Fortune*, March 6, 2000, pp. F 84–F 86.
2. Brian O'Rielly, "The Mechanic Who Fixed Continental," *Fortune*, December 20, 1999, p. 176.
3. Dana James, "Don't Forget Staff in Marketing Plan," *Marketing News*, March 13, 2000, pp. 10–11.
4. Bob Cox, "General Motors Plans Chain of Dealerships," *Fort-Worth Star Telegram*, September 29, 1999.
5. Paul McDougall, "Compaq Catches Flak For Direct-Sales Push—Resellers Say Commercial PC Strategy Could Backfire on Struggling Desktop Vendor," *Information Week*, February 7, 2000, p. 32.
6. Kevin Hogan, "Not the Agents of Change," *Business2.0* Magazine, http://www.business2.com/content/magazine/indepth/2000/06/01/11 008 (June 1, 2000).
7. Dale Buss, "The Dimmer Side of Sears," *Business2.0* Magazine, http://www.business2.com/content/magazine/indepth/2000/06/01/13 061 (June 1, 2000).
8. "Success of First Live Interactive Career Fair Leads to Nationwide Program Expansion for 2000," *Business Wire*, February 8, 2000.
9. Henry Mintzberg, "The Manager's Job: Folklore and Fact," *Harvard Business Review*, July/August 1975, pp. 49–61.
10. Robert Kreitner, *Management*, 8th ed. (Boston: Houghton Mifflin, 2001), p. 467.
11. Ricky W. Griffin, *Fundamentals of Management*, 2nd ed. (Boston: Houghton Mifflin, 2000), p. 96.
12. Dale Buss, "Not So Magical Kingdom," *Business2.0* Magazine, http://www.business2.com/content/magazine/indepth/2000/06/01/13 048 (June 1, 2000).
13. Kim Girard, "Unlike a Virgin," *Business2.0* Magazine, http://www. business2.com/content/magazine/indepth/2000/06/01/13060 (June 1, 2000).
14. "Kellogg Abandons Bagels," *Grocer*, October 2, 1999, p. 12.
15. "BI Earns Prestigious Malcolm Baldrige National Quality Award," PR Newswire, November 23, 1999.
16. Michael Petrou, "Striking a Nerve," *Financial Post*, July 8, 2000, p. D7.
17. Based on information from "Herbert D. Kelleher," *Business Week*, January 8, 2001, p. 73; Katrina Brooker, "Can Anyone Replace Herb?" *Fortune*, April 17, 2000, pp. 186+; Katherine Yung, "Dallas-Based Southwest Airlines Named Number One in Quality Ratings," *Dallas Morning News*, April 10, 2000, http://www.dallasnews.com; Shelly Branch, "So Much work, So Little Time," *Fortune*, February 3, 1997, pp. 115–117; Jim Barlow, "Southwest Puts Employees First," *Houston Chronicle*, November 24, 1996, p. B1; Matthew Ball, "Only Five Ways to Run a Company," *Corporate Finance*, March 1996, pp. 24–27; Amy Malloy, "On the Job: Southwest Airlines," *Computerworld*, June 1996, p. 47; Southwest Airlines, http://www.iflyswa.com; and Kevin Freiberg and Jackie Freiberg, *Nuts! Southwest Airlines' Crazy Recipe for Business and Personal Success* (Austin, Tex.: Bard Press, 1996), pp. 300–301.

CHAPTER 8

1. Based on information from Justin Fox, "Nokia's Secret Code," *Fortune*, May 1, 2000, pp. 160–174; Manoj Gairola and Sharad Goel, "Interview With Nokia CEO," *The Times of India*, February 9, 2000, http://wapsight. com/info/2000/02/09/232248.html (March 21, 2000); Steve Silberman, "Just Say Nokia," *Wired*, September 1999, http://www.wired.com/wired/archive/7.09/nokia.html?pg=5&topic=&topic_set= (May 31, 2000).
2. "Canada Life Financial Corporation Press Release," *Canadian Corporate Newswire*, January 27, 2000.
3. "Executive Suite: Iomega Announces Strategic Organizational Changes to Position Company for 1999 and Beyond: Company to Align Along Functional Lines Prompting Management Changes," *EDGE: Work Group Computing Report*, January 25, 1999, p. 170–171.
4. Jeremy Kahn, "The Hottest Way to Rewire Old Landmarks: Hotels With No Beds," *Fortune*, June 26, 2000, p. 60.
5. Henry Unger, "Draft Outlines Decentralized Coke," *The Atlanta Journal and Constitution*, January 29, 2000, p. 1B.
6. Zhenya Gene Senyak, "Talk Shops," *Business2.0* Magazine, http://www. business2.com/content/magazine/marketing/2000/06/01/12980 (June 1, 2000).
7. Robert Kreitner, Management, 8th ed. (Boston: Houghton Mifflin, 2001), p. 307.
8. Peter Burrows, "The Second Coming of Software," *Business Week*, June 19, 2000, p. 88.
9. Ricky Griffin, *Fundamentals of Management* (Boston: Houghton Mifflin, 2000), pp 167–168 and Robert Kreitner, *Management*, 8th ed. (Boston: Houghton Mifflin, 2001), pp. 318–319.

10. Ricky Griffin, *Fundamentals of Management* (Boston: Houghton Mifflin, 2000), p. 168.
11. Licensing Agreement Brings Starbucks Coffee to Marriott International, Inc. Properties," *Business Wire*, March 21, 2000, p. 181.
12. "Tricks of E*Trade," *Business Week*, February 7, 2000, p.EB18.
13. Rob Goffee and Gareth Jones, "The Character of a Corporation: How Your Company's Culture Can Make or Break Your Business," *Jones Harper Business*, p. 182.
14. Arthur Ciancutti and Thomas Steding, "Trust Fund," *Business2.0* Magazine, http://www.business2.com/content/magazine/ebusiness/2000/06/01/12910 (June 1, 2000).
15. Kreitner, *Management*, p. 92.
16. Alan T. Saracevic, "Bricks For the Clicks," *Business2.0* Magazine, http://www.business2.com/content/magazine/indepth/2000/06/01/12082 (June 1, 2000).
17. Based on information from "T.G.I. Friday's to Open Fifth Site in Japan," *Dallas Business Journal*, December 7, 2000, http://www.bizjournals.com/dallas/stories/2000/12/04/daily21.html; "New Brands, New Products, New International Locations All on the Agenda for Carlson Restaurants Worldwide," *Hotels*, November 2000, pp. S20+; Katie Fairbank, "Celebrity Chef Cuts Most Ties with Dallas-Based Restaurant Chain," *Dallas Morning News*, October 17, 2000, http://www.dallasnews.com; Andy Battaglia, "Wally Doolin," *Nation's Restaurant News*, January 2000, pp. 68+; "U.S. Restaurant Chains Learn to Adapt," *The Nikkei Weekly*, October 4, 1999, p. 8; Donna Hood Crecca, "Models for Success in Foodservice 2005," *Restaurants and Institutions*, May 1, 1997, pp. 117–131; "T.G.I. Friday's Is First to Open in Russia," http://www.prnewswire.com/0728MNM016 (July 28, 1997); "Guatemala: TGI Friday's Franchise," *Caribbean Update*, April 1, 1997; "Friday's® Continues Aggressive Global Expansion: Three New International Development Agreements Signed," http://www.prnewswire.com/0227DATH004 (February 27, 1997); and T.G.I. Friday's, http://www.tgifridays.com (September 10, 1997, and September 22, 1997).

CHAPTER 9

1. Based on information from the Campbell Soup web site at www.campbellsoup.com (May 22, 2000); Dan Beucke, "Great Performers and How to Spot Them," Table data: Compustat. Provided by Standard and Poor's Institutional Market Services, *Business Week*, March 27, 2000, pp. 131, 136; *Hoover's Handbook of American Business 2000, A Profile of 750 Major U.S. Companies* (Austin, Texas, Hoover's Inc., 2000) pp. 310–311; "A 'Loved Label,' " *Maclean's*, September 6, 1999, p. 8, copyright 1999 Maclean Hunter Canadian Publishing Ltd.; Richard Turcsik, "Soup to Go," *Progressive Grocer*," July 1999, p. 18.
2. U.S. Department of Labor, Bureau of Labor Statistics, *Monthly Labor Review*, March, 2000, p. 76.
3. Robert Kreitner, *Management*, 8th ed. (Boston: Houghton Mifflin, 2001), pp. 535–536.
4. Zhenya Gene Senyak, "Talk Shops," *Business2.0* Magazine, http://www.business2.com/content/magazine/marketing/2000/06/01/12980 (June 1, 2000).
5. Anthony Paul and Cindy Kano, *Fortune*, December 6, 1999, p. 190.
6. The 3M Company web site at www.3M.com (June 10, 2000).
7. Dale Buss, "Not So Magical Kingdom," *Business2.0* Magazine, http://www.business2.com/content/magazine/indepth/2000/06/01/13048 (June 1, 2000).
8. Robert Kreitner, *Management*, 7th ed. (Boston: Houghton Mifflin, 1998), p. 527.
9. Steve Bennett, "Wings and a Prayer," *Business2.0* Magazine, http://www.business2.com/content/magazine/indepth/2000/06/01/13040 (June 1, 2000).
10. Derek Reveron, "The Race to Reach Critical Mass," *Hispanic Business*, January/February, 2000, p. 18.
11. *Ibid.*, p. 22.
12. Mark Gimein, "Cool Companies 2000," *Fortune*, June 26, 2000, p.122.
13. The Dell Corporation web site at www.dell.com (June 12, 2000).
14. Justin Martin, "Give 'Em Exactly What They Want," *Fortune*, November 10, 1997, p. 283+.
15. Tyler Maroney, "An Air Battle Comes to the Web," *Fortune*, June 26, 2000, p. 315.
16. "U.S. and Foreign Productivity and Unit Labor Costs," *Monthly Labor Review*, February, 1997, pp. 26–27.
17. Ricky W. Griffin, *Management*, 6th ed. (Boston: Houghton Mifflin, 1999), p. 650.
18. Based on information from Saturn Corporation, "A Different Kind of Company," www.saturn.com (June 12, 2000); Kathleen Kervin, "A Different Kind of Saturn," *Business Week Online*, July 5, 1999, www.businessweek.com (June 12, 2000); Randolph Heaster, "Corporation Pays Off, Saturn Executive Says," *Kansas City Star*, July 17, 1997, p. B1; Susan Karlin, "Musing for Fun and Profit," *Working Woman*, February, 1997, p. 45; "Road Hazzard," *Advertising Age*, May 5, 1997, p. 30; and Keith Bradsher, "GM Announces Two Steps to Streamline Its Operations," *New York Times*, March 11, 1997, p. D4.

CHAPTER 10

1. Based on information from Tom Fowler, "Nation Starving For Technology Workers," *Austin Business Journal*, January 31, 2000, http://www.bizjournals.com/austin/stories/2000/01/31/story2.html(May 24, 2000); Chuck Salter, " 'There's a War Going On, and We're Right in the Middle of It,' " *Fast Company*, December 1999, pp. 216–222; Eibhir Mulqueen, "Demands of Dell Keep Casey Running Just to Stand Still," *The Irish Times*, December 23, 1999, p. 53; "Dell Recruits TV To Fill Vacancies," *The Irish Times*, December 16, 1999, p. 21; John Byrne, "The Search for the Young and Gifted: Why Talent Counts," *Business Week*, October 4, 1999, http://www.businessweek.com/1999/99_40/b3649012.htm (April 24, 2000).
2. Diane Rezendes Khirallah, "Vendors Team to Offer Comprehensive Skills Testing," *Information Week*, January 24, 2000, p. 109.
3. Peter Burrows, "Technology on tap," *Business Week*, June 19, 2000, p. 82.
4. Statistical Abstract of the United States, 1999, p.403.
5. Texas Instruments: TI Recognized as Outstanding Employer for Asians, Blacks, and Hispanics, M2 Presswire, July 2, 1999.
6. "Ericcson's Dallas Site Hiring RS Wireless Network Engineers, *Electronic Engineering Times*, April 13, 1998, p.1.
7. Staff writers, "Plus Ca Change: Job Boards Search for Work" *Business2.0* Magazine, http://www.business2.com/content/magazine/filter/2000/06/01/12973 (June 01, 2000).
8. Michael Schrage, "You're Nuts If You're Not Certifiable," *Fortune*, June 26, 2000, p. 338.
9. "America's Best Company Benefits," *Money*, October 1, 1999, page 116.
10. U.S. Department of Labor, Bureau of Labor Statistics, News Release, June 24, 1999.
11. "Not Your Usual Perks," *Fortune*, January 10, 2000, p.92.
12. Kip Tindel, "Who Said the Trash Can Can Make You Smile? Transcending Value at the Container Store." *Arthur Andersen Retailing Issues Letter*, Center for Retailing Studies, Texas A&M University, January 2000, p. 3.
13. Phone Interview, Sue Weiss, Motorola University, March 6, 2000.
14. Sandra Dillich, "Training or Learning," *Computing Canada*, June 23, 2000, p. 25.
15. *Ibid.*
16. Cynthia D. Fisher, Lyle F. Schoenfeldt, and James B. Shaw, *Human Resource Management* (Boston: Houghton Mifflin, 1999) pp. 534–535.
17. Susan J. Wells, "A New Road, Traveling on 360-Degree Evaluation," *HRMagazine*, September 1999, p. 82.
18. "Study Reveals Increase in Federal Court Cases," LRP Publications, Feb. 11, 2000.
19. Based on information from http://www.Headhunter.net/JobSeeker/Index.htm (January 15, 2001); "Headhunter.net," *PC Magazine*, January 16, 2001, p. 188; "Headhunter.net Launches International Gateway," Headhunter.net press release, http://www.headhunter.net (December 19, 2000); Jennifer Weitzman, "Career Tracks: From On-Line Banking to On-Line Recruiting," *American Banker*, May 4, 1999, p. 5; Sarah Fister, "Online Recruiting: Good, Fast and Cheap?" *Training*, May 1999, pp. 26+.

CHAPTER 11

1. Based on information from Stephen Swoyer, "BMC Rounds Out Its Line For E-Business," *Information Week*, May 8, 2000, pp. 182+; Dwight Silverman, "Houston-Based BMC Software Offers Money-Back Guarantee to Corporations," *Houston Chronicle*, April 5, 2000, http://www.lexis-nexis.com (April 25, 2000), Claire Poole, "Leadership To the Max," *Texas Monthly*, March 2000, pp. S12+; Jerry Useem, "Welcome to the New Company," *Fortune*, January 10, 2000, pp. 62–70; "Benefits," BMC Software, n.d., http://www.bmc.com/careers/benefits.cfm (April 5, 2000).
2. Cora Daniels, "This Man Wants to Help You. Seriously," *Fortune*, June 26, 2000, pp.327–330.
3. Michelle Conlin and Kathy Moore, "Dr. Goodnight's Company Town," *Business Week*, June 19, 2000, p. 192.
4. Michael Petrou, "Striking a Nerve," *Financial Post*, July 8, 2000, p. D7.
5. Douglas McGregor, *The Human Side of Enterprise* (New York: McGraw-Hill, 1960).
6. William Ouchi, *Theory Z* (Reading, MA: Addison-Wesley, 1981).
7. Ricky W. Griffin, *Fundamentals of Management*, 2nd ed. (Boston: Houghton Mifflin, 2000), p. 281.
8. "GiftCertificates.com provides corporate customer incentive program for Boston Beer Company," *PR Newswire Association*, February 22, 2000.
9. Ricky W. Griffin, *Management*, 6th ed. (Boston: Houghton Mifflin, 1999), p. 223.
10. Profile America, Radio Service of the U.S. Census Bureau, February 29, 2000.
11. John Berndt, "Do You Offer Flexible Time Schedules?" *Baltimore Business Journal*, January 21, 2000, p.23.
12. Stephanie Armour, "Parttimers Reap Benefits of Tight Market," *USA Today*, November 1, 1999, p.1B.
13. Nancy Wong, "The Key Is To Find the Right Partner," *Workforce*, April, 1999, p. 112.
14. Daniel M. Hirak, "Millions Move to Home Office," *Strategic Finance* Magazine, December 1999, pp.54–57.
15. Reid Goldsborough, "Making Telecommuting Work," *Commercial Law Bulletin*, January/February 2000, pp.34–35.
16. Jill Elswick, "Puttin' on the Ritz: Hotel Chain Touts Training to Benefit Its Recruiting and Retention," *Employee Benefit News*, February 2000, pp.1, 34–35.
17. Richard C. Kearney and Steven W. Hayes, "Labor Management Relations and Participative Decision-Making: Toward a New Paradigm," *Public Administration Review*, January/February 1994, pp. 44–51.
18. Steward L. Strokes, Jr., "Moving Toward Self-Directed Teams: An Action Plan for Self-Managed Teams," *Information Systems*, winter 1994, pp.40–44.
19. The National Center for Employee Ownership (NCEO), *Statistical Profile of Employee Ownership*, (Oakland, CA: NCEO, www.nceo.org/library).
20. Shawn Tully, "The Party's Over," *Fortune*, June 26, 2000, p.156.
21. Based on information from Jennifer Gormanus Burke, "A Sweet Deal," *Bostonia*, May 12, 2000, http://web.bu.edu/alumni/bostonia/spring2000/leblanc.html; Valerie Morris, "Harbor Sweets Founder," *CNNfn Business Unusual*, August 16, 1999, transcript 99081603FN–112; "LeBlanc Buys Harbor Sweets," *Candy Industry*, November 1998, p. 12; "Harbor Sweets: What a Great Place to Work," *National Association of Working People*, October 1996, http://www.beachworks.com/nawp/greatplace/harbor.html.

CHAPTER 12

1. Based on information from Ann Zimmerman, "Wal-Mart Butchers Burned in Battle," *Houston Chronicle*, April 16, 2000, business section, p. 3; Wendy Zellner, "Up Against the Wal-Mart," *Business Week*, March 13, 2000, pp. 76–78; Frank Swoboda, "Wal-Mart Ends Meat-Cutting Jobs; Shutdown at 180 Stores Comes After a Union Victory," *Washington Post*, March 4, 2000, p. E1.
2. "Workers Are Winning More Elections," www.aflcio.org (June 11, 1999).
3. David Morgan, "Tech Boom Still Driving the Economy," *Financial Post*, July 12, 2000, p. C11.
4. Robert B. McKersie, "Labour-Management Partnerships: U.S. Evidence and Implications for Ireland," *Ibar*, vol. 17, 1996, pp. 1–13.
5. Bill Leonard, "The New Face of Organized Labor," *HRMagazine*, July 1999, p. 54.
6. "Union and Management Look for New Ways of Doing Business," *Canadian Corporate News*, February 15, 2000.
7. William Trolan, "Stretching Your Limits," *Business2.0* Magazine, http://www.business2.com/content/magazine/getalife/2000/06/01/10947 (June 01, 2000).
8. Saul A. Rubinstein, "The Impact of Co-Management on Quality Performance: The Case of the Saturn Corporation," *Industrial and Labor Relations Review*, January 2000, pp. 197–218.
9. "Unfair Labor Practices Charges Filed Against Battle Creek Health Systems by SIEU Local," *PR Newswire*, January 29, 1999.
10. David Morgan, "Tech Boom Still Driving the Economy," *Financial Post*, July 12, 2000, p. C11.
11. Jeffrey H. Birnbaum, "Death to Bureaucrats, Good News for the Rest of Us," *Fortune*, June 26, 2000, pp. 241–242.
12. U.S. Department of Labor, Bureau of Labor Statistics, www.bls.gov/news.release, February 24, 2000.
13. Claire Mencke, "Boeing's Strike Raises New Issue," *Investers Business Daily*, March 14, 2000.
14. David Field, "Airlines Battle Union in Court Slowdown, Sickout Acts are Targets" *USA Today*, January 10, 2000, p. 1B.
15. "Texas Congressman Criticizes Crown Central Petroleum for Lockout of Union Workers," *Newswire*, February 2, 2000.
16. Based on information from "Xerox Will Abolish 2000 U.S. Jobs by Moving Production to Mexico," *Wall Street Journal Interactive*, http://interactive.wsj.com/archive/ (January 5, 2001); Michael R. Zimmerman, "Xerox Zeros in on Savings," *eWeek*, November 27, 2000, p. 31; Daniel Eisenberg, "An Image Problem At Xerox," *Time*, October 30, 2000, pp. 63+; Peter Lazes et al., "Xerox and the ACTWU: Using Labor-Management Teams to Remain Competitive," *National Productivity Review*, summer 1991, pp. 339–349; Norman E. Richard, Jr., "The Quest for Quality: A Race Without a Finish," *Industrial Engineering*, January 1991, pp. 25–27; Anne Ritter, "Are Unions Worth the Bargain Power?" *Personnel*, February 1990, pp. 12–14; Dan Dordtz, "Listening to Labor," *Financial World*, September 2, 1991, pp. 44–47; "Company-Union Partnership Turns Xerox Around," *Personnel Journal*, January 1994, p. 61; Dawn Anfuso, "Xerox Partners with the Union to Regain Market Share, *Personnel Journal*, August 1994, pp. 46–53; Roberta C. Yafie, "Pass the 10Q, Partner," *Journal of Business Strategy*, January/February 1996, pp. 53–56; Martha A. Gephart and Mark E. VanBuren, "Building Synergy: The Power of High Performance Work Systems," *Training & Development*, October 1996, pp. 21–32; George Sutton and James R. Talbot, eds., *Hoover's 500 Profiles of America's Largest Business Enterprises* (Austin, TX: Hoover's Business Press, 1996), p. 528; Xerox Corporation, http://www.xerox.com (January 21, 1997); and Xerox Corporation, The High Road: Union Management Partnership, videocassette, 1994.

CHAPTER 13

1. Based on information from "USAA Expresses Interest in Arizona," *Business Wire*, September 17, 1999, http://web.lexis-nexis.com (April 17, 2000); "Banks Integrate Channels To Support One-To-One Marketing," *Retail Delivery News*, April 28, 1999; Mary E. Thyfault, "Customer Service Drives Upgrade," *Information Week*, October 5, 1998, p. 52; F. W. Timmerman Jr., "ECHO System Helps USAA Listen—And Respond—To Customer Feedback," *Journal of Retail Banking Services*, Summer 1998, pp. 29–33; Edward E. Furash, "Values As a Strategy," *Journal of Lending and Credit Risk Management*, November 1996, pp. 9–13; William M. Pride and O.C. Ferrell, *Marketing: Concepts and Strategies* (Boston: Houghton Mifflin, 2000), p. 320.
2. Jathon Sapsford, "New Jersey's Commerce Bancorp Stretches Hours, Cuts Service Fees," *Wall Street Journal*, Interactive Edition, p.1
3. "Marriott Revamped Mileage Awards," Colloquy, www.colloquy.org/news (March 22, 2000).
4. "It's (Still) Time to Make the Donuts," *Sales and Marketing Management*, June 2000, p. 135.
5. Teresa Howard, "18–34 Adults; Opposites Attract," *Media Week*, May 10, 1999, p.8.

6. Peter Burrows, "Technology on Tap," *Business Week*, June 19, 2000, p. 80.
7. *Ibid.*
8. William M. Pride and O.C. Ferrell, *Marketing: Concepts and Strategies* (Boston: Houghton Mifflin Company, 2000), p.195.
9. Kay Parker, "Old-Line Goes Online," *Business2.0* Magazine, http://www.business2.com/content/magazine/marketing/2000/06/01/12979 (June 1, 2000).
10. Chad Kaydo, "A Position of Power," *Sales and Marketing Management*, June 2000, p. 106.
11. Del Jones, "Some Schools to Surf Net to Cut Costs of Supplies," *USA Today*, March 20, 2000, p.B1.
12. U.S. Department of Labor, Bureau of Labor Statistics, Office of Pricing and Living Conditions, ftp://ftp.bls.gov/pub/specialrequests (March 2000).
13. "Kick It Up," *American Demographics*, June 2000, p. 26.
14. Ira P. Schneiderman, "Rich Boomers Prove to be Savers, Not Spenders," *DNR*, January, 2000, p.11.
15. Alex Frew McMillan, "Net Shopping Differs by Sex," CNN FN, April 19, 2000.
16. Melanie Warner, "Cool Companies 2000," *Fortune*, June 26, 2000, p. 108.
17. Amy Kover, "The Hot Idea of the Year," *Fortune*, June 26, 2000, p. 129.
18. Based on information from Marty Jerome, "E-Commerce," *Ziff Davis Smart Business for the New Economy*, December 1, 2000, pp. 104+; Ken Burke and Chris McCann, "Ask the Experts," *Catalog Age*, August 2000, p. 1S5; Jeff Sweat, "The Well-Rounded Customer," *Information Week*, April 10, 2000, pp. 44+; Stephen Boey, "1–800–Flowers.com Seek Partners to Expand," *Business Times* (Malaysia), February 15, 2000; "Company Overview," http://www.1800flowers.com/flowers/welcome.asp (January 12, 2001).
19. Kay Parker, "Old-Line Goes Online," *Business2.0* Magazine, http://www.business2.com/content/magazine/marketing/2000/06/01/12979 (June 1, 2000).

CHAPTER 14

1. Based on information from "Two Local Companies on List of Fastest-Growing Firms," *Denver Post*, April 6, 2000; Ilan Mochari, "Passing Fancy," *1999 Inc. 500*, p. 84; Rebecca Landwehr, "Manufacturer Continues Winning Streak," *Denver Business Journal*, April 30, 1999, pp. 14B–15B; Rebecca Landwehr, "Incubator Graduates Big Tenant," *Denver Business Journal*, January 1, 1999; Robert Baun, "CSU Grads Staying on the Ball," *Coloradoan*, October 26, 1999, p. B2.
2. Anne Marie Owens, "Mad About Harry," National Post, July 10, 2000, p. D1.
3. Brian Palmer, "Cool Companies 2000," *Fortune*, June 26, 2000, p. 112.
4. Eric Schmuckler, "The Bandwidth Blues," *Forbes*, May 22, 2000, p. 32.
5. "GE Launches GE Financial Network to Deliver True Consumer-Driven Financial Services Through the Internet," *Limitless Wire*, February 8, 2000.
6. Lisa Campbell, "Why Unilever B-Brands Must Be Cast Aside," *Marketing*, June 10, 1999, p. 13.
7. Keith Naughton, "Crunch Time at Kellogg," *Newsweek*, February 14, 2000, p. 52–53.
8. Elana Harris, "Digital Face Off," *Sales and Marketing Management*, July 2000, p. 17.
9. Peter D. Bennett, ed., *Dictionary of Marketing Terms* (Chicago: American Marketing Association and NTC Publishing Group, 1995), p. 27.
10. Tom Prendergast, Manager of Research Services, Private Label Manufacturers Association, Telephone Interview, May 3, 2000.
11. "The $1 Billion Brands League," Interbrand, www.interbrand.com (April 13, 2000).
12. Kay Parker, "Old-Line Goes Online," *Business2.0* Magazine, http://www.business2.com/content/magazine/marketing/2000/06/01/12979 (June 1, 2000).
13. Annual Report, U.S. Patent and Trademark Office, www.uspto.gov, June 15, 2000.
14. David Provost, "Up, Up, and Away," *Business2.0* Magazine, http://www.business2.com/content/magazine/numbers/2000/06/01/10982 (June 1, 2000).
15. Leonard L. Berry, "Retailers with a Future," *Marketing Management*, spring 1996, pp. 38–46.
16. Jennifer Gilbert, "AOL's Marketing Builds Service into Powerhouse," *Advertising Age*, March 6, 2000, pg. S16.
17. Micheline Maynard, "In a Search for Hot Wheels, Buyers Hit a Dead End," *New York Times*, May 7, 2000, Section 3, p. 12.
18. Based on information from "Gillette to Fire 2,700, Close 8 Plants Next Year," *Boston Business Journal*, December 19, 2000, http://www.bizjournals.com/boston/stories/2000/12/18/daily4.html; Mercedes M. Cardona, "No New CEO, But Gillette Does Have a New Product," *Advertising Age*, November 2000, http://www.adage.com; "Gillette to Spend $100 Million to Promote Electric Toothbrush," *Boston Business Journal*, November 29, 2000, http://www.bizjournals.com/boston/stories/2000/11/27/daily9.html; Gillette Introduces Proprietary Clear Stick Technology into Gillette Series and Right Guard Anti-Perspirants and Deodorants," http://www.businesswire.com/7101069 (July 10, 1996); Chris Reidy and Alex Pham, "Gillette Makes $7.8b Deal for Battery King Duracell," *Boston Globe*, September 13, 1996, p. A1; "Gillette Plans Spate of Introductions," *Chain Drug Review*, February 3, 1997, pp. 53–54; Chantal Tode, "Gillette Cleans Up Men's Grooming," *WWD*, April 4, 1997, p. 10; Linda Grant, "Gillette Knows Shaving—and How to Turn Out Hot New Products," *Fortune*, October 14, 1996, p. 207–209; and Pablo Galarza, "Shave and a Lawsuit . . . ," *Financial World*, April 8, 1996.

CHAPTER 15

1. Based on information from Herb Greenberg, "Dead Mall Walking," *Fortune*, May 1, 2000, p. 304; Tom Andel, "Logistics@Barnesandnoble.com," *Material Handling Management*, January 2000, p. 39; "Mezzanines Help Support Store and Web Demand," *Material Handling Management*, January 2000, p. 14SCF.
2. Patricia Seybold, "Niches Bring Riches," *Business2.0* Magazine, http://www.business2.com/content/magazine/ebusiness/2000/06/01/10681 (June 1, 2000).
3. Jay Greene, "The Man Behind All Those E-Ads," *Business Week*, June 26, 2000, p. 76.
4. U.S. Department of Commerce, Bureau of the Census, *Statistical Abstract of the United States*, 1999, p. 782.
5. *Ibid.*, p. 769
6. *Ibid.*
7. *Ibid.*
8. William M. Pride and O.C. Ferrell, *Marketing: Concepts and Strategies*, 2000/e (Boston: Houghton Mifflin, 2000) p. 406.
9. *Chain Store Age/Supermarkets*, July 1983, p. 11.
10. Jonathan Fuerbringer, "A Miffed Moscow Means Headaches for IKEA," *New York Times*, April 9, 2000, Section 3, p. 4.
11. World Federation of Direct Selling Association, "Worldwide Direct Sales Data," June 27, 2000.
12. Dale Buss, "The Dimmer Side of Sears," *Business2.0* Magazine, http://www.business2.com/content/magazine/indepth/2000/06/01/13061 (June 1, 2000).
13. Ken Ibold, "Take This Job and Love It," *Florida Trend*, February 2000, p. 40.
14. Susan Kuchinskas, "By Invitation Only," *Business2.0* Magazine, http://www.business2.com/content/magazine/indepth/2000/06/01/12927?page=1 (June 1, 2000).
15. Stanley C. Hollander, "The Wheel of Retailing," *Journal of Marketing*, July 1960, p. 37.
16. Peter Burrows, "Technology on Tap," *Business Week*, June 19, 2000, p. 80.
17. Todd Murphy, "Developers Rush to Meet Demands of E-Commerce," *New York Times*, January 23, 2000, Section 3, p. 3.
18. Based on information from "Dash Celebrates Key Milestone: Over One Billion Served," Dash.com press release, August 15, 2000, http://www.dash.com; David McGuire, "Regulate Thyself, Warns Dash.com," *Newsbytes*, January 28, 2000, http://www.newsbytes.com; Kathryn Kranhold, "Omnicom Extends Internet Push with a 20% Stake in Dash.com," *Wall Street Journal*, December 6, 1999, http://www.wsj.com; "Dash Announces Strategic CRM Partnership with United Airlines," Dash.com press release, November 1, 2000, http://www.dash.com; http://www.dash.com (January 19, 2001).

CHAPTER 16

1. Based on information from Kate MacArthur, "Burger Giants Dig Up Dinos for Summer Movie Tie-Ins," *Advertising Age*, April 17, 2000, p. 3; "Segmenting the Message," *Adweek Eastern Edition*, April 17, 2000, p. 20; Chua Lee Hoong, "Take A Cue From McDonald's On Good PR," *Straits Times (Singapore)*, February 9, 2000, p. 36; Shareem Amry, "The Cute, The Cuddly, The Ugly," *New Straits Times (Malaysia)*, January 23, 2000, p. 3; Louise Kramer, "McD's Steals Another Toy From BK," *Advertising Age*, November 15, 1999, p. 1; Greg Hernandez, "Burger King Plays For Deep Pockets With 'Pokemon,'" *Los Angeles Times*, November 9, 1999, part C, p. 1+.
2. Terence A. Shimp, *Advertising, Promotion, and Supplemental Aspects of Integrated Marketing Communications*, (Ft. Worth, TX: Dryden Press, 2000) pp. 22–23.
3. Mercedes M. Cardona, "Coen's '99 Tally: Cable, Radio, Net Drive Ad Revenue, *Ad Age*, May 22, 2000, p. 20.
4. "Direct E-Mail Keeps Them Coming Back," www.pccomputing.com, February 2000, p. 163.
5. Nielsen Media Research. May 1999.
6. "NPC Marketing Group Renews Copy Protection Agreement with Macrovision," *Business Wire*, March 21, 2000.
7. Steve Raabe, "The Denver Post Advertising and Marketing Column," *Denver Post*, January 30, 2000.
8. Mercedes M. Cardona, p. 20.
9. "Top 25 Internet Advertisers," *Advertising Age*, September 27, 1999, p. S41.
10. Janet Ginsberg, "The Great Portal Purge," *Business Week*, June 26, 2000, p.152.
11. Susan Kuchinskas, "Fair Gamers," *Business2.0* Magazine, http://www.business2.com/content/magazine/marketing/2000/06/01/12914 (June 1, 2000).
12. "Cyber-caster is Sold," *The Montreal Gazette*, July 6, 2000, p. C2.; "Ananova is Bought by Orange," http://www.ananova.com/news/story/sm_9317.html (May 7, 2000); http://www.ananova.com/about/about_ananova.html.
13. "America's 500 Largest Sales Forces," *Selling Power*, October 1999, pp. 68–69.
14. Terence A. Shimp, *Advertising, Promotion, and Supplemental Aspects of Integrated Marketing Communications* (Ft. Worth, TX: Dryden Press, 2000), pp. 514–518.
15. 20th Annual Survey of Promotional Practices, (Largo, Florida: Cox-direct, 1998), p. 74.
16. "Snipping Coupons = Increasing Profits," *Canadian Grocer*, August 1999, p. S1–S6.
17. Ann Smith, "Promote Profits," *Progressive Grocer*, February 1997, p. 101.
18. "Smile! With Clearly Canadian's Trident Gum Trial Offer," *Canadian Corporate Newswire*, August 30, 1999.
19. Jason Compton, "Reward Your Customers," *Smartbusiness.com*, May 2000, pp. 196–199.
20. Stephanie Thompson, "Kellogg Concept Turns Aisles into Breakfast-land," *Advertising Age*, July 3, 2000, pg. 3.
21. Jane Applegate, "Size Doesn't Matter If You Have a Trade Show Booth," *The Arizona Republic*, February 22, 2000, p. D2.
22. "Kids in Virginia and California Will Learn to Love Books and Reading with Help from RIF and Best Buy," *Business Wire*, March 28, 2000.
23. Colleen O'Connor, "Getting Religion," *Business2.0* Magazine, http://www.business2.com/content/magazine/ebusiness/2000/06/01/12908 (June 1, 2000).
24. Based on information from Richard Linnett and Wayne Friedman, "No Gain: Super Bowl Ad Pricing Is Flat," *Advertising Age*, January 15, 2001, http://adage.com/news_and_features/features/20010115/article5.html; Jennifer Gilbert, "Running on Empty," *Advertising Age*, 2000, http://adage.com/i20/srmain.html; "There's No Escaping the Dot.Com Ad Blitz," *ZDNet.com U.K.*, 1999, http://www.zdnet.co.uk/news/1999/47/ns-11785.html; "The Net Goes Guerilla," 1999, http://www.zdnet.co.uk/news/1999/47/ns-11783.html.

CHAPTER 17

1. Based on information from "Fact City and iWon.com Launch Internet's First Comprehensive Facts-on-Demand Service," *Business Wire*. September 18, 2000, p. 2315; Timothy J. Mullaney, "Web Lotto: It Ain't Pretty," *Business Week*, May 15, 2000, p. #B 122; Christopher Palmeri, "You May Already Be a Winner.Com!," *Business Week* April 24, 2000, p. 132; J. William Gurley, "If iWon Wins, Do Portals Lose?," *Fortune*, February 7, 2000, p. 190; and Karissa S. Want, "CBS Enters Portal Lottery," *Electronic Media*, October 11, 1999, p. 16.
2. Daniel Roth, "Meet e-Bay's Worst Nightmare," *Fortune*, June 26, 2000, p. 200.
3. Peter Burrows, "Technology on Tap," *Business Week*, June 19, 2000, p. 76.
4. Julie Creswell, "Cool Companies 2000," *Fortune*, June 26, 2000, p. 101.
5. Based on information from CSX Corporation web site, www.csx.com (December 13, 2000); CSX Corporation at http://finance.yahoo.com (December 13, 2000); James A. Anderson, "A Risky Ride on the Railroads, *Business Week Online* (April 10, 2000); Joseph Weber, "CSX-Conrail: How Shareholders Would Get Railroaded," *Business Week*, November 9, 1996, p. 44; and George Sutton and James R. Talbot,eds., *Hoover's 500 Profiles of America's Largest Business Enterprises*, (Austin, TX: Hoover's Business Press, 1996), p. 156.

CHAPTER 18

1. Based on information from The Arthur Andersen web site, www.arthurandersen.com (July 14, 2000); *Hoover's Handbook of American Business 2000, A Profile of 750 Major U.S. Companies*, Copyright 1999 by Hoover's Inc. (Austin, Texas 2000), pp.154–155, 1164–1165; George Shaheen, "Andersen's Androids," *The Economist*, May 4, 1996, p. 72.
2. The Bureau of Labor Statistics web site, www.bls.gov (July 20, 2000).
3. Jim Griffin, "Rethinking Internet Valuation," *Business2.0* Magazine, http://www.business2.com/content/magazine/vision/2000/06/01/10989 (June 1, 2000).
4. Bethany McLean, "Hocus-Pocus: How IBM Grew 27 Percent a Year," *Fortune*, June 26, 2000, pp. 165–168.
5. Peter Burrows, "Technology on Tap," *Business Week*, June 19, 2000, p. 74.
6. Kim Girard, "Middle Management," *Business2.0* Magazine, http://www.business2.com/content/magazine/ebusiness/2000/06/01/12966 (June 1, 2000).
7. Based on information from http://www.officedepot.com (January 12, 2001); and *Hoover's Handbook of American Business 2000, A Profile of 750 Major U.S. Companies*, Copyright 1999 by Hoover's Inc. (Austin, Texas 2000), pp. 1058–1059.

CHAPTER 19

1. Based on information from Manual Schooners, "Double Identity," *Kiplinger's Personal Finance Magazine*, June 2000, p. 84; "Virtual Rivals," *The Economist*, May 20, 2000, p. NA; "Wingspan Sputters, Seeks Options," *Future Banker*, May 2000, p. 18S; Mercedes M. Cordon, "Wingspan Takes Flight," *Advertising Age*, November 1, 1999, p.S46; Wingspan.com web site, www.wingspan.com (July 10, 2000); and Gomez.com web site, www.gomez.com (July 14, 2000).
2. *Federal Reserve Bulletin*, June, 2000, p. A8.
3. *Ibid*, p. A7.
4. David Morgan, "Tech Boom Still Driving the Economy," *Financial Post*, July 12, 2000, p. C11.
5. The Federal Reserve Bank web site, www.federalreserve.gov (July 15, 2000).
6. Robert Farmighetti, ed., *The World Almanac and Book of Facts 2000* (Mahwah, NJ: K-III Reference Corporation, 1999), p. 116.
7. Office of Thrift Supervision web site, www.ots.treas.gov (July 15, 2000).
8. *Ibid*.
9. The Federal Deposit Insurance Corporation web site, www.fdic.gov (July 16, 2000).
10. U.S. Department of Commerce, Economics and Statistics Administration, and U.S. Census Bureau, *Statistical Abstract of the United States, 1999* (119th ed.), p. 524.
11. *Ibid.*, p. 527.
12. Staff writers, "Plus Ca Change: Fraud Fund" *Business2.0* Magazine, http://www.business2.com/content/magazine/filter/2000/06/01/12973?page=5 (June 1, 2000).

13. Susan Kuchinskas, "By Invitation Only," *Business2.0* Magazine, http://www.business2.com/content/magazine/indepth/2000/06/01/12927?page=1 (June 1, 2000).
14. Farmighetti, *op.cit.*, p. 116.
15. The Federal Deposit Insurance Corporation web site, www.fdic.gov (July 12, 2000).
16. The Dun & Bradstreet web site, www.dnb.com (July 16, 2000).
17. Mindy Charski, "Online Bill Paying Is Still Waiting for the Big Payoff," *U.S. News & World Report*, March 6, 2000, p. 57.
18. Based on information from the Stokes Interactive, "Interactive Services," "Client List," "Team Members," "Awards," "Samples," "CD-ROM," "CD-I," "Video CD," "RealTime MPEG Encoding," "Pitchman," "Web Page Development," "Production Services," (September 25, 1997), "Stokes Has Moved" and "The Stokes Group: A Word from the President," http://www.stokesfx.com/index.html (January 22, 2000).

CHAPTER 20

1. Based on information from Pamela L. More, "Name Your Price—For Everything?" *Business Week*, April 17, 2000, p. 72; Gary Cohen, "Why Captain Kirk Sings for Priceline," *U.S. News & World Report*, March 6, 2000, p. 38; Irene Gashurov and Noshua Watson, "The Big Score," *Fortune*, February 7, 2000, p. 134+; J. William Gurley, "The Great Art of Storytelling," *Fortune*, November 8, 1999, p. 300+; Peter Elkind, "The Hype Is Big, Really Big, at Priceline," *Fortune*, September 6, 1999, p. 193; Robert D. Hof, "Inside an Internet IPO," *Business Week*, September 6, 1999, p. 60+; Daniel Eisenberg, "Internet IPOs, What Goes Up," *Time*, June 21, 1999, p. 50; and Anne Tergeson, "IPOs: On the Outside Looking In," *Business Week*, April 19, 1999, p. 172.
2. Stuart F. Brown, "Good Bye Test Tubes, Hello Labs on a Chip," *Fortune*, October 11, 1999, p. 282(C)+.
3. *Advertising Age* web site, www.adage.com (June 28, 2000).
4. Nelson D. Schwartz, "Trial By Fire," *Fortune*, June 26, 2000, pp. 141–146.
5. *Mergent Handbook of Common Stocks*, Winter 1999–2000. (New York: Mergent FIS, Inc., 2000).
6. *Ibid.*
7. Susanne Koudsi, "Why Is This Sock Puppet Still Smiling?" *Fortune*, June 26, 2000, p. 54.
8. "Business Brief—Rite-Aid Corporation: Corporate Credit Rating Is Dropped a Notch by Standard & Poor's," *The Wall Street Journal*, October 8, 1999, p. A12.
9. "Business Brief—Reebok International Ltd: Standard & Poor's Lowers Long-Term Debt Ratings," *The Wall Street Journal*, January 28, 1998, p. B2.
10. Barnaby J. Feder, "Outsider Put at the Helm of Mercury," *New York Times*, February 4, 1997, p. D1.
11. *General Electric Annual Report*, General Electric Corporation web site, www.ge.com (June 28, 2000).
12. *Exxon/Mobil Annual Report*, Exxon/Mobil Corporation web site, www.exxonmobil.com (June 28, 2000).
13. Lee Clifford, "Anatomy of a Tech IPO," *Fortune*, June 26, 2000, p. 302.
14. Robert J. Samuelson, "Internet Joyride Can't Go on Forever," *Financial Post*, July 13, 2000, p. A18.
15. Nicholas Siropolis, *Small Business Management*, 6th ed. (Boston: Houghton Mifflin, 1997), p. 264.
16. Roger Fillion, "Rocky Mountain High Tech," *Business2.0* Magazine, http://www.business2.com/content/magazine/ebusiness/2000/06/01/12934 (June 1, 2000).
17. Based on information from Physician Sales & Service web site, www.pssd.com (July 2, 2000); Yahoo! Finance web site, http://finance.yahoo.com (July 3, 2000); Patrick Kelly, "Physician Sales & Service—Keys to Hypergrowth," http://www.fed.org/leadingcompanies/Nov96/case—study.html (October 2, 1997); and John Case, "The 10 Commandments of Hypergrowth," *Inc.*, September, 1996, p. 12.

CHAPTER 21

1. Based on information from Adam Cohen, "Wireless Summer," *Time*, May 29, 2000, p. 58; Christine Y. Chen, "Qualcomm Hits the Big Time," *Fortune*, May 15, 2000, p. 213+; Chana R. Schoenberger, "Eyes in the Skies," *Forbes*, May 15, 2000, p. 348; Amy Barrett, "The Best Performers," *Business Week*, March 27, 2000, p. 125; and Laura Washington, "Hitting the Jackpot," *Money*, March 1, 2000, p. 92; and "Qualcomm Incorporated," *Hoover's Handbook of American Business 2000*, p. 1186.
2. The Learning Center: Basics of Smart Investing, The Standard & Poor's personal wealth web site, www.personalwealth.com (June 24, 2000), Standard & Poor's Corporation, 25 Broadway, New York, NY 10004.
3. America Online Corporation web site, www.aol.com (June 20, 2000).
4. Brenon Daly, "Venture Forth," *Business2.0* Magazine, http://www.business2.com/content/magazine/investing/2000/06/01/12932 (June 1, 2000).
5. The New York Stock Exchange web site, www.nyse.com (June 20, 2000).
6. Rachel Lehmann-Haupt, "Following the Money Trail," *Business2.0* Magazine, http://www.business2.com/content/magazine/ebusiness/2000/06/01/10600 (June 1, 2000).
7. Mark Gimein, "Cool Companies 2000," *Fortune*, June 26, 2000, pp. 118–120.
8. Susanne Koudsi, "Why Is This Sock Puppet Still Smiling?," *Fortune*, June 26, 2000, p. 54.
9. Paul Bagnell, "Chip Outlook Keeps Investors on Knife-Edge," *Financial Post*, July 12, 2000, p. D1.
10. Based on information from http://www.csfbdirect.com (February 3, 2001); Steven T. Goldberg, Courtney McGrath, Christine Pulfrey, "Online Trading's Agony & Ecstasy," *Kiplinger's Personal Finance Magazine*, October 2000, p. 40; David Fairlamb, "This Bank Keeps Growing and Growing . . ." *BusinessWeek*, September 11, 2000, p. 134; Stephane Fitch, "Brokers," *Forbes*, September 11, 2000, p.120; and Margaret Popper, "Brokers Clicks of the Trade," *BusinessWeek*, May 22, 2000, p. 154.

APPENDIX B

1. *U.S. Industry and Trade Outlook*, 1999 (Washington DC: U.S. Department of Commerce, 1999), pp. 44–42 and 43.

credits

BOX CREDITS

Chapter 1 **p. 3** Feliciano Garcia, "The Lists," *Fortune*, April 17, 2000, pp. 289+; Carol J. Loomis, "Sam Would Be Proud," *Fortune*, April 17, 2000, pp. 130+; Amy Barrett, "The Best Performers," *Business Week*, March 27, 2000, pp. 124+; Robert Frick, "Shootout on Wall Street," *Kiplinger's Personal Finance Magazine*, March, 2000. p. 50; Geoffrey Colvin, "America's Most Admired Companies," *Fortune*, February 21, 2000, pp. 108+; Jennifer Reingold and Marcia Stepanek, with Diane Brady, "Why the Productivity Revolution Will Spread," *Business Week*, February 14, 2000, pp. 112+; and Lisa DiCarlo, "America's Most Wired Companies," *PC Computing*, December, 1999, p. 108. **p. 12** Based on information from Campbell Soup Company, "Welcome to Campbell's Labels for Education 2000," http://www.labelsforeducation.com/welcome.asp (accessed April 15, 2000), "Good Neighbor Program," http://www.tomthumb.com/goodneighbor.htm (accessed April 15, 2000), Ronald McDonald House Charities, "RMHC Press Releases" http://www.rmhc.com/press/2000releases/04062000/0406200release.html, April 6, 2000; "RMHC Press Releases," http://www.rmhc.com/press/1999releases/092499/092499rmhc.html, September 24, 1999; "About RMHC—Education and Social Responsibility," http://www.rmhc.com/about/programs/education/rmh/rmh.html (accessed April 12, 2000), "McDonald's U.S.A. Earth Effort," http://www.com/mcdonaldland/helpingout/environ.html (accessed April 12, 2000), Michael Ryan, "They Lead the Way," *The Dallas Morning News Parade Magazine*, April 9, 2000, pp. 4–6; Geoffrey Colvin, "America's Most Admired Companies," *Fortune*, February 21, 2000, p. 110. **p. 25** John Huey, Jr. "Heavy Lifting," *Fortune*, April 17, 2000, p. 40, Nicholas Stein, "Fortune 5 Hundred," *Fortune*, April 17, 2000, p. 126, Feliciano Garcia, "The Lists," *Fortune*, April 17, 2000, p. 294; "Fortune 500 Largest Corporations," *Fortune*, April 17, 2000, pp. F-1, F-3, F-29; "Fortune 1 Thousand Ranked With Industries, *Fortune*, April 17, 2000, pp. F-29, F-78; and *Hoover's Guide to American Business 2000, A Profile of 750 Major U.S. Companies*, (Austin, TX, Hoovers, Inc., 1999), pp. 406–407, pp. 482–483, pp. 724–725, pp. 774–775.

Chapter 2 **p. 40** Based on information from "Doing Well By Doing Good," *The Economist*, April 22, 2000, pp. 65–67; Allen L. White, "Sustainability and the Accountable Corporation," *Environment*, October 1999, pp. 30+. **p. 41** Based on information from Pamela Sebastian Ridge, "Business Bulletin: Ethics Programs Aren't Stemming Employee Misconduct, a Study Indicates," *Wall Street Journal*, May 11, 2000, p. A1; Susan J. Wells, "Turn Employees Into Saints?" *HR*Magazine, December 1999, pp. 49+; Marsha Austin, "Startups Overlooking Ethics Training," *Denver Business Journal*, November 5, 1999, p. 3A. **p. 48** Based on information from Dawn Stover, "The Business of Education," *Popular Science*, November 1999, pp. 80+; Edvaldo Pereira Lima, "Seeding a World of Transformation," *Industry Week*, September 6, 1999, p. 30.

Chapter 3 **p. 80** Based on information from Bill Roberts, "Stratton Sclavos," *Internet World*, January 15, 2000, http://www.iw.com/print/2000/01/15/features/20000115-interview.html (May 23, 2000); Matthew W. Beale, "CyberTrust OK to Export Crypto Worldwide," *E-Commerce Times*, September 27, 1999, http://www.ecommercetimes.com/news/articles/990927-3.shtml (May 23, 2000); Matthew W. Beale and Robert Conlin, "China's Central Bank Leads Quest for E-Commerce Security," *E-Commerce Times*, September 1, 1999, http://www.ecommercetimes.com/news/articles/990901-1.shtml (May 23, 2000). **p. 85** Based on information from Paul Magnusson, "China Trade: Will Clinton Pull It Off?" *Business Week*, May 29, 2000, pp. 74, 76; Keith Bradsher, "Rallying Round the China Bill, Hungrily," *New York Times*, May 21, 2000, sec. 3, pp. 1, 18–19; David L. Aaron, "PNTR and WTO Accession for China: Good for the U.S. and Good for American Small Businesses," speech before the Economic Strategy Institute's Panel on China/Permanent Normal Trade Relations, March 2, 2000, http://www.ita.doc/gov/media/ChinaWto.htm (May 14, 2000). **p. 88** Based on information from John Schacht, "Manufacturers Go Global to Expand Market Share," *The Charlotte Business Journal*, April 24, 2000, http://www.bizjournals.com/charlotte/stories/2000/04/24/focus2.html (May 23, 2000); "Export Readiness Prerequisites," *International Business Academy*, (n.d.), http://iba.tradecompass.com/eras/content.asp (May 23, 2000); "Developing an Export Strategy," *Unz & Company*, (n.d.), http://www.unzco.com/basicguide/c1.html (May 14, 2000).

Strategic Case I **p. 100** Based on information from the Orbis Fiscal Year 1999 Annual Report; Orbis web site (http://www.orbis.com).

Chapter 4 **p. 115** Based on information from Heather Green, Mike France, Marcia Stepanek, and Amy Borrus, "Online Privacy: It's Time for Rules in Wonderland," *Business Week*, March 20, 2000, pp. 83–96.

Chapter 5 **p. 130** Based on information from the Procter & Gamble web site at www.pg.com accessed April 30, 2000; "2000: The Power of Invention: How We Live," *Newsweek*, Winter, 1997, p. 39; and *Hoover's 500: Profiles of America's Largest Business Enterprises*, Hoover's Business Press, (Austin, Texas), copyright 1996, p. 401. **p. 141** Nicholas Stem, "Winning the War to Keep Top Talent," *Fortune*, May 29, 2000, p. 132+; Erin J. Walter, "Finders and Keepers," *Austin American-Statesman*, April 30, 2000, http://dallasnews.com/technology/71540_perks_30rec.AR.html.; John Byrne, with Andy Reinhardt and Robert D. Hof, "The Search for the Young and the Gifted," *Business Week*, October 4, 1999, p. 28. **p. 148** Based on information from Doug Halonen, "AOL's Ad Interruptus?" *Advertising Age*, April 3, 2000, p. 34; Steward Alsop, "Good News," *Fortune*, February 7, 2000, p. 56; Margaret Boitano, "These Guys Want It All," *Fortune*, February 7, 2000, pp. 70+; Doug Donovan, "Golden Hairball," *Forbes*, February 7, 2000, p. 53; Brett Pulley, "Morning After," Forbes, February 7, 2000, p. 54; and William J. Holstein, "AOL Vows Openness," *U.S. News & World Report*, March 13, 2000, p. 45.

Chapter 6 **p. 159** Based on information from Daniel McGinn, "'It's All About Acceleration': Incubators," *Newsweek*, March 20, 2000, p. 74B; James Lardner, "Ideas On the Assembly Line," *U.S. News & World Report*, March 20, 2000, p. 48. **p. 165** Based on information from Rochelle Sharpe, "Teen Moguls," *Business Week*, May 29, 2000, pp. 108–118; "High-Tech Teens," *Mclean's*, June 7, 1999, p. 9. **p. 179** Based on information from Amy Zuber, "Minority Franchisees Prosper With Help From McD Support Groups," *Nation's Restaurant News*, February 14, 2000, p. 26; Milford Prewitt, "Minority Franchisees Make Gains at Chains," *Nation's Restaurant News*, February 7, 2000, p. 1; Hala Moddelmog, "Increased Number of Women Entrepreneurs Does Not Equal More Female Franchisees," *Nation's Restaurant News*, May 24, 1999, p. 68.

Strategic Case II **p. 181** Based on information from http://www.awards.com, accessed January 31, 2001; Victor Godinez, "Online Shopping World Expanding at Staggering Rate," *The Dallas Morning News*, October 13, 2000, p. K2067; Julia King, "Mom-and-Pop Shops Gain Clout on Web," *Computerworld*, July 31, 2000, p. 8; Stephanie Neil, "Employees Benefit—It Takes More Than Cash to Make Workers Happy," *eWeek*, May 8, 2000, p. 80; and Richard Metters, Michael Kentzenberg, and George Gillen, "Welcome Back, Mom and Pop," *Harvard Business Review*, May 2000, p. 24.

Chapter 7 **p. 191** Based on information from Steve Hamm, "The E.Biz 25: Larry Ellison," *Business Week*, May 15, 2000, p. EB 40; "He's No Techie, But He Loves the Web," *Business Week*, January 31, 2000, p. 22+; Jennifer Reingold, "In Search of Leadership," *Business Week*, November 15, 1999, pp. 172, 176; John R. Darling and Thomas M. Box, "Keys for Success in the Leadership of Multinational Corporations, 1990 Through 1997," *SAM Advanced Management Journal*, August 1999, p. 16+; Michael Barrier, "Leadership Skills Employees Respect," *Nation's Business*, January 1999, pp. 28+. **p. 193** Based on information from Debra Sparks, "The Buck Stops Where?" *Business Week*, May 15, 2000, p. 154; Bernard Condon, "Conseco on the Ropes," *Forbes*, May 15, 2000, http://www.forbes.com/forbes/00/0529/6511058a.htm (May 18, 2000); Jennifer Reingold, "Executive Pay," *Business Week*, April 17, 2000, pp. 100–112; David Barboza, "Taking the Starch Out of an American Icon," *New York Times*, March 19, 2000, sec. 3, pp. 1, 16. **p. 201** Based on information from Greg Dalton, "Ford Explorer," *The Industry Standard*, May 1, 2000, p. 206; Kathleen Melymuka, "Survey Finds Companies Lack E-Commerce Blueprint; Established Businesses, Management Slow to Adapt to Online Requirements," *Computerworld*, April 17, 2000, p. 38; Don Tapscott, "Minds Over Matter," *Business 2.0*, March 2000, pp. 220–227; Jim Highsmith, "There Are Projects and There Are Internet Projects," *Computerworld*, March 27, 2000, http://www.computerworld.com/home/print.nsf/all/000327CDCE (May 19, 2000); Lisa Hamm-Greenawalt, "Careers in 2000: Labor Crunch," *Internet World*, January 1, 2000, http://www.iw.com/print/2000/01/01/business/20000101-crunch.html (May 19, 2000).

Chapter 8 **p. 219** Based on information from John Mariotti, "On Management: Strategic Outsourcing Can Be Powerful Medicine," *Industry Week*, April 19, 1999, http://www.industryweek.com/columns/asp/columns.asp?ColumnId=440 (May 31, 2000); David Raths, "Let the Net Do It," *Inc. Tech 1999*, no. 1, pp. 52–58; Bruce Caldwell, "Web Host Appeal," *Information Week*, December 21, 1998, pp. 18–20. **p. 226** Based on information from Lance Secretan, "Spirit At Work: Values-Centered Leadership Emphasizes Compassion, Not War," *Industry Week*, July 12, 1999, http://www.industryweek.com/IWGC/columns.asp?ColumnID=284; Paul Orfalea, "My Biggest Mistake," *Inc.*, March 1999, p. 88; Leah Curtin and Roy Simpson, "You Want Me To Do What?" *Health Management Technology*, October 1999, p. 30; "Small Virtues," *Business Week*, February 28, 2000, p. F 4. **p. 228** Based on information from Malcolm Fleschner, "Change Agent," *Selling Power*, March 2000, pp. 78–81; Peter F. Drucker, "Change Leaders," *Inc.*, June 1999, pp. 65–72; Jeffrey L. Seglin, "The Future of Business," *Inc.*, May 1999, p. 102.

Chapter 9 **p. 241** Based on information from the Rubbermaid web site at www.rubbermaid.com (accessed May 21, 2000); *Hoover's Handbook of American Business 2000, A Profile of 750 Major U.S. Companies*, copyright 1999 by Hoover's Inc. (Austin, Texas, 2000) pp. 1026–1027; Andrew Osterland, "Fixing Rubbermaid is No Snap," *Business Week*, September 20, 1999, pp. 108+, copyright 1999 by the McGraw-Hill Companies, Inc. **p. 247** Based on information from Cisco Systems, www.cisco.com (June 12, 2000); *Hoover's Handbook of American Business 2000* (Austin, Texas, 2000), Cisco Systems, Inc., pp. 370–371; Irene Gashurov and Angela Key, "There's Something About Cisco," *Fortune*, May 15, 2000, pp. 114+; and Cisco Systems 1999 Annual Report. **p. 261** Based on information from Jennifer Reingold and Marcia Stepanek, with Diane Bradey, "Why the Productivity Revolution Will Spread," *Business Week*, February 14, 2000, pp. 112+; "Robotics," *The Cutting Edge, An Encyclopedia of Advanced Technologies*, (New York: Oxford University Press, Inc.), copyright 2000, pp. 231–234; Robert Heller, "Thing-making Has a Future Too," *Management Today*, August 1999, pp. 32+; John Teresko, "New Eyes in Manufacturing," *Industry Week*, April 19, 1999, pp. 47+.

Strategic Case III **p. 267** Based on information from Trevor Delaney, "Luring Back the Leery Investor," *SmartMoney*, February 2001, p. 48; "Online Bank Tops $1B in New Net Deposits," *Washington Business Journal*, January 4, 2001, http://www.bizjournals.com/washington/stories/2001/01/01/daily14.html; Michael Mahoney, "E*Trade Soars after Beating the Street," *E-Commerce Times*, October 20, 2000, http://www.ecommercetimes.com/news/articles2000/001020-3.shtml; "E*Trade Cautiously Enters Japan," *Redherring.com*, September 25, 2000, http://www.redherring.com/industries/2000/0925/ind-etrade092500.html; Maria Trombly, "E*Trade Fined for Slow Complaint Response; Company Cites High Growth Rate," *Computerworld*, May 8, 2000, p. 8; Maria Trombly, "E*Trade Makes Move from Clicks to Bricks; Acquisition Makes Brokerage No. 3 ATM Operator," *Computerworld*, March 20, 2000, p. 4; Chet Dembeck, "Latest Hacker Attack Cripples Online Brokerage," *E-Commerce Times*, February 25, 2000, http://www.ecommercetimes.com/news/articles2000/000225-6.shtml; Andy Wang, "Another Day, Another Outage," *E-Commerce Times*, February 25, 1999, http://www.ecommercetimes.com/news/articles/990225-stock.shtml; "The Story of E*Trade," http://www.etrade.com, accessed January 22, 2000.

Chapter 10 **p. 279** Based on information from Andrea C. Poe, "Face Value," *HRMagazine*, May 2000, http://www.shrm.org/hrmagazine/articles/0500poe.htm#acp (May 26, 2000); Chuck Salter, "Jeff Daniel," *Fast Company*, December 1999, pp. 206–212; "Finding the Next Generation," *PC Week*, February 22, 1999, p. 98. **p. 284** Based on information from Daniel Roth, "My Job At the Container Store," *Fortune*, January 10, 2000, pp. 74–78; Diana Kunde, "Magazine Ranks Three Dallas Firms Among Nation's Best Employers," *Dallas Morning News*, December 21, 1999, http://web.lexis-nexis.com (April 17, 2000). **p. 288** Based on information from "Groom Your Workforce," *PC Computing.com*, March 2000, pp. 137–138; Sally Roberts, "Training Starts to Click," *Business Insurance*, January 17, 2000, pp. 3+; Kim Kiser, "10 Things We Know So Far About Online Training," *Training*, November 1999, pp. 66–72.

Chapter 11 **p. 304** Based on information from Patricia Chisolm, "What the Boss Needs To Know," *Maclean's*, May 29, 2000, http://www.macleans.ca/pub-doc/2000/05/29/cover/35015.shtml (June 6, 2000); Michelle Conlin and Peter Coy, "The Wild New Workforce," *Business Week*, December 6, 1999, pp. 39–44; Andrea C. Poe, "When In Rome," *HR Magazine*, November 1999, pp. 61+; John Russell, "Working Overseas Can Cloud Benefits Picture," *Houston Chronicle*, May 16, 1999, p. 3+. **p. 310** Based on information from Gertie Ampil Tirona, "Women Power Making Inroads in the Workplace," *BusinessWorld*, January 5, 2000; H. Hammonds, "Work and Life: Helen Wilkinson," *Fast Company*, December 1999, pp. 187–196; Meg Lundstrom, "Mommy, Do You Love Your Company More Than Me?" *Business Week*, December 20, 1999, p. 175; Peter York, "The Gender Agenda," *Management Today*, October 1999, pp. 56+; Mary Hale, "He Says, She Says: Gender and Worklife," *Public Administration Review*, September 1999, pp. 410+. **p. 313** Based on information from Michael A. Verespej, "Stressed Out," *Industry Week*, February 21, 2000, http://www.industryweek.com/currentarticles/asp/articles.asp?ArticleID=751 (March 9, 2000); Regis Coccia, Shelly Reese, "Healthy Minds Have Great Ideas," *Business and Health*, December 1999, p. 16; Diane McDougall, "Feeling Stressed?" *CMA Management*, November 1999, p. 14.

Chapter 12 **p. 339** Based on information from David Field, "Boeing Engineers End Weeks-Long Strike," *USA Today*, March 20, 2000, p. 12A; "Boeing, Union Reach Pact," *CNNfn*, March 17, 2000, http://cnnfn.com/2000/03/17/companies/boeing; Jeff Cole, "Striking Boeing Workers Warn Regulators of Plane-Safety Risks," *Wall Street Journal*, March 17, 2000, http://interactive.wsj.com/archive/retrieve.cgi?id-SB95322689434602809.djm; Jeff Cole, "Boeing Halts Research Effort on New Jet Line Amid Strike," *Wall Street Journal*, March 15, 2000, http://interactive.wsj.com/archive/retrieve.cgi?id-SB953077722920548480.djm (March 17, 2000); Jane Lii and Margaret Steen, "Boeing Strike Puts Engineers in Unusual Position," *San Jose Mercury News*, March 14, 2000, http://www.sjmercury.com (April 5, 2000). **p. 341** Based on information from "GE Has Mixed Plans for Indiana Refrigerator Plant," *Industrial Maintenance and Plant Operation*, October, 1999, p. 6; Bill Koenig, "Bloomington, Ind., Suffers Bumpy Transition from Old Manufacturing Base," *Indianapolis Star*, August 29, 1999, http://web.lexis-nexis.com; (April 24, 2000); "GE To Shutter Two U.S. Plants," *Ozone Depletion Network Online Today*, August 4, 1999, http://web4.insite2.gale.com (April 24, 2000). **p. 346** Based on information from Robyn Meredith, "Five Questions For Roy S. Roberts," *New York Times*, January 23, 2000, sec. 3, p. 3; Charlotte W. Craig, "Ford Names Leader For Parts Unit; Spin-Off Possible," *Detroit Free Press*, November 13, 1999, http://web.lexis-nexis.com (April 18, 2000); Ted Evanoff, "General Motors, UAW Show Progress on Agreements with Locals," *Detroit Free*

Press, October 28, 1999, http://web.lexis-nexis.com (April 18, 2000); Joann Muller, "The Auto Talks," Who Really Won," *Business Week*, October 25, 1999, pp. 98, 102.

Strategic Case IV **p. 351** Based on information from Ed Duggan, "Layoffs to Hit Motorola's Boynton Facility," *South Florida Business Journal*, December 6, 2000, http://www.bizjournals.com/southflorida/stories/2000/12/04/daily49.html; John C. Tanner, "Get Organized! Centralized Recruitment in a Global World," *Telecom Asia*, July 2000, p. 79; "Talent Bank," *Malaysian Business*, May 10, 2000; "What's in It for You?" and "HR 2000," http://www.motorola.com (January 18, 2001); Robert W. Galvin, "Quality Thinking," *Executive Excellence*, February 1997, pp. 15–16; David Kirkpatrick, "Child-Free Employees See Another Side of Equation," *Wall Street Journal*, interactive edition, April 2, 1997; Motorola, Inc., "What is HR 2000?" http://www.mot.com (October 8, 1997); Motorola, Inc., "Motorola Timeline-Highlights," http://www.mot.com (December 3, 1997); Richard Koonce, "The Motorola Story: An Interview," *Training & Development*, August 1997, pp. 26–27; Elizabeth Sheley, "High Tech Recruiting Methods," *HRMagazine*, September 1995; and Motorola, Inc., "Lifesteps" (Motorola benefits package).

Chapter 13 **p. 361** Based on information from "Global Activists Raise Concerns About Tobacco Industry Political Influence in Tobacco Treaty Discussions," *PR Newswire*, January 26, 2000, p. 386; William M. Pride and O.C. Ferrell, *Marketing: Concepts and Strategies* (Boston: Houghton Mifflin, 2000), p. 280; Marianne C. Delpo, "Tobacco Abroad: Legal and Ethical Implications of Marketing Dangerous United States Products Overseas," *Business and Society Review*, Summer 1999, pp. 147–162; "WHO Repeats Call For Worldwide Tobacco Ad Ban," *Advertising Age International*, June 1, 1998, http://www.adage.com (June 23, 2000); "Tobacco Ads, Sponsorship To Be Outlawed in Europe," *Advertising Age International*, May 14, 1998, http://www.adage.com (June 23, 2000). **p. 365** Based on information from Bill Donahue, "Embracing the Lizard," *Convenience Stores Decisions*, April 2000, http://www.sobebev.com/healthyrefreshment/news_co040100A.htm (June 23, 2000); Susan Hansen, "Herbal-Tonic Bottler Has Healthy Start," *Inc.*, June 1999, pp. 21–22; "SoBe Succeeds By Selling Lifestyle," *Food Processing*, September 1999, p. 28; Steve Dwyer, "Shooting From the 'Hip,' " *Prepared Foods*, October 1999, p. 21. **p. 372** Based on information from Michael Grebb, "Behavioral Science," *Business 2.0*, March 2000, pp. 112–114; Steve Hamm, "An Eagle Eye on Customers," *Business Week*, February 21, 2000, pp. 66–76; Judith Mottl, "Customer Tracking: It's Not Just Web-Site Hits—Tools and Services Help E-Retailers Monitor Customer Behavior Online and Tailor Advertising," *Information Week*, February 7, 2000, p. 104.

Chapter 14 **p. 390** Based on information from David Evans, "Nicolas Hayek Sees Affinities in Making Movies and Watches, David Evans Finds Swatch Head Stages Timely Job Switch," *South China Morning Post*, April 3, 2000; Carol Matlack, "Swatch: Ready For Net Time?" *Business Week*, February 14, 2000, p. 61. **p. 395** Based on information from "Nike Losing Ground in the Fickle Worlds of Teen Cool," *United Press International*, April 10, 2000; Louise Lee, "Take Our Swoosh, Please," *Business Week*, February 21, 2000, p. 128; Louise Lee, "Can Nike Still Do It?" *Business Week*, February 21, 2000, pp. 120–128; Jo Wrighton, "Just Do It: Nike Rebounds," *Institutional Investor*, January 2000, p. 22. **p. 401** Based on information from Pamela L. Moore, "Name Your Price—For Everything?" *Business Week*, April 17, 2000, pp. 72–78; David Orgel, "The Priceline Proposition," *Supermarket News*, February 14, 2000, pp. 1+.

Chapter 15 **p. 429** Based on information from "Shakeout Seen in E-Commerce Players," *Los Angeles Times*, April 12, 2000, part C, p. 3; Janet Ginsburg, "Extreme Retailing," *Business Week*, December 20, 1999, pp. 120–128; Joshua Macht, "Mortar Combat," *Inc. Tech 1999*, no. 3, pp. 102–110. **p. 430** Based on information from "7-Eleven Japan To Sell Online With Net Start-up," *Asia Pulse News*, April 12, 2000, p. 51; Irene M. Kunii, "From Convenience Store to Online Behemoth?" *Business Week*, April 10, 2000, pp. 64+; "7-Eleven Japan Forms Online-Sales Joint Venture," *Japan Weekly Monitor*, February 7, 2000; Tokihiko Umezu, "Convenient Tickets Strike Chord with Music Fans," *Mainichi Daily News*, January 27, 2000. **p. 439** Based on information from Candace Goforth, "Akron, Ohio-Based Shipping Firm Takes FedEx Name," *Akron Beacon Journal*, January 20, 2000; Victoria Reynolds Harrow, "King of the Road," *Inside Business*, November 1999.

Chapter 16 **p. 461** Based on information from Rekha Balu, "Whirlpool Gets Real With Customers," *Fast Company*, December 1999, pp. 74, 76; "New Products At the Touch of a Button," *Commerce Business* Magazine, July 1, 1999. **p. 464** Based on information from Michelle Jeffers and Evantheia Schibsted, "Sample This," *Business 2.0*, March 2000, p. 124; "Ingredients.com and Bluefly Team Up on Holiday Promotion," Ingredients.com news release, December 21, 1999, http://www.prnewswire.com (April 19, 2000): Sloane Lucas, "Dot Shops," *Adweek*, November 8, 1999, pp. IQ66–IQ72. **p. 466** Based on information from Stephen Manes, "Software, Lies, and Videotape," *PC World*, May 1999, p. 316; Tobi Elkin, "Microsoft Tries Soft Sell, Plays Hardball with DOJ; Spokesmen Gates, Ballmer Battle Bad PR About Breakup," *Advertising Age*, May 8, 2000, p. 26; "Microsoft Hires Community PR Chief," *Marketing*, February 3, 2000, p. 5; "Microsoft: Crafting Image Through Public Relations," *Marketing 2000e* (Boston: Houghton Mifflin, 2000), pp. 481–482.

Strategic Case V **p. 475** Based on information from "K'NEX Industries," *Discount Store News*, March 20, 2000, p. 23; "New Toy Ploy from Pizza Hut," *Advertising Age*, March 25, 1999, http://www.adage.com; Elizabeth Bennett, "Its K'NEX with Education," "*Philadelphia Business Journal*, August 27, 1999, pp. 25+; T. L. Stanley, "K'Nex Logs Link to Lincoln Logs," *Brandweek*, February 1, 1999, p. 12; Joseph Pereira, "Toys: Slighted in U.S., Whimsical Toy Is a Wow in Europe," *Wall Street Journal*, May 21, 1998, pp. B1+; Lisa Friedman Miner, "They're All K'nected," *Chicago Daily Herald*, January 23, 1997, pp. 4–1, 4–3; Jane M. Von Bergen, "Success Is Nothing to Play At," *Philadelphia Inquirer*, Aug. 25, 1997, pp. F1, F12; John T. George, "Joel Glickman: Hatfield Toymaker Connects with K'nex," *Business Ledger*, April 1997, p. 8; and K'NEX Industries, Inc., press kit.

Chapter 17 **p. 485** Based on information from Alan Goldstein, "All work, no PLAY," *The Dallas Morning News*, September 20, 2000, E-commerce Section H, pp. 1H, 6H; Michael Schrage, "E-Mail or E-Sting? Your Boss Knows, But He's Not Telling," *Fortune*, March 20, 2000, p. 240; Michael Barrier, "What Message Is Your E-Mail Really Sending?" *Nation's Business*, May 1999, p. 13; and "The Ins and Outs of E-Mail," *USA Today*, August 1998, p. 12. **p. 489** Based on information from Jeremy Kahn, "Proving Napster Legal Is a Tough Job for Boies," *Fortune*, October 2, 2000, p. 50+; Dimitry Elias Leger, "Pop Blows Up; Whither Web Film," *Fortune*, October 2, 2000, p. 62; James Lardner, "The Empire Strikes Back," *U.S. News & World Report*, September 18, 2000, p. 54; James Evans and Cathleen Moore, "MP3.com Faces the Music in Legal Battle," *InfoWorld*, September 11, 2000, p. 3; Sean M. Dugan, "Net Prophet," *InfoWorld*, September 4, 2000, p. 108; Calvin Reid, "Hollywood vs. 2600.com," *Publishers Weekly*, September 4, 2000, p. 47; Ron White, "How It Works: Napster," *Ziff Davis Smart Business for the New Economy*, September 1, 2000, p. 162; Lev Grossman, "Digital Divisiveness," *Time*, August 28, 2000, p. 40; Thomas Claburn, "The End of the Web as You Know It," *Ziff Davis Smart Business for the New Economy*, July 1, 2000, p. 46; Janathan Takiff, "While Some Musicians Decry New Technology, Others Experience Deja Vu," *Knight-Ridder/Tribune News Service*, June 6, 2000, p. k5866; Steven V. Brull, "The Record Industry Can't Stop Music," *Business Week*, May 15, 2000, p. 50; Patricia L. Casey, "Be Your Own Copyright Cop," *AV Video Multimedia Producer*, May, 2000, p. 57; and "Piracy on the Net: Why It Needs More Policing," *Business Week*, January 24, 2000, p. 28. **p. 497** Based on information from Amy Zuckerman, "Standards Bodes Struggle to Stay Current," *Electronic News*, July 31, 2000, p. 16; Walter Wingo, "Standards Update," *Design News*, July 17, 2000, p. 20; Amy Zuckerman, "Standards Efforts Offer Glimpse into Future," *Electronic News*, January 3, 2000, p. 14; and the web sites for www.iso.ch; www.iec.ch; and www.itc.ch accessed on December 13, 2000.

Chapter 18 **p. 515** Based on information from Elizabeth McDonald, "Are Those Revenues for Real?" *Forbes*, May 29, 2000, p. 108; Karen Kroll, "SEC Chief Scrutinizes (Mis)Reporting," *Industry Week*, April 17, 2000, p. 20; and Carol J. Loomis, et al., "Lies, Damned Lies, and Managed Earnings," *Fortune*, August 2, 1999, p. 74+. **p. 522** Inventory values for The Goodyear Tire & Rubber Company and J.C. Penney were based on information from The Yahoo! Marketguide Finance web site at http://yahoo.marketguide.com on July 31, 2000. **p. 531** Based on information from "Tomorrow's Stock Markets," *The Economist*, June 17, 2000, p. 19; John S. McClenahen, "Accounting for Global Change," *Industry Week*, June 12, 2000, p. 135; Mike McNamee, "Can the SEC Make Foreign Companies Play by Its Rules?" *Business Week*, March 6, 2000, p. 46; Thomas K. Grose, "Balancing the Books," *Time International*, February 14, 2000, p. 62+;

Emily Thornton, "The Secret Pour Out," *Business Week*, August 2, 1999. p. 50+; and Jeffrey E. Garten, "Global Accounting Rules? Not So Fast," *Business Week*, April 5, 1999, p. 26.

Strategic Case VI **p. 541** Based on information from http://www.ups.com accessed January 12, 2001; *Hoover's Handbook of American Business 2000, A Profile of 750 Major U.S. Companies*, Copyright 1999 by Hoover's Inc. (Austin, Texas 2000), pp. 1444–1445; "Those Who Can . . . Those Who Cannot: Winners and Losers in the Digital Age," Address by Jim Kelly, Chairman, UPS, *Vital Speeches*, Copyright 1998, November 15, 1998, p. 89.

Chapter 19 **p. 555** Based on information from the About.com web site at www.about.com on July 7, 2000; "U.S. Seeks Curbs on 'Predatory' Lending," *The New York Times*, June 21, 2000, p. C10; Nicholas Kulish, "Policy Makers to Scrutinize Predatory-Lending Abuses," *The Wall Street Journal*, May 24, 2000, p. A8(E); Michael Schroeder, "Summers Calls for Legislation to Curb Predatory Lending in Mortgage Markets," *The Wall Street Journal*, April 13, 2000, p. A2(E); Michael Schroeder, "Fannie Mae Sets Campaign to Improve Lending Image, Curbing Predatory Lending," *The Wall Street Journal*, April 11, 2000, p. A28(E). **p. 561** Based on information from the Consumer Credit Counseling Credit Service web site at www.cccs.com on July 15, 2000; the Debt Conselors of America web site at www.dca.org on July 15, 2000; Ellen Stark, "The Truth About Credit Counselors," *Money*, December 1997, p. 51; Deborah Collins, "We're Drowning in Debt," *Good Housekeeping*, January 1997, p. 56; Tracey Longo, "Credit Crunched," *Kiplinger's Personal Finance Magazine*, August 1996, p. 61. **p. 571** Based on information from Daniel Tynan, "Privacy 2000 in Web We Trust?" *PC World*, June 2000, p. 103; Harry Wessel, "Consumer News and Notes," *The Orlando Sentinel*, June 27, 2000, p. K4759; and Catherine Siskos, "Making History," *Kiplinger's Personal Finance Magazine*, May 2000, p. 96; The Experian Credit Bureau web site at www.experian.com on July 10, 2000, The Trans Union Corporation web site at www.transunion.com on July 10, 2000, and Equifax Information Services web site at www.equifax.com on July 10, 2000.

Chapter 20 **p. 582** Based on information from Sabrina Tavernise in Moscow, "I Want The Market to Work," *Business Week*, April 17, 2000, p. 158; Katrina Vanden Heuvel, "Who Is Putin?", *The Nation*, April 17, 2000, p. 3; Paul Starobin with Sabrina Tavernise in Moscow, "A New Home for Russian Capital—Russia," *Business Week*, March 6, 2000, p. 58; Andrew Meier, "In from the Cold: Western Investors Are Returning to Russia," *Time International*, February 7, 2000, p. 46+. **p. 594** Based on information from "Rampant Abuse," *The Economist*, May 20, 2000, p. 10; William Giese, "Painting the Tape," *Kiplinger's Personal Finance Magazine*, April, 2000, pp. 80+; Amy Feldman, "The Seedy World of Online Stock Scams: Stock Fraud Is One of the Net's Fastest-Growing Industries. Here's What You Need to Know to Protect Yourself," *Money*, February 1, 2000, pp. 143+. **p. 598** Based on information from Bank of America web site (www.bankofamerica.com/small business) accessed June 22, 2000; Sharon Nelton, "Widening The Web Of Resources," *Nation's Business*, June 1999, p. 37; David R. Evanson; Art Beroff, "Ready, set . . . ," *Entrepreneur*, February 1998, pp. 58+; Wendy M. Beech, "Businesses Get Help Going High-tech: Microsoft and Compaq Partner with SBA to Introduce New Technology Program." *Black Enterprise*, June 1997, p. 41.

Chapter 21 **p. 615** Based on information from Paul J. Lim, Sage Dillon, James M. Pethokoukis, Mindy Charski, "Online Investors Need Help Surfing Through the Shoals," *U.S. News & World Report*, May 8, 2000, pp. 54+; James M. Pethokoukis and Fred Vogelstein, "Market Mania," *U.S. News & World Report*, April 3, 2000, p. 34; and Robert Safian, "Brokerages' Brave New World," *Money*, April 1, 2000, p. 140+. **p. 617** Based on information from Richard Huff, "Against 'Millionaire' Rivals Can Only Bide Their Time," *New York Daily News*, May 24, 2000, p. K2391; Andrew Phillips, "Who Doesn't Want to Watch Regis?" *Maclean's*, April 10, 2000, p. 63.; and Raymond A. Schroth, "Quiz Shows," *National Catholic Reporter*, February 11, 2000, p. 12. **p. 634** Based on information from Michael Sivy, "Select Stocks: Trying to Reach Your Financial Goals and Still Stay on Safe Ground? A Portfolio of the Blue Chips Most Popular with Investing Clubs Can Help." *Money*, May 15, 2000, pp. 70+; Nanette Byrnes in New York, "Sifting for Clues," *Business Week*, March 27, 2000, pp. 138, 140; Kathy Jones and James Ramage, "Remember Dividends?" *Kiplinger's Personal Finance Magazine*, October 1999, p. 86.

Strategic Case VII **p. 645** Based on information from http://www.worldlyinvestor.com accessed on February 4, 2001; http://www.money.com accessed on January 15, 2001; and Daniel Kadlec, "How to Navigate the Storm," *Time*, January 8, 2001, pp. 23–25.

Appendix A **p. A8** Based on information from Jack R. Kapoor, Les Dlabey, and Robert J. Hughes, *Personal Finance*, Sixth Edition, p. 47. Copyright © 2001 by the McGraw-Hill Companies. Adapted by permission.

PHOTO CREDITS

Part I (top) David Young Wolff/Photoedit; (bottom) Hugh Setton/Tony Stone Images.

Chapter 1 **Page 3** David R. Frazier/Photolibrary. **Page 5** John Chapple/Online USA. **Page 7** AP Photo/Nati Harnik. **Page 10** Robert McClaran/SABA. **Page 12** Jeff Greenberg/Photoedit. **Page 13** Rhoda Sidney/Stock Boston. **Page 21** © AFP/Corbis. **Page 27** Mark Richards/Photoedit.

Chapter 2 **Page 36** Courtesy of Texas Instruments. **Page 38** AP Photo/Ron Edmonds. **Page 40** Andrew Holbrooke/Sipa. **Page 45** © John Abbott. **Page 50** Mark Burnett/Stock Boston. **Page 55** Kim Rultsh/SABA. **Page 58** Spencer Grant/Photoedit. **Page 59** Myrleen Ferguson.

Chapter 3 **Page 68** Courtesy of JLG Industries, Inc. **Page 70** Lonnie Duka/Tony Stone Images. **Page 75** Peter Menzel/Stock Boston. **Page 77** Mark Richards/Photoedit. **Page 79** © AFP/Corbis. **Page 84** Mark Renders/Isopress/Liaison. **Page 85** Robman/Sipa. **Page 87** Les Stone/Sygma.

Part II (top) Mark Richards/Photoedit; (bottom) Deborah Davis/Photoedit.

Chapter 4 **Page 103** © AFP/Corbis. **Page 107** David Young Wolff/Photoedit. **Page 109** Michael Newman/Photoedit. **Page 112** Courtesy Nervewire. **Page 114** © AFP/Corbis. **Page 115** Erik Freeland/SABA. **Page 118** Andy Freeberg. **Page 119** Courtesy Motorola.

Chapter 5 **Page 126** Associated Press, AP. **Page 128** Tony Freeman/PhotoEdit. **Page 134** Associated Press, AP. **Page 139** Tony Freeman/PhotoEdit. **Page 141** Michael Newman/PhotoEdit. **Page 143** Associated Press, AP. **Page 145** Associated Press, AP. **Page 147** AP Photo/Lucent Technologies/Court Mast.

Chapter 6 **Page 156** Francisco Rangel. **Page 160** AP Photo/Nick Ut. **Page 163** AP Photo/Charles Krupa. **Page 164** AP Photo/David J. Phillip. **Page 165** Stock Market. **Page 166** Bob Thomas/Tony Stone Images. **Page 169** Michael Newman/PhotoEdit. **Page 175** David H. Wells/Corbis.

Part III (top) Kaluzny/Thatcher/Tony Stone Images; (bottom) Fisher/Thatcher/Tony Stone Images.

Chapter 7 **Page 185** Ed Kash/Corbis. **Page 188** AP Photo/Mike Derer. **Page 189** David Young Wolff/PhotoEdit. **Page 190** Liane Enkelis/Stock Boston. **Page 191** Thierry Boccon-GIBOO/Liaison. **Page 194** Paul Chesley/Tony Stone Images. **Page 197** Reuters New Media Inc./Corbis. **Page 198** Chris Casabary/Liaison. **Page 200** AP Photo/Kent Gilbert.

Chapter 8 **Page 210** Joel W. Roberts/Corbis. **Page 211** (left) John Nebauer/PhotoEdit; (right) Rob Crandall/Stock Boston. **Page 214** Tony Page/Tony Stone Images. **Page 215** Billy Hustace/Tony Stone Images. **Page 219** Reprinted by permission of onlinebenfits.com. **Page 223** Rudi Von Briel/PhotoEdit. **Page 227** Bob Daemmrich/Stock Boston. **Page 230** Spencer Grant/PhotoEdit.

Part IV (top) Charles Gupton/Tony Stone Images; (bottom) Michael Rosenfeld/Tony Stone Images.

Chapter 10 **Page 271** Bob Daemmrich/Stock Boston. **Page 273** AP Photo/Tom Strattmann. **Page 279** Reprinted by permission of College-hire.com. **Page 280** Mark Richards/PhotoEdit. **Page 284** Reprinted by permission of The Container Store, 2000 Valwood Parkway, Dallas, TX 75234, 800-786-7315. **Page 286** Seth Resnick/Stock Boston. **Page 288** Davis Barber/PhotoEdit. **Page 294** Richard Pasley/Stock Boston.

Chapter 11 **Page 302** Courtesy BMC Software. **Page 303** AP Photo/George Nikitin. **Page 304** Margaret Ross/Stock Boston. **Page 305** Brown Brothers. **Page 313** David Young Wolff/PhotoEdit. **Page 317** (left) Michael Newman/PhotoEdit; (right) Bonnie Kamin/PhotoEdit. **Page 319** Spencer Grant/PhotoEdit. **Page 320** AP Photo/Daily Southtown, Chris Sweda.

Chapter 12 **Page 326** James Leynse/SABA. **Page 328** Library of Congress. **Page 334** The Archives of Labor and Urban Affairs. **Page 339** AP Photo/Barry Sweet. **Page 344** Robert Kusel/Tony Stone Images. **Page 345** AP Photo/Monique Brunsberg.

Part V (top) Hugon Sitton/Tony Stone Images; (bottom) Alan Schein/the Stock Market.

Chapter 13 **Page 355** Courtesy USAA. **Page 359** Courtesy Northwest Airlines, Inc. Creative by Carmichael Lynch. **Page 360** Courtesy Staples, Inc. **Page 361** David Simson/Stock Boston. **Page 363** Tina Finenberg/AP Photo. **Page 368** Courtesy PricewaterhouseCoopers. **Page 373** Stephen Frame/Stock Boston. **Page 374** Courtesy Tropicana.

Chapter 14 **Page 382** Courtesy Classic Sport Companies, Inc. **Page 384** © Don and Pat Valenti/Tony Stone Images. **Page 385** John Boykin/PhotoEdit. **Page 386** AFP/Corbis. **Page 388** Tony Freeman/PhotoEdit. **Page 389** Bonnie Kamin/PhotoEdit. **Page 392** Reuters New Media, Inc., Corbis. **Page 395** Will Hart/PhotoEdit. **Page 396** Courtesy Campbell Soup Company. **Page 397** Tony Freeman/PhotoEdit. **Page 406** David R. Frazier/Photolibrary. **Page 408** Bonnie Kamin/PhotoEdit.

Chapter 15 **Page 418** Spencer Grant/PhotoEdit. **Page 420** Spencer Grant/PhotoEdit. **Page 422** Tony Freeman/PhotoEdit. **Page 431** (top) David Young Wolff/PhotoEdit; (bottom) Myrleen Cate/PhotoEdit. **Page 433** Gail Albert Haliban/SABA. **Page 436** Tony Freeman/PhotoEdit. **Page 438** Michael Newman/PhotoEdit. **Page 439** Michael Newman/PhotoEdit. **Page 440** Deborah Davis/PhotoEdit.

Chapter 16 **Page 448** Francisco Rangel. **Page 450** David Young Wolff/PhotoEdit. **Page 453** Carmichael Lynch of Minneapolis developed the creative and media strategy. AAP is a nonprofit trade association that acts as the unifying voice for advertising and has as its members advertising agencies, advertisers, and media organizations. "Great Brands" ads have been shown in *The New York Times, Wall Street Journal, USA Today, Fortune, Advertising Age, AdWeek, BrandWeek, MediaWeek* and *Brand Marketing.* **Page 454** Michael Newman/PhotoEdit. **Page 457** Courtesy Liz Claiborne, Inc. **Page 460** Matthew Gilson. **Page 461** David Young Wolff/PhotoEdit. **Page 463** Courtesy Sound Installations. **Page 465** Jeff Greenberg/PhotoEdit.

Part VI (top) Lester Lefkowitz/Stock Market; (bottom) Frank Siteman/Tony Stone Images.

Chapter 17 **Page 479** Reprinted with permission. **Page 482** Karen Moskowitz. **Page 484** Dennis Kleiman. **Page 487** Mark Richards/PhotoEdit. **Page 495** Courtesy Verio, Inc. Advertisement is for illustrative purposes only and may no longer contain a valid promotional offer. **Page 497** Copyright © International Organization for Standardization. All rights reserved. **Page 501** Hosea L. Johnson. **Page 503** Reprinted by permission of Peachtree Software.

Chapter 18 **Page 512** Jonathan Kim/Liaison. **Page 513** Courtesy Ernst & Young LLP. **Page 518** Courtesy NetLedger, Inc. **Page 520** Nathan Benn/Stock Boston. **Page 522** Michael Newman/PhotoEdit. **Page 526** Ron Sherman/Tony Stone Images. **Page 527** Phyllis Picardi/Stock Boston. **Page 529** Courtesy Robert Half International.

Part Opener VII (top) Mark Burnett/Stock Boston; (bottom) Jon Riley/Tony Stone Images.

Chapter 19 **Page 545** David R. Frazier/Photolibrary. **Page 546** AP Photo/Fotomontage/fru. **Page 556** David Young Wolff/PhotoEdit. **Page 559** Courtesy Wilmington Trust Corporation. Creative by Korey Kay & Partners, New York; Chuck Kuhn, Photographer. **Page 561** Myrleen Cate/PhotoEdit. **Page 564** Phil Borden/PhotoEdit. **Page 566** Tony Freeman/PhotoEdit. **Page 567** Bob Daemmrich/Stock Boston.

Chapter 20 **Page 578** Associated Press, AP. **Page 580** Copyright © 2001 Getty Images. **Page 583** Reuters News Media, Inc./Corbis. **Page 587** Brian Bentrim @ cyber-stop.net/photo by Bill Bentrim. **Page 592** Copyright © 2001 Getty Images. **Page 595** AP Photo/Jim Walker. **Page 597** Dan Dry. **Page 599** David R. Frazier/Photolibrary.

Chapter 21 **Page 608** Lee Cleano/Liaison. **Page 611** Lois Ellen Frank/Corbis. **Page 616** Courtesy Phoenix Home Life Mutual Insurance Company. **Page 617** Liaison/Newsmakers/Online USA. **Page 621** Courtesy Dreyfus Service Corp. **Page 630** Reprinted with permission. **Page 633** Courtesy Motley Fool.

Name Index

subject index